THE FACTS ON FILE
COMPANION TO

CLASSICAL DRAMA

JOHN E. THORBURN, JR.

☑®
Facts On File, Inc.

Dedicated to
Penny, Alexis, and Chloe

The Facts On File Companion to Classical Drama

Copyright © 2005 by John E. Thorburn, Jr.

Facts On File, Inc.
132 West 31st Street
New York NY 10001

Library of Congress Cataloging-in-Publication Data
Thorburn, John E.
   The Facts On File companion to classical drama / written by John E. Thorburn, Jr.
     p. cm.
   Includes bibliographical references and index.
   ISBN 0-8160-5202-6 (hardcover : alk. paper)
   1. Classical drama—Encyclopedias. 1. Title: Companion to classical drama. II. Title.

PA3024.T48 2005
880'.09—dc22   2004016803

Text design adapted by James Scotto-Lavino
Cover design by Cathy Rincon

Printed in the United States of America

VB Hermitage 10 9 8 7 6 5 4 3 2 1

This book is printed on acid-free paper.

CONTENTS

ACKNOWLEDGMENTS

Thanks to Henry Rasof for introducing me to this project and assisting in constructing the original proposal. I would also like to express my appreciation to Anne Saverese for her help and advice in the early stages of this project. My deep appreciation also to Jeff Soloway for his help and guidance with this work. I am extremely grateful to the following colleagues, who were kind enough to read sections of this work: Antonios Augoustakis, Anne-Marie Bowery, Julia Dyson, Brent Froberg, John Nordling, Phillip Donnelly, Niall Slater, Alden Smith, DeAnna Toten Beard, and Amy Vail. Thanks to my students Andrew Alwine and Candace Spain, who read substantial portions of the manuscript. Special gratitude goes to Thelma Mathews, our departmental assistant, who not only helped with proofreading, but also helped compile the appendices and selected books on classical drama. Any faults and errors that remain are mine alone.

INTRODUCTION

If the experience of today's American students is the same as my own was, a student's first encounter with the world of drama will be to read a play of Shakespeare, perhaps *Romeo and Juliet* or *Julius Caesar,* and possibly also Arthur Miller's *The Crucible* or Tennessee Williams' *A Streetcar Named Desire.* At some point during their midteens, students may also read a play or two by Sophocles, *Oedipus Tyrannus* and *Antigone,* or perhaps Euripides' *Medea.* What teenage students may not be aware of (I certainly was not at that age) is that several dozen other classical plays exist and that the Greeks and Romans enjoyed watching comedies as well as tragedies. Although students may soon realize that the ideals and issues dealt with in plays such as *Antigone* and *Medea* are no different from the ones we face today, they may not know that the plays of the Greeks and Romans can also tell us much more.

This book has arisen from undergraduate courses I teach in classical drama and mythology. I like having my students read classical dramas because, after no more than 90 minutes of reading by them, I can present a complete work, beautiful poetry, and ideas that are powerful and enduring. Within this brief period of reading, they meet with issues of culture, politics, religion, history, and educational philosophy. Students of classical drama face questions such as "What is justice?" and "What is the relationship between human beings and the divine?" Furthermore, these critical questions are embedded within a world of fantastic

creatures, magical powers, unpredictable divinities, heroes of superhuman strength and endurance, and people who contrive fiendish or fantastic schemes. I hope that this work will inspire students to challenge themselves to go beyond the classical plays they encounter in their formative studies and read not only additional classical plays (one could read all the surviving plays within three months at the pace of one per day) but other works produced by two of world's greatest cultures.

The Facts On File Companion to Classical Drama was written for those without any previous introduction to classical studies or the ancient Greek or Latin language. I would be delighted, however, if scholars also benefited from this work. In this book, *classical drama* is taken to refer primarily to plays (tragedies, comedies, and satyr plays) written by Greek and Roman authors between the sixth century B.C.E. and the second century C.E. Understanding classical drama is a daunting task. Of the thousands of plays written during this period, only about 85 survive in more or less complete form, and though we know the names of some 300 classical playwrights, the surviving 85 plays can be attributed to only eight writers: Aeschylus, Sophocles, Euripides, Aristophanes, Menander, Plautus, Terence, and Seneca. The works of the other playwrights are known only from references made to them by other ancient authors or from partial manuscripts that have survived. Similarly, many other plays written by the eight major authors have also been lost and exist today only in fragments or references.

HOW TO USE THIS BOOK

The Facts On File Companion to Classical Drama focuses on the eight major classical playwrights, all their surviving plays, the major characters in the important tragedies (e.g., Agamemnon, Heracles, Electra, Orestes) and Aristophanic comedies, and the names of persons, places, and things important to understanding classical drama. For example, one cannot begin to understand most of Aristophanes' plays without a working knowledge of the Peloponnesian War or of the historical figures Cleon and Alcibiades. Similarly, one cannot understand Aeschylus' *Oresteia* without knowing about mythological characters such as Tantalus, Pelops, Atreus, and Thyestes. Accordingly, the *Companion to Classical Drama* provides entries for such items. The book also provides a number of terms connected with drama (such as chorus, parody, supplication) as well as entries on most of the major figures in ancient mythology, many of whom were the subjects of lost dramas. I have not provided individual entries for the characters in the comedies of Menander, Plautus, and Terence, works that employ stock characters such as prostitutes, pimps, and slaves. Instead, I have included individual entries on the broader categories into which these characters fall. In the course of an entry, the reader will find words in small capital letters (e.g., EURIPIDES, HERACLES). Words thus capitalized have corresponding entries elsewhere in the book. Only the first occurrence of such words in an entry is capitalized.

The *Companion to Classical Drama*'s most extensive entries are on individual plays. For each of the surviving plays, the book provides a plot summary, a commentary, and a few bibliographical references for further study. Given the format and audience of this series, the number of bibliographical references for each entry is limited, and preference has been given to works in English that attempt to provide an extensive treatment of a particular topic. Because translations of the plays are widely available, I have listed in Selected Books on Classical Drama only a select few, giving preference to those that might not be readily known to the average student (e.g., Lloyd-Jones' translation of Sophocles' fragments).

Readers should also note that the interpretations provided in the commentary section can highlight only a few of the major themes or issues in a particular play. Students unfamiliar with classical scholarship should be advised that in some cases scholars have written hundreds of articles and books about a single play (e.g., Sophocles' *Antigone,* Euripides' *Bacchae*). Students should also be aware that much of what we "know" about classical drama is based on information that cannot be verified, since so many classical plays have been lost. Thus, the phrases *may be, seem to be,* and *appear to be* occur frequently in this work.

Information on some of the fragmentary plays from antiquity is present in the *Companion to Classical Drama* and may be listed in the entry for a particular mythological or historical figure or, on rare occasions, in an entry on a particular place. Thus, information about Euripides' *Philoctetes* (of which only fragments exist) can be found under the entry for the figure Philoctetes. Information about plays entitled *Women of Lemnos* may be found under the entry on the island of Lemnos.

Many entries conclude with a list of ancient sources. These lists cannot cite every reference to a particular topic in classical literature but should allow readers to check what some of the major Greek or Roman writers have said about a particular topic. These lists focus on references to the surviving plays of the major playwrights but also include references to fragments of the ancient playwrights. In these cases, a reference such as the following appears: "Cratinus, fragment 85.1 Kock." Here, Cratinus is the ancient author; 85.1 refers to fragment 85, line 1; and Kock is the last name of one of the modern editors of Cratinus' fragments. Because Kock edited several volumes of ancient fragments, readers will sometimes find a number after his name or the name of other editors of fragments, such as Philemon, fragment 42.1 Kock 2. The number after Kock's name refers to the second volume of fragments edited by Kock. An additional remark should be made regarding Kock. Whereas Kock's work on the fragments has now been superseded by R. Kassel and C. Austin's *Poetae Comici Graeci,* Liddell and Scott's *Greek-English Dictionary* (the dictionary most widely used by classicists) follows Kock's numbering of the fragments. Additionally, the *Thesaurus Linguae Graecae* computer database of Greek texts has not yet incorporated Kassel and Austin's edition of the Greek comic fragments. Therefore, I have followed Kock's numbering because it seems the most commonly available edition of the Greek comic fragments.

The ancient sources section also includes references to other ancient authors who are not playwrights. In some cases, these authors (e.g., Homer) may have influenced the playwrights. In other cases, the playwrights may have influenced them (e.g., Ovid). Frequently cited also are the works of Apollodorus (*Library* and *Epitome*) and Hyginus (*Fables*), both of which provide brief summaries of stories from classical mythology. The most frequently cited authors from literature other than the plays are Apollodorus, Aristotle, Herodotus, Hesiod, Homer, Hyginus, Ovid, Pausanias, Plato, Pollux, and Thucydides.

For those unfamiliar with the method of citing ancient authors, a few explanatory remarks may be in order. For example, the citation "Euripides, *Medea* 25–30" refers to lines 25 through 30 in Euripides' *Medea;* "Homer, *Iliad* 2.176" refers to Book 2, line 176, of Homer's *Iliad;* "Apollodorus, *Library* 1.9.15" refers to Book 1, section 9, subsection 15, of Apollodorus' *Library.* In the case of an author who has only one surviving work, only the author's name and the reference numbers are given. Thus, "Herodotus 8.7" refers to Book 8, section 7, of Herodotus' *Histories.*

References to Greek texts in the *Companion to Classical Drama* follow those found in version E of the *Thesaurus Linguae Graecae* compact disk. References to Latin texts follow those found in version 5.3 of the Packard Humanities Institute compact disk. Students reading translations of the plays should note that the book, section, and line numbers given in this book may not match the numbering systems in their particular translation.

Regarding the spelling of Greek proper names, although the current trend in classical scholarship is to give literal transliterations of Greek names (e.g., Aischylos rather than Aeschylus), I have chosen to follow cultural habit and actual usage. Thus, in contrast to those who write Asklepios, Hektor, and Herakles, I have adopted spellings that might be more recognizable to someone who is unfamiliar with classical literature (Asclepius, Hector, and Heracles). A more difficult issue has been the choice of how to list the titles for the various plays, because translations often deviate from the ancient title. Because this work is designed primarily for use by those who will be working from translations, entries for such plays are found under a widely accepted English translation for a play's title. Where the appended English translation of a Greek or Latin work is not italicized, this indicates that the work does not appear in a published English-language edition. Cross-references are also provided to help alleviate confusion. As an additional aid, the appendices list all the 85 surviving plays, grouped by author, with the titles used in the text of this book.

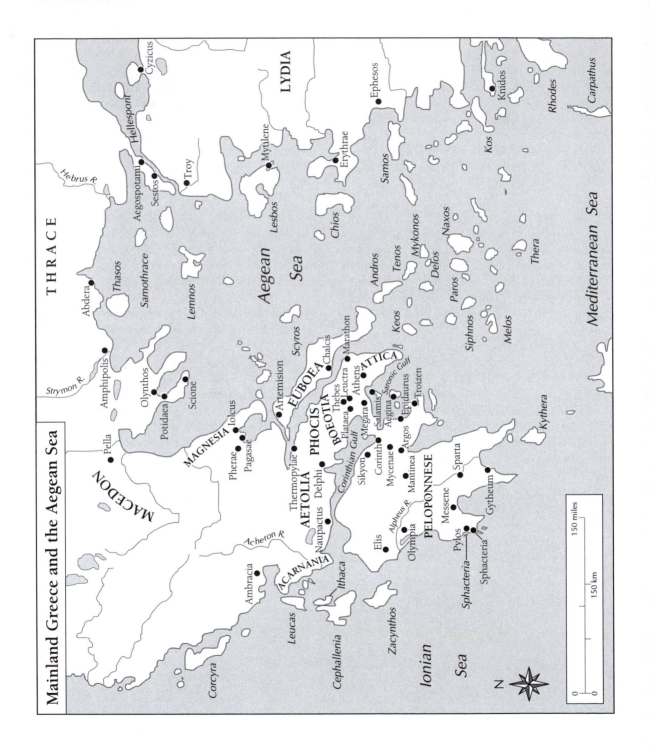

Mainland Greece and the Aegean Sea

A

ABAE In the northwest part of the region of PHO-CIS, Abae was the location of an oracle of APOLLO. The Persian XERXES severely damaged the sanctuary at Abae during his invasion of Greece. [ANCIENT SOURCES: Pausanias, 10.35.1–2; Sophocles, *Oedipus Tyrannos* 900]

ABSYRTUS (APSYRTUS) Absyrtus, the son of AEETES and Eidyia or the Caucasian nymph Asterodeia, was the younger brother of MEDEA. When JASON and Medea escaped from COLCHIS, Aeetes pursued them. To counter the pursuit, Medea, accompanied by Absyrtus aboard the ship, killed her brother by cutting up his body and scattering his limbs upon the sea, an action that caused Aeetes to break off his pursuit. EURIPIDES also makes Medea the killer of her brother, but according to the fourth century B.C.E. epic poet Apollonius Rhodius, Medea lures Absyrtus, pursuing the *Argo,* into an ambush by which Jason kills him. Hyginus reports that Jason kills Absyrtus without the use of trickery. Apollodorus makes Absyrtus' burial site a place in the Black Sea region called Tomi, meaning "cut" and referring to the manner of his death, whereas Hyginus says Medea buries her brother at Absoros, an island in the Adriatic Sea. [ANCIENT SOURCES: Apollodorus, *Library* 1.9.23; Apollonius Rhodius, *Argonautica* 4.303–481; Hyginus, *Fables* 23; Seneca, *Medea* 131–32, 911–12]

BIBLIOGRAPHY
Edgeworth, R. J. "The Eloquent Ghost: Absyrtus in Seneca's *Medea," Classica et Mediaevalia* 41 (1990): 151–61.

ABYLA See CALPE.

ACAMAS A son of THESEUS and brother of DEMOPHON. See also *CHILDREN OF HERACLES.*

ACASTUS (AKASTOS) The son of Pelias and Anaxibia (or Phylomache), and the brother of ALCESTIS, Pisidice, Pelopia, and Hippothoe, Acastus was a king of IOLCUS. Acastus was also the father of Sthenele, LAODAMEIA, and Sterope by either Astydameia or CRETHEUS' daughter, Hippolyte. Acastus accompanied JASON and the Argonauts on their quest for the Golden Fleece. After the murder of his father through the treachery of MEDEA and Jason, Acastus became king of Iolcus and drove them from the town. SENECA suggests that after Jason and Medea went to Corinth Acastus sought them for punishment. EURIPIDES suggests that Acastus might retaliate against ADMETUS for the death of Alcestis.

According to Euripides, Acastus has banished PELEUS, the father of ACHILLES, from THESSALY. The circumstances are as follows: According to Apollodorus, Acastus' wife, Astydameia, fell in love with Peleus and tried to seduce him. When Peleus rejected her, Astydameia told Peleus' wife (his spouse before his union with Thetis) that Peleus was going to marry Acastus' daughter Sterope. Hearing this, Peleus' wife hanged herself. Astydameia also informed Acastus that Peleus had attempted to rape her. Acastus took Peleus to hunt on Mount PELION, and when Peleus fell asleep, Acastus, hoping Peleus would be killed, hid Peleus' sword and left him on the mountain. The defenseless Peleus awoke and the CENTAURS attacked, but the centaur CHIRON saved him and gave him back his sword.

Acastus also appears in one version of the tragic events associated with his daughter Laodameia. After the death of PROTESILAUS, Laodameia's husband, a statue of him was made and the grieving Laodameia was accustomed to holding and kissing it. A servant saw her do so and told Acastus, who thought Laodameia was having intercourse with another man. When Acastus found the statue, he had it burned. The sorrowful Laodomeia then committed suicide by throwing herself into the same fire. [ANCIENT SOURCES: Apollodorus, *Library* 1.9.10, 3.13.3; Euripides, *Alcestis* 732–33, *Trojan Women* 1,127–38; Hyginus, *Fables* 103–4; Seneca, *Medea* 257, 415, 521, 526]

ACCIUS (CA. 170–90 B.C.E.)

Accius, a Roman writer, produced several types of literature. The content of one work, *Parerga,* is unknown. Two works, *Didascalica* and *Pragmatica,* both dealt with various aspects of literature, especially drama. Accius' *Sotadica* seems to have been a collection of erotic poetry. Accius was the author of about 45 tragedies. At least one-quarter of these were probably modeled on plays by EURIPIDES; SOPHOCLES and AESCHYLUS (in that order) were also drawn upon. Titles of two historical dramas (see FABULA PRAETEXTA) are known: *Aeneadae* (or *Decius*) and *Brutus.*

BIBLIOGRAPHY
Slater, N. W. "Two Republican Poets on Drama: Terence and Accius." In *Antike Dramentheorien und ihre Rezeption.* Edited by Bernhard Zimmermann. Stuttgart: M&P Verl. Für Wiss. & Forsch., 1992.

ACCLAMATIO

A Latin term (plural: *acclamationes*) that refers to groups of people (arranged for by a person connected with a play, such as an actor) placed in the crowd to applaud rhythmically or to shout. [ANCIENT SOURCES: Ovid, *Art of Love* 1.113; Plautus, *Amphitruo* 65–85]

ACESTOR

A tragic poet from ATHENS whom a few comic poets mention in the last three decades of the fifth century B.C.E.; he was "widely accused of being of foreign birth" (Sommerstein). His mother may have been an Athenian; his father may have been from MYSIA. Acestor's nickname was Sacas, a reference to a tribe called the Sacae (the Scythians who lived in Asia). [ANCIENT SOURCES: Aristophanes, *Birds* 31–32, *Wasps* 1221; Athenaeus 6.237a; Cratinus, fragment 85.1 Kock; Eupolis, fragment 159.14 Kock; Theopompus, fragment 60.2 Kock]

BIBLIOGRAPHY
Dunbar, Nan. *Aristophanes: Birds.* New York: Oxford University Press, 1995, 146–47.
Kock, T. *Comicorum Atticorum Fragmenta.* Vol. 1. Leipzig: Teubner, 1880.
Sommerstein, A. H. *The Comedies of Aristophanes.* Vol. 4, *Wasps.* Warminster, U.K.: Aris & Phillips, 1983, 228.

ACHAEANS

The group of people who inhabited Achaea, a region in the northwestern part of the Peloponnese on mainland Greece. EURIPIDES, *ION,* 1,591–94, derives the region's name from Achaeus, a son of XUTHUS and CREUSA, who eventually ruled over the region. Poets more often use the name Achaeans as a synonym for the Greeks of the Peloponnese or for the Greeks as a whole, especially the coalition of Greeks who fought during the Trojan War. MENANDER wrote a play entitled *Achaeans* (Greek: *Achaioi*) from which a single three-line fragment survives (fragment 113 Austin).

BIBLIOGRAPHY
Austin, C. *Comicorum Graecorum Fragmenta in Papyris Reperta.* Berlin: De Gruyter, 1973.

ACHAEUS (BORN CA. 484–481 B.C.E.)

A Greek tragedian from ERETRIA who may have written as many as 44 plays, although only 19 or 20 titles survive and fewer than five dozen fragments remain. At least seven of the surviving titles are recorded as SATYR PLAYS, and Diogenes Laertius reports that the philosopher Menedemus considered only Aeschylus' satyr plays as superior to those of Achaeus. In the first century B.C.E., the Alexandrian scholar Didymus wrote a commentary on Achaeus, and the Alexandrian scholars included him in their canon (a list of the best classical poets). Athenaeus comments that Achaeus' style of composition was "polished," but that he expressed ideas darkly and that he often wrote enigmatically. Achaeus' first play appeared around 447 B.C.E., and he won first prize in a competition on one occasion. Athenaeus states that Euripides borrowed a line from Achaeus' satyr play *Aethon* ("Cypris exists in satiety, not in a hungry man"). [ANCIENT SOURCES: Athenaeus, 6.270b, 10.451c; Diogenes Laertius, 2.133]

BIBLIOGRAPHY
Snell, B. *Tragicorum Graecorum Fragmenta.* Vol. 1. Göttingen, Ger.: Vandenhoeck & Ruprecht, 1971.

ACHARNAE An Athenian DEME. The chorus of ARISTOPHANES' *ACHARNIANS* are from Acharnae.

ACHARNIANS ARISTOPHANES (425 B.C.E.)
This COMEDY defeated offerings from the veteran playwrights CRATINUS and EUPOLIS and captured the first prize at the LENAEA (see line 504) in ATHENS. The play's setting shifts several times but is primarily Athens and its outlying areas. The play deals with the struggles of an Athenian farmer, DICAEOPOLIS (honest citizen), in the sixth year of the PELOPONNESIAN WAR between ATHENS and SPARTA. One cause of this war, the MEGARIAN DECREE, banned the people of MEGARA, a town several miles west of Athens, from trading in Athenian ports. The decree caused hardship not only for Megarians but also for Athenians such as Dicaeopolis, who counted on trade with the Megarians to supplement their income. Furthermore, because the Spartans ravaged territory outside the walls of Athens during the war, people such as Dicaeopolis, who lived in the countryside, were brought within the city walls for safety: a situation that made the country folk unhappy.

As the *Acharnians* opens, the audience listens to Dicaeopolis, who, waiting for the Athenian assembly to begin its business, longs for his country home and complains of the war and its economic hardships and the apparent unwillingness of the Athenian assembly to discuss peace. When the assembly opens, a divinity, Amphitheus (whose name means "divine on both sides"), tells the assembly that the gods have sent him to make a treaty with the Spartans. After the Athenian magistrates indicate that they will not provide Amphitheus with money to make his journey, the divinity is thrown out of the assembly. An Athenian

ambassador to the king of Persia next enters the assembly. The ambassador's report indicates that he has done nothing but waste Athenian money. The ambassador, however, has with him Pseudartabas, whose name means "false Artabas" and who serves as the "Eye" of the king of Persia. Pseudartabas, whose speech Aristophanes casts partly in Greek, partly in gibberish, tells the Athenians that they will not receive any financial backing from the Persians, despite the ambassador's interpretation to the contrary. With no hope of peace in sight, Dicaeopolis summons Amphitheus and pays the divinity to arrange a peace treaty between his family and the Spartans, a treaty that will allow him to trade with the Megarians and other allies of the Spartans. When the next visitors to the assembly, a group of Odomantian mercenaries from Thrace, steal Dicaeopolis' lunch, Dicaeopolis pretends that he feels a drop of rain and calls for the assembly to be dismissed.

As the assembly breaks up, Amphitheus returns from Sparta with the peace treaties, actually wineskins. Because the Greek verb *spendein* can mean both "to conclude a peace treaty" and "to pour a drink offering," ARISTOPHANES takes literal advantage of this double meaning. Dicaeopolis delights in the taste of the 30-year treaty and accepts it. Amphitheus runs out, because some Acharnian veterans (who compose the play's chorus) from the battle of MARATHON have smelled his peace treaties and start to chase him. The Acharnians, whose grapevines the Spartans destroyed during their incursions into Athenian territory, favored the war with Sparta (compare Thucydides 2.21.3).

At first, Dicaeopolis distracts the Acharnians by leading his family's own procession in honor of Dionysus. As Dicaeopolis ends the festivities, the aged Acharnians, who have learned that Dicaeopolis has made peace with the Spartans and their allies, attempt to stone Dicaeopolis. To hold off the Acharnians, Dicaeopolis takes hostage some charcoal—the Acharnians were known for their production of charcoal—and threatens to "kill" it if they do not put down their rocks. This scene parodies a nonextant play by EURIPIDES, *Telephus,* in which TELEPHUS apparently took AGAMEMNON's son, ORESTES, hostage and threatened to kill him. After the Acharnians drop their stones, Dicaeopolis persuades them to allow him to costume himself appropriately for the speech. At this point, Dicaeopolis goes to the house of the tragic poet Euripides and borrows the tattered costume of Telephus. Dicaeopolis hopes that his wearing Telephus' rags will draw sympathy and understanding from the Acharnian chorus.

Dressed as Telephus, Dicaeopolis makes his argument to the Acharnian chorus. Dicaeopolis reduces the causes of the war to the denunciation of Megarians who try to trade in Athenian ports, the abduction of a Megarian PROSTITUTE by some drunken Athenians, and the retaliatory abduction of two Athenian prostitutes by the Megarians; the ensuing Megarian decree; and the Megarians' eventual plea to the Spartans for help. Dicaeopolis' argument divides the opinion of the chorus, and they summon the Athenian general LAMACHUS for help. When Lamachus arrives, he and Dicaeopolis insult one another, mainly arguing that whereas a young man such as Lamachus always receives his military pay, the old men who serve in the army do not get theirs. At this point, Dicaeopolis and Lamachus exit, leaving the chorus to deliver the PARABASIS, in which they praise Aristophanes' concern for and instruction of the state, and they promise that Aristophanes will serve the audience well in the future. The chorus also condemn the Athenians for their treatment of aged war veterans.

After the parabasis, Dicaeopolis sets up his own marketplace and begins to trade wares with various merchants who enter. He trades garlic and salt with a Megarian for "piggies," in fact the Megarian's daughters dressed as pigs. Next, when Dicaeopolis encounters a Theban merchant, a market informant tries to denounce the pair; Dicaeopolis has the informant packed up and trades him to the Theban for some eels, a delicacy from that region.

After the transaction with the Theban, a servant from Lamachus enters and summons Dicaeopolis to the PITCHER FEAST. As Dicaeopolis prepares for this feast, various people ask him for some of his "peace." The farmer Dercetes, blind as a result of weeping for his two oxen destroyed during a Boeotian incursion, wants Dicaeopolis to heal his eyes. Dicaeopolis, however refuses. Next, a bridegroom sends one of his groomsmen to ask for some "peace" so that he can stay home and have intercourse with his new bride rather

than go off to war. Dicaeopolis agrees to this request and provides the bride with some wine with which to anoint her husband's penis.

At this point, the Pitcher Feast is interrupted by the arrival of a messenger who summons Lamachus to war, while another messenger calls Dicaeopolis to drink, dinner, and dancing girls. The play ends by showing a side-by-side view of the two men in their various environments. Dicaeopolis experiences all the pleasures of peace (warm weather, wine, and women), while Lamachus suffers the hardships of war (cold, soldiers' rations, and injury).

COMMENTARY

As shown by its victory at the Lenaea, *Acharnians* achieved critical acclaim in its own day. Modern scholars also regard the play highly. Whitman calls it "one of [Aristophanes'] greatest works." *Acharnians* contains a number of noteworthy features. First, Aristophanes uses dialect more extensively in this play than in any other extant drama. Other than Aristophanes' own Attic Greek, spoken by the play's Athenian characters, Aristophanes gives the Persian Pseudartabas a sort of gibberish Greek to speak (100–104); the Megarian merchant speaks his regional dialect (729–835), as does the Boeotian merchant (860–954).

Aristophanes' use of multiple settings in the play is also remarkable, especially because his audience would have seen a simple backdrop that Dover thinks makes use of no more than two doors—one representing the entrance to Dicaeopolis' house, the other the door to Lamachus' house. Thus, peace and war literally live next door to one another in this play. As the play opens, Dicaeopolis is at the Pnyx near the Athenian acropolis. After the assembly breaks up, the audience must now imagine that Dicaeopolis goes to his home in the countryside, which Aristophanes seems to place next door to the home of Lamachus. After his confrontation with the Acharnians and Lamachus, Dicaeopolis goes to Euripides' home, traditionally on the island of Salamis, but for the purposes of the play conveniently located beside Dicaeopolis' home. Dicaeopolis then returns to his own home, outside which he eventually sets up his marketplace. The play's final scene is a tour de force, and the audience must imagine that Dicaeopolis basks in the sunshine outside his own house, while Lamachus labors in the snows of Thrace.

The *Acharnians* is also noteworthy for the use of tragic parody to enhance comedy. In addition to Aristophanes' employment of Euripides' *Telephus,* the wounding of Lamachus that occurs at the end of the play may also allude to *Telephus,* because Telephus' wound prompted him to journey to Greece and seek a cure. Aristophanes commonly uses and abuses Euripidean poetry in his repertoire and appears to do so to an even greater extent in his THESMOPHORIAZUSAE and FROGS.

Acharnians also provides an excellent example of a typical Aristophanic play and a typical Aristophanic hero. It is one of three extant Aristophanic plays (compare also PEACE and LYSISTRATA) that focus on the Peloponnesian War. As in *Peace* and *Lysistrata,* so in *Acharnians* the hero contrives, as Sommerstein describes it, a "fantastic project" to achieve peace with the Spartans and their allies. Unlike events in the other two extant peace plays, in the *Acharnians* the hero's peace involves only himself and a select few (his family, those who trade with him, the bride and groom) upon whom he chooses to confer the benefits of his peace. As is typical in Aristophanic comedy, the hero's plan must overcome obstacles. In this play, Dicaeopolis must overcome the Acharnians themselves and Lamachus. Ultimately, the hero triumphs and reaps the rewards of peace often mentioned by Aristophanes: wine, women, and song. The final scene of *Acharnians* brilliantly conveys Aristophanes' message to his fellow Athenians: By accepting the ways of peace, one can enjoy the sunshine, drink wine, eat fine foods, and enjoy the company of women; by choosing war, one must suffer through cold, eat soldiers' rations, and risk injury and perhaps even death. As Reckford writes, "This comedy, like the *Peace,* not only plays out a recovery of the good things of peace . . . before the audience, but gives them an experience of recovery, of participation in the delights of peace, that must remind them feelingly of what they have lost."

BIBLIOGRAPHY

Carey, C. "The Purpose of Aristophanes' *Acharnians,*" *Rheinisches Museum* 136 (1993): 245–63.

Dover, K. J. *Aristophanic Comedy.* Berkeley: University of California Press, 1972, 78–88.

Edmunds, Lowell. "Aristophanes' *Acharnians,*" *Yale Classical Studies* 26 (1980): 1–41.

Foley, H. P. "Tragedy and Politics in Aristophanes' *Acharnians,*" *Journal of Hellenic Studies* 108 (1988): 33–47.

MacDowell, D. M. "The Nature of Aristophanes' *Akharnians,*" *Greece & Rome* 30 (1983): 143–62.

Reckford, Kenneth J. *Aristophanes' Old-and-New Comedy.* Chapel Hill: University of North Carolina Press, 1987, 162–215.

Sommerstein, A. *The Comedies of Aristophanes.* Vol. 1, *Acharnians.* Warminster, U.K.: Aris & Phillips, 1980, 11.

Whitman, Cedric H. *Aristophanes and the Comic Hero.* Cambridge, Mass.: Harvard University Press, 1964, 59–79.

ACHELOAN CITIES   Places of uncertain location either near the Thracian coast or on islands off the coast from THRACE. [ANCIENT SOURCES: Aeschylus, *Persians* 867]

ACHELOUS (ACHELOOS)   Achelous was the divinity who ruled over the river (of the same name) that divides the regions of AETOLIA and Acarnania in southwestern Greece and flows into the Ionian Sea. Hesiod makes him the child of Oceanus and Tethys. EURIPIDES calls Achelous the father of DIRCE. Several sources make him the father of the Sirens by the MUSE Melpomene. Apollodorus also makes him the father of Hippodamas and ORESTES by Perimede; Pausanias says the river fathered Pirene and the CASTALIAN SPRING. Achelous became a suitor for DEIANEIRA of CALYDON. Despite Achelous' ability to alter his shape from a river to a bull, a serpent, or a creature that was part ox, part man, HERACLES defeated him in a wrestling match for Deianeira's hand in marriage when Heracles broke off one of his horns. Achelous recovered his horn, however, by trading Heracles the horn of AMALTHEA, the cornucopia, which had the ability to produce as much food or drink as a person could want.

Achelous is also connected with the story of ALCMEON. After he killed his mother, ERIPHYLE, Alcmeon eventually went to Achelous' springs. The river purified Alcmeon of the murder and gave him his daughter, Callirrhoe, in marriage. Alcmeon later colonized the land formed by the silt of the Achelous. [ANCIENT SOURCES: Apollodorus, *Library* 1.3.4, 1.7.3, 2.7.5, 3.7.5; Aristophanes, *Lysistrata* 381; Euripides, *Bacchae* 519–20; Hesiod, *Theogony* 337–40; Hyginus, *Fables* 141; Pausanias, 2.2.3, 9.34.3, 10.8.9; Sophocles, *Trachinian Women* 3–25; Seneca, *Hercules Oetaeus* 299–304, 495–500]

ACHERON   While two rivers in the upper world were called Acheron, one in Greece that passes through Lake Acherusia to the Ionian Sea and one in southern Italy, Acheron, a word that means "lacking in joy," is best known as the name of a river in the UNDERWORLD. According to HOMER, two other rivers, the COCYTUS and the Pyriphlegethon, flow into the Acheron. Whereas some ancient writers say that the souls of the dead had to cross the river Styx to enter the underworld, others have souls crossing the Acheron. PLATO says the Acheron flows in the opposite direction from Oceanus, passes through desert regions, and eventually flows into the underworld, where it empties into Lake Acherusia. Plato later says that souls who have lived neither a good nor a bad life go by the Acheron and travel by boat to the lake, where they are purified and pay penalties if they have committed some wrong while alive. Some writers make Acheron synonymous with the underworld. [ANCIENT SOURCES: Aeschylus, *Seven against Thebes* 854–60; Aristophanes, *Frogs* 471; Homer, *Odyssey* 10.513–15; Plato, *Phaedo* 112e; Plautus, *Amphitruo* 1078, *Carthaginian* 431, *The Three-Dollar Day* 525; Seneca, *Hippolytus* 198, *Oedipus* 578]

ACHILLES   Achilles was the son of the mortal PELEUS and the goddess THETIS. ZEUS himself was attracted to Thetis until a prophecy revealed that Thetis would produce a son destined to be more powerful than his father. Desiring to avoid this fate, Zeus arranged for Thetis to marry Peleus. Some sources say that Thetis attempted to make her son immortal by dipping him into the river STYX, but that she failed because she did not immerse the child's heel, by which she was holding him. Others say that every day and night Thetis anointed Achilles with ambrosia and placed him in the embers of a fire. Peleus, however, discovered Thetis anointing their son. His interruption

not only broke the magic spell, but also angered Thetis, who left Peleus and returned to the sea. As a young boy, Achilles was trained by the CENTAUR CHIRON. Peleus gave PHOENIX as a tutor to Achilles as a young man. When Menoitius, father of PATROCLUS, who accidentally caused a friend's death, traveled to Phthia seeking purification for his son, Patroclus and Achilles soon became inseparable friends.

Thetis knew her son would die at TROY if he fought there, so Achilles, disguised as a woman, was taken to the island of SCYROS, where he lived at the court of King LYCOMEDES. While on Scyros, Achilles became the father of NEOPTOLEMUS (also known as Pyrrhus) by Lycomedes' daughter Deidamia. When the Greeks were gathering to sail to Troy, ODYSSEUS went to Scyros in search of Achilles. Odysseus tricked Achilles into revealing himself by visiting Lycomedes' palace and offering the women of the court some gifts. Among the gifts, Odysseus had placed a shield and spear. As the women of the palace were gazing at the gifts, Odysseus arranged for a battle trumpet to be sounded. The disguised Achilles, thinking the island was under attack, grabbed the implements of war, thus revealing his identity. Despite Thetis' warning, Achilles accompanied the Greeks to war at Troy. Physically, he was the most powerful of the Greek warriors in the Trojan War, and in EURIPIDES' *IPHIGENIA AT AULIS* he is described as outrunning a four-horse chariot.

The accounts of the Greeks' voyage to Troy vary greatly. According to one account, the Greeks' first attempt to sail there failed, as they landed in Mysia. Achilles, fighting against the natives, wounded their leader, TELEPHUS. The Greeks then returned to Greece in need of someone to guide them to Troy. Later, when Telephus' wound would not heal, Telephus traveled to Greece in accordance with an oracle, which stated that only the one who wounded him could heal him. Ultimately, Telephus found Achilles, who healed him with the rust from his spear. In thanks, Telephus agreed to guide the Greeks to Troy.

The Greeks' successful voyage to Troy started from Aulis; when adverse weather prevented them from sailing and an oracle declared that the sacrifice of Agamemnon's daughter IPHIGENIA, was the only remedy for the bad weather, Iphigenia was lured to Aulis under the pretext that she would marry Achilles, who knew nothing about the plot until Iphigenia arrived at Aulis. In Euripides' *Iphigenia at Aulis,* Achilles offers to save Iphigenia, but she eventually agrees to be sacrificed to save her country. After the Greeks left Aulis, they landed on and stormed the island of Tenedos, just off the coast of Troy. In the fighting, Achilles killed Tenes, a son of APOLLO. Thetis had warned Achilles to avoid Apollo's sons, because any harm to a son of Apollo would invite retaliation from the god. Achilles, however, apparently did not know Tenes' lineage. Immediately upon arriving at Troy, Achilles made his presence known as he encountered POSEIDON's son CYCNUS. Despite the supposed invulnerability of Poseidon's son Achilles managed to choke Cycnus to death. When the Trojans saw the havoc that Achilles was wreaking on their army, they retreated to the safety of their city and made every effort to avoid engaging the Greeks in open battle. Occasionally, Achilles managed to pick off a few Trojans who ventured outside the walls, most notably PRIAM's son Troilus.

Otherwise, the Greeks had to content themselves with making raids on the towns in the surrounding countryside and nearby islands that were allied with the Trojans. Such raids continued for the first nine years of the war. Achilles was instrumental in the sacking of almost two dozen towns. After a successful attack on Lyrnessus, Achilles was awarded a female captive, Briseis. In the 10th year of the war, Achilles refused to fight any longer when Agamemnon took Briseis for himself. With Achilles out of the fighting, the Trojans began to engage the Greeks in open warfare. The Trojans' success prompted Agamemnon to try to appease Achilles' wrath. Agamemnon sent a few Greeks to Achilles' tent to win him over with a vast amount of gifts and money, but Achilles refused Agamemnon's offer and stated that the following morning he planned to sail home to Greece.

The next day, however, the Trojans smashed their way into the Greek camp and the Trojan HECTOR was threatening to burn the Greek ships. Achilles' comrade, Patroclus, was so distressed by these circumstances that he begged Achilles to allow him to lead their troops into battle. Patroclus persuaded Achilles to allow him to wear Achilles' armor, in the hope that the

Trojans would be frightened and retreat, thinking that Achilles had returned to the battle. Hector, however, killed Patroclus and stripped off Achilles' armor. After HEPHAESTUS made Achilles a new suit of armor, Achilles and Agamemnon were reconciled and Achilles returned to battle. Achilles killed numerous Trojans and dumped their bodies into the river Xanthus, causing the river itself to rise up against Achilles. Fortunately for Achilles, Hephaestus came to his aid and with his flames drove the river back. Soon, Achilles killed Hector, defiled his body by dragging it behind his chariot, and held funeral games for Patroclus. Eventually, at the insistence of the gods, Achilles ransomed Hector's body, which was returned to Priam.

After the death of Hector, Achilles killed several other notable Trojans or Trojan allies. After Achilles killed the Amazon Penthesileia, some sources say that he fell in love with her. When his fellow Greek Thersites made fun of him for this, Achilles killed Thersites. Achilles also killed MEMNON, the son of EOS and Tithonus. Before the fall of Troy, an Apollo-guided arrow from the Trojan Paris' bow killed Achilles. As the Greeks left the conquered city of Troy, Achilles' ghost appeared and demanded a sacrifice at his grave: Polyxena, the daughter of Priam and Hecabe.

Achilles was an important figure in TRAGEDY, COMEDY, and the SATYR PLAY, although he appears as a character in only one extant work—Euripides' *Iphigenia at Aulis.* As mentioned previously, in this play Agamemnon lures his daughter Iphigenia to Aulis by pretending that she is to marry Achilles, when she is actually to be sacrificed to Artemis. When Achilles discovers this plan, he is outraged (primarily because he has been used in Agamemnon's scheme without his knowledge) and tries to persuade the Greeks not to sacrifice Iphigenia. When he tries to do so, however, the Greek army shouts him down. Achilles notes that even his own troops turned against him. Although Achilles nobly tries to defend Iphigenia, one notes that when she is sacrificed Achilles is present and even offers a prayer before the sacrifice (1568–76).

Numerous ancient dramas would have had Achilles as a character or would have dealt with some aspect of Achilles' life. Greek playwrights who wrote dramas entitled *Achilles* are Aristarchus, Iophon, Astydamas, the younger Carcinus, Diogenes, and Cleophon. Chaeremon wrote *Achilles Thersitoktonos* (Achilles, the killer of Thersites). Aeschylus wrote an Achilles trilogy (*Myrmidons,* fragments 131–42 Radt; *Nereids,* fragments 150–54 Radt; *Phrygians* or *The Washing of Hector,* fragments 263–72 Radt), of which survive several fragments; the work treated Patroclus' death, Achilles' killing of Hector, and the ransom of Hector's body from Achilles. Athenaeus says Aeschylus introduced the subject of love between males (Achilles and Patroclus) in *Myrmidons.* SOPHOCLES wrote *Lovers of Achilles* (Greek: *Achilleos Erastai*), whose roughly 20 surviving lines reveal that it was a satyr play and that Peleus and Phoenix were characters. Both Ennius (fragments 1–9 Jocelyn) and ACCIUS wrote Latin tragedies entitled *Achilles* that may have concerned the embassy to Achilles. [ANCIENT SOURCES: Athenaeus, 13.601a–b; Euripides, *Iphigenia at Aulis;* Homer, *Iliad;* Hyginus, *Fables* 96–98, 106–14; Ovid, *Metamorphoses* 12.580–628; Seneca, *Trojan Women;* Sophocles, *Philoctetes*]

BIBLIOGRAPHY

Jocelyn, H. D. *The Tragedies of Ennius.* Cambridge: Cambridge University Press, 1969.

Kiso, A. *The Lost Sophocles.* New York: Vantage Press, 1984.

Radt, S. *Tragicorum Graecorum Fragmenta.* Vol. 3. Göttingen, Ger.: Vandenhoeck & Ruprecht, 1985.

Snell, B. *Tragicorum Graecorum Fragmenta.* Vol. 1. Göttingen, Ger.: Vandenhoeck & Ruprecht, 1971.

Sutton, D. F. *The Lost Sophocles.* Lanham, Md.: University Press of America, 1984.

Warmington, E. H. *Remains of Old Latin: Ennius and Caecilius.* Vol. 1. Cambridge, Mass., and London: Harvard University Press, 1935.

Warmington, E. H. *Remains of Old Latin: Livius Andronicus, Naevius, Pacuvius, and Accius.* Vol. 2. Cambridge, Mass.: Harvard University Press, 1936.

ACRAEA   A title given to the goddess HERA. According to EURIPIDES, MEDEA buried her children near the sanctuary of Hera Acraea. Because the play's setting is CORINTH, this title would refer to a shrine on the Corinthian ACROPOLIS, or Acrocorinth as it is usually called. [ANCIENT SOURCES: Euripides, *Medea* 1379]

ACRISIUS   A king of ARGOS, Acrisius was the son of Abas and Aglaia. He was also the brother of Proetus and husband of Eurydice. Acrisius had no male offspring and so he consulted an oracle, who told him that he would not have a son, but that a son produced by his daughter, DANAE, would kill him. To prevent his own death, Acrisius imprisoned Danae in a bronze chamber. Zeus, however, saw Danae, transformed himself into a golden shower, and impregnated her. Acrisius then placed both Danae and her child, PERSEUS, in a wooden chest, which was thrown into the sea. Perseus and Danae survived, landing on the island of SERIPHUS. Many years later, when Acrisius heard that Perseus was returning to Argos, Acrisius went to LARISA in northern Greece. According to Pausanias, Perseus heard that Acrisius was living in Larisa and went to see his grandfather. When Perseus was giving a demonstration of the discus, which Pausanias says Perseus invented, Acrisius was struck dead when he happened to walk into the path of the discus. Apollodorus differs slightly, saying that Perseus was participating in the pentathlon when he struck Acrisius (in the foot). SOPHOCLES wrote a play entitled *Acrisius,* from which some brief fragments survive (see fragments 60–76 Radt). According to Sutton, the usual view is that the play treated the "earlier phases" of the Acrisius legend. Lloyd-Jones is inclined to think that Sophocles' *Acrisius* and *Danae* were actually the same play. [ANCIENT SOURCES: Apollodorus, 2.2.1–2, 2.4.1–2.4.4; Hyginus, *Fables* 63; Pausanias, 2.16.2, 3.13.8]

BIBLIOGRAPHY

Kiso, A. *The Lost Sophocles.* New York: Vantage Press, 1984.

Lloyd-Jones, H. *Sophocles: Fragments.* Cambridge, Mass.: Harvard University Press, 1996, 29.

Radt, S. *Tragicorum Graecorum Fragmenta.* Vol. 4. Göttingen, Ger.: Vandenhoeck & Ruprecht, 1977.

Sutton, Dana. *The Lost Sophocles.* Lanham, Md.: University Press of America, 1984, 4.

ACROPOLIS   An acropolis, by definition, is the high point of a city. When one thinks of an acropolis, one usually thinks of the Athenian acropolis, the rocky rise upon which the Parthenon stands. Along with the Parthenon, the Theater of DIONYSUS, the place where the plays of dramatists such as AESCHYLUS, Sophocles,

EURIPIDES, and ARISTOPHANES were performed, was located on the slopes of the Athenian acropolis. Sometimes the Athenian acropolis serves as a location in drama. In Euripides' *ION,* APOLLO sexually assaulted CREUSA near the Athenian acropolis and near the same place Creusa abandoned the child who resulted from that union. In Aristophanes' *LYSISTRATA,* the women seize the Athenian acropolis so that they can gain control of the money kept in the Parthenon.

ACTAEON   The son of Aristaeus and AUTONOE, Actaeon was a Theban prince. Taught to hunt by CHIRON, Actaeon died while he was hunting on Mount CITHAERON. According to another tradition, ZEUS caused Actaeon's destruction because the young man tried to court SEMELE. The more common version is that Actaeon angered ARTEMIS. In *BACCHAE,* EURIPIDES says Actaeon boasted that he was a better hunter than Artemis was, while the most common tradition is that Actaeon merely saw the goddess bathing (although Hyginus says that Actaeon wanted to assault the goddess sexually). The enraged Artemis caused Actaeon to appear as a stag, which his own hunting dogs tore apart. To the Greek playwrights PHRYNICHUS, Cleophon, and Iophon are attributed plays entitled *Actaeon.* [ANCIENT SOURCES: Apollodorus, 3.4.3; Euripides, *Bacchae* 337–40; Hyginus, *Fables* 180; Ovid, *Metamorphoses* 3.138–252; Pausanias, 9.2.3; Seneca, *Oedipus* 756–63]

BIBLIOGRAPHY
Snell, B. *Tragicorum Graecorum Fragmenta.* Vol. 1. Göttingen, Ger.: Vandenhoeck & Ruprecht, 1971.

ACTE   Acte was a former slave who became NERO's mistress. [ANCIENT SOURCES: Seneca, *Octavia* 195; Tacitus, *Annals* 13.12, 42, 14.2]

ACTOR   The brother of Hyperbius, Actor defended one of THEBES' seven gates in the famous invasion led by POLYNEICES. [ANCIENT SOURCES: Aeschylus, *Seven against Thebes* 553–62]

ACTORS   In the Greek theater, men played all the roles, even those of women. In the early days of Greek drama, tradition states, only the CHORUS took the stage.

Later, a single actor joined the chorus. The usual Greek word for actor, *hupokrites,* means "answerer" or "explainer," and this term points to the relationship between the chorus and the actor. ARISTOTLE reports that AESCHYLUS introduced a second actor and that SOPHOCLES introduced a third, although clearly three actors are needed at certain points in Aeschylus' *ORESTEIA.* In COMEDY, certain plays of ARISTOPHANES (*ACHARNIANS, BIRDS, THESMOPHORIAZUSAE*) seem to require more than three actors.

One should also keep in mind that the Greek tragedians often put on a TETRALOGY (four plays) with the same group of actors in each play. Thus, the actor who played CLYTEMNESTRA in Aeschylus' *Agamemnon* and *Libation Bearers* (see *ORESTEIA*) could conceivably play ATHENA in *Eumenides* (see *ORESTEIA*) and PROTEUS in the satyr play that concluded the *Oresteia* tetralogy. Additionally, some playwrights, such as Aeschylus and Sophocles, performed in their own plays. Athenaeus reports that Sophocles played the lyre in his *Thamyras* and played some sort of ball game on stage in his *Nausicaa.*

While the number of actors eventually increased to three, two major acting styles, the "grand style" and the "realistic style," emerged in Greek drama. As the names imply, the grand style employed more extravagant language and costuming than the realistic style. The contrast in these two styles can be seen in the debate between Aeschylus and EURIPIDES in ARISTOPHANES' *FROGS.* Aeschylus is characterized as using extremely complex vocabulary, dressing his characters in extravagant clothing, and having his heroes speak and behave in a manner that is "larger than life." Euripides, in contrast, often put rags on his heroes and heroines and had them speak in a much simpler fashion.

Around 450 B.C.E., actors began competing for a prize in the dramatic festivals, and, with occasional exceptions, this ended the practice of poets' acting in their own plays. This development seems to have contributed to the rise of the importance of the actor and the decrease in the importance of the chorus. Actors became increasingly professionalized; by the fourth century B.C.E., they were more prominent than the playwrights themselves, and around 330 B.C.E. Greek actors would begin to form guilds known as the Artists of Dionysus. Acting guilds also existed in Rome as early as the second century B.C.E.

Whereas in Greek drama the actors were usually citizens, in Roman drama the actors (Latin: *histriones;* singular: *histrio*) were typically slaves and as such could be punished as slaves were (by whipping) if their performance was not satisfactory. Most Roman citizens considered acting a vile profession, although that attitude did not prevent them from going to see the various performances. As on the Greek stage, in the plays of PLAUTUS and TERENCE men would have played both male and female roles. In Rome, women could appear as dancers onstage or in MIMES and PANTOMIMES. [ANCIENT SOURCES: Aristophanes, *Acharnians* 404–34, *Frogs* 907–26, 959–67, 1058–69; Aristotle, *Poetics* 1449a15–19, *Problems* 956b11, *Rhetoric* 1403b31–35, 1404b18–25, 1405a23; Athenaeus, 1.20f: Suetonius, *Augustus* 45.3; Tacitus, *Annals* 1.77, *Histories* 2.62.2; see especially Csapo]

BIBLIOGRAPHY
Csapo, E., and W. J. Slater. *The Context of Ancient Drama.* Ann Arbor: University of Michigan Press, 1995, 221–85.
Knox, B. M. W. "Aeschylus and the Third Actor," *American Journal of Philology* 93 (1972): 104–24.

ADAMANT   A mythical dense, black substance considered the hardest of all metals. In AESCHYLUS' *PROMETHEUS BOUND,* shackles made of this material bind PROMETHEUS. According to SENECA, HERACLES used chains of this material to bind CERBERUS. PERSEUS used a sickle made of adamant to behead MEDUSA. [ANCIENT SOURCES: Aeschylus, *Prometheus Bound* 6, 64, 148; Apollodorus, *Library* 2.4.2; Seneca, *Hercules Furens* 808]

ADEIMANTUS   The cousin of ALCIBIADES, Adeimantus was an Athenian commander at the battle of Aegospotami in 406/405 B.C.E. The Spartans defeated the Athenians in this battle, and Adeimantus "was widely regarded as a traitor and responsible for the disaster" (Dover). After the battle, the Spartans were killing the Athenian captives, but they spared Adeimantus because he had opposed a decree of the Athenian Assembly regarding severing captives' hands. [ANCIENT SOURCES: Aristophanes, *Frogs* 1513; Lysias, 14.38; Xenophon, *Hellenica* 2.1.30–32]

BIBLIOGRAPHY
Dover, Kenneth. *Aristophanes: Frogs.* Oxford: Clarendon Press, 1993, 76.

ADEUES   A Persian who took part in the battle of SALAMIS. [ANCIENT SOURCES: Aeschylus, *Persians* 312]

ADITUS MAXIMUS   A Latin phrase that means "the main entrance," *aditus maximi* (plural) are the two entrance paths, usually vaulted, into the ORCHESTRA from the sides of a Roman theater. In the Greek theater, this entrance path is called a PARODOS (2).

ADMETUS   The son of PHERES and Periclymene, Admetus became king of Pherae while his father was still alive. Admetus was the husband of ALCESTIS, and by her he fathered Eumelus and Perimele. Tradition says that Admetus took part in both the quest for the Golden Fleece and the hunt for the Calydonian boar. Admetus is best known for his relationship with APOLLO, whose host he became after ZEUS sentenced Apollo to serve a mortal master for one year as punishment for Apollo's killing of some Cyclopes. Apollo was so impressed with Admetus' hospitality that the god helped Admetus gain Alcestis as his wife. Because Alcestis' father, Pelias, would allow only the man who yoked a lion and a boar to a chariot to marry her, Apollo accomplished the task for Admetus and then allowed Admetus to drive this unusual team in Pelias' presence. On Admetus and Alcestis' first night as husband and wife, Admetus forgot to sacrifice to ARTEMIS, who consequently put snakes in their bedroom. Apollo, however, helped Admetus appease his sister, Artemis. Apollo, by tricking the FATES (AESCHYLUS says he made them drunk), also arranged for Admetus to avoid death, provided that he could find someone to die in his place. Alcestis gave up her life for that of Admetu but was restored to her husband either when HERACLES wrestled her away from Thanatos, the god of death (see EURIPIDES' *ALCESTIS*), or when PERSEPHONE sent her back to the upper world. The fate of Admetus and Alcestis after this event is unknown.

Two comic poets, Aristomenes and Theopompus, wrote plays entitled *Admetus,* but no fragments survive from either play. To SOPHOCLES is attributed an *Adme-*

tus, from which no fragments survive. Admetus may have been the speaker in Sophocles, fragment 851 (Radt), who refers to a rooster that is summoning someone (Apollo?) to a mill (belonging to Admetus?).

Most of our knowledge about Admetus comes from Euripides' *Alcestis,* and modern scholars have vigorously debated the character of Admetus in this play. Is Admetus a virtuous man? In the course of the *Alcestis,* both Apollo and Heracles call Admetus the best of hosts, and in the prologue Apollo uses the same epithet, *hosios* (pious), to describe himself and Admetus. Elsewhere in the play, Admetus appears in a negative light. Admetus deceives Heracles about Alcestis' death, although the chorus seem satisfied with Admetus' explanation that he did not want to turn Heracles away because then his house would be considered unfriendly to guests. The encounter between Admetus and his father, Pheres, becomes unpleasant when Admetus essentially renounces Pheres as his father, while Pheres offers the view that some in Euripides' audience must have been considering—that Admetus was a coward and the actual cause of Alcestis' death. [ANCIENT SOURCES: Aeschylus, *Eumenides* 727–28; Apollodorus, *Library* 1.9.15; Euripides, *Alcestis;* Hyginus, *Fables* 51–52]

BIBLIOGRAPHY
Burnett, Anne Pippin. "The Virtues of Admetus," *Classical Philology* 60 (1965): 240–55.
Dyson, M. "Alcestis' Children and the Character of Admetus," *Journal of Hellenic Studies* 108 (1988): 13–23.
Kiso, A. *The Lost Sophocles.* New York: Vantage Press, 1984.
Lloyd-Jones, H. *Sophocles: Fragments.* Cambridge, Mass.: Harvard University Press, 1996.
Radt, S. *Tragicorum Graecorum Fragmenta.* Vol. 4. Göttingen, Ger.: Vandenhoeck & Ruprecht, 1977.
Sutton, D. F. *The Lost Sophocles.* Lanham, Md.: University Press of America, 1984.

ADONIA   A Greek festival (usually lasting two days) that honored ADONIS. The first day of the festival involved mourning for Adonis' disappearance; the second day was devoted to a search for his body by the community's women, with whom the Adonia was quite popular. This ritual search celebrated Adonis' return to life and a six-month reunion with his lover, APHRODITE (compare the arrangement among HADES, PERSEPHONE, and DEMETER). The festival first appears in the fifth century B.C.E. but may not have been officially sanctioned by the Athenian government during that time. [ANCIENT SOURCES: Aristophanes, *Peace* 420; Plato, *Phaedrus* 276b]

BIBLIOGRAPHY
Detienne, M. *The Gardens of Adonis: Spices in Greek Mythology.* Translated from the French by Janet Lloyd. Introduction by J. P. Vernant. Hassocks, U.K.: Harvester Press, 1977.
Simms, R. "Mourning and Community at the Athenian Adonia," *Classical Journal* 93, no. 2 (1997–1998): 121–144.
Sommerstein, A. H. *The Comedies of Aristophanes.* Vol. 5, *Peace.* Warminster, U.K.: Aris & Philips, 1985, 152.

ADONIS   The son of either Phoenix and Alphesiboea, or Cinyras and Metharme, or Cinyras (or Theias) and Myrrha (also called Smyrna), Adonis was a handsome young mortal with whom APHRODITE fell in love. Bizarre details surround the story of his birth. Myrrha, who fell in love with her father, Cinyras, managed to trick him into having sexual relations with her. When Cinyras learned what had happened, he tried to kill Myrrha, but she was transformed into a myrrh tree by the gods. Cinyras split the tree open with his sword and the infant Adonis emerged.

In one account of the story Adonis was so beautiful when he was born that Aphrodite, immediately captivated by the child, put him into a chest and gave him to PERSEPHONE with instructions not to look into the chest. Persephone's curiosity got the better of her, however, and she, also being captivated by Adonis, refused to give up the child to Aphrodite. When the dispute between the goddesses was referred to ZEUS, he decided that Adonis should spend part of the year with Aphrodite, part of the year with Persephone, and part of the year alone—an arrangement similar to the one HADES and DEMETER had regarding Persephone. Other sources say Zeus turned over the arbitration to the Muse Calliope, who decided that Adonis should spend half the year with Aphrodite and the other half with Persephone. Some say that the angered Aphrodite killed Calliope's son ORPHEUS in retaliation. Adonis, however, died young, fatally wounded by a boar.

Other sources say that Adonis was a young man when he first captured Aphrodite's attention, that she fell in love with him, and she spent much of her time with him. Adonis, however, enjoyed hunting, and Aphrodite warned him about the dangers of such sport. Unfortunately, Adonis disregarded Aphrodite's warning and was killed by a boar. The red anemone sprang up from his blood. The comic poet Nicophon wrote an *Adonis,* of which only the title survives. [ANCIENT SOURCES: Apollodorus, *Library* 3.14.3–4; Aristophanes, *Lysistrata* 389; Hyginus, *Fables* 58, 248, 251, *Poetica Astronomica* 2.7; Ovid, *Metamorphoses* 10.519–59]

BIBLIOGRAPHY

Kock, T. *Comicorum Atticorum Fragmenta.* Vol. 1. Leipzig: Teubner, 1880.

ADRASTEIA   Adrasteia, which means "she who cannot be escaped," was the daughter of ZEUS and NECESSITY. Some sources consider Adrasteia synonymous with the goddess Necessity or Nemesis. Others consider Adrasteia as a goddess who rewards those who act in a proper manner but punishes those who are proud and arrogant. Apollodorus mentions an Adrasteia as one of the nymphs who cared for Zeus when he was an infant. [ANCIENT SOURCES: Aeschylus, *Prometheus Bound* 936; Apollodorus, *Library* 1.1.6; Euripides, *Rhesus* 342–43, 468; Menander, *Girl with the Shaven Head* 304, *Samia* 503, fragment 321 Kock]

ADRASTUS   A king of ARGOS, Adrastus was the son of Talaus and Lysimache (or Eurynome). Adrastus married Amphithea and by her fathered three daughters, Argia, Deipyle, and Aegialeia, and two sons, Aegialeus and Cyanippus. An oracle of APOLLO told Adrastus to arrange the marriages of two of his daughters, one to a lion and one to a boar. When POLYNEICES of THEBES and TYDEUS of CALYDON, both exiles from their native land, fought over a place to sleep in Adrastus' palace, Adrastus noticed Polyneices had a lion on his shield and Tydeus had a boar on his shield. Realizing the oracle must be referring to Tydeus and Polyneices, Adrastus married his daughters to the two princes: Argia (or Aegialeia) to Polyneices, Deipyle to Tydeus.

Adrastus' new sons-in-law were both exiles from their native town and barred from kingdoms that they claimed. When Polyneices claimed the Theban throne held by his brother ETEOCLES, Adrastus provided Polyneices with an army and allies. The subsequent expedition became known as the Seven against Thebes. On the way to Thebes, at NEMEA, Adrastus and the other leaders competed in funeral games for Opheltes. Adrastus was champion in the horse race. Upon arrival at Thebes, each of the seven commanders assaulted one of Thebes' seven gates. Adrastus and his troops were positioned near the Homoloidian Gate. After the defeat of Polyneices and his allies, Adrastus became the sole survivor of "the Seven."

In EURIPIDES' *SUPPLIANT WOMEN,* Adrastus went to THESEUS and the Athenians for help in recovering the dead for burial. Theseus defended Adrastus and the Argives from the Thebans, who opposed Adrastus' claim. Before Theseus turned over the bodies for burial, however, ATHENA appeared and arranged for Adrastus and his citizens to swear that they would not wage war against Athens and would assist the Athenians if they were attacked. Regarding the ultimate fate of Adrastus, Pausanias reports a story from the Megarians that he died in their territory on the way back from Thebes as a result of old age and grief over the death of his son Aegialeus.

Other than in Euripides' *Suppliant Women,* Adrastus does not take the stage in any extant drama. Adrastus, however, would have appeared in other dramas that have not survived. To AESCHYLUS is attributed an Adrastus TETRALOGY that included *Nemea, Women* (or *Men*) *of Argos,* and *Men of Eleusis.* Adrastus also may appear in SOPHOCLES' *Epigonoi.* Fragment 187 suggests an encounter between Adrastus and ALCMEON in which Alcmeon reproaches Adrastus with being the brother of ERIPHYLE, whose actions brought about the death of her husband, AMPHIARAUS, and Adrastus retorts that Alcmeon killed his mother, Eriphyle. The tragedian Achaeus also wrote a play entitled *Adrastus,* from which a single word survives. [ANCIENT SOURCES: Apollodorus, 1.9.13, 3.6.1–3.7.1; Euripides, *Phoenician Women, Suppliant Women;* Hyginus, *Fables* 69–71; Pausanias, 1.43.1, 9.5.13]

BIBLIOGRAPHY

Kiso, A. *The Lost Sophocles*. New York: Vantage Press, 1984.

Lloyd-Jones, H. *Sophocles: Fragments*. Cambridge, Mass.: Harvard University Press, 1996.

Radt, S. *Tragicorum Graecorum Fragmenta*. Vol. 4. Göttingen, Ger.: Vandenhoeck & Ruprecht, 1977.

Snell, B. *Tragicorum Graecorum Fragmenta*. Vol. 1. Göttingen, Ger.: Vandenhoeck & Ruprecht, 1971.

Sutton, D. F. *The Lost Sophocles*. Lanham, Md.: University Press of America, 1984.

ADRIA Poets use the name Adria to refer to both a region in northern Italy and the Adriatic Sea.

ADULESCENS The *adulescens* (plural: *adulescentes*), a stock character in Roman COMEDY, is a young man usually in his late teens or twenties and usually unmarried. Typically, the *adulescens* spends his time either pursuing the love of a PROSTITUTE or a slave girl, who eventually turns out to be a freeborn woman, or helping another *adulescens* acquire the object of his affection. The *adulescens* must usually either avoid having his father find out about the woman with whom he is in love or find money to pay off the PIMP who owns her. The *adulescens* is most often aided by a clever slave, who will try to prevent the young man's father from finding out about the love affair and try to find money to pay off the pimp. Whereas Plautus' plays usually feature one *adulescens* in love, most of Terence's plays have two *adulescentes*. Whereas PARASITES often make comments about their desire for food, the *adulescens* frequently comment on the grief and hardship that being in love is causing him. In some instances, the *adulescens* expresses thoughts of suicide when he thinks he will be unable to have his beloved, but this extreme action never comes to pass. Duckworth remarks that "the youths of Terence as a rule are more respectful and respectable than those of Plautus, they are also less amusing and somewhat less colorful."

BIBLIOGRAPHY

Duckworth, G. E. *The Nature of Roman Comedy*. Princeton, N.J.: Princeton University Press, 1952, 242.

AEACUS The son of ZEUS and Aegina, Aeacus married Endeis and by her had PELEUS and Telamon. By the NEREID Psamathe, he had another son, Phocus. When Aeacus was born, the island where he lived was uninhabited. After Aeacus prayed to Zeus to populate the island, the god transformed the island's ants into humans. Aeacus named the people Myrmidons, from the Greek word for "ant" (*myrmex*). Other sources say that the people were born from the earth or that they appeared after a plague had wiped out the island's people. After the island was populated, Aeacus renamed it after his mother and became the island's ruler. Aeacus gained fame for his piety and his sense of justice. When Nisus and Sciron quarreled about the kingship of MEGARA, Aeacus arbitrated the dispute and made Nisus the king but put Sciron in charge of military affairs. Sciron was so pleased that he gave his daughter, Endeis, to Aeacus as his wife. When Greece suffered from barrenness because of PELOPS' killing of Stamphylus, an oracle declared that the barrenness would end if Aeacus prayed for Greece. Aeacus did, and the famine ended. When Peleus and Telamon killed their brother, Phocus, Aeacus exiled his two surviving sons. Because of his just decisions in the upper world, Aeacus was rewarded by becoming a judge in the UNDERWORLD or being allowed to keep Hades' keys. Aeacus appears as a character in ARISTOPHANES' *Frogs,* in which he tortures DIONYSUS and Xanthias to determine which of them is a god and which a slave. Aeacus also had a speaking role in Euripides' *Peirithous,* which dealt with the title character's entrapment in the underworld. [ANCIENT SOURCES: Apollodorus, *Library* 3.12.6; Aristophanes, *Frogs;* Hesiod, *Theogony* 1003–4; Hyginus, *Fables* 52; Isocrates, 9.13–15; Ovid, *Metamorphoses* 7.472–660; Pausanias, 1.44.9, 2.29.2–2.30.5]

BIBLIOGRAPHY

Page, D. L. *Select Papyri*. Vol. 3. 1941. Reprint, London: Heinemann, 1970.

AEDILE In Roman society, the aedile was a magistrate who oversaw the finances required to organize theatrical productions. [ANCIENT SOURCES: Plautus, *Persian* 160]

AEETES   A king of COLCHIS, Aeetes was the son of Helios, god of the SUN, and Persa. Aeetes was the husband of Chalciope and by her became the father of MEDEA and ABSYRTUS, although some sources call Medea the daughter of Aeetes and Idyia. When JASON traveled to Colchis and asked for the Golden Fleece, Aeetes told Jason he would give him the fleece if he yoked a pair of fire-breathing bulls and plowed a field with the teeth of a dragon. Jason was successful, thanks to the help of Medea, but Aeetes did not turn over the fleece. Instead, Aeetes plotted to kill Jason and burn his ship. With Medea's help, Jason made off with the fleece. Afterward, Aeetes lost his kingdom to his brother Perses but he regained it with Medea's help when she returned to Colchis after her expulsion from Athens. Some sources say that Medea herself killed Perses and restored Aeetes to the throne; others report that Medea had her son MEDUS kill Perses and then take the kingdom for himself. [ANCIENT SOURCES: Apollodorus, *Library* 1.9.23; Apollonius Rhodius, 2.1140–4.241; Hyginus, *Fables* 22–23]

AEGEAN SEA   The sea located to the east of mainland Greece and the west of modern-day Turkey. According to the myth, the sea got its name when AEGEUS, the father of THESEUS, committed suicide by hurling himself into it.

AEGEIRA   A town near the coast of the region of Achaea, Aegeira is mentioned in AESCHYLUS, fragment 284 (Radt).

BIBLIOGRAPHY
Radt, S. *Tragicorum Graecorum Fragmenta.* Vol. 3. Göttingen, Ger.: Vandenhoeck & Ruprecht, 1985.

AEGEUS   The son of Pandion (or Scyrius) and Pylia, Aegeus was a king of ATHENS. Because Aegeus had no children by either his first wife, Meta, or his second wife, Rhexenor, he consulted the DELPHIC ORACLE. According to EURIPIDES' *MEDEA,* the oracle told him not to loose the mouth of his wineskin until he reached Athens. The hidden meaning of the oracle was that Aegeus was not supposed to have sexual intercourse until he returned to Athens. Any child conceived before Aegeus returned to Athens would cause Aegeus' doom. Aegeus, however, not understanding the oracle, decided to ask his friend Pittheus about the meaning. According to EURIPIDES' *Medea,* Aegeus passed through CORINTH on his way to Pittheus' home in TROEZEN. En route through Corinth, Aegeus met Medea and mentioned the oracle to her. Medea did not interpret the oracle for Aegeus but promised she would help him have children through her skills in magic if he would grant her asylum in Athens after she left Corinth. Aegeus agreed to Medea's proposal and then set out for Pittheus' home. Pittheus did understand the oracle, but his desire for grandchildren apparently outweighed his friendship with Aegeus. Accordingly, Pittheus made Aegeus drunk and arranged for him to have intercourse with his daughter Aethra. On the same night, POSEIDON also had intercourse with Aethra, who became pregnant and eventually gave birth to THESEUS. The next morning, Aegeus departed Pittheus' house and left a sword and a pair of sandals under a large rock. Aegeus instructed Aethra that if she gave birth to a son and the son were ever able to lift the rock and retrieve these items, that child should be sent to him at Athens.

After Aegeus returned to Athens, he married Medea and fathered MEDUS by her. Many years later, when Theseus grew up, he retrieved the sword and sandals and traveled to Athens. When Theseus arrived, Medea realized that he would replace her son Medus as heir to the Athenian throne. To prevent this, Medea, having convinced Aegeus that Theseus was planning to kill him, plotted to have Aegeus give Theseus a poisoned cup of wine at a banquet. When Aegeus recognized the sword and sandals that Theseus wore as his own, Aegeus caused the poisoned wine to be spilled. Medea was then driven from Athens.

The reunion of Aegeus and Theseus was brief. Many years earlier, some Athenians had killed Androgeus, the son of MINOS, king of CRETE, during his visit to Athens. In retaliation, Minos waged war against Athens, defeated its soldiers, and imposed a severe penalty upon its citizens: The Athenians were obligated to send seven young men and seven maidens to be sacrificed to the MINOTAUR every nine years. Not long after Theseus arrived in Athens, this tribute fell due. Theseus volunteered to be one of the victims. Although Theseus survived his journey to Crete, Aegeus believed that Theseus was killed during the mission. When Theseus had left Athens, the ship was flying a dark-colored sail. Aegeus told Theseus to change the sail to a light-colored one if he had been successful on Crete. Upon returning to Athens, Theseus forgot to change the ship's sail. When Aegeus, anxiously awaiting Theseus' return from Crete, saw Theseus' ship flying a dark-colored sail, he assumed Theseus had died and threw himself into the sea, which was then named the AEGEAN after him.

SOPHOCLES wrote an *Aegeus* that appears to have dealt with the arrival of Theseus in Athens and his subsequent reunion with his father (see fragments 19–25a Radt). Euripides also wrote an *Aegeus* (fragments 1–13 Nauck). [ANCIENT SOURCES: Apollodorus, *Library* 3.15.6–7; Euripides, *Medea;* Hyginus, *Fables* 37, 43]

BIBLIOGRAPHY
Kiso, A. *The Lost Sophocles.* New York: Vantage Press, 1984.
Nauck, A. *Tragicorum Graecorum Fragmenta.* 1889. Reprint, Hildesheim, Ger.: Olms, 1964.
Radt, S. *Tragicorum Graecorum Fragmenta.* Vol. 4. Göttingen, Ger.: Vandenhoeck & Ruprecht, 1977.
Sutton, D. F. *The Lost Sophocles.* Lanham, Md.: University Press of America, 1984.
Webster, T. B. L. *The Tragedies of Euripides.* London: Methuen, 1967.

AEGINA   This small island, off the coast of ATHENS in the Saronic Gulf, was the home of AEACUS and the birthplace of PELEUS and Telamon. The island took its name from Aeacus' mother, Aegina, with whom ZEUS had sexual relations. [ANCIENT SOURCES: Aristophanes, *Acharnians* 653, *Frogs* 353, *Wasps* 122]

AEGIPLANCTUS   Mount Aegiplanctus, west of ATHENS near MEGARA, was one of the points by which CLYTEMNESTRA's signal fires (indicating the end of the Trojan War) were relayed. [ANCIENT SOURCES: Aeschylus, *Agamemnon* 303 (see ORESTEIA)].

AEGIS   The aegis (Greek for "goatskin"), described as either a breastplate or a shawllike garment worn over the head and shoulders, had the scales of a serpent, may have been ringed with serpents, and had the face of a gorgon on it. In EURIPIDES' *ION,* we hear that Athena killed a certain gorgon and then used its skin as the aegis. Other sources said that the aegis was the skin of the goat Amalthea, who had suckled the infant ZEUS. The aegis is most associated with Zeus and ATHENA, who often caused fear by shaking it. In a story about a fight between Athena and Pallas, Zeus tries to part the combatants by putting the aegis between them. [ANCIENT SOURCES: Apollodorus, *Library* 3.12.3; Aristophanes, *Clouds* 603; Euripides, *Ion* 989–96; Seneca, *Agamemnon* 528–32]

AEGISTHUS   Aegisthus' birth resulted from the incestuous union of THYESTES and his daughter Pelopea. Not long after Thyestes impregnated Pelopea—he sexually assaulted her—Pelopea married Thyestes' brother, ATREUS. As soon as Aegisthus was born, Pelopea left the child to die, but he was found by a shepherd, who allowed him a she goat to suckle him. The name Aegisthus means "strength from a goat." When Atreus learned that the child had been left to die, Atreus, believing that he was the child's father, retrieved Aegisthus. A number of years later, Atreus, who hated Thyestes, captured his brother and imprisoned him at his house. Atreus, wanting to kill Thyestes, sent the young Aegisthus to kill him. Thyestes, however, recognized the sword that Aegisthus carried as one that he had dropped when he had sexually assaulted Pelopea. Thyestes asked Aegisthus from whom he had received the sword, and when Thyestes learned that the boy's mother had given it to him, Thyestes asked to see the boy's mother. When Pelopea was face to face with Thyestes and realized that she had produced a child by her father, she committed suicide with the sword. Thyestes then revealed to Aegisthus that he, not Atreus, was his father. Aegisthus, instructed by Thyestes, took the sword and killed Atreus. Thyestes again became king of Argos but was soon driven out by Atreus' son AGAMEMNON. Thyestes and Aegisthus then went into exile, after which apparently Thyestes died. After Thyestes' death, Aegisthus tried to avenge his father. While Agamemnon was fighting at Troy to recover HELEN, Aegisthus seduced Agamemnon's wife,

CLYTEMNESTRA, and then plotted with her to murder Agamemnon when he returned from the Trojan War. Aegisthus died at the hands of Agamemnon's son, ORESTES, who avenged his father's murder.

Aegisthus appears as a character in AESCHYLUS' *Agamemnon* and *Libation Bearers* (see ORESTEIA), EURIPIDES' *ELECTRA*, SOPHOCLES' *ELECTRA*, and SENECA's *AGAMEMNON*. ACCIUS wrote a tragic *AEGISTHUS*, from which survive several fragments. That play seems to have dealt with Orestes' killing of Aegisthus and Clytemnestra. [ANCIENT SOURCES: Aeschylus, *Agamemnon, Libation Bearers* (see ORESTEIA); Euripides, *Electra*; Hyginus, *Fables* 87–88, 119; Seneca, *Agamemnon*; Sophocles, *Electra*]

AEGOCERUS Aegocerus, "goat-horned," is another name for the constellation Capricorn. [ANCIENT SOURCES: Seneca, *Thyestes* 864]

AEGYPTUS As his name indicates, Aegyptus was a mythical king of Egypt and the brother of Danaus. Aegyptus wanted his 50 sons to marry Danaus' 50 daughters, known as the DANAIDS. The women refused and fled to Greece with their father. The sons of Aegyptus pursued the Danaids to Greece and forced the women to marry them. Danaus persuaded his daughters to murder their new husbands. With the exception of one son, Lynceus, all Aegyptus' sons died. [ANCIENT SOURCES: Aeschylus, *Suppliant Women*; Aristophanes, *Frogs* 1206]

AENEAS The son of Anchises and APHRODITE, Aeneas was one of the greatest of the Trojan warriors during the Trojan War. He was also one of the few Trojan males to survive the fall of TROY. With his son Ascanius (also called Iulus), Aeneas eventually made his way to Italy, where he founded a settlement. Among the Greek dramas, Aeneas appears as a character in one extant play, EURIPIDES' *RHESUS*. Here, Aeneas cautions Hector against rushing hastily into battle against the Greeks and advises instead that they send a spy to determine the Greeks' intentions. Among Roman authors, ACCIUS wrote a historical drama (see *FABULA PRAETEXTA*), *Sons of Aeneas* (Latin: *Aeneadae*), a play about the victory of Decius Mus over the Samnites

and Gauls in 295 B.C.E. (see lines 1–16 Warmington). [ANCIENT SOURCES: Homer, *Iliad* 5, 17, 20; Hyginus, *Fables* 112, 273; Ovid, *Metamorphoses* 14.75–608; Vergil, *Aeneid*]

BIBLIOGRAPHY
Warmington, E. H. *Remains of Old Latin: Livius Andronicus, Naevius, Pacuvius, and Accius.* Vol. 2. Cambridge, Mass.: Harvard University Press, 1936.

AENIANES A tribe who lived in northeastern Greece near TRACHIS.

AEOLUS The son of Hellen and Orseis, Aeolus was the brother of Dorus and XUTHUS. When Hellen divided Greece among his sons, Aeolus acquired Thessaly and called its inhabitants Aeolians. Aeolus had numerous sons and daughters by his wife, Enarete; some sources name ATHAMAS, CRETHEUS, SALMONEUS, and SISYPHUS among them. Another of Aeolus' sons, Macareus, raped his sister Canace, who tried to conceal the birth of their child by pretending to be sick. Macareus persuaded his father to let Macareus and his brothers marry their sisters. Aeolus agreed and drew lots, but Canace's lot fell to someone other than Macareus. After Aeolus learned of the incestuous relationship of Macareus and Canace, he sent Canace a sword, with which she committed suicide. Macareus then committed suicide. EURIPIDES wrote the play *Aeolus* (fragments 14–41 Nauck), which Webster thinks was staged before 423 B.C.E. and appears to have dealt with the incest and deaths of Canace and Macareus.

BIBLIOGRAPHY
Casali, Sergio. "Ovid's Canace and Euripides' *Aeolus*: Two Notes on *Heroides* 11," *Mnemosyne* 51, no. 6 (1998): 700–10.
Webster, T. B. L. *The Tragedies of Euripides*. London: Methuen, 1967.

AEROPE When Catreus, king of CRETE, learned from an oracle that he would be killed by one of his children, he gave NAUPLIUS his daughter Aerope (and some add her sister, Clymene), to sell in a foreign country (or to kill). Nauplius, however, spared the girl or girls. Some sources say Aerope came to MYCENAE and married PLEISTHENES, the son of ATREUS. When Pleisthenes died, Aerope married Atreus. Aerope had a daughter, Anaxibia, and two sons, Atreus and THYESTES; however, the ancient sources differ as to whether the children's father was Pleisthenes or Atreus. Aerope, however, had an affair with Atreus' brother, Thyestes, and gave to Thyestes a golden lamb that belonged to Atreus. The people of Argos had agreed that whoever possessed this lamb would be king. After Atreus discovered Aerope's betrayal, he had her drowned.

Aerope does not appear as a character in any surviving plays, although her story was dealt with in several fragmentary works. Euripides' *Cretan Women,* produced in 438 B.C.E., appears to have treated Aerope's encounter with Nauplius. AGATHON wrote an *Aerope,* from which a single word survives (fragment 1 Snell). The younger Carcinus also wrote an *Aerope,* of which only the title survives. [ANCIENT SOURCES: Apollodorus, *Library* 3.2.1–2, *Epitome* 2.10; Euripides, *Helen* 390–92, *Orestes* 18; Hyginus, *Fables* 87]

BIBLIOGRAPHY
Snell, B. *Tragicorum Graecorum Fragmenta.* Vol. 1. Göttingen, Ger.: Vandenhoeck & Ruprecht, 1971.

AESCHIINADES
An otherwise unknown person mentioned by ARISTOPHANES at *Peace* 1154.

AESCHINES
A minor Athenian statesman prominent in the 420s and 410s B.C.E. who falsely claimed to be wealthy. In the year 423, he may have accompanied AMYNIAS "on an embassy to Pharsalus in 423" (Sommerstein), and in 418/417 he served on the board that oversaw the contributions made by members of the Athenian empire. [ANCIENT SOURCES: Aristophanes, *Birds* 823, *Wasps* 325, 459, 1220, 1243]

BIBLIOGRAPHY
Sommerstein, A. H. *The Comedies of Aristophanes.* Vol. 4, *Wasps.* Warminster, U.K.: Aris & Phillips, 1983, 185.
Storey, I. C. *Komodoumenoi and Komodein in Old Comedy.* Toronto: University of Toronto, 1977, 150.

AESCHYLUS (AISCHYLOS) (525/524–456/455 B.C.E.)
Because the oldest extant dramas are those of Aeschylus, this playwright is often called the father of Greek TRAGEDY. Written more than a quarter-century after Aeschylus' death, ARISTOPHANES plays (especially *FROGS*) portray Aeschylus as the best of the Athenian tragedians, especially in the view of the elders and conservative thinkers in the Athenian society of the fifth century. Moreover, during Aristophanes' career, Aeschylus was the only tragedian whose dramas were restaged in ATHENS. At the opening of Aristophanes' *ACHARNIANS,* produced in 425, the hero recalls his disappointment when an expected tragedy from Aeschylus is not staged. At the conclusion of Aristophanes' *Frogs,* produced 20 years later, DIONYSUS takes Aeschylus back to the upper world because he is best able to instruct the Athenians.

Aeschylus, the son of Euphorion, and a native of Eleusis, also served alongside his fellow countrymen in their battles against the Persians at MARATHON, Artemisium, and SALAMIS (Pausanias 1.14.5). Little information exists about the nature of Aeschylus' youth and education; his first play was produced between 500 and 496. The anonymous *Life of Aeschylus* (*Vita Aeschyli 13*) reports that Aeschylus won 13 first prizes at dramatic competitions at the CITY DIONYSIA in Athens, the first victory in 484, according to *Parian Marble.* The article on Aeschylus in the *Suda* (a historical encyclopedia written in Greek in the 10th century) adds another 15 victories, presumably at other festivals than the City Dionysia.

Aeschylus visited SICILY twice. In 476/475, he went to the island as the guest of King Hiero of Syracuse. During Aeschylus' stay there, he wrote *Aitnaiai* (*Women of Aetna*) to honor that city, which Hiero had recently founded. During Aeschylus' second visit to Sicily, his life ended at the town of Gela. For obvious reasons, modern scholars do not give credence to the popular story that Aeschylus died when an eagle dropped a tortoise onto his head. More than 80 dramas are attributed to Aeschylus, of which only seven survive: *PERSIANS* (472 B.C.E.), *THE SEVEN AGAINST THEBES* (467), *SUPPLIANT WOMEN* (ca. 466–459), and the *ORESTEIA* trilogy, which consisted of *Agamemnon, Libation Bearers,* and *Eumenides* (458). The authorship and date of the seventh drama, *PROMETHEUS BOUND,* are disputed. Although Aeschylus is best known as a writer of tragedies, a SATYR PLAY would normally conclude a tragedian's TETRALOGY, and Pausanias says Aeschylus' satyr plays were popular, though none survives today.

Aeschylus' plays reveal the following characteristics: First, Aeschylus had a reputation for visually stimulating costumes. Pausanias writes that Aeschylus (in *Eumenides*) was the first to show the Furies with snakes in their hair. Aeschylus was also noted for complex imagery and diction. Aristophanes (*FROGS* 926) exaggerates that the spectators could not understand much of what Aeschylus said, but in *Agamemnon* (827–28), for example, the Greek army's destruction of TROY is described as a savage lion's leaping over its walls and lapping up royal blood. Aeschylean drama is also characterized by prologues that are either brief or not present at all. Aeschylean choruses also have a prominent role. Of the six surviving plays regarded as genuinely Aeschylean, the CHORUS speak almost half of the lines. Contrast the seven extant plays of SOPHOCLES, in which the chorus deliver a little more than one-third of the lines. Thus, Aeschylean choral odes are generally longer than what we find later in Sophocles or EURIPIDES. The first choral passage in *Agamemnon* approaches 225 lines; the chorus open *Suppliant Women* with 175 lines of song. Often, Aeschylean scenes consist of a single actor's speaking to the chorus (e.g., *Suppliant Women* 176–907) or two actors' addressing one another. In fact, at *Poetics* 1449a, Aristotle says Aeschylus was the first to increase the number of actors from one to two. In *Suppliant Women*, only three other characters besides the chorus speak in the play. The largest number of speaking characters, seven, are in *Libation Bearers* (see ORESTEIA). At *Frogs* 911–15, Aristophanes also suggests that Aeschylus had a habit of having characters on stage who would remain silent for an inordinately long period.

As for themes commonly treated by Aeschylus, Ferguson states that "they are found in the great moral problems at the heart of the universe." In the *Oresteia*, for example, Agamemnon and Orestes must choose between obedience to the gods and killing of a family member. The ultimate triumph of justice over HUBRIS, violent arrogance, also commonly occurs in Aeschylus' extant plays. At *Persians* 749, Aeschylus has Xerxes' own father, Darius, portray his son as someone who tried to defeat even the gods themselves. Xerxes fails because the gods will not allow a violent and wicked man to triumph. In *Suppliant Women,* the daughters of DANAUS pray to ZEUS to deliver them from the hubris of the sons of AEGYPTUS. At *Agamemnon* 944–57, the title character's fate is sealed when he walks on the purple tapestries—an act that he himself realizes should be reserved only for divinities. Acts of hubris that violate the customs of HOSPITALITY (*xenia*) are also highlighted in Aeschylus. PARIS' abduction of HELEN and ATREUS' slaughter of THYESTES' children at a banquet are central to the events of *Agamemnon*, and both violators are ultimately punished.

At *Frogs* 913–27, Aristophanes suggests that Aeschylus taught his fellow citizens how to behave properly in times of peace or war, and that the most noble achievement to which a citizen could aspire was to triumph over one's enemies. Because Aeschylus had a reputation for dramas that dealt with war, Aristophanes (*Frogs* 1045) not surprisingly suggests Aeschylus' works had nothing to do with Aphrodite, that is, love. With less than 10 percent of Aeschylus' work surviving, it is difficult to say to what extent Aristophanes' claim is true. Aeschylus certainly wrote about women with whom gods such as Zeus (compare the title character of *Semele*) and Poseidon (compare the title character of the satyric *Amymone*) had affairs. Aeschylus does not, however, seem to have put on stage women such as PHAEDRA or STHENEBOEA (as Euripides did), who actively attempted to seduce men forbidden to them. In Aeschylus' *Agamemnon,* adulterous CLYTEMNESTRA is motivated to kill her husband, Agamemnon, more because of her love for the daughter whom Agamemnon sacrificed than of any passion she has for her lover, AEGISTHUS. Although Euripides may have had a reputation for writing plays about evil women, the younger playwright certainly had a model to draw on in Aeschylus' Clytemnestra.

Ultimately, Aeschylus celebrates the Athenian way of life, the triumph of civilization over barbarism. At *Persians* 1025–26, the defeated enemy acknowledge the valor of the Athenian people. In *Eumenides* (see ORESTEIA) bloodshed over several generations in the house of Tantalus is resolved ultimately through the agency of Athens' patron goddess, ATHENA, and her citizens. Athena even manages to calm the wrath of the

Furies and incorporate them into the city that Aeschylus himself served both on the battlefield and in the theater. [ANCIENT SOURCES: Herodotus, 2.156.1; Pausanias, 1.2.3, 1.28.6, 2.13.6, 2.24.4, 8.37.6; Plutarch, *Cimon* 8.8]

BIBLIOGRAPHY

Conacher, D. J. *Aeschylus: The Earlier Plays and Related Studies.* Toronto: University of Toronto Press, 1996.

Ferguson, J. *A Companion to Greek Tragedy.* Austin: University of Texas Press, 1972, 33.

Gargarin, M. *Aeschylean Drama.* Berkeley, Los Angeles, and London: University of California Press, 1976.

Otis, B. *Cosmos and Tragedy: An Essay on the Meaning of Aeschylus.* Chapel Hill: University of North Carolina Press, 1981.

Podlecki, A. J. *The Political Background of Aeschylean Tragedy.* Ann Arbor: University of Michigan Press, 1966.

Rosenmeyer, T. G. *The Art of Aeschylus.* Berkeley: University of California Press, 1982.

Sommerstein, A. H. *Aeschylean Tragedy.* Bari, Italy: Levante, 1996.

Taplin, O. *The Stagecraft of Aeschylus.* Oxford: Oxford University Press, 1977.

West, M. L. *Studies in Aeschylus.* Stuttgart: B. G. Teubner, 1990.

Winnington-Ingram, R. P. *Studies in Aeschylus.* Cambridge: Cambridge University Press, 1983.

AESCULAPIUS   See ASCLEPIUS.

AESIMUS   An Athenian statesman prominent between 403 and the 370s B.C.E. Aesimus led the forces for democracy in the Athenian civil war of 403, went on an embassy to CHIOS in 384, and served the Second Athenian League in 378/377 by leading a tour of the AEGEAN for the purpose of, among other things, swearing in new members of the league. ARISTOPHANES mentions him at *ECCLESIAZUSAE* 208 as someone badly treated by the Athenian public. [ANCIENT SOURCES: Lysias, 13.80]

BIBLIOGRAPHY

Sommerstein, A. H. *The Comedies of Aristophanes.* Vol. 10, *Ecclesiazusae.* Warminster, U.K.: Aris & Phillips, 1998, 158.

AESOP   Living on the island of SAMOS during the first half of the sixth century B.C.E., Aesop was a famous fabulist (especially telling stories involving animals). [ANCIENT SOURCES: Aristophanes, *Birds* 471, 651, *Peace* 129, *Wasps* 566, 1259; Herodotus, 2.134.3–4]

AETHRA   See THESEUS.

AETNA (ETNA)   At approximately 3,350 meters high, Aetna, on SICILY, is the highest active volcano in Europe. In mythology, Aetna was often considered the home of the CYCLOPES and the location of HEPHAESTUS' forge. ZEUS ended the fire-breathing monster TYPHON's reign of terror by throwing Aetna on top of the monster. AESCHYLUS wrote the play *Women of Aetna* (fragments 6–10 Radt), which appears to have dealt with a Sicilian woman named Aetna (or Thaleia), who, after having become pregnant with twin sons by Zeus, prayed that the Earth would swallow her so that she could avoid punishment by HERA. Aetna's prayer was answered, but the Earth opened again and her sons emerged. The boys were called the Palici (those who come back) and people who lived near Mount Aetna worshiped them. EURIPIDES' *CYCLOPS* has a cave beneath Aetna as its setting. [ANCIENT SOURCES: Aeschylus, *Prometheus Bound* 351–65; Aristophanes, *Peace* 73; Euripides, *Cyclops*; Macrobius, 5.19.17; Seneca, *Medea* 410; Servius on Vergil, *Aeneid* 9.584]

BIBLIOGRAPHY

Smyth, H. W., and H. Lloyd-Jones. *Aeschylus.* Vol. 2. 1926. Reprint, Cambridge, Mass.: Harvard University Press, 1971, 381–82.

AETOLIA   A region in northwestern Greece east of the ACHELOUS RIVER. In mythology, OENEUS, MELEAGER, and DEIANEIRA were all Aetolians. In SENECA's *HERCULES OETAEUS*, a chorus of Aetolian women appear. The Greek comic poet Philemon wrote a play titled *Aetolian* (*Aitolos*), of which only a single word survives: "light" (*elaphros*) (see fragment 6 Kock).

BIBLIOGRAPHY

Kock, T. *Comicorum Atticorum Fragmenta.* Vol. 2. Leipzig: Teubner, 1884.

AFRANIUS (BORN CA. 150 B.C.E.)   Lucius Afranius produced more comedies whose characters wore native (Roman) dress (see *FABULA TOGATA*) than any other Roman poet. Some 430 fragments (most no more than two lines long) survive and 42 titles are known. Afranius' poetry focuses on the "middle" classes of society and life in the family. The poetry of TERENCE influenced him, and Horace compares him with MENANDER; he himself indicates his debt to Menander in a fragment from the prologue of his *Compitalia*. Quintilian thought Afranius excelled in the *fabulae togatae* but wished that he "had not defiled his plots" with tales of love affairs of males. [ANCIENT SOURCES: Horace, *Epistle* 2.1.57; Quintilian, 10.1.100]

BIBLIOGRAPHY

Beare, W. *The Roman Stage.* London: Methuen, 1950, 128–136.
Ribbeck, O. *Tragicorum Romanorum Fragmenta.* Leipzig, 1897.

AGAMEMNON

The son of ATREUS (or Plisthenes) and AEROPE, Agamemnon became the king of MYCENAE. Agamemnon was the husband of CLYTEMNESTRA, and by her he became the father of ORESTES, IPHIGENIA, ELECTRA, and Chrysothemis. When HELEN, the wife of Agamemnon's brother MENELAUS, was abducted by the Trojan PARIS, Agamemnon joined his brother in the military efforts to recover Helen. Agamemnon served as the commander in chief of the Greek expedition during the Trojan War and before the Greek fleet sailed for Troy was forced to make a decision whose full effect would not be felt until many years later. When the Greek fleet gathered at AULIS, poor weather conditions prevented them from sailing. When the prophet CALCHAS was consulted as to the reason, the problem was blamed on Agamemnon, who had offended the goddess ARTEMIS. The only way to remedy the situation, according to the prophet, was for Agamemnon to sacrifice his daughter Iphigenia to the goddess. Fearing repercussions from the Greek army if he failed to act, Agamemnon had Iphigenia taken to Aulis with the pretext that she was to marry Achilles. According to EURIPIDES' *IPHIGENIA AT AULIS,* when Iphigenia discovered the reason she had been taken to Aulis, she willingly sacrificed herself. Whereas AESCHYLUS' Agamemnon states that he sacrificed his daughter, Euripides' plays about Iphigenia portray Artemis as rescuing Iphigenia at the last moment. In either case, the adverse weather subsided, and the Greek fleet was able to sail for Troy.

After the war begins, we hear relatively little about Agamemnon, despite his lofty position as commander of the Greek army. Because the Trojans generally avoided direct confrontation, the Greeks had to content themselves with raiding towns in the areas around Troy. During one of these raids, Agamemnon was awarded a female captive, Chryseis. According to Homer's *Iliad,* during the 10th year of the war, Chryseis' father, Chryses, a priest of APOLLO, went to the Greek camp to try to ransom his daughter from Agamemnon. When Agamemnon angrily refused, the priest prayed to Apollo for vengeance. The god obliged his priest by sending a plague upon the Greek camp. When the Greek prophet Calchas announced that Agamemnon's rejection of Chryses' request was the cause of the plague and that the situation could be remedied by his daughter's return, Agamemnon reluctantly agreed to return the girl but demanded that he be given another to replace her. As Achilles had been the primary supporter of the effort to restore Chryseis to her father, he had angered Agamemnon, who decided to take for himself Achilles' female war captive, Briseis. This action so enraged Achilles that he refused to fight any longer.

With Achilles out of the fighting, the Trojans took hope and made renewed assaults on the Greeks and their camp. As the Trojans were successful, Agamemnon offered Achilles a huge reward to return to the fighting, but Achilles rejected this offer. After Achilles' comrade PATROCLUS was killed in battle, Achilles returned to the fighting and settled his quarrel with Agamemnon, who restored Briseis to him. In Aeschylus' *Agamemnon* (see *ORESTEIA*), Agamemnon returns from Troy with the Trojan prophetess CASSANDRA as his concubine and is killed by his wife, Clytemnestra, and her lover, Aegisthus.

Agamemnon appears as a character in Aeschylus' *Agamemnon*, SOPHOCLES' *AJAX,* Euripides' *HECABE* and *Iphigenia at Aulis,* and SENECA's *AGAMEMNON*. Agamemnon would also have appeared as a character in numerous other plays that no longer survive. We also know that he appeared in Euripides' *Telephus*. Agamemnon was known for his skill with a spear, but he does not have the superior fighting power of Achilles, Ajax, or Diomedes. Agamemnon's function in classical drama is usually that of a decision maker or arbiter, and on the classical stage Agamemnon is often placed in situations in which the decision he must make is a difficult one. His most difficult choice, of course, is whether to sacrifice his daughter Iphigenia. In Sophocles' *Ajax*, Agamemnon and Menelaus oppose the burial of their comrade Ajax, who had attempted to kill them in a fit of rage when he was not given the armor of Achilles. Agamemnon's role in Euripides' *Hecabe* is minor, as he acts as an arbiter in the grievance between Hecabe and Polymestor. He sides with Hecabe though she is the wife of his enemy.

AGAMEMNON   A Play by AESCHYLUS. See also ORESTEIA.

AGAMEMNON SENECA (WRITTEN BETWEEN 49 AND 65 C.E.?)   As is AESCHYLUS' play of the same name, SENECA's drama is set at AGAMEMNON's palace at ARGOS. Unlike Aeschylus' play, whose prologue is delivered by the mortal watchman of the house, Seneca's play opens supernaturally as the ghost of THYESTES (cf. the ghost of Tantalus in the opening of Seneca's *THYESTES*), whose brother ATREUS served him his own children for dinner, predicts AEGISTHUS' revenge against Atreus' son Agamemnon. Seneca also changes the makeup of the CHORUS, replacing Aeschylus' Argive elders with Argive women. Their opening song on Fortune has little thematic connection to Thyestes' prologue or the ensuing conversation between CLYTEMNESTRA and her nurse, in which the queen ponders the course of action she will take against her husband when he returns from Troy. Clytemnestra, moved by Agamemnon's sacrifice of IPHIGENIA at Aulis and the fact that Agamemnon takes home with him the war captive CASSANDRA, appears to decide to kill both her husband and his concubine. Soon, however, Clytemnestra begins to waver because of her feelings for Agamemnon. Aegisthus, however, tries to persuade her otherwise.

After the exit of Clytemnestra and Aegisthus, the chorus sing a hymn invoking APOLLO, Juno (Greek: HERA), Minerva (Greek: ATHENA), Diana (Greek: ARTEMIS), and Jove (Greek: ZEUS). After their song, a herald, Eurybates, enters and makes a lengthy speech

(15 percent of the play) describing the journey of the Greek fleet from TROY—a voyage in which many lost their lives. Soon, a new chorus, composed of captive Trojan women and led by Cassandra, a priestess of Apollo, advance. They lament their fate and describe the final hours of their city and the stratagem of the wooden horse that led to its destruction. After further lamentation by Cassandra and the chorus, Cassandra feels herself beginning to be seized upon by the spirit of Apollo. In her frenzy, Cassandra predicts Agamemnon's and her death. Cassandra then faints and is restored to consciousness by Agamemnon, who has just entered. Cassandra warns Agamemnon that he has much to fear, but the unsuspecting king enters the palace.

Next, the chorus sing an ode to Hercules (Greek: HERACLES), alluding to many of his labors. The ode seemingly has little relevance to Agamemnon or his situation, except that Hercules was also connected with the town of Argos and that, as the chorus mention in the ode's last five lines, Hercules also waged a successful military campaign against Troy. After the choral ode, Cassandra emerges from the palace and describes Agamemnon's death at the hands of Aegisthus and Clytemnestra.

After Cassandra's description, Electra and her young brother, Orestes (who are not seen in Aeschylus' *Agamemnon* [see ORESTEIA]), Agamemnon, and Clytemnestra's children emerge from the palace, fearful for their lives. Their fear is remedied by the sudden arrival of Strophius and his son, Pylades (characters who also do not appear in Aeschylus' play). Electra urges Strophius to take Orestes and keep him in hiding.

As Strophius and Pylades depart with Orestes, Clytemnestra emerges from the palace. Clytemnestra wonders what Electra is doing outside the palace. Electra reproaches her mother for her actions and informs her that Orestes is safely in exile. Clytemnestra threatens to kill Electra, but the plan of Aegisthus, who also emerges from the palace, that Electra be imprisoned is followed instead. Cassandra, who has witnessed the entire scene, is taken back into the palace to be slaughtered. The play ends with Cassandra's prediction of Orestes' vengeance against Clytemnestra.

COMMENTARY

In addition to the comparisons of the plays of Seneca and Aeschylus, many of which have been mentioned, Seneca's *Agamemnon* draws attention to fathers, children, and altars. Because of the sins of Agamemnon's father, Atreus, the ghost of Atreus' brother Thyestes will attack Atreus' son, just as Atreus destroyed the sons of Thyestes. To take vengeance on Atreus, Thyestes' ghost recalls how Fortune defiled him as a father by compelling him to rape his daughter to produce a son, Aegisthus, who would avenge the wrongs done to him by Atreus (28–36).

The horrific deeds of the fathers Atreus and Thyestes are paralleled when Agamemnon, before sailing for Troy, stood before sacred altars and sacrificed his daughter (166); when Clytemnestra begins to waver in her resolve to kill Agamemnon (236), whose blood Clytemnestra's nurse imagines will defile Clytemnestra's altars (219), Aegisthus reminds her of that deed. Aegisthus also suggests that Agamemnon is planning to divorce Clytemnestra and that if he rejects her, then she will also be rejected if she tries to return to her father's house (282).

Upon Agamemnon's return from Troy, before his death by treachery, Clytemnestra orders that sacrifices of thanksgiving be made at the altars (585). This action parallels the glad sacrifices that Trojan fathers made before the fall of Troy through the treachery of the Greeks (645). Agamemnon takes with him captive Trojan women, who recall seeing the fall of their fatherland (611). Among the Trojan captives is Cassandra, whose fatherland and father Agamemnon's army destroyed (699). Additionally, she declares that Troy's altars have drunk her blood (700). Not only did both her father and brother die while taking refuge at altars: During the fall of Troy Cassandra also sought refuge at an altar of Athena, was torn from that altar, and then was raped by AJAX, the son of Oileus. As Eurybates indicates in his speech, Minerva attacked the Greek fleet at sea and in imitation of her father (537) struck Ajax with a lightning bolt. Father Neptune (553) then drowned Ajax. For the desecration of her altar, Pallas (using her father's weapons) takes revenge upon the Greeks; Eurybates reports that another father, the father of Palamedes (568)—who was treacherously killed by his fellow Greeks at Troy—used false signal beacons to cause many Greek ships to run aground on deadly rocks.

After Cassandra arrives at Agamemnon's palace, she predicts that she will follow her father in death (742). When Cassandra's frenzied prophecy apparently causes her to faint, her fellow Trojan captives compare the fallen girl to a bull sacrificed at an altar (776–77). This comparison is paralleled and echoed later as Cassandra predicts that Agamemnon will fall as a bull does at an altar (898). When Agamemnon enters, he rejoices to see his father's house (*patrios lares,* 782), which not only echoes the greeting of the messenger Eurybates upon his return home (*patrios lares,* 392), but also both echoes and contrasts with the ghost of Thyestes, who shuddered to see the house of his father and brother (*paternos . . . fraternos lares,* 6). As Agamemnon urges Cassandra to kneel at an altar and pray before they enter the house, the daughter Cassandra recalls that her father was killed at an altar (792)—a memory that recalls the father Agamemnon's sacrifice of his daughter Iphigenia at an altar (166). Cassandra's presence at the altar is also ironic given her experience during the fall of Troy of being raped at Minerva's altar.

Ultimately, Agamemnon's death is facilitated by the woman who made him a father. Because the father sacrificed the daughter, the mother causes the father's death. Two of the father's children survive, and the daughter, Electra, makes sure that the son, Orestes, will live to avenge the death of their father (910). Electra hands over Orestes to Strophius, who will act as a surrogate father to him. Strophius, whose name means "nurturer," is appropriately named for this task. As Strophius departs (940), he urges his own son, Pylades, to learn steadfastness through his example. After Strophius leaves with Orestes, Electra makes her way to an altar and prepares to face death (951), thus creating a parallel between her and her sister, Iphigenia. When Clytemnestra enters and demands her son, Orestes, Electra demands that Clytemnestra restore her father to her (968). Upon Aegisthus' arrival, Clytemnestra complains about Electra's treatment of her. When Aegisthus tells Electra to speak respectfully to her mother, Electra scoffs at him as one who, among other things, is the grandson of his father (985).

BIBLIOGRAPHY

Boyle, A. J. "*Hic epulis locus:* The Tragic Worlds of Seneca's *Agamemnon* and *Thyestes.*" In *Seneca Tragicus: Ramus Essays on Senecan Drama.* Edited by A. J. Boyle. Berwick. Australia: Aureal, 1983, 199–228.

Fantham, E. "Seneca's *Troades* and *Agamemnon:* Continuity and Sequence," *Classical Journal* 77 (1981–82): 118–29.

Shelton, J. A. "Revenge or Resignation: Seneca's *Agamemnon,*" *Ramus* 12 (1983): 159–83.

AGATHON   A writer of TRAGEDY in the last quarter of the fifth century B.C.E. Six titles of Agathon's plays are known: *Aerope, Alcmeon, Antheus, Thyestes, Mysoi* (*The Mysians*), and *Telephus.* Although only the title of Agathon's *Antheus* is known, the play was thought to be the first tragedy whose characters did not originate in mythology and were the author's own invention. Agathon is also credited with giving the CHORUS songs that served as interludes, rather than being connected to the play's plot in some way. Agathon's first victory in a drama competition onstage occurred in 416 B.C.E., a victory celebrated in Plato's *Symposium.* In ARISTOPHANES' *THESMOPHORIAZUSAE,* staged in 411, Agathon appears as an extremely effeminate character. When the women at the Thesmophoria decree death for EURIPIDES, Euripides goes to Agathon's house and begs Agathon, because of his effeminate appearance, to plead his case before the women. Agathon refuses but does provide Euripides with some stage props with which he can dress his cousin, Mnesilochus. Early in *FROGS,* staged in 405, Aristophanes mentions that Agathon had left Athens to live at the court of King Archelaus of Macedonia.

AGAVE   The daughter of CADMUS and Harmonia, Agave was the sister of AUTONOE, INO, SEMELE, and Polydorus. Agave became the wife of Echion and the mother of PENTHEUS. In EURIPIDES' *Bacchae,* DIONYSUS drives her mad and in her delusion she kills her son, Pentheus, thinking that he is a lion. After the death of Pentheus, she goes into exile in Illyria; marries the local king, Lycotherses; and then kills him, an act that allows her father, Cadmus, to take over the kingdom. In SENECA's *OEDIPUS* (616), her spirit is conjured from the UNDERWORLD. [ANCIENT SOURCES: Apollodorus, *Library* 3.4.2; Euripides, *Bacchae;* Hesiod, *Theogony* 975–78; Ovid, *Metamorphoses* 511–733]

AGBATANA   See ECBATANA.

AGENOR   The son of POSEIDON and Libya, Agenor was a king of Phoenicia. He was the father of CADMUS and EUROPA. [ANCIENT SOURCES: Aristophanes, *Frogs* 1226; Euripides, *Bacchae* 171, *Phoenician Women* 217, 281, 291; Seneca, *Oedipus* 715]

AGLAUROS   The wife of CECROPS, a king of ATHENS. Aglauros was the mother of Herse, Pandrosus, and Aglauros the younger. Athena had entrusted Aglauros' daughters with a box that contained a child named ERICTHONIUS. Although the goddess had told the girls not to look into the box, they violated her command. The goddess had put two serpents into the box to protect the child, and when the girls saw the serpents, they were terrified and hurled themselves down from the Athenian ACROPOLIS and died. [ANCIENT SOURCES: Aristophanes, *Thesmophoriazusae* 533; Euripides, *Ion* 23, 496; Hyginus, *Fables* 166, 213]

AGON   In general, an *agon* is any sort of competition; in drama the *agon* is a debate between two characters. For example, the argument in EURIPIDES' *ALCESTIS* between ADMETUS and his father, PHERES, is an *agon* between father and son over whether it was proper for Alcestis to give up her life for Admetus. The *agon* is a standard feature in the COMEDY of ARISTOPHANES. In the *CLOUDS,* for example, an *agon* regarding the proper way of training and educating young people takes place between Stronger Argument and Weaker Argument.

BIBLIOGRAPHY

Lloyd, Michael. *The Agon in Euripides.* Oxford: Clarendon Press, 1992.

AGONOTHETES   In Greek society, the *agonothetes* (plural: *agonothetai*) was the person who sponsored, administered, and to some extent funded a festival.

AGORA   Although this Greek word is usually translated "market" or "marketplace," the agora in a Greek city was home, not only to various markets, but also to certain government buildings and served as a town's civic center. In some cases, an agora could be a staging ground for a festival. References to the agora are not especially frequent in Greek TRAGEDY, although the altar to which HERACLES' children take refuge in EURIPIDES' CHILDREN OF HERACLES is located in the agora at MARATHON. In Greek COMEDY, however, in which the focus is often on the mundane, references to the agora are frequent and the agora becomes a focal point for comic activity. In ARISTOPHANES' ACHARNIANS, DICAEOPOLIS arranges a peace treaty between him and the Spartans so that he can create his own personal agora for trade. In two of Aristophanes' extant plays, the heroes have the word *agora* in their name. In KNIGHTS, AGORACRITUS (the market's choice), a sausage seller for the Athenian agora, saves the Athenian people from the clutches of the politician Paphlagon (a caricature of Cleon). In ECCLESIAZUSAE, PRAXAGORA ("effective in the assembly") leads the women's takeover of the Athenian government. In general, Aristophanes characterizes the Athenian agora of his day as a place where idle chatter took place, one to be avoided by persons of modest behavior. As shown by *Acharnians,* an agora where produce and useful products were abundant was a sign of peaceful conditions, of which Aristophanes saw little in his own lifetime.

BIBLIOGRAPHY
Joyner, G. "The Agora in Athens: Literary Sources." In *Hellenika: Essays on Greek History and Politics.* Edited by G. H. R. Horsley. North Ryde, Australia: Macquarie University Ancient History Association, 1982, 97–120.
Thompson, H. A., and R. E. Wycherley. *The Agora of Athens: The History, Shape, and Uses of an Ancient City Center.* Princeton, N.J.: American School of Classical Studies at Athens, 1972.
Wycherley, R. E. *How the Greeks Built Cities.* 2d ed. London, Melbourne: Macmillan, 1967.

AGORACRITUS

A character in ARISTOPHANES *KNIGHTS,* Agoracritus, whose name means approximately "the market's choice" (see AGORA), is a fictional sausage seller who defeats Paphlagon in a contest to win the favor of Demos, who represents the Athenian people. Like Aristophanic heroes such as DICAEOPOLIS, STREPSIADES, or TRYGAEUS, Agoracritus is neither sophisticated nor especially virtuous. Agoracritus defeats Paphlagon (a caricature of the Athenian demagogue CLEON) by being more crude and more flattering than his opponent and thus wresting Demos from the control of the evil Paphlagon. Unlike Dicaeopolis, Strepsiades, or Trygaeus, Agoracritus does not instigate the reform that he achieves but is enlisted by two of Paphlagon's fellow slaves to defeat Paphlagon.

BIBLIOGRAPHY
Bennett, L. J., and W. B. Tyrrell. "Making Sense of Aristophanes' *Knights,*" *Arethusa* 23 (1990): 235–54.
Edmunds, Lowell. "The Aristophanic Cleon's 'Disturbance' of Athens," *American Journal of Philology* 108 (1987): 233–63.

AGRIPPINA THE ELDER (CA. 14 B.C.E.–33 C.E.)

Agrippina I was the daughter of Marcus Vipsanius Agrippa and the emperor AUGUSTUS' daughter, Julia. Agrippina I was the mother of numerous children but was survived by only four of them (including the future emperor CALIGULA and AGRIPPINA THE YOUNGER). The emperor Tiberius suspected that Agrippina was involved in the death of her husband, Germanicus (Tiberius' adopted son), and in the year 29 had Agrippina arrested. She died in exile on the island of PANDATERIA. [ANCIENT SOURCES: Seneca, *Octavia* 932; Suetonius, *Augustus* 64–65, *Caligula* 7–8; Tacitus, *Annals* 14.63]

BIBLIOGRAPHY
Balsdon, J. *Roman Women.* Rev. ed. London: Bodley Head, 1974.

AGRIPPINA THE YOUNGER (15–59 C.E.)

The daughter of Germanicus and AGRIPPINA THE ELDER, the younger Agrippina was the sister of the emperor Caligula and the mother of NERO by Gnaeus Domitius Ahenobarbus. She later married Crispinus Passienus and eventually married the emperor CLAUDIUS in 49 C.E. The next year, Agrippina persuaded Claudius to adopt Nero, although Claudius already had a son, Britannicus. In 54, Claudius died (perhaps poisoned by Agrippina), and Nero became emperor. Nero, however, grew tired of his domineering mother's interference and in 59 had her assassinated. Agrippina's ghost appears in SENECA's OCTAVIA and complains of her son's crimes against her. [ANCIENT SOURCES: Seneca, *Octavia*; Suetonius, *Claudius, Nero*; Tacitus, *Annals* 12–14, 16]

BIBLIOGRAPHY

Balsdon, J. *Roman Women*. Rev. ed. London: Bodley Head, 1974.

Barrett, A. *Agrippina: Sex, Power, and Politics in the Early Empire*. New Haven, Conn.: Yale University Press, 1996.

Flach, D. "Seneca und Agrippina im antiken Urteil," *Chiron* 3 (1973): 265–76.

AGYIEUS   See APOLLO.

AGYRRHIUS

A wealthy Athenian leader who rose to prominence in the first two decades of the fourth century B.C.E. He is mentioned several times in ARISTOPHANES' *ECCLESIAZUSAE* and in the 390s is connected with introducing pay for attendance at the Athenian assembly. Under Agyrrhius' proposal, those who attended the assembly would receive one OBOL. By the time *Ecclesiazusae* was staged, Agyrrhius had managed to increase the pay to three obols, the same amount that jurors were paid for a day's service. Between 389 and 387, Agyrrhius was elected general at least once, and perhaps twice. [ANCIENT SOURCES: Aristophanes, *Ecclesiazusae* 102, 184, *Wealth* 176; Philemon, fragment 42.1 Kock 2; Plato Comicus, fragment 185.2 Kock 1]

BIBLIOGRAPHY

Kock, T. *Comicorum Atticorum Fragmenta*. Vol. 1. Leipzig: Teubner, 1880.

———. *Comicorum Atticorum Fragmenta*. Vol. 2. Leipzig: Teubner, 1884.

Sommerstein, A. H. *The Comedies of Aristophanes*. Vol. 11 *Wealth*. Warminster, U.K.: Aris & Phillips, 2001, 147.

AIAS   See AJAX (1).

AJAX (1) (Greek: AIAS)

The son of TELAMON and Periboea (or Eriboea), Ajax was a native of the island of SALAMIS. Ajax accompanied the Greeks on their expedition to TROY to rescue HELEN. While there, Ajax served well and proved himself the most powerful warrior after ACHILLES. For Ajax's valor in combat, he was awarded a captive, TECMESSA, by whom he fathered EURYSACES. In the seventh book of Homer's *Iliad*, Ajax fought the Trojan HECTOR to a draw. After Ajax and Hector's duel, the two exchanged gifts—Ajax gave Hector a sword belt, and Hector gave Ajax a sword. After the death of Achilles, a contest was held to determine who would receive the hero's armor. Ajax and ODYSSEUS emerged as the contestants for this reward, but despite Ajax's valor the armor was awarded to Odysseus. Ajax was enraged and tried to kill Odysseus, AGAMEMNON, and MENELAUS. ATHENA, however, caused Ajax to go mad and Ajax killed some cattle instead. After Ajax realized what he had done, SOPHOCLES relates that Ajax committed suicide with the sword that Hector had given him. Other sources say that Ajax was invulnerable over most of his body and that when he tried to stab himself the sword recoiled from his body. Eventually, Athena had to show Ajax a place beneath his arm where he could position the sword and kill himself. Some sources also report that from Ajax's blood there sprang up a flower whose petals bore the first two letters of Ajax's name, Ai (in Greek), which is a Greek word meaning "alas" or "woe."

Ajax appears as a character in one extant play, Sophocles' *AJAX*, in which he is portrayed as clinging to a code of behavior that seems outdated compared with the code of Odysseus. To Ajax's way of thinking, the best warrior was someone who excelled in deeds rather than words. After the death of Achilles, Ajax believed that he should have been considered the best of the Greek warriors at Troy. As such, he expected to receive the armor of Achilles as his reward instead of Odysseus. Unable to abide by this decision, Ajax struck out against his former friends and comrades. He not only transformed his friends into enemies, but he also treated them as inferiors as he lashed them with his whip. In the course of the play, however, we learn that Ajax's trouble had started some time earlier. When he left for the Trojan War, Ajax rejected his father's advice on how he should conduct himself in battle. Additionally, while in battle on one occassion, Ajax rejected Athena's offer of help when she stood behind him. Having ignored both his father and the goddess, Ajax had put himself in a dangerous position even before his attack on his comrades. Thus, after Ajax's attempt on his comrades' lives and the Athena-sent madness that prevented him from killing them, Ajax reasoned that his best course of action would be suicide. In keeping with the play's emphasis on the reversal of roles between friends and enemies, Ajax used the sword of his enemy Hector to take his own life. Unfortunately for Ajax, he did not anticipate that his former friends, Agamemnon and Menelaus, would oppose his burial. Ultimately, Ajax had to rely on the help of another former friend whom he tried to kill, Odysseus, to rise above the traditional code of ethics (help friends and harm enemies) and secure burial for him in spite of the opposition of Agamemnon and Menelaus.

In addition to Sophocles in the extant *Ajax,* several ancient authors wrote plays about this hero. Aeschylus wrote a tetralogy; Astydamas wrote *Ajax Mainomenos* (Ajax mad), of which only the title survives. This title would suggest, however, that the play dealt with Ajax's insanity. The younger Carcinus wrote the play *Ajax,* in whose one surviving fragment Ajax laughs at Odysseus' statement "It is necessary to do just things." Theodectas also wrote a play with the title *Ajax,* to which Aristotle refers (*Rhetoric* 1399b29, 1400a27–28), of which only the title survives. Polemaeus wrote a satyric *Ajax,* of which only the title is extant. ENNIUS wrote a tragic *Ajax,* from which a few lines survive (fragments 10–13 Jocelyn).

BIBLIOGRAPHY
Jocelyn, H. D. *The Tragedies of Ennius.* Cambridge: Cambridge University Press, 1969.

Warmington, E. H. *Remains of Old Latin: Ennius and Caecilius.* Vol. 1. Cambridge, Mass.: Harvard University Press, 1935.

AJAX (2)

AJAX (2) The son of Oileus, Ajax, who also fought in the Trojan War, was from the region of Locria. During the fall of TROY, Ajax dragged CASSANDRA away from the statue of ATHENA, to which Cassandra was clinging for refuge. SOPHOCLES wrote *Ajax the Locrian* (fragments 10a–18 Radt), which may have been about Ajax's rape of Cassandra and subsequent trial by his fellow Greeks. Fragment 10c indicates that Athena was a character in the play.

BIBLIOGRAPHY
Kiso, A. *The Lost Sophocles.* New York: Vantage Press, 1984.

Lloyd-Jones, H. *Sophocles: Fragments.* Cambridge, Mass.: Harvard University Press, 1996, 29.

Radt, S. *Tragicorum Graecorum Fragmenta.* Vol. 4. Göttingen, Ger.: Vandenhoeck & Ruprecht, 1977.

Sutton, D. F. *The Lost Sophocles.* Lanham, Md.: University Press of America, 1984.

AJAX SOPHOCLES (CA. 450–440 B.C.E.) The date of the play is uncertain, although *Ajax* is often considered the earliest extant Sophoclean play. Modern scholars usually date it before ANTIGONE (442 or 441) and during the 440s. The action of the play occurs before the tent of AJAX near the coast of TROY during the 10th year of the Trojan War. After ACHILLES' death, his mother, THETIS, decided to award her son's armor to the warrior who had done the most to retrieve Achilles' body from the battlefield. The contest for Achilles' armor narrowed to two Greeks, ODYSSEUS and Ajax, the son of Telamon. When Odysseus was chosen, the furious Ajax tried to kill not only Odysseus, but also AGAMEMNON and MENELAUS, who Ajax thought favored Odysseus.

As the play opens, ATHENA addresses Odysseus, who is attempting to find Ajax. Odysseus has learned that some of the Greeks' cattle were slaughtered. Athena informs Odysseus that Ajax was responsible for killing the animals but that he had intended to kill Odysseus, Menelaus, and Agamemnon. When Athena summons Ajax from his tent, the goddess then explains to Odysseus that she caused Ajax to become insane and attack the cattle, rather than Odysseus and the others. Athena urges Odysseus to mock Ajax, but Odysseus refrains. When Athena summons Ajax from his tent, Odysseus hides. Ajax, still suffering from madness, emerges from the tent and tells Athena that Menelaus and Agamemnon are dead and that he has Odysseus tied up inside the tent and is preparing to kill him. When Ajax reenters the tent, Odysseus emerges from his hiding place and expresses his pity for Ajax. Athena warns Odysseus not to behave as Ajax has, because the gods hate evil.

After the departure of Athena and Odysseus, the CHORUS, consisting of Ajax's comrades from SALAMIS, enter. They have heard of the horrific deeds of their leader. They wonder which divinity Ajax could have offended and what he did to create offense. They pray that the gods will save them from implication in this crime. After the chorus' song, TECMESSA, a female war prize of Ajax, leaves from the tent and describes Ajax's madness to the chorus. When she relates how Ajax tortured and brutally killed the cattle, Ajax's comrades expect that the army will stone them. Tecmessa also informs them that Ajax's madness has now passed; he realizes the terrible atrocities he has committed and sits in dejection amid the slaughtered cattle. After Tecmessa concludes her account of Ajax's actions and current behavior, Ajax can be heard wailing from within the tent and calling for his son, EURYSACES.

Soon Tecmessa opens the entrance to the tent, and probably by means of the ECCYCLEMA, Ajax, spattered with blood and gore, is revealed sitting amid slaughtered cattle. The chorus express horror and pity for their leader, who continues to hope for the death of Odysseus, Menelaus, and Agamemnon. As the scene continues, Ajax begins to express thoughts of suicide. He realizes that the gods hate him; he wonders how he could face his father if he returned home. The chorus and Tecmessa realize that Ajax wants to take his own life and try to dissuade him. In a speech modeled on that of ANDROMACHE to HECTOR in *Iliad* 6, Tecmessa makes a tearful plea to her husband not to abandon her and their son, Eurysaces. As with the encounter between Hector and Andromache, Ajax calls for his young son and addresses him for the last time. Ajax declares that his half brother, TEUCER, will become the boy's guardian and gives the child his shield. As will Hector, Ajax will soon meet his fate, despite further pleas from Tecmessa. Ironically, Ajax will kill himself with a sword that Hector had given him.

After this, Ajax reenters the tent. Next, the chorus sing an ode asking their native land to pity their plight; they lament Ajax's situation and predict the grief of Ajax's mother and father. After the choral ode, Ajax emerges from the tent and gives one of the most controversial speeches in classical drama. In the presence of Tecmessa and his comrades, Ajax's words (at least on the surface) indicate that he has changed his attitude completely. He says that he will bury his sword in the earth and that he will obey both the gods and Menelaus and Agamemnon. As Ajax departs, he instructs Tecmessa and his comrades to pray that events turn out for him as he wishes. He asks that when Teucer arrives he take care of matters as he (Ajax) would wish and says that when next they hear of Ajax, his suffering will be over and he will be safe. When Ajax makes his exit, the chorus praise the gods for Ajax's new attitude and hope for reconciliation among Ajax, Menelaus, and Agamemnon. The chorus do not realize that they have just seen Ajax alive for the last time.

After the chorus' joyful ode, a messenger enters and announces that Teucer has returned and that he was threatened with death by a mob from the army. When the messenger says Ajax should be told about this, the chorus say that he has left the tent. The messenger is troubled by this news because Teucer had been told by the Greeks' prophet, CALCHAS, that Ajax should not leave his tent that day because Athena's anger would fall upon him. The messenger goes on to relate that Ajax had angered Athena by rejecting her direction on the battlefield. The chorus, worried by this news, summon Tecmessa from the tent, and the messenger informs her of Calchas' warning. Tecmessa then sends some of the chorus to summon Teucer, while others search for Ajax.

With the stage empty (a rare occurrence in classical drama), Ajax appears. He states that Hector's sword has been fixed in the ground. He prays to ZEUS that the news of his death will be reported to Teucer, so that he can take up Ajax's body. Ajax prays to HERMES that he will guide him to the UNDERWORLD. He prays that the FURIES will take vengeance on the Greek army for him, and that Helios (see SUN) will report the news of his death to his father and family in his native land. After bidding farewell to his native land and Troy, he falls on his sword.

After this, the chorus enter searching for Ajax. They are joined by Tecmessa, who points out his body. The chorus lament their fallen leader and Tecmessa covers him with a cloth. The chorus and Tecmessa then continue to mourn for Ajax, expecting that Odysseus, Menelaus, and Agamemnon will mock him. The group is then joined by Teucer, who with the chorus expresses his grief. Teucer sends Tecmessa to find Eurysaces so that their enemies will not harm the child. After Tecmessa departs, Teucer utters a lengthy lamentation over Ajax's body. Teucer worries that his father, Telamon, will not welcome him home if he returns without Ajax. Teucer also notes that Hector's sword killed Ajax though Hector had died already, when the sword belt that Ajax gave Hector was used to bind Hector to a chariot rail and drag him until he died.

After Teucer's speech, the play's action recalls that of SOPHOCLES' ANTIGONE. In *Antigone,* Creon had refused to allow the burial of POLYNEICES, because Polyneices, although a Theban by birth, had waged war against Thebes. In *Ajax,* Menelaus now enters and declares that Teucer must not bury Ajax. Menelaus explains that because of Ajax's attempt against their lives, his body will be left for the birds to pick over. Menelaus then talks about the need for people to yield to authority and the law. He concludes by warning Teucer not to bury Ajax; if he does, he too may be killed. Teucer argues that Menelaus has no authority over Ajax and that he will not obey Menelaus. The argument between the two continues, and no compromise or solution is reached. After an angry Menelaus exits, the chorus urge Teucer to go to prepare a grave for Ajax. At this point, Tecmessa and Eurysaces enter. Teucer urges Eurysaces to sit as a suppliant by his father's corpse and cling to the body until he returns.

After Teucer's exit, the chorus sing an ode expressing their desire to know when their labors at Troy will end. They lament the invention of war and the loss of their defender, Ajax, and wish that they could return to their native land. After the choral ode, Teucer enters and announces that Agamemnon is approaching. Agamemnon immediately begins to attack Teucer verbally with insults about Teucer's birth of a woman who was a war captive. Because Teucer is of low birth, Agamemnon claims, he should not speak so arrogantly to free men. Teucer responds that Agamemnon has forgotten how often Ajax helped the Greeks in battle, and that Agamemnon himself is a descendant of a barbarian and that his mother was an adulterous Cretan. Teucer also defends his own birth, saying that his mother was a Trojan princess, who was a war prize given to his father by Heracles.

The arrival of Odysseus, who intercedes on Ajax's behalf and persuades Agamemnon to relent, interrupts the argument of Teucer and Agamemnon. As ANTIGONE does in Sophocles' play, Odysseus argues that denying Ajax burial would violate the laws of the gods. Agamemnon expresses hatred for Ajax but allows Odysseus to have his way. After Agamemnon departs, Odysseus becomes reconciled with Teucer, who had expected him to behave much differently with respect to Ajax. Odysseus even offers to help Teucer bury Ajax, but Teucer rejects his offer, saying that Ajax would not have wanted this. With this rejection, Odysseus exits and Teucer, Eurysaces, and Ajax's comrades begin to prepare Ajax for burial.

COMMENTARY

Ajax has attracted a fair amount of attention from critics but is surely not as popular with the general mass of readers as *Antigone* or *Oedipus Tyrannos.* One of the play's major issues is Ajax's suicide, which may have taken place on stage. First, the change of scene for Ajax's suicide, which apparently moves from his tent to an isolated spot on the shore, is rare in Greek TRAGEDY (cf. AESCHYLUS' *Eumenides* [see ORESTEIA]). It is not clear whether SOPHOCLES' audience would simply have to imagine this change or whether some sort of painted screen representing a seashore was put on the stage. Second, how the suicide would have been achieved before the audience is not clear. The body is clearly on stage during the last third of the play, as it becomes the focal point for the other characters. Scholars have proposed a variety of solutions to this problem. Most of these involve Ajax' pretending to fall on his sword behind something (such as a painted screen) that would conceal his prostrate body from the audience's view. At some point, the actor playing Ajax would stealthily move back into the stage building and a dummy would have been put in his place (perhaps by using the eccyclema).

In addition to problems of staging, Ajax's speech in which he deceives his comrades and the relevance of last third of the play have troubled critics. Regarding Ajax's "deception speech," some scholars have thought Ajax is lying; others have thought his character has changed. Sicherl, however, argues that Ajax neither lies nor has a change in character, but that Ajax's words are ambiguous and deceive his comrades. As for the play's structure, after Ajax's death, a substantial part of the play remains. In some ways, *Ajax* is constructed in reverse of *Antigone*. In *Antigone,* the audience hears a debate about the burial of Polyneices and then is presented with the suicides of Antigone, Haemon, and EURYDICE. In *Ajax,* the audience is presented with the suicide of Ajax and then listens to a debate over his burial. The unity of *Ajax,* however, may be found in the play's major themes, such as the reversal in the roles of friends and enemies.

Ajax is another Sophoclean hero who has become entangled in the Greek ethical practice of helping one's friends and harming one's enemies (see Blundell's study). His friends, the Greek army, become his enemies when they award Achilles' arms to Odysseus. Ajax tries to kill three of his new enemies, but he is prevented by the goddess Athena, whose help, we are told, he had rejected earlier in the war (thus transforming Athena from a friend to an enemy). While some of Ajax's friends become his enemies, some of his enemies become his friends. Tecmessa, whose country Ajax destroyed with his spear (515), was his enemy. Although she is his spear prize from battle, she seems concerned for his welfare and appears to have some feeling for the man. Even if Tecmessa is motivated by self-preservation, she is certainly not his enemy. Another Trojan, to some extent, changes from enemy to friend in *Ajax*. Earlier in the war, when the single combat between Hector and Ajax had resulted in a draw, the two men had exchanged gifts. The sword of Ajax's enemy Hector becomes the weapon with which he kills himself.

While Trojans have become Ajax's friends, the Greeks have become Ajax's enemies. The final instance of a person who moves between friend and enemy is Odysseus. From Ajax's perspective, Odysseus has become his enemy. Odysseus, however, does something unusual with respect to the Greek ethical code of helping one's friends and harming one's enemies in opposing this code. Contrast Agamemnon and Menelaus, who, after discovering that Ajax has tried to kill them, are ready to deny Ajax burial. The sons of Atreus adhere to the traditional code of ethics as they try to harm the man who once was their friend but now is their enemy. Odysseus, in contrast, rejects Athena's invitation to mock Ajax and pities the man

who has become his enemy (121–22). Furthermore, Odysseus later opposes his friends Agamemnon and Menelaus with respect to the issue of burying Ajax and even offers to help bury the body of the man who tried to kill him (1376–80). Odysseus has shown an ability and a willingness to move beyond the bounds of the traditional ethical code in his society, whereas even in death, Ajax cannot. Accordingly, Teucer rejects Odysseus' offer because he believes that Ajax would be offended (1395).

Sophocles' *Ajax* is a play filled with the unexpected: Ajax's attack against his enemies, Ajax's apparent change of heart toward his enemies (716), and Odysseus' intervention in the burial of Ajax (1382). At the end of the play, however, Ajax continues to behave in accordance with the traditional code of ethics, while Odysseus adapts to the world as it changes around him. Ajax is a man who has isolated himself from the civilized community but fails to anticipate that after his death this community has the power to allow or refuse him burial. Were it not for the intervention of a person Ajax considered his enemy, Ajax's corpse would have remained unburied. Thus, the reversal in the roles of friends and enemies not only serves as a major theme in the drama but also helps unify the play.

BIBLIOGRAPHY
Blundell, M. W. *Helping Friends and Harming Enemies: A Study in Sophocles and Greek Ethics.* Cambridge: Cambridge University Press, 1989, 60–105.
Garvie, A. F. *Sophocles. Ajax.* Warminster, U.K.: Aris & Phillips, 1998.
March, J. R. "Sophocles' *Ajax:* The Death and Burial of the Hero," *Bulletin for the Institute of Classical Studies* 38 (1991–93): 1–36.
Segal, Charles. "Catharsis, Audience, and Closure in Greek Tragedy." In *Tragedy and the Tragic: Greek Theatre and Beyond.* Edited by M. S. Silk. Oxford and New York: Oxford University Press, 1996, 149–81.
Sicherl, M. "The Tragic Issue in Sophocles' *Ajax,*" *Yale Classical Studies* 25 (1977): 67–98.

ALCAEUS (1) (BORN CA. 620 B.C.E.) A writer of poetry, especially lyric poetry, from the island of LESBOS. ARISTOPHANES, at *THESMOPHORIAZUSAE* 161, associates Alcaeus with delicate behavior and soft clothing.

ALCAEUS (2) A Greek comic poet, whose *Pasiphae* was defeated in a drama competition by ARISTOPHANES' *WEALTH* in 388 B.C.E.

BIBLIOGRAPHY
Kock, T. *Comicorum Atticorum Fragmenta.* Vol. 1. Leipzig: Teubner, 1880.

ALCESTIS The daughter of Pelias and Anaxibia, Alcestis was the wife of ADMETUS and mother of EUMELUS and Perimele. She had one brother, ACASTUS, and several sisters: Amphinome, Asteropeia, Evadne, Hippothoe, Medusa (not the GORGON), Peisidice, and Pelopia. Alcestis' father, Pelias, refused to marry Alcestis to anyone who could not yoke a lion and a boar to a chariot. Admetus wanted to marry Alcestis, and the god APOLLO, who was on good terms with Admetus, yoked the lion and boar for him to take the yoked pair to Pelias. In this way, Admetus was able to marry Alcestis. Some time later, Apollo arranged for Admetus to avoid death provided that he could find someone to die in his place. Admetus' parents refused, but Alcestis agreed to give up her life for her husband. Alcestis died but was rescued from death by HERACLES (according to EURIPIDES' *ALCESTIS*) or by PERSEPHONE, who allowed Alcestis to be restored to Admetus. Because of her sacrifice, Alcestis became a model for virtuous behavior among Greek women.

In addition to Euripides' extant *Alcestis,* dramas with the same title were written by several other playwrights. The tragedian PHRYNICHUS' *Alcestis* predated Euripides' play, and presumably Euripides drew on it in his own work. Although only a few words survive of Phrynichus' play, those that do hint at the wrestling match between Heracles and Death. [ANCIENT SOURCES: Apollodorus, 1.9.10, 15; Euripides, *Alcestis*]

BIBLIOGRAPHY
Nielsen, R. M. "Alcestis: A Paradox in Dying," *Ramus* 5 (1976): 92–102.
O'Higgins, Dolores. "Above Rubies: Admetus' Perfect Wife," *Arethusa* 26 (1993): 77–97.

ALCESTIS EURIPIDES (438 B.C.E.) *Alcestis* was the final play of a TETRALOGY that included *Alcmeon in Psophis, Cretan Women,* and *Telephus,* three plays of which only fragments survive. The drama's setting is PHERAE, a small town near the coast of northeastern Greece. The play opens with the departure of APOLLO from the house of ADMETUS, the king of Pherae. Apollo tells the audience that had been forced by his father, ZEUS, to become a servant to Admetus, because Apollo had killed some of the CYCLOPES, the giant one-eyed creatures who make lightning bolts for Zeus. Apollo had killed the Cyclopes because Zeus had killed Apollo's son, ASCLEPIUS. During Apollo's servitude, he found Admetus most hospitable, and accordingly he tricked the Moirae (FATES) to allow Admetus to avoid death by finding someone to die in his place. The encounter between Apollo and Admetus in which the god reveals his gift to Admetus does not occur in the play itself; therefore, the audience does not know whether Admetus tried to reject this gift. Apollo does tell the audience, however, that Admetus asked his parents whether they would be willing to die in his place. Admetus' parents, despite their advanced age, were unwilling to die for their son. Admetus' wife, Alcestis, was. The encounter of Admetus and Alcestis when she agrees to die for her husband is also not seen in the play.

Apollo then explains that with Alcestis on the verge of death, he must leave the house to avoid the pollution caused by the presence of death. No sooner are these words out of Apollo's mouth than he encounters Thanatos, Death himself, who is there to take Alcestis' life. Apollo tries to persuade Thanatos to let Alcestis live, but Thanatos refuses. As Apollo leaves, he predicts that Thanatos will be defeated and Alcestis will survive.

After Apollo's departure, the chorus of elders from Pherae approach the house looking for some indication of whether Alcestis is still alive. Soon a female servant emerges from the house and tells the chorus of Alcestis' actions inside. Subsequently, Admetus emerges from the house with Alcestis, who is near death. Before Alcestis dies, she requests that Admetus not remarry after her death, a request to which Admetus accedes.

After Admetus reenters the house with the now-deceased Alcestis, the hero HERACLES arrives in town, hoping to stay with Admetus for a brief time before continuing on to Thrace. After Heracles discusses his mission (to fetch the horses of the Thracian Diomedes) with the chorus, Admetus, wearing dark clothing and having cut his hair as a sign of mourning, emerges from the house. Heracles recognizes that Admetus is in mourning, but Admetus, not wanting Heracles to stay with another host, does not tell Heracles that Alcestis has died. Heracles wants to go to another host, but Admetus insists that he stay. Won over, Heracles reluctantly enters the house. The chorus question Admetus' decision to take in a guest during a time of mourning, but Admetus argues that Heracles has always been a good host to him when he visited him and that he does not want to have his home labeled as unfriendly to guests.

At this point, Admetus reenters the house to prepare for Alcestis' funeral. During Admetus' absence, the chorus sing an ode to Admetus' house, recalling that the presence of Apollo brought peace and prosperity to the kingdom, and that Admetus remains hospitable even in the face of the present misfortune. After the choral ode, Admetus emerges from the house. He is soon met by his father, Pheres, who has arrived to pay his respects to Alcestis. Admetus, however, does not welcome his father, who did not offer to die for him and allowed Alcestis to die instead. Admetus criticizes his father and mother's refusal to die and states that he is no longer their child. Pheres, in turn, lashes back at Admetus and calls him a coward for clinging to life. After further angry words, Pheres departs, presumably to his home, and Admetus exits to bury Alcestis.

While Admetus conducts Alcestis' funeral outside the house, Heracles becomes drunk inside, as the audience is informed by a servant who claims Heracles is the worst guest he has ever served. Heracles himself, quite intoxicated, soon emerges from the house, criticizes the servant for his gloomy expression and attitude, and proceeds to philosophize on the inevitability of death, the pleasure of wine, and the power of APHRODITE. Heracles then learns from the servant that Alcestis has died. Heracles declares he will ambush Thanatos and rescue Alcestis from him.

Just as Heracles departs to the gravesite to rescue Alcestis, Admetus returns from the same site (perhaps a problem for the staging of the play because the two men would presumably pass one another). When Admetus returns, he laments the loss of his wife and expresses the realization that his continued existence will be painful. Soon, however, Heracles returns from the burial site with a silent young woman (Alcestis) whose face is not visible to Admetus. Heracles tells Admetus that he won the girl in an athletic competition and asks Admetus to take care of her for him while he is on his mission. Because Admetus had promised Alcestis that he would not remarry, he does not wish to take the young woman into his home. Eventually, Heracles persuades Admetus to take her. When Admetus takes the young woman's hand, he recognizes his wife, who continues to be silent. As the play ends, Admetus thanks the hero, who continues on his journey, and then declares a celebration in his kingdom. What happens between Admetus and Alcestis after the drama's conclusion is unknown.

COMMENTARY

Alcestis is one of EURIPIDES' most controversial plays. Much of the debate centers on the play's genre. In Euripides' tetralogy of 438, an ancient HYPOTHESIS to the play lists *Alcestis* as the fourth play. The fourth play was reserved for a SATYR PLAY, but no satyrs appear in the drama. Satyr plays were comic in tone, and the tone of the *Alcestis* is tragic for the most part. A few humorous elements are present in the text—the servant's account of Heracles' drunkenness and Apollo's encounter with Thanatos have some wry moments. Otherwise, the play's text, dominated by Alcestis' death, is largely devoid of humor. The play's intermingling of TRAGEDY and COMEDY has led some scholars to label it a TRAGICOMEDY. Other scholars prefer to attribute the play's enigmatic tone to its derivation from a folktale, a genre in which a typical pattern is that the husband rescues his bride from a terrible ogre. In *Alcestis,* Thanatos is the terrible ogre, and Heracles replaces Admetus in the battle with the ogre.

Another of the play's major issues concerns the respective characters of Admetus and Alcestis. Few have found Admetus worthy of Alcestis' sacrifice, and some even regard Alcestis as manipulative and lacking in feeling. Scholars have also debated the purpose of the statue of Alcestis that Admetus proposes to have made and placed in Alcestis' bed after her death. Admetus says he will put his arms around the statue and call it by Alcestis' name. Some scholars have found this perversely sexual; others have suggested that it is meant to recall the story of LAODAMEIA and her husband, PROTESILAUS. After Protesilaus died, Laodameia commissioned a statue of her husband. Just as Admetus declares that he will place the statue of Alcestis in their marriage bed, wrap his arms around it, and call it by her name, Laodameia placed the statue in their marriage bed and embraced it.

Another much-discussed issue in the play is the silence of Alcestis after her return from the grave. Heracles explains her silence as a product of her recent return from the dead—Admetus is not permitted to hear her speak until she is purified from her encounter with the gods below and two full days have passed. Modern scholars, however, have usually dismissed Heracles' remark, pointing out that evidence for such a ritual purification does not exist. Others have argued that when *Alcestis* was staged, other than the chorus, commonly only two speaking actors would be on stage at one time. Because Admetus and Heracles are the speaking actors in this scene, Alcestis' character remains silent.

BIBLIOGRAPHY

Burnett, A. P. *Catastrophe Survived: Euripides' Plays of Mixed Reversal.* Oxford: Oxford University Press, 1971.

Conacher, D. J. *Euripides. Alcestis.* Warminster, U.K.: Aris & Phillips, 1988.

Dale, A. M. *Euripides: Alcestis.* Oxford: Oxford University Press, 1954.

Lesky, Albin. *Alkestis, der Mythus und das Drama.* Vienna and Leipzig: Holder Pichler Temsky, 1925.

Segal, Charles, *Euripides and the Poetics of Sorrow: Art, Gender, and Commemoration in Alcestis, Hippolytus, and Hecuba.* Durham, N.C., and London: Duke University Press, 1993.

Wilson, J. R. *Twentieth Century Interpretations of Euripides' Alcestis.* Englewood Cliffs, N.J.: Prentice-Hall, 1968.

ALCIBIADES (CA. 450–404 B.C.E.)

Alcibiades was one of the most charismatic yet outrageous Athenian military commanders and statesmen of the last quarter of the fifth century B.C.E. After his father died in 447, Alcibiades grew up in his uncle, PERICLES',

house. Alcibiades' first major military action occurred in 418, when he led an unsuccessful Athenian force against the Spartans at Mantinea. In 415, Alcibiades persuaded his fellow Athenians to launch the SICILIAN EXPEDITION. Alcibiades, along with LAMACHUS and NICIAS, was elected one of the generals to lead the Athenians' expedition to SICILY. Shortly after the expedition sailed in 415 B.C.E., the Athenians recalled Alcibiades because he was suspected of participating in a mockery of the Eleusinian mysteries and in the mutilation of various statues of Hermes (called Herms) before the expedition's departure. Alcibiades, however, evaded the Athenian ship sent to take him back. He escaped to Sparta and began providing the spartans with military advice that would help them against the Athenians. In particular, Alcibiades advised the Spartans to establish a permanent garrison in Athenian territory (at Decelea), from which they could strike out against Athens all year. In addition to creating this garrison, the Spartans sent Alcibiades to the region of Ionia (in western Turkey) to help stir up rebellion among the Athenian allies there. Because some leading Athenians began to favor oligarchy over democracy, Alcibiades, using a promise of Persian financial backing, began to work with the oligarchic group in hopes that he might be recalled to Athens.

Despite the hardship that Alcibiades had caused his fellow Athenians, many recognized his abilities as a military leader, and after a few years Alcibiades had worn out his welcome in Sparta. His relationship with the Persians troubled the Spartans, and Alcibiades' seduction of the wife of Agis, one of the Spartan kings, did not help matters. In 411, the prooligarchic party managed to overthrow the Athenian democracy. Although this initial coup was in turn replaced by a mixture of oligarchy and democracy, by the end of 411 the new government had voted to recall Alcibiades. In 410, at Cyzicus, Alcibiades led the Athenians to victory over the Spartans, who then offered to make peace with Athens. The Athenians refused, and the Spartans eventually rebuilt their fleet. In 406, the Spartan fleet defeated the Athenians at the battle of Notion. Alcibiades, although not present at the battle, was considered responsible for the Athenian fleet, and thus he was exiled again by the Athenians. The conclusion of

ARISTOPHANES' *FROGS,* produced in 405, suggests that the Athenians were still considering allowing Alcibiades to return, but the recall did not come to pass. Retiring to a castle he owned on the shores of the HELLESPONT, Alcibiades advised the Athenian fleet of a Spartan attack at Aegospotami; he was ignored and this setback paved the way for the ultimate defeat of Athens in 404. After the Athenians surrendered to the Spartans, the Spartan naval commander and statesman Lysander arranged for Alcibiades to be killed by the Persian satrap Pharnabazus.

Although Alcibiades does not appear as a character in any extant dramas, the comic poets mentioned him by name several times. Fragments from PHERECRATES (155 Kock 1) and Eupolis (158 Kock 1) refer to Alcibiades' relations with numerous women; a fragment from an unknown comic poet mentions Alcibiades' affair with the Spartan queen (fragment 3–5 Kock 3). In Aristophanes' *Banqueters* of 427 B.C.E., Alcibiades' name appears, and five years later Aristophanes makes fun of his lisp in *WASPS.* At least two characters in Aristophanes' plays, PHEIDIPPIDES in *CLOUDS* and PEISETAERUS in *BIRDS,* are thought to be modeled on Alcibiades.

Vickers, in his 2000 article, has suggested parallels between Alcibiades and several characters in extant tragedies. Vickers argues that the potentially incestuous relationship between PHAEDRA and HIPPOLYTUS in EURIPIDES' *HIPPOLYTUS* may have been influenced to some extent by a charge made against Alcibiades in a fragment from the works of the philosopher Antisthenes (fragment 29a Caizzi), which accuses Alcibiades of having sexual relations with his mother, daughter, and sister. Vickers suggests that Euripides' portrait of Hippolytus has parallels in Alcibiades and that Euripides' portrait of Phaedra may have been influenced by the prostitute Aspasia, the lover of Alcibiades' uncle, Pericles, who would then represent THESEUS in the play. Writing in 1987, Vickers finds similarities between Alcibiades and PHILOCTETES (Sophocles' *Philoctetes* was staged in 409 B.C.E.), who, as did Alcibiades, experienced exile and recall for military motives. Vickers equates ODYSSEUS, Philoctetes' enemy, with the orator Andocides, an opponent of Alcibiades'. Regarding Euripides' *CYCLOPS,* which Vickers dates to 408, Vickers links Alcibiades with the Odysseus of Euripides' play because both "were aristocrats in exile, articulate, and eager to return home." Vickers also links the drunken satyr SILENUS with "Alcibiades the archboozer." For Vickers, the blinded CYCLOPS represents either "a gross caricature of a Spartan" or an important ambassador of the king of Persia, an official known as the King's Eye. [ANCIENT SOURCES: Aristophanes, *Banqueters,* fragment 198.6 Kock, *Frogs* 1422ff, *Wasps* 44–46; Cornelius Nepos, *Alcibiades;* Plato, *Alcibiades, Gorgias, Symposium;* Plutarch, *Alcibiades, Nicias;* Thucydides, *Histories*]

BIBLIOGRAPHY

Bloedow, E. F. *Alcibiades Reexamined.* Wiesbaden, Ger.: Steiner, 1973.

Caizzi, F. D. *Antisthenis Fragmenta.* Milan: Istituto Editoriale Cisalpino, 1966.

Ellis, Walter M. *Alcibiades.* London: Routledge, 1989.

Forde, Steven. *The Ambition to Rule: Alcibiades and the Politics of Imperialism in Thucydides.* Ithaca, N.Y.: Cornell University Press, 1989.

Kock, T. *Comicorum Atticorum Fragmenta.* Vol. 1. Leipzig: Teubner, 1880.

———. *Comicorum Atticorum Fragmenta.* Vol. 3. Leipzig: Teubner, 1888.

Rhodes, P. J. *What Alcibiades Did or What Happened to Him.* Durham, N.C.: Durham University, 1985.

Tompkins, D. P. "Stylistic Characterization in Thucydides: Nicias and Alcibiades," *Yale Classical Studies* 22 (1972): 181–214.

Vickers, M. "Alcibiades on Stage: *Philoctetes* and *Cyclops,*" *Historia* 36 (1987): 171–97.

———. "Alcibiades and Aspasia: Notes on the *Hippolytus,*" *Dialogues d'histoire ancien* 26, no. 2 (2000): 7–17.

ALCIDES Another name for HERACLES, who was a "descendant of Alcaeus."

ALCMENA (ALCMENE or ALCUMENA) The daughter of Electryon and Anaxo (or AMPHIARAUS and ERIPHYLE), Alcmena is best known as the mother of HERACLES (Roman: Hercules). When Alcmena's brothers were killed attempting to repel a cattle raid by the TELEBOANS, her father, Electryon, left Mycenae to wage war against the raiders. Electryon left the kingdom and Alcmena under the care of his nephew AMPHITRYON. When Electryon returned,

Amphitryon accidentally killed his uncle. When Amphitryon went into exile, Alcmena accompanied her cousin to THEBES. In Thebes, Amphitryon and Alcmena married, but Alcmena would not consummate their marriage until Amphitryon avenged the death of her brothers. While Amphitryon was away fighting the Teleboans, ZEUS, disguised as Amphitryon, arrived at Alcmena's house and pretended to return victorious from battle. Alcmena slept with Zeus and became pregnant with Heracles. Not long after Zeus left, Amphitryon returned home. Alcmena was baffled by Amphitryon's appearance, and he was equally puzzled when she claimed to have had sexual relations with him a few hours earlier. The confusion was eventually resolved by the prophet TEIRESIAS, who explained what Zeus had done. Once Amphitryon and Alcmena learned the truth, they became reconciled and they too slept together. Thus, Alcmena became pregnant with fraternal twins. By Zeus, Alcmena had Heracles; by Amphitryon, she produced Iphicles.

When it was time for Alcmena to deliver her children, HERA delayed the birth so that EURYSTHEUS could be born first and receive a blessing (the kingship of ARGOS) that Zeus had intended for Heracles. After Heracles and Iphicles were born, some sources say that Alcmena, fearing that Hera would harm her, left Heracles to die. Athena, however, retrieved Heracles and returned him to Alcmena. Athena told Alcmena that she herself should not fear Hera, and that Heracles himself would be the target of any assault by Hera. After the birth of Heracles, we hear little of Alcmena. In EURIPIDES' HERACLES, she is not living in Thebes with Amphitryon, but some sources say that she returned to Tiryns and was living with some of Heracles' children. In Euripides' CHILDREN OF HERACLES, Alcmena has accompanied some of Heracles' children to MARATHON, where they took refuge from Eurystheus, who was trying to kill them. After Eurystheus was defeated in battle and captured, he was taken before Alcmena. The end of Euripides' play is lost; other sources say that Alcmena either demanded Eurystheus' execution or gouged out the eyes from Eurystheus' severed head, sent to her by HYLLUS, son of Heracles. Little is known about Alcmena's death except that the ancient sources usually say that Amphitryon preceded her in death.

Some sources say that after Amphitryon died, Alcmena married RHADAMANTHYS of CRETE, and that she and Rhadamanthys were buried in Haliartus.

Besides *Children of Heracles,* Euripides also wrote *Alcmena* (fragments 88–104 Nauck), which was probably staged before 428 B.C.E. and dealt with the circumstances surrounding Heracles' birth. Aeschylus also wrote a play titled *Alcmena,* from which one word survives (see fragment 12 Radt). The Greek tragedian Astydamas' *Alcmena* (fragment 1d Snell) survives only as a title.

Among the Romans, Alcmena became the prime example of a virtuous wife. Alcmena also appears as a character in Plautus' *Amphitruo,* in which she experiences much confusion about Zeus' being disguised as her husband. Although the words from Alcmena's mouth are often noble, Christenson argues that the presentation of Alcmena in this play is farcical, as she is portrayed as a sex-starved wife and, because she is pregnant during most of the play, she would have appeared in a heavily padded costume. We should also keep in mind that her part would have been played by a man. [ANCIENT SOURCES: Apollodorus, *Library* 2.4.5; Homer, *Iliad* 19.96–133; Ovid, *Metamorphoses* 9.280–323; Pausanias, 5.17.1]

BIBLIOGRAPHY

Christenson, David. "Grotesque Realism in Plautus' *Amphitruo,*" *Classical Journal* 96, no. 3 (2000–1): 243–60.

Nauck, A. *Tragicorum Graecorum Fragmenta.* Leipzig: Teubner. 1889. Reprint, Hildesheim, Ger.: Olms, 1964.

Snell, B. *Tragicorum Graecorum Fragmenta.* Vol. 1. Göttingen, Ger.: Vandenhoeck & Ruprecht, 1971.

Webster, T. B. L. *The Tragedies of Euripides.* London: Methuen, 1967.

ALCMEON (Latin: ALCMEO)

The son of AMPHIARAUS and ERIPHYLE, Alcmeon was the brother of Amphilochus. Ten years after the destruction of the expedition by the Seven against THEBES, the sons of the fallen leaders, known collectively as the EPIGONI, again undertook an attack on Thebes to avenge their fathers' deaths. In the earlier war, Eriphyle had been bribed by POLYNEICES with a necklace to persuade Amphiaraus to go to a war that took his life. In the expedition of the Epigoni, Polyneices' son Thersander bribed Eriphyle with a robe to persuade Alcmeon to go to war. An oracle had declared that the Epigoni would be victorious if Alcmeon led the army. Alcmeon did lead the Epigoni to victory and killed ETEOCLES' son Laodamas in the battle.

After the battle, Alcmeon learned of his mother's bribery. At this point, Alcmeon's story becomes similar to that of ORESTES. The angry Alcmeon, in accordance with another oracle, killed his mother, Eriphyle, and was subsequently tormented by her FURIES. Seeking purification from his crime, Alcmeon went to Oicles of Arcadia and then Phegeus of Psophis. Phegeus purified Alcmeon and then married him to his daughter ALPHESIBOEA (or Arsinoe). When a plague fell upon the town and an oracle revealed Alcmeon's presence as the cause, Alcmeon left Psophis and, at the instruction of the oracles, went to the river ACHELOUS for purification. After purification, Achelous married his daughter Callirrhoe to Alcmeon. Later, Callirrhoe refused to remain with Alcmeon unless he gave her the robe and necklace. Alcmeon then returned to Psophis to retrieve them and told Phegeus that his, Alcmeon's, madness would be healed if Phegeus gave him the robe and necklace. Phegeus handed over the items, but when he learned the truth about them, he told some of his sons to ambush and kill Alcmeon. When Alphesiboea accused the young men of this act, they sold her into slavery to Agapenor and claimed that she had murdered Alcmeon.

The legend of Alcmeon was apparently popular with dramatists, although no extant drama based on this subject survives. EURIPIDES wrote *Alcmeon in Corinth* and *Alcmeon in Psophis*. From the former play, only a single fragment survives (73a Snell). This fragment, perhaps the words of APOLLO, mentions the sons of Alcmeon. *Alcmeon in Psophis* was followed to the Athenian stage in 438 B.C.E. by *Cretan Women, Telephus,* and *Alcestis.* SOPHOCLES also wrote a play called *Alcmeon,* which may have dealt with Alcmeon's time in Psophis (fragments 108–10 Radt). Of Ennius' *Alcmeon* (Latin: *Alcmeo*) about 15 lines survive; the lines suggest that Ennius' play dealt with Alcmeon's Fury-induced madness.

Other tragedians who wrote plays entitled *Alcmeon* are AGATHON (fragment 2 Snell), Astydamas (fragment 1c Snell), Theodectas (fragments 1a–2 Snell), Timotheus (see Snell), Euaretus (fragment 2 Snell), and Nicomachus of Alexandria (fragment 2). A SATYR PLAY entitled *Alcmeon* is attributed to Achaeus (fragments 12–15 Snell). In Ennius' *Alcmeo* (fragments 14–16 Jocelyn), Alcmeon appears to have been tormented by the Furies. [ANCIENT SOURCES: Apollodorus, *Library* 3.7; Hyginus, *Fables* 73]

BIBLIOGRAPHY
Jocelyn, H. D. *The Tragedies of Ennius.* Cambridge: Cambridge University Press, 1969.
Snell, B. *Tragicorum Graecorum Fragmenta.* Vol. 1. Göttingen, Ger.: Vandenhoeck & Ruprecht, 1971.
Warmington, E. H. *Remains of Old Latin: Ennius and Caecilius.* Vol. 1. Cambridge, Mass.: Harvard University Press, 1935.

ALCYONE   See CEYX.

ALETES (ALEITES)

At least three characters of classical mythology have the name Aletes. One Aletes, the son of Icarius and Periboea, was the brother of ODYSSEUS' wife, PENELOPE. Another Aletes, a son of AEGISTHUS and CLYTEMNESTRA, usurped the kingdom of Argos from ORESTES. After returning from the land of the Taurians, Orestes killed Aletes and reclaimed the throne. Stobaeus attributed to SOPHOCLES a play entitled *Aleites,* which may have been about Orestes' killing of Aletes. A descendant of Heracles, also named Aletes, defeated the descendants of SISYPHUS at CORINTH and reestablished the rule of his family there. [ANCIENT SOURCES: Apollodorus, *Library* 3.10.6; Hyginus, *Fables* 122; Pausanias, 2.4.1; Strabo, 8.8.5]

ALEUS

This king of TEGEA was the husband of Neaera, by whom he had four children: three sons, Amphidamas, Cepheus, and LYCURGUS, and a daughter, AUGE. An oracle had said that Aleus would be killed by a son born to Auge. To prevent this death, Aleus made Auge one of ATHENA's priestesses, who had to be virgins, and threatened to kill her if she had intercourse. HERACLES, however, passing through the region, became drunk and had intercourse with Auge. When Aleus learned that Auge was pregnant, he gave her to the sailor Nauplius with instructions to drown her.

Before Nauplius could carry out these orders, Auge gave birth to a son. At this point, Nauplius disobeyed Aleus' instructions and gave Auge and her son to the Mysian king Teuthras. The latter married Auge and named the son TELEPHUS. Sophocles wrote a play entitled *The Sons of Aleus* (Greek: *Aleadae*). [ANCIENT SOURCES: Apollodorus, *Library* 2.7.4]

ALEXANDER   See PARIS.

ALEXANDRIA

Established in 331 B.C.E. and named after its founder, Alexander the Great, this port city became the capital of Egypt and an unsurpassed center of Greek culture. Alexandria was the home to the most substantial library in the ancient world. In addition to holding a collection of works that numbered in the hundreds of thousands and included manuscripts of the plays of the great dramatists, the library provided employment for poets and scholars. It was damaged by fire on several occasions, the most well known being in 47 B.C.E.

BIBLIOGRAPHY
Alexandria and Alexandrianism. Malibu, Calif.: J. Paul Getty Museum, 1996.
Forster, E. M. *Alexandria: A History and a Guide.* Garden City, N.Y.: Anchor Books, 1961.

ALEXICACUS

A title of the god HERMES and other divinities. Alexicacus means "he who wards off evil." [ANCIENT SOURCES: Aristophanes, *Peace* 422]

ALIS   See ELIS.

ALOPE

Not only is Alope the name of a town north of TRACHIS on the coast of northeastern Greece, it is also that of a daughter of the Eleusinian king CERCYON. Alope became the mother of Hippothoon by POSEIDON. Hyginus provides the most detailed source of her myth. After giving birth, Alope ordered her nurse to leave the child to die. A shepherd, however, found a mare nursing the child. When a second shepherd asked that the child be given to him, the first shepherd handed over the child, but not the regal clothing that the infant wore. When the two shepherds argued over the clothing, their dispute was taken

before Cercyon, king in the region of ARCADIA. Cercyon, recognizing the infant's clothing as his daughter's handiwork, again ordered the child to be left to die, but a mare and shepherds saved the child's life a second time. Alope, however, did not have the same good fortune when Cercyon killed her, although Poseidon transformed her into a fountain. THESEUS killed Cercyon and turned over his kingdom to Hippothoon when he learned that Hippothoon, as he was, was Poseidon's son. Several plays entitled *Alope* survive. Nine brief fragments survive from Euripides' *Alope* (105–13 Nauck), staged, Ferguson thinks, in 414 along with *Ion* and *Heracles.* Aristotle mentions an *Auge* by Carcinus; Pausanias knew of one written by Choerilus. [ANCIENT SOURCES: Aristophanes, *Birds* 559; Aristotle, *Nichomachean Ethics* 1150b10; Hyginus, *Fables* 187; Pausanias, 1.14.3]

BIBLIOGRAPHY
Ferguson, J. "Tetralogies, Divine Paternity, and the Plays of 414," *Transactions and Proceedings of the American Philological Association* 100 (1969): 109–117.
Nauck, A. *Tragicorum Graecorum Fragmenta.* Leipzig: Teubner. 1889. Reprint, Hildesheim, Ger.: Olms, 1964).
Snell, B. *Tragicorum Graecorum Fragmenta.* Vol. 1. Göttingen, Ger.: Vandenhoeck & Ruprecht, 1971.
Webster, T. B. L. *The Tragedies of Euripides.* London: Methuen, 1967.

ALPHESIBOEA

The daughter of Phegeus, Alphesiboea (also known as Arsinoe) married ALCMEON, who had gone to PSOPHIS after he had killed his mother, ERIPHYLE. After an oracle from Apollo prompted Alcmeon to leave Psophis and marry another woman, ACHELOUS' daughter Callirrhoe, Alphesiboea continued to love Alcmeon. After Alphesiboea's brothers killed Alcmeon, she was angry with them. Accordingly, they enclosed her in a box; took her to Agapenor, king of Tegea; and claimed she had killed Alcmeon. Alphesiboea died in Tegea after she arranged for her brothers to be killed by Alcmeon's sons. Among the Greek dramatists, the tragedian Achaeus wrote an *Alphesiboea,* whose three surviving words (fragment 16 Snell) refer to someone who is raving mad. The single seven-line fragment extant from Chaeremon's *Alphesiboea* (fragment 1 Snell) describes the skin and hair of a beautiful woman (Alphesiboea?). Timotheus also wrote an *Alphesiboea,* of which only the title survives. [ANCIENT SOURCES: Pausanias, 8.24.8–10]

BIBLIOGRAPHY
Snell, B. *Tragicorum Graecorum Fragmenta.* Vol. 1. Göttingen, Ger.: Vandenhoeck & Ruprecht, 1971.

ALTHAEA   The daughter of Thestius and Eurythemis, Althaea was the sister of Euippus, Eurypylus, Hypermnestra, Iphiclus, LEDA, Plexippus, and Prothous. Althaea became the wife of the Calydonian king OENEUS, by whom she had four sons, Clymenus, MELEAGER, Thyreus, and Toxeus, and two daughters, DEIANEIRA and Gorge. The best known of her children are Deianeira, who eventually married HERACLES, and Meleager, who killed the Calydonian boar. Althaea, having learned through prophecy that Meleager would live as long as a certain log remained intact, hid it in a chest. Many years later, after Meleager killed Althaea's brothers, Althaea burned the log completely. In her grief, Althaea committed suicide. [ANCIENT SOURCES: Apollodorus, *Library* 1.7.10–1.8.3; Homer, *Iliad* 9.543–99; Hyginus, *Fables* 129; Ovid, *Metamorphoses* 8.260–456]

AMAZONS   The Amazons are depicted as a female-dominated tribe of warriors who frequently live on the fringes of the Greek world, most often near the Black Sea region. Numerous Greek heroes fought against Amazon women. BELLEROPHON battled some Amazons during his stay with Iobates of Lycia. HERACLES defeated an attack of Amazon women during his quest for an Amazon's girdle. THESEUS, who accompanied Heracles on his mission and abducted the Amazon Hippolyta (or ANTIOPE), eventually fought and defeated the Amazons on Athenian soil. By Hippolyta Theseus fathered HIPPOLYTUS, but eventually divorced her (and killed her) in favor of PHAEDRA. In the final year of the Trojan War, Achilles killed the Amazon Penthesileia, who had allied herself and her women with the Trojans. Three Greek comic poets wrote plays entitled *Amazons:* Dinolochus (fragment 2 Kaibel), Cephisodorus (fragment 1 Kock 1), and Epicrates (fragment 1 Kock 2). Only the title of Dinolochus' play survives and the fragments from the plays of Cephisodorus and Epicrates are too brief to be informative. [ANCIENT SOURCES: Apollodorus, 2.5.9; Aristophanes, *Lysistrata* 679; Diodorus Siculus, 4.16; Euripides, *Heracles* 374, 408, *Hippolytus* 10, 307, 351, 581, *Ion* 1145; Herodotus, 4.110–17; Homer, *Iliad* 6.186; Hyginus, *Fables* 30; Pausanias, 1.17.2, 1.41.7, 5.10.2; Plutarch, *Theseus* 27, 31, 33; Quintus Smyrnaeus, 1.18–47]

BIBLIOGRAPHY
duBois, Page. *Centaurs and Amazons: Women and the Pre-History of the Great Chain of Being.* Ann Arbor: University of Michigan Press, 1982.
Kaibel, G. *Comicorum Graecorum Fragmenta.* Vol. 1.1 [*Poetarum Graecorum Fragmenta.* Vol. 6.1]. Berlin: Weidmann, 1899.
Kock, T. *Comicorum Atticorum Fragmenta.* Vol. 1. Leipzig: Teubner, 1880.
———. *Comicorum Atticorum Fragmenta.* Vol. 2. Leipzig: Teubner, 1884.
Von Bothmer, Dietrich. *Amazons in Greek Art.* Oxford: Clarendon Press, 1957.

AMEIPSIAS   An Athenian comic poet who was a contemporary and rival of ARISTOPHANES. In 423 B.C.E., a work by Ameipsias placed second in dramatic competition, ahead of Aristophanes' CLOUDS; in 414, Ameipsias' work was victorious and defeated Aristophanes' BIRDS. He also won a victory at the LENAEA in the late fifth or early fourth century. [ANCIENT SOURCES: Aristophanes, *Frogs* 14]

BIBLIOGRAPHY
Austin, C. *Comicorum Graecorum Fragmenta in Papyris Reperta.* Berlin: De Gruyter, 1973.
Sommerstein, A. H. *The Comedies of Aristophanes.* Vol. 9, *Frogs.* Warminster, U.K.: Aris & Phillips, 1996, 158.

AMMON   The ram-headed Egyptian god whom the Greeks identified with Zeus. Ammon had an oracle in the Libyan desert whose "fame had come to rival that of Delphi and Dodona" (Dunbar). [ANCIENT SOURCES: Aristophanes, *Birds* 619, 716; Euripides, *Alcestis* 116, *Electra* 734]

BIBLIOGRAPHY
Dunbar, Nan. *Aristophanes: Birds.* New York: Oxford University Press, 1995, 407.

Parke, H. W. *Greek Oracles.* London: Hutchinson, 1967.
———. *The Oracles of Zeus: Dodona, Olympia, Ammon.* Oxford: Blackwell, 1967.

AMPHIARAUS

Amphiaraus, son of Oicles (or APOLLO) and Hypermestra, daughter of Thestius, was a prophet and nobleman of ARGOS. He participated in the hunt for the Calydonian boar but is best known for his association with the famous Seven against THEBES expedition. Amphiaraus married ERIPHYLE, sister of the Argive king ADRASTUS. Amphiaraus foresaw that everyone (except Adrastus) who participated in the war against Thebes would die but was eventually persuaded to participate in it by his wife, Eriphyle, whom Polyneices had bribed with the notorious necklace of Cadmus' daughter Harmonia. At Thebes, Amphiaraus died, swallowed up by the earth.

Although Amphiaraus does not appear as a speaking character in any complete extant tragedies, he played a significant role in EURIPIDES' *Hypsipyle* (cf. Bond, Page). In *Hypsipyle,* the title character has been charged with care of the infant OPHELTES. When Amphiaraus arrives he asks Hypsipyle to show him a spring of pure water so that he can make a libation for the army (on its way to Thebes). When Hypsipyle does so, leaving the infant unattended, the child is bitten by a snake and dies. The child's mother, EURYDICE, thinking Hypsipyle has murdered the child, orders Hypsipyle to be killed. At this point in the drama, Amphiaraus plays a role comparable to that played by ARTEMIS in Euripides' *HIPPOLYTUS.* As Hypsipyle is being led away to die, Amphiaraus arrives to explain the truth of Opheltes' death. Upon hearing Amphiaraus, Eurydice decides to spare Hypsipyle's life.

Among other tragedians, Cleophon wrote an *Amphiaraus,* of which only the title survives. The younger Carcinus also composed an *Amphiaraus,* of which the single stage direction that survives tells us nothing about the play's plot. From among the work of the comic poets, the single line of Philippides' *Amphiaraus* that survives indicates nothing of the plot. ARISTOPHANES' *Amphiaraus* was performed in 414 B.C.E. at the LENAEA (fragments 1–19, Meineke 2.2); [ANCIENT SOURCES: Apollodorus, *Library* 3.6.2; Hyginus, *Fables* 68, 73, 128]

BIBLIOGRAPHY

Bond, G. W. *Euripides: Hypsipyle.* Oxford: Clarendon Press, 1963.

Meineke, A. *Fragmenta Comicorum Graecorum.* Vol. 2.2. 1841. Reprint, Berlin: De Gruyter, 1970.

———. *Fragmenta Comicorum Graecorum.* Vol. 4. Berlin: 1841. Reprint, De Gruyter, 1970.

Page, D. L. *Select Papyri.* Vol. 3. 1941, Reprint, London: Heinemann, 1970.

Snell, B. *Tragicorum Graecorum Fragmenta.* Vol. 1. Göttingen, Ger.: Vandenhoeck & Ruprecht, 1971.

AMPHITHEATER

Although the structures are known by the Greek word that means "double theater" or "a place to view on both sides," the first amphitheaters, built in the first century B.C.E., are credited to the Romans. Amphitheaters are best known as the sites of gladiatorial matches and wild animal hunts, rather than of performances of plays.

AMPHITHEUS

A fictional divinity who appears early in ARISTOPHANES' *ACHARNIANS* and arranges for DICAEOPOLIS a peace treaty with the Spartans. The god's name literally means "divine on both sides." Sommerstein translates the god's name as "Godschild." The name Amphitheus was known in ATHENS. Griffith tried to identify Aristophanes' divinity with one of the playwright's contemporaries.

BIBLIOGRAPHY

Dow, S. "Some Athenians in Aristophanes," *American Journal of Archaeology* 73 (1969): 234–35.

Griffith, J. G. "Amphitheos and Anthropos in Aristophanes," *Hermes* 102 (1974): 367–69.

Sommerstein, A. H. *The Comedies of Aristophanes.* Vol. 1, *Acharnians.* Warminster, U.K.: Aris & Phillips, 1980.

AMPHITRUO PLAUTUS (AFTER 201 B.C.E.)

The circumstances surrounding the birth of Hercules (Greek: HERACLES) are the subject of this play, set in THEBES. The action takes place before the house of Amphitruo (see AMPHITRYON). As the play opens, Mercury (Greek: HERMES), in a lengthy PROLOGUE (152 lines), calls for the audience's attention and informs them that the subject of the play is tragic, but that he will change it into a TRAGICOMEDY. Mercury also says he is going to send inspectors into the audience to make sure no one has been stationed to support or disrupt any of the actors unfairly. After these preliminary remarks, the audience is informed that Amphitruo, the husband of Alcumena (see ALCMENA), led the Theban people to war against the TELEBOANS, and that Alcumena was pregnant. After Amphitruo departed for war, Jupiter (see ZEUS), king of the gods, disguised himself as Amphitruo, slept with Alcumena, and impregnated her. Furthermore, Mercury relates that his father remains in the house and has lengthened the night. He adds that he has disguised himself as Amphitruo's SLAVE, Sosia, and that he and Jupiter will be wearing little gold tassels on their hats so that the audience will be able to distinguish them from the real Sosia and Amphitruo. These tassels will be unnoticed by the other people on stage, however.

In the opening act, Sosia, carrying a lantern, arrives from the harbor to inform Alcumena of his success in battle. He tells the audience of the Thebans' victory and Amphitruo's success. Before entering the house, Sosia rehearses the speech that he will deliver to Alcumena. He relates the battle between the Thebans and Teleboans and notes that Amphitruo killed the opposing king, PTERELAS, and then was given a golden bowl as a prize of victory. After rehearsing his speech, Sosia prepares to enter the house, but Mercury blocks his access. Mercury/Sosia and the real Sosia quarrel, and Mercury forcefully drives a bewildered Sosia from the house. As Sosia leaves, he declares that he will go to the harbor to tell Amphitruo what has happened. After Sosia exits, Mercury declares that he will trick Sosia and Amphitruo when they return, he also says that the trickery of the two gods will cause trouble between Amphitruo and Alcumena, but that Jupiter will eventually smooth out matters. Additionally, Mercury notes that today Alcumena will give birth to twins, one the son of Jupiter, the other the son of Amphitruo, and says Amphitruo will learn the truth about Jupiter's sleeping with Alcumena. Mercury then steps aside as Jupiter and Alcumena emerge from the house. Jupiter tells an unhappy Alcumena that he must return to his troops. To soothe Alcumena's ruffled feelings at so sudden a departure, Jupiter gives Alcumena the golden bowl that he says he won as spoil in the war.

The second act opens with the return of the real Sosia and the real Amphitruo. Sosia tries, unsuccessfully, to convince Amphitruo that he, Sosia, was driven from the house by Sosia. The befuddled and angry Amphitruo soon becomes more confused after he sees Alcumena. He expects that she will be glad to see him, but Alcumena is puzzled that Amphitruo has returned so soon after leaving. Alcumena is also upset because she thinks Amphitruo's sudden, unannounced return is an attempt to test her fidelity. Alcumena stirs up further anger and confusion in Amphitruo when she tells him all about the battle he just fought and produces the golden bowl that Jupiter gave to her. Amphitruo is astonished, and when Sosia opens the box where he was keeping the bowl, the box is empty. Amphitruo is further horrified when Alcumena declares that they have slept together. Amphitruo expresses his belief that Alcumena has been seduced, but Alcumena swears (ironically by Jupiter and Juno) that she has slept with no one except him. Amphitruo is still baffled and ponders divorcing Alcumena. Eventually, Amphitruo decides to invite Alcumena's relative, Naucrates, who sailed with Amphitruo on his journey, to arbitrate the couple's dispute.

In the third act, Jupiter appears and tells the audience that he has arrived to help Alcumena out of her predicament. He also announces that he will eventually help Alcumena and Amphitruo to reconcile and Alcumena to give birth to her twins painlessly. Alcumena then emerges from the house and declares that she will leave Amphitruo if he does not apologize to her. When Jupiter/Amphitruo approaches her and tells her that he was just testing her, she is not persuaded. Only when he swears by Jupiter and calls a curse upon Amphitruo if he is lying does Alcumena finally relax. With Alcumena appeased, Jupiter asks her to prepare for a sacrifice (to Jupiter). With Alcumena busy in the house, Jupiter calls Amphitruo's Sosia out to invite Blepharo, the pilot of Amphitruo's ship, to lunch. However, Jupiter says Blepharo will not have lunch, because Amphitruo will know nothing about the invitation. After Sosia, thinking Jupiter is Amphitruo, sets out to find Blepharo, Jupiter summons Mercury and orders him to trick Amphitruo. Mercury, still disguised as Sosia, agrees to do so; he says he will climb onto the roof of the house and pretend to be drunk.

In the fourth act, Amphitruo arrives, unable to find Naucrates. When Amphitruo tries to gain entrance to his house, he is met from above by Mercury/Sosia, who begins to wrangle verbally with him. As their argument begins, a gap occurs in the manuscript (after line 1034), and most of the remainder of the act is lost. The surviving fragments from the missing section suggest that Mercury and Amphitruo's quarrel caused Alcumena to emerge from the house. After Alcumena and Amphitruo again quarrel, Amphitruo leaves the house, perhaps to get help from some friends. When Amphitruo returns, he encounters Sosia returning with Blepharo. Another argument between Amphitruo and Sosia apparently takes place, after which Sosia exits. Jupiter then emerges from the house and argues with Amphitruo. Near the end of the fourth act, the manuscript resumes with Amphitruo's appealing to Blepharo for help, but Blepharo leaves because he does not know which Amphitruo he is being asked to help. Jupiter/Amphitruo then enters the house because Alcumena is about to deliver her twins. Amphitruo laments what has happened to him and declares he will enter the house and kill everyone he sees. Before he can enter, a thunderclap occurs and knocks him to the ground.

The play's final act opens with the arrival of a maidservant, Bromia, who announces that she heard the thunderclap and heard the voice of Jupiter declare that he had arrived to give aid to Alcumena. Bromia also announces that Alcumena has given birth to twin sons. Bromia then finds Amphitruo lying on the ground, helps him up, and tells him about what has happened inside the house. Bromia tells Amphitruo that when the twins were in their cradles, two serpents attacked the children, but the bigger of the twin boys (see HER-ACLES) killed the serpents with his bare hands. Bromia also tells Amphitruo that she heard Jupiter's voice declare that the child who had killed the snakes was his son, and the other child was Amphitruo's son. Upon hearing this, Amphitruo makes no complaint about sharing his bed with Jupiter and orders that a sacrifice be prepared for the god. He also announces his intention to consult the prophet TIRESIAS about what he should do. Another thunderclap occurs, and Jupiter appears and tells Amphitruo not to consult

Tiresias; Jupiter explains his actions to Amphitruo and tells him to resume his life with Alcumena. As Jupiter departs for the skies, Amphitruo promises to do as the god has commanded him.

COMMENTARY

Amphitruo is one of PLAUTUS' most interesting plays, and its influence on drama in modern times has been significant. The French playwright Molière wrote an *Amphitryon* and Plautus' use of two sets of identical twins may have influenced Shakespeare's *Comedy of Errors.* As in BACCHIDES and MENAECHMI, in *Amphitruo* the humor of twins is exploited. In *Amphitruo,* however, Plautus has created two sets of twins rather than one. Furthermore, the divine nature of the twins usually allows them to control the situation totally.

Amphitruo shares some similarities with plays such as *Bacchides* and *Menaechmi;* it also resembles HAUNTED HOUSE, in that one of the primary functions of the wily slave in the play is to prevent others from entering the house. In *Haunted House,* the slave Tranio tries to prevent the father from entering the house because he will find that his son is having a party with his friends and a prostitute. In *Amphitruo,* the divine slave Mercury tries to prevent a mortal slave and the mortal owner of the house from entering and catching the king of the gods with the wife of the owner of the house. Mercury, as a god, can use the threat of physical violence to repel anyone who might interrupt his father's fun. Tranio, in *Haunted House,* must rely on elaborate trickery to prevent the father from spoiling the son's pleasure.

Plautus' *Amphitruo* is also intriguing because it is the only extant comedy among the works of Plautus or TERENCE that humorously renders an event from mythology. Unlike in other Roman comedies in which wily members of the lower or servile classes trick members of the upper classes, in *Amphitruo* the king of the gods authorizes and orchestrates the trickery. Whereas Hermes (Mercury) appears in several surviving Greek dramas, this is the only extant play in which Zeus (Jupiter) does.

In addition to including a unique, humorous dramatization of a mythological event, *Amphitruo* is an atypical Roman comedy with no fathers or pimps to be tricked, no lovesick men, no quest to acquire money to buy the man's beloved. Amphitruo is a soldier, but he is not the overconfident, braggart warrior seen in other Roman comedies. Amphitruo's war exploits are fact, not exaggerations. Amphitruo also plays an unusual comic male role, for he actually loves his wife. Husbands in Roman comedy typically either express no feelings for their wife or seek some younger woman with whom to have an affair. Additionally, Amphitruo loves his wife but does not display the obsessed anguish of other lovers in Roman comedy.

Alcumena is also not the usual matron one finds in Roman comedy. She is not, for example, like the nameless wife in *Menaechmi* who constantly watches her husband and questions his every action. As do several young women in Roman comedy, Alcumena gives birth during the play, but she becomes pregnant not as the result of a drunken young man's violence, but through the actions of the king of the gods, disguised as her husband. Alcumena's words in this play are often noble, but Christenson (2000) argues that the presentation of Alcumena in *Amphitruo* is farcical, as she is characterized as a sex-starved wife and, because she is pregnant during most of the play, she would have appeared in a heavily padded costume.

BIBLIOGRAPHY

Baier, T., ed. *Studien zu Plautus' Amphitruo*. Tubingen, Ger.: Narr, 1999.

Bond, R. P. "Plautus' *Amphitryo* as Tragi-Comedy," *Greece and Rome* 46, no. 2 (1999): 203–19.

Christenson, D. *Plautus: Amphitruo*. Cambridge: Cambridge University Press, 2000.

————. "Grotesque Realism in Plautus' *Amphitruo*," *Classical Journal* 96, no. 3 (2001): 243–60.

Schmidt, E. A. "Die Tragikomodie *Amphitruo* des Plautus als Komodie und Tragodie," *Museum Helveticum* 60, no. 2 (2003): 80–104.

AMPHITRYON (Latin: AMPHITRUO)

Amphitryon, the son of Alcaeus, was a descendant of PERSEUS. The sources differ as to the identity of Amphitryon's mother (Astydameia, Hipponome, Laonome, or Lysidice). Amphitryon became the husband of ALCMENA and by her the father of Iphicles. Amphitryon was the foster father of HERACLES, whose real father was ZEUS. After a raid on his uncle, ELEC-TRYON's, cattle by the Teleboans, Amphitryon's uncle entrusted him to watch over the kingdom while he searched for the cattle. Electryon also entrusted Amphitryon with the care of his daughter, Alcmena. Not only did Amphitryon watch over the kingdom and Alcmena, but also he managed to recover Electryon's cattle during his uncle's absence. When Electryon returned, Amphitryon presented him with the cattle. According to some sources, the cattle stampeded and killed Electryon. Other sources say that Amphitryon threw a stick at the cattle, which ricocheted off one of the cow's heads, struck Electryon, and killed him. In either event, after Electryon's death, Amphitryon left Argos and went into exile at THEBES. Because all of Alcmena's male relatives were dead, she accompanied Amphitryon.

In Thebes, CREON purified Amphitryon of killing Electryon. Amphitryon also helped Creon rid Thebes of a dangerous fox that was ravaging the land. Amphitryon and Alcmena also appear to have been married around this time. Alcmena, however, refused to consummate their marriage until Amphitryon avenged the deaths of her brothers, who had been killed defending their father's cattle. With military backing from Creon, Amphitryon waged war successfully against the Teleboans. While Amphitryon was at war, Zeus disguised himself as Amphitryon and had intercourse with Alcmena, who became pregnant with Heracles. Amphitryon returned from war after Zeus left, and he also had intercourse with Alcmena, who became pregnant with Iphicles.

Amphitryon appears as a character in EURIPIDES' *HERACLES*, SENECA's *HERCULES FURENS*, and PLAUTUS' *AMPHITRUO*. In Euripides' play, Amphitryon is the aged defender of HERACLES' wife and children against the evil LYCUS, who threatens to kill them. As a defender of children, Amphitryon most recalls IOLAUS, who performs that role for the hero's children in Euripides' *CHILDREN OF HERACLES*. Also as Iolaus does, Amphitryon witnesses the overthrow of the evil tyrant who oppresses the children. In *Children,* however, Heracles' offspring are saved by the sacrifice of their sister and Iolaus' miraculous rejuvenation, which allows him to capture the evil king EURYSTHEUS. In *Heracles,* Amphitryon himself gives Heracles advice and helps lure

Lycus to a doom that Heracles inflicts on him. In *Heracles,* the evil king is dead halfway through the play, and Amphitryon's role seems to change in the second half of the play. After Heracles' madness and destruction of his family, Amphitryon becomes more like Euripides' ELECTRA in ORESTES, who must care for the hero who has been tormented by madness and has committed a horrific crime.

Amphitryon's presence in Euripides' *Heracles* also serves as a constant reminder of the dual paternity with which Heracles struggles. Doubts about Heracles' divine paternity are mentioned throughout the play—by Lycus (148–49), Amphitryon (339–47), the Theban chorus (803–6), and eventually Heracles himself (1258–65), who declares that he considers Amphitryon his father rather than Zeus. Thus, in the first half of the play, Heracles rescues his mortal father Amphitryon, and in the second half of the play he denies that he has a divine father and embraces Amphitryon as his true father.

In Seneca's *Hercules Furens,* Amphitryon's contribution to the plot is essentially the same as in Euripides' play. As in *Heracles,* Seneca's Amphitryon does try to soothe MEGARA's fears Hercules will not return. Additionally, Seneca's Amphitryon defends to Lycus the story of Hercules' divine birth and his wondrous labors, although the two do not argue about the nature of the bow as in Euripides' play. After the madness of Senecan Hercules, Amphitryon (see EURIPIDES) is first to face his son and tries to dissuade him from committing suicide. One difference between Euripidean Amphitryon and Senecan Amphitryon is that Senecan Amphitryon does not attribute Hercules' servitude to Eurystheus as being due to an effort to help Amphitryon return to his native land of ARGOS. Additionally, unlike Euripides' Amphitryon, Seneca's Amphitryon asks Lycus to kill him before he kills Megara and the children. Also, unlike in Euripides' play, in which an anonymous messenger tells of Heracles' destruction of his wife and children, in Seneca's Amphitryon describes these gory details. Finally, in contrast to Euripides' Amphitryon, Seneca's Amphitryon threatens to kill himself after his son's madness, but his son prevents him.

In Plautus' *Amphitruo,* the title character is portrayed as a victorious warrior, but he is unlike the braggart warriors whom Plautus usually brings to stage. Indeed, Amphitruo is one of the few warriors in Plautus' plays whose deeds can actually match his words and who is not mocked behind his back by those who consider his actions in war a joke or even a complete fiction. Whereas other warriors in Plautus gain little sympathy from audiences, people can actually sympathize with Amphitruo as he is tricked, not by a wily slave as in other Plautine works, but by the gods themselves.

Sophocles wrote an *Amphitryon,* which may have dealt with Amphitryon's killing of Electryon. Three other playwrights wrote plays titled *Amphitryon:* the tragedian Aeschylus of Alexandria (fragment 1 Snell) and two comic poets, Archippus (fragments 1–7 Kock) and Rhinthon (fragment 1 Kaibel). Of Rhinthon's play, only the title survives. The two surviving lines of Aeschylus' play tell nothing about the plot. Athenaeus (10.426b) indicates that Archippus' *Amphitryon* apparently had a second production and fragment 2 indicates that drinking of wine occurred in the play.

BIBLIOGRAPHY

Gregory, J. W. "Euripides' *Heracles*," *Yale Classical Studies* 25 (1977): 259–75.

Kaibel, G. *Comicorum Graecorum Fragmenta.* Vol. 1.1 [*Poetarum Graecorum Fragmenta.* Vol. 6.1]. Berlin: Weidmann, 1899.

Kock, T. *Comicorum Atticorum Fragmenta.* Vol. 1. Leipzig: Teubner, 1880.

Snell, B. *Tragicorum Graecorum Fragmenta.* Vol. 1. Göttingen, Ger.: Vandenhoeck & Ruprecht, 1971.

AMYCLAE

AMYCLAE   A town just south of SPARTA in southern Greece. [ANCIENT SOURCES: Aristophanes, *Lysistrata* 1299]

AMYMONE   The daughter of Danaus, Amymone went to search for water near ARGOS, after POSEIDON had caused the region's springs to dry up. Seeing a deer, she attempted to hit the animal with a spear but instead struck a SATYR, who attempted to assault her sexually. When Poseidon happened to pass by, the satyr ran away; Amymone then had intercourse with Poseidon, who showed to her LERNA's springs. AESCHYLUS wrote an *Amymone* (fragments 13–15 Radt), which may have been a SATYR PLAY. [ANCIENT SOURCES: Apollodorus, *Library* 2.1.4; Hyginus, *Fables* 149a]

BIBLIOGRAPHY
Smyth, H. W., and H. Lloyd-Jones. *Aeschylus.* Vol. 2. 1926.
Reprint, Cambridge, Mass.: Harvard University Press, 1971.

AMYNIAS (1)   An unknown person mentioned by ARISTOPHANES at *CLOUDS* 31 as someone to whom STREPSIADES owes money.

BIBLIOGRAPHY
Dover, Kenneth. *Aristophanes: Frogs.* Oxford: Clarendon Press, 1993, 97.

AMYNIAS (2)   The son of Pronapes, Amynias was mocked by several comic poets for being effeminate or for being a braggart or avoiding military service. He may have been wealthy at one time but lost his money by gambling. In 423/2 B.C.E., Amynias may have served as a general for the Athenian military. ARISTOPHANES and HERMIPPUS suggest that Amynias may have been a Spartan sympathizer or have been involved in some scheme with the Spartan general BRASIDAS. [ANCIENT SOURCES: Aristophanes, *Clouds* 691, *Wasps* 74, 1266; Cratinus, fragment 213 Kock; Eupolis, fragment 209 Kock; Hermippus, fragment 71 Kock]

BIBLIOGRAPHY
MacDowell, D. M. *Aristophanes: Wasps.* Oxford: Clarendon Press, 1971, 139.
Sommerstein, A. H. *The Comedies of Aristophanes.* Vol. 4, *Wasps.* Warminster, U.K.: Aris & Phillips, 1983, 159.

AMYNON   A person mentioned only by ARISTOPHANES at *ECCLESIAZUSAE* 365 and by the ancient commentators on that line. Aristophanes suggests he was "a passive homosexual" (Sommerstein) and the ancient commentators indicate that Amynon may have been a male prostitute before he became an Athenian politician.

BIBLIOGRAPHY
Sommerstein, A. H. *The Comedies of Aristophanes.* Vol. 10, *Ecclesiazusae.* Warminster, U.K.: Aris & Phillips, 1998, 172.

ANACREON (BORN CA. 570 B.C.E.)   A Greek poet from Teos (on the western coast of modern Turkey). Anacreon wrote elegiac, iambic, and lyric poetry. [ANCIENT SOURCES: *Thesmophoriazusae* 161]

ANAGNORISIS   A Greek word meaning "recognition," *anagnorisis* refers to an event in drama in which characters recognize or learn something that they did not previously know. Probably the most famous example of *anagnorisis* in drama occurs when OEDIPUS discovers that he has killed his father and married his mother. *Anagnorisis* also occurs in COMEDY, as, for example, in PLAUTUS' *MENAECHMI,* when the twin Menaechmus brothers recognize one another. [ANCIENT SOURCES: Aristotle, *Poetics* 1452a29–b13]

ANAGYROUS   A DEME on the coast south of ATHENS, Anagyrous took its name from a foul-smelling plant that grew in this marshy area. Both ARISTOPHANES (fragments 41–63 Kock 1) and DIPHILUS (fragment 11 Kock 2) wrote plays that bear the name of this DEME's local hero, Anagyrus. Only the title of Diphilus' *Anagyrus* survives. Aristophanes' *Anagyrus* appears to have been staged about 418 or 417 B.C.E. and contained an attack on the comic playwright EUPOLIS. [ANCIENT SOURCES: Aristophanes, *Lysistrata* 67–68; Plato Comicus, fragment 160]

BIBLIOGRAPHY
Henderson, J. *Aristophanes: Lysistrata.* Oxford: Clarendon Press, 1987, 76.
Hofmann, H. "Ein Kommentar zum Anagyros des Aristophanes (P. Oxy. 2737)," *Zeitschrift für Papyrologie und Epigraphik* 5 (1970): 1–10.
Kock, T. *Comicorum Atticorum Fragmenta.* Vol. 1. Leipzig: Teubner, 1880.
———. *Comicorum Atticorum Fragmenta.* Vol. 2. Leipzig: Teubner, 1884.
Luppe, W. "Der Anagyros-Kommentar Pap. Oxy. 2737," *Archiv für Papyrusforschung und verwandte Gebiete* 21 (1971): 93–110.
———. "Ein neues Lemma im Anagyros-Kommentar (Fr. 56 Austin)," *Zeitschrift für Papyrologie und Epigraphik* 30 (1978): 20–22.

ANALEMMA   This Greek word (plural: *analemmata*) refers to a support wall on the side of Greek theaters. *Analemmata* were built out from the slope of a hill.

ANAPHLYSTUS   A DEME on the coast of Athenian territory that was southeast of ATHENS. ARISTOPHANES mentions this deme because its name is similar to the Greek verb *anaphlan,* which means "to masturbate" or "to achieve an erection." [ANCIENT SOURCES: Aristophanes, *Ecclesiazusae* 979, *Frogs* 427]

BIBLIOGRAPHY
Sommerstein, A. H. *The Comedies of Aristophanes.* Vol. 10,
   Ecclesiazusae. Warminster, U.K.: Aris & Phillips, 1998, 222.

ANAPIESMA   The Greek word *anapiesma* means "that which presses upward." In ancient drama, the *anapiesma* was some type of trap door to allow characters such as the FURIES to rise up from below the ground level of the theater. An *anapiesma* did not exist in every theater and its use probably did not begin until the latter half of the fourth century B.C.E. [ANCIENT SOURCES: Pollux, *Onomasticon* 4.127, 132]

ANCAEUS   A son of LYCURGUS of Arcadia, Ancaeus participated in the hunt for the Calydonian boar and was killed by the boar during the course of the hunt. [ANCIENT SOURCES: Apollodorus, *Library* 1.8.2; Ovid, *Metamorphoses* 8.401–7; Seneca, *Medea* 643]

ANDRIA (THE GIRL FROM ANDROS)
TERENCE (166 B.C.E.)   Traditionally, this play has been considered the earliest of TERENCE's surviving works. In the play's prologue, Terence admits that he has combined elements from MENANDER's *Andria* and *Perinthia* for his play. The action takes place in ATHENS before the houses of Simo, an Athenian gentleman, and Glycerium, the woman from ANDROS.

As the play opens, Simo informs his freedman, Sosia, that the anticipated wedding of his son, Pamphilus, and Chremes' daughter, Philumena, will not take place. Simo explains that Chrysis, a woman from the island of Andros, moved to Athens and became a prostitute. When the companions of Simo's son Pamphilus took him along to her house, Pamphilus did not partake of her sexual favors. Simo's neighbor, Chremes, was so impressed by Pamphilus' behavior that he arranged with Simo for his daughter Philumena to marry Pamphilus. A few days after this arrangement, Chrysis died and at the funeral Pamphilus became attracted to Chrysis' sister, Glycerium. When Glycerium moved too close to the funeral pyre, Pamphilus

stopped her, and she fell weeping into his arms. When Chremes learned of Pamphilus' actions with Glycerium, he broke off Pamphilus' engagement to Philumena. At this point, Simo tells Sosia that he himself will try to patch up matters with Chremes; Sosia's job will be to prevent Pamphilus and Davus, another of Simo's slaves, from carrying out any plot.

After Sosia exits, Simo encounters Davus and threatens him with torture if he does anything to stop the marriage of Pamphilus and Philumena. When Simo departs, Davus puzzles over whether to help Pamphilus or obey Simo. Davus also reveals that Pamphilus has impregnated Glycerium and that Pamphilus and Glycerium have invented a story that Glycerium was an Athenian and that she was raised by Chrysis' father after he discovered her as an infant washed up on Andros. After his soliloquy, Davus goes to the FORUM to find Pamphilus.

Next, Mysis, a maidservant of Simo's, emerges from Simo's house to fetch the midwife Lesbia, as Glycerium's labor is beginning. Mysis is interrupted by a highly agitated Pamphilus, who has just learned of his arranged marriage to Philumena. Just as Davus was torn between obeying his master, Simo, and helping Pamphilus, Pamphilus is torn between obedience to his father, Simo, and his love for Glycerium. Mysis informs Pamphilus of Glycerium's condition and her concern that Pamphilus will abandon her. Pamphilus reassures Mysis that he will not abandon Glycerium and reveals that Chrysis, on her deathbed, had entrusted Pamphilus with care of Glycerium. Given this assurance, Mysis continues on her errand to fetch the midwife.

As Pamphilus remains on stage pondering his problems, the young man Charinus and his slave, Byrria, enter from the forum and discuss Pamphilus' marriage to Philumena. This news upsets Charinus because he is in love with Philumena. Charinus then approaches Pamphilus, tells him of his love for Philumena, and begs him not to marry her. Pamphilus urges Charinus and Byrria to do whatever they can to ensure that Philumena will be given to Charinus instead.

At this point, Davus rushes in and informs Pamphilus and Charinus that Chremes has decided to cancel the marriage of Pamphilus and Philumena. Simo, angered at Chremes, refuses to accept this situation. Davus, knowing that Chremes will refuse the union, urges Pamphilus to agree to marry Philumena to prevent conflict. Pamphilus agrees but makes Davus promise not to reveal Glycerium's pregnancy to Simo.

Next, Simo and Byrria enter separately. Byrria eavesdrops on the ensuing conversation between Simo and Pamphilus in which the son agrees to marry Philumena. Byrria, hearing this and thinking Pamphilus has reneged on his earlier words to Charinus, runs off to report to his master. After Pamphilus has returned to Simo's house, Davus tells Simo that Pamphilus is upset that Simo has spent little money on the wedding. Simo, who realizes that Davus is engaged in trickery, nevertheless agrees to rectify the situation.

The play's third act begins with the entrance of Mysis and the midwife, Lesbia. Davus and Simo eavesdrop as Mysis tells the midwife that Pamphilus has agreed to raise the child. Simo, however, thinks that this is a trick to induce Chremes to break off the engagement. Even when Simo hears Glycerium, in the throes of labor, crying out inside the house, he thinks that her cries are part of the charade. As further chaos and confusion surround Glycerium's delivery, Simo accuses Davus of trickery. Davus, however, blames the deceit on Glycerium, asserting that she is in love with Pamphilus and is falsely claiming that the baby is Pamphilus' to stop the wedding.

After Simo orders Davus to go back into their house, Chremes arrives and Simo tries to smooth matters over with his friend. Simo persuades Chremes that Pamphilus will be committed to Philumena and calls Davus from the house to attest to this. Davus pretends he is eager for the wedding to begin, but then Simo tells Davus that the wedding was a sham in order to test how Davus would react. To throw Davus off track further, Simo then says, however, that he has in fact arranged the wedding of Pamphilus and Philumena, that it will take place immediately, and that Davus should make sure that Pamphilus is prepared.

After Chremes and Simo depart to their various houses to prepare for the wedding, a baffled and frightened Davus realizes that he has done just the opposite of what Pamphilus wanted. Pamphilus, who has apparently just heard about his wedding, storms out-

side his house and confronts Davus, who promises to rectify matters. Next, Charinus arrives, angry at Pamphilus about the developments regarding Philumena. Charinus and Pamphilus argue, but Davus tells the two young men that he will try to resolve the problem.

At this point, Mysis arrives from Glycerium's house in search of Pamphilus, who again promises that he will not abandon her. As Pamphilus enters Glycerium's house and Charinus departs for his own house, Davus enters Glycerium's house, carries out a baby, and then places it on the doorstep of Glycerium's house. When Davus sees Chremes approaching, he urges Mysis to support his story when the need arises and then dashes off. As soon as Chremes enters and sees the baby, Davus rushes back in, pretending he has arrived from the forum. Davus, pretending not to know about the baby, asks Mysis whether she placed it on the step. As Chremes watches and listens, Davus instructs Mysis to state that the child belongs to Pamphilus and that the child's mother is an Athenian citizen. Overhearing all these things, Chremes goes into Simo's house to call off the wedding of Pamphilus and Philumena. The act concludes with the arrival of Chrysis' cousin, Crito, from the harbor. Crito has arrived to claim his cousin's possessions. Crito is met by Mysis and Davus, and soon the trio enter Glycerium's house.

The play's final act begins with the entrance of Chremes and Simo, who are arguing about the wedding. Simo urges Chremes not to trust anything that he has seen or heard from Davus and Mysis. Next, Davus emerges from Glycerium's house and informs Simo and Chremes of Crito's arrival and states that Crito knows Glycerium is an Athenian citizen. When Simo hears this, he becomes angry and calls his slave, Dromo, out of his house to take Davus to be whipped. After Davus is hauled away, Simo summons Pamphilus from Glycerium's house and questions his son about Glycerium's social status. When Pamphilus does not deny the statement that Glycerium is an Athenian citizen, Simo is enraged, thinking that his son has called in Crito to make this statement and that his son plans to marry Glycerium against his wishes. Chremes, however, tries to intercede on Pamphilus' behalf and to calm Simo's temper. Soon, the situation is resolved as Crito enters from Glycerium's house and explains to Simo that

Glycerium is actually the daughter of a man (Phania) who was shipwrecked on Andros with a young girl (Glycerium). When Chremes hears the name Phania, he excitedly states that Phania is his brother. Crito also reveals that Glycerium is not Phania's daughter, but the daughter of Phania's brother. Thus, the girl with whom Pamphilus is in love turns out to be Chremes' daughter, whose name was originally Pasibula. When Simo learns this, he is more than happy to agree to the marriage of Pamphilus and Glycerium.

After Chremes and Crito reenter Glycerium's house to reunite father and daughter, Simo tells Pamphilus to invite Glycerium to Simo's house. Pamphilus agrees and says he will have tell Davus to make the arrangements. When Pamphilus learns that Davus is being punished, he pleads for Davus' release and Simo relents. After Simo's exit into his house, Charinus enters and eavesdrops on Pamphilus, who is soon joined by Davus. Pamphilus tells Davus about Glycerium's discovery of her father and his imminent marriage to Glycerium. Eventually, Charinus approaches Pamphilus and offers his congratulations. The play ends as Pamphilus and Charinus enter Glycerium's house, while Davus is sent off to gather people to form the wedding procession.

COMMENTARY

The main focal points of Terence's *Andria* are marriage and the acquisition of a wife. This play contains more than half of the references to marriage in Terence's works. Intertwined with the focus on marriage are the themes of knowledge and anxiety. Simo arranges for his son to marry Chremes' daughter, but when Simo learns that his son, Pamphilus, feels love for another girl, he fabricates a false marriage with Chremes' daughter to discover his son's true feelings. Because Pamphilus does not know about his father's plan, he and his beloved Glycerium concoct a plan of their own so that they can marry. Rumors of Simo's false marriage make Davus fear (*timeo,* 210) for Pamphilus and propel him into action as the slave wants to make sure Pamphilus is aware of what his father is doing.

Before Pamphilus can be informed, the young lover expresses his uninformed worries (*curae,* 260) about what his father and Chremes have in mind for him.

These uninformed opinions are overheard by Mysis and she fears (*timeo,* 264) that Pamphilus will abandon Glycerium. Mysis also relates that Glycerium's knowledge of Pamphilus' supposed marriage to Chremes' daughter is causing Glycerium to fear (*timet,* 269) that Pamphilus will abandon her. Pamphilus tries to allay Mysis' anxiety but does not want her to tell Glycerium about the wedding because of the anxiety it might cause her.

The anxiety about Pamphilus' supposed marriage has not only caused Davus, Pamphilus, Mysis, and Glycerium to worry, but troubled Charinus as well (*cura,* 304), because he loves Chremes' daughter. Charinus' worries are somewhat slackened by the acquisition of accurate knowledge from Pamphilus himself, who informs Charinus that he does not love Chremes' daughter and does not want to marry her. Not only are Charinus' worries diminished, but when Davus appears on the scene he declares that he has information that will take away Pamphilus' fear (*metum,* 339). Hearing this, the citizen Pamphilus begs the slave Davus to free him from fear (*metu,* 351). Pamphilus is relieved when Davus tells him that observing the lack of marriage preparations at Chremes' house has led him to conclude that Pamphilus is not going to marry Chremes' daughter.

Upon learning this, Pamphilus and Davus enter a counterplot to deceive the father, Simo, and to ensure that Pamphilus will marry Glycerium. From Pamphilus' viewpoint, the key to his success is preventing his father from acquiring knowledge (400) of his child by Glycerium. As for Davus, the deception of Simo depends on Pamphilus' appearing not to be worried by marriage to Chremes' daughter (403).

Simo, however, soon learns of Pamphilus' child, and this knowledge, if true, causes Simo to worry (465). Once Simo thinks that the child is meant to scare off (*absterreant,* 472) Chremes, that anxiety is relieved. Davus, however, becomes anxious that his plans are unraveling. When Simo accuses Davus of trickery, Davus realizes that Simo has incorrectly interpreted the information about the baby. Thus, Davus' worries are relieved and Davus claims Glycerium is spreading false information about the baby to stop the wedding. The anxiety is again reversed when Simo tells Davus that he had given

Davus false information about the wedding because he feared (*veritus sum,* 582; *metuens,* 585) that Davus would try to trick him. The wedding of Pamphilus and Philumena will, in fact, take place, according to Simo. Again Davus enters a state of high anxiety (600–6).

Information of this wedding also agitates both Pamphilus and Charinus. Davus, however, promises to relieve their anxieties. After Pamphilus again tries to calm Glycerium's fear that he will abandon her (693–97), Davus puts a halt to the wedding of Pamphilus and Philumena by creating a false situation (the abandonment of the baby) that will supply Chremes with true information (Pamphilus has a child by Glycerium, who is actually an Athenian citizen) that will lead Chremes to break off the wedding. Davus' alleged abandonment is rendered all the more tense because Mysis' knowledge is incomplete: She does not understand what Davus is doing (791).

As Davus' scheme has relieved the tension between Pamphilus and Charinus, it has also created tension between Chremes and Simo. When Davus gives Simo accurate information about Glycerium's citizenship, Simo is further angered and demands that the slave be punished. When Pamphilus confirms the information that Davus has revealed, Simo continues to think that the information is false. Not only is Simo in torment (886–87), but Pamphilus is sorely vexed as well by his father's accusations of deception. The anxieties of father and son are soon resolved when Pamphilus reveals his true feelings about Glycerium and summons out Crito to tell his story (896–900). Crito's information is confirmed as accurate by Chremes, and when Glycerium's true father is revealed, Chremes and Simo agree to the marriage of Pamphilus and Chremes' daughter, albeit a different daughter. Thus, by the end of the play, Glycerium's citizenship and true identity have been revealed. The tension between Chremes and Simo has been alleviated; that between father and son has been removed; that between the young men Charinus and Pamphilus has also been eliminated, and as Pamphilus will marry one of Chremes' daughters, the audience expects that Charinus will marry the other. Even Davus' anxiety is eliminated as Pamphilus intercedes on the slave's behalf and integrates him into the wedding festivities.

BIBLIOGRAPHY
Goldberg, S. M. "The Dramatic Balance of Terence's *Andria,*" *Classica et Mediaevalia* 33 (1981–82): 135–43.
McGarrity, T. K. "Thematic Unity in Terence's *Andria,*" *Transactions of the American Philological Association* 108 (1978): 103–14.
Richardson, L. "The Moral Problems of Terence's *Andria* and Reconstruction of Menander's *Andria* and *Perinthia,*" *Greek, Roman, and Byzantine Studies* 38, no. 2 (1997): 173–85.
Valgiglio, E. "Sul prologo Terenziano," *Annali della Facoltà di Lettere e Filosofia, Università di Macerata* 3–4 (1970–71): 69–96.
Victor, B. A. "A New Critical Edition of Terence's Andria." Ph.D. diss., University of Michigan at Ann Arbor, 1988.

ANDROCLES (DIED 411 B.C.E.) A statesman from the DEME of COLONUS, Androcles was a staunch supporter of the democratic government in ATHENS. He appears to have served as a military commander in the 420s, and in 415 he vigorously supported the attempt to prosecute ALCIBIADES. When the oligarchs overthrew the democracy in 411, they killed Androcles, perhaps because of his earlier opposition to Alcibiades, who favored the oligarchic revolution. As early as the 430s, the comic poets in Athens had branded Androcles as someone who had recently acquired wealth, who was a ruthless legal prosecutor, was a thief, was born a slave, and had once been a male prostitute. In ARISTOPHANES' *WASPS,* BDELYCLEON associates Androcles with the behavior of up-and-coming young statesmen. [ANCIENT SOURCES: Andocides, 1.27; Aristophanes, *Wasps* 1187; Cratinus, fragments 263, 458 Kock; Ecphantides, fragment 4 Kock; Telecleides, fragment 15 Kock; Thucydides, 8.65.2]

BIBLIOGRAPHY
Sommerstein, A. H. *The Comedies of Aristophanes.* Vol. 4, *Wasps.* Warminster, U.K.: Aris & Phillips, 1983, 225.

ANDROMACHE The daughter of Eëtion, Andromache was the wife of HECTOR, by whom she produced a son, ASTYANAX. In the early years of the Trojan War, Achilles killed Andromache's father. After the fall of TROY, the Greeks killed Astyanax, and Andromache became the war prize of ACHILLES' son, NEOPTOLEMUS. After the war, Andromache returned to

Greece with Neoptolemus and gave birth to at least one son (EURIPIDES mentions only MOLOSSUS), and perhaps as many as three (other sources add Pergamus and Pielus). Neoptolemus' wife, HERMIONE, became jealous of Andromache, because Hermione herself had borne no children. Hermione persecuted Andromache and accused her of using magic to make her barren. Andromache took refuge at an altar, and Neoptolemus' grandfather, Peleus, rescued her. After Neoptolemus was killed at DELPHI, Andromache married the Trojan prophet Helenus, the brother of her first husband, Hector; Apollodorus says Helenus left Troy with Neoptolemus and founded a city in the region of Molossia (in northern Greece). By Helenus Andromache had a son, Cestrinus.

Andromache appears as a character in EURIPIDES' *ANDROMACHE* and has a brief role in the same author's *TROJAN WOMEN*. In addition to Euripides' extant play, several other playwrights produced plays entitled *Andromache*. SOPHOCLES may have written one, although Lloyd-Jones notes that the single fragment that survives may have been an incorrect attribution from Sophocles' *Andromache*. ENNIUS wrote a tragic *Andromache Aechmalotis* (Andromache the captive), of which about three dozen lines survive and whose action may have been similar to that in Euripides' *Trojan Women*. Some of the play's fragments refer to the deaths of POLYXENA and Astyanax, events that occur in Euripides' play (see fragments 27–44 Jocelyn). Naevius also wrote an *Andromache,* the two surviving lines of which reveal nothing about its plot. [ANCIENT SOURCES: Apollodorus, *Library* 3.12.6, *Epitome* 5.23, 6.12; Homer, *Iliad* 6.369–529, 22.437–515, 24.723–45; Pausanias, 1.11.1; Vergil, *Aeneid* 3]

BIBLIOGRAPHY

Lloyd-Jones, H. *Sophocles: Fragments.* Cambridge, Mass.: Harvard University Press, 1996.
Warmington, E. H. *Remains of Old Latin: Ennius and Caecilius.* Vol. 1. Cambridge: Harvard University Press, 1935.
———. *Remains of Old Latin: Livius Andronicus, Naevius, Pacuvius, and Accius.* Vol. 2. Cambridge, Mass.: Harvard University Press, 1936.

ANDROMACHE EURIPIDES (430–424 B.C.E.)

The action of *Andromache* takes place before the palace of NEOPTOLEMUS, king of Phthia, a town in northeastern Greece. As Andromache informs the audience in the prologue, she is the widow of the Trojan hero HECTOR and now the slave and concubine of Neoptolemus, by whom she has produced a son, MOLOSSUS. Ironically, Neoptolemus was the son of ACHILLES, the man who killed her husband, Hector. Thus, Andromache has produced a son by the son of the man who killed her husband. Some time after Molossus' birth, Neoptolemus married Hermione, the daughter of MENELAUS and HELEN. When Hermione was unable to produce any children, she claimed that Andromache used magic to prevent her from becoming pregnant. Hermione threatened to kill Andromache, causing her to take refuge at an altar of THETIS, the grandmother of Neoptolemus. Andromache relates that she has sent Molossus from town in fear for his life. She notes that Hermione's efforts are aided by Menelaus, who has arrived in Phthia. Neoptolemus himself is unable to help Andromache because he has gone to DELPHI to consult APOLLO about Achilles' death and to gain Apollo's friendship.

After Andromache's opening monologue, an aged female SLAVE, who served Andromache in TROY, arrives from the palace and informs Andromache that Hermione and Menelaus are planning to kill Molossus and that Menelaus has gone to take the child back to the palace. Andromache worries about her child's fate but holds out a glimmer of hope that Achilles' father, Peleus, for whom she has sent, will aid her. Andromache begs the old servant to go ask Peleus again for help. After the slave's departure, Andromache laments her sufferings and sings an ode that recalls Helen's abduction by PARIS and Hector's death at Achilles' hands.

Andromache's song is followed by the entrance of the CHORUS, a group of women from Phthia. Although Hermione is a Greek (from SPARTA) and Andromache is a barbarian (from Troy), the chorus of Greek women sympathize with Andromache. They urge her to leave the altar and accept her status as Hermione's servant. After the chorus' opening statement, Hermione, dressed in Spartan rather than Phthian finery, enters. Hermione claims Andromache's witchcraft has made her barren and Andromache should learn to be a servant. Hermione criticizes Andromache's fellow Trojans for committing incest and murder and having more than one wife—a critique that is ironic given the mythological traditions about Hermione's family and the situations already mentioned (e.g., Neoptolemus' sleeping with both Andromache and Hermione; Menelaus and Hermione's efforts to kill Andromache and Molossus). Andromache admits that she is Hermione's slave but denies that she is taking Hermione's place as a wife or that she is practicing witchcraft. Andromache blames Hermione's barrenness on her hateful character and suggests that she is like her mother, Helen. After this, Andromache and Hermione's argument deteriorates into single-line barbs at one another. Hermione threatens to kill Andromache before Neoptolemus returns, but Andromache remains defiant. After Hermione's exit, the chorus sing an ODE about the judgment of Alexander (see PARIS) and lament that he was allowed to live. If Alexander had been killed as an infant, in accordance with the prophecies, Troy and Andromache would not have suffered.

After the choral ode, Menelaus and his henchman enter with Molossus. Menelaus threatens to kill the child unless Andromache leaves her station at Thetis' altar. Andromache argues that Hermione and Menelaus will be considered murderers, Neoptolemus will divorce Hermione, and Menelaus will be unable to marry her to anyone else. Menelaus, of course, rejects this line of reasoning and again threatens that if she does not leave the altar, Molossus will die. Andromache wonders what she has done to Menelaus to deserve such treatment but leaves the altar. The chorus express pity for Andromache and urge Menelaus to persuade Hermione to reach some accord with Andromache. After Andromache leaves the altar, Menelaus orders his men to seize Andromache and threatens to allow Hermione to decide Molossus' fate. Andromache protests Menelaus' treachery and the lies of his people, the Spartans. After the exit of Menelaus, Andromache, and Molossus into the palace, the chorus sing an ode about the dangers of two women's sharing one man.

The chorus' song is followed by the entry of Andromache, Molossus, and Menelaus. In a moving exchange, Andromache and Molossus anticipate their deaths. Andromache urges Molossus to beg Menelaus for mercy, but Menelaus rejects the child. The tense situation is relieved with the unexpected arrival of Peleus. Andromache explains the situation and Peleus demands that Andromache be set free. Menelaus refuses, and Peleus threatens to strike him with his walking stick. Peleus labels Menelaus a coward and his wife Helen a whore. Peleus also criticizes Menelaus because he urged the sacrifice of IPHIGENIA and did not kill Helen after the war. Menelaus retorts that Peleus should not side with a barbarian over a Greek. He states that Helen's situation was caused by the gods, not her own free will; that the war with Troy brought about advances in military operations and resulted in the unification of many different Greeks; and that not killing Helen was an act of self-control. Peleus continues the verbal assault on Menelaus, who he claims has achieved glory for a war in which he had little front-line experience. Peleus also warns Menelaus to take Hermione and leave Neoptolemus' house. Peleus then unties Andromache's bonds and states that he will take care of Andromache and Molossus at his house. With this, Menelaus declares that he is going back to Sparta. After Menelaus leaves, Peleus, Andromache, and Molossus also exit. Their departure is followed by a choral ode that praises the life of those who have wealth and honor, the exercise of power in moderation, and the valor of Peleus.

Andromache's rescue marks the beginning of the play's second segment. Once Andromache is rescued, Hermione now fears for her own life. After the choral ode, Hermione's nurse arrives from the house and says Hermione was just prevented from hanging herself by some other servants. Hermione, in a suicidal frenzy, emerges from the palace. She laments that her father has left her, and her nurse advises her not to take extreme actions. The earlier despair and rescue of Andromache are now repeated in the case of HERMIONE as ORESTES arrives on his way to consult ZEUS' oracle at Dodona. When Hermione sees her cousin Orestes, she clings to him and begs for his help. Hermione explains the situation to Orestes, and he agrees to help her because, as he says, Menelaus had promised to marry Hermione to him before Neoptolemus but had reneged on the agreement when Orestes suffered from the FURIES after he killed his mother, CLYTEMNESTRA. Before Orestes and Hermione depart, Orestes reveals that he has a plot ready to spring on Neoptolemus at Delphi that will result in his death. The departure of Orestes and Hermione is followed by a choral ode that wonders why APOLLO and POSEIDON allowed Troy, whose walls they built, to be destroyed. They lament the deaths of many Trojans, but also the deaths of many Greeks, especially that of AGAMEMNON, whose killing at the hands of Clytemnestra was avenged by Orestes at Apollo's command.

After the choral ode, Peleus returns and asks about the rumor he has heard that Hermione has left. The chorus confirm the rumor and explain what happened. The women also inform Peleus that Orestes mentioned a plot to kill Neoptolemus. Peleus sends an attendant off to Delphi to warn Neoptolemus, but a messenger arrives from Delphi and reports that Neoptolemus has been killed there—ambushed by Orestes and some of his henchmen. As Andromache did earlier in the play, Neoptolemus initially took refuge at an altar but eventually left and tried to fight against his attackers. The messenger who makes the announcement ends his speech by attributing the death to Apollo, who held a grudge against Neoptolemus for his earlier criticism of Apollo for Achilles' death. After the messenger's speech, the chorus see the body of Neoptolemus being carried in. Peleus, who is onstage during this announcement, laments the loss of his grandson, Neoptolemus, and his son, Achilles. Peleus' lament, however, is interrupted by the appearance of the goddess THETIS, Peleus' estranged wife. Thetis tells Peleus to bury Neoptolemus at Delphi as a reproach to its people. She predicts that Andromache will marry a Trojan named Helenus and raise her son, Molossus, who will pass on his name to the people of Molossia. Thetis announces that she will make Peleus immortal and live with him in the house of her father, NEREUS, and that Peleus will see their son, Achilles, living on the Island of the Blessed. After Thetis' speech, Peleus announces his intention to follow her instructions and points out the importance of marrying someone of noble blood. The chorus conclude the play with a comment on the unexpected events that gods bring to pass. The same choral remark ends Euripides' *ALCESTIS, HELEN,* and *BACCHAE.* The ending of *MEDEA* is the same except the first line.

COMMENTARY

Andromache is one of EURIPIDES' most puzzling plays. Its structure has some similarities to that of Euripides' *HERACLES.* Andromache opens as an altar siege (as does *Heracles*); the siege gives way to a rescue (as in *Heracles*), which is followed by another rescue; the report of the death of a hero, who has not taken the stage, occurs next, and then a divine appearance that promises the reunion of goddess with mortal man dispels the sadness of Neoptolemus' death.

Because Euripides' fellow Athenians were involved in the PELOPONNESIAN WAR with SPARTA and its allies when *Andromache* was presented, the play has often been viewed as an attack against the Spartans. The Spartan Hermione threatens to burn, mangle, and torture the innocent Andromache. Hermione's Spartan father, Menelaus, is characterized as equally violent, threatening Andromache and her son with death, luring Andromache from the altar under the pretense that he will save Molossus, and even having some role in the death of Neoptolemus. Orestes, although born at ARGOS, eventually became a king of Sparta according to some traditions and is said to have incited the Delphians to kill Neoptolemus.

In addition to being critical of the Spartans, *Andromache,* as is *Iphigenia in Aulis* at the end of Euripides' career, is quite concerned with the subject of marriage, which provides a unifying theme for a play that seems structurally unconnected. Euripides' reasons for concentrating on marriage in this play are disputed, but according to one line of thought, the Athenians, because of a war-depleted population, allowed their citizens to take multiple wives for a brief time. Thus, just as the Peloponnesian War disrupted Athenian marriages, the mythical Trojan War affected the marriages in *Andromache.*

The Trojan War resulted from Paris' disruption of the marriage of Menelaus and Helen. The war also disrupted the marriage of Menelaus' brother, Agamemnon, whose wife, as the chorus recall later in the play (1028–30), killed him on his return from Troy. The same war led to the death of Andromache's husband, Hector, and the death of her child by him. Now Andromache has produced a child for the son of the man who killed her husband, and Andromache's child by Neoptolemus has caused the disintegration of the marriage of Neoptolemus and Hermione. Hermione blames the problems in her marriage on Andromache's magic, but Andromache claims Hermione has failed to adapt herself to her husband and behaves as her mother, Helen (213–31), did. Andromache predicts Neoptolemus will divorce Hermione and Menelaus will not be able to find another husband for her. At the height of Andromache's despair, she calls upon her deceased husband, Hector (523), but although Hector does not return, the aged Peleus provides a temporary and sufficient substitute as he rescues Andromache and Molossus.

With the rescue of Andromache, Hermione becomes suicidal. She knows she has wronged her husband (835) and fears he will divorce her (808) or kill her (857). Her nurse thinks Hermione's husband will forgive her (840, 869), but Hermione cannot be calmed. Just as the distressed Andromache was saved by Peleus, Orestes saves Hermione.

Upon his arrival, Orestes quickly guesses that Hermione's husband prefers another woman's bed to Hermione's (907) and Hermione tells him of her fears that her husband will kill her (919, 926). Hermione claims the gossip of her female companions led her to be jealous of her husband (939). Orestes is more than happy to help Hermione, because he says Menelaus had promised her to him before Neoptolemus. Thus, Orestes will rescue Hermione, will become her new husband, and will arrange for her former husband to be killed.

When Peleus hears of Neoptolemus' death, he laments the marriage (to Hermione) that destroyed both his house and his city (1186). Although the gods themselves attended Peleus' own wedding, the chorus declare that Peleus has received little benefit from them (1218). Just as Andromache and Hermione both reached the height of despair and then were rescued, now Thetis appears and rescues Peleus from his grief. Thetis predicts Andromache's marriage to Helenus will be happy and prosperous and announces that her own marriage to Peleus will be repaired. After the goddess departs, Peleus praises the marriages of noble men and women.

BIBLIOGRAPHY

Allan, W. *The Andromache and Euripidean Tragedy.* Oxford: Oxford University Press, 2000.

Kovacs, P. D. *The Andromache of Euripides: An Interpretation.* Chico, Calif.: Scholars Press, 1980.
Lloyd, M. *Euripides: Andromache.* Warminster, U.K.: Aris & Phillips, 1994.
Phillippo, S. "Family Ties: Significant Patronymics in Euripides' *Andromache,*" *Classical Quarterly* 45, no. 2 (1995): 355–71.
Steven, P. T. *Euripides: Andromache.* Oxford: Clarendon Press, 1971.
Storey, I. C. "Domestic Disharmony in Euripides' *Andromache,*" *Greece & Rome* 36 (1989): 16–27.

ANDROMEDA The daughter of Cepheus and Cassiopeia, Andromeda became the wife of PERSEUS. After Cassiopeia boasted that her beauty surpassed that of the NEREIDS, POSEIDON sent a sea monster that began destroying Ethiopia and its inhabitants. An oracle from AMMON declared that they would be rid of the monster if Cepheus sacrificed Andromeda to it. Andromeda was chained on the shore and left for the monster to devour. Fortunately for Andromeda, Perseus, flying past on his way back from beheading the GORGON MEDUSA, saw the young woman, fell in love with her, rescued her from the monster, and killed the creature by revealing Medusa's head. Andromeda left her home with Perseus, and they returned to Greece, after which little is heard about Andromeda. She and Perseus had a son named Perses. After Andromeda's death, she became a constellation.

Several playwrights wrote a play with the title *Andromeda.* EURIPIDES' version, produced in 412 B.C.E., is the best known, as ARISTOPHANES parodies it in his *THESMOPHORIAZUSAE.* SOPHOCLES also wrote an *Andromeda.* ENNIUS wrote a tragic *Andromeda,* from which eight lines are extant (see fragments 45–51 Jocelyn). These few lines indicate that the play was about Andromeda's exposure to the sea monster and her rescue by Perseus. ACCIUS' *Andromeda,* which appears to have treated the same subject, has some two dozen extant lines. Warmington suggests the probability that the action of Accius' play "began earlier than the exposing of Andromeda to the monster." Cepheus' brother, Phineus, may have been a character in Accius' play. [ANCIENT SOURCES: Apollodorus, *Library* 2.4.3–5; Hyginus, *Fables* 64, *Poetica Astronomica* 2.11; Ovid, *Metamorphoses* 4.670–803]

BIBLIOGRAPHY

Bubel, F. *Euripides, Andromeda*. Stuttgart: Steiner, 1991.

Falcetto, R. "L'Andromeda di Euripide: proposta di ricostruzione." In *Quaderni del Dipartimento di filologia, linguistica e tradizione classica 1997*. Bologna: Pàtron, 1998, 55–71.

Resta Barrile, A. *Ennio e il mito di Andromeda*. Bologna: Tip. Compositori, 1998.

Warmington, E. H. *Remains of Old Latin: Ennius and Caecilius*. Vol. 1. Cambridge, Mass.: Harvard University Press, 1935.

———. *Remains of Old Latin: Livius Andronicus, Naevius, Pacuvius, and Accius*. Vol. 2. Cambridge, Mass.: Harvard University Press, 1936.

ANDROS An island in the central AEGEAN SEA, just off the southern end of EUBOEA. In TERENCE's *ANDRIA,* Glycerium is from Andros. Terence's play was influenced by a play of MENANDER by the same name (fragments 33–45 Körte).

BIBLIOGRAPHY

Körte, A., Thierfelder, A. *Menandri Quae Supersunt*. Vol. 2, 2d ed. Leipzig: Teubner, 1959.

ANGIPORTUM In Roman COMEDY, the *angiportum* was a space between two houses where characters could hide to eavesdrop on conversations by other characters. [ANCIENT SOURCES: Plautus, *Comedy of Asses* 741, *Haunted House* 1044–46, *Persians* 444, 678, *Pseudolus* 971; Terence, *Phormio* 891]

ANTAEUS The son of POSEIDON, Antaeus was a king in LIBYA who challenged strangers to his land to wrestle him. Antaeus, having killed all his opponents, was roofing his father, Poseidon's, temple with their skulls. Antaeus' reign of terror ended when he encountered HERACLES. Antaeus posed a great challenge to Heracles, however, because as long as Antaeus remained in contact with the EARTH (who some say was his mother), his strength increased. When Heracles realized this, he lifted Antaeus off the ground and crushed the life from him. PHRYNICHUS and Aristias wrote plays (no longer extant) with the title *Antaeus*. Archestratus may also have written an *Antaeus*. [ANCIENT SOURCES: Apollodorus, *Library* 2.5.11; Pindar, *Isthmian* 3/4 70–73; Seneca, *Hercules Oetaeus* 1899]

BIBLIOGRAPHY

Snell, B. *Tragicorum Graecorum Fragmenta*. Vol. 1. Göttingen, Ger.: Vandenhoeck & Ruprecht, 1971.

ANTAGONIST A term derived from Greek words meaning "one who struggles against," in drama an antagonist is the main character who opposes the PROTAGONIST. In EURIPIDES' *HELEN,* the Egyptian king Theoclymenus would be the antagonist as he tries to force Helen to marry him. In ARISTOPHANES' *KNIGHTS,* PAPHLAGON opposes the goals of the sausage seller, AGORACRITUS. In PLAUTUS' comedies, the PIMP is commonly the antagonist of the young man who seeks to be with his beloved. In some plays, the protagonist might struggle against multiple opponents; in others protagonists might struggle against themselves (e.g., OEDIPUS).

ANTENOR A respected Trojan who served as host to MENELAUS and ODYSSEUS when they requested the release of HELEN prior to the outbreak of the Trojan War. Antenor favored the release of Helen and even protected the two Greeks from the Trojans who wanted to kill them. Because of Antenor's kindness, when the Greeks destroyed TROY, Menelaus and Odysseus, by hanging a leopard's skin over Antenor's door, signaled to their comrades that they should spare the lives of Antenor and his family. Both SOPHOCLES and ACCIUS wrote plays entitled *The Sons of Antenor* (*Antenoridae*). The seven surviving lines from Accius' play indicate that it had Troy as its setting, and that the action may have started early in the morning. One fragment is spoken by someone who has apparently arrived to be an ally to the Trojans. In another fragment, the speaker boasts that he will rout the Greeks on land, burn their ships, or drive their camp into the sea. [ANCIENT SOURCES: Homer, *Iliad* 3.203–24, 7.344–53; Pausanias, 10.26.7–8, 27.3–4; Pindar, *Pythian* 5.80–87; Vergil, *Aeneid* 1.242–49.]

BIBLIOGRAPHY

Warmington, E. H. *Remains of Old Latin: Livius Andronicus, Naevius, Pacuvius, and Accius*. Vol. 2. Cambridge, Mass.: Harvard University Press, 1936.

ANTIDOSIS A Greek word meaning "exchange," *antidosis* refers to the legal process by which an Athenian who was a candidate for a LITURGY would trade property with someone he thought was better able to carry out the liturgy. The second person would then use the proceeds from the property to perform the liturgy. If the second person did not want to perform the liturgy, then he could give his property to the first person and the first person would perform the liturgy.

BIBLIOGRAPHY
Csapo, E., and W. J. Slater. *The Context of Ancient Drama.* Ann Arbor: University of Michigan Press, 1995, 126, 140, 145–46.

ANTIGONE   The daughter of OEDIPUS and JOCASTA, Antigone was the sister of ETEOCLES, POLYNEICES, ISMENE, and even Oedipus himself, because Jocasta was both mother and wife to Oedipus. When Oedipus blinded himself and left THEBES, Antigone and Ismene accompanied their father/brother into exile. Eventually, the trio made their way to COLONUS, just outside Athens. When it was discovered that the Thebans could not win their war with Polyneices and his Argive allies unless Oedipus was buried in Theban territory, CREON and Eteocles went to Colonus and tried to persuade Oedipus to return to Thebes. Antigone and Ismene were even taken prisoner by the Thebans to force Oedipus to return; THESEUS, the Athenian king, rescued them from the Thebans. After Oedipus' death, Antigone and Ismene returned to Thebes. After the war between Eteocles and Polyneices, in which the brothers killed each other, Creon became king of THEBES and declared that anyone who buried Polyneices—who had waged war against Thebes—should be put to death. When Antigone managed to bury Polyneices, Creon sealed her in a rocky cavern and left her to die, although she was engaged to marry Creon's son HAEMON. Creon later reversed his decision and went to release Antigone, who had hanged herself.

Antigone is one of the most admired figures of ancient drama. Her defiant stance against an unyielding tyrant is inspirational, as is her willingness to give up her life to ensure that her brother receive a proper burial, a ritual the Greeks believed was necessary to allow the deceased to reach his or her proper resting place in the UNDERWORLD. Antigone regards laws established by the gods as taking precedence over laws established by humans.

Besides dramas entitled *Antigone* by SOPHOCLES and SENECA, plays with this title were produced by numerous other authors. EURIPIDES wrote an *Antigone* about 413 B.C.E. ACCIUS' *Antigone,* from which about 10 lines survive, surely dealt with the same subject as Sophocles' play. The fragments indicate that Antigone, Ismene, and a guard assigned to guard Polyneices' body were all characters in Accius' play.

BIBLIOGRAPHY
Sconocchia, S. "L'Antigona di Accio e l'Antigone di Sofocle," *Rivista di Filologia e di Istruzione Classica* 100 (1972): 273–82.

ANTIGONE SOPHOCLES (442 OR 441 B.C.E.)
The play's setting is the palace of CREON at THEBES. The action takes place after the battle between two sons of OEDIPUS, ETEOCLES and POLYNEICES, for the right to rule Thebes. In the battle, the brothers had killed each other. As the play opens, Oedipus' daughters, ANTIGONE and ISMENE, discuss what to do about their brother, Polyneices, whom Creon, the new king of Thebes, has decreed should not be buried because he attacked Thebes to retake the throne. Furthermore, Creon has decreed death for anyone who buries Polyneices. Antigone declares her intention to bury Polyneices despite Creon's edict, while Ismene suggests that women should obey men and obey the city's laws.

As Antigone and Ismene end their argument, Ismene returns to the palace while Antigone exits to bury Polyneices. After their exit, the CHORUS, composed of elderly Theban men, enter. They recall the Theban victory over Polyneices and the other commanders of the Seven against Thebes force. The elders propose that they go to the temples of the gods and dance in celebration of the victory. As their song concludes, Creon enters and thanks the elders for their loyalty and service throughout the years. He also reiterates his decree regarding Polyneices and asks the chorus for their support in this matter. The elders agree, because they do not want to die.

After Creon's remarks, a fearful guard enters from the countryside and informs Creon that someone has sprinkled dust upon the body of Polyneices. Creon is outraged and thinks that some of his political enemies hired someone to do this. He threatens the guard and his comrades with death if they do not find out who buried Polyneices. As the guard leaves, he declares that Creon will never see him again. After the guard's exit, Creon reenters the palace. The chorus then sing a now-famous ode about the wonders of human beings. The elders remark that humans have managed to tame sea and earth, animals on land and sea, and protect themselves against the elements, but that they have not yet learned to overcome death. They note that if people honor the laws of men and gods, then their city will prosper, but that a person who does not has no city.

As the chorus conclude their song, they see Antigone being led in by the guard who left a little earlier. When Creon arrives from the palace, the guard describes for the king how he and his fellow guards caught Antigone burying Polyneices. After Creon dismisses the guard, he interrogates Antigone about her actions. Antigone does not deny the deed and declares that she was acting in accordance with the laws of the gods, rather than Creon's laws. Creon declares that Antigone will pay the penalty for her actions even though she is his niece. Creon also orders Ismene to be taken from the palace. Creon and Antigone continue to argue about what Antigone has done and both remain firm in the position that they are acting in accordance with what is right.

Soon Ismene arrives from the palace and says she is ready to accept some guilt in the burial of Polyneices. Antigone refuses to allow Ismene to have a share in her actions and suggests that Ismene has sided with Creon by not helping her bury Polyneices. Ismene wonders what her life will be like without Antigone and wonders whether Creon really intends to kill the woman who is supposed to marry his son HAEMON. Creon's mind is made up, however, and he orders his servants to take the young women into the palace. After the exit of Creon and his nieces, the chorus sing of the endless evils that have fallen upon Oedipus' family generation after generation. They note that ruin often follows greatness and that hope can either bless or deceive human beings.

After the choral ode, Haemon enters. Haemon declares his loyalty to his father, who urges him to reject Antigone, preaches to him about the need for obedience to authority, and declares that they must not accept defeat by a woman. Haemon does not deny some truth in what his father says but notes that from the city's people he has heard comments of sympathy for Antigone. Haemon urges his father to follow a more moderate course and take some advice from a younger man. Creon, however, refuses to be advised by someone younger or to be subject to the will of the city. The conversation then breaks down and father and son begin to exchange angry words. Creon threatens to summon Antigone and kill her before Haemon's eyes, but the young man exits. Creon then declares that he will kill both Antigone and Ismene, but the chorus persuade him not to do that. Finally, Creon declares that Antigone's punishment will be to be placed in a cavern with a small amount of food.

After Creon concludes his remarks, the Theban elders sing of the power of Love, which has caused relatives to be in conflict. Antigone, who has been taken from the palace, sings that her marriage will take place in the underworld. The chorus sing in response that she has won distinction and praise, but that the choice to oppose Creon was hers. Antigone compares herself to NIOBE, who was transformed into an ever-weeping stone, but the chorus suggest that Antigone's death will carry greater fame because she is a mortal and Niobe was born of divine stock. Antigone thinks the Theban elders are mocking her and calls on them for pity. They suggest that her trouble may be the result of Oedipus' crimes, but they also point out that Antigone opposed Creon and that her own temper has led her to ruin. Creon, who has remained onstage during Antigone's remarks, now breaks in and orders that she be led away. Antigone anticipates encountering her family, all of whom she helped to bury, in the underworld. She laments going to meet her death without having married, had children, or had friends. She wonders what divine law she has violated and hopes that Creon and his people will suffer a fate equal to hers if they are in the wrong.

After Antigone's departure to her cavern prison, the chorus sing an ode that compares the situation between Antigone and Creon to that between ACRISIUS and his daughter, DANAE, whom Acrisius imprisoned, but whom ZEUS impregnated in the form of a golden rain shower. They also compare Antigone's situation to the encounter of LYCURGUS and DIONYSUS, in which Lycurgus tried to persecute Dionysus and his followers but was eventually imprisoned himself in a rocky dungeon. Finally, they compare the harsh fate of Antigone with that of the children of PHINEUS, whose wife blinded them and caused them to live out their life in misery.

After this, the prophet TIRESIAS informs Creon that the gods will not accept their prayers or sacrifices because of Creon's actions toward Polyneices. Creon rejects Tiresias' advice that he reverse his decision and accuses him of being interested in financial gain. An angered Tiresias then predicts that soon Creon and his household will suffer disaster and suggests that his refusal to bury the dead will start a similar trend in other towns that will lead to universal anger against him. After Tiresias' departure, Creon begins to question his actions and turns to the chorus for advice. The Theban elders advise him to release Antigone and give Polyneices a proper burial. Creon agrees and, accompanied by servants, sets out for the place where he has entombed Antigone. After Creon's exit, the Theban elders pray for Dionysus to come and heal their town.

After their prayer, a messenger enters and informs the Theban elders that Haemon has committed suicide. News of this swiftly reaches to Creon's wife, EURYDICE, who leaves the palace to hear the messenger's full report. The messenger tells Eurydice and the elders that after Creon and his attendants buried Polyneices, they set out for the prison. Inside, they saw that Antigone had hanged herself and that Haemon was weeping and embracing her body. Haemon, upon seeing his father, was enraged, drew his sword, and attempted to stab him. Creon avoided the blow and Haemon, apparently ashamed of his attempt on his father's life, turned the sword on himself.

Upon hearing this news, Eurydice returns in silence to the interior of the palace. As the chorus expresses concern the messenger decides to follow Eurydice. Next, Creon, with the body of Haemon, enters. No sooner has Creon blamed himself for his son's death than a messenger emerges from the palace and informs Creon that Eurydice has stabbed herself to death. As Creon gazes upon the face of his dead son, the corpse of Eurydice is also brought into view. Creon laments

the fate of his family, wishes that he himself were dead, and accepts responsibility for their deaths. The play ends with Creon being led away into the palace.

COMMENTARY

Antigone is usually considered one of the finest of all ancient dramas. Other than the problem that Polyneices is apparently buried three times (seemingly twice by Antigone, 245–58, 422–31; once by Creon, 1197–1204), a detail for which many different explanations have been advanced, the staging of the play seems relatively uncomplicated and its issues seem clear. Charles Segal has compared the narrative pattern of Antigone to the story of PERSEPHONE. Just as Antigone's marriage was arranged by Creon and a male member of Antigone's household, Persephone's marriage was arranged by her father, ZEUS, and HADES. To the underworld, Hades carried off Persephone against her will, as in an underground chamber Antigone is imprisoned by Creon against her will. At one point, Antigone even likens her marriage to one with the powers of the underworld (809–14). Eventually, complaints and threats of world famine by Persephone's mother, Demeter, lead to a change in the arrangement between Zeus and Hades. Persephone will spend part of the year with her mother in the upper world and part of the year with Hades. As Zeus does, Creon tries to modify the arrangement and take Antigone from her rocky chamber into the upper world, but Antigone has already committed suicide. She will not become a second Persephone.

In addition to similarities with the story of Persephone, *Antigone* shares some common themes with SOPHOCLES' *AJAX,* which may have been staged just a few years earlier. Both plays deal with the issue of allowing a friend-turned-enemy to have a proper burial. Unlike in *Ajax,* in which the debate occurs between male warriors, in *Antigone* the character of Antigone changes the dynamics of the debate and allows a male-versus-female aspect to emerge—especially from Creon's perspective, as the king is determined not to allow a woman to defeat him on the question of Polyneices' burial.

Whereas the argument over Ajax's burial focuses on his value to the Greek army before his madness, the debate in *Antigone* centers on mortal law versus divine law. Creon, who advocates obedience to the authority of the city that he represents and adherence to laws established by humans, is pitted against Antigone, who is committed to upholding laws transmitted by the gods themselves. Creon and Antigone both believe firmly that their position is correct and that they are acting in accordance with piety. Although Sophocles shows that the Thebans are sympathetic to Antigone, Creon's position is not without merit and the chorus tell her that she has caused her own destruction (872–76).

The issue of Polyneices' burial is complicated by the fact that those involved in the conflict are related to or will be related to one another. Caught between the extremes established by Antigone and Creon are Ismene and Haemon. As Chrysothemis does in Sophocles' ELECTRA, Ismene provides an opposing female perspective to her sister's determination. Ismene does not want to participate in the burial of her brother, an act that would oppose the law established by the city's ruler. Ismene urges her sister to realize that they are only women and must be obedient to men (61–64). Antigone, however, refuses to obey Creon. She rejects the reasoning of one loved one, her sister, and buries another loved one despite a mortal law to the contrary.

The conflict between the two sisters is paralleled by the conflict between Creon and Haemon, father and son. In Greek society, sons were expected to honor their father, but Haemon cannot respect his father's demand that he turn his back on Antigone. Haemon tries to steer a course between his father and the laws of the city and his allegiance to Antigone, the woman who could eventually produce children for his house. Thus, *Antigone* reveals the aftermath of a conflict between two brothers that has disastrous effects on two sisters, father and son, husband and wife, uncle and niece, father-in-law and potential daughter-in-law. By the end of the play, one sister has lost the other, and a father has lost his son, wife, niece, and potential daughter-in-law. The city of Thebes had been ravaged by war before the play's opening, but *Antigone* reveals the utter destruction of an individual house and family.

BIBLIOGRAPHY

Foley, Helene. "Tragedy and Democratic Ideology: The Case of Sophocles' *Antigone*." In *History, Tragedy, Theory: Dialogues on Athenian Drama*. Edited by B. Goff. Austin: University of Texas Press, 1995, 131–50.

Griffith, Mark. *Sophocles: Antigone*. New York: Cambridge University Press, 1999.

Johnson, Patricia. "Woman's Third Face: A Psycho-Social Reconsideration of Sophocles' *Antigone*," *Arethusa* 30, no. 3 (1997): 369–98.

Segal, Charles. "*Antigone*: Death and Love, Hades and Dionysus." In *Tragedy and Civilization: An Interpretation of Sophocles*. Cambridge, Mass.: Harvard University Press, 1981, 179–88.

Tyrrell, W. B., and L. J. Bennett. *Recapturing Sophocles' Antigone*. Lanham, Md.: Rowman & Littlefield, 1998.

ANTILABE A Greek word meaning "a thing to hold by" or "a handle," in drama *antilabe* is a line of dialogue that is broken and shared by multiple speakers. In the plays of AESCHYLUS, with the possible exception of PROMETHEUS BOUND (line 980), this phenomenon does not occur. Because *antilabe* is not common in TRAGEDY, it is often thought to be used for special effect. For example, in EURIPIDES' ALCESTIS (390–91), *antilabe* occurs twice as ADMETUS speaks his final words to his dying wife. In SOPHOCLES' ELECTRA (1502–3), *antilabe* occurs as ORESTES tries to induce AEGISTHUS to enter the house so that Orestes can kill him.

BIBLIOGRAPHY

Bonaria, Mario. "L'antilabé nella tragedia greca antica." In *Studi di filologia classica in onore di Giusto Monaco*. I, *Letteratura greca*. Palermo: University di Palermo Fac. di Lettere e Filosofia, 1991, 173–88.

McDevitt, A. S. "*Antilabe* in Sophoclean *Kommoi*," *Rheinisches Museum* 124 (1981): 19–28.

ANTILOCHUS The son of NESTOR, Antilochus died in the Trojan War trying to rescue his father from MEMNON. Antilochus' name appears in fragments from both AESCHYLUS' MYRMIDONS and ACCIUS' *Myrmidons*. In the fragment from Aeschylus (138 Radt), the speaker (probably ACHILLES) tells Antilochus to mourn for him rather than someone who has just died (probably PATROCLUS), because the death of Achilles has caused him to lose everything. In the fragment from Accius (lines 452–57 Warmington), Achilles appears to be responding to a charge of stubbornness leveled against him by Antilochus. [ANCIENT SOURCES: Aristophanes, *Ecclesi-*

azusae 392; Homer, *Iliad* 23, 423, 541, 556, *Odyssey* 4.188; Hyginus, *Fables* 112; Sophocles, *Philoctetes* 425]

BIBLIOGRAPHY

Radt, S. *Tragicorum Graecorum Fragmenta*. Vol. 3. Göttingen, Ger.: Vandenhoeck & Ruprecht, 1985.

Warmington, E. H. *Remains of Old Latin: Livius Andronicus, Naevius, Pacuvius, and Accius*. Vol. 2. Cambridge, Mass.: Harvard University Press, 1936.

ANTIMACHUS   An Athenian and a "member of one or more of the many special boards that were appointed to draft complex pieces of legislation" (Sommerstein). The CHORUS of ARISTOPHANES' ACHARNIANS curse Antimachus, who has not invited them to a post-production dinner. Several men named Antimachus were active in the 420s B.C.E., and it is uncertain which Antimachus Aristophanes has in mind. In CLOUDS, Aristophanes links Antimachus with the style of logic practiced by SOCRATES. [ANCIENT SOURCES: Aristophanes, *Acharnians* 1150, *Clouds* 1022]

BIBLIOGRAPHY

Sommerstein, A. H. *The Comedies of Aristophanes*. Vol. 1, *Acharnians*. Warminster, U.K.: Aris & Phillips, 1980, 210–11.

ANTIOPE (1)   Also called Hippolyta, Antiope was an AMAZON woman whom THESEUS abducted from her land and took back with him to ATHENS. By Antiope, Theseus became the father of HIPPOLYTUS. Theseus divorced Antiope to marry PHAEDRA and the angry Amazon tried to kill Theseus for this insult. Theseus, however, killed Antiope. [ANCIENT SOURCES: Apollodorus, *Epitome* 1.16; Euripides, *Children of Heracles* 215–19; Hyginus, *Fables* 30, 241, 250; Seneca, *Hippolytus* 227, 927]

ANTIOPE (2)   The daughter of Nycteus and Polyxo, Antiope lived in BOEOTIA. ZEUS impregnated Antiope, who became the mother of twin boys, AMPHION and ZETHUS. When Antiope's father, angry at her pregnancy out of wedlock, threatened her with violence, Antiope ran away. Later, she married Epopeus (or Epaphus), a man from SICYON. Nycteus was angry at the marriage, but before he could punish Antiope, he died; before his death he made his brother LYCUS promise to punish Antiope. Accordingly, Lycus went to Sicyon, killed Epopeus, and led Antiope back to Boeotia. Along the way, Antiope gave birth and left the children to die, but a shepherd rescued them. Upon reaching Boeotia, Antiope lived under constant torment by Lycus' wife Dirce. After many years of imprisonment, Antiope finally escaped and managed to make her way to the home of Amphion and Zethus. Dirce traveled there and began to drag Antiope back to Boeotia. When the shepherd who had raised Amphion and Zethus informed the young men that the persecuted woman was their mother, the twins caught Dirce and killed her by binding her hair to a wild bull.

EURIPIDES wrote an *Antiope* that dates to between 410 and 408 B.C.E., of which more than 200 lines survive (fragments 179–227 Nauck). The play appears to have been set at a rocky cavern that was home to the shepherd who raised the twins. *Antiope* probably opened with the twins' shepherd father's explaining that he raised the twins and that he knows Antiope is their mother but does not know Zeus is their father. The chorus was made up of shepherds, who had arrived to hear Amphion play the lyre and to converse with him about music and the lyre's invention. At some point, Amphion and Zethus debated whether the state was better served by artists and philosophers or soldiers and statesmen. Eventually, Antiope would have arrived on the scene, told the twins about her oppression, and eventually been recognized by them. The happy reunion would be cut short by the arrival of Dirce and a group of women worshiping DIONYSUS. They would have carried off Antiope to punish her, but the twins would have rescued her and killed Dirce. A lengthy fragment of some 111 lines from the end of the play shows that after Dirce's death, the twins and Antiope plotted to kill Lycus, who arrived in search of them. As in Euripides' HERACLES, in which AMPHITRYON lured the Theban king Lycus into the house to be killed by Heracles, in *Antiope* the shepherd lured Lycus into his cavern, where the twins awaited him. A confrontation ensued and Amphion told Lycus of Dirce's death. Before the twins could kill Lycus, Hermes appeared, explained Zeus' affair with Antiope, and told Lycus to turn over the throne to Amphion and Zethus and, after burning Dirce's bones, to throw the ashes into the spring of Ares, thus causing the spring to overflow and create the stream of Dirce. Hermes told the twins to establish a seven-gated city near the Ismenus River. Amphion's musical skills would help build the city by moving stones and trees magically into place. Hermes also announced that the twins would marry, Zethus to a Theban, Amphion to a daughter of TANTALUS (see NIOBE). The fragment concludes with Lycus' inviting the twins to remain and rule the land and declaring that he would be obedient to Hermes' commands.

The Greek comic poet Eubulus also wrote an *Antiope* (fragments 10–13 Kock), but other than a reference to Amphion and Zethus in fragment 10, we have little idea of the play's content. Among Roman authors, ENNIUS also wrote a tragic *Antiope,* as did PACUVIUS. Pacuvius' play, from which 28 short fragments survive, apparently contained a debate by Amphion and Zethus about music and wisdom (as in Euripides' *Antiope*), and in it the twins also encountered Antiope and Dirce. [ANCIENT SOURCES: Apollodorus, *Library* 3.5.5; Hyginus, *Fables* 7–8]

BIBLIOGRAPHY

Kambitsis, J. *L'Antiope d'Euripide.* Athens: Hourzamanis, 1972.

Kock, T. *Comicorum Atticorum Fragmenta.* Vol. 2. Leipzig: Teubner, 1884.

Nauck, A. *Tragicorum Graecorum Fragmenta.* 1889. Reprint, Hildesheim, Ger.: Olms, 1964.

Page, D. L. *Select Papyri.* Vol. 3. 1941. Reprint, London: Heinemann, 1970.

Podlecki, Anthony J. "Had the *Antiope* of Euripides Political Overtones?" *Ancient World* 27, no. 2 (1996): 131–46.

Rubatto, Stefania. "L'Antiope di Euripide: proposta di ricostruzione." In *Quaderni del Dipartimento di filologia, linguistica e tradizione classica 1997.* Bologna: Pàtron, 1998, 73–84.

Slings, Simon R. "The Quiet Life in Euripides' *Antiope.*" In *Fragmenta Dramatica: Beiträge zur Interpretation der griechischen Tragikerfragmente und ihrer Wirkungsgeschichte.* Unter Mitarb. von Harder M. Annette; hrsg. von Hofmann Heinz. Göttingen, Ger.: Vandenhoeck & Ruprecht, 1991, 137–51.

Warmington, E. H. *Remains of Old Latin: Livius Andronicus, Naevius, Pacuvius, and Accius.* Vol. 2. Cambridge, Mass.: Harvard University Press, 1936.

ANTIPHON (480–411 B.C.E.) A person mentioned by ARISTOPHANES at *WASPS* 1270 and 1301, this Antiphon, Sommerstein thinks, was the famous orator who was a leader during the oligarchic revolution in Athens in 411 B.C.E. After the oligarchs were driven from power, Antiphon was put to death. Antiphon was also mocked for his wealth, greed, and enjoyment of "good food and comfortable living" (Sommerstein). [ANCIENT SOURCES: Plato Comicus, fragment 103 Kock; Xenophon, *Memorabilia* 1.6]

BIBLIOGRAPHY

Sommerstein, A. H. *The Comedies of Aristophanes.* Vol. 4, *Wasps.* Warminster, U.K.: Aris & Phillips, 1983, 232.

ANTISTHENES Mentioned by ARISTOPHANES at *ECCLESIAZUSAE* 366 and 806, three Athenians of this name are known to have lived at the time this play was produced. Demosthenes mentions a banker named Antisthenes, who retired from business in 394/3 B.C.E. Antisthenes, son of Antiphates, was a CHOREGUS, landowner, priest, and commander of a warship. Xenophon also mentions a wealthy Antisthenes who won many victories as a choregus and who on one occasion served as a general although he had never served as an infantryman. Sommerstein thinks that all three men are the same person. [ANCIENT SOURCES: Demosthenes, 36.43; Xenophon, *Memorabilia* 3.4.1–4]

BIBLIOGRAPHY

Sommerstein, A. H. *The Comedies of Aristophanes.* Vol. 10, *Ecclesiazusae.* Warminster, U.K.: Aris & Phillips, 1998, 173.

ANTISTROPHE A Greek word meaning "turning the other way," an antistrophe is a section of a lyric ode that follows a STROPHE. In terms of metrical pattern, the antistrophe matched the strophe. In the antistrophe, the chorus sang while moving to the left.

ANTONIUS (CA. 83–30 B.C.E.) Marcus Antonius, better known as Marc Antony, was a Roman soldier and statesman who rose to prominence during his service with Julius Caesar in the middle of the first century B.C.E. After Caesar's assassination, Antony helped Lepidus and Octavian (Caesar's adopted son and the future emperor AUGUSTUS) in their military operations against Caesar's assassins. By 42, the assassins' defeat was accomplished and Antony and Octavian took up the task of reorganizing the Roman empire. Because Antony was in charge of the eastern part of the empire, his work took him to Egypt, where in 41 he met the Egyptian queen Cleopatra, became her lover, and eventually became her husband (ca. 37), although he was married to Octavian's sister, OCTAVIA. In addition to his relationship with the Egyptian queen, Antony's buildup of military assets in the region led to a showdown between him and Octavian's force at the battle of Actium in September 31. Antony and his forces were defeated and 11 months later Octavian entered the Egyptian capital of Alexandria. Both Antony and Cleopatra had committed suicide before they could be taken prisoner by Octavian. [ANCIENT SOURCES: Plutarch, *Antony*; Seneca, *Octavia* 518; Suetonius, *Julius Caesar, Augustus*]

APATURIA An Athenian festival (lasting at least three days) held in the early autumn (October–November). The name Apaturia means "the feast of common fatherhood" (Parke), the major functions of the festival were that male infants were registered as members of their phratries (see PHRATRY) and young men who had reached puberty were recognized as full members of the phratry. For each child presented, the child's father had to offer a sacrificial animal to provide the food for the feast. [ANCIENT SOURCES: Aristophanes, *Acharnians* 146, *Thesmophoriazusae* 558]

BIBLIOGRAPHY
Parke, H. W. *Festivals of the Athenians*. Ithaca, N.Y.: Cornell University Press, 1977, 88–92.
Sommerstein, A. H. *The Comedies of Aristophanes*. Vol. 1, *Acharnians*. Warminster, U.K.: Aris & Phillips, 1980, 164.

APHRODITE A love goddess, Aphrodite (Roman: Venus) was referred to in some sources as the daughter of ZEUS and a goddess named Dione and in others as born from the foam that surrounded the genitalia of URANUS, after his son CRONUS castrated him and threw his severed members into the sea. The name Aphrodite means "she who comes from foam." The new goddess floated along in an easterly direction past the southern tip of Greece and the island of CYTHERA. For this reason, Aphrodite is called Cytherean. Eventually, she went ashore on CYPRUS. As did Cythera,

Cyprus became sacred to her, and it was considered her birthplace. Accordingly, she was also called Cypris or the Cyprian. Mount ERYX in SICILY was sacred to her and she is sometimes called Erycina.

As a love goddess, Aphrodite had numerous sexual relationships with both gods and mortals. She is often named as the wife of HEPHAESTUS; she was unfaithful to him with ARES, by whom she became the mother of HARMONIA, who became CADMUS' wife. Aphrodite is also said to have produced by DIONYSUS a child named Priapus. By the mortal Anchises, she became the mother of AENEAS. Aphrodite also had a love affair with the mortal ADONIS. Some ancient sources considered her the mother of EROS.

Aphrodite appears as a character in EURIPIDES' HIP-POLYTUS, in which she delivers the opening monologue and reveals her plans to destroy HIPPOLYTUS, who refuses to worship her. Aphrodite appeared as a character in AESCHYLUS' *Danaids* (fragment 44 Radt) and may appear in Euripides' *Alexander* (fragment 45 Snell). Two Greek comic poets, Nicophon (fragments 1–4 Kock 1) and Antiphanes (fragment 55 Kock 2), wrote plays entitled *The Birth of Aphrodite*. The plots of these plays are unknown. [ANCIENT SOURCES: Apollodorus, *Library* 3.14.3–4; Apollonius Rhodius, 4.914–19; Hesiod, *Theogony* 203–4; Homer, *Odyssey* 8.266–367; *Homeric Hymn to Aphrodite*; Hyginus, *Fables* 58, 94, 164; Seneca, *Hippolytus* 199]

BIBLIOGRAPHY
Kock, T. *Comicorum Atticorum Fragmenta*. Vol. 1. Leipzig: Teubner, 1880.
———. *Comicorum Atticorum Fragmenta*. Vol. 2. Leipzig: Teubner, 1884.
Radt, S. *Tragicorum Graecorum Fragmenta*. Vol. 3. Göttingen, Ger.: Vandenhoeck & Ruprecht, 1985.
Snell, B. *Euripides Alexandros und andere Strassburger Papyri mit Fragmenten griechischer Dichter*. [*Hermes Einzelschriften* 5 (1937)].

APIA Another name for the region where ARGOS was located. According to AESCHYLUS, Apia took its name from the healer and prophet Apis, a son of APOLLO, who rid the land of various plagues and monsters. [ANCIENT SOURCES: Aeschylus, *Suppliant Women* 117, 128, 260–70]

APOLLO   The son of ZEUS and Leto and the twin brother of ARTEMIS. He is also called Agyieus, Loxias, Phoebus, and Smithean. Apollo is sometimes called the Sun god, but he is most associated with prophecy, archery, and music. Apollo did not seem to have any one, lasting love interest but had several sexual encounters with both females and males. Apollo had numerous children, among the most famous ASCLEPIUS by Coronis (or Arsinoe), ION by CREUSA, and Mopsus by TIRESIAS' daughter Manto. Apollo unsuccessfully pursued CASSANDRA, daughter of PRIAM, and Daphne, daughter of the river Ladon. Apollo accidentally killed his male lover Hyacinthus with a discus toss.

Apollo is one of the most frequently mentioned divinities in ancient drama and is best known as the god who responds to questions about the future through the DELPHIC ORACLE. Apollo's earliest appearance in extant drama (458 B.C.E.) occurs in AESCHYLUS' *Eumenides* (see ORESTEIA), in which he champions ORESTES, whom Apollo had commanded to kill his mother. In this play, Aeschylus describes Apollo as a deity who is incapable of telling a lie and who stands firmly by Orestes when the FURIES pursue him and argues on Orestes' behalf when the Furies prosecute him in Athens. In EURIPIDES' *ORESTES*, however, Apollo does not appear to testify on Orestes' behalf when the assembly at Argos debates his fate. Only at the conclusion of *Orestes* does Apollo appear, and at that point he has rescued HELEN from being killed by Orestes and prevents Orestes from killing HERMIONE.

Euripides' *Ion* offers a rather controversial view of Apollo. Apollo does not take the stage in this play but is the most talked-about divinity and the force that impels the other characters. He sexually assaults and impregnates CREUSA, who, fearing her father's anger about her having a child out of wedlock, leaves her baby to die. At Apollo's command, however, the infant is rescued and taken to DELPHI, where the child, Ion, is raised at Apollo's temple.

In Euripides' *ALCESTIS,* Apollo appears in a less than serious light. In this play, Apollo delivers the prologue and tells of his servitude to the mortal king ADMETUS, a result of Apollo's killing of some Cyclopes. Apollo announces that he is leaving Admetus' house to avoid the pollution caused by ALCESTIS' impending death, but

as he leaves he encounters Thanatos (Death himself). Apollo tries to persuade Death to let Alcestis live, but Death refuses. Apollo then predicts that HERACLES will take Alcestis from him. [ANCIENT SOURCES: Apollodorus, *Library* 1.4.1–2, 1.3.3–4, 1.7.6, 1.7.9, 3.1.2, 3.10.3–4; Aristophanes, *Acharnians* 875; Homer, *Iliad* 1.603–4, *Odyssey* 9.576; *Homeric Hymn to Apollo;* Hyginus, *Fables* 140, 165, 191, 203; Ovid, *Metamorphoses* 1.416–567, 2.531–632, 10.162–219, 11.194–220, 12.580–628; Pausanias, 2.7.7, 2.30.3, 3.1.3, 8.20.2, 10.5.3, 10.6.5, 10.16.3, 10.17.3]

ARABES   The people who lived in ARABIA. SENECA connects them with the worship of the SUN and with the use of poisonous arrows. [ANCIENT SOURCES: Seneca, *Hercules Oetaeus* 793, *Medea* 711, *Oedipus* 117]

ARABIA   Situated at the southwestern corner of Asia, Arabia had the Red Sea as its western border, the Persian Gulf as its northeastern border, and the Arabian Sea as its south and southeastern borders. Ancient Arabia included not only the entire peninsula that is now occupied largely by modern Saudi Arabia, but also the modern regions of Jordan, Syria, and western Iraq. In EURIPIDES' *BACCHAE,* DIONYSUS claims his worship has extended all the way to Arabia. [ANCIENT SOURCES: Aeschylus, *Prometheus Bound* 420; Euripides, *Bacchae* 16; Plautus, *Persa* 506, 522, 541, *Three-Dollar Day* 845, 933–34, *Truculentus* 539]

ARACHNAEUS   A mountain northeast of MYCENAE. [ANCIENT SOURCES: Aeschylus, *Agamemnon* 309 (see ORESTEIA); Pausanias, 2.25.10]

ARAI   See CURSES.

THE ARBITRATION (EPITREPONTES) **MENANDER (CA. 304 B.C.E.)**   Only about half the text of this play survives. The drama's setting is ATHENS, and the action occurs before the houses of Charisius (on the audience's left) and Chairestratus (on the audience's right), both of whom are young Athenian gentlemen. Roughly 40 lines survive from the first act, which would have revealed that Charisius married Pamphile, who had a baby after five months of marriage. Charisius, upset by this, moved into Chairestra-tus' house and began to drink heavily. The child was left outside to die but was rescued by one of Chaire-stratus' servants. The lines that survive from the first act consist of a conversation between Chairestratus and a music girl (musician/prostitute), Habrotonon, about Charisius' drinking. In another dozen lines from the first act Smicrines, Pamphile's father, announces to Habrotonon and Chairestratus some sort of scheme against Charisius.

In the second act, Syrus, a servant of Chairestratus, Syrus' wife, and Daos, a shepherd, enter. Syrus' wife is carrying a child (that of Charisius). Syrus and Daos are involved in a quarrel over the baby and call upon Smi-crines to arbitrate their dispute. Daos tells Smicrines that he found the baby while he was shepherding and took the child home. Afterward, Daos began to wonder whether he could afford to raise a child, so while he was with his flocks the next day, he encountered Syrus and told him of the problem. Syrus begged to have the child, for his wife's own child had just died, and finally persuaded Daos. Because Daos also found some trin-kets with the infant, Syrus wanted those as well, but Daos refused to turn those over. Syrus, on the other hand, argued that he represented the interests of the child, for whom the trinkets are a source of identifica-tion. Smicrines declares that the trinkets belong to the child, and that the child should remain in Syrus' cus-tody. Daos hands over the trinkets and Syrus tells his wife to take them to Chairestratus. As Syrus is handing over a ring to his wife, one of Charisius' servants, Onesimus, enters and recognizes the ring as belonging to Charisius, who lost the ring once when he was drunk. After some discussion, the ring is given to Onesimus.

The third act opens with an encounter between Onesimus and Syrus. Onesimus still has not had an opportunity to show his master the ring. Onesimus tells Syrus his suspicion that Charisius raped a girl, she had his baby, and she left the child to die. Onesimus is convinced that if they could find the girl and the ring, they would confirm his theory. Habrotonon, who has been onstage and listening to this conversation, says she met a young woman who had been raped at a cer-tain festival. Onesimus urges that they search for the girl, but Habrotonon does not want to become involved until she knows the name of the rapist. Habrotonon does suggest, however, that she wear the ring, speak to Charisius, and pretend that she was raped and gave birth to a child. Onesimus approves of this plan and suggests that Charisius will buy Habrotonon's freedom if he thinks she is the child's mother. Onesimus then gives Habrotonon the ring and she enters Charisius' house. Onesimus worries, how-ever, that Charisius will desert Pamphile and marry Habrotonon. When Onesimus sees Smicrines approaching, he goes into Charisius' house to avoid the old man. In the next 50 lines, the manuscript is damaged, but at this point Smicrines and a cook, Car-ion, both hear of the commotion caused by Habrotonon's story and believe it to be true. When the manuscript resumes, Smicrines considers taking Pam-phile back home if Charisius is going to behave in such a wild manner.

In the next act, Pamphile and Smicrines discuss the recent turn of events. The manuscript is heavily dam-aged, but apparently Pamphile refused to go home with her father. At some point, Smicrines leaves and Habrotonon, carrying the child, arrives from Charisius' house. Habrotonon tells Pamphile that she pretended the child was hers and states that she recognizes Pam-phile as the girl she saw at the festival. When the two women see Onesimus approach from Chairestratus' house, they go into Charisius' house, where Habrotonon promises to explain the whole story to Pamphile. After the women's departure, Onesimus describes Charisius' depression about recent events and worries that Charisius may kill him. Charisius emerges from the house and worries aloud about his problems as Onesimus eavesdrops. Eventually, Habrotonon arrives from Charisius' house, and, although the text breaks off for about 15 lines, appar-ently she reveals the truth to Charisius—that Charisius and Pamphile are the child's parents.

The play's final act begins with two fragments from a speech of Chairestratus, in which he confesses having fallen in love with Habrotonon. After Chairestratus exits, Smicrines enters. Pamphile's father still does not know the truth about Charisius and Pamphile and knocks on Charisius' door. Smicrines is met by Onesimus, who starts to reveal the truth about Charisius and Pamphile. Although the rest of the manuscript is lost, Smicrines would have learned the truth and become reconciled with Charisius, and the play probably ended with a celebration.

BIBLIOGRAPHY

Anderson, W. S. "Euripides' *Auge* and Menander's *Epitrepontes*," *Greek, Roman, and Byzantine Studies* 23 (1982): 165–77.

Arnott, W. G. "The Time-Scale of Menander's *Epitrepontes*," *Zeitschrift fur Papyrologie und Epigraphik* 70 (1987): 19–31.

Iversen, P. A. "Coal for Diamonds: Syriskos' Character in Menander's *Epitrepontes*." *American Journal of Philology* 122, no. 3 (2001): 381–403.

Primmer, A. "Karion in den *Epitrepontes*," *Weiner Studien* 20 (1986): 123–41.

Sisti, Francesco, ed. *Menandro, Epitrepontes*. Genova: Univ. di Genova Fac. di Lettere, 1991.

Stockert, W. "Metatheatralisches in Menanders *Epitrepontes*," *Weiner Studien* 110 (1997): 5–18.

ARCADIA　A mountainous region in the northern part of southern Greece. ATALANTA, PARTHENOPAEUS, and TELEPHUS were born in this region and ORESTES is said to have died there. The gods PAN and HERMES are often associated with Arcadia. In one tradition the Arcadians were the earliest people on Earth. [ANCIENT SOURCES: Apollodorus, *Library* 1.8.2, *Epitome* 6.28, 7.38; Euripides, *Electra* 1273, *Telephus* fragment 696.2 Nauck; Seneca, *Hercules Oetaeus* 1883, *Phaedra* 786; Strabo, 12.8.4, 13.1.3]

BIBLIOGRAPHY

Nauck, A. *Tragicorum Graecorum Fragmenta*. 1889. Reprint, Hildesheim, Ger.: Olms, 1964.

ARCADIAN BOAR　Also known as the Erymanthean boar, this dangerous creature had to be captured and taken back alive as one of HERACLES' labors for EURYSTHEUS. [ANCIENT SOURCES: Apollodorus, *Library* 2.5.4; Seneca, *Agamemnon* 832, *Hercules Furens* 229, *Hercules Oetaeus* 1536]

ARCADY　See ARCADIA.

ARCHEDEMUS　An Athenian statesman mocked for not being (allegedly) a native Athenian and for being "bleary-eyed." Archedemus prosecuted ERASI-NADES, one of the Athenian commanders at the Battle of ARGINUSAE, for embezzlement Archedmus may have been instrumental in securing the death penalty for Erasinades and his fellow commanders at Arginusae. [ANCIENT SOURCES: Aristophanes, *Frogs* 417, 588; Lysias, 14.25; Xenophon, *Hellenica* 1.7.2, 1.7.35]

BIBLIOGRAPHY

Kock, T. *Comicorum Atticorum Fragmenta*. Vol. 1. Leipzig: Teubner, 1880.

Lang, M. L. "Theramenes and Arginousai," *Hermes* 120, no. 3 (1992): 267–79.

Sommerstein, A. H. *The Comedies of Aristophanes*. Vol. 9, *Frogs*. Warminster, U.K.: Aris & Phillips, 1996, 193.

ARCHEGETIS　A title of ATHENA. The name, which means "founder," refers to Athena's role as the "patron of a city or colony" (Henderson). [ANCIENT SOURCES: Aristophanes, *Lysistrata* 644]

BIBLIOGRAPHY

Henderson, J. *Aristophanes: Lysistrata*. Oxford: Clarendon Press, 1987, 156.

ARCHELAUS　Classical mythology mentions at least two men named Archelaus. One, the son of AEGYPTUS, married Anaxibia, daughter of DANAUS. The other Archelaus was the son of ELECTRYON and therefore the brother of ALCMENA. EURIPIDES wrote an *Archelaus* (fragments 1–38 Austin) that dates to 407 B.C.E. Euripides' play seems to have concerned Archelaus' killing of Cisseus, king of Macedon. After the killing Archelaus left and founded Aegae ("goats"), named after the goat that led him to the site. [ANCIENT SOURCES: Apollodorus, *Library* 2.1.5, 2.4.5; Hyginus, *Fables* 219]

BIBLIOGRAPHY

Austin, C. *Nova Fragmenta Euripidea in Papyris Reperta*. Berlin: De Gruyter, 1968.

Webster, T. B. L. *The Tragedies of Euripides*. London: Methuen, 1967.

ARCHENOMUS　An otherwise unknown person on whom ARISTOPHANES wishes death at *Frogs* 1507.

ARCHEPTOLEMUS　The son of Hippodamus of MILETUS, Archeptolemus was an Athenian politician whom Aristophanes mentions favorably in *Knights* (424

B.C.E.). In this play, Archeptolemus, of foreign birth himself, seems to have opposed CLEON with respect to the treatment of non-Athenians. In 411 B.C.E., Archeptolemus helped lead the oligarchic revolution in ATHENS. After the oligarchs were forced from power, Archeptolemus was convicted of treason and executed. [ANCIENT SOURCES: Aristophanes, *Knights* 327, 794]

BIBLIOGRAPHY
Sommerstein, A. H. *The Comedies of Aristophanes.* Vol. 2, *Knights.* Warminster, U.K.: Aris & Phillips, 1981, 161.

ARCHITEKTON   A Greek word meaning "primary builder," *architekton* refers to the person who served as the manager for a Greek theater. By at least 270 B.C.E., the *architekton* appears to have been an elected official. [ANCIENT SOURCES: Demosthenes, *On the Crown* 28.5; *Inscriptiones Graecae* ii² 500.20–36]

ARCHMIME   A Greek word meaning "primary mime," the archmime would have the leading role in a MIME but also served as the leader of the troupe of mimes. [ANCIENT SOURCES: *Corpus Inscriptionum Latinarum* 6.1064, *Inscriptiones Latinae Selectae* 5209a, 5211]

BIBLIOGRAPHY
Csapo, E., and W. J. Slater. *The Context of Ancient Drama.* Ann Arbor: University of Michigan Press, 1995, 373–75.

ARCHON   The archon (Greek: leader or ruler) archons was a man who served as a public magistrate in various Greek towns. In ATHENS, an archon was supposed to hold the office only once and for only one year. After the year in office, the archon, if he had performed his duty honorably, became a lifetime member of a judicial board called the AREOPAGUS. Each year the Athenians selected nine archons by lot from the upper classes of society. Three of the nine archons had special titles and functions. Before 490 B.C.E., the *archon polemarchos* (war ruler) was in charge of military affairs. The *archon basileus* (king) was in charge of religious matters and legal matters connected with religion. Finally, the eponymous archon presided over lawsuits involving issues of inheritance and property. The Athenians also named each year after the name of the eponymous archon.

ARCTOPHYLAX   A constellation (also known as BOÖTES), Arctophylax (the bear's guardian) was originally a person named Arcas, the son of ZEUS and CALLISTO. After his death, he was transformed into a constellation. [ANCIENT SOURCES: Hyginus, *Fables* 176; Ovid, *Metamorphoses* 2.468; Seneca, *Thyestes* 874]

ARCTOS   From the Greek word *arktos* (bear), Arctos can refer to either Ursa Major (the Greater Bear) or Ursa Minor (the Lesser Bear), or both constellations. [ANCIENT SOURCES: Ovid, *Metamorphoses* 2.401–530; Seneca, *Hercules Furens* 6, 1326, *Medea* 405, 683, *Octavia* 234, *Oedipus* 507, 606, *Thyestes* 477]

ARCTURUS   A star in the constellation Boötes, Arcturus, whose name means "watcher of the bear," "watches" Ursa Major (the greater bear) move around the pole. In PLAUTUS' *ROPE,* the god Arcturus delivers the prologue. [ANCIENT SOURCES: Plautus, *Rope* 1–82; Sophocles, *Oedipus Tyrannos* 1137]

AREOPAGUS   Near the Athenian ACROPOLIS, this place, whose name means "ARES' hill," was a well-known site for murder trials both in legend and in history. According to mythology, the first murder trial, POSEIDON's prosecution of ARES for the murder of his son, Halirrhothius, occurred on this hill. ORESTES' trial for killing his mother also took place on the Areopagus. Not only was Areopagus the name of the geographical site, but in historical times the court that sat to hear murder cases there was also called the Areopagus. The site is also famous in the Christian tradition as the place where the apostle Paul first preached about Jesus Christ to the people of ATHENS in the middle of the first century C.E.

BIBLIOGRAPHY
Carawan, E. M. "*Apophasis* and *Eisaggelia:* The Role of the Areopagus in Athenian Political Trials," *Greek, Roman, and Byzantine Studies* 26 (1985): 114–40.
Gagarin, M. "The Vote of Athena," *American Journal of Philology* 96 (1975): 121–27.
Ostwald, Martin. "The Areopagus in the *Athenaion Politeia.*" In *Aristoteles and Athens: [actes de la table ronde "Centenaire de l'Athenaion politeia"], Fribourg (Suisse), 23–25 mai 1991.* Edited by M. Piérart. Fribourg: Séminaire

d'Histoire ancienne de l'Université de Fribourg; Paris: de Boccard, 1993, 139–53.

Sealey, R. "The Athenian Courts for Homicide," *Classical Philology* 78 (1983): 275–96.

Wallace, R. W. *The Areopagus Council, to 307 B.C.* Baltimore: Johns Hopkins University Press, 1989.

ARES The son of ZEUS and HERA, Ares is the Roman god Mars (also called Mavors or Gradivus). Ares is a god of war, but unlike ATHENA, who seems to be associated with the glories of war, Ares appears to represent war's savage and bloody side. Ares' primary love was APHRODITE, although she was married to HEPHAESTUS, who eventually caught the adulterous couple making love by snaring them in an invisible net. Although caught by Hephaestus, Ares and Aphrodite had a daughter, HARMONIA, who became the wife of CADMUS. Ares had numerous other children by various women. The most famous of these are MELEAGER by ALTHAEA; two sons named CYCNUS, one by Pyrene, one by Pelopia; DIOMEDES of Thrace by Cyrene; PARTHENOPAEUS by ATALANTA; TEREUS; and the Amazon PENTHESILEIA by Otrere. Although one of the major divinities, Ares plays a prominent role in relatively few myths. His name is mentioned frequently in tragedies, especially those dealing with war; however, Ares does not appear as a character in any extant Greek dramas. The Golden Fleece was placed in a grove sacred to Ares; the Amazon Hippolyte had her golden belt from Ares. Ares was imprisoned in a bronze pot for 13 months by Otos and Ephialtes but was eventually rescued by HERMES. The serpent that CADMUS killed was a child of Ares'. To atone for this action, Cadmus served Ares for a year, after which Ares married his daughter Harmonia to Cadmus. In EURIPIDES' *PHOENICIAN WOMEN*, MENOECEUS sacrifices himself to Ares to ensure victory for the Thebans against POLYNEICES and the Argives, as well as to atone further for Cadmus' killing of Ares' serpent. At the conclusion of EURIPIDES' *ELECTRA*, Euripides seems to draw a connection between ORESTES and Ares, as the DIOSCOROI mention that ORESTES' trial will take place at the AREOPAGUS, the place where POSEIDON prosecuted ARES for the killing of Halirrhothius, the son of Poseidon who had raped Ares' daughter Alcippe. Ares was acquitted of murder, just as Orestes would be acquitted of killing his mother. [ANCIENT SOURCES: Apollodorus, *Library* 1.7.4, 1.8.2, 3.4.1, 3.6.7, 3.9.2; 3.14.2, 3.14.8, *Epitome* 5.1; Euripides, *Electra* 1258–61; Seneca, *Hippolytus* 125]

ARGINUSAE Three small islands southeast of LESBOS and just off the coast of modern-day Turkey. In 406 B.C.E., Arginusae was the site of a famous naval battle during the PELOPONNESIAN WAR. Although the Athenians defeated the Spartans in this battle, adverse weather prevented them from recovering those who sailed on ships that had been wrecked during the battle. Upon returning to Athens, the Athenian commanders were prosecuted in a mass trial (contrary to usual Athenian practice) and condemned to die. [ANCIENT SOURCES: Aristophanes, *Frogs* 33, 191; Xenophon, *Hellenica* 1.6.22–1.7.35]

BIBLIOGRAPHY
Hunt, P. "The Slaves and the Generals of Arginusae," *American Journal of Philology* 122 (2001): 359–80.

Skoczylas Pownall, F. "Shifting Viewpoints in Xenophon's *Hellenica:* The Arginusae Episode," *Athenaeum* 88 (2000): 499–513.

ARGIVE See ARGOS.

ARGO The name of the ship in which JASON and the Argonauts sailed to fetch the Golden Fleece. The ship was built by ARGUS (1), whose name means "fast." Thus, *Argo* is the "fast" boat, built by the "fast" man, and its crew are "those who sail on the fast boat." The ship was constructed of timber gathered from Mount PELION and was equipped with an oracular beam for ZEUS' shrine at DODONA. Thus, the ship could give prophecies. Jason was killed when a piece of the *Argo* struck him in the head. AESCHYLUS wrote an *Argo* (fragments 20–21 Radt), but nothing of its plot is known. A satyric *Argo* is also attested, but its author is unknown and only the title survives (see Kannicht). [ANCIENT SOURCES: Apollodorus, *Library* 1.9.16; Euripides, *Medea* 1, 1386–88; Seneca, *Medea*]

BIBLIOGRAPHY
Kannicht, R., and Snell, B. *Tragicorum Graecorum Fragmenta.* Vol. 2. Göttingen, Ger.: Vandenhoeck & Ruprecht, 1981.

Radt, S. *Tragicorum Graecorum Fragmenta.* Vol. 3. Göttingen, Ger.: Vandenhoeck & Ruprecht, 1985.

ARGOS   A town near the southeastern coast of Greece between NEMEA and LERNA. The region where Argos is located is called the Argolid and the inhabitants are called Argives, although poets often use the name Argives as a synonym for Greeks in general. Argos is only a few miles away from MYCENAE and TIRYNS, and poets often refer to these three towns interchangeably. Several of the most famous figures in classical mythology lived in Argos—AGAMEMNON, ADRASTUS, AMPHITRYON, CLYTEMNESTRA, ELECTRA, EURYSTHEUS, ORESTES, to name a few. AESCHYLUS wrote a *Men of Argos* (fragments 16–18 Radt); nothing about its plot is known.

BIBLIOGRAPHY

Radt, S. *Tragicorum Graecorum Fragmenta.* Vol. 3. Göttingen, Ger.: Vandenhoeck & Ruprecht, 1985.

ARGUS (1)   The builder of the ship ARGO, on which JASON and the Argonauts sailed. [ANCIENT SOURCES: Apollodorus, *Library* 1.9.16; Apollonius Rhodius, 1.18–19, 1.321–26]

ARGUS (2)   The son of AGENOR (or Arestor or Inachus, or an elder Argus) and Ismene, or perhaps even born from the earth, Argus was a creature who had numerous eyes. Ancient sources number those eyes between four and 1,000, and artists often depicted them as covering his body. Because not all of Argus' eyes ever slept at one time, he was an ideal shepherd. Various sources say that Argus killed a bull that was ravaging ARCADIA, a cattle-stealing SATYR, the killer of Apis, and the monster Echidna, who had abducted a traveler. Argus is best known as the guardian of IO, one of ZEUS' lovers. After Io was transformed into a cow, HERA arranged for Argus to keep constant watch over her. Zeus freed Io from Argus by sending HERMES, who managed to lull all Argus' eyes to sleep and then kill Argus. Argus' eyes were placed in the feathers of Hera's favorite bird, the peacock. Despite Argus' death, his enraged spirit inhabited the body of a gadfly that continued to pursue Io after she was freed. Eventually Zeus put an end to this torment as well by restoring Io to her human form. [ANCIENT SOURCES: Aeschylus, *Prometheus Bound* 566 ff.; Apollodorus, *Library* 2.2.2–3; Ovid, *Metamorphoses* 1.622–723]

ARIADNE   The daughter of MINOS and PASIPHAE, Ariadne was the sister of PHAEDRA and Deucalion. Ariadne lived on the island of CRETE, and when THESEUS was there to be sacrificed to the MINOTAUR, Ariadne fell in love with Theseus, gave him a magical thread that allowed him to escape from the labyrinth where the Minotaur was kept, and then fled the island with him. On the return voyage to Theseus' home in Athens, Theseus and Ariadne stopped on the island of NAXOS. When Theseus left Naxos, however, Ariadne did not accompany him. Various reasons are given for this, and most involve the god DIONYSUS. The earliest account, in HOMER's *Odyssey,* indicates that ARTEMIS killed Ariadne at the request of Dionysus, in whose sacred cave Ariadne and Theseus may have had sexual relations. Others indicate that Dionysus commanded Theseus to leave her so that the god could have her or that Dionysus took her away from Theseus and married her. The best-known accounts say that Theseus simply abandoned her. After Ariadne's abandonment, either she committed suicide or, the more usual version, Dionysus married her. By Dionysus Ariadne had several sons: Euanthes, Oenopion, Peparethus, Phlias, Staphylus, Tauropolis, and THOAS.

One quite different tradition, however, suggests that Theseus returned to Crete after the death of Minos; killed the new king, Deucaliona; and then married Ariadne. On their return to Athens, a storm drove Theseus and Ariadne, who by now was pregnant with Theseus' child, toward the island of Cyprus. Apparently, the storm at sea caused Ariadne to fear that the child would be miscarried, so she asked to go ashore. Ariadne went ashore at Amathus, but the storm swept Theseus and his ship back out to sea. The women of Amathus cared for Ariadne, who died in childbirth and was buried there. The usual tradition, however, is that Ariadne was buried in a temple of Dionysus in ARGOS and that Dionysus placed the crown he gave her as a wedding present in the heavens as the constellation Corona.

Ariadne is not a character in any surviving dramas, although fragment 730a (Radt) from SOPHOCLES indicates that Ariadne appeared in a play that dealt with Theseus' experience on Crete. [ANCIENT SOURCES: Apollodorus, *Library* 3.15.8, *Epitome* 1.8–10; Catullus, 64;

Diodorus Siculus, 4.61, 5.51; Euripides, *Hippolytus* 399; Hesiod, *Theogony* 947–49, *Catalogues of Women* 76; HOMER, *Odyssey* 11.324; Hyginus, *Fables* 42, 43, *Poetic Astronomy* 2.5; Ovid, *Heroides* 10, *Metamorphoses* 7.456, 8.175, Pausanias, 1.20.2, 1.27.9, 1.44.5, 9.40.2, 10.29.2; Plutarch, *Theseus* 15, 19, 20; Seneca, *Hercules Furens* 18, *Oedipus* 448, 497, *Hippolytus* 245, 662–65; Stephanus Byzantium, "Phlious"]

BIBLIOGRAPHY
Armstrong, Rebecca. Cretan Women: Pasiphae, Ariadne and Phaedra in Latin Literature. D. Phil., Oxford University, 2001. (Index to Theses 52-5464)
Mills, Sophie. Theseus and the Ideals of Athens in Literature from Homer to Euripides. D. Phil., Oxford University, 1992. (Index to Theses 42-5183)
Radt, S. *Tragicorum Graecorum Fragmenta*. Vol. 4. Göttingen, Ger.: Vandenhoeck & Ruprecht, 1977.

ARIAN   Of or pertaining to the district of Aria in Persia. [ANCIENT SOURCES: Aeschylus, *Libation Bearers* 423 (see ORESTEIA)]

ARIGNOTUS   The son of AUTOMENES, Arignotus was a talented and well-known lyre player in ATHENS. [ANCIENT SOURCES: Aristophanes, *Knights* 1278, *Wasps* 1277–78; Athenaeus, 220b]

BIBLIOGRAPHY
Sommerstein, A. H. *The Comedies of Aristophanes*. Vol. 2, *Knights*. Warminster, U.K.: Aris & Phillips, 1981, 210.

ARIMASPIANS   A mythical tribe who were said to live beyond the region of SCYTHIA, to have only one eye, and to steal gold from creatures called GRIFFINS, with whom they were frequently at war. [ANCIENT SOURCES: Aeschylus, *Prometheus Bound* 804–7; Herodotus, 3.116, 4.13, 4.27; Pausanias, 1.24.6]

ARIPHRADES   An Athenian mentioned a few times by ARISTOPHANES as someone who enjoyed the secretions of women. He may have been a student of Anaxagoras, and Degani thinks that Aristophanes did not like Ariphrades because of his philosophical and political views, but little evidence exists to confirm Degani's opinion. ARISTOTLE mentions a comic poet named Ariphrades, and MacDowell suggests that

Aristophanes might have disliked him because he was a rival dramatist. [ANCIENT SOURCES: Aristophanes, *Ecclesiazusae* 128, *Knights* 1285, *Peace* 883, *Wasps* 1283; Aristotle, *Poetics* 1458b31; Athenaeus, 220b]

BIBLIOGRAPHY
Degani, E. "Arifrade L'Anassagoreo," *Maia* 12 (1960): 190–217.
MacDowell, D. M. *Aristophanes: Wasps*. Oxford: Clarendon Press, 1971, 298.

ARISTAEUS   The father of ACTAEON by CADMUS' daughter, AUTONOE. [ANCIENT SOURCES: Euripides, *Bacchae* 1227, 1371]

ARISTARCHUS (FIFTH CENTURY B.C.E.)   A Greek tragedian from the town of Tegea, Aristarchus is said to have written 70 plays and have recorded two victories, although only three titles are known (*Asclepius, Achilles, Tantalus*). In the opening lines of PLAUTUS' CARTHAGINIAN, the speaker of the prologue claims to be imitating Aristarchus' *Achilles*. [ANCIENT SOURCES: Plautus, *Carthaginian* 1–4; *Suda*, "Aristarchus"]

BIBLIOGRAPHY
Snell, B. *Tragicorum Graecorum Fragmenta*. Vol. 1. Göttingen, Ger.: Vandenhoeck & Ruprecht, 1971.

ARISTIDES (DIED CA. 463 B.C.E.)   The son of Lysimachus, Aristides was an Athenian statesman and military leader. He fought at the battle of MARATHON against the Persians but opposed THEMISTOCLES and was exiled from Athens in 483/482 B.C.E. When the Persians threatened to invade Greece again, Aristides was recalled and served as a commander at the battles of SALAMIS and PLATAEA. [ANCIENT SOURCES: Aristophanes, *Knights* 1325; Plutarch, *Aristides*]

ARISTOPHANES (CA. 450–385 B.C.E.)   The son of Philippus and Zenodora, Aristophanes, from the DEME of Cydathenaeum, is considered the greatest comic poet of ancient Greece (with the possible exception of MENANDER). Aristophanes had three sons, Araros, Philippus, and Nicostratus (or perhaps Philetaerus), all of whom became comic poets.

   Aristophanes wrote about 40 plays, of which 11 survive: *ACHARNIANS* (425 B.C.E.), *KNIGHTS* (424), *CLOUDS*

(423), WASPS (422), PEACE (421), BIRDS (414), LYSIS-
TRATA (411), THESMOPHORIAZUSAE (411), FROGS (405),
ECCLESIAZUSAE (392/391), and WEALTH (388). The first
nine plays in the list are considered examples of Old
Comedy; last two are often cited as examples of Middle Comedy (see COMEDY). Almost all of Aristophanes'
plays were produced either at the City DIONYSIA
(Clouds, Peace, Birds, and perhaps Thesmophoriazusae)
or at the LENAEA (Acharnians, Knights, Wasps, Frogs, and
perhaps Lysistrata), although he is known to have produced a comedy at a festival at ELEUSIS. Aristophanes'
first three plays, Banqueters (427), Babylonians (426),
and Acharnians, were produced under the name of his
friend CALLISTRATUS. Callistratus also produced Birds
and Lysistrata for Aristophanes, and a certain
Philonides produced Frogs and two other plays.
Aristophanes claims to have had his first three plays
produced by others because of his own young age, but
it is not clear why others produced his plays after
Aristophanes had become a well-established veteran of
the theater. Walton suggests that perhaps Aristophanes
"saw himself primarily as a writer and preferred to pass
the staging to some specialist in that field."

Of Aristophanes' first four plays, all but the Banqueters appear to have won the prize in their respective
competitions (cf. also Knights). Although the first four
years of Aristophanes' career were successful, compet-
itively speaking, Aristophanes finished first only three
other times over the next four decades (a play in 422,
perhaps the Proagon; Frogs in 405; Cocalus in 387).
Banqueters, Wasps, Peace, and Birds are known to have
finished second, and the first production of Clouds to
have finished last (third place).

Most of Aristophanes' plays are highly topical, often
dealing with actual persons (e.g., EURIPIDES, CLEON,
SOCRATES, ALCIBIADES) and issues of his own day, such as
the PELOPONNESIAN WAR, the Athenian court system, or
current trends in intellectual thought. During most of
Aristophanes' career as a dramatist, his native city of
Athens was at war with the people of SPARTA and their
allies. Nine of Aristophanes' 11 extant plays were written during the Peloponnesian War, a conflict that unde-
niably shaped his writing. Acharnians (425 B.C.E.), Peace
(421), and Lysistrata (411) all deal directly with the war
and its effects on the Athenian people. In each of these

plays, the hero conceives a highly unusual plan to
achieve peace. Thus, modern scholars have labeled
these works peace plays. In 404 B.C.E., Athens finally
surrendered to Sparta and the two surviving Aristophanic plays, Ecclesiazusae and Wealth, which appear
after 404, both lack the spirit of Aristophanes' earlier
plays. In these last two plays, the role of the chorus is
greatly diminished and extended attacks on political
figures decrease, an aspect evident in the plays after the
death of Cleon in 422. One should also note that by
404 Aristophanes' other favorite target, Euripides, had
died. Thus, with the major military conflict over and
both Cleon and Euripides dead, Aristophanes' later
comedies (not surprisingly) took on a rather different
tone. Similar changes might be observed in modern
humor, as comics have altered their material and style
to go with the politicians in office at the time.

In some instances, Aristophanes' attacks on public
figures had effects that carried beyond the stage.
Regarding the trial of Socrates in 399 B.C.E., in Plato's
Apology Socrates himself mentions that these charges
are not new and alludes to Aristophanes' characterization of him in the Clouds, whose first production was
24 years earlier. Despite the role Aristophanes' caricature of Socrates may have played in the charges against
Socrates, who was found guilty and sentenced to
death, Plato's Symposium, written after the deaths of
both Socrates and Aristophanes, shows Aristophanes,
at least on the surface, to be on good terms with not
only Socrates, but the others at the symposium.

Aristophanes' Babylonians, produced in 426, put the
playwright in conflict with Cleon, who made some sort
of legal charge against Aristophanes for slandering "the
magistrates, councillors and people of Athens in the
presence of foreigners" (Sommerstein). Although
Aristophanes' attacks on Cleon had some impact on
the playwright personally, they apparently did not have
much effect on the public's opinion of Cleon, as the
Athenian people continued to entrust him with military commands. Likewise, despite Aristophanes'
embarrassing portrayal of the general LAMACHUS in
Acharnians, Lamachus continued to hold military commands until his death a decade later.

In addition to criticizing the political and intellectual extremists of his day, Aristophanes shows no

sympathy for people who make their living by exploiting certain situations or taking advantage of other people. Those who profit from the war with Sparta, people who manipulate religion or popular superstition for their own benefit, and professional INFORMANTS are frequently barred from enjoying the fruits of the reforms created by Aristophanes' heroes, who are usually the common people of Athenian society, such as DICAEOPOLIS (*Acharnians*) and TRYGAEUS (*Peace*), both of whom make their living by working the land. Although most of Aristophanes' plays are highly topical, the desires of his leading characters are universal: a life free of war and political corruption, clothing, sufficient food and drink, and a satisfying love life.

BIBLIOGRAPHY

Bowie, A. M., *Aristophanes: Myth, Ritual and Comedy.* Cambridge: Cambridge University Press, 1996.

Dover, K. J. *Aristophanic Comedy.* Berkeley: University of California Press, 1972.

Henderson, J. *The Maculate Muse: Obscene Language in Attic Comedy.* 2d ed. New Haven, Conn.: Yale University Press, 1991.

Konstan, D. *Greek Comedy and Ideology.* New York: Oxford University Press, 1995.

MacDowell, D. *Aristophanes and Athens.* Oxford: Oxford University Press, 1995.

Segal, Erich, ed. *Oxford Readings in Aristophanes.* Oxford: Oxford University Press, 1996.

Sommerstein, A. H. *The Comedies of Aristophanes.* Vol. 1, *Acharnians.* Warminster, U.K.: Aris & Phillips, 1980, 3.

Walton, J. M. *Living Greek Theatre.* New York: Greenwood Press, 1987, 176.

ARISTOTLE (384–322 B.C.E.)

Born at Stagirus in northeastern Greece, the young Aristotle was sent to ATHENS to study after his father's death. There Aristotle studied with PLATO for two decades and became the leader of a philosophical school in Athens known as the Academy. Aristotle wrote numerous works, whose subjects included politics, ethics, rhetoric, and scientific matters of the time. Numerous references to classical drama are found throughout Aristotle's works; only two segments are discussed here. The first occurs in Aristotle's *Politics* (8.7), in which the author speaks briefly about the educational and emotional (see CATHARSIS) benefits of

music (which includes dramatic poetry), especially on the different classes who make up the spectators in the theater. Aristotle's most famous remarks on drama appear in his *Poetics,* a short incomplete treatise that may consist of notes for one of Aristotle's lectures and may not even have been written by Aristotle at all. Despite the problems concerning the text itself and its authorship, *Poetics* has had a profound influence on the way Greek TRAGEDY, even up to the present day, is read. In its own day, in many places *Poetics* responded to and challenged some of Plato's views on drama that appear in *Republic.* Although Aristotle's *Poetics* indicates that its intent was to discuss epic poetry, tragedy, and COMEDY, the section on comedy is missing and the section on epic poetry may be incomplete. Some scholars believe that a certain document known as the Tractatus Coislinianus contains a summary of the missing section on comedy. Most of the material contained in *Poetics,* as we have it, deals with tragedy. Thus, Aristotle's *Poetics* provides information about the origins of tragedy, comedy, and epic poetry; the development of tragedy; what Aristotle considers the six constituent parts of tragedy (plot, character, diction, reasoning, spectacle, song); and similarities of and differences between tragedy and epic poetry.

BIBLIOGRAPHY

Bremer, J. M. *Hamartia: Tragic Error in the Poetics of Aristotle and in Greek Tragedy.* Amsterdam: Hakkert, 1969.

Halliwell, S. *Aristotle's Poetics.* Chapel Hill: University of North Carolina Press, 1986.

Janko, R. *Aristotle on Comedy.* London: Duckworth, 1984.

Lucas, D. W. *Aristotle. Poetics.* Oxford: Clarendon Press, 1968.

Rorty, A. O., ed. *Essays on Aristotle's Poetics.* Princeton, N.J.: Princeton University Press, 1992.

ARISTYLLUS

A person whom Aristophanes ridicules for taking pleasure in fecal material. He may have enjoyed licking or kissing the anus. [ANCIENT SOURCES: Aristophanes, *Ecclesiazusae* 647, *Wealth* 314]

BIBLIOGRAPHY

Sommerstein, A. H. *The Comedies of Aristophanes.* Vol. 11, *Wealth.* Warminster, U.K.: Aris & Phillips, 2001, 159.

ARTAPHRENES (1)   Also called Artaphernes, Artaphrenes, according to AESCHYLUS, killed the fifth Persian king, MARDUS. Aeschylus also names an Artaphrenes as the seventh Persian king, who was followed to the throne by DARIUS. An Artaphrenes is known to have governed Sardes, part of the Persian empire. Artaphrenes also had a son by the same name. [ANCIENT SOURCES: Aeschylus, *Persians* 776, 778]

ARTAPHRENES (2)   Also called Artaphernes, Artaphrenes, the son of Artaphrenes the elder, was one of the losing Persian commanders (his colleague was named Datis) at the battle of MARATHON in 490 B.C.E. [ANCIENT SOURCES: Aeschylus, *Persians* 21; Herodotus, 6.94–7.74]

ARTEMIS   The daughter of ZEUS and LETO and the twin sister of APOLLO, Artemis has the Roman counterpart Diana and is also called Britomartis, Cynthia, Delia, Dictynna, Phoebe, or Trivia. Delia refers to DELOS, the island where she was born. Dictynna points to the Greek word for net (*diktuon*). Because Greek hunters often used nets to catch their prey, Artemis, who is associated with hunting, is the goddess of the net. The name Trivia means "three roads," and Artemis appears to have been worshiped at crossroads. As her brother, Apollo, is associated with the SUN, Artemis is connected with the MOON. She is associated with wilderness, virginity, human sacrifice, and death of women. Despite the association with the death of women, Artemis was especially revered by women and in COMEDY women often swear by Artemis. She is also associated with childbirth and is even said to have helped deliver her twin brother, Apollo. As a virgin goddess, Artemis has no children, although the Roman Cicero says she produced Cupid (EROS) by Mercury (HERMES). As a virgin goddess, Artemis also required those devoted to her to be virgins. When Artemis discovered that her follower Callisto was pregnant (the result of a sexual assault by Zeus), ancient sources say that Artemis either shot her or changed her into a bear.

Artemis did not lack men who were attracted to her; when Artemis' chastity was threatened, she protected herself with force. The river Alphaeus tried to pursue her, and she eluded him by covering herself with mud.

The giant Otus tried to assault her sexually, and she killed him. Artemis brought about the destruction of ACTAEON when he saw her bathing, although in EURIPIDES' *Bacchae* we hear that Actaeon boasted that he was a better hunter than Artemis was. Some sources say that when the great hunter ORION tried to rape Artemis, she sent a huge scorpion to kill him. Other sources say that Artemis cared for Orion and that he became one of her followers. Apollo, fearing that Artemis would fall in love with Orion, arranged for GAIA to send the scorpion to attack Orion. Apollo then tricked Artemis into killing Orion. In both traditions, Artemis transformed Orion and the scorpion into constellations.

As is the punishment wreaked upon those who attempted to enjoy Artemis' sexual favors, other appearances of Artemis in myth and drama are marked by violence. The sacrifice of IPHIGENIA at AULIS was demanded by Artemis in AESCHYLUS' *Agamemnon* (see *ORESTEIA*) and EURIPIDES' *IPHIGENIA AT AULIS*; in Euripides' *IPHIGENIA IN TAURIS*, the audience hear that the Taurians sacrifice strangers to Artemis.

In the *HIPPOLYTUS* plays by EURIPIDES and SENECA, she is the divinity most worshiped by HIPPOLYTUS, who maintains his own chastity in honor of her. She appears at the conclusion of Euripides' play to reveal Hippolytus' innocence to THESEUS. Artemis also promises to take revenge on one of APHRODITE's favorites for her destruction of Hippolytus. When NIOBE boasted that she had produced more children than Artemis' mother, Leto, Artemis helped Apollo destroy Niobe's children.

The Greek comic poet Ephippus wrote a play entitled *Artemis,* but the two lines that survive (about a bread-eating fellow from Thessaly named Alexander) tell little about the play's content (fragment 1 Kock). [ANCIENT SOURCES: Apollodorus, *Library* 1.4.1, 1.8.2, 1.9.15, 2.5.3, 3.4.4, 3.5.6, 3.8.2, 3.14.4, *Epitome* 2.2, 2.10, 3.21–22; Cicero, *On the Nature of the Gods* 3.23; Ovid, *Metamorphoses* 2.401–530, 3.138–252]

BIBLIOGRAPHY
Kock, T. *Comicorum Atticorum Fragmenta.* Vol. 2. Leipzig: Teubner, 1884.

ARTEMISIA   A queen of Caria who was an ally of the Persian king XERXES. Although Artemisia advised Xerxes against attacking SALAMIS in 480 B.C.E., she led five ships against the Greek forces and even sank an enemy ship. After the Persian defeat, she advised Xerxes to retreat. He accepted this advice and arranged for Artemisia to transport some of his sons (whom he had with him at Salamis) to Ephesus. [ANCIENT SOURCES: Aristophanes, *Lysistrata* 675, *Thesmophoriazusae* 1200; Herodotus, 7.99, 8.68–69, 8.87–93, 101–107]

ARTEMISIUM   A town at the northern end of the island of EUBOEA. In 480 B.C.E., a coalition of allied Greeks fought an important naval battle (most of the ships were supplied by ATHENS) against the Persians off the coast of Artemisium. [ANCIENT SOURCES: Aristophanes, *Lysistrata* 1251; Herodotus, 7.175–78, 8.1–2, 8.14.1]

BIBLIOGRAPHY
Henderson, J. *Aristophanes: Lysistrata.* Oxford: Clarendon Press, 1987, 211–12.

ARTEMON   A contemporary of the Greek lyric poet ANACREON (who was born around 570 B.C.E.), who labeled him as morally corrupt. [ANCIENT SOURCES: Aristophanes, *Acharnians* 850; Anacreon, fragment 43.5 Page]

BIBLIOGRAPHY
Page, D. L. *Poetae Melici Graeci.* 1962, Reprint, Oxford: Clarendon Press, 1967.
Sommerstein, A. H. *The Comedies of Aristophanes.* Vol. 1, *Acharnians.* Warminster, U.K.: Aris & Phillips, 1980, 199.

ASCLEPIUS (Latin: AESCULAPIUS)
Asclepius was the son of APOLLO and Coronis (or Arsinoe). Asclepius was especially revered and worshiped at the Greek town of EPIDAURUS. When Apollo found that Coronis preferred the mortal Ischys to him, Apollo killed Coronis but snatched the infant from her body on the funeral pyre. Apollo took Asclepius to the centaur CHIRON, who trained him in hunting and medicine. Asclepius became so skilled at medicine that he was able to raise the dead. Among those Asclepius was said to have raised from the dead was THESEUS' son, HIPPOLYTUS, but no hint of this exists in EURIPIDES' *HIPPOLYTUS.* ZEUS, fearing that more people might acquire the ability to raise the dead, killed Asclepius. Asclepius had several children: Machaon, Podalirius, IASO

(Cure), Hygeia (Health), and Panacea (Cure). Asclepius does not appear as a character in any surviving dramas, but the Greek tragic poet Aristarchus wrote a play called *Asclepius* (only the title is known; cf. Snell). Among the Greek comic poets, both Antiphanes (fragment 45 Kock) and Philetaerus (fragment 1 Kock) wrote plays entitled *Asclepius,* and Alexis (fragment 24 Kock) wrote *Asclepiokleides;* only one brief fragment survives from each play. [ANCIENT SOURCES: Apollodorus, 3.10.3–4; Aristophanes, *Wealth* 411, 640; Diodorus Siculus, 4.71.2–4; Euripides, *Alcestis* 3–6, 970; Hyginus, *Fables* 49; Ovid, *Metamorphoses* 15.622–744]

BIBLIOGRAPHY
Edelstein, Emma, and Ludwig Edelstein. *Asclepius: A Collection and Interpretation of the Testimonies, with a New Introduction by Gary B. Ferngren.* 2d ed. Baltimore: Johns Hopkins University Press, 1998.
Kock, T. *Comicorum Atticorum Fragmenta.* Vol. 2. Leipzig: Teubner, 1884.
Snell, B. *Tragicorum Graecorum Fragmenta.* Vol. 1. Göttingen, Ger.: Vandenhoeck & Ruprecht, 1971.

ASCONDAS   A Greek, perhaps from BOEOTIA, who apparently lived during the middle of the fifth century B.C.E. and was a champion pancratiast (skilled in a sport similar to modern kickboxing). [ANCIENT SOURCES: Aristophanes, *Wasps* 1191, 1383]

BIBLIOGRAPHY
Sommerstein. A. *The Comedies of Aristophanes.* Vol. 4, *Wasps.* Warminster, U.K.: Aris & Phillips, 1980, 226.

ASIA   From the perspective of the ancients, a reference to Asia usually denoted the western half of what is today Turkey. In AESCHYLUS' *PERSIANS,* the whole of Asia is considered Persian territory. The wanderings of DIONYSUS and IO took them through Asia. Playwrights sometimes refer to the Trojans as Asians. [ANCIENT SOURCES: Aeschylus, *Prometheus Bound* 735; Euripides, *Bacchae* 17, 64, 1168]

ASINARIA   See COMEDY OF ASSES.

ASOPUS   A river that flows south of THEBES. Poets sometimes refer to THEBES as the land of Asopus. The personification of the Asopus is said to have had a daughter, AEGINA, who produced AEACUS by ZEUS. [ANCIENT SOURCES: Aeschylus, *Persians* 805; Euripides, *Suppliant Women* 383, 571, 1149, *Heracles* 1163, *Bacchae* 749, 1044, *Iphigenia at Aulis* 697; Hyginus, *Fables* 52, 155]

ASPASIA A freeborn intelligent woman from MILETUS, Aspasia lived with the Athenian statesman PERICLES for some time, although she was not his wife. Rumor labeled her a "madam" who arranged sexual liaisons between Pericles and other freeborn women or someone who trained prostitutes. Aristophanes jokes that the reason behind the PELOPONNESIAN WAR was that some young Athenians stole a Megarian prostitute and the Megarians retaliated by stealing two of Aspasia's prostitutes. [ANCIENT SOURCES: Aristophanes, *Acharnians* 524–27; Plutarch, *Pericles* 24.3–5]

BIBLIOGRAPHY
Henry, M. M. *Prisoner of History: Aspasia of Miletus and Her Biographical Tradition.* New York: Oxford University Press, 1995.
Loraux, Nicole. "Aspasia: la straniera, l'intellettuale." In *Grecia al femminile.* Edited by N. Loraux. Roma: Laterza, 1993, 123–54.
Vickers, M. J. "Alcibiades and Aspasia: Notes on the *Hippolytus*," *Dialogues d'histoire ancienne* 26, no. 2 (2000): 7–17.
Wilkins, John. "Aspasia in Medea?" *Liverpool Classical Monthly* 12 (1987): 8–10.

ASPIS See THE SHIELD.

ASSEMBLYWOMEN ARISTOPHANES See *ECCLESIAZUSAE.*

ASTACUS The father of MELANIPPUS, who was one of the SEVEN AGAINST THEBES. [ANCIENT SOURCES: Aeschylus, *Seven against Thebes* 407; Apollodorus, *Library* 3.6.8]

ASTRAEA A daughter of ZEUS and THEMIS, Astraea, the sister of Shame (Greek: Aidos; Latin: Pudicitia) was a goddess of justice. She and her sister lived among human beings until their wicked behavior drove her to the heavens. Astraea became the constellation Virgo. [ANCIENT SOURCES: Ovid, *Metamorphoses* 1.150; Seneca, *Hercules Furens* 1068, *Hercules Oetaeus* 69, *Octavia* 424, *Thyestes* 857]

ASTYANAX Also called Scamandrius, Astyanax, the son of HECTOR and ANDROMACHE, was killed by the Greeks after the fall of TROY. Astyanax appears as a silent character in EURIPIDES' TROJAN WOMEN, in which he is taken away to be killed. Later, his body is taken back to be buried by his grandmother, HECABE. Among Roman authors, ACCIUS wrote a tragic *Astyanax,* whose approximately two dozen surviving lines indicate that the play was set at Troy and that Hecuba (Hecabe) and the prophet CALCHAS, and probably Ulysses (ODYSSEUS) and MENELAUS, had speaking parts. [ANCIENT SOURCES: Apollodorus, *Epitome* 5.23; Euripides, *Andromache* 9–10, *Trojan Women* 577ff.; Homer, *Iliad* 6.390–493, 22.482–507; Hyginus, *Fables* 109; Ovid, *Metamorphoses* 13.415; Seneca, *Agamemnon* 634, *Trojan Women* 369ff.]

BIBLIOGRAPHY
Warmington, E. H. *Remains of Old Latin: Livius Andronicus, Naevius, Pacuvius, and Accius.* Vol. 2. Cambridge, Mass.: Harvard University Press, 1936.

ATALANTA (ATALANTE) The tradition about the famous female hunter Atalanta is a confusing one, because two regions, BOEOTIA and ARCADIA, both claimed to be home to an Atalanta. Her mother is usually named Clymene; her father is named Iasus, Maenalus, or Schoeneus. Atalanta's father wanted a son and therefore exposed his infant daughter to die. As was PARIS, Atalanta was suckled by a she bear. Hunters rescued Atalanta and raised her. She herself became a great hunter and remained a virgin, either because she wanted to continue her hunting activities or because she had heard an oracle that marriage would mean disaster for her. Although some writers say Atalanta sailed with the Argonauts, her most famous adventure occurred when she joined the hunt for the Calydonian boar. Atalanta struck the boar first, and MELEAGER, who eventually killed it, awarded her the animal's pelt.

Now that Atalanta had become famous, her father invited her home. Hoping for grandchildren, he tried to find a husband for Atalanta. She, however, wanted to stay unmarried, and so she told her father that she would only marry someone who could defeat her in a footrace. If the prospective suitor lost the race, he also lost his life. Several suitors challenged Atalanta, but she defeated them all until the arrival of Melanion (or Hippomenes). This suitor, helped by Aphrodite, defeated Atalanta by luring her off the racecourse with three golden apples that the goddess had given him. Each time Atalanta ran ahead of the suitor, he would throw an apple, which Atalanta would leave the course to retrieve. Because Atalanta lost the race, she married Melanion. Unfortunately, the newlyweds chose the sacred precinct of a divinity (ZEUS or CYBELE, depending on the source) to consummate their marriage. The angered divinity changed the lovers into lions.

Atalanta's marriage to Melanion was brief, but she is said to have had a son, PARTHENOPAEUS. Some, however, make Meleager or ARES the father of the boy. Atalanta exposed Parthenopaeus on Mount Parthenius, but shepherds rescued him. Coincidentally, the same shepherds rescued TELEPHUS and the two young men became comrades.

Although Atalanta does not appear as a character in any extant classical dramas, she would have appeared in several plays that have not survived. AESCHYLUS is said to have written an *Atalanta,* of which only the title survives (Mette). Aristias produced an *Atalanta,* of which only four, uninformative words exist (fragment 2 Snell). Several Greek comic poets wrote a play titled *Atalanta,* of which fragments that survive give no information about the plot: *Alexis* (title only; Kock), *Callias* (fragment 1 Kock 1), *Euthycles* (fragments 2–4 Kock), *Philyllius* (title only; Kock), *Strattis* (fragments 3–9 Kock 1). In the lone fragment that survives from Philetaerus' *Atalanta,* someone speaks of his or her ability in running, labors, and eating (fragment 3 Kock). Among Roman authors, PACUVIUS wrote an *Atalanta* (lines 49–78 Warmington), which appears to have treated a search by Parthenopaeus for his mother. One of the fragments (lines 68–69) mentions someone's running past Parthenopaeus. Perhaps Parthenopaeus entered the race with Atalanta, was defeated by her, and before he was killed was recognized by his mother. [ANCIENT SOURCES: Apollodorus, *Library* 3.9.2; Callimachus, *Hymn to Artemis* 216–21; Hyginus, *Fables* 99, 185;

Ovid, *Metamorphoses* 3.318, 10.565; Pausanias, 3.24.2, 5.9.1, 8.45.4]

BIBLIOGRAPHY
Kock, T. *Comicorum Atticorum Fragmenta.* Vol. 1. Leipzig: Teubner, 1880.
Mette, H. J. *Die Fragmente der Tragödien des Aischylos.* Berlin: Akademie-Verlag, 1959.
Snell, B. *Tragicorum Graecorum Fragmenta,* Vol. 1. Göttingen, Ger.: Vandenhoeck & Ruprecht, 1971.
Warmington, E. H. *Remains of Old Latin: Livius Andronicus, Naevius, Pacuvius, and Accius.* Vol. 2. Cambridge, Mass.: Harvard University Press, 1936.

ATÊ   The Greek word *atê* has many meanings, including "delusion," "error," "curse," and "woe." Thus, the goddess Atê, the daughter of ERIS (strife) or ZEUS, personifies these entities. On one occasion, Atê even deluded Zeus into taking an oath that resulted eventually in EURYSTHEUS' becoming the master of HERACLES. This delusion led Zeus to cast Atê from OLYMPUS. Atê took up residence on the Earth, where she caused delusions among human beings. In AESCHYLUS' *ORESTEIA,* Atê appears to be associated with revenge. [ANCIENT SOURCES: Aeschylus, *Libation Bearers* 68, 381 (see *ORESTEIA*); Euripides, *Children of Heracles* 607, *Electra* 1307; Hesiod, *Theogony* 230; Homer, *Iliad* 9.503, 10.391, 19.85, 126; Sophocles, *Ajax* 123, *Antigone* 1097, *Electra* 1298, *Oedipus Tyrannos* 1284]

ATELLANA   See *FABULA ATELLANA.*

ATHAMAS   The son of Aeolus and Enarete, Athamas was a king of BOEOTIA. Athamas was the brother of CRETHEUS. Athamas' first wife, Nephele, was of divine stock, and by her he fathered a son and a daughter—PHRIXUS and Helle. For some reason, Nephele and Athamas parted ways. After the divorce, Athamas married either INO or Themisto. By Ino, daughter of CADMUS and HARMONIA, Athamas fathered Learchus and Melicertes (or Melicerta). By Themisto, daughter of Hypseus, Athamas had two sons, Orchomenus and Sphincius. According to Hyginus, Ino left Athamas and he, thinking she had died, married Themisto. When Athamas later learned that Ino was alive, he had her taken back to the palace.

Themisto, thinking she was a captive, employed Ino as a nurse not only to her children, but also to Ino's children, who still lived in the palace. Themisto later confided to Ino that she wanted to kill Ino's children. Ino, pretending to be loyal to Themisto, entered the plot with her and told Themisto to dress one woman's children in black clothing and the other woman's children in white. Ino, however, later switched the clothing and Themisto killed her own children. When Themisto realized what she had done, she committed suicide. Athamas became mad and killed Learchus, and Ino jumped into the sea with Melicertes.

Another story connected with Athamas deals with Ino's plot against Athamas' children by Nephele. Ino wanted her own children to succeed to the kingship, so she plotted to destroy Nephele's son, Phrixus, first in line to inherit the throne. Another tradition says that both Athamas and Ino plotted to kill Phrixus. Ino's plot was extremely clever and would not cast suspicion on her. Ino persuaded the women of the town to parch their town's grain supply, so that the crops would fail during the upcoming season. After the crops failed, Athamas sent a messenger to consult the Delphic oracle to learn a solution for the poor harvest. Ino, however, arranged for the messenger to tell Athamas that the only remedy for the situation would be to sacrifice Phrixus. According to Hyginus, Athamas refused to kill Phrixus, but Phrixus volunteered to give up his life. As the sacrifice was about to occur, Hyginus says a servant revealed to Athamas the plot of Ino, which ended the threat to Phrixus. Athamas, however, then decided to kill Ino and her son Melicertes, but DIONYSUS prevented this. According to John Tzetzes, HERACLES rescued Phrixus before he could be sacrificed. Other sources say that Nephele sent a ram with golden fleece to rescue Phrixus. Helle, who also happened to be present, also climbed aboard the ram. Phrixus flew away to safety. Helle, however, fell off the ram and died. The sea into which Helle plunged was called the Hellespont (the sea of Helle). Hyginus says Dionysus drove Phrixus and Helle mad, and Nephele sent the ram to rescue them in their wanderings.

One version of Phrixus' near sacrifice relates that when Phrixus' aunt, Demodice, the wife of Cretheus, was unsuccessful in her efforts to seduce Phrixus, she told Cretheus falsely that Phrixus had attempted to assault her sexually. Cretheus demanded that Athamas kill Phrixus; Athamas agreed to do so, but Nephele sent the golden-fleeced ram to rescue Phrixus.

Another story about Athamas makes him and Ino caretakers of the young Dionysus. HERA, angry that Dionysus was Zeus' child by SEMELE, tried to destroy Dionysus by causing Athamas to become insane. In his insanity, Athamas imagined that his son Learchus was a deer and killed him. Ino, also driven mad, killed Melicertes by putting him into a boiling cauldron and then hurling herself and the cauldron into the sea. Ino was changed into the sea divinity Leucothea. Another tradition states that Athamas persecuted Ino's children because of Ino's plot against Phrixus.

Athamas himself was exiled from Boeotia because of the killing of his son. After hearing an oracle that he should live where wild animals received him as a guest, Athamas traveled north to Thessaly, where he encountered wolves, who fled when he approached. Athamas then established his home in that region and called it Athamantia (the land of Athamas). Strabo calls the place Halus and says the Pharsalians later took over that land. Athamas then married Hypseus' daughter, Themisto, and fathered four sons by her: Leucon, Erythrius, Schoeneus, and Ptous. Another tradition says that Athamas adopted Haliartus and Coronus, the sons of his brother, Thersander.

Several playwrights wrote dramas entitled *Athamas*. A few brief fragments from Aeschylus' play of this name survive, one of which may refer to the cauldron into which Melicertes was thrown (fragment 1 Radt). To SOPHOCLES are attributed two plays entitled *Athamas* (fragments 1–10 Radt), but whether these deal with two different events in Athamas' life or whether one is a reworking of the earlier play is not clear. The Greek tragedian Astydamas wrote an *Athamas,* of which only the title is extant. XENOCLES wrote a satyric *Athamas,* of which only the title survives. Among the Roman playwrights, ENNIUS and ACCIUS both composed an *Athamas*. Of Ennius' play survives a single five-line fragment that refers to the revelry of some worshipers of Dionysus. Four extensive fragments from Accius' *Athamas* that exist indicate that the play seems to have treated Demodice's false accusation of Phrixus.

[ANCIENT SOURCES: Apollodorus, *Library* 1.7.3, 1.9.1–2, 3.4.3; Herodotus 7.197; Hyginus, *Fables* 1–3; Pausanias, 1.44.7–8, 9.23.6–24.1, 9.34.6–7; Strabo, 9.5.8]

BIBLIOGRAPHY

Antò, V. d'. "L'Athamas di Ennio e di Accio," *BStudLat* 1 (1971): 371–78.

Jocelyn, H. D. *The Tragedies of Ennius.* Cambridge: Cambridge University Press, 1969.

Warmington, E. H. *Remains of Old Latin: Ennius and Caecilius.* Vol. 1. Cambridge, Mass., and London: Harvard University Press, 1935.

ATHENA (Latin: MINERVA)

Athena is also called Pallas or Pallas Athena. A virgin goddess, Athena is associated with weaving, wisdom, and war. She was born fully armed from the head of ZEUS after Zeus swallowed the pregnant goddess METIS ("wisdom") in order to avoid a prophecy that he would be overthrown by a child of Metis'. The meaning of Metis' name and Athena's method of birth help explain the wisdom of both Zeus and Athena. Some sources place Athena's birth near a body of water (either a river or a lake, usually in Libya) called TRITON. Because of her birthplace, Athena is sometimes called Tritonia, Tritonis, or Tritogeneia (Triton-born). Athena is usually thought of as wearing a war helmet, carrying a spear, and having some sort of covering over her shoulders or chest. This covering, called the AEGIS, had on it the image of a GORGON. Most sources say this was the Gorgon MEDUSA, whom PERSEUS killed. EURIPIDES, however, in the *ION*, says Athena's aegis was from the skin of another Gorgon that was produced by Mother EARTH and that Athena destroyed.

Athena became the patron divinity of ATHENS by defeating POSEIDON in a contest for this honor. When Athena created an olive tree and Poseidon produced a salt spring, CECROPS, the king of Athens, decided Athena was the divinity who would be more beneficial to his city and she was chosen. After she became patron divinity of Athens, Athena asked HEPHAESTUS to create for her some new armor. Hephaestus created the armor but also tried to rape Athena. When the goddess fought off the aroused god, Hephaestus ejaculated on Athena's leg. The disgusted goddess wiped off the semen with a piece of wool, which she threw onto the ground. This caused Mother Earth to become pregnant and subsequently produce ERICHTHONIUS, who later became a king in Athens and whom Athena raised at her temple.

As a goddess of wisdom and war, Athena can often be found at the side of classical mythology's great heroes such as ACHILLES, ODYSSEUS, HERACLES, THESEUS, and even ORESTES. In the Trojan War, Athena favored the Greek side because the Trojan PARIS had not chosen her as more beautiful than HERA or APHRODITE. Athena is sometimes mentioned as the inspiration for the stratagem of the wooden horse, which gave the Greeks victory at TROY. After the Trojan War, however, Athena was angry with the Greeks because Locrian AJAX raped CASSANDRA at a shrine of Athena. Accordingly, Athena arranged for a terrible storm to destroy many of the Greek ships as they returned from Troy.

Athena appears as a character in several extant plays. In AESCHYLUS' *Eumenides* (see ORESTEIA), Athena presides over the trial of Orestes and ultimately casts her vote in his favor. She then negotiates with the FURIES and persuades them to take up residence in Athens, where they will continue to be honored. In SOPHOCLES' *AJAX,* Athena appears at the beginning of the play and reveals to Odysseus that she has driven Ajax mad, preventing him from killing AGAMEMNON, MENELAUS, and Odysseus. Athena urges Odysseus to mock AJAX, but Odysseus declines this opportunity. A fragment from Sophocles' *Ajax the Locrian* indicates that Athena appeared in that play to complain about Ajax's rape of Cassandra (fragment 10c Radt). Athena drove AJAX mad but put an end to Heracles' madness in EURIPIDES' *HERACLES* by knocking him unconscious.

Athena appears at the conclusions of Euripides' *SUPPLIANT WOMEN, ION,* and *IPHIGENIA IN TAURIS,* as well as the beginning of his *TROJAN WOMEN.* In *Suppliant Women,* Athena urges Theseus not to let the Argives leave without swearing that they will not attack Athens and that they will help defend Athens should others attack the city. Athena also predicts the future victory of the Argives' sons over the Thebans. In *Ion,* Athena prevents ION from asking APOLLO embarrassing questions about his (Ion's) birth and orchestrates a plan between Ion and CREUSA that will keep XUTHUS in the dark about Apollo's paternity of ION (2). In *Iphigenia in*

Tauris, Athena prevents King Thoas from pursuing Orestes, Pylades, and Iphigenia and tells Orestes and Iphigenia about their respective futures.

Athena also appears in Euripides' *Rhesus.* In this play, Athena tells Odysseus and Diomedes that the Greeks will be victorious in the war provided that they kill Rhesus before dawn. Athena directs them to Rhesus' camp spot and suggests that they capture his magnificent horses. After she has sent Odysseus and Diomedes off to tend to Rhesus, the Trojan Paris approaches, and Athena, who disguises herself as Aphrodite, tells Paris about Rhesus' arrival and says that Hector has gone to help him settle his encampment. After Paris exits, Athena calls to Odysseus and Diomedes, who have by now killed Rhesus and captured his horses, to take care to avoid the Trojans, who are pursuing them. [ANCIENT SOURCES: Apollodorus, *Library* 1.3.6, 1.4.2, 1.6.1–2, 2.1.4–5, 2.4.1–3, 2.5.6, 3.4.1–2, 3.6.7–8, 3.12.3, 3.14.1, 3.14.6, *Epitome* 5.22–6.6, 6.20–22; Hesiod, *Theogony* 886–900, 924–930; Homer, *Iliad, Odyssey; Homeric Hymn to Aphrodite* 5.8–15; Hyginus, *Fables* 142, 165, 168; Pausanias 1.24.1–7, 2.30.6, 8.26.6, 9.11.2, 9.33.7; Pindar, *Olympian Odes* 13.63–82, *Pythian Odes* 12.6–27]

BIBLIOGRAPHY
Radt, S. *Tragicorum Graecorum Fragmenta.* Vol. 4. Göttingen, Ger.: Vandenhoeck & Ruprecht, 1977.

ATHENS   The principal city in Greece and the home of most Greek dramatists during the classical period. In mythology, Athens was the home of Aegeus, Creusa, Ion, and Theseus, to name but a few. In Greek tragedy, Athens is often characterized as a place of refuge for the outcast and downtrodden. Heracles, Heracles' children, Medea, Oedipus, and the mothers from Argos grieving the loss of their sons (killed in battle at Thebes) all benefit from the kindness of Athens' rulers and people. Athens is also a common setting for comedy, and most of the plays of Aristophanes, Plautus, and Terence are set there.

ATHMONIA   Also called Athmone, this deme was about five miles north of Athens. In Aristophanes' *Peace* (line 190), Trygaeus states that he is from this deme.

ATHOS   A mountain (almost 6,400 feet high) in the Greek region of Macedonia. [ANCIENT SOURCES: Aeschylus, *Agamemnon* 285 (see Oresteia); Seneca, *Medea* 720; *Hercules Oetaeus,* 145, 1048, 1158, 1383, 1730]

ATLANTIDES   Children of Atlas.

ATLAS   The son of Iapetus and Clymene (or Asia), Atlas was the father (by Pleione) of seven daughters known as the Pleiades. He was also the father of Calypso, with whom Odysseus lived for several years. Additionally, Atlas fathered Maia, the mother of Hermes. Atlas sided with Cronus and the Titans in their war against Zeus and his brothers and sisters. After the war, Zeus punished Atlas by compelling him to hold up the sky throughout eternity. During Heracles' quest for the golden apples of the Hesperides, some sources say that Heracles held up the sky for Atlas, so that Atlas could retrieve the apples for Heracles (the Hesperides were Atlas' daughters). When Atlas returned, he did not want to take back the sky; accordingly, Heracles had to trick Atlas to do so, by asking him to hold the sky momentarily, so that he could get a cushion for his neck. Atlas agreed. Heracles took the apples, Atlas took back the sky, and Heracles walked away with the apples. Atlas does not appear as a character in any extant dramas, but he is mentioned many times. A few satyr plays entitled *Atlas* were written by Greek authors, but the names of those authors are unknown. From one of these anonymous plays, a fragment (655 Kannicht) of more than 50 lines that survives preserves a conversation between Heracles and Atlas that appears to occur when Atlas has returned with the apples and refuses to take the sky back from Heracles. [ANCIENT SOURCES: Aeschylus, *Prometheus Bound* 350–53, 425–30; Apollodorus, *Library* 1.2.2, 2.5.11, 3.10.1; Euripides, *Ion* 1–4; Hesiod, *Theogony* 507–20, 938–39; Ovid, *Metamorphoses* 4.621–662; Seneca, *Hercules Oetaeus* 12, 1599, 1905]

BIBLIOGRAPHY
Kannicht, R., and B. Snell. *Tragicorum Graecorum Fragmenta.* Vol. 2. Göttingen, Ger.: Vandenhoeck & Ruprecht, 1981.

ATOSSA The daughter of Cyrus the Great, who became the wife of DARIUS, king of Persia, and mother of XERXES, Achaemenes, Hystasptes, and Masistes. Xerxes succeeded his father as king of Persia. Atossa appears as a character in AESCHYLUS' PERSIANS, in which she is simply called Queen. In Aeschylus' play, Atossa is characterized as the worried mother of Xerxes, who is waging war against the Greeks. Atossa has had disturbing dreams about her son, and when she learns that Xerxes and the Persians have been defeated at SALAMIS, she and the chorus summon the spirit of her dead husband, Darius, from his tomb. After Darius explains the reasons for Xerxes' fall, Atossa goes to comfort him. Although Aeschylus' Persians is one of the least-read Greek tragedies in modern times, the figure of Atossa probably influenced later playwrights' portraits of aging and suffering queens such as the Trojan HECABE. [ANCIENT SOURCES: Herodotus, 3.68, 3.88, 3.133–34, 7.2–3, 7.64, 7.82]

BIBLIOGRAPHY

Harrison, T. "Aeschylus, Atossa and Athens." In Ancient Iran and the Mediterranean World. Edited by E. Dabrowa. Krakow: Jagiellonian University Press, 1998, 69–86.

Karamitrou, C. "Atossa, a 'Barbarian' Melancholic Queen; Sparagmos: Identity of Passions in Aischylos," Parnassos 38 (1996): 124–30.

Moreau, A. "Le songe d'Atossa: Perses, 176–214: Éléments pour une explication de textes," Cahiers du Groupe Interdisciplinaire du Théâtre Antique 7 (1992–93): 29–51.

Sancisi-Weerdenburg, H. "Exit Atossa: Images of Women in Greek Historiography on Persia." In Images of Women in Antiquity. Edited by A. Cameron and A. Kuhrt. London: Croom Helm, 1983, 20–33.

Sider, D. "Atossa's Second Entrance: Significant Inaction in Aeschylus' Persai," American Journal of Philology 104 (1983): 188–91.

ATREUS The son of PELOPS and HIPPODAMEIA, Atreus was the father of AGAMEMNON and MENELAUS. Atreus constantly feuded with his brother THYESTES over the kingdom of ARGOS. The gods showed their favor to Atreus by giving him a lamb with golden fleece. When the people of Argos decided that the possessor of this lamb would become their king, Atreus' brother Thyestes seduced Atreus' wife, AEROPE, who helped Thyestes gain possession of the lamb. Thyestes became king, but this act ran against the will of the gods, who apparently induced Thyestes to agree that he would give up the kingdom if the Sun reversed course in the sky. After this improbable event occurred, Atreus became king. Atreus then exiled Thyestes but later invited him back to Argos under pretense of a reconciliation banquet. The main course for the dinner, however, was Thyestes' own children, whom Thyestes unwittingly ate. At this point, Thyestes again went into exile and fathered AEGISTHUS. When Aegisthus grew up, he and his father returned to Argos. Aegisthus killed Atreus and Thyestes became king.

Atreus is mentioned numerous times in drama, but often only as the father of Agamemnon and Menelaus. Atreus does appear as a character in SENECA's THYESTES, in which he serves his brother the gruesome feast described earlier. SOPHOCLES wrote a play entitled Atreus (or perhaps The Mycenaean Women), of which the dozen words that survive give no hint as to its plot. ACCIUS wrote a tragic Atreus, from which about three dozen lines survive. The play, set at Atreus' palace, appears to have dealt with Atreus' killing of Thyestes' sons and the gruesome banquet, as several of the fragments allude to this. One fragment refers to Pelops' acquisition of Hippodameia as his bride; two fragments refer to Thyestes' affair with Atreus' wife, Aerope; another refers to the golden-fleeced ram that appeared in Atreus' flocks.

BIBLIOGRAPHY

Radt, S. Tragicorum Graecorum Fragmenta. Vol. 4. Göttingen, Ger.: Vandenhoeck & Ruprecht, 1977.

Warmington, E. H. Remains of Old Latin: Livius Andronicus, Naevius, Pacuvius, and Accius. Vol. 2. Cambridge, Mass.: Harvard University Press, 1936.

ATTENDANTS These are usually silent characters in drama who accompany important mortals, such as kings, queens, princes, and religious officials. Attendants (Greek: prospoloi, douloi, doulai) are sometimes called upon to perform various menial tasks, such as transporting a corpse, opening doors, or escorting various persons. [ANCIENT SOURCES: Euripides, Alcestis 607, Bacchae 1217, Electra 1007, Heracles 332, 724, ION 510, 1250, Iphigenia in Tauris 638, 1205, Medea 1314,

ORESTES 629, *Trojan Women* 1047; Sophocles, *Antigone* 1214, 1320]

ATTIC   See ATTICA.

ATTICA   A triangle-shaped region on the eastern coast of central Greece where such places as ATHENS, ELEUSIS, and MARATHON are located. The dialect of Greek spoken by the inhabitants of this region is Attic Greek.

ATTIS   According to one version of Attis' story, the gods cut off the male member of a powerful hermaphrodite named Agdistis and from his blood an almond tree arose. A river divinity named Nana was impregnated by one of these almonds and gave birth to Attis. After Attis grew up, the same Agdistis fell in love with Attis. Attis, however, rejected Agdistis and, to avoid the union, castrated himself. In another version of the story a boar kills Attis. Agdistis, sorry about what had happened to Attis, prayed that ZEUS would not allow Attis' body to decay. Zeus answered Agdistis' prayer and Attis' body was kept in the sacred precinct of the goddess Cybele (see RHEA) on a mountain named after Agdistis. In honor of Attis, Cybele's priests had to undergo castration. In the springtime, a ceremonial mourning and search for Attis' body were held by worshipers of Cybele. On the third day of this search, the worshipers celebrated the discovery of his body. [ANCIENT SOURCES: Catullus, 63; Ovid, *Fasti* 2.221–44; Pausanias, 7.17.10–12; Seneca, *Agamemnon* 686]

AUGE   The daughter of ALEUS of Tegea, Auge was the mother of TELEPHUS by HERACLES (see Aleus and Telephus). EURIPIDES wrote an *Auge* (fragments 265–81 Nauck) that probably dates to the last five years of his life. SOPHOCLES also may have written an *Auge*, of which only the title survives. Two Greek comic poets, Philyllius (fragments 3–6 Kock 1) and Eubulus (fragment 15 Kock 2), wrote plays entitled *Auge*, surviving fragments of which give little indication of the content. [ANCIENT SOURCES: Apollodorus, *Library* 2.7.4; Hyginus, *Fables* 99–100; Pausanias, 8.4.9; Seneca, *Hercules Oetaeus* 367]

BIBLIOGRAPHY
Anderson, W. S. "Euripides' *Auge* and Menander's *Epitrepontes*," *Greek, Roman, and Byzantine Studies* 23 (1982): 165–77.
Huys, Marc. "Euripides, *Auge*, fr. 265, 272, 278, 864 N. and the Role of Herakles in the Play," *Sacris Erudiri: Jaarboek voor Godsdienstwetenschappen* 31 (1989–90): 169–85.
Kock, T. *Comicorum Atticorum Fragmenta*. Vol. 1. Leipzig: Teubner, 1880.
———. *Comicorum Atticorum Fragmenta*. Vol. 2. Leipzig: Teubner, 1884.
Nauck, A. *Tragicorum Graecorum Fragmenta*. 1889. Reprint, Hildesheim, Ger.: Olms, 1964.
Webster, T. B. L. *The Tragedies of Euripides*. London: Methuen, 1967.

AUGEAN STABLES   One of HERACLES' labors was to clean (in one day) the extremely filthy stables of Augeas, a king of ELIS in southwestern Greece. Because Augeas did not believe Heracles could accomplish the task in a single day, he agreed to give Heracles some of his cattle if he were successful. When Heracles accomplished the task by diverting two rivers through the stables, Augeus refused to give him the agreed-upon reward. Accordingly, Heracles later returned to Elis and destroyed Augeas' kingdom and, according to some sources, Augeas himself. [ANCIENT SOURCES: Apollodorus, *Library* 2.5.5, 2.7.2; Pausanias, 5.1.9–5.3.3; Seneca, *Hercules Furens* 247]

AUGUSTUS (SEPTEMBER 23, 63 B.C.E.–AUGUST 19, 14 C.E.)   The son of Gaius Octavius and Atia, the niece of Julius Caesar, Augustus was originally known by the same name as his father. The title Augustus (consecrated, majestic) was added to his name after he became the sole ruler of the Roman empire in 27. Augustus' father died in the year 59 and Augustus was later adopted by Julius Caesar. When Caesar was assassinated by his political enemies March 15, 44, Augustus worked with Marcus ANTONIUS and others to wage war against the conspirators and their military forces. By 36, Augustus and his allies had defeated the assassins and various other rebels. By this time, though, the relationship between Augustus and Antonius had deteriorated significantly and Antonius, who had allied himself politically and emotionally with

the queen of Egypt, Cleopatra, was indicating that he intended to control the Roman empire. Thus, Augustus now began to wage war against Antonius and his forces. By the year 30, Antony's forces had been defeated and Antony and Cleopatra had committed suicide. Although Augustus officially returned control of the Roman state to Rome's seneate and people in 27, he, aided greatly by Marcus Vipsanius Agrippa, continued to operate in a position of exceptional power. The death of Agrippa in 12 left Augustus the most powerful man in the empire. Because Augustus did not have a male heir by his wife, Livia, he adopted sons, including Gaius, Lucius, and Agrippa Postumus, the sons of Agrippa and Augustus' daughter, Julia. Gaius and Lucius, however, died and Augustus had a major falling out with Agrippa Postumus, who later died in exile. Augustus also adopted Tiberius, the son of Augustus' wife, Livia, by a previous marriage. Tiberius eventually succeeded Augustus as ruler of the Roman empire after Augustus died in 14 C.E. After Augustus' death, the Roman senate decreed that Augustus should be recognized as a god. [ANCIENT SOURCES: Appian, *Civil War*; Augustus, *Res Gestae*; Suetonius, *Augustus*; Dio Cassius, 45ff.; Seneca, *Octavia* 477, 505, 528; Velleius Paterculus, 2.36–127]

BIBLIOGRAPHY
Bowersock, G. W. *Augustus and the Greek World.* Oxford: Clarendon Press, 1965.
Eck, W. *The Age of Augustus.* Translated by Deborah Lucas Schneider. New material by Sarolta A. Takacs. Malden, Mass.: Blackwell, 2003.
Hammond, M. *The Augustan Principate in Theory and Practice during the Julio-Claudian Period.* Cambridge, Mass.: Harvard University Press, 1933.
Raaflaub, K. A., and M. Toher, eds. *Between Republic and Empire: Interpretations of Augustus and his Principate.* Contributions by G. W. Bowersock et al. Berkeley: University of California Press, 1990.
Southern, P. *Augustus.* London: Routledge, 1998.

AULAEUM

A Latin word (plural: *aulaea*) that denotes the curtain in the Roman theater. Unlike modern curtains, which open and close horizontally or drop downward vertically, the Roman curtain moved up and out from a slot in the stage.

AULIS

A town northeast of Athens on the coast of Greece, in drama Aulis was the place where the Greek fleet gathered to set sail for TROY in their expedition to rescue HELEN. Before the fleet set sail, however, they had to sacrifice IPHIGENIA, the daughter of AGAMEMNON, to appease the wrath of ARTEMIS, who had generated violent winds that prevented the fleet from sailing. EURIPIDES' play *IPHIGENIA AT AULIS* deals with these events.

AULOS (Plural: AULOI)

A wind instrument that accompanied the songs in Greek drama. The *aulos* was played in times of joy or sadness. In EURIPIDES' *HERACLES,* the Libyan pipe is used to praise HERACLES. Elsewhere in Euripides, we find the *aulos* ringing out the end of the Trojan War, consoling despair, and played in celebration of the marriage of PELEUS and THETIS. Wedding processions advanced to the tune of the *aulos.* Lucian, writing in the second century C.E., suggests that the music of the *aulos* is typically played at funerals. *Auloi* made in different countries may have been used for different moods and circumstances. In EURIPIDES' *ALCESTIS,* ADMETUS declares that he will not sing to the Libyan *aulos* after ALCESTIS dies. In Euripides' *BACCHAE,* however, the Phrygian *aulos* accompanies the revelry associated with DIONYSUS. [ANCIENT SOURCES: Euripides, *Alcestis* 347, *Bacchae* 128, 380, *Helen* 170, 1351, *Heracles* 684, *Iphigenia at Aulis* 1036, *Trojan Women* 544; Lucian, *On Funerals* 19; Sophocles, *Trachinian Women* 641]

BIBLIOGRAPHY
Bélis, A. "L'aulos phrygien," *Revue Archéologique* (1986): 21–40.
Oakley, J. H., and R. H. Sinos. *The Wedding in Ancient Athens.* Madison: University of Wisconsin Press, 1993, 15.

AULULARIA

See THE POT OF GOLD.

AUTOLYCUS

The son of HERMES (or Baedalion) and Chione (or Philonis), Autolycus was a famous thief who had the power to make himself invisible. He could also make invisible the things that he stole or change the stolen items so that their owners could not recognize them. Autolycus also taught HERACLES to wrestle and was the grandfather of ODYSSEUS (his mother, Anticleia, was Autolycus' daughter). HOMER says Autolycus gave Odysseus his name. It was while hunting with Autolycus on Mount PARNASSUS that Odysseus received the scar by which Odysseus' nurse identified him when he returned from TROY. EURIPIDES wrote a SATYR PLAY entitled *Autolycus,* of which four fragments survive (282–84 Nauck, 282a Snell). The plot of Euripides' play is unknown; fragment 282 is a rather famous 27-line speech on the evils of athletes and the need to reward noble and wise men rather than athletes. The Greek comic poet EUPOLIS wrote two plays entitled *Autolycus,* of which the two dozen brief fragments that survive (42–67 Kock) provide little help in reconstructing the plot. [ANCIENT SOURCES: Apollodorus, *Library* 1.9.16, 2.4.9; Homer, *Odyssey* 11.85, 19.392–466; Ovid, *Metamorphoses* 11.301–15; Pausanias, 8.4.6, 10.8.8; Plautus, *Bacchides* 275]

BIBLIOGRAPHY
Diggle, James. "Notes on Fragments of Euripides," *Classical Quarterly* 47, no. 1 (1997): 98–108.
Kock, T. *Comicorum Atticorum Fragmenta.* Vol. 1. Leipzig: Teubner, 1880.
Nauck, A. *Tragicorum Graecorum Fragmenta.* 1889. Reprint, Hildesheim, Ger.: Olms, 1964.
Snell, B. *Tragicorum Graecorum Fragmenta. Supplementum.* Hildesheim, Ger.: Olms, 1964.

AUTOMENES   An otherwise unknown person mentioned by ARISTOPHANES, at *WASPS* 1275, as someone to be envied (the remark is sarcastic) for his three sons, one of whom is the sexual pervert ARIPHRADES.

BIBLIOGRAPHY
Sommerstein. A. *The Comedies of Aristophanes.* Vol. 4, *Wasps.* Warminster, U.K.: Aris & Phillips, 1980, 233.

AUTONOE   The daughter of CADMUS and HARMONIA, Autonoe was the sister of AGAVE, INO, and SEMELE. Autonoe became the wife of Aristaeus and the mother of ACTAEON. Pausanias says Autonoe left THEBES after Actaeon's death, but in EURIPIDES' *BACCHAE,* she participates in the killing of her nephew, PENTHEUS. [ANCIENT SOURCES: Apollodorus, *Library* 3.4.2, 3.4.4; Euripides, *Bacchae* 230, 681, 1130, 1228; Hesiod, *Theogony* 975–78; Hyginus, *Fables* 179, 180; Pausanias, 1.44.5]

AUXILIUM   A Roman divinity who personifies help or aid. Auxilium delivers a delayed PROLOGUE in PLAUTUS' *CASKET COMEDY.*

THE AWARD OF ARMS OR *THE JUDGMENT OF ARMS* (Greek: *HOPLON KRISIS;* Latin: *ARMORUM IUDICIUM)*

Several dramatists took up the subject of the decision by which the armor of ACHILLES was awarded to ODYSSEUS, rather than to AJAX, in the 10th year of the Trojan War. AESCHYLUS, PACUVIUS, and ACCIUS composed plays about this contest. The six lines that survive from Aeschylus' play suggest that THETIS, Ajax, and Odysseus appeared as characters, and that a debate occurred between Ajax and Odysseus over which of them deserved Achilles' armor. Some 20 short fragments exist from Pacuvius' play, in which AGAMEMNON seems to have held a contest between Ajax and Odysseus, taken advice from ATHENA about how to judge the contest, and on that advice impaneled a group of judges. Accius' play, from which almost three dozen lines survive, also dealt with this topic. As in SOPHOCLES' *AJAX,* Ajax, Odysseus (Latin: Ulysses), TECMESSA, the child EURYSACES, and Agamemnon appear in the play. Unlike in Sophocles' play, in Accius' play, Ajax and Odysseus seem to have debated their respective valor, a possibility that suggests that the play's action began before Achilles' armor had been awarded. As Sophocles did, Accius may have had Agamemnon refuse to grant burial to Ajax, only to have Odysseus persuade him otherwise.

BIBLIOGRAPHY
Radt, S. *Tragicorum Graecorum Fragmenta.* Vol. 3. Göttingen, Ger.: Vandenhoeck & Ruprecht, 1985.
Warmington, E. H. *Remains of Old Latin: Livius Andronicus, Naevius, Pacuvius, and Accius.* Vol. 2. Cambridge, Mass.: Harvard University Press, 1936.

AXIUS   A river in the Greek region of Macedonia that arises from Mount Scardus and flows into the Gulf of Thermaicus. [ANCIENT SOURCES: Euripides, *Bacchae* 569]

B

BABYLON   This famous city, located on the banks of the Euphrates River, served as a capital city for the Assyrians; in 539 B.C.E., the Persians captured the city. The city, built in a square shape, was famous among the Greeks for, among other things, the huge walls made of sun-baked bricks that surrounded the city.

At the City DIONYSIA of 426 B.C.E., ARISTOPHANES produced a play entitled *Babylonians,* of which numerous brief fragments survive (64–99 Kock 1). Little is known about the play's plot; however, *Babylonians* prompted CLEON to indict (apparently unsuccessfully) Aristophanes "for ridiculing the elected magistrates of the city in front of an audience . . . containing many foreign visitors" (Dover). The Greek comic poet PHILEMON wrote a play called *Babylonian;* the two lines that survive (which contain a reference to the famous prostitute Pythonice) tell us nothing about the play's plot (fragments 16 Kock 2). [ANCIENT SOURCES: Aeschylus, *Persians* 52; Aristophanes, *Birds* 552; Athenaeus, 13.595c; Herodotus, 1.178–79]

BIBLIOGRAPHY

Dover, K. J. *Aristophanic Comedy.* Berkeley: University of California Press, 1972, 13.

Kock, T. *Comicorum Atticorum Fragmenta.* Vol. 1. Leipzig: Teubner, 1880.

———. *Comicorum Atticorum Fragmenta.* Vol. 2. Leipzig: Teubner, 1884.

BACCHAE   Also known as Bacchants, Bacchanals, or MAENADS, the Bacchae were women who worshiped the god DIONYSUS (also known as Bacchus). During their worship, the women often wore animal skins, held snakes, and carried a THYRSUS. In classical TRAGEDY, the activities of Bacchae were notorious for turning violent, as in EURIPIDES' *BACCHAE,* in which women under the influence of Dionysus tear apart PENTHEUS.

Euripides was not the first tragedian to write a play entitled *Bacchae.* AESCHYLUS' *Bacchae* preceded Euripides' play to the stage; however, the single two-line fragment (about swift-footed evil's coming upon mortals) that survives reveals nothing about the play's content (fragment 22 Radt). In addition to the work of Aeschylus, Aelian (2.8) reports that XENOCLES' tetralogy of 415 B.C.E., which included a *Bacchae,* defeated Euripides' performances of that year. Unfortunately, only the title of Xenocles' work survives so it is not known whether the play dealt with the downfall of Pentheus (fragment 1 Snell). SOPHOCLES also may have written a *Bacchae,* but modern scholars have questioned this. At any rate, only the title survives and we do not know the date of this play if it did exist. Sophocles' son Iophon, who competed against Euripides at least once (428 B.C.E.), also wrote a *Bacchae* (or *Pentheus*), in which AGAVE is the speaker of the only surviving fragment ("Even though I am a woman I understand that one who seeks to know especially the things of the gods will be far less than such a person"; fragment 2 Snell). Cleophon also wrote a *Bacchae,* of which only the title survives (see Snell). Among Roman authors, ACCIUS wrote a

Bacchae, whose several fragments (see verses 201–26 Warmington) indicate significant influence of Euripides' *Bacchae,* although Warmington says Accius' *Bacchae* "departed widely from that poet [Euripides] in the lyric parts."

In addition to the work of the tragic poets, several Greek comic poets wrote plays entitled *Bacchae:* Antiphanes (fragment 56 Kock 2), Diocles (fragments 1–3 Kock 1), Epicharmus (fragment 19 Kaibel), and Lysippus (fragments 1–5 Kock 1). The fragments of these plays are brief and are uninformative about the plots of the respective plays, although it is known that Lysippus' *Bacchae* made an attack on the seer LAMPON.

BIBLIOGRAPHY

Kaibel, G. *Comicorum Graecorum Fragmenta.* Vol. 1.1 [*Poetarum Graecorum Fragmenta,* Vol. 6.1]. Berlin: Weidmann, 1899.

Kock, T. *Comicorum Atticorum Fragmenta.* Vol. 1. Leipzig: Teubner, 1880.

————. *Comicorum Atticorum Fragmenta.* Vol. 2. Leipzig: Teubner, 1884.

Radt, S. *Tragicorum Graecorum Fragmenta.* Vol. 3. Göttingen, Ger.: Vandenhoeck & Ruprecht, 1985.

Snell, B. *Tragicorum Graecorum Fragmenta.* Vol. 1. Göttingen, Ger.: Vandenhoeck & Ruprecht, 1971.

Warmington, E. H. *Remains of Old Latin: Livius Andronicus, Naevius, Pacuvius, and Accius.* Vol. 2. Cambridge, Mass.: Harvard University Press, 1936.

BACCHAE EURIPIDES (405 B.C.E.)

The play's name, which means "Women of Bacchus," was first staged in the year after EURIPIDES' death. Euripides' son produced the play, which appeared in the same TETRALOGY as *IPHIGENIA IN AULIS* and *Alcmeon in Corinth,* the latter of which is no longer extant. Which SATYR PLAY completed the tetralogy is unknown. The setting is the palace of PENTHEUS at THEBES. In the PROLOGUE, DIONYSUS recalls his travels through the eastern part of the world and declares that in those lands he has established himself as a god. He states that THEBES is the first Greek city to which he has traveled and that he has driven the town's women mad because the sisters of his mother, SEMELE, did not believe that Dionysus was the child of ZEUS and Semele. As in Euripides' *HIPPOLYTUS,* in which APHRODITE announces that she will destroy Hippolytus because of his refusal to worship her, in the *Bacchae,* Dionysus announces the destruction of Pentheus for his refusal to acknowledge that he is a divinity.

After Dionysus' opening monologue, the CHORUS, made up of women who have followed Dionysus from the East, enter and sing an ODE in which they praise him, recall his birth, and express the delight they feel in worshiping him. After the choral ode, the prophet TIRESIAS and Pentheus' grandfather, CADMUS, enter and prepare to set out for the countryside to worship Dionysus. Because the two are quite old (and Tiresias is blind), their efforts to practice the energetic dances of Dionysus are amusing. The light tone ends, though, with the entrance of King Pentheus, who declares that he has arrested some of the female worshipers of Dionysus and that he intends to capture the god himself. When Pentheus sees Cadmus and Tiresias dressed as worshipers of Dionysus, he scoffs at them and the worship of the new god. Tiresias and Cadmus try to persuade Pentheus to acknowledge Dionysus as a divinity, but Pentheus refuses and orders some of his men to go out and apprehend Dionysus. After the exit of Cadmus and Tiresias to the countryside and the worship of Dionysus, the chorus sing an ode that condemns Pentheus' behavior and predicts his downfall. They also long to visit Cyprus, an island sacred to APHRODITE, who is sympathetic to the worship of Dionysus, a god whose blessings fall upon the rich and poor alike.

After the choral ode, one of Pentheus' soldiers enters with Dionysus, who speaks as if he is not the god himself, but simply an unnamed stranger. Pentheus proceeds to interrogate the stranger about the worship and rituals of Dionysus. Pentheus threatens to put the stranger in prison, but the stranger says that Dionysus will release him whenever he wishes. The stranger warns Pentheus not to imprison him, but Pentheus does so anyway. After the exit of Dionysus, Pentheus, and the guards, the chorus complain about Pentheus' treatment of Dionysus and call upon the god to punish Pentheus.

In the next EPISODE, the chorus' pleas are rewarded as Dionysus, after escaping from Pentheus and causing his palace to shake, appears and reports to the chorus how he escaped from Pentheus by transforming himself into a bull and then a phantom. Soon, an exasperated Pentheus arrives and asks the stranger how he escaped. Their conversation is interrupted by a herdsman from Mount CITHAERON, who reports the activities of the female worshipers of Dionysus. At first, the women's behavior was peaceful and strangely beautiful; when, however, they perceived that the herdsman and his friends were going to try to apprehend them, the women went into such a frenzy that the herdsman and his comrades fled in fear. The women proceeded to ravage the countryside and even caused other men to flee. Pentheus, troubled by the herdsman's report, prepares to call out his full army to battle against the god's worshipers. The stranger warns Pentheus against this and persuades him to dress as a female worshiper, go out into the countryside, and spy on the women. As the stranger and Pentheus enter the palace, the stranger informs the chorus and the audience that Pentheus will soon meet his doom. After this, the chorus sing an ode that raises questions about the nature of wisdom. They point out the foolishness of fighting against the gods and suggest that the best way to live is day by day.

After the choral ode, Dionysus and Pentheus, who is dressed as a female worshiper of Dionysus, emerge from the palace. A humorous yet sinister scene follows as Pentheus, who leaves the palace imagining that he sees double and thinking that the stranger now appears to be a bull, proceeds to fuss with his dress. After the stranger helps Pentheus arrange his garb, the two exit for Mount Cithaeron. Upon their departure, the chorus sing an ode calling for the destruction of Pentheus. They call for justice and urge that Dionysus strike down Pentheus.

In the next episode, a messenger arrives and informs a delighted chorus that Pentheus is dead. The messenger explains that Dionysus led Pentheus to the woods to spy on the women. So that Pentheus could see the women, Dionysus placed him high in a tree. Unfortunately for Pentheus, the women could now see him. The Dionysus-possessed women, imagining that Pentheus was a lion, tore down the tree with their bare hands and then went on to tear apart Pentheus himself. Chief among the women who killed Pentheus were his mother, AGAVE, and his aunts, INO and AUTONOE.

After the departure of the messenger, Agave, still possessed with the frenzy of Dionysus, returns from the wilderness to the city as a triumphant hunter who has killed a lion, proudly displaying her son's head on her THYRSUS. Next, Agave's father, Cadmus, accompanied by servants who carry the remains of Pentheus, enters. Agave rejoices in her kill, but Cadmus soon restores Agave to her senses by pointing out that the head she carries is that of her son. Having realized that she has killed her son, Agave and Cadmus mourn the loss of Pentheus and the fate that awaits them. After line 1329, the play's manuscript has a gap of about 50 lines, but it is clear that in this missing section Dionysus appeared, revealing himself clearly as a divinity, and began to tell Agave and Cadmus of the exile that awaited them. When the manuscript resumes, Dionysus tells Cadmus that in exile both he and his wife will lead a barbarian tribe and eventually be transformed into snakes. Dionysus notes, however, that ARES will give them a new, everlasting existence after their life on Earth. Cadmus begs Dionysus for mercy, but the god refuses. The play ends as Cadmus and Agave lament their fate and prepare to go into exile, to different lands.

COMMENTARY

Euripides was not the first tragedian to take up the subject of the Bacchae or Pentheus and Euripides' play is often thought to have been influenced by the earlier works by AESCHYLUS. Aeschylus also wrote a *Bacchae* (fragment 22 Radt); little is known about the play's content. Aeschylus also wrote a *Pentheus* (fragment 183 Radt), whose surviving fragment is uninformative. Aeschylus composed a tetralogy that dealt with Dionysus' travels through THRACE and focused primarily on the god's encounter with LYCURGUS, whose story (as preserved in Apollodorus, *Library* 3.5.1) has a number of similarities with that of Pentheus. As did Pentheus, Lycurgus rejected Dionysus, tried to capture the god and failed, persecuted the god's followers, was driven mad by the god, and then was torn apart through the god's agency. A few of the fragments of Aeschylus' *Edonians,* which dealt with Lycurgus' encounter with Dionysus, recall Euripides' *Bacchae.* The shaking of *Pentheus'* palace in Euripides is reminiscent of a line from *Edonians* ("Lo, the house is frenzied with the god, the roof revels, Bacchant-like"; fragment 58 Radt, Lloyd-Jones translation). Another fragment (61 Radt) of *Edonians* mentions the effeminate appearance of Dionysus, as does Euripides several times in *Bacchae*.

In addition to the work of Aeschylus, which preceded Euripides' *Bacchae* to the stage, accordingly to Aelian (2.8), XENOCLES' tetralogy of 415 B.C.E., which included a *Bacchae,* defeated Euripides' performances of that year. Unfortunately, only the title of Xenocles' work survives so we do not know whether the play treated Pentheus' death (fragment 1 Snell). Sophocles also may have written a *Bacchae,* of which only the title survives, and we do not know the date of this play, whose existence modern scholars have questioned. Sophocles' son Iophon, who competed against Euripides on at least one occasion (428 B.C.E.), also wrote a *Bacchae* (or *Pentheus*); in the only surviving fragment Agave states, "Even though I am a woman I understand that one who seeks to know especially the things of the gods will be far less than such a person" (fragment 2 Snell). Cleophon also wrote a *Bacchae,* of which only the title survives (see Snell); it is not certain whether Euripides could have known this play.

Having considered some other tragedians who wrote plays entitled *Bacchae,* let us now turn to Euripides' play. According to J. Michael Walton, "The sheer power and mystery of the *Bacchae* is so startling that it rightly belongs in the forefront of the greatest plays ever written." At first, one winces in anticipation of divine punishment as Pentheus clearly sins against the god by refusing to admit his worship in Thebes and persecuting those who worship him. Later, however, one may shudder at the cruelty of the god, who leads Pentheus to destruction.

Bacchae is a play of numerous reversals. In the first half of the play, Pentheus is characterized as the hunter, as he tracks down Dionysus and attempts to control him (cf. 434–35). In the last half of the play, the tables are turned as the hunter becomes the hunted. For instance, at line 848, Dionysus notes that Pentheus is moving into *his* net. Likewise, the women whom Pentheus was hunting in the first half of the play become the hunters of Pentheus in the second half. When Pentheus is killed, the language Euripides uses

to describe the women in this scene evokes images of hunting dogs (1122–36). Euripides thus wants to create a link between the death of Pentheus and Pentheus' cousin ACTAEON, the son of AUTONOE. Early in the play (337–40), Cadmus warns Pentheus about becoming like Actaeon, who angered Artemis by claiming that he was a better hunter than she and was eventually torn apart by his own hunting dogs. Just as Pentheus' kinsman, the hunter Actaeon, after offending ARTEMIS, was torn apart by dogs that he himself raised, Pentheus is torn apart by the woman who raised him after he has offended the god Dionysus. We should also note that Pentheus' death occurs in the same location (Mount Cithaeron) where Actaeon was killed, as Cadmus notes at line 1291. Furthermore, we should notice that Actaeon's mother, Autonoe, also takes part in the destruction of Pentheus (1130). Finally, it is interesting that when Pentheus dies, he would have been wearing a fawn skin (cf. 835), which would make him resemble a deer, the animal into which tradition says that Artemis changed Actaeon before his hunting dogs killed him.

The play also shows reversals of gender. In the first half, Pentheus comments on Dionysus' effeminate appearance; in the latter half it is Pentheus who is dressed as a woman. The female followers of Dionysus also experience a gender reversal as they engage in activities that the Greeks associated with males. Their presence outside the home and away from their usual activities as weavers of cloth leads them to the outskirts of the city, a space typically visited by males. During their rampage through the Theban countryside, the women are described as being like warriors (752ff.) as they rout the men who oppose them. After Agave's destruction of Pentheus, whom she thinks to be a lion, the messenger notes that she describes Dionysus as her fellow hunter (1146). Later, she proudly announces to her father, Cadmus, that she has given up weaving for hunting wild animals (1235–37).

In addition to changes of gender, *Bacchae* offers literal, figurative, and imagined changes of species. Both Cadmus and Tiresias dress in fawn skins, appearing to be animals. By the play's end, Dionysus predicts that Cadmus will, in fact, become a snake (1330, 1358). The play's women, also dressed in fawn skins, are described as birds (748) and dogs (731), and their tearing apart of Pentheus has a canine aspect (1122–36). Dionysus also moves from human to animal form. When Pentheus tries to imprison Dionysus, he finds instead a bull (618), with which he wrestles in vain. Once Pentheus is under the god's spell, he imagines that Dionysus has become a bull (920–22). Later, the chorus call upon Dionysus to appear to them in the form of a bull, hundred-headed serpent, or fire-breathing lion (1017–19). Such an invocation is also noteworthy because both Dionysus and Cadmus are linked to serpents, and both Dionysus and Pentheus are associated with lions. Not only is Pentheus imagined as a lion by his frenzied mother; he is also connected with the serpent when the chorus recall the birth of Pentheus' father, Echion, who was born from the teeth of Ares' serpent (539–40, 1155), a serpent that Cadmus killed. Finally, we note that before Pentheus went to spy on the Bacchae, he not only disguised himself as a woman, but, as do all the other characters in the play, put on the fawn skin (835).

Finally, role reversals on a "cosmic" level also exist. Dionysus is a god, but he has gone to Thebes in the guise of a mortal. Pentheus, although mortal, sets himself on a level above a god by opposing Dionysus. In the previously mentioned rampage through the countryside, the messenger notes that the god's power was the driving force behind the mortal women's ability to accomplish this. Thus, in the course of *Bacchae*, we see most of the major characters (with the exception of Cadmus and Tiresias) experience changes between hunter and hunted, male and female, human and animal, and divine and mortal.

BIBLIOGRAPHY

Dodds, E. R. *Euripides: Bacchae.* 2d ed. Oxford: Clarendon Press, 1960.
Kirk, G. S. *The Bacchae.* Cambridge: Cambridge University Press, 1979.
Kock, T. *Comicorum Atticorum Fragmenta.* Vol. 1. Leipzig: Teubner, 1880.
———. *Comicorum Atticorum Fragmenta.* Vol. 2. Leipzig: Teubner, 1884.
Oranje, H. *Euripides' Bacchae: The Play and Its Audience.* Leiden: Brill, 1984.
Radt, S. *Tragicorum Graecorum Fragmenta.* Vol. 3. Göttingen, Ger.: Vandenhoeck & Ruprecht, 1985.
Seaford, R. *Euripides: Bacchae.* Warminster, U.K.: Aris & Phillips, 1996.
Segal, C. *Dionysiac Poetics and Euripides' Bacchae.* Princeton, N.J.: Princeton University Press, 1982.
Smyth, H. W., and H. Lloyd-Jones. *Aeschylus.* Vol. 2. 1926. Reprint, Cambridge, Mass.: Harvard University Press, 1971.
Snell, B. *Tragicorum Graecorum Fragmenta.* Vol. 1. Göttingen, Ger.: Vandenhoeck & Ruprecht, 1971.
Walton, J. M. *Living Greek Theatre.* New York: Greenwood Press, 1987, 166–70.
Warmington, E. H. *Remains of Old Latin: Livius Andronicus, Naevius, Pacuvius, and Accius.* Vol. 2. Cambridge, Mass.: Harvard University Press, 1936.

BACCHIDES (THE TWO BACCHISES)

PLAUTUS (189 B.C.E.)   The Greek model for PLAUTUS' play was MENANDER's *Dis Exapaton.* The action of Plautus' play takes place before the houses of two Athenians, the prostitute Bacchis (woman of Bacchus) and Pistoclerus, the son of Philoxenus. The play's opening section is missing except some 30 lines of fragments, in which we learn that Bacchis of ATHENS has a twin sister (another prostitute named Bacchis), who has just arrived from her home on the island of SAMOS.

In the first intact scene, Athenian Bacchis and her sister try to devise a way that the sister can return to Samos when her time of service to the soldier Cleomachus ("famous warrior") is concluded. Athenian Bacchis tries to persuade Pistoclerus to help her sister, but Pistoclerus is reluctant. As Cleomachus is due to arrive soon, Athenian Bacchis wants Pistoclerus to protect them and pretend to be her boyfriend. Pistoclerus realizes this plan will cause him trouble but agrees and at Athenian Bacchis' prompting even agrees to host and pay for a dinner party in the sister's honor. Later, as Pistoclerus and his TUTOR, Lydus, return with provisions for the dinner, Lydus warns Pistoclerus about associating with prostitutes and tries to lead the young man away from Bacchis' house, but Pistoclerus eventually enters the house despite the tutor's objections.

Next, Chrysalus, the slave of Nicobulus, and Nicobulus' son, Mnesilochus, enter after a two-year absence in Ephesus. Pistoclerus emerges from Bacchis' house and greets Chrysalus. In the course of their conversation, we hear that Pistoclerus, Mnesilochus' friend, was supposed to be watching out for Mnesilochus' interest in Bacchis of Samos. Pistoclerus advises Chrysalus, whose name means "goldy," that Mnesilochus had better get some gold before Cleomachus arrives and steals Bacchis of Samos from him.

Soon, Nicobulus enters from his house, wondering why his son, Mnesilochus, has not arrived from the harbor. Chrysalus joins Nicobulus and tries to trick his master in order to induce Nicobulus to leave town so that Mnesilochus will be free to pursue his love affair with Bacchis. Chrysalus tells Nicobulus that Nicobulus' supposed friend, Archidemides, had tried to steal the gold they had acquired in Ephesus. Chrysalus states that Mnesilochus took some of the money with them to Athens but deposited most of it with Theotimus, a priest at Diana's temple at Ephesus. He informs Nicobulus that if he wants the rest of his money, he must travel to Ephesus. After Nicobulus dashes off to the FORUM to find Mnesilochus, Chrysalus rejoices that his trickery will allow Mnesilochus to use and dispense the gold however he sees fit. Chrysalus then runs to the forum to let Mnesilochus know about his deception.

Chrysalus' departure is followed by the emergence of Lydus from Bacchis' house. Shocked by Pistoclerus' behavior in the house, Lydus runs off to tell Pistoclerus' father, Philoxenus. When Lydus returns, he tells Philoxenus of Pistoclerus' behavior. Mnesilochus, who has just returned, eavesdrops and hears what Pistoclerus has been doing on his behalf. Soon Lydus sees Mnesilochus and praises his behavior as opposed to that of Pistoclerus. Mnesilochus tells Lydus that Pistoclerus is just acting this way to help a friend (not mentioning that he is the friend) and then promises to look after Pistoclerus for Lydus and Philoxenus. Having heard from Lydus, however, that how Pistoclerus and Bacchis were flirting with one another, Mnesilochus has become angered and decides to give the money he took from Ephesus to his father rather than let Bacchis have it. Mnesilochus goes into his father's house and gives him the money, then reemerges and tells the audience that he was able to persuade his father to pardon Chrysalus. Next, Pistoclerus, arrived from Bacchis' house, approaches Mnesilochus. Mnesilochus, thinking that Pistoclerus has betrayed him, treats him with

contempt, and Pistoclerus has no idea why Mnesilochus is upset. Mnesilochus accuses Pistoclerus of being in love with Bacchis. When Pistoclerus declares that there are two Bacchises in the house, Mnesilochus is skeptical but follows him into Bacchis' house for proof.

In the fourth act, Cleomachus' PARASITE and one of Cleomachus' attendants enter. The parasite has been sent to ask Bacchis whether she will pay back the money she owes Cleomachus or go with him. At Bacchis' door, the parasite is met by Pistoclerus, who angrily informs him that Bacchis loves someone else and that she will not go with him. After Pistoclerus chases off the parasite with threats of violence, Mnesilochus emerges from Bacchis' house and expresses remorse for doubting Pistoclerus and handing over all his money to his father. Pistoclerus tries to console Mnesilochus, but Mnesilochus is convinced that Cleomachus will carry off Bacchis. As the two young men converse, Chrysalus approaches. They eavesdrop on Chrysalus as he congratulates himself on helping Mnesilochus acquire the money he needed. Soon, Mnesilochus approaches Chrysalus and informs him that he has handed over the money to his father. Chrysalus is upset but agrees to help Mnesilochus find money to pay off Cleomachus by tricking Nicobulus. Accordingly, Chrysalus sends Pistoclerus to get some writing materials. When Pistoclerus returns, Chrysalus persuades Mnesilochus to write a letter to Nicobulus warning his father that Chrysalus will try to trick him out of some money and to tie up Chrysalus with ropes if he does so. Mnesilochus is puzzled as to how such a letter will help him get the money, and Chrysalus tells him not to worry. After the letter is sealed, Chrysalus prepares to take it to Nicobulus. The slave sends the two young men to Bacchis' house for dinner with the sisters.

Next, Chrysalus goes to Nicobulus' house and delivers the letter. Nicobulus, who has read the letter, summons a slave to tie up Chrysalus. Nicobulus declares that Chrysalus will never get his money, but Chrysalus predicts that soon Nicobulus will beg him to take the money. Indeed, Nicobulus' attitude is given incentive for change when the doors of Bacchis' house open and he sees his son and Pistoclerus dining with the two

Bacchises. The situation is further complicated by the arrival of Cleomachus, who Chrysalus claims is married to Mnesilochus' Bacchis. To prevent Mnesilochus from being caught with Bacchis by Cleomachus, Nicobulus unbinds Chrysalus. When Nicobulus and Chrysalus overhear Cleomachus' making threats against Mnesilochus and Bacchis unless he receives a large sum of money, Nicobulus agrees to pay off the soldier. After Nicobulus and Cleomachus make their financial arrangement, Chrysalus tells Cleomachus falsely that Mnesilochus is on the family farm and that Bacchis is at the temple of Minerva (Greek: ATHENA). After Cleomachus' departure to search for Bacchis, Chrysalus begs Nicobulus to allow him to go into Bacchis' house and chastise Mnesilochus for his behavior.

Several minutes later, Chrysalus emerges from Bacchis' house with another letter, which he claims is like a Trojan horse prepared to destroy the city of PRIAM (with Nicobulus representing Priam or the city itself). In a lengthy speech Chrysalus continues to compare his exploits to the Trojan War and indicates that he needs to trick Nicobulus out of more money so that Mnesilochus, Pistoclerus, and the Bacchises can celebrate their "triumph." Next, Nicobulus arrives from his house and Chrysalus informs him that his encounter with Mnesilochus was productive. Nicobulus reads the letter from Mnesilochus, in which he expresses regret for his behavior and begs that Chrysalus be given money that he (Mnesilochus) has sworn he would give to Bacchis, so that he will not have to break his oath to her. Nicobulus does not want his son to have a reputation as a liar, so he agrees to pay the money. After Chrysalus receives the money and goes into Bacchis' house, Pistoclerus' father, Philoxenus, enters in search of Mnesilochus, who was supposed to be guiding Pistoclerus toward a modest way of life.

In the final act, Nicobulus, who has just learned that Bacchis is a prostitute and not Cleomachus' wife, expresses rage that he was tricked by Chrysalus. Philoxenus, who has overheard Nicobulus' tirade, approaches, and the two fathers commiserate about regarding their sons' behavior. When the fathers go to Bacchis' house, the two Bacchises answer the door, make fun of the old men, and call them sheep. The two women then change their attitude, however, and

decide to lure them inside. After a bit of flattery from the Bacchises, the two fathers' passions are aroused and they join in the party alongside their sons.

COMMENTARY

As do AMPHITRUO, THE BRAGGART WARRIOR, and MENAECHMI, BACCHIDES deals with the complications of the lives of twins. In *Amphitruo,* one set of twins (divine) prevents the second set of twins (mortal) from interfering in the seduction of ALCMENA. In *Menaechmi,* one twin reaps various benefits when he is mistaken for his twin brother. *The Braggart Warrior* is more similar to *Bacchides* in that the two twins are female, although in *Braggart Warrior,* Philocomasium does not really have a twin but pretends she does to trick the soldier's slave, Sceledrus. The trickery in *Braggart Warrior* is orchestrated by a clever slave, Palaestrio, just as in *Bacchides* the clever slave Chrysalus orchestrates much of the deception. We should note, however, that the two Bacchis twins take an active role in trying to fulfill their desires in contrast with Philocomasium, who primarily runs back and forth between two houses under Palaestrio's direction. In both plays, the BRAGGART WARRIOR is an object of deception; in *Bacchides* Mnesilochus' father is also deceived. Bacchides is also a "quest for cash" play, whereas in *Braggart Warrior* the financial arrangements for the prostitute have already been made.

One point of interest in *Bacchides* is the play's double plot, a feature common in TERENCE, but not in Plautus. Usually, Plautine plays focus on one love affair, whereas the *Bacchides* deals with both the love affair of Mnesilochus and Bacchis of Samos and that of Pistoclerus and Athenian Bacchis. According to Clark, "The secondary love plot of Pistoclerus and the Athenian Bacchis provides a delaying action in the first half of the play." Thus, the seduction of Pistoclerus in the play's first half is balanced by the seduction of the two fathers in the second half.

Much of the scholarship on Plautus' *Bacchides* has focused on comparisons of Plautus' play and Menander's *Dis Exapaton.* In particular, scholars have been concerned to determine how far Plautus deviated from Menander's play and to discover, if possible, original elements of Plautus' work. The lines from *Dis Exapaton* that survive reveal that Plautus changed the names of Menander's characters, used different METER in some places, and made his dialogue more lively and aimed at garnering laughs as opposed to smiles at subtle wit. One element of Plautus' originality appears to have been an expanded role for the clever slave Chrysalus (Syrus in Menander's play), whose actions "dominate the stage action" (Clark). Because only about 50 lines of Menander's play survive, the content of that play is uncertain.

With Palaestrio, as well as Pseudolus (PSEUDOLUS) and Tranio (HAUNTED HOUSE), Chrysalus is among the more delightful characters in Roman COMEDY. In some ways, Chrysalus resembles ODYSSEUS. As Odysseus has, Chrysalus has made a lengthy journey at sea and is full of craftiness. His letter becomes like the Trojan horse (a stratagem for which Odysseus often receives credit) prepared to destroy the city of PRIAM (with Nicobulus' representing Priam or the city itself). At one point, Chrysalus even declares that he is Odysseus (946). Chrysalus goes further, declaring that he is AGAMEMNON and this comic Agamemnon will overcome Cleomachus ("famous warrior"), whom Chrysalus calls MENELAUS (946). In addition to being a trickster and a warrior, Chrysalus is in effect a playwright as he orchestrates a deception that will allow Mnesilochus to acquire Bacchis. At the same time, Athenian Bacchis is also producing her own play, which aims to deceive the soldier. Accordingly, Slater says that Chrysalus "is the playwright of the inner play . . . [while] the outer play is controlled by Bacchis."

As several Roman comedies do, Bacchides contains many references to the concept of fides, a Latin word that can mean "trustworthiness," "credibility," and "faithfulness." In Bacchides, Nicobulus runs into trouble when he trusts his slave rather than his fellow citizen. Chrysalus himself declares himself a person full of treachery (perfidia, 226) and therefore the very person to trick Nicobulus. Chrysalus, the last person with whom someone should enter into a bond of fides, concocts a story that makes Nicobulus distrust Archidemides (275, 283, 285) and trust Chrysalus.

Whereas Chrysalus' plot leads Nicobulus to trust him, the plans of Athenian Bacchis lead Mnesilochus to distrust his friend, Pistoclerus. When Mnesilochus hears of Pistoclerus' flirting with Bacchis, his bond of fides with Pistoclerus is disrupted and he wonders how to know who is trustworthy (fidelem, 491) and who is not. This rupture in the bond of fides between the young men leads Mnesilochus to give the money back to his father. This action, of course, causes the bond of fides between Chrysalus and Nicobulus to be shattered. The alleged temporary breach of fides between Mnesilochus and Pistoclerus comes to a head when Mnesilochus accuses Pistoclerus of being in love with Bacchis, and an indignant Pistoclerus drags him into Bacchis' house to prove the firmness of his bond of fides (570) with Mnesilochus. After Mnesilochus discovers the truth, he is angry with himself for distrusting his friend (629), especially since his distrust led him to give the gold back to his father.

Mnesilochus, who has repaired his bond of fides with Pistoclerus, informs Chrysalus that he must repair his bond of fides with Nicobulus. Chrysalus cannot imagine how he can induce Nicobulus to trust him (697), and Mnesilochus even indicates that it will be harder than Chrysalus thinks: Nicobulus would not believe Chrysalus if the slave said that the Sun was the Sun (699–700). Hearing this, Chrysalus is supremely confident and declares that he will trick Nicobulus. Now, Chrysalus relies on Nicobulus' lack of fides with him to carry out the deception. Chrysalus again establishes a bond of fides with Nicobulus, who considers him untrustworthy, by preying on Nicobulus' belief. Not only does Chrysalus reestablish his bond with Nicobulus, but to accomplish his scheme he must induce Nicobulus to enter a bond of fides with Cleomachus. Chrysalus also establishes a bond of fides with Cleomachus when he swears that Mnesilochus is not having an affair with Bacchis. Ironically, Nicobulus, in the midst of being deceived by Chrysalus, is able to recognize that Chrysalus is lying to Cleomachus. After Cleomachus and Chrysalus exit, Nicobulus expresses thanks for Chrysalus' help, but says he still will not trust the slave (922), although he does trust the letter (924) that he does not realize the slave has fabricated.

Having duped the old man out of one pile of money, Chrysalus has a second letter written that will lead Nicobulus to hand over additional money. When Nicobulus wants Chrysalus to take the money to Mnesilochus, Chrysalus declares that he does not want the money to be entrusted to him (1062, 1064). Even as Chrysalus tells Nicobulus not to trust him, the old man, who has declared that he will not trust him, insists that he take the money. This insistence, however, will lead to Chrysalus' being caught as Nicobulus encounters Cleomachus in the forum and discovers that again Chrysalus' bond is false. Nicobulus and Philoxenus, who have both been fooled by the slave, end the play in a display of further gullibility as the two Bacchises lure them into their house. Nicobulus, who has already entered into treacherous bonds of *fides* with his slave, ends the play trusting in a prostitute. Earlier, Lydus had declared the door to Bacchis' house a gateway to the UNDERWORLD (368); Nicobulus now enters that part of the underworld reserved for those who do not respect the bonds of *fides*.

BIBLIOGRAPHY

Barsby, J. *Plautus: Bacchides.* Warminster, U.K.: Aris & Phillips, 1986.

Clark, J. R. "Structure and Symmetry in the *Bacchides* of Plautus," *Transactions of the American Philological Association* 106 (1976): 85–96.

Damen, Mark L. "'By the Gods, Boy . . . Stop Bothering Me!: Can't You Tell Menander from Plautus?': or How *Dis exapaton* Does Not Help Us Understand *Bacchides*," *Antichthon* 29 (1996): 15–29.

Owens, W. M. "The Third Deception in *Bacchides: Fides* and Plautus' Originality," *American Journal of Philology* 115 (1994): 381–407.

Slater, N. W. *Plautus in Performance.* Princeton, N.J.: Princeton University Press, 1985, 94–117.

BACCHUS   See DIONYSUS.

BACIS

An influential prophet from BOEOTIA who lived during the fifth century B.C.E., Bacis was said to be inspired by NYMPHS. Aristophanes mentions Bacis several times in connection with oracles. [ANCIENT SOURCES: Aristophanes, *Birds* 962, 970, *Knights* 123–24, 1003–4, *Peace* 1070–72; Herodotus, 8.20, 77, 96, 9.43; Pausanias, 4.27.4, 10.12.11]

BACTRA   See BACTRIA.

BACTRIA

A province in the Persian empire comprising the territory of what is today northern Afghanistan. Bactra was the capital of Bactria. In EURIPIDES' *BACCHAE*, DIONYSUS says his journey has taken him through Bactria. [ANCIENT SOURCES: Aeschylus, *Persians* 306, 318, 732; Euripides, *Bacchae* 15]

BANKER

A stock character in NEW COMEDY, the banker, or *trapezita*, is usually a villain. In PLAUTUS' *CURCULIO*, Curculio compares the banker Lyco to a PIMP. [ANCIENT SOURCES: Plautus, *Captives* 193, 449, *Comedy of Asses* 438, *Curculio* passim, *Epidicus* 143, *Pseudolus* 757, *Three-Dollar Day* 424]

BARBARIAN

In Greek drama, a barbarian is someone who is not a Greek or someone who behaves in a way that is repugnant to civilized Greeks. For example, the Greeks regarded as barbarians people such as MEDEA, the Phrygian messenger in EURIPIDES' *ORESTES*, the Scythian archer in ARISTOPHANES' *THESMOPHORIAZUSAE*, the AMAZONS, the Persians, and the Trojans. One of the most emphatic statements on the contrast between Greeks and barbarians is in Euripides' *IPHIGENIA AT AULIS*. In this play, the title character decides to allow herself to be sacrificed so that the Greeks can sail to wage war against the Trojans. Iphigenia should give up her own life because, as she reasons, "It is fitting for Greeks to rule barbarians, but not for barbarians to rule Greeks. . . . Barbarians are slaves, but Greeks are free." As among the Greeks, among the Romans those who were not Romans or did not behave in manner considered civilized were regarded as barbarians (though the Romans are more flexible with the term). Interestingly, at the conclusion of *OCTAVIA*, the chorus regard the treatment of the Roman OCTAVIA as less merciful than that which occurs in barbaric lands, thus suggesting that the Roman emperor Nero was more cruel than those he would consider barbarians. The connotation of the term *barbarian* was not always pejorative, however: In EURIPIDES' *BACCHAE*, Dionysus addresses the women who follow him as "barbarian women" (*barbaroi gunaikes*). [ANCIENT SOURCES: Aeschylus, *Persians;* Euripides, *Helen, Iphigenia in Tauris, Iphigenia at Aulis* 1400, *Bacchae* 604; Plautus, *Bacchides* 121, 123; Seneca, *Octavia* 43]

BARCA

A town on the coast of northern Africa. In the middle of the sixth century B.C.E., it was colonized by Greeks from Cyrene. Barca was famous for chariot driving and the training of horses. [ANCIENT SOURCES: Sophocles, *Electra* 727]

BARCAEAN   See BARCA.

BASSARAI
As were the BACCHAE, the Bassarai were a group of women who worshiped DIONYSUS. The Bassarai lived in Thrace, Phrygia, or Lydia. When ORPHEUS, who considered Helios (see SUN) the greatest divinity, refused to worship Dionysus, the scorned wine god sent the Bassarai to tear him apart. AESCHYLUS also wrote a *Bassarai*, or *Bassarides* (fragments 23–25 Radt), which was part of the Lycurgus trilogy, which included *EDONIANS* and *Youths* (Greek: *Neaniskoi*). Aeschylus' play seems to have been about Orpheus' fatal encounter with Dionysus.

BIBLIOGRAPHY
Radt, S. *Tragicorum Graecorum Fragmenta.* Vol. 3. Göttingen, Ger.: Vandenhoeck & Ruprecht, 1985.

BASSARIDES   See BASSARAI.

BATTUS
In the seventh century B.C.E., Battus colonized Cyrene with people from the island of Thera. For 200 years after Battus' death, his name continued to be used as a title for every other king of Cyrene. [ANCIENT SOURCES: Aristophanes, *Wealth* 925; Herodotus 4.150–63]

BIBLIOGRAPHY
Sommerstein, A. H. *The Comedies of Aristophanes.* Vol. 11, *Wealth.* Warminster, U.K.: Aris & Phillips, 2001, 195.

BDELYCLEON
The son of PHILOCLEON in ARISTOPHANES' *WASPS,* his name means "hater of CLEON." Like Pheidippides in *CLOUDS,* the son, Bdelycleon, appears sensible whereas his father, Philocleon, is out of control. After convincing Philocleon that he is a pawn of politicians such as Cleon, Bdelycleon attempts to put an end to his father's practice of sitting on jury panels by setting up a court for his father at his own home. Bdelycleon tricks his father into acquitting the first defendant at the "home court." Later, Bdelycleon tries to introduce his father to refined society by taking him to a dinner party; however, Philocleon becomes drunk, tells boorish jokes, runs off with the party's flute girl, and assaults someone on the way home.

BIBLIOGRAPHY
Sidwell, Keith. "Was Philokleon Cured?: The *Nosos* Theme in Aristophanes' *Wasps*," *Classica & Mediaevalia* 41 (1990): 9–31.

BELIAS
A female descendant of Belus. Belus, the son of POSEIDON and LIBYA, was the father of Danaus, whose daughters, the DANAIDS, killed their husbands. [ANCIENT SOURCES: Seneca, *Hercules Oetaeus* 960]

BELLEROPHON
The son of Glaucus and Eurymede, Bellerophon was a Corinthian nobleman. After Bellerophon killed his own brother, whose name was Deliades, Piren, or Alcimenes, he went to Proetus for purification. Proetus' wife, STHENEBOEA (or Anteia), conceived a passion for Bellerophon and made sexual advances to him. After Bellerophon rejected her, Stheneboea told Proetus that Bellerophon had tried to assault her sexually. Proetus, wanting to get rid of Bellerophon but not to kill the young man himself, wrote a letter to King IOBATES of Lycia. This letter apparently requested that Iobates should kill Bellerophon. Proetus sealed the letter and instructed Bellerophon to deliver it to Iobates. Iobates first tried to kill Bellerophon by having him battle the CHIMAERA, a creature that was part a lion, part a goat, and part a serpent. With the aid of the winged horse PEGASUS, a gift from ATHENA, Bellerophon destroyed the Chimaera. Next, Bellerophon defeated the tribes of the Solymi and Amazons. Finally, after Bellerophon killed the Lycians, who had ambushed him, Iobates, apparently convinced of the young man's nobility, married Bellerophon to his daughter, named Philonoe, Anticlia, or Cassandra. At some point, Bellerophon had a daughter, Laodamia (not the wife of PROTESILAUS). Eventually, Bellerophon became king of the Lycians. Some sources relate that Bellerophon tried to ride Pegasus to Mount Olympus, but the winged horse fought him, and Bellerophon fell off, crashed to the ground, and became lame. Then, Bellerophon somehow wandered

the plain of Aleios and avoided contact with other humans.

Bellerophon occasionally turns up in ancient drama, both TRAGEDY and COMEDY. EURIPIDES' *Bellerophon,* produced around 430 B.C.E., has more than 100 lines that survive (fragments 285–312 Nauck). This play's setting is Lycia, and its highlight seems to be Bellerophon's ill-fated flight to Mount Olympus to confront the gods; the reason for the confrontation is uncertain. From ARISTOPHANES' remarks in *ACHARNIANS,* it is known that Bellerophon appeared onstage lame and dressed in rags. Aristophanes' *Peace* contains a parody of Bellerophon's flight on Pegasus, when the hero, TRYGAEUS, flies to Olympus on a dung beetle. Bellerophon was also a character in Euripides' *Stheneboea* (staged before 422 B.C.E.). The tragedian Astydamas also wrote a play called *Bellerophon,* of which only the title survives. On the comic stage, Eubulus wrote a *Bellerophon,* from which a two-line fragment survives (fragment 16 Kock). [ANCIENT SOURCES: Apollodorus, *Library* 1.9.3; 2.3.1–2; Aristophanes, *Acharnians* 427–29; Aristophanes, *Peace* 60–179; Hesiod, *Theogony* 319–25; Homer, *Iliad* 6.155–202; Hyginus, *Fables* 57; Pausanias, 2.4.1; Pindar, *Olympian Odes* 13.63–90]

BIBLIOGRAPHY

Collard, C., M. J. Cropp, and K. H. Lee. *Euripides: Selected Fragmentary Plays.* Vol. 1. Warminster, U.K.: Aris & Phillips, 1995. 98–120.

Kock, T. *Comicorum Atticorum Fragmenta.* Vol. 2. Leipzig: Teubner, 1884.

Nauck, A. *Tragicorum Graecorum Fragmenta.* 1889. Reprint, Hildesheim, Ger.: Olms, 1964.

Webster, T. B. L. *The Tragedies of Euripides.* London: Methuen, 1967.

BELLONA   The sister or wife of Mars (Greek: ARES), Bellona is a Roman divinity associated with war. Her name is related to a Latin word for war, *bellum.* Bellona is sometimes equated with the Greek divinity Enyo. [ANCIENT SOURCES: Plautus, *Amphitruo* 43, *Bacchides* 847; Seneca, *Agamemnon* 82, *Hercules Oetaeus* 1312]

BIA   *Bia,* a Greek word meaning "strength," "force," or "violence," in AESCHYLUS' *PROMETHEUS BOUND* is personified as a divinity who assists in the binding of PROMETHEUS. Bia does not speak in Aeschylus' play.

BIRDS (Greek: *ORNITHES*; Latin: *AVES*) ARISTOPHANES (414 B.C.E.)   The play was performed at the City DIONYSIA and finished second to AMEIPSIAS' *Revelers.* ARISTOPHANES had Callistratus produce the play for him. Set in an imaginary land beyond the city of ATHENS, Aristophanes' *Birds* opens with the appearance of two Athenians, PEISETAERUS (he who persuades his comrades) and Euelpides (son of good hope), each of whom carries a bird, which he hopes will lead him to another bird named TEREUS. Euelpides reveals that they have decided (because of the constant legal wrangling in Athens) to find a place where they may live in peace. They hope that Tereus will be able to advise them about the existence of such a city. Soon, the two men approach a rock, from which emerges a bird (the Plover Page) that serves Tereus. The bird frightens the Athenians so much that they let go of their own birds. Eventually, Plover Page summons Tereus, who is dressed as a featherless Hoopoe.

When the two Athenians ask Tereus whether he knows of a peaceful city where they can live, they reject his suggestions as being unpleasant places. Peisetaerus then proposes that Tereus and the birds found their own city in the air and argues that it could rival the gods' home on Mount Olympus. Peisetaerus also suggests that unless the gods pay tribute to the birds, the birds should not allow the smoke from sacrifices to reach the gods. Delighted by the suggestion, Tereus summons the rest of the birds so that Peisetaerus can explain his plan to them. This prompts the entrance of the chorus, composed of various birds. Initially, the birds do not want to have any association with humans and threaten to kill the two Athenians. After Tereus explains their plan, however, the birds relax and promise not to harm them. Peisetaerus convinces the birds that their lineage is older and more noble than that of the gods themselves and that birds once ruled the world. Peisetaerus suggests that the birds build a city and reclaim their empire from the gods. The birds are skeptical that mortals would accept them as gods, but Peisetaerus argues that because the birds have ample powers to harm or help humans (for example, destroying their crops or protecting the crops from insects), human beings will accept them as divinities.

After hearing Peisetaerus, the birds decide to implement his plan. Tereus then invites Peisetaerus and Euelpides into his "house." Before they exit, however, the birds beg Tereus to summon his wife the nightingale. When she appears, the Athenians admire her beauty and then enter Tereus' house. The chorus then begin the PARABASIS with a praise of the nightingale. The birds narrate that the entire universe was brought forth from an egg and that winged EROS, love, was first to spring forth. In turn, Eros gave birth to the birds. The birds then mention some of the blessings that they offer to humans and urge the audience to accept them as divinities and thus receive even greater benefits. The birds then invite people, particularly those whose behavior was despised in Athens, to live with them and suggest some of the advantages of being able to fly.

After the parabasis, Peisetaerus and Euelpides enter, now equipped with wings. In consultation with the bird chorus, they decide to name their city Nephelokokkugia ("cloud-cuckooland" or "cloud-cuckoobury"). After naming the city, Peisetaerus sends Euelpides off to help the birds build a wall for their city. Next, Peisetaerus calls for a priest so that he can make a sacrifice to the birds. When a raven priest enters, Peisetaerus and this winged priest begin to pray to the various birds. Their ritual is interrupted by the arrival of a pitifully dressed human poet, who has come to sing a song of celebration for the new city. After hearing some of his awful verses, Peisetaerus decides to get rid of this "cold" poet by giving him some clothing (thus warming the poet and ideally his poetry).

Peisetaerus attempts to resume the sacrifice to the birds, but he is again interrupted, this time by an oracle monger, who wants to offer prophecies about the new city in exchange for food and clothing. Peisetaerus, however, claims he has a prophecy that predicts the destruction of any scam artist who tries to interrupt his sacrifice. After Peisetaerus drives off the oracle monger, the astronomer METON enters, hoping to perform a survey of Peisetaerus' airspace. Peisetaerus tells Meton that their new city has a practice of driving out all "quacks" and then proceeds to drive Meton away with blows. The interruptions continue as a commissioner and statute seller enter and try to make money

in the new city. In each instance, Peisetaerus drives them away with blows. Finally, Peisetaerus decides to move to a different location to make the sacrifice.

After Peisetaerus' exit, the bird chorus deliver a second parabasis. They sing of how mortals will worship them and how anyone who mistreats birds will surely be punished. They also address the judges of the dramatic competition and describe the blessings that they will receive should the play win first prize, but say that they will defecate on them if they do not rank the play first.

After this parabasis, a MESSENGER enters and informs Peisetaerus that the birds have completed construction of the city's wall. Next, a guard enters to tell Peisetaerus that one of the Olympian gods is approaching. Soon, the goddess IRIS enters, and immediately Peisetaerus has the birds seize her, as he threatens to have her put to death. Iris declares that she is traveling to Earth with a message from ZEUS, namely, that mortals should make sacrifice to the gods. Peisetaerus, however, scoffs at this statement and declares that the birds are the gods now, thus threatening to attack Zeus if he bothers him again. Peisetaerus then angrily sends Iris away. After her exit, a herald enters and offers Peisetaerus a golden crown from the people of Earth, who the herald says have started to imitate the ways of birds. The herald also says thousands of mortals will soon be making their way to the new city to acquire wings and the birds' way of life. Accordingly, Peisetaerus tells the birds to get baskets of wings in preparation for the new arrivals.

The first person who tries to gain access is a young man who beats his father. Peisetaerus notes that birds do have the custom of attacking their fathers, but that birds also have the custom of caring for their elders. The young man is disappointed, and so Peisetaerus, after telling him not to beat his father, suggests that he work out his aggression by joining the fighting in THRACE. After the father beater agrees and exits, a dithyrambic poet named CINESIAS enters, desiring wings. Peisetaerus listens to his lofty verses and presumably drives him away, but the text is uncertain at this point. Next, a sycophant (see INFORMANT), dressed in rags, enters in search of wings so that he can inform on people in numerous cities. Peisetaerus tries to urge the man to practice a more honest occupation, but when the sycophant refuses, he flogs him with a whip and sends him away wingless. As the sycophant departs, Peisetaerus makes the man help him gather up the wings and they exit. Next, the bird chorus sing a brief ode about what they have seen recently while flying over Earth. After the choral song, PROMETHEUS enters to tell Peisetaerus that the rise of the birds' city has prevented sacrifices by humans from reaching the gods and thus puts Zeus' existence in jeopardy. Furthermore, the gods of foreign lands have threatened to attack Zeus unless he resolves the situation. Prometheus says that Zeus and the foreign gods will send representatives to ask for a peace treaty, but that Peisetaerus should not make one unless Zeus agrees to allow him to marry Basileia (the personification of sovereignty) and hand over the scepter of power to the birds.

The exit of Prometheus is followed by the entrance of POSEIDON; a foreign god, Triballos (see TRIBALLIAN); and HERACLES, who have been sent to arrange peace with the birds. Peisetaerus is ready to make peace provided that Zeus restore power to the birds. Poseidon is initially reluctant, but when Peisetaerus explains that the gods will benefit from having the birds as allies, Poseidon and the other two agree. After Peisetaerus mentions the marriage to Basileia, however, Poseidon again balks. Heracles, whose only concern is the food he will obtain through the restoration of sacrifices, is ready to agree, but Poseidon argues that if Zeus hands over his kingdom, then Heracles will lose his inheritance because Zeus is his father. Peisetaerus, however, argues that because Heracles' mother was mortal, he will not inherit anything (a joke on the laws of inheritance among the Athenians, who did not recognize bastards as legitimate heirs), and that Zeus' inheritance will go to Poseidon. Accordingly, Heracles votes to allow Basileia to marry Peisetaerus; Poseidon, however, votes against the marriage. Peisetaerus turns to Triballos to cast the tie-breaking vote. As a foreigner, Triballos speaks gibberish, but Peisetaerus interprets his response as voting for Heracles' position. Although Poseidon objects, he relents and agrees to all of Peisetaerus' terms.

At this point, preparations for Peisetaerus' wedding and a feast begin. After a brief choral interlude, a messenger enters and announces that Peisetaerus is approaching with his new bride, Basileia. The play ends as Peisetaerus and Basileia enter and the bird chorus sing a wedding hymn and the power of the birds is acknowledged.

COMMENTARY

With more than two dozen costumes of birds of various types, Aristophanes' *Birds* must have been one of the finest visual spectacles to grace the Athenian stage. Aristophanes' poetry in this play is also quite imaginative, especially when the sounds of birds are represented in Greek. Nowhere else in classical drama can one find words such as *tiotiotiotinx, totototototototototinx,* and *torotorotorolililix*. Despite these wonderful elements, however, one should note that Aristophanes was not the first Greek playwright to compose such a play. His predecessors Magnes (see Kock) and Crates (see Kock) had both composed a play named *Birds,* of which only the title remains. The notion of leaving current society and finding a better society was also not original to Aristophanes, as PHERECRATES' *Savages* had explored a similar premise just four years earlier. Aristophanes' *Birds* also exhibits a structure much like that of his earlier plays, especially *PEACE,* staged seven years earlier. As in Aristophanes' *Peace,* the hero of *Birds* makes a journey toward the heavens. Instead of a quest for peace and a subsequent return to Earth, however, in *Birds* no return to Earth is planned and the foundation of a new city in the skies is realized. In both *Peace* and *Birds,* the heroes manage to induce the gods to allow them to proceed with their plans, and both plays conclude with a sacred marriage of the hero and a divine female.

As in *Peace* and other Aristophanic plays, in *Birds* the hero experiences various challenges to the fantastic solution he has proposed. The heroes of *Peace* and *Birds* both exclude oracle mongers from the benefits of their social reforms; as DICAEOPOLIS does in *ACHARNIANS* or Chremylus does in the later *Wealth,* Peisetaerus drives off an informant. In *Acharnians* and *Peace,* many of those excluded from the heroes' social reforms are driven away because they are in conflict with the heroes' reforms. In *Birds,* admittance to the perfect world that Peisetaerus is trying to create depends on whether the prospective citizen will fit in with Peisetaerus' vision of the proper citizen to inhabit his new city. Bad poets, corrupt religious and governmental officials, and vile criminals are all rejected from the city in the clouds.

Whereas in other Aristophanic plays the Athenian heroes try to reform the existing city of Athens, in *Birds* the Athenian hero tries to create a completely new city— a city, however, that probably resembles a Persian city as much as it does the Athenians' city. One major difference between Athens and the new city of the birds is that Athens was a democracy. In Peisetaerus' city, he may convince the birds that they will be the rulers (cf. 467, 482) whose new city can rival that of Zeus Basileus (sovereign), but in reality Peisetaerus is the ruler and he is the one who, in accordance with Zeus' agreement, marries Basileia (the personification of sovereignty). Thus, Peisetaerus will become the new Basileus (sovereign), a title not only added to Zeus' name, but elsewhere in Aristophanes, especially in *Acharnians*, used to denote the king of Persia.

Several times in *Birds*, Aristophanes mentions Persian elements in the city. At line 277, one of the birds of the chorus is described as being a Median (i.e., Persian) bird. Although Athens was famed for its fortification walls, the walls that Peisetaerus proposes building he compares to those surrounding the Persian city of Babylon (552). At one point, Peisetaerus and Euelpides even discuss similarities between the sovereign birds and the Persians and suggest that the tiara worn by the Persian Basileus is similar to the plumage of a bird (481–87). Peisetaerus also describes the Persian king's rule as a tyranny (*eturannei,* 483). Elsewhere in the play both the rule of Zeus (*urannidos,* 1605) and the new kingdom of the birds (*urannida,* 1643) are called tyrannies. Finally, as the play concludes, Peisetaerus is called a tyrant (*urannon,* 1708). So, at the conclusion of *Birds,* Peisetaerus is addressed joyfully by the birds as the same sort of ruler whom the Athenians had overthrown some hundred years earlier in favor of creating democracy.

The notion that Athenian democracy might be replaced with tyranny was probably not out of the realm of possibility when Aristophanes put on *Birds.* Three years later the democracy would be overthrown and an oligarchy of 400 leading citizens would replace it. If Athens could revert to tyranny, it certainly had a possible candidate in ALCIBIADES, who bears some resemblance to Peisetaerus, although Dunbar rejects such a comparison on the grounds of insufficient textual evidence. Because Aristophanes' fellow Athenians had undertaken an ambitious military expedition to the far-away island of SICILY in 415 B.C.E., the basic premise of *Birds* (staged in 414) would have had obvious parallels to their own situation. One of the military commanders of the Athenians' SICILIAN EXPEDITION was Alcibiades, who had been instrumental in persuading the Athenians to undertake the expedition; the Greek word root in the first part of Peisetaerus' name is derived from a Greek verb meaning "to persuade."

The *Birds* begins with two Athenians' desire to find a new place to live in peace and quiet but soon develops into one man's desire for absolute control over a city and even for power that rivals that of the gods themselves. Peisetaerus claims to want to restore power to the birds, but the audience see Peisetaerus reap most of the benefits while Euelpides and the birds carry out his commands. In the case of Alcibiades, shortly after the expedition sailed in 415 B.C.E., the Athenians recalled him because he was suspected of participating in a mockery of the Eleusinian Mysteries and of participating in the mutilation of various statues of HERMES before the expedition's departure. THUCYDIDES also says the Athenian people suspected that those involved in these evil deeds were conspiring to overthrow the democracy and install either an oligarchy or a tyranny (6.60.1). Thucydides reports that Alcibiades was the primary suspect in a conspiracy against the Athenian people (6.61.1). Alcibiades, however, evaded the Athenian ship sent to take him back, and the Athenians condemned Alcibiades to death. He escaped to SPARTA and began to give military advice that would help the Spartans against the Athenians. Thus, as Thucydides confirms and Aristophanes suggests, talk of revolution and tyranny was in the air when Aristophanes produced *Birds* in 414 and the ambitious and persuasive Peisetaerus is not completely unlike Alcibiades.

BIBLIOGRAPHY
Arrowsmith, W. "Aristophanes' *Birds:* The Fantasy Politics of Eros," *Arion* 1 (1973): 119–67.

Dunbar, N. *Aristophanes: Birds*. New York: Oxford University Press, 1995.

Konstan, D. "A City in the Air: Aristophanes' *Birds*," *Arethusa* 23 (1990): 183–207.

Sommerstein, A. H. *The Comedies of Aristophanes*. Vol. 6, *Birds*. Warminster, U.K.: Aris & Phillips, 1987.

Vickers, M. "Alcibiades on Stage: Aristophanes' *Birds*," *Historia* 38 (1989): 267–99.

BOEOTIA

A region in central Greece whose principal city was THEBES.

BOÖTES

Another name for the constellation ARCTOPHYLAX. [ANCIENT SOURCES: Seneca, *Agamemnon* 69–70, *Medea* 315, *Octavia* 233]

BOREAS

A god who represents the north wind, Boreas abducted Oreithyia, daughter of ERECHTHEUS, from ATHENS and took her to his home in THRACE. By Oreithyia, Boreas became the father of two daughters, Chione and CLEOPATRA, and two sons, Zetes and Calais, who joined the quest for the Golden Fleece. Boreas does not appear as a character in any extant dramas, but he certainly had a speaking role in AESCHYLUS' *Oreithyia* (fragments 280–81b Radt). [ANCIENT SOURCES: Apollodorus, *Library* 1.9.16, 3.15.1–2; Ovid, *Metamorphoses* 6.675–721; Pausanias, 1.19.5, 1.38.2]

BORRHAEAN GATE

One of the seven gates of THEBES. In AESCHYLUS' *SEVEN AGAINST THEBES*, this gate is defended by the Theban Actor and attacked by PARTHENOPAEUS.

BOSPORUS

Two straits are called by this name. The Thracian Bosporus connects the Propontis (another body of water) to the southern part of the Black Sea. Near the southern end of the Thracian Bosporus, the cities of Byzantium and Chalcedon were situated on shores opposite one another. The Cimmerian Bosporus is located at the northern end of the Black Sea and connects this sea with what is now the Sea of Azov and in ancient times was known as Lake Maeotis. The name Bosporus, which means "cow [*bos*] passage [*porus*]," is derived from the time when IO, a cow at the time, crossed the strait.

BRAGGART WARRIOR (Latin: *MILES GLORIOSUS*)

Although the braggart warrior is a stock character in New Comedy, such military buffoons can be seen as early as ARISTOPHANES' character LAMACHUS in ACHARNIANS (425 B.C.E.). The braggart warrior typically exaggerates his military conquests. In BRAGGART WARRIOR, Pyrgopolynices claims to have killed 7,000 men in a single day; in CARTHAGINIAN Antamoenides claims to have taken 60,000 lives in one day. These warriors also assume a tough facade but usually back down when confronted. The play's other characters usually dislike the warrior, who is often a rival lover or another character in the play. Several such warriors appear in Plautus' plays: Therapontigonus (CURCULIO), Cleomachus (BACCHIDES), Pyrgopolynices (*Braggart Warrior*), Antamoenides (*Carthaginian*), Stratophanes (TRUCULENTUS), and an unnamed warrior in EPIDICUS. The most extensive role for such a warrior occurs in *Braggart Warrior*, in which Pyrgopolynices' belief in his good looks leads to him lose one woman and then be fooled into thinking a married woman wants to have an affair with him. Only one braggart warrior appears in the six plays of TERENCE: Thraso in EUNUCH, a warrior who considers his words, rather than his deeds, as the key to his popularity. Not all warriors in surviving New Comedy are unsympathetic figures and lose the women in whom they are interested. In MENANDER'S *THE MAN SHE HATED* (*Misoumenos*) Thrasonides eventually marries his beloved. Likewise, in Menander's *THE GIRL WITH THE SHAVEN HEAD* (*Perikeiromene*), the warrior Polemon is reconciled with Glycera after he has cut off her hair in a jealous rage.

BIBLIOGRAPHY

Duckworth, G. *The Nature of Roman Comedy*. Princeton, N.J.: Princeton University Press, 1952. 264–65.

THE BRAGGART WARRIOR (Latin: *MILES GLORIOSUS*) PLAUTUS (CA. 205 B.C.E.)

The author of the Greek original is not known, but its title, *Alazon* (*The Braggart*), is mentioned at line 86. PLAUTUS' play has EPHESUS as its setting (the only Roman COMEDY set in this city), and the action occurs before the adjoining houses of the soldier Pyrgopolynices and Periplectomenus, an elderly Ephesian citizen—the only such configuration (private citizen living next door to a soldier) in extant Roman comedy. The play's opening act is an unusual one, in that it consists of a single scene, 78 lines long, involving Pyrgopolynices and his PARASITE Artotrogus. As the play opens, Pyrgopolynices is boasting about his prowess in battle, and Artotrogus is flattering him to get a free meal. The act concludes with Atrotrogus' praising the soldier's good looks.

After Pyrgopolynices and Artotrogus exit for the FORUM to pay recruits for King Seleucus, the next act begins with the arrival of Palaestrio, the current slave of Pyrgopolynices and former slave of Pleusicles, a young Athenian gentleman. Palaestrio delivers a delayed prologue. Palaestrio informs the audience that his master, Pleusicles, was in love with a PROSTITUTE, Philocomasium, who was in love with him. When Pleusicles was away from ATHENS, Pyrgopolynices saw Philocomasium, fell in love with her, became good friends with the woman's mother, and managed to have Philocomasium shipped off to Ephesus. When Palaestrio set sail to inform Pleusicles of the woman's loss, Palaestrio was captured by pirates, who turned him over to Pyrgopolynices. When Palaestrio arrived at Pyrgopolynices' house, he encountered Philocomasium and learned that she was still in love with Pleusicles. Palaestrio managed to send a message to Pleusicles to return to Ephesus immediately. Upon arriving in Ephesus, Pleusicles became the guest of Periplectomenus, who lives next door to the soldier. Palaestrio also informs the audience that he has created a way for the young lovers to communicate by digging a hole through a wall shared by the two houses. Because Periplectomenus supports Palaestrio's scheme, their only obstacle other than the soldier himself is the servant, Sceledrus, whom the soldier has placed as a guard for Philocomasium. Palaestrio tells the audience that during the course of the play Philocomasium will pretend to be another woman so that they can trick Sceledrus.

In the next scene, Periplectomenus informs Palaestrio that Sceledrus, while on the roof of Pyrgopolynices' house, had looked through the skylight of their house and seen Pleusicles and Philocomasium kissing. Palaestrio then tells Periplectomenus to summon Philocomasium and tell her to prepare to trick Sceledrus. After considerable thought, Palaestrio tells Periplectomenus that they will pretend that Philocomasium has an identical twin sister, who has recently arrived for a visit from Athens. After Periplectomenus goes inside to coach Philocomasium on her role in the deception, Palaestrio encounters Sceledrus, who tells him about Philocomasium's kissing of Pleusicles. Palaestrio tells Sceledrus that he himself would get into trouble if he were to give false information about Philocomasium. Furthermore, because Sceledrus is supposed to be guarding Philocomasium, he will only be reporting that he failed in his duty. When Sceledrus informs Palaestrio that Philocomasium is at Periplectomenus' house, Palaestrio goes inside to see for himself. When Palaestrio returns, he claims that Philocomasium is still at the soldier's house. Sceledrus, who does not know about the passageway that Palaestrio created between the two houses, is amazed when Palaestrio soon leads Philocomasium from Pyrgopolynices' house. Philocomasium denies Sceledrus' accusations, claims her name is Dicea (the just woman), and says that she has arrived from Athens to look for her twin sister. Even when Philocomasium threatens Sceledrus with the punishment the soldier will give him for spreading lies about her, Sceledrus still insists that he saw her at Periplectomenus' house. When Philocomasium turns to leave, Sceledrus tries to grab her. Philocomasium struggles, manages to get away from him, and darts into Periplectomenus' house. Palaestrio then tells Sceledrus to go into the soldier's house and get him a sword so that he can go into Periplectomenus' house and kill anyone who is kissing Philocomasium. By this time, however, Philocomasium has used the passageway to cross back over to the soldier's house. Thus, when Sceledrus returns, he is embarrassed to tell Palaestrio that Philocomasium is at the soldier's house. Then Palaestrio returns to Periplectomenus' house and Sceledrus continues his guard duty at the soldier's house.

In the next scene, Periplectomenus, knowing about Sceledrus' accusation of Philocomasium, enters and complains at the way his "guest" (Dicea/Philocomasium) has been treated, while also threatening Sceledrus with severe punishment. Periplectomenus suggests that Sceledrus look inside his (Periplec-tomenus') house to see proof of his guest. When Sceledrus does so, he finds Dicea/Philocomasium inside. Periplectomenus then suggests that Sceledrus look inside the soldier's house to check on Philocomasium. In the meantime, Philocomasium has returned to the soldier's house. Having seen these things, Sceledrus admits to Periplectomenus that he must have been mistaken. Sceledrus, thinking that Periplectomenus will inform the soldier of his behavior and that he will be punished, decides to hide for a few days until the commotion dies down.

The play's third act opens with the appearance of Palaestrio, Periplectomenus, and Pleusicles. After a lengthy discussion about love and Periplectomenus' congenial nature, Palaestrio reveals a plan for tricking Pyrgopolynices and allowing Pleusicles to have Philocomasium for himself. Palaestrio borrows a ring from Periplectomenus and says they will find an attractive woman and her maidservant, dress the woman as a married woman, and have her pretend to be in love with Pyrgopolynices. Palaestrio will give the ring to Pyrgopolynices and pretend that it is a gift from the "married woman." Palaestrio also reminds Pleusicles to call Philocomasium "Dicea" when Pyrgopolynices returns home.

In the following scene, Palaestrio calls Sceledrus from Pyrgopolynices' house but learns from another slave, Lucrio, that Sceledrus is off drinking somewhere. Lucrio is quite drunk, and when Palaestrio threatens to tell Pyrgopolynices, Lucrio goes off to hide. After Lucrio's exit, Palaestrio sees Periplectomenus approaching with the prostitute Acroteleutium and her maidservant, Milphidippa. Palaestrio then schools the two women about their role in this scheme. He informs Acroteleutium that she will pretend to be Periplectomenus' wife. When the women have received their instructions, they enter Periplectomenus' house to complete their preparations. Palaestrio, in turn, sets out for the forum to find the soldier.

In the fourth act, Palaestrio returns from the forum with Pyrgopolynices. Palaestrio gives the soldier the ring and tells him it is from a beautiful married woman. Pyrgopolynices is excited by the prospect of

the affair but wonders what he should do about Philocomasium. Palaestrio suggests that Pyrgopolynices allow Philocomasium to return to Athens with her twin sister, who has just arrived in Ephesus. Palaestrio even persuades the soldier to agree to allow Philocomasium to keep any jewelry or clothing given to her. As Palaestrio prepares the soldier for the deception, Milphidippa emerges from Periplectomenus' house and, pretending not to notice the soldier, speaks of her mistress' love for the soldier. Soon, Palaestrio approaches Milphidippa and has a few words in private with her about how best to trick the soldier. After Palaestrio tells her to continue building him up with talk of her mistress' love, Palaestrio returns to the soldier and continues the flattery. Then, Milphidippa approaches Pyrgopolynices and plies him with flattery. Palaestrio even arranges to have Milphidippa's mistress pay a substantial amount of money for the soldier's "services." The soldier quickly agrees to the affair and urges Milphidippa to have her mistress come out. Before Milphidippa leaves, Palaestrio tells her to make sure Philocomasium goes over to Periplectomenus' house. Milphidippa informs Palaestrio that Philocomasium is already in the house and that she and Acroteleutium have been eavesdropping on the conversation with the soldier.

After Milphidippa's exit, Palaestrio advises the soldier about how to dismiss Philocomasium as his girlfriend. After Pyrgopolynices returns to his house to carry out this task, Acroteleutium, Milphidippa, and Pleusicles emerge from Periplectomenus' house. Palaestrio informs them of how their scheme is progressing and gives the group further instructions about how he wants to proceed. Acroteleutium is to pretend that she is divorcing Periplectomenus and that Periplectomenus' house was part of Acroteleutium's dowry on their marriage (thus, the house is Acroteleutium's property). Pleusicles is instructed to dress as a ship master and summon Philocomasium to the harbor to take her to Athens. Palaestrio will help Philocomasium take her luggage to the harbor, and then he, together with Philocomasium and Pleusicles, will sail for Athens. Pleusicles agrees to the plan and promises to set Palaestrio free in return for his efforts.

After Pleusicles, Acroteleutium, and Milphidippa return to their house, Pyrgopolynices enters from his house, informs Palaestrio that he has broken off his relationship with Philocomasium, and says that he has given Palaestrio to Philocomasium at her request. Soon, Acroteleutium and Milphidippa return. They see the soldier and, without going up to him, begin to praise him and his good looks. After they have built up the soldier's ego, they at last approach him in awe and in almost divine reverence. Milphidippa informs the soldier that Acroteleutium wants the soldier to live with her in her house. The soldier rejects this because he thinks she is married, but when Milphidippa tells him that Acroteleutium has divorced her husband and that the house belongs to her, the soldier agrees. After the exit of Milphidippa and Acroteleutium into Periplectomenus' house, Pleusicles, disguised as a ship master, enters and pretends to seek Philocomasium. Palaestrio goes into the soldier's house and returns with Philocomasium, who pretends to weep bitterly about having to leave the soldier. After much ado, the tearful Philocomasium departs for the harbor with Pleusicles. Palaestrio, who will follow them, pretends to shed similar tears at having to part with Pyrgopolynices. Eventually, Palaestrio sets out for the harbor. Next, an unnamed servant emerges from Periplectomenus' house and summons Pyrgopolynices into the house to be with Acroteleutium. After the soldier enters the house, the slave informs the audience that Periplectomenus is inside prepared to accuse the soldier of adultery.

The play's final act begins as Pyrgopolynices is dragged from the house by some of Periplectomenus' slaves. Periplectomenus accuses the soldier of adultery, which Pyrgopolynices, of course, denies. Still, Periplectomenus threatens to have his slaves beat Pyrgopolynices. Ultimately, however, Periplectomenus releases Pyrgopolynices and makes him swear not to engage in such behavior again. After having been set free, Pyrgopolynices asks whether Philocomasium has already left. He is informed that she has and learns that the sailor who took her was actually her lover. The play ends with Pyrgopolynices' suggesting that adultery would decrease if all adulterers were treated the way he was.

COMMENTARY

Braggart Warrior falls into two halves that have not been linked with the greatest care, as some modern scholars note. Despite its structural problems, this play is usually considered one of Plautus' more amusing works because of depictions of both the soldier and the slave Palaestrio. The Latin title of the play, *Miles Gloriosus,* was used as the name of the braggart warrior in the modern musical *A Funny Thing Happened on the Way to the Forum.*

Although the title of Plautus' play suggests that the focal point is the braggart warrior, the onstage action is dominated by the wily slave Palaestrio. As shown by Frangoulidis' article, *Braggart Warrior,* as can several other Roman comedies, can be read with a metatheatrical perspective, with Palaestrio as the producer and director of the plays within the play. Palaestrio's audience for his "plays" consist of the slave Sceledrus and Pyrgopolynices. In the deception of Sceledrus, Palaestrio employs Philocomasium herself as his actress to make Sceledrus believe that he has seen her twin. In the deception of the soldier, Palaestrio employs a different prostitute to play the role of a wife. A stage property (the ring) is acquired and Palaestrio acts in his own play as he uses it to convince the soldier that a married woman is in love with him. The goal of Palaestrio's second play is to secure the release of Philocomasium from the soldier and reunite her with Pleusicles, who takes on the role of the ship's captain and costumes himself appropriately.

Although the play's structural unity has been criticized, one common factor that runs throughout the play is the theme of sight. About 20 percent of Plautine references to the eyes occur in this play. This theme links nicely with the metatheatrical analysis to the play, because successful playwrights can manipulate skillfully their audience's senses of hearing and sight. In the first half of the play, Palaestrio speaks of his trickery of Sceledrus in terms of affecting his eyes (148). When Sceledrus insists on the reliability of his eyesight (290), Palaestrio wants to have Sceledrus' eyes gouged out (315). Palaestrio tells Sceledrus that he has not employed his eyes properly (336), and Sceledrus, the eager spectator, is curious to know how Palaestrio will convince him that he did not see what he insists he has seen (347). Despite Palaestrio's attempted trickery with the twin Philocomasium, Sceledrus continues to insist on what he has seen (368); eventually, however, Palaestrio's tricks prevail and Sceledrus supposes that a mist must have covered his eyes (405). The play's second act ends with Periplectomenus' declaring that Sceledrus' eyes, ears, and mind have all gone over to their side (589), and in the third act Sceledrus' eyes are closed in a drunken stupor (827).

As Palaestrio's goal in the play's opening half was to make Sceledrus believe he did not see what he saw, in the second half of the play Palaestrio relies on the soldier's conceit about the way women look at him for the success of this deception. In the first half of the play, Palaestrio's trickery transformed one woman into two women. In the second half, Palaestrio will create a woman so alluring that the soldier will give up Philocomasium before he has even seen the other woman. First, Palaestrio tells the soldier that this new woman loves him more than she loves her own eyes (984), which is to say her own life. When the prostitute's maid, Milphidippa, enters, the soldier is immediately impressed with Milphidippa's looks, but Palaestrio tells him that the beauty of her mistress is even greater. While Palaestrio is manipulating the soldier's eyes, Milphidippa also uses her eyes to great advantage, and Palaestrio observes that she is becoming a hunter with her eyes and a bird catcher with her ears (990). Additionally, when Milphidippa enters she alters her eyesight as she pretends not to see her intended audience, the soldier (992). So convinced is the soldier of the beauty of a woman he has not seen that Palaestrio marvels that the soldier can have feelings for a woman he has not yet seen with his eyes (1005).

Palaestrio and Milphidippa so manipulate the soldier that he agrees to send Philocomasium away before he has seen Acroteleutium. Palaestrio convinces the soldier that Philocomasium will be safe because her mother and twin sister are at the harbor waiting to take her home. Palaestrio tells the soldier that he has seen the twin with his own eyes (1104) but says the mother remained aboard the ship because of problems with her eyes (1108). In keeping with the theme of faulty eyesight, when Palaestrio instructs Pleusicles how to

dress as a ship's captain, he tells him to wear a patch over his eye (1178).

When Acroteleutium finally arrives on the scene, Milphidippa instructs her mistress to pretend that they do not see the soldier (1217). As the women flatter the soldier, the unwitting spectator is further drawn into Palaestrio's play. Acroteleutium worries that the soldier's eyes may change his mind when he sees her (1234), because she may not be beautiful enough. Amusingly, when Acroteleutium pretends that she has caught the soldier's scent, the soldier remarks that her nose is keener than her eyesight. Hearing this, Palaestrio quips, "She is blinded by love" (1259). When Acroteleutium pretends that she has finally seen the soldier, she claims she is going to faint because of what her eyes have seen (1261). What Acroteleutium has seen also affects her speech. Initially, she remains silent and Milphidippa explains to the soldier that her "eyes have cut off her tongue" (1271). Soon, the soldier is completely under Acroteleutium's spell and the prostitute has no trouble in convincing him that her eyes have been affected by his looks.

Interestingly, when the disguised Pleusicles enters to retrieve Philocomasium, the soldier immediately asks Pleusicles about what happened to his eye (1306). The soldier's interest in Pleusicles' falsely impaired sight makes one think of Jesus' question in the New Testament "Why do you see the speck in your neighbor's eye, but you do not see the beam in your own eye?" The soldier, whose perception of himself and his situation is completely warped, is immediately drawn to the false patch that covers Pleusicles' properly functioning eye. Even more amusing is Pleusicles' response to the soldier's question, literally, "By Hercules, because of the sea I do not use this eye; for if I had abstained from love, I would also use this one." Of course, the soldier thinks that Pleusicles means that if it were not for his love of the sea, then his eyesight would not be impaired. The audience, however, realize that Pleusicles means that if it were not for his love of Philocomasium, he would not have to disguise himself in such a way.

When Philocomasium finally emerges from the house and moves toward the harbor, she too distorts her eyes as she pretends to weep over leaving the soldier. The soldier tells her not to cry, but she says she cannot stop crying when she looks at him (1324–25). In keeping with the theme of eyesight, as Philocomasium continues to bid farewell to the soldier, she addresses him as, literally, "my eye, my soul" (once again *eye* is used in the sense of "life"). Eventually, Philocomasium and Pleusicles begin to move off, and she pretends to faint, thus allowing Pleusicles to catch her and steal a quick kiss. As did his slave earlier in the play, the soldier now sees Pleusicles kissing Philocomasium, but Pleusicles quickly makes up an excuse so that the soldier will not think he has seen what he thinks he has seen. Thus, Philocomasium leaves one man whose vision is warped by conceit for a man whose vision has been altered in accordance with the instructions of the slave-playwright Palaestrio. The soldier soon discovers that Acroteleutium is a false vision with which Palaestrio has tempted his eyes and that the man who had the patch over his left eye (1430) was actually Philocomasium's lover. When the soldier asks how his slave knows this, the slave fittingly reports that he saw them kissing and hugging (1432–33). To which the soldier responds, "I see [*video*] that I have been tricked" (1434). Finally, no one will contest the sight of Philocomasium and Pleusicles' kissing.

BIBLIOGRAPHY

Frangoulidis, Stavros A. "Palaestrio as Playwright." In *Studies in Latin Literature and Roman History*. Vol. 7. Edited by C. Deroux. Bruxelles: Latomus, 1994, 72–86.

Hammond, M., A. M. Mack, and W. Moskalew. *T. Macci Plauti. Miles Gloriosus.* Revised by M. Hammond. Cambridge, Mass.: Harvard University Press, 1997.

Leach, E. W. "The Soldier and Society: Plautus' *Miles Gloriosus* as Popular Drama," *Rivista di Studi Classici* 27 (1979): 185–209.

Lefèvre, E. "Plautus-Studien IV: Die Umformung des ALAZON zu der DoppelKomödie des *Miles Gloriosus,*" *Hermes* 112 (1984): 30–53.

Saylor, C. F. "Periplectomenus and the Organization of the *Miles Gloriosus,*" *Eranos* 75 (1977): 1–13.

BRASIDAS   The son of Tellis, Brasidas was a successful general of SPARTA during the first decade of the PELOPONNESIAN WAR, when the Athenians considered him the leading warmonger of the Spartans. Brasidas died fighting against the Athenians at the battle of Amphipolis in 422 B.C.E. (a battle that the Spartans won). [ANCIENT SOURCES: Aristophanes, *Wasps* 475, *Peace* 274–84; Thucydides, 2.25–5.18]

BRAURON   A town about 15 miles east of ATHENS. Brauron was an important center for the worship of ARTEMIS, and a feast (called the Brauronia) devoted to the goddess was held there every four years. [ANCIENT SOURCES: Aristophanes, *Lysistrata* 645, *Peace* 874; Euripides, *Iphigenia in Tauris* 1463]

BIBLIOGRAPHY

Antoniou, A. *Brauron.* Athina: Kardamitsa, 1990.

Lloyd-Jones, H. "Artemis and Iphigeneia," *Journal of Hellenic Studies* 103 (1983): 87–102.

Parke, H. W. *Festivals of the Athenians.* Ithaca, N.Y.: Cornell University Press, 1977, 139–40.

BRIAREUS   One of the three 100-handed creatures who were the children of URANUS and Gaia (see EARTH). SENECA includes him among the GIANTS who tried to overthrow the Olympian gods. [ANCIENT SOURCES: Apollodorus, *Library* 1.1.1; Homer, *Iliad* 1.404; Seneca, *Hercules Oetaeus* 167]

BRISEIS   The daughter of Briseus, Briseis (also called Hippodameia) was captured by the Greeks during the Trojan War. She became the war prize of ACHILLES but was taken from him by AGAMEMNON during the 10th year of the war because of a quarrel between the two men. After the quarrel ended, Agamemnon restored Briseis to Achilles. [ANCIENT SOURCES: Homer, *Iliad* 1, 9, 18; Ovid, *Heroides* 3; Seneca, *Trojan Women* 194, 220, 318]

BRITOMARTIS   See Artemis.

BRITTANICUS (FEBRUARY 12, 44–55 C.E.) The son of the Roman emperor CLAUDIUS and MESSALINA, Tiberius Claudius Brittanicus Caesar was in line to become emperor of Rome, but his stepmother, AGRIPPINA, persuaded Claudius to promote her own son, NERO, instead. Britannicus died in 55, probably of poisoning arranged by Nero. [ANCIENT SOURCES: Seneca,

Octavia 47, 67, 166, 242, 269; Suetonius, *Claudius, Nero;* Tacitus, *Annals* 11–14.3]

BROMIUS See DIONYSUS.

BRONTEION A device used for making the sound of thunder. Pollux says the *bronteion* was a bag of pebbles that were rolled into copper pots behind the stage. [ANCIENT SOURCES: Pollux, *Onomasticon* 4.127, 130]

THE BROTHERS (Greek: *ADELPHOI*) TERENCE (160 B.C.E.) Staged at the funeral games of Aemilius Paullus, TERENCE's sixth and final play was based on a Greek original by MENANDER entitled *Adelphoi*. The play's setting is ATHENS, and the action occurs before two houses, one belonging to Micio, an elderly Athenian citizen, the other belonging to Sostrata, the mother of Pamphila. In the prologue, the speaker defends Terence against the charge of using in *Brothers* a scene that PLAUTUS deleted from one of his plays. The prologue's speaker also mentions, but does not deny, the accusation that members of the nobility assist Terence in the writing of his plays.

In the opening act, Micio emerges from his house searching for Aeschinus (his nephew and his son by adoption from his brother, Demea). Aeschinus has not returned home from a party the previous night, and Micio worries that something has happened to the young man. Micio explains that he himself is an unmarried easygoing city fellow, whereas his brother, Demea, is married and strict and lives in the country. Micio explains that he adopted Demea's elder son, Aeschinus, and raised him in the city. Micio admits that he has not been strict with Aeschinus and claims that he therefore has created a bond of friendship and trust with Aeschinus. Demea, however, does not approve of such a lax approach and Micio is ruining the boy.

Soon, Demea himself approaches and tells Micio that Aeschinus has recently broken down the door of someone's house and stolen a girl. Micio dismisses Aeschinus' actions as typical youthful behavior. Micio tells Demea that Aeschinus is his (Micio's) responsibility and that any wrong he does reflects on Micio.

Micio's casual attitude angers Demea, who storms off to his house in the country. After Demea leaves, Micio states that Aeschinus' behavior does trouble him but says that he did not want to admit this to his brother. Micio then sets out for the FORUM to find Aeschinus.

The play's second act begins with the entrance of a PIMP, Sannio, who is calling upon the citizens to help him against Aeschinus, the kidnapper of Bacchis, one of his girls (Aeschinus has stolen her for his brother). Sannio threatens to take Aeschinus to court, but the young man ignores him and, with the help of his slave, Parmeno, begins to take Bacchis into Micio's house. Sannio tries to drag Bacchis away, but Aeschinus tells Parmeno to strike Sannio and Bacchis eventually is taken into Micio's house. Aeschinus tells Sannio that he will pay him the same price that he paid for her but declares that Sannio has no right to sell someone who was born free. After Aeschinus exits into Micio's house, Sannio says he is willing to accept the price he paid for Bacchis but worries that he will not be paid anything. Next, Syrus, another of Aeschinus' slaves, arrives from the house and tells Sannio not to worry so much about the money for one woman, especially since Sannio has several women that he intends to sell on the island of Cyprus. Sannio, realizing that he will miss his business opportunity on Cyprus if he does not settle the matter quickly with Aeschinus, urges Syrus to try to arrange some payment with Aeschinus. As Syrus and Sannio are talking, Demea's son, Ctesipho, enters and praises his brother, Aeschinus, for his help. Soon, Aeschinus enters, informs Ctesipho that Bacchis is waiting for him inside, and says that he and Syrus will go to make sure Sannio receives his money.

In the third act, Sostrata and a nurse, Canthara, enter. Their conversation reveals that Sostrata's daughter, Pamphila, who was raped, is about to have a baby. The women hope that Aeschinus, who is in love with Pamphila and wants to marry her, will come to their house. Next, Sostrata's slave, Geta, enters. Sostrata and Canthara eavesdrop as Geta complains that Aeschinus has betrayed them and fallen in love with Bacchis. Geta is wrong about this, but he saw Aeschinus carry off Bacchis from Sannio's house, so he assumes the worst. Sostrata is upset at this news and tells Geta to inform her relative, Hegio, about Aeschinus' behavior. Sostrata also sends Canthara to find a midwife to help Pamphila deliver her baby.

After Geta and the women exit, an angry Demea enters. He has heard that his son, Ctesipho, was involved in the abduction of Bacchis. When Demea sees Syrus approaching, the old man eavesdrops on the slave. Demea listens as Syrus explains that Aeschinus told Micio about Bacchis, that Micio handed over the money to pay for Bacchis, and that he even gave them some money to spend on supplies for a party. An enraged Demea then emerges, addresses Syrus, and criticizes Micio for his extravagant mode of life. Demea is horrified to learn that Micio intends to allow Bacchis to remain in his house. When Demea asks about Ctesipho, Syrus lies; he tells him that he saw Ctesipho at Demea's farm in the country. Syrus lies again, telling Demea that Ctesipho criticized Aeschinus for abducting Bacchis. Demea expresses his pride in his son when he hears this and attributes Ctesipho's behavior to his strict upbringing. After listening to Demea's self-congratulations, Syrus excuses himself to tend to his duties in the house.

After Syrus' departure, Sostrata's relative, Hegio, approaches with Geta. Hegio expresses his outrage about Aeschinus' behavior and indicates that he intends to help Sostrata and her family. When Demea greets Hegio, Hegio informs him that Aeschinus has raped and impregnated Pamphila and then abandoned her for the music girl-prostitute Bacchis. Demea is shocked by Aeschinus' behavior and promises to speak to Micio about the young man. Hegio, satisfied by Demea, enters Sostrata's house, where the cries of Pamphila, who is in labor, can be heard. Demea exits toward the forum to tell Micio what he has heard.

In the fourth act, Syrus informs Ctesipho that his father has gone to the country. Ctesipho also tries to find some excuse to stay at Micio's house. Suddenly, however, Syrus and Ctesipho see Demea, who is approaching. Syrus tells Ctesipho to hide and says he will take care of Demea. Syrus and Ctesipho eavesdrop as Demea expresses his frustration that he cannot find Micio and that he has also learned that Ctesipho is not at the farm. Ctesipho, worried that his father may find him, begs Syrus to help him and then exits into the house. When Demea approaches Micio's house, Syrus

pretends that Ctesipho has beaten him and has claimed that the purchase of the music girl was Syrus' fault. Demea is delighted by Ctesipho's behavior and asks Syrus whether Micio is at home. Syrus gives Demea false, lengthy, and impossibly complicated directions to Micio's location. After Demea sets out, Syrus reenters Micio's house to enjoy the party.

Next, Micio enters with Hegio; he tells Hegio that he will help smooth over the misunderstanding about Aeschinus and Bacchis, and the two men exit into Sostrata's house. Soon, Aeschinus enters from the forum, worried because his most recent effort to see how Pamphila was doing has been refused. Aeschinus realizes that the women suspect that he is having an affair with Bacchis, but he does not want to reveal his brother, Ctesipho's, secret. Aeschinus decides that he must resolve this problem and goes to Sostrata's house. Just as Aeschinus knocks on the door, his adoptive father, Micio, emerges. Micio, realizing that Aeschinus is on the verge of confessing his mistakes, decides to tease his son by pretending that Pamphila is going to marry one of her relatives and live with him in Miletus. When Aeschinus hears this, he begins to cry. Micio then tells Aeschinus that he knows the truth, and he tells Aeschinus that he has arranged for him to marry Pamphila.

After Micio and a joyful Aeschinus exit into their house to prepare for the wedding, Demea, exhausted from searching for Micio, enters and announces his intention to wait for Micio. When Micio emerges from his house, Demea immediately complains to him about Aeschinus' behavior. Micio tells his brother that he knows everything and that Aeschinus will marry Pamphila. Demea is outraged by the purchase of the music girl and is more appalled when he hears that she and Pamphila will both live under Micio's roof. Micio, however, tells Demea to control his temper and prepare to celebrate Aeschinus' marriage.

The play's final act begins with the appearance of an intoxicated Syrus, who encounters Demea. When another slave, Dromo, opens the door and tells Syrus that Ctesipho wants him to go back inside, Demea hears and forces his way into Micio's house. Next, Micio, followed by Demea, emerges from the house. Demea demands to know what Ctesipho is doing at Micio's house and why Micio bought Bacchis for Ctesipho.

Micio defends his actions, but Demea worries that Micio's carefree attitude will ruin the youths. Demea declares that he will take Ctesipho and Bacchis to the farm the next day and will give Bacchis difficult chores.

After Micio reenters the house, Demea expresses his desire to be easygoing and loved as Micio is. Demea decides that if being loved results from being easygoing and free with his money, then he will do that. Accordingly, Demea begins by acting friendly to the slaves he encounters, Syrus and Geta. Next, Aeschinus, anxious to get the wedding under way, arrives from the house. Demea urges him to knock down the wall that separates Micio and Sostrata's houses and put Pamphila's entire household under Micio's roof. Aeschinus is delighted by this idea and Demea is delighted by the annoyance it will cause Micio. Demea then orders Syrus to knock down the wall and Geta to fetch Sostrata and her household.

When Micio hears what is happening, he goes out and confronts Demea, who argues that this uniting of the two families is the proper thing to do. Furthermore, Demea suggests that Micio should marry Pamphila's mother. The bachelor Micio is horrified by this suggestion, but Aeschinus urges him to marry Sostrata. After Micio agrees to the marriage proposal, Demea suggests that Micio do something nice for Sostrata's kinsman, Hegio, namely, give him a plot of land that Micio owns. Again, Micio agrees, egged on by Aeschinus' begging. Next, Demea suggests that Syrus be given his freedom. When Aeschinus indicates his approval, Micio frees Syrus. Additionally, when Syrus expresses the desire that his wife be freed as well, Micio is compelled to free her. Demea also arranges for Micio to give Syrus some money so that he can support himself as a freedman. When Micio asks Demea why he is behaving so generously, Demea says that it is to teach Micio a lesson. Aeschinus agrees that Demea knows what is in his sons' best interest. The play ends as Demea declares that Ctesipho may keep Bacchis, but that she must be his last such indulgence.

COMMENTARY

Brothers is considered Terence's best play and one of the finest ancient comedies. The primary issue in *Brothers* is how the respective characters and parenting styles of the two brothers will affect the two sons. Demea has been strict with Ctesipho, who has rewarded his father by deceiving him and by having a secret love affair. Micio has not been strict with Aeschinus, who has been honest with his father. Although Micio's style of parenting initially appears to be superior, at the play's conclusion Demea exposes the weaknesses of being too liberal with one's children. Clearly, a style of parenting between the two extremes is needed.

Duckworth classifies *Brothers* as one of five extant Roman comedies (see also POT OF GOLD, STICHUS, THREE-DOLLAR DAY, and TRUCULENTUS) that focus on character. One may pass over comparison with *Stichus,* because this play bears little resemblance to anything else in Roman COMEDY. The no-nonsense Demea has some similarity to Euclio in *Pot of Gold,* but the grouchy Euclio is more concerned about his pot of gold than about his pregnant daughter. Demea is concerned with the behavior of his sons. *Three-Dollar Day* is similar to *Brothers* in that both plays are about young men who are engaged in riotous living and who are under the care of men who are not their biological father. Unlike Lesbonicus in *Three-Dollar Day,* Aeschinus has not squandered his fortune, and therefore the young men have entirely different problems. As for *Truculentus,* the young Diniarchus is somewhat like Ctesipho in that both men have had sexual relations with freeborn women and eventually are allowed to stay with them. As *Brothers* does, *Truculentus* also features a "country" boy who is in love with a woman of slave status and who ultimately will enjoy her favors. The young men in *Truculentus* are not brothers, however, and the fathers of the young men are relegated to the background.

Although *Brothers* shares some common ground with these plays, this play is most similar to Terence's own SELF-TORMENTOR, which appeared three years earlier. In both plays, the two sons are involved in love affairs, one with a freeborn woman, the other with a slave. Both plays focus on the relationship between two fathers and two sons. As in *Brothers,* one of the fathers is strict with his son and the other is more lenient. In *Self-Tormentor,* however, the strict father has repented of his earlier behavior at the beginning of the play, whereas in *Brothers* the strict father modifies his attitude at the end of the play. Also, in *Self-Tormentor* the more lenient father tries to prevent the more strict father from becoming overly indulgent with his sons. Ultimately, as in *Brothers,* the more lenient father in *Self-Tormentor* discovers that his son has been deceiving him. In both plays, the son of the more strict father will marry the freeborn woman; however, whereas in *Brothers* the son of the more indulgent father will be allowed to keep his slave-concubine, in *Self-Tormentor* the son of the more indulgent father must also marry a freeborn woman. Both *Self-Tormentor* and *Brothers* have the message that fathers must seek a middle ground in dealing with sons. One major difference between the two plays, as indicated in the title of the later play, is the concept of brotherhood. In *Self-Tormentor,* the two young men and the two older men are friends and neighbors, but not brothers. In the later play, the brotherhood of Aeschinus and Ctesipho, and Demea and Micio, creates a more complex dynamic. Demea is concerned about his brother and his two sons. Aeschinus is concerned about the feelings of his father, brother, future wife, and future mother-in-law.

In addition to the complexities of two sets of brothers, other major differences between *Self-Tormentor* and *Brothers* occur in the roles of the slave Syrus, the young man Aeschinus, and the fathers. The Syrus in *Self-Tormentor* spends much of the play trying to acquire money so that the young man Clitipho can carry on his love affair. The Syrus in *Brothers* does not attempt to orchestrate deception but aids Aeschinus in dealing with the pimp and misdirects Demea by telling him that Ctesipho is in the country and then sending him on a wild search for Micio. In *Brothers,* Syrus is given his freedom; in *Self-Tormentor,* Syrus is merely pardoned for his mischief.

In *Brothers,* we find no such scheming as in *Self-Tormentor,* but two instances of misdirection from Syrus and force from Aeschinus. Aeschinus' high level of activity in the second act is unusual for Roman comedy in that the young male citizen does not ordinarily take charge in the pursuit of his love affairs. Typically, the young man sits back while his slave does the work for him. Aeschinus, however, is vigorous in helping his brother's love affair succeed. Aeschinus appears rather

violent as he breaks into the pimp's house, steals the woman, and then forcefully drives off the pimp. Although Aeschinus appears to be a rather tough character with respect to his brother's affair, he behaves in a much milder fashion about his own affair. He keeps his word about his intention to marry Pamphila, he shows concern for the distress he is causing Sostrata and Pamphila, and he tells them the truth despite the difficulties doing so will cause for his brother. He also tells his father the truth after bursting into tears. Indeed, in the fourth act, Aeschinus appears very different from the young man who smashed his way into a pimp's house and abducted a woman.

As for the fathers, in *Self-Tormentor,* Chremes schemes with his contemporary, Menedemus, to fund his son's love affair. In *Brothers,* neither Demea nor Micio takes this sort of role in his son's love affairs. Not only are Demea and Micio separated by educational philosophy, they are also separated physically during most of the middle three acts of the play. In *Brothers,* the fathers' educational philosophy regarding their sons is established in the opening act and then the audience witnesses how the sons behave. In *Self-Tormentor,* the sons are largely kept occupied with their women offstage, while Syrus and Chremes are busying forming plots onstage. *Self-Tormentor* is, as its name indicates, rather tormenting for the audience, because the plots that Syrus and Chremes have spent most of the play concocting have little direct role in the final resolution. The conclusion of *Brothers* is imminently more satisfying, as Demea's reversal of behavior allows him to have the last laugh. He gives away property, frees slaves, and arranges marriages. Demea has gone from playing the angry old man to playing the indulgent old man—and all at his brother's expense.

BIBLIOGRAPHY

Fantham, E. "*Hautontimoroumenos* and *Adelphoe:* A Study of Fatherhood in Terence and Menander," *Latomus* 30 (1971): 970–98.

Goldberg, S. M. *Understanding Terence.* Princeton, N.J.: Princeton University Press, 1986, 22–29, 97–105, 211–16.

Grant, J. N. "The Ending of Terence's *Adelphoe* and the Menandrian Original," *American Journal of Philology* 96 (1975): 42–60.

Gratwick, A. S. *Terence: The Brothers.* 2d ed. Warminster, U.K.: Aris & Phillips, 2000.

Johnson, W. R. "Micio and the Perils of Perfection," *California Studies in Classical Antiquity* 1 (1968): 171–86.

Lord, C. "Aristotle, Menander, and the *Adelphoe* of Terence," *Transactions of the American Philological Association* 107 (1977): 183–202.

Martin, R. H. *Terence: Adelphoe.* Cambridge and New York: Cambridge University Press, 1976.

BRUTTIUM   The region that occupies the "toe" of Italy's "boot." [ANCIENT SOURCES: Seneca, *Hercules Oetaeus* 651, *Thyestes* 578]

BRUTUS (CA. 85–OCTOBER 42 B.C.E.)   Marcus Iunius Brutus was one of the principal assassins of JULIUS CAESAR. Although Brutus fought against Caesar in his war with Pompey in the early 40s, Caesar pardoned him. In 46, Brutus governed the Roman province of Cisalpine Gaul and two years he later participated in the plot to kill Caesar. After this, civil war broke out between the assassins and their supporters and those who favored Caesar, who were led by Marcus ANTONIUS and Octavian (the future emperor AUGUSTUS). The final showdown between the two armies occurred at Philippi (northeastern Greece) on October 23, 42. Brutus' forces were defeated and Brutus committed suicide after the battle. [ANCIENT SOURCES: Appian, *Civil Wars* 2–4; Cicero, *Brutus, Letters, Phillipics;* Plutarch, *Marcus Brutus, Comparison of Brutus and Dion;* Seneca, *Octavia* 498; Suetonius, *Julius Caesar* 49–85]

BIBLIOGRAPHY
Clarke, M. L. *The Noblest Roman: Marcus Brutus and his Reputation.* London: Thames & Hudson, 1981.

Radin, M. *Marcus Brutus.* New York and London: Oxford University Press, 1939.

Syme, R. *The Roman Revolution.* London: Oxford University Press, 1962.

BUPALUS   The son of Archermus, Bupalus was a sculptor from the island of CHIOS. Bupalus' statue of Hipponax, a writer of iambic verse, led to his being attacked in Hipponax's writings. [ANCIENT SOURCES: Aristophanes, *Lysistrata* 361]

BIBLIOGRAPHY
Henderson, J. *Aristophanes: Lysistrata.* Oxford: Clarendon Press, 1987, 113.

BUSIRIS   A son of POSEIDON and Lysianassa (or Anippe), Busiris was a mythical king of Egypt. When Egypt experienced famine for nine years, a certain prophet stated that the famine would end if every year the Egyptians sacrificed a stranger to ZEUS. Busiris began by sacrificing the prophet himself and continued to sacrifice strangers who traveled to his land. Eventually, HERACLES arrived in Busiris' kingdom, was captured, and was prepared for sacrifice. Heracles, however, escaped and killed Busiris; his son, Amphidamas (or Iphidamas); and Busiris' attendants at the sacrifice.

EURIPIDES wrote a satyric *Busiris* of which three brief fragments survive. In fragment 312a (Snell), a person named LAMIA may be the speaker. Two women named Lamia are known from mythology. Two sources mention a Libyan Lamia, the daughter of Poseidon and the first woman to chant oracles. The better known Lamia, also from Libya, was the daughter of Belus. Zeus had an affair with her that HERA discovered. Hera took Lamia's children away from her, causing Lamia to become insane and begin to kill other children. It is unknown how Euripides might have integrated the story of Lamia with that of Busiris.

Several comic poets wrote plays entitled *Busiris.* Only the title survives from the younger Cratinus' play and a single, uninformative line remains from the elder Cratinus' *Busiris* (fragment 21 Kock 1). In the single fragment of Mnesimachus' *Busiris* Heracles is the speaker and notes his substantial appetite (fragment 2 Kock 2). In the lone fragment from Ephippus' *Busiris,* Heracles identifies himself as being an Argive and says that Argive men fight all their battles while drunk (fragment 2 Kock 2). Antiphanes also wrote a *Busiris,* whose fragments are too brief to provide information about the play's content (fragments 65–67 Kock 2). [ANCIENT SOURCES: Apollodorus, *Library* 2.5.11; Isocrates, *Speeches and Letters* 11; Scholiast on Apollonius Rhodius, *Argonautica* 4.1396; Seneca, *Hercules Furens* 483, *Hercules Oetaeus* 26, 1787, *Trojan Women* 1106]

BIBLIOGRAPHY

Kock, T. *Comicorum Atticorum Fragmenta.* Vol. 1. Leipzig: Teubner, 1880.

———. *Comicorum Atticorum Fragmenta.* Vol. 2. Leipzig: Teubner, 1884.

Nauck, A. *Tragicorum Graecorum Fragmenta.* 1889. Reprint, Hildesheim, Ger.: Olms, 1964.

Snell, B. *Tragicorum Graecorum Fragmenta:* Supplementum. Hildesheim, Ger.: Olms, 1964.

BUSKIN   A boot (as high as the calf) worn by actors in TRAGEDY, although perhaps not during the fifth century B.C.E. Henderson says this boot "fitted either foot and was worn mainly by women." The comic poet Philonides, who produced three of ARISTOPHANES' plays, staged a *Buskins* (Greek: *Kothornoi*), of which a few fragments survive (1–6 Kock). The Roman term for this boot is *Soccus* (plural: *socci*). [ANCIENT SOURCES: Aristophanes, *Frogs* 47, 557, *Lysistrata* 657; Herodotus, 1.155, 6.125]

BIBLIOGRAPHY

Dover, Kenneth. *Aristophanes: Frogs.* Oxford: Clarendon Press, 1993, 195.

Henderson, J. *Aristophanes: Lysistrata.* Oxford: Clarendon Press, 1987, 158.

Kock, T. *Comicorum Atticorum Fragmenta.* Vol. 1. Leipzig: Teubner, 1880.

BYBLINE MOUNTAINS   A mountain range through which the NILE flows in Africa. [ANCIENT SOURCES: Aeschylus, *Prometheus Bound* 811]

BYRSINE   A pseudonym for Myrsine or Myrrhine, the wife of the Athenian tyrant HIPPIAS. [ANCIENT SOURCES: Aristophanes, *Knights* 449]

BIBLIOGRAPHY

Sommerstein, A. H. *The Comedies of Aristophanes.* Vol. 2, *Knights.* Warminster, U.K.: Aris & Phillips, 1981, 167–68.

BYZANTIUM   A famous city on the European side of the strait that guards the southern entrance to the Black Sea. In 478 B.C.E., a coalition of Greeks under the command of the Spartan Pausanias retook the city from the Persians. The Greek comic poet Antiphanes wrote a play called *Byzantios* (The Byzantine man), of which three words survive (69 Kock). [ANCIENT SOURCES: Aristophanes, *Clouds* 249, *Wasps* 236; Thucydides 1.94.2, 1.131.1]

BIBLIOGRAPHY

Kock, T. *Comicorum Atticorum Fragmenta.* Vol. 2. Leipzig: Teubner, 1884.

C

CABEIRI Four divinities worshipped by the Pelasgians. The name Cabeiri usually referred to HADES, DEMETER, PERSEPHONE, and HERMES, and as with the Greek worship of Demeter and Persephone, one could be initiated into the MYSTERIES of the Cabeiri. Initiation into these mysteries "was supposed to be a guarantee that the initiate's prayers would be answered, especially when he was in danger at sea" (Sommerstein). The worship of the Cabeiri was prominent in the islands of the northern AEGEAN, especially on Imbros, LEMNOS, and SAMOTHRACE. [ANCIENT SOURCES: Apollonius Rhodius, 1.916–21; Aristophanes, *Peace* 277; Herodotus, 2.51]

BIBLIOGRAPHY
Sommerstein, A. H. *The Comedies of Aristophanes.* Vol. 5, *Peace.* Warminster, U.K.: Aris & Philips, 1985, 145–46.

CADMEIDES The daughters of CADMUS. [ANCIENT SOURCES: Seneca, *Hercules Furens* 758]

CADMUS (KADMOS) The son of AGENOR and Argiope, Cadmus was originally from the region near Tyre and Sidon. After the abduction of his sister, EUROPA, by ZEUS, Cadmus went in search of her. He eventually made his way to Greece and the DELPHIC ORACLE, who told him not to continue his search for Europa, but to found a town on the spot where he saw a certain cow rest. After departing from the oracle, Cadmus saw the cow, followed it, and founded the town that would eventually become THEBES on the spot

where it lay down. After a serpent that guarded a nearby spring killed some of Cadmus' men, Cadmus killed it. As Cadmus stood marveling at the dead creature, ATHENA appeared and ordered Cadmus to plant half of the serpent's teeth in the ground. When Cadmus did so, a crop of armed warriors sprang up. On Athena's advice, Cadmus threw a rock at the warriors. The warriors, accusing each other of having thrown the rock, began to fight among themselves. All the warriors, with the exception of five, died. The survivors helped Cadmus establish his new town. Because the serpent was sacred to ARES, Cadmus had to atone to the war god for his actions. After Cadmus had atoned for the serpent's death, Ares married his daughter HARMONIA to him. They had four daughters (INO, SEMELE, AGAVE, AUTONOE) and a son (Polydorus). After the disaster involving PENTHEUS, Cadmus and Harmonia were exiled from Thebes and traveled to Illyria, where they ruled over a tribe called the Encheleans and led them to victory in several wars. The Encheleans lost favor with Apollo, however, because they raided some of his shrines. The Encheleans began to be unsuccessful in war, and Ares turned Cadmus and Harmonia into serpents.

Cadmus is frequently mentioned in ancient drama but appears as a character in only one surviving play—EURIPIDES' *BACCHAE.* In that play, Cadmus is characterized as the aged former Theban king, who is willing to accept the worship of DIONYSUS. At the end of *Bacchae,* however, Dionysus announces that Cadmus and his wife must go into exile and will eventually be turned into serpents. Euripides may have written a play titled *Cadmus,* from which three lines survive (fragment 448 Nauck). Webster is convinced the fragment is a forgery. [ANCIENT SOURCES: Hyginus, *Fables* 6; Ovid, *Metamorphoses* 3.1–137, 4.563–603; Seneca, *Oedipus* 712, *Hercules Furens* 261, 392, 917, *Phoenician Women* 125, 644]

BIBLIOGRAPHY
Devereux, G. "The Psychotherapy Scene in Euripides' *Bacchae,*" *Journal of Hellenic Studies* 90 (1970): 35–48.
Nauck, A. *Tragicorum Graecorum Fragmenta.* 1889. Reprint, Hildesheim, Ger.: Olms, 1964.
Webster, T. B. L. *The Tragedies of Euripides.* London: Methuen, 1967.

CAECIAS

A name for a wind from the northeast. The Paphlagonian (CLEON) is compared to such a wind in ARISTOPHANES' *KNIGHTS* (437).

CAECILIUS (DIED 168 B.C.E.)

As TERENCE was, Caecilius, who was born in Gaul, was taken to Rome as a slave (perhaps around the year 223 or 222) and became a writer of comedies that were adapted from Greek comic poets such as MENANDER. Some ancient critics ranked Caecilius ahead of Terence in skill, and Caecilius is said to have listened to Terence's *ANDRIA* and to have had a positive opinion of it. Because *Andria* was not produced until two years after Caecilius' death, this story has been doubted.

None of Caecilius' plays has survived intact, but some 280 lines exist and 42 titles are known. About a third of these titles indicate that Caecilius drew on Menander as his model. The most extensive fragments in Caecilius are from his *Plocium* (The little necklace), which was based on a Menandrian play of the same name. The 45 lines that survive show that the play dealt with a young man and woman who planned to get married. The woman, however, was pregnant and gave birth to a child. The young man's mother thought her husband was the culprit, and the young man's paternity was proved by means of a necklace. [ANCIENT SOURCES: Cicero, *Letters to Atticus* 7.3; Horace, *Epistles* 2.1.59; Quintilian, 10.1.99; Suetonius, *De Poetis* 11.27–34; Terence, *Mother-in-Law* 9–27; Volcacius Sedigitus, fragment 1.5]

BIBLIOGRAPHY
Ooms, C. W. "Studies on the Language of Caecilius Statius." Dissertation, University of Minnesota, 1977.
Warmington, E. H. *Remains of Old Latin: Ennius and Caecilius.* Vol. 1. Cambridge, Mass., and London: Harvard University Press, 1935.

CAENEUS

Caeneus was born a woman of the Lapith tribe, but after POSEIDON had sexual intercourse with her, she asked him to make her an invulnerable male. Poseidon granted her request, and when THESEUS and PIRITHOUS battled the centaurs, Caeneus was uninjured by those who struck him and killed numerous centaurs. He died, however, when some surviving centaurs surrounded him and buried him beneath a pile of fir trees and rocks, which caused him to suffocate.

Two Greek comic poets, Antiphanes (fragment 112 Kock) and Araros (fragments 4–7 Kock), wrote plays entitled *Caeneus.* The fragment from Antiphanes refers to the famous drinking cup of NESTOR. Araros fragment 4 refers to a maiden who may be Caeneus, for the speaker of the fragment appears to be surprised that the person is wearing women's clothing; fragment 5 ("your daughter, when he cut her with [his] axe") may be a reference to Poseidon's intercourse with Caeneus as the verb here is used in an obscene sense. The other two fragments from Araros' *Caenus* provide little insight into the play's content. [ANCIENT SOURCES: Apollodorus, *Epitome* 1.22; Hyginus, *Fables* 14; Ovid, *Metamorphoses* 12.459–532]

BIBLIOGRAPHY
Kock, T. *Comicorum Atticorum Fragmenta.* Vol. 2. Leipzig: Teubner, 1884.

CAESAR, GAIUS JULIUS (100–MARCH 15, 44 B.C.E.)

The son of Gaius Caesar and Aurelia, Julius Caesar rose to prominence in Rome in the 50s by his conquests when he was a governor of the provinces of Cisalpine Gaul and Transalpine Gaul. The Roman Senate became fearful of Caesar's power and on January 1, 49, voted that he should give up his command. Caesar refused and with his armies intact crossed the Rubicon River in northern Italy. This hostile action caused a civil war to break out between the forces of Caesar and Pompey, who had been married to

Caesar's daughter, Julia (who died in 54). By 48, Caesar had defeated Pompey's forces in Egypt (Pompey was also killed), where Caesar's mistress, Cleopatra, had been firmly installed in her position by Caesar. Although Pompey was dead, Caesar continued to face military resistance from pro-Pompeian forces and he continued to fight until 45 B.C.E., when he finally defeated Pompey's sons and his own former legate, Titus Labienus. In the early 40s, the Roman Senate had appointed Caesar to a series of temporary dictatorships; in 44 they made him dictator for life. Caesar's life, however, did not last long: He was assassinated by political rivals (led by BRUTUS and Cassius) on March 15, 44. In 45, Caesar adopted his nephew, Octavian (see AUGUSTUS), as his heir. Octavian went on to avenge Caesar's assassination and eventually became emperor of Rome. [ANCIENT SOURCES: Anonymous, *Bellum Africum, Bellum Alexandrinum, Bellum Hispaniense;* Caesar, *Bellum Gallicum, Bellum Civile;* Lucan, *Bellum Civile;* Seneca, *Octavia* 500; Plutarch, *Caesar;* Suetonius, *Augustus, Caesar*]

BIBLIOGRAPHY
Adcock, F. E. *Caesar, as Man of Letters.* Cambridge: Cambridge University Press, 1956.
Balsdon, J. P. V. D. *Julius Caesar: A Political Biography.* New York, Atheneum, 1967.
Grant, M. *Julius Caesar.* London: Weidenfeld & Nicolson, 1969.
Holmes, T. Rice. *The Roman Republic and the Founder of the Empire.* New York: Russell & Russell, 1923.
Yavetz, Z. *Julius Caesar and His Public Image.* Ithaca, N.Y.: Cornell University Press, 1983.

CALAIS   A son of BOREAS and the brother of ZETES.

CALCHAS   The son of Thestor, Calchas of MEGARA was the main prophet of the Greek army who fought at TROY to rescue HELEN. Calchas was the brother of Leucippe and Theonoe. Before the Greeks sailed to Troy, Calchas determined that Troy could not be captured without ACHILLES' help. When the Greeks made a sacrifice to APOLLO at Aulis, a snake emerged from the altar, slithered up a nearby plane tree, and, after consuming eight sparrows and their mother, turned to stone. Calchas said that ZEUS gave them this sign and declared that Troy was destined to be taken in a period of 10 years (the birds represented nine years; the serpent's turning to stone after consuming them indicated victory in the 10th year). While still at Aulis, when AGAMEMNON offended ARTEMIS before the Greek fleet sailed to Troy, Calchas prophesied that Artemis could be appeased by the sacrifice of IPHIGENIA. When Apollo struck the Greek camp with a plague in the 10th year of the war, Calchas correctly predicted that Agamemnon's restoration of Chryseis to her father would end the plague. In SOPHOCLES' *AJAX,* Calchas predicted that AJAX would die if he left his tent on the day after Ajax had tried to kill ODYSSEUS, AGAMEMNON, and MENELAUS. Later, Calchas predicted that Troy could not be captured without the help of Achilles' son NEOPTOLEMUS and the weapons of HERACLES, which were in the possession of PHILOCTETES. Calchas may also have issued a prophecy that prompted the building of the wooden horse. When the Greeks had sacked Troy and were preparing to sail away, Calchas prevented them from leaving, saying that ATHENA was angry with them because of the Locrian Ajax's rape of CASSANDRA. Ironically, prophecy eventually brought about Calchas' death, as it was prophesied that he would die when a better prophet appeared. When Calchas lost a contest in prophecy to TIRESIAS' son, Mopsus, Calchas died of grief and was buried at Notium. [ANCIENT SOURCES: Apollodorus, *Library* 3.13.8, *Epitome* 3.15, 5.8, 6.4; Euripides, *Iphigenia at Aulis, Iphigenia in Tauris* 16–21; Homer, *Iliad* 1–2; Hyginus, *Fables* 97, 98, 128, 190; Plautus, *Menaechmi* 748, *Merchant* 945; Seneca, *Agamemnon* 167, *Trojan Women* passim; Sophocles, *Ajax* 748–83; Strabo, 14.1.27; Vergil, *Aeneid* 2.100–185]

BIBLIOGRAPHY
Degener, J. M. "The *Caesura* of the *Symbolon* in Aeschylus' *Agamemnon,*" *Arethusa* 34, no. 1 (2001): 61–95.
Elata-Alster. G. "The King's Double Bind: Paradoxical Communication in the Parodos of Aeschylus' *Agamemnon,*" *Arethusa* 18 (1985): 23–46.
Tyler, J. "Sophocles' *Ajax* and Sophoclean Plot Construction," *American Journal of Philology* 95 (1974): 24–42.

CALLIAS   The son of HIPPONICUS, Callias was a wealthy Athenian who was mocked as being extravagant, as having a sexual appetite for both men and women (even his mother-in-law), and as being preyed upon by flatterers. Callias fought at the battle of MARATHON and may have been the architect behind a peace treaty between ATHENS and Persia around 450, as well as one between Athens and SPARTA in 446/445. Callias had a son named Hipponicus. [ANCIENT SOURCES: Andocides, 1.124–27l; Aristophanes, *Birds* 283–84, *Ecclesiazusae* 810, *Frogs* 428; Cratinus, fragments 12, 81 Kock; Eupolis, fragment 161 Kock; Herodotus, 7.151; Plato, *Protagoras*; Xenophon, *Symposium*]

BIBLIOGRAPHY
Dunbar, Nan. *Aristophanes: Birds.* New York: Oxford University Press, 1995, 235–36.

Kock, T. *Comicorum Atticorum Fragmenta.* Vol. 1. Leipzig: Teubner, 1880.

CALLIMACHUS   At *ECCLESIAZUSAE* 809, ARISTOPHANES calls Callimachus a chorus trainer (see DIDASKALOS). The ancient commentators on the line say he had little money, but there is no other evidence to support this claim.

BIBLIOGRAPHY
Sommerstein, A. H. *The Comedies of Aristophanes.* Vol. 10, *Ecclesiazusae.* Warminster, U.K.: Aris & Phillips, 1998, 208.

CALLISTO   The daughter of Nycteus (or Ceteus or Lycaon), Callisto (most beautiful) was a young woman devoted to ARTEMIS. Callisto attracted the attention of ZEUS, who, disguising himself as APOLLO or Artemis, sexually assaulted her. Callisto became pregnant and gave birth to a son, Arcas. Later, Zeus changed Callisto into a bear to trick his wife, HERA. Hera learned that Zeus had slept with Callisto and persuaded Artemis to shoot her. Another tradition says that Artemis killed Callisto when the goddess learned that the woman was no longer a virgin. Ovid relates that when Arcas was 15 he encountered the bear Callisto and would have killed her, but Zeus took both Callisto and Arcas in to the heavens and changed them into constellations. Callisto became Ursa Major (the bigger bear), and Arcas became Ursa Minor (the smaller bear). Other sources say that Zeus turned Callisto into a constellation, rescued the unborn Arcas from Callisto's body, and gave the child to MAIA to raise.

AESCHYLUS wrote a *Callisto,* whose surviving two words tell nothing about its plot. Among the Greek comic poets, Amphis wrote a *Callisto,* of which only the title survives (fragment 23 Kock vol. 2). Two brief fragments (17–18 Kock vol. 1) survive from Alcaeus' *Callisto,* but neither gives a clue to the play's plot or characters. [ANCIENT SOURCES: Apollodorus, *Library* 3.8.2; Hyginus, *Fables* 177; Ovid, *Metamorphoses* 2.401–530; Pausanias, 1.25.1, 8.3.5; Seneca, *Hercules Furens* 6–7, 1139]

BIBLIOGRAPHY
Kock, T. *Comicorum Atticorum Fragmenta.* Vol. 1. Leipzig: Teubner, 1880.

———. *Comicorum Atticorum Fragmenta.* Vol. 2. Leipzig: Teubner, 1884.

Radt, S. *Tragicorum Graecorum Fragmenta.* Vol. 3. Göttingen, Ger.: Vandenhoeck & Ruprecht, 1985.

Smyth, H. W., and H. Lloyd-Jones. *Aeschylus.* Vol. 2. 1926. Reprint, Cambridge, Mass.: Harvard University Press, 1971.

Sutton, D. F. "A Handlist of Satyr Plays," *Harvard Studies in Classical Philology* 78 (1974): 107–43.

CALPE   A mountain on the southern coast of Spain opposite the African coast. [ANCIENT SOURCES: Seneca, *Hercules Furens* 237, *Hercules Oetaeus* 1240, 1253, 1569]

CALYDON   A town near the coast of the Gulf of CORINTH in northwestern Greece. Calydon was the home of OENEUS, ALTHAEA, MELEAGER, DEIANEIRA, and TYDEUS and the site of the legendary hunt for the Calydonian boar. PLAUTUS' CARTHAGINIAN has Calydon as its setting.

CALYPSO   The daughter of ATLAS, Calypso (the concealer) was a goddess who lived on the mythical island of Ogygia. During ODYSSEUS' return home from the Trojan War, he landed on the island and spent several years (five or seven, depending on the source) with Calypso, who offered to make him immortal. Apollodorus says Calypso produced a son, Latinus, by

Odysseus. Other sources mention two sons. Eventually, the gods arranged for Odysseus to leave Calypso's island by raft.

Calypso does not appear as a character in any extant dramas. The Greek comic poet Anaxilas wrote a *Calypso,* of which two lines survive (fragments 10–11 Kock). Fragment 10 ("first the old woman will taste your drink for you") may refer to Odysseus or one of his men. It is difficult to see how fragment 11 ("Then I realized I had a pig's snout") would fit in with the story of Calypso because Odysseus was not changed into a pig by CIRCE, and all his men who had been with him on Circe's island were dead by the time Odysseus reached Calypso's island. [ANCIENT SOURCES: Apollodorus, *Epitome* 7.24; Homer, *Odyssey* 1, 5]

BIBLIOGRAPHY
Kock, T. *Comicorum Atticorum Fragmenta.* Vol. 2. Leipzig: Teubner, 1884.

CAMARINA   A town on the southwest coast of SICILY. [ANCIENT SOURCES: Aristophanes, *Acharnians* 605]

CANCER   The zodiacal constellation representing the crab. HERACLES killed this crab during his battle against the Hydra, and HERA put the crab's image in the heavens. [ANCIENT SOURCES: Seneca, *Hercules Oetaeus* 41, 67, 1219, 1573, *Hippolytus* 287, *Thyestes* 854]

CANNONUS   The son of Sibyrtius from the DEME of Lamptrae, Cannonus was active in Athenian politics during the first quarter of the fifth century B.C.E. Cannonus initiated "a decree making regulations for the trial of those charged with 'injuring the Athenian people'" (Sommerstein). Defendants who were under the provisions of this decree had to remain in prison until their trial, which was presented before the public as a whole. During the trial, these defendants had to stand in their bonds and have two guards. If convicted of the charges, the defendants were executed by being thrown down into the *barathron,* a deep and rocky ditch outside ATHENS. No instance in which Cannonus' decree was put into practice is known. In 406 B.C.E., an effort to try the Athenian naval commanders at the battle of ARGINUSAE by employing Cannonus' decree did

not succeed. The commanders were tried as a group and were executed. [ANCIENT SOURCES: Aristophanes, *Ecclesiazusae* 1089; Xenophon, *Hellenica* 1.7.20–21, 34]

BIBLIOGRAPHY
Sommerstein, A. H. *The Comedies of Aristophanes.* Vol. 10, *Ecclesiazusae.* Warminster, U.K.: Aris & Phillips, 1998, 230.

CANOPUS   Also spelled Canobus, Canopus is an African town about a dozen miles east of ALEXANDRIA near the westermost mouth of the NILE River. ZEUS restored IO to human form at Canopus. [ANCIENT SOURCES: Aeschylus, *Prometheus Bound* 846, *Suppliant Women* 311]

CANTHARUS   Usually called the PEIRAEUS, Cantharus was the official name for the primary harbor at ATHENS. [ANCIENT SOURCES: Aristophanes, *Peace* 145]

BIBLIOGRAPHY
Sommerstein, A. H. *The Comedies of Aristophanes.* Vol. 5, *Peace.* Warminster, U.K.: Aris & Philips, 1985, 141.

CAPANEUS   The son of Hipponous, Capaneus was the husband of EVADNE, by whom he had a son, Sthenelus. Capaneus fought on the Argive side in the famous battle of the Seven against THEBES. While attempting to scale the walls of Thebes with a ladder, Capaneus boasted that he would take the town whether or not the gods were willing. ZEUS, hearing this boast, struck Capaneus dead with a lightning bolt. The tragedian Timesitheus wrote a *Capaneus,* of which only the title survives. [ANCIENT SOURCES: Aeschylus, *Seven against Thebes* 422–56; Apollodorus, *Library* 3.6.3–7, 3.10.8; Euripides, *Phoenician Women* 1128–86, *Suppliant Women* 861–71; Pausanias, 9.8.7; Statius, *Thebaid*]

BIBLIOGRAPHY
Snell, B. *Tragicorum Graecorum Fragmenta.* Vol. 1. Göttingen, Ger.: Vandenhoeck & Ruprecht, 1971.

CAPHEREUS   A rocky promontory on the southeast end of the Greek island of EUBOEA. In mythology, the Greek fleet, returning from the Trojan

War, was wrecked off Caphereus. [ANCIENT SOURCES: Euripides, *Trojan Women* 90; Hyginus, *Fables* 116; Pausanias, 2.23.1, 4.36.6; Seneca, *Agamemnon* 560]

CAPITOLINE   One of the famous seven hills of ROME, between the Campus Martius and the Palatine hill. [ANCIENT SOURCES: Plautus, *Three-Dollar Day* 84]

***CAPTIVES* PLAUTUS (CA. 189 B.C.E.)**   The Greek original on which PLAUTUS' play is based is unknown. The action takes place before the house of Hegio in an Aetolian town. As the play opens, the audience see two male war captives from ELIS, Philocrates and Tyndarus, chained to the front of Hegio's house. Hegio, a rich Aetolian, had two sons, Philopolemus and a child later named Tyndarus, the latter of whom was stolen when he was four by Hegio's SLAVE, Stalagmus, and sold in Elis. Theodoromides Polyplusius, the person who bought Tyndarus, was the father of Philocrates, one of the war prisoners from Elis. In turn, Philocrates' father gave Tyndarus to Philocrates to be his personal servant. Years later, during a war between AETOLIA and Elis, Hegio's second son, Philopolemus (whose name means "lover of war"), was taken captive in Elis. Therefore, Hegio began buying war captives so that he could find one to exchange for Philopolemus.

After the play's prologue and a monologue by the PARASITE Ergasilus, Hegio comes from the house, unchains Philocrates and Tyndarus from the wall, and allows them to walk around the grounds of his home. After a guard takes the prisoners into the house, Ergasilus, who has been eavesdropping, emerges and complains to Hegio about his lack of food because Philopolemus was captured. After the exit of Hegio and Ergasilus, a guard enters with the two prisoners. Philocrates and Tyndarus move out of earshot of the guards and discuss their plan to reverse their roles. Tyndarus will pretend to be the master, while Philocrates will act as his slave.

Next, Hegio arrives from the house and interrogates Philocrates and Tyndarus about their respective backgrounds. Hegio does not realize that Tyndarus is his long-lost son. Hegio tells Tyndarus that if he helps him ransom back his son, Philopolemus, then he will arrange for Tyndarus and Philocrates to be freed. When

Hegio reveals that Philopolemus is in the hands of a doctor named Menarchus, Philocrates blurts out that Menarchus is known to Tyndarus, and Tyndarus agrees to help arrange for Philopolemus to be ransomed. Hegio agrees to allow Philocrates to go to Elis to arrange for the ransom. Tyndarus agrees to pay Hegio a large sum of money if Philocrates does not return.

After Philocrates departs for Elis, a glum Ergasilus returns from the town, complaining of not being able to find a free meal. His departure is followed by the arrival of Hegio, who returns from town with a newly bought captive, Aristophontes, who happens to know Philocrates. When Tyndarus, who is pretending to be Philocrates, sees Aristophontes, Tyndarus fears their deception will be revealed. Aristophontes, seeing Tyndarus, addresses him by that name. Tyndarus tells Hegio that Aristophontes is insane, denies that he is the slave Tyndarus, and claims he is a free man. Eventually, Hegio interrogates Aristophontes and discovers that Tyndarus and Philocrates have tricked him. The angered Hegio then orders Tyndarus to be bound and threatens to send him to the stone quarries.

After the exit of Hegio and the captives, an excited Ergasilus enters from the harbor and joyfully reveals to Hegio that he has seen his son, Philopolemus; Philocrates; and Stalagmus, the slave who abducted the child Tyndarus. A hopeful Hegio promises Ergasilus a lifetime of free meals if his information is true. At this point, Ergasilus enters the house to dine, while Hegio exits for the harbor.

Soon Hegio returns with Philopolemus, Philocrates, and Stalagmus. Hegio, delighted by his reunion with his son, Philopolemus, agrees to turn Tyndarus over to Philocrates. As Philopolemus and Philocrates enter Hegio's house, Hegio questions Stalagmus, who reveals to him that he abducted Tyndarus, and sold him to Philocrates' father. After Hegio summons Philocrates from the house, Stalgmus reveals that the child he abducted and the child who became Philocrates' servant, Tyndarus, are one and the same. As Philocrates confirms this, Hegio realizes that he has sentenced his son to the quarries. At that moment, a chained and disheveled Tyndarus enters. Tyndarus is baffled when Hegio addresses him as his son, but Philocrates soon explains the truth to him. As the action concludes,

Hegio calls for Tyndarus' chains to be removed and threatens to put Stalagmus in them.

COMMENTARY

Many scholars have admired *Captives* because it has a higher moral tone than Plautus' other plays. This tone has led some scholars to question whether the play was actually written by Plautus. Others have defended it as Plautine and noted the usual Plautine elements of trickery, farce, and word-play and the usual comic structure. Clearly, however, the play is different from other Plautine comedies. As is noted in the prologue, the play has no pimp or prostitutes (or any female characters, for that matter). *Captives* also lacks the lovesick young man usually found in New Comedy (see COMEDY). The introduction of the role of the parasite, Ergasilus, is considered a Plautine innovation and many scholars consider it an intrusive innovation. The willingness of Tyndarus to help his master is reminiscent of the friendship of ORESTES and PYLADES. One wonders whether PACUVIUS' *Orestes as Slave,* in which Orestes and Pylades were captured and Pylades claimed that he was Orestes so that he might be executed instead of his friend (see Cicero, *De Amicitia* 24), might have been produced in time to have influenced Plautus' *Captives.* Pacuvius would have been about 30 years old when *Captives* was staged. Even if Pacuvius' play was unknown to Plautus, the relationship between Tyndarus and Philocles does have a quality reminiscent of the relationship between Orestes and Pylades, and their friendship had been portrayed on stage as early as the fifth century B.C.E. (see especially EURIPIDES' *IPHIGENIA IN TAURIS*).

Two of the more prominent features of *Captives* are irony and role reversal. For a play that lacks the clever slave found in so many other Plautine comedies, *Captives* has numerous references to slaves and slavery. Of course, in opposition to the slave is the master, but the master-slave relationship is further complicated in *Captives* by the father-son relationship, and in this play these relationships become reversed, confused, and then untangled. Hegio's son, Tyndarus, who was born free, abducted by a slave, sold to Philocrates as a slave, and later captured in war, will pretend to be the master of Philocrates. Thus, Tyndarus will pretend to be a free person, as, in fact, he is. Philocrates, also born free and captured in war, will pretend to be the slave of his slave, Tyndarus. Hegio's son, Philopolemus, as was his brother, Tyndarus, was born free but has also become a captive. When Tyndarus agrees to arrange for the ransom of Philopolemus, he unwittingly is arranging to help ransom his brother. When Tyndarus pledges money if Philocrates does not return, he is unwittingly negotiating with his father, but he is also pledging money that, as a slave, does not belong to him, but to his master, Philocrates.

When Hegio discovers the deception, he is angry with Tyndarus, who, ironically, argues that after a single day Hegio should not have expected him to be more loyal to a stranger than to the master he has served since childhood (717–19). Even more ironic is that this is exactly what will happen once Tyndarus discovers that he is Hegio's son. As soon as Tyndarus' slave status ends and his freedom begins, he will become more loyal to his father, Hegio, than to his master, Philocrates. Hegio, after hearing Tyndarus' remark, unwittingly sends his own son off to the stone quarries.

Eventually, Hegio discovers the identities of his sons. Interestingly, before Ergasilus informs Hegio that that he has seen his son, Philopolemus, and Philocrates and Stalagmus, Ergasilus says he will behave as the slaves do in comedies (778) so that Hegio will reward him. Captive Philopolemus is transformed from captive into a free person and is reunited with his father. Slave Tyndarus regains his freedom, becomes a former captive, and is reunited with his father. Ultimately, the little freedom in life that the slave Stalagmus does have is further curtailed as he is threatened with chains at the play's conclusion.

BIBLIOGRAPHY

Benz, L., and Lefèvre, E., eds. *Maccus Barbarus: Sechs Kapitel zur Originalität der Captivi des Plautus.* Tübingen, Ger.: Narr, 1998.

Konstan, D. "*Captivi:* City-State and Nation." In *Roman Comedy.* Ithaca, N.Y.: Cornell University Press, 1983, 57–72.

Lowe, J. C. B. "Prisoners, Guards, and Chains in Plautus, *Captivi*," *American Journal of Philology* 112 (1991): 29–44.

McCarthy, K. *Slaves, Masters and the Art of Authority in Plautine Comedy.* Princeton, N.J.: Princeton University Press, 2000.

Segal, Erich. "Is the *Captivi* Plautine?" In *Roman Laughter: The Comedy of Plautus.* New York: Oxford University Press, 1987, 191–214.
Thalmann, W. G. "Versions of Slavery in the *Captivi* of Plautus," *Ramus* 25, no. 2 (1996): 112–45.

CARCINUS (1)

The son of Xenotimus, Carcinus, from the DEME of Thoricus, was an Athenian military commander (in 432/431 B.C.E.), dancer, and playwright. Carcinus had produced plays at least as early as 446 B.C.E. and had claimed a victory at the City DIONYSIA. Because Carcinus' name means "crab" in Greek, in WASPS ARISTOPHANES uses this as an opportunity to make fun of the way Carcinus' sons danced. One of Carcinus' sons (also named CARCINUS) was a playwright. Virtually nothing of the elder Carcinus' poetry survives (fragments 1–2 Snell). [ANCIENT SOURCES: Aristophanes, *Clouds* 1261, *Peace* 781, 866, *Thesmophoriazusae* 441, *Wasps* 1501–12; *Inscriptiones Graecae* i² 296.30–40; Plato Comicus, fragment 134.2 Kock; Thucydides, 2.23]

BIBLIOGRAPHY
MacDowell, D. M. *Aristophanes: Wasps.* Oxford: Clarendon Press, 1971, 326–27.
Olson, S. D. "Was Carcinus I a Tragic Playwright? A Response," *Classical Philology* 92, no. 3 (1997): 258–60.
Rothwell, K. S. "Was Carcinus I a Tragic Playwright?" *Classical Philology* 89 (1994): 241–45.
Sommerstein. A. *The Comedies of Aristophanes.* Vol. 4, *Wasps.* Warminster, U.K.: Aris & Phillips, 1980, 246.

CARCINUS (2)

One of the sons of CARCINUS, grandson of Carcinus, and son of the elder Carcinus' son, XENOCLES. The younger Carcinus was, as were his father and grandfather, a dancer and a dramatist. About a dozen fragments and 10 or 11 titles survive from the younger Carcinus' plays. [ANCIENT SOURCES: Aristophanes, *Wasps* 1501–12]

BIBLIOGRAPHY
Snell, B. *Tragicorum Graecorum Fragmenta.* Vol. 1. Göttingen, Ger.: Vandenhoeck & Ruprecht, 1971.

CARDOPION

A mythological character about whom nothing is known. [ANCIENT SOURCES: Aristophanes, *Wasps* 1178]

BIBLIOGRAPHY
MacDowell, D. M. *Aristophanes: Wasps.* Oxford: Clarendon Press, 1971, 283.

CARIA

A region along the western coast of what is modern Turkey. [ANCIENT SOURCES: Aristophanes, *Knights* 173; Plautus, *Curculio*]

CARTHAGE (Greek: CARCHEDON; Latin: CARTHAGO)

A powerful city-state on the coast of northern Africa. In the latter part of the fifth century B.C.E., some Athenians eyed Carthage as a possible addition to their own empire. During the third and second centuries B.C.E., Carthage was Rome's greatest rival. Several of PLAUTUS' plays were written during the last six or seven years of Rome's second major war with Carthage (218–201): ASINARIA, MERCHANT, BRAGGART WARRIOR, and CASKET COMEDY. Plautus' CARTHAGINIAN deals with the fate of some Carthaginian children who were abducted from Carthage and taken to CALYDON. Plautus' play may have been modeled on MENANDER's *Carthaginian* (*Carchedonius*), but little of Menander's play survives (fragments 226–31 Körte). The Greek comic poet Alexis also wrote a *Carthaginian* (*Carchedonius*), of which only two words ("You are a eunuch of Cybele") survive (fragment 100 Kock). [ANCIENT SOURCES: Aristophanes, *Knights* 174, 1303; Plautus, *Casina* 71]

BIBLIOGRAPHY
Kock, T. *Comicorum Atticorum Fragmenta.* Vol. 2. Leipzig: Teubner, 1884.
Körte, A., and A. Thierfelder. *Menandri Quae Supersunt.* Vol. 2, 2d ed. Leipzig: Teubner, 1959.

THE CARTHAGINIAN (Latin: POENULUS) PLAUTUS (CA. 194 OR 193 B.C.E.)

The play's date is very tentative. The author of the Greek original may have been MENANDER. Plautus' prologue reveals that the original title of the Greek play was *Carchedonius* (Carthaginian). The action of the play takes place in Calydon (the only occurrence of this setting in extant Roman drama) before the houses of Agorastocles, a young gentleman (see ADULESCENS), and Lycus, a PIMP. The prologue invites the audience to hurry and take their seats. Interestingly, the prologue suggests that women were in the audience.

As the prologue's unnamed speaker informs the audience, a certain Carthaginian had his seven-year-old son, Agorastocles, stolen, and he, Antidamas, died six years later. The person who stole Agorastocles took him to CALYDON and sold him to a childless bachelor. A similar fate happened to Hanno, the cousin of Agorastocles' father. He had two young daughters, Adelphasium and Anterastilis, who with their nurse, Giddenis, vanished near Carthage. Their abductor took them to Anactorium and sold them to a pimp named Lycus, who later moved with them and their nurse to Calydon. When the pimp moved in next door to Agorastocles, the young man fell in love with Adelphasium. Antamonides, a soldier, fell in love with Anterastilis and wanted to buy her as his concubine. The prologue also informs the audience that Hanno has been searching for his lost daughters for years and has just arrived in Calydon.

In the opening act, Agorastocles and his slave, Milphio, enter, and Agorastocles tells him of his love for Adelphasium. Milphio tells Agorastocles that he will help him acquire Adelphasium from the pimp by sending Agorastocles' bailiff, Collybiscus, to the pimp's house to hire the prostitute. While Collybiscus is inside Lycus' house, Agorastocles will ask Lycus whether his slave is there. Because Lycus does not know Collybiscus, Lycus will think that Agorastocles means Milphio; when Lycus says Agorastocles' servant is not in his house, Agorastocles will then accuse the pimp of stealing his slave. Milphio predicts that Lycus will be taken to court and judged liable to Agorastocles. They believe Lycus will have to turn over his entire house to Agorastocles.

Before Agorastocles and Milphio go off to make plans with Collybiscus, Adelphasium and Anterastilis approach with offerings for that day's festival of Venus (see APHRODITE). The two men eavesdrop as Adelphasium enters discussing the difficulties of caring for two women and sermonizing on the virtues of moderation. While the two women discuss going to Venus' temple, where Lycus is waiting, the two men make jokes about Agorastocles' love for Adelphasium. As Adelphasium speaks further of moderation, Agorastocles continues raving about her. Finally, Agorastocles approaches Adelphasium to ask where she is going. Adelphasium says she is going to show herself at a sale of prostitutes that is taking place at Venus' temple. In vain, Agorastocles tries to fondle and kiss Adelphasium. Agorastocles pleads with Milphio to smooth over matters with Adelphasium, but Agorastocles becomes jealous when his slave sweetly talks to Adelphasium. Milphio is unsuccessful, and Adelphasium leaves for the temple. After the women's departure, Agorastocles begs Milphio to help him defeat Lycus. Milphio tells Agorastocles to get some witnesses, while he goes inside to prime Collybiscus for the plot.

The brief second act opens with the arrival of Lycus from Venus' temple. Lycus is upset because his sacrifices to Venus were not met with favorable omens. The pimp is soon joined by the soldier Antamonides, who boasts of his military exploits. Lycus tries to get away from Antamonides, but the soldier demands that Anterastilis be turned over to him that same day. Lycus and the soldier then enter the house.

The next act begins with Agorastocles awaiting the arrival of his witnesses. Finally, the slow-moving fellows enter and explain for the audience's benefit, as the witness point out, the plan to trick the pimp. Then, Milphio and Collybiscus enter. Collybiscus is dressed as a mercenary soldier serving in SPARTA. In the presence of Agorastocles and his witnesses, Milphio reviews the scheme with Collybiscus, who then sends Milphio and Agorastocles into the house to avoid the pimp. Collybiscus and the witnesses then encounter Lycus, who is leaving his house. After the witnesses and Lycus insult one another for some time, Lycus asks who the disguised Collybiscus is. They tell Lycus they just met him that morning leaving a merchant's ship and took him to Lycus' house, because he said he wanted to find a place where he could drink and find some "romance." They also tell Lycus that the man has plenty of money with him. Lycus, delighted by the prospect of making a profit, gladly urges the foreigner to go into his house. As Lycus moves off toward his house with Collybiscus, the witnesses move off to a distance to observe.

The witnesses then call Agorastocles out of his house to watch the proceedings. Agorastocles watches as Collybiscus hands over the money to Lycus. After Collybiscus and Lycus enter his house, Agorastocles asks the witnesses to recite what they saw take place. Agorastocles, planning how to confront Lycus, emerges from his house and announces his plans to spend the money. As the witnesses cover their faces so that Lycus will not recognize them, Agorastocles approaches and accuses Lycus of allowing his (Agorastocles') slave into his house. When Lycus denies the accusation, Agorastocles calls the witnesses to take note of the denial. Lycus, recognizing the witnesses, realizes the plot against him. Soon, Agorastocles enters Lycus' house to retrieve Collybiscus. Lycus, worrying what he should do next, departs to seek advice from his friends. After Agorastocles and Collybiscus emerge from Lycus' house, the witnesses inform Agorastocles that Lycus has gone. Agorastocles then tells Collybiscus to change back into his usual clothes and asks the witnesses to meet him the following day so that he can bring a suit against Lycus.

In the fourth act, Milphio sees Lycus' slave, Syncerastus, who is returning from making a sacrifice to Venus, and eavesdrops on him as he complains about having to serve the pimp. Syncerastus notes that the prostitutes' sacrifices found favor with Venus, but those of Lycus did not. Milphio then approaches Syncerastus, who reveals to him that both Adelphasium and Anterastilis are freeborn women from Carthage. Milphio is delighted to hear this and notes that Agorastocles himself was born in Carthage.

In the fifth act, Hanno of Carthage enters from the harbor in search of his daughters and his now-deceased friend, Antidamas (Agorastocles' father). Hanno wants to meet with Agorastocles, who soon appears talking with Milphio. Hanno eavesdrops on the pair and hears them talking about the kidnapping of Adelphasium and Anterastilis. Eventually, Hanno steps forward and soon learns about Agorastocles' identity. Hanno and Agorastocles also figure out that Hanno is Agorastocles' maternal uncle. Upon hearing this, Milphio makes a plan that Hanno will tell Lycus that he is the father of Adelphasium and Anterastilis. Hanno is happy to play along and notes, coincidentally, that he had two daughters, who, along with their nurse, were kidnapped when they were young. The nurse, Gidennis, emerges from Lycus' house and recognizes her old master, Hanno.

Next, Adelphasium and Anterastilis enter, and Hanno and Agorastocles eavesdrop on their conversation, which concludes with Anterastilis' remark that a prophet mentioned that soon the two women would be free. When Hanno approaches Adelphasium and Anterastilis, father and daughters are reunited. Hanno also agrees to allow Agorastocles to marry Adelphasium.

As the joyful reunion continues, Antamonides enters from Lycus' house, sees Hanno hugging Anterastilis, and, thinking Hanno is a rival lover, threatens the old man. The soldier calms down after he learns that Hanno is the woman's father. After this, Lycus enters and is immediately confronted by Hanno, who informs the pimp that Adelphasium and Anterastilis are his daughters. Because the women are freeborn, Lycus cannot employ them as prostitutes. He realizes that he must give them up and agrees to make financial restitution to Agorastocles. The play ends with Agorastocles' planning to auction his property and return to Carthage with Hanno and his daughters.

COMMENTARY

P. W. Harsh, living up to his name, delivered an unequivocal condemnation of Plautus' play: "The *Carthaginian* is miserably constructed and is a poor play in every respect." Most of the scholarly attention paid to this play has focused on the passages written in the Carthaginian language. Since the 1990s, however, *Carthaginian* has received some fresh consideration by Franko and Starks, who have considered the play in terms of the relationship between the Romans and the Carthaginians during the period when the play was staged (the decade after the end of Rome's second major war with Carthage).

As does BRAGGART WARRIOR, *Carthaginian* deals with two men, a young freeborn gentleman and a professional soldier, who are in love with prostitutes (or prospective prostitutes). In *Warrior,* the two men are in love with the same woman; the situation leads to much humor as the tricky slave in that play must outwit the soldier's slave to allow his master to be with his beloved. Whereas the soldier (Pyrgopolynices) and the young man (Pleusicles) are in love with the same woman in *Warrior,* in *Carthaginian,* the soldier and the young gentleman are in love with different women; as a result, little humor develops from this plot line. The most significant humor surrounding the soldier to arise occurs when he accuses Hanno of embracing his beloved. Of course, the soldier soon finds out that Hanno is her father and not his rival.

Whereas *Warrior* focuses on the utter defeat and embarrassment of the soldier, defeat of the pimp is the focal point of *Carthaginian*. As in *Warrior,* in *Carthaginian* a tricky slave engineers the deception, and slaves in both plays employ disguised accomplices to trick their opponents. Milphio's first deception of the pimp in the third act appears to be a waste of time because the legal action proposed by Agorastocles does not come to pass as a result of this trick. Furthermore, in the fourth act, Milphio devises a new intrigue with the pimp's slave, but this deception is never implemented. In the play's final act, Milphio at last engineers a plan whose results are seen as he tells the women's father to declare to Lycus that they are his freeborn daughters and therefore cannot be sold into slavery.

Thus, as do *Curculio* and ROPE, *Carthaginian* ends with the ruin of the pimp. At the conclusion of *Rope,* however, the pimp is forgiven and invited to dinner. The conclusion of *Carthaginian* is more like that of *Curculio,* in which the soldier apprehends the pimp, to whom no forgiveness or participation in feasting will be granted. The planned sale of goods and departure from the town are parallelled in MENAECHMI.

BIBLIOGRAPHY

Franko, G. F. "The Characterization of Hanno in Plautus' *Poenulus,*" *American Journal of Philology* 117, no. 3 (1996): 425–52.

Harsh, P. W. *A Handbook of Classical Drama.* Stanford, Calif.: Stanford University Press, 1944, 364.

Heidelberg, M. G. *Poenulus.* Heidelberg: Winter, 1975.

Rosivach, V. J. "The *Advocati* in the *Poenulus* and the *Piscatores* in the *Rudens,*" *Maia* 35 (1983): 83–93.

Starks, J. "*Nullus me est hodie poenus poenior:* Balanced Ethnic Humor in Plautus' *Poenulus,*" *Helios* 27, no. 2 (2000): 163–86.

Zwierlein, O. *Zur Kritik und Exegese des Plautus.* Vol. I, *Poenulus und Curculio.* Stuttgart: Steiner, 1990.

CARYSTIAN ALLIES

The people of Carystus were allies of the Athenians during the 420s and 410s B.C.E. In 425, they helped ATHENS invade CORINTH, and they participated in the SICILIAN EXPEDITION of 415–13. They also aided in replacing the Athenian democracy with the oligarchy of 400 in the year 411. [ANCIENT SOURCES: Aristophanes, *Lysistrata* 1058, 1182; Thucydides, 4.42, 7.57.4, 8.69.3]

BIBLIOGRAPHY

Henderson, J. *Aristophanes: Lysistrata.* Oxford: Clarendon Press, 1987, 191.

CASINA PLAUTUS (185 OR 184 B.C.E.)

The play's prologue (lines 31–34) reveals that Plautus adapted the play from *Kleroumenoi* (Lot drawers) of DIPHILUS, the author whose original PLAUTUS used in composing ROPE. The prologue (lines 13–14) also indicates that *Casina* had been staged successfully at an earlier time. The play's action occurs in ATHENS (the most common setting for Roman comedies) before the houses of two elderly gentlemen, Lysidamus and Alcesimus.

As the prologue informs us, 16 years earlier one of the slaves, who had seen a woman abandon the baby Casina, asked her whether he might have the infant. The slave then took the infant to his mistress, who raised the child. After Casina grew up, both Lysidamus and his son fell in love with her. Unknown to each other, Lysidamus and his son had been attempting to arrange a union with Casina. Because Casina was raised as a slave, the two noblemen could not marry her, but they did want to enjoy her sexual favors. Therefore, Lysidamus and his son were trying to induce their own male slaves to marry Casina but allow Lysidamus and his son to enjoy her also. Thus, the son's slave, Chalinus, was commissioned to ask Casina to marry him, and Lysidamus' slave, Olympio, was commissioned to arrange his own marriage to Casina. To complicate matters more, Lysidamus was already married to Cleostrata. Because Cleostrata knew that her husband loved Casina, she was trying to help her son get her. After Lysidamus learned his son was in love with Casina, he sent him abroad. Cleostrata, however, continued to help her son in his absence.

In the brief opening act, Chalinus and Olympio argue over who will get Casina. In the second act, after the departure of the slaves, Cleostrata encounters Myrrhina, the wife of her neighbor, Alcesimus. Cleostrata complains to Myrrhina about the way Lysidamus has been treating her, but Myrrhina tells Cleostrata she should tolerate her husband's affair because otherwise he might divorce her.

After Myrrhina returns to her house, Lysidamus enters, drunk and ecstatic from feelings of love for Casina. Cleostrata eavesdrops while Lysidamus speaks of love. Lysidamus sees Cleostrata and tries to soothe her, but she knows what he has been doing. When the conversation turns to Casina, Lysidamus and Cleostrata argue about whether Casina should marry Chalinus or Olympio. Lysidamus and Cleostrata decide to try to persuade one of the slaves to give up his attempt to marry Casina, but neither is successful. Finally, they agree that Casina's marriage will be decided by the drawing of lots—a lottery that Olympio wins.

After Olympio's victory, a dejected Chalinus listens in while Lysidamus and Olympio plan a rendezvous between Lysidamus and Casina. Because Olympio lives in the countryside, Lysidamus can enjoy Casina without his wife's knowledge. Lysidamus reveals that while preparations for the wedding are going on, Myrrhina will stay at Lysidamus' house to help Cleostrata. Alcesimus, whom Lysidamus has informed of his love for Casina, will help Lysidamus by allowing him to use his house for a sexual encounter with Casina that night. Then Alcesimus sends Olympio to the FORUM to buy some food. As Olympio departs for the forum and Lysidamus enters Alcesimus' house, Chalinus gleefully plans to gain revenge by telling Cleostrata what her husband has in mind.

In the play's third act, Lysidamus and Alcesimus confirm their plans for the rendezvous with Casina. Lysidamus departs for the forum, while Alcesimus returns to his house. Next, Cleostrata, who has learned of Lysidamus' scheme, encounters Alcesimus and says that she does not need Myrrhina's help after all. As Cleostrata pretends to enter her house, she listens as Alcesimus worries that Lysidamus' plans will be spoiled.

In the next scene, Lysidamus returns from the forum and finds Cleostrata, who tells him that Alcesimus would not allow his wife to go to their house. After Cleostrata returns to the house, Lysidamus meets Alcesimus. The two men accuse each other of deviat-

ing from the agreed-upon plan. Eventually, Alcesimus calms and agrees to send Myrrhina to Lysidamus' house. Before Lysidamus can return to his house, the maidservant, Pardalisca, rushes from the house in a terror. Pardalisca's fear, however, is an element of Cleostrata and Myrrhina's plot to trick Lysidamus. Pardalisca tells Lysidamus that Casina has become mad, is waving two swords, and is threatening to kill herself, Lysidamus, and Olympio. Pardalisca claims Casina will not put down the swords unless the marriage to Olympio is called off. Lysidamus fears for his life, but he insists that the wedding occur and begs Pardalisca to go back into the house and try to calm Casina. In the following scene, Olympio returns with some cooks and food for the wedding feast. Lysidamus informs him of Casina's madness, but Olympio thinks her actions are nonsense, and eventually both men enter the house.

Pardalisca opens the fourth act by reporting the events inside Lysidamus' house. She informs the audience that all those inside, including the cooks, are doing their best to prevent Lysidamus from having dinner. Cleostrata and Myrrhina have dressed Chalinus as a woman and plan to pass him off as Casina. Soon, Lysidamus, unable to have dinner, claims he want to take his meal at his farm outside. He calls for Olympio and Casina, and after the two old men sing the wedding song, Chalinus, disguised as Casina, emerges from the house. After the departure of those attending the "bride," Lysidamus and Olympio begin to fight over the "girl." As the two men attempt to kiss and caress her, she gives them all sorts of punches and kicks. Eventually, the two men persuade the cross-dressed Chalinus to enter Alcesimus' house.

The play's final act opens with the appearance of Cleostrata, Myrrhina, and Pardalisca, who anxiously await news of what has happened between "Casina" and the men. The three women eavesdrop as a bewildered and bruised Olympio emerges from Alcesimus' house. Olympio begins to tell of his efforts to make love to "Casina," when Cleostrata and Myrrhina approach and ask him to continue with his story. Olympio goes on to explain that "Casina" beat him when he tried to make love to her. Lysidamus, in a condition similar to Olympio's, arrives from Alcesimus' house. Lysidamus is soon followed by Chalinus, who mockingly invites him to return to bed. Lysidamus tries to get away from Chalinus, but Cleostrata blocks his path. Lysidamus eventually realizes that he cannot escape. He begs his wife for forgiveness and says she can beat him should he try to make love to Casina again. Cleostrata agrees to forgive Lysidamus, and Chalinus jokingly complains that he married two men but consummated neither relationship. The play's epilogue reveals that the real Casina is discovered to be the daughter of Alcesimus, and she finally marries Lysidamus' son, Euthynicus.

COMMENTARY

As do COMEDY OF ASSES and MERCHANT, *Casina* involves a father and son who are in love with the same woman. Unlike in *Comedy of Asses,* the son does not appear in *Casina.* Additionally, in *Comedy of Asses,* the father does not fall in love with the woman until later in the play. In *Casina,* Lysidamus' love of Casina is known from the play's outset, and in *Merchant,* Demipho falls in love with Pasicompsa in the first act. In all three plays, the wife, upon discovering her husband's plans for a secret love affair, prevents it. In Casina, the prologue reveals that Cleostrata knows of Lysidamus' love, whereas the wives in *Comedy of Asses* and *Merchant* discover their husband's mischief late in the play. Also, in *Comedy of Asses* and *Casina,* the young woman eventually marries the son when she is discovered to be freeborn. In *Merchant,* Charinus is allowed to keep Pasicompsa as his mistress, but plans for marriage are not evident. In *Comedy of Asses,* the wife's treatment of the husband at the end of the play is harsher than in *Casina.* In *Comedy of Asses,* the husband is not permitted to join in the closing celebration, whereas in *Casina* and *Merchant* the wife forgives her husband.

As is frequent in Roman COMEDY, the humor in these plays depends on role reversal. Olympio's discovery of Chalinus' gender role reversal is one of the funniest scenes in ancient comedy. Unfortunately, the ancient manuscripts of the play are riddled with small gaps during the description of Olympio's discovery, but the scene remains amusing. As Slater notes, Lysidamus elevates himself to a divine level. At line 230, he calls Cleostrata Juno (see HERA) and himself Jove (see ZEUS).

Lysidamus uses this description of himself again with Olympio (331–37, 406–7). Of course, as is the Jove of mythology, Lysidamus is interested in having sexual relations with a woman other than his wife. As was often the case in mythology, Juno discovered her husband's affairs. In mythology, however, Juno rarely, if ever, seems to have been able to retaliate directly against Jove. Instead, the brunt of Juno's anger was felt by the mistress or the offspring of the mistress. In the case of Juno/Cleostrata, Cleostrata is able to prevent her Jove from enjoying Casina, although Olympio suffers the physical hardship of Cleostrata's counterplot.

The power wielded by the wife Cleostrata is another unusual feature of *Casina.* Usually, wives in Roman comedy do not become involved in trickery or deception. Cleostrata is a notable exception. Slater, applying a metatheatrical methodology to some of Plautus' comedies, has discussed Cleostrata as a trickster and poet. Cleostrata replaces the usual clever slave who produces a "play" within the play. Not only is Cleostrata Juno to Lysidamus' Jove, but she is also his rival playwright. One round of dramatic competition emerges when Lysidamus tries to enlist his neighbor's help in consummating the affair with Casina. His play fails, however, as Chalinus overhears Lysidamus' constructing his plot and informs Cleostrata of her rival playwright's intent. Accordingly, Cleostrata has the cooks and Pardalisca serve as actors in an additional play whose aim is to prevent the union of Lysidamus and Casina. The cooks do everything they can to prevent Lysidamus from having his fun, and Cleostrata (with the aid of her neighbor's wife) has instructed Pardalisca to create a story about Casina's madness. In this instance, however, Cleostrata's play is not completely successful, as Lysidamus is frightened by the woman's madness but will not call off the wedding. Cleostrata's next play is more successful, as she dresses her male actor (Chalinus) as a woman and produces a play in which her rival playwright's actor (Olympio) is humiliated. Thus, in the contest of rival playwrights, the wife defeats the husband in Plautus' *Casina.*

BIBLIOGRAPHY

Franko, G. F. "Imagery and Names in Plautus' *Casina,*" *Classical Journal* 95, no. 1 (1999–2000): 1–17.

MacCary, W. T., and M. M. Willcock. *Casina.* Cambridge: Cambridge University Press, 1976.

O'Bryhim, S. "The Originality of Plautus' *Casina,*" *American Journal of Philology* 110 (1989): 81–103.

Slater, N. W. "The Pilots of Penance or the Slave of Lust." In *Plautus in Performance.* Princeton, N.J.: Princeton University Press, 1985, 70–93.

Way, M. L. "Violence and the Performance of Class in Plautus' *Casina,*" *Helios* 27, no. 2 (2000): 187–206.

Williams, B. "Games People Play: Metatheatre as Performance Criticism in Plautus' *Casina,*" *Ramus* 22 (1993): 33–59.

THE CASKET COMEDY (Latin: *CISTELLARIA*) PLAUTUS (CA. 203 OR 202 B.C.E.)

The play may have been staged at the end of the Romans' second war with the Carthaginians. Discovery of fragments of MENANDER's *Synaristosai* (Women at luncheon) and other archaeological evidence reveal that PLAUTUS' play was based on Menander's earlier work. The action of the play occurs in SICYON (the only time this city is used as a setting in extant Roman COMEDY) before two houses, one belonging to two gentlemen, one young, Alcesimarchus, the other elderly, Demipho.

The play's opening remarks occur in the form of a conversation of two PROSTITUTES, Selenium and Gymnasium, with Syra, Gymnasium's rather intoxicated mother, who also acts as the "madam" for the two prostitutes. In the course of their conversation, Selenium reveals that although she is a prostitute, she has only had a single customer, Alcesimarchus, with whom she is desperately in love. Alcesimarchus had promised Selenium's mother that he would marry her, but his father was forcing him to marry a relative of Demipho's. When Selenium's mother learned that Alcesimarchus is going to marry someone else, she ordered Selenium to return home for a few days. Selenium asks Gymnasium to look after her home while she is away.

After the two prostitutes exit, Gymnasium's mother delivers a delayed PROLOGUE. She explains that she found Selenium (an infant) abandoned in an alley. She then gave Selenium to another prostitute, who pretended that she had given birth to Selenium and raised the child as her own. At this point, Gymnasium's mother staggers offstage, and the god AUXILIUM, whose name means "help" or "aid," enters, and continues the prologue.

Auxilium explains that at a festival of DIONYSUS, a merchant from LEMNOS became intoxicated, sexually assaulted a young woman, and then returned to Lemnos. We later learn that this merchant's name is Demipho and that the young woman's name is Phanostrata. Phanostrata gave birth to Selenium; the infant was abandoned and eventually fell into the hands of the prostitute (Melaenis). Auxilium adds that when the first wife of the merchant Demipho died, he moved to Sicyon and married Phanostrata, the woman whom he had assaulted years earlier. When Demipho learned that Phanostrata had a daughter, he tried to discover who had raised the child. Demipho sent out a slave, Lampadio, to seek Selenium's caregiver.

After the exit of Auxilium, the play's second act opens with a soliloquy by Alcesimarchus, who laments his inability to be with Selenium, whom he loves dearly. Unfortunately, the rest of Alcesimarchus' soliloquy has not survived and the play's manuscript is in fragmentary condition for several hundred lines. Alcesimarchus, however, would have learned of Selenium's departure and discovered the true reason why Selenium left. Some of the surviving fragments indicate that the distraught Alcesimarchus is eventually encouraged to ask Melaenis for information about Selenium.

After the departure of Alcesimarchus, his father enters, sees Gymnasium, and expresses his attraction for her. He also suspects that Gymnasium is the woman with whom Alcesimarchus is in love. Gymnasium, realizing she has been mistaken for Selenium, decides to play along with the old man's delusion. At this point, the manuscript again has some gaps. Apparently, Alcesimarchus' father, after he had had sexual relations with Gymnasium, arranged to marry her through Gymnasium's mother and took her to his house. At some point, Demipho's slave, Lampadio, would have recognized Gymnasium's mother as the one who took the infant Selenium. Lampadio then followed her back to her house. Selenium and her mother, accompanied by Alcesimarchus, also would have returned.

Alcesimarchus begs Selenium and Melaenis for understanding but is rejected. Before Alcesimarchus goes into his father's house, he says he will kill Melaenis, Selenium, and himself, if Melaenis does not send Selenium to him. Melaenis decides to watch Alcesimarchus to make sure he does not do anything rash, but before she can act, Lampadio enters to tell Phanostrata that he saw Gymnasium's mother pick up the infant Selenium; Melaenis overhears and thinks that she herself will be in trouble. Phanostrata encourages Lampadio to seek out Melaenis.

After Phanostrata departs into Demipho's house, Melaenis emerges from her hiding place and speaks with Lampadio, who, not knowing who she is, tells her about Selenium's background and says he was the one who abandoned the infant. Lampadio dashes off, not wanting to be delayed by a woman whom he perceives as a nuisance. Melaenis decides to restore Selenium to her rightful family.

As the third act opens, Melaenis, Selenium, and Melaenis' maid, Halisca, enter. Melaenis leads Selenium toward Demipho's house to reunite her with her true family. Melaenis carries a small box filled with toys, which were left by Selenium's real parents when she was abandoned as an infant. When they knock on Demipho's door, however, Alcesimarchus, still distraught, rushes from the house with sword in hand. The women try to prevent him from doing anything foolish, but he carries Selenium into his house. Melaenis and Halisca follow him. In the confusion, Halisca drops the box of toys on the ground.

The play's fourth act begins with Lampadio's return from the house of Gymnasium's mother and finding the box. Phanostrata, to whom Lampadio is reporting, recognizes the box as Selenium's own. Halisca, emerging from Alcesimarchus' house, laments dropping the box of toys. Lampadio, seeing Halisca, realizes that she is looking for the box. Phanostrata then calls to Halisca, and she and Lampadio question Halisca about the box. Eventually, they tell her they have the box, and in the course of further questioning Phanostrata realizes that Selenium is her own daughter. Then, Phanostrata, Lampadio, and Halisca go back into Alcesimarchus' house.

The play's final act and epilogue are a little more than a dozen lines. Demipho returns, is informed by Lampadio that Selenium has been discovered as his daughter, and enters Alcesimarchus' house. Several members of the acting troupe tell the audience not to expect those within the house to reappear and then invite the audience's applause.

COMMENTARY

Given the large gaps in the manuscript of *Casket Comedy,* this has been one of the least-discussed Plautine plays over the past 30 years. The most-discussed scholarly issue that has emerged regarding the play has been the identification of Menander's *Synaristosai* as Plautus' model. The delivery of the prologue by the divinity Auxilium (who does not appear as a character elsewhere in surviving classical drama) is relatively unusual in extant Roman comedy but has parallels in AMPHITRYO and ROPE. A delayed prologue given by a divinity does not occur elsewhere in extant Roman comedy but does occur in Menander's *Aspis* (SHIELD).

Casket lacks the energetic fun of some of Plautus' other plays, perhaps because it does not have a clever slave such as Pseudolus or Tranio (HAUNTED HOUSE) and because it has a madam rather than a PIMP. Unlike in *Comedy of Asses,* in which a madam also appears, Syra is thought to be the mother of one of the prostitutes, and unlike others who keep prostitutes, she lacks the vile qualities of other Plautine flesh peddlers. The madam in *Casket* is more concerned with the young man's credibility than his cash.

As is evident from *Casina,* comic potential does exist in having both father and son in love with the same woman, but in *Casket* the father has mistaken Gymnasium for Selenium and father and son are not actually attracted to the same woman, as in *Casina.* Furthermore, in *Casket* we do not enjoy the comic results of the wife's discovery of her husband's infatuation with the prostitute as we do in *Casina.* Any further humor that might arise from the father-son rivals does not appear in *Casket,* and the love affair of father and prostitute is not developed.

In addition to the rather serious madam, Alcesimarchus, who Harsh declares is "the most violent lover of New Comedy," contributes to *Casket*'s less festive tone. In a manner that somewhat anticipates the situation between Demea and Ctesipho in TERENCE's BROTHERS (a play that also employs a Menandrian model),

Alcesimarchus' father tries to deliver his son from temptation by keeping him in the country. Alcesimarchus has been sent to the country but has obviously violated his father's wishes by returning to town and his beloved. As Ctesipho has, Alcesimarchus has been sent to the country, but he also has the physical aggressiveness of Ctesipho's brother, Aeschinus, who forcibly takes a prostitute from a pimp's house. Alcesimarchus is more violent than the unarmed Aeschinus. Although Plautine characters occasionally talk about using weapons such as swords, the playwright's audience rarely see them brandished. In *Casina,* Lysidamus is told (falsely) that Casina has a sword and is threatening to kill the man with whom she sleeps that night. In PSEUDOLUS, the distraught young lover, Calidorus, asks Pseudolus for a sword to kill himself, but his request is not taken seriously, and the audience never sees the sword. In *Casket,* however, Alcesimarchus' sword is actually seen by the audience as he drags Selenium from the house and threatens to kill himself.

Although the tone of *Casket* is not as light as that of other Plautine plays, the play is not without interesting features. As Konstan and others have noted, the plot of *Casket* involves two threads, one involving romance, the other recognition. Eventually, the recognition of Selenium as a freeborn woman will clear the way for the romance. Just as the play's plot has two strands, the young lover in *Casket* faces two obstacles. Whereas either a pimp or a father is usually the young lover's obstacle, in *Casket,* the young man is opposed by both his father and a madam. Not only is the young man caught between his father and the madam, he is also caught between two opposing classes and the laws that prevented unions between those classes, as Konstan shows. On one hand, Alcesimarchus' father has every reason to believe that Selenium, a prostitute, is beneath his son socially and thus does not want his freeborn son to marry a prostitute. On the other hand, the madam opposes the young man because she thinks he has broken his promise to Selenium. Though the prostitute and the madam are of lower social status than the young man, the madam will not allow the young man to treat her in such a way. Thus, unlike other plays involving young men who need to outmaneuver pimps, *Casket* is not a "quest for cash" play in which

money must be acquired to purchase the prostitute. Unlike in these other Roman comedies, the young man in *Casket* must prove to the prostitute's owner that he possesses something more valuable than cash: If he wants his beloved, he must prove his credibility.

BIBLIOGRAPHY

Gaiser, K. "Ein Fragment aus Menander *Synaristosai?*" *Zeitschrift fur Papyrologie und Epigraphik* 39 (1980): 99–111.

Harsh, P. W. *A Handbook of Classical Drama.* Stanford, Calif.: Stanford University Press, 1944, 352.

Konstan, D. "*Cistellaria:* Noncitizen Order." In *Roman Comedy.* Ithaca, N.Y.: Cornell University Press, 1983, 96–114.

Lange, D. K. "The Identification of Plautus' *Cistellaria* with Menander's *Synaristosai,*" *Classical Journal* 70, no. 3 (1975): 30–32.

Paratore, E. "La Struttura della *Cistellaria* di Plauto," *Atti dell'Accademia Pontaniana* 30 (1981): 429–45.

Rosivach, V. J. "The Stage Settings of Plautus' *Bacchides, Cistellaria* and *Epidicus,*" *Hermes* 114 (1986): 429–42.

Thamm, G. *Zur Cistellaria des Plautus.* Ph.D. dissertation, Freiburg, Germany, 1971.

CASSANDRA   Also called Alexandra, Cassandra was the daughter of PRIAM and HECABE and the sister of HECTOR, PARIS, POLYXENA, TROILUS, and many others. APOLLO became attracted to Cassandra and promised to teach her to be a prophet in exchange for her sexual favors. Initially Cassandra agreed, but after learning the prophetic arts, she rejected Apollo's advances. In *Agamemnon* (see ORESTEIA), AESCHYLUS describes their encounter as being like a wrestling match. The angry Apollo then cursed Cassandra by making sure that people did not believe her prophecies. The Trojans especially would come to regret not heeding Cassandra's prophecies. Although Cassandra is usually considered younger than Paris is, in EURIPIDES' ANDROMACHE there is a report that Cassandra declared that her brother Paris should be destroyed or else he would become the ruin of TROY. Before the fall of Troy, Cassandra also warned the Trojans about the Greeks' hiding in the wooden horse. During the fall of Troy, Cassandra was raped by Locrian AJAX while she was clinging to a statue of ATHENA. In EURIPIDES' TROJAN WOMEN, ATHENA considers Cassandra's rape the primary reason for her wanting POSEIDON to raise a deadly storm against the Greek fleet on their way back from Troy. Because, after Troy fell, Cassandra became the slave and concubine of AGAMEMNON, in *Trojan Women* Euripides has the frenzied Cassandra appear carrying torches as if in celebration or her marriage to Agamemnon. During this mockery of the wedding ritual, Cassandra predicts her own death as well as that of Agamemnon. She also prophesies the wanderings of ODYSSEUS after the war. In Aeschylus' *Agamemnon*, the audience see that Cassandra has returned with Agamemnon to ARGOS. Again, Cassandra is shown as the frenzied prophetess who predicts her own death as well as that of Agamemnon. Ultimately, CLYTEMNESTRA kills Cassandra, whose body is displayed beside that of the slain Agamemnon.

Cassandra does not appear as a character in SENECA'S *TROJAN WOMEN*, although she does appear in Seneca's *AGAMEMNON*, in which her role is more extensive than in Aeschylus' *Agamemnon*. In Aeschylus' play, Clytemnestra's primary motive for revenge against her husband is his sacrifice of IPHIGENIA. Seneca does not overlook this motive but adds to Clytemnestra's motivation the emphasis of Cassandra's role as a rival for the love of Agamemnon. As in Aeschylus' play, Cassandra predicts her own death and Agamemnon's. Unlike Aeschylus, however, Seneca has Cassandra and Agamemnon converse before they are killed. Seneca's Agamemnon even tries to reassure Cassandra that she has nothing to fear. After Agamemnon enters the palace, Cassandra describes in detail the way in which Agamemnon is killed. In contrast to Aeschylus' play, Seneca's *Agamemnon* ends with Clytemnestra's driving Cassandra into the palace. [ANCIENT SOURCES: Apollodorus, *Library* 3.12.5, *Epitome* 5.17, 5.22–23, 6.23; Euripides, *Andromache* 297, *Hecabe, Trojan Women*; Homer, *Odyssey* 11.420; Hyginus, *Fables* 93, 117; Seneca, *Agamemnon, Trojan Women* 37, 61, 967, 977; Vergil, *Aeneid* 2.344, 425]

BIBLIOGRAPHY

Calder, W. M. "Seneca's *Agamemnon*," *Classical Philology* 71 (1976): 27–36.
Leahy, D. M. "The Role of Cassandra in the *Oresteia* of Aeschylus," *Bulletin of the John Rylands Library* 52 (1969): 144–77.
Morgan, K. A. "Apollo's Favorites," *Greek, Roman, and Byzantine Studies* 35 (1994): 121–43.
Papadopoulou, T. "Cassandra's Radiant Vigour and the Ironic Optimism of Euripides' *Troades*," *Mnemosyne* 53, no. 5 (2000): 513–27.
Taplin, O. "Aeschylean Silences and Silences in Aeschylus," *Harvard Studies in Classical Philology* 76 (1972): 57–98.

CASTALIA   This spring arises at DELPHI and is noted for the purity of its waters. APOLLO's priestess at Delphi, the Pythia, as well as those who wanted to consult the oracle, were said to bathe in the Castalian spring. According to legend, Castalia was the daughter of the Achelous River or the spring was a gift to Castalia from the river. [ANCIENT SOURCES: Euripides, *Iphigenia in Tauris* 1256, *Ion* 95, 149, *Phoenician Women* 222; Pausanias, 10.8.9; Seneca, *Oedipus* 229, 276, 712; Sophocles, *Antigone* 1130]

CASTOR AND POLLUX (POLYDEUCES)

Castor and Pollux were the sons of LEDA, queen of SPARTA. They were the brothers of HELEN and CLYTEMNESTRA. Because Leda was impregnated on the same night by both ZEUS and her husband, TYNDAREUS, one boy (Pollux) was the son of the god, the other (Castor) the son of a mortal. Although only one of them was actually Zeus' son, the two boys were called the Dioscoroi, the "sons of Zeus." Castor is said to have trained HERACLES in the art of swordplay. Pollux appears to have had great skill in boxing. The two brothers married daughters of Leucippus of Messene. Castor married Hilaira and had a son, Anagon; Pollux married Phoebe and had a son, Mnesileus. When THESEUS kidnapped Helen, they rescued her and took Theseus' mother, Aethra, as a captive. Tradition says that they took part in the hunt for the Calydonian boar, as well as the quest for the GOLDEN FLEECE.

Castor and Pollux met their demise after a cattle raid in which they were accompanied by Aphareus' son, Idas, and LYNCEUS. When Idas tricked the brothers out of their share of the cattle and drove the animals to Messene, Castor and Pollux followed, recaptured the cattle, and then set up an ambush for Idas and Lynceus. Lynceus, having exceptional powers of sight, saw Castor and told Idas. After Idas killed Castor, Lynceus was slain by Pollux. Having suffered a head wound in his fight, Pollux fainted before he could attack Idas. Zeus, however, struck Idas with a lightning bolt and transported Pollux to heaven. Because Castor was dead, Pollux refused to accept immortality. Eventually, Zeus allowed the brothers to live in heaven and on Earth on alternate days. As divinities, they are usually considered protectors of sailors.

In extant drama, they appear at the conclusion of EURIPIDES' *ELECTRA* and *HELEN*. In both plays, the brothers appear as divinities to resolve the dramas. In *Electra,* they arrange the marriage of ELECTRA and PYLADES and tell ORESTES of his wanderings, his torment by the FURIES, and his eventual acquittal of his crimes in ATHENS. In *Helen,* the brothers stop Theoclymenus from pursuing their sister, Helen, and her husband, MENELAUS. [ANCIENT SOURCES: Apollodorus, *Library* 1.8.2, 1.9.16, 2.4.9, 3.10.7, 3.11.2, *Epitome* 1.23; Apollonius Rhodius, 1.146–47, 2.20, 62, 100–2, 756, 916, 4.588–89; Seneca, *Octavia* 208, *Thyestes* 628]

CATAMEITUS   See GANYMEDE.

CATHARSIS   One of the most controversial words in the history of literary criticism. According to ARISTOTLE's *Poetics* (1449b24–28), TRAGEDY, through pity and fear, produces a catharsis of those emotions. The Greek word for "emotions" (*pathemata*) is also disputed, and some scholars have argued that it means "events." Thus, Aristotle's passage says that tragedy brings about a catharsis of such "emotions" or of such "events." Most scholars, however, seem to take *pathemata* as meaning "emotions." If interpreted in this way, tragedy, through pity and fear, yields catharsis of emotions. Still, modern scholars do not agree on what the word *catharsis* means in this context. Some, such as Golden, have argued that *catharsis* refers to an intellectual clarification either of the emotions or of the play's events among the members of the audience. Others think that tragedy brings about a "purification" (catharsis) of the emotions of pity and fear. Others, such as Yates, have noted that elsewhere in Aristotle's works (especially *Politics* 8.7) *catharsis* can mean purgation in a biological sense. Charles Segal seems to have combined some of these views by describing *catharsis* as "a cleansing release . . . of pity and fear."

Segal suggests that in *OEDIPUS TYRANNOS,* for example, the audience experience catharsis in the Aristotelian sense "at the moment of recognition, when the chorus first looked with horror on their blinded king." Thus, the pity and fear of the characters in the play invite the audience to experience communally an emotional response of pity and fear themselves.

BIBLIOGRAPHY
Else, G. F. *Aristotle: Poetics.* Ann Arbor: University of Michigan Press, 1967.
Golden, L. "Epic, Tragedy, and Catharsis," *Classical Philology* 71 (1976): 77–85.
Oksenberg, R. A., ed. *Essays on Aristotle's Poetics.* Princeton, N.J.: Princeton University Press, 1992.
Segal, Charles. "Catharsis, Audience, and Closure in Greek Tragedy." In *Tragedy and the Tragic: Greek Theatre and Beyond.* Edited by Michael Stephen Silk. Oxford: Oxford University Press, 1996, 149–81.
Yates, V. "A Sexual Model of Catharsis," *Apeiron* 31, no. 1 (1998): 35–57.

CAUCASUS   A mountain range and a specific mountain in that range, which extends from the eastern shore of Black Sea to the western shore of the Caspian Sea. Usually, Mount Caucasus is named as the location of PROMETHEUS' binding. [ANCIENT SOURCES: Aeschylus, *Prometheus Bound* 422, 719; Appian, *The Foreign Wars* 12.15.103; Apollodorus, *Library* 1.7.1, 2.5.11; Pausanias, 5.11.6; Seneca, *Hercules Oetaeus* 1378, *Medea* 709]

CAVEA   A Latin word literally meaning "hollow space," *cavea* (plural: *caveae*) refers to that part of an ancient theater where the spectators sit. *Theatron* and *auditorium* are synonyms for *cavea.* The size of the cavea differed from town to town. Some *caveae* could have accommodated a few hundred spectators; others would have seated several thousand. In many instances, especially in Roman theaters during the imperial period, certain sections of the cavea were reserved for specific segments of the population: senators, women, young men, and the like.

BIBLIOGRAPHY
Cicu, Luciano. "*Spectator in fabula: ut aeque mecum sitis gnarures (Poen.* 47)," *Sandalion* 18 (1995): 67–113.

Small, D. B. "Social Correlations to the Greek *Cavea* in the Roman Period." In *Roman Architecture in the Greek World.* Edited by Sarah Macready and F. H. Thompson. London: The Society of Antiquaries of London, 1987, 85–93.

CAYSTRIAN PLAINS   Between EPHESUS and SARDIS in what is today Turkey, these plains created the first part of a route between the Persian capital, SUSA, and the AEGEAN SEA. [ANCIENT SOURCES: Aristophanes, *Acharnians* 68]

BIBLIOGRAPHY
Sommerstein, A. H. *The Comedies of Aristophanes.* Vol. 1, *Acharnians.* Warminster, U.K.: Aris & Phillips, 1980, 160.

CEBRIONE (CEBRIONES)   A son of PRIAM, Cebrione was killed during the 10th year of the Trojan War. [ANCIENT SOURCES: Aristophanes, *Birds* 553; Homer, *Iliad* 16.775–76]

BIBLIOGRAPHY
Dunbar, Nan. *Aristophanes: Birds.* New York: Oxford University Press, 1995, 375–77.

CECROPIA   Another name for the city of ATHENS. See also CECROPS.

CECROPS   The son of HEPHAESTUS and Mother EARTH (Gaia) or the Earth alone, Cecrops had an unusual physique: He was human from the waist up and serpent from the waist down. Cecrops was the first king of ATHENS, but during his reign he named the city after himself, CECROPIA, a name that poets sometimes used for Athens. Similarly, poets sometimes call the Athenians the descendants or sons of Cecrops. Cecrops' wife was Actaeus' daughter, Agraulos (or Aglauros); by Agraulos Cecrops had three daughters, Agraulos the younger (or Aglauros), Herse, and Pandrosos), and a son, Erysichthon. The most significant event of Cecrops' reign occurred when ATHENA and POSEIDON quarreled over possession of the city. According to one tradition, Cecrops was appointed to judge which divinity would be of greater benefit to the city. Poseidon stuck the Athenian ACROPOLIS with his trident and produced a salt spring, while Athena planted an olive tree. Cecrops judged Athena's gift to be more beneficial to the city. Consequently, she became the patron divinity and the city was named after her. Poseidon, the angry loser, flooded Athena's new town. [ANCIENT SOURCES: Apollodorus, *Library* 3.14.1; Euripides, *Ion* 1136; Hyginus, *Fables* 48; Ovid, *Metamorphoses* 2.555, 784, 797, 806; Seneca, *Medea* 76, *Thyestes* 1049]

CEDALION   A smith from the island of NAXOS from whom HEPHAESTUS learned the craft. Another tradition makes Cedalion the servant of Hephaestus. When ORION sexually assaulted Merope, the daughter of Dionysus' son, Oenopion, DIONYSUS and his satyrs blinded Orion. The sightless Orion made his way to LEMNOS, where Hephaestus sent Cedalion with Orion to be his guide. Orion had learned that if he met the rising sun, he would regain his sight. With Cedalion as his guide—Orion placed Cedalion on his shoulders—Orion was successful. SOPHOCLES wrote a satyric *Cedalion,* but the seven surviving fragments (none longer than two lines) reveal little about the plot. The blinding of Orion recalls the blinding of POLYPHEMUS in the only extant SATYR PLAY, EURIPIDES' *CYCLOPS.*

BIBLIOGRAPHY
Lloyd-Jones, H. *Sophocles: Fragments.* Cambridge, Mass.: Harvard University Press, 1996.
Radt, S. *Tragicorum Graecorum Fragmenta.* Vol. 4. Göttingen, Ger.: Vandenhoeck & Ruprecht, 1977.
Yoshida, A. "Mythe d'Orion et de Cédalion, II." In *Hommages à Marcel Renard.* Edited by J. Bibauw. Bruxelles: 60 rue Colonel Chaltin, 1969, 828–44.

CELEUS   A king at ELEUSIS, Celeus was husband of Metaneira and father of TRIPTOLEMUS and Demophon. Celeus became the first priest of DEMETER at Eleusis. His daughters were the goddess' first priestesses. ARISTOPHANES, apparently for the purposes of a comic genealogy, changes the genealogy and makes Celeus the son of Demeter and Triptolemus. [ANCIENT SOURCES: Aristophanes, *Acharnians* 49; *Homeric Hymn to Demeter;* Pausanias, 1.14.2]

CENAEUM   A promontory at the northwest end of the island of EUBOEA. [ANCIENT SOURCES: Apollodorus, *Library* 2.7.7; Seneca, *Hercules Oetaeus* 102, 782; Sophocles, *Trachinian Women* 238, 753, 993]

CENTAUR   The centaurs were a race of creatures that had the head and upper body of a human being attached to the body and legs of a horse. According to one tradition, IXION produced the first centaur when he had intercourse with a cloud that ZEUS had made into the form of HERA, whom Ixion was trying to seduce. Another tradition says that IXION's son, Centaurus, produced the first centaurs when he mated with some mares on Mount PELION. With the exception of the hospitable centaur Pholus and of Chiron, who raised and trained heroes such as ACHILLES and JASON, centaurs are usually characterized as uncivilized and savage creatures who pose a sexual threat to Greek females and whom Greek males must defeat. HERACLES battled successfully against centaurs on more than one occasion. He killed the centaur Eurytion, to whom Dexamenus was going to betroth his daughter. Heracles also killed the centaur NESSUS, who had attempted to rape his wife, DEIANEIRA. THESEUS had helped the Lapiths defeat some centaurs that had attempted to violate PIRITHOUS' bride. ATALANTA killed some centaurs that tried to rape her.

Just as the centaur's nature was dual, centaurs were suited for TRAGEDY or COMEDY. The Greek tragedian Chaeremon wrote a play entitled *Centaur*, from which two brief fragments survive (10–11 Snell). Fragment 10 refers to a group of women searching for flowers in a meadow. Such women might have been the sexual targets of a lusty centaur. Greek comedies entitled *Centaur* are known from ARISTOPHANES (fragments 267–77 Kock 1), Lynceus (fragment 1 Kock 3), Nicochares (fragments 7–8 Kock 1), Theognetus (see Kock 3), Timocles (fragment 19 Kock 2). Only the title of Theognetus' play survives and the few fragments of Aristophanes' and Nichochares' plays that survive are uninformative. From Lynceus' *Centaur*, a 22-line fragment is extant in which the speaker refuses to be served a dish of several kinds of food and demands a dish with only one kind. Timocles' *Centaur* may have dealt with Heracles' rescue of Dexamenus' daughter from the centaur Eurytion. The comic poet Apollophanes wrote a *Centaurs*, of which only the title remains (see Kock 1). [ANCIENT SOURCES: Apollodorus, *Library* 2.5.4–5, 2.7.6, 3.9.2; Euripides, *Andromache* 792, *Heracles* 181, 365, 1273, *Iphigenia at Aulis* 706, 1047, 1060; Ovid, *Metamorphoses* 12.219, 536; Seneca, *Hercules Furens* 778, *Hercules Oetaeus* 503, 1049, 1195, 1925; Sophocles, *Trachinian Women* 680, 831, 1141, 1162]

BIBLIOGRAPHY
duBois, Page. *Centaurs and Amazons: Women and the Pre-History of the Great Chain of Being*. Ann Arbor: University of Michigan Press, 1982.

Kock, T. *Comicorum Atticorum Fragmenta*. Vol. 1. Leipzig: Teubner, 1880.

———. *Comicorum Atticorum Fragmenta*. Vol. 2. Leipzig: Teubner, 1884.

———. *Comicorum Atticorum Fragmenta*. Vol. 3. Leipzig: Teubner, 1888.

Osborne, Robin. "Framing the Centaur: Reading Fifth-Century Architectural Sculpture." In *Art and Text in Ancient Greek Culture*. Edited by Simon Goldhill and Robin Osborne. Cambridge and New York: Cambridge University Press, 1994, 52–84.

Scobie, A. "The Origins of Centaurs," *Folklore* 89 (1978): 142–47.

Snell, B. *Tragicorum Graecorum Fragmenta*. Vol. 1. Göttingen, Ger.: Vandenhoeck & Ruprecht, 1971.

Stern, F. van K. "Heroes and Monsters in Greek Art," *Archaeological News* 7 (1978): 1–23.

CEPHALE   A DEME in the region of Attica, Cephale was the site of "a large cemetery" known to ARISTOPHANES. [ANCIENT SOURCES: Aristophanes, *Birds* 476]

BIBLIOGRAPHY
Dunbar, Nan. *Aristophanes: Birds*. New York: Oxford University Press, 1995, 327.

CEPHALLENIA   An island just off the western coast of mainland Greece and close to the island of ITHACA. Some sources regard Cephallenia as part of the kingdom of ODYSSEUS. [ANCIENT SOURCES: Euripides, *Cyclops* 103; Seneca, *Trojan Women* 518; Sophocles, *Philoctetes* 264, 791]

CEPHALUS (1)   From the DEME of Collytus, Cephalus was active in Athenian politics in the first quarter of the fifth century B.C.E. Cephalus argued in favor of Athenian military operations during this time and in the year 384 led a diplomatic mission to confirm an alliance with the island of CHIOS. Comic poets such as ARISTOPHANES and Plato labeled him as being mentally unstable and having a vile smell, but the orators Aeschines, Deinarchus, and Demosthenes show respect to him "as a great democrat and patriot" (Sommerstein). [ANCIENT SOURCES: Aeschines, 3.194; Andocides, 1.115, 150; Aristophanes, *Ecclesiazusae* 248; Deinarchus, 1.38–39, 76; Demosthenes, 18.219, 251; Pausanias, 3.9.8; Plato Comicus, fragment 201 Kock]

BIBLIOGRAPHY

Kock, T. *Comicorum Atticorum Fragmenta.* Vol. 1. Leipzig: Teubner, 1880.

Sommerstein, A. H. *The Comedies of Aristophanes.* Vol. 10, *Ecclesiazusae.* Warminster, U.K.: Aris & Phillips, 1998, 161.

CEPHALUS (2)

This Cephalus attracted the attention of the goddess EOS, who carried him off to her bed. By Eos, Cephalus became the father of PHAETHON. [ANCIENT SOURCES: Euripides, *Hippolytus* 455–56; Hesiod, *Theogony* 886–91; Pausanias, 1.3.1]

CEPHALUS (3)

The son of Deion and Diomede, Cephalus became suspicious that his wife, PROCRIS, would be unfaithful to him. Therefore, disguising himself as a stranger, he tried to seduce her. Procris acquiesced after Cephalus offered her a substantial bribe. When Cephalus revealed his true identity, however, Procris left him and went to the house of MINOS on CRETE. Eventually, fearing the wrath of Minos' wife, PASIPHAE, Procris returned to ATHENS and became reconciled with Cephalus. She gave Cephalus two gifts that she had received from Minos: a spear that never missed its mark and a dog that always caught what it chased.

After some time, Procris began to suspect that Cephalus was being unfaithful to her. Therefore, when Cephalus went out hunting, Procris followed him. Cephalus, hearing a rustling in a thicket, threw his spear and unwittingly struck and killed Procris. Cephalus was put on trial in the AREOPAGUS, condemned, and sent into permanent exile. At some point during his life, Cephalus became a friend and ally of HERACLES' mortal father, AMPHITYRON, who borrowed Cephalus' famous dog to hunt a dangerous fox whose destiny was that it could never be caught. Because the dog was fated to catch anything it chased, the result was a stalemate, which ZEUS resolved by changing both animals into stone. After Cephalus went into exile, he fought alongside Amphitryon in his victory over the Taphians. For this service Amphitryon gave Cephalus and Heleus (another of the allies) the islands of the Taphians, where both men founded towns that they named after themselves. Cephalus was the founder of CEPHALLENIA. The Greek comic poet Philetaerus wrote a *Cephalus,* of which only the title survives (see Kock). [ANCIENT SOURCES: Apollodorus, *Library* 1.9.4, 2.4.7; 3.15.1; Hyginus, *Fables* 189; Ovid, *Metamorphoses* 7.661–865; Strabo 10.2.14, 20, 24]

BIBLIOGRAPHY

Kock, T. *Comicorum Atticorum Fragmenta.* Vol. 2. Leipzig: Teubner, 1884.

CEPHISODEMUS

An Athenian who was the father of EUATHLUS. [ANCIENT SOURCES: Aristophanes, *Acharnians* 705]

CEPHISOPHON

A friend of EURIPIDES' who was said to have helped him with his writing (especially the lyric segments) and to have acted in his plays. Cephisophon was also rumored to have seduced Euripides' wife. In ARISTOPHANES' *ACHARNIANS,* the slave who answers the door of Euripides' house is often identified as Cephisophon in marginal annotations in the ancient manuscripts. [ANCIENT SOURCES: Aristophanes, *Acharnians* 393–403, *Frogs* 944, 1408, 1452–53, fragment 580 Kock]

BIBLIOGRAPHY

Dover, Kenneth. *Aristophanes: Frogs.* Oxford: Clarendon Press, 1993, 53–54.

Kock, T. *Comicorum Atticorum Fragmenta.* Vol. 1. Leipzig: Teubner, 1880.

Sommerstein, A. H. *The Comedies of Aristophanes.* Vol. 9, *Frogs.* Warminster, U.K.: Aris & Phillips, 1996, 239–40.

CEPHISUS

Several rivers in Greece were known by this name, but in classical drama Cephisus usually seems to refer to a river in Athenian territory that flowed past the town of ELEUSIS. [ANCIENT SOURCES: Euripides, *Medea* 835, *Ion* 1261; Sophocles, *Oedipus at Colonus* 687]

CERAMEICUS   The potter's district of ATHENS, where, among other things, those who died in battle received a public burial. There were actually two places in Athens called Cerameicus, one inside and one outside the Dipylon or Thriasian Gate. [ANCIENT SOURCES: Aristophanes, *Knights* 772, *Birds* 395, *Frogs* 129, 1093; Pausanias, 1.3.1]

CERBERUS   The offspring of Typhon and Echidna, Cerberus is a dog with multiple heads (three or 50) that guards the UNDERWORLD. In addition to having multiple heads, some sources state, Cerberus had "hair" on these heads that consisted of snakes. Some sources also give the Cerberus a snake for a tail. In HERACLES' final labor, he traveled to the underworld and dragged the Cerberus to the upper world. After Heracles showed the dog to EURYSTHEUS, Heracles took the dog back to the underworld. SOPHOCLES wrote a *Cerberus,* whose single surviving fragment (Radt 327a) tells nothing about the play's plot and gives no indication whether the play was a tragedy or a SATYR PLAY. [ANCIENT SOURCES: Apollodorus, *Library* 2.5.12; Hesiod, *Theogony* 306–12; Seneca, *Hercules Furens* 782–829; Sophocles, *Trachinian Women* 1114]

BIBLIOGRAPHY
Radt, S. *Tragicorum Graecorum Fragmenta.* Vol. 4. Göttingen, Ger.: Vandenhoeck & Ruprecht, 1977.
Sutton, D. F. "A Handlist of Satyr Plays," *Harvard Studies in Classical Philology* 78 (1974): 107–43.

CERCHNIA   A river in southeastern Greece near the town of LERNA. [ANCIENT SOURCES: Aeschylus, *Prometheus Bound* 676]

CERCOPES   The Cercopes were two men who, according to one tradition, were turned into apes by ZEUS. Their name appears to be related to the Greek word *kerkos,* which means "tail." Thus, the Cercopes may have had the tails of monkeys. During HERACLES' servitude to OMPHALE, Heracles captured the Cercopes near the town of EPHESUS. The Cercopes appear to have been a favorite subject of comic writers as the Greek poets Eubulus (fragments 53–54 Kock 2), HERMIPPUS (fragments 35–40 Kock 1), and Menippus (fragment 1

Kock 3) and the comic poet Plato (fragments 88–90 Kock 1) all wrote plays with titles that bear the name of these creatures. Only the title of Menippus' play exists and the brief fragments of Plato's *Cercopes* indicate nothing of the play's plot. Regarding Hermippus' *Cercopes,* DIONYSUS was a character and drinking was involved in the play. As for Eubulus' *Cercopes,* the speaker of the first fragment mentions going to CORINTH and losing his shirt to a prostitute. In fragment 2, the speaker tells of going to THEBES, where people dine all day and all night and have toilets beside the doors of their houses. [ANCIENT SOURCES: Apollodorus, *Library* 2.6.3; Athenaeus, 10.417d, 12.551a, 13.567b–c; Herodotus 7.216.1]

BIBLIOGRAPHY
Kock, T. *Comicorum Atticorum Fragmenta.* Vol. 1. Leipzig: Teubner, 1880.
———. *Comicorum Atticorum Fragmenta.* Vol. 2. Leipzig: Teubner, 1884.
———. *Comicorum Atticorum Fragmenta.* Vol. 3. Leipzig: Teubner, 1888.

CERCYON   A mythical king of ELEUSIS, Cercyon was the father of ALOPE. Cercyon challenged all strangers to his town to a wrestling match, during which he would kill them. Cercyon's reign of terror ended when THESEUS killed him in a wrestling match. AESCHYLUS wrote a satyric *Cercyon* that may have dealt with THESEUS' encounter with the king; only about 10 words survive from this play. ARISTOTLE indicates that Cercyon's defeat was dealt with in Carcinus' *Alope.* See also ALOPE. [ANCIENT SOURCES: Apollodorus, *Epitome* 1.3; Aristotle, *Nichomachean Ethics* 1150b10; Hyginus, *Fables* 187]

BIBLIOGRAPHY
Smyth, H. W., and H. Lloyd-Jones. *Aeschylus.* Vol. 2. 1971. Reprint, Cambridge, Mass.: Harvard University Press, 1971.

CERES   See DEMETER.

CEYX   The son of the morning star, Ceyx was a hospitable king of TRACHIS who welcomed two exiles, PELEUS and HERACLES, into his kingdom. With Heracles' help Ceyx was able to defeat his enemies. Ceyx drowned on a journey by sea to DELPHI; his wife, Alcyone, was saddened by his death. Some sources say that the gods took pity on Ceyx and Alcyone and changed them into birds; others say that the gods changed them into birds because they were calling each other ZEUS and HERA. Ceyx became a seagull (the meaning of his name in Greek), and Alcyone became a halcyon. [ANCIENT SOURCES: Apollodorus, *Library* 1.7.3–4; Hyginus, *Fables* 65; Ovid, *Metamorphoses* 11.268–748; Pausanias, 1.32.6; Seneca, *Agamemnon* 681, *Hercules Oetaeus* 197, *Octavia* 7]

CHAEREAS   An unknown effeminate man whom ARISTOPHANES makes fun of at WASPS 687. Sommerstein thinks that the Chaereas mentioned in Eupolis (fragment 80) "is probably unconnected" with the person ridiculed by Aristophanes.

BIBLIOGRAPHY
Sommerstein. A. *The Comedies of Aristophanes.* Vol. 4, *Wasps.* Warminster, U.K.: Aris & Phillips, 1980, 200.

CHAEREPHON   From the DEME of Sphettus in the region of ATTICA, Chaerephon was a friend of SOCRATES'. Though some scholars doubt the truth of the story, PLATO and Xenophon report that Chaerephon's inquiry of the ORACLE at DELPHI regarding who was the wisest man propelled Socrates to discover the truth behind this oracle. After the Spartans defeated the Athenians in 404 B.C.E., Chaerephon was banished from ATHENS, but he returned in 403. He died before Socrates' trial and execution in 399. In *CLOUDS*, ARISTOPHANES portrays Chaerephon as being Socrates' "star" pupil, as having pale skin, and as showing an interest in silly knowledge such as how far a flea could jump. At the conclusion of *Clouds*, STREPSIADES sets fire to Socrates' school and expresses a desire to kill Socrates and Chaerephon. Chaerephon appears as a silent character at the end of Aristophanes' WASPS. Here, he serves as a witness for a woman baker who is assaulted by PHILOCLEON. In *Memorabilia*, Xenophon defends Chaerephon and some of Socrates' other companions as men who never did anything wrong, truly wanted to be good men, and behaved properly with everyone they encountered. [ANCIENT SOURCES: Aristophanes,

Clouds 104, 144–47, 156, 503–4, 1465, *Wasps* 1408–15; Plato, *Apology* 20e–21, *Charmides* 153–54, *Gorgias* 447–48, 458d, 481b; Xenophon, *Apology* 14, *Memorabilia* 1.2.48]

BIBLIOGRAPHY
Kraut, Bruce H. "The Reappearance of Chaerephon in Aristophanes' *Wasps,*" *Text and Presentation* 8 (1988): 129–36.
Montuori, Mario. "The Oracle Given to Chaerephon on the Wisdom of Socrates: An Invention by Plato," *Kernos* 3 (1990): 251–59.
Strycker, E. de. "The Oracle Given to Chaerephon about Socrates (Plato, *Apology* 20e–21)," In *Kephalaion: Studies in Greek philosophy and Its Continuation offered to C. J. de Vogel.* Edited by J. Mansfeld and L. M. de Rijk. Assen, Netherlands: Van Gorcum, 1975, 39–49.

CHAERETADES   A probably fictional Athenian mentioned by ARISTOPHANES at ECCLESIAZUSAE 51. No historical Athenian of this name is known.

BIBLIOGRAPHY
Sommerstein, A. H. *The Comedies of Aristophanes.* Vol. 10, *Ecclesiazusae.* Warminster, U.K.: Aris & Phillips, 1998, 143.

CHAERIS   A musician whom several comic poets considered unskilled. He appears to have been active between 431 and 414 B.C.E. [ANCIENT SOURCES: Aristophanes, *Acharnians* 15–16, 857, *Birds* 857, *Peace* 950; Cratinus, fragment 118 Kock; Pherecrates, fragment 6 Kock]

BIBLIOGRAPHY
Dunbar, Nan. *Aristophanes: Birds.* New York: Oxford University Press, 1995, 507–8.
Kock, T. *Comicorum Atticorum Fragmenta.* Vol. 1. Leipzig: Teubner, 1880.
Sommerstein, A. H. *The Comedies of Aristophanes.* Vol. 5, *Peace.* Warminster, U.K.: Aris & Philips, 1985, 178.

CHALCIDIAN   See CHALCIS.

CHALCIS   This Athenian colony, located on the southwestern shore of the island of EUBOEA opposite the region of BOEOTIA, was one of the most important towns on the island. The people of Chalcis were called

Chalcidians. The CHORUS of women in EURIPIDES' *IPHI-GENIA IN AULIS* state that they are from this town. [ANCIENT SOURCES: Aristophanes, *Knights* 238; Euripides, *Iphigenia in Aulis* 168]

CHALCODON   The husband of Alcyone (or Melanippe) and the father of Elephenor, Chalcodon was a king on the island of EUBOEA. Pausanias says AMPHITYRON killed Chalcodon during a battle between the Thebans and Euboeans. [ANCIENT SOURCES: Apollodorus, *Epitome* 3.11; Pausanias, 9.19.3; Sophocles, *Philoctetes* 489]

CHALYBES   A savage (from the Greek perspective) race of people who lived along the coast of the region of Pontus in northern Asia Minor, who were famous for their work with iron. [ANCIENT SOURCES: Aeschylus, *Prometheus Bound* 715]

CHAONIA   A region along the coast of northwestern Greece. Chaonia was home to the Chaonian Oaks, a grove of trees sacred to ZEUS. Some sources regarded this grove as the oldest oracle in Greece, and the trees themselves (or the doves that lived in them) were supposed to deliver the prophecies. [ANCIENT SOURCES: Aristophanes, *Acharnians* 613, *Knights* 78, Seneca, *Oedipus* 728, *Hercules Oetaeus* 1623]

CHAOS   According to classical tradition, Chaos was the first thing to exist in the universe. The ancients disagreed, however, about exactly what chaos was and where it was located. Some considered it a state of confusion that existed before the ordering of the world, others as a huge void in the universe from which EARTH emerged, others as a part of the UNDERWORLD. [ANCIENT SOURCES: Aristophanes, *Birds* 691; Hesiod, *Theogony* 116–23, 814]

CHARACTER   This word can refer to a person portrayed in a play, such as CREON or ANTIGONE, but also to the combination of features and qualities that distinguish one character from another. When attempting to define the character of a person in a classical drama, one must notice what the person does, what the person says or reveals about him- or herself,

and what the other people in the play say about him or her. In some instances, the audience can quickly determine a person's character, especially in new COMEDY, which employs stock characters. The title of MENANDER'S *DYSCOLUS* (*The Grouch*) indicates immediately how Knemon will behave, and when he wants to be left alone and tries to drive away everyone who goes near his house it is no surprise. Similarly, in the plays of PLAUTUS and TERENCE, the audience expects a PIMP to be evil or a soldier to be a braggart, and when these characters go onstage, they quickly behave in a way that confirms expectations. In *ORESTEIA*, AESCHYLUS clearly shows AEGISTHUS is an unpleasant character and has an unpleasant character by describing him as a wolf and a cowardly lion and by clearly condemning his adultery with AGAMEMNON'S wife. EURIPIDES' Athenian audience would have had little sympathy for the Spartan MENELAUS in that playwright's *ANDROMACHE* as the Spartan treats Andromache and her young son with deception and brutality.

Many times, however, playwrights deliberately create ambiguities about a person's character. In EURIPIDES' *ALCESTIS,* APOLLO, HERACLES, and the CHORUS praise the hospitality of ADMETUS, but elsewhere in the play Admetus' father calls him a coward for allowing his wife to give up her life for him. In Aeschylus' *PROMETHEUS BOUND,* Prometheus portrays himself as someone who has given human beings great benefits and who has taught them many things, but other characters in the play criticize him for his stubbornness and unwillingness to be taught. In SOPHOCLES' *OEDIPUS TYRANNOS,* one can approach the character of OEDIPUS by examining what the people of THEBES say about him, what Oedipus says about himself, and what the gods (namely, APOLLO) and their representatives (i.e., TIRESIAS) say about him (through oracles). Whereas Oedipus thinks that he is a newcomer to Thebes, the god knows that he is a native Theban. Whereas Oedipus regards himself as skilled in the solving of riddles, the god knows that Oedipus has not yet unraveled the riddle of his own identity. Whereas the people of Thebes regard Oedipus as their savior, they later discover that he is also the cause of their current misery.

In addition to evaluating a person's character through his or her deeds and words and others' judgments, we can gain information about character from the stage properties, images, and symbols with which a person is associated. In Aeschylus' SEVEN AGAINST THEBES, information about the character of various warriors is provided by the decorations on their shields. In Sophocles' AJAX, the title character is associated with a whip during his madness; however, when ODYSSEUS first looks for AJAX, he describes him as "shield-bearing" Ajax, an epithet that evokes his past valor rather than his present madness. In Euripides' HERACLES, one of the weapons by which HERACLES gained fame, the bow, helps provide some understanding of his character. From the perspective of the evil king Lycus, the bow is the weapon of a coward. From the perspective of Heracles' mortal father, AMPHITRYON, the bow is the weapon of the clever person as it can unleash numerous arrows from a position of unseen safety.

BIBLIOGRAPHY

Easterling, P. E. "Character in Sophocles," *Greece and Rome* 24 (1977): 121–29.
Pelling, C. B. R., ed. *Characterization and Individuality in Greek Literature*. Oxford: Clarendon Press, 1990.

CHARES

A person of low intelligence who may have been a "relative of the Chares who served on an embassy to Sparta to negotiate peace in 446/445." [ANCIENT SOURCES: Aristophanes, *Acharnians* 603; Diodorus Siculus, 12.7]

BIBLIOGRAPHY

Sommerstein, A. H. *The Comedies of Aristophanes*. Vol. 1, *Acharnians*. Warminster, U.K.: Aris & Phillips, 1980, 186.

CHARINADES

The name of a fictional Athenian male. [ANCIENT SOURCES: Aristophanes, *Peace* 1155, *Wasps* 232]

CHARITES

See GRACES.

CHARIXENE

An Athenian woman whose name became proverbial for the distant past. She may have been a prostitute, who "may have lived in the late sixth century [B.C.E.]" (Sommerstein). Sommerstein speculates that Charixene might have been the mistress of the tyrant Hipparchus or his brother, HIPPIAS. [ANCIENT

SOURCES: Aristophanes, *Ecclesiazusae* 943; Cratinus, fragment 153 Kock; Hesychius, e5413; Theopompus Comicus, fragment 51]

BIBLIOGRAPHY

Sommerstein, A. H. *The Comedies of Aristophanes*. Vol. 10, *Ecclesiazusae*. Warminster, U.K.: Aris & Phillips, 1998. 220.

CHARMINUS

An Athenian naval commander who lost a battle to the Spartans off the southwestern coast of modern Turkey in 412/411 B.C.E. Charminus participated in the oligarchic revolution on the island of Samos in 411 and the subsequent assassination there of the exiled democratic leader Hyperbolus. After the oligarchic revolution failed, Charminus lost his post but did manage to keep his life. [ANCIENT SOURCES: Aristophanes, *Thesmophoriazusae* 804; Thucydides, 8.41.3–43.1, 8.73.3, 8.76.2]

BIBLIOGRAPHY

Sommerstein, A. H. *The Comedies of Aristophanes*. Vol. 8, *Thesmophoriazusae*. Warminster, U.K.: Aris & Phillips, 1994, 206.

CHARON

The son of EREBUS and NIGHT, Charon was a gruff, raggedly dressed sailor with a penetrating gaze. For a small fee (placed in the mouth of the deceased), Charon would transport people across the body of water in the UNDERWORLD that separated them from their final destination. He appears as a character in ARISTOPHANES' FROGS and carries DIONYSUS in his boat. [ANCIENT SOURCES: Aristophanes, *Frogs* 180–84, *Lysistrata* 606, *Wealth* 278; Euripides, *Alcestis* 254, 361, *Heracles* 432; Seneca, *Agamemnon* 752, 764, 770, *Hercules Furens* 555, *Hercules Oetaeus* 1072, *Oedipus* 166]

CHARONIAN STEPS

As described by Pollux, some theaters (not earlier than the fourth century B.C.E.) had underground passages between the orchestra's center and the stage building. Such a passage would have allowed supernatural characters such as ghosts or FURIES to appear to rise up from the stage or from the orchestra. The theater at ERETRIA has such a passageway preserved. [ANCIENT SOURCES: Pollux, *Onomasticon* 4.128, 4.132]

BIBLIOGRAPHY
Csapo, E., and W. J. Slater. *The Context of Ancient Drama.* Ann Arbor: University of Michigan Press, 1995, 82.

CHARYBDIS A whirlpool that spouted water and sucked that water down again three times a day, Charybdis was encountered during the adventures of both ODYSSEUS and JASON. Opposite the Charybdis was another deadly obstacle, the monster SCYLLA. Some ancient sources believed the Charybdis was located between SICILY and the toe of Italy's boot. In ARISTOPHANES' *KNIGHTS,* the politician CLEON is compared to the Charybdis. [ANCIENT SOURCES: Apollodorus, *Library* 1.9.25; *Epitome* 7.21; Apollonius Rhodius, 4.789, 825, 923; Aristophanes, *Knights* 248; Euripides, *Trojan Women* 436; Homer, *Odyssey* 73–110; 235–59; 430–44; Seneca, *Hercules Oetaeus* 235, *Medea* 408, *Thyestes* 581; Strabo, 6.2.3; Thucydides, 4.24.5]

CHERRONESUS Also called the CHERSONESE, this is a long, slender peninsula that extends into the AEGEAN SEA from Thrace and is opposite the northwestern coast of modern Turkey. [ANCIENT SOURCES: Aristophanes, *Knights* 262]

***CHILDREN OF HERACLES* (Greek: *HERACLEIDAI*) EURIPIDES (430 B.C.E.)** This TRAGEDY deals with the persecution of HERACLES' children by Heracles' enemy EURYSTHEUS. AESCHYLUS also wrote a *Children of Heracles* (fragments 73b–77 Radt); little is known about this play and how it might have influenced EURIPIDES' own treatment of the myth. Euripides sets his play at MARATHON, a small town some 25 miles northeast of ATHENS. The CHORUS consist of old men from Marathon. The action of the drama takes places after the death of Heracles.

As the play opens, the audience see that the children of Heracles and their relative IOLAUS have taken refuge at an altar of ZEUS in Marathon. The PROLOGUE begins with a monologue by IOLAUS, who sits with Heracles' sons on the steps of the altar. Iolaus notes that ALCMENA and Heracles' daughters have taken refuge inside the temple. As exiles, Iolaus and Heracles' children have traveled from town to town, seeking a place that will grant them asylum. Wherever they go, however, they are pursued by Heracles' enemy, Eurystheus, who threatens to punish any town that receives them. Iolaus' monologue ends with the arrival of Eurystheus' herald, Copreus ("dung man"), who demands that Iolaus and Heracles' children return to ARGOS for punishment. When Iolaus refuses, Copreus tries to drag them from the altar. Iolaus' cries for help are answered by the old men of Marathon. Iolaus explains the situation to the aged Marathonians, who offer their support. When Copreus confronts the chorus, they inform him that he should take up the issue with the king in the region, THESEUS' son, DEMOPHON.

The chorus' mention of Demophon's name heralds his arrival. Demophon's brother, Acamas, accompanies him but remains silent. When Demophon arrives, the chorus explain the situation. Copreus defends his right to take Iolaus and Heracles' children because he claims that the people of Argos have passed a sentence of death against them. Copreus warns Demophon that any interference will provoke a war between Argos and Demophon's people. Iolaus, in contrast, argues that Demophon's people have a reputation for aiding those in need and even argues that Theseus and Heracles were relatives, and therefore Demophon's people are obligated to Heracles' descendants as well. Demophon, swayed by Iolaus' argument, agrees to help Heracles' children. An angry Copreus leaves and threatens to begin a war when he returns.

After the departure of Copreus, Iolaus praises Demophon and his people. Demophon urges Iolaus and the children to leave the altar, but Iolaus says they will not leave until Demophon and his people are victorious. When Demophon leaves to make preparations for war with the Argives, the chorus sing an ode in praise of their city and their determination to resist violence against suppliants. The choral ode is followed by the return of Demophon, who announces to Iolaus that he has seen Eurystheus and his army. Furthermore, Demophon notes that through his consultation of oracles he has learned that he will gain victory only by sacrificing his own daughter to PERSEPHONE. Demophon, however, states that he will not sacrifice his daughter nor ask any of his citizens to make such a sacrifice. Upon hearing this, Iolaus says he cannot blame Demophon and despairs that he and Heracles' children will die. Iolaus soon decides to offer himself to Eurystheus in order to save Heracles' children. Demophon responds that Eurystheus cares little about Iolaus but wants to kill the children. Demophon suggests that they find some other remedy for their difficulty.

At this point, Heracles' daughter, Macaria, enters from the temple and asks what is happening. When Iolaus explains about the sacrifice, Macaria offers to give up her life. Iolaus suggests that lots should be drawn from among Macaria and her sisters, but Macaria rejects this idea. Before Macaria exits to be sacrificed, she bids farewell to Demophon, urging him to teach Heracles' sons well and to honor Iolaus, Alcmena, and the elders of Marathon. As Macaria exits, Iolaus praises her courage and nobility. The chorus then sing a brief ode about how it is impossible to avoid one's destiny. They urge Iolaus to endure the gods' will and they predict that Heracles' daughter will be glorified for her actions.

After the choral ode, a servant of Heracles' son HYL-LUS enters and asks Iolaus about events. The servant says that he has good news, so Iolaus calls Alcmena from the temple. The servant informs them that Hyllus has arrived and is arranging his troops in preparation for the battle with Eurystheus. Iolaus then announces that he will go with the servant to the battle front and take part in the fighting. The servant is skeptical because Iolaus is an old man, but Iolaus insists and decides to wear into battle armor from the temple. The chorus and Alcmena also urge Iolaus not to engage in the fighting. After the servant returns from the temple with the armor, he helps Iolaus as the old man totters off to battle. After the servant and Iolaus depart, the chorus sing an ode in which they pray to the gods, especially ATHENA, for assistance.

After the chorus' prayer, the servant enters and announces victory over Eurystheus. The servant tells Alcmena that initially Hyllus challenged Eurystheus to a one-on-one combat to settle the dispute, but that Eurystheus was too cowardly to accept the challenge. Then, after the battle began, a miracle occurred as Iolaus prayed to HEBE and Zeus that he might be young again. Iolaus' prayer was answered and the servant relates that the spirits of Hebe and Heracles appeared over Iolaus' chariot. Iolaus then pursued Eurystheus

and captured him. Hearing the servant's message, Alcmena rejoices and predicts that Eurystheus will soon die. Alcmena wonders why Iolaus did not kill Eurystheus. The servant tells her that Iolaus wanted to allow her to meet her family's enemy face to face. At this, the servant departs and the chorus sing an ode of joy. The old men note that the gods punish the pride of wicked persons; they rejoice that Heracles has become a god; and they observe that Athena's people have aided Alcmena's family just as Athena herself once aided Heracles.

The choral ode is followed by the return of the servant with the captive Eurystheus. Alcmena threatens him with death, but the chorus declare that their country's law does not permit people captured in battle to be put to death. Despite the chorus' remark, Alcmena states her intention to kill Eurystheus. Eurystheus himself then speaks, blaming his enmity with Heracles on Hera. Eurystheus warns Alcmena that his spirit will haunt her if she kills him. Despite Eurystheus' warning, Alcmena persists. Eurystheus does not beg for mercy but reveals an oracle stating that if he is buried in Athenian territory, then his spirit will protect the Athenians against future attack by the offspring of Heracles' children. Upon hearing this, Alcmena urges that Eurystheus be led out to death. At this point, the ancient manuscript of the play breaks off and it is uncertain what happens to Eurystheus.

COMMENTARY

One recurrent theme in *Children of Heracles* is the superiority of Athenian policy over that of other cities, especially those of the Peloponnesians, with whom Athens was at war when Euripides' play was staged. In Euripides' play, Heracles' children find themselves on Athenian soil, and the Athens of drama and myth was proverbial for helping those who found themselves in difficult circumstances. In AESCHYLUS' *Eumenides* (see *ORESTEIA*), ORESTES was acquitted of killing his mother with the help of Athena and her citizens. In Euripides' *MEDEA,* the Athenian king Aegeus had offered asylum to Medea, faced with exile from Corinth. In Euripides' *HERACLES,* staged a decade or so after *Children of Heracles,* Aegeus' son, THESEUS, offers Heracles asylum after Heracles kills his own wife and children. In SOPHOCLES'

OEDIPUS AT COLONUS, the Athenians grant asylum to the title character. In Children of Heracles, Theseus' son, Demophon, the current ruler of Athens, will act as protector.

Children of Heracles has a different theme, however, from the protective role usually played by Athens, as Demophon is faced with the possibility of sacrificing his daughter to save the lives of strangers to his land. Unlike the AGAMEMNON of Aeschylus' Agamemnon (see ORESTEIA), who sacrifices IPHIGENIA to put an end to the adverse weather that prevented the Greeks from sailing to TROY and rescuing MENELAUS' wife, HELEN, Demophon himself will not make a similar sacrifice nor ask that of any of his citizens. Whereas another Athenian ruler who appears in drama, ERECHTHEUS, was willing to sacrifice his daughter to save Athens, Demophon will not do that on behalf of outsiders. Fortunately for Demophon, one of Heracles' daughters steps forward and relieves him of this burden.

The sacrifice of one who dies before her time commonly occurs in Euripidean drama. Macaria's self-sacrifice has a predecessor in that of ALCESTIS, in Euripides' play of 438 B.C.E. Yet unlike Alcestis, Macaria has neither husband nor children. Thus, among extant Euripidean works, Macaria, the sacrificial maiden, is the forerunner of Erechtheus' daughter in Euripides' Erechtheus (no longer extant), POLYXENA in HECABE, and Iphigenia in IPHIGENIA AT AULIS. Unlike in the latter plays, in Children of Heracles, there is no mention of actual sacrifice. Macaria declares her intention to give up her life, and presumably she does, but no description of her death is given as in other Euripidean plays that have sacrificial victims.

BIBLIOGRAPHY

Allan, W. Euripides: The Children of Heracles. Warminster, U.K.: Aris & Phillips, 2001.
Burian, P. "Euripides' Heraclidae: An Interpretation," Classical Philology 72 (1977): 1–21.
Burnett, A. P. "Tribe and City, Custom and Decree in Children of Heracles," Classical Philology 71 (1976): 4–26.
Rehm, R. "The Staging of Suppliant Plays," Greek, Roman, and Byzantine Studies 29 (1988): 263–307.
Wilkins, J. Euripides: Heraclidae. Oxford: Clarendon Press, 1993.

CHIMAERA   The offspring of Typhon and Echidna, the Chimaera lived in LYCIA and was a fire-breathing monster whose body comprised a lion (front), goat (middle), and serpent (tail). A certain Amisodaurus raised the Chimaera to torment his fellow mortals; BELLEROPHON eventually killed the monster. [ANCIENT SOURCES: Apollodorus, Library 1.9.3, 2.3.1; Hesiod, Theogony 319–25; Homer, Iliad 6.178–83; Seneca, Medea 828]

CHIOS   An island, famed for its marble and wine, off the western coast of modern Turkey. From 494 to 479 B.C.E., Persians controlled Chios. After the defeat of the Persians, Chios became a staunch ally of the Athenians until their unsuccessful revolt in 412 B.C.E. [ANCIENT SOURCES: Aeschylus, Persians 882; Aristophanes, Birds 879–80, Ecclesiazusae 1139, Peace 171, 835; Herodotus, 6.31; Thucydides, 8.6–64]

CHIRON   When CRONUS transformed himself into a horse and impregnated Philyra, the resulting child was the immortal CENTAUR Chiron. Chiron, whose name means "hand," was skilled in medicine and restored PHOENIX's sight after he was blinded. Chiron trained several heroes (ACTAEON, ASCLEPIUS, JASON, ACHILLES) in the arts of healing and/or hunting. Chiron saved PELEUS when ACASTUS abandoned him on Mount Pelion and hid his spear. He also advised Peleus on how to seize THETIS and gave Peleus a famous spear of ash. At the marriage of Peleus and Thetis, Chiron predicted the birth of their great son, Achilles, and his heroism against PRIAM and the Trojans. Heracles accidentally wounded Chiron with one of his arrows, which normally caused instant death, but because Chiron was immortal, he did not die. Eventually Chiron was able to die when PROMETHEUS offered to trade his mortality for Chiron's immortality. After Chiron's death, he was placed in the sky as the constellation Sagittarius. A Chiron is attributed to the Greek comic poet PHERECRATES (145–153 Kock). [ANCIENT SOURCES: Apollodorus, Library 1.2.4, 2.5.4, 3.13.3–8; Euripides, Iphigenia at Aulis 162–75; HOMER, Iliad 16.143–44; Seneca, Hercules Furens 971, Trojan Women 832, Thyestes 860]

BIBLIOGRAPHY

Kock, T. Comicorum Atticorum Fragmenta. Vol. 1. Leipzig: Teubner, 1880.

CHITON   The primary garment worn by the Greeks, the *chiton* generally had one of two styles, Doric and Ionic. The Doric *chiton* was simpler in its appearance that the Ionic *chiton*. A woman's *chiton* descended from her neck and covered her ankles; a man's was worn to just above the knee. For both sexes, the chiton could be draped to leave the arms bare.

BIBLIOGRAPHY
Brooke, Is. *Costume in Greek Classic Drama.* New York: Theatre Arts Books, 1962, 18–25.

CHLAMUS   A short cloak worn primarily by Greek messengers and warriors.

BIBLIOGRAPHY
Brooke, I. *Costume in Greek Classic Drama.* New York: Theatre Arts Books, 1962, 28.

CHLOE   A title (meaning "tender plant") for DEMETER. In the second century C.E., the traveler Pausanias noted in ATHENS a shrine dedicated to Demeter Chloe. [ANCIENT SOURCES: Aristophanes, *Lysistrata* 835; Pausanias, 1.22.3]

CHOAE   See PITCHER FEAST.

CHOEPHOROI   See LIBATION BEARERS (ORESTEIA).

CHOREGIA   The Greek word that refers to the duties performed by the *CHOREGUS*. [ANCIENT SOURCES: Thucydides, 6.16.3]

CHOREGUS (Latin: *CHORAGUS*)   The Athenian *choregus*—the name literally means "chorus driver"—was a citizen whose role involved paying for outfitting the CHORUS and/or players with costumes. In ATHENS, either a citizen might volunteer financial resources for this duty or a public official called an ARCHON might nominate him. In his speech against Timarchus, Aeschines says the Athenian *choregus* had to be older than 40 years old, and thus presumably mature enough not to sponsor entertainment inappropriate for the youth. This law does not seem to have been strictly enforced, however. Once a *choregus* volunteered or was appointed, he was assigned a chorus

instructor (*chorodidaskalos* or DIDASKALOS) with whom to work and an Athenian tribe from whom the chorus would be drawn. Because the chorus had to have a place to practice, the choregus would probably arrange for this as well. Antiphon, a contemporary of SOPHOCLES and EURIPIDES', says that he provided a teaching room (*didaskaleion*) in his house.

Among the Romans, during the time of PLAUTUS and TERENCE, an official called an aedile contracted with a *choragus,* who provided costumes and other stage equipment to the playwright and performers. In Plautus' *CURCULIO,* the choragus speaks (461–86), lamenting that one character is so tricky that he fears he will not return the costume he rented for the production. Later, in the time of SENECA, a *procurator summi choragi* (manager of the chief chorus supplier) seems to have been an emperor-appointed position within the government. [ANCIENT SOURCES: Aeschines, *Against Timarchus* 11–12; Antiphon, *On the Choreutes*]

CHORODIDASKALIA   See DIDASKALIA.

CHORODIDASKALOS   See DIDASKALOS.

CHORUS   The Greek word *choros* can refer to a place for dancing, a dance in a ring, or the people who participate in such a dance (i.e., the chorus). In DITHYRAMB, a chorus had 50 members. The chorus of Greek TRAGEDY consisted of 12 members in the early days, but this number was increased to 15 around the middle of the fifth century B.C.E. The Greek comic chorus of ARISTOPHANES' day had 24 members. In both tragedy and COMEDY, there are some instances of the chorus' dividing into two groups and singing responsively to one another. In a few plays, we find an auxiliary chorus (*parachoregema*) with the primary chorus. In AESCHYLUS' *Eumenides* (see ORESTEIA), produced in 458, the FURIES make up the primary chorus; at the end of the play a group of Athenian women sing a song in praise of them. In EURIPIDES' *HIPPOLYTUS* (produced in 428), the title character enters the play with a group of hunters who are praising ARTEMIS. Soon, however, HIPPOLYTUS sends the hunters off and the main chorus, composed of women from TROEZEN, enter.

In all Greek drama, the persons who served as members of the chorus were male (even if playing female characters) and wore masks as the actors on stage did. The main function of the chorus was to sing and dance the odes dividing a play's EPISODES. Occasionally, the chorus and the actors would chant or sing in lyric dialogue. The chorus had musical accompaniment on the AULOS, and one of their formations for dance may have been rectangular (either three lines of four or three lines of five). In his speech against ALCIBIADES, Andocides, a contemporary of ARISTOPHANES', notes that members of a chorus in competition had to be Athenian citizens.

In Greek tragedy of the late sixth and early fifth centuries, the chorus members constituted the principal characters in a play. So important was the chorus that originally the term for playwright was *chorodidaskalos* ("teacher of the chorus"); in *Poetics*, ARISTOTLE says the chorus should be regarded as one of the play's actors and should participate in a drama's action. As time went on, the chorus' role diminished and the chorus became less integral to the play's action. In the last three surviving plays of AESCHYLUS (see ORESTEIA), dated to 458 B.C.E., the chorus speak more than 45 percent of the lines. In the following decade, however, in SOPHOCLES' *Ajax* and *ANTIGONE,* the chorus deliver about 25 percent of the lines. This percentage remains consistent with slight decreases until the 410s, when in Euripides' *Orestes,* IPHIGENIA AT AULIS, and *BACCHAE* and Sophocles' PHILOCTETES and OEDIPUS AT COLONUS, the choruses recite roughly 20 percent.

The same decreasing involvement of the chorus can be seen in Aristophanes' plays and is even more pronounced. In Aristophanic plays of the 420s, the chorus delivered as many as a quarter of the lines, but by the time of ECCLESIAZUSAE and WEALTH, Aristophanes' last two extant plays (392 and 388, respectively), the chorus would have had no more than 10 percent of the lines (one choral passage from *Ecclesiazusae* has been lost from the play's manuscripts and six choral passages are missing from *Wealth*). Although the last extant Greek tragedies have choral passages, the ancient manuscripts of MENANDER'S comedies (first produced in the late fourth and early third centuries) do not contain choral passages, but only a note indicating at what points the chorus sang. In several of Menander's plays, this indication is preceded by a character

remarking that a group of drunken men are approaching. This chorus of drunken rowdies would have sung "stock" songs as sort of a musical interlude between acts. This use of readily transferable songs is attributed to the Greek tragedian AGATHON, active in the last two decades of the fifth century. The Roman comedies of PLAUTUS and TERENCE do not have choral parts at all, although some traces of the chorus from the Greek originals can be found in Plautus' *BACCHIDES* (based on Menander's *Twice Deceived*) and *ROPE* (the group of fishermen who appear and then disappear).

In a SATYR PLAY, the chorus would consist of satyrs, who commonly seem to have described themselves as servants to someone (e.g., the CYCLOPS in Euripides' *CYCLOPS*). An exception to this rule occurs in Euripides' *ALCESTIS,* which was staged in place of a satyr play. There, the chorus is much like a typical chorus in tragedy, as it consists of elder males from the town of PHERAE. As in tragedy, the chorus in a satyr play had 12 members.

In tragedy, the makeup of the chorus would vary more widely. The tragic chorus generally represent the point of view of the common person. In some plays, the chorus are women (e.g., Aeschylus' SUPPLIANT WOMEN, Sophocles' TRACHINIAN WOMEN, Euripides' PHOENICIAN WOMEN); in others, men (Aeschylus' *Agamemnon* [see ORESTEIA], Sophocles' *Antigone,* Euripides' *Alcestis*). The male choruses tend to consist of older men, and the female choruses tend to consist of younger women who are either free women or slaves.

Among the comic poets of Aristophanes' day, the common people's voice could still be heard in comic choruses, as the men who make up the choruses of ACHARNIANS, PEACE, and *Wealth* demonstrate. Comedy, however, had far greater license for choral identity than tragedy, as the titles of some of Aristophanes' plays indicate: *Acharnians,* KNIGHTS, CLOUDS, WASPS, BIRDS, *Ecclesiazusae.* Additionally, the choruses in fifth-century comedy would be more physically involved in the action of the play than in tragedy of the same period. The Acharnians threaten to stone DICAEOPOLIS at one point; the old men and old women in LYSISTRATA actually do have an onstage skirmish in which the men are doused with water. The Clouds claim that they led

STREPSIADES into foolish behavior to teach him a lesson. As is also indicated in the titles of Aristophanes' plays, the costumes of the comic choruses would often have been wondrous to see. It must have been a delight to see two dozen of Aristophanes' cloud-women waft into the orchestra, not to mention the two dozen different birds in costumes that were enjoyed by the spectators at Aristophanes' *Birds*. [ANCIENT SOURCES: Andocides, *Against Alcibiades* 20; Aristotle, *Poetics*; Plautus, *Bacchides* 105–8, *Rope* 284–324]

BIBLIOGRAPHY

Buxton, R. W. B. *The Chorus in Sophocles' Tragedies*. New York: Oxford University Press, 1980.

Csapo, E., and W. J. Slater. *The Context of Ancient Drama*. Ann Arbor: University of Michigan Press, 1995, 349–68.

Kranz, Walther. *Stasimon: Untersuchungen zu Form und Gehalt der griechischen Tragodie*. Berlin: Weidmann, 1933.

Sifakis, G. M. *Parabasis and Animal Choruses: A Contribution to the History of Attic Comedy*. London: Athlone Press, 1971.

Webster, T. B. L. *The Greek Chorus*. London: Methuen, 1970.

Wilson, Peter. *The Athenian Institution of the Khoregia: The Chorus, the City and the Stage*. Cambridge: Cambridge University Press, 2000.

CHRYSE (1) An island in the northern AEGEAN near LEMNOS. PHILOCTETES was bitten by a serpent while on Chryse. [ANCIENT SOURCES: Sophocles, *Philoctetes* 270]

CHRYSE (2) The name of a divinity who protected the island of Chryse. PHILOCTETES angered this divinity and was bitten by a serpent that guarded the divinity's shrine. [ANCIENT SOURCES: Sophocles, *Philoctetes* 194, 1327]

CHRYSEIS See CHRYSES.

CHRYSES King of the island of Sminthe and a priest of APOLLO, Chryses was the father of Chryseis, who was taken prisoner during the Trojan War by the Greeks and became the war prize of AGAMEMNON. When Chryses went to the Greek camp to try to ransom his daughter, Agamemnon harshly drove him away. The angered Chryses prayed for revenge from APOLLO, who caused a plague to descend upon the Greeks. When the Greeks learned the reason for the plague, they persuaded Agamemnon to restore Chryseis to her father. Many years later, when ORESTES, PYLADES, and IPHIGENIA were returning to Greece with a statue of ARTEMIS they had stolen from Tauris, they landed on Chryses' island. When the Taurian king THOAS, who had pursued them, demanded that Chryses hand over the three, Chryses initially decided to do so, but when he learned that Orestes and Iphigenia were Agamemnon's children, he chose to help the trio instead and they killed Thoas. SOPHOCLES wrote a *Chryses*, of which virtually nothing is known (fragments 726–30 Radt). Among Roman authors, PACUVIUS wrote a *Chryses* that dealt with Thoas' pursuit of Orestes and Pylades (lines 79–118 Warmington). [ANCIENT SOURCES: Homer, *Iliad* 1; Hyginus, *Fables* 120–21; Seneca, *Trojan Women* 223]

BIBLIOGRAPHY

Kiso, A. *The Lost Sophocles*. New York: Vantage Press, 1984.

Lloyd-Jones, H. *Sophocles: Fragments*. Cambridge, Mass.: Harvard University Press, 1996.

Radt, S. *Tragicorum Graecorum Fragmenta*. Vol. 4. Göttingen: Vandenhoeck & Ruprecht, 1977.

Sutton, D. F. *The Lost Sophocles*. Lanham, Md.: University Press of America, 1984.

Warmington, E. H. *Remains of Old Latin: Livius Andronicus, Naevius, Pacuvius, and Accius*. Vol. 2. Cambridge, Mass.: Harvard University Press, 1936.

CHRYSIPPUS The son of PELOPS and Astyoche (or Axioche), Chrysippus was a handsome young man whom the Theban king LAIUS abducted. Because of this act, Pelops cursed Laius and his descendants. According to some sources, his stepbrothers, ATREUS and THYESTES, rescued Chrysippus; other sources say Pelops rescued him after attacking THEBES. Accounts of Chrysippus' death also vary. Some say he committed suicide; others state that his stepmother, HIPPODAMEIA, fearing that he might become king rather than her sons, Atreus and Thyestes, persuaded Atreus and Thyestes to kill him. After Pelops blamed Hippodameia for Chrysippus' death, she committed suicide.

Among the Greek dramatists, Diogenes and Lycophron wrote plays entitled *Chrysippus*. From Lycophron's play, only the title survives; the five remaining lines from Diogenes' play provide no information about that play's content. EURIPIDES wrote a tragic *Chrysippus,* of which about two dozen lines remain and which may date to before 428 B.C.E. Euripides' play appears to have treated the relationship between Laius and Chrysippus, and in the course of its action the young man seems to have committed suicide. The comic poet Strattis also wrote a play called *Chrysippus;* the six surviving lines tell little about its content.

Among Roman authors, ACCIUS wrote a *Chrysippus,* from which about six lines survive; the subject matter of the play is unknown. In one fragment, the speaker refers to the possible surrender of SPARTA and Amyclae, territories that would have been under Pelops' control. [ANCIENT SOURCES: Apollodorus, *Library* 3.5.5; Hyginus, *Fables* 85]

BIBLIOGRAPHY
Kock, T. *Comicorum Atticorum Fragmenta.* Vol. 1. Leipzig: Teubner, 1880.
Snell, B. *Tragicorum Graecorum Fragmenta.* Vol. 1. Göttingen, Ger.: Vandenhoeck & Ruprecht, 1971.
Webster, T. B. L. *The Tragedies of Euripides.* London: Methuen, 1967.

CHRYSOTHEMIS The daughter of AGAMEMNON and CLYTEMNESTRA, Chrysothemis is the sister of ORESTES, ELECTRA, and IPHIGENIA. She appears as a character in SOPHOCLES' *ELECTRA,* in which she performs a function similar to that of ISMENE in Sophocles' *ANTIGONE,* as she provides a contrast with the attitudes of her sister Electra. Electra decides that she will make an attempt to kill AEGISTHUS, but Chrysothemis does not want to be involved in this plot and advises her sister to be sensible. Electra, in turn, accuses Chrysothemis of being a coward. [ANCIENT SOURCES: Apollodorus, *Epitome* 2.16; Euripides, *Orestes* 23; Homer, *Iliad* 9.145]

CHYTROI In ATHENS, the third and final day of the feast of Anthesteria was called the Chytroi (the Pot Feast). This part of the festivities took place "at the sanctuary of Dionysus *in Limnais.*" On this day the participants sacrificed to HERMES "as the god in charge of the passage of souls to the UNDERWORLD, and there was strong awareness of the presence of the dead" (Dover). [ANCIENT SOURCES: Aristophanes, *Frogs* 218]

BIBLIOGRAPHY
Dover, Kenneth. *Aristophanes: Frogs.* Oxford: Clarendon Press, 1993, 223–24.

CICYNNA A DEME in ATHENS. In ARISTOPHANES' *Clouds* (134, 210), STREPSIADES says he is from this deme.

CILICIA A region along the coast of what is today southern Turkey. [ANCIENT SOURCES: Plautus, *Miles Gloriosus* 42, *Three-Dollar Day* 599; Terence, *Phormio* 66]

CILISSA In AESCHYLUS' *Libation Bearers* (see *ORESTEIA*), Cilissa is the name given to ORESTES' nurse.

CILLICON A "semilegendary traitor" whose name became synonymous with evil actions. When suspected that he was planning to betray his city (MILETUS or SAMOS) to its enemies, he was asked what he was planning to do. His response was "It's all good." [ANCIENT SOURCES: Aristophanes, *Peace* 363]

BIBLIOGRAPHY
Sommerstein, A. H. *The Comedies of Aristophanes.* Vol. 5, Peace. Warminster, U.K.: Aris & Philips, 1985, 150.

CIMMERIA A land located in the northern part of the Black Sea region. In AESCHYLUS' *PROMETHEUS BOUND,* PROMETHEUS tells Io that she will have to pass across the Cimmerian ISTHMUS in her wanderings. [ANCIENT SOURCES: Aeschylus, *Prometheus Bound* 730]

CIMOLUS An island in the southern AEGEAN (just northeast of MELOS) that was famous for its chalky soil (Cimolian earth), which was used by barbershops and bathhouses and in medicine. [ANCIENT SOURCES: Aristophanes, *Frogs* 712]

CIMON The son of Miltiades and Hegesipyle, Cimon was an important Athenian statesman and military commander during the second quarter of the fifth century B.C.E. His most important victory occurred around 468, when his forces wiped out the Persian navy in a military operation near the river Eurymedon in what is today southern Turkey. Cimon was exiled from ATHENS in 461 but eventually returned and died some time after 450 while leading a military expedition to retake the island of CYPRUS from the Persians. [ANCIENT SOURCES: Aristophanes, *Lysistrata* 1144]

CINESIAS (1)   (CA. 450–CA. 390 B.C.E.)   A dithyrambic poet whom ARISTOPHANES mocks on several occasions for writing poems with "airy" diction, but lacking in substance. In Aristophanes' BIRDS, Cinesias is driven away from the new city of the birds. The Greek comic poet Strattis, a contemporary of Aristophanes', wrote a *Cinesias,* whose fragments give no indication of the play's plot (fragments 13–14 Kock). [ANCIENT SOURCES: Aristophanes, *Birds* 1372, *Ecclesiazusae* 330, *Frogs* 153, 1437]

BIBLIOGRAPHY
Kock, T. *Comicorum Atticorum Fragmenta.* Vol. 1. Leipzig: Teubner, 1880.

CINESIAS (2)   A fictional Athenian who appears as the love-starved husband of Myrrhine in ARISTOPHANES' *LYSISTRATA* (838ff.). Cinesias' name is derived from the Greek verb *kinein,* which can denote the motion used during sexual intercourse.

CIRCE   The daughter of Helios (see SUN) and Perse, Circe was an immortal witch who lived on the island of Aeaea. During their wanderings, ODYSSEUS and his men arrived on her island. As HOMER tells the story in *Odyssey* 10, Odysseus and half of his men remained with the ship, while the other half went out to explore the island. During their exploration, they entered the house of Circe, who turned them into pigs. Eurylochus, who did not enter the house, returned to the ship and reported what had happened. Odysseus then set out alone to investigate the situation for himself. On the way to Circe's house, he was met by HERMES, who gave him a remedy, moly, to counteract the effects of Circe's drugs. When Circe tried to transform Odysseus, her magic failed. He drew his sword on her and she invited him to sleep with her (an invitation that Odysseus accepted). Circe later changed Odysseus' comrades back into humans. After they had spent a year on Circe's island, Odysseus and his crew received her advice about how to reach their home, including the news that Odysseus would have to travel to the UNDERWORLD to accomplish his homecoming. One of Odysseus' comrades, Elpenor, died after falling asleep on the roof of Circe's house and then tumbling off. Odysseus did not know this at the time and later encountered Elpenor's spirit in the underworld. Elpenor begged Odysseus to return to Circe's house, find his body, and bury it (Odysseus did). By Odysseus, Circe also gave birth to a son, named Telegonus.

Circe does not appear as a character in any extant dramas but would have been a character in several plays that no longer survive. AESCHYLUS wrote a satyric *Circe,* from which three brief, uninformative fragments survive (113a–115 Radt). The comic poet Anaxilas also wrote a *Circe,* whose two surviving fragments (12–13 Kock) indicate that the play dealt with the transformation of Odysseus' men. The comic poet Ephippus also wrote a play entitled *Circe;* the two lines that survive give no indication of plot (fragment 11 Kock). [ANCIENT SOURCES: Apollodorus, *Epitome* 7.14–18; Homer, *Odyssey* 10]

BIBLIOGRAPHY
Kock, T. *Comicorum Atticorum Fragmenta.* Vol. 2. Leipzig: Teubner, 1884.
Radt, S. *Tragicorum Graecorum Fragmenta.* Vol. 3. Göttingen, Ger.: Vandenhoeck & Ruprecht, 1985.
Smyth, H. W., and H. Lloyd-Jones. *Aeschylus.* Vol. 2. 1926, Reprint, Cambridge, Mass.: Harvard University Press, 1971.

CIRCUS   The Latin word *circus* literally means "circle" and refers to a course for racing, especially chariot racing. The most famous *circus* is the Circus Maximus in Rome, which, although primarily used as a racing course, was sometimes adapted for use in theatrical productions. [ANCIENT SOURCES: Polybius, 30.14]

CIRRHA   A Greek town southwest of DELPHI on the northern coast of the Gulf of CORINTH. [ANCIENT SOURCES: Seneca, *Hercules Oetaeus* 92, 1475, *Oedipus* 269]

CISTHENE   A place where the PHORCIDES were supposed to live. At *PROMETHEUS BOUND* 793, PROMETHEUS tells Io that she will have to pass Cisthene. See also CRATINUS, fragment 309 Kock.

BIBLIOGRAPHY
Kock, T. *Comicorum Atticorum Fragmenta*. Vol. 1. Leipzig: Teubner, 1880.

CITHAERON

This mountain, located near THEBES, was the site of many tragic occurrences in drama. It was on Cithaeron that the infant OEDIPUS was to be left to die. ACTAEON was torn apart there by his own hunting dogs and PENTHEUS by his own mother in EURIPIDES' *BACCHAE*. The dead from the expedition of the Seven against Thebes are buried on Cithaeron, and APOLLO killed NIOBE's male children as they hunted there.

BIBLIOGRAPHY
Buxton, Richard. "News from Cithaeron: Narrators and Narratives in the *Bacchae*," *Pallas* 37 (1991): 39–48.
Kubota, T. "On the Relation between the Scenes on Cithaeron and the Stage Actions in Euripides' *Bacchae*," *Classical Studies* (1980): 23–40.

CLASHING ROCKS

Also known as the Symplegades (those that clash together) or the Cyaneae (the dark-blue ones), this dangerous pair of rocks guarded the southern entrance to the Black Sea. Homer calls them the Planktai (wandering ones), although Apollonius of Rhodes makes the Symplegades and the Planktai two different sets of rocks. Typically, the rocks smashed anything that tried to pass between them, but JASON and Argonauts, armed with advice from PHINEUS and the help of the gods, were able to make it through the rocks. One tradition is that after Jason passed through these rocks they no longer smashed together, but in EURIPIDES' *IPHIGENIA IN TAURIS*, ORESTES is also said to have passed through them and Euripides implies that they remained dangerous. [ANCIENT SOURCES: Apollodorus, *Library* 1.9.22; Apollonius of Rhodes, 2.601; Euripides, *Medea* 2, 1263, *Andromache* 795, 863, *Iphigenia in Tauris* 241, 260, 355, 392, 746, 889–90, 1389; Homer, *Odyssey* 12.61–72; Hyginus, *Fables* 19, 21; Pindar, *Pythian* 4.371; Seneca, *Hercules Furens* 1211, *Medea* 456, *Hercules Oetaeus* 1273, 1380]

BIBLIOGRAPHY
Pickard, William F. "The Symplegades," *Greece and Rome* 34 (1987): 1–6.
Pocock, L. G. "The *Odyssey*, the Symplegades, and the Name of Homer," *Studi micenei ed egeoanatolici* 4 (1967): 92–104.

CLAUDIUS (10 B.C.E.–54 C.E.)

The son of Drusus the elder and Antonia the lesser, Tiberius Claudius Nero Germanicus was the Roman emperor who reigned between CALIGULA and NERO. By his wife, Valeria Messalina, Claudius became the father of OCTAVIA and Britannicus. After Messalina's death, Claudius married his niece, AGRIPPINA, who may have helped kill him by giving him a dish of poisoned mushrooms. [ANCIENT SOURCES: Seneca, *Octavia* 26, 45, 269, *Apocolocyntosis*; Suetonius, *Claudius, Nero*; Tacitus, *Annals* 11–12]

CLEAENETUS

The father of CLEON. [ANCIENT SOURCES: Aristophanes, *Knights* 574]

CLEIDEMIDES

A person mentioned by ARISTOPHANES at *FROGS* 791 about whom nothing certain is known. One ancient commentator on this line thought Cleidemides was a son of SOPHOCLES', and another thought that he acted in Sophocles' plays.

BIBLIOGRAPHY
Dover, K. J. *Aristophanes: Frogs*. Oxford: Clarendon Press, 1993, 289.
Sommerstein, A. H. *The Comedies of Aristophanes*. Vol. 9, *Frogs*. Warminster, U.K.: Aris & Phillips, 1996, 225.

CLEIGENES

Mentioned in ARISTOPHANES' *FROGS*, Cleigenes, according to Dover, may have operated bathhouses. A Cleigenes served as a secretary for the council in ATHENS in 410/409 B.C.E., but this person is otherwise unknown. [ANCIENT SOURCES: Aristophanes, *Frogs* 709–13]

BIBLIOGRAPHY
Dover, K. J. *Aristophanes: Frogs*. Oxford: Clarendon Press, 1993, 280.
Sommerstein, A. H. *The Comedies of Aristophanes*. Vol. 9, *Frogs*. Warminster, U.K.: Aris & Phillips, 1996, 218.

CLEINARETE

A woman mentioned by ARISTOPHANES at *ECCLESIAZUSAE* 41. She is not identified with any historical person.

CLEINIAS

The father of ALCIBIADES. [ANCIENT SOURCES: Aristophanes, *Acharnians* 716]

CLEISTHENES An Athenian political leader in the last quarter of the fifth century B.C.E. mocked for his effeminacy. ARISTOPHANES mentions him by name in most of his extant plays, and in his *THESMOPHORIAZUSAE*, Cleisthenes is able to gain access to the female-only worshipers at the THESMOPHORIA without disguising himself as a woman. Cleisthenes is also mentioned by Aristophanes' contemporary comic poets, CRATINUS (fragment 195 Kock), who says Cleisthenes would look ridiculous playing dice, and PHERECRATES (fragment 135 Kock), who compares Cleisthenes to a pigeon. [ANCIENT SOURCES: Aristophanes, *Acharnians* 118, *Birds* 831, *Clouds* 355, *Frogs* 48, 422, *Knights* 1374, *Lysistrata* 1092, *Thesmophoriazusae* 709–13, *Wasps* 1187; Cratinus, fragment 195.1 Kock; Pherecrates, fragment 135.1 Kock]

BIBLIOGRAPHY
Kock, T. *Comicorum Atticorum Fragmenta.* Vol. 1. Leipzig: Teubner, 1880.

CLEOCRITUS ARISTOPHANES calls Cleocritus' mother an ostrich and thus indicates that Cleocritus' body shape was like that of animal. Dunbar tentatively suggests that Cleocritus may have been ARCHON in 413/412 "and/or the Herald of the (Eleusinian) Initiates . . . whose speech in 403, after the battle of Munychias between democrats and supporters of the Thirty Tyrants, helped to end civil strife." [ANCIENT SOURCES: Aristophanes, *Birds* 873, *Frogs* 1437; Xenophon, *Hellenica* 2.4.20–2]

BIBLIOGRAPHY
Dunbar, Nan. *Aristophanes: Birds.* New York: Oxford University Press, 1995, 512–13.

CLEOMENES From about 519 to 490 B.C.E., Cleomenes I was one of the kings of SPARTA (the Spartans had a two-king system). In 510, Cleomenes helped the Athenians drive out the tyrant HIPPIAS. Two years later Cleomenes, backing the Athenian Isagoras' effort to establish an oligarchy in ATHENS, returned to Athens with an armed force and occupied the ACROPOLIS. Those opposed to Isagoras rallied successfully, however, and Cleomenes left Athens under a truce. Many years later, after managing to have his fellow-king removed from office and stirring up the Arcadians against his fellow Spartans, Cleomenes was recalled to Sparta. Cleomenes committed suicide soon after his return. [ANCIENT SOURCES: Aristophanes, *Lysistrata* 274; Herodotus, 5.39ff.]

BIBLIOGRAPHY
Henderson, J. *Aristophanes: Lysistrata.* Oxford: Clarendon Press, 1987, 103.

CLEON The son of Cleaenetus, a wealthy tanner, Cleon was an Athenian political leader and general who seems to have evoked extreme emotions from those who encountered him. People either liked Cleon or hated him. Cleon moved to the forefront of Athenian politics in 431–430 by attacking the policies of PERICLES and gaining favor with the masses by orchestrating such measures as increased pay for jurors. After Pericles' death in 429, Cleon became the foremost political leader in ATHENS, and the historian Thucydides labeled him the most violent of Athens' citizens. In 427, Cleon orchestrated a decree that would have put to death all the male inhabitants of MYTILENE, a town on the island of Lesbos that had tried unsuccessfully to revolt against Athens. Fortunately for the Mytilenians, the Athenians decided not to carry out this decree, but in 423, Cleon proposed a similar decree for the Macedonian town of SCIONE and its people. In Scione, the decree was enforced out—the men were killed, the women and children sold into slavery.

Several comic poets made fun of Cleon (DIPHILUS, EUPOLIS, HERMIPPUS, Machon, and PHILEMON), but our knowledge of the feud between ARISTOPHANES and Cleon is the most extensive. Aristophanes had no love for Cleon, because Cleon tried to prosecute Aristophanes on charges of slandering Athenian citizens, councilors, and magistrates before the foreigners who attended Aristophanes' *Babylonians* at the City DIONYSIA in 426 B.C.E. Cleon's prosecution failed, however, and Aristophanes ridiculed him mercilessly in his plays. In *KNIGHTS*, Aristophanes caricatures Cleon in PAPHLAGON ("the blusterer"), whose evil tactics and flattery allow him to control DEMOS, who represents the people of Athens. Cleon again tried to prosecute Aristophanes after *Knights*, but the grounds on which the charge was based is not known. In Aristophanes'

WASPS, the playwright depicts a father named Philocleon (lover of Cleon) and a son named Bdelycleon (hater of Cleon); Bdelycleon demonstrates to Philocleon that Cleon has enslaved him, not empowered him. Even after Cleon's death, Aristophanes continued to express his dislike of Cleon. In PEACE (261–73), Aristophanes calls Cleon a pestle that war would use to grind up the cities of Greece. Later in the same play (313–15), Cleon is labeled a CERBERUS who will prevent the goddess of Peace from being raised out of the pit into which the god War has cast her.

Cleon's greatest success occurred in 425 B.C.E. at Sphacteria, a small island off the coast of PYLOS in southwestern Greece. When the Athenian army managed to trap on Sphacteria some of the Spartans' best fighters, the Athenian commander NICIAS did not pursue the action against the Spartans vigorously enough to satisfy Cleon. When Cleon criticized Nicias, Nicias unexpectedly gave up his command and offered it to Cleon. Challenged in this way, Cleon had little choice but to accept the generalship. Not only did Cleon do so, but he also boasted that he would resolve the matter within 20 days. Ultimately, Cleon confirmed his boast and the Athenians captured a large number of the Spartans. Cleon's success was short lived, however, as he was killed at the battle of Amphipolis in 422. Thucydides makes a point of noting that Cleon died with his back to the battle. [ANCIENT SOURCES: Aristophanes, *Acharnians, Knights, Wasps, Peace;* Diodorus Siculus, 12.72–76; Plutarch, *Nicias, Pericles;* Thucydides, *Histories* 3.36–5.16]

BIBLIOGRAPHY

Andrews, James A. "Cleon's Ethopoetics," *Classical Quarterly* 44 (1994): 26–39.

Edmunds, Lowell. *Cleon, Knights and Aristophanes' Politics.* Lanham, Md.: University Press of America, 1987.

Lang, M. L. "Cleon as the Anti-Pericles," *Classical Philology* 67 (1972): 159–69.

Marshall, M. H. B. "Cleon and Pericles: Sphacteria," *Greece and Rome* 31 (1984): 19–36.

McGlew, James F. "Everybody Wants to Make a Speech: Cleon and Aristophanes on Politics and Fantasy," *Arethusa* 29, no. 3 (1996): 339–61.

CLEONAE A town in southeastern Greece between CORINTH and ARGOS. Because of Cleonae's

proximity to NEMEA, the home of the lion that HERACLES killed in his first labor, the Nemean lion is sometimes called the Cleonaean lion. [ANCIENT SOURCES: Apollodorus, *Library* 2.5.1; Seneca, *Hercules Furens* 798]

CLEONYMUS A minor political figure in ATHENS during the last quarter of the fifth century B.C.E. In the first half of ARISTOPHANES' career the playwright makes fun of Cleonymus numerous times, but after BIRDS (414 B.C.E.) references to him end, possibly an indication that Cleonymus had died. On one occasion, Aristophanes brands Cleonymus a glutton, but most often the playwright mocks him for having thrown away his shield (through cowardice) in battle ("probably some time in 425," according to MacDowell). In 426/425 B.C.E., Cleonymus is known to have proposed "a major decree enforcing stricter procedures for collecting tribute from the allied states," and in 415 he proposed "a reward of 1,000 drachmas for information about sacrilegious mock-celebrations of the Eleusinian mysteries" (Sommerstein). [ANCIENT SOURCES: Aristophanes, *Acharnians* 88, 844, *Birds* 289–90, 1475, *Clouds* 353, 400, 673–80, *Knights* 958, 1293, 1372, *Peace* 673–78, 1295, *Wasps* 19–20, 822]

BIBLIOGRAPHY

Dunbar, Nan. *Aristophanes: Birds.* Oxford: Clarendon Press, 1995, 238–39.

MacDowell, D. M. *Aristophanes: Wasps.* Oxford: Clarendon Press, 1971, 130.

Sommerstein, A. II. *The Comedies of Aristophanes.* Vol. 1, *Acharnians.* Warminster, U.K.: Aris & Phillips, 1980, 161–62.

CLEOPATRA Not to be confused with the queen of Egypt who had relationships with Julius CAESAR and Marcus ANTONIUS in the first century B.C.E., Cleopatra was the daughter of the wind god BOREAS and the Athenian king ERECHTHEUS' daughter Oreithyia. By the Thracian king and prophet PHINEUS, Cleopatra had two sons. When Phineus had an affair with Idaea and she had produced two sons for him, Idaea, jealous of Cleopatra, falsely claimed that Cleopatra's sons had tried to seduce her. Phineus blinded these two boys and then imprisoned them and Cleopatra. Cleopatra was later freed by her brothers, Zetes and Calais, the sons of Boreas, when the Argonauts arrived. Cleopatra's fate after this time is unknown. [ANCIENT SOURCES: Apollodorus, *Library* 3.15.3; Diodorus Siculus, 4.44; Hyginus, *Fables* 19; Scholiast on Sophocles, *Antigone* 973; Sophocles, *Antigone* 966–87]

CLEOPHON (DIED 404 B.C.E.) A maker of lyres and an Athenian statesman, Cleophon was the son of Cleippides and a Thracian mother; as a result Cleophon's right to Athenian citizenship was questioned (an earlier law required that both parents of citizens be from ATHENS). ARISTOPHANES' reference to him in THESMOPHORIAZUSAE indicates that his was a recognizable name by 411. Cleophon became prominent after the restoration of democracy in Athens in 410, was an adversary of Critias and ALCIBIADES', and opposed Spartan offers of peace after their defeat at the battles of Cyzicus (410) and Aegospotami (405). The comic poet Plato wrote a *Cleophon* from which about five lines survive (fragments 56–63 Kock). [ANCIENT SOURCES: Aeschines, *Against Ctesiphon* 148, *The Speech on the Embassy* 75; Andocides, *On the Mysteries* 145; Aristophanes, *Frogs* 678–79, 1504, 1532, *Thesmophoriazusae* 805]

BIBLIOGRAPHY
Baldwin, B. "Notes on Cleophon," *Acta Classica* 17 (1974): 35–47.
Kock, T. *Comicorum Atticorum Fragmenta.* Vol. 1. Leipzig: Teubner, 1880.
Renaud, R. "Cléophon et la guerre du Péloponnèse," *Les Études Classiques* 38 (1970): 458–77.
Romilly, J. De. "L'assemblée du peuple dans l'Oreste d'Euripide, I," In *Studi Classici in Onore di Quintino Cataudella.* Catania: Fac. di Lett. e Filos., 1972, 237–51.

CLEPSYDRA A Greek word meaning "concealer of water," Clepsydra is the name of several springs in Greece. In ARISTOPHANES' LYSISTRATA, Myrrhine speaks of purifying herself in the Athenian Clepsydra, which was "at the foot of the cliff at the [northwest] angle of the ACROPOLIS, in a cleft converted into a fountain house in the [fifth century B.C.E.]" (Dunbar). The word *clepsydra* also denotes the water clock (a sort of hourglass) that the Athenians used to time speakers' remarks in court. The Greek comic poet Eubulus wrote a play entitled *Clepsydra,* of which only the title has survived (Kock). [ANCIENT SOURCES: Aristophanes, *Acharnians* 693, *Birds* 1695, *Lysistrata* 913, *Wasps* 93, 857–58; Pausanias, 2.38.2]

BIBLIOGRAPHY
Dunbar, Nan. *Aristophanes: Birds.* New York: Oxford University Press, 1995, 740–41.
Kock, T. *Comicorum Atticorum Fragmenta.* Vol. 2. Leipzig: Teubner, 1884.

CLOACINA An epithet of Venus (see APHRODITE). According to Servius, the name is from the verb *cloare,* "to purge" or "to purify." [ANCIENT SOURCES: Plautus, *Curculio* 471; Servius Honoratus on *Aeneid,* 1.720]

CLOTHO The name of one of the FATES.

CLOUDS ARISTOPHANES (423 B.C.E.) The play originally placed third of the three at the DIONYSIA. The first prize went to CRATINUS, whose *Putine* (*Wine Flask* or *The Bottle*) made fun of Cratinus' own alleged drinking problem. In the PARABASIS of WASPS, ARISTOPHANES expresses his disappointment in the audience's reaction to *Clouds,* claiming that it was his most clever play to date. It is not surprising that Aristophanes would have been disappointed, because his plays had finished in first place the previous two years.

The setting of *Clouds* is ATHENS. The stage building makes use of at least two doors, with one representing the house of the main character, STREPSIADES, the other the school run by SOCRATES. The play opens just before dawn at the house of Strepsiades. Onstage Strepsiades and his son, PHEIDIPPIDES, are in bed. Strepsiades is awake, but Pheidippides continues to sleep. The audience first hears Strepsiades complain that he has fallen into debt because of the expenses his son, Pheidippides, has incurred through his love of horses. Plagued by creditors, Strepsiades plots to cheat them by having Pheidippides learn a clever manner of arguing, called "Wrong Logic," from Socrates. When Pheidippides refuses to go to Socrates' school, the Phrontisterion (Thinkateria or Pondeterium), Strepsiades himself decides to become Socrates' pupil.

When Strepsiades goes to the school he initially meets one of the students, who tells him of Socrates' astonishing mental feats and shows him some of the subjects studied by the school's students, who look like prisoners of war, according to Strepsiades. Finally, Strepsiades' student guide leaves and Socrates himself appears. Socrates enters above the stage level in the MECHANE and claims he is walking on air and contemplating the sun. When Strepsiades tells Socrates that he has come to learn the sort of argumentation that can help him avoid payment of his debts, Socrates agrees to instruct him. Socrates also introduces Strepsiades to his patron divinities, the Clouds, who constitute the play's chorus. Socrates informs Strepsiades that the Clouds are divinities, and that ZEUS does not rule the gods, but, rather, a divinity named Dinos (Vortex), a pun on *Dios* (Zeus or God), does. Strepsiades is made to swear that he will reject the traditional gods and acknowledge as divinities Chaos, Clouds, and Tongue. After Strepsiades takes this oath, the Clouds promise Strepsiades that he will become a clever speaker. Socrates tries to teach the old man about rhythm in poetry and the gender of nouns, but Strepsiades is unable to grasp these subjects. Because Strepsiades is never able to satisfy him, Socrates refuses to teach him any longer. Strepsiades turns to the Clouds for advice, and they urge him to send his son to the Phronesterion. Although Pheidippides had earlier rejected this idea, he now agrees to study at the Phrontesterion.

At the school, Pheidippides is instructed not by Socrates, but by Stronger and Weaker Logic (or Argumentation). Pheidippides' initial lessons take the form of a debate between the two Logics, with the winner of the debate getting the privilege of instructing Pheidippides. In this debate, Stronger Logic represents the traditional Athenian system of education and values, while Weaker Logic represents the opposite. When Weaker Logic, through his crafty means of argument, manages to convince Stronger Logic that some of the most "successful" people in society are also the most corrupt and immoral, he wins the debate and Pheidippides becomes his pupil.

Pheidippides' mastery of the new learning occurs quickly, and soon, with his son's backing, Strepsiades is able to drive away two of his creditors. After the two creditors are gone, Strepsiades and Pheidippides enter their house to have dinner. The chorus, however, predict that Strepsiades will soon repent of his son's new learning. Their prediction comes true as Strepsiades, being beaten by his son, then rushes from his house. As it turns out, not only can Pheidippides foil Strepsiades' creditors, but by using "weaker logic" he also argues that beating his father is proper. Strepsiades is unable to refute his son's argument, but when Pheidippides claims he will prove he would be in the right to beat his mother as well, Strepsiades decides that this behavior has gone far enough. Thus, Strepsiades proceeds to attack the problem at its root by burning down the Phrontesterion. The drama concludes with Strepsiades' setting fire to Socrates' school and Socrates himself calling out for help.

COMMENTARY

The version of *Clouds* that survives to this day was revised a few years after it was written but does not seem to have been performed in competition. In the second version of the play, Aristophanes apparently altered the parabasis, made some modification to the encounter between Stronger and Weaker Logic, and added the burning of Socrates' school.

Reconstructing the staging of the *Clouds* poses some challenges. Because ancient plays were presented during the daytime, the audience of *Clouds* would have to imagine that it is night when the play opens. Also, the ancient stage is limited in its capacity to represent the interior of a house, so Strepsiades and his son would lie on beds outside the stage building. Thus, the audience must imagine that they are inside Strepsiades' house.

Usually, ancient drama made use of only three actors, but at two places in *Clouds* four are needed. When Stronger and Weaker Logic debate, Pheidippides and Strepsiades are both onstage. At the play's conclusion during the burning of the house, Strepsiades, Socrates, and two students speak.

The burning of house poses the greatest challenge to staging the play. How was this accomplished? The ancient stage building was wooden, and so Strepsiades could not have actually set fire to it. Strepsiades and his slave may have carried real torches and pretended to touch them to the building, while people hidden behind the stage building held torches or smoking braziers behind the building in such a way that the smoke and/or flames gave the illusion of the building's being set ablaze.

Regarding the subject matter of the play, one of the focal points of *Clouds* is the concept of *logos* (plural: *logoi*), whose basic meanings are "word" and "speech." Strepsiades believes that the power of *logos* is the key to solving his problems (see O'Reagan's study). When Strepsiades fails to master the new *logos* taught by Socrates, his son Pheidippides witnesses as the weaker *logos* defeats the stronger *logos*. The weaker *logos* subverts traditional values in Athenian society. The argument weaker *logos* uses to defeat his opponent allows people to justify adultery by taking Zeus and the most prominent members of society as their models. Pheidippides' new understanding of *logos* proves intolerable to his father, as it runs contrary to the traditional values upon which Strepsiades' life rests. Using weaker *logos*, Pheidippides convinces his father that the son should be permitted to beat the father. At the end of the play, Strepsiades rejects the weaker *logos* and turns to brute force as he sets fire to the Phrontesterion.

In addition to the play's concern with the power of *logos*, *Clouds* presents the audience with the contrast between *nomos* (what is permitted by established custom) and *phusis* (which means "nature," "condition," or "constitution"). Aristophanes shows that the danger of the weaker form of argumentation is that it seeks to overturn what has been established by custom (cf. line 1040). Strepsiades wants to use the "weaker logic" to avoid paying his debts when they are customarily due by creating a clever loophole to show that this custom is not valid. Because Strepsiades' son initially refuses to study with Socrates, Strepsiades decides that he himself will. The Clouds, who are able to change their *phusis* (352), praise Strepsiades for his willingness to change his *phusis* (515). However willing the old man may be, he proves unable to change his nature and forces his son, who he claims is clever by nature (*phusis*, 877), to study with Socrates. Pheidippides then listens to the argument between Stronger and Weaker Logos, in which the Weaker Logos argues (among other points) that men can use his form of argumenta-

tion to indulge their nature (*phusis*, 1078) by committing acts that violate established custom, such as adultery. All men need to do is appeal to the example of Zeus. If the king of the gods commits adultery, then why should mortal men not follow his example?

In contrast to Strepsiades, who is not able to change his *phusis*, Pheidippides has a *phusis* that is able to grasp this new type of argumentation. Unfortunately for Strepsiades, his son not only has the ability to argue his way out of the customary date for the payment of debts, but also declares that he enjoys the power of being able to look down upon other established customs (*nomoi*, 1400). When Strepsiades runs from his house in horror at being beaten by his son, he declares that nowhere is it customary for sons to beat their father (1420). His son, however, reasons that because it was a man who first established this custom, he as a man should be allowed to establish a new custom (1421–26). Because humans do not observe the custom of sons' beating fathers, Pheidippides appeals to the world of nature, in which he claims that the offspring of animals retaliate against their fathers. Thus, he should be allowed to beat his father.

One final point of interest for this play is that it provides us with a comic caricature of an actual figure from history: Socrates. Although the play was staged first in 423 B.C.E., when the real Socrates was brought to trial in 399, in PLATO's *Apology* Socrates alludes to Aristophanes' portrayal of him. Some of the points that Aristophanes' mentions in his portrayal of Socrates are the same charges made against him in Plato's *Apology*, as well as Xenophon's account of Socrates' defense. The three charges against the real Socrates are that he was corrupting the youth of Athens, that he did not believe in the divinities customarily worshiped by the Athenians, and that he was introducing new divinities of his own. All these charges can be found in Aristophanes' portrayal of Socrates. Of course, Aristophanes makes the same suggestions about EURIPIDES in *FROGS*, and a few links between Euripides and the Weaker Logic ascribed to Socrates are established in the *Clouds*. In the latter part of the play, when Strepsiades and Pheidippides dine together, Strepsiades asks Pheidippides to sing a song or recite some poetry. Pheidippides rejects the poets of old such as SIMONIDES and AESCHY-

LUS and instead recites some lines from Euripides about the incest of a brother and sister (lines 1371–72). By the time *Frogs* was produced, however, Euripides was already dead, having left Athens for the court of the Macedonian king Archelaus a few years earlier. Euripides did not live to see the defeat of Athens by SPARTA in 404 and the brief reign of terror imposed by the Spartan conquerors. Although democracy had been restored by the time Socrates was on trial, Athens was not the same and Socrates became a victim of the city he loved so much.

BIBLIOGRAPHY

Dover, K. J. *Aristophanes: Clouds.* Oxford: Clarendon Press, 1989.

Havelock, E. A. "The Socratic Self as It Is Parodied in Aristophanes' *Clouds*," *Yale Classical Studies* 22 (1972): 1–18.

Marianetti, M. C. *Religion and Politics in Aristophanes' Clouds.* Hildesheim and New York: Olms-Weidmann, 1992.

O'Regan, D. E. *Rhetoric, Comedy, and the Violence of Language in Aristophanes' Clouds.* New York: Oxford University Press, 1992.

Segal, Charles, "Aristophanes' Cloud-Chorus," *Arethusa* 2 (1969): 143–61.

Vander Waert, P. A., "Socrates in the *Clouds*." In *The Socratic Movement.* Edited by Paul A. Vander Waert. Ithaca, N.Y.: Cornell University Press, 1994, 48–86.

CLYTEMNESTRA (CLYTAEMESTRA)

The daughter of TYNDAREUS and LEDA, Clytemnestra was the sister of Phoebe, CASTOR, POLLUX, and HELEN. Clytemnestra was first married to THYESTES' son, TANTALUS, a prince at MYCENAE. Clytemnestra had a child by Tantalus, but when AGAMEMNON assumed the rule of Mycenae, he killed Tantalus and the child. After this, Clytemnestra became Agamemnon's wife. For some time, Agamemnon and Clytemnestra seem to have lived in relative harmony. They had four children together: ELECTRA, IPHIGENIA, CHRYSOTHEMIS, and ORESTES. Clytemnestra's happiness ended, however, when Agamemnon sacrificed IPHIGENIA to gain fair winds for sailing to TROY. After this tragic event, Clytemnestra began to plot revenge against her husband. She had an affair with AEGISTHUS, who also had grievances against Agamemnon and his father, ATREUS. When Agamemnon, accompanied by the prophetess

CASSANDRA, returned from Troy, Clytemnestra and Aegisthus killed him and Cassandra and Clytemnestra became Aegisthus' queen. When Agamemnon was killed, his son, Orestes, was living with STROPHIUS in the region of PHOCIS. Eventually, Orestes would return from Phocis, arrange for a false announcement of his death, and kill Clytemnestra and Aegisthus. Clytemnestra's FURIES pursued and tormented Orestes until he was acquitted of his crime by ATHENA and the people of ATHENS.

Clytemnestra, both an adulteress and a murderer, is one of the most notorious female characters in ancient drama. She appears as a character in AESCHYLUS' ORESTEIA, SOPHOCLES' ELECTRA, EURIPIDES' ELECTRA and IPHIGENIA AT AULIS, and SENECA's AGAMEMNON. In Aeschylus' *Agamemnon,* (see ORESTEIA), she is depicted as an intelligent woman who is underestimated by the men of Argos and her husband. Aeschylus also describes her in animalistic or subhuman terms—as a lioness who beds with a wolf, a serpent, and a Fury. Clytemnestra's ghost makes a brief appearance in Aeschylus' *Eumenides* (see ORESTEIA) as she rouses the sleeping Furies and urges them to pursue and persecute her son, Orestes.

In IPHIGENIA AT AULIS, Euripides shows Clytemnestra as a stern but somewhat sympathetic matron who upsets Agamemnon's plan to sacrifice Iphigenia. Clytemnestra also appears in both SOPHOCLES' ELECTRA and EURIPIDES' ELECTRA. In both plays, Clytemnestra argues that she was justified in murdering Agamemnon because Agamemnon had sacrificed Iphigenia. Euripides' Clytemnestra also condemns Agamemnon for taking CASSANDRA home as a concubine. When Electra argues against her mother, Clytemnestra offers no defense and even expresses understanding and forgiveness toward Electra. Euripides' portrait of Clytemnestra is also more sympathetic than that of Sophocles because Euripides' Electra lures Clytemnestra to her death with the pretext of helping her make a sacrifice for the birth of a son who does not exist. Once inside the hut where Electra lives, Clytemnestra is killed by Orestes, who is waiting inside, and Electra reports that her hand was on the blade with his. In Sophocles' *Electra,* Clytemnestra threatens to have Aegisthus punish Electra for her criticism of and impudence toward her. Sophocles also has both

Clytemnestra and Electra on hand when the announcement of Orestes' "death" is made. Upon hearing that her son is dead, Clytemnestra expresses relief at the news and continues to show no sympathy to Electra. In contrast to Euripides' play, when Orestes kills Clytemnestra, Electra remains outside the house.

Sophocles wrote a *Clytemnestra,* of which a single line survives that reveals nothing about the play's plot. The Greek tragedian Polemaeus also wrote a *Clytemnestra,* of which only the title survives. Among Roman authors, ACCIUS wrote a *Clytemnestra* (234–47 Warmington), whose handful of surviving lines indicate that the play probably culminated in the murder of Agamemnon and Cassandra; the latter appears to be the speaker in two fragments. Unlike Aeschylus' *Agamemnon* (see ORESTEIA), Accius' play may have had Electra as a character, as she is in Seneca's *Agamemnon.* [ANCIENT SOURCES: Apollodorus, *Library* 3.10.7, *Epitome* 2.15–16, 3.22; Homer, *Odyssey* 11.421–39]

BIBLIOGRAPHY
Betensky, A. "Aeschylus' *Oresteia:* The Power of Clytemnestra," *Ramus* 7 (1978): 11–25.
MacEwen, S., ed. *Views of Clytemnestra, Ancient and Modern.* Lewiston, N.Y.: Edwin Mellen Press, 1990.
Mader, G. "*Fluctibus variis agor:* An Aspect of Seneca's Clytemnestra Portrait," *Acta Classica* 31 (1988): 51–70.
Radt, S. *Tragicorum Graecorum Fragmenta.* Vol. 4. Göttingen, Ger.: Vandenhoeck & Ruprecht, 1977.
Snell, B. *Tragicorum Graecorum Fragmenta.* Vol. 1. Göttingen, Ger.: Vandenhoeck & Ruprecht, 1971.
Warmington, E. H. *Remains of Old Latin: Livius Andronicus, Naevius, Pacuvius, and Accius.* Vol. 2. Cambridge, Mass.: Harvard University Press, 1936.

COCALUS After DAEDALUS' son, Icarus, died, Daedalus journeyed to the court of Cocalus in the Sicilian town of Camicus. MINOS, king of CRETE, pursued Daedalus, and everywhere Minos searched he took along a spiral shell and promised to reward the person who could pass a thread through the shell, thinking that only Daedalus would be clever enough to do this. Finally, Minos reached Camicus and showed the shell to Cocalus, who gave it to Daedalus. The inventor threaded the shell by boring a hole through it, tying a thread to an ant, and then letting the ant go through the hole. When Cocalus returned and gave the threaded shell to Minos, Minos realized that Daedalus was nearby and demanded that he be surrendered to him. Cocalus said he would hand over Daedalus but delayed Minos with the customary hospitality offered to strangers. Cocalus' daughters killed Minos by pouring boiling water on him as he bathed.

ARISTOPHANES wrote a play entitled *Cocalus,* from which about 50 words survive. The play was produced after 388 B.C.E. by one of Aristophanes' sons. SOPHOCLES wrote a *Men of Camicus* that may have dealt with Minos' death at Camicus. Whether the play was a TRAGEDY or SATYR PLAY is not known. [ANCIENT SOURCES: Apollodorus, *Epitome* 1.14–15; Hyginus, *Fables* 44; Pausanias, 7.4.6; Strabo 6.2.6]

BIBLIOGRAPHY
Cassio, A. C. "Un frammento del Cocalo di Aristofane (351 K.)," *Rivista di Filologia e di Istruzione Classica* 102 (1974): 164–69.
Dover, K. J. *Aristophanic Comedy.* Berkeley: University of California Press, 1972, 14.
Kock, T. *Comicorum Atticorum Fragmenta.* Vol. 1. Leipzig: Teubner, 1880.
Radt, S. *Tragicorum Graecorum Fragmenta.* Vol. 4. Göttingen, Ger.: Vandenhoeck & Ruprecht, 1977.

COCYTUS According to HOMER, this river in the UNDERWORLD, whose name means "shrieking" or "wailing," flowed into the ACHERON and was a branch of the STYX. There was also a river named Cocytus in northern Greece, which Pausanias describes as "very unpleasant." Pausanias thought Homer applied the name of this actual river to the one in the underworld. [ANCIENT SOURCES: Aeschylus, *Agamemnon* 1160 (see ORESTEIA), SEVEN AGAINST THEBES 690; Aristophanes, *Frogs* 472; Euripides, *Alcestis* 458; Homer, *Odyssey* 10.513–14; Pausanias, 1.17.5; Seneca, *Hercules Furens* 686, 870, *Hercules Oetaeus* 1963]

COESYRA The mother of MEGACLES, who may have been one of the Alcmeonids, an aristocratic Athenian family. Coesyra, who claimed to be descended from ZEUS, was famous for her pride and displays of wealth. [ANCIENT SOURCES: Aristophanes, *Acharnians* 614, *Clouds* 48, 800]

BIBLIOGRAPHY
Dover, K. J. *Aristophanes: Clouds.* Oxford: Clarendon Press, 1968, 99–100.
Sommerstein, A. H. *The Comedies of Aristophanes.* Vol. 1, *Acharnians.* Warminster, U.K.: Aris & Phillips, 1980, 187.

COLAENIS   A title of the goddess ARTEMIS at Myrrhinous, about 12 miles southeast of ATHENS. [ANCIENT SOURCES: Aristophanes, *Birds* 872; Pausanias, 1.31.4]

BIBLIOGRAPHY
Dunbar, Nan. *Aristophanes: Birds.* New York: Oxford University Press, 1995, 511–12.

COLCHIAN BULLS   Fire-breathing bulls that JASON had to yoke and with which he had to plow a field in COLCHIS. MEDEA, having fallen in love with Jason, gave him a potion to protect him from the bulls' fiery breath. [ANCIENT SOURCES: Seneca, *Medea* 829]

COLCHIS   A town located near the southeastern coast of the Black Sea in what is today the region of Georgia. In drama, Colchis is best known as the home of ABSYRTUS, AEETES, and MEDEA and the location of the Golden Fleece. No extant play has Colchis as its setting, but some classical dramas would have been set there, particularly those dealing with JASON and Medea.

SOPHOCLES wrote a *Colchides* (Women of Colchis) [fragments 336–49 Radt], which treated the tasks imposed on Jason by Aeetes and Jason's acquisition of the Golden Fleece. A scholiast's remark on Apollonius Rhodius (*Argonautica* 3.1040c) informs us that in Sophocles' play Medea instructs Jason about the tasks that Aeetes gave to Jason. In fragment 341, Aeetes questions a messenger about armed warriors that sprang up from the ground (after Jason had sown the dragon's teeth). In fragment 339, Medea apparently questions Jason about whether he will swear to do her a favor in exchange for the one she is going to do him.

BIBLIOGRAPHY
Braund, D. C. *Georgia in Antiquity: A History of Colchis and Transcaucasian Iberia, 550 BC–AD 562.* New York: Oxford University Press, 1994.
Lloyd-Jones, H. *Sophocles: Fragments.* Cambridge, Mass.: Harvard University Press, 1996.

Radt, S. *Tragicorum Graecorum Fragmenta.* Vol. 4. Göttingen, Ger.: Vandenhoeck & Ruprecht, 1977.

COLIAS   A title of the goddess APHRODITE, who had a temple on Cape Colias (in Athenian territory). Henderson notes that the priestess of Aphrodite Colias had a reserved seat in the theater at ATHENS. [ANCIENT SOURCES: Aristophanes, *Clouds* 52, *Lysistrata* 2; Herodotus, 8.96; Pausanias, 1.1.5]

BIBLIOGRAPHY
Dover, K. J. *Aristophanes: Clouds.* Oxford: Clarendon Press, 1968, 100.
Henderson, J. *Aristophanes: Lysistrata.* Oxford: Clarendon Press, 1987, 67.

COLONUS   A DEME a little more than a mile northwest of ATHENS, Colonus was the birthplace of SOPHOCLES and the setting for Sophocles' last extant play, *OEDIPUS AT COLONUS.* At the end of his life, OEDIPUS took refuge at Colonus.

COLOSSEUM   Construction of the Colosseum at Rome, properly known as the Flavian amphitheater, was started under the emperor Vespasian and finished under Titus and Domitian. The Colosseum was dedicated in 80 C.E. and could seat as many as 50,000 people.

COMEDY   Our word *comedy* is from a Greek word, *komoidia,* which is a combination of two words, *komos,* meaning "revel," "merrymaking," or "festal procession," and *oidos,* which means "song." Thus, comedy is a "*komos* song." How comic performances originated is unknown, but the theories fall along the following lines and some theorists combine elements of them. First, comedy emerged from certain fertility rituals in which the dancers were dressed as animals or fertility rituals in which the dancers were dressed as SATYRS. Second, comedy emerged from religious rituals that involved the exchange of jests or obscenities by participants. Third, comedy evolved from PHALLUS wearers or phallus bearers in dances or processions (cf. Aristotle, *Poetics* 1449a10).

Not only are the origins of comedy unknown, we do not know when comedy first began to be performed. Susarion of MEGARA was credited with inventing comedy and introducing it in Attica (the region where ATHENS is located) between 580 and 564 B.C.E. No existing evidence corroborates this tradition, however. Better evidence exists in a vase produced in Attica around 550 B.C.E., which shows men dressed as horses and carrying riders on their backs. A person playing the pipes can also be seen. Such an illustration suggests a comic performance (cf. ARISTOPHANES' *KNIGHTS*). Other vase paintings from the sixth century B.C.E. show men who are dressed as satyrs and dancing about. This, too, suggests some sort of comic performance, but we cannot be certain. Thus, although some archaeological evidence for comic performances does exist in the mid-sixth century, the first known comic performances in competition in Athens are said to have occurred around 486 B.C.E. at the City DIONYSIA. As with Greek TRAGEDY, the surviving Greek comedies were performed at festivals that honored DIONYSUS. Unlike the three Greek tragedians, who put on three tragedies and a SATYR PLAY at the Dionysia, five comic poets presented a single play. Beginning around 442 B.C.E., tragedies and comedies began to be performed at the LENAEA, another Athenian festival honoring Dionysus. In contrast to the format of the City Dionysia, at the Lenaea only two tragedians competed and each presented two tragedies.

Tragedy and comedy were performed in the same theater structure and used the same special effects devices, such as the ECCYCLEMA (a rolling platform used to show interior scenes) and the MECHANE (a crane used to suspend characters above the ground). Aristophanic comedy sometimes uses these devices in parody of tragedy (cf. especially *ACHARNIANS*, *PEACE*, *THESMOPHORI-AZUSAE*). As did tragedy, comedy had a CHORUS (24 members) who sang and danced during the performance. Dance styles in comedy differed from those in tragedy and could be wilder and more sexually suggestive. Usually, no more than three actors were needed to perform a play. Thus, actors would play multiple roles. This system could have posed quite a challenge for comic actors because comedies tend to have more speaking roles than tragedies. Aristophanes' *Knights* has only five speaking roles besides the chorus; Aristophanes' *BIRDS* has 20 speaking roles. Greek tragedies seldom have more than 10 speaking roles in addition to the chorus. As with tragedy, males played the speaking roles of both genders.

As in tragedy, in comedy the chorus and the actors wore MASKS, but comic masks would have expressions designed to evoke laughter from the audience rather than the response appropriate to tragedy. Obviously, comic costumes would also differ from tragic costumes, especially with respect to the chorus, whose members might dress as the men or women of Athens in some plays and in others dress as ant-people, birds, clouds, goats, or various bizarre creatures. Comic costumes also were padded to provide additional humor to the physique. Male comic costumes before the end of the fourth century B.C.E. also included an exaggerated PHALLUS. As in tragedy, in comedy the words the actors and chorus spoke or sang followed a fixed pattern of rhythm (see METER) rather than rhyme and were accompanied by musical pipes (see AULOS). Although the metrical patterns of comedy could be just as complex as those found in tragedy, the language of comedy was less formal. In comparison to that in tragedy, comic diction employed more extensive use of alliteration, play on words, puns, invented words, and obscenity.

Modern scholars have divided classical comedy into three periods: Old Comedy (ca. 500–400 B.C.E.), Middle Comedy (ca. 400–325 B.C.E.), and New Comedy (ca. 325 B.C.E.–250 C.E.). Of these three periods, the most is known about New Comedy (represented by the roughly 30 complete plays and fragments of MENANDER, PLAUTUS, and TERENCE) and the least about Middle Comedy (represented by two plays, *ECCLESI-AZUSAE* and *Wealth*, of Aristophanes). Our knowledge of Old Comedy rests on the nine other surviving plays of Aristophanes and the fragments of such playwrights as CRATINUS, EUPOLIS, and PHERECRATES. Although only about 40 complete plays from four comic poets have survived, the names of at least 150 comic playwrights are known.

Old Comedy is known for its sexual humor and obscenity, fantasy-filled story lines (e.g., men going to live with the birds in Aristophanes' *Birds*; famous politicians being raised from the dead in Eupolis' *Demes*), as well as commentary on current events, intellectual trends, and the political affairs of fifth-century Athens. The sort of humor found in the television program *Saturday Night Live* provides a modern parallel to Old Comedy. Just as satire of political leaders is seen on the program, in the last four decades of the fifth century B.C.E., Athenian leaders such as PERICLES, CLEON, ALCIBIADES, and HYPERBOLUS were often the object of comic satire in the plays of such writers as Aristophanes, Cratinus, and Eupolis. The Athenians of this period also enjoyed the sort of humor that transplanted people from their usual station in life into situations that were completely foreign to them. In Old Comedy, simple folk are face to face with wily politicians, intellectuals, or even the gods themselves. The playwrights of Old Comedy also produced plays that offered a humorous take on stories or characters from mythology, such as Aristophanes' *Women of Lemnos,* Crates' *Lamia,* and Cratinus' *Dionysus as Alexander.* In some of these plays, mythological figures may have represented political leaders. In Cratinus' *Dionysus as Alexander,* Dionysus may have represented Pericles. Pericles may also have been behind the figure of Zeus in Cratinus' *Nemesis.* Another feature of Old Comedy was that the choruses sometimes represented unusual beings (e.g., Pherecrates' *Ant-People*) or animals (e.g., birds, frogs, goats, wasps). Aristophanes' early comedies also have a feature called the PARABASIS, in which the chorus address the audience as if they are the playwright himself. Old Comedy also featured an AGON, which was essentially a debate between two characters (e.g., the debate between Stronger Logic and Weaker Logic in Aristophanes' CLOUDS).

Middle Comedy represents a transitional period between Old and New Comedy. The two so-called Middle Comedies of Aristophanes show a marked decrease in attacks on public figures and a diminished role for the chorus. The parabasis disappeared in this period. One of the leading representatives of this period was Alexis (ca. 370–270 B.C.E.), who is said to have written 245 plays. As his predecessors in Old Comedy did, Alexis wrote comedies about events and characters from mythology (e.g., *Hesione, Orestes, Sciron, Tyndareus*), but also titles that show a greater concern with the stereotypical figures in everyday life of the time. Some of Alexis' titles—*Brothers, Parasite, Twins*—are echoed in the characters or plays of Plautus or Terence. Eubulus, a contemporary of Alexis', shows

a similar pattern with mythological titles such as *Antiope, Auge,* and *Daedalus,* and titles that hint at New Comedy, such as *Pamphilus,* the *Pimp,* and *Chrysilla.*

In the period known as New Comedy, mention of political or contemporary persons has almost completely vanished, mythological references have diminished, obscenity has greatly decreased, and the chorus' appearance has been restricted to occur between a play's five acts. In New Comedy, the plays' plots and characters become stereotypical. New Comedy usually focuses on a subject to which everyone can relate, love and marriage. The players involved in this type of comedy were the common figures of society of that period: the freeborn father, his nagging wife, his son, the freeborn "girl next door," the PROSTITUTE, the PIMP, the BRAGGART WARRIOR, the PARASITE, and SLAVES, COOKS, and NURSES. New Comedy generates its humor from character and situation. "Getting the girl" is often the object in these comedies; the father and son are the characters who appear most frequently and the effect of the love affair on the relationship of father and son or son and birth family is of major interest. Many of the story lines in New Comedy are similar to that of EURIPIDES' ION, in which CREUSA is raped, she abandons her child (ION), the child is raised by someone else, and eventually mother and child recognize one another through items left with the infant. Compare Menander's *Arbitration,* in which Pamphile is raped, becomes pregnant, marries Charisius, and exposes the child during Charisius' absence from home. The child is found by slaves and by means of items left with the infant the baby is shown to be Pamphile's and Charisius is shown to be the rapist.

Beginning in the last half of the third century B.C.E., Roman playwrights began to adapt the Greek plays of authors such as Menander for Roman audiences. Such a play, called a FABULA PALLIATA, is a Greek play in which the characters wear Roman clothing. The plays of PLAUTUS and TERENCE are of this type. Such comedies continued to be written until the first century B.C.E., but other kinds of comedy began to be written and performed as well, such as MIMES, FABULA ATELLANA, and FABULA TOGATA (Latin comedy in Roman dress). The *fabula togata* were not especially popular; however, performances of mimes and the *fabula atellana* eclipsed those of the *palliata* in popularity. [ANCIENT SOURCES: Aristotle, *Poetics* 1448a31–33, 1449a10, 1449b2; Aristophanes, *Birds* 262–308; Athenaeus, *Deipnosophists* passim; Demosthenes, 21.10; *Inscriptiones Graecae,* ii² 2318; *Parian Marble* 71]

BIBLIOGRAPHY

Beare, W. *The Roman Stage.* London: Methuen, 1950.
Pickard-Cambridge, A. W. *Dithyramb, Tragedy, and Comedy.* 2d ed. Revised by T. B. L. Webster. Oxford: Clarendon Press, 1962.
———. *The Dramatic Festivals of Athens.* 2d ed. Revised by J. Gould and D. M. Lewis. Oxford: Clarendon Press, 1968.
Sandbach, F. H. *The Comic Theatre of Greece and Rome.* New York: Norton, 1977.
Webster, T. B. L. *Studies in Later Greek Comedy.* 2d ed. Manchester: Manchester University Press, 1970.

COMEDY OF ASSES (Latin: *ASINARIA*)

PLAUTUS   The play's date is unknown; Duckworth has dated it to the early part of PLAUTUS' career. The play's setting is ATHENS, and the action occurs before the houses of Demaenetus, an elderly Athenian gentleman, and Cleareta, a madam (see PIMP). The prologue reveals that the source of Plautus' play was Demophilus' *Onagos*. As the play opens, Demaenetus and his slave, Libanus, discuss the love affair of Argyrippus ("silver horse"), Demaenetus' son, and Philaenium ("lover of bronze"), the daughter of Cleareta. Argyrippus has asked his father for some 20 MINAE (which Demaenetus wants to provide) to help him in his love affair. Demaenetus asks Libanus to cheat him of the money, so that the money can be provided without arousing suspicion from Demaenetus' wife, Artemona.

After both Libanus and Demaenetus depart for the FORUM, Argyrippus emerges from Cleareta's house and expresses his anger that Philaenium has rejected him because his gifts are not of great value, although in earlier times they were satisfactory. Cleareta follows the young man and tosses Argyrippus' claims of unfairness back in his face and says that if he wants Philaenium for a single night then he must pay an exorbitant price. When Argyrippus asks Cleareta how much it would cost to have Philaenium for the next year, she names a price of 20 minae, provided that someone else not pay that amount before Argyrippus does.

After Argyrippus sets out to try to find the money, Libanus returns from the forum and his fellow servant, Leonida, soon joins him. Together they plot how to trick Demaenetus out of the 20 minae. As it turns out, the house steward, Saurea, had sold some asses and a MERCHANT was on his way to Demaenetus' house to pay him (20 minae) for them. Leonida proposes that he pose as Saurea, take the money for the asses, and then use that money to help Argyrippus.

When the merchant arrives at Demaenetus' house, Libanus describes Saurea and characterizes him as a hot-tempered man who beats those with whom he is angry. At that moment, Leonida, posing as Saurea, arrives, angry that Libanus has not met him at the barber's shop. The merchant attempts to calm Leonida as he tries to strike Libanus. After Leonida rants for some time, he pretends at last to notice the merchant and says he will take the money owed to Demaenetus. The merchant, however, insists upon paying the money in Demaenetus' presence. Despite the efforts of Libanus and Leonida to persuade the merchant to hand over the money, the merchant persists. Eventually, Leonida leads the merchant off to the forum to find Demaenetus.

Next, Cleareta and her daughter, Philaenium, emerge from their house and argue about the arrangement that Cleareta has made with Argyrippus. Philaenium loves the young man, but her mother does not want her attached to someone who offers sweet talk instead of money. After the women exit into their house, Libanus and Leonida return from the forum with the 20 minae that they have swindled from the merchant, thanks to help from Demaenetus, who played along with their charade.

As Libanus and Leonida talk, Argyrippus and Philaenium arrive from Philaenium's house. The two servants listen as the two lovers tearfully part company. Eventually, the two servants greet the lovers and Argyrippus suggests that he will end his life if he cannot raise the 20 minae required by Cleareta, and which another young Athenian gentleman, Diabolus (whose name means "the enemy"), has promised to provide. Upon hearing this, Leonidas tells Argyrippus that he and Libanus will give him the 20 minae if Argyrippus frees them from slavery. Argyrippus readily agrees, but then Leonida teases Philaenium with the money, saying that he will not hand it over until she flirts with him and Libanus. Then, Libanus makes Argyrippus carry him on his back as a horse carries a jockey. Next, the two slaves playfully suggest that their master should set up statues and altars and worship them as the gods Salvation and Fortune. Finally, the two slaves hand over the money under one condition—Argyrippus' father, Demaenetus, wants to have dinner and spend the night with Philaenium. Argyrippus is so desperate to have Philaenium that he agrees to this request.

After the two lovers enter Cleareta's house and the two slaves enter Demaenetus' house, Diabolus and his unnamed PARASITE arrive with a contract between Diabolus and Cleareta. The contract guarantees that Philaenium will have no other male company than Diabolus for a year. No sooner does Diabolus enter Philaenium's house, however, than he reemerges, angry that Argyrippus has paid for Philaenium before he could. Diabolus and his parasite decide to cause trouble for Demaenetus, whom they have apparently seen inside Cleareta's house, by telling his wife that he and Argyrippus are carousing with Philaenium.

After the departure of Diabolus and his parasite, Demaenetus, Argyrippus, and Philaenium are seen in the midst of a banquet at Cleareta's house. Argyrippus, however, is unhappy because his father rather than he is enjoying Philaenium. The fun is soon interrupted when Diabolus' parasite leads Demaenetus' wife, Artemona, past Cleareta's house, where Artemona sees her husband hugging and kissing Philaenium. Artemona also hears Demaenetus make derogatory comments about her. Eventually Artemona is unable to tolerate the verbal abuse. She bursts into Cleareta's house and drags off her husband to their house. Argyrippus, however, returns to Cleareta's house and the waiting arms of Philaenium. After the actors exit, the entire cast appears to ask the audience to save Demaenetus from a beating by giving loud applause.

COMMENTARY

Comedy of Asses is not one of Plautus' most popular plays with modern critics. Harsh branded it one of "least interesting" works. Duckworth classified *Comedy of Asses* as a play of "guileful deception" and grouped it

with BACCHIDES, CASINA, THE MERCHANT, MILES GLORIOSUS, THE HAUNTED HOUSE, THE PERSIAN, and PSEUDOLUS. In recent years, the play has found more admirers and Konstan considered *Comedy of Asses* "an ingenious variation on the comic archetypes." Slater has approached *Comedy of Asses* as a play in which most of the characters function as playwrights who are trying to gain control of the action. Ultimately, Slater concludes that the play is "a tale of failed improvisation, for no one gets what he wants in full."

Unlike in other plays about young male lovers in which the slave tries to trick the father to get the money to purchase the prostitute with whom the young man is in love (e.g., *The Haunted House*), in *Comedy of Asses* the father already knows about the love affair because the son has told him about it. Indeed, the father in *Comedy of Asses* supports the love affair; perversely, however, he helps his son because he also wants to have sexual relations with the woman (compare Plautus' *Casina* and *Merchant*).

The agreement of the young lover to allow his father to have sexual relations with his beloved recalls to some extent the mythical story of PELOPS and MYRTILUS. Myrtilus agreed to help Pelops kill HIPPODAMEIA's father, OENOMAUS, in exchange for the promise that after Pelops married Hippodameia, Pelops would allow Myrtilus to have sexual relations with her. In the case of Hippodameia, who was unaware of this arrangement, Pelops killed Myrtilus after he tried to assault the woman sexually. Myrtilus, just before he died, put a curse on Pelops and his descendants. As does Myrtilus, Plautus' Demaenetus gives his son, who functions as the Pelops figure, assistance so that he can acquire the woman. In exchange, the son will allow him to have sexual relations with her. In some ways, the COMEDY is more perverse than the tragic myth because instead of two male stranger's agreeing to share the woman, a father and son agree. In both the myth and the comedy, trickery is involved: Myrtilus sabotaged the chariot of Hippodameia's father to bring about the man's death, and Demaenetus allowed himself to be tricked in order to supply his son with money and to deceive his wife. Artemona, however, who functions as the Oenomaus figure, does not "perish" in the deception and instead is able to triumph over her scheming husband. Thus, just as the mythical Pelops was able to enjoy his beloved, so too the comic Argyrippus does. As Pelops killed Myrtilus, Artemona (with help from Diabolus' parasite) will bring about the destruction of Demaenetus. Although Demaenetus does not literally die, all the same, at line 911, after Artemona's arrival, Pardalisca announces that "Demaenetus is dead."

Although *Comedy of Asses* has some similarities with the story of Pelops and Myrtilus, this play is unique in that the mother will be the ultimate source of the money for the young lover, although the trickery involves the mother in an indirect way. In fact, *Comedy of Asses* is the most "mother-centered" Roman comedy. Roman comedy often involves an inversion of societal roles (especially as concerns slaves); in *Comedy of Asses* we find the mother playing a role usually reserved for fathers. Even the father, Demaenetus, admits that the tight rein that his wife keeps on their son is usually held by the father (78–83). Not only will Argyrippus have to elude his mother to gain his beloved, but instead of the usual male pimp a lover must defeat, he has to contend with a female who is both the mother and the madam of his beloved (147). To gain access to the daughter of one mother the lover must deceive his own. The presence of the two mothers also creates an interesting dynamic for the prostitute Philaenium. As Cleareta's child, she owes her mother a certain allegiance and dutifulness (505–44). As a young woman in love with a man who cannot meet the financial demands of her mother the madam, Philaenium struggles against this allegiance and dutifulness. Once the money from one mother, Artemona, is acquired, the barriers posed by the second mother, Cleareta, are eliminated. Thus, the celebratory banquet with the prostitute begins. Just as the dutifulness of the daughter Philaenium was tested earlier, the dutifulness of the son is now tested as Argyrippus agrees to allow his father a share in his beloved because his duty as a son requires that he do so (831). Typically in a Roman COMEDY we expect a deceived father to interrupt a young man's festivities with his beloved. In *Comedy of Asses,* however, the father joins the party and the mother interrupts it. Usually, the father forgives a repentant son and allows him to marry his beloved, but in this play the son becomes

of secondary concern as the mother Artemona drags her delinquent husband from the party. As for Argyrippus, no marriage with his beloved appears to be imminent as it so often is for young men in Roman comedy; instead, apparently he will have to share Philaenium with Diabolus. Argyrippus has paid for the right to enter the mother Cleareta's house, but he apparently does not have permission to take his beloved as his wife into the mother Artemona's house.

BIBLIOGRAPHY

Bertini, F. *Asinaria.* Genova: Univ. di Genova Ist. di Filol. class. e medioev., 1968.

Duckworth, G. E. *The Nature of Roman Comedy.* Princeton, N.J.: Princeton University Press, 1952, 55, 165.

Harsh, P. W. *A Handbook of Classical Drama.* Stanford Calif.: Stanford University Press, 1944, 342.

Konstan, D. "*Asinaria*: The Family." In *Roman Comedy.* Ithaca, N.Y.: Cornell University Press, 1983. 47–56.

Lowe J. C. B. "Aspects of Plautus' Originality in the *Asinaria,*" *Classical Quarterly* 42 (1992): 152–75.

Slater, N. W. "Six Authors in Search of a Character: *Asinaria* as Guerrilla Theatre." In *Plautus in Performance.* Princeton, N.J.: Princeton University Press, 1985, 55–69.

Vogt-Spira, Gregor. "Asinaria oder Maccus vortit Attice." In *Plautus barbarus: sechs Kapitel zur Originalität des Plautus.* Edited by E. Lefèvre et al. Tübingen, Ger.: Narr, 1991, 11–69.

COMITIUM   The place where the Roman assembly met. [ANCIENT SOURCES: Plautus, *Carthaginian* 807, *Curculio* 403, 470]

CONISALUS   A mythical creature with a large erect PHALLUS. The Greek comic poet Timocles wrote a *Conisalus,* in whose two surviving lines (fragment 20 Kock 2), one person threatens to force another to tell the truth. [ANCIENT SOURCES: Aristophanes, *Lysistrata* 982; Athenaeus, 430ff.; Plato Comicus, fragment 174.13 Kock 1]

BIBLIOGRAPHY

Henderson, J. *Aristophanes: Lysistrata.* Oxford: Clarendon Press, 1987, 185–86.

CONNUS   The son of Metrobius, Connus was a once-successful musician who "was unable to make a living by playing and teaching" (Sommerstein). This failure was apparently a result of his lack of intelligence, and the name of Connus became synonymous with ignorance. Two Greek comic poets, PHRYNICHUS (fragments 6–8 Kock) and AMEIPSIAS (fragments 7–12 Kock), wrote plays entitled *Connus*. Only a few uninformative words survive from Phrynichus' play, but the fragments of Ameipsias' play are quite interesting. Ameipsias' *Connus* placed ahead of ARISTOPHANES' *CLOUDS* in 423 B.C.E. and fragment 9 reveals that SOCRATES was a character in the play (as in Aristophanes' *Clouds*) and was depicted on stage in a ragged cloak. Fragment 10 makes fun of DIOPEITHES, another person whom Aristophanes mocks. [ANCIENT SOURCES: Aristophanes, *Knights* 534, *Wasps* 675; Cratinus, fragment 317 Kock; Diogenes Laertius, 2.28]

BIBLIOGRAPHY

Kock, T. *Comicorum Atticorum Fragmenta*. Vol. 1. Leipzig: Teubner, 1880.

Sommerstein, A. H. *The Comedies of Aristophanes*. Vol. 4, *Wasps*. Warminster, U.K.: Aris & Phillips, 1983, 198–99.

CONTAMINATIO   The precise meaning of this Latin word is debated by modern scholars. Kujore has argued that with respect to TERENCE's dramas, *contaminatio* refers to the omission of details from a play from which Terence borrowed. In other instances, *contaminatio* may involve either the fusing of two or more Greek plays to create one play or the importation into a play of "a small portion from a second original" (Duckworth). In three of Terence's plays (*ANDRIA*, *BROTHERS*, and *EUNUCH*), the playwright combined elements from two plays of MENANDER. Many plays of PLAUTUS also show evidence of *contaminatio* (e.g., *AMPHITRUO*, *THE BRAGGART WARRIOR*, *CASINA*, *THE CARTHAGINIAN*, *PSEUDOLUS*, and *STICHUS*), but the degree to which Plautus' plays are "contaminated" is vigorously debated. [ANCIENT SOURCES: Terence, *Andria* 16, *Eunuch* 552, *Self-Tormentor* 17]

BIBLIOGRAPHY

Duckworth, G. *The Nature of Roman Comedy*. Princeton, N.J.: Princeton University Press, 1952, 202–8.

Kujore, O. "A Note on *Contaminatio* in Terence," *Classical Philology* 59 (1974): 39–42.

COOK (Latin: *COCUS*)   Because COMEDY often portrays weddings, celebrations, or feasting, cooks are stock characters in plays by authors such as MENANDER and PLAUTUS. Cooks are typically contract laborers, people hired from the outside to cook in one's house. These cooks are not wealthy individuals, and because they or their helpers move in and out of people's houses with great freedom, they are frequently suspected of stealing from the houses where they work. In some plays, the cooks have amusing names, such as Anthrax ("charcoal") and Congrio ("conger eel") in PLAUTUS' *POT OF GOLD* or Cylindrus ("mixing bowl") in PLAUTUS' *MENAECHMI*. In other plays, unnamed cooks appear: MENANDER's *SHIELD*, Plautus' *CASINA*, *CURCULIO*, *MERCHANT*, and *PSEUDOLUS*.

BIBLIOGRAPHY

Duckworth, G. *The Nature of Roman Comedy*. Princeton, N.J.: Princeton University Press, 1952, 262.

Hallett, J. P. "Plautine Ingredients in the Performance of the *Pseudolus*," *Classical World* 87, no. 1 (1993–94): 21–26.

Lowe, J. C. B. "Cooks in Plautus," *Classical Antiquity* 4 (1985): 72–102.

Lowe, J. C. B. "The Cook Scene of Plautus' *Pseudolus*," *Classical Quarterly* 35 (1985): 411–16.

COPAIS   A lake in north central Greece (BOEOTIA) that was famous for its eels, which the Greeks considered a delicacy. [ANCIENT SOURCES: Aristophanes, *Acharnians* 880, *Knights* 546, *Peace* 1005]

COPREUS   A herald who served EURYSTHEUS. See EURIPIDES' *CHILDREN OF HERACLES*.

CORDAX   A sexually suggestive dance performed in COMEDY. [ANCIENT SOURCES: Aristophanes, *Clouds* 540, 555; Athenaeus, 1.20e, 14.631d; Lucian, *On Dance* 22, 26; Pausanias, 6.22.1; Theophrastus, *Characters* 6.3]

CORINTH   A Greek town located at the isthmus joining the northern and southern parts of mainland Greece. The Corinthians supported SPARTA during the PELOPONNESIAN WAR. The mythical hero BELLEROPHON was from Corinth; in classical drama Corinth is the setting for EURIPIDES' *MEDEA, Alcmeon through Corinth* (fragment 8 Page), SENECA'S *MEDEA*, and MENANDER'S *GIRL WITH THE SHAVEN HEAD*. Corinth was famous for its prostitutes and the Greek comic poet Poliochus wrote a *Corinthiastes* (The whoremonger), whose sole extant fragment (fragment 1 Kock) gives no indication of the play's plot.

BIBLIOGRAPHY
American School of Classical Studies at Athens. *Corinth: A Brief History of the City and a Guide to the Excavations.* Rev. ed. Athens, 1969.

Kock, T. *Comicorum Atticorum Fragmenta.* Vol. 3. Leipzig: Teubner, 1888.

Page, D. L. *Select Papyri.* Vol. 3. 1941, Reprint, London: Heinemann, 1970.

CORINTHUS A son of ZEUS. The expression "Corinthus, son of Zeus," means "'the same old thing over again' or . . . 'back to square one'" (Dover). [ANCIENT SOURCES: Aristophanes, *Frogs* 439]

BIBLIOGRAPHY
Dover, K. J. *Aristophanes: Frogs.* Oxford: Clarendon Press, 1993, 250.

CORYBANTES The children of APOLLO and the MUSE Thalia (or CRONUS or ZEUS and the Muse Calliope), the Corybantes were priests or devotees of the goddess CYBELE. Some sources make them synonymous with the CURETES. Their worship activities involved frenzied dance and wild music. The Corybantes are also connected with the worship of DIONYSUS and are said to have created the timbrel (a percussion instrument like a tambourine) for that god. In EURIPIDES' *HIPPOLYTUS*, PHAEDRA's lovesickness is compared to possession by the Corybantes. [ANCIENT SOURCES: Apollodorus, *Library* 1.3.4; Aristophanes, *Lysistrata* 558, *Ecclesiazusae* 1069; Euripides, *Hippolytus* 143, *Bacchae* 124–25; Hyginus, *Fables* 139; Seneca, *Hercules Oetaeus* 1877; Strabo, 10.3]

BIBLIOGRAPHY
Dignas, B. "Priestly Authority in the Cult of the Corybantes at Erythrae," *Epigraphica Anatolica* 34 (2002): 29–40.

Ustinova, Y. "Corybantism: The Nature and Role of an Ecstatic Cult in the Greek Polis," *Horos* 10–12 (1992–93): 503–20.

CORYCIAN This adjective is derived from the name of a NYMPH, Corycia, the mother of Lycorus by APOLLO. A cave on Mount PARNASSUS was called Corycian after her and the nymphs who lived in that cave were also called Corycian. [ANCIENT SOURCES: Aeschylus, *Eumenides* 22 (see *ORESTEIA*); Euripides, *Bacchae* 559; Pausanias, 10.6.5; Sophocles, *Antigone* 1127]

CORYPHAEUS Derived from a Greek word for "head" (*koruphe*), the coryphaeus was the leader of the CHORUS in Greek drama. [ANCIENT SOURCES: Aristophanes, *Wealth* 953; Aristotle, *Politics* 1277a11; Demosthenes, 21.60]

COTHOCIDAE A DEME about 10 miles northwest of ATHENS. [ANCIENT SOURCES: Aristophanes, *Thesmophoriazusae* 622]

COTHURNUS See BUSKIN.

COURTESAN See PROSTITUTE.

CRANAAN CITY Another name for ATHENS. See also CRANAUS.

CRANAUS A king of ATHENS who followed CECROPS to the throne and was in turn driven from the kingship by Amphictyon. In drama, the name of Cranaus is often used as a synonym for Athens or the Athenians. [ANCIENT SOURCES: Aeschylus, *Eumenides* 1011 (see *ORESTEIA*); Apollodorus, *Library* 1.7.2, 3.14.1, 5–6; Aristophanes, *Acharnians* 75, *Birds* 123, *Lysistrata* 481; Euripides, *Suppliant Women* 713; Pausanias, 1.2.6]

CRATES A comic poet who was an elder contemporary of ARISTOPHANES, Crates' first victory at the City DIONYSIA appears to have occurred in 450 B.C.E., and he won two other times at this festival. ARISTOTLE credits Crates as the first comic poet to write plays with a broad appeal in contrast to highly topical or narrowly focused subjects, such as the attacks on CLEON in some of Aristophanes' plays. About 15 plays by Crates are known, including *Birds* (compare Aristophanes' play of

414 B.C.E.) and *Wild Animals* (Greek: *Theria*), in which utensils and tools performed their various tasks without being powered by human beings (fragments 14–15 Kock) and animals apparently refused to allow human beings to eat them (fragment 17 Kock). [ANCIENT SOURCES: Aristophanes, *Knights* 536; Aristotle, *Poetics* 1449b7–9; Athenaeus, 3.119c]

BIBLIOGRAPHY

Kock, T. *Comicorum Atticorum Fragmenta*. Vol. 1. Leipzig: Teubner, 1880.

Sommerstein, A. H. *The Comedies of Aristophanes*. Vol. 2, *Knights*. Warminster, U.K.: Aris & Phillips, 1981, 172–73.

CRATHIS   A river located near the toe of Italy's boot. According to legend, its waters would make one's hair blond. [ANCIENT SOURCES: Euripides, *Trojan Women* 228]

CRATINUS   Along with ARISTOPHANES and EUPOLIS, Cratinus was considered one of the greatest Athenian comic poets of his era. Cratinus' plays appeared as early as 450 B.C.E. and his last datable play was staged in 423. In *Dionusalexandros*, staged around 430 or 429, Cratinus made fun of PERICLES' head. Aristophanes, in *KNIGHTS* (424 B.C.E.), accused Cratinus of being a drunkard and a washed-up poet. The next year, Cratinus parodied his alleged drinking problem in *Putine* (Wine flask), which, much to Aristophanes' chagrin, defeated his *CLOUDS*. More than 460 fragments and 27 titles are known from Cratinus' works, which won nine victories in competition (six at the City DIONYSIA, three at the LENAEA). Aristophanes' *Peace* (421 B.C.E.) mentions that Cratinus has died, but this reference may be a joke. [ANCIENT SOURCES: Aristophanes, *Acharnians* 849, 1173, *Frogs* 357, *Knights* 400, 526, *Peace* 700; Athenaeus 2.39c]

BIBLIOGRAPHY

Amado Rodriguez, M. T. "Cratino en Ateneo," *Euphrosyne* 24 (1996): 53–76.

Dworacki, S. "The *Putine* and the Date of Cratinus' Death." In *Vetustatis Amore et Studio*. Edited by I. Lewandowski and A. Wojcik. Poznan, Poland: Wydawnictwo Naukowe Uniwersytetu im. Adama Mickiewicza, 1995, 117–19.

Luppe, W. "The Rivalry between Aristophanes and Cratinos." In *The Rivals of Aristophanes: Studies in Athenian Old Comedy*. Edited by D. Harvey and J. Wilkins. London: Duckworth and the Classical Press of Wales, 2000, 15–21.

Revermann, M. "Cratinus' *Dionusalexandros* and the Head of Pericles," *Journal of Hellenic Studies* 117 (1997): 197–200.

Rosen, R. "Cratinus' *Pytine* and the Construction of the Comic Self." In *The Rivals of Aristophanes: Studies in Athenian Old Comedy*. Edited by D. Harvey and J. Wilkins. London: Duckworth and the Classical Press of Wales, 2000, 23–39.

CREON (1)   The son of MENOECEUS (1), Creon was the brother of JOCASTA and the brother-in-law of OEDIPUS. Creon married Eurydice and by her fathered HAEMON and MENOECEUS (2). On at least two separate occasions, Creon reigned as king of THEBES. After the death of King LAIUS, Creon appears to have been king. When the SPHINX plagued the Thebans, Creon offered the kingship and his sister, Jocasta, to anyone who could solve the Sphinx's riddle. When Oedipus solved the riddle, he became king. Thus, in SOPHOCLES' *OEDIPUS TYRANNOS*, Creon appears as the loyal brother-in-law of Oedipus and is wrongly accused of trying to usurp the throne from Oedipus. After the fall of Oedipus and the deaths of ETEOCLES and POLYNEICES, Creon again becomes king. In Sophocles' *ANTIGONE*, Creon is characterized as the stubborn king who decrees death for anyone who buries Polyneices. When ANTIGONE, Creon's future daughter-in-law, buries Polyneices, Creon nevertheless declares that she must die. Creon later changes his mind (too late, as Antigone has committed suicide).

In EURIPIDES' *PHOENICIAN WOMEN*, Creon first is seen as a rather hapless father caught up in the problems of Oedipus' household. When the Argive army marches against Thebes, Creon is told that for Thebes to be victorious, his son, Menoeceus, must be sacrificed. As with other parents in classical TRAGEDY who face the sacrifice of their children, the Euripidean Creon tries to prevent the loss of his child and urges him to go into exile. Without Creon's knowledge, however, Menoeceus sacrifices himself. At the conclusion of *Phoenician Women*, Creon behaves in a different way, appearing more like the Creon of Sophocles' *Antigone*. Upon the deaths of Eteocles and Polyneices, Creon has become the new king of Thebes. He decrees exile for Oedipus, refuses burial to Polyneices, and rages against the defiance of Antigone.

BIBLIOGRAPHY
Linforth, I. M. "Antigone and Creon," *University of California Publications in Classical Philology* 15, no. 5 (1961): 183–260.

CREON (2)   Creon, king of CORINTH and son of Lycaethus, was the father of Creusa (or Glauce, as she is called by some). Creon appears as a character in EURIPIDES' *MEDEA* and SENECA'S *MEDEA*. When JASON decides to divorce MEDEA and marry Creon's daughter, Creon declares that Medea must immediately leave Corinth. Creon grants Medea's request to stay in Corinth for one more day, however, unwittingly allowing her time to plot the destruction of his own daughter. After Medea sends her a poisoned robe and diadem, she dies in agony, much as Heracles does in SOPHOCLES' *TRACHINIAN WOMEN*. Creon, hearing the cries of his daughter, rushes to her aid, but he too becomes entangled in the deadly clothing and dies. [ANCIENT SOURCES: Apollodorus, *Library* 1.9.28; Euripides, *Medea;* Hyginus, *Fables* 25; Seneca, *Medea*]

CRESPHONTES (KRESPHONTES)

Along with his brothers, Aristodemus and Temenus, Cresphontes, the son of Aristomachus, conquered the Peloponnese in the generation after HERACLES. Cresphontes and his brothers divided the rule of the Peloponnese by lottery. Cresphontes wanted Messenia as his territory, and when the brothers decided that Messenia would fall to the person whose lot was drawn third, Cresphontes gained it through trickery. A pitcher of water, in which to cast the lots, was used, after his two brothers put their lots into the pitcher, Cresphontes put a clod of dirt, which dissolved and ensured that the lots of his brothers would rise first. In this way, Cresphontes became ruler of Messenia. The Messenians eventually killed Cresphontes and two of his sons. The Messenian Polyphontes married Cresphontes' widow, Merope.

One of Cresphontes' sons, also called Cresphontes (some also call him Aepytus), who was smuggled off to safety in Aetolia, eventually returned to Messenia to avenge his father's death. The younger Cresphontes gained entrance to the palace by disguising himself and claiming to have killed Cresphontes. Polyphontes allowed the younger Cresphontes to stay in the palace. While Cresphontes was asleep, Merope, upon hearing that the sleeping man had killed Cresphontes, tried to kill Cresphontes, not realizing that he was her son. Before she could do so, an old man, who had delivered messages between Merope and Cresphontes while he was in exile, entered, recognized Cresphontes, and prevented the killing. Subsequently, Cresphontes killed Polyphontes while he performed some sort of religious ritual.

EURIPIDES wrote a *Cresphontes,* from which some 150 lines exist, and which was staged no later than 421 B.C.E. Euripides' play deals with the return of the younger Cresphontes to Messenia and his vengeance against Polyphontes. The chorus consisted of old men from Messenia and the play was set at Polyphontes' palace, formerly the house of the elder Cresphontes. At some point early in the play, a servant at the palace met the disguised Cresphontes at the door. Merope also appeared as a character. ENNIUS also wrote a tragic *Cresphontes,* of which about 15 lines are extant. Two of the fragments appear to be spoken by Merope. One fragment seems to refer to Polyphontes' marriage to Merope; another contains a lament about the inability of Merope (?) to weep over, clothe, or bury the bodies of her loved ones. [ANCIENT SOURCES: Apollodorus, 2.8.4–5; Hyginus, *Fables* 137]

BIBLIOGRAPHY
Collard, C., M. J. Cropp, and K. H. Lee. *Euripides: Selected Fragmentary Plays.* Vol. 1. Warminster, U.K.: Aris & Phillips, 1995, 121–47.
Jocelyn, H. D. *The Tragedies of Ennius.* Cambridge: Cambridge University Press, 1969, 96–98, 270–81.
Warmington, E. H. *Remains of Old Latin: Ennius and Caecilius.* Vol. 1. Cambridge, Mass., and London: Harvard University Press, 1935.

CRETE   A large island due south of mainland Greece, Crete is best known as the home of MINOS and his family (PASIPHAE, ARIADNE, PHAEDRA). The infant ZEUS was hidden in a cave on Crete when his father, CRONUS, was trying to kill him. Several playwrights

wrote plays entitled *Cretans* or *Cretan Women*. In 438 B.C.E., EURIPIDES' *Cretan Women* (fragments 460–70 Nauck) led off the TETRALOGY and was followed by *Alcmeon in Psophis, Telephus,* and ALCESTIS. The surviving fragments of *Cretan Women* suggest that the play dealt with the affair of THYESTES and ATREUS' wife, AEROPE, and the gruesome feast that Atreus served to Thyestes. Euripides also wrote a *Cretans* (fragments 471–72 Nauck), about Pasiphae's sexual union with the bull and the birth of the MINOTAUR. SOPHOCLES may have written a play titled *Cretans,* of which only the title survives (fragment 359 Radt). The Greek comic poets Apollophanes (fragments 5–8 Kock) and Nicochares (fragment 9 Kock) each wrote a *Cretans,* but the fragments give little indication of the content of these plays.

BIBLIOGRAPHY

Kock, T. *Comicorum Atticorum Fragmenta.* Vol. 1. Leipzig: Teubner, 1880.

Nauck, A. *Tragicorum Graecorum Fragmenta.* 1889. Reprint, Hildesheim, Ger.: Olms, 1964.

Radt, S. *Tragicorum Graecorum Fragmenta.* Vol. 4. Göttingen, Ger.: Vandenhoeck & Ruprecht, 1977.

Webster, T. B. L. *The Tragedies of Euripides.* London: Methuen, 1967.

CREUSA (1) The daughter of ERECHTHEUS and Praxithea, Creusa is an Athenian queen and the wife of XUTHUS. After APOLLO sexually assaulted her, Creusa gave birth to a male child, but she eventually abandoned the infant (who was rescued by HERMES at Apollo's command). In EURIPIDES' *ION,* Creusa travels to DELPHI with her husband, Xuthus, and meets a young man, ION, who, unknown to her, is her son. When Xuthus decides to adopt Ion, Creusa is persuaded that the young man will threaten her position as queen of Athens. Accordingly, Creusa arranges to have Ion poisoned. When the plot fails, Ion threatens to kill Creusa. The crisis is averted when Apollo's priestess reveals some items that were found with Ion when he was an infant. Creusa recognizes the items as things she left with the baby, and mother and son are reunited. SOPHOCLES wrote two plays that may have treated the story of Creusa: one entitled *Creusa* (fragments 350–59 Radt), the other entitled *Ion.* Some

scholars think these may have been the same play. The two dozen lines that survive reveal nothing about the plot. The chorus was composed of women, an old man seems to have been a character, and there was a conversation between husband and wife in which the woman defends her desire to keep her wealth.

BIBLIOGRAPHY

Kiso, A. *The Lost Sophocles.* New York: Vantage Press, 1984.

Lloyd-Jones, H. *Sophocles: Fragments.* Cambridge, Mass.: Harvard University Press, 1996.

Radt, S. *Tragicorum Graecorum Fragmenta.* Vol. 4. Göttingen, Ger.: Vandenhoeck & Ruprecht, 1977.

Sutton, D. F. *The Lost Sophocles.* Lanham, Md.: University Press of America, 1984.

CREUSA (2) Also called Glauce, Creusa was daughter of the Corinthian king CREON. Creusa was the princess to whom JASON was to be married after his divorce of MEDEA. EURIPIDES does not indicate her name in his *MEDEA,* but SENECA does in his *MEDEA.* Medea kills Creusa by means of a poisoned gown and diadem. [ANCIENT SOURCES: Apollodorus, *Library* 1.9.28; Hyginus, *Fables* 25; Pausanias, 2.3.6]

CRIOA A DEME in Athenian territory. [ANCIENT SOURCES: Aristophanes, *Birds* 645]

CRISA A town a few miles southwest of DELPHI. In SOPHOCLES' *ELECTRA* (730), ORESTES' death is falsely reported as having occured on a racing course at Crisa.

CRONUS (Latin: SATURN) The son of URANUS and GAIA (see EARTH), Cronus became ruler of the gods when he overthrew his father by castrating him. Cronus married his sister, RHEA, and their children were ZEUS, POSEIDON, HADES, DEMETER, HERA, and HESTIA. Cronus had heard a prophecy that he would be overthrown by one of his children, so as soon as they were born he swallowed them. Cronus had eaten five of his children when Rhea, pregnant with Zeus, devised a trick. Rhea smuggled away the newborn Zeus to the island of CRETE for safekeeping, then gave Cronus a rock wrapped in swaddling clothes, which the careless god swallowed. After Zeus grew up, he returned unrecognized to the house of Cronus and gave his father a potion that caused him to vomit his brothers, sisters, and the stone, which Zeus placed at Delphi to mark the center of the Earth (according to the Greeks). After this, Zeus and his siblings waged war (known as the Titanomachy) against Cronus and his allies. After Zeus' side won the war, Cronus was banished to the UNDERWORLD. AESCHYLUS relates, however, that after his fall Cronus cursed Zeus to suffer a similar fate, but this never comes to pass. In SENECA's *HERCULES FURENS,* the title character threatens to release Cronus from the underworld unless Zeus makes him a god. In ARISTOPHANES, things or ideas that are considered old-fashioned are sometimes referred to as being from the time of Cronus. The Greek comic poet PHRYNICHUS wrote a *Cronus,* whose surviving fragments indicate nothing about the plot (fragments 9–13 Kock). [ANCIENT SOURCES: Aeschylus, *Prometheus Bound* 199–223, 910–14, *Eumenides* 641 (see ORESTEIA); Apollodorus, *Library* 1.1.4–7; Aristophanes, *Clouds* 398, 929, 1070; Hesiod, *Theogony;* Hyginus, *Fables* 118, 139; Seneca, *Hercules Furens* 965–68]

BIBLIOGRAPHY
Kock, T. *Comicorum Atticorum Fragmenta.* Vol. 1. Leipzig: Teubner, 1880.

CTESIAS   An unidentifiable person mentioned by ARISTOPHANES at *ACHARNIANS* 839. He is spoken of in the same breath as some INFORMANTS, so he may have been one himself.

***CUNEUS* (Plural: *CUNEI*)**   A Latin word meaning "wedge," a *cuneus* is a wedge-shaped area of seating in the part of the Roman theater called the CAVEA. Stairways divided the Roman theater into six or more *cunei.* The Greek equivalent of the *cuneus* is the *kerkis* (plural: *kerkides*).

BIBLIOGRAPHY
Csapo, E., and W. J. Slater. *The Context of Ancient Drama.* Ann Arbor: University of Michigan Press, 1995, 84, 86.

CUPID   See EROS.

***CURCULIO* PLAUTUS (CA. 193 B.C.E.)**   The action of the play occurs in EPIDAURUS (it is the only

surviving Roman COMEDY set in this city) before the two houses of Cappadox, a PIMP, and Phaedromus, a young gentleman (see ADULESCENS). A temple of the god Aesculapius (see ASCLEPIUS) can also be seen. This configuration of buildings (house of respectable citizen, house of pimp, and temple) occurs only here in extant Roman comedy.

In the opening act, the audience must imagine a nocturnal setting as Phaedromus, who is in love with Planesium, enters carrying a candle. Phaedromus reveals to his slave, Palinurus, that Planesium belongs to a pimp named Cappadox, whose asking price for her keeps changing. Phaedromus has sent his PARASITE, Curculio (weevil), to CARIA to acquire money with which Phaedromus can purchase Planesium from Cappadox. Phaedromus approaches Cappadox's house with the intention of luring out Cappadox's old slave woman, Leaena, with a bribe of wine. In exchange for the wine, Leaena agrees to arrange a meeting between Phaedromus and Planesium. Soon, Leaena returns with Planesium. Phaedromus and Planesium express their mutual feelings of love, while Palinurus comments on their behavior.

In the second act, Cappadox emerges from the temple of Aesculapius, where he has been staying during an illness. He is met by Palinurus, who is leaving Phaedromus' house. Palinurus offers Cappadox no sympathy as the pimp complains about his ailment. When Cappadox asks Palinurus to interpret a dream for him, as if on cue, an unnamed cook, who happens to be skilled in such matters, appears from Phaedromus' house. Cappadox tells the cook that he dreamed that Aesculapius would not approach him. The cook interprets this as indicating that the other gods also will not give Cappadox any favor. The cook then advises Cappadox to return to Aesculapius' temple and ask the god for Peace.

After the departure of Cappadox, Curculio, who has returned from Caria, enters. In a manner typical of a parasite, Curculio acts as if he is starving and asks for food. Phaedromus promises Curculio that lots of food has been prepared for him, but Phaedromus himself is crushed when Curculio tells him that his friend in Caria was not able to lend him the money to buy Planesium. Curculio reports, however, that while in Caria he encountered a soldier who claims to have bought a woman from Cappadox and has deposited the money, some clothes, and jewelry with a banker, Lyco, in Epidaurus. The soldier told Curculio that when Lyco received a letter, sealed with the soldier's ring, Lyco would arrange for the bearer of the letter to acquire Planesium. Later, Curculio and the soldier had dinner together, and the soldier became drunk and fell asleep. While he was sleeping, Curculio stole the soldier's seal ring. Upon learning this, a delighted Phaedromus, accompanied by Curculio, enter Phaedromus' house to dine and write a letter on which to use this seal.

As the third act opens, the banker Lyco, enters and is soon met by Curculio, who claims he is the freedman Summanus ("dripper" or "trickler"), of a soldier named Therapontigonus Platagidorus (his last name Nixon translates as Smackahead). Curculio hands Lyco the letter that he and Phaedromus have written. When Lyco wants to know why the soldier himself did not go to Epidaurus, Curculio makes up a story about the soldier's staying behind in Caria to have a statue of himself made. Lyco believes the story, and he and Curculio prepare to depart to settle their business. Before they can leave, Cappadox enters from Aesculapius' temple. Lyco tells Cappadox to send Planesium with Curculio.

The play's fourth act begins in an unusual way, as the play's CHORAGUS, or property manager, gives a speech of some 20 lines. In the first half of the speech, the *choragus* commends Phaedromus for his trickery; in the speech's second half, the *choragus* mentions various places in Rome (although the play's setting is Epidaurus) where one can find specific kind of people: Perjurers are found at the COMITIUM, liars and braggarts at the temple of Venus CLOACINA, and so on. The sound of Phaedromus' door's creaking sends the *choragus* off. From the house emerge Curculio, his servant, Cappadox, Lyco, and Planesium. Lyco reminds Cappadox that if Planesium should be discovered to be a freeborn woman, Lyco would get his money back. After Curculio and his slave depart with Planesium, Lyco and Cappadox make arrangements for payment for Planesium. Upon Lyco's exit, Cappadox returns to Aesculapius' temple.

In the next scene, the soldier Therapontigonus enters with Lyco and demands the money that he had

deposited with Lyco. The soldier soon discovers, however, that Lyco has given the money to Summanus (Curculio). Despite the soldier's dissatisfaction, Lyco has carried out his part of the agreement and departs. Soon Cappadox appears from the temple, encounters Therapontigonus, and tells him that Planesium has been handed over to Summanus. At this point, the soldier realizes Curculio has stolen his ring and decides to search for the parasite.

In the play's final act, Curculio begins by noting that Planesium has seen the ring that he has stolen from the soldier. Planesium and Phaedromus emerge from the house, and Planesium declares that her father had worn the same ring. Curculio tells Planesium that he won the ring playing dice with a soldier. When the soldier enters, he demands his money from Curculio or Planesium. Phaedromus, however, declares that Planesium is a freeborn woman and that the trading of freeborn women is illegal; he threatens to take the soldier to court and calls upon Curculio to serve as a witness. The situation calms when Phaedromus asks the soldier where he got the ring. When Therapontigonus reveals that his father, Periphanes, gave it to him, Planesium recognizes Periphanes as the name of her father and greets the soldier as her brother. As Planesium subsequently reveals, when she was a little girl, she was carried off by an unknown man during a storm at a festival of DIONYSUS. Planesium shows that she has a ring that matches the soldier's.

After the reunion of brother and sister, Cappadox returns from the FORUM after collecting money from Lyco. As Cappadox prepares to go home, he is confronted by both Therapontigonus and Phaedromus, who want to punish him for trying sell Planesium. Eventually, Phaedromus decides to play the role of arbiter between Therapontigonus and Cappadox. Therapontigonus reminds Cappadox that he had promised to refund the money for Planesium if she was discovered to be freeborn. Despite Cappadox's denial, Phaedromus decrees that Cappadox must refund the soldier's money. Cappadox, faced with threats of physical violence from the soldier and Phaedromus, finally hands over the money. The play ends with Phaedromus' inviting Therapontigonus to dinner and announcing his wedding to Planesium.

COMMENTARY

At 729 lines, *Curculio* is the shortest surviving Roman comedy and one that has received relatively little attention from modern scholars. The play has an interesting topographical inconsistency in its fourth act. Although the play's setting is Epidaurus, at one point the choragus mentions various places in Rome, such as the Comitium and the temple of Venus Cloacina. This passage exemplifies how PLAUTUS would adapt a Greek play for his Roman audience.

As for the rest of the play, *Curculio* has some of the typical features of Plautine comedy (a love-sick young man and his beloved PROSTITUTE, an evil pimp, a BRAGGART WARRIOR). Among the more novel features of *Curculio* are the absence of a father as a stumbling block to the young man's love affair, the discovery that the prostitute is the sister of the soldier (compare the modern production of *A Funny Thing Happened on the Way to the Forum*), and the use of the parasite (rather than a wily slave) as the primary trickster in the play.

Although Curculio is a parasite, he does many of the same things that slaves do in other Roman comedies such as impersonating someone else (compare *PSEUDOLUS*) and writing a deceptive letter (compare Chrysalus in *BACCHIDES*). Curculio is also noteworthy for his ability to adapt to changing circumstances. Although the story begins under the assumption that this will be a "quest for cash" play, Curculio's initial attempt to secure funds for Phaedromus fails. Curculio quickly adapts, however, and steals the soldier's ring, has a false letter written, impersonates the soldier's freedman, and secures Planesium.

BIBLIOGRAPHY
Arnott, W. G. "The Opening of Plautus' *Curculio*: Comic Business and Mime." In *Plautus und die Tradition des Stegreifspiels: Festgabe für Eckard Lefèvre zum 60. Geburtstag*. Edited by B. Lore, S. Ekkehard, and G. Vogt-Spira. Tübingen, Ger.: Narr, 1995, 185–92.
Goldberg, S. M. "Improvisation, Plot, and Plautus' *Curculio*." In *Plautus und die Tradition des Stegreifspiels: Festgabe für Eckard Lefèvre zum 60. Geburtstag*. Edited by B. Lore, S. Ekkehard, and G. Vogt-Spira. Tübingen, Ger.: Narr, 1995, 33–41.
Kruschwitz, P., J. Mulberger, and M. Schumacher. "Die Struktur des 'Curculio,'" *Gymnasium* 108, no. 2 (2001): 113–21.
Monaco, G. *Curculio*. Palermo: Palumbo, 1969.
Slater, N. W. "The Dates of Plautus' *Curculio* and *Trinummus* Reconsidered," *American Journal of Philology* 108 (1987): 264–69.

CURETES Mythical warriors who guarded the infant ZEUS. They clashed their shields so that Zeus' father, CRONUS, would not hear his voice. When IO gave birth to EPAPHUS, HERA had the Curetes steal the child. Zeus, however, discovered this and killed the Curetes. [ANCIENT SOURCES: Apollodorus, *Library* 1.1.6–7, 2.1.3; Euripides, *Bacchae* 121, *Hypsipyle* fragment 12.76 (Page); Hyginus, *Fables* 139; Pausanias, 4.33.1; Seneca, *Hercules Oetaeus* 1877]

BIBLIOGRAPHY
Page, D. L. *Select Papyri*. Vol. 3. 1941. Reprint, London: Heinemann, 1970.

CURSE The calling of evil or misfortune upon someone or something. Curses often play an important role in classical TRAGEDY. In EURIPIDES' *HIPPOLYTUS*, the title character is killed when his father, THESEUS, calls down a curse upon him. The deaths of ETEOCLES and POLYNEICES were a result of a curse that their father, OEDIPUS, had put on them. The misfortunes that AGAMEMNON and his family suffered were also supposed to be the result of curses on them by people of earlier generations. Curses can also be personified. In AESCHYLUS' *Eumenides* (417) (see *ORESTEIA*), the chorus of FURIES indicate that they are the embodiment of "Curses."

CYANEAE See CLASHING ROCKS.

CYBELE (CYBEBE) See RHEA.

CYCLOBORUS A torrential stream in the region where ATHENS is located. At *KNIGHTS* 137, ARISTOPHANES compares CLEON's voice to the Cycloborus.

CYCLOPS (Plural: CYCLOPES) The Cyclopes ("circle-eyed") were the giant, one-eyed offspring produced by URANUS and Gaia (see EARTH). Ancient writers often located their home beneath the volcanic mountain AETNA on SICILY. Uranus had imprisoned them in the UNDERWORLD, but ZEUS released them, and in gratitude they helped Zeus overthrow his father, CRONUS, by giving Zeus thunder and lightning. After Zeus became ruler of the gods, the Cyclopes continued to supply him with thunder and lightning; these three Cyclopes, the children of Uranus and Gaia, were named Arges, Brontes, and Steropes. Other Cyclopes existed, however, such as the tribe whom ODYSSEUS encountered upon his return from TROY. One of these Cyclopes, POLYPHEMUS, was the son of POSEIDON, and Odysseus' blinding of him resulted in Poseidon's punishment, which condemned Odysseus to 10 years of wandering after the Trojan War. Apollo also killed some Cyclopes (perhaps the children of one of the original Cyclopes), for which Zeus forced him to serve a mortal (ADMETUS) for a year. In addition to providing Zeus with thunder and lightning, the Cyclopes were said to have built the walls of TIRYNS and MYCENAE.

Among the Greek dramatists, the comic poets Callias and Diocles wrote plays entitled *Cyclopes*. Only the title survives from Diocles' play (see Kock 1), and several short, uninformative fragments (3–10 Kock 1) from Callias'. In addition to EURIPIDES' satyric *CYCLOPS*, we know of a few other plays entitled *Cyclops*. As did Euripides' play, these plays probably dealt with Odysseus' encounter with the Cyclops Polyphemus. The Greek tragedian Aristias produced a satyric *Cyclops* that would have predated Euripides' play by several decades. The single fragment (4 Snell) that survives preserves a remark about wine's potency and was spoken by the Cyclops to Odysseus. The comic poet Epicharmus' *Cyclops* also appeared before Euripides' play, but the three brief fragments that survive (81–83 Kaibel) give little indication of the play's plot. In the first quarter of the fourth century B.C.E., the comic poet Antiphanes also produced a *Cyclops*. The surviving fragments (131–33 Kock 2) primarily comprise a list of foods. [ANCIENT SOURCES: Apollodorus, *Library* 1.1.2, 1.2.1, *Epitome* 7.3–9; Aristophanes, *Wealth* 290, 296; Euripides, *Alcestis* 1–7, *Cyclops, Electra* 1158, *Heracles* 15, 944, 998, *Iphigenia at Aulis* 152, 265, 534, 1501, *Iphigenia in Tauris* 845, *Orestes* 966, *Trojan Women* 1088; Hesiod, *Theogony* 139–46; Homer, *Odyssey* 9; Ovid, *Metamorphoses* 13.738–897; Hyginus, *Fables*

125; Pausanias, 2.16.5, 7.25.5; Seneca, *Hercules Furens* 997, *Thyestes* 407, 582; Vergil, *Aeneid* 3.680]

BIBLIOGRAPHY

Nieto Hernández, Pura. "Back in the Cave of the Cyclops," *American Journal of Philology* 121, no. 3 (2000): 345–66.

Kaibel, G. *Comicorum Graecorum Fragmenta.* Vol. 1.1 [Poetarum Graecorum fragmenta. Vol. 6.1]. Berlin: Weidmann, 1899.

Kock, T. *Comicorum Atticorum Fragmenta.* Vol. 1. Leipzig: Teubner, 1880.

———. *Comicorum Atticorum Fragmenta.* Vol. 2. Leipzig: Teubner, 1884.

Scott, Shirley Clay. "Man, Mind, and Monster: Polyphemus from Homer through Joyce," *Classical and Modern Literature* 16, no. 1 (1995): 19–75.

Snell, B. *Tragicorum Graecorum Fragmenta.* Vol. 1. Göttingen, Ger.: Vandenhoeck & Ruprecht, 1971.

CYCLOPS EURIPIDES (BETWEEN 425 AND 408 B.C.E.)

Recent scholarly opinion, based primarily on statistical analysis of certain metrical tendencies over the course of EURIPIDES' career, suggests a date of production of the play closer to 408 than 425. At only 709 lines, *Cyclops* is one of the shortest surviving classical dramas, and the only SATYR PLAY extant in its entirety. The play's action occurs before the cave (cf. SOPHOCLES' *PHILOCTETES*) of the Cyclops POLYPHEMUS near Mount AETNA on SICILY. SATYRS make up the chorus. Euripides' play is a comic version of ODYSSEUS' encounter with the CYCLOPS, which is also preserved in the ninth book of HOMER's *Odyssey*.

The play opens with the satyr SILENUS sweeping the cave of the Cyclops, whom he and his SATYR children serve. Silenus relates that when DIONYSUS was abducted by pirates, Silenus and his sons set sail to find Dionysus. A storm blew up and sent them off course to Sicily, where Silenus and his sons were captured and enslaved by the Cyclops Polyphemus. Silenus' PROLOGUE is followed by the entrance of the satyr chorus, whose opening song indicates that they are driving Polyphemus' flocks from the pasture. The audience also hears them lament the absence of Dionysus. After the choral song, Silenus sees a Greek ship and soon Odysseus and his men arrive. Odysseus informs Silenus that they are returning from TROY and attempting to reach their native island of ITHACA. Silenus tells Odysseus that they are on the island of Ithaca and near the cave of the cannibalistic Cyclops. Odysseus tries to barter with Silenus for food and drink, and the chief satyr is delighted that Odysseus' payment will be in the form of wine. As Silenus drinks some of the wine and begins to dance about in delight, his satyr sons ask Odysseus about HELEN and whether the soldiers took turns having sexual relations with her.

The light mood soon changes when Silenus sees the Cyclops approaching. Silenus directs Odysseus and his men to hide in the Cyclops' cave, but Euripides' Odysseus, unlike his Homeric counterpart, refuses to do so. When the Cyclops enters and demands to know what is happening, Silenus lies, telling the Cyclops that he was trying to prevent Odysseus and his men from taking the Cyclops' goods. Hearing this, the Cyclops threatens to eat Odysseus and his men. At this point, Odysseus explains that he and his men were trying to trade for food and that Silenus is lying. Silenus, of course, denies this. When the Cyclops goes on to question Odysseus about his journey, Odysseus answers truthfully. Odysseus also begs the Cyclops not to eat him or his men, because they have well served the Cyclops' father, POSEIDON. Silenus, however, urges the Cyclops to eat Odysseus. The Cyclops responds by giving a short speech in which he boasts that his own power rivals that of the gods. He also states that the gifts of hospitality that he will give to Odysseus and his crew are a nice pot in which he will boil them. Hearing this, Odysseus prays to ATHENA and ZEUS for protection.

The Cyclops drives Odysseus and his men into the cave. Inside, the chorus of satyrs sing an ode about the impending "meal" of which the Cyclops is about to partake and note that the monster will violate the customs of hospitality by his killing and eating of Odysseus' men. After the choral ode, Odysseus emerges from the cave and reports the horrific slaughter and consumption of his men by the Cyclops. Odysseus also tells the satyrs that he gave the Cyclops some wine and made him drunk. When Odysseus tells the satyrs that he has a plan to blind the Cyclops, the satyrs are delighted and offer to help.

Before the plot unfolds, the drunken Cyclops, supported by Silenus, emerges from the cave. When the Cyclops says he wants to share some of the wine with his fellow Cyclopes, Odysseus persuades him not to do this, because it will thwart Odysseus' plan. As in HOMER, when the Cyclops asks Odysseus what his name is, Odysseus replies, "Nobody." While Odysseus and the Cyclops converse, Silenus tries to steal some of the Cyclops' wine. The Cyclops, however, becoming aroused sexually, begins to grope for Silenus and eventually drags him into his cave.

After the exit of the Cyclops and Silenus, Odysseus urges the satyrs to be bold and help him blind the monster. After Odysseus prays to HEPHAESTUS and SLEEP to aid him in his efforts, he reenters the cave. When the time arrives for the satyrs to assist Odysseus, however, they offer a variety of excuses why they cannot help him. The satyrs do sing a lyric cheer as they urge him to blind the monster. Soon, the blinded Cyclops emerges from the cave and laments his fate. As in Homer, when the Cyclops complains that Nobody has ruined him, the amused chorus responds, "Nobody has done wrong to you." After other similar jokes, the Cyclops begins to grope for the satyrs but bumps his head on a rock. Afterward Odysseus and his remaining men leave the cave. As in Homer, Odysseus reveals his true identity to the Cyclops. The Cyclops recalls the prophecy that Odysseus would blind him but also notes that Odysseus would suffer many years at sea as a result. Odysseus, however, departs for the beach to sail away. The play ends with the Cyclops' threatening to throw boulders at Odysseus' ship and the satyrs' declaring that they will sail away with Odysseus.

COMMENTARY

As alluded to previously, Euripides' *Cyclops* is intriguing because one may compare it with Homer's earlier version of the story in Odyssey. Other classical dramas, such as AESCHYLUS' *Libation Bearers* (see ORESTEIA) expand on events mentioned in the Odyssey; Euripides' *Cyclops* is the only surviving play to dramatize a complete episode from the Homeric epic. Both Homer and Euripides focus on violations of hospitality in the Odysseus-Cyclops encounter; however, conventions of the stage and the satyric genre require Euripides to alter Homer's story in certain respects. Homeric

Odysseus was trapped in the Cyclops' cave, whereas Euripidean Odysseus must be able to move back and forth between the interior and exterior of the "cave." Because Euripides is writing a satyr play, he must also create a story line that puts the satyrs on the Cyclops' island. Obviously, Euripides' Odysseus-Cyclops encounter ends on a happier note, as Odysseus and the satyrs sail away without any allusion to the trials that await Odysseus at the hands of Poseidon.

In addition to points of comparison between Homer and Euripides, Euripides' *Cyclops* is most valuable for the information it provides about the Greek satyr play. As it is the only complete satyr play from antiquity, however, we cannot tell whether it was "typical." *Cyclops* does contain several elements that appear to have been common in this genre: attention to the theme of hospitality (although this is also an element in TRAGEDY), the frequent references to and consumption of wine, jokes of a sexual nature (the satyrs' asking about the Greeks' having sexual relations with Helen; the Cyclops' sexual attraction to Silenus), the satyrs' seeking freedom from an oppressive master (in this case, the Cyclops), the presence of unusual creatures or beings with unusual powers. After one reads Euripides' surviving tragedies, it is difficult to imagine that the same author composed the *Cyclops,* but this play shows that such a feat could be accomplished.

BIBLIOGRAPHY

Katsouris, A. G. "Euripides' *Cyclops* and Homer's *Odyssey:* An Interpretative Comparison," *Prometheus* 23, no. 1 (1997): 1–24.
Konstan, D. "An Anthropology of Euripides' *Cyclops,*" *Ramus* 10 (1981): 87–103.
Seaford, R. *Euripides: Cyclops.* Oxford: Oxford University Press, 1984.
Vickers, M. "Alcibiades on Stage: *Philoctetes* and *Cyclops,*" *Historia* 36 (1987): 171–97.
Willink, C. W. "Notes on the *Parodos* and Other *Cantica* of Euripides' *Cyclops,*" *Mnemosyne* Ser. 4, 54, no. 5 (2001): 515–30.

CYCNUS (1)   The son of Sthenelus, Cycnus was a king of the Ligurians. When Cycnus died, he was changed into a swan; appropriately, his name means "swan" in Greek. [ANCIENT SOURCES: Pausanias, 1.30.3]

CYCNUS (2)   The son of POSEIDON and Calyce, Cycnus was king of Colonae, a town near TROY. Cycnus married Proclia and their children were Hemithea and Tenes, although some sources make Tenes a son of APOLLO. Later, Cycnus married Philonome, who fell in love with Tenes and tried to seduce him. When Tenes rejected her advances, Philonome told Cycnus that Tenes had tried to rape her. She even arranged for a flute player, Eumolpus, to corroborate her claim. Cycnus believed Philonome and put Tenes and Hemithea into a box and cast them out into the sea. The castaways survived, landing on the island of Leucophyrs, which Tenes later ruled, also changing its name to Tenedos (Tenes' island). Eventually, after Cycnus learned that Tenes was innocent, Cycnus ordered Eumolpus stoned to death and Philonome buried alive. After that, the tradition regarding Cycnus becomes unclear. Some say that he went to Tenedos to apologize to his son and that although Tenes initially rejected his father, eventually Cycnus settled on the island. Ovid suggests that Cycnus fought ACHILLES at TROY in the early days of the war, and that despite Cycnus' invulnerability to conventional weapons, Achilles killed him by strangling him with the strap of his own helmet. At Cycnus' death, Poseidon transformed him into a swan.

SOPHOCLES may have written a *Cycnus,* although this play may have been the same as Sophocles' *Shepherds* (*Poimenes*), in which the death of Cycnus may have played some role and that Lloyd-Jones thinks was produced no later than 460 B.C.E. Whether Sophocles' *Shepherds* was a TRAGEDY or SATYR PLAY is not known, but some of the 20 lines that survive have an informal tone. The play's setting would probably have been the shore near Troy, and Trojan shepherds may have composed the chorus. The scholiast on Lycophron 530 reports that HECTOR killed PROTESILAUS in this play, and fragment 498 is spoken by Hector. Fragment 500 appears to refer to Cycnus' invulnerability; in fragment 501 Cycnus boasts that he will kill an opponent and almost literally "kick his ass." [ANCIENT SOURCES: Apollodorus, *Epitome* 3.22–25; Ovid, *Metamorphoses* 64–145]

BIBLIOGRAPHY

Lloyd-Jones, H. *Sophocles: Fragments.* Cambridge, Mass.: Harvard University Press, 1996.

Radt, S. *Tragicorum Graecorum Fragmenta.* Vol. 4. Göttingen, Ger.: Vandenhoeck & Ruprecht, 1977.

CYCNUS (3) Tradition gives ARES two sons named Cycnus, both of whom fought with HERACLES. In the pseudo-Hesiodic *Shield of Heracles,* Heracles encounters ARES and Cycnus while on the way to TRACHIS, in southern THESSALY, and the kingdom of Ceyx, whose daughter, Themistinoe, was married to Cycnus. After Heracles killed Cycnus, Ares attacked Heracles, who gave Ares a wound that sent him retreating to Mount Olympus. In EURIPIDES' *ALCESTIS,* Heracles, while on the way to fetch the mares of Diomedes (his eighth labor), seems to allude to this battle with Cycnus; in Euripides' *HERACLES,* the chorus mention a Cycnus—seemingly the same as mentioned in pseudo-Hesiod and the *Alcestis*—who lived in Thessalian Amphanae and murdered his guests. The chorus recall that Heracles killed this Cycnus with his arrows, whereas pseudo-Hesiod has Heracles run Cycnus through with his spear. Apollodorus seems to have the same Cycnus in mind when he mentions Cycnus, the son of Ares and Pelopia, whom Heracles fought and killed near Itonus in Thessaly. Apollodorus, in describing Heracles' return from his 11th labor, says that a different Cycnus, the son of Ares and Pyrene, challenged Heracles to fight near the river Echedorus in Macedonia, but that the battle was broken off when a lightning bolt (presumably thrown by Heracles' father, ZEUS) fell between the two combatants. [ANCIENT SOURCES: Apollodorus, *Library* 2.5.11, 2.7.7; Euripides, *Alcestis* 503, *Heracles* 389–93; Hesiod, *Shield of Heracles;* Hyginus, *Fables* 31; Seneca, *Hercules Furens* 486]

CYLLENE (1) The highest mountain in southern Greece (in the region of ARCADIA), Cyllene is traditionally the birthplace of HERMES and the Pleiades. SOPHOCLES' *SEARCHERS,* which deals with Hermes' birth, is set on Mount Cyllene. PAN was also associated with Cyllene. [ANCIENT SOURCES: Apollodorus, *Library* 3.10.1–2]

CYLLENE (2) A NYMPH who lived on Mount CYLLENE. In SOPHOCLES' *SEARCHERS,* she informs the SATYRS of the birth of HERMES and his invention of the lyre. She also defends the young god against the satyrs' accusation that he stole APOLLO's cattle.

CYLLENE (3) A port in southwestern Greece that served the town of ELIS. [ANCIENT SOURCES: Aristophanes, *Knights* 1081]

CYNALOPEX A nickname ("dog-fox") for PHILOSTRATUS, whom ARISTOPHANES labels a PIMP. [ANCIENT SOURCES: Aristophanes, *Knights* 1069 and the scholiast on the line, *Lysistrata* 957]

BIBLIOGRAPHY
Henderson, J. *Aristophanes: Lysistrata.* Oxford: Clarendon Press, 1987, 183.
Sommerstein, A. H. *The Comedies of Aristophanes.* Vol. 2, *Knights.* Warminster, U.K.: Aris & Phillips, 1981, 201.

CYNNA A well-known PROSTITUTE in ATHENS. [ANCIENT SOURCES: Aristophanes, *Lysistrata* 765, *Peace* 755]

BIBLIOGRAPHY
Sommerstein, A. H. *The Comedies of Aristophanes.* Vol. 5, *Peace.* Warminster, U.K.: Aris & Philips, 1985, 169.

CYNTHIA Another name for ARTEMIS.

CYPRIS Another name for APHRODITE.

CYPRUS An island in the eastern Mediterranean Sea that was considered the birthplace of APHRODITE and thus was especially sacred to her. AJAX's brother, TEUCER, went to Cyprus when banished by his father after the Trojan War. [ANCIENT SOURCES: Aristophanes, *Lysistrata* 833; Euripides, *Bacchae* 402–3; Hesiod, *Theogony* 193–99]

CYRENE A well-known PROSTITUTE in ATHENS. [ANCIENT SOURCES: Aristophanes, *Frogs* 1328, *Thesmophoriazuae* 98]

CYRUS The son of Cambyses, Cyrus was the king of Persia who ascended to the throne in 550/549 B.C.E. [ANCIENT SOURCES: Aeschylus, *Persians* 767, 773; Arrian, *Anabasis* 6.29.8; Herodotus, 1.71ff.; Strabo, 15.730; Xenophon, *Cyropaedia*]

CYTHERA   An island off the southern tip of Greece. The island was associated with the birth of APHRODITE, who had a temple there. Aphrodite is sometimes called Cytherea or the Cytherean.

CYZICUS   A city on a half-peninsula of the same name. Cyzicus was located northeast of TROY in what is today northwestern Turkey. [ANCIENT SOURCES: Aristophanes, *Peace* 1176]

DAEDALUS A builder and creator from the island of CRETE, Daedalus ("clever") was the father of ICARUS. When MINOS' wife, PASIPHAE, was in love with a bull, Daedalus built a hollow wooden cow to help her satisfy her lust. Daedalus also built the mazelike labyrinth to house the offspring of Pasiphae and the bull, the MINOTAUR. When THESEUS and his fellow Athenians were taken to Crete and imprisoned in the labyrinth, Daedalus gave Minos' daughter, ARIADNE, (who had fallen in love with Theseus), a thread that would allow them to find their way out of the labyrinth. After the Athenians and Ariadne escaped from the labyrinth, Minos blamed Daedalus for their escape and threatened to kill him. To escape the island, Daedalus constructed two pairs of wings, for himself and his son, Icarus. Equipped with these wings, Daedalus and Icarus flew from Crete; despite Daedalus' instructions, Icarus flew too close to the Sun, the wax that was holding his wings together melted, and Icarus plunged into the sea to his death.

After Icarus died, Daedalus went to the court of COCALUS in the Sicilian town of Camicus. Minos pursued Daedalus, and everywhere Minos searched he took along a spiral shell and promised to reward to the person who could pass a thread through the shell, thinking that only Daedalus would be clever enough to do this. Finally, Minos reached Camicus and showed the shell to Cocalus, who gave it to Daedalus. Daedalus threaded the shell by boring a hole through it, tying a thread to an ant, and then letting the ant go through the hole. When Cocalus returned and gave the threaded shell to Minos, Minos realized that Daedalus was nearby and demanded that he be turned over to him. Cocalus said he would hand over Daedalus but delayed Minos with the customary hospitality offered to strangers. Cocalus' daughters killed Minos by pouring boiling water on him.

SOPHOCLES wrote a *Daedalus*, but the fragments (158–64a Radt) are too brief to be informative. Aristophanes' *Daedalus* (fragments 184–97 Kock) may have satirized the SICILIAN EXPEDITION and cast ALCIBIADES as Icarus. The Greek comic poets Plato (fragments 19–20 Kock 1) and Eubulus (fragment 21 Kock 2) also wrote plays entitled *Daedalus,* whose brief fragments tell us nothing about their plots. [ANCIENT SOURCES: Euripides, *Hecabe* 838; Hyginus, *Fables* 39–40, 44; Ovid, *Metamorphoses* 8.183–235; Seneca, *Hercules Oetaeus* 684, 687, *Oedipus* 900, *Phaedra* 120, 1171]

BIBLIOGRAPHY

Kock, T. *Comicorum Atticorum Fragmenta.* Vol. 1. Leipzig: Teubner, 1880.
———. *Comicorum Atticorum Fragmenta.* Vol. 2. Leipzig: Teubner, 1884.
Radt, S. *Tragicorum Graecorum Fragmenta.* Vol. 4. Göttingen, Ger.: Vandenhoeck & Ruprecht, 1977.

DANAANS Often used by the dramatists as a synonym for the Greeks as a whole, the term *Danaans* technically refers to the descendants of Danaus, an African king who went to Greece and later became ruler of ARGOS. See also DANAIDS.

DANAE   For the story of Danae, see ACRISIUS. SOPHOCLES wrote a *Danae*, which may have dealt with Acrisius' exposure of Danae and her infant son, PERSEUS. EURIPIDES also composed a *Danae,* which Webster thinks was staged between 438 and 431 B.C.E. Among Roman authors, NAEVIUS wrote a play called *Danae,* which may have had the same subject matter as Sophocles' play. Fragment 11 indicates that Danae has been discovered to be pregnant; fragment 14, apparently spoken by Danae, reads, "I, innocent, have been driven unworthily from my fatherland."

BIBLIOGRAPHY
Kiso, A. *The Lost Sophocles.* New York: Vantage Press, 1984.
Lloyd-Jones, H. *Sophocles: Fragments.* Cambridge, Mass.: Harvard University Press, 1996.
Radt, S. *Tragicorum Graecorum Fragmenta.* Vol. 4. Göttingen, Ger.: Vandenhoeck & Ruprecht, 1977.
Sutton, D. F. *The Lost Sophocles.* Lanham, Md.: University Press of America, 1984.
Webster, T. B. L. *The Tragedies of Euripides.* London: Methuen, 1967.

DANAIDS   The daughters of Danaus, a king of Egypt. Danaus' brother, AEGYPTUS, wanted his 50 sons to marry Danaus' 50 daughters. The women refused and fled to Greece with their father. The sons of Aegyptus pursued the Danaids and forced the women to marry them. Danaus persuaded his daughters to murder their new husbands. The Danaids married Aegyptus' sons and killed them on their wedding night (with one exception—Hypermnestra did not kill Lynceus). In the UNDERWORLD, the Danaids were punished by being required to fill vessels with holes in them throughout eternity. The Danaids make up the chorus of AESCHYLUS' *SUPPLIANT WOMEN.* Aeschylus also wrote a *Danaids* (fragments 43–46 Radt), which probably dealt with the Danaids' killing of their husbands, in which APHRODITE may have been a character. The Greek comic poet DIPHILUS wrote a *Danaids,* of which only the title survives. [ANCIENT SOURCES: Hyginus, *Fables* 168; Ovid, *Heroides* 14; Seneca, *Hercules Furens* 500, *Hercules Oetaeus* 948]

BIBLIOGRAPHY
Kock, T. *Comicorum Atticorum Fragmenta.* Vol. 2. Leipzig: Teubner, 1884.

DANAUS   See DANAIDS.

DANISTA   See USURER.

DARDANUS   A son of ZEUS and Electra (not AGAMEMNON's daughter), Dardanus was a king of TROY and the father of Tros, who gave his name to Troy. Poets sometimes call the Trojans Dardanians and Troy Dardania. The Greek comic poet MENANDER wrote a *Dardanus,* whose surviving 11 words give no indication of the plot (fragments 93–94 Körte). [ANCIENT SOURCES: Apollodorus, *Library* 3.12.1]

BIBLIOGRAPHY
Körte, A., and A. Thierfelder. *Menandri Quae Supersunt.* Vol. 2, 2d ed. Leipzig: Teubner, 1959.

DATIS   One of the Persian generals (ARTAPHRENES was his colleague) defeated at the battle of MARATHON in 490 B.C.E. [ANCIENT SOURCES: Aristophanes, *Peace* 289; Herodotus, 6.94]

BIBLIOGRAPHY
Molitor, M. V. "The Song of Datis," *Mnemosyne* 39 (1986): 128–31.

DAUGHTERS OF HELIOS (HELIADES)
After the death of PHAETHON, his sisters, the daughters of Helios (see SUN) and Rhode, wept so much that ZEUS, taking pity on them, changed them into poplar trees. The trees continued to "weep," and their "tears" became drops of amber. Authors differ as to the number of the Heliades. Hesiod mentions seven daughters, but AESCHYLUS names only three—Aegle, Lampetie, and Phaethousa. In Aeschylus' *Heliades* (fragments 68–72 Radt), the daughters of Helios probably formed the chorus and the play may have dealt with Phaethon's death.

DAULIS   West of DELPHI, Daulis (or Daulia) is a town in north central Greece. [ANCIENT SOURCES: Seneca, *Hercules Oetaeus* 192, *Thyestes* 275; Sophocles, *Oedipus Tyrannos* 734]

DAWN   See EOS.

DEIANEIRA The daughter of OENEUS and ALTHAEA, Deianeira became the wife of HERACLES and the mother of HYLLUS. Immediately after Deianeira's marriage to Heracles, the CENTAUR NESSUS attempted to rape her. Wounded by Heracles' arrow, the centaur, with his dying words, told Deianeira that his blood could be used as a charm to ensure Heracles' love for her. When Heracles sent home a female captive (Iole), Deianeira gave her husband a robe smeared with this "love charm," hoping to win him back. What Nessus knew, but Deianeira did not realize, was that Nessus' blood was mingled with a lethal poison that tipped Heracles' arrows. Upon discovering that the robe stuck to Heracles' body and burned his skin, she committed suicide.

Deianeira appears as a character in two extant plays, SOPHOCLES' TRACHINIAN WOMEN and SENECA'S HERCULES OETAEUS. In Sophocles' play, Deianeira is a figure worthy of pity. Unlike CLYTEMNESTRA, who in AESCHYLUS' *Agamemnon* (see ORESTEIA) deliberately murders her husband, Deianeira destroys Heracles accidentally and through love, not revenge. Whereas MEDEA gives her rival a poison robe with the intent of destroying her and causing her former husband, JASON, extreme grief, Deianeira expresses sympathy for her rival, Iole, and does not intend the robe to injure Heracles. Deianeira commits suicide when he realizes she has harmed Heracles.

In *Hercules Oetaeus,* Deianeira initially appears angrier than she does in Sophocles' play. In the Roman play, on learning of the capture of Iole, she utters threats of violence against her husband. Yet, she later decides not to kill him and to try, as Sophocles' Deianeira does, to win back his love by using the centaur's blood as a charm. Ultimately, as her Sophoclean counterpart does, Seneca's Deianeira commits suicide when she learns of the injury the love charm has caused her husband.

BIBLIOGRAPHY

Bergson, L. "Herakles, Deianeira und Iole," *Rheinisches Museum* 136, no. 2 (1993): 102–15.
Hoey, T. F. "The *Trachiniae* and the Unity of Hero," *Arethusa* 3 (1970): 1–22.
McCall, M. "The *Trachiniae*: Structure, Focus, and Herakles," *American Journal of Philology* 93 (1972): 142–63.
Ryzman, M. "Deianeira's Moral Behaviour in the Context of the Natural Laws in Sophocles' *Trachiniae*," *Hermes* 119 (1991): 385–98.
Scott, M. "The Character of Deianeira in Sophocles' *Trachiniae*," *Acta Classica* 40 (1997): 33–47.

DEIGMA Its name the Greek word meaning "sample" or "specimen," the Deigma in ATHENS was a location at that city's main harbor (see PIRAEUS) where merchants displayed and sold samples of their merchandise. [ANCIENT SOURCES: Aristophanes, *Knights* 979]

DEIPHOBUS A son of PRIAM and HECABE, Deiphobus married HELEN after the death of PARIS. Deiphobus was killed by MENELAUS during the fall of TROY. Vergil says Helen hid Deiphobus' weapons and then opened the doors of the house for Menelaus, who was accompanied by ODYSSEUS. His attackers horribly mutilated Deiphobus' body, and Vergil suggests that Helen herself may have done some of the damage.

The Roman playwright ACCIUS wrote a *Deiphobus,* from which eight lines survive. Accius' play was clearly set at Troy. The speaker of one fragment is a fisherman; another fragment seems to refer to the capture of SINON; another contains the dedicatory inscription to Athena on the wooden horse; another speaks unfavorably about Odysseus. The nature of the play is otherwise unknown. [ANCIENT SOURCES: Apollodorus, *Epitome* 5.9, 22; Seneca, *Agamemnon* 749; Vergil, *Aeneid* 6.495–534]

DELIA See ARTEMIS.

DELOS Also called Ortygia, Delos is a tiny island in the AEGEAN SEA (southeast of ATHENS and north of NAXOS), the traditional birthplace of APOLLO and ARTEMIS and a major center for their worship. According to SENECA, Delos was a floating mass that later became stationary at Artemis' command. During the second quarter of the fifth century B.C.E., Delos was also home to the treasury of the Delian League, an alliance of Greek cities formed after the Persian invasions of the first quarter of the century, whose purpose was to defend the allied Greeks from further Persian threats. The Greek comic poets CRATINUS (fragments 22–30 Kock 1) and Sophilus (fragment 2 Kock 2) wrote plays entitled *Delian Women,* and nothing is known about either play. The comic poet Antiphanes wrote a *Delian Woman,* of which only four words, which deal with vegetables being shredded or chopped up, survive (fragment 79 Kock). The comic poet Philostephanus wrote the play *Delian Man,* from which a four-line fragment about famous cooks survives (fragment 1 Kock 3). [ANCIENT SOURCES: Aeschylus, *Eumenides* 9 (see ORESTEIA); Aristophanes, *Birds* 869–70, *Clouds* 596, *Thesmophoriazusae* 333–34; Athenaeus, 9.373a; Euripides, *Hecabe* 462, *Heracles* 687, *Ion* 167, *Iphigenia in Tauris* 1235, *Trojan Women* 89; Seneca, *Agamemnon* 384, *Hercules Furens* 453]

BIBLIOGRAPHY
Kock, T. *Comicorum Atticorum Fragmenta.* Vol. 1. Leipzig: Teubner, 1880.
———. *Comicorum Atticorum Fragment.* Vol. 2. Leipzig: Teubner, 1884.
———. *Comicorum Atticorum Fragmenta.* Vol. 3. Leipzig: Teubner, 1888.
Laidlaw, W. A. *A History of Delos.* Oxford: B. Blackwell, 1933.
Themelis, P. *Mykonos-Delos: Archaeological Guide.* 2d ed. Athens: Apollo Editions, 1977.
Zaphiropoulou, P. *Delos: Monuments and Museum.* Athens: Krene Editions, 1983.

DELPHI See DELPHIC ORACLE.

DELPHIC ORACLE
When people in the ancient Mediterranean region wanted to learn the future or the answer to a particularly difficult question, they consulted an ORACLE. The most famous oracle was the one at DELPHI, located northwest of ATHENS in central Greece. Those who consulted the oracle believed that they were receiving the wisdom of APOLLO, the god who presided over the Delphic oracle. Apollo's words were delivered through a priestess called the Pythia. Apollo's oracles are ambiguous and enigmatic but always true. In extant drama, the pronouncements of the Delphic oracle frequently form the backdrop of a drama. It was the Delphic oracle who made HERACLES perform numerous labors to atone for killing his wife and children. OEDIPUS attempts to run away from his parents because of an oracle from Delphi that said he would kill his father and marry his mother. Often people consulted the Delphic oracle about having children, as AEGEUS does in EURIPIDES' MEDEA, or XUTHUS does in Euripides' ION.

BIBLIOGRAPHY
Parke, H. W. *Greek Oracles.* London, Hutchinson, 1967.

DELPHUS
The son of APOLLO and Thyia (or Melaena), Delphus was a mythical king of DELPHI. One tradition gives him a son named Castalius, whose name is preserved in the spring of CASTALIA at Delphi. Another tradition said Delphus' son was Pythes, who became king of the town of PYTHO (often synonymous with Delphi). [ANCIENT SOURCES: Aeschylus, *Eumenides* (see ORESTEIA); Pausanias, 7.18.9, 10.6.3–5]

DEME
The region of Attica, of which ATHENS was the principal city, was divided into more than 100 demes, most of which were outside the walls of Athens proper. ARISTOPHANES' ACHARNIANS takes its name from the deme of Acharnae. In addition to those performed at the major festivals in Athens proper, the City DIONYSIA and the LENAEA, ancient dramas were performed at local festivals held in particular demes such as ACHARNAE, ELEUSIS, SALAMIS, and THORICUS.

BIBLIOGRAPHY
Csapo, E., and W. J. Slater. *The Context of Ancient Drama.* Ann Arbor: University of Michigan Press, 1995, 121–22.

DEMETER (Latin: CERES)
The daughter of CRONUS and RHEA, Demeter (also known as Deo) is the sister of ZEUS, POSEIDON, HADES, HESTIA, and HERA. Demeter is sometimes given the title Euchlous. Demeter is a goddess associated with the Earth, agriculture, and grain. Because she supplies mortals with food, in EURIPIDES' BACCHAE, Demeter is called one of the two greatest divinities among humans (DIONYSUS is the other). By Zeus Demeter was the mother of PERSEPHONE, who was abducted by Hades and taken to the UNDERWORLD. Demeter withdrew from the gods and wandered the Earth, fasting, in search of her daughter. When she learned that Persephone was in the underworld, Demeter caused the Earth to become barren. Eventually, Zeus, Hades, and Demeter reached an agreement whereby Persephone would spend part of

every year in the underworld and the remaining part with Demeter. Euripides' SUPPLIANT WOMEN opens at the temple of Demeter at ELEUSIS, the best-known site for the worship of Demeter and Persephone, where throughout antiquity pilgrims traveled to be initiated into the Eleusian MYSTERIES. [ANCIENT SOURCES: Apollodorus, *Library* 1.1.5–1.2.1, 1.5.1–3, 2.5.12, 3.6.8, 3.12.1, 3.14.7; Apollonius Rhodius, 4.986–90; Aristophanes, *Thesmophoriazusae*; Euripides, *Helen* 1301–68; Hesiod, *Theogony* 453–506, 912–14, 969–74; Homer, *Odyssey* 5.125–28; *Homeric Hymn to Demeter* 2; Hyginus, *Fables* 141, 146, 147; Ovid, *Metamorphoses* 5.341–571, 642–61, 6.118–19, 8.738–78, 9.422–23; Pausanias, 1.14.1–3, 1.37.2, 2.5.8]

BIBLIOGRAPHY

Foley, H. P. *The Homeric Hymn to Demeter.* Princeton, N.J.: Princeton University Press, 1994.

DEMOPHON   The son of THESEUS and PHAEDRA, Demophon was the brother of ACAMAS. As had his father, Theseus, Demophon became a king of ATHENS. He fought in the Trojan War and rescued Theseus' mother, AETHRA, who had become a servant of HELEN's. During Demophon's return from TROY, he landed among the Bisaltians of THRACE and set a date to marry Phyllis, the king's daughter. Before the wedding, Demophon told Phyllis that he had to leave Thrace to visit his home in Athens but that he would return by the appointed date. Phyllis gave him a box and told him that inside was a sacrament of the goddess RHEA and that he should not open the box until he had given up hope that he would return to her. When Demophon, delaying for some unknown reason, did not return to Thrace at the appointed time, Phyllis cursed Demophon and committed suicide. At some point, Demophon opened the box, was terrified by what he saw, jumped onto his horse (who was also terrified), and, on being thrown from his horse, fell on his sword and died.

In EURIPIDES' CHILDREN OF HERACLES, Demophon functions as other Athenian kings do in Greek TRAGEDY as he goes to the aid of the oppressed. When his prophets advise him that he must sacrifice a maiden of noble birth to defeat EURYSTHEUS, Demophon refuses to sacrifice one of his own children or to ask one of his fellow Athenians to do so. After one of Heracles' daughters offers to give up her life, Demophon praises her courage, and at line 573 he exits and does not appear again. [ANCIENT SOURCES: Apollodorus, *Epitome* 1.18, 1.23, 5.22; Hyginus, *Fables* 59; Pausanias, 10.25.7–8]

DEMOS   A Greek word meaning "people," the term *demos* in ATHENS usually referred to male citizens who had the right to vote. Although the Athenians during the heyday of classical drama often followed the advice of leading citizens such as PERICLES, CLEON, or ALCIBIADES, Athens was a direct democracy (the term means "rule by the people"), and the people, the *demos,* were the city's rulers. In ARISTOPHANES' KNIGHTS, a character named Demos personifies the citizens of Athens. Aristophanes describes Demos as a grumpy master who is easily fooled by his slaves (political leaders such as Cleon) and whose favor can be gained by the slave who promises or gives him the most pleasant things. Aristophanes has Demos claim that he uses the flattering slaves to get what he wants from them, but this remark may be an attempt to flatter the members of the *demos* who were the spectators and judges of his play.

DEMOSTRATUS   An Athenian orator who advocated the SICILIAN Expedition of 415 B.C.E. [ANCIENT SOURCES: Aristophanes, *Lysistrata* 391, 393; Plutarch, *Alcibiades* 18, *Nicias* 12]

DENOUEMENT   A French word meaning "an untying," denouement refers to the resolution of a play after its climax.

DEO   See DEMETER.

DEUCALION   The son of PROMETHEUS, Deucalion is the Noah of classical mythology. Deucalion married Pyrrha, the daughter of Epimetheus and Pandora. Prometheus, upon learning that ZEUS was planning to wipe out the human race, advised Deucalion to build a boat. When Zeus sent heavy rains to flood the Earth, Deucalion and Pyrrha managed to ride out the storm, floating along for nine days and nights and finally landing on Mount PARNASSUS. When Deucalion made a sacrifice to Zeus, Zeus granted him a wish. Deucalion's wish was to restore the human race. When told to throw the bones of their mother behind them, Deucalion and Pyrrha were initially horrified at this impious act, but they soon realized that their mother's bones were the stones of mother Earth. The stones that Deucalion threw turned into men, and Pyrrha's became women. Deucalion had several children by Pyrrha: a daughter named Protogenia and two sons, Amphictyon, who became a king in Attica, and Hellen, after whom the Hellenic people are named. Deucalion does not appear as a character in any extant dramas, although several comic poets wrote plays about him. The Greek comic poet Ophelio wrote a *Deucalion,* of which only the title survives. Epicharmus wrote a *Deucalion* (also entitled *Pyrrha and Prometheus*), whose fragments contain a reference to the marriage of Deucalion and Pyrrha (fragments 114–18 Kaibel). The *Myrmekanthropoi* (Ant-People) of the comic poet PHERECRATES dealt with Deucalion and Pyrrha's adventures (fragments 113–25 Kock). The fragments that survive from the Deucalion plays by Antiphanes (fragments 77–78 Kock) and Eubulus (fragment 24 Kock) are uninformative regarding their subject matter. [ANCIENT SOURCES: Apollodorus, *Library* 1.7.2; Ovid, *Metamorphoses* 1.262–415; Pindar, *Olympian* 9.40–56; Seneca, *Trojan Women* 1039]

BIBLIOGRAPHY
Kock, T. *Comicorum Atticorum Fragmenta.* Vol. 2. Leipzig: Teubner, 1884.

DEUS EX MACHINA See MECHANE.

DEUTERAGONIST An actor who played the supporting roles in Greek drama. [ANCIENT SOURCES: Hesychius, d741]

DEXINICUS A person mentioned by ARISTOPHANES at WEALTH 800 as being at the play and eager to grab some of the figs tossed out among the spectators. He is not otherwise known, although Sommerstein speculates that he may have been a minor politician.

The ancient commentators on the passage suggested that Dexinicus was either a glutton, a poor man, or a military commander, but no other sources corroborate these speculations.

BIBLIOGRAPHY
Sommerstein, A. H. *The Comedies of Aristophanes.* Vol. 11, *Wealth.* Warminster, U.K.: Aris & Phillips, 2001, 186–87.

DEXITHEUS A lyre player who had won a contest at the Pythian games, although some Greeks considered his playing uninspired. [ANCIENT SOURCES: Aristophanes, *Acharnians* 14]

BIBLIOGRAPHY
Sommerstein, A. H. *The Comedies of Aristophanes.* Vol. 1, *Acharnians.* Warminster, U.K.: Aris & Phillips, 1980, 158–59.

DIANA See ARTEMIS.

DIASIA Held on Anthesterion 23 (February–March), the Diasia was a festival honoring ZEUS Meilichois (kindly or open to propitiation) with bloodless offerings. [ANCIENT SOURCES: Aristophanes, *Clouds* 408, 864; Thucydides, 1.126.6]

BIBLIOGRAPHY
Parke, H. W. *Festivals of the Athenians.* Ithaca, N.Y.: Cornell University Press, 1977, 95, 120–22, 189–90.

DIAZOMA See PRAECINCTIO.

DICAEOPOLIS The hero of ARISTOPHANES' *ACHARNIANS* (425 B.C.E.), Dicaeopolis ("honest citizen") arranges a personal peace for himself and his family with the Spartans and their allies. As the hero of Aristophanes' earliest surviving play, Dicaeopolis is often cited as a model for other Aristophanic heroes. He is a seemingly ordinary Athenian citizen, a farmer living in the countryside, but with a common sense that allows him to outwit or outmaneuver urban opponents who threaten or oppose him. As other Aristophanic heroes (especially Trygaeus in PEACE) do, Dicaeopolis longs for peace and a return to the simple life that he enjoyed before the war between ATHENS and SPARTA. For Dicaeopolis, the good life means the freedom to worship his gods and the freedom to sell products from his farm and enjoy products he acquires through trade. In Dicaeopolis' case, wine is the embodiment of peace, and by the end of *Acharnians* he is nicely intoxicated and accompanied by two attractive women who will help him as he staggers home.

BIBLIOGRAPHY

Compton-Engle, G. L. "From Country to City: The Persona of Dicaeopolis in Aristophanes' *Acharnians*," *Classical Journal* 94, no. 4 (1998–99): 359–73.

Fisher, N. R. E. "Multiple Personalities and Dionysiac Festivals: Dicaeopolis in Aristophanes' *Acharnians*," *Greece and Rome* 40 (1993): 31–47.

Olson, S. D. "Dicaeopolis' Motivations in Aristophanes' *Acharnians*," *Journal of Hellenic Studies* 111 (1991): 200–3.

Parker, L. P. E. "Eupolis or Dicaeopolis?" *Journal of Hellenic Studies* 111 (1991): 203–8.

Slater, N. W. "Aristophanes' Apprenticeship Again," *Greek, Roman, and Byzantine Studies* 30 (1989): 67–82.

DICTYNNA   See ARTEMIS.

DICTYS

The son of Magnes, the fisherman Dictys was the brother of Polydectes, the king of the island of SERIPHUS. After the box into which PERSEUS and DANAE had been placed washed ashore on Seriphus, Dictys, whose name means "net," found the child and mother and took them to his brother's palace. After the death of Polydectes, Dictys became king of Seriphus. EURIPIDES wrote a *Dictys*, staged in 431 B.C.E. as the third play of the tetralogy that included MEDEA, *Philoctetes*, and THERISTAI. Webster thinks the play may have resembled in structure Euripides' later HERACLES, in which HERACLES returned to rescue AMPHITRYON, MEGARA, and Heracles' children, who were being besieged at an altar by LYCUS. Webster suggests that in *Dictys*, Dictys and Danae were besieged at an altar by Polydectes (who was in love with Danae) and that Perseus returned to rescue Danae, killed Polydectes, and then made Dictys king. AESCHYLUS wrote a SATYR PLAY, DICTYULCI, about Dictys' rescue of Perseus and Danae. [ANCIENT SOURCES: Apollodorus, *Library* 1.9.6, 2.4.1; Hyginus, *Fables* 63; Strabo, 10.5.10]

BIBLIOGRAPHY

Webster, T. B. L. *The Tragedies of Euripides*. London: Methuen, 1967.

DICTYULCI   See DICTYS.

DIDASKALIA

A Greek word (plural: *didaskaliai*) meaning "teaching," this term can refer to (1) the process of training a CHORUS, which was also known as *chorodidaskalia*, (2) the plays that are produced, or (3) lists of dramas that include such information as the plays' titles, the names of the playwrights, the names of actors, the dates of production, and the dramas' placement in competition. [ANCIENT SOURCES: Diogenes Laertius, 5.26; Plato, *Alcibiades* 125e, *Gorgias* 501e; Plutarch, *Cimon* 8, *Pericles* 5, *Moralia* 839d, 1096a; scholia on Aristophanes, *Frogs* 1155]

BIBLIOGRAPHY

Csapo, E., and W. J. Slater. *The Context of Ancient Drama.* Ann Arbor: University of Michigan Press, 1995, 41–43, 136–37, 227–29.

DIDASKALOS

A Greek word (plural: *didaskaloi*) meaning "teacher" or "master," the term *didaskalos* can refer to the chorus trainer or the play's producer. The term *chorodidaskalos* (chorus teacher) is also used of the person who trained the chorus. Originally, the playwright himself would have been the *chorodidaskalos*, but even in the fifth century B.C.E. this role had become separate from that of the poet. [ANCIENT SOURCES: Antiphon 6.13; Aristophanes, *Birds* 628, *Ecclesiazusae* 809; Plato, *Laws* 655a, 812e; *Sylloge Inscriptionum Graecarum* 450.5]

BIBLIOGRAPHY

Csapo, E., and W. J. Slater. *The Context of Ancient Drama.* Ann Arbor: University of Michigan Press, 1995, 44, 136–37.

DIEITREPHES

An Athenian of a rather prominent family (despite ARISTOPHANES' claims to the contrary) during the latter half of the fifth century B.C.E., Dieitrephes held positions of military authority, related to Thracian mercenaries and in THRACE from 413 to 411. In 411, Dieitrephes supported an overthrow of the democracy on the island of Thasos by oligarchs. [ANCIENT SOURCES: Aristophanes, *Birds* 798, 1442; Thucydides, 7.29–30, 8.64.2]

BIBLIOGRAPHY

Dunbar, Nan. *Aristophanes: Birds.* New York: Oxford University Press, 1995, 484–85.

DIKE See JUSTICE.

DIOCLES A Greek from the town of MEGARA, Diocles was a hero at both Megara and ELEUSIS. The Megarians honored him with an annual festival, the Diocleia. [ANCIENT SOURCES: Aristophanes, *Acharnians* 774; *Homeric Hymn to Demeter,* 153, 474; Plutarch, *Theseus* 10.3; Theocritus, 12.27–33]

BIBLIOGRAPHY
Sommerstein, A. H. *The Comedies of Aristophanes.* Vol. 1,
  Acharnians. Warminster, U.K.: Aris & Phillips, 1980, 196.

DIOMEA The Athenian DEME Diomea, south of the ACROPOLIS, had a place of worship for HERACLES and the site for a festival to that hero. [ANCIENT SOURCES: Aristophanes, *Frogs* 651]

BIBLIOGRAPHY
Dover, Kenneth. *Aristophanes: Frogs.* Oxford: Clarendon
  Press, 1993, 53–54.

DIOMEDES (1) The son of ARES and Cyrene, Diomedes was the evil king of the Bistones, a Thracian tribe. He fed strangers to his man-eating horses, until HERACLES put an end to the terror by feeding the horses the king himself. [ANCIENT SOURCES: Apollodorus, *Library* 2.5.8; Euripides, *Alcestis* 483; Seneca, *Agamemnon* 842, *Hercules Furens* 226, 1170, *Hercules Oetaeus* 20, 1538, 1790, *Trojan Women* 1108]

DIOMEDES (2) A prince of ARGOS, Diomedes was the son of TYDEUS and Deipyle. After the sons of a certain Agrius usurped the kingdom of OENEUS, imprisoned and tortured him, and turned over his kingdom to Agrius, Diomedes, accompanied by ALCMAEON, traveled from Argos and killed most of Agrius' sons. Because Oeneus was an old man, Diomedes turned over the kingdom to Oeneus' son-in-law, Andraemon, and took Oeneus himself to Argos. The surviving sons of Agrius ambushed and killed Oeneus in ARCADIA; Diomedes took his body to Argos and buried him on the site that later became the city of Oenoe. Upon returning to Argos, Diomedes married Aegialia, the daughter of the Argive king Adrastus (or Aegialeus). Diomedes fought in two major wars.

Accompanied by the sons (the EPIGONI) of those who died in the famous Seven against Thebes expedition, Diomedes helped wage a second war against the Thebans. He also accompanied the Greek forces to Troy in their effort to rescue HELEN. In book five of Homer's *Iliad,* Diomedes fights against APHRODITE and ARES. Diomedes takes the stage in one extant Greek drama, *RHESUS,* in which he accompanies ODYSSEUS on his nocturnal incursion into the Trojan camp to kill RHESUS.

After the death of ACHILLES, Diomedes is said to have accompanied Odysseus to the island of LEMNOS to take back PHILOCTETES, although SOPHOCLES, in *PHILOCTETES,* has Achilles' son NEOPTOLEMUS accompany Odysseus. Diomedes also accompanied Odysseus when the two journeyed to Troy to steal the statue known as the Palladium. After the fall of Troy, Diomedes was one of the few Greek warriors to reach his native land in a timely fashion. At some point, he eventually made his way to Italy, where he founded the town of Arpi. [ANCIENT SOURCES: Appian, *The Foreign Wars* 7.5.31; Apollodorus, *Library* 1.8.5–6, 3.7.2, *Epitome* 3.12, 4.2, 4.4, 5.8, 5.13; Euripides, *Rhesus* 564–641; Homer, *Iliad;* Servius on *Aeneid* 8.9 and 11.246]

BIBLIOGRAPHY
Stagakis, George. "Dolon, Odysseus and Diomedes in the
  Doloneia," *Rheinisches Museum* 130 (1987): 193–204.
Walton, J. M. "Playing in the Dark: Masks and Euripides'
  Rhesus," *Helios* 27, no. 2 (2000): 137–47.

DIONYSIA An Athenian festival honoring DIONYSUS. One Dionysia, known as the Rural Dionysia, was held in the month of POSEIDON (late December or early January). In ARISTOPHANES' *ACHARNIANS,* DICAEOPOLIS holds his own personal Rural Dionysia after he establishes his peace treaty with SPARTA. Another Dionysia, first held in ATHENS around the middle of the sixth century B.C.E., was called the Great Dionysia or City Dionysia. This festival occurred in the month of Elaphebolion (late March). The Great or City Dionysia was a festival that included a major drama competition. According to tradition, the first dramatic performances, tragedies under the direction of THESPIS, appeared at this festival in 534 B.C.E. Competition in DITHYRAMB was established by 590; comedies did not appear until 486.

In contrast to the LENAEA, held two months earlier, the City Dionysia would have been attended by a significant number of non-Athenians because the weather for travel was better at this time of year.

During the sixth and fifth centuries, playwrights who wanted to compete in the City Dionysia were chosen by a public official called the eponymous ARCHON; later an official called the Agonothete made the selections. Once the playwrights were determined, at some point not long before the competition a lottery was held to determine the order in which they would compete. No later than Elaphebolion 8, the chosen playwrights participated in a precontest event called the Proagon, at which they, their actors, and their choruses appeared unmasked and without costume to gave a preview (see PROAGON) of their upcoming productions.

The next two days of the festival were occupied with a procession, the sacrifice of hundreds of animals, and dancing and singing in honor of Dionysus. In addition to transporting food, drink, and items for sacrifice, the procession carried a statue of Dionysus and large *phalloi* (penises), a symbol of fertility. The Rural Dionysia also included the carrying of a PHALLUS in procession. On arrival at the precinct of Dionysus Eleuthereus, a feast in honor of the god was held.

Elaphebolion 10 also marked the festival's first day of competition. Before the performances, the theater underwent a purification ritual: The 10 military commanders elected for that year poured out an offering of wine to Dionysus; various dignitaries and those who had served Athens well were presented to the crowd; the male orphans of Athenians who had died in war were honored with armor and allowed to sit in the front row of the theater, along with Dionysus' priest and the god's statue; and judges for the plays were selected by lot (one judge from each of the 10 Athenian tribes). Before the fall of Athens to SPARTA in 404 B.C.E., this time was also used to display to the spectators the various tributes that the members of the Athenian empire had offered.

The order of competition for the dithyrambs, tragedies, and comedies is uncertain. For dithyramb, each of the 10 Athenian tribes supplied two choruses of 50 (one of men, one of boys) for the event. The CHOREGUS and the poet of the winning chorus received

prizes and were escorted home in a victory procession. Some scholars believe the dithyrambic competition occurred on Elaphebolion 10 and that the comic competition (with five comic poets each presenting a single play) took place on Elaphebolion 11. It is often thought that during the PELOPONNESIAN WAR (431–404) the number of comedies was reduced to three as a result of financial hardships in the city; a day of COMEDY was followed by three days devoted to TRAGEDY, with three playwrights each staging three tragedies and a SATYR PLAY during a single day.

Other scholars think that the first day of competition featured the boys' dithyramb and some comedies; the second day the men's dithyramb and the remaining comedies were staged; the final three days presented the tragedies. On the last day of competition, after all the plays were concluded, each judge ranked the productions on a tablet. It is usually thought that not all of the judges' ballots were taken into account, and that the eponymous archon selected five of the ballots from a jar. After the judges' rankings were tallied, crowns of oak leaves were given to the victorious playwrights, and a victory parade escorted them home.

BIBLIOGRAPHY

Connor, W. R. "City Dionysia and Athenian Democracy," *Classica et Mediaevalia* 40 (1989): 7–32.

Csapo, E., and W. J. Slater. *The Context of Ancient Drama.* Ann Arbor: University of Michigan Press, 1995, 103–32.

Goldhill, S. D. "The Great Dionysia and Civic Ideology," *Journal of Hellenic Studies* 107 (1987): 58–76.

Parke, H. W. *Festivals of the Athenians.* Ithaca, N.Y.: Cornell University Press, 1977, 125–36.

Pickard-Cambridge, A. W. *Dithyramb, Tragedy, and Comedy,* 2d ed. Revised by T. B. L. Webster. Oxford: Clarendon Press, 1962, 41–126.

DIONYSIUS I From 405 B.C.E. until his death in 367, Dionysius I ruled the city of SYRACUSE (on SICILY). By 392 Dionysius had gained control of eastern Sicily, and by 389/398 he had added most of the toe of Italy's "boot." Dionysius was disliked in ATHENS because he was a longtime ally of the Spartans. Not long after the year 388 Dionysius' ships reinforced a Spartan fleet whose blockade of the HELLESPONT was causing hardship for the Athenians during the so-called Corinthian

War (395–86). The Athenians eventually had to accept a peace treaty on their enemies' terms. Despite the Athenian dislike of Dionysius, he appears to have been popular enough with his own people. Not only did he rule Syracuse, but he also wrote tragedies and even won a victory in Athens at the LENAEA. The titles of five of his plays are known (see fragments 1–12 Snell): *Adonis, Alcmena, The Ransoming of Hector, Leda,* and a SATYR PLAY entitled *Hunger.* [ANCIENT SOURCES: Aristophanes, *Wealth* 550; Diodorus Siculus, 14.109.1–3; 15.74.1–4; Lysias, 33; Xenophon, *Hellenica* 5.1.26–28]

BIBLIOGRAPHY

Caven, Brian. *Dionysius I, War-Lord of Sicily.* New Haven, Conn.: Yale University Press, 1990.

Sanders, L. J. *Dionysius I of Syracuse and Greek Tyranny.* London: Croom Helm, 1987.

Snell, B. *Tragicorum Graecorum Fragmenta.* Vol. 1. Göttingen, Ger.: Vandenhoeck & Ruprecht, 1971.

Sommerstein, A. H. *The Comedies of Aristophanes.* Vol. 11, *Wealth.* Warminster: Aris & Phillips, 2001, 174.

Stroheker, K. F. *Dionysios I.* Wiesbaden, Ger.: F. Steiner, 1958.

DIONYSUS   The son of ZEUS and the mortal SEMELE, Dionysus (also called Bacchus, Bromius, and, by the Romans, Liber) is best known as the god of wine, but he is also the god of drama.

After Semele became pregnant with Dionysus, HERA discovered Zeus' affair and, disguised as Semele's maidservant, tricked Semele into asking Zeus to have intercourse with her in the same way that he did with Hera. Semele, not knowing that Zeus and Hera's lovemaking involved thunder and lightning, asked Zeus for an unspecified favor. After Zeus promised to grant whatever she asked, Semele made her request. Zeus could not fail to honor his word, and Semele was killed. Zeus, however, rescued the unborn child and stitched him inside his thigh, from which Dionysus was eventually born. The name Dionysus may mean something like "he who was sewn in."

After Dionysus' birth, Zeus still feared Hera's wrath, so he instructed HERMES to take Dionysus to live with INO and ATHAMAS of BOEOTIA. Dionysus was disguised as a woman to fool Hera, who saw through the disguise and drove Athamas insane in the hope that he would kill Dionysus. Dionysus escaped when Zeus changed Dionysus into a young goat. Hermes then took Dionysus to the nymphs of Mount Nysa in what is now western Turkey.

After Dionysus grew up, he wandered throughout the world, seeking to prove his divinity to humans. During the course of his wanderings, the young god experienced many adventures. At one point, he was captured by pirates, but he escaped by entwining their ship with vines and making them hallucinate so that they jumped overboard and were changed into dolphins. During a pass through the island of NAXOS, Dionysus found (or abducted) MINOS' daughter, ARIADNE, and made her his bride.

Dionysus' entrances into various towns usually followed a similar pattern. Initially he would be rejected, but he would be accepted after he caused some sort of trauma to those who rejected him. When Dionysus entered the realm of the Thracian king LYCURGUS, the god's followers were captured, but Dionysus escaped by leaping into the AEGEAN SEA. Dionysus later returned and inflicted madness on Lycurgus, who mistook his son for a vine and killed him. This crime caused the gods to generate hardship for Lycurgus' kingdom until Lycurgus' subjects had him killed and accepted Dionysus as a divinity. The same pattern is played out in EURIPIDES' *Bacchae:* Dionysus gives to Thebes; King PENTHEUS attempts to apprehend the god; Dionysus escapes and then brings about Pentheus' destruction at the hands of his mother and his aunts.

Dionysus appears on stage in several dramas, the most notable Euripides' *Bacchae* and ARISTOPHANES' *Frogs.* Both of these plays were first staged in Athens in 405 B.C.E., and they give completely different portrayals of the god. In *Bacchae,* TIRESIAS describes Dionysus as being one of the two greatest gifts (DEMETER is the other) that mortals have, because Dionysus (wine) frees humans from their cares. Despite Tiresias' efforts to rationalize the god with soothing, beneficent wine, Pentheus' attempts to apprehend the god and suppress his worship draw out a cunning, vengeful, and even malicious side in him. Dionysus toys with Pentheus and ultimately lures him to a grisly death at the hands of his own mother. In *Frogs,* we see the comic side of Dionysus. Dionysus' effeminate nature is alluded to in *Bacchae* and is witnessed more clearly in *Frogs.*

Several other ancient dramatists wrote plays entitled *Dionysus*. In that of the Greek tragedian Chaeremon the first of four brief fragments (4–7 Snell) suggest that the play dealt with the god's encounter with Pentheus. [ANCIENT SOURCES: Apollodorus, *Library* 3.4.3; Euripides, *Bacchae;* Ovid, *Metamorphoses* 3.253–315, 511–700, 4.1–54, 416–562]

BIBLIOGRAPHY

Snell, B. *Tragicorum Graecorum Fragmenta.* Vol. 1. Göttingen, Ger.: Vandenhoeck & Ruprecht, 1971.

DIOPEITHES A person of questionable sanity according to comic poetry, Diopeithes is described by Dunbar as "a minor political figure known for his active interest in oracles." [ANCIENT SOURCES: Ameipsias, fragment 10 Kock; Aristophanes, *Birds* 988, *Knights* 1085, *Wasps* 380; Plutarch, *Pericles* 32.2]

BIBLIOGRAPHY

Dunbar, Nan. *Aristophanes: Birds.* New York: Oxford University Press, 1995, 549–50.
Kock, T. *Comicorum Atticorum Fragmenta.* Vol. 1. Leipzig: Teubner, 1880.

DIPHILUS (BORN CA. 355 B.C.E.) A poet of New Comedy (see COMEDY), Diphilus was born at Sinope in the Black Sea region but spent most of his life in ATHENS, where he was victorious three times at the LENAEA. He is said to have written about 100 plays, of which about 60 titles are known but only some 130 fragments survive. Most of Diphilus' titles sound like the typical stuff of New Comedy (e.g., *Brothers, Eunuch, Merchant, Parasite,* and *Treasure*); a few indicate mythological topics (e.g., *Danaids, Hecate, Heracles,* and *Theseus*). Two of PLAUTUS' plays were adapted from plays by Diphilus, CASINA from his *Kleroumenoi* (Lotdrawers) and ROPE from a play of unknown title. Diphilus' *Sunapathneskontes* (Suicide pact) provided the basis for a lost Plautine play (*Commorientes*) and the first scene in the second act of TERENCE'S BROTHERS.

BIBLIOGRAPHY

Astorga, J. A. "The Art of Diphilus: A Study of Verbal Humor in New Comedy." Dissertation, University of California Berkeley, 1990.
Damen, M. L. "The Comedy of Diphilos Sinopeus in Plautus, Terence and Athenaeus." Dissertation, University of Texas, 1985.
Friedrich, W. *Euripides und Diphilos: Zur Dramaturgie der Spatformen.* Munchen: Beck, 1953.
Lefevre, E. *Diphilos und Plautus: Der Rudens und sein Original.* Mainz: Akademie der Wissenschaften und der Literatur, 1984.

DIPOLIA Also called the Bouphonia ("ox sacrifice"), this annual Athenian feast honored ZEUS Polieus. Younger Athenians may have considered it as "overladen with archaic ritual and devoid of the athletic and artistic contests which made other festivals interesting" (Dover). [ANCIENT SOURCES: Aristophanes, *Clouds* 984, *Peace* 420; Pausanias, 1.28.11]

BIBLIOGRAPHY

Dover, K. J. *Aristophanes: Clouds.* Oxford: Clarendon Press, 1989.

DIRCE The daughter of ACHELOUS, Dirce was the wife of LYCUS, who later became king of THEBES. Dirce persecuted ANTIOPE, the daughter of Lycus' brother Nycteus. When Antiope's sons, AMPHION and ZETHUS, discovered Dirce's cruelty, they tied Dirce to a bull that dragged her to death. Dirce's body was thrown into a nearby stream, which bore her name after that time. The demise of Dirce would have been dramatized in EURIPIDES' *Antiope* and PACUVIUS' *Antiopa.* [ANCIENT SOURCES: Apollodorus, *Library* 3.5.5; Hyginus, *Fables* 7–8; Euripides, *Bacchae* 519–20, *Heracles* 27, 573, 784; Plautus, *Pseudolus* 199–200; Seneca, *Hercules Furens* 916, *Oedipus* 177, 234, 531, 588, 714, *Phoenician Women* 19, 126]

BIBLIOGRAPHY

Kambitsis, J. *L'Antiope d'Euripide.* Athens: Hourzamanis, 1972.
Warmington, E. H. *Remains of Old Latin: Livius Andronicus, Naevius, Pacuvius, and Accius.* Vol. 2. Cambridge, Mass.: Harvard University Press, 1936.

DIS See HADES.

DISCORD In SENECA'S *HERCULES FURENS,* this is the name of the FURY whom Juno (see HERA) calls upon to drive the title character insane.

DISTEGIA   A second story of a theater building. Pollux says that *distegia* could be used for scenes like the one in EURIPIDES' *PHOENICIAN WOMEN* in which ANTIGONE observes the approach of the Argive army. Pollux also states that sometimes the *distegia* was made of tiles and that tiles were thrown down from it. [ANCIENT SOURCES: Pollux, *Onomasticon* 4.127, 129–30]

DITHYRAMB   A lyric hymn sung by a CHORUS in honor of DIONYSUS, who was sometimes called Dithyrambos. The dithyramb received musical accompaniment by the *AULOS*. Tradition says that Arion of CORINTH perfected the form of the dithyramb around the year 600 B.C.E. and from Corinth the dithyramb made its way to ATHENS (taken there by Lasus of Hermione), where it became a part of the competition at festivals honoring DIONYSUS. In *Poetics*, ARISTOTLE claims that TRAGEDY itself evolved from some aspect of dithyrambic poetry. How this evolution took place—if it did—is unclear. The earliest known victory in competition at Athens was that in 509/508 of Hypodicus of Chalcis. Until the first quarter of the fifth century, the dithyramb had a corresponding STROPHE and ANTISTROPHE as in the choral odes of tragedy, but after this time the form began to change. Soloists supplemented the chorus and the musical component of the dithyramb began to take precedence over the words, which may have become increasingly complex and lofty in their diction. In ARISTOPHANES' *BIRDS*, the dithyrambic poet CINESIAS is rejected when he tries to gain entrance to the new city of the birds, and Aristophanes mocks the "airy" quality of his poetry. Although dithyrambic poets continued to compete around the AEGEAN region well into the second century B.C.E., the popularity of this poetic form had already started to decline two centuries earlier. [ANCIENT SOURCES: Archilochus, fragment 77; Aristophanes, *Peace* 829; Aristotle, *Poetics* 1447a14, 1447b26, 1449a11, *Politics* 1342b7; Euripides, *Bacchae* 526; Herodotus, 1.23.1; Pindar, *Olympian* 3.19; Plato, *Laws* 700b]

BIBLIOGRAPHY
Pickard-Cambridge, A. W. *Dithyramb, Tragedy and Comedy.* Oxford: Clarendon Press, 1962.

DIVINATION   See PROPHET.

DOCTOR (Latin: *MEDICUS*)   A stock figure in New and Roman COMEDY. In PLAUTUS' *TWO MENACHMUSES*, the Medicus is summoned when Menaechmeus is thought to be insane.

DODONA   A town in northern Greece that was famous for its oracle of ZEUS. Unlike the DELPHIC ORACLE, in which the god spoke through a single priestess, at Dodona, Zeus issued his oracles through an ancient oak tree. When the wind blew through the leaves of this oak, two priestesses called Peleiades interpreted the rustling of the leaves. An oracle from Dodona plays a part in SOPHOCLES' *TRACHINIAE,* in which we twice hear of an oracle from Dodona about HERACLES' ultimate fate. [ANCIENT SOURCES: Aeschylus, *Prometheus Bound* 658, 830–31; Aristophanes, *Birds* 716; Euripides, *Andromache* 886; Seneca, *Hercules Oetaeus* 1473, *Medea* 349; Sophocles, *Trachinian Women* 172, 1159–73]

BIBLIOGRAPHY
Parke, H. W. *Greek Oracles.* London: Hutchinson, 1967.
———. *The Oracles of Zeus: Dodona, Olympia, Ammon.* Oxford: B. Blackwell, 1967.

DOLON   The son of Eumedes (or Eumelus), Dolon (whose name is derived from the Greek word for "trickery") was a Trojan who fought against the Greeks in the Trojan War. He appears in one extant play, *RHESUS,* in which he volunteers to spy on the Greek camp in exchange for the horses of ACHILLES. During Dolon's mission, the Greeks capture him, and in exchange for his life, he gives the Greeks information about the Trojan camp. After he does, the Greeks kill him anyway. [ANCIENT SOURCES: Apollodorus, *Epitome* 4.4; Euripides, *Rhesus;* Homer, *Iliad* 10.299–464]

DOLOPIANS   The Dolopians were a tribe who lived in northern Greece, who HOMER says were ruled by PHOENIX. SOPHOCLES wrote a *Dolopians* (Greek: *Dolopes*), of which two brief fragments survive (174–75 Radt). Lloyd-Jones thinks that Sophocles' *Dolopians* may have been identical to his *Phoenix,* which may have dealt with the blinding of Phoenix by his father, Amyntor; his subsequent healing by CHIRON;

and his establishment as king of the Dolopians by PELEUS. The fragments assigned under the title *Dolopians,* however, give us little hint of the play's content.

BIBLIOGRAPHY
Lloyd-Jones, H. *Sophocles: Fragments.* Cambridge, Mass.: Harvard University Press, 1996.
Radt, S. *Tragicorum Graecorum Fragmenta.* Vol. 4. Göttingen, Ger.: Vandenhoeck & Ruprecht, 1977.

DOMITIUS   The father of the Roman emperor NERO. [ANCIENT SOURCES: Seneca, *Octavia* 249]

DORIANS   A group of people who the ancient Greeks believed invaded Greece from the north between 1100 and 950 B.C.E. Legend says the Dorians invaded to restore the children of HERACLES to power in southern Greece. The Dorians settled in the southern part of Greece in such places as ARGOS, CORINTH, and SPARTA, and the term *Dorian* is sometimes synonymous with Peloponnesian or Spartan. According to one mythical tradition, the Dorian people took their name from a certain Dorus, the son of XUTHUS (see *ION*) and CREUSA of ATHENS. Whereas the Athenians spoke a dialect of Greek called Attic, the Dorians spoke in the Doric dialect. The name Dorian also has a connection with music and the Dorian mode was "one of the most important of the melodic patterns . . . in which Greek music was composed" (Sommerstein). The Dorian mode, with its dignified and somber tones, was employed in various types of music. [ANCIENT SOURCES: Aeschylus, *Persians* 183, 486, 817; Aristophanes, *Knights* 989; Euripides, *Electra* 819, 836, *Hecabe* 450, 934, *Ion* 1590, *Orestes* 1372, *Trojan Women* 234; Herodotus, 1.56; Pausanias, 2.12–13; Sophocles, *Oedipus at Colonus* 696, 1301, *Oedipus Tyrannos* 775; Strabo, 8.1.2; Thucydides, 1.12.3]

BIBLIOGRAPHY
Sommerstein, A. H. *The Comedies of Aristophanes.* Vol. 2, *Knights.* Warminster: Aris & Phillips, 1981, 196.

DRACHMA   A Greek coin worth six OBOLS.

DRACONTIDES   The name of several Athenians active in public life between 450 and 400 B.C.E. In *WASPS* (422 B.C.E.), ARISTOPHANES mentions one as a

person against whom legal action was impending. One Dracontides was present when the Athenians and the people of CHALCIS ratified a treaty, but the date of this treaty is not certain (either 446/445 or 424/423); a second Dracontides was a military commander in 443/442; a third challenged PERICLES' management of public funds in the 430s; a fourth (from Bate) had a daughter, Lysimache, who was a priestess of ATHENA Polias; a fifth Dracontides (from Aphidna) was one of the Thirty Tyrants installed by SPARTA in 404/403 to rule Athens. Some of these Dracontides may have been the same person, but which, if any, Aristophanes had in mind is unknown. [ANCIENT SOURCES: Aristophanes, *Wasps* 157, 438; *Inscriptiones Graecae* i³ 306.24, i³ 364.20; Plutarch, *Pericles* 32.3]

BIBLIOGRAPHY
MacDowell, D. M. *Aristophanes: Wasps.* Oxford: Clarendon Press, 1971, 153.
Sommerstein, A. H. *The Comedies of Aristophanes.* Vol. 4, *Wasps.* Warminster, U.K.: Aris & Phillips, 1983, 166.

DRACYLLUS   A fictional name for one of the chorus members in ARISTOPHANES' *ACHARNIANS* (line 612). Some editors use instead the name Anthracyllus ("little charcoal"), a name more fitting given the occupation of the Acharnians, who were known for their production of charcoal.

BIBLIOGRAPHY
Sommerstein, A. H. *The Comedies of Aristophanes.* Vol. 1, *Acharnians.* Warminster, U.K.: Aris & Phillips, 1980, 187.

DRAMATIC FOIL   A character in drama who provides a sharp contrast to another character to highlight the latter's views. In SOPHOCLES' *ANTIGONE,* for example, the unwillingness of ISMENE to oppose CREON's edict against the burial of POLYNEICES contrasts sharply with the attitude of her sister, ANTIGONE, who favors burying Polyneices even if it means that she will be executed.

DRAMATIC IRONY   See IRONY.

DREAMS   In drama, dreams are always taken seriously and are often regarded as messages sent by the gods or by the dead. Often dreams point to future events. In AESCHYLUS' *Libation Bearers* (see ORESTEIA), a troubling dream compels CLYTEMNESTRA to send libations to AGAMEMNON's grave. Clytemnestra's dream that she was suckling a snake that drew both blood and milk from her breast was proved to refer to the return of ORESTES and his killing of Clytemnestra. In EURIPIDES' HECABE, the ghost of POLYDORUS sends his mother, HECABE, a dream that leads her to the discovery of his unburied body and points to Polydorus' murder by POLYMESTOR. In some cases, the dreams are interpreted incorrectly. In Aeschylus' PERSIANS, ATOSSA's dream about her son, XERXES, falling from his chariot is downplayed by the CHORUS, but it does come to pass. In Euripides' IPHIGENIA IN TAURIS, IPHIGENIA incorrectly interprets her dream as indicating that Orestes has died. One of the most important remarks about dreams is in SOPHOCLES' OEDIPUS TYRANNOS, when JOCASTA converses with her husband, OEDIPUS, who has told her about an oracle that warned him that he would marry his mother (he does not yet realize it is Jocasta). At lines 980–82, Jocasta tells Oedipus that he should not worry about marrying his mother because many men, in their dreams, have had sexual relations with their mother. Jocasta's remark later contributed to SIGMUND FREUD's theory of the Oedipus complex. As dreams often have important functions in TRAGEDY, comic poets also make use of them in their plays. ARISTOPHANES' WASPS opens with two slaves discussing dreams that they had about CLEONYMUS and CLEON, respectively. In PLAUTUS' MERCATOR, Demipho's dream about two she goats and a monkey parallels the events of the play. In Plautus' AMPHITRUO, the confusion caused by the presence of twins leads some of the characters to think that they or others in the play are dreaming.

BIBLIOGRAPHY
Devereux, G. *Dreams in Greek Tragedy: An Ethno-Psycho-Analytical Study.* Berkeley: University of California Press, 1976.
Lewis, N. *The Interpretation of Dreams and Portents.* Toronto: Hakkert, 1976.
Lieshout, R. G. A. van. *Greeks on Dreams.* Utrecht: HES, 1980.
Nussbaum, M. C. "The 'Oedipus Rex' and the Ancient Unconscious." In *Freud and Forbidden Knowledge.* Edited by P. L. Rudnytsky and E. H. Spitz. New York and London: New York University Press, 1994, 42–71.
Valakas, K. "Dreams and Tragedy: The Problem of Predictions in Euripides' *Iphigenia in Tauris*," *Ariadne* 6 (1993): 109–39.

DRUSUS (CA. 13 B.C.E.–23 C.E.) Julius Drusus was the son of the Roman emperor Tiberius and Vipsania. Drusus had a successful military career and might have succeeded Tiberius as emperor but died of poisoning, of which Drusus' wife, Claudia LIVIA, and her lover, Sejanus, were suspected. [ANCIENT SOURCES: Seneca, *Octavia* 887, 942]

DRYADS See NYMPHS.

DRYAS The father of the Thracian king LYCURGUS. [ANCIENT SOURCES: Sophocles, *Antigone* 955]

DYSCOLUS (OLD CANTANKEROUS, THE BAD-TEMPERED MAN, OR *THE MISANTHROPE*) MENANDER (316 B.C.E.)
This play won first prize at the LENAEA in ATHENS when Demogenes was ARCHON, and its principal actor was Aristodemus of Scarphe. The play's action occurs in a village outside ATHENS called Phyle. On the audience's left is the house of Knemon, a bad-tempered old farmer; on their right is the house of Gorgia, Knemon's stepson. Between the two houses stands a shrine dedicated to PAN and the NYMPHS. A statue of APOLLO stands near Knemon's door.

The PROLOGUE is delivered by Pan, who informs the audience about the bad-tempered Knemon, who married a widow and had a daughter by her. Because Knemon was so unpleasant, his wife eventually left him and went back to live with her son, Gorgias, Knemon's neighbor. Pan tells the audience that he has cast a spell on Sostratus, a rich young man from the city, who has fallen in love with Knemon's daughter, Myrrhine.

After the prologue, Pan returns to his shrine. His exit is followed by the entrance of Sostratus and the PARASITE Chaireas. Sostratus tells Chaireas that he is in love and has sent his huntsman, Pyrrhias, to ask Knemon about his daughter. Soon Pyrrhias himself enters, arriving from Knemon's house, and reports that his encounter with Knemon was unsuccessful—the old man drove him away from the farm with a barrage of clods, stones, and pears. Hearing this, Chaireas volunteers to go to talk to Knemon the next day. After Chaireas exits, Sostratus accuses Pyrrhias of doing something to make Knemon mad, but Pyrrhias swears that he did nothing wrong. Pyrrhias then sees Knemon approach and exits.

Sostratus is fearful as Knemon approaches and moves away from him. Knemon enters and complains about people who go on his land and talk to him. Sostratus hesitantly addresses Knemon, but when the old man maintains his surly attitude, Sostratus decides that he should tell his servant, Getas, who is experienced in such conversations, to talk to Knemon. As Sostratus ponders these matters, Sostratus' daughter enters from Knemon's house and laments that a female servant has just dropped the bucket into the well while drawing water. Sostratus approaches her and offers to fill a jug of water for her in the shrine of the Nymphs. She accepts his offer, and Sostratus soon returns with the water from the shrine. This exchange is seen by Gorgias' servant, Daos, who worries about the young woman's safety and suggests that he should tell Gorgias about this.

The second act opens with the entry of Daos and Gorgias, who scolds his servant because he has not confronted Sostratus about his intentions. As they discuss the situation, Sostratus approaches, unsuccessful in his efforts to find Getas, and decides to knock on Knemon's door. Before he does so, Gorgias suggests that Sostratus is trying to seduce an innocent girl. Sostratus declares that he has nothing but honest intentions toward her; when Gorgias hears this, he offers to help Sostratus. Gorgias suggests that Sostratus help him with some farming so that Knemon will think Sostratus is an industrious country boy rather than a rich, lazy fellow from the city. Sostratus agrees to do whatever is necessary to be with her.

Next, Sikon, a cook who works for Sostratus' mother, carries in a sheep for sacrifice to Pan. Sikon encounters Getas and tells him that his mistress dreamed that Pan was binding Sostratus and making him perform hard labor. Sikon says the sacrifice is being performed to prevent this.

In the third act, Knemon emerges from his house, but because he hates crowds he goes back inside when he sees that Sostratus' mother and her party are approaching. Next, Getas enters from the shrine and indicates that he needs to borrow a pot. When he knocks on Knemon's door, the old man gives him a hostile reception. Sikon also tries the door, but Knemon drives him away. Sostratus then enters exhausted from the hard work. He is soon met by Getas, emerging from the shrine. When Sostratus hears of the sacrifice, he decides to invite Gorgias to the sacrificial feast. After Sostratus exits, Knemon's aged maidservant, Simiche, enters after having dropped her bucket and mattock into their well. An angry Knemon threatens to throw Simiche down the well also. After Knemon drives Simiche into the house, Getas sees Sostratus, Gorgias, and Daos, who are approaching and preparing to attend the sacrificial feast.

The fourth act begins with the appearance of a frantic Simiche, who calls for help, as Knemon has fallen down the well. After Gorgias hears of this, he calls Sostratus out of the shrine and the two men follow Simiche into Knemon's house. Soon Sostratus leaves Knemon's house and reports the efforts to rescue Knemon from the well. Sostratus notes that as he was helping to pull Knemon out of the well, he took the opportunity to lust after Knemon's daughter, in anguish over her father's predicament. The old man is rescued, but when he next appears, he has to be helped from the house. Knemon's experience has caused him to regret his past behavior. Knemon then adopts Gorgias as his son and asks Gorgias to find a husband for Myrrhine. Gorgias quickly arranges to have Sostratus marry her. The act concludes with the arrival of Sostratus' father, Callipides, who has arrived for the sacrificial feast.

In the fifth act, Sostratus pleads with his father to arrange the marriage of Sostratus' sister and Gorgias. Callipides does not want his daughter to marry a poor farmer, but Sostratus eventually wins him over. Gorgias, however, is also reluctant to marry someone who is above his social status, but Sostratus also persuades him to agree. After the arrangements for the marriages are made, the men prepare for a party to celebrate the upcoming marriages. In the next scene, Sikon learns from Getas that Knemon is asleep inside the house and unable to get out of bed. Sikon proposes that Knemon be taken outside Sikon can torment Knemon with requests to borrow various items. Getas then takes a turn and vexes Knemon with requests for rugs and curtains. After Sikon and Getas have a little more fun pestering the old man, they pull him to his feet and try to make him dance. Finally, they carry Knemon into the house to join the others in celebrating.

COMMENTARY

MENANDER'S DYSCOLUS is a play that focuses on character and social status. On one hand, we have the grouchy lower-class Knemon, who desires to be alone. On the other hand, we have affable upper-class Sostratus, who does not want to be alone but must prove he is worthy of marrying Knemon's daughter although he is higher in rank than Knemon socially.

One of the primary themes of Dyscolus is loneliness; intertwined with loneliness is the image of the door. Dyscolus makes use of three doors, one belonging to Knemon, the other belonging to the shrine of Pan and the nymphs, the third belonging to Knemon's stepson; the most used doors are those of Knemon and Pan's shrine. Knemon, who wants to be left alone, hopes to keep people away from his door, whereas the shrine constantly welcomes worshipers through its door. Pyrrhias is the first to be driven from Knemon's door (97) and advises Sostratus to keep away from Knemon's door as well (87). After hearing Knemon's yelling, Sostratus decides to move away from his door (149), and after encountering the grouchy man, who expresses annoyance at Sostratus' proximity to his door (167, 174), Sostratus thinks about having Getas intercede with Knemon on his behalf. The emergence of Knemon's beautiful daughter from the door (188) makes Sostratus delay his exit.

After Sostratus returns from his unsuccessful search for Getas, he decides to knock on Knemon's door (267). Daos, however, prevents him from doing this and he and Gorgias give Sostratus advice on how to win over Knemon. After Sostratus is sent to labor for Knemon, Sikon and Getas enter the shrine. The next time Knemon appears, he emerges from his door and orders his old maidservant to make sure no one enters through it (427). He reverses his command and

demands that she open the door (454) when Sostratus' mother and her party enter the shrine. Knemon experiences further annoyance when Sikon arrives from the shrine and knocks on his door asking to borrow a pot. Once again, Knemon drives a visitor from his door and threatens violence for anyone else he finds near it (482). Sikon will not give up, and, because he considers himself a master in the art of borrowing pots from neighbors, he again knocks at Knemon's door. The "master," however, is again driven away from the door by Knemon and reenters the shrine. When Sostratus returns from his labor, he indicates that he will soon enter the shrine and join in the sacrificial feast.

While people continue to be driven from Knemon's door and take welcome refuge inside the doors to the shrine, an additional and unlikely portal (Knemon's well) begins to become a point of focus near the end of act 3. Earlier in the play, Sostratus and Knemon's daughter had a pleasant encounter there (191). The well becomes rather unpleasant, however, when Simiche drops her bucket and mattock into it. Knemon suggests that Simiche throw herself down the well; Getas wants to lower her down on a rope. Finally, Knemon decides to climb down the well on his own (598) but falls in (625). When Sikon hears, he refuses to go down into the well (634) and returns to the shrine. Eventually, Gorgias rescues Knemon, thus letting Sostratus have his second encounter with Knemon's daughter at the well.

Knemon's near-death experience in the well softens the grouch, and in his next appearance, he asks Gorgias to ask his former wife to come to the house. He realizes that he was wrong to keep Gorgias away from his door (724) and decides to adopt him. This move clears the way for the marriage of Sostratus and Knemon's daughter. Knemon has not completely reformed, however. After Gorgias, his mother, and Knemon's daughter exit the house and prepare to go into the shrine, Gorgias tells Sostratus that Knemon wanted Simiche to go out as well, so that Knemon could be alone (869). When Simiche complies, she declares that he can lie inside the house all alone (874–75). Thus, while everyone else in the play has gone into the shrine or is planning to go there, Knemon remains in his house alone.

Knemon's loneliness is soon shattered by the emergence of Getas and Sikon from the shrine. They decide to have some fun with the man and torment him by knocking on his door and asking to borrow various things. To end his isolation and their torment, Knemon must respond to their knocks. When he does, the two jokers drag the grouch of his house, make him dance, and finally persuade him enter Pan's shrine. Thus, at the end of *Dyscolus*, Knemon's loneliness and isolation end when he can no longer drive people from his door and agrees to enter the divine door that he had scorned for so long.

BIBLIOGRAPHY

Anderson, M. "Knemon's *Hamartia*," *Greece and Rome* 17 (1970): 199–217.

Goldberg, S. M. "The Style and Function of Menander's *Dyskolos* Prologue," *Symbolae Osloenses* 53 (1978): 57–68.

Keuls, E. "Mystery Elements in Menander's *Dyscolus*," *Transactions of the American Philological Association* 100 (1969): 209–20.

Traill, A. E. "Knocking on Knemon's Door: Stagecraft and Symbolism in the *Dyskolos*," *Transactions of the American Philological Association* 131 (2001): 87–108.

Zagagi, N. "Sostratos as a Comic, Over-Active and Impatient Lover: On Menander's Dramatic Art in his Play *Dyskolos*," *Zeitschrift für Papyrologie und Epigraphik* 36 (1979): 39–48.

E

EARTH This goddess was called Gaia or Ge by the Greeks and Tellus or Terra by the Romans. According to Hesiod's *Theogony,* Earth was one of the first divinities in existence. In addition to being the goddess of the earth, she was associated with oracles, and the famous ORACLE at DELPHI was under her control before Apollo's arrival.

Earth produced Sea, Mountains, and Sky (URANUS) without mating with anyone. With the Sea, Earth produced Ceto, Eurybia, NEREUS, Phorcys, and Thaumas. With her son, Uranus, Earth produced numerous offspring, including the CYCLOPES, the Hecatoncheires, and the Titans (among whom were CRONUS and RHEA). When Uranus put his children by Earth back into her womb, Earth made a sickle, with which one of her children, Cronus, castrated Uranus. Blood from Uranus' wound fell onto Earth, who produced the FURIES, GIANTS, and some NYMPHS who inhabited ash trees. Earth is also called the mother of the giants ANTAEUS and TITYUS, TRIPTOLEMUS, and the Athenian king ERICHTHONIUS (after HEPHAESTUS' semen had contact with her).

After the castration of Uranus, Earth's activities seem somewhat contradictory. Both she and Uranus warned Cronus that he would be overthrown by one of his own sons. Earth, however, helped her daughter, Rhea, act against her son, Cronus, by hiding ZEUS (the son who would overthrow Cronus) from his father. After Zeus overthrew Cronus, Earth then turned against Zeus and with the aid of Tartarus (see UNDERWORLD) produced the monster Typhoeus, whom she sent to attack Zeus. When Zeus destroyed Typhoeus, Earth then sent the Giants to attack Zeus and his fellow divinities. The Giants were destroyed with the aid of HERACLES. [ANCIENT SOURCES: Apollodorus, *Library* 1.1.1–5, 1.2.1, 1.2.6, 1.3.6, 1.5.2, 1.6.1–3, 2.1.2, 2.5.11, 3.8.1; Hesiod, *Theogony* 116–87, 233–39, 459–97, 820–22, 881–85; Hyginus, *Fables* 203; Pausanias, 1.2.6, 1.14.3, 5.14.10, 7.25.13, 8.25.8–10, 10.5.6, 10.6.6]

ECBATANA A city (modern Hamadan, Iran) that served as the capital of Media (part of the Persian empire). Ecbatana's location at a high elevation made it a good refuge for the Persian kings seeking to escape the summer heat of SUSA. [ANCIENT SOURCES: Aeschylus, *Persians* 16, 535, 961; Aristophanes, *Acharnians* 64, *Wasps* 1143]

***ECCLESIAZUSAE (WOMEN IN ASSEMBLY)* ARISTOPHANES (392/391 B.C.E.)** The date of the play is not precise and is based on references to contemporary political and military events in it, especially the reference at lines 823–29 to a tax that had recently been proposed by HEURIPPIDES and that had failed. Unlike for many of ARISTOPHANES' other plays, we do not know how *Ecclesiazusae* ranked in competition or at which festival it was staged. The play's action occurs before two houses, one to Blepyros and Praxagora, the other to an unnamed neighbor and his wife, who is also unnamed.

The play's action begins before dawn as PRAXAGORA ("effective in the assembly"), carrying a lamp, emerges from her house to deliver the prologue. She relates that she and the women of Athens had convened at a recent festival, the SCIROPHORIA, and planned to go to the assembly disguised as men. Soon, other women enter, with their husband's cloaks, walking sticks, men's shoes, and false beards. After the women arrive, they put on the clothing and practice talking and behaving as men. When one woman demands to know the details of the plot, Praxagora explains that the men's rule of the city has become so poor that the women should take charge. After all, she argues (as did LYSISTRATA in the play that bears her name), women manage their household efficiently, so they should be able to run the city as well. Because women produce children, they will be sensitive to sending their sons off to war. After some further discussion about what action they will take if certain speakers object to Praxagora's remarks, the women exit for the assembly. In theory, under the new government, all citizens will share everything.

After the women's exit, the chorus, composed of women pretending to be men, approach the assembly. Half the women represent the people of the city, the other half people from the countryside. They complain that in "the good old days" citizens attended the assembly because it was their civic duty, but now they attend merely because they are paid. After the chorus' song, the women exit the orchestra as if going to the assembly. Next, Praxagora's husband, Blepyrus, enters dressed in his wife's clothing. He has left his house to "use the bathroom." Blepyrus is soon met by one of his fellow citizens, to whom he explains (while defecating) that his wife left with his clothing. Both men were planning to go to the assembly, but soon they encounter another citizen, Chremes, who is returning from the assembly. Chremes informs them that the assembly was packed with many pale-skinned men (the disguised women). Chremes relates that one speaker (the disguised Praxagora) proposed that women are better suited to run the government and that the assembly approved this proposal. Chremes also reveals that the men will now perform the duties women usually perform.

After Chremes' exit, the chorus of women return from the assembly. They watch carefully for men, because they worry that their disguises will be discovered. As the chorus remove their manly disguises, they see Praxagora, who is returning from the assembly. After Praxagora removes her disguise, her husband, Blepyrus, emerges from the house. When Blepyrus questions Praxagora about why she left the house and took his clothing, she claims she had to hurry out to help a friend who was giving birth. Praxagora then listens as Blepyrus informs her that the assembly has handed over the government to the women. Praxagora expresses her pleasure and describes some of the benefits that the city will receive with women in charge.

Praxagora goes on to propose that the people should share everything. All goods and property will be deposited in the public treasury and then be redistributed equally. Even marriage and sexual favors will be regulated. People will be required to have sexual relations with unattractive people before they can have relations with attractive people. Children will not know who their parents are, and the entire community will take care of the children; the children, once they have grown up, will take care of any parent who happens to be in need once the parents have become elderly. People will always have plenty of food and clothing; dining will occur at communal banquets; lawsuits, debt, and theft will end. One of the only institutions that will not change is slavery. After Praxagora outlines her proposal, she exits for the AGORA so that she can began to arrange for people to take their property the public treasury and prepare for the first communal banquet. Praxagora also announces that she is going to make sure that prostitutes do not prevent free women from having the first opportunity to sleep with men.

After Praxagora's exit, Blepyrus and Chremes depart to take their property to the public treasury. Some time later, Chremes reappears with his property. He is met by a citizen who refuses to contribute his goods. The two men argue at length about whether the new system of government will work. By the end of their argument, the unnamed citizen has not changed his mind. Their argument is broken off by the arrival of a herald, who announces that the communal banquet is ready and invites everyone to attend. When the reluctant citizen hears this, he, not wanting to be excluded from the banquet, indicates a change of heart. After Chremes exits for the banquet, however, the citizen announces that he wants to find a way to keep his property and still attend the banquet.

In the next EPISODE, an ugly old woman and a pretty young woman enter. Both women are seeking to attract a lover. The two women then sing songs in rivalry to achieve their aim. When a young man approaches, the two women withdraw to watch him. When the young man expresses his interest in finding a beautiful lover, the young woman appears and sings a song to attract him. The young man sings a song that calls for the young woman to come to him. Before the young woman can, the old woman appears and declares that Praxagora's new laws state that the young man must have sexual relations with her before he can go to the young woman. The young man is horrified at this prospect, but the tough old woman begins to drag him off to her house. When the young woman tries to intervene, an even uglier old woman enters and tries to drag the young man away. Then, a third old woman, the ugliest of all, appears and also tries to carry off the young man. Eventually, the three old women drag the young man away.

As the young woman laments the loss of her young lover, Blepyrus and his children, on their way to the communal banquet, approach. The young woman tells Blepyrus that her mistress told her to accompany him to the banquet. After Blepyrus, the young woman, and the children prepare to move off for the banquet, the chorus sing a song asking the judges of the comic contest for victory. They conclude their song by asking Blepyrus to perform a dance. As Blepyrus dances, the chorus sing of all the good food that will be served at the banquet. The play ends with the chorus' urging Blepyrus to hurry off to the banquet and hoping for victory in the comic competition.

COMMENTARY

As did LYSISTRATA, produced almost 20 years earlier, *Ecclesiazusae* deals with women taking over the government of Athens. Since *Lysistrata,* however, Aristophanes' Athens had undergone tremendous turmoil.

The Athenians had lost the PELOPONNESIAN WAR to the Spartans in 404 and the Spartans had made the Athenians dismantle their fortifications and their powerful fleet. Many Athenians had died during the oppressive regime of the Thirty Tyrants whom SPARTA had installed after the war. These tyrants were overthrown within a year and democracy was restored, but Athens continued to have problems with Sparta, and when *Ecclesiazusae* was staged the Athenians were still involved in military hostilities with the Spartans.

Thus, as did both the Athenians themselves and *Lysistrata* of 411, the Athenians and *Ecclesiazusae* of 392/391 lacked their former vigor and exuberance. Praxagora, though an admirable figure, does not seem to have quite the same spark as Lysistrata. The attacks on and caricatures of contemporary political figures, which were so common in Aristophanes' early plays, have disappeared to a great extent and the role of the chorus has been diminished. These and other factors have led some scholars to describe *Ecclesiazusae* as a transitional play between the Old COMEDY of such plays as ACHARNIANS and KNIGHTS and the New Comedy of MENANDER, which would emerge in the last quarter of the fourth century B.C.E. Thus, along with WEALTH, *Ecclesiazusae* is often cited as an example of Middle Comedy.

Although *Ecclesiazusae* has often been classified as a transitional play, it still manifests many of the same elements found in Aristophanes' earlier plays, such as the unlikely hero (or heroine), the fantastic plan to deal with a pressing social issue or crisis, and the implementation of and challenges to that fantastic plan. Also, as in many Aristophanic plays, the action ends with the enjoyment of food, drink, and sex of those who embrace the hero or heroine's reforms.

Given the prominence of women in the play, *Ecclesiazusae* is most comparable to such plays as *Thesmophoriazusae* and *Lysistrata.* EURIPIDES, however, and not the women, is the focal point of *Thesmophoriazusae.* The governmental change that occurs in *Lysistrata* is most comparable to that in *Ecclesiazusae.* In contrast, in *Ecclesiazusae* the motivation for the overthrow of the government differs from that in *Lysistrata.* In *Lysistrata,* the women take over the government to create peace in all of Greece. In *Ecclesiazusae,* the women persuade the men to hand over the government to them because men cannot manage the city's affairs properly. The effects of Praxagora's revolution will be local, not national. In addition, because the men in *Ecclesiazusae* offer little opposition to Praxagora's revolution, we do not find the battles of the sexes that occur throughout the *Lysistrata*. Finally, unlike in *Lysistrata*, Praxagora's reforms in *Ecclesiazusae* cause revolutionary changes in the laws (*nomoi*) of the city.

In *Lysistrata*, the major crisis revolves around the effects of war on the whole of Greece. In *Ecclesiazusae*, there is much greater concern with the basic needs of life (food, shelter, and clothing) in a single city. The word root *deipn-*, which appears in Greek words meaning "dine" and "dinner," occurs 24 times in *Ecclesiazusae*. This same word root occurs no more than nine times in any other Aristophanic play. Unlike in Aristophanes' BIRDS, in which the hero abandons Athens and builds a fantastic new city in the clouds, which will exclude the elements that make Athens unbearable, in *Ecclesiazusae* the heroine has a fantastic plan to reshape Athens and allow all its elements to coexist.

Whereas Lysistrata's goal was to save Greece (41, 525), Praxagora aims to save the city (Greek: *polis*). Praxagora proposes that the women take over the city's affairs so that they can do the city some good (107–8). Praxagora is troubled by everything that is going on in the city (175) and feels that women should run affairs because they already manage households efficiently (210–12). When the assembly begins, the topic of how to save the city and its citizens is immediately taken up (396–97, 414). After a proposal to provide clothing and bedding to the poor is made, the disguised Praxagora makes her proposal about handing over the city to the women (430), and this proposal wins the day because it is the only solution that has never been tried (455–56).

The men worry that conditions will change for them once the women are in charge, but Chremylus suggests that the men should cooperate with the women's plans, as they will be of advantage to the city (471–72). Once Praxagora informs the men of her plans of how to rule the city, much of which involves the fulfillment of needs for clothing and basic finances (565–66), the men indicate that they are willing to agree, provided that Praxagora's proposed reforms turn out successfully.

At least one man appears on the scene to argue against Praxagora's plan and points out that it was not long ago that HEURIPPIDES had had a plan to save the city (824). This dissenting voice, however, is reminded that men were in charge of the city then, but that the women will "now" manage the city's affairs (830–31). Now that the women are in charge, everyone's basic needs will be met. The remainder of the play, while gratifying the audience with scenes of amusing sexual humor, most often focuses on the banquet of which all cooperative citizens will partake. The warring factions alluded to in the first part of the play, such as the rich and the farmers (198), will now be found side by side at the communal banquet that Praxagora's reforms have provided for the city.

Thus, although *Ecclesiazusae* itself may lack the spark of *Lysistrata* and other plays, the communistic type of government proposed in the play probably predated a similar form of government described in the fifth book of Plato's *Republic*. Thus, "it may well be claimed that *Ecclesiazusae* has been in the long run the most intellectually influential of all ancient comedies" (Sommerstein).

BIBLIOGRAPHY

Foley, H. P. "The Female Intruder Reconsidered: Women in Aristophanes, *Lysistrata* and *Ecclesiazusae*," *Classical Philology* 77 (1982): 1–21.

Rothwell, K. S. *Politics and Persuasion in Aristophanes' Ecclesiazusae.* Leiden: Brill, 1990.

Sommerstein, A. H. *The Comedies of Aristophanes.* Vol. 10, *Ecclesiazusae.* Warminster, U.K.: Aris & Phillips, 1998, 144.

Taaffe, L. K. "The Illusion of Gender Disguise in Aristophanes' *Ecclesiazusae*," *Helios* 18 (1991): 91–112.

Ussher, R. G. *Aristophanes: Ecclesiazusae.* Oxford: Clarendon Press, 1973.

ECCYCLEMA (EKKUKLEMA)

Also called the *exostra*, the *eccyclema*, as its name ("that which is wheeled out") indicates, was a wooden platform on some sort of rollers used in the Greek theater. This platform, probably made of wood and perhaps no more than two square meters in size, allowed something and/or someone behind the SKENE to be moved into the view of the spectators (cf. Pollux 4.128). For example, because the death of a person typically occurred out of the spectators' sight on the ancient stage, the corpse could be taken out by using the *eccyclema*. Whether AESCHYLUS made use of the *eccyclema* is debated; its use is clear in ARISTOPHANES' *ACHARNIANS* (425 B.C.E.). When DICAEOPOLIS goes to the house of the playwright EURIPIDES, he calls for the poet to wheel himself out (line 408), to which Euripides responds, "I'll wheel myself out" (*ekkuklesomai*). Another explicit reference to its use occurs in Aristophanes' *THESMOPHORIAZUSAE* (411 B.C.E.). At line 96, in response to Mnesilochus' question "What sort of man is he [Agathon]?" Euripides says, "That's him; the one being wheeled out" (*ekkukloumenos*).

BIBLIOGRAPHY
Csapo, E., and W. J. Slater. *The Context of Ancient Drama.* Ann Arbor: University of Michigan Press, 1995, 270–72.
Dale, A. M. "Seen and Unseen on the Greek Stage." In *Collected Papers.* Cambridge: Cambridge University Press, 1969, 119–29.
Walton, J. M. *Living Greek Theatre.* New York: Greenwood Press, 1987, 22.

ECHINUS A town on the coast of northeastern Greece on the shore opposite the northwestern end of EUBOEA. The Spartans controlled Echinus when ARISTOPHANES' *LYSISTRATA* was produced in 411 B.C.E. [ANCIENT SOURCES: Aristophanes, *Lysistrata* 1169]

ECHION When CADMUS planted dragon's teeth near the future site of the town of THEBES, a crop of armed men sprang up from the ground. Cadmus threw a stone at these men, and they began to fight one another. Five survived the battle: Chthonius, Hyperenor, Pelorus, Udaeus, and Echion. Echion helped Cadmus establish his town and because of Echion's valor, Cadmus rewarded him with marriage to his daughter AGAVE, by whom Echion became the father of PENTHEUS. Echion does not appear as a character in any surviving ancient dramas, although his name is frequently mentioned in EURIPIDES' *BACCHAE*. [ANCIENT SOURCES: Aeschylus, fragment 731a Mette; Apollodorus, *Library* 3.4.1–2; Ovid, *Metamorphoses* 3.1–137; Pausanias, 9.5.3–4]

BIBLIOGRAPHY
Mette, H. J. *Die Fragmente der Tragödien des Aischylos.* Berlin: Akademie-Verlag, 1959.

ECHO Echo was a talkative NYMPH who had a sexual affair with ZEUS. HERA cursed Echo by allowing her only to repeat speech she heard. Echo fell in love with NARCISSUS, who rejected her advances. So lovesick was Echo that her body wasted away to the point that only her voice remained. Echo's voice is heard in ARISTOPHANES' *THESMOPHORIAZUSAE*, in which she echoes the words of the captive Mnesilochus and his guardian, a Scythian archer. Echo's presence in *Thesmophoriazusae* parodies her appearance in EURIPIDES' *ANDROMEDA*, in which she would have echoed the title character. The comic poet Eubulus wrote an *Echo* of which a single fragment (regarding the approach of a beautiful bride) survives (fragment 35 Kock). [ANCIENT SOURCES: Aristophanes, *Thesmophoriazusae* 1056–96; Ovid, *Metamorphoses* 3.339–510]

BIBLIOGRAPHY
Kock, T. *Comicorum Atticorum Fragmenta.* Vol. 2. Leipzig: Teubner, 1884.

EDONIANS The Edonians were a Thracian tribe who lived near the river Strymon. AESCHYLUS wrote an *Edonians* (fragments 57–67 Radt) that may have dealt with LYCURGUS' rejection of DIONYSUS and the subsequent destruction of Lycurgus by Dionysus.

BIBLIOGRAPHY
Griffith, J. "The Myth of Lycurgus, King of the Edonian Thracians, in *Literature and Art.*" In *Ancient Bulgaria.* Vol. I. Papers presented to the International Symposium on the Ancient History and Archaeology of Bulgaria, University of Nottingham, 1981. Edited by A. G. Poulter. Nottingham, U.K.: University of Nottingham Press, 1983, 217–32.

EGYPT From the perspective of the ancient Greeks and Romans, Egypt consisted of the northeastern half of what is modern Egypt. According to legend, the wanderings of IO began in Greece and ended in northern Egypt, and one of her son EPAPHUS' descendants AEGYPTUS, gave his name to the country. Aegyptus' 50 sons later pursued the daughters of their uncle,

DANAUS, to Greece. Thus, the Egyptian descendants of the Greek Io eventually returned to Greece, and Danaus' descendants became a dominant presence in Greece.

EURIPIDES' HELEN is set in Egypt, and several Greek playwrights (including Euripides) wrote plays about BUSIRIS, a mythical Egyptian king. Several Greek dramatists wrote plays entitled *Egyptians* (*Aiguptoi*). The Greek tragedian PHRYNICHUS wrote an *Egyptians* (fragment 1 Snell) that may have been about the same subject as AESCHYLUS' SUPPLIANT WOMEN. Aeschylus wrote an *Egyptians,* of which only a single word (Zagreus; another name for HADES) is extant (fragment 5 Radt). The Greek comic poet Antiphanes wrote an *Egyptians,* only a single word of which survives (fragment 17 Kock 2). A single four-line fragment—dealing with the futility of worshiping Egyptian gods—survives of Timocles' *Egyptians* (fragment 1 Kock 2). The comic poet Callias wrote an *Egyptian,* of which only the title is extant (fragment 1 Kock 1).

BIBLIOGRAPHY

Kock, T. *Comicorum Atticorum Fragmenta.* Vol. 2. Leipzig: Teubner, 1884.

Radt, S. *Tragicorum Graecorum Fragmenta.* Vol. 3. Göttingen, Ger.: Vandenhoeck & Ruprecht, 1985.

Snell, B. *Tragicorum Graecorum Fragmenta.* Vol. 1. Göttingen, Ger.: Vandenhoeck & Ruprecht, 1971.

EILEITHYIA   The daughter of ZEUS and HERA, Eileithyia is goddess of childbirth. Her name is related to the Greek noun *eleuthia* (the coming): This goddess visits women who are in labor. [ANCIENT SOURCES: Aristophanes, *Ecclesiazusae* 369, *Lysistrata* 742; Seneca, *Agamemnon* 385, *Medea* 2, 61]

BIBLIOGRAPHY

Henderson, J. *Aristophanes: Lysistrata.* Oxford: Clarendon Press, 1987, 166.

EISODOS   See PARODOS (2).

ELECTRA   One of the daughters of AGAMEMNON and CLYTEMNESTRA, Electra was the sister of ORESTES, IPHIGENIA, and Chrysothemis. After Iphigenia was sacrificed at AULIS and Clytemnestra's affair with AEGISTHUS began to unfold, the lives of Electra and Orestes were at risk. Some sources say that Electra, who was several years older than Orestes, helped the young Orestes avoid being killed by Aegisthus and Clytemnestra by smuggling Orestes out of ARGOS and sending him to stay with his uncle, Strophius of Phocis. With Orestes away from home, Electra seems to have felt the brunt of her evil stepfather Aegisthus' abuse. To prevent Electra from producing offspring who might one day rise up against Aegisthus, either she is not allowed to marry or, as EURIPIDES' ELECTRA presents it, she is married to a local peasant so that she will not produce a son of noble blood (in this play Euripides considers the issue of whether nobility is a result of nature or social status). In addition to the difficulties connected with her marital status or lack thereof, Electra grows to hate her mother. In Euripides' *Electra* and SOPHOCLES' ELECTRA especially, this hatred becomes apparent as she argues with her mother about why Clytemnestra killed Agamemnon.

Given her hatred of Clytemnestra, Electra supports Orestes in his efforts to kill Aegisthus and Clytemnestra. How much Electra helps him in the effort to kill them depends on the source. In AESCHYLUS' LIBATION BEARERS (see ORESTEIA) and Sophocles' *Electra,* Electra offers verbal support to Orestes. In *Libation Bearers,* she is inside the house when the killings take place, but she does not speak any lines in the second half of the play. In Sophocles' play, Electra informs her sister, Chrysothemis, of her plan to kill Aegisthus, but this plan never comes to pass, and when Orestes kills Clytemnestra, Electra remains outside the house. As for Aegisthus' death, Sophoclean Electra urges Orestes to kill him, but the text gives no indication that she will actually take a physical part in the killing. In Euripides' *Electra,* the title character is not present when Orestes kills Aegisthus. Euripidean Electra plays an active role, however, in her mother's death, as she lures Clytemnestra to her (Electra's) home under the pretext that Clytemnestra is to participate in a birth ritual and thus brings her to Orestes, who is waiting inside. Electra also follows her mother into the house, so the audience is well aware of her presence when Clytemnestra dies. Furthermore, Euripides' Electra states that once inside she urged Orestes to kill

Clytemnestra and notes that her hand was beside Orestes' when he did so (1224–26). In Euripides' *Orestes,* Electra also says she held the sword that killed Clytemnestra (1235).

Electra's actions after the deaths of Aegisthus and Clytemnestra also differ in the sources, and, in Euripides' case, her actions differ from one play to the next. At the end of Euripides' *Electra,* the Dioscuri (CASTOR AND POLLUX) dissolve her marriage to the peasant and arrange for her to marry Orestes' comrade, PYLADES. They also inform her that she will go to Pylades' home in Phocis. In Euripides' *Orestes,* the action of which takes place seven days after the deaths of Aegisthus and Clytemnestra, Electra is still engaged to marry Pylades, but she remains in Argos to care for Orestes, as his torment by the Furies has exhausted him and the people of Argos have prevented them from leaving the town and are working to bring about his death. Eventually, the people of Argos sentence both Orestes and Electra to take their own life, but they (along with Pylades) decide to try to kill HELEN. Electra's role in that plot will be to help take Helen's daughter HERMIONE as a hostage, an action in which Electra successfully and ruthlessly participates. When APOLLO and the gods thwart the effort to kill Helen, Apollo reestablishes the planned union between Electra and Pylades and states that a fortunate life awaits him (1658–59).

Euripides, however, in his *Orestes,* postpones the wedded bliss of Electra and Pylades, which Apollo predicts. In Euripides' IPHIGENIA IN TAURIS, Pylades travels with Orestes to Tauris to retrieve a statue of Artemis. With Orestes gone, Aegisthus' son ALETES had taken over the kingdom. When Electra went to DELPHI to consult the ORACLE, she encountered Iphigenia, who had returned from Tauris with Orestes and Pylades. At Delphi, someone mistakenly told Electra that Iphigenia had killed Orestes. Electra, grabbing a firebrand from Apollo's altar, tried to strike Iphigenia, whom she did not realize was her long-lost sister. Fortunately, Orestes arrived in time to prevent her. Iphigenia went on to serve as a priestess of ARTEMIS at Brauron, and Electra returned to Argos with Orestes. Once back in Argos, Orestes killed Aletes, and Pylades and Electra, who had two sons, Medon and STROPHIUS, appear to have lived happily ever after. [ANCIENT SOURCES: Aeschylus,

Libation Bearers (see ORESTEIA); Euripides, *Electra;* Hyginus, *Fables* 109, 122, 240; Pausanias, 2.16.7; Sophocles, *Electra*]

BIBLIOGRAPHY
Halporn, J. W. "The Skeptical Electra," *Harvard Studies in Classical Philology* 87 (1983): 101–18.

ELECTRA EURIPIDES (CA. 415 B.C.E.)

The play's date has been deduced from statistical analyses of EURIPIDES' metrical patterns and a possible allusion to the SICILIAN EXPEDITION at lines 1347–48. The play deals with the same event as AESCHYLUS' *Libation Bearers* (see ORESTEIA), the killing of AEGISTHUS and CLYTEMNESTRA. Euripides, however, differs in his treatment of the story in numerous places. The play's setting remains ARGOS, as in Aeschylus' *Libation Bearers,* but instead of the grave of AGAMEMNON and his palace, the area outside the hut of an unnamed peasant and his wife, who happens to be Electra, is the site of the action. Euripides' introduction of the peasant adds a different dimension to the story. Unlike Aeschylus' distressed but regal Electra, a princess in rags, who lives in the hut of a peasant with whom her marriage has been arranged to prevent her begetting a noble son, is presented by Euripides to the audience. Furthermore, as the peasant reveals in the monologue that opens the play, he has not had sexual relations with Electra because of respect for her nobility and in consideration of his own impoverished condition.

In contrast to Aeschylus' Electra, who takes libations to her father's grave, the Euripidean Electra begins the play prepared to perform the menial task of collecting the daily water. After Electra sets out for the spring, ORESTES and PYLADES appear. Orestes' first glimpse of his sister, Electra, whom he mistakes for a maidservant, occurs as she is returning from the spring. Orestes and Pylades move into a hiding place to watch Electra, who laments the nature of her life. Soon Electra is joined by a chorus of women who live in the Argive countryside, in contrast with Aeschylus' chorus of women from the royal palace. The Argive women invite Electra to Hera's temple with the other maidens to attend a sacrifice, but Electra claims she is too pitiful and has nothing to wear.

Electra's conversation with the chorus is cut off when she sees Orestes and Pylades. Orestes recognizes Electra as his sister but does not reveal his identity to her. He does tell her, however, that he knows Orestes is alive. Electra tells Orestes of her wretched life and asks that he inform Orestes of it. Soon Electra's husband returns from his work, and the courteous peasant invites the men into his home for a meal. Electra criticizes her husband for inviting noblemen into their hut when they have little to offer. She then sends him off to find an old servant of her father's so that he can provide food suitable for Orestes and Pylades.

After the peasant departs, the chorus sing an ode about ACHILLES and his wondrous armor. One of the figures described on the shield is Perseus' triumph over the Gorgon Medusa, a reference that foreshadows the similarity between Orestes' killing of his mother and Perseus' killing of Medusa. The chorus note that HECTOR saw Achilles' shield before he died, and the corselet's depiction of BELLEROPHON and Pegasus triumphing over the CHIMAERA. The chorus end their ode with their hope eventually to witness the death of HELEN, whose adultery caused the deaths of many noble warriors.

After the choral ode, Agamemnon's aged tutor enters with food and drink for the guests. In front of the hut, Electra meets him and the old man tells her that on his way he passed by Agamemnon's grave, where he saw a sacrificed sheep and a lock of hair. The discussion between the old man and Electra that follows pokes fun at the tokens of recognition used by Aeschylus in *Libation Bearers* (see ORESTEIA). In Aeschylus' play, Electra had compared the lock of hair to her own. When Euripides' old man suggests that Electra make such a comparison, Electra dismisses that idea as foolish. When the old man suggests that Electra compare the footprints on the grave with her own (another comparison made by Aeschylus' Electra), Euripides' Electra again rejects the idea as foolish—men have bigger feet than women. Finally, the old man suggests that if Electra were to be face to face with Orestes, she might be able to recognize him by clothing he wore when he was a little boy—the means by which Electra finally does recognize him in *Libation Bearers*. Electra again dismisses this notion: A person's body grows, but one's clothes do not. At this point, the old man says he wants

to question the two strangers about Orestes. When Orestes and Pylades emerge from the hut, the old man quickly recognizes Orestes by a scar on his brow.

After expressions of joy by Electra and the chorus, Orestes and Electra immediately begin planning their revenge. The old man gives Orestes advice on how and where to approach Aegisthus, while Electra informs Orestes and the old man about how she will trick Clytemnestra into entering her hut.

In contrast to Aeschylus' *Libation Bearers* (see ORESTEIA), in which Aegisthus' death barely receives mention, Euripides' drama has a detailed description of his death. Euripides places Aegisthus not in his palace, as Aeschylus does, but in the countryside preparing to make a sacrifice to the nymphs. In *Libation Bearers,* Orestes altered his speech and claimed to have news of Orestes' death to gain access to the palace. Euripides also makes Orestes deceptive. In *Electra,* a messenger reports that Orestes saw Aegisthus while he was making sacrifice. Aegisthus invited Orestes and Pylades to join in the sacrifice. Orestes told Aegisthus that he and Pylades were Thessalians, on their way to the river Alphaeus to sacrifice to Zeus of Olympia. When slaughtering the sacrificial victim posed difficulty for Aegisthus' man, Orestes stepped forward and killed the beast quickly and expertly. Upon inspecting the victim's entrails, Aegisthus was disturbed by irregularities in the animal's internal organs, which he interpreted as an omen of Orestes' presence. At this point, Orestes struck Aegisthus dead. After hearing the messenger's report of Aegisthus' death, Electra and the chorus hail Orestes as if he were a victor in an athletic competition.

Clytemnestra's death, which occurs next, is also treated differently in *Electra* and in *Libation Bearers.* Euripides makes Electra much more involved in her mother's death. Whereas Aeschylus had made Orestes the primary deceiver, Euripides gives Electra the spotlight in his play, as she lures Clytemnestra to her hut with a false story about having her mother offer sacrifice for Electra's fictitious newborn child.

When Clytemnestra arrives at the hut, she and Electra argue about Clytemnestra's killing of Agamemnon. Clytemnestra tries to justify her actions, but Electra pleads her father's case. Eventually, Clytemnestra enters the hut, where Orestes is waiting. After Clytemnestra enters, the chorus listen as Clytemnestra's cries from within the hut are soon heard. Some members of the chorus express pity for the woman killed by her children; other members suggest that Clytemnestra got what she deserved for killing her husband. Next, Electra and Orestes emerge from the house. Orestes is horrified that he has killed both Aegisthus and Clytemnestra. Both Orestes and Electra wonder how they will be received by society now that they have killed their mother. The chorus express some criticism of Electra for forcing Orestes to kill Clytemnestra and wonder how she could have endured watching her mother die. Electra notes that she held Orestes' hand while he stabbed his mother with the sword.

As does the rest of the play, Euripides' conclusion differs significantly from Aeschylus', in which Orestes hastily departs as soon as he perceives that the FURIES are beginning to torment him. Euripides ends his play with an epiphany by CASTOR AND POLLUX, the now-divine brothers of Helen and Clytemnestra. Castor and Polydeuces criticize Apollo's command to kill Clytemnestra as unwise. They also dissolve the marriage of Electra and the peasant and arrange the union of Electra and Pylades. They announce Orestes' torment by the Furies, his eventual journey to ATHENS to seek ATHENA's protection, his ultimate acquittal after a trial in the AREOPAGUS, and the incorporation of the Furies into Athenian worship. Unlike Aeschylus, however, Euripides has Castor and Pollux announce that Orestes will settle in the region of Arcadia and have a city named after him. The divine twins also state that Aegisthus will be buried in Argos, and Helen and Menelaus will bury Clytemnestra. They then tell Pylades to take Electra and the peasant with him to PHOCIS, and for Pylades to reward the peasant handsomely.

Although the appearance of divinity and their pronouncements usually lead to a quick conclusion to a Euripidean drama, in *Electra,* the chorus ask Castor and Polydeuces why they, as Clytemnestra's brothers, did not save Clytemnestra. They answer that Apollo's oracle and Necessity could not be averted. Castor and Polydeuces then reiterate that both Electra and Orestes will have to go into exile and express pity that brother and sister must be parted after so brief a reunion. As a tearful Electra and Orestes depart, Castor and Polydeuces state that they will leave to assist ships sailing for SICILY.

COMMENTARY

As evidenced by the preceding paragraphs, Euripides' *Electra* provides us with an opportunity to compare how a later playwright dealt with the material of an earlier playwright (here, Aeschylus). Scholars have also been challenged to determine whether SOPHOCLES' *Electra* was influenced by Euripides' play or vice versa. This question has not been settled, however, because neither play can be dated securely and the dramas are thought to have been staged within a decade of each other.

Another noteworthy aspect of Euripides' *Electra* is its concern with the violation of ritual or civic institutions. As in several other plays, Euripides likes to involve his leading characters in rituals or institutions that have been disrupted or perverted. The death of Aegisthus occurs while he is making a sacrifice to some NYMPHS and Orestes slaughters Aegisthus with a blade that was meant for the sacrificial victim.

In addition to the killing of Aegisthus during a sacrificial ritual, Euripides has Electra involved in a marriage that runs contrary to custom and ritual. The marriage was arranged by the man who murdered her father with the aim of making sure that Electra did not produce a noble son who could grow up to avenge his grandfather's death. Electra's marriage is made even more strange because her husband has not had sexual relations with her. Not only will Electra not have noble children, she will apparently not have any children with her peasant husband. Unlike in modern U.S. culture, in which it is not uncommon for husband and wife to choose not to have children, in a Greek household this choice would have been virtually unthinkable. Thus, Electra's marital status is ambiguous at best: She is a wife, yet not a wife. When the chorus of Argive women enter, they invite Electra to a sacrifice and note that all of the maidens (*parthenikai,* 174) are going to go to Hera's temple. The chorus' use of the term *parthenikai* calls attention to Electra's strange marriage. Twice in her husband's opening monologue, the peasant notes that Electra was still a *parthenos* (44, 51), a maiden or virgin. Electra refuses to go to the temple with the other maidens, however. Not only does Electra not participate in the usual activities of other married women; she also does not participate in the activities of other unmarried women. Later in the play, Electra perverts another custom of married women. Electra lures her mother to her house by asking her to help her with a purification ritual that would have been performed after the birth of a child. As a virgin, however, Electra could not have a child. Thus, lured to the house with a pretense she will assist with a purification ritual, Clytemnestra is killed by Orestes and Electra.

In addition to the perversion of ritual in the play, we find a concern with the question of what it means to be noble. In the first half of the play, Euripides introduces into the story the figure of the peasant, whom the audience will quickly admire for his work ethic, his reverence for the custom of hospitality, and his respect for a wife who seems to have done little to merit it. As noted, Aegisthus married Electra to the peasant because he feared she would produce a child of noble blood (26) who would avenge Aegisthus' killing of Agamemnon. The peasant is from a "good" family, but he himself says that poverty negates the benefits of a noble birth (37–38; see also 362–63). Electra echoes his comments later as she describes her husband as poor, but noble (253). After hearing Electra's description of the peasant, Orestes agrees that he appears noble and should be rewarded (262).

After Orestes meets the peasant, he fully recognizes the nobility of the man and remarks that one cannot determine a person's nobility by one's parents, wealth, clothing, or home and implies that nobility should be judged only after one meets a person and observes the way he or she behaves. Orestes declares that the peasant may be one of the common people, but his character shows him to be one of the best (382). When the peasant invites Orestes and Pylades into his hut for a meal, Electra objects because the two strangers are far above the peasant's social level. The peasant persists, however, and says that if they are as noble as they seem to be (406), then they will be comfortable in a hut or in a palace. Surely, this peasant is the noblest individ-

ual in the play and arguably the noblest in all of Euripides' surviving works.

By establishing the peasant as a model of nobility, Euripides invites the audience to compare his nobility with the supposed nobility of Electra, Orestes, Clytemnestra, or Aegisthus, all of whom were the offspring of nobles or kings and were born in palaces. Thus, Euripides prompts the audience to ask, Just how noble are these so-called nobles? In the case of Orestes, Electra regards him as a nobleman (528). The old man (played by the same actor who played the peasant) observes that Orestes and Pylades appear to be nobly born, but that some who are noble are wicked (550–51). After this point, however, references to nobility are largely absent and for the most part Euripides leaves the audience to judge the characters by their actions. Aegisthus invites Orestes to participate in a sacrifice to some nymphs but then is slaughtered by him. Clytemnestra is lured into the peasant's hut under false pretenses and is cut down by Orestes and Electra. Eventually, Orestes and Electra's maternal uncles, Castor and Pollux, appear and declare somewhat cryptically that Clytemnestra's punishment was just, but that their actions in the matter were not just (1244). Castor and Pollux go on to explain the various trials and tribulations that Orestes will face, but we should also note the provisions they make for the peasant. Not only do they free him from marriage to Electra (1249–50), but they also declare that Pylades must take him to his (Pylades') native land and make the peasant a rich man. Thus, the reward for the peasant's nobility is perhaps the finest given in Greek TRAGEDY: He is freed of his connection with the house of Atreus.

BIBLIOGRAPHY
Arnott, W. G. "Double the Vision: A Reading of Euripides' *Electra*," *Greece & Rome* 28 (1981): 179–92.
Cropp, M. J. *Euripides: Electra.* Warminster, U.K.: Aris & Phillips, 1988.
Denniston, J. D. *Euripides: Electra.* Oxford: Clarendon Press, 1954.
Halporn, J. W. "The Skeptical Electra," *Harvard Studies in Classical Philology* 87 (1983): 101–18.
Raeburn, David. "The Significance of Stage Properties in Euripides' *Electra*," *Greece & Rome* 47, no. 2 (2000): 149–68.

ELECTRA SOPHOCLES (BETWEEN 420 AND 410 B.C.E.)   The date of SOPHOCLES' play is uncertain; scholars generally agree that it was written about the same time as EURIPIDES' ELECTRA, but whether Sophocles' or Euripides' play appeared first is a matter of debate. The play deals with the same events as AESCHYLUS' *Libation Bearers* (see ORESTEIA)—the killing of AEGISTHUS and CLYTEMNESTRA—but Sophocles, as does Euripides, dramatizes the events in a different way than Aeschylus. As Aeschylus does and Euripides does not, Sophocles sets his play at AGAMEMNON's palace at MYCENAE. Sophocles' prologue also differs from those of Aeschylus and Euripides, in that ORESTES' tutor leads in Orestes and PYLADES, whereas in Aeschylus' *Agamemnon* Orestes is sent to live with Strophius of PHOCIS. Sophocles' Tutor informs the audience that it was he who took Orestes away from Mycenae on the day that Agamemnon was killed. The Tutor also states that he raised Orestes to manhood.

Orestes tells the Tutor that he must find out what is happening at Agamemnon's palace and then report to him and Pylades. Orestes tells the Tutor to pretend that he is Pantheus of Phocis, one of Aegisthus and Clytemnestra's friends, and that Orestes has died in a chariot accident at the Pythian games. This method of approaching Aegisthus and Clytemnestra differs from that of both Aeschylus and Euripides, as Aeschylus' Orestes disguises his voice and informs Clytemnestra that Orestes has died in an unspecified way and Euripides' Orestes approaches Aegisthus pretending to be a traveler from Thessaly and does not mention Orestes' death. Sophocles' Orestes, however, tells the Tutor that he and Pylades will make an offering at Agamemnon's grave and then take back to the palace a bronze urn, which supposedly contains Orestes' ashes.

Before the Tutor, Orestes, and Pylades exit, they hear the sound of lamentation from inside the palace. As they leave, Electra enters from the palace and laments the woes that have fallen upon her since the death of Agamemnon. The chorus of Mycenaean women, who sympathize with Electra's plight, soon join her. They reveal that Electra has two sisters, Chrysothemis and Iphianassa, who are alive, and they wonder where Orestes may be. Electra hopes that Orestes will return, and the chorus urge her not to give up hope. As Euripides' Electra does, Sophocles' Electra indicates that she lives a life of poverty, but she has not been forced into marriage, as Euripides' Electra has. Sophocles' Electra continues to talk about the oppressive behavior of Aegisthus and Clytemnestra and informs the chorus that Aegisthus is presently away from the home. When the chorus hear this, they ask about news of Orestes. Electra says she has his promises that he will come, but that they are only promises.

Next, Electra's sister, Chrysothemis, emerges from the palace and criticizes Electra for her bitter lamentation. As does Ismene in Sophocles' ANTIGONE, Chrysothemis provides a stark contrast to Electra. Electra responds by condemning Chrysothemis' obedience to Aegisthus and Clytemnestra. As is Antigone, Electra is a woman of action, whereas Chrysothemis, like Ismene, is a woman of words only. After the chorus intervene to end the quarrel, Chrysothemis informs Electra that (as with Antigone) a decree of death has been passed against her, and (as with Antigone) Electra will be imprisoned alive. As Antigone does, Electra boldly faces her doom, in the face of Chrysothemis' advice to be obedient to Aegisthus and Clytemnestra.

When Chrysothemis turns to leave, Electra notices that her sister has some offerings. Chrysothemis tells Electra that they are libations sent by Clytemnestra for Agamemnon's grave. Unlike Aeschylus' Electra, who takes libations to the grave on Clytemnestra's behalf in *Libation Bearers* (see ORESTEIA), Sophocles' Chrysothemis takes the libations. Furthermore, Sophocles changes the content of the dream that prompted the Aeschylean Clytemnestra to send the libations. In contrast to Aeschylus, whose Clytemnestra dreams that she is suckling a snake that draws blood from her breast, Sophocles' Clytemnestra says she has dreamed that Agamemnon has returned to life and that his scepter, which Aegisthus was carrying, sprouted into a bough that provided shade for Mycenae. When Electra hears this dream, she persuades Chrysothemis to put away the libations and take instead a lock of her own hair, as well as a lock of Electra's and her girdle. Chrysothemis agrees to Electra's request and departs for the grave. After Chrysothemis' exit, the chorus sing an ode in which they predict that vengeance is not far away, and they lament the generations of sorrow that Mycenae has witnessed.

After the choral ode, Clytemnestra enters from the palace and addresses Electra, whereas in Aeschylus' *Libation Bearers* Clytemnestra and Electra do not engage in dialogue onstage. Clytemnestra reproaches Electra for her treatment of her and defends her own part in the killing of Agamemnon. Clytemnestra claims her actions were performed in retaliation for Agamemnon's sacrifice of their daughter Iphigenia. Electra responds by defending her father's sacrifice, saying that ARTEMIS gave Agamemnon no other choice. Electra also points out that Clytemnestra has since given birth to Aegisthus' children. The two argue further, and eventually Clytemnestra threatens Electra with punishment when Aegisthus returns. Next, Clytemnestra prays to Apollo and asks for her own safety in light of her recent dream and in the face of Electra's hatred.

After Clytemnestra's prayer, the Tutor, pretending to be a messenger from Phanoteus of Phocis, enters and informs Clytemnestra of Orestes' death. The Tutor gives an elaborate description of Orestes' death in a chariot race at Delphi. After Clytemnestra hears this news, she is torn between joy and grief. She tells the Tutor that she wants proof of Orestes' death. As Clytemnestra expresses relief over the news of Orestes, Electra laments her brother's loss and its effect on her own fate. When the Tutor turns to leave, Clytemnestra invites him into the palace. After they enter the palace, Electra continues her lamentation and the chorus attempt to console her. Electra's grief is interrupted by the arrival of Chrysothemis from Agamemnon's grave. In contrast to Aeschylus' *Libation Bearers,* in Sophocles' drama Chrysothemis announces that she has found at the grave offerings and a lock of hair, which she assumes Orestes has left. Electra, however, tells Chrysothemis the news of Orestes' death. Next Electra, behaving much more forcefully than her Aeschylean or Euripidean counterparts, tries to persuade Chrysothemis to help her kill Aegisthus. Chrysothemis, however, in a manner again reminiscent of Sophocles' Ismene, cites the weakness of women and the certainty of their own death if they fail and refuses to help her sister. Electra then decides that she will act alone. After the departure of Chrysothemis, the chorus sing an ode about the wis-

dom of humans, the quarrel between Chrysothemis and Electra, and Electra's plan to kill Aegisthus.

After the choral ode, the audience witness the entry of Orestes and Pylades, the latter of whom carries a funeral urn. Orestes asks the chorus to announce to those in the palace that some men from Phocis are looking for Aegisthus. Electra, not recognizing Orestes, approaches and learns that they have the ashes of Orestes. When Orestes allows Electra to hold the urn, she gives a lengthy speech lamenting Orestes and his death. By the time Electra finishes her speech, Orestes realizes that this is his sister. Before Orestes reveals his identity, however, he questions her about her suffering. Eventually Orestes tells her who he is and proves his identity by showing her a seal ring of Agamemnon's.

After their joyful reunion, Orestes informs Electra of the plot against Aegisthus and Clytemnestra. Electra gladly agrees to cooperate with his plan. Before they can enter the house, however, the Tutor emerges and informs them that Clytemnestra is without male protection in the house and that they should act against her quickly. While Orestes, Pylades, Electra, and the Tutor enter the house, the chorus wait outside in anticipation of what will happen. Soon Electra emerges, announces that the men will soon attack Clytemnestra, and says that she has gone outside to watch for Aegisthus. Unlike Aeschylus, who has an extended encounter between Clytemnestra and Orestes that the audience sees, Sophocles creates an encounter of mother and son outside the audience's view. Sophocles has Electra, outside the house, respond to cries from Clytemnestra within the house. Orestes and Pylades go out to announce the death of Clytemnestra, then reenter the house when the chorus see that Aegisthus is approaching. Aegisthus enters and asks about the strangers from Phocis and about Orestes' death. Electra tells him that the men are inside. When Aegisthus asks to see proof of Orestes' death, he sees Orestes and Pylades, the latter of whom he does not recognize, who are standing near Clytemnestra's body, which is covered so that Aegisthus cannot see her. Aegisthus calls for Clytemnestra, but Orestes tells her that she is already nearby. When the corpse is uncovered, Aegisthus sees Clytemnestra. Immediately Aegisthus realizes that he is in the presence of Orestes. With Electra urging Orestes to kill Aegisthus, Orestes forces Aegisthus to enter the house, where he will meet his doom. After some struggle, Aegisthus, accompanied by Orestes and Pylades, enters. At this point, the chorus conclude the play by announcing that the house of Atreus has been released from its suffering.

COMMENTARY

As alluded to previously, one of the major issues concerning the play is whether Sophocles' *Electra* appeared before Euripides' *Electra,* or vice versa. Our present state of knowledge does not allow us to be certain about this, but most modern scholars think that Euripides' play was the earlier of the two.

Some scholars have taken Sophocles' play as an expansion on the references to Orestes' killing of Aegisthus in HOMER's *Odyssey.* These interpreters view Sophocles' interpretation of Orestes' vengeance as an act of justice that shows no signs of the pessimism that undercuts the Euripidean Orestes and Electra. Other scholars have found Sophocles' play more pessimistic. Winnington-Ingram, for example, calls Electra "a woman (like her mother) of violence in word and deed; she is a Fury, a wrathful agent of infernal powers; she is a willing matricide. She is a Sophoclean hero." Woodard sees the play as a conflict between words and deeds, in which Orestes represents the male world of action, and Electra represents the more feminine world of speech. In the course of the play, Electra enters Orestes' world of deeds.

Blundell has described thoroughly how Sophocles' *Electra,* as other Sophoclean plays do, deals with the issue of helping one's friends and harming one's enemies. For Blundell, Orestes' revenge against Clytemnestra and Aegisthus is "performed in a world where the legitimacy of such revenge passes unchallenged" (p. 150). Despite opposition to Orestes' revenge, the issue is complicated because the vengeance occurs between family members. Son and daughter seek revenge against mother, while their mother defends what she has done to their father by claiming that her actions were retaliation for Agamemnon's killing of Electra's sister, Iphigenia.

Most recently, scholars such as Batchelder and Ringer have advocated studying Sophocles' *Electra*

with a metatheatrical perspective. Batchelder views Orestes and Aegisthus as "two rival dramatists, each competing to gain, or maintain, political control through poetic art. Each uses the power of words and the illusions of the theater to establish his authority in the community" (p. 2). Batchelder and Ringer both view the opening of the Electra as a sort of "rehearsal," in which the Tutor functions as an elder playwright, who directs Orestes on how to construct his "play" (the destruction of Clytemnestra and Aegisthus). The next segment of the play, according to Batchelder, shows Clytemnestra and Electra "as rival poets of praise and blame, each trying to establish as true her own version of the past, the story of Agamemnon's death" (pp. 3–4). Ringer views Chrysothemis as an actor caught between the plays that Clytemnestra and Electra are trying to produce. The victor in the verbal contest between Clytemnestra and Electra, however, will be determined by the poetic contest between Orestes and Aegisthus.

The third phase in *Electra* involves Orestes' "play." With the Tutor as the principal actor and Clytemnestra and Aegisthus as the audience, that play must convince Orestes' mother and her lover that Orestes is dead. For Ringer, the Tutor's speech is a "tragedy-within-a-tragedy" (p. 162), and the urn is a stage property that serves to introduce her in Orestes' play (p. 184). For Batchelder, the dramatic contests reach a resolution when Orestes and Electra recognize one another. After Orestes and Electra are reunited, Orestes then integrates Electra into his play as a mourner so that he can destroy Clytemnestra. Unlike Aeschylus' or Euripides' version of Orestes' return, in which the death of Aegisthus precedes that of Clytemnestra, Sophocles' drama postpones Aegisthus' death so that the play will end with "the defeat of Orestes' rival dramatist" (Batchelder p. 125). At the play's end, Orestes gains control of Aegisthus and drives him from the stage. "At the moment that Orestes forces Aegisthus, his political and poetic rival, off the stage to meet his death, he has achieved, through the playwright's art, final and complete control over the kingdom of Mycenae" (Batchelder p. 140).

BIBLIOGRAPHY

Batchelder, A. G. *The Seal of Orestes: Self-Reference and Authority in Sophocles' Electra.* Lanham, Md.: Rowman & Littlefield, 1995.

Blundell, M. W. *Helping Friends and Harming Enemies: A Study in Sophocles and Greek Ethics*. Cambridge: Cambridge University Press, 1989, 149–83.

Davidson, J. F. "Homer and Sophocles' *Electra*," *Bulletin for the Institute of Classical Studies* 35 (1989): 45–72.

Ringer, Mark. *Electra and the Empty Urn: Metatheater and Role Playing in Sophocles*. Chapel Hill: University of North Carolina Press, 1998, 127–212.

Winnington-Ingram, R. P. *Sophocles: An Interpretation*. Cambridge: Cambridge University Press, 1980, 246.

Woodard, T., ed. *Sophocles: A Collection of Critical Essays*. Englewood Cliffs, N.J.: Prentice Hall, 1966.

ELECTRAN GATE   One of the seven gates at THEBES. Pausanias says the entrance to Thebes from PLATAEA is by this gate. AESCHYLUS says CAPANEUS of ARGOS made his assault on this gate during the battle of the Seven against Thebes, but Apollodorus has PARTHENOPAEUS attack this gate. [ANCIENT SOURCES: Aeschylus, *Seven against Thebes* 423; Apollodorus, *Library* 3.6.6; Euripides, *Bacchae* 780; Pausanias, 9.8.7]

ELECTRYON   The son of PERSEUS and ANDROMEDA, Electryon was the husband of Anaxo and the father of numerous sons, including LICYMNIUS, and one daughter, ALCMENA, who became the mother of HERACLES. When Electryon was king of MYCENAE, PTERELAS' sons, accompanied by some Taphians, went to Mycenae and claimed their maternal grandfather Mestor's kingdom. When Electryon ignored their claim, they drove off his cattle. Electryon's sons (with the exception of the young Licymnius) tried to prevent this and were killed. The Taphians sailed away with the cattle and entrusted them to Polyxenus, the king of ELIS. Electryon, hoping to avenge the death of his sons, departed to wage war against these murderous thieves. Before he left, Electryon entrusted his kingdom and daughter to AMPHITRYON. While Electryon was away, Amphitryon paid Polyxenus ransom for the cattle and took them back to Mycenae. When Electryon returned from the war, Amphitryon gave him the cattle. During this transaction, one of the cows charged and Amphitryon threw a club at the animal. The club struck the cow's horns, rebounded, hit Electryon in the head, and killed him. [ANCIENT SOURCES: Apollodorus, *Library* 2.4.5–6; Euripides, *Heracles* 17; Hesiod, *Shield* 1–19; Pausanias, 9.11.1]

ELEOS   According to Pollux, in the days before Thespis (ca. 550 B.C.E.?), the *eleos* was a table on which a man would stand and converse with the CHORUS. [ANCIENT SOURCES: Pollux, *Onomasticon* 4.123]

ELEUSIN   See ELEUSIS.

ELEUSIS   A town several miles west of ATHENS, Eleusis was famous as the site of the Eleusinian Mysteries, a ritual initiation devoted to DEMETER and PERSEPHONE. According to EURIPIDES, during HIPPOLYTUS' pilgrimage to Eleusis to be initiated into these mysteries THESEUS' wife, PHAEDRA, first conceived a passion for Hippolytus (her stepson). Euripides' SUPPLIANT WOMEN has Eleusis as its setting. AESCHYLUS wrote *Eleusinioi* (Eleusinian men), of which two brief fragments survive (53a–54 Radt), which was presumably set at Eleusis and may have had the same subject as Euripides' *Suppliant Women*. [ANCIENT SOURCES: Euripides, *Hippolytus* 24–28]

ELIS   A town in southwestern Greece north of OLYMPIA. PLAUTUS calls this town Alis in *CAPTIVES*. [ANCIENT SOURCES: Plautus, *Captives* passim; Seneca, *Trojan Women* 850]

ELYMNIUM   A rocky place near the northwest coast of the island of EUBOEA. [ANCIENT SOURCES: Aristophanes, *Peace* 1126; Sophocles, fragments 437, 888 Radt]

BIBLIOGRAPHY
Radt, S. *Tragicorum Graecorum Fragmenta*. Vol. 4. Göttingen, Ger.: Vandenhoeck & Ruprecht, 1977.

ELYSIUM   See UNDERWORLD.

EMMELEIA   A type of dance performed in TRAGEDY that acted out the words being spoken. [ANCIENT SOURCES: Athenaeus, 1.20e, 14.631d; Lucian, *On Dance* 26; Herodotus, 6.129; Plato, *Laws* 816b]

EMPUSA A bizarre female goblin that was thought to eat humans and was able to take on different forms. In ARISTOPHANES' *FROGS,* she is imagined as changing into a cow, a mule, a beautiful woman, and then a dog, whose face blazes with fire and who has a bronze leg. Empusa either is sent by HECATE or is synonymous with Hecate. [ANCIENT SOURCES: Aristophanes, *Ecclesiazusae* 1056, Frogs 289–94]

BIBLIOGRAPHY
Heil, Andreas. "Herakleiodionysos am Scheideweg: Die Empusa-Szene (Aristophanes, *Ranae* 285–311)," *Grazer Beitrage* 23 (2000): 53–58.

ENCELADUS A son of EARTH and Tartarus, Enceladus was one of the GIANTS who tried to overthrow ZEUS and the other gods but was defeated and buried beneath SICILY. [ANCIENT SOURCES: Apollodorus, *Library* 1.6.2; Euripides, *Cyclops* 7, *Heracles* 908, *Ion* 209; Seneca, *Hercules Furens* 79, *Hercules Oetaeus* 1140, 1145, 1159, 1735]

ENETOI See VENETI.

ENNIUS (239–169 B.C.E.) Born in the Italian town of Rudiae in the region of Calabria, this Roman poet produced both comedies and tragedies, as well as several other types of literature, including satiric poems, a poem about the Roman general Scipio Africanus, and an epic poem (*Annals*) about the history of Rome from the fall of TROY to Ennius' own time. Only four lines survive from Ennius' comedies, from *Caupuncula* (little hostess) and *Pancratiastes*. A few brief fragments also survive of two *fabulae praetextae*. The *Ambracia* treated Marcus Fulvius' capture of Ambracia; Ennius' *Sabine Women* surely dealt with the rape of the Sabine women (only seven words survive). We have numerous fragments from at least 20 of Ennius' tragedies: *Achilles, Ajax, Alcmaeon, Alexander, Andromache, Andromeda, Athamas, Cresphontes, Erechtheus, Eumenides, The Ransom of Hector, Hecuba, Iphigenia, Medea, Melanippe, Nemea, Phoenix, Telamon, Telephus, Thyestes*. Most of these plays appear to have been adapted from EURIPIDES; a few seem to have been derived from the works of AESCHYLUS. Ennius' *Achilles*

was adapted from a play by Aristarchus of Tegea, a contemporary of Euripides.

BIBLIOGRAPHY
Jocelyn, H. D. *The Tragedies of Ennius: The Fragments.* London: Cambridge University Press, 1967.
Norden, Eduard. *Ennius und Vergilius: Kriegsbilder aus Roms grosser Zeit.* Leipzig: Teubner, 1915.
Skutsch, O. *Studia Enniana.* London: Athlone, 1968.
Warmington, E. H. *Remains of Old Latin.* Vol. 1. London: W. Heinemann and Cambridge, Mass.: Harvard University Press, 1935.

ENNOSIS See POSEIDON.

ENYALIUS The son of ARES and ENYO, Enyalius, whose name means "warlike," is a god associated with war. Some sources used the word *enyalius* as an epithet for Ares. [ANCIENT SOURCES: Aristophanes, *Peace* 457; Sophocles, *Ajax* 179]

ENYO Enyo was a goddess associated with war. Some sources call her the daughter of ARES; others make her the wife of Ares, by whom she became the mother of ENYALIUS. [ANCIENT SOURCES: Aeschylus, *Seven against Thebes* 45]

EOS The daughter of Hyperion and Theia, Eos (called Aurora by the Romans) is the goddess of the dawn. She is the sister of the SUN, Helios, and the MOON, Selene. By Astraeus ("starry"), Eos produced the winds and the stars. When Eos had intercourse with ARES, a favorite lover of APHRODITE's, Aphrodite cast a spell on Eos that caused her to be in love constantly. Accordingly, Eos became one of the most sexually aggressive females in classical mythology. Eos carried off ORION to the island of DELOS; she abducted HERMES' son, CEPHALUS, and made him her lover. By Cephalus Eos had a son, Tithonus. Eos is also said to have had sexual relations with Tithonus and by him borne MEMNON, who fought in the Trojan War. [ANCIENT SOURCES: Apollodorus, *Library* 1.2.2, 1.2.4, 1.4.4, 3.14.3, *Epitome* 5.3; Hyginus, *Fables* 125, 160, 189, 270]

EPAPHUS The son of ZEUS and IO. Epaphus was born near the Nile River; married Memphis, daughter of the Nile; and had a daughter named Libya. [ANCIENT SOURCES: Aeschylus, *Prometheus Bound* 851, *Suppliant Women* 47–48, 315–16, 589; Apollodorus, *Library* 2.1.3–4; Euripides, *Phoenician Women* 678; Hyginus, *Fables* 145, 149–150]

EPEUS   A Greek from the region of PHOCIS, Epeus went to TROY and is credited with building the wooden horse. EURIPIDES wrote a play entitled *Epeus,* of which only the title survives (see Nauck). [ANCIENT SOURCES: Apollodorus, *Epitome* 5.14; Euripides, *Trojan Women* 10; Homer, *Odyssey* 8.493, 11.523; Hyginus, *Fables* 108; Plautus, *Bacchides* 937]

BIBLIOGRAPHY
Nauck, A. *Tragicorum Graecorum Fragmenta.* 1889. Reprint, Hildesheim: Olms, 1964.

EPHUDION   A person mentioned by ARISTOPHANES as engaging successfully in the pancratium (a sport similar to modern kickboxing), despite his advanced age. [ANCIENT SOURCES: Aristophanes, *Wasps* 1191, 1383]

EPICHARMUS   A comic playwright from SICILY, Epicharmus appears to have been active between 500 and 475 B.C.E. About 200 fragments from Epicharmus' works exist, and some 30 titles are known. Many of Epicharmus' titles indicate that he focuses on comic versions of mythological events (e.g., *Amycus, Bacchae, Busiris, Sciron, Sirens, Sphinx, Philoctetes*). [ANCIENT SOURCES: Aristotle, *Poetics* 1448a32; Diogenes Laertius, 3.9–15; *Parian Marble* 71; Plutarch, *Numa* 8; Theocritus, *Epigram* 18]

EPICRATES   From the DEME of Cephisia, Epicrates was active in Athenian politics during the first decade of the fourth century B.C.E. Comic poets made fun of his long beard. Epicrates supported war with SPARTA in 396/395 and went on a diplomatic mission to Persia around 393. Epicrates' mission to Persia resulted in accusations of his taking bribes from the Persians; he was also put on trial for and acquitted of charges of embezzlement and bribery that allegedly occurred during his tenure as a financial officer around the time of his mission to Persia. After he served as a delegate at a peace conference in Sparta in 392, Epicrates' troubles continued. When Epicrates and his fellow Athenian delegates rejected the peace treaty (which had already been agreed upon), they were tried on charges of taking bribes, being disobedient, and giving false information to the Athenian Council. To escape the trial, Epicrates and the others went into exile. In their absence, the Athenians condemned them to death. [ANCIENT SOURCES: Aristophanes, *Ecclesiazusae* 71; Athenaeus, 6.251a; Demosthenes, 19.277; Lysias, 27.3–6; Pausanias, 3.9.8; Plato Comicus, fragment 119, 122 Kock; Plutarch, *Pelopidas* 30.12]

BIBLIOGRAPHY
Kock, T. *Comicorum Atticorum Fragmenta.* Vol. 1. Leipzig: Teubner, 1880.
Sommerstein, A. H. *The Comedies of Aristophanes.* Vol. 10, *Ecclesiazusae.* Warminster, U.K.: Aris & Phillips, 1998, 144.

EPICURUS   Mentioned by ARISTOPHANES at *ECCLESIAZUSAE* 645, Epicurus was apparently an Athenian and, according to Tuplin, the son of an Athenian military commander, Paches, during the PELOPONNESIAN WAR (428/427 B.C.E.). Sommerstein, however, regards this identification as "highly speculative" because Paches had been dead for more than three decades when *Ecclesiazusae* was staged. Nothing else of this Epicurus is known.

BIBLIOGRAPHY
Sommerstein, A. H. *The Comedies of Aristophanes.* Vol. 10, *Ecclesiazusae.* Warminster, U.K.: Aris & Phillips, 1998, 195.
Tuplin, C. J. "Fathers and Sons: *Ecclesiazusae* 644–45," *Greek, Roman, and Byzantine Studies* 23 (1982): 325–30.

EPIDAMNUS   A town on the eastern coast of the Adriatic Sea. PLAUTUS' *MENAECHMI* has Epidamnus as its setting.

EPIDAURUS   A town in the southeastern part of Greece between CORINTH and TROEZEN. The town, a center for the worship of ASCLEPIUS, is the location of one of the best-preserved ancient theaters. PLAUTUS'

CURCULIO is set at Epidaurus. A character from Plautus' EPIDICUS, Philippa, is also said to be from Epidaurus, where Periphanes sexually assaulted her. Three Greek comic poets wrote plays entitled *Epidaurios* (The Epidaurian): Alexis (fragment 77 Kock), Antiphanes (fragments 92–93 Kock), and Theophilus (fragment 3 Kock). The fragments tell us nothing about the plots of these plays, however. [ANCIENT SOURCES: Seneca, *Hippolytus* 1022]

EPIDICUS PLAUTUS (CA. 292–289 B.C.E.)

References in *Epidicus* to a military campaign by Athens against Thebes that appears to have occurred in either 293 or 290 would date the original to about 292 or 289 B.C.E. The Greek model for PLAUTUS' play is unknown, although the name of the actor who played Epidicus is (Titus Publilius Pellio). The action of the play occurs in ATHENS (the most common setting for Plautus' and TERENCE's plays) before the two houses of Periphanes and Chaeribulus, the former an elderly gentleman, the latter a young gentleman.

The play opens as Epidicus, the SLAVE of Periphanes, encounters Thesprio, the slave of Stratippocles. Thesprio has returned from the battlefront, where his master purchased a young woman from the spoils of the war. Epidicus is surprised to learn this, because before Stratippocles went to war, he commissioned Epidicus to purchase a MUSIC GIRL (unnamed) with whom he was in love. To make matters worse, the Theban moneylender from whom Stratippocles borrowed the money to buy her girl has arrived to collect his money. This situation distresses Epidicus because Stratippocles did not want to see his father until after he had repaid the interest charged by the moneylender. After the departure of Thesprio, Epidicus reveals that he had tricked Stratippocles' father, Periphanes, into thinking that the woman being purchased was his long-lost daughter. Epidicus fears that if Periphanes finds out that he has been tricked, he will beat him.

As Epidicus considers his next move, Stratippocles and his friend, Chaeribulus, approach. Epidicus listens in as the two friends discuss Stratippocles' financial situation. Stratippocles asks Chaeribulus to lend him the money, but Chaeribulus has his own financial problems. As Stratippocles states that he would pay for

Epidicus' help, Epidicus emerges from his hiding place and greets his master. When Epidicus tells his master that he has purchased the music girl, Stratippocles informs his slave that he no longer cares about her. Stratippocles then tells Epidicus that unless he raises the money by sundown, Epidicus will be punished. Epidicus promises his help and suggests that they may be able to sell the music girl to a rich soldier from Euboea whom he knows. As Stratippocles and Chaeribulus leave with plans to enjoy the day, Epidicus decides to wage his own little war against Stratippocles' father.

The second act begins with the arrival of Periphanes and his elderly friend, Apoecides. The two gentlemen are discussing Periphanes' upcoming marriage to a poor woman who was the mother of his long-lost daughter. As the two men talk, Epidicus begins to enter from Charibulus' house, prepared to "gut" Periphanes' moneybag. Epidicus listens to the men as Periphanes reveals that he knows about Stratippocles' business concerning the music girl. At this point, Epidicus realizes how to get the money from Periphanes and appears, acting as if he has been searching for Periphanes. Epidicus reports that the troops have returned from Thebes, and that Epidicus noticed that the music girl was waiting near the city gate for Stratippocles. Epidicus then claims he overheard some women saying that Stratippocles had borrowed some money to buy the music girl's freedom. This news stuns Periphanes, who asks for Apoecides' advice. Epidicus, however, breaks in and suggests that Periphanes should find a bride for Stratippocles before he marries the music girl. Epidicus also tells Periphanes that Stratippocles has not yet returned from the war, and that Periphanes himself should pretend to be in love with the music girl and set her free. Epidicus also suggests that once the music girl is freed, she should be sent from the city. Epidicus suggests that Apoecides carry the money to her owner. Epidicus also says that Periphanes will be able to sell her to a soldier from Rhodes. Periphanes agrees to the plan; Apoecides says he will go to the FORUM and tells Epidicus to meet him there. As Periphanes enters his house to get the money, Epidicus rejoices in the success of his plan but wonders how he will find a music girl to fool

Periphanes. Epidicus then remembers that Periphanes had told him to hire a music girl to play while Periphanes was making a sacrifice. Epidicus says that he will use the same person to fool Periphanes and tell her about the scheme.

As the third act begins, Stratippocles and Chaeribulus despair about whether they will receive help from Epidicus. Stratippocles also moans that he is getting no help from Chaeribulus. Next, Epidicus enters from Periphanes' house with a bag of money, which he soon hands over to Stratippocles. Epidicus then informs Stratippocles of his plan to fool Periphanes. Epidicus also tells Stratippocles that he has already paid off the PIMP for the music girl, but that he will return to the pimp's house and will make sure the pimp says, if necessary, that the money he took was for Stratippocles' war captive. Stratippocles, delighted by Epidicus' plan, returns to his house with Chaeribulus. Epidicus departs to hire a music girl to fool Periphanes and Apoecides.

After some time passes, Periphanes encounters Apoecides and the music girl Epidicus hired to fool the old men. Periphanes has the girl taken inside his house but gives instructions that she be kept away from Periphanes' daughter. Apoecides tells Periphanes of their encounter with the pimp, the masterful way in which Epidicus deceived the pimp, and the way that he himself played along as if he was a simpleton. At this point, Apoecides departs for the forum. Periphanes, however, soon sees a soldier and his slave approaching. The soldier is searching for Periphanes. The soldier tells Periphanes that he has heard that Periphanes bought the soldier's mistress, Acropolistes, and says that he wants to buy her from him. Periphanes agrees to sell her to him and makes a profit in the transaction as well. When the music girl is taken out, however, the soldier realizes she is not the person he expected. The soldier tells Periphanes that he must have been tricked into paying money for her. At this, the soldier exits with the intent of finding his mistress. Upon the soldier's exit, Periphanes questions the music girl about how she was hired, and she tells him the story about being hired to play during a sacrifice. Periphanes next asks the music girl about Acropolistes and where she lives. The music girl reports that she

knows Acropolistes but does not know where she lives because Stratippocles recently set her free.

As the furious Periphanes sends the music girl from his house, Philippa, a woman from EPIDAURUS, enters and laments that her daughter has been captured. It turns out that the daughter, Telestis, is the captive woman with whom Stratippocles is in love. Periphanes and Philippa also recognize one another. Many years before, Periphanes had sexually assaulted Philippa while he was in Epidaurus, she had become pregnant, and, unknown to him, she had given birth to Telestis. Periphanes tells Philippa not to worry: When he heard that the girl was captured, Periphanes had Epidicus pay ransom money for her. At this point, Periphanes summons the girl to greet her mother. The girl who emerges from the house, however, is not Philippa's daughter, but Acropolistis, the girl with whom the soldier was in love. As this strange girl baffles both Periphanes and Philippa, Acropolistis reveals that Epidicus had instructed her to say that she was Periphanes' daughter, Telestis. Periphanes had been fooled because Epidicus told him that she was his daughter. At this, a tearful Philippa enters Periphanes' house while Periphanes promises to find their real daughter and destroy Epidicus.

The play's final act concludes with the arrival of Epidicus from the forum. He has seen Periphanes and Apoecides searching for him and has learned that they mean to torture him. Epidicus encounters Stratippocles, whom Epidicus begs for help. Their discussion is interrupted by the arrival of a moneylender and the captive, Telestis, whom Stratippocles had purchased. The usurer wants to square accounts with Stratippocles. After the young man goes into his house to get the money, Epidicus recognizes Telestis as the daughter of Periphanes and Philippa and thus the sister of Stratippocles (compare MENANDER's *THE GIRL WITH THE SHAVEN HEAD*). After some prompting, Telestis remembers Epidicus, who informs her that she has been purchased by her half brother (they had the same father, but a different mother). As Telestis excitedly asks about her father, Stratippocles returns from his house, hands over the money to the usurer, and sends the man on his way. Stratippocles is eager to embrace Telestis, but she greets him as her brother. After the bittersweet reunion, Epidicus lifts Stratippocles' spirits when he tells him that he has the music girl whom Stratippocles had loved originally. Epidicus sends Stratippocles and Telestis back into the house but begs them to assist him if Periphanes and Apoecides try to lay hands on him.

Soon the two old men return, searching for Epidicus and uttering threats against him. Epidicus emerges from the house and immediately and willingly offers to be bound. The baffled Periphanes, however, hesitates to bind Epidicus, who demonstrates a false bravado. Finally, Periphanes binds his hands. No matter how tight he binds Epidicus, the slave pretends to feel no pain (compare Xanthias in ARISTOPHANES' FROGS). Periphanes interrogates Epidicus, who admits that he tricked the old man and gave the money to Stratippocles. Epidicus sends Periphanes into the house, claiming that what he finds inside will convince him that Epidicus deserves to be freed from slavery. After Periphanes returns, he begs Epidicus' forgiveness and grants him his freedom.

COMMENTARY

Whereas in BACCHIDES (214), Plautus suggests that *Epidicus* was one of his favorite plays, modern scholars have not shown the same affection for the play. Most of the attention given to the play has been related to determining its Greek model, and this issue remains unsettled. Plautus' play has some similarities to Menander's *Girl with the Shaven Head* in that in both the young man discovers that his love interest is actually his sister (however, there is no suggestion this was the model for Plautus' play). Although modern scholars have not paid much attention to Epidicus for its own merits, this brief play (only 733 lines) is not without its charm. As with PSEUDOLUS, the play's dominant figure is the wily slave. Whereas Pseudolus must overcome both an evil pimp and a watchful father to help his master acquire his beloved prostitute, Epidicus' primary obstacle is his young master's father, whom Epidicus must trick twice to carry out his young master's wishes.

As for several other Roman comedies, a metatheatrical approach (see Slater) may be employed successfully with *Epidicus*. In this methodology, Epidicus would be viewed as a playwright who is trying to produce a play within a play. As the playwright, Epidicus is charged with the task of convincing an audience (in this case, Periphanes), and he casts the other characters for his play within the play and even takes on roles himself. Acting is the business of pretending to be someone or something else, and numerous instances of pretense are found in *Epidicus*.

At line 195, Epidicus pretends (*adsimulato*) that he has been searching for Periphanes all over town. At line 238, Epidicus tells the two old men that he pretended (*dissimulabam*) to hear a conversation that, in fact, he never actually heard, but that is part of the illusion he is using to fool the two men. Not only does Epidicus himself play roles in his play, but he enlists the aid of many others as well. Some of Epidicus' "actors" are aware that they are involved in his play, but others are not. In the case of the first music girl, Epidicus integrates her into his play by instructing her to pretend to be Periphanes' daughter (88, 357). Unlike several Plautine comedies, *Epidicus* does not have an evil pimp who takes the stage. There is mention of Epidicus' having dealings with a pimp, however, and in an interesting twist on the usual slave-versus-pimp theme, in *Epidicus* the title character apparently has the pimp under his control and integrates him into his play within the play. At lines 364–70, Epidicus tells Stratippocles that he will instruct the pimp to say, if necessary, that the money he took was for Stratippocles' war captive. Epidicus also tells Stratippocles that he will hire a clever music girl who will pretend (*simulet*, 373) that she has been bought and will help trick the old men.

Whereas the music girl and pimp would be coached by Epidicus on their role in his play, the old gentlemen Periphanes and Apoecides would not be fully aware of the role they would take on in Epidicus' play. After the music girl is acquired, Apoecides tells Periphanes how Epidicus tricked her to think that she was purchased for Periphanes, and he seems to take great pride in relating how, as a participant in Epidicus' scheme, he pretended (*assimulabam*, 420) to be an ignorant simpleton. The irony, of course, is that Apoecides is a simpleton and that it is not so much that Apoecides has assimilated himself into Epidicus' scheme, as that

Epidicus has assimilated Apoecides into his play within the play.

In the case of Periphanes, Epidicus assimilates him into his play as he directs the old man to pretend to be in love with the music girl. Although it is not unusual in Roman COMEDY for a young man and his father both to have a love interest, Epidicus' scheme that the father himself should pretend to be in love with the music girl is a novel twist on such deceptions. Epidicus not only directs Periphanes to play the role of the aged lover, but transforms Periphanes into a pimp (contrast Slater, who likens Periphanes to a BRAGGART WARRIOR). At lines 299–301, Epidicus suggests to Periphanes that he will be able to sell the music girl to the soldier. When the soldier appears, the soldier tells Periphanes that he wants to buy the girl from him. In a manner worthy of a pimp, Periphanes agrees, knowing he stands to turn a profit as well. When the soldier's mistress is supposed to be taken out, however, Epidicus' play begins to unravel and Periphanes begins to understand the unwitting role he and the music girl have played. After further investigation, Periphanes learns about the role of the other girl in Epidicus' drama as Acropolistis reveals that Epidicus had instructed her to say that she was Periphanes' daughter, Telestis. Upon discovering this second strange young woman in his house, Periphanes wonders whether he is playing the pimp (551), given all of the women and money that seem to be flowing in and out of his house.

With Periphanes' discovery of Epidicus' tricks, the COMEDY has collapsed into TRAGEDY (as Slater notes), and Epidicus (as is Pseudolus near the conclusion of his play) is in danger of severe punishment by the old master, but the arrival of Periphanes' real daughter saves him from a beating. As in the case of Pseudolus, his master forgives Epidicus. Pseudolus is forgiven but does not receive the bonus of freedom as Epidicus does (although he appears reluctant to accept it). Unlike in *Pseudolus,* though, in which the young man is eventually united with his beloved, the arrival of Telestis diffuses the young man Stratippocles' love intrigue. The woman with whom he was in love turns out to be his sister and the woman that he had arranged for Epidicus to purchase in the first part of the play has been dismissed.

BIBLIOGRAPHY

Auhagen, Ulrike, ed. *Studien zu Plautus' Epidicus.* Script-Oralia Series 125, Reihe A, Altertumswissenschaftliche Reihe 33. Tübingen: Narr, 2001.

Fantham, E. "Plautus in Miniature: Compression and Distortion in the *Epidicus.*" In *Papers of the Leeds International Latin Seminar.* Edited by Francis Cairnes. Liverpool: Cairns, 1981, 1–28.

Goldberg, S. M. "Plautus' *Epidicus* and the Case of the Missing Original," *Transactions of the American Philological Association* 108 (1978): 81–91.

Slater, N. W. "Epidicus." In *Plautus in Performance.* Princeton, N.J.: Princeton University Press, 1985, 19–36.

Willcock, M. M. "Plautus and the *Epidicus,*" In *Papers of the Leeds International Latin Seminar.* Edited by R. Brock and A. J. Woodman. Leeds: Cairns, 1995, 19–29.

EPIGONI (EPIGONOI)   This term, which means "those born afterward," denotes the sons of the chieftains who participated in the famous Seven against THEBES expedition. At the end of EURIPIDES' SUPPLIANT WOMEN, ATHENA predicts that the Epigoni will avenge their fathers' defeat by marching on Thebes again. The leader of this second expedition was ALCMEON. AESCHYLUS (fragments 55–56 Radt, vol. 3) wrote an *Epigoni,* whose extant 20 words indicate virtually nothing about it. The fragments (185–98 Radt, Vol. 4) of SOPHOCLES' *Epigoni* are more extensive; they indicate a hostile encounter between ERIPHYLE and her son, Alcmeon, as well as an argument between Alcmeon and ADRASTUS. The tragedian Astydamas also wrote an *Epigoni,* of which only the title survives (see Snell 1971). Among Roman authors, ACCIUS staged a play called *Epigoni.* Alcmeon, Amphilochus, Eriphyle, and Eriphyle's daughter Demonassa, appear to have had speaking roles in Accius' play, which dealt, at least in part, with Alcmeon's killing of Eriphyle. [ANCIENT SOURCES: Apollodorus, *Library* 3.7.2–3]

BIBLIOGRAPHY

Kiso, A. "Notes on Sophocles' *Epigoni,*" *Greek, Roman, and Byzantine Studies* 18 (1977): 207–26.

Lloyd-Jones, H. *Sophocles: Fragments.* Cambridge, Mass.: Harvard University Press, 1996.

Radt, S. *Tragicorum Graecorum Fragmenta.* Vol. 3. Göttingen, Ger.: Vandenhoeck & Ruprecht, 1985.

———. *Tragicorum Graecorum Fragmenta,* Vol. 4. Göttingen, Ger.: Vandenhoeck & Ruprecht, 1977.

Snell, B. *Tragicorum Graecorum Fragmenta*. Vol. 1. Göttingen, Ger.: Vandenhoeck & Ruprecht, 1971.

Sutton, D. F. *The Lost Sophocles*. Lanham, Md.: University Press of America, 1984.

Warmington, E. H. *Remains of Old Latin: Ennius and Caecilius*. Vol. 1. Cambridge, Mass.: Harvard University Press, 1935.

———. *Remains of Old Latin: Livius Andronicus, Naevius, Pacuvius, and Accius*. Vol. 2. Cambridge, Mass.: Harvard University Press, 1936.

EPIGONUS   A man mentioned by ARISTOPHANES, at *ECCLESIAZUSAE* 167, as having an effeminate appearance. The ancient commentators on this line suggest that other comic poets ridiculed Epigonus as commonly found in the company of women and as being a passive homosexual.

BIBLIOGRAPHY
Sommerstein, A. H. *The Comedies of Aristophanes*. Vol. 10, Ecclesiazusae. Warminster, U.K.: Aris & Phillips, 1998, 152.

EPIRUS   A region near the coast of far northwestern Greece.

EPISKENION   A Greek word meaning "on top of the *skene*," the term *episkenion* refers to the second level of the stage building (*SKENE*).

EPISODE   ARISTOTLE defines an episode as the part of a drama that takes place between choral songs. Most extant Greek tragedies have three episodes, a few have four episodes, and SOPHOCLES' *ANTIGONE* has five episodes. Regarding extant Greek COMEDY, four of Aristophanes' 11 plays have five episodes, *PEACE* has only two, and *WEALTH* has eight. [ANCIENT SOURCES: Aristotle, *Poetics* 1452b20–21]

EPITREPONTES   See THE ARBITRATION.

EPODE   From the Greek word *epodos*, meaning "after song," the epode was the part of a lyric song that followed the STROPHE and ANTISTROPHE. Multiple strophes and antistrophes could precede an epode, as in SOPHOCLES', *ANTIGONE* 806–82, in which three strophes and their corresponding antistrophes precede the epode (876–82). In contrast to their role in the strophe and antistrophe, during an epode the CHORUS is thought to have stood still.

ERASINADES   An Athenian general tried and executed after the battle of ARGINUSAE in 406 B.C.E. Dover notes that "the trouble in fact started when [Erasinades] was individually prosecuted by Archedemos for embezzlement." [ANCIENT SOURCES: Aristophanes, *Frogs* 1196]

BIBLIOGRAPHY
Dover, K. J. *Aristophanes: Frogs*. Oxford: Clarendon Press, 1993, 337.

EREBUS   According to HESIOD, Erebus was the child of CHAOS and the brother of NIGHT. Erebus mated with Night and produced Aether and Day. Often, the name Erebus is used as a synonym for the UNDERWORLD or a part of the underworld. [ANCIENT SOURCES: Aristophanes, *Birds* 691; Hesiod, *Theogony* 123–25]

ERECHTHEUS (Latin: ERECTHEUS)
Ancient sources differ as to the birth and parents of this Athenian king. Some sources make him the son of Pandion and Zeuxippe, and the earliest reference to Erechtheus says that he was born from EARTH (GAIA) and raised by ATHENA. Erechtheus' wife was Praxithea; they had three sons (Cecrops, Metion, and Pandorus) and numerous daughters—CREUSA, Oreithyia, and PROCRIS are the best known.

When a war broke out between the Athenians and their neighbors the Eleusinians, Erechtheus consulted the DELPHIC ORACLE about how to win the war. The oracle told Erechtheus to sacrifice one of his daughters. When Erechtheus did so, some of the girl's sisters killed themselves. According to EURIPIDES' *ION*, Erechtheus' daughter, Creusa, did not die. In the ensuing battle, Erechtheus killed the Eleusinian champion Eumolpus, son of POSEIDON. Poseidon retaliated by making the Earth swallow Erechtheus.

Euripides wrote an *Erechtheus*, staged about 422 B.C.E., from which roughly 200 lines survive. The setting was Athens and old men of Athens made up the chorus. POSEIDON appeared in the prologue and mentioned his rescue of Eumolpus. A lengthy fragment remains from Praxithea's speech in which she rationalizes her reasons for offering her daughter for sacrifice. In another lengthy fragment, Erechtheus, apparently on the verge of departing for the battle, gives an unnamed male heir advice on how a virtuous and noble person should behave. In the battle, Erechtheus killed Eumolpus and Poseidon killed Erechtheus, and a fragment from a choral speech indicates that the old men experience a Poseidon-caused earthquake. The play ended with an appearance by Athena. Some 45 lines survive from her speech, in which Athena demands that Poseidon put an end to his threat to her city; she instructs Praxithea about the burial of her sacrificed daughter; she informs her that the daughters who committed suicide have been transported to heaven and will be called the Hyacinthids; she orders the building of a sacred precinct that will honor Poseidon Erechtheus; and she makes Praxithea one of her priestesses. As the fragment breaks off, Athena begins to make a pronouncement about Eumolpus' son, also named Eumolpus.

Among Roman authors, ENNIUS also wrote an *Erectheus,* of which two short fragments survive. [ANCIENT SOURCES: Apollodorus, *Library* 3.15.4–5; Euripides, *Ion* 277–80; Hyginus, *Fables* 46; Lycurgus, *Against Leocrates* 98–101]

BIBLIOGRAPHY
Austin, C. *Nova Fragmenta Euripidea in Papyris Reperta.* Berlin: De Gruyter, 1968.
Calder, W. M., "The Date of Euripides' *Erechtheus,*" *Greek, Roman, and Byzantine Studies* 10 (1969): 147–56.
Collard, C., M. J. Cropp, and K. H. Lee. *Euripides: Selected Fragmentary Plays.* Vol. 1. Warminster, U.K.: Aris & Phillips, 1995, 148–94.
Jocelyn, H. D. *The Tragedies of Ennius.* Cambridge: Cambridge University Press, 1969.
Mikalson, J. D. "Erechtheus and the Panathenaia," *American Journal of Philology* 97 (1976): 141–53.

ERETRIA A Greek town south of CHALCIS on the western coast of the island of EUBOEA. [ANCIENT SOURCES: Plautus, *Merchant* 646, *Persian* 259, 322–23]

ERGASION A fictional person—his name means "workman"—mentioned in ARISTOPHANES' *WASPS* (1201) as having his vine props (stakes) stolen by PHILOCLEON.

BIBLIOGRAPHY
Sommerstein, A. H. *The Comedies of Aristophanes.* Vol. 4 *Wasps.* Warminster, U.K.: Aris & Phillips, 1983, 226.

ERGINUS The son of Clymenus, Erginus was a king of the Minyans and lived in the town of Orchomenus. When Clymenus was killed by a Theban named Perieres, Clymenus, with his dying words, ordered Erginus to avenge his death. Accordingly, Erginus waged war against the Thebans, defeated them, and imposed a penalty upon them (every year for 20 years the Thebans were to send 100 cattle to him). Once, when HERACLES was returning from hunting the lion of CITHAERON, Heracles encountered some heralds from Erginus who were on their way to Thebes to ask for this tribute. Heracles, apparently not liking the idea that his fellow townspeople would have to pay the tribute, cut off the noses, ears, and hands of the heralds and hanged these body parts around their necks. When the mutilated heralds returned to Erginus, the angry king immediately marched on the Thebans, who should have been slaughtered because the Minyans had disarmed them after their previous war. In this conflict, however, Heracles fought on the Theban side. Heracles killed Erginus, drove away the Minyans, and forced them to pay the Thebans twice that tribute. Some sources say that Heracles' mortal father, AMPHITRYON, died in the battle against the Minyans. Among the Greek dramatists, the tragedian Achaeus may have written an *Erginus,* of which only the title survives. [ANCIENT SOURCES: Apollodorus, *Library* 2.4.11; Euripides, *Heracles* 47–50, 220–21, 560; Pausanias, 9.17.2]

BIBLIOGRAPHY
Snell, B. *Tragicorum Graecorum Fragmenta.* Vol. 1. Göttingen, Ger.: Vandenhoeck & Ruprecht, 1971.

ERICHTHONIUS The son of HEPHAESTUS and Mother EARTH. The circumstances surrounding Erichthonius' birth are unusual. When ATHENA requested that Hephaestus create armor for her, he attempted to assault her sexually. Hephaestus' effort failed, but he ejaculated on Athena, who wiped off the semen with a piece of wool and then threw the wool onto the ground (Earth). Mother Earth became pregnant and Erichthonius was born. Earth returned Erichthonius to Athena, who raised him at her temple in ATHENS, where he eventually became king after driving out Amphictyon. Erichthonius is credited with instituting the festival of the Panathenaea. He married Praxithea and by her had a son, PANDION. The story of Erichthonius figures in EURIPIDES' ION, in which the title hero's life experience has some similarities to that of Erichthonius. [ANCIENT SOURCES: Apollodorus, *Library* 3.14.6–7; Euripides, *Ion* 21, 268, 999, 1429; Hyginus, *Fables* 166]

BIBLIOGRAPHY
Robertson, N. "The Origin of the Panathenaea," *Rheinisches Museum* 128 (1985): 231–95.

ERIDANUS   A river west of Greece that was eventually equated with the Po. PHAETHON was supposed to have died near the Eridanus and his sisters' tears over their brother to have turned into amber, which could supposedly be found near the river's mouth. [ANCIENT SOURCES: Euripides, *Hippolytus* 737; Hesiod, *Theogony* 338; Seneca, *Hercules Oetaeus* 186]

ERIGONE (Latin: ERIGONA)   The daughter of AEGISTHUS and CLYTEMNESTRA, Erigone was the brother of ALETES and had at least one child, Penthilus, by her half brother, ORESTES. Some sources say she also produced Tisamenus by him. After a false report of the deaths of Orestes and PYLADES reached Aletes, he tried to take over the kingdom. When ELECTRA went to DELPHI to learn whether this was true, Orestes and Iphigenia also happened to be there. Before Electra saw Orestes, she saw IPHIGENIA, and the same deceitful messenger told Electra that Iphigenia had killed Orestes (Electra had not seen her for years and did not realize she was her sister). Electra, hearing this, attacked Iphigenia with a burning log from a nearby altar. Orestes, however, arrived in time to stop Electra. When the brother and sisters recognized one another, they returned to MYCENAE. Orestes killed Aletes and

tried to kill Erigone, but, just as ARTEMIS had with Iphigenia at AULIS in EURIPIDES' play, the goddess rescued Erigone and transported her to Attica, where she became her priestess. Apollodorus cites some unnamed sources, which stated that Erigone prosecuted Orestes for killing his mother. SOPHOCLES wrote an *Erigone,* whose two surviving fragments reveal little about the play. Other Greek playwrights who wrote an *Erigone* that is known only by title are Cleophon, PHILOCLES, and Phrynichus II. Among Roman authors, ACCIUS composed an *Erigona,* of which about eight lines survive. This play may have dealt with Orestes' attempt on Erigona's life. [ANCIENT SOURCES: Apollodorus, *Epitome* 6.25, 28; Hyginus, *Fables* 122]

BIBLIOGRAPHY
Kiso, A. *The Lost Sophocles.* New York: Vantage Press, 1984.
Lloyd-Jones, H. *Sophocles: Fragments.* Cambridge, Mass.: Harvard University Press, 1996.
Merkelbach, R. *Hestia und Erigone: Vorträge und Aufsätze.* Hrsg. v. W. Blümel, B. Kramer, J. Kramer, C. E. Römer. Stuttgart: Teubner, 1996.
Radt, S. *Tragicorum Graecorum Fragmenta.* Vol. 4. Göttingen, Ger.: Vandenhoeck & Ruprecht, 1977.
Sutton, D. F. *The Lost Sophocles.* Lanham, Md.: University Press of America, 1984.

ERINYES   See FURIES.

ERIPHYLE (Latin: ERIPHYLA)   The daughter of Talaus and Lysimache (or Lysianassa), Eriphyle was the sister of ADRASTUS, king of ARGOS, and the wife of AMPHIARAUS, a prophet of Argos. Once upon a time, when AMPHIARAUS and Adrastus had an argument, Amphiaraus agreed to allow Eriphyle to decide any future disagreement he might have with Adrastus. When Adrastus and Amphiaraus, whose prophetic powers told him that he would die in battle against THEBES, disagreed about whether help POLYNEICES to wage war against Thebes, Polyneices gave Eriphyle a necklace as a bribe so that she would persuade Amphiaraus to participate in the expedition against Thebes. Amphiaraus did so and died in the fighting. Amphiaraus and Eriphyle had two daughters (Demonassa and Eurydice) and two sons (Amphilochus and ALCMEON). Alcmeon avenged the death of his

father by killing Eriphyle. SOPHOCLES wrote an *Eriphyle,*
although this play may have been another name for his
Epigoni. The Greek tragedian Nichomachus also wrote
an *Eriphyle,* of which only the title survives (fragment
4 Snell). Among Roman authors, ACCIUS wrote an *Eriphyla;* only a single line survives: "Double-bodied Pallas draws the coils of serpents" (line 326 Warmington).
[ANCIENT SOURCES: Apollodorus, *Library* 1.9.3, 3.6.2,
3.7.2; Homer, *Odyssey* 11.326, 15.247–48; Hyginus,
Fables 73; Pausanias, 1.34.2, 3.15.6, 5.17.4; Pindar,
Nemean Odes 9.57, *Olympian Odes* 6.21]

BIBLIOGRAPHY
Kiso, A. *The Lost Sophocles.* New York: Vantage Press, 1984.
Lloyd-Jones, H. *Sophocles: Fragments.* Cambridge, Mass.:
    Harvard University Press, 1996.
Radt, S. *Tragicorum Graecorum Fragmenta.* Vol. 4. Göttingen,
    Ger.: Vandenhoeck & Ruprecht, 1977.
Snell, B. *Tragicorum Graecorum Fragmenta.* Vol. 1. Göttingen,
    Ger.: Vandenhoeck & Ruprecht, 1971.
Sutton, D. F. *The Lost Sophocles.* Lanham, Md.: University
    Press of America, 1984.
Warmington, E. H. *Remains of Old Latin: Livius Andronicus,
    Naevius, Pacuvius, and Accius.* Vol. 2. Cambridge, Mass.:
    Harvard University Press, 1936, 438–39.

ERIS (Latin: DISCORDIA)   The daughter of
NIGHT or of ZEUS and HERA, Eris personifies strife. She
is often found in the company of her brother, ARES.
The start of the Trojan War can be traced to Eris, who,
angered at not being invited to the wedding of PELEUS
and THETIS, threw an apple inscribed "To the fairest"
into a group of goddesses. HERA, ATHENA, and
APHRODITE all claimed the apple and asked ZEUS to
determine which of them was the fairest. Not wanting
to choose among his wife and two of his daughters,
Zeus turned over the choice to the Trojan PARIS, who
eventually chose Aphrodite as the fairest. Paris' judgment angered the other two goddesses, who began to
prepare their revenge against Paris and the Trojans.
With Aphrodite's backing, Paris ran off with MENELAUS'
wife, HELEN, and soon afterward the Trojan War began.
[ANCIENT SOURCES: Euripides, *Iphigenia at Aulis* 1302;
Herodotus, 6.86; Hesiod, *Theogony* 225; Homer, *Iliad*
4.441–45, 5.518, 11.3, 11.73, 20.48; Hyginus, *Fables*
92; Pausanias, 5.19.1]

EROS (Latin: CUPID or AMOR)   Accord-
ing to HESIOD, Eros is one of the earliest divinities to
exist. Along with Chaos, Tartarus (see UNDERWORLD),
and Gaia (see EARTH), Eros appears at the beginning of
existence and has no parent or parents. Other sources
make him the son of APHRODITE. Eros is usually
depicted as a handsome young male who has wings. He
carries a bow and those whom his arrows strike are
filled with feelings of love or passion. Eros does not
appear as a character in any extant dramas, but his
power is often mentioned and is evident in many plays,
especially EURIPIDES' *HIPPOLYTUS* (which deals with PHAE-
DRA's passion for her stepson) and SOPHOCLES' *TRACHIN-
IAN WOMEN* (which focuses on several loves of HERACLES
and DEIANEIRA's attempt to maintain Heracles' love).
[ANCIENT SOURCES: Euripides, *Hippolytus* 525–41,
1268–82, *Iphigenia at Aulis* 548–51, *Medea* 529–30,
Trojan Women 840; Hesiod, *Theogony* 120–22, 201;
Menander, fragment 198 Körte; Plato, *Symposium*;
Sophocles, *Antigone* 781–800]

BIBLIOGRAPHY
Körte A., and A. Thierfelder. *Menandri Quae Supersunt.* Vol.
    2, 2d ed. Leipzig: Teubner, 1959.

EROTES   This Greek term can refer either to the
twin sons of APHRODITE, EROS (Roman: Cupid) and
Anteros, or the winged male creatures that are frequently found in situations (such as weddings) in
which love may be flourishing or about to flourish.
The Greek comic poet Myrtilus wrote an *Erotes,* of
which only the title survives (fragment 1 Kock).
[ANCIENT SOURCES: Euripides, *Bacchae* 405, *Medea* 843;
Seneca, *Hippolytus* 275]

BIBLIOGRAPHY
Kock, T. *Comicorum Atticorum Fragmenta.* Vol. 1. Leipzig:
    Teubner, 1880.

ERYCINA   See APHRODITE.

ERYTHRAE   A Greek town south of THEBES.
[ANCIENT SOURCES: Euripides, *Bacchae* 751]

ERYX (1)   The son of Aphrodite and Butes, Eryx
was a mighty boxer who challenged all strangers to his

land (SICILY) to a boxing match. Usually Eryx killed all his opponents, but he himself was killed when HERACLES defeated him. [ANCIENT SOURCES: Hyginus, *Fables* 260; Seneca, *Hercules Furens* 481]

ERYX (2) A mountain of western SICILY that was supposed to have been named after APHRODITE's son, ERYX. Aphrodite is sometimes called Erycina, the goddess of Eryx. [ANCIENT SOURCES: Seneca, *Hippolytus* 199, *Medea* 707, *Oedipus* 600]

ERYXIS The son of PHILOXENUS, Eryxis was someone who enjoyed eating and drinking. In Greek, his name means "belch" or "burp." [ANCIENT SOURCES: Aristophanes, *Frogs* 934; Aristotle, *Eudemian Ethics* 1231a17]

ETEOCLES The son of JOCASTA and the son and brother of OEDIPUS, Eteocles was the brother of POLYNEICES, ANTIGONE, and ISMENE. After Oedipus blinded himself, Eteocles and Polyneices were in line for the kingship of THEBES. Oedipus, because of some disrespect his sons had shown him, had cursed the brothers to kill one another. To avoid this, Eteocles and Polyneices agreed to take turns ruling Thebes, each serving for a year at a time. Eteocles ruled first but refused to give up power after a year. Polyneices then gathered an army and marched on Thebes. In the battle, Eteocles and Polyneices killed each other in single combat.

Eteocles appears as a character in AESCHYLUS' *SEVEN AGAINST THEBES,* EURIPIDES' *PHOENICIAN WOMEN,* and SENECA's *PHOENICIAN WOMEN.* Each of these plays tells of the struggle between Eteocles and his brother. Polyneices does not have a speaking role in Aeschylus' play, although some of his words are reported and his corpse is carried in at the play's conclusion, along with that of Eteocles, who delivers almost one-quarter of the lines in the play. Thus, Eteocles is the focal point in *Seven against Thebes,* in which he is seen as a somewhat coldhearted political and military leader. Eteocles shows little sympathy toward the Theban women who worry about the impending war and threatens with death anyone who disobeys him. Much of the play shows Eteocles as the military strategist who matches

the various Theban champions with the enemies' champions. When Eteocles learns that Polyneices' shield bears the image of Justice leading a golden warrior and an inscription that states that Justice will restore Polyneices to his rightful kingdom of Thebes, Eteocles scoffs at the notion that Polyneices has Justice as an ally and declares that he himself will go out to face his brother. The chorus warn Eteocles about the implications of killing one's brother, but Eteocles is determined to gain victory even if it means the destruction of his own brother and his own household. The chorus suggest that a sacrifice might appease the gods that oppose Eteocles' house, but Eteocles believes the gods have forsaken him and his family. The Theban women beg Eteocles not to go out into battle against his brother, but he refuses. Ultimately, Eteocles and Polyneices kill one another in battle.

In Euripides' play, the speaking parts of Eteocles and Polyneices are almost equal. Euripides portrays Eteocles as hungry for power, but Polyneices is criticized as well and neither brother will compromise. Eteocles arranges for the marriage of Antigone and CREON's son, Haemon; notes that the prophet TIRESIAS should be consulted; orders Creon not to allow Polyneices to be buried on Theban soil if he dies in battle; and decrees death for anyone who tries to bury him in Thebes. Eventually, Jocasta goes to the battlefield to attempt to effect the reconciliation of the brothers, but that effort fails and the brothers kill one another.

In Seneca's *Phoenician Women,* Eteocles is characterized in roughly the same way as in Euripides' play. As in Euripides' play, Jocasta tries to persuade the brothers to make peace on the battlefield, but Eteocles declares that Polyneices must continue in exile. Because the text of Seneca's play breaks off after only 664 lines, how the debate between the two brothers continued or how Seneca dealt with the battle between the two is unknown.

SOPHOCLES' *OEDIPUS AT COLONUS* (401 B.C.E.) also deals with the events before the battle, but Polyneices, rather than Eteocles, appears as a character in this play. Sophocles' ANTIGONE (442/441 B.C.E.) deals with the events after the battle, but focuses on the edict by Creon not to bury Polyneices. Eteocles is mentioned by name a few times in Euripides' *SUPPLIANT WOMEN,* which is about the Argive attempt to recover the bodies of their fallen champions from the Thebans. [ANCIENT SOURCES: Apollodorus, *Library* 3.6.5–6; Hyginus, *Fables* 67–72; Pausanias, 9.5.11–13]

ETEOCLUS   The son of Iphis, Eteoclus was from ARGOS and one of the Seven against THEBES. His platoon attacked the Neistan Gate at Thebes. Eteoclus was killed in battle by the Theban Leades. [ANCIENT SOURCES: Aeschylus, *Seven against Thebes* 458; Apollodorus, *Library* 3.6.3, 3.6.8; Euripides, *Suppliant Women* 872, 1037; Pausanias, 10.10.3]

ETHIOPIA   The lands in Africa south of Egypt, but north of the equator, were often referred to as Ethiopia. SOPHOCLES wrote an *Ethiopians,* whose content is unknown (see fragments 28–33 Radt). Because two famous figures of mythology, ANDROMEDA and MEMNON, were from Ethiopia, some scholars think *Ethiopians* was an alternate title for Sophocles' *Andromeda* or *Memnon*. [ANCIENT SOURCES: Apollodorus, *Library* 2.4.3; Pausanias, 1.42.3; Seneca, *Hercules Furens* 38; Terence, *Eunuch* 165, 471]

BIBLIOGRAPHY
Kiso, A. *The Lost Sophocles.* New York: Vantage Press, 1984.
Kock, T. *Comicorum Atticorum Fragmenta.* Vol. 2. Leipzig: Teubner, 1884.
Lloyd-Jones, H. *Sophocles: Fragments.* Cambridge, Mass.: Harvard University Press, 1996.
Radt, S. *Tragicorum Graecorum Fragmenta.* Vol. 4. Göttingen, Ger.: Vandenhoeck & Ruprecht, 1977.
Sutton, D. F. *The Lost Sophocles.* Lanham, Md.: University Press of America, 1984.

ETNA   See AETNA.

EUAEON   A man mentioned by ARISTOPHANES, at *ECCLESIAZUSAE* 408, as being a clever public speaker, but apparently so poor that he did not have a cloak. His proposal in the public assembly was that people should be provided free cloaks and blankets for their bed. Euaeon is not mentioned elsewhere in the ancient sources.

BIBLIOGRAPHY
Sommerstein, A. H. *The Comedies of Aristophanes.* Vol. 10, *Ecclesiazusae.* Warminster, U.K.: Aris & Phillips, 1998, 177.

EUATHLUS   An Athenian who prosecuted THUCYDIDES, the son of Melesias, just before 425 B.C.E. and may have brought a charge of impiety against the sophist Protagoras, who may have been his teacher. [ANCIENT SOURCES: Aristophanes, *Acharnians* 710, *Wasps* 592, fragment 411.2 Kock; Diogenes Laertius, 9.56; Quintilian, 3.1.10]

BIBLIOGRAPHY
Kock, T. *Comicorum Atticorum Fragmenta.* Vol. 1. Leipzig: Teubner, 1880.
MacDowell, D. M. *Aristophanes: Wasps.* Oxford: Clarendon Press, 1971, 213.
Sommerstein, A. H. *The Comedies of Aristophanes.* Vol. 1, *Acharnians.* Warminster, U.K.: Aris & Phillips, 1980.

EUBOEA   A large island that lies roughly parallel to the eastern coast of Greece. Some of HERACLES' final hours on Earth were spent on the northern end of this island. The evil king LYCUS, who persecuted Heracles' family, is said to have been from Euboea. [ANCIENT SOURCES: Aristophanes, *Clouds* 211, *Wasps* 715; PLAUTUS, *Epidicus* 153; Seneca, *Hercules Oetaeus;* Sophocles, *TRACHINIAN WOMEN*]

EUBOULE   The personification of "Good Counsel." [ANCIENT SOURCES: Aristophanes, *Thesmophoriazusae* 808]

EUCHARIDES   All that is known about this person is that he was apparently a seller of vegetables. [ANCIENT SOURCES: Aristophanes, *Wasps* 680]

EUCHLOUS   See DEMETER.

EUCRATES   Several Athenians of this name are known during the last quarter of the fifth century B.C.E. NICIAS had a brother Eucrates; another Eucrates, from the deme of Melite, was a minor Athenian statesman who made a living selling bran and hemp. The identity of the Eucrates ARISTOPHANES mentions in *LYSISTRATA* is uncertain, but Aristophanes indicates that he was a military commander in Thrace when that play was produced in 411. [ANCIENT SOURCES: Aristophanes, *Knights* 129, 254, *Lysistrata* 103, fragment 696 Kock]

BIBLIOGRAPHY
Henderson, J. *Aristophanes: Lysistrata.* Oxford: Clarendon Press, 1987, 79.
Kock, T. *Comicorum Atticorum Fragmenta.* Vol. 1. Leipzig: Teubner, 1880.
Sommerstein, A. H. *The Comedies of Aristophanes.* Vol. 2, *Knights.* Warminster, U.K.: Aris & Phillips, 1981, 150.

EUDAMUS (EUDEMUS)   A seller of medicine, magical charms, and poison. [ANCIENT SOURCES: Aristophanes, *Wealth* 884; Plato Comicus, fragment 217 Austin; Theophrastus, *History of Plants* 9.17.2]

BIBLIOGRAPHY
Austin, C. *Comicorum Graecorum Fragmenta in Papyris Reperta.* Berlin: De Gruyter, 1973.

EUELPIDES   A character in ARISTOPHANES' *BIRDS,* Euelpides has a name that means "son of good hope." Euelpides joins Peisetaerus in leaving ATHENS and pursuing a life among the birds. About halfway through the play, Peisetaerus sends Euelpides to build walls for their city in the clouds and perform various other administrative tasks necessary for the city's operation. Euelpides does not return to the stage after this point.

EUMELUS   The son of ADMETUS and ALCESTIS, Eumelus married Icarius' daughter, Iphthime. He fought at TROY and competed in the chariot race at PATROCLUS' funeral games. SOPHOCLES wrote a *Eumelus,* whose content is unknown (fragment 205 Radt). [ANCIENT SOURCES: Apollodorus, *Epitome* 3.14, 5.5; Euripides, *Iphigenia at Aulis* 217–26; Homer, *Iliad* 2.713–15, 23.287–565; Hyginus, *Fables* 97]

BIBLIOGRAPHY
Kiso, A. *The Lost Sophocles.* New York: Vantage Press, 1984.
Lloyd-Jones, H. *Sophocles: Fragments.* Cambridge, Mass.: Harvard University Press, 1996.
Radt, S. *Tragicorum Graecorum Fragmenta.* Vol. 4. Göttingen, Ger.: Vandenhoeck & Ruprecht, 1977.
Sutton, D. F. *The Lost Sophocles.* Lanham, Md.: University Press of America, 1984.

EUMENIDES   See ORESTEIA.

EUMOLPIDAE   The descendants of Eumolpus, the son of POSEIDON. At the town of ELEUSIS, the Eumolpidae served as priests for the Eleusinian MYSTERIES. [ANCIENT SOURCES: Demosthenes, 59.117; Plutarch, *Alcibiades* 22, 33; Sophocles, *Oedipus at Colonus* 1053; Thucydides, 8.53.2]

EUNUCH TERENCE (161 B.C.E.?)   The date of the play is in some dispute as the play's production notice and all its manuscripts say that it was TERENCE's second. The play's production notice, however, gives a date of 161 B.C.E., which would date it after *ANDRIA* and *SELF-TORMENTOR.* Terence drew upon MENANDER for the original. The action takes place on an Athenian street before the houses of Demea, an Athenian gentleman, and Thais, a prostitute. In the play's prologue, Terence warns an unnamed rival poet (who was, in fact, Luscius Lanuvinus) not to attack him for staging a play that had already been produced by NAEVIUS and PLAUTUS, as well as transferring characters from Menander's *Flatterer* into Menander's *Eunuch,* the latter of which was the primary model for Terence's play. The prologue speaker does not deny transferring the characters but does deny stealing from the work of Naevius or Plautus.

In the opening act, Demea's son, Phaedria, and his middle-aged servant, Parmeno, discuss Phaedria's love of Thais. Soon, Thais emerges from her house and tells Parmeno and Phaedria that once a merchant had given Thais' mother a young girl (who turns out to be Pamphila), whom pirates had stolen from SUNIUM (near Athens). When Thais' mother died, Thais' greedy brother sold Pamphila (who people thought was Thais' sister). A male friend of Thais', the soldier Thraso, whose name means "bold" or "confident," happened to buy Pamphila and planned to give her to Thais as a present, but has not yet done so. Thais, who loves Phaedria, asks him to allow the soldier to spend a few days with her so that she can receive the young woman and restore her to her real family, whom she claims to have found. Phaedria reluctantly agrees to this but complains because he typically gives Thais anything she wants. Phaedria points out that when Thais said she wanted a eunuch, he bought her one. Phaedria says that he will leave town for a few days and spend time at his house in the country. Thais praises Phaedria for his attitude, but before he leaves he tells Parmeno to watch over his interests while he is away.

After Phaedria leaves, Parmeno witnesses the arrival of Gnatho ("jaw"), PARASITE to the soldier Thraso, and a beautiful woman named Pamphila. Parmeno listens as Gnatho explains how he flatters people to get invitations to dinner. Gnatho also says that he is taking Pamphila to Thais' house. After a brief conversation with Parmeno, Gnatho enters Thais' house with Pamphila. After Gnatho delivers Pamphila, he emerges from her house and exits. Next, Parmeno watches as a breathless Chaerea, the brother of Phaedria, enters in search of Pamphila. Chaerea has seen Pamphila, has fallen in love with her, and was following her but was delayed by one of their relatives, Archidemides. When Chaerea sees Parmeno, he confesses his feelings for the young woman to Parmeno, who realizes that he must be looking for Pamphila. Parmeno tells Chaerea where Pamphila is and informs him of the situation between Thraso and Thais. Upon hearing that Phaedria was giving a eunuch to Thais, Chaerea expresses envy, because the eunuch will be in close proximity to Pamphila. Parmeno jokingly suggests that Chaerea should switch clothes with the eunuch so that he can be close to her. Chaerea is delighted by this idea and drags Parmeno into their house to make the change.

In the play's third act, Gnatho and Thraso arrive. After some initial bragging by Thraso about his greatness and wit, they discuss how Thraso should deal with Thais' jealousy that Thraso is attracted to Pamphila. Thraso knows that Thais does not love him, but Gnatho tries to encourage him. Soon, Thais herself enters. Gnatho tries to persuade Thais and Thraso to leave so that they can have dinner. Parmeno, who has arrived on the scene, tries to prevent them from moving inside by telling her to wait for the gifts (an Ethiopian maidservant and the eunuch) that Phaedria has for her. Thais agrees and the maid, Pythias, and Chaerea, dressed as a eunuch named Dorus, are taken over to Thais' house. With this exchange taken care of, at last Thraso, Gnatho, and Thais set out for Thraso's house to dine.

The play's fourth act opens with the arrival of a young Athenian gentleman named Chremes, who suspects that Thais wants to cause him some trouble. From Chremes' speech, it becomes clear that Thais has

been questioning Chremes about Pamphila, who Thais must suspect is Chremes' brother. Soon, Chremes is taken to see Thais at Thraso's house. After Chremes' departure, Antipho, a young Athenian gentleman, enters in search of Chaerea, because they had agreed to have dinner together and Chaerea was in charge of the arrangements. Antipho is amazed to see Chaerea, dressed as a eunuch, appear at the door of Thais' house. When Antipho questions Chaerea about what he is doing, Chaerea explains his scheme and also informs Antipho that he has just sexually assaulted Pamphila. Stunningly, Antipho's immediate response to this announcement is to wonder whether Chaerea has taken care of their dinner arrangements. Chaerea states that he has, and the two then exit for Antipho's house so Chaerea can change his clothes.

After the departure of Antipho and Chaerea, Dorias, one of Thais' maidservants, enters and reports that trouble broke out at Thraso's house at the arrival of Chremes, who Thraso believed Thais had taken in as a rival to him for Thais' affections. Thus, to make Thais jealous, Thraso asked for Pamphila to be taken over to entertain the party. Thais, upset by this suggestion, took some trinkets that were found with Pamphila when she was a young girl and gave them to Dorias to take home (a gesture that Dorias took as indicating Thais would soon be leaving Thraso's house). After Dorias' entry into Thais' house, Phaedria, longing to see Thais, returns from the country. Next, Pythias and Dorias enter; Phaedria listens in horror as Pythias tells Dorias that the eunuch raped Pamphila. Phaedria, not knowing that the eunuch was his brother in disguise, approaches the two maidservants and asks about the trouble. When Phaedria hears that the eunuch whom he gave to Thais has assaulted Pamphila, he does not believe such a thing could happen. Still, Phaedria goes out to find the eunuch. Soon, he returns with the real eunuch dressed in Chaerea's clothes. When Phaedria shows the eunuch to Thais' maidservants, they claim they have never seen the man before. Dorus then explains that Chaerea switched clothes with him, but Phaedria, hearing of his brother's misbehavior, does not believe the eunuch and soon, threatening to torture him to find out the truth, drags him off to his house.

After Phaedria's exit, Pythias and Dorias wonder what they should do next. Dorias takes the box with Thais' jewelry into the house, while Pythias remains outside and talks to an intoxicated Chremes, who is on his way back from Thraso's house. Chremes tells Pythias of the quarrel between Thraso and Thais, who soon arrives on the scene. Thais tells Chremes that the quarrel involves him, because it concerned his long-lost sister, who, Thais says, is inside her house. Thais also tells Chremes that Thraso is on his way to the house to take the young woman to his house. Chremes wants to get some other men to help him against Thraso, but Thais tells him that Chremes should simply tell Thraso that the woman is his sister and show him the trinkets that Thais has saved.

After the exit of Thais and Chremes into her house, Thraso, accompanied by Gnatho and a band of servants armed with items such as crowbars and sponges, enters and threatens to storm Thais' house, take Pamphila, and punish Thais. When Thais and Chremes appear at a window on the second floor of the house, Thraso complains to her that she took in someone as a rival to him and threatens to carry off Pamphila by force. Chremes, however, declares that Pamphila is his sister and a freeborn Athenian. Chremes also says that he will soon produce evidence to prove his claim.

After the departure of Thraso and his "army," the play's final act begins with a quarrel between Thais and Pythias, who has informed Thais about Chaerea's sexual assault of Pamphila. Thais chastises Pythias for allowing this to happen, but Pythias hopes they will have some measure of revenge, as she sees Chaerea approaching. Chaerea is still dressed as a eunuch because he was prevented from changing his clothes by various mishaps. Thais approaches him and chastises him as if he were the eunuch Dorus. Soon, however, she drops her pretense and confronts him with his actions. Chaerea explains his love for Pamphila and his desire to marry her. Thais agrees to this and Chaerea, despite Pythias' objection, enters the house with Thais.

In the next scene, Chremes arrives with a nurse, Sophrona, who will help prove that Pamphila is Chremes' sister. Pythias approaches them and learns that Sophrona has recognized the items that confirm Pamphila's identity. As they discuss these things,

Pythias sees Parmeno approaching and decides to scare him, because she has suspected that Parmeno had some role in Chaerea's earlier scheme. Accordingly, Pythias begins complaining loudly about the outrage caused by the eunuch and Parmeno. When Parmeno asks Pythias to explain, she tells him that the eunuch has sexually assaulted an Athenian citizen (a crime that would have carried a heavier penalty than assault on a slave). Pythias also says that Chremes learned of it, tied up the eunuch, and threatened to punish him in the way that adulterers are punished (probably castration in this instance, an ironic punishment because eunuchs were already assumed to be castrated). At this point, Parmeno informs Pythias that Chaerea is the culprit and that no harm had better come to him. Pythias suggests, however, that Parmeno himself may find trouble because people may think that he planned Chaerea's dressing as a eunuch.

As Parmeno considers his own trouble, his master, the father of Chaerea and Phaedria, approaches. Parmeno, though he realizes he may receive a beating, decides to tell his master the truth about what has happened. When the father hears of the threat to Chaerea, he enters Thais' house to intervene. Soon, Pythias emerges from the house and laughs about the joke she has played on Chaerea's father. She also informs Parmeno of the joke she has played on him. After Pythias' return to Thais' house, Parmeno eavesdrops as Thraso and Gnatho approach. Thraso states his intent to "surrender" to Thais. Before Thraso can enter Thais' house, Chaerea emerges and declares to Parmeno his delight at learning that Pamphila has been discovered to be an Athenian citizen and that she will marry him. Chaerea also announces that Phaedria's relationship with Thais is stable and that Thais will reject Thraso. After Parmeno goes to inform Phaedria of this, Phaedria emerges from his house and expresses his joy to Chaerea. Thraso, who has been eavesdropping on this conversation, begs Gnatho to create a scheme to win over Thais. Gnatho agrees to try but recognizes the difficulty of fulfilling the soldier's desire. At this point, Thraso and Gnatho step forward and address the brothers. Phaedria threatens the soldier to expect trouble if he ever goes to Thais' house again. Gnatho intervenes, however, and takes the brothers aside. Gnatho proposes that Phaedria "use" Thraso to keep Thais supplied with expensive gifts (because Phaedria has little money for such things) and that they allow Gnatho himself to spend time with them rather than Thraso. Gnatho tells Phaedria that he need not fear that Thais will fall in love with Thraso, and that they can get rid of the soldier whenever they like. The brothers agree to this proposal and, as the play ends, welcome the unwitting soldier to join them at Thais' house.

COMMENTARY

As do most of Terence's other plays, *Eunuch* has a double plot in which two lovers are ultimately united with the women they desire. Phaedria's relationship with Thais, however, is relegated to the background as Terence somewhat clumsily sends him off to the country. Although Terence's prologue denies stealing from Plautus, this play is Terence's most Plautine work. No other Terentian play contains a prominent BRAGGART WARRIOR, and Thraso's eventual defeat, although of secondary importance in the play, recalls Plautus' BRAGGART WARRIOR. Thraso's army of kitchen-tool-equipped slaves provides an amusing scene and is reminiscent of Plautus' lighter comic touch. Although the title character of Terence's PHORMIO is called a parasite, Phormio bears little resemblance to the usual food-obsessed parasites of Plautus' comedies. In *Eunuch,* however, Gnatho's strategy of success through flattery and his obsession with food show him to be a parasite more in the Plautine tradition.

Terence's use of cross-dressing also seems to embrace the bawdier style of Plautus. The dressing of the young man as a genderless eunuch is reminiscent of Plautus' CASINA, in which Chalinus dresses as a bride and tricks Olympio, who tries to consummate a relationship with the person he thinks is the slave-woman Casina. In Terence's play, however, Chaerea is a freeborn male, whereas in Plautus' Chalinus is a slave. In Roman COMEDY, freeborn men may behave foolishly, but they do not subject themselves to such an extreme change of costume as Chaerea's. Such overt role playing is usually done by slaves, as in the example of Chalinus. Perhaps the closest example would be Pleusicles, who in Plautus' *Braggart Warrior* disguises himself as a ship's captain so that he can escape with his

beloved. We may also consider Philocrates, in Plautus' CAPTIVES, who is a freeborn male but pretends to be a slave. This role, however, does not involve such an extreme change of costume.

Not only is Chaerea's change of costume extreme, but his rape of the music girl seems unusually violent, despite his professed love for her and desire to marry her. Of course, several Roman comedies make reference to freeborn males' raping women, but the playwrights seem to try to mitigate the violence of these acts by placing them in a distant past when the man was young, intoxicated, and at some festival at which wild behavior would not be surprising. Chaerea is not at a festival, he is not intoxicated, and the rape takes place in the present, not in the distant past. Instead of the usual mitigating elements that accompany such rapes, in Terence's play blame for Chaerea's actions is placed on the slave Parmeno (1007–8) for convincing Chaerea to dress as a eunuch (of course, Parmeno did not tell Chaerea to commit rape). Another effort to mitigate Chaerea's violence may be Terence's introduction of the roles of the parasite and braggart warrior.

The theme of altered clothing appears later in the play as well. At lines 646 and 820, we learn that Chaerea tore Pamphila's hair and ripped her clothing (646, 820). Thus, Chaerea has radically altered not only his clothing but the young woman's as well. Chaerea's actions also lead to the false accusation of the real eunuch, who is wearing Chaerea's clothes (671); because the eunuch is no longer wearing colorful clothing, his appearance is unpleasant (683). Besides tearing Pamphila's clothing, Chaereas exchanges clothing with the eunuch, an exchange also described in somewhat violent language as the eunuch responds in the affirmative to Phaedria's question, "Did Chaerea take your clothing from you?" (707). The Latin verb used here, *detrahere,* can literally be translated "to drag away." Thus, it seems Chaerea has done violence to the eunuch's clothing as well as Pamphila's. The false accusation of the real eunuch becomes even more perilous for the eunuch when Pamphila is discovered to be an Athenian citizen. When Chaerea raped Pamphila, she was supposed to be a slave, but when the eunuch is alleged to have raped her, her status had changed to freeborn, and, as noted, in Athenian law the rape of a freeborn woman was considered a more serious offense than the rape of a slave.

Some measure of revenge is taken against Chaerea later in the play when he, still dressed as a eunuch, is chastised by Thais as if he were the eunuch Dorus. After Chaerea confesses his wrongdoings to her, he is able to return to shed his eunuch's clothing. Chaerea's change of clothing occurs just in time, too, as he avoids having his future brother-in-law (907) see him dressed in such a shameful fashion. Thus, although Terence's *Eunuch* may contain more Plautine elements than any of his other plays, Terence may have needed these elements to offset the extreme violence of his young lover Chaerea.

BIBLIOGRAPHY
Brothers, A. J. *The Eunuch: Terence.* Warminster, U.K.: Aris & Phillips, 2000.
Dessen, C. S. "The Figure of the Eunuch in Terence's *Eunuchus,*" *Helios* 22, no. 2 (1995): 123–39.
Konstan, D. "Love in Terence's *Eunuch:* The Origins of Erotic Subjectivity," *American Journal of Philology* 107 (1986): 369–93.
Saylor, C. F. "The Theme of Planlessness in Terence's *Eunuchus,*" *Transactions of the American Philological Association* 105 (1975): 297–311.
Smith, L. P. "Audience Response to Rape: Chaerea in Terence's *Eunuchus,*" *Helios* 21 (1994): 21–38.

EUPHEMIUS   An otherwise unknown person mentioned by ARISTOPHANES at WASPS 599.

EUPHORIDES   A fictional character named as one of the chorus members in ARISTOPHANES' ACHARNIANS (612). His name means "son of good carrier."

EUPOLIS (D. CA. 411 OR 410 B.C.E.)   Eupolis was a rival of ARISTOPHANES and was considered one of the best comic poets of his era. Eupolis' first play, *Men of Prospalta,* was produced in 429, just two years before Aristophanes' first play. His *Days of the New Moon* (*Noumeniai*) was defeated by Aristophanes' ACHARNIANS at the LENAEA in 425, and his *Flatterers* (which attacked CALLIAS' relationship with SOPHISTS) competed against Aristophanes' PEACE at the City DIONYSIA in 421. Also in 421, at the Lenaea, Eupolis' *Maricas* took aim at the

politician HYPERBOLUS. Eupolis' other datable plays include *Autolycus* (420), *Cities* (420), *Dippers* (*Baptai;* 424–15), and *Demes* (417–12). Eupolis also wrote plays entitled *Abusers of Law* (*Hubristodikai*), *Commanders* (*Taxiarchoi*), *Friends, Goats, The Golden Race, Laconians,* and *Thefts.* As Aristophanes did in WASPS, Eupolis dealt with corrupt jurors in *Abusers of Law,* and his *Men of Prospalta* seems to have concerned litigation. In *Commanders,* DIONYSUS seems to have been trained under the Athenian naval commander PHORMIO. In FROGS (405), Aristophanes may have adapted this idea as Dionysus has difficulties in rowing for CHARON in the UNDERWORLD. Eupolis' *Demes* may also have had some influence on *Frogs,* as this play deals with the four deceased leaders returning from the underworld to save Athens from ruin. [ANCIENT SOURCES: Aristophanes, *Clouds* 553, scholia on *Clouds* 551, argument to *Acharnians,* Peace; *Athenaeus,* 5.216d; Horace, *Satire* 1.4.1; *Inscriptiones Graecae* ii² 2325.59, 126]

BIBLIOGRAPHY
Harvey, D., and J. Wilkins, eds. *The Rivals of Aristophanes: Studies in Athenian Old Comedy.* London: Duckworth and the Classical Press of Wales, 2000, 159–246.
Kock, T. *Comicorum Atticorum Fragmenta.* Vol. 1. Leipzig: Teubner, 1880.
Sidwell, K. "Aristophanes' *Acharnians* and Eupolis," *Classica et Mediaevalia* 45 (1994): 71–115.

EURIPIDES (CA. 484–406 B.C.E.)   The date of Euripides' birth is uncertain. One ancient source places it in 484; another tradition says that he was born in the year of the battle of SALAMIS, 480. Although comic poets characterized Euripides as having parents of little wealth and low birth (they said Euripides' mother sold vegetables), these slanders cannot be confirmed, and other information about Euripides suggests that his parents were respectable and had a healthy income. Inscriptions record that Euripides served as wine pourer for well-born young males who honored APOLLO, and on another occasion he served as torch bearer in a procession for Apollo. Euripides is said to have been an athlete early in his career, then to have taken up painting, and finally become a poet. Euripides was a member of the DEME of PHYLA, but his family had property on the island of Salamis and he is said to have done some of his writing there. Ancient sources often stated that Euripides studied with thinkers such as Protagoras and SOCRATES. Euripides' writing also shows that he knew something of the work of Anaxagoras and Prodicus, and after his lifetime Euripides was called the philosopher of the stage. Tradition reports that Euripides was married twice (to Melito and Choirile) and had three sons, Euripides the younger, Mnesarchides, and Mnesilochus. After Euripides died, the younger Euripides produced his IPHIGENIA AT AULIS and BACCHAE for competition in Athens.

According to one rumor, Euripides' slave Cephisophon, who was said to have helped Euripides compose his plays, seduced Euripides' wife. This cannot be confirmed, however, and the rumor may have evolved from another stereotype about Euripides, namely, that he hated women (compare ARISTOPHANES' THESMOPHORIAZUSAE). This stereotype arises from statements made by characters in some of Euripides' plays, both male and female, who make remarks about the evils of women. Euripides has an equal number of negative remarks about men, however, and one later writer, Athenaeus, calls him not a hater, but a lover of women. Euripides died at the court of the Macedonian king Archelaus, where he spent the last two years of his life. One tradition says that Euripides died after being torn apart by dogs. This story, however, should be dismissed as being modeled on the death of ACTAEON, a character in mythology who died in that manner. SOPHOCLES, who himself would die within another year, is said to have honored Euripides by wearing mourning clothes and by summoning his chorus before the play without their usual garlands.

Although Euripides did not gain as much critical acclaim as AESCHYLUS or SOPHOCLES during his lifetime (Euripidean dramas had only four victories, more than three times fewer than those of Aeschylus), after his death Euripides' plays continue to enjoy more popularity than those of Aeschylus or Sophocles. Euripides' first known play, *Peliades* (The daughters of Pelias), was staged in 455 (the year after Aeschylus' death), and he had his first victory in 442 (with which plays is unknown). Euripides put some 90 plays on the stage, of which 19 survive (five more than the combined surviving plays of Aeschylus and Sophocles): ALCESTIS

(438), MEDEA (431), THE CHILDREN OF HERACLES (ca. 430), HIPPOLYTUS (428), ANDROMACHE (ca. 426), HECABE (ca. 424), SUPPLIANT WOMEN (ca. 422), HERACLES (ca. 417), TROJAN WOMEN (415), ELECTRA (ca. 415), IPHIGENIA IN TAURIS (414 or 413), HELEN (412), ION (ca. 410), PHOENICIAN WOMEN (ca. 410), ORESTES (408), Bacchae (405), Iphigenia at Aulis (405), CYCLOPS (a SATYR PLAY), and *Rhesus* (which some scholars do not believe Euripides wrote).

Not only did Euripides write plays, but, as alluded to, a fictional Euripides appeared as a character in several plays. Three of Aristophanes' surviving plays have Euripides as a character. In ACHARNIANS, Aristophanes satirizes Euripides' practice of having major characters on stage dressed in rags when Dicaeopolis goes to the tragedian's house to borrow the costume of Telephus from Euripides' play of the same name. In THESMOPHORIAZUSAE, Aristophanes portrays Euripides as a hater of women and has the women at the Thesmophoria decree death for the tragedian. Finally, in FROGS, DIONYSUS goes to the UNDERWORLD with the intention of taking back Euripides because all of the other good poets have left Athens or are dead. At the play's conclusion, however, Dionysus decides to take Aeschylus back to the upper world because he judges him better able to advise the Athenians than Euripides.

If one compares Aristophanes' portrayal of Socrates in CLOUDS and of Euripides' in *Frogs,* one finds a great number of similarities and none of them speaks well of Euripides. Both are described as worshiping unusual divinities, corrupting people with their ideas, and expressing themselves in ways that were difficult for people to understand. On several occasions, Aristophanes quotes lines from Euripides' plays that the comic playwright found bizarre (e.g., "My tongue has sworn, my mind remains unsworn"; "What is shameful unless it seems so to those who do it?"; "Who knows if life is death or death is life?").

Although much of Aristophanes' criticism of Euripides is exaggerated, in contrast to Aeschylus and Sophocles, Euripides definitely seems to have tested the limits of dramatic art. His expository prologues, in which a single character appears at the beginning and "sets the stage" for the events that will ensue, were criticized as rather bland, but we find the same sort of prologues in PLAUTUS. Euripides is also criticized for not integrating the chorus skillfully into the action of his plays, but in some cases (e.g., *Orestes*) this may have been done to create a particular dramatic effect or emphasize a particular theme. Critics have often noted the artificial or contrived endings of many of his plays through a deus ex machina (see MECHANE). Women, common people, and slaves receive more attention in Euripides' plays than in those of the other two great playwrights. ELECTRA's peasant husband has more lines than CLYTEMNESTRA in Euripides' *Electra,* and in *Iphigenia in Tauris* a cowherd's speaking role is more extensive than that of the Taurian king, THOAS. Euripides was interested in the psychological motivation of his characters, and sometimes his characters seem inconsistently drawn as they waver back and forth between courses of action (e.g., MEDEA in *Medea,* AGAMEMNON in *Iphigenia at Aulis*). They often express a cynical attitude toward the behavior of their fellow humans and the divinities that control the world. [ANCIENT SOURCES: Aristophanes, *Acharnians, Frogs, Thesmophoriazusae;* Aristotle, *Poetics* passim; Athenaeus, *Deipnosophists* passim; Dio Chrysostomus, *Oration* 52; Suda, e3695; see especially Kovacs]

BIBLIOGRAPHY

Burnett, A. P. *Catastrophe Survived: Euripides' Plays of Mixed Reversal.* Oxford: Clarendon Press, 1971.

Conacher, D. J. *Euripidean Drama.* Toronto: University of Toronto Press, 1967.

Kovacs, D. *Euripidea.* Leiden: Brill, 1994.

Mossman, J., ed. *Oxford Readings in Classical Studies: Euripides.* Oxford: Oxford University Press, 2003.

Webster, T. B. L. *The Tragedies of Euripides.* London: Methuen, 1967.

EURIPUS   The narrow strait between the island of EUBOEA and mainland Greece.

EUROPA   The daughter of AGENOR (or Phoenix), Europa was the sister of CADMUS, Cilix, Phoenix, and Thasus. She was seduced by ZEUS (disguised as a bull), who carried her from her home (TYRE) to the island of CRETE, where he sexually assaulted her. She gave birth to several sons by Zeus: MINOS, RHADAMANTHYS, and Sarpedon. After her experience with Zeus, Europa married Asterius, a Cretan prince. The continent of EUROPE takes its name from her. [ANCIENT SOURCES: Apollodorus, *Library* 2.5.7, 3.1.1; Homer, *Iliad* 14.321, *Odyssey* 4.564; Hyginus, *Fables* 178; Ovid, *Metamorphoses* 2.833–75; Seneca, *Hercules Furens* 9, *Hercules Oetaeus* 550, *Octavia* 206, 766, *Oedipus* 715, *Trojan Women* 896]

EUROTAS   A river in southern Greece on which the town of SPARTA is located.

EURYALUS (1)   The son of Mecisteus, Euryalus gained fame for sailing with the Argonauts, as well as serving on the Greek side during the Trojan War.

EURYALUS (2)   According to Parthenius' *Erotica,* ODYSSEUS, after he left TROY, went to Epirus and, while staying with KING Tyrimmas, impregnated his daughter, Euippe, who produced Euryalus. When Euryalus grew up, he traveled to ITHACA in search of his father. When Euryalus arrived at his father's house, he was met first by Odysseus' wife, PENELOPE, who immediately became jealous of Odysseus' child. When Odysseus arrived on the scene, Penelope convinced him that Euryalus planned to kill him and that Odysseus should kill Euryalus, and he did. SOPHOCLES wrote a *Euryalus,* of which only the title survives. Because Mecisteus' son, EURYALUS (1), does not seem to be a character suited for drama, scholars generally agree that Sophocles' play was about Odysseus' son, Euryalus.

BIBLIOGRAPHY

Kiso, A. *The Lost Sophocles.* New York: Vantage Press, 1984.

Lloyd-Jones, H. *Sophocles: Fragments.* Cambridge, Mass.: Harvard University Press, 1996.

Radt, S. *Tragicorum Graecorum Fragmenta.* Vol. 4. Göttingen, Ger.: Vandenhoeck & Ruprecht, 1977.

Sutton, D. F. *The Lost Sophocles.* Lanham, Md.: University Press of America, 1984.

EURYBATES   A herald from ITHACA who aided AGAMEMNON and ODYSSEUS during the Trojan War. Agamemnon sent Eurybates on embassies to take BRISEIS from ACHILLES and to try to persuade Achilles to continue fighting in the war. [ANCIENT SOURCES: Homer,

Iliad 1.318–48, 9.170, *Odyssey* 19.244–48; Seneca, *Agamemnon* 392, 421]

EURYCLES Either a prophet or a spirit who gave prophecies through other people. [ANCIENT SOURCES: Aristophanes, *Wasps* 1019; Plato, *Sophist* 252c; Plutarch, *Moralia* 414e]

EURYDICE (1) The wife of CREON in SOPHO-CLES' *ANTIGONE*. She appears at the end of the play (1180ff.) and learns that her son, HAEMON, has committed suicide. In grief, Eurydice hangs herself.

EURYDICE (2) The wife of ORPHEUS, Eurydice died of a snakebite on the day she was married. Orpheus went to the UNDERWORLD to recover her, but as they were leaving, Orpheus looked back (in violation of HADES' command) and Eurydice returned to the land of the dead. [ANCIENT SOURCES: Apollodorus, 1.3.2; Hyginus, *Fables* 164, 251; Ovid, *Metamorphoses* 10.1–85; Pausanias, 9.30.6; Seneca, *Hercules Furens* 569, *Hercules Oetaeus* 1084]

EURYDICE (3) The wife of Lycurgus, king of NEMEA. She appears as a character in EURIPIDES' *HYP-SIPYLE* and threatens HYPSIPYLE with death because Eurydice blames her for the death of her son, OPHELTES.

BIBLIOGRAPHY
Page, D. L. *Select Papyri*. Vol. 3. 1941. Reprint, London: Heinemann, 1970, 77–109.

EURYPYLUS The son of TELEPHUS and Astyoche, Eurypylus went as an ally to the Trojans in the 10th year of the war after the deaths of ACHILLES and HECTOR. Initially, Eurypylus did not want to fight, but in a situation similar to the story of AMPHIARAUS and ERIPHYLE, PRIAM, the brother of Eurypylus' mother, Astyoche, bribed his sister with a golden vine to persuade Euryalus to enter the war. Eurypylus did so and achieved some success but eventually was killed by Achilles' son, NEOPTOLEMUS. SOPHOCLES wrote a *Eurypylus*, of which 121 fragments exist, most of them extremely brief. One of the fragments appears to refer to the duel between Eurypylus and Neoptolemus.

BIBLIOGRAPHY
Kiso, A. *The Lost Sophocles*. New York: Vantage Press, 1984.
Lloyd-Jones, H. *Sophocles: Fragments*. Cambridge, Mass.: Harvard University Press, 1996.
Radt, S. *Tragicorum Graecorum Fragmenta*. Vol. 4. Göttingen, Ger.: Vandenhoeck & Ruprecht, 1977.
Sutton, D. F. *The Lost Sophocles*. Lanham, Md.: University Press of America, 1984.

EURYSACES The son of AJAX and TECMESSA, Eurysaces was a child no more than 10 years old when his father committed suicide at TROY. Eurysaces was taken back to Ajax's native island of SALAMIS and eventually became king there. Justin 44.3 relates that Eurysaces' uncle, TEUCER, founded the town of Salamis on CYPRUS and later returned to the island. Repelled by Eurysaces, Teucer left and later established the town of Galicia in Spain.

SOPHOCLES wrote a *Eurysaces,* of which one quotation survives; Lloyd-Jones thinks the play may have been the same as Sophocles' *Teucer.* Among Roman authors, ACCIUS wrote a *Eurysaces,* of which some 40 lines survive. Several of the fragments, which describe someone who appears to be an exile and wandering over land and sea, may refer to Teucer. Fragment 363 mentions taking someone to Salamis. Fragment 367 mentions a possible attack on a king, but which king is unknown. In fragment 368, the speaker (Eurysaces?) orders two or more people, apparently servants or guards, to drag someone (Teucer?) away quickly.

BIBLIOGRAPHY
Kiso, A. *The Lost Sophocles*. New York: Vantage Press, 1984.
Lloyd-Jones, H. *Sophocles: Fragments*. Cambridge, Mass.: Harvard University Press, 1996.
Radt, S. *Tragicorum Graecorum Fragmenta*. Vol. 4. Göttingen, Ger.: Vandenhoeck & Ruprecht, 1977.
Sutton, D. F. *The Lost Sophocles*. Lanham, Md.: University Press of America, 1984.
Warmington, E. H. *Remains of Old Latin: Livius Andronicus, Naevius, Pacuvius, and Accius*. Vol. 2. Cambridge, Mass.: Harvard University Press, 1936.

EURYSTHEUS The son of Sthenelus and PELOPS' daughter, Nicippe, Eurystheus is called the king of ARGOS, MYCENAE, or TIRYNS. He became famous for his persecution of HERACLES, who would have become king of the land were it not for the trickery of HERA. Eurystheus and Heracles were related: ALCMENA, Heracles' mother, was the daughter of ELECTRYON; Electryon's brother, Sthenelus, was the father of Eurystheus. Also, Eurystheus' father, Sthenelus, and Alcaeus, the father of Heracles' mortal father, AMPHITRYON, were both sons of PERSEUS, who was a son of ZEUS, as was Heracles. When Hera discovered that Alcmene was pregnant with Zeus' child, she persuaded her husband to swear that the next of his descendants to be born would inherit the kingdom. Zeus, knowing that Heracles would soon be born, agreed to the oath. At this, Hera delayed the birth of Heracles and sped up the birth of Eurystheus. Because Eurystheus was born before Heracles, the kingdom became his. Many years later, after Heracles killed his wife and children in a fit of Hera-induced insanity, the DELPHIC ORACLE made Heracles perform 10 (or usually 12) labors to atone for his crime. The oracle required that Heracles perform these tasks for Eurystheus. Eurystheus was ultimately killed by either Iolaus, Heracles' nephew, or Heracles' son HYLLUS. Eurystheus appears as a character in EURIPIDES' CHILDREN OF HERACLES and is taken before Heracles' mother, Alcmena. His fate in this play is unclear because of the ancient manuscript breaks off before the conclusion. [ANCIENT SOURCES: Apollodorus, 2.8.1; Diodorus, 4.57.6; Euripides, *Children of Heracles* 843 ff.; Isocrates, *Panathenaicus* 194, *Panegyricus* 58, 60; Pausanias, 1.44.9; Pindar, *Pythian Ode* 9.79 ff.]

EURYTUS A king of the town of Oechalia on the island of EUBOEA. Eurytus was the father of, among others, IPHITUS and IOLE. Heracles wanted to marry Iole, but Eurytus declared that he could marry her only if he defeated Eurytus and his sons in an archery contest. Heracles defeated them, but Eurytus still refused to marry Iole to Heracles. For a time, Heracles left Eurytus, but just before the end of Heracles' life, Heracles returned and destroyed Eurytus and his kingdom and took Iole as a captive in the process. [ANCIENT SOURCES: Seneca, *Hercules Furens* 477, *Hercules Oetaeus* 100, 207, 221, 1490; Sophocles, *Trachinian Women*]

EUTHYMENES An Athenian who held the office of ARCHON in 437/436 B.C.E. [ANCIENT SOURCES: Aristophanes, *Acharnians* 67]

BIBLIOGRAPHY
Sommerstein, A. H. *The Comedies of Aristophanes*. Vol. 1, *Acharnians*. Warminster, U.K.: Aris & Phillips, 1980, 160.

EXARCHON A Greek term for the leader of a chorus. [ANCIENT SOURCES: Demosthenes, 18.260]

EXECESTIDES A person mocked by ARISTOPHANES as a slave and a barbarian. MacDowell thought Execestides' father may have disowned his son in infancy as a bastard and that later Execestides, when he became an adult, may have sued to gain recognition as a legitimate son. Dunbar suggests that Execestides may have been an Athenian who was raised abroad and then returned to ATHENS and tried to reclaim status as his father's legitimate son. [ANCIENT SOURCES: Aristophanes, *Birds* 764, 1527]

BIBLIOGRAPHY
Dunbar, Nan. *Aristophanes: Birds*. New York: Oxford University Press, 1995, 137–38.
MacDowell, D. M. "Foreign Birth and Athenian Citizenship in Aristophanes." In *Tragedy, Comedy, and the Polis: Papers from the Greek Drama Conference, Nottingham, 18–20 July 1990*. Edited by A. H. Sommerstein, S. Halliwell, J. Henderson, and B. Zimmermann. Bari: Levante Editori, 1993.

EXODOS The Greek word *exodos* means "exit song." The *exodos* is the part of a drama that is not followed by a choral song; thus, it is the play's conclusion. [ANCIENT SOURCES: Aristotle, *Poetics* 1452b21–22]

EXOSTRA Another name for the ECCYCLEMA. [ANCIENT SOURCES: Pollux, *Onomasticon* 4.127, 129]

EXTRAS Minor participants in a drama. The Greek expression for "extras" is *kopha prosopa* ("mute persons"). SOPHOCLES' *AJAX,* for example, has three *kopha prosopa:* the child Eurysaces, the child's tutor, and a herald. This expression is somewhat misleading, however, because sometimes *kopha prosopa* do speak. Pylades has three important lines in AESCHYLUS' *Libation Bearers* (see ORESTEIA), in which he gives ORESTES advice on the question of killing Orestes' mother. In most cases, however, the extras consisted of slaves (who might carry things on- or offstage), ATTENDANTS on important persons, or those who played children's parts. In several plays (EURIPIDES' ALCESTIS, ANDROMACHE, and SUPPLIANT WOMEN, to name a few), children have brief remarks. Even divine beings could be extras. HERMES does not speak in Aeschylus' *Eumenides* (see ORESTEIA) and in PROMETHEUS BOUND Force remains silent. Greek COMEDY made more extensive use of extras than TRAGEDY. Although surviving tragedies usually have no more than 10 *prosopa,* only one of ARISTOPHANES' 11 plays (*KNIGHTS*) has fewer than 10 *prosopa.* In *WASPS,* certain boys guide the CHORUS into the orchestra. In *CLOUDS,* extras would have been needed to play the various students of SOCRATES' whom STREPSIADES is shown. Certain attractive women in Aristophanes' plays at whom men gawk and grab were played by extras. In Roman comedy, the extras primarily represent the lower classes (slaves, prostitutes, and cooks). Plautus' *CARTHAGINIAN* has a group of counselors and his *ROPE* has a group of fishermen.

BIBLIOGRAPHY

Stanley-Porter, D. P. "Mute Actors in the Tragedies of Euripides," *Bulletin for the Institute of Classical Studies* 20 (1973): 68–93.

Zweig, B. "The Mute Nude Female Characters in Aristophanes' Plays." In *Pornography and Representation in Greece and Rome.* Edited by A. Richlin Amy. Oxford: Oxford University Press, 1991, 73–89.

F

FABULA ATELLANA   Also known as Atellana, Atellan farce, or Oscan farce (Oscan was a dialect in Italy), *Fabula Atellana* was a type of drama that was said to have originated in the town of Atella, near Italy's western coast between Rome and Naples. Although no complete Atellan play has survived, we do know of some 120 titles and 300 lines of fragments from the works of Lucius Pomponeius of Bononia and a certain Novius, both of whom were active during the first two decades of the first century B.C.E. The subject matter of the *Atellana* usually appears to have revolved around the humorous situations of everyday life in "small-town" central Italy. In contrast to that of the plays of MENANDER, PLAUTUS, and TERENCE, the language of the *Atellana* appears to have been more coarse and obscene. As did the comedies of the authors mentioned, *Atellana* employed broad humor and stock characters who wore MASKS. Atellan stock characters, however, were often different from those found in the works of those playwrights. Six titles from Pomponius and three from Novius contain the name of a character named Maccus ("buffoon"). Four titles from Pomponius' plays and one from Novius' include the name of a character named Pappus ("grandfather"). Fullers and their trade (the pressing and cleaning of cloth) also appear to have been popular subjects, as two of Pomponius' plays and three of Novius' mention fullers or their trade in the title. A few of the titles indicate some similarity to Greek SATYR PLAYS (Pomponius' *Agamem-non Suppositus* and *The Judgment of Arms;* Novius' *Andromache, Hercules Coactor,* and *Phoenician Women*).

BIBLIOGRAPHY
Beare, W. *The Roman Stage.* London: Methuen, 1950, 137–48.
Frassinetti, P. *Fabula Atellana.* Genova: Istituto di filologia classica, 1953.
Lowe, J. C. B. "Plautus' Parasites and the Atellana." *In Studien zur vorliterarischen Periode im frühen Rom.* Edited by Gregor Vogt-Spira. Tübingen: Narr, 1989.

FABULA PALLIATA   "A play in Greek clothing" (the *pallium*), *fabulae palliatae* are comedies that Roman playwrights adapted or translated from Greek plays by such playwrights as APOLLODORUS of Carystus, DIPHILUS, MENANDER, and PHILEMON. Although these plays were performed for Roman audiences, their characters dressed in Greek clothing. All of the comedies of PLAUTUS and TERENCE are examples of *fabulae palliatae.* Other writers of *fabulae palliatae* include CAECILIUS Statius, Gnaeus NAEVIUS, Luscius Lanuvinus, and Sextus Turpilius (died 103 B.C.E.), but only fragments of their plays survive. In Rome, *fabulae palliatae* were popular during the last three centuries B.C.E.

BIBLIOGRAPHY
Duckworth, G. *The Nature of Roman Comedy.* Princeton, N.J.: Princeton University Press, 1952.
Warmington, E. H. *Remains of Old Latin: Livius Andronicus, Naevius, Pacuvius, and Accius.* Vol. 2. Cambridge, Mass.: Harvard University Press, 1936.

FABULA PRAETEXTA   Plays written in Latin that dramatized historical events. The only extant example is *Octavia,* attributed to the younger Seneca. Several other *fabulae praetextae* are known, however. Naevius wrote a play called *Clastidium,* which appears to have dealt with Marcus Claudius Marcellus' return to Rome after a victory over Viridomarus in 222 B.C.E. Naevius also put on a *Romulus* (also entitled *The Wolf;* Latin: *Lupus*), which seems to have treated Romulus' exposure at birth and suckling by the she wolf.

BIBLIOGRAPHY
Flower, Harriet I. *"Fabulae Praetextae* in Context: When Were Plays on Contemporary Subjects Performed in Republican Rome?" *Classical Quarterly* 45 (1995): 170–90.

FABULA TOGATA   Comedies written in Latin in which the characters dressed in Roman clothing (i.e., the toga). This type of COMEDY emerged in the second century B.C.E. A poet named Titinius is credited with inventing this type of comedy, and some 180 verses and a dozen titles of his plays have survived. Writers of *togata* include Lucius Afranius and Titus Quinctius Atta (who died in 77 C.E.). Some five dozen titles and more than 600 lines (two-thirds of which are from Afranius) survive from the *togata,* but no single play can be reconstructed. Women apparently played greater roles in *togata* than in FABULA PALLIATA, but the clever slaves of the *palliata* were apparently not permitted in the *togata.* The *togata* not only presented "love affairs between young people of respectable families" (Duckworth), but also referred to same-sex relationships between men.

BIBLIOGRAPHY
Duckworth, G. *The Nature of Roman Comedy.* Princeton, N.J.: Princeton University Press, 1952, 68–70.

FATES   These female divinities, usually three in number, are also called the Moerae (or Moirai) by the Greeks or the Parcae by the Romans. In both languages, their individual names are Clotho ("spinner"), Lachesis ("assigner of lots"), and Atropos ("unavoidable"). In *Theogony,* HESIOD called them the daughters of Night (Greek: Nyx) in one place (217–22), and the daughters of ZEUS and THEMIS in another (901–6).

Whether the gods controlled the Fates or vice versa depends on the source. In AESCHYLUS' *PROMETHEUS BOUND* 515–18, Zeus himself must abide by what the Fates decree. The Fates could be tricked, and both AESCHYLUS, at *Eumenides* (see *ORESTEIA*) 723–24, and EURIPIDES, in *ALCESTIS,* mention Apollo's deception of the Fates, which resulted in ADMETUS being able to avoid his death provided that he could find someone to die in his place.

FESCENNINE VERSES   Named after the Italian town of Fescennium, these coarse verses were sung at weddings. They were an early form of dramatic entertainment in Italy in which masked performers engaged in improvised conversations with rude or crude language. [ANCIENT SOURCES: Catullus, 61.126–55; Seneca, *Medea* 113]

FIDICINA   See MUSIC GIRL.

FLUTE   See AULOS.

FORTUNE   Among the Greeks, this goddess, who personified chance or luck, was named TYCHE; the Romans called her Fortuna.

FORUM   In Roman culture, the forum was a center for commercial and civic business. The Greek counterpart is the AGORA. According to Erich Segal, business in the forum is an obstacle to the enjoyment of the festival atmosphere created in Plautine COMEDY.

BIBLIOGRAPHY
Segal, Erich. *Roman Laughter: The Comedy of Plautus.* New York: Oxford University Press, 1987.

FRAGMENTS   Of the thousands of plays written by the ancient Greeks and Romans, about 85 complete plays survive. In many cases, however, fragments of incomplete plays survive. The majority of these fragments are no more than two lines; many times a fragment may only be a single word. Occasionally, the fragments of a play amount to more than 100 lines. In some cases, a play's fragments are in an ancient manuscript that has been damaged or broken off. In most instances, however, they are from quotations from other ancient authors. For example, the philosopher Plato might quote a line from a play by EURIPIDES. Athenaeus of Naucratis, living in the second century C.E., preserves hundreds of quotations from Greek TRAGEDY and COMEDY.

FREUD, SIGMUND (MAY 6, 1856–SEPTEMBER 23, 1939)

Born in Freiburg, Moravia, Sigmund Freud is credited with the establishment of psychoanalytic theory. Freud's theories have exerted considerable influence on the interpretation of classical drama. Freud published numerous works, but his work that has had the most impact on classical drama, *The Interpretation of Dreams,* in which Freud discussed this theory of the oedipus Complex, appeared in 1900. This theory was based upon his reading of a passage in SOPHOCLES' *OEDIPUS TYRANNOS,* in which JOCASTA remarks to OEDIPUS that in their dreams many men have had sexual relations with their mother. Freud concluded that the reason Sophocles' play had such a tremendous impact on the audience was that all men have a desire (which is repressed in most people) to have sexual relations with their mother and kill their father (as Oedipus did). Because sons want and need the love of their mother, they come to view their father as a sexual rival. Thus, to eliminate the sexual rival, Freud believed, sons harbor a desire to kill their father.

Freud also advanced a corresponding theory with respect to daughters, the Electra complex, named after ELECTRA, the daughter of AGAMEMNON and CLYTEMNESTRA. In plays such as AESCHYLUS' *Libation Bearers* (see *ORESTEIA*), SOPHOCLES' *ELECTRA,* and EURIPIDES' *ELECTRA,* Electra has feelings of hatred toward her mother and love toward her father, in whose murder her mother participated. In the Electra complex, daughters want to produce children by their father. Daughters also experience an envy of the father's penis, desire to have a penis of their own, and blame their mother for, as it were, castrating them.

Although most modern psychologists regard Freud's theories in this area as simplistic, Freud's work has influenced modern interpreters of classical drama, who have tried to apply psychoanalytic methodology to some ancient dramas. In addition to *Oedipus Tyrannos,*

Freud's psychoanalitic theories have been applied to Euripides' MEDEA, HIPPOLYTUS, and BACCHAE, and Aeschylus' PROMETHEUS BOUND, just to name a few.

BIBLIOGRAPHY

Derrida, J. *The Post Card: From Socrates to Freud and Beyond.* Translated by A. Bass. Chicago: University of Chicago Press, 1987.
Rudnytsky, P. L., and E. H. Spitz, eds. *Freud and Forbidden Knowledge.* New York: New York University Press, 1994.
Santas, G. X. *Plato and Freud: Two Theories of Love.* Oxford: Blackwell, 1988.

FROGS (Greek: *BATRACHOI*; Latin: *RANAE*) ARISTOPHANES (405 B.C.E.)

The play won first prize at the LENAEA over PHRYNICHUS' *Muses* and Plato's *Cleophon.* The play opens as DIONYSUS, the god of wine and drama, and his slave, Xanthias, make their way to HERACLES' house. Dionysus, who is on foot, wears not only his yellow robe and the boots that are traditionally worn by tragic actors, but over his robe, in imitation of Heracles, he wears a lion skin and carries a club. The slave Xanthias carries his master's luggage but rides on a donkey. Heracles, upon arriving at his house, is amused to see Dionysus dressed as he dresses and questions him about the reason. Dionysus tells Heracles that he intends to travel to the UNDERWORLD (as Heracles did) and take back the tragic poet EURIPIDES, because no "good" poets are left in ATHENS. Dionysus goes on to ask Heracles' advice about how best to reach the underworld and what he might expect to encounter along the way.

After receiving advice from Heracles, Dionysus and Xanthias set out for the underworld. Failing to hire a corpse to carry their baggage, they continue until they encounter CHARON, who agrees to ferry Dionysus across the lake to the underworld. Charon refuses to carry a slave in his boat, so Dionysus tells Xanthias that he must walk around the lake on foot. After Charon and Dionysus embark, Dionysus must help row the boat. As he rows, a CHORUS, composed of the spirits of dead frogs, sing a hymn to Dionysus and intermittently croak out a rhythm to which Dionysus rows (*brekekekex koax koax*). Dionysus complains about the pains of rowing and the noise of the frogs, which refuse to stop their croaking.

Eventually, Dionysus arrives at the opposite side of the lake and Xanthias joins him. After the pair again set out, they encounter the monster EMPUSA, which causes Dionysus to soil his clothing. Next, another chorus, composed of the souls of those who have been initiated into the Eleusinian Mysteries (see *Eleusis*), enter and sing a hymn to IACCHUS. They also ward off all things profane and sing processional hymns to PERSEPHONE, DEMETER, and Iacchus. Before their departure, the chorus inform Dionysus that he has arrived at the house of Pluto (see HADES).

Soon, Dionysus, still dressed as Heracles, knocks on the door to Pluto's house. When AEACUS answers and sees a man who he thinks is Heracles, he threatens to have him torn to pieces. After Aeacus leaves to fetch some monsters to attack "Heracles," Dionysus tells Xanthias to wear the Heracles disguise. No sooner does Xanthias put on the disguise than a maidservant from Pluto's house appears at the door, sees "Heracles," and invites him in to a huge banquet at which several attractive women will provide the entertainment. After the maidservant returns to the interior of the house, Dionysus makes Xanthias give him back the disguise. Next, the female keeper of a bake shop and her partner, Plathane, appear, see Heracles (Dionysus), and charge him with gobbling down some of their food during his previous trip to the underworld and terrifying them. When the two women run off to find their male patrons, CLEON and HYPERBOLUS, who will bring lawsuits against Heracles, Dionysus again makes Xanthias wear the Heracles costume.

At this point, Aeacus returns with some attendants and tells them to seize "Heracles." Xanthias/Heracles declares his innocence and says that he will allow his slave (Dionysus) to be examined under torture to prove his innocence. Hearing this, Dionysus declares his own true identity and claims that Xanthias/Heracles is the slave and should be flogged as well. Because Xanthias is a slave and is accustomed to being beaten, he has no objection to this proposal. Thus, Aeacus flogs both Xanthias and Dionysus to determine which is telling the truth about being a god. Unfortunately for Aeacus, both the slave and the god prove themselves resistant to pain and Aeacus decides to take the two inside to Pluto and Persephone to determine the truth.

After the exit of Aeacus, Dionysus, and Xanthias to Pluto's house, the chorus deliver the PARABASIS. They urge the people of Athens to restore the rights of citizenship to those who had been disenfranchised by the oligarch rulers a few years earlier. They also advise the Athenians to reverse their practice of making use of worthless men for important tasks.

After the parabasis, Aeacus and Xanthias enter. Xanthias questions Aeacus about the commotion inside Pluto's house. Aeacus informs Xanthias that AESCHYLUS and Euripides are quarreling over who should be recognized as the greatest tragic poet. Aeacus also relates that Pluto has proposed a competition between the two tragedians and that Dionysus will serve as the judge. After the exit of Aeacus and Xanthias and a brief comment by the chorus in anticipation of the upcoming contest, Dionysus, Aeschylus, and Euripides enter. After the two poets verbally abuse each other and pray to their respective gods (Aeschylus to Demeter, Euripides to Ether), Dionysus begins the contest.

Euripides complains that Aeschylus would customarily bring onto stage a character dressed as a mourner, who not say anything for a long time, but when such characters did finally speak, no one could understand what they were saying because the language was so complex. Euripides claims he himself put the language of TRAGEDY on a diet and slimmed it down. Furthermore, he explained matters clearly in the opening prologue and allowed characters from every social class to speak, to speak at length, and to examine the hows and whys of things.

Aeschylus responds by declaring that his own plays, such as *SEVEN AGAINST THEBES* and *PERSIANS*, made people seek to behave more virtuously and with greater zeal to fight on behalf of their country. He declares that it is a poet's duty to teach his audience something useful, and not to present onstage, as Euripides does, women who behave wickedly. Aeschylus claims Euripides' poetry has led to moral decline in society and even to a lack of physical fitness, because young men now sit around all day and argue about philosophical quibbles instead of exercising.

After a brief choral comment on the state of the competition thus far and the intellectual ability of the audience to comprehend the points that the poets are making, the two poets examine each other on the quality of their prologues. Euripides complains that Aeschylus' prologues contain statements that are illogical and redundant, and Aeschylus argues that Euripides' prologues contain statements that are factually inaccurate and that his metrical patterns are so predictable that the phrase "he lost his bottle of oil" can frequently be inserted at the end of a line. Similarly, Euripides charges Aeschylus with writing choral passages that are monotonous metrically and contain bizarre words. Aeschylus responds by claiming that whereas his Muse is pure, Euripides' is a wanton woman who plays castanets rather than a lyre and whose lyrics violate the rules of meter. After this contest, scales with two pans are carried out and the poets compete to see whose verses have most "weight." Aeschylus wins this event because he includes things such as rivers, chariots, and death in his verses, whereas Euripides speaks of "lighter" topics.

In the play's final contest each poet gives advice on how the people of Athens should deal with the statesman ALCIBIADES and how the Athenians can be saved militarily. Eventually, Dionysus must make a choice, and, despite his earlier desire to restore Euripides, the god chooses Aeschylus. After Dionysus, Aeschylus, and Pluto go back into Pluto's house for a banquet, the chorus praises the person of intelligence who does not engage in philosophical babble as Socrates does (and Euripides). Soon, Pluto and Aeschylus emerge from the house and Aeschylus is sent on his way back to the upper world. Before Aeschylus leaves, he tells Pluto to give his chair (as best tragedian among the dead) to SOPHOCLES. The play ends with the chorus' praising Aeschylus and hoping that he can provide Athens with good advice.

COMMENTARY

Frogs is one of Aristophanes' finest plays and contains an excellent blend of humor and seriousness. The idea of raising someone from the dead to remedy a social crisis in Athens was not new with Aristophanes, as EUPOLIS had done something similar with the great political leaders of Athens in his *Demes* in the previous decade. The expanded role of the wisecracking slave, Xanthias, is a new feature in comparison to Aristo-

phanes' earlier plays, and Xanthias' role has often been regarded as a precursor to the clever slaves of New Comedy. The switching of costumes and roles by Xanthias and Dionysus is also extremely funny and fits in with the theatrical theme of the play. Dionysus and Xanthias are characters in a play about the quest for a good poet, but they also play different roles within that play (e.g., Heracles).

The interaction of Dionysus and the chorus of croaking frogs is brilliant, although whether the audience would have actually seen a chorus dressed as frogs or whether the frogs were only heard is debated. At line 205, Charon says that Dionysus will hear the frogs, a statement that would imply that he will not see them. On one hand, some have thought that the Athenian economy was so pressed by the war that the cost of equipping two choruses would have been too great at this time. On the other hand, the main chorus in *Frogs* is dressed in rags (presumably inexpensive to produce), so perhaps money would have available to provide for the presumably more expensive frog costumes.

In addition to the fun of the croaking frogs, that scene also involves the use of a boat. Certainly a boat on wheels must have been employed, but how such a boat would have been propelled along the orchestra is not clear. Dover suggests the possibility that men hidden out of sight in the wings pulled the boat from one wing to the other. This would not have taken long, however, unless the boat were pulled at a very slow pace. The distance from one wing to the other was less than 100 feet and the choral ode itself is some 60 lines long. Are we to expect that this boat crept along at one foot per line? Perhaps the boat around the perimeter of the orchestra was either pulled around the perimeter by an unobtrusive extra or propelled by the foot power of the person who played Charon. The Athenians were familiar with the construction of boats on wheels, as they used one in the procession to their ACROPOLIS at the City DIONYSIA, so the boat in which Dionysus travels would not have been a vessel whose construction was completely foreign to those who built it.

Another problem of staging is the donkey that Xanthias rides. Dover thinks that a real donkey was used and then led off by a slave at line 44 when Dionysus tells Heracles to approach him. One wonders how wise it would have been to employ a real donkey onstage, because these animals can be rather temperamental and before thousands of spectators the animal might become more unpredictable. A "stick donkey" might have been used to more humorous effect. At line 32, Dionysus apparently tells Xanthias to pick up the donkey and carry the animal, because Xanthias complains that the donkey is not helping him bear his load. At line 35, when Dionysus tells Xanthias to dismount, Xanthias could pretend to dismount the "stick donkey" and then placed the stick donkey over his shoulder, thus picking up the donkey and carrying him as Dionysus suggested.

Although *Frogs* is filled with laughs, when the play appeared in 405 B.C.E., the political situation in Athens was a tense one. The Athenians had been at war with the Spartans and their allies since 431, and the Athenian political and military fortunes had been especially difficult during the decade before *Frogs*. The oligarchic revolution of 411 had defeated and democracy had been restored. Athens' most skilled military commander, Alcibiades, had been condemned to die in 415, had escaped the Athenians and gone over to the Spartan side, had been taken back to Athens, and then, in 406, after an Athenian loss at the battle of Notion, been exiled again. Also of importance to *Frogs* was the battle of ARGINUSAE in 406. Here, the Athenians defeated the Spartans, but adverse weather prevented the Athenians from recovering those who sailed on ships that had been wrecked. Upon returning to Athens, the Athenian commanders were tried as a group (contrary to usual Athenian practice) and condemned to die.

In addition to the political background of *Frogs*, another important aspect of this play is that it provides some of the earliest extant comments on the role and value of the poet and poetry in society. Just as in our own times some think the subject matter of certain television programs, motion pictures, or popular music can have a negative effect on society, in the same way Aristophanes suggests (although in a manner that is perhaps not altogether serious) that the poets can corrupt the morals of society or even influence people to behave in a certain way. As Aristophanes has Aeschylus say at lines 1034–36, children have their teachers, but

poets are the teachers of adults and poets should say things that benefit people.

With its educational focus, *Frogs* has much in common with Aristophanes' *CLOUDS*, and the Euripides of *Frogs* has much resemblance to the Socrates of *Clouds*. Aristophanes links both men with babbling (*lalia*) nonsensically; expressing thoughts that are difficult for others to understand; having associations with some of the more vile people in society; regarding Ether and the Tongue as divinities; teaching people to use tricky rhetoric; corrupting those who listen to them; and even being responsible for poor physical fitness of the society (because people no longer exercise, but sit and argue about philosophical nonsense). Aeschylus, in contrast, argues that his poetry has taught people how to be brave in battle and loyal to one's country and to behave in a morally upright fashion. Ultimately, when Dionysus chooses Aeschlyus, he does on the basis of who can give Athens the best advice in its time of crisis. As Aeschylus begins his journey to the upper world, the chorus praise him as someone who is intelligent (1490) but take a parting shot at both Euripides and Socrates by saying that sitting around and babbling (*lalein,* 1492) with Socrates both contributes to the corruption of tragedy and is the mark of a person who is mentally unstable.

One final aspect of *Frogs* that we should not neglect is Dionysus' role in the play. If Dionysus is to be considered the hero of the play, he certainly seems different from other Aristophanic heroes. Aristophanic heroes are typically common mortals who try to rise up against some social crisis and devise a novel plan to bring about reform. Although Dionysus does have a plan to reform a social crisis, he is the only divine hero in Aristophanes' extant plays. One helpful approach to understanding Dionysus' role is that taken by Moorton, who analyzes Dionysus' journey in terms of a rite of passage. Ancient rites of passage include traveling to a strange land, crossing a threshold, and returning across that threshold. During this journey, the traveler must undergo various tests or challenges. If the traveler is successful in his or her journey, society will be regenerated on the traveler's return. Dionysus' journey to the underworld, his crossing of the lake of frogs, his flogging by Aeacus, and his judging of the contest between

Euripides and Aeschylus reflect elements of such rites of passage. Dionysus begins his journey with the desire to bring back Euripides, and in the course of his journey, he discovers that Aeschylus will be of more value to the city of Athens than Euripides. Just as Heracles traveled to the underworld and rescued the Athenian Theseus from that realm and restored him to the Athenians, Dionysus, disguised as Heracles, travels to the underworld, rescues Aeschylus, and restores him to the Athenians. According to Euripides' HERACLES, staged about a decade before FROGS, Theseus later returned the favor by granting that hero asylum in Athens after his madness. In the case of Aeschylus, his return to Athens would not only regenerate Dionysus' favorite artistic medium, tragedy, but regenerate Athens as well.

BIBLIOGRAPHY

Dover, K. J. *Aristophanes: Frogs.* Oxford: Clarendon Press, 1993.

Moorton, R. F. "Rites of Passage in Aristophanes' *Frogs*," *Classical Journal* 84 (1988–89): 308–24.

Moorton, R. F. "Aristophanes on Alcibiades," *Greek, Roman and Byzantine Studies* 29 (1988): 345–59.

Padilla, Mark. "The Heraclean Dionysus: Theatrical and Social Renewal in Aristophanes's *Frogs*," *Arethusa* 25 (1992): 359–84.

Sommerstein, A. H. *The Comedies of Aristophanes.* Vol. 9 *Frogs.* Warminster, U.K.: Aris & Phillips, 1996.

FURIES Also known as the Erinyes or Semnae, the Furies, according to HESIOD's *Theogony*, were born as a result of the spilling of blood onto the ground from the wound of the castrated divinity URANUS. In *Eumenides* (see ORESTEIA), AESCHYLUS calls them the daughters of Night. Ancient vase paintings depict them as having wings, but in *Eumenides* Aeschylus says they do not have wings. Aeschylus goes on to describe them as being black, breathing heavily, and having eyes that give off a discharge. The Furies were invoked in curses and called upon to punish unavenged crimes, especially those involving the killing of parents by children. In classical drama, the Furies are best known for their pursuit and persecution of ORESTES after he killed his mother, CLYTEMNESTRA. In Aeschylus' *Eumenides*, the Furies make up the chorus and pursue Orestes to Delphi and ATHENS, where they submit their grievance to ATHENA and the judgment of her citizens. After the judgment rules against the Furies, they threaten to attack Athens, but Athena manages to persuade them to live in her city and enjoy the worship of her people. After the Furies agree to Athena's proposal, they change their name to Eumenides, which means "the kindly ones."

The Furies are frequently mentioned in other Greek dramas but do not appear as characters. In EURIPIDES' ORESTES, the title character appears to suffer from their torment as the play opens, but they never take the stage. In IPHIGENIA IN TAURIS, Euripides represents some of the Furies as refusing to accept the judgment of Athena and continuing to torment Orestes. In Roman TRAGEDY (SENECA's THYESTES), a Fury appears from the UNDERWORLD to compel the ghost of TANTALUS to drive ATREUS to kill the sons of his brother, THYESTES, and cause Thyestes to eat his own children.

G

GAIA See EARTH.

GALATEA The sea NYMPH Galatea, whose name means "milk-white" in Greek, was the daughter of Nereus and Doris. Galatea was in love with Acis, and the CYCLOPS Polyphemus was in love with Galatea. In a jealous rage, POLYPHEMUS killed Acis with a boulder and Galatea changed Acis into a river in SICILY. The comic poet Nicochares wrote a *Galatea*, whose two surviving fragments indicate nothing about the play's subject matter. [ANCIENT SOURCES: Apollodorus, *Library* 1.2.7; Hesiod, *Theogony* 251; Homer, *Iliad* 18.45; Ovid, *Metamorphoses* 13.738–897]

BIBLIOGRAPHY
Kock, T. *Comicorum Atticorum Fragmenta*. Vol. 1. Leipzig: Teubner, 1880.

GAMOS A Greek word meaning "marriage." Many dramas, especially comedies, end with some sort of union, real or symbolic, of a male and female. For example, at the conclusion of ARISTOPHANES' BIRDS, the main character, PEISETAERUS, is married to Basileia, the personification of sovereignty. EURIPIDES' HELEN concludes with a sort of remarriage of HELEN and MENELAUS; in SOPHOCLES' ANTIGONE, the title character experiences a figurative marriage with death.

GANYMEDE (Latin: CATAMEITUS)
Born at TROY, Ganymede is called the son of various Trojan kings (Assaracus, Erichthonius, Tros). Accius makes him the brother of Ilus and Assaracus. Ganymede was abducted by ZEUS, who some sources say had taken on the form of an eagle. Other sources say a whirlwind whisked Ganymede away. Zeus took Ganymede to Mount OLYMPUS, where Ganymede became Zeus' cupbearer. Zeus compensated Ganymede's father for the loss by giving him a golden grapevine, which HEPHAESTUS made, or a team of mares. Among the constellations, Ganymede represents the water carrier Aquarius. Ganymede also became one of Zeus' sexual partners, and his name is often synonymous with the submissive partner in intercourse between males. In EURIPIDES' CYCLOPS, the drunken and sexually aroused CYCLOPS tells SILENUS that he will turn him into his Ganymede. Three Greek comic poets wrote plays entitled *Ganymede*: Alcaeus (fragments 2–9 Kock 1), Antiphanes (fragments 73–74 Kock 2), and Eubulus (fragments 17–18 Kock 2). In each case, however, the fragments are too brief to inform us of the play's content. [ANCIENT SOURCES: Accius, fragment 653b; Aristophanes, *Peace* 724; Euripides, *Cyclops* 582–85, *Trojan Women* 820–58, *Orestes* 1392, *Iphigenia at Aulis* 1053; Hyginus, *Fables* 224, 271; Plautus, *Menaechmi* 143–46]

BIBLIOGRAPHY
Ambrose, Z. Philip. "Ganymede in Euripides' *Cyclops*: A Study in Homosexuality and Misogyny," *New England Classical Newsletter* 23, no. 3 (1995–96): 91–95.

Burnett, A. "Trojan Women and the Ganymede Ode," *Yale Classical Studies* 25 (1977): 291–316.

Kock, T. *Comicorum Atticorum Fragmenta*. Vol. 1. Leipzig: Teubner, 1880.

———. *Comicorum Atticorum Fragmenta*. Vol. 2. Leipzig: Teubner, 1884.

GARGETTUS   A DEME in Athenian territory near Mount HYMETTUS. [ANCIENT SOURCES: Aristophanes, *Thesmophoriazusae* 898]

GE   See EARTH.

GELA   A town on the southwestern coast of SICILY. AESCHYLUS died at Gela in 456 B.C.E. [ANCIENT SOURCES: Aristophanes, *Acharnians* 606]

GENETYLLIS   Either a goddess associated with childbirth or a title of APHRODITE. [ANCIENT SOURCES: Aristophanes, *Clouds* 52, *Lysistrata* 2, *Thesmophoriazusae* 130]

GERAESTUS   A cape at the southern end of the island of EUBOEA. POSEIDON is sometimes called the god of Geraestus. [ANCIENT SOURCES: Aristophanes, *Knights* 561; Euripides, *Cyclops* 295, *Orestes* 993]

GERANOS   Pollux says the *geranos* could be lowered from above the stage building (see SKENE) and used for raising a body from the ground, as when the goddess EOS raises up the body of MEMNON. This device was probably not in use until after the fifth century B.C.E. [ANCIENT SOURCES: Pollux, *Onomasticon* 4.127, 130]

GERES   It is uncertain whether this person was merely a fictional character (his name hints at a Greek word for "old man," *geron*) or a man active in Athens between the 420s and 390s B.C.E. The ancient commentators on ARISTOPHANES, *ECCLESIAZUSAE* 932, claim there was a historical Geres who had little money or hair. At *ACHARNIANS* 605, Aristophanes also mentions a Geres, and a historical Geres (who was bald) is known to have participated in an embassy to northwestern Greece in the 420s. The possibility also exists that there may have been two different persons named Geres. [ANCIENT SOURCES: Aeschines, 1.75 and the scholia; Lysias, 14.25–28 and the scholia]

BIBLIOGRAPHY
Sommerstein, A. H. *The Comedies of Aristophanes*. Vol. 10, *Ecclesiazusae*. Warminster, U.K.: Aris & Phillips, 1998, 218–19.

GERON   An otherwise unknown man mentioned by ARISTOPHANES at *ECCLESIAZUSAE* 848. His name means "old man" in Greek. Because Geron is mentioned in the same sentence as a young man who is enjoying the communal banquet, Aristophanes may be suggesting that young and old alike could exist happily side by side under the new system of government.

BIBLIOGRAPHY
Sommerstein, A. H. *The Comedies of Aristophanes*. Vol. 10, *Ecclesiazusae*. Warminster, U.K.: Aris & Phillips, 1998. 212.

GERYON   The son of Chrysaor and Callirrhoe, Geryon had three heads and six arms, and his three upper torsos met at a single waist that branched out into six legs. ARISTOPHANES calls him "four-feathered" (*tetraptilôi*), but no other tradition mentions this attribute and modern scholars are at a loss to explain it. Geryon ruled over Erytheia (or Erythrea), which has been identified with the town of Cadiz in Spain, or some unknown island west of Spain. While in search of Geryon's cattle, HERACLES battled with this bizarre humanoid, killed him, and took his cattle. The tragedian Nichomachus wrote a *Geryon,* of which only the title survives. The comic poet Ephippus also wrote a play called *Geryon,* from which about three dozen lines survive. [ANCIENT SOURCES: Aeschylus, *Agamemnon* 870 (see *ORESTEIA*); Apollodorus, *Library* 2.5.10; Aristophanes, *Acharnians* 1082; Euripides, *Heracles* 423–24; Plautus, *Pot of Gold* 554; Seneca, *Agamemnon* 841, *Hercules Furens* 487, 1170, *Hercules Oetaeus* 26, 1900]

BIBLIOGRAPHY
Burkert, W. "Le mythe de Géryon: Perspectives préhistoriques et tradition rituelle," *Il mito greco: Atti del Convegno internazionale (Urbino 7–12 maggio 1973)*. Edited by B. Gentili and G. Paioni. Roma: Ed. dell' Steneo e Bizzarri, 1977, 273–83.

Davies, M. "Stesichorus' Geryoneis and Its Folk-Tale Origins," *Classical Quarterly* 38 (1988): 277–90.

GERYONES   See GERYON.

THE GHOST   See THE HAUNTED HOUSE.

GIANTS   The offspring of EARTH, the Giants tried to overthrow ZEUS and the other Olympian divinities. Zeus and his allies discovered that they could not defeat the Giants without the help of a mortal, and so they enlisted the aid of HERACLES, who was part mortal. With Heracles as their ally, Zeus and the Olympians destroyed the Giants. The Greek comic poet Cratinus the younger wrote a *Giants;* the brief fragments that survive (fragments 1–2 Kock) give no indication of the play's content. [ANCIENT SOURCES: Apollodorus, *Library* 1.6.1–2; Euripides, *Heracles* 179, 1191, 1272, *Ion* 207, 988; Hesiod, *Theogony* 185–86; Hyginus, *Fables* prologue section 4; Seneca, *Hercules Furens* 976, *Oedipus* 91, *Thyestes* 806, 1084; Sophocles, *Trachinian Women* 1059]

BIBLIOGRAPHY

Kock, T. *Comicorum Atticorum Fragmenta.* Vol. 2. Leipzig: Teubner, 1884.

THE GIRL WITH THE SHAVEN HEAD (Greek: *PERIKEIROMENE*) MENANDER (CA. 302 B.C.E.)   About half of this play survives, and more than 100 lines are missing from its opening act. The play's setting is CORINTH, and the action occurs before two houses, one belonging to the soldier Polemon, the other to Myrrhine, the foster mother of a young man named Moschion. The play's text picks up in the prologue, which is delivered by a divinity, Misapprehension. The goddess informs the audience that the wife of an old man named Pataikos had twins, Glycera and Moschion. When Pataikos' wife died during childbirth, Pataikos exposed the children so they would die. An old woman found the children and raised Glycera, and she gave Moschion to a wealthy woman named Myrrhine. The goddess' speech also reveals that before her appearance, Glycera, the mistress of Polemon, appeared onstage with her hair cut off. The reason for Glycera's hair's being cut off was that

Polemon, who had returned from war, was informed by his slave, Sosias, sent ahead to the house, that Glycera was embracing another man. What Sosias and Polemon did not know, however, was that the other man was Glycera's twin brother, Moschion. Apparently, Glycera knew that Moschion was her brother but did not want to inform him of this. Not only did Moschion not know that Glycera was his sister, but he was also in love with her. After Polemon was led to believe that his mistress was taking up with another man, he apparently became enraged and cut off Glycera's hair. Not much of the first act survives after the departure of Misapprehension. It would appear, however, that Glycera took refuge at Myrrhine's house.

The play's second act begins with the arrival from the city of Moschion and his slave, Daos, who tells his master that Glycera is in his foster mother Myrrhine's house. Moschion then tells Daos to serve as his "spy," enter Myrrhine's house, and keep him informed of what is happening. Daos soon emerges and reports that Glycera is bathed and appears to be waiting for him. Moschion orders Doas to go back inside and announce his presence. When Daos returns, he reports that Moschion's mother is angry at Daos because she thinks he has told Moschion that Glycera took refuge in their house. Upon hearing this, Moschion is also angry at Daos, as he believes the slave has ruined his chances with his sister. Eventually, Daos calms Moschion and persuades him to go inside Myrrhine's house and try to correct the situation.

After Moschion exits, Polemon's servant, Sosias, arrives; sees Daos; and demands that Glycera be returned to Polemon. Sosias threatens Daos and his household with violence if she is not returned, and this threat sends an unnerved Daos back into Myrrhine's house. The last part of the act is missing; apparently Sosias leaves to tell Polemon where Glycera has taken refuge.

The opening of the play's third act is also missing; however, Sosias and Polemon have returned with a ragtag band of slaves (and a music girl, Habrotonon) to make their assault on Myrrhine's house. Pataikos, who will turn out to be Glycera and Moschion's father, is present and tries to calm the soldier and Sosias. Eventually, Polemon enlists Pataikos' help and persuades him to talk to Glycera on his behalf. Before this takes place, however, Pataikos escorts Polemon back into his (Polemon's) house. As they leave, Moschion emerges from Myrrhine's house and shouts after them. He also begins to complain about what occurred inside the house, but the last part of the act is missing. Apparently, Myrrhine revealed to him that he could not marry Glycera but does not appear to have told him why.

The fourth act's beginning is also missing, and the text picks up with a conversation between Pataikos and Glycera, who claims she was not trying to seduce Moschion. Glycera also tells Pataikos about some items she has that will ultimately help reveal her parents' identity. Glycera calls in to her maid Doris and asks her to carry out the box in which these items are kept. While Pataikos is looking over the items, Moschion enters from Myrrhine's house. Not noticing Glycera and Pataikos, Moschion reveals that he has learned that his mother exposed both him and his sister. The continuing conversation between Glycera and Pataikos causes Pataikos to realize that he is Glycera's father and to explain why he had abandoned her and her brother. Moschion overhears their conversation and realizes that Pataikos must be his father. The last part of the act is lost, but brother, sister, and father must have recognized one another.

The opening of the play's final act is also missing; when the text resumes Polemon is relating his continued distress about Glycera to Doris, although he has learned that Moschion and Glycera are brother and sister. Doris tries to cheer up Polemon and tells him that he and Glycera will be reunited. When Polemon hears Glycera and Pataikos leaving the house, he panics and runs off into his own house. Soon Polemon reemerges, acting composed and declaring that he is going to make a sacrifice in thanks for Glycera's good luck. The play ends with Pataikos' arranging the wedding of Polemon and Glycera and then exiting to set up a marriage for Moschion. A few lines from the play's ending that are lost probably dealt with preparations for a celebration.

COMMENTARY

Readers of TERENCE and especially PLAUTUS, in whose plays a BRAGGART WARRIOR sometimes appears, may be surprised by the fairly sympathetic portrayal of the

soldier in MENANDER's play. Although his violent act carries both injustice and misfortune, as Fortenbaugh has shown, Pataikos intervenes on his behalf and Glycera ultimately forgives him. Furthermore, one notes that in Menander's play, the soldier "gets the girl" at the play's conclusion. Contrast Plautus' CURCULIO, in which the soldier and girl discover that they are brother and sister and the young freeborn male will become the girl's husband. The opposite occurs in Menander's play. Glycera's role in the play is also noteworthy, and Konstan has discussed how throughout much of the play she has a status in between that of wife and citizen. This status gives Glycera a sort of freedom that she will no longer enjoy once she becomes the wife of Polemon.

BIBLIOGRAPHY
Fortenbaugh, W. W. "Menander's *Perikeriomene:* Misfortune, Vehemence, and Polemon," *Phoenix* 28 (1974): 430–43.
Karnezis, J. E. "Comments on Menander's *Perikeiromene* and *Epitrepontes,*" *Platon* 31 (1979): 111–22.
Konstan, D. "Between Courtesan and Wife: Menander's Perikeiromene," *Phoenix* 41 (1987): 122–39.

GLAUCETES
An Athenian who had a ravenous appetite that earned him nicknames such as "whale" and "turbot" (fish). He may have been the son of Peisander of ACHARNAE. [ANCIENT SOURCES: Aristophanes, *Peace* 1008, *Thesmophoriazusae* 1035; Plato Comicus, fragment 106 Kock]

BIBLIOGRAPHY
Kock, T. *Comicorum Atticorum Fragmenta.* Vol. 1. Leipzig: Teubner, 1880.
Sommerstein, A. H. *The Comedies of Aristophanes.* Vol. 5, *Peace.* Warminster, U.K.: Aris & Philips, 1985. 181.

GLAUCUS (1) (GLAUKOS)
The son of Nereus, Glaucus was a fisherman who, after eating a certain grass, was changed into a sea divinity able to prophesy. Glaucus fell in love with the maiden Scylla. When she rejected him, he went for advice to CIRCE, who fell in love with him. When Glaucus rejected Circe, the angered goddess poisoned the waters where Scylla bathed and she was transformed into a monster. AESCHYLUS wrote a play, probably satyric, entitled *Glaucus Pontius* (fragments 25c–34 Radt).

BIBLIOGRAPHY
Smyth, H. W., and H. Lloyd-Jones. *Aeschylus.* Vol. 2. 1926.
Reprint, Cambridge, Mass.: Harvard University Press,
1971.

GLAUCUS (2) (GLAUKOS)

The son of SISYPHUS and Merope, Glaucus had mares that he had fed human flesh so that they would charge enemies more quickly and eagerly. When this bizarre food supply was exhausted, the mares ate Glaucus himself while he was attending funeral games for Pelias. A scholiast on EURIPIDES' ORESTES 318 says that the horses had eaten a type of grass that caused them to become mad and turn on Glaucus. Other sources say that APHRODITE caused them to attack Glaucus because, hoping to make his mares run faster, he would not allow them to mate. AESCHYLUS wrote a play entitled *Glaucus Potneius* (fragments 36–42a Radt), which was the third play of a tetralogy produced in 472 B.C.E. that included *Phineus, Persians,* and *Prometheus.* [ANCIENT SOURCES: Pausanias, 9.22.7; Plutarch, *Life of Cicero* 2]

BIBLIOGRAPHY
Smyth, H. W., and H. Lloyd-Jones. *Aeschylus.* Vol. 2. 1926.
Reprint, Cambridge, Mass.: Harvard University Press,
1971.

GLYCE

The name of a fictional Greek slave woman. [ANCIENT SOURCES: Aristophanes, *Ecclesiazusae* 430, *Frogs* 1343]

GODSCHILD See AMPHITHEUS.

GOLDEN AGE

The earliest time when human beings lived, when no strife or evil existed. [ANCIENT SOURCES: Seneca, *Medea* 329, *Hippolytus* 525, *Octavia* 395]

GOLDEN FLEECE See JASON.

GORGIAS (CA. 483–376 B.C.E.)

A sophist and rhetorician from the town of Leontini on the eastern coast of SICILY. In 427, Gorgias traveled to ATHENS on a diplomatic mission whose purpose was to gain aid for his town against the people of SYRACUSE. Gorgias' mission was a success, but he later returned to Athens, took up residence, and became a teacher of the art of persuasion. Two works that survive are attributed to Gorgias, *The Apology of Palamedes* and *The Encomium of Helen.* [ANCIENT SOURCES: Aristophanes, *Birds* 1701; Pausanias, 6.17.9; Plato, *Gorgias*]

GORGON

The Gorgons were creatures who lived on the fringes of the known world. The Gorgons' head was wreathed with serpents and their large tusks were similar to those of a wild boar. Their hands were made of bronze and they had wings of gold. Those who looked directly at them were turned to stone. In AESCHYLUS' *Libation Bearers* and *Eumenides* (see ORESTEIA), the FURIES are said to resemble Gorgons. Ancient sources usually mention three Gorgon sisters (Euryale, Stheno, and MEDUSA), who were the daughters of Phorcys and Ceto (or Typhon and Echidna) and the sisters of the PHORCIDES. In some sources the first two Gorgon sisters were immortal, and Medusa was mortal. In EURIPIDES' *ION,* the author speaks of a Gorgon born from the earth, which ATHENA killed. Usually, however, PERSEUS is said to have killed the Gorgon Medusa and then presented the creature's head to Athena. Given the Gorgons' terrifying appearance, ancient warriors often had the face of a Gorgon on their shield. In ARISTOPHANES' *ACHARNIANS,* the Athenian statesman and commander LAMACHUS is said to have such an image on his shield. The AEGIS of the goddess Athena was made from the skin of a Gorgon and had the Gorgon's face on it. In Euripides' *Ion,* CREUSA mentions that she possesses two drops of that Gorgon's blood, one of which can heal, the other destroy. Creusa tries to kill Ion with the latter drop of blood but fails. Near the end of Euripides' *ALCESTIS,* when ADMETUS is about to reach out and take the hand of an unfamiliar woman after his wife has died, he compares the experience to reaching out to kill a Gorgon. The Gorgons do not appear in any surviving plays from antiquity but may have taken the stage in some dramas about Perseus. Perseus may have carried a Gorgon's head onto the stage in Euripides' *Andromeda.* The Greek comic poet Heniochus wrote a *Gorgons;* the three lines that survive reveal only that someone is demanding a drink (fragment 1 Kock). [ANCIENT SOURCES: Aeschylus, *Libation Bearers* 1048 (see ORESTEIA), *Eumenides* 48–49 (see ORESTEIA), *Prometheus Bound* 799–802; Apollodorus, *Library* 2.4.2, 2.7.3; Aristophanes, *Thesmophoriazusae* 1101–3; Euripides, *Ion* 988–1006].

BIBLIOGRAPHY
Kock, T. *Comicorum Atticorum Fragmenta.* Vol. 2. Leipzig: Teubner, 1884.

GRACCHI   Tiberius Sempronius Gracchus and his younger brother, Gaius Sempronius Gracchus, were Roman statesmen who were killed. Tiberius was killed in 133 B.C.E. by opponents of a controversial property reform law that he had proposed. After the elder Gracchus' death, his brother took up his political program. Gaius managed to have a few important laws passed, but his political work was controversial and he was killed in a riot in the year 121. [ANCIENT SOURCES: Appian, *Civil Wars* 1; Plutarch, *Gaius and Tiberius Gracchus*; Seneca, *Octavia* 882]

BIBLIOGRAPHY
Earl, Donald C. *Tiberius Gracchus: A Study in Politics.* Bruxelles-Berchem: Latomus, 1963.

GRACES   Also known by the Greek name Charites (the Romans called them Gratiae), the Graces were goddesses who were usually said to be daughters of ZEUS (several different women are named as their mother), although APOLLO or DIONYSUS was occasionally named as their father. The Graces are usually three in number (usually named Aglaia, Euphrosyne, and Thalaia); sometimes two Graces are mentioned. As their name indicates, the Graces personified grace and beauty and their presence conferred joy. They are sometimes found in the company of the MUSES or love divinities such as APHRODITE and EROS. Despite the Graces' love of pleasure and joy, they do not seem to have produced children. [ANCIENT SOURCES: Apollodorus, *Library* 1.3.1, 3.15.7; Hesiod, *Theogony* 64, 907; Pausanias, 4.24.5, 9.35.1, 9.38.1; Pindar, *Olympian Odes* 13.8, 14.7, 15; Statius, *Thebaid* 2.286]

GRADIVUS   See ARES.

GREAT DIONYSIA   See DIONYSIA.

GREAT GODDESSES   See DEMETER and PERSEPHONE.

GRIFFINS   Large mythical creatures with a lion's body, eagle's wings, and four feet, the griffins were famous as guardians of gold in the land of the ARIMASPIANS (in the Black Sea region), who constantly tried to steal the gold. The Greek comic poet Plato wrote a play entitled *Griffins* (Greek: *Grupes*), from which a few brief fragments survive (15–18 Kock). These fragments give us little insight into the play's content, however. [ANCIENT SOURCES: Aeschylus, *Prometheus Bound* 804–7; Herodotus, 3.116, 4.13]

BIBLIOGRAPHY
Kock, T. *Comicorum Atticorum Fragmenta.* Vol. 1. Leipzig: Teubner, 1880.
Reed, Nancy B. "Griffins in Post-Minoan Cretan Art," *Hesperia* 45, no. 4 (1976): 365–79.

GRYTTUS (GRYPUS)   An otherwise unknown person whom ARISTOPHANES names at KNIGHTS 877 as being someone who enjoyed being the active partner in anal intercourse.

GYAS   A giant who battled against ZEUS and his allies. [ANCIENT SOURCES: Seneca, *Hercules Oetaeus* 167, 1139]

HADES The son of CRONUS and RHEA, Hades was the brother of ZEUS, POSEIDON, DEMETER, HESTIA, and HERA. Also known by the name Pluto or Orcus, he was the master of UNDERWORLD and his name was synonymous with the place over which he rules. Hades possessed a cap that allowed its wearer to be invisible. In Hades' best-known appearance in mythology, he abducted Zeus and Demeter's daughter, PERSEPHONE. Although Demeter tried to retrieve Persephone from the underworld, Hades ensured that she had to stay at least part of the year with him by feeding her some seeds of a pomegranate. Hades does not appear as a character in extant drama, although he is mentioned many times. The death of a woman who perishes before her time, such as ALCESTIS, ANTIGONE, or IPHIGENIA, is often referred to as marriage with Hades. [ANCIENT SOURCES: Aristophanes, *Acharnians* 390; *Homeric Hymn 2 (to Demeter)*; Ovid, *Metamorphoses* 5.346–571]

HAEMON The son of CREON and Eurydice, Haemon (whose name is derived from a Greek word for blood) was a Theban prince. He appears as a character in SOPHOCLES' *ANTIGONE,* in which he is engaged to be married to ANTIGONE at the same time that she has been condemned to death by Haemon's father, CREON. Haemon tries to urge his father to reconsider Antigone's death sentence, but Creon angrily accuses him of siding with a woman against his own father. After Antigone is sealed in a rocky tomb and left to die, Haemon goes to this place and finds that she has

hanged herself. Creon, having reconsidered his decision, also goes to the tomb and finds Haemon. Haemon, angry at his father, draws his sword and tries to kill him. The father, however, sidesteps the attempted blow. Haemon, ashamed of his effort, then turns the sword on himself and dies. Another tradition says that Haemon died attempting to solve the riddle of the SPHINX. [ANCIENT SOURCES: Apollodorus, *Library* 3.5.8; Sophocles, *Antigone*]

BIBLIOGRAPHY
Johnson, P. "Woman's Third Face: A Psycho-Social Reconsideration of Sophocles' *Antigone*," *Arethusa* 30, no. 3 (1997): 369–98.

HAEMUS A mountain in THRACE where ZEUS battled against TYPHON. The mountain takes its name from Typhon's blood (Greek: *haima*), which was shed on the mountain. [ANCIENT SOURCES: Apollodorus, *Library* 1.6.3; Seneca, *Hercules Oetaeus* 1280, 1383, *Medea* 590]

HALIMUS A DEME on the coast a few miles south of ATHENS. EUELPIDES is said to have been from Halimus. [ANCIENT SOURCES: Aristophanes, *Birds* 496]

HALIRRHOTHIUS The son of POSEIDON, Halirrhothius raped ARES' daughter, Alcippe. Ares killed him and then had to stand trial in ATHENS before the court of the AREOPAGUS. According to tradition, Ares was the first to be tried for shedding another's blood. [ANCIENT SOURCES: Apollodorus, *Library* 3.14.2; Euripides, *Electra* 1260; Pausanias, 1.21.4, 1.28.5]

HAMARTIA A Greek word used by ARISTOTLE in his *Poetics* that has become famous and controversial in the history of literary criticism. In describing what he considers the best way to construct the plot of a TRAGEDY, Aristotle observes that tragedies with the best plots involve a person who does not fall into misfortune because of badness or villainy, but is like OEDIPUS, THYESTES, or a person of similar family, has good fortune and is well thought of, but experiences misfortune due to *hamartia* (*Poetics* 1453a7–12). Modern scholars, however, do not agree about what Aristotle means by *hamartia* in this passage and have offered several possible meanings, such as "mistake of fact," "ignorance of fact," or "moral defect."

BIBLIOGRAPHY

Bremer J. M. *Hamartia: Tragic Error in the Poetics of Aristotle and in Greek Tragedy.* Amsterdam: Hakkert, 1969.

Golden, L. "Hamartia, Ate, and Oedipus," Classical World 72 (1978): 3–12.

Østerud, S. "*Hamartia* in Aristotle and Greek Tragedy," *Symbolae Osloenses* 51 (1976): 65–80.

Schuetrumpf, Eckart. "Traditional Elements in the Concept of *Hamartia* in Aristotle's *Poetics*," *Harvard Studies in Classical Philology* 92 (1989): 137–56.

Stinton, T. C. W. "*Hamartia* in Aristotle and Greek Tragedy," *Classical Quarterly* 25 (1975): 221–54.

HANGER-ON See PARASITE.

HARMODIUS In 514 B.C.E., Harmodius and Aristogeiton assassinated the brother (Hipparchus) of the Athenian tyrant HIPPIAS. They became famous as liberators of the Athenian people from tyranny. The Athenians erected bronze statues of Harmodius and Aristogeiton in the center of their main marketplace (see AGORA). A drinking song, "Harmodius," became popular after this act and various versions of this song survive. [ANCIENT SOURCES: Aristophanes, *Acharnians* 980, 1093, *Ecclesiazusae* 682, *Knights* 786, *Wasps* 1225]

BIBLIOGRAPHY

Sommerstein, A. H. *The Comedies of Aristophanes.* Vol. 1, *Acharnians.* Warminster, U.K.: Aris & Phillips, 1980, 204.

———. *The Comedies of Aristophanes.* Vol. 10, *Ecclesiazusae.* Warminster, U.K.: Aris & Phillips, 1998, 199.

HARMONIA A daughter of ARES and APHRODITE (or sometimes the daughter of ZEUS and ATLAS' daughter, Electra), Harmonia became the wife of CADMUS and had several children with him: AGAVE, AUTONOE, INO, SEMELE, and POLYDORUS. After the death of her grandson, PENTHEUS, Harmonia and Cadmus left THEBES and became rulers in ILLYRIA, where they had another son, Illyrius. Eventually, Harmonia and Cadmus were changed into serpents (or dragons) and taken by the gods to ELYSIUM or the ISLANDS OF THE BLESSED.

Perhaps more important than Harmonia herself were a necklace and robe that she was given as a wedding present when she married Cadmus. These items later passed into the hands of POLYNEICES, who used them as a bribe to induce ERIPHYLE to persuade her husband, AMPHIARAUS, to go to war against Thebes. After Amphiaraus died in battle, his son, ALCMEON, was so angry at Eriphyle that he killed her. When Alcmeon went into exile at PSOPHIS, he gave the items to Phegeus' daughter, ARSINOE. After Alcmeon was driven from Psophis, he went to the river ACHELOUS and married his daughter, Callirrhoe, who also wanted the items and threatened to divorce Alcmeon if he did not give them to her. Alcmeon retrieved the items from Phegeus, but when Phegeus learned that Alcmeon was taking them to Callirrhoe, he had his sons kill Alcmeon. When Phegeus' sons took the necklace and robe to DELPHI to dedicate them to APOLLO, Alcmeon's sons killed Phegeus' sons and then dedicated the items to the god. [ANCIENT SOURCES: Apollodorus, *Library* 3.4.2, 3.6.1–2, 3.7.5–7; Aristophanes, *Peace* 810–11; Euripides, *Bacchae* 1332–57, *Phoenician Women* 7, 822; Hyginus, *Fables* 6, 73, 148, 240; Ovid, *Metamorphoses* 4.562–602; Pausanias, 5.17.7, 8.24.8–10, 9.41.2–3]

HARPIES The daughters of Thaumas and Electra (other parents named by the ancient sources are EARTH, Pontus, POSEIDON, TYPHON, and PHINEUS), the Harpies, usually named Aello, Celaeno, and Podarge (other names include Aellopos, Acholoe, Nichothoe, Ocypode, and Ocythoe), were the sisters of IRIS. The Harpies had the head of a woman and the body of a bird, and, judging by AESCHYLUS' comparison of their appearance to the Furies' were not attractive creatures. Their name means "snatchers" and the gods appointed them to punish

234 THE HAUNTED HOUSE

PHINEUS by snatching away his food anytime he tried to eat. The Harpies eventually were driven away by the winged Argonauts Zetes and Calais. Some sources say that they died trying to escape the winged Argonauts or arranged a truce with them whereby they would no longer harass Phineus. [ANCIENT SOURCES: Aeschylus, *Eumenides* 50–52 (see *ORESTEIA*); Apollodorus, *Library* 1.2.6, 1.19.21, 3.15.2; Apollonius Rhodius, 2.298; Hesiod, *Theogony* 267; Homer, *Iliad* 16.149, *Odyssey* 1.24, 14.371, 20.66, 77; Hyginus, *Fables* 14, 19; Ovid, *Metamorphoses* 7.4; Vergil, *Aeneid* 3.210–16]

THE HAUNTED HOUSE (Latin: *MOSTELLARIA*) PLAUTUS (BETWEEN 215 AND 184 B.C.E.)

The Greek model for PLAUTUS' play is unknown, although Philemon, MENANDER, and Theognetus wrote comedies entitled *Phasma* that involved ghosts. Plautus' play has Athens as its setting; the action takes place before the houses of Theopropides, an Athenian merchant, and Simo. In the opening act, Grumio and Tranio, who are slaves of Theopropides', argue about Tranio's corruption of Theopropides' son, Philolaches. Theopropides himself has been away from home for three years in Egypt. After their argument, Grumio departs for the family's farm in the countryside, while Tranio leaves for the harbor to buy fish.

In the next scene, Philolaches arrives and gives a wonderful monologue in which he compares a person to a recently built house. The parents are the builders, who lay the foundation and raise the structure, but once the child is left in charge, the house becomes ruined. In Philolaches' case, his "house" is in disrepair because of his love for a prostitute named Philematium. Soon, Philematium herself and her aged attendant, Scapha, emerge from Simo's house. Although Philolaches has spent all his money on Philematium and claims he is penniless, Philematium still love him, and before long the two sit down to dinner and drinks. They are joined by Philolaches' friend, Callidamates, and his girlfriend, Delphium, who is also a prostitute. Both Callidamates and Delphium are somewhat intoxicated. As the four continue their party, Tranio returns from the harbor and informs Philolaches that his father has returned from his trip abroad. As Philolaches despairs about what his father will say about the party

and the women, Tranio promises to scare Theopropides away from the house. Tranio sends the two young men and their women into Theopropides' house and then prepares for the arrival of Theopropides.

When Theopropides arrives, he finds his house locked. When he knocks on the door, he is met by Tranio, who informs him that his house has been haunted by the ghost of a guest once murdered there by the previous owner. Tranio claims Philolaches and the others have left the house empty for seven months. When sounds from the drunken young people inside the house are heard, Tranio pretends that this is voice of the ghost and urges Theopropides to leave quickly. Tranio, claiming that he has made his peace with the ghost, says he will remain. After Theopropides leaves, Tranio enters the house.

At this point, an unpleasant moneylender named Misargyrides enters. When Tranio leaves the house, he worries because Misargyrides lent money to Philolaches for Philematium. As Tranio approaches Misargyrides, Theopropides also approaches and tells Tranio that he has met with the man who sold him the house. Theopropides informs Tranio that the man denied any knowledge of the crimes alleged by Tranio. While Tranio ponders what to do about Theopropides, he approaches Misargyrides, who wants the money he is owed. Tranio tells Misargyrides that he will give him the money later in the day. Misargyrides, however, insists on being paid the interest he is owed and refuses to leave. Theopropides, who hears the argument, approaches and discovers that Philolaches owes Misargyrides money. When Theopropides asks the purpose of the money, Tranio lies: He tells him that he has used the money as a deposit to buy a house. Theopropides is delighted to hear that his son is making a wise investment and agrees to pay Misargyrides the following day.

After Misargyrides leaves, Theopropides wants to know the location of the house that Philolaches bought. Again Tranio lies, saying that he purchased the next-door neighbor, Simo's, house. Hearing this, Theopropides wants to go inside and have a look at the house. As Tranio stalls for time, Theopropides takes a stroll away from the house. When the house's owner, Simo, emerges, Tranio eavesdrops on the man. Hearing

Simo complain about his wife, Tranio approaches Simo, who knows about Philolaches' affairs, and begs him for help. Tranio tells Simo that Theopropides wants to add on to his own house and wants to look at Simo's house as a model. When Simo has no objections, Tranio goes to get Theopropides. Tranio informs Theopropides that Simo is upset about having sold the house and wants him to persuade Philolaches to sell the house back to him. Theopropides, however, refuses. Soon, with Simo's permission, Theopropides and Tranio begin inspecting his house. While Theopropides continues to inspect the house, Simo informs them that he has to leave to go to town on business.

After the departure of Simo for the town and of Theopropides and Tranio into Simo's house, a slave, Phaniscus, arrives. Phaniscus has been sent to take Callidamates back to his own house. Before Phaniscus can knock on Theopropides' door, one of his fellow slaves, Pinacium, arrives and knocks on the door first. Because nobody answers the door, Pinacium continues to knock. As he does, Tranio and Theopropides emerge from Simo's house and discuss the fine investment that Philolaches has made. Tranio, however, tells Theopropides that Simo's asking price for the house is twice as much as Philolaches owes Misargyrides. Tranio suggests that Theopropides give him the money so that he can give it to Simo, but Theopropides, knowing Tranio's tricks, rejects this idea. Instead, Theopropides tells Tranio to go to the family farm, inform Philolaches that he has returned, and take him back to the house. Tranio departs, as if to go to the country, but then returns to Theopropides' house.

As Tranio leaves, Phaniscus and Pinacium have remained at Theopropides' house, where they are met by Theopropides himself, who wonders what the two men are doing. Theopropides, however, does not reveal to them that he is the house's owner. Phaniscus tells him that his master, Callidamates, is inside the house drinking and that they have arrived to fetch him. When Theopropides claims the house has been empty for months, Phaniscus thinks the old man is crazy and says that Callidamates has been enjoying frequent parties with Philolaches. An alarmed Theopropides probes Phaniscus further and discovers that Philolaches has bought Philematium

for a substantial sum of money and then freed her. Furthermore, Phaniscus informs Theopropides that Philolaches has not put down a deposit on Simo's house. Eventually, the two slaves give up on finding Callidamates and leave. After their departure, Theopropides laments the financial ruin that his son has caused him. He is soon joined by Simo. Theopropides asks him about the deposit that Philolaches paid him for his house, but Simo denies having received any money from Philolaches or Tranio. Soon, Theopropides realizes that Tranio has tricked him and asks Simo to let him borrow some of his slaves and some whips.

Not long afterward, Tranio enters from Theopropides' house and informs the audience that he has removed Philolaches and his friends from the house, but that they had rejected him as a participant in their fun. As Tranio considers confessing to Theopropides, Theopropides emerges from Simo's house and announces to the audience that he is going to punish Tranio. Theopropides confronts Tranio with his lies, but Tranio maintains his pretense about the deposit on Simo's house. Theopropides suggests that they interrogate some of Simo's slaves under torture. Tranio agrees to hear their testimony, but as Theopropides summons the slaves from Simo's house, Tranio seats himself at a nearby altar and says that he is sitting there to prevent the slaves from seeking refuge at it. Theopropides, knowing that Tranio is trying to take refuge, tells him that he wants the slaves to try to seek refuge, as it will make proving his case easier. Soon Theopropides confronts Tranio about his trickery and threatens to punish him.

As their confrontation continues, Callidamates enters to tell the audience that Philolaches has appointed him as peacemaker between Philolaches and his father. Theopropides continues to threaten Tranio, while Callidamates invites Theopropides to dinner. Theopropides, intent on punishing Tranio, refuses the offer. Tranio continues to plead for clemency, and after some time Callidamates switches places with Tranio at the altar. Callidamates takes the blame for Philolaches' reckless behavior and offers to repay the money he owes. Callidamates also pleads for Tranio and persuades the old man not to punish him.

COMMENTARY

The Haunted House is one of Plautus' more delightful plays, thanks largely to Tranio's masterful handling of the deception. As Leach and Grimal have discussed, *The Haunted House* is organized around the image of the house. Indeed, words for house are three times more frequent in this play than in any other Roman COMEDY. In Philolaches' opening song (84–156), he compares raising a child to building and caring for a house. He notes that the parents lay the foundations for a child, raise the structure, and spare no expense in maintaining the "house" that is their child. Because Philolaches' father, Theopropides, has been away, however, the "house" that is Philolaches has fallen on ruin. The prostitute, Philematium, and the love Philolaches has for her are described as a torrential rainstorm on his heart (142–43) and a storm that stripped the roof of modesty from his house (162–65).

In addition to the ruin of Philolaches caused by Philematium, the slave Tranio, who has taken the place of the young man's father during Theopropides' absence, has played a significant part in the young man's downfall, as Grumio notes in the play's opening (29–33). Whereas the return of Theopropides is viewed as disastrous by both Tranio and Philolaches, the more modest in Plautus' audience, whose view is well expressed by Grumio (76–78), will see the father's return as a blessing from the gods, because this may signal the restoration of the "house" that is Philolaches.

To prevent Philolaches and his friends from being caught while they enjoy their drinking party, Tranio decides to transform Theopropides' house into a haunted one. Not only has Tranio helped transform the house that is Philolaches from a sturdy one to one that is corrupted; now the slave also tries to transform Theopropides' house into one in which a horrific crime has been committed. The imaginary dead man Tranio says haunts Theopropides' house will become a real dead person if Theopropides discovers the Tranio-aided mode of life that Philolaches has been enjoying.

The arrival of the moneylender Misargyrides poses another threat to Tranio's plans. Furthermore, while Tranio has been in the house trying to manage Philolaches and his friends, Theopropides has questioned the person who sold him the house. He reports to

Tranio that the seller has completely denied the stories of haunting. To throw Theopropides off the trail and appease the moneylender, Tranio invents another story about a house. This time Tranio pretends that Philolaches has bought a house and needs money to pay off the moneylender. Of course, the irony is that Philolaches needs this money to support the mode of life that has resulted in the ruin of Philolaches' "house of self." Theopropides believes that Philolaches' decision to buy this house is a wise one, so he gladly agrees to pay the moneylender.

Unfortunately for Tranio, Theopropides wants to see the house that Philolaches has bought, so now Tranio must make his imaginary house become a reality. In desperation, Tranio claims that Philolaches has bought the house belonging to Theopropides' neighbor, Simo. Given this lie, Tranio must create yet another imaginary house. So that Theopropides can look over Simo's house, Tranio tells Simo that Theopropides is planning to add on to his own house and wants to look at Simo's house as a model because, according to Tranio, Theopropides has heard from an architect (760) that Simo's house is well shaded in every season (a rumor that Simo denies). Of course, Tranio is the imaginary architect for the imaginary addition that Theopropides is alleged to have in mind. Additionally, Tranio's remark that Theopropides wants to use Simo's house as a model (*exemplum,* 762, 763, 773) is somewhat ironic because the calm of Simo's house would be the sort of setting Theopropides would wish for in his own house. Philolaches had used the same word for model, *exemplum* (103), in his opening song as he observed that a well-built house is one that each person wants to use as a model for his or her own. Of course, once Philolaches' "house of self" has become ruined, he has become a model that no one would want to copy and not the sort of "house" that Theopropides would want to show off to his neighbors.

After Theopropides inspects the house that he thinks Philolaches has purchased, he is quite pleased with his son's imaginary purchase. After he sends Tranio off to his house in the country to take Philolaches back to town, Theopropides encounters Phaniscus and Pinacium knocking at his door in search of Callidamates. Theopropides declares that they have arrived at the wrong house. Soon, however, Theopropides learns that his perception of his house is incorrect and that the house that he has been told has been empty for six months has actually been occupied constantly by Philoloches and his party companions. Theopropides also learns that the purchase of Simo's house was also a lie. Theopropides now feels he is a stranger at his own house (993–96). When Simo confirms the stories of Phaniscus and Pinacium, Theopropides considers himself a dead man (1030–31). Before Theopropides reclaims his house, he enters Simo's house to borrow some of his slaves and whips so that he can retaliate against Tranio.

By this time, Tranio has restored Theopropides' house to its original condition. He has entered the house through a backdoor and evacuated the partygoers from the house. Tranio's feeling of safety is short lived, however, as Theopropides confronts him with his lies. Before Theopropides can apprehend him and make an example (*exemplum,* 1116) of him, Tranio, who has manipulated physical space throughout the play, now takes refuge at an altar. In typical comic fashion, both prodigal son and wily slave are forgiven, but perhaps most important is that the house of Theopropides has been reclaimed by its rightful owner and Tranio's construction of imaginary houses has ended—at least until the next day.

BIBLIOGRAPHY

Felton, D. *Haunted Greece and Rome: Ghost Stories from Classical Antiquity.* Austin: University of Texas Press, 1999.

Grimal, P. "La maison de Simon et celle de Théopropidès dans la *Mostellaria.*" In *L'Italie préromaine et la Rome républicaine: Mélanges offerts à Jacques Heurgon.* Paris: de Boccard, 1976, 371–86.

Leach, E. W. "*De exemplo meo ipse aedificato:* An Organizing Idea in the *Mostellaria,*" *Hermes* 97 (1969): 318–32.

Merrill, F. R. *Mostellaria.* London: Macmillan, 1972.

Stärk, Ekkehard. "*Mostellaria* oder Turbare statt sedare." In *Plautus barbarus: sechs Kapitel zur Originalität des Plautus.* Edited by Eckard Lefèvre, Ekkehard Stark, and Gregor Vogt-Spira. Tübingen: Narr, 1991, 107–40.

HEAUTON TIMORUMENOS   See THE SELF-TORMENTOR.

HEBE   A daughter of ZEUS and HERA, Hebe is a goddess who personifies youth. After HERACLES' death, he ascended to Mount OLYMPUS and married Hebe. [ANCIENT

SOURCES: Apollodorus, 1.3.1; Euripides, *Children of Heracles* 851, 857, *Orestes* 1687; Hesiod, *Theogony* 949; Homer, *Iliad* 4.2, 5.722, 905, *Odyssey* 11.603; Ovid, *Metamorphoses* 9.400; Seneca, *Octavia* 211]

HEBRUS   A river in THRACE that flows into the sea between the towns of Doriscos and Ainos. ORPHEUS' head was thrown into the Hebrus after his death. [ANCIENT SOURCES: Aristophanes, *Birds* 774]

HECABE (Latin: HECUBA)   The wife of PRIAM, king of TROY during the Trojan War, Hecabe, according to Homer, was the mother of 19 of Priam's 50 sons, the most famous of whom are HECTOR and PARIS. Before the birth of Paris, Hecabe dreamed that she gave birth to a flaming piece of wood that destroyed TROY. The local prophets declared that the child should be killed and Paris was taken to the wilds outside Troy and left to die, but he was suckled by a she-bear and later retrieved by the herdsman who had been told to abandon him. Paris, of course, grew up and eventually returned to Troy. The surviving fragments of EURIPIDES' *Alexander* (see Page) indicate that upon Alexander/Paris' return to Troy Hecabe participated in a plot to kill Paris, who she did not realize was her son. The plot was thwarted, however, and Paris' true identity was revealed. Paris' abduction of HELEN led to the Trojan War and the fall of Troy. In the course of the war, Hecabe's sons were killed in battle; after the war, Hecabe and her daughters were enslaved by the Greeks or suffered other horrible fates.

The end of Hecabe's life is dealt with in Euripides' *HECABE* and *TROJAN WOMEN*, as well as SENECA's *TROJAN WOMEN*. After the fall of Troy, Hecabe became the slave of ODYSSEUS. In both *Trojan Women* plays, Hecabe is characterized as the suffering survivor of the Trojan War, who must face the added trauma of seeing her daughters enslaved or, in the case of Polyxena, sacrificed to appease ACHILLES' spirit. In these plays, Hecabe also has to deal with the horror of her grandson ASTYANAX being killed by the Greeks. In Euripides' *Hecabe,* she becomes like Odysseus in his encounter with the Cyclops POLYPHEMUS as she lures the Thracian king POLYMESTOR into her tent and blinds him. Polymestor had killed one of Hecabe's sons, Polydorus. As Polymestor predicts at the conclusion of *Hecabe,* Hecabe leaps to her death from Odysseus' ship after their departure from Troy. According to another tradition, Hecabe was attacked by some of Polymestor's fellow Thracians. During the attack, she was transformed into a snarling dog, which the Thracians then killed. The place where she was buried on the Thracian coast became a landmark for sailors, called Cynosema ("the dog's grave"). Among Roman authors, ACCIUS wrote a *Hecuba,* from which a single line survives about a limit set by the FATES (375 Warmington). [ANCIENT SOURCES: Apollodorus, 3.12.5, 8; Homer, *Iliad* 2.817, 16.716, 22.234, 24.495; Hyginus, *Fables* 91, 111; Ovid, *Metamophoses* 13.423–575; Plautus, MENAECHMI 714, 716, BACCHIDES 963]

BIBLIOGRAPHY

Daitz, S. G. "Concepts of Freedom and Slavery in Euripides' *Hecuba,*" *Hermes* 99 (1971): 217–26.

Mossman, J. *Wild Justice: A Study of Euripides' Hecuba.* New York: Oxford University Press, 1995.

Segal, C. "Violence and the Others: Greek, Female, and Barbarian in Euripides' *Hecuba,*" *Transactions and Proceedings of the American Philological Association* 120 (1990): 109–31.

Warmington, E. H. *Remains of Old Latin: Livius Andronicus, Naevius, Pacuvius, and Accius.* Vol. 2. Cambridge, Mass.: Harvard University Press, 1936.

HECABE EURIPIDES Staged in the mid-420s B.C.E., *Hecabe* is set before AGAMEMNON'S tent on the coast opposite TROY after its fall. The prologue is delivered by the ghost of POLYDORUS, the youngest son of PRIAM and HECABE. Polydorus tells the audience that during the war, his father sent him to live with the Thracian king, POLYMESTOR. Priam sent with him a large sum of gold so that if Troy fell, any surviving members of Priam's family would have money to live. After Troy fell, however, Polymestor killed Polydorus to acquire his gold. Polydorus' spirit now hovers over his mother, Hecabe, in the hope that she will provide burial for his corpse, thrown out on the shore by Polymestor. Polydorus' ghost also reveals that as the Greek fleet was sailing from Troy, Achilles' ghost appeared above his tomb and demanded the sacrifice of Polydorus' sister, Polyxena.

With this, Polydorus' spirit vanishes and Hecabe, having seen Polydorus' spirit in a dream, emerges from Agamemnon's tent. The aged queen relates her dream about Polydorus and Polyxena. After the queen's speech, the chorus of captive Trojan women enter. They recall that when Achilles' spirit appeared and demanded Polyxena as a sacrifice, Agamemnon rejected the idea out of love for Hecabe's daughter, CASSANDRA. In a statement that must have provoked some unsettling feelings among some in EURIPIDES' Athenian audience, the chorus note that it was two Athenians, the sons of Theseus, who championed the view that Polyxena should be sacrificed. That the two Athenians' view was supported by ODYSSEUS, frequently characterized in a negative light in Euripidean drama, also would have indicated to Euripides' audience that such a sacrifice should be regarded as horrific. The captive women tell Hecabe that soon Odysseus will take Polyxena away from her and urge her to beg Agamemnon for help.

Upon hearing this news, Hecabe despairs about what she should do and then summons Polyxena from the tent. Hecabe informs Polyxena that the Greeks have decided to sacrifice her, but the young woman expresses her belief that death is a more fortunate lot than her current life of shame and misery. When Odysseus enters, Hecabe tries to persuade him not to take Polyxena. Hecabe reminds Odysseus of a time when he arrived in Troy as a spy and was found out by Hecabe, who allowed him to leave. Hecabe now claims that Odysseus owes her similar consideration and becomes a supplicant to him as he had been to her. Odysseus, however, refuses, claiming that Achilles' grave deserves to be honored and that he himself wants his grave to be viewed reverently when he dies. Hecabe urges Polyxena to plead with Odysseus, but the young woman says that she prefers death as a free person to life as a slave. Hecabe offers her own life for Polyxena's, but Odysseus rejects her offer. After Odysseus takes Polyxena away to Achilles' tomb, the captive Trojans sing an ODE in which they wonder where they will end up as slaves.

After the choral ode, the herald, Talthybius, enters and informs Hecabe and the chorus of the sacrifice of Polyxena, the noble way in which she died, and the admiration of the Greeks for her nobility. Hecabe then laments the death of Polyxena and wonders whether nobility is a product of one's heredity or upbringing. She asks Talthybius to tell the Greek soldiers not to touch Polyxena and asks one of her servants to get sea water so that she can wash the corpse. At this, Hecabe returns to Agamemnon's tent. The chorus then sing an ode in which they suggest that their doom was sealed from the time that PARIS sailed to Greece for HELEN.

The song of the captive Trojans is followed by the entrance of a servant, who reveals to the chorus and Hecabe that Polydorus is dead (the corpse of Polydorus has also been carried in). Hecabe recalls her dream about Polydorus and realizes that Polymestor must have killed her son. Next, Agamemnon enters and wonders why Polydorus' corpse is near his tent. Hecabe, after some debate with herself, then kneels before Agamemnon and begs him to help her avenge the murder of Polydorus. She asks Agamemnon to take pity on her as a woman who is without a city, friends, or children. Because Agamemnon has taken Cassandra as his slave and concubine, Hecabe appeals to Agamemnon as a kinsman to Polydorus. Agamemnon is sympathetic but does not want to do anything that would be criticized by his fellow Greeks. Hecabe promises Agamemnon that she will release him from any risk in her plot, but Agamemnon is doubtful that a woman can deal with Polymestor. Hecabe, however, assures Agamemnon that she and her fellow Trojan captives will handle him. Hecabe then sends her attendant out to summon Polymestor to the Greek camp. After the exit of the attendant, Hecabe, and Agamemnon, the Trojan women lament their departure from Troy. They recall their activities on the night that Troy fell and how they saw their husbands killed by the Greeks. They also curse Helen and hope she does not reach her home.

After the choral song, Polymestor, accompanied by his two sons, enters. When questioned about Polydorus, Polymestor lies, saying that the young man is still alive. Hecabe tells Polymestor that she knows of an additional cache of gold and that Polymestor should tell Polydorus about it. Hecabe also says she has some things in Agamemnon's tent that she wants Polymestor to take with him. With this, Polymestor and his sons follow Hecabe into the tent. Before long, cries for help are heard within the tent as Hecabe and some of the

women are blinding Polymestor and killing his sons. Hecabe emerges from the tent and is soon followed by the blinded Polymestor, who threatens to destroy her. He calls for his fellow Thracians to help him but receives no assistance. Agamemnon, however, does return upon hearing Polymestor's cries. Polymestor tells him what Hecabe has done and demands justice. At this point, Agamemnon agrees to act as arbiter between Polymestor and Hecabe.

Polymestor explains how he killed Polydorus and claims he did so out of fear that eventually Polydorus would gather together those who survived Troy's fall and overrun Thrace. In Polymestor's view, his killing of Polydorus was a favor to the Greeks. Polymestor then explains how Hecabe and the other women attacked him. After Polymestor's remarks, Hecabe offers a rebuttal and claims that Polymestor had no intention of helping the Greeks, but killed Polydorus out of greed for his gold. After hearing the two speeches, Agamemnon judges in favor of Hecabe and states that Polymestor must endure his fate. Before the play ends, however, Polymestor predicts that Hecabe will be killed by falling from the mast of Odysseus' ship, that she will be transformed into a dog, and that her grave will serve as a marker for sailors. Polymestor also predicts the deaths of Cassandra and Agamemnon at the hands of CLYTEMNESTRA. When Agamemnon hears this, he orders Polymestor to be silenced and left on a deserted island. Agamemnon then tells Hecabe to go and bury her two children and the other women to prepare to sail from Troy.

COMMENTARY

Euripides' Hecabe has garnered more critical attention in recent years. Readers of the play should keep in mind that when the play was staged Athens had been at war with Sparta and its allies since 431 B.C.E. Furthermore, the question of how a conqueror should treat the conquered was an issue with which the Athenians had dealt during the years before the production of Hecabe. One thinks, in particular, of the Athenians' suppression of the revolt from their empire of the people of Mytilene on the island of Lesbos, an island not far from Hecabe's Troy. In 427, after the Athenians had conquered the Mytileneans, the Athenian assembly decided to put to death Mytilene's entire male population and enslave their women and children. Fortunately, the Athenians reversed their decision the following day and decided to execute only the primary leaders of the revolt. Judith Mossman has noted the political language in Hecabe and has indicated that when the chorus enter they report a debate among the Greek army regarding the sacrifice of Polyxena that must have sounded rather familiar to Euripides' Athenian audience. Interestingly, Agamemnon opposed the sacrifice of Polyxena, and his opinion is contrasted with that of two Athenians, who argued in favor of the sacrifice (122–28). Eventually, it appears that Odysseus persuades the assembled Greeks to sacrifice Polyxena; Odysseus, whom, in the chorus' report of the debate, Euripides describes as a wily, sweet-talking liar, curries favor with the mob (131–32). Such a description surely would have reminded Euripides' Athenian audience of their own CLEON, who had been the primary advocate of the proposal to execute the entire male population of Mytilene and who was notorious for currying favor with the Athenian masses (cf. ARISTOPHANES' KNIGHTS and WASPS).

As does Euripides' later TROJAN WOMEN, Hecabe treats the horrors of war and its effects on the innocent. Unlike in Trojan Women, the presence of the unsympathetic barbarian Polymestor lightens the tone of Hecabe. Additionally, the theme of revenge, which plays a dominant role in the last third of Hecabe, is not present in Trojan Women. Furthermore, Cassandra and HECTOR's wife, Andromache, do not take the stage. Nor do we hear of the killing of Hector's son, ASTYANAX, as we do in Trojan Women. Both plays contain the slaughter of Trojan children, but Hecabe deals more extensively with Polyxena's death than does Trojan Women, and Polydorus has no part or mention in the latter play. Both plays end with burials, but in Trojan Women the burial of Astyanax by Hecabe is dealt with at some length. Unlike the debate in Trojan Women between Hecabe and Helen, judged by MENELAUS, in which the audience would sympathize with Hecabe but know that Menelaus would not punish his wife, the debate between Hecabe and Polymestor, which Agamemnon judges, has a more satisfactory result. Agamemnon finds the argument of his enemy Hecabe more com-

pelling than that of Polymestor, who claims to be helping him.

One of the themes treated by both Hecabe and Trojan Women is the idea of freedom versus slavery and how quickly one's fortune can change from one extreme to the other. Hecabe is transformed from the queen of Troy into a slave. In Hecabe's debate with Odysseus, she reminds him that she had set him free when he had been captured during a mission to Troy. She points out that in that instance he was her slave (249) and Odysseus admits as much. After the fall of Troy, however, the roles are reversed and now the former queen Hecabe has literally become Odysseus' slave. The clever words that Odysseus used to persuade Hecabe to release him earlier are not present in Hecabe's speech to Odysseus, who rejects his new slave's pleas to spare her daughter. Polyxena, however, boldly faces her death and even welcomes it. She states that even her new name of *slave* makes her long for death (357–58). Polyxena would rather die free, a Trojan princess, than live as a slave (550–52). The Trojan women are not the only ones who have fallen from freedom to slavery, however. After Hecabe's supplication of Agamemnon, she notes that even Agamemnon, commander in chief of the Greek army, is enslaved to the opinion of his troops. She concludes that no mortal is free (864). By the end of the play, however, Hecabe proves that a woman who is a slave still has some ability to strike out at her enemies as she blinds Polymestor. At line 1253–54, the barbaric Thracian king laments that he has been bested by someone who is a woman and a slave.

Although the theme of slavery versus freedom runs throughout the play, some scholars have criticized the structural unity of Hecabe. Although Odysseus appears only in the play's opening half, the figure of Odysseus looms throughout the play and provides additional unity. In the play's first half, Hecabe encounters Odysseus and begs him for her daughter's life. She recalls that when she discovered him in Troy he was a suppliant to her and became her slave (line 249). Although Odysseus was successful in his appeal to Hecabe, Hecabe fails with Odysseus in the play's opening half. In the second half of the play, however, she continues her Odysseus-like tactics of supplication in her encounter with Agamemnon. Here, she is more successful and gains Agamemnon's permission to take revenge on Polymestor. Hecabe's attack on Polymestor is modeled on Odysseus' attack on the Cyclops POLYPHEMUS, which was most famous from the ninth book of Homer's *Odyssey*. Some scholars also believe that Euripides' CYCLOPS was the SATYR PLAY that concluded the TETRALOGY in which *Hecabe* appeared. This notion, however attractive, cannot be confirmed, for statistical analysis of Euripides' metrical tendencies dates *Cyclops* to the last decade of Euripides' career.

Thus, in *Hecabe*, the title character becomes like Odysseus in his encounter with the Cyclops. Agamemnon's tent substitutes for the Cyclops' cave; the Trojan women replace Odysseus' men. Both Polymestor and Polyphemus have violated the customs of hospitality by killing a guest—Polymestor has killed Polydorus; Polyphemus kills some of Odysseus' men. Both villains are blinded by an opponent from whom they expect little opposition. When Polymestor emerges from the tent, he calls for help but receives none (the same result experienced by the Cyclops). After Polymestor's blinding, he, as the Cyclops does, gropes about for his attackers and threatens further violence. Polymestor even echoes the cannibalistic behavior of the Cyclops as he threatens to eat the Trojan women if he catches them (lines 1071–74). Finally, whereas the blinded Cyclops recalls a prophecy that he would be blinded by Odysseus, Polymestor becomes a prophet at the conclusion of *Hecabe* and predicts the death of not only Hecabe, but Cassandra and Agamemnon.

BIBLIOGRAPHY
Collard, C. *Euripides: Hecuba*. Warminster, U.K.: Aris & Phillips, 1991.
Gregory, J. W. *Hecuba: Euripides*. Atlanta: Scholars Press, 1999.
Kovacs, D. *The Heroic Muse: Studies in the Hippolytus and Hecuba of Euripides*. Baltimore: Johns Hopkins University Press, 1987.
Mossman, J. *Wild Justice: A Study of Euripides' Hecuba*. New York: Oxford University Press, 1995.
Segal, Charles. *Euripides and the Poetics of Sorrow: Art, Gender, and Commemoration in Alcestis, Hippolytus, and Hecuba*. Durham, N.C.: Duke University Press, 1993.

HECATE   The daughter of Perses and Asteria (or LETO), Hecate is a goddess associated with the MOON. She is often described as having three forms or as holding torches. Hecate was thought to visit crossroads frequently, and people often left offerings for her or built sanctuaries to her in these locations. She is frequently connected with women and witchcraft. In the plays of EURIPIDES and SENECA, MEDEA is linked with Hecate as she considers the revenge she will take on JASON. Hecate is also associated with madness or delusion. In EURIPIDES' *HELEN*, when MENELAUS sees in Egypt the HELEN whom he thought he had taken from Troy, he calls on Hecate to send him favorable visions. The Greek comic poets Diphilus (fragment 29 Kock) and Nicostratus (fragments 11–12 Kock) each wrote a *Hecate,* but the fragments reveal nothing about their content. [ANCIENT SOURCES: Apollodorus, *Library* 1.2.4; Aristophanes, *Frogs* 1362; Euripides, *Helen* 569, *Medea* 396–99, *Phoenecian Women* 109–10; Hesiod, *Theogony* 404–52; Seneca, *Hercules Oetaeus* 1519, *Medea* 6, 577, 833, 841, *Oedipus* 569, *Phaedra* 412, *Trojan Women* 389]

BIBLIOGRAPHY
Berg, W. "Hecate, Greek or Anatolian," *Numen* 21 (1974): 128–40.
Kock, T. *Comicorum Atticorum Fragmenta*. Vol. 2. Leipzig: Teubner, 1884.
Marquardt, P. A. "A Portrait of Hecate," *American Journal of Philology* 102 (1981): 243–60.
Rabinowitz, J. D. *The Rotting Goddess: The Origin of the Witch in Classical Antiquity*. Brooklyn, N.Y.: Autonomedia, 1998.

HECATEA   At the end of a month, Greeks would leave food offerings "at places where three roads met" (Sommerstein). Such crossroads were sacred to HECATE and the offerings were called Hecatea. [ANCIENT SOURCES: Aristophanes, *Frogs* 366]

BIBLIOGRAPHY
Sommerstein, A. H. *The Comedies of Aristophanes*. Vol. 9, *Frogs*. Warminster, U.K.: Aris & Phillips, 1996, 189.

HECTOR   The son of PRIAM and HECABE, Hector was the husband of ANDROMACHE and the father of Astyanax. Hector was the greatest of the Trojan warriors who fought against the Greeks in their war to recover HELEN. Hector killed numerous Greeks, including

ACHILLES' comrade, PATROCLUS. In the seventh book of HOMER's *Iliad,* Hector fought a single combat with AJAX to decide the outcome of the war, but the combat was declared a draw. The two warriors exchanged gifts after the combat, and according to SOPHOCLES' *AJAX,* Ajax committed suicide with the sword Hector gave him. Hector's killing of Patroclus in the 10th year of the war prompted the return of Achilles to the fighting, and eventually Achilles killed Hector. Achilles defiled Hector's body by dragging it behind his chariot. Priam eventually persuaded Achilles to accept ransom for Hector's body so that it could be given a proper burial.

Although Hector appears only once as a character in extant drama, EURIPIDES' *RHESUS,* he was the subject of several plays. The ransom of Hector's body was treated in AESCHYLUS' *Phrygians,* which is alternatively titled *Ransom of Hector* (fragments 263–72 Radt). The Greek playwrights Dionysius I (2a Snell) and Timesitheus (title 2 Snell) also wrote plays entitled *Ransom of Hector,* of which only the titles survive. Among Roman authors, Ennius wrote a *Ransom of Hector* (lines 162–201 Warmington 1). NAEVIUS wrote a TRAGEDY entitled *Hector's Departure* (Latin: *Hector Proficiscens*), which presumably dramatizes Hector's departure from Troy before his fatal encounter with Achilles (lines 17–18 Warmington 2).

Whereas Homer's *Iliad* generally depicts Hector in a positive light, Euripides' *Rhesus* offers a negative portrayal of the hero. In the early part of play, Hector incorrectly thinks that the activity in the Greek camp is due to their preparation to leave Troy. Accordingly, Hector's initial response is to launch an immediate attack. AENEAS, however, provides a more cautious suggestion (which also will fail), namely, that the Trojans send a spy to discover precisely what the Greeks are doing. Later, after the arrival of RHESUS as an ally to the Trojans, Hector initially wants to reject Rhesus' help. After the Greeks kill Rhesus, Hector blames the Trojan troops who were assigned to guard the army and threatens to punish them severely. Hector does agree to take in Rhesus' wounded charioteer and arrange for his healing. Hector also declares his intent to provide a proper burial for Rhesus. [ANCIENT SOURCES: Euripides, *Andromache, Hecabe, Trojan Women;* Homer, *Iliad;* Hyginus, *Fables* 106, 112; Ovid, *Metamorphoses* 12–13; Seneca, *Trojan Women;* Vergil, *Aeneid* 2.268–97, 3.294–489]

BIBLIOGRAPHY

Radt, S. *Tragicorum Graecorum Fragmenta.* Vol. 3. Göttingen, Ger.: Vandenhoeck & Ruprecht, 1985.

Redfield, J. M. *Nature and Culture in the Iliad: The Tragedy of Hector.* Chicago: University of Chicago Press, 1975.

Romilly, Jacqueline de. *Hector.* Paris: de Fallois, 1996.

Rosivach, V. J. "Hector in the Rhesus," *Hermes* 106 (1978): 54–73.

Snell, B. *Tragicorum Graecorum Fragmenta.* Vol. 1. Göttingen, Ger.: Vandenhoeck & Ruprecht, 1971.

Warmington, E. H. *Remains of Old Latin: Ennius and Caecilius.* Vol. 1. Cambridge, Mass.: Harvard University Press, 1935.

———. *Remains of Old Latin: Livius Andronicus, Naevius, Pacuvius, and Accius.* Vol. 2. Cambridge, Mass.: Harvard University Press, 1936.

HECUBA   See HECABE.

HECYRA   See THE MOTHER-IN-LAW.

HEGELOCHUS   Active during the last quarter of the fifth century B.C.E., Hegelochus was an actor who made a famous mistake during the performance of EURIPIDES' *ORESTES.* Hegelochus' incorrect accenting of a word in line 279 changed ORESTES' statement "I see a calm after the storm" into "I see a weasel after the storm." Several comic poets made fun of this mistake in their plays. [ANCIENT SOURCES: Aristophanes, *Frogs* 304; Sannyrion, fragment 8; Strattis, fragments 1, 60 Kock]

BIBLIOGRAPHY

Kock, T. *Comicorum Atticorum Fragmenta.* Vol. 1. Leipzig: Teubner, 1880.

HELEN   Considered the most beautiful of women in classical mythology, as well as one of the most hated, Helen was the daughter of ZEUS and LEDA, or Zeus and NEMESIS. Helen's mortal father was TYNDAREUS. She was the sister of CLYTEMNESTRA, CASTOR, and POLLUX (Polydeuces). Helen became the wife of MENELAUS and they had a daughter, HERMIONE. Helen was abducted twice in her lifetime, first by THESEUS, later by the Trojan PARIS. In the case of Theseus, Helen's brothers rescued her. Helen's second abduction sparked the Trojan War, in which her husband, Menelaus, spent 10 years trying to free her. Sources differ as to whether Helen went with Paris willingly or unwillingly.

Helen appears as a character in EURIPIDES' TROJAN WOMEN, HELEN, and ORESTES, as well as SENECA'S TROJAN WOMEN. The portrayal of Helen's character differs, of course, from play to play. In *Orestes* and the two *Trojan Women* plays, Helen is viewed as an object of hatred, even by some of her own relatives. In Euripides' *Orestes*, ORESTES, PYLADES, and ELECTRA enter a plot to kill Helen. If they succeed, they reason, they will be considered heroes throughout Greece for having killed such a hated woman. Their plot fails, however, and ironically, the woman they considered so vile is rescued by the gods and transformed into a divinity.

In Euripides' *Helen*, however, Helen is depicted as a cunning damsel in distress and a victim of misperception. In this play, we learn that Paris kidnapped a phantom of Helen, while the real Helen was transported by the gods to Egypt, where she suffers the unwanted advances of King Theoclymenus, who is trying to marry her. After Helen's long-lost husband, Menelaus, washes ashore in Egypt, Helen concocts the scheme that allows them to escape from Egypt. [ANCIENT SOURCES: Apollodorus, *Library* 3.10.7–11.1, *Epitome* 1.23, 6.29; Gorgias, *Encomium of Helen*; Herodotus, 2.112–20; Homer, *Iliad* 3, *Odyssey* 4; Pausanias, 2.22.6–7, 3.19.9–3.20.1]

BIBLIOGRAPHY
Holmberg, I. E. "Euripides' Helen: Most Noble and Most Chaste," *American Journal of Philology* 116, no. 1 (1995): 19–42.

HELEN EURIPIDES (412 B.C.E.) Evidence

from ARISTOPHANES' *THESMOPHORIAZUSAE*, which was produced in 411 B.C.E. and preserves a parody of *Helen*, helps date EURIPIDES' play. Euripides' TETRALOGY also included *Andromeda*, which is no longer extant, but was also parodied by Aristophanes in *Thesmophoriazusae*. The action of *Helen* occurs in the seventh year after the sack of Troy by the Greeks and takes place in Egypt before the palace of King Theoclymenus. A structure representing the tomb of Theoclymenus' father, Proteus, is visible. Helen, who delivers the play's opening monologue, informs the audience that the gods transported her to Egypt, while a phantom in her likeness was at Troy. Helen has taken refuge at the tomb of Proteus, whose son, Theoclymenus, is attempting to force her to marry him.

After Helen's monologue, TEUCER, the son of TELAMON and brother of AJAX, arrives on the scene. Teucer encounters Helen and is horrified to see the woman for whom he and the Greeks spent so many years fighting at Troy. Teucer informs her that his father banished him from home. He even notes that he saw Helen's husband, Menelaus, dragging her away from Troy, but that Menelaus has not yet reached home, having been driven far off course by a storm. Teucer tells Helen that her mother, LEDA, and her brothers, CASTOR and POLLUX, are dead, but that her brothers have become gods. All three, according to Teucer, killed themselves because of shame about Helen's behavior. Teucer then states that he has gone to Egypt to consult the prophetess Theonoe, Theoclymenus' sister, about how to reach CYPRUS, where APOLLO told him he should settle. Helen shows Teucer the path but warns him to beware of Theoclymenus, who usually kills all Greeks he encounters.

After Teucer's exit, Helen laments her fate and summons the chorus, composed of captive Greek women who serve as her attendants, to join in her lament. With the chorus' offering sympathetic responses, Helen sings of the news about her deceased mother and brothers, ALEXANDER's abduction of her phantom, and her divine transportation to Egypt. Helen goes on to wish that her whole life had been different; she has lost her native land and her status and suspects that her husband is now dead; her unmarried daughter is growing old. Helen even expresses the notion that suicide might be the best way to preserve her sense of shame. The chorus, urging her not to give up hope, suggest that Menelaus may still be alive and advise her to consult Theonoe about this possibility. Helen states that if she learns that her husband is dead, she will kill herself and laments the loss of life that the war over her caused. After Helen concludes her lament, accompanied by the chorus, she enters the palace to consult Theonoe. From the perspective of staging, this is unusual, as the chorus typically does not leave the stage once they have entered. What is most unusual here, however, is that not only do they leave, but also they enter the palace, a move that does not occur elsewhere in classical drama.

After the exit of Helen and the chorus, Menelaus enters dressed in rags. He has been wandering the seas since the fall of Troy and has been shipwrecked on Egypt's shores. He tries to gain some hospitality from Theoclymenus' house, but a bad-tempered old woman, meeting him at the gate, drives him away; she does, however, inform Menelaus of where he is and warns him about Theoclymenus' hatred of Greeks. She also tells an astonished Menelaus that Helen is inside the palace. After the old woman returns to the interior of the palace, Menelaus expresses his amazement at the news about Helen. He also states his intention to wait for Theoclymenus and make some effort to gain some help from him. Menelaus then moves into a place of hiding from which he can watch what happens.

Next, the chorus and Helen enter with the news from Theonoe that Menelaus is not dead. Menelaus, seeing Helen, is amazed and approaches Helen, who has resumed her position at Proteus' tomb. Helen does not recognize Menelaus at first because of his ragged appearance but soon realizes that he is her husband. Husband and wife then discuss the confusion about the phantom Helen, whom Menelaus took aboard his ship and believed he was currently hiding in a cave on the Egyptian coast. Menelaus, however, is not sure that the woman standing before him is the real Helen. Menelaus' opinion changes when one of his men enters and informs him that Helen has vanished into the air. After Menelaus and Helen express their mutual joy at being reunited and then lament the hardships caused by the events precipitated by Helen. Menelaus then sends the messenger back to the ship to inform the crew to be ready for action so that they can escape from Egypt.

After the messenger departs, Helen warns Menelaus of the danger to Greeks posed by Theoclymenus and tells him that Theoclymenus intends to marry her. At this point, Helen and Menelaus begin to consider their escape from Egypt. They decide to consult Theonoe about this matter and pledge to commit suicide together should they fail to escape. Before they can consult Theonoe, she emerges from the palace and

informs Helen that she is going to send someone to tell her brother, Theoclymenus, that Menelaus has arrived in their land. Both Helen and Menelaus plead for help and mercy from Theonoe. Menelaus tells Theonoe that if she prevents him from being reunited with Helen, he will try to kill Theoclymenus; failing that, he declares that he will kill Helen and himself. Their pleas are successful and Theonoe agrees not to interfere with their efforts to escape. She tells them, however, that they themselves must discover a way to flee.

After Theonoe exits, Helen and Menelaus begin to plot their flight. Helen conceives the idea of dressing in mourning clothes, telling Theoclymenus that she has just heard Menelaus has died, and conducting a false burial for him at sea. After Menelaus agrees to this plan, Helen goes into the palace to prepare herself to look as if she is in mourning while Menelaus takes refuge at Proteus' tomb. After Helen's exit, the chorus sing an ode that recalls the abduction of Helen and the woe that it visited on the Trojans and Greeks. The chorus sing that they consider those who seek virtue through war to be madmen.

After the chorus' song, Theoclymenus enters, having returned from a hunting expedition. He is surprised to see that Helen has left her place of refuge at Proteus' tomb and soon sees her emerge from the palace made up as a mourner. Helen tells Theoclymenus that she will marry him, but that she must first perform a burial at sea for her husband, Menelaus, of whose death, she says she has just learned from both Theonoe and one of Menelaus' shipmates (who Menelaus now pretends to be). Theoclymenus questions Menelaus, who informs him of the things they will need to perform the ritual. Theoclymenus agrees to supply Helen with everything she needs for the ritual, including a ship. After the exit of Menelaus, Helen, and Theoclymenus to attend to the preparations for the ritual, the chorus sing an ode about DEMETER and her search for her daughter, PERSEPHONE, whom HADES abducted, and Demeter's eventual reconciliation with Zeus and end to her grief over the loss of her daughter.

After the choral ode, Helen enters and informs the chorus that Theonoe has not revealed the plot to Theoclymenus. Helen also notes that Menelaus has bathed and put on fresh clothing. Soon Theoclymenus and

Menelaus enter from the palace. After Theoclymenus bids what he thinks is a temporary farewell to his soon-to-be bride, Menelaus and Helen exit for the shore. Next, the chorus sing an ode in which they anticipate the return of Helen to her home in Sparta.

The chorus' song is followed by the arrival from the shore of a messenger, who informs Theoclymenus that Menelaus and his men have overpowered and killed many Egyptians and sailed away with Helen. When Theoclymenus learns the truth, he considers punishing his sister, Theonoe, for not revealing Menelaus' presence to him, but this action is averted by the appearance of the divine CASTOR and POLLUX. The twin divinities inform Theoclymenus that Helen's destiny requires that she return to her home in Greece. They also call to Helen and tell her that eventually she herself will become a goddess and that an island not far off the coast from Athenian territory will be named after her because she first stopped there when taken from Sparta. The divinities announces that Menelaus will be rewarded with a home on the ISLAND OF THE BLESSED after his death. The play ends with Theoclymenus' responding that he will comply with the will of the gods.

COMMENTARY

Euripides' *Helen,* which has become one of the more popular ancient dramas among classical scholars in recent years, is another of Euripides' more puzzling dramas, as it contains a blend of tragic and comic elements. The plot of Helen has several similarities to that of IPHIGENIA IN TAURIS, which was staged the year before. As has IPHIGENIA, Helen has been transported by the gods into a land populated by barbarians who customarily do violence to Greek males. Just as Iphigenia is reunited with her brother, Orestes, Helen is reunited with her husband, Menelaus. Orestes and Menelaus have both experienced considerable trauma: Orestes has killed his mother, has been hounded by her FURIES, and has suffered a dangerous sea voyage past the CLASHING ROCKS to reach Tauris. Similarly, Menelaus had fought for 10 years at Troy and then wandered the sea for an additional seven years before being shipwrecked in Egypt. In both plays, after having been reunited with their women, the Greeks must escape from the barbaric land. Just as Iphigenia contrived a

plot to escape from Tauris, Helen creates a plan to escape from Egypt. In both cases, the plot involves the falsification of a ritual (purification in the case of Iphigenia, burial in the case of Helen). After the Greeks escape, the respective barbarian kings (Thoas, Theoclymenus) threaten violence but are prevented from carrying it out by the appearance of divinities (Athena, Castor and Pollux). In both plays, the Greeks return to their native land with expectation of a "happy" life.

Although *Helen* has serious themes, this play lacks the tension and pathos of such Euripidean plays as *MEDEA* and *HIPPOLYTUS*. We hear of threats of violence from Theoclymenus, death and suffering caused in the past as a result of Helen's abduction, and even Helen's own consideration of suicide, but the only deaths that occur in the play are those of some nameless Egyptians and a bull. Theoclymenus' attempt to force Helen to marry him fails, Theoclymenus' reputation for killing strangers to his land never manifests itself, and his threat to punish his sister, Theonoe, is also averted.

Indeed, *Helen* even has a few comic elements at work. The appearance of Menelaus in rags may have garnered some laughs. Fourteen years earlier, in ACHARNIANS, Aristophanes had joked about Euripides' putting nobles in rags onstage in his tragedies. In *Helen,* however, the presence of rags on a mythical king of Sparta may have seemed fitting and amusing to many of Euripides' fellow Athenians, who had been at war with the Spartans for two decades by this time. The scene between the female gatekeeper of Theoclymenus' palace and Menelaus, in which the old hag repels the pitiful wanderer, is reminiscent of the exchange between Dionysus and the gatekeeper of the UNDERWORLD in Aristophanes' *FROGS* several years later, or of other such slapstick exchanges in New Comedy. The tricking of the barbarian Theoclymenus by Helen and her Greek countrymen echoes not only the deception of the barbarian Thoas by Iphigenia in Euripides' *Iphigenia in Tauris,* but Odysseus' blinding of the barbaric CYCLOPS in Euripides' *CYCLOPS,* a SATYR PLAY. The reunion and figurative remarriage of Helen and Menelaus, rather than the death of a member of this married couple, anticipate the happy endings of new comedy, in which long-separated loved ones are frequently reunited.

Perhaps adding to the play's humor are its metatheatrical elements, namely that *Helen* contains a play within a play. After the reunion of Helen and Menelaus, the couple must find a way to escape from Egypt. The same phenomenon occurs in *Iphigenia in Tauris* with Iphigenia and Orestes, but in *Helen* the metatheatricality is more pronounced. As Iphigenia does, Helen functions as the poet and creates a plot line that will deceive her barbarian audience. In Iphigenia's case, however, Orestes already has a ship. Menelaus' ship has been lost and Helen's plot must ensure that Theoclymenus provide them with a ship, Egyptian rowers who will move the ship into position and take orders from Menelaus, and even the bull needed for the false sacrifice. In addition to the extensive stage properties required for Helen's "play," Helen tells Menelaus that he must pretend to be dead, perhaps borrowing a tactic from Orestes, who pretends that he is dead to trick Clytemnestra and Aegisthus in AESCHYLUS' ORESTEIA. Helen also informs Menelaus that he must play the role of the shipwreck's sole survivor and tell Theoclymenus that Menelaus is dead. Menelaus will not need a costume because the rags with which he entered this play will serve him in this internal play. Helen, however, will need a costume that will convince Theoclymenus that she is now in a state of mourning. Accordingly, she must go into the palace and exchange her light-colored clothing for dark, mar her face with her fingernails, and cut her hair in a sign of mourning. The beauty that Helen complains has destroyed so many she will now destroy. The cutting of Helen's hair is an interesting phenomenon from a theatrical point of view because ancient vase paintings that show actors' MASKS also reveal that the masks have hair. Thus, whereas an ancient actor's mask usually remains static in expression and appearance, Euripides now has Helen enter the palace and alter that mask. Furthermore, the fact that Helen of all people would cut her hair seems amazing. In EURIPIDES' ORESTES, performed a few years after *Helen*, Helen cuts only the tips of her hair in a show of mourning for her dead sister, Clytemnestra. In *Helen*, the title character has properly shorn her fabled locks and only five lines after Helen's next entrance Theoclymenus mentions her short hair (1187–88). Helen recalled earlier in the play that the

Trojan maidens cut their hair in mourning for their dead brothers (368–69a). At last, she herself has made a gesture of mourning that parallels the gestures that her phantom prompted.

The presence of two Helens in this play calls attention to another of the play's themes, appearance versus reality and the effects of this dual nature of one human being on others. In Euripides' *Helen,* the title character and those who encounter her and are connected with her must deal with her dual nature. Hera caused a wicked, phantom Helen to be taken to one barbarian land, while a virtuous, corporeal Helen was taken to another barbarian land but was placed in the home of a person whom Zeus considered the most honest of mortal men. In Egypt, the corporeal Helen preserved her marriage to Menelaus, whereas for the phantom Helen, the Trojan War was fought and countless lives were lost. People curse the Helen of Troy. When Teucer encounters her, he says he would have killed her, for his exile can be attributed to her. Teucer further informs the virtuous Helen that the reputation of the wicked Helen caused Helen's mother to commit suicide and that her brother's deaths can also be linked to the evil Helen. We also learn later that the phantom Helen's reputation has cost her daughter the chance of marriage. Of course, Teucer also tells Helen that her husband, Menelaus, is dead. The chorus warn her, however, that she should not believe everything she hears and their advice turns out to be true, as Menelaus eventually appears.

When the once regal king of Sparta arrives in Egypt, however, he certainly does not appear to be a king and is dressed in rags. When Helen first encounters him, even she does not recognize her husband. Once Helen and Menelaus recognize one another, however, a messenger arrives to announce that the phantom Helen has vanished and that the evil rumors that the real Helen had heard about herself were untrue. Once the phantom Helen is gone, we perhaps begin to see a wholly integrated Helen, a Helen who has much in common with the trickster Odysseus. Eventually, the real Helen, whose phantom caused immense hardship, will create the illusion of a dead Menelaus to occupy Theoclymenus' mind. The reality, however, will not match the appearance. The real Menelaus will be before Theoclymenus' eyes, and the fictional, dead Menelaus will captivate Theoclymenus' mind and give him hope of marriage to Helen. Ultimately, Theoclymenus is deceived by the phantom of Menelaus that Helen created in his mind. Helen and Menelaus will return to their native Sparta and Helen herself will become a goddess at the end of her mortal life.

Despite the play's comic elements, one cannot help but feel that some members of Euripides' audience must have felt a certain sadness and heartache while watching this play. Euripides' *Helen* deals with the futility of war. After 10 years of war, Menelaus discovers that the real Helen was never at Troy. Countless lives, both Greek and Trojan, were lost, fighting over a phantom. Helen's daughter remains unmarried and childless because of her mother's poor reputation. Helen's mother committed suicide because of Helen's supposed affair with PARIS. The Athenians themselves had experienced a similar futility between 415 and 413 as they witnessed the almost total annihilation of the mighty fleet and the forces that their SICILIAN EXPEDITION comprised. The illusion of the prize of SICILY did not match the reality of the crushing defeat that they suffered. A similar discouraging note to an Athenian audience may have been found in the reversal of fortune of the Spartans in the play: The situation of Helen and Menelaus, both Spartans, in the first half of the play was desperate; by the end of the play the Spartans gain the upper hand. The Spartans trick the barbarians through a false ritual and escape. The divinities who prevent Theoclymenus from further violence were Spartans while they lived. Furthermore, these divinities promise the Spartan Helen that she will become a divinity, and that her husband, the king of Sparta, will be honored with a life on the Island of the Blessed in the afterlife. As a further reminder to the Athenians of the Spartans' good fortune, an island within sight of their territory would be named after Helen. Unlike the Spartans of *Helen*, who return home safely from a foreign land, very few of the Athenians who fought in the Sicilian Expedition returned home.

BIBLIOGRAPHY

Austin, N. *Helen of Troy and Her Shameless Phantom.* Ithaca, N.Y.: Cornell University Press, 1994.

Dale, A. M. *Euripides: Helen.* Oxford: Clarendon Press, 1967.

Foley, H. P. *Female Acts in Greek Tragedy.* Princeton, N.J.: Princeton University Press, 2001, 303–31.

Podlecki, A. J. "The Basic Seriousness of Euripides' *Helen,*" *Transactions of the American Philological Association* 101 (1970): 401–18.

Segal, C. P. "The Two Worlds of Euripides' *Helen,*" *Transactions of the American Philological Association* 102 (1971): 553–614.

Wolff, C. "On Euripides' *Helen,*" *Harvard Studies in Classical Philology* 77 (1973): 61–84.

HELENUS   The son of PRIAM and HECABE, Helenus was the brother of CASSANDRA, DEIPHOBUS, HECTOR, PARIS, POLYDORUS, POLYXENA, TROILUS, and many others. As his sister Cassandra was, Helenus was a prophet of APOLLO. Unlike those of Cassandra, however, Helenus' prophecies seem to have been believed. After the death of Paris, Helenus and his brother, Deiphobus, became rivals for Helen. When Deiphobus won Helen, Helenus became angry and left TROY. Captured by the Greeks, Helenus revealed to them the secret of Troy's success, a statue called the Palladium, and told them that if they could gain possession of this statue, they could overthrow Troy.

HELIAEA   A law court located in the AGORA at ATHENS. [ANCIENT SOURCES: Aristophanes, *Knights* 897; Pausanias, 1.28.8]

HELICON   A mountain or range of mountains near the Gulf of CORINTH in the western part of BOEOTIA. The mountain was sacred to the MUSES and APOLLO. [ANCIENT SOURCES: Euripides, *Heracles* 240, 791; Hesiod, *Theogony* 1–2, 23; Pausanias, 9.29.5; Sophocles, *Oedipus Tyrannos* 1108–9]

HELIUS   See SUN.

HELLAS   The name usually used by the ancient Greeks for their country.

HELLE   The daughter of ATHAMAS and Nephele and the brother of PHRIXUS. When Helle and her brother were rescued by the ram with the Golden Fleece, Helle fell into the sea and died. The sea was named Hellespont after her. [ANCIENT SOURCES: Apollodorus, *Library*

1.9.1; Aristophanes, *Wasps* 309; Hyginus, *Fables* 3; Seneca, *Thyestes* 851, *Trojan Women* 1034]

HELLENES In the works of the dramatists, the name Hellenes is usually synonymous with the Greeks. The name Hellenes is from Hellen, the name of one of the sons of DEUCALION. ACCIUS wrote a play entitled *Hellenes,* of which two lines survive (376–77 Warmington) but the plot unknown.

BIBLIOGRAPHY
Warmington, E. H. *Remains of Old Latin: Livius Andronicus, Naevius, Pacuvius, and Accius.* Vol. 2. Cambridge, Mass.: Harvard University Press, 1936.

HEMIKUKLION A Greek word meaning "semicircular," the *hemikulion,* according to Pollux, was placed near the ORCHESTRA in the ancient theater with the purpose of showing objects or persons in the distance. This device was probably not in use until after the fifth century B.C.E. [ANCIENT SOURCES: Pollux, *Onomasticon* 4.127, 131]

HEPHAESTUS (Latin: VULCAN, MULCIBER) Best known as the craftsman of the gods and a god associated with fire, Hephaestus was the son of ZEUS and HERA according to some, or, according to others, the child of Hera alone, born from her thigh. Hephaestus was the husband of APHRODITE, according to some; of Charis, according to others. He may have fathered the Argonaut Palaemon. By Anticlia, Hephaestus is said to have fathered Periphetes, whom THESEUS killed. He suffered an injury to his legs either at birth or when he was thrown from Mount OLYMPUS by Zeus or Hera. Hephaestus landed on the island of LEMNOS, an island that became sacred to him. The injured god was cared for by the sea nymph THETIS, as Hephaestus and Thetis recall in *Iliad* 18 when Thetis arrives to request that the god make armor for her son, ACHILLES. Despite Hephaestus' injuries early in life, he seems to have been reconciled to Zeus and Hera later and tradition says that DIONYSUS made Hephaestus drunk and took him back to Olympus. After Hephaestus' return, he was recognized as a divinity. Hephaestus helped the Olympian gods in their fight against the GIANTS. In *Iliad,* Hephaestus also helps save Achilles when the Scamander River attacks him. In Vergil's *Aeneid,* Hephaestus makes armor for Aeneas. Hephaestus is also said to have supplied Heracles with a breastplate. Hephaestus may have given MINOS the bronze giant Talos.

Hephaestus appears in the opening of AESCHYLUS' *PROMETHEUS BOUND* as one who is assigned the task of overseeing Prometheus' binding to a peak of the Caucasus. Among the Greek dramatists, Achaeus wrote a satyric *Hephaestus* that may have dealt with Hephaestus' return to Olympus, as the single fragment (17 Snell) that survives preserves five lines of a conversation of Hephaestus and Dionysus in which the wine god promises Hephaestus a banquet and says that he will anoint him with myrrh. [ANCIENT SOURCES: Apollodorus, *Library* 1.6.2, 1.9.16, 26, 2.4.1; Homer, *Iliad* 18; Vergil, *Aeneid* 8]

BIBLIOGRAPHY
Snell, B. *Tragicorum Graecorum Fragmenta.* Vol. 1. Göttingen, Ger.: Vandenhoeck & Ruprecht, 1971.

HERA The goddess Hera, whose Roman counterpart is Juno, is a daughter of CRONUS and RHEA. She is both the sister and the wife of ZEUS. She is also the sister of HADES, POSEIDON, HESTIA, and DEMETER. Some sources make Hera and Zeus the parents of HEPHAESTUS; others say that Hera produced Hephaestus from her thigh. Hera is considered the queen of the sky and is particularly concerned with the preservation of the marriage bond. She is also connected with childbirth, and in TERENCE's *ANDRIA* (473), Glycerium calls upon Juno Lucina as she goes into labor. She seldom appears as a character in extant dramas. In PLAUTUS' *Amphitruo,* Juno (Hera) is reported to have sent serpents to destroy the infant Hercules (HERACLES). In EURIPIDES' *HERACLES,* Iris reports that Hera arranged for Madness to persecute Heracles; in SENECA's *HERCULES FURENS,* Juno herself speaks of her grievances against the hero.

HERACLES The greatest of the classical heroes, Heracles (Roman: Hercules) was the son of ZEUS and the mortal ALCMENA. His mortal father was AMPHITRYON. Heracles also had a brother, Iphicles, who was the son of Amphitryon and Alcmena. After Amphitryon was exiled to THEBES for the killing of his uncle,

ELECTRYON, he married Electryon's daughter, Alcmena. Amphitryon's new bride refused to consummate the marriage until Amphitryon avenged the deaths of her brothers, who had been killed during a raid on their father's cattle. When Amphitryon left Thebes to battle the enemy, Zeus disguised himself as Amphitryon, had intercourse with Alcmena, and impregnated her. Almost immediately after Zeus left the house, the real Amphitryon returned from the war. Successful in the battle, Amphitryon wanted to sleep with Alcmena, but Alcmena was puzzled by Amphitryon's presence, because she thought he had left her bed a little earlier. Amphitryon was also troubled because he knew that he had not slept with his wife, despite her claims to the contrary. Eventually, after the prophet TIRESIAS informed the couple of what had happened, Alcmena welcomed Amphitryon to her bed, was again impregnated, and thus became the mother of twins. Zeus was Heracles' father, and Amphitryon was Iphicles' father.

Before Heracles was born, Zeus had boasted that his next descendant to be born would become a powerful king. Zeus thought that Heracles would be the beneficiary of this claim. HERA, hearing this boast, decided to thwart Zeus. She delayed the birth of Heracles and accelerated the birth of his cousin, EURYSTHEUS. Hera's hatred of Heracles continued after he was born, as the goddess sent two serpents to kill the child. Heracles proved his might by strangling the serpents with his tiny hands.

Heracles' next challenge occurred when he was 12 years old, and in a fit of anger he killed his music teacher, LINUS. Heracles was acquitted of murder when he successfully argued that he was only retaliating for being struck wrongfully. Amphitryon, however, thought both Heracles and his fellow Thebans might be better off if this dangerous young man spent some time herding cattle in the countryside. When Heracles was 18, he gained fame for killing a lion that was ravaging the herds of Amphitryon and Thespius, king of Thespiae. As Heracles was returning from hunting the lion, he encountered ambassadors from a certain king, ERGINUS, who had defeated his fellow Thebans in battle and had imposed a tribute on them. Having learned the ambassadors' business, Heracles took offense at the tribute imposed on his native town and assaulted the ambassadors, cutting off their ears, nose, and hands and hanging these body parts around their neck.

Erginus, on learning of the attack on his ambassadors, set out immediately to punish the Thebans. The total destruction of Thebes seemed unpreventable. After the previous war, Erginus had forced the Thebans to disarm. This time, however, the Thebans had a weapon that they had not had before—Heracles. In the ensuing battle, the Heracles-led Thebans achieved a decisive victory over Erginus and his people. In gratitude, the Theban king, CREON, gave Heracles his daughter, MEGARA, in marriage. Life for Heracles and Megara was happy until Hera caused Heracles to become mad and kill Megara and his children by her. Heracles journeyed to the DELPHIC ORACLE to ask what he could do to atone for his crimes; the oracle commanded him to serve EURYSTHEUS, king of Mycenae, and perform 10 (some sources say 12) labors for him. In EURIPIDES' *HERACLES*, however, Euripides reverses the order of Heracles' madness and labors. In this play, Heracles performs his labors for Eurystheus and then becomes mad and kills Megara and his children.

Heracles was, of course, successful in all of his labors. He killed the invulnerable lion of NEMEA by strangling it. Heracles killed the hydra of Lerna by cutting off its multiple heads and then burning the severed places. He used the hydra's venom to make his own arrows extremely lethal. He diverted the courses of the rivers Alpheus and Peneus to cleanse the stables of Augeas, king of ELIS. He used a bronze rattle to drive away the birds that plagued the region around Lake Stymphalus. He subdued and took back to Eurystheus the stag of Cerynea, the Erymanthean boar, the bull of Crete, the flesh-eating mares of Diomedes, the cattle of the triple-bodied creature GERYON, and CERBERUS, the multiheaded dog who guarded the UNDERWORLD. Heracles also retrieved for Eurystheus the belt of the AMAZON Hippolyte and the apples of the HESPERIDES. During this latter adventure, he performed ATLAS' task of holding the sky on his shoulders. In the course of Heracles' labors, he performed numerous additional deeds (or *parerga*). Heracles battled and defeated centaurs on several occasions; he killed ARES' son, CYCNUS, who killed strangers near the town of Amphanae; he wrestled Death himself to raise ADMETUS' wife, ALCES-TIS, from the dead; he rescued the maiden HESIONE of Troy from a sea monster; he wrestled to death several villains, such as ANTAEUS and BUSIRIS, who killed all who wrestled with them. At some point in his career, he sacked the towns of Troy and Elis. Some sources state that after his destruction of Elis Heracles established the Olympic games to honor his father, Zeus. Heracles even fought alongside the gods to defend them from the Giants.

After Heracles completed his labors for Eurystheus, he decided to marry again. His first choice was IOLE, daughter of EURYTUS, king of OECHALIA. Eurytus, however, refused to marry Iole to Heracles. For the time being, Heracles seems to have put aside this rejection and traveled to CALYDON, where he became a suitor for DEIANEIRA, the daughter of OENEUS and sister of MELEA-GER. Heracles was not the only suitor interested in Deianeira, however, and he had to wrestle the river god ACHELOUS for the right to marry her. Heracles, after defeating Achelous, took his new bride to Argos. On the way to Argos, Heracles and Deianeira had to cross the river Evenus, which was treacherous. At the banks of the Evenus, the CENTAUR NESSUS offered to carry Deianeira across the river. While Heracles made his way across the stream, the centaur tried to assault Deianeira sexually. Heracles shot the centaur with one of his venom-tinged arrows. Before Nessus died, however, he convinced Deianeira that his blood (now poisoned with hydra venom) could be used as a love charm if Deianeira suspected Heracles of loving another woman. Deianeira managed to collect some of the centaur's blood and kept it with her.

After Heracles and Deianeira arrived in Argos, they seem to have had a happy life for a number of years. They had at least one child together, HYLLUS. At some point during Heracles' time in Argos, he received a visit from IPHITUS, the son of Eurytus, who was searching for cattle that had been stolen from their land. Heracles helped Iphitus look for the cattle, but during their search madness (caused by Hera, according to some sources) struck Heracles, and he killed Iphitus. Heracles consulted the Delphic oracle about what he should do to atone for this crime, but the oracle refused to answer him. The angered Heracles snatched the ora-

cle's sacred tripod and left to establish his own oracle. This act of sacrilege prompted the appearance of APOLLO, the god of DELPHI. Heracles and Apollo would have fought, but their father, Zeus, stopped them and resolved this tense situation. Heracles returned Apollo's tripod, and Apollo told Heracles how he could atone for his crime.

Heracles again had to become a slave, this time of a woman, OMPHALE, the queen of Lydia. Before Heracles went into exile, he moved his family to TRACHIS, in northeastern Greece. After Heracles' servitude to Omphale, he returned to Greece; sacked the town of Eurytus, on whom he blamed his troubles; and took Eurytus' daughter, Iole, prisoner. While Heracles remained on Eurytus' island to make a sacrifice to Zeus, Iole was sent ahead to Trachis. When Deianeira saw the young captive, she rightly suspected that Heracles would make the young woman his concubine. Remembering the centaur Nessus' love charm, she placed some of this substance on a robe that Heracles would wear while making sacrifice and sent it to him via the messenger Lichas. When Heracles put on the robe, it became stuck to his body; trying to remove the robe only tore off his skin. Later, after Deianeira discovered her love charm's true power, she committed suicide. Heracles managed to have himself ferried to Trachis, where he begged his son, Hyllus, to put him out of his misery. Hyllus took his father to the top of Mount Oeta, where a funeral pyre was built and Heracles, still alive, was placed on top. He could not make himself light his father's pyre, and a passing shepherd, PHILOCTETES, agreed to help Heracles. In exchange for this service, Heracles gave Philoctetes his bow and arrows. Once the pyre was ignited, Heracles' mortal part was burned away and his divine part ascended to Mount OLYMPUS, where he was welcomed as a god and married to HEBE, the daughter of Zeus and Hera.

Heracles appears as a character in several extant dramas and would have appeared as a character in dozens of other dramas, both tragedies and comedies, that are no longer extant. In EURIPIDES' *ALCESTIS*, he appears as the enduring but somewhat uncouth hero who becomes drunk during the funeral of Alcestis, but later rescues Alcestis from THANATOS, the god of death. In Euripides' *Heracles*, he returns from the UNDERWORLD and is characterized as the savior of Thebes, Greece, and even the gods themselves. He rescues his family from persecution by the evil king Lycus but then is dashed violently from the pinnacle of his success by Hera, who sends Madness to drive him insane—and his insanity leads him to kill his wife and sons. After Heracles recovers from his madness, Euripides shows him as a broken man, who rejects the idea that Zeus was his father.

Euripides' portrayal of Heracles in *Heracles* recalls SOPHOCLES' treatment of AJAX in the earlier play of the same name. As is Ajax, Heracles is stricken with temporary madness and attacks those who pose no violent threat to him. Heracles' madness leads him to his kill his harmless wife and children, thinking he is attacking his enemy, Eurystheus; Ajax's madness leads to the destruction of harmless cattle, rather than ODYSSEUS, AGAMEMNON, and MENELAUS, as Ajax had intended. Special weapons play important roles in the portrayals of Ajax and Heracles. Sophocles' Ajax mistakenly kills the cattle and then himself with a sword given to him by his enemy, HECTOR. Euripides portrays Heracles' bow as the primary weapon that helped him accomplish his labors, but the same bow is one of the weapons used to destroy his family. Ajax rid himself of the weapon of his madness by burying that weapon in his own body; in the last part of Euripides' *Heracles,* the hero debates whether he should rid himself of the bow or continue to carry it. Eventually, Heracles decides that he cannot bear to discard his bow, though it destroyed his family. Finally, both Ajax and Heracles have a special connection with ATHENS. In Sophocles' play, Ajax is frequently linked with the city and, in fact, worshiped as a hero throughout Athenian territory. At the conclusion of Euripides' *Heracles,* Theseus, the Athenian king, promises to take Heracles to Athens, give him a home and land there, and, after his death, establish the worship of Heracles in Athens.

In Sophocles' *Trachiniaen Women,* Heracles is characterized as someone who constantly uses violence to achieve his goals. He wrestles and defeats ACHELOUS for the right to marry Deianeira. He kills Iphitus suddenly and without explanation. Heracles destroys Eurytus' kingdom with apparently little more motivation than a desire to enslave Eurytus' daughter, IOLE, and make her

his concubine. Heracles' killing of the centaur Nessus, although justifiable, eventually leads to his own death, as the venom from Heracles' arrow that tainted Nessus' blood will provide the poison with which Deianeira will accidentally destroy Heracles.

HERACLES EURIPIDES (CA. 420–415 B.C.E.)

EURIPIDES' *Heracles* has HERACLES' house at THEBES as its setting. As the play opens, Heracles' mortal father, AMPHITRYON, relates in the PROLOGUE that the current king of Thebes, LYCUS, arrived there from EUBOEA; killed the Theban king, CREON (father of Heracles' wife, MEGARA); and usurped his throne. Amphitryon states that he himself went to Thebes after he was exiled from ARGOS for killing his uncle, ELECTRYON. Additionally, he says that Heracles offered EURYSTHEUS, king of Argos, to rid the earth of various monsters in exchange for allowing Amphitryon to return to Argos. At present, Heracles is in the UNDERWORLD, there to take CERBERUS back to the upper world. While Heracles has been in the underworld, Lycus has begun to persecute Heracles' family and threatens to kill them. To save themselves, Amphitryon, Heracles' wife, and his three children have taken refuge at Zeus' altar.

After Amphitryon's opening monologue, Megara addresses Amphitryon, wondering how they are going to escape their situation. Amphitryon is uncertain but encourages her to be hopeful. Next, the chorus, composed of old Theban men, enter. They sing of their weak old age, their once glorious youth, and the great resemblance of Heracles' children to their father. The old men's entry is followed by the arrival of Lycus, who scoffs at the group for continuing to hope for salvation. Lycus also downplays Heracles' valor because his chief weapon is the bow, a coward's weapon in Lycus' view. He intends to prevent Heracles' children from growing up and taking revenge on him for the killing of Creon. Amphitryon defends Heracles' valor and suggests that the bow is a clever weapon that allows the warrior to fight safely from a distance. Amphitryon wonders what Heracles' children have done to Lycus and criticizes the people of Thebes for not helping them, especially because Heracles once saved their city from the Minyans.

Lycus does not try to refute Amphitryon's arguments; he calls on his servants to pile wood around the altar to burn Amphitryon and Heracles' family. At this, the old Thebans raise their staffs and threaten Lycus. Megara, however, feels that their death is a certainty and states that if they must die, they should die with dignity. Amphitryon asks Lycus to kill him and Megara before the children die so that they will not have to watch their death. Megara also asks that they be allowed to wear funeral garments before they perish. Lycus agrees to both these requests and then departs. Megara takes the children into the palace and is followed by Amphitryon, who questions the value of Zeus' being Heracles' father because the god has not aided Heracles' family.

While Heracles' family is inside the palace clothing themselves for their imminent death, the Theban elders sing a lengthy ode that celebrates the various labors of Heracles. They conclude the song by wondering where Heracles is. They long for the strength of their youth, which might allow them to rescue Heracles' children. After their song, Amphitryon and Heracles' family emerge from the palace wearing garments appropriate for their impending death. As their despair reaches its height, Heracles suddenly returns from the underworld. Megara explains the situation to Heracles, who quickly decides to destroy Lycus. Amphitryon, advising Heracles on how best to attack the king, suggests that he enter the palace and wait for Lycus there. Amphitryon also questions Heracles about his journey to the underworld. After this, Heracles, Amphitryon, and the family reenter the palace.

After their exit, the aged Thebans sing an ode wishing for a second youth. They sing of Heracles' victories, they declare him Zeus' son (a relationship that Heracles himself will later renounce), and praise the hero for securing peace and tranquility for them. Their song is followed by Lycus' arrival. Amphitryon, who has emerged from the palace, then lures the unsuspecting king into the palace. Soon, Lycus' cries are heard from the palace and the chorus begin to dance in celebration of the tyrant's death. They rejoice in the triumph of Heracles and express their present certainty (previously they had doubts) that Zeus was Heracles' father.

The chorus' celebration, however, is interrupted by the appearance of the goddess IRIS, whom Madness accompanies. The appearance of divinities in the mid-

dle of a play is unusual in classical drama. Euripides frequently sends divinities into his dramas, but they usually appear at the beginning or end. The unexpected appearance of Iris and Madness both marks and initiates the play's second half. Heracles has reached the height of his accomplishments as a hero by this point in the play. Now, as was Job in the Old Testament, he will be toppled from the pinnacle of success. Iris tells the chorus that neither Zeus nor fate would allow Hera to assault Heracles during his labors. With the completion of the labors, however, Hera will make Heracles kill his children. The unfairness of this action is voiced by Madness herself, who notes that Heracles has helped not only humankind, but the gods themselves. Iris dismisses Madness' sympathy and tells her to carry out her assignment. As with the exchange between Power and HEPHAESTUS in PROMETHEUS BOUND, in which Hephaestus is reluctant to affix PROMETHEUS to the mountain, Madness is reluctant to attack Heracles but says that she will do so.

The chorus' earlier joy is now turned to sadness as the old men of Thebes mourn the loss of Heracles and describe for the audience the looming attack of Madness and a sort of storm that shakes Heracles' house. After the choral ode, a messenger enters and describes Heracles' killing of his wife and children. This MESSENGER speech is one of the most horrific in extant drama. The perversity and horror of Heracles' madness are intensified by the fact that his madness occurs while Heracles is leading his family in a religious ceremony to purify their house of the killing of Lycus. The messenger notes that Heracles was stricken with insanity in the midst of this ceremony. In Heracles' madness, he imagined that he was climbing into a chariot to go to MYCENAE and kill Eurystheus. As Heracles imagined passing through various towns on his way to Mycenae, he stopped and prepared to eat an imaginary meal; he then removed his clothing and engaged in a wrestling match with no one. Upon arriving at the imaginary Mycenae, Heracles snatched up his bow and began to take aim at his own sons, thinking that they were Eurystheus' sons. Heracles killed one child with his bow, a second with his club; with another arrow he killed Megara and his third son. Heracles' rampage ends when the phantom of ATHENA knocks out the hero with a massive boulder. While Heracles is unconscious, Amphitryon and servants tie him to a pillar.

After the messenger's speech, the doors of the palace are opened and Heracles is revealed, tied to a pillar and sleeping. Amphitryon urges the chorus to be quiet so that they will not wake him. Eventually, Heracles awakens from his slumber and wonders at the corpses of his family nearby. When Amphitryon explains to Heracles what he has done, Heracles wonders why he does not take his own life. His self-questioning is cut short, however, by the entrance of the Athenian king THESEUS, who has traveled to Thebes because he had received news that Lycus had overthrown the government there and because Heracles has rescued Theseus from the underworld. Heracles covers his head with his cloak so that he will not be seen by Theseus, who coaxes him to uncover his head. Heracles is in great despair: He speaks of suicide, denies that he is Zeus' son, and rejects the stories told by poets about the gods' immoral behavior. Theseus does manage to persuade Heracles not to take his own life and to go with him to Athens.

Before Heracles leaves, he arranges for Amphitryon to bury his family. Heracles then bids farewell to his wife and sons. He considers abandoning the bow with which he killed his family but decides that he cannot part with it. Heracles requests that Theseus accompany him to verify for Eurystheus that Heracles restored Cerberus from the underworld. As Theseus and Heracles leave, Heracles is weeping. He promises Amphitryon that he will send for him to go to Athens.

COMMENTARY

Euripides' *Heracles* is not regarded as one of the author's best plays. The drama moves slowly at its beginning and end but is fast-paced during its central part. Thus, much of the criticism of the play is related to its structure. As does Euripides' earlier ANDROMACHE, *Heracles* begins with the seige of innocent people at an altar (ANDROMACHE and child; Amphitryon, Megara, and children) and is followed by the rescue of the innocents and the repulsion of the beseiger (PELEUS saves Andromache and child and repels MENELAUS and HERMIONE; Heracles saves his family and kills Lycus); that is in turn followed by a terrible killing (NEOPTOLEMUS is killed; Heracles kills his wife and children).

Also unusual, as noted, is the appearance of the divinities in the middle of the play. As unexpected and unconventional as this may seem, it does fit in with one of the play's themes, which Padilla has well detailed. Among the important concepts of Euripides' *Heracles* are the notions of "the seen" and "the unseen." When the play opens, Heracles is in Hades, whose name means "unseen." During Amphitryon and Lycus' argument in the first half of the play, Amphitryon defends Heracles' use of the bow because this weapon allows the person who wields it to strike at enemies from an unseen position. When Heracles returns from the land of the unseen, he tells Amphitryon that he entered Thebes unseen (598). Soon, Heracles will enter the house and strike out at Lycus, who will not see his assailant. The unseen Heracles who kills Lycus is in turn driven insane by Madness, who states that she will enter Heracles' house unseen (873). After Heracles kills his wife and children, he becomes unseen again, this time in shame for his actions, as he covers his head with his cloak. Near the play's conclusion, Heracles considers leaving behind his bow, the weapon of the unseen warrior, but cannot bear to part with the weapon that has served him through so many labors, although he destroyed his family with this same weapon.

Also prominent among the themes of *Heracles* is the idea of friendship, as Barlow and many other scholars have pointed out. In the first half of the play, it appears that other than Amphitryon and Heracles' family, Heracles has no friends. The people of Thebes, whom Heracles liberated from the Minyans, provide no help to him. Amphitryon accuses Zeus, Heracles' father, of not being a friend to Heracles (341) and claims he himself is a better friend than the mighty god. Heracles defeats Lycus, but once this threat is eliminated, he is overthrown by Madness, an agent of his enemy, Hera. After Heracles' madness, the hero himself believes that he has become friendless. Theseus, the king of Athens, however, proves himself a friend and promises Heracles asylum in his land.

In addition to the theme of friendship, another of the play's focal points is fatherhood. The play opens with a prologue by Heracles' mortal father, who notes that Heracles became a slave to Eurystheus so that his father (Amphitryon) could return to his native land. The audience also learns that Amphitryon must function as a father figure to Heracles' wife and children. The father of Heracles' wife was killed in the overthrow of the Theban government and Heracles' labors cause the children to miss their father.

Whereas attention is constantly drawn to Heracles' role as a father, the oppressor of Heracles' family is seemingly fatherless and no mention is made of his having a wife or children, a highly unusual condition for a Greek male. We learn that Lycus is a descendant of a former Theban king, but his father's name is never given. Amphitryon even scoffs that Lycus' fatherland (*patran,* 187) would not be able to provide anyone who could testify that Lycus had ever performed a noble deed. Because Lycus has killed Megara's father and his male children, he now wants to put his rule of Thebes on firmer ground by killing Heracles' father and children. Lycus feels he has nothing to fear from Heracles, who is surely dead in the underworld, but he does not want the father's children to grow up and take vengeance on him. Lycus will not become another AEGISTHUS, whose murder of AGAMEMNON was avenged by his son, ORESTES.

Father Heracles does, however, return from the underworld and destroy the man who threatened his father and threatened to take away his own identity as a father by killing his children. Unfortunately, the victorious return of the father is quickly countered by the appearance of Madness, who, in her opening line, maintains the paternal theme by noting that she was born of a noble mother and father (843). Madness is reluctant to act against Heracles because of the help he has given the gods. Still, she carries out the wishes of Hera, the wife of Heracles' divine father, and causes father Heracles to kill his children. In his madness, Heracles thinks that he is killing the children of his enemy, Eurystheus, an ironic parallel to what Lycus planned for the children of his enemy, Heracles.

After Heracles kills his wife and children, not only can he no longer be called a father, but his relationship with his divine father is changed in his mind. Heracles wonders who Zeus is and declares that he considers Amphitryon his father and not Zeus (1265). Not only does Heracles reject his immortal father, but as a killer he must leave his fatherland. Heracles' exile also means that he will leave his mortal father Amphitryon. Thus, having no children, being rejected by his fatherland, and having rejected his ties to his divine father and been compelled to leave his mortal father behind, Heracles is beginning to resemble Lycus.

Finally, the issue of how Euripides has changed the order of events with respect to Heracles' killing of his wife and children seems worthy of consideration. In another version of the story Heracles kills his wife and children before he performs his labors and atonement for these killings is the reason for his performance of the labors for Eurystheus. Presenting Heracles' killing of his wife and children after the completion of his labors allows Euripides to take Heracles to the pinnacle of his achievements and then push him over the edge. If Heracles kills his wife and children before his labors, he remains a powerful figure, but he is still relatively unknown. By the time Heracles commits these murders in Euripides' play, he has saved his city, his country, the world, and even the gods. Madness herself has great respect for Heracles and what he has done. After the murders, Heracles falls from almost divine status to that of a mere mortal. Theseus, on hearing Heracles' laments and thoughts of suicide, observes that Heracles is talking as an ordinary person does (1248). Thus, in Euripides' *Heracles,* the title character moves from hero to mortal.

BIBLIOGRAPHY

Barlow, S. A. *Heracles: Euripides.* Warminster, U.K.: Aris & Phillips, 1996.

Bond, G. W. *Euripides: Heracles.* London: Oxford University Press, 1981.

Gregory, J. W. "Euripides' *Heracles,*" *Yale Classical Studies* 25 (1977): 259–75.

Padilla, M. "The Gorgonic Archer: Danger of Sight in Euripides' *Heracles,*" *Classical World* 86 (1992): 1–12.

Vickers, M. "Heracles Lacedaemonius: The Political Dimensions of Sophocles' *Trachiniae* and Euripides' *Heracles,*" *Dialogues d'Histoire Ancien* 21, no. 2 (1995): 41–69.

Worman, Nancy. "The Ties That Bind: Transformations of Costume and Connection in Euripides' *Heracles,*" *Ramus* 28, no. 2 (1999): 89–107.

HERCULES FURENS SENECA (WRITTEN BETWEEN 49 AND 65 C.E.?)   The basic story of the play is the same as that of EURIPIDES' *HERACLES.* The

play's setting is the house of Hercules (Greek: HERA-CLES) at THEBES. Unlike in Euripides' play, in which AMPHITRYON speaks the prologue, in SENECA's play Juno (Greek: HERA), who does not appear in Euripides' play, delivers the prologue. In Juno's lengthy speech, she complains that she has left heaven because her place has been taken by women with whom her husband, Jove (Greek: ZEUS), has had affairs. Juno has attempted to take revenge on Hercules, the child of ALCMENA by Zeus. Hercules, however, has destroyed all the monsters that Juno has put in his path. Juno notes that now Hercules has gone to and returned from the UNDERWORLD with the guardian dog, CERBERUS. Juno worries that because Hercules has conquered, figuratively, the underworld, he may next attempt to overthrow heaven, his father, Zeus', kingdom. Juno announces that she will prevent Hercules from doing this by causing him to become mad. She concludes by rousing the female demons of the underworld to attack Hercules with madness.

Next, the chorus of Thebans enter. They greet the approaching dawn and describe the various labors the people of Thebes will undertake during the day. Whereas the common people labor in relative peace, they note, other people, who strive after wealth and the like, are faced with constant cares. The chorus point out that all people die, and even Hercules' time will come. As the chorus end their speech, Hercules' father, Amphitryon; his wife, MEGARA; and his children emerge from Hercules' house. Amphitryon recalls many of the labors that Hercules has had to endure and announces that now another challenge faces him. Amphitryon goes on to relate that CREON, king of Thebes, has been killed by LYCUS, who now persecutes Hercules' family. Amphitryon and Megara express their fervent hope that Hercules will return soon to help them, because they have had to take refuge at an altar in fear of Lycus.

The conversation of Amphitryon and Megara is interrupted by the arrival of Lycus, who (unlike his Euripidean counterpart) declares that his new kingship can be established firmly if he marries Hercules' wife, Megara. When Lycus invites Megara to become his queen, she refuses. Lycus, however, persists and threatens to kill her if she will not marry him. Megara

believes that Hercules will return from the underworld and eventually ascend to heaven. When Lycus wonders who Hercules' father is to make Megara have such a belief, Amphitryon defends the idea that the king of the gods is Hercules' father. Lycus, however, wonders whether beings who were once enslaved or persecuted themselves can be gods. Lycus questions Hercules' bravery, noting that he behaved in an unmanly fashion during his servitude to OMPHALE. Lycus also notes that when Hercules destroyed EURYTUS and his kingdom, he did not do so at the command of Juno or EURYSTHEUS.

Amphitryon defends Hercules against these accusations and declares that Lycus will meet the same fate that many of Hercules' victims did. Lycus, however, ignores this threat and declares his intention to marry Megara, by force if necessary. When Megara continues to refuse, Lycus orders his servants to pile up logs around the altar and prepare to burn Amphitryon, Megara, and the children. Lycus then exits to make a sacrifice to Neptune (Greek: POSEIDON). After the king departs, Amphitryon prays that Hercules will save them. Next, the chorus sing a lengthy song in which they recall some of Hercules' successes. They pray that the hero will return from the underworld and recall that ORPHEUS was almost able to make a successful journey back from the underworld. They hope that although Orpheus' music failed, Hercules' strength will succeed.

After the choral ode, Hercules, accompanied by the Athenian king, THESEUS (and perhaps the dog Cerberus), returns from the underworld. When Amphitryon informs Hercules what Lycus is planning for his wife and family, Hercules immediately exits to kill Lycus. During Hercules' absence, Amphitryon questions Theseus about their adventures in the underworld. Theseus gives a long description of the geography of the underworld, the condition and its inhabitants, how Hercules made the journey and what he saw on the way, and how Hercules subdued Cerberus. As Theseus concludes his speech, the chorus approach, celebrate Hercules' successful return, and hope that they themselves will not see the underworld any time soon. The chorus also rejoice that Hercules has produced peace in Thebes.

After the chorus' song, Hercules enters, announces that he has killed Lycus, and begins to give thanks to the gods. As Hercules prays, however, madness (caused by Juno) strikes him. Unlike in Euripides' play, Hercules begins to have visions of overthrowing his father, Jove. The hero also sees his own children, imagines that they are Lycus' children, and attacks them. As Hercules drags off his children to kill them, a horrified Amphitryon describes what Hercules is doing. Megara, who leaves the stage to protect her children, is also killed by Hercules, who imagines that she is his enemy, Juno. Amphitryon, seeing these horrors, wishes to die and offers himself to Hercules for slaughter. At this point, however, the madness leaves Hercules and he falls to the ground in exhausted slumber. His weapons are removed to prevent further bloodshed. After this, the chorus lament Hercules' misfortune, pray that sleep will comfort him, and hope that his madness will depart. They also pray that Hercules' slain children will reach their final destination in the underworld.

After the choral ode, Hercules, now in his right mind, awakens to find that he has killed his wife and children. He wants to kill himself and suggests that he will destroy his weapons as well. Amphityron urges Hercules to seek pardon for his crime, but the hero doubts that Jove will forgive him. He calls for his weapons so that he can kill himself, but Theseus urges him to endure his adversity. When Hercules threatens to hurl the entire city of Thebes onto himself, Amphitryon gives him back his weapons. At this point, Amphitryon threatens to kill himself. Because Hercules' hands are stained with his family's blood, he does not want to touch his father, so he calls for Theseus to help Amphitryon. After Amphitryon's suicide is prevented, Hercules calls upon Theseus to help him. As does Euripides, Seneca ends the play with Theseus' promise to grant Hercules asylum in Athens.

COMMENTARY

During the first half of the first century B.C.E., Seneca witnessed the further solidification of Rome's transition from a republic governed by many to an empire ruled by one man. When the lives of these emperors ended, or sometimes even during their lifetime, Rome's emperors were worshiped as gods. Seneca himself served as tutor to the emperor NERO, who himself would be deified. Thus, unlike in Euripides' *Heracles*,

with its concern with friendship and the contrast between the seen and the unseen, in Seneca's play one of the focal points is the possible transformation of a man into a god, with the disruption of the vertical axis (heaven–earth–underworld) that would result were such a transformation to take place.

As Hercules' father had left heaven to impregnate Hercules' mother (265), Hercules' stepmother has also left heaven for the Earth as the play opens. Juno has descended the vertical axis because the population of heaven produced by Jove's concubines has driven her out (4–5). Juno claims to be concerned that Hercules, who has already demonstrated his ability to hold heaven on his shoulders (69, 73) and whose fame has reached heaven (194), scorning the things of Earth (89), will seize heaven's throne (64). To prevent Hercules from being admitted to heaven, she will drive him to commit a horrific crime on Earth.

Despite Juno's fears and plans, when the play begins Hercules is as far from heaven as he can be. As Juno notes that Hercules held the weight of heaven on his shoulders, Megara declares to Lycus that although Hercules is in the underworld, the man who held up heaven will not be pressed down by the weight of the Earth (425). In contrast to heaven's queen, who worries that Hercules will usurp Jove's throne, the earthly king, Lycus, doubts that Hercules has the lineage to claim a place in heaven (438), does not believe that those who dwell in heaven have sexual relations with those who dwell on Earth (448), and does not believe that Hercules will return to Earth from the underworld.

Lycus' skepticism will soon be refuted, however, when Hercules ascends the vertical axis and moves from underworld to upper world. After emerging from darkness, Hercules addresses his first words to APOLLO, who rules the light and the glory of heaven (592), and Jove, who rules the heavenly gods (597). Although the hero has triumphed over the lower world, he returns to find trouble in the upper world and regaining control of his family's situation on Earth becomes his first priority. Killing Lycus will accomplish this. Soon, Hercules causes the evil king to descend the vertical axis to the land from which Hercules just returned.

After killing Lycus, Hercules plans to honor the heavenly gods with prayers and sacrifices. Hercules' prayers (926–38) show that he does not intend to usurp Jove's throne, as Juno had feared. In the midst of these prayers, however, the vertical axis seems to be reversed in Hercules' mind. The light is replaced by darkness and night's stars appear during the day. As Amphitryon observes, Hercules' perception of heaven is changing (954), and in the hero's madness, he declares that he will seek heaven (957) and the stars his father promised him. He even threatens to take Saturn from the underworld to help him overthrow heaven and to pile mountains on top of one another to reach heaven (972).

As a result of Hercules' madness, he kills his wife and children and thus sends them to the underworld. Amphitryon is so distraught by Hercules' actions that he wants to descend the vertical axis as well, either by his son's hand or by his own. When Hercules awakens from his madness, he is unsure where he is. He imagines that Jove has descended from heaven (1157) and begotten a new son, who has overcome him. When Hercules realizes what he has done, the hero whose fame had touched the stars wishes that he could return to the depths of the underworld. His crime is so great that earth and sky move away from him (1332–34). He begs Theseus to take him back to the underworld (1338–39), but instead Theseus will take him to Athens, a place on Earth where even the gods above can be cleansed of bloodshed (1344).

BIBLIOGRAPHY

Billerbeck, M. *Seneca: Hercules Furens*. Leiden: E. J. Brill, 1999.

Lawall, G. "*Virtus* and *Pietas* in Seneca's *Hercules Furens*," In *Seneca Tragicus: Ramus Essays on Senecan Drama*. Edited by A. J. Boyle. Berwick, Australia: Aureal, 1983, 6–26.

Motto, A. L., and J. R. Clark. "*Maxima Virtus* in Seneca's *Hercules Furens*," *Classical Philology* 76 (1981): 100–17.

Rose, A. "Seneca's *HF*: A Politico-Didactic Reading," *Classical Journal* 75 (1979–80): 135–42.

Shelton, J. A. *Seneca's Hercules Furens: Theme, Structure and Style*. Göttingen, Ger.: Vandenhoeck & Ruprecht, 1978.

HERCULES OETAEUS SENECA (?) (WRITTEN BETWEEN 49 AND 65 C.E.?)

Although tradition attributes the authorship of the play to SENECA, most modern scholars doubt this. The main plot of the story is the same as that of SOPHOCLES' TRACHINIAN WOMEN. Unlike Sophocles' play, which is set TRACHIS, the play apparently begins near the town of OECHALIA on the island of EUBOEA. In Sophocles' play, DEIANEIRA delivers the PROLOGUE, whereas Seneca has Hercules (Greek: HERACLES) recite it. Hercules begins with a prayer to his father, Jove (Greek: ZEUS), wondering why he has not yet ascended to heaven: He has completed his labors and overcome all obstacles placed in his path. Next, the hero tells his herald, LICHAS, to proclaim abroad that he has overthrown Oechalia, the kingdom of EURYTUS, and to prepare for a sacrifice to Jove.

After Hercules' exit, the CHORUS enter. Unlike in Sophocles' play, in which women from Trachis constitute the chorus, in this drama the chorus is a group of captive women from Oechalia. They lament their captivity and complain about the cruelty of Hercules. The chorus' song is followed by a lament by another captive, Eurytus' daughter, IOLE, whom Hercules intended to make his concubine. Whereas Sophocles' Iole does not speak, Seneca's Iole gives a lengthy speech in which she compares her fate to that of other unhappy women in mythology. She recalls with horror Hercules' killing of her father and other family members.

Next, the NURSE of Hercules' wife, DEIANEIRA, enters. The nurse relates the behavior of Deianeira when she learned that Hercules was going to take Iole to their home as a concubine. Unlike Sophocles' Deianeira, who looks upon Iole with some pity, Seneca's Deianeira has virtually become insane with anger and jealousy. When Deianeira enters, she calls on Juno (Greek: HERA) to take vengeance against Hercules. She worries that Iole's children by Hercules will become rivals to her own children. Deianeira's nurse asks her how she is planning to avenge herself. The nurse warns Deianeira that any violent act she commits will result in her death, but Deianeira is not swayed by this argument. The nurse also points out that Hercules has encountered many women in his life, but has not loved them intensely. She suggests that Hercules will not prefer Iole, a slave and the daughter of his enemy, to her. Deianeira, however, is convinced that Hercules seeks a new woman to love and declares that she will kill Hercules. The nurse suggests that a magic charm might make Hercules love Deianeira. In turn, Deianeira informs the nurse that she has a potion that she acquired from blood of the centaur NES-SUS, who had once tried to rape her. When Hercules killed the centaur with an arrow tinged with venom from the Lernaean hydra, the venom became intermingled with Nessus' blood. Nessus, knowing that deadly hydra venom was in his blood, told Deianeira that she could use that blood as a love charm for Hercules by placing it on one of Hercules' garments.

Deianeira then sends the nurse to get the centaur's blood, which she keeps in a hidden place, and smear it on one of Hercules' robes. After this is done, Hercules' herald, Lichas, enters, and Deianeira gives the robe to Lichas and instructs him to give it to Hercules. After Lichas' exit, Deianeira returns to the palace to pray to Venus.

As Deianeira departs, she instructs a second chorus, composed of women who accompanied her from her native land of AETOLIA, to lament her misfortune. Not only do the Aetolian women express sorrow about Deianeira's situation, they also complain about the greed of humankind and the brevity of life. They suggest that women who do not have extravagant weddings are more likely to be happy because those who stray from the "middle course" are likely to suffer ruin. As they end their ode, Deianeira and her nurse enter. Deianeira worriedly reveals that she has now discovered that the potion that she put on Hercules' robe ignites when exposed to sunlight. At this point, Deianeira's son, HYLLUS, enters and informs his mother that Hercules is being tormented by the ravages of the poison. Hyllus describes in detail how the poison attacked Hercules while he was making a sacrifice to Jove and how Hercules, in his madness, hurled Lichas, who gave the poisoned robe to Hercules, into the sea. Hyllus notes that at present Hercules is being taken to the palace. Upon hearing this, Deianeira begins to consider suicide. Unlike Sophocles' Hyllus, who is angry at his mother for what she has done to her husband, Hyllus tries to persuade Deianeira not to kill herself. Deianeira cannot be swayed from her purpose, however, and even begs Hyllus to kill her. Eventually, in a burst of passion, Deianeira rushes out, still voicing her suicidal intent. Hyllus, hoping to prevent this act, hurries after her.

After Hyllus' exit, the chorus sing a lengthy ode in which they recall the powerful and magical songs of Orpheus and his failed journey to the UNDERWORLD to rescue his wife. They go on to suggest that Hercules' fall indicates that someday the gods, heaven, and Earth will collapse. The chorus conclude their song by wondering what single place will contain the realms of heaven, Earth, and underworld when this happens.

After the choral ode, Hercules enters in extreme anguish. As in Sophocles' play, Seneca's Hercules laments the irony that he was able to overcome so many monsters and difficult labors, but that he is ultimately being destroyed by a mortal woman. Hercules also complains that his death will not be a glorious one, wonders about the actual cause of his torment, and wonders why his pain has caused him to shed tears. He also prays to his father, Jove, to have pity on him and put him out of his misery. At this point, unlike in Sophocles' play, Hercules' mother, ALCMENA, enters and questions her son about what has happened to him. Hercules informs her of Deianeira's treachery and the poisoned robe. He says that he has given up hope that he will live any longer. Alcmena tries to encourage her son, but Hercules cannot be consoled and even moves to kill himself with his own weapons. After Alcmena has them moved out of his reach, she herself begins to feel despair and expresses thoughts of suicide.

At this point, Hyllus enters and informs Hercules that Deianeira has committed suicide in grief over what she has done. Hyllus also tells his father that the centaur Nessus had tricked Deianeira to use the poison. Hercules then realizes that this must be true, because an oracle once told him that he would be killed by one whom he had killed. Next, Hercules orders that a pyre be built on Mount Oeta so that he can place his poison-ravaged body on it and have it consumed by fire. Unlike Sophocles' play, in which Hyllus is ordered to carry out this horrible task, the Latin play removes the possibility of a son's killing his father by having this order given to PHILOCTETES, who appears to have been onstage, although no indication of his presence has been given up to this point. As in Sophocles' play, however, Hyllus' father orders him to marry Iole. Hercules then bids farewell to Alcmena and sets out for the pyre.

After Hercules' departure, the chorus sing an ode in which they wonder who will protect the world once

Hercules is gone. They predict that the hero's spirit will achieve high status in the underworld and that his image will be placed among the stars. They also pray to Jove for protection from the monsters and tyrants of the world. Their ode concludes as the chorus hear a sound that they interpret as Jove's mourning for his son. Next, Philoctetes enters and describes to the chorus how Hercules faced his death on the pyre. Philoctetes also reports that Hercules gave him his bow and arrows as a gift for his assistance and that his club and lion skin were burned with him. He describes Hercules' prayer to his father, Jupiter, and then states that the hero called for him to give him a torch. Though he was reluctant to do so, Philoctetes tells them, he applied the torch to the pyre and watched as Hercules calmly and bravely allowed the fire to burn his body.

After Philoctetes' speech, Alcmena enters, carrying an urn that contains Hercules' ashes. She laments her son and wonders what she herself will do and where she will go. Upon hearing this, Hyllus tries to comfort his grandmother, but Alcmena continues her lamentation and calls upon all the nations of the world to mourn the loss of Hercules. After Alcmena concludes, the voice of the dead Hercules is heard. He tells his mother not to lament because he has arrived at the kingdom of heaven. She doubts the reality of what she has heard, but Hercules again encourages her to cease mourning, for he has triumphed once again over the underworld. Alcmena, finally convinced, decides to depart for Thebes to announce the existence of a new divinity. The play concludes with the chorus rejoicing and praying that Hercules be with them and protect them.

COMMENTARY

Unlike Sophocles' play on this subject, which focuses on the failure of communication between mortals, *Hercules Oetaeus* is much more concerned with the vertical axis along which the ancient cosmos is ordered (heaven–earth–underworld). Hercules has overcome all the obstacles that have been placed in his path and believes that he should ascend to heaven. Unlike Seneca's *HERCULES FURENS*, in which Hercules is in the underworld most of the play, Hercules Oetaeus shows the hero on earth and wondering why he has not yet reached heaven. In *Hercules Furens,* Hercules' step-

mother, Juno, is concerned that Hercules will rise to heaven; only in Hercules' madness does the hero imagine reaching the pinnacle of the vertical axis. In *Hercules Oetaeus,* the title character has overcome creatures on land, on sea, and beneath the earth. Now, he aims for the sky.

Hercules is prevented from reaching heaven because, in some sense, the vertical axis has been inverted. Juno has transformed into stars the animals that Hercules defeated so that Hercules might fear heaven (75–76). She tries to make heaven worse than both Earth and the underworld (77–78). Whereas Juno opposes Hercules' reaching heaven, his wife, Deianeira, wavers between wanting to send him to the underworld and wanting to send herself to the underworld. Although Hercules is a man who held heaven on his shoulders (282) and whose fame reaches the sky (316), Deianeira's passion rages to heaven (285). She declares that whereas the wrath of the gods will make a person miserable, the wrath of a human being (her own wrath) will destroy him or her completely (441). Although Deianeira's anger appears to outstrip even that of the queen of heaven herself, Deianeira wavers about the course of action she wants to follow. Thus, Deianeira turns to her nurse's magic arts for help. In some ways, the nurse is even more powerful than Hercules. Hercules has conquered land, sea, and underworld; the nurse boasts that her magic arts have conquered land, sea, underworld, and heaven (461).

Deianeira agrees to her nurse's plan, but her ruin is foreshadowed in the chorus' song about those who fail to pursue a middle course, such as Phaethon and Icarus, both of whom did not follow a path between heaven and Earth (675–91). Light from the sky touches some wool on which the centaur's blood has been smeared and Deianeira realizes that she will destroy her husband. Once again the vertical axis is inverted as the dead (Nessus) will destroy the living (Hercules). The report of Hercules' being afflicted by the poison produces another inversion of this axis. When Hercules kills Lichas, he hurls the man to the stars and spatters the clouds with his blood (816–17). Hercules seeks the stars, but Lichas reaches them before he does.

Deianeira, upon hearing news of Hercules' demise, decides that she wants to descend the vertical axis, in order, she believes, to join her husband. The fall of Hercules also makes the chorus think that the world itself is vulnerable and that someday the sky itself will sink into the underworld (1112). If Hercules can fall, they imagine, eventually the stars, sea, and underworld will all become one (1126–27). When the agonized Hercules enters, he too speaks as if the vertical axis is being inverted and the heavens are being cast into the underworld (1131–50). Hercules wishes that, if he had to be destroyed by a woman's hand, he would have fallen at the hands of a woman who rules heaven (1183). Hercules began the play thinking he was worthy of the stars, but now he shows his earthly side. He doubts that the ruler of heaven, Jove, is his father and says Amphitryon will be thought to be his father (1247–48). Hercules calls upon Jove to release him from his torment, or, if Jove is unwilling to do so, then he asks that the powers of the underworld be allowed to kill him (1311–12). He even prays to Juno to end his misery (1317–19).

Even if Seneca is not the author of *Hercules Oetaeus,* modern scholars have detected Stoic elements in the play. Upon the arrival of Hercules' mother, Hercules begins to speak in the manner of a Stoic. He invites Death to attack him (1373) and declares he would not cry out even if he suffered the torments of PROMETHEUS, were crushed by the famous Clashing Rocks, or the sky itself fell onto him (1377–88). After hearing that Deianeira has descended the vertical axis, Hercules perceives that he is being called to ascend the axis, but then he imagines that the stars are being withheld again (1431–47). Hercules seems to move away from the ideal Stoic as his anger at Deianeira boils over, but his emotions come under control when his son explains the centaur's treachery.

As Hercules regains his composure, he commands his mother to do likewise (1507). He orders his son to prepare a pyre for him, as he expects to descend to the underworld (1514). Philoctetes attests to Hercules' bravery in death when the chorus ask him whether Hercules joyously faced the fires (1609–10). Hercules' fearlessness is contrasted with the emotional breakdown of Alcmena, whose cries of lamentation contrast with Hercules' composed silence. Faced with the flames of his funeral pyre, Hercules again calms his

mother's emotional outburst. Once again, Hercules prays to Jove to admit his spirit to the stars (1703–4) or allow him to enter the underworld (1711–12).

After the pyre's flames consume Hercules' mortal body, his mother returns to her emotional state and wonders what will become of her. As his father did, Hyllus tries to persuade Alcmena to compose himself. She mourns her son and wonders why Hercules has not inherited the heavenly realms that Jove promised him (1910). She imagines that Hercules' spirit is now throwing the underworld into confusion. Finally, Alcmena's emotional outbursts end when Hercules himself addresses her from heaven (1940–44). She believes his voice is from the underworld, but he declares that again he has conquered the land below. Finally, Alcmena is convinced and exits to announce a new god in heaven (1980). Thus, in true Stoic fashion, the virtue of Hercules triumphs over the underworld (1982) and Hercules' expectations about his place in the vertical axis have come to pass. The inversions of the vertical axis have not occurred, despite the best efforts of the nurse, Deianeira, the centaur, and Juno.

BIBLIOGRAPHY

Etman, A. M. *The Problem of Heracles' Apotheosis in the Trachiniae of Sophocles and in Hercules Oetaeus of Seneca: A Comparative Study of the Tragic and Stoic Meaning of the Myth.* Athens: University of Athens, 1974.

King, C. M. "Seneca's *Hercules Oetaeus:* A Stoic Interpretation of the Greek Myth," *Greece & Rome* 18 (1971): 215–22.

Larson, V. T. "The *Hercules Oetaeus* and the Picture of the *Sapiens* in Senecan Prose," *Phoenix* 45 (1991): 39–49.

Marcucci, S. *Analisi e interpretazione dell'Hercules Oetaeus.* Pisa: Istituti Editoriali e Poligrafici Internazionali, 1997.

HERMES The son of ZEUS and the goddess Maia, daughter of ATLAS and Pleione. Hermes (Latin: Mercury) is best known as the messenger of the gods. He also functioned as a guide both above and below the ground. He gained fame for killing the multieyed Argus, who guarded IO. As indicated in the opening lines of PLAUTUS' AMPHITRUO, Hermes is also a god associated with commerce. Hermes is associated with thieves, because the day he was born he stole some of APOLLO's cattle. On the same day, the infant Hermes killed a tortoise and used its shell to invent the lyre and plectrum. Eventually, Apollo tracked down the infant thief, who mischievously denied stealing the cattle. Apollo then took the infant to Zeus for arbitration of the dispute. Zeus ordered Hermes to return the cattle, and he eventually did, trading Apollo the lyre he had invented for the cattle.

Hermes frequently aided various gods and heroes. Occasionally, Hermes kept the young DIONYSUS safe from HERA. Hermes gave HERACLES a sword and guided him in the UNDERWORLD. He also provided PERSEUS with the sickle that the hero used to cut off the head of the GORGON MEDUSA.

Hermes had numerous children by different women, both mortal and immortal. Two of his sons, Eurytus and AUTOLYCUS, joined Jason's quest for the Golden Fleece. His son Cephalus (by Herse) became the lover of EOS, goddess of the dawn. Another son, MYRTILUS, played an important role in the death of OENOMAUS and the curse on the house of PELOPS.

Hermes takes the stage in five surviving dramas. In AESCHYLUS' EUMENIDES (see ORESTEIA), Hermes does not speak, but is called upon by Apollo to escort ORESTES to ATHENS. In Aeschylus' PROMETHEUS BOUND, Hermes, on behalf of Zeus, appears at the end of the play to demand that Prometheus reveal who will overthrow Zeus. In EURIPIDES' Ion, Hermes delivers the prologue and reports that, acting at the behest of Apollo, he transported the infant Ion to DELPHI. In ARISTOPHANES' PEACE, Hermes encounters Trygaeus on Mount OLYMPUS and informs him that the gods have left for a higher region of heaven. In Aristophanes' WEALTH, Hermes goes to Chremylus' house as a beggar, because the result of Plutus' redistribution of wealth is that no one makes offerings to the gods anymore.

The surviving fragments of Euripides' Antiope indicate that Hermes appeared at the conclusion of that play to prevent Amphion from killing Lycus, to explain what should be done with Dirce's body, and to give instructions to Amphion and Zethus about their respective futures. SOPHOCLES' SEARCHERS provides a comic dramatization of the search for Apollo's cattle, which Hermes stole as an infant. The fragments of the satyric Inachus of Sophocles indicate that Hermes had a significant stage presence in attempting to acquire for Zeus IO, who had been changed into a cow. In PLAUTUS'

AMPHITRUO, Mercury acts as the servant of Jupiter (see ZEUS) and helps him carry out his father's seduction of ALCMENA. The Greek playwright Astydamas wrote a Hermes, possibly a SATYR PLAY, whose four surviving lines tell us little about its subject matter. [ANCIENT SOURCES: Apollodorus, Library 1.9.16, 2.4.2, 2.4.11, 3.4.3, 3.10.2, 3.14.3; Epitome 2.6; Euripides, Antiope 64–97; Page, Ion 1–81; Homeric Hymn 4 to Hermes; Sophocles, Searchers 278 ff.]

HERMIONE The daughter of MENELAUS and HELEN. According to Apollodorus, when Menelaus was fighting at TROY, he promised to marry Hermione to ACHILLES' son, NEOPTOLEMUS. ORESTES, however, married Hermione, but, when Orestes became mad after killing his mother, Neoptolemus carried off Hermione, who became his wife. After Orestes regained his sanity, he again regained Hermione as his wife, for Neoptolemus was killed at DELPHI (Orestes may have had some role in Neoptolemus' death). Hermione appears as a character in Euripides' ANDROMACHE and ORESTES. In Andromache, she has not produced children for Neoptolemus and accuses his Trojan slave, ANDROMACHE, who has, of using witchcraft against her. Andromache, fearing that Hermione intends to have her killed, takes refuge at an altar. When Neoptolemus' grandfather, Pelias, goes to Andromache's rescue, Hermione begins to fear for her own life. Accordingly, when her cousin, Orestes, passes through the town, Hermione begs him to take her with him, and he does. [ANCIENT SOURCES: Apollodorus, Epitome 6.14; Euripides, Andromache]

HERMIPPUS A Greek comic poet who was an elder contemporary of ARISTOPHANES. Hermippus was victorious at the City DIONYSIA at least once (436/435 B.C.E.) and four times at the LENAEA (one victory around 430). As Aristophanes did in his early career, Hermippus, in his plays, touched upon contemporary politics and politicians such as PERICLES, CLEON, and HYPERBOLUS. Hermippus also staged humorous versions of stories of mythology, such as his Fates (Moirae), Cercopes, and Gods. About 100 fragments survive and 10 titles are known. [ANCIENT SOURCES: Aristophanes, Clouds 557]

BIBLIOGRAPHY

Kock, T. *Comicorum Atticorum Fragmenta*. Vol. 1. Leipzig: Teubner, 1880.

HESIOD (LATE EIGHTH OR EARLY SEVENTH CENTURY B.C.E.)

A Greek farmer who lived in the town of Ascra in the region of BOEOTIA, Hesiod was one of Greece's greatest epic poets. His best-known poems are *Theogony* and *Works and Days*. In only 1,022 lines, *Theogony* deals with the origin of the divinities and Zeus' rise to power. The subject matter of *Works and Days* ranges from advice on when to do various agricultural activities to justice. Both of these poems have stories about PROMETHEUS that could have provided source material for AESCHYLUS' *PROMETHEUS BOUND*. A poem entitled *Shield,* which deals with HERACLES' shield and his battle with ARES' son CYCNUS, is also attributed to Hesiod, but this attribution was proved incorrect even in ancient times by Aristophanes of Byzantium. Another poem, *Catalogue of Women* (or *Ehoiae*), on which tragic poets may have drawn for material about their female subjects, was also attributed to Hesiod in ancient times, but in reality seems to have been written no earlier than the sixth century B.C.E. Other works attributed to Hesiod are *Astronomy (Astronomia)*, *Divination by Birds (Ornithomanteia)*, *Precepts of Chiron (Cheironos Hupothekai)*, *Great Works (Megala Erga)*, *Idaean Dactyls (Idaioi Daktuloi)*, *The Great Eoiae (Megalai Eoiae)*, *The Marriage of Ceyx (Keukos Gamos)*, *Melampodia (Melampodeia)*, and *Aegimius (Aigimios)*.

BIBLIOGRAPHY

Edwards, G. P. *The Language of Hesiod in Its Traditional Context*. Oxford: Blackwell, 1971.

Lamberton, R. *Hesiod*. New Haven, Conn.: Yale University Press, 1988.

Nelso, S. A. *God and the Land: The Metaphysics of Farming in Hesiod and Vergil*. With a translation of Hesiod's *Works and Days* by David Grene. New York: Oxford University Press, 1998.

Pucci, P. *Hesiod and the Language of Poetry*. Baltimore: Johns Hopkins University Press, 1977.

Solmsen, F. *Hesiod and Aeschylus*. With a new foreword by G. M. Kirkwood. Ithaca, N.Y.: Cornell University Press, 1995.

HESIONE (1)

A daughter of OCEANUS and TETHYS, Hesione was the wife of PROMETHEUS. [ANCIENT SOURCES: Aeschylus, *Prometheus Bound* 560]

HESIONE (2)

The daughter of LAOMEDON and sister of PRIAM, Hesione was offered as a sacrifice to a sea monster that harassed TROY. HERACLES, on his return from the land of the AMAZONS, rescued Hesione and killed the sea monster. Laomedon had promised Heracles horses in exchange for his help, but he rescinded the offer after Heracles succeeded. Some time later, the angered Heracles returned to Troy, sacked the town, and gave Hesione to his comrade, Telamon, as a prize of war. The hero put to death most of the Trojan males, but spared Priam at Hesione's request. She later produced for Telamon a son, TEUCER.

Among the Greek dramatists, the tragedian Demetrius wrote a SATYR PLAY entitled *Hesione*, no longer extant (see SNELL); the comic poet Alexis wrote a *Hesione*, of which two brief fragments survive (85–86 Kock). These reveal that Heracles was depicted eating and drinking heavily in the play. Among Roman authors, Naevius wrote a TRAGEDY entitled *Hesione*, which may have been about the events surrounding Hesione's sacrifice and rescue. The single surviving line appears to be spoken by Hercules: "so that I may not seem to do my will by word rather than the sword." [ANCIENT SOURCES: Apollodorus, *Library* 2.5.9, 3.12.7; Athenaeus, 9.367f. 11.470e; Hyginus, *Fables* 89]

BIBLIOGRAPHY

Kock, T. *Comicorum Atticorum Fragmenta*. Vol. 2. Leipzig: Teubner, 1884.

Snell, B. *Tragicorum Graecorum Fragmenta*. Vol. 1. Göttingen, Ger.: Vandenhoeck & Ruprecht, 1971.

Warmington, E. H. *Remains of Old Latin: Livius Andronicus, Naevius, Pacuvius, and Accius*. Vol. 2. Cambridge, Mass.: Harvard University Press, 1936.

HESPERIDES

Ancient sources offered numerous possible parents of the Hesperides, whose name means "the daughters of evening." Some call them the children either of NIGHT or of Erebus; others, the children of ATLAS and Hesperis, Phorcys and Ceto, or even ZEUS and THEMIS. The number of Hesperides also varies: three, four, or seven. They lived in a garden near the western edge of the world and guarded golden apples that Mother EARTH had given to HERA as a wedding present. After HERACLES took the golden apples as one of his labors, the Hesperides themselves changed into trees. This transformation seems to have been temporary, however, because they later helped JASON and the Argonauts by showing them a spring that Heracles had made in the desert. [ANCIENT SOURCES: Apollodorus, *Library* 2.5.11; Euripides, *Hippolytus* 742; Hyginus, *Fables* 30, *Poetica Astronomica* 2.3]

HESPERUS

The son of EOS and Astraeus (or CEPHALUS), Hesperus represented the evening star; some equated him with the morning star as well. [ANCIENT SOURCES: Seneca, *Medea* 72, 878, *Phaedra* 750, *Hercules Furens* 821, 883, *Hercules Oetaeus* 149, *Phoenician Women* 87]

HESTIA (Latin: VESTA)

The daughter of CRONUS and RHEA, Hestia was the sister of ZEUS, POSEIDON, HADES, HERA, and DEMETER. The Greek word *hestia* means "hearth" and Hestia is the goddess of the hearth, the fire on the hearth, and activities within the house. A virgin goddess, Hestia does not have offspring. Hestia does not appear as a character in any extant drama, although ALCESTIS has a close affinity with her in EURIPIDES' play. [ANCIENT SOURCES: Euripides, *Alcestis* 162; Hesiod, *Theogony* 453–506; *Homeric Hymn to Aphrodite* 5.21–32; *Homeric Hymns to Hestia* 24, 33; Pausanias, 5.14.4; Vergil, *Georgics* 1408]

HETAIRA

A Greek word meaning "female companion," *hetaira* (plural: *hetairai*) is a euphemism for "prostitute" or "courtesan." The *hetaira* becomes a stock character in New Comedy (see PROSTITUTE). [ANCIENT SOURCES: Alciphron, *Epistles* 4; Aristophanes, *Wealth* 149; Athenaeus, *Deipnosophists* 13; Lucian, *Dialogues of the Courtesans*]

HEURIPPIDES

A person mentioned by ARISTOPHANES at *ECCLESIAZUSAE* 825, Heurrippides was an Athenian statesman active in the last decade of the fifth century and the first decade of the fourth century B.C.E. Heurrippides' father was Adeimantus and he was from the DEME called Myrrhinus. Not long before the production of *Ecclesiazusae,* Heurrippides proposed a $2^{1}/_{2}$ percent tax that was supposed to bolster the Athenian treasury.

BIBLIOGRAPHY
Sommerstein, A. H. *The Comedies of Aristophanes.* Vol. 10, *Ecclesiazusae.* Warminster, U.K.: Aris & Phillips, 1998, 210.

HIERO

A man mentioned at *ECCLESIAZUSAE* 757, Hieron is called a herald (*kerux*) by ARISTOPHANES. Nothing else is known about him.

BIBLIOGRAPHY
Sommerstein, A. H. *The Comedies of Aristophanes.* Vol. 10, *Ecclesiazusae.* Warminster, U.K.: Aris & Phillips, 1998, 206.

HIERONYMUS (1)

A composer of tragedies and dithyrambs. ARISTOPHANES makes fun of Hieron, son of Xenophantus, for his wild, tangled hair. Hieron was known for plots that were emotionally charged to an excessive degree and for the terrifying masks that some of his characters wore. [ANCIENT SOURCES: Aristophanes, *Acharnians* 389, *Clouds* 349]

BIBLIOGRAPHY
Sommerstein, A. H. *The Comedies of Aristophanes.* Vol. 1, *Acharnians.* Warminster, U.K.: Aris & Phillips, 1980, 172.

HIERONYMUS (2)

A military commander who served the Athenians during the latter half of the 390s B.C.E. Hieronymus was opposed to the Athenians' making peace with SPARTA in the year 392/391. [ANCIENT SOURCES: Aristophanes, *Ecclesiazusae* 201; Diodorus Siculus, 14.81.4]

BIBLIOGRAPHY
Sommerstein, A. H. *The Comedies of Aristophanes.* Vol. 10, *Ecclesiazusae.* Warminster, U.K.: Aris & Phillips, 1998, 156.

HIPPIAS

From 527 to 510 B.C.E., Hippias, the son of Pisastratus, was the absolute ruler, or tyrant, of ATHENS. His rule began peacefully enough, as he lowered taxes and made reconciliatory gestures toward various prominent clan groups. As Hippias' rule grew harsher, however, his enemies multiplied and tried to remove him from power. These enemies assasinated his brother, Hipparchus, in 514. One of the clan groups who opposed Hippias, the Alcmaeonidae, orchestrated a Spartan-backed military assault on Hippias and his forces that eventually resulted in Hippias' political downfall. He and his family went into exile and eventually found refuge at the court of the Persian king, Darius. When the Persians invaded Greece in 490 B.C.E., Hippias guided them to MARATHON, where they were defeated. [ANCIENT SOURCES: Aristophanes,

Knights 448, *Lysistrata* 617, 1153, *Wasps* 502; Herodotus, 5.55–96, 6.102–21]

HIPPOCRATES (1)
The son of Ariphon, Hippocrates was the nephew of PERICLES and served the Athenians as a military commander in the 420s B.C.E. He was killed at the battle of Delion in 424 B.C.E. [ANCIENT SOURCES: Aristophanes, *Clouds* 1001, *Thesmophoriazusae* 273; Diodorus Siculus, 12.66–69, 13.66; Eupolis, fragment 103 Kock; Thucydides, 4.66–101]

BIBLIOGRAPHY
Dover, K. J. *Aristophanes: Clouds.* Oxford: Clarendon Press, 1989, 221.
Kock, T. *Comicorum Atticorum Fragmenta.* Vol. 1. Leipzig: Teubner, 1880.

HIPPOCRATES (2)
A man mentioned by ARISTOPHANES at *THESMOPHORIAZUSAE* 273. If this Hippocrates was not same as HIPPOCRATES, son of Ariphon (and he does not appear to be, because Ariphon's son had died some 13 years earlier), then he is not otherwise known. Aristophanes indicates that this Hippocrates was the wealthy owner of a run-down block of housing.

BIBLIOGRAPHY
Kock, T. *Comicorum Atticorum Fragmenta.* Vol. 1. Leipzig: Teubner, 1880.
Sommerstein, A. H. *The Comedies of Aristophanes.* Vol. 8, *Thesmophoriazusae.* Warminster, U.K.: Aris & Phillips, 1994, 174–75.

HIPPODAMEIA
The daughter of OENOMAUS, king of Pisa. Hippodameia became the bride of PELOPS after he defeated (and killed) her father in a chariot race. By Pelops, Hippodameia became the mother of ATREUS and THYESTES. Sophocles is said to have written a *Hippodameia,* but this appears to have been an alternate title for his *Oenomaus.* [ANCIENT SOURCES: Euripides, *Iphigenia in Tauris* 825; Hyginus, *Fables* 84–85]

HIPPODAMUS
The son of Euryphon, Hippodamus of Miletus lived during the fifth century B.C.E., gained fame for his designs of city layouts, and was especially noted for his grid pattern for streets. Around 450 B.C.E., he created the design for the main harbor at ATHENS (see PIRAEUS). In 443, Hippodamus went as a colonist to the Italian town of Thurii, where he was probably responsible for the design of that town. [ANCIENT SOURCES: Aristophanes, *Knights* 327; Aristotle, *Politics* 1267b22–30; Strabo, 14.2.9]

BIBLIOGRAPHY
Burns, A. "Hippodamus and the Planned City," *Historia* 25 (1976): 414–28.

HIPPOLYTUS
The son of THESEUS and an AMAZON woman named ANTIOPE (or Hippolyta), Hippolytus was devoted to the goddess ARTEMIS. He therefore rejected the love of women and thus the goddess APHRODITE. Some sources say Hippolytus lived in ATHENS; others make his home TROEZEN. Because of Hippolytus' devotion to Artemis, Aphrodite decided to destroy him. She brought this about by causing Hippolytus' stepmother, PHAEDRA, to fall in love with him. When Phaedra made a sexual proposition to Hippolytus, he rejected her advances. Phaedra then hanged herself and wrote a note accusing Hippolytus of raping her. After Theseus read the note, he cursed his son and sent him into exile. As Hippolytus drove away in his chariot, a bull roared up out of the sea and scared his horses. The terrified animals galloped wildly and tossed Hippolytus from the chariot. Hippolytus became tangled in the reins and was dragged to his death. EURIPIDES says that maidens from Troezen dedicated locks of their hair to Hippolytus before they married. Some sources indicate that APOLLO's son, ASCLEPIUS, raised Hippolytus from the dead and that he went on to become a king in the Italian town of Aricia. The people of SPARTA had a hero shrine dedicated to Hippolytus, and the people of Troezen claimed that Hippolytus was transformed into the constellation Auriga (the "charioteer").

Hippolytus appears as a character in two extant plays, the *HIPPOLYTUS* plays by EURIPIDES and SENECA. Several classical myths deal with young men as the victims of sexual advances by married women; Hippolytus may be the only one among them who rejected the woman's advances because of devotion to Artemis. The Greek tragedian Lycophron (fragment 1g Snell) also

wrote a *Hippolytus,* as did the Greek comic poet Sopa-
ter (fragment 8 Kaibel). [ANCIENT SOURCES: Apollodorus, *Epitome* 1.18–19; Euripides, *Hippolytus;*
Hyginus, *Fables* 47; Ovid, *Metamorphoses* 15.497–546;
Seneca, *Hippolytus;* Pausanias, 1.22.1–3, 2.27.4,
2.32.1–4; Vergil, *Aeneid* 7.761–82]

BIBLIOGRAPHY

Kaibel, G. *Comicorum Graecorum Fragmenta.* Vol. 1.1 [*Poet-
    arum Graecorum Fragmenta.* Vol. 6.1]. Berlin: Weidmann,
    1899.
Snell, B. *Tragicorum Graecorum Fragmenta.* Vol. 1. Göttingen,
    Ger.: Vandenhoeck & Ruprecht, 1971.

HIPPOLYTUS EURIPIDES (428 B.C.E.)

The
version of *Hippolytus* that is extant was staged in 428
B.C.E. as part of one of the few Euripidean productions
to win first place in competition. EURIPIDES also presented *Hippolytus* onstage at an earlier date (see fragments 428–47 Nauck). The first production of the
play, however, seems to have met with little success,
perhaps because of Euripides' shocking characterization of PHAEDRA, who was apparently much more
brazen and direct in her attempts to seduce HIPPOLYTUS
(as was the Phaedra of SENECA's HIPPOLYTUS) than in the
second version of the play. The second production of
the drama apparently shows Phaedra in a much more
sympathetic light. In antiquity, the first version of the
play was called *Hippolytus Kaluptomenos* (Hippolytus
veiled), because Hippolytus may have covered his face
in shame after Phaedra tried to seduce him. The second production of the play was called *Hippolytus
Stephanephoros* (Hippolytus the bringer of garlands),
because Hippolytus carries garlands for Artemis when
he enters.

The play's setting is the home of Theseus at TROEZEN,
a small town opposite ATHENS on the shores of the
Saronic Gulf. *Hippolytus* opens with a monologue by
APHRODITE, who explains that Hippolytus, the illegiti-
mate son of THESEUS and an AMAZON, is a devoté of the
goddess ARTEMIS. As such, Hippolytus remains chaste
and refuses to worship Aphrodite, who therefore
intends to punish him. While Hippolytus was in
Athens to witness and to be initiated into the mysteries of DEMETER, Aphrodite caused Theseus' wife, Phaedra, to fall in love with her stepson, Hippolytus. When

Theseus went into exile at Troezen, after his destruction of the sons of Pallas (one of Theseus' political
rivals in Athens), Phaedra went with him and now is
wasting away with love for Hippolytus. Before her
monologue concludes, Aphrodite announces that Theseus will learn of Phaedra's love, Phaedra will perish,
and Theseus will cause Hippolytus' death by employing one of three wishes that his father, POSEIDON,
granted him.

Upon the approach of Hippolytus, Aphrodite leaves
the ORCHESTRA. Hippolytus, attended by a group of
hunters, enters and offers a greeting and a garland to
Artemis, whose statue stands before the house. A statue
of Aphrodite stands opposite that of Artemis, and one
of Hippolytus' servants urges him to pay his respects to
Aphrodite as well. Hippolytus, however, says that he
greets Aphrodite from a distance. The servant advises
Hippolytus not to scorn Aphrodite, but the prince
ignores his advice. As Hippolytus enters the palace, the
servant asks Aphrodite to forgive Hippolytus.

Next, the CHORUS, composed of women from
Troezen, enter. They sing of the sufferings of Phaedra
and wonder whether they were caused by a divinity,
specifically, Artemis; or whether Theseus has been
unfaithful; or, whether perhaps Phaedra has received
bad news from her homeland of Crete. The choral ode
is followed by the arrival of Phaedra and her NURSE
from the palace. Phaedra's lovesickness causes her to
speak wildly about going to the hills and hunting. The
Nurse, baffled by Phaedra's words, tries to discover
what is causing them. When the chorus question the
Nurse about Phaedra's sickness, she tells them that she
has not eaten in three days and that she intends to
commit suicide. The Nurse also notes that Phaedra has
hidden her sufferings from Theseus, who is not in
Troezen at the present time.

The Nurse then turns her attention to Phaedra, and
questions her about the cause of her sufferings. Phaedra does not want to tell the Nurse her secret, but the
persistent nurse finally compels Phaedra to admit that
she is in love with Hippolytus. The Nurse and the chorus are horrified when they hear the truth. Phaedra
then explains that she attempted to control her passions but finding that they were too strong, decided
that suicide was the best course of action for her. The

Nurse, however, having had time to consider the situation, decides that because the gods themselves do not resist illicit love, Phaedra also should yield to her passion. Phaedra is shocked by the advice but eventually agrees to let her approach Hippolytus on her behalf.

After the Nurse goes into the house, the chorus sing an ode about the deadly power of love and its mastery over people such as HERACLES and ZEUS. After the choral ode, Phaedra listens in horror as she hears Hippolytus shouting at the Nurse, who apparently has revealed Phaedra's love for him. Soon Hippolytus and the Nurse emerge from the house. Their conversation indicates that Hippolytus has sworn not to reveal Phaedra's proposition to his father. Hippolytus then delivers a lengthy speech about the evils of women. He regrets giving his word not to tell his father but says that he will keep his oath. After Hippolytus' tirade, he exits. The chorus and Phaedra then lament the situation. Phaedra realizes that she is doomed if Theseus or Pittheus finds out about the situation. The Nurse apologizes to Phaedra for her attempt to proposition Hippolytus. Phaedra then angrily dismisses the Nurse from her sight. After the Nurse's exit, Phaedra tells the chorus to remain silent about what they have heard. The chorus swear (ironically, by Artemis) that they will keep silent. Phaedra then states her intention to kill herself and exits into the palace.

After Phaedra's departure, the chorus wonder where they can go to escape the horrific situation that has developed. They also describe how Phaedra will hang herself, a description that is soon confirmed by a cry from within the house. As the chorus wonder what to do, Theseus arrives and wonders what is happening. After the chorus inform him of Phaedra's death, the doors of the house are opened and Phaedra's corpse is revealed. Theseus and the chorus then lament Phaedra's death. Upon closer examination of her body, Theseus finds in her hand a note that accuses Hippolytus of trying to assault her sexually. Upon reading this, Theseus uses one of the wishes that Poseidon has given him and curses his son. The chorus urge Theseus to reconsider his words, but just as Hippolytus earlier refused to acknowledge Aphrodite, Theseus refuses to retract his words and states that he will send Hippolytus into exile. Soon Hippolytus himself enters, won-

ders at Phaedra's death, and asks Theseus to explain the situation. When Theseus accuses Hippolytus of betraying him by trying to seduce Phaedra, Hippolytus tries to explain himself to his father. He reminds his father of his chastity and his devotion to Artemis and swears by Zeus that he did not assault Phaedra. Theseus, however, refuses to believe Hippolytus and orders him to leave Troezen. Hippolytus pleads, but to no avail. After Theseus exits, Hippolytus laments his fate and bids farewell to Athens and Troezen. The chorus then sing an ode about the ever-changing fortunes of humans. They lament the loss of Hippolytus, the hunting he enjoyed, and the music of his lyre, expressing anger at the gods for Hippolytus' exile.

After the choral ode, a MESSENGER enters to tell Theseus and the chorus that Hippolytus is near death. The messenger relates that as Hippolytus was driving his chariot along the coast outside Troezen, a bellowing bull rose from the sea and frightened his horses. Hippolytus was thrown from his chariot and dragged for some distance after becoming tangled in the reins. After hearing the messenger's story, Theseus expresses mixed feelings about the news of his son's accident. Theseus orders the messenger to have Hippolytus taken to the palace. Subsequently, the chorus sing a brief ode about the all-conquering power of Aphrodite and EROS. After the chorus' song, Artemis appears and reveals to Theseus the truth about the incident between Phaedra and Hippolytus, namely, that Phaedra's accusation was false and that Hippolytus was innocent of wrongdoing. Artemis explains that the situation was caused by Aphrodite, and that she herself will retaliate against one of Aphrodite's favorites. After Artemis' announcement, Hippolytus, on the verge of death, is carried in on a litter. Hippolytus, lamenting his fate, longs for death. His lamentation then alternates with sympathetic responses from Artemis and her comments about Aphrodite's wrath. Hippolytus expresses sorrow for Theseus' error. He even wishes that the curses of humans could work against the gods, but Artemis rebukes this speech, consoling him with her vengeance against one for whom Aphrodite cares. Artemis also tells Hippolytus that the women of Troezen will honor him in the future by cutting off a lock of their hair before they marry. Before Artemis departs, she urges Hippolytus not to hate his father. Hippolytus obeys the goddess, and just before he dies, he forgives his father.

COMMENTARY

Not only was *Hippolytus* highly regarded when it was produced in 428, it remains universally considered one of Euripides' finest plays. The story of Phaedra's sexual advances toward her stepson has often been compared to the story in Genesis 39 of the sexual advances of Potiphar's wife to Joseph. In both stories, the married woman's attempt to seduce the young man fails and the rejected woman claims the young man has tried to rape her. In both stories, the husband drives the young man from his household. Hippolytus is exiled from Troezen, and Joseph is imprisoned. On the other hand, Joseph is later released from prison and becomes even more powerful than before, and whereas Phaedra commits suicide, the fate of Potiphar's wife is not mentioned in Genesis 39.

Similar stories can be found in other cultures. Among the Egyptians, Anubis' wife tried unsuccessfully to seduce Anubis' brother, Bata, and claimed that he tried to rape her. Anubis tried to kill his brother, but the god Ra prevented him. Bata swore that he had not raped Anubis' wife and cut off his penis to confirm his assertion. Bata then bled to death and a saddened Anubis returned to his house and killed his wife. Several other similar stories appeared in Greek mythology as early as the time of HOMER, who in *Iliad* 6 tells the story of Anteia, the wife of Proetus, who failed to seduce BELLEROPHON and then claimed that he raped her. PROETUS himself did not want to kill Bellerophon, so he sent off Bellerophon to Lycia to the court of Iobates, who was instructed to kill Bellerophon. Bellerophon overcame all of the dangerous tasks that Iobates imposed on him and eventually Iobates gave him his daughter in marriage. Euripides himself took up the story of Bellerophon but changed Anteia's name to STHENEBOEA, and Euripides' play (staged before 422 B.C.E.) about their conflict bore her name.

As for Euripides' *Hippolytus,* the play's structure is exceptionally well balanced. Aphrodite's appearance at the play's opening is matched by Artemis' epiphany at the play's end. This balance is also seen in one of the play's major themes, speech versus silence. Phaedra's concern with revealing too much through speech is echoed by Hippolytus' silence about her proposition. Ironically, the letter that Phaedra writes accusing Hippolytus of raping her is a silent witness that Theseus accepts and one that, unlike a human witness, cannot be cross-examined. Phaedra's breaking of silence leads to an indecent proposal; Hippolytus' oath to remain silent about that proposal prevents him from refuting the silent yet vocal testimony that condemns him. Theseus' assumption that the letter's testimony must be true prompts him also to violate the bounds of moderate speech and thus curse his own son.

The crossing of boundaries or borders is a prominent theme in the play. Phaedra's lust for Hippolytus compels her to long for the wilds of Troezen, a place where Artemis and Hippolytus are comfortable, but where one would not expect to find a married Greek woman. The spatial boundary she desires to cross is matched by a boundary of moral law that she tries to avoid crossing. As a married woman, Phaedra should not have such feelings for another man, much less her stepson. Phaedra initially considers suicide, but her nurse temporarily prevents her from entering the realm of the dead by persuading her to cross the boundary of moral decency and make an advance toward Hippolytus. Hippolytus wishes that such speech had never passed the boundary of his ears and has taken an oath that this proposal will not breech the boundary of his lips. Interestingly, Theseus, whose temporary exile from Athens has led him to take up residence in Troezen and thus put Phaedra in closer contact with Hippolytus, returns to find that his wife has crossed over into the land of the dead. Thinking that Hippolytus has corrupted his wife, Theseus, the exile, banishes his son beyond the borders of Troezen. Once outside Troezen, Hippolytus is mortally injured. On the verge of passing into the UNDERWORLD, Hippolytus is taken back into Troezen, forgives his father, and dies.

Linked with and underlying the themes of speech versus silence and the crossing of figurative and literal borders is the Greek concept of *sophrosune,* whose meanings include "chastity," "discretion," "moderation," and "self-control." No extant Euripidean play has more references to *sophrosune* than *Hippolytus* and in some ways Euripides' *Hippolytus* probes this range of meanings as Hippolytus' concept of *sophrosune* conflicts with Aphrodite's attitude toward his *sophrosune* and Phaedra's desire to maintain her sense of *sophrosune*.

In *Hippolytus,* the title character goes to the extreme of avoiding love and embracing chastity, and Aphrodite drives an unwilling Phaedra to the extreme of illicit love. Phaedra struggles to maintain her sense of *sophrosune* (399), but when she realizes that the power of love is too great she decides to end her life. She declares that she hates people who are moderate in their words, but not in their deeds (413–14). Whereas Phaedra wants to maintain her sense of discretion or end her life, the Nurse advises a more expedient course and persuades her to continue living and to try to have love. The Nurse advises Phaedra to violate *sophrosune*.

Once Phaedra oversteps the bounds of moderation, Hippolytus wishes that someone could teach women to be moderate (667). Phaedra curses her nurse, who laments that she did not act in a moderate fashion (704). As Hippolytus wished that women could learn to have *sophrosune*, Phaedra's last spoken remarks on stage are a declaration that her revenge against Hippolytus will cause him to learn to be moderate (731).

In Theseus' subsequent accusation that Hippolytus has crossed the bounds of moderation by raping Phaedra, Theseus scoffs at Hippolytus' moderation and purity (949) and exiles him, despite the young man's declaration that no person on Earth has more *sophrosune* than he (995; see also 1100, 1365). Hippolytus realizes, however, that his *sophrosune* does not convince Theseus that he did not rape Phaedra (1007), so he tries to defend himself on other grounds. As Hippolytus ends his defense, he laments that Phaedra was unable to exercise *sophrosune* despite her efforts to do so and that he himself, who does have *sophrosune*, has not profited from it. After Hippolytus' accident and the appearance of Artemis, the goddess tells the dying man that Aphrodite hated Hippolytus' *sophrosune*. Ultimately, Hippolytus discovers his mortal understanding of *sophrosune* is not the same as the divine understanding of *sophrosune*. For Hippolytus, *sophrosune* means complete abstinence from sexual relations with women. For Aphrodite, *sophrosune* connotes behavior that respects and accepts her divine power.

BIBLIOGRAPHY

Barrett, W. S. *Euripides: Hippolytus.* Oxford: Clarendon Press, 1964.

Goff, B. E. *The Noose of Words: Readings of Desire, Violence and Language in Euripides' Hippolytus.* Cambridge: Cambridge University Press, 1990.

Kovacs, D. P. *The Heroic Muse: Studies in the Hippolytus and Hecuba of Euripides.* Baltimore: Johns Hopkins University Press, 1987.

Segal, Charles. *Euripides and the Poetics of Sorrow: Art, Gender, and Commemoration in Alcestis, Hippolytus, and Hecuba.* Durham, N.C.: Duke University Press, 1993.

Zeitlin, F. I. "The Power of Aphrodite: Eros and the Boundaries of the Self in the *Hippolytus*." In *Directions in Euripidean Criticism: A Collection of Essays.* Edited by Peter Burian. Durham, N.C.: Duke University Press, 1985, 52–111.

HIPPOLYTUS SENECA (WRITTEN BETWEEN 49 AND 65 C.E.?)

This TRAGEDY, sometimes entitled *Phaedra,* follows essentially the same plot as EURIPIDES' *HIPPOLYTUS,* although SENECA does differ in several places from his Greek predecessor. Seneca's setting is THESEUS' palace at ATHENS, not TROEZEN, as in the Euripidean play. Unlike Euripides, Seneca does not have the divinities APHRODITE and ARTEMIS take the stage in his play. HIPPOLYTUS, who delivers the prologue in Seneca's play (contrast Aphrodite in Euripides), opens with instructions to those who will hunt with him that day and a prayer to Diana (Greek: Artemis) to assist him in his hunting.

As Hippolytus sets out for the forest, Phaedra emerges from the palace. Her husband, Theseus, is in the UNDERWORLD (contrast Euripides, in which Theseus is away consulting an oracle) with his friend, PEIRITHOUS. The queen indicates that she is in love and has traded her work at the loom for a hunting spear. She recalls her mother PASIPHAE's illicit love for a bull and wonders whether any cure exists for her own affliction, which she attributes to Venus (Greek: Aphrodite). Unlike the Nurse in Euripides' *Hippolytus,* Seneca's Nurse tries to persuade Phaedra not to yield to her passion. Phaedra knows the Nurse is right but claims the illogic of love drives her to these feelings. The Nurse correctly argues that Hippolytus, being devoted to chastity, will never yield to temptation, but Phaedra says she will pursue him to the ends of the Earth. She even states that if she fails to win Hippolytus' love, she will commit suicide. Ultimately, the Nurse agrees to approach Hippolytus on Phaedra's behalf and persuade him to accept this horrific union. After the Nurse and Phaedra's conversation, the CHORUS, composed of Athenian citizens (unlike Euripides' chorus of Troezenians), sing an ode about the power of Venus and Cupid (Greek: EROS). The chorus note that love has mastered many divinities and nature's mightiest creatures.

The second act begins with a conversation between the Nurse and chorus. The Nurse tells the chorus that Phaedra's passion allows her no comfort or satisfaction. Soon, Phaedra is seen in the interior of the house, expressing her wish to have her hair unbound and to take up a spear and bow. The Nurse prays to Diana and HECATE that Hippolytus will yield to Phaedra's love for him. Now, Hippolytus enters and the Nurse approaches him. He realizes that something is bothering her. She claims she is worried about his chaste mode of life and urges him to seek the joys of Venus. Hippolytus argues that his life in the country allows him to avoid the worries and burdens of life in the city, and that his present life rivals that of those who lived in the GOLDEN AGE. Hippolytus eventually declares that women are the cause of all evil and cites MEDEA as an example. The Nurse wonders that Hippolytus can condemn all women on the basis of one woman's behavior, and Hippolytus declares that he despises women. The Nurse points out that Hippolytus' mother knew love, but Hippolytus coldly notes that his mother's death means that he no longer has any women whom he is required to love.

At this point, Phaedra emerges from the palace and asks to speak with Hippolytus in private. She offers herself to Hippolytus as a servant and asks that he take pity on a widow. Hippolytus claims Theseus will return from the underworld, but Phaedra does not believe him. She then tells him that a mad love is raging in her heart, which Hippolytus assumes is love for Theseus. Soon, however, Phaedra confesses to Hippolytus that she loves him. This admission differs much from that of the Euripidean play, in which the

Nurse acts as Phaedra's go-between, although in Euripides' first staging of *Hippolytus* the playwright apparently had Phaedra herself approach Hippolytus.

When Seneca's Hippolytus hears this confession, he is horrified. He wishes that he were dead and curses Phaedra, who declares that she will follow him wherever he goes. Hippolytus even draws his sword and threatens to kill Phaedra, but he refrains from doing so. At this point, the Nurse, realizing Phaedra's situation is out of control, decides the best way to save Phaedra's honor is to accuse Hippolytus of a crime. Accordingly, she cries out for help and claims Hippolytus is trying to rape Phaedra, who has fainted by this time. At some point, Hippolytus has fled the scene and left behind his sword, which the Nurse claims is evidence of his assault on Phaedra. After the Nurse arranges for Phaedra to be carried back inside the palace, the chorus sing a lengthy ode about beauty. They praise the beauty of the goddess Diana and of Bacchus (Greek: DIONYSUS) but lament that mortal beauty fades with time and pray that the gods will spare Hippolytus, whose beauty has caused him nothing but trouble.

The play's third act opens with Theseus' arrival from the underworld. The king notes that he has been away from home for four years and that Hercules (Greek: HERACLES) rescued him from the underworld. His joy at his return soon turns to grief when the Nurse tells him that Phaedra has decided to kill herself. Soon, the palace doors open and Phaedra converses with Theseus, who begs her to tell him of her problems. She claims Hippolytus has raped her and reveals Hippolytus' sword as proof (contrast Euripides' Phaedra, who hangs herself first and leaves a note accusing Hippolytus of rape). Theseus is enraged and, as in Euripides' play, uses one of the three wishes granted to him by his father, Neptune (Greek: POSEIDON), to request the death of Hippolytus. After Theseus' remarks, the chorus sing a brief ode in which they wonder why the gods do not help the good or punish those who are evil and why people should live a virtuous life when sinners are unpunished.

In the fourth act, a MESSENGER arrives with news of Hippolytus' death. As in Euripides' play, Hippolytus has left town, driving his chariot along the coast road. His horses were terrified by a creature (part bull and part sea monster) that cast up from the sea and pulled the chariot off the path. Hippolytus, thrown from the car, became tangled in the reins and was dragged and torn apart (unlike in Euripides' play). Also, unlike the Theseus of Euripides' play, Seneca's Theseus immediately expresses remorse that his curse caused Hippolytus' death.

The play's final act begins with the emergence of a maddened Phaedra from the palace. Unlike Euripides' Phaedra, Seneca's Phaedra laments Hippolytus' death and mourns over his broken body, which has now been taken back to the palace. She declares that she will follow Hippolytus in death. Whereas Euripides' Phaedra hanged herself before Hippolytus' death and made no such lamentation over his body, Seneca's Phaedra falls on a sword after her lamentation. Theseus, witnessing this, now mourns for his dead wife, wishes that he himself were dead, and wonders how he might accomplish the deed. The chorus, however, interrupt Theseus and urge him to bury Hippolytus. He mourns over his son's torn body, while the chorus tell him that he must reassemble the body parts in the proper order. After Theseus does so, he calls upon the people of Athens to mourn, prepare a pyre, and search for any other parts of Hippolytus that have not yet been found. Whereas Hippolytus' body will be cremated, he announces that Phaedra will be buried in the ground.

COMMENTARY

Whereas Seneca's *MEDEA* focuses on the consequences of passion contaminated by anger, Seneca's *Hippolytus* highlights passion that is intertwined with madness. Seneca's *Hippolytus* has more references to madness than any other Senecan play, including *HERCULES FURENS,* in which the title character is afflicted by madness and kills his wife and children. As a proponent of STOICISM, Seneca, as did his fellow Stoics, contended that intense emotion must be controlled to achieve happiness. In Seneca's *Hippolytus,* Phaedra and Hippolytus suffer from different kinds of madness that ultimately cause disaster for both.

Phaedra is not the only person in *Hippolytus* afflicted by madness. At line 96, Phaedra notes that her husband has gone to the underworld as an accomplice to

his friend Pirithous' mad attempt to acquire Hades' wife. The madness that has compelled Pirithous and Theseus to cross this forbidden boundary is paralleled in that of Phaedra, whose love madness drives her from the house and into the forests (112). Phaedra knows that following her nurse's advice is correct, but madness compels her to ignore it (178), for mad passion has overcome the ability to reason properly (184). For the Stoics, people could be truly happy only when their lives were guided by reason (*ratio*), so clearly Phaedra's emotions are leading her away from any sort of happiness.

The Nurse argues that mad passion has caused people to transform Venus and Cupid into divinities (197–202) and urges Phaedra to help herself by putting an end to this madness (248; cf. also 268). Despite the Nurse's prudent advice, Phaedra's madness persists. At 361, the Nurse declares that there will be no end to the insane flames (*flammis . . . insanis*) that engulf Phaedra and notes that her face betrays her madness (*furor,* 363). The image of fire returns later as Phaedra reveals to Hippolytus that love scorches her mad heart (*pectus insanum,* 640) and declares she will follow Hippolytus even over the mad sea (*mare insanum,* 700).

Unfortunately for Phaedra, the object of her mad passion suffers from his own madness. Earlier in the play, Hippolytus had declared that someone who, as he does, leads the solitary life of a hunter is unaffected by the madness (*furor,* 486) of greed. Later, however, he admits that his hatred of women may be madness (*furor,* 567), reason (*ratio*), or just part of his nature. Phaedra hopes confessing her love will cure her of madness (*sanas furentem,* 711). Phaedra's confession only serves to inflame Hippolytus' own madness, however, and when Hippolytus flees his stepmother for the sane refuge of the forest, the chorus compare him to a raging (*insanae,* 736) storm. The chorus conclude this lengthy ode by wondering what Phaedra's madness (*furor,* 824) would leave untried.

The chorus' question is soon answered when Phaedra tells Theseus that Hippolytus tried to rape her. A shocked Theseus marvels at his son's alleged behavior and the madness (*furor,* 909) of the Amazon race (a part of Hippolytus' heritage), as these female warriors reject the customs of Venus. Theseus, believing Phaedra's accusation, curses Hippolytus, and this curse results in the young man's horses' being afflicted by madness (*furor*, 1070) that leads to Hippolytus' death. This death leads to another death and at 1156 Theseus wonders what madness (*furor*) drives Phaedra to emerge from the palace, a sword in hand. Before Phaedra commits suicide, she confesses to Theseus the madness (*demens*) of her insane behavior (*insano*, 1193). Phaedra ends the flames of her madness with a suicidal blade; the play concludes with Theseus' composing the scattered limbs of Hippolytus and preparing to consign his body to the flames of a funeral pyre (1274, 1277).

BIBLIOGRAPHY

Boyle, A. J. "In Nature's Bonds: A Study of Seneca's *Phaedra*," *Aufstieg und Niedergang der römischen Welt* 32, no. 2 (1985): 1,284–1,347.

Leeman, A. D. "Seneca's *Phaedra* as a Stoic Tragedy." In *Miscellanea Tragica in Honorem J. C. Kamerbeek*. Edited by J. M. Bremer, S. L. Radt, and C. J. Ruijgh. Amsterdam: Hakkert, 1976, 199–212.

Paschalis, M. "The Bull and the Horse: Animal Theme and Imagery in Seneca's *Phaedra*," *American Journal of Philology* 115 (1994): 105–28.

Segal, Charles. *Language and Desire in Seneca's Phaedra*. Princeton, N.J.: Princeton University Press, 1986.

HIPPOMEDON Hippomedon's father was TALAUS (or Aristomachus); his mother is usually called Metidice. Hippomedon of ARGOS married Evanippe and by her fathered Polydorus. Hippomedon was one of the Seven against THEBES; Ismarus killed him in the battle. [ANCIENT SOURCES: Aeschylus, *Seven against Thebes* 488; Euripides, *Phoenician Women* 126, 1113, *Suppliant Women* 881; Sophocles, *Oedipus at Colonus* 1317]

HIPPONAX (SIXTH CENTURY B.C.E.) A writer of iambic poetry from the town of EPHESUS. [ANCIENT SOURCES: Aristophanes, *Frogs* 661]

HIPPONICUS The name of the father of CALLIAS as well as of Callias' son. The younger Hipponicus served ATHENS as a military commander during the first part of the PELOPONNESIAN WAR and was killed at the battle of Delium in 424 B.C.E. [ANCIENT SOURCES: Aristophanes, *Birds* 283]

HIPPONOUS This king of OLENUS had a daughter, Periboea, who became pregnant when she was not married and gave birth to a son, Tydeus. Hipponous sent Periboea away (and perhaps the child as well) to be killed. Both Periboea and Tydeus survived. What eventually became of Hipponous is not known. SOPHOCLES wrote a *Hipponous,* of which about five lines survive (fragments 300–4 Radt), but the play's overall content is unknown. One fragment (300) is spoken by someone (perhaps Periboea) from Olenus. [ANCIENT SOURCES: APOLLODORUS, *LIBRARY* 1.8.4; Pausanias, 9.8.7]

BIBLIOGRAPHY

Kiso, A. *The Lost Sophocles*. New York: Vantage Press, 1984.

Lloyd-Jones, H. *Sophocles: Fragments*. Cambridge, Mass.: Harvard University Press, 1996.

Radt, S. *Tragicorum Graecorum Fragmenta*. Vol. 4. Göttingen, Ger.: Vandenhoeck & Ruprecht, 1977.

Sutton, D. F. *The Lost Sophocles*. Lanham, Md.: University Press of America, 1984.

HISTER Now called the Danube, this river originates in Germany and flows into the Black Sea. [ANCIENT SOURCES: Sophocles, *Oedipus Tyrannos* 1227]

HISTRIO See ACTOR.

HOMER (EIGHTH CENTURY B.C.E.) Little is known about the life of Homer, whom the Greeks consider their greatest poet. Dates for his life vary by as much as 500 years, though he does not appear to have lived later than 700 B.C.E. His place of birth also is disputed, but two places along the western coast of Turkey (Smyrna and the island of Chios) remain the most likely candidates. Tradition says that Homer was blind. This cannot be verified but neither can it be disproved.

Two surviving epic poems, *Iliad* and *Odyssey,* are attributed to Homer, although many scholars believe that two different poets wrote these poems. *Iliad* deals with a period of some 40 days during the 10th year of the Trojan War, focusing on a violent argument between ACHILLES and AGAMEMNON; Achilles' withdrawal from the war; the killing of Achilles' friend, PATROCLUS, by HECTOR; Achilles' return to the battle; and the latter's killing of Hector. *Odyssey* deals with the return of ODYSSEUS from the Trojan War and hardships faced by his family as a result of his absence.

Numerous ancient dramas, especially tragedies, were influenced by the two Homeric epics. EURIPIDES' *RHESUS* is based on the 10th book of *Iliad* and Euripides' *Cyclops* used as its source the ninth book of *Odyssey*. Although only two surviving plays are based directly on *Iliad* and *Odyssey*, numerous other dramas drew upon Homer's works or his characters (e.g., AESCHYLUS' ORESTEIA; SOPHOCLES' AJAX, PHILOCTETES; Euripides' ANDROMACHE, HECABE, IPHIGENIA AT AULIS, TROJAN WOMEN; SENECA'S AGAMEMNON, TROJAN WOMEN). Additionally, at least 10 ancient dramas contain the name of Achilles in their title; two of them are by comic poets (Anaxandrides and Philetaerus). About the same number of ancient dramas contain Odysseus' name in the title, equally divided between tragic and comic poets.

BIBLIOGRAPHY

Camps, W. A. *An Introduction to Homer.* London: Oxford University Press, 1980.

Griffin, J. *Homer.* 2d ed. London: Bristol Classical, 2001.

Kirk, G. S. *Homer and the Oral Tradition.* Cambridge: Cambridge University Press, 1976.

McAuslan, I., and P. Walcot, eds. *Homer.* Oxford: Oxford University Press, 1998.

Wace, A. J. B., and F. H. Stubbings, eds. *A Companion to Homer.* New York: Macmillan, 1962.

HOMOLOEAN GATE

One of THEBES' seven gates. The gate was defended by LASTHENES and attacked by AMPHIARAUS, according to AESCHYLUS, but attacked by Tydeus, according to EURIPIDES. [ANCIENT SOURCES: Aeschylus, *Seven against Thebes* 570; Euripides, *Phoenician Women* 1119]

HORACE (DECEMBER 65–NOVEMBER 27, 8 B.C.E.)

Quintus Horatius Flaccus (Horace) was a Roman poet who wrote, among other works, a brief letter (476 lines) entitled *Ars Poetica* (The art of poetry). Composed in the 10s B.C.E., this letter, addressed to certain members of the Piso family, gives advice on how plays should be constructed. The letter discusses the unity of plays, diction, meter, consistency of story and character, methods to set forth a play's events, the use of the chorus and music, SATYR PLAYS, the origins of drama, the sort of educational training a poet should have, the level of excellence for which a poet should strive, and the necessity for poets to behave in a moderate fashion. *Ars Poetica* is an important document in the history of classical drama because it preserves remarks on writing poetry by a poet. The accuracy of Horace's remarks on the history and origins of Greek drama is generally doubted by modern scholars, who prefer that such statements be corroborated by inscriptional or archaeological evidence.

BIBLIOGRAPHY

Brink, C. O. *Horace on Poetry.* II, *The Ars Poetica.* Cambridge, Mass.: Cambridge Univeristy Press, 1971.

Frischer, B. *Shifting Paradigms: New Approaches to Horace's Ars Poetica.* Atlanta: Scholars Press, 1991.

Golden, Leon. "*Ars* and *Artifex* in the *Ars Poetica:* Revisiting the Question of Structure," *Syllecta Classica* 11 (2000): 141–61.

Trimpi, W. "Horace's *Ut Pictura Poesis:* The Argument for Stylistic Decorum." *Traditio* 34 (1978): 29–73.

HOUSEHOLD GODS

In Roman religion, each household had a set of family gods known as the Penates and Lares. In TERENCE'S PHORMIO (lines 311–12), when Demipho returns from abroad, he announces that he will enter his home and greet his Penates.

HUBRIS

A common reason that characters are punished in TRAGEDY is an act of hubris, a word that connotes extreme arrogance or outrageous behavior. Acts of hubris would include committing rape, persecuting innocent people, injuring a guest, mistreating one's parents, claiming that one is better than a divinity, or refusing to worship a divinity. In EURIPIDES' HIPPOLYTUS, for example, the title character's refusal to worship APHRODITE would be considered hubris; consequently, Aphrodite causes Hippolytus' death. Probably the most famous remark about hubris occurs in SOPHOCLES' OEDIPUS TYRANNOS (872): "Insolence [*hubris*] breeds the tyrant." Sophocles wrote a SATYR PLAY entitled *Hubris,* of whose only five words survive (fragment 670 Radt).

BIBLIOGRAPHY
Kiso, A. *The Lost Sophocles.* New York: Vantage Press, 1984.
Lloyd-Jones, H. *Sophocles: Fragments.* Cambridge, Mass.: Harvard University Press, 1996.
Radt, S. *Tragicorum Graecorum Fragmenta.* Vol. 4. Göttingen, Ger.: Vandenhoeck & Ruprecht, 1977.
Sutton, D. F. *The Lost Sophocles.* Lanham, Md.: University Press of America, 1984.

HYADES Originally seven NYMPHS whom ZEUS transformed into stars. According to one tradition, they cared for the young DIONYSUS until they (and the god) were chased into the sea by LYCURGUS; another tradition is that the death of their brother, Hyas, caused them to die of sorrow. The ancients associated the setting of these stars (located in the head of the constellation Taurus) with rain and storms. [ANCIENT SOURCES: Apollodorus, *Library* 3.4.3; Euripides, *Electra* 468, *Ion* 1156; Homer, *Iliad* 18.486; Hyginus, *Fables* 192; Seneca, *Medea* 312, 769, *Thyestes* 853]

HYBRISTES A mythical river past which Io wandered. [ANCIENT SOURCES: Aeschylus, *Prometheus Bound* 717]

HYDRA See LERNA.

HYLAS (1) The son of Thiodamaus, Hylas was a handsome young man who accompanied JASON and the Argonauts on the quest for the Golden Fleece. Hylas was the beloved of HERACLES but vanished after he was abducted by water nymphs in the land of Mysia. Heracles left the journey to continue looking for Hylas but never found the young man. [ANCIENT SOURCES: Apollodorus, *Library* 1.9.19; Apollonius Rhodius, 1.1207–1357; Hyginus, *Fables* 14; Seneca, *Hippolytus* 780, *Medea* 647; Theocritus, 13]

HYLAS (2) The name of a fictional slave at ARISTOPHANES, *KNIGHTS* 67. Historical slaves of that name are known.

HYLLUS In the most common tradition Hyllus is the son of HERACLES and DEIANEIRA; Apollonius of Rhodes makes him the son of Heracles and the nymph Melite, who lived among the Phaeacians. When Hyllus grew up, he led a band of Phaeacians to the northeastern coast of the Adriatic Sea, founded a city, and called the people Hylleans. Hyllus was killed defending his cattle against a raid by the Mentores. The best-known tradition is found in SOPHOCLES' TRACHINIAN WOMEN and SENECA's HERCULES OETAEUS, in which Hyllus promises his father, Heracles, that he will marry Heracles' concubine, IOLE, and kill Heracles himself, who was being tormented by the poisoned robe sent to him by Deianeira. Although Hyllus took the pain-wracked Heracles to the top of Mount Oeta and had a funeral pyre built for him, he could not make himself light his father's pyre; PHILOCTETES performed that task. Hyllus did, however, marry Iole, and, according to one tradition, she produced for him a son, Cleodaeus. Some sources indicate that Hyllus, rather than IOLAUS, killed EURYSTHEUS in a battle to protect Heracles' children. In EURIPIDES' CHILDREN OF HERACLES, we find that Hyllus challenged Eurystheus to a single combat, but that Eurystheus was too cowardly to accept the challenge. Hyllus himself was killed by Echemus when Hyllus led Heracles' children in an attempt to reclaim Heracles' kingdom in MYCENAE. [ANCIENT SOURCES: Apollodorus, *Library* 2.7.7–2.8.2; Euripides, *Children of Heracles*; Pausanias, 1.4.2, 1.4.10, 3.15.10, 4.2.1, 8.5.1; Sophocles, *Trachinian Women*]

HYMEN (HYMENAEUS) Hymen is the god of marriage and the marriage song, which is called the *hymenaeus.* Various divinities are named as his parents: APOLLO and one of the MUSES, DIONYSUS and APHRODITE, a mortal named Magnes and the Muse Calliope. The marriage hymn was sung when the bride left her house for the house of her future husband. In EURIPIDES' TROJAN WOMEN, CASSANDRA, in frenzied anticipation of becoming AGAMEMNON's concubine, sings a hymn to Hymen and then predicts Agamemnon's death. At the conclusion of ARISTOPHANES' PEACE, a hymn to Hymen is sung in anticipation of TRYGAEUS' marriage. See also PLAUTUS' CASINA, in which Olympio and Lysidamus sing a hymn to Hymen before Olympio's marriage to Casina (Chalinus in disguise). [ANCIENT SOURCES: Aristophanes, *Peace* 1332–59; Euripides, CHILDREN OF HERACLES 917, *Trojan Women*

310–42; Plautus, *Casina* 799–809; Seneca, *Medea* 116, 300; Terence, *Brothers* 905, 907]

HYMN   Derived from the Greek *humnos,* the word *hymn* refers to a song, often of praise or thanksgiving, to a divinity. The best-known hymns from antiquity are the so-called *Homeric Hymns,* which are written in a style similar to that of HOMER and praise various Greek divinities. These poems range in length from just a few lines to several hundred. In classical drama, hymns sung by the CHORUS, such as the famous hymn to ZEUS in the opening choral song of AESCHYLUS' *Agamemnon* (see ORESTEIA), are not uncommon. In SOPHOCLES' *OEDIPUS TYRANNOS,* the chorus of Theban elders enter singing a hymn to APOLLO, ARTEMIS, and ATHENA, in which they pray for help in the face of the plague that afflicts their city. In EURIPIDES' *IPHIGENIA IN TAURIS,* at lines 1234–57, the chorus sing a hymn about Apollo's triumph over the Python and the establishment of his power at DELPHI.

BIBLIOGRAPHY
Furley, W. D. "Praise and Persuasion in Greek Hymns," *Journal of Hellenic Studies* 115 (1995): 29–46.
Smith, P. M. *On the Hymn to Zeus in Aeschylus' Agamemnon.* Chico, Calif.: Scholars Press, 1980.

HYPERBIUS   The son of Oenops, Hyperbius (whose name means "passionate" or "excessive" in Greek) was a Theban nobleman who sided with ETEOCLES against his brother, POLYNEICES. In the battle of the Seven against THEBES, Hyperbius was matched against HIPPOMEDON and defeated him. [ANCIENT SOURCES: Aeschylus, *Seven against Thebes* 504–18]

HYPERBOLUS (DIED 411 B.C.E.)   An Athenian political leader mentioned negatively by the historian Thucydides, ARISTOPHANES, and other comic poets. The Greek comic poet Hermippus attacked Hyperbolus and his mother in a play entitled *Artopolides* (Baker women). Another Greek comic poet, Plato, who Plutarch suggests was sympathetic to Hyperbolus, wrote a *Hyperbolus* (fragments 166–72 Kock).

In 417 (or 415) B.C.E., Hyperbolus tried to engineer the ostracism of ALCIBIADES or NICIAS (or PHAEAX), but the two joined forces and managed to have Hyperbo-

lus ostracized instead. Apparently, the Athenians considered the process of ostracism so corrupt that after this time they no longer resorted to the process. Thus, Hyperbolus became the last Athenian to be ostracized. In exile, Hyperbolus went to the island of SAMOS, where political revolutionaries killed him. [ANCIENT SOURCES: Aristophanes, *Acharnians* 846, *Knights* 1304, 1363, *Clouds* 551, 557, 558, 623, 876, 1065, *Frogs* 570, *Peace* 681, 921, 1319, *Thesmophoriazusae* 840, *Wasps* 1007; Plutarch, *Alcibiades* 13, *Nicias* 11; Thucydides, 8.73]

BIBLIOGRAPHY
Kock, T. *Comicorum Atticorum Fragmenta.* Vol. 1. Leipzig: Teubner, 1880.
Woodhead, A.G. "I.G., I2, 95, and the Ostracism of Hyperbolus," *Hesperia* 18 (1949): 78–83.

HYPERMESTRA   See DANAIDS.

HYPNOS   See SLEEP.

HYPOCRITES   See ACTOR.

HYPORCHEME   A song or hymn (accompanied by dance and pantomimic action) in honor of APOLLO. The hyporcheme was thought to have originated on CRETE. Occasionally, SOPHOCLES inserts one of these lively hymns immediately before the CATASTROPHE. [ANCIENT SOURCES: Plato, *Ion* 534c; Sophocles, *Ajax* 693–717, *Antigone* 1115–54; *Oedipus Tyrannos* 1086–1109]

HYPOTHESIS   A hypothesis usually contains a brief summary of the play's plot and sometimes includes additional useful information about the play. In the case of some classical plays, one or more hypotheses accompany the play's text. ARISTOPHANES' *BIRDS,* for example, has four hypotheses that range between 10 and 40 lines. EURIPIDES' *ALCESTIS* is accompanied by two hypotheses. One contains a summary of the play's plot; the other not only has a plot summary, but also reveals when the play was produced, which playwright won first place in the competition, and titles of the other plays that Euripides staged in that festival. It also includes some comments on the tone of Euripides' *Alcestis.*

HYPSIPYLE The daughter of THOAS, Hypsipyle was the ruler of LEMNOS. When JASON and the Argonauts went to Lemnos, Jason slept with Hypsipyle and by her had two sons, Euneus and Nebrophonus (or Deipylus). When Hypsipyle became queen, she and the women of her island killed almost all of the island's male inhabitants. The lone male survivor of this slaughter was Hypsipyle's father, whom she herself saved by putting him in a vessel and setting him adrift in the AEGEAN SEA. When the Lemnians learned she had saved Thoas, they sold her into slavery or pirates captured her. The king of NEMEA, Lycurgus (or Lycus), bought her and she served as nurse to his son Opheltes, who was killed by a deadly snake while she was showing a spring to those who participated in the Seven against THEBES expedition. EURIPIDES wrote a *Hypsipyle,* which was staged about 410 B.C.E. [ANCIENT SOURCES: Apollodorus, *Library* 1.9.17]

BIBLIOGRAPHY
Webster, T. B. L. *The Tragedies of Euripides.* London: Methuen, 1967.

HYSIAE A village on the outskirts of THEBES. [ANCIENT SOURCES: Euripides, *Bacchae* 751]

I

IACCHUS A divinity sometimes equated with DIONYSUS. In the Eleusinian Mysteries, Iacchus "was the god who was carried in procession from his sanctuary in Athens to Eleusis when the Mysteries were celebrated, and his name is the name of the processional song" (Dover). In ARISTOPHANES' *FROGS* (323–400), Iacchus is found in the UNDERWORLD, "called upon to come and dance with his worshippers . . ., brandish his torches . . . and lead them to the flowery plain . . ., and summoned to join the procession 'to the goddess'" (Dover).

BIBLIOGRAPHY
Dover, K. J. *Aristophanes: Frogs.* Oxford: Clarendon Press, 1993, 61.

IAPETUS The brother of CRONUS and the father of PROMETHEUS, Iapetus' name became synonymous with "old-fashioned" things. [ANCIENT SOURCES: Aristophanes, *Clouds* 998]

IASO One of the daughters of ASCLEPIUS (Panacea is the other). Iaso's name means "healer." [ANCIENT SOURCES: Aristophanes, *Wealth* 701]

IBERIA Either a name (after the river Iberus) used by the ancients for Spain or an Asian country along the southern shores of the Black Sea (occupying now what is Russian Georgia). SOPHOCLES (or perhaps his son) wrote an *Iberians* (see Radt), of which only the title survives. [ANCIENT SOURCES: Seneca, *Hercules Oetaeus* 1522]

BIBLIOGRAPHY
Radt, S. *Tragicorum Graecorum Fragmenta.* Vol. 4. Göttingen, Ger.: Vandenhoeck & Ruprecht, 1977.
Sutton, Dana. *The Lost Sophocles.* Lanham, Md.: University Press of America, 1984, 62–63.

IBYCUS A Greek lyric poet from Rhegium in southern Italy. Ibycus was active in the middle of the sixth century B.C.E. and known for his love poetry and love of nature. [ANCIENT SOURCES: Aristophanes, *Thesmophoriazusae* 161]

BIBLIOGRAPHY
Bowra, C. M. *Greek Lyric Poetry from Alcman to Simonides.* 2d rev. ed. Oxford: Clarendon Press, 1961.

ICARUS See DAEDALUS.

ICHNEUTAE See THE SEARCHERS.

IDA (1) A mountain or mountain range near the town of TROY. PARIS was a shepherd on Ida when he judged the beauty of the goddesses HERA, ATHENA, and APHRODITE. This event, known as the JUDGMENT OF PARIS, led to the Trojan War. Paris chose Aphrodite as the most beautiful after she promised him HELEN. Hera and Athena, angered at not being selected, joined forces and sided against the Trojans in the war.

IDA (2) A mountain in central CRETE, Ida claimed to be the birthplace of ZEUS. [ANCIENT SOURCES: Aristophanes, *Frogs* 1355]

IDMON   The son of APOLLO and Asteria, Idmon was a prophet who accompanied JASON and the Argonauts in the search for the Golden Fleece. According to Seneca, Idmon died of a bite from a serpent; other sources report that a boar killed him. [ANCIENT SOURCES: Hyginus, *Fables* 18; Seneca, *Medea* 652]

ILION   See TROY.

ILIONA   A daughter of PRIAM and HECABE, Iliona was the wife of POLYMESTOR of Thrace. When Iliona's brother POLYDORUS was sent to live with Polymestor and Iliona, Polymestor killed Polydorus for the fortune that he took with him. PACUVIUS wrote an *Iliona*, from which about two dozen lines survive and the events of which would have overlapped to some extent those of EURIPIDES' HECABE (although Iliona is not mentioned in Euripides' play). One fragment from Pacuvius' play recalls the opening of Euripides' play, as Pacuvius has the ghost of the deceased Polydorus call upon Hecabe to awaken and bury him. In another fragment, Iliona may express the wish to gouge out Polymestor's eyes, a deed performed by Hecabe in Euripides' play. The fragments do suggest, however, that Iliona did take revenge on Polymestor. [ANCIENT SOURCES: Hyginus, *Fables* 109]

BIBLIOGRAPHY
Warmington, E. H. *Remains of Old Latin: Livius Andronicus, Naevius, Pacuvius, and Accius.* Vol. 2. Cambridge, Mass.: Harvard University Press, 1936.

ILIUM   See TROY.

IMAGERY   With respect to the craft of the ancient dramatist, imagery is use of vivid descriptions to create in or suggest to the audience's mind objects or events that they could ordinarily perceive with the five senses. In the plays, imagery most commonly occurs in passages containing lyric poetry (such as choral passages) or in messenger speeches (especially those of EURIPIDES). Images of animals, especially serpents, bulls, and birds, are common. In SOPHOCLES' ANTIGONE, for example, the poet evokes in his audience's mind the image of an eagle as he describes POLYNEICES' attack on THEBES as being like the flight of that bird over the city. Images of

light and darkness pervade AESCHYLUS' ORESTEIA, SOPHOCLES' AJAX, and SENECA's OEDIPUS. In PLAUTUS' COMEDY, military imagery is common, as that author's slaves often become like commanders who marshal their troops for attack against an opponent such as a PIMP.

BIBLIOGRAPHY
Barlow, S. A. *The Imagery of Euripides.* London: Methuen, 1970.
Fowler, B. H. "Aeschylus' Imagery," *Classica et Mediaevali* 28 (1967): 1–74.
Mastronarde, D. J. "Iconography and Imagery in Euripides' *Ion*," *California Studies in Classical Antiquity* 8 (1975): 163–76.
Paschalis, M. "The Bull and the Horse: Animal Theme and Imagery in Seneca's *Phaedra*," *American Journal of Philology* 115 (1994): 105–28.
Stanford, W. B. "Light and Darkness in Sophocles' *Ajax*," *Greek, Roman, and Byzantine Studies* 19 (1978): 189–97.

IMBROS   An island in the northeastern AEGEAN and located east of LEMNOS. MENANDER wrote a play entitled *Imbrians,* whose fragments reveal little about the content (212–14 Körte).

BIBLIOGRAPHY
Körte, A., and A. Thierfelder. A. *Menandri Quae Supersunt.* Vol. 2, 2d ed. Leipzig: Teubner, 1959.

IMITATION   See MIMESIS.

INACHUS   The son of Oceanus and Tethys, the river Inachus flows through ARGOS. Inachus fathered Io by Melia, the nymph of an ash tree. According to AESCHYLUS' PROMETHEUS BOUND, when Io told her father about the sexually charged dreams that ZEUS had been causing her to have, Inachus banished her from the house. Zeus then impregnated Io; she was transformed into a cow (by Zeus or HERA); and in that form she was guarded by the multieyed ARGUS.

SOPHOCLES wrote a satyric *Inachus* from which numerous fragments survive. In fragment 269a, Inachus and the chorus appear to be discussing Zeus' rape of Io and Io's transformation into a cow. In fragment 269c the chorus encounter HERMES, who appears in the play, probably to battle Argus. The scholiast on *Prometheus Bound* 574a says Argus enters the stage singing. Lloyd-Jones suspected that Hermes might challenge Argus in a musical contest. Tradition says that Hermes charmed Argus' eyes to sleep by his music. Fragment 272 suggests that IRIS may appear in the play. [ANCIENT SOURCES: Aeschylus, *Libation Bearers* 6 (see ORESTEIA), *Prometheus Bound* 590, 663, 705, *Suppliant Women* 497; Apollodorus, *Library* 2.1.1–4; Euripides, *Suppliant Women* 372, 629, 645, 890; Ovid, *Metamorphoses* 1.568–746]

BIBLIOGRAPHY
Kiso, A. *The Lost Sophocles.* New York: Vantage Press, 1984.
Lloyd-Jones, H. *Sophocles: Fragments.* Cambridge, Mass.: Harvard University Press, 1996.
Radt, S. *Tragicorum Graecorum Fragmenta.* Vol. 4. Göttingen, Ger.: Vandenhoeck & Ruprecht, 1977.
Sutton, D. F. *The Lost Sophocles.* Lanham, Md.: University Press of America, 1984.

INDIA For the ancient Greeks and Romans, the land of India represented one of the eastern boundaries of the world as they knew it. The Greek playwrights knew that gold could be found in India, and Roman playwrights knew that the people of India had darker skin than theirs and that India possessed its share of elephants. DIONYSUS was also said to have introduced the people of India to his worship. [ANCIENT SOURCES: Apollodorus, *Library* 3.5.2; Catullus, 11.2, 45.6, 61.109a; Hyginus, *Fables* 131, 133; Plautus, *Curculio* 439, *Miles Gloriosus* 25; Seneca, *Hippolytus* 345, 392, 753, *Medea* 484; Sophocles, *Antigone* 1038; Terence, *Eunuch* 413]

INFORMANT A stock character in ancient COMEDY, an informant (Greek: *sycophantes;* Latin: *sycophanta*) was usually someone who made a living by revealing to the local authorities the illegal importation of goods. Such people are always excluded from the benefits that result from the fantastic plans of the heroes in ARISTOPHANES' plays. In ACHARNIANS, for example, the poet suggests that informants are so prevalent in ATHENS that they themselves could serve as an export. Indeed, in this play DICAEOPOLIS packs up one of the informants who appear in *Acharnians* and trades him to a Boeotian merchant. In Aristophanes' *Birds,* the informant who tries to infiltrate the new city

of the birds is driven away by whips. In Aristophanes' WEALTH, the informant is wrapped up in the ragged cloak of a honest man who has now become wealthy and has the honest man's old shoes nailed to his forehead. In PLAUTUS' THREE-DOLLAR DAY, a *sycophanta* appears. His role, however, is not that of an informant; instead, he has been hired to swindle Charmides out of some money.

BIBLIOGRAPHY
Muecke, F. "Names and Players: The Sycophant Scene of the *Trinummus* (*Trin.* 4.2)," *Transactions of the American Philological Association* 115 (1985): 167–86.

INO The daughter of CADMUS and HARMONIA, Ino was the sister of AGAVE, AUTONOE, SEMELE, and Polydorus. Ino married ATHAMAS, a king in the central part of northern Greece. With Athamas, Ino helped raise the young Dionysus. (For more on Ino's marriage, see ATHAMAS.) In EURIPIDES' BACCHAE, Ino, in a Bacchic frenzy, helps kill her nephew, PENTHEUS. Euripides wrote an *Ino* of which some 80 lines survive (fragments 398–423 Nauck). Webster thought Euripides' play dealt with Ino's divorce of Athamas, his marriage to Themisto, Ino's subsequent return to Athamas' house, her employment as a nurse to the children of Athamas, and Ino's trickery, which resulted in Themisto's killing her own children. In ARISTOPHANES' ACHARNIANS, reference is made to the rags in which Euripides apparently costumed his Ino. [ANCIENT SOURCES: Euripides, *Bacchae;* Hyginus, *Fables* 2, 4]

BIBLIOGRAPHY
Webster, T. B. L. *The Tragedies of Euripides.* London: Methuen, 1967.

IO The daughter of Inachus and Melia, Io was a priestess of HERA. Io had the misfortune of being one of ZEUS' many lovers. After Zeus impregnated Io, Hera discovered the relationship. According to some sources, such as Ovid, Zeus changed Io into a cow to hide her from Hera. Other sources, such as PROMETHEUS BOUND, state that Hera transformed her into a cow. After Io's transformation, she was placed under the watch of a multieyed creature named ARGUS. When HERMES (at Zeus' instigation) killed Argus, Io was freed, but then Argus' FURY tormented her. In a state of frenzy, the cow Io wandered the earth. Eventually she reached Egypt, where Zeus restored her to human form. There, she gave birth to Zeus' son, EPAPHUS, who became king of Egypt.

In PROMETHEUS BOUND, Io's wanderings lead her past the site where PROMETHEUS is chained. Prometheus tells Io of her impending wanderings and ultimate release from torment. He also prophesies that one of her descendants, HERACLES, will release him from his torment. Eventually, Io will make her way to Egypt, be restored to human form by Zeus' touch, and give birth to a son named EPAPHUS. Although Io does not appear as a character in AESCHYLUS' SUPPLIANT WOMEN, the name and image of Io are evoked frequently in the play by the chorus of DANAUS' daughters, who liken Io's sufferings to their own.

Io's sufferings at the hands of Zeus and Hera certainly made her a fitting subject for TRAGEDY, as exemplified by the plays cited, and by an Io by the Greek tragedian Chaeremon (fragment 9 Snell). Additionally, several Greek comic poets wrote an Io: Titles only survive from Anaxilas and Anaxandrides; a single line (fragment 55 Kock) from Plato the comic poet; four words from Sannyrion (fragments 10–11 Kock). We know nothing about the plots of these plays, however. Among Roman authors, ACCIUS wrote an Io, from which three lines survive. One fragment refers to Argus' guarding Io; another refers to Io's expulsion from home by her father.

BIBLIOGRAPHY

Kock, T. Comicorum Atticorum Fragmenta. Vol. 1. Leipzig: Teubner, 1880.

———. Comicorum Atticorum Fragmenta. Vol. 2. Leipzig: Teubner, 1884.

Snell, B. Tragicorum Graecorum Fragmenta. Vol. 1. Göttingen, Ger.: Vandenhoeck & Ruprecht, 1971.

IOBATES   The king of LYCIA, Iobates fathered STHENEBOEA (also called Anteia), who became the wife of Proetus, king of TIRYNS. After Stheneboea accused BELLEROPHON of raping her, Proetus sent Bellerophon to Iobates in the hope that Iobates would kill him. Iobates created several challenges for Bellerophon, all of which Bellerophon overcame. Eventually, Iobates married

Bellerophon to his daughter and gave his new son-in-law half his kingdom. Sophocles wrote an Iobates; the few surviving lines do not give any indication of the play's content. [ANCIENT SOURCES: Apollodorus, Library 2.3.1–2; Hyginus, Fables 57, 243; Servius Honoratus on Aeneid, 5.118]

BIBLIOGRAPHY

Kiso, A. The Lost Sophocles. New York: Vantage Press, 1984.

Lloyd-Jones, H. Sophocles: Fragments. Cambridge, Mass.: Harvard University Press, 1996.

Radt, S. Tragicorum Graecorum Fragmenta. Vol. 4. Göttingen, Ger.: Vandenhoeck & Ruprecht, 1977.

Sutton, D. F. The Lost Sophocles. Lanham, Md.: University Press of America, 1984.

IOCASTA   See JOCASTA.

IOLAUS   The son of HERACLES' son Iphicles, Iolaus accompanied his uncle, Heracles, on some of his labors as his charioteer. Iolaus is best known for helping Heracles kill the HYDRA of Lerna. Apollodorus wrote that after Heracles completed his labors he gave his wife, MEGARA, to Iolaus to be his wife. Euripides and Seneca, however, in their plays on Heracles' madness, say that Heracles killed Megara while she was still his wife. In EURIPIDES' CHILDREN OF HERACLES, after the death of Heracles, Iolaus serves as the protector of Heracles' children, a role similar to that played by AMPHITRYON later in Euripides' HERACLES. Unlike Amphitryon, however, in Euripides' Children of Heracles, during a battle with Eurystheus and his army, the aged Iolaus prays to HEBE and ZEUS that he will regain his youth for a single day so that he can take vengeance against his enemies. Amazingly, Iolaus regains his youth and captures EURYSTHEUS. Eurystheus' ultimate fate is not clear in Euripides' Children (because the conclusion of that play is lost). Pausanias, however, says Iolaus killed Eurystheus. Pausanias also reports that Iolaus himself died at Sardis in Asia Minor. [ANCIENT SOURCES: Apollodorus, Library 2.5.2, 2.6.1; Euripides, Ion 194–200; Hesiod, Shield of Heracles, Theogony 316–18; Ovid, Metamorphoses 9.394–401; Pausanias, 1.44.10, 5.8.4, 9.23.1]

IOLCUS   A town on the northeastern coast of mainland Greece, Iolcus was the birthplace of Pelias,

ACASTUS, ALCESTIS, and JASON. It was at Iolcus that Jason and the Argonauts began their quest for the Golden Fleece. [ANCIENT SOURCES: Euripides, *Alcestis* 249, *Medea* 7, 484, 551; Seneca, *Medea* 457, *Trojan Women* 819]

IOLE The daughter of EURYTUS, king of OECHALIA. HERACLES sacked Eurytus' town and took Iole captive with the intent of making her his concubine. Heracles died before he was able to enjoy her, and one of his dying wishes was to have his son HYLLUS marry the princess. Iole appears as a silent character in SOPHOCLES' *TRACHINIAN WOMEN*; she has a brief speaking role in SENECA's *HERCULES OETAEUS,* in which she laments her fate as a captive and recalls seeing her father and brother killed. [ANCIENT SOURCES: Apollodorus, *Library* 2.6.1, 2.7.7, 2.8.2; Euripides, *Hippolytus* 545; Hyginus, *Fables* 35; Ovid, *Heroides* 9]

ION (1) (CA. 480–BEFORE 421 B.C.E.) A Greek poet from the island of CHIOS who wrote several different types of poetry. Ion competed in ATHENS in both TRAGEDY and DITHYRAMB. His first competition in tragedy was around 451. In 428 EURIPIDES' production (which included *HIPPOLYTUS*) defeated Ion's offerings. About 75 fragments of Ion's plays survive, none longer than five lines. The play titles attributed to Ion are *Agamemnon, Alcmene, Argeioi, Eurytidai, Laertes, Mega Drama, Omphale* (a SATYR PLAY), *Teucer, Phoenix,* and *Phrouroi* (Guards). [ANCIENT SOURCES: Aristophanes, *Peace* 835]

BIBLIOGRAPHY

Dover, K. J. "Ion of Chios: His Place in the History of Greek Literature." In *Chios: A Conference at the Homereion in Chios 1984.* Edited by J. Boardman and C. E. Vaphopoulou-Richardson. Oxford: Clarendon Press, 1986, 27–37.

Snell, B. *Tragicorum Graecorum Fragmenta.* Vol. 1. Göttingen, Ger.: Vandenhoeck & Ruprecht, 1971.

West, M. L. "Ion of Chios," *Bulletin of the Institute of Classical Studies* 32 (1985): 71–78.

ION (2) The son of APOLLO and CREUSA, Ion was born in ATHENS after Apollo raped Creusa near the Athenian ACROPOLIS. Creusa exposed Ion in the place where she was raped. At Apollo's command, HERMES took the infant Ion to DELPHI, where Ion was raised by Apollo's priestess. Many years later, Ion, who became a servant of Apollo's at Delphi, encountered Creusa and her husband, XUTHUS, at the ORACLE. The couple had traveled to consult the oracle about the possibility of having children. Xuthus, told that the first person he encountered after exiting the shrine would be his son, encountered Ion. When Creusa, however, discovered Xuthus' intention to adopt Ion, she arranged to have Ion poisoned. Her plot failed and then Ion threatened to kill her. This catastrophe was averted when Apollo's priestess carried out some items that had been found with Ion when he was taken to Delphi as an infant. Creusa recognized the items and convinced Ion that she was his mother. After their joyful reunion, Ion returned to Athens with Creusa and Xuthus. Ion married Helice and had four sons, Aegicores, Argades, Geleon, and Hoples, from whom the four Ionian tribes were descended. When Helice's father, Selinus, a king of Aegialea in the Peloponnese, died, Ion ruled the Aegialeans. Just as his foster father Xuthus had gone to Athens as an ally of the Athenians, Ion went to the Athenians' aid in one of their wars with the people of ELEUSIS. Upon defeating the Eleusinians, Ion also became king of Athens.

Ion appears as a character in EURIPIDES' *ION,* which deals with Ion's adoption by Xuthus, his near death through Creusa's plot, his near killing of Creusa, and his discovery that Creusa was his mother and Apollo his father. To SOPHOCLES is attributed an *Ion* of which four brief, uninformative fragments survive (319–22 Radt), but this play may have been confused with Sophocles' *Creusa.* The Greek comic poet Eubulus also wrote an *Ion,* about nine of whose lines survive (fragments 37–39 Kock). The fragments contain references to various foods and banqueting but reveal nothing about the play's plot. [ANCIENT SOURCES: Apollodorus, *Library* 1.7.3, *Epitome* 3.15.1; Pausanias, 1.31.3]

BIBLIOGRAPHY

Kiso, A. *The Lost Sophocles.* New York: Vantage Press, 1984.

Kock, T. Comicorum *Atticorum Fragmenta.* Vol. 2. Leipzig: Teubner, 1884.

Lloyd-Jones, H. *Sophocles: Fragments.* Cambridge, Mass.: Harvard University Press, 1996.

Radt, S. *Tragicorum Graecorum Fragmenta.* Vol. 4. Göttingen, Ger.: Vandenhoeck & Ruprecht, 1977.

Sutton, D. F. *The Lost Sophocles.* Lanham, Md.: University Press of America, 1984.

Zeitlin, F. I. "Mysteries of Identity and Designs of the Self in Euripides' *Ion,*" *Proceedings of the Cambridge Philological Society* 35 (1989): 144–97.

ION EURIPIDES (CA. 420–410 B.C.E.) The play's date is uncertain and based primarily on metrical and thematic tendencies compared with those of other Euripidean plays of the same period. The drama's setting is the temple of APOLLO at DELPHI (compare the opening of AESCHYLUS' *Eumenides* [see ORESTEIA]. The play opens with a monologue by HERMES, who explains that Apollo had raped CREUSA, the daughter of the Athenian king, ERECHTHEUS. Creusa gave birth to a male child and exposed the child in a basket at the foot of the Athenian ACROPOLIS. At Apollo's instruction, Hermes rescued the child and took him to Delphi, where Apollo's priestess raised him. When the child grew up, the Delphians made him guardian of Apollo's treasury. As Hermes' monologue ends, the god reveals that the young man's name is ION (2). Hermes also informs the audience that Creusa later married XUTHUS, who had served as an Athenian ally during a recent war. Because Creusa and Xuthus did not have children of their own, they were traveling to Delphi to inquire about the possibility of offspring. Hermes tells the audience that Apollo will give Ion to Xuthus as his son, and that Ion's descendants will eventually found the Ionian race, who would live in what is today western Turkey.

After Hermes' monologue, Ion emerges from Apollo's temple and sings a joyful MONODY about his service at Apollo's temple. He sweeps the temple area, pours cleansing water on it, and chases away birds that threaten to soil the shrine. Next, the CHORUS, consisting of Athenian women, enter and begin describing the mythological images they see carved on Apollo's temple. They see a portrayal of HERACLES killing the Hydra, BELLEROPHON killing the CHIMAERA, and the gods, including their own patron divinity Athena, battling the GIANTS. The women want to enter the sanctuary, but Ion prevents them, because they have bare feet. The chorus question Ion about the temple and he asks them where they are from. Soon Creusa enters, and Ion addresses her, wondering why she has tears on her face when most people take pleasure at Apollo's temple. Creusa responds by alluding to the outrage Apollo committed against her. Ion does not understand what she means, but goes on to question her about her name and background. When Ion asks about the "Long Rocks," the place in Athens where POSEIDON killed Creusa's father, Erechtheus, this question prompts Creusa's memory that Apollo had attacked her there. Creusa does not explain further but goes on to tell Ion about her marriage to Xuthus and points out that her husband has stopped at the oracular shrine of TROPHONIUS before going to Delphi. When Ion pities their childlessness, Creusa asks about Ion's parents, but he says he does not know his parents' identity. He wonders whether he was born of some shameful act, and Creusa again recalls her own injury. When she tells Ion of a "friend" of hers who claims to have had sexual relations with Apollo and to have produced a child by the god, Ion dismisses this suggestion as impossible. Creusa says she wants to find out whether the child is still alive. Ion, however, suggests that no one will take such a question to Apollo's oracle, because the god would be offended. Creusa, however, maintains that Apollo has wronged this unknown woman and her child. Creusa's reproach of the god ends as her husband, Xuthus, enters.

Xuthus tells Creusa that Trophonius' oracle had told him that he and Creusa would not leave Apollo's oracle without a child. Xuthus soon enters the temple, while Ion and Creusa remain outside. When Creusa steps off to the side of the temple, Ion wonders aloud at Creusa's questions and comments. Ion himself chides Apollo for assaulting a maiden. After Ion's exit, the chorus pray to ATHENA and ARTEMIS for fertility for Creusa. They praise having children but lament Apollo's rape of Creusa and imagine that the exposed child was killed by animals. Soon after the choral ode, Xuthus emerges from Apollo's temple and immediately greets Ion as his son. Ion is puzzled by Xuthus' remarks, and Xuthus reveals that Apollo's oracle has told him that Ion is his son. Xuthus recalls that many years earlier he traveled to Delphi, became drunk at a festival of DIONYSUS, and had intercourse with a young

Delphian woman. Xuthus assumes that Ion was born of this union. Ion accepts the god's oracle but worries about how he will be accepted by the Athenians and Creusa. He asks Xuthus to allow him to continue living at Delphi. Xuthus, however, rejects this idea. He tells Ion that he will take him to Athens as a "sightseer," and will reveal the truth about him when the time is right. Xuthus then tells Ion to prepare a sacrifice and tells the chorus not to reveal any of this to Creusa.

After Ion's departure, the chorus predict the Creusa will be upset by the news that Ion is Xuthus' son, although she herself remains childless. They wonder about Ion's true origin, state that they will tell Creusa about what Xuthus is doing, and pray that Xuthus may come to ruin. They also pray Ion will not go to Athens and pray for his death. After the choral ode, Creusa enters with an old man, who was once the TUTOR of her father, Erechtheus. The chorus inform Creusa that Apollo has given Ion to Xuthus as his son. Creusa is disturbed by this news, and the old tutor predicts that the young man will eventually go to Athens. The tutor says that Xuthus probably had the child in secret when he realized that Creusa could not have children, arranged for a Delphian woman to raise the child, and then decided to take the child to Athens when he grew up. The tutor tells Creusa that she should kill Xuthus and Ion before she herself is killed. At this point, Creusa sings a monody in which she recalls Apollo's assault on her. She recalls giving birth to her son, and exposing him, expresses anger at Apollo, and, as did the chorus earlier, imagines that animals killed the child. The tutor is puzzled by Creusa's outburst, but then she explains to him in plain language about Apollo's assault on her and its consequences. The tutor suggests that Creusa burn down Apollo's temple or kill Xuthus, but she rejects these ideas. Creusa does, however, agree to the tutor's urging that she kill Ion. She decides that she will use some GORGON's poison, contained in a bracelet passed down by Athena to her ancestor, ERICHTHONIUS, who eventually gave it to her father, Erechtheus. The tutor agrees to put the poison into Ion's cup during the offering of libations at the sacrifice.

After the departure of Creusa and the tutor, the chorus sing an ode in which they pray that Ion never become the ruler in Athens. They predict that if her plot fails, she will commit suicide. They express shame that a foreigner should witness in Athens the celebration of the MYSTERIES of Dionysus, DEMETER, and PERSEPHONE. Finally, the women vent their wrath at those who sing of women's love affairs, and reproach men for their love affairs. The chorus' ode is followed by the arrival of a servant, who relates that the plot against Ion has failed. After a lengthy description of the images on the tent in which the ceremony took place, the slave relates that during the ceremony Ion poured some of his wine onto the ground as a libation, and a bird drank some of the wine and died. Ion realized that someone had poisoned the wine and was trying to kill him. Ion apprehended the aged tutor and forced him to reveal Creusa's plot. At that point, the prominent citizens of Delphi voted that Creusa should be stoned to death, but Creusa herself could not be found.

When the chorus hear this news, they fear for their own lives and wonder where they can go to escape. Next, Creusa, trying to escape, enters. The chorus advise her to take refuge at Apollo's altar. Ion enters and threatens to pull her from the altar and throw her down the slopes of Mount Parnassus. Before Ion can commit this violent act, Apollo's priestess emerges from the temple, carrying the basket in which Ion was found when he was an infant. The priestess states that Apollo had inspired her to take out the basket at this particular time. She urges Ion to seek out his mother and then returns to the temple. As Ion wonders what he should do with the basket, Creusa sees the vessel and recognizes it. She leaves Apollo's altar and proceeds to describe the items that she put inside the basket when she exposed Ion years earlier—a weaving with a Gorgon, a golden snake necklace, and a garland of olive. As soon as Ion realizes that she has described the items correctly, he greets Creusa as his mother. Creusa explains that he was born as a result of her union with Apollo and that she had exposed him when he was an infant.

Ion, however, is still troubled by the combination of Creusa's story and Apollo's giving him to Xuthus as his son, so he decides to enter the temple and question Apollo about his real father's identity. At this point, however, Athena appears and prevents Ion from asking Apollo potentially embarrassing questions. Athena tells Ion that Apollo arranged for his rescue from Creusa's plot and that eventually he would have revealed Ion's true parentage in Athens. Athena tells Creusa and Ion to go to Athens and says that eventually Ion will become king, and from him will be born four sons who will be the ancestors of the four tribes of Athens. Athena also predicts that Xuthus and Creusa will have two sons, Doris, founder of the Dorian race, and Achaeus, founder of the Achaean race. Athena then tells Creusa and Ion that they should keep secret the fact that Ion is Creusa's son. Ion accepts that he is Creusa's son by Apollo, and Creusa now expresses her approval of Apollo's actions. The play concludes as Creusa and Ion plan to return to Athens.

COMMENTARY

In recent years, *Ion* has become one of the more popular plays among Euripidean scholars. The action is fast-paced, the characters of Ion and Creusa are compellingly drawn, and the play's imagery is perhaps the most vibrant of any Euripidean drama, with exquisite detail given especially to Apollo's temple at Delphi and the tent in which Ion will celebrate his adoption. Controversy regarding the play has surrounded Euripides' portrayal of Apollo as well as the play's genre: Some consider it a COMEDY, others a TRAGEDY, and others a blending of the two.

The figure of Xuthus is quite comic. His efforts to embrace Ion after discovering that the young man will be his son and Ion's homophobic reaction to Xuthus' actions could have been quite amusing. A touch of humor may be found in Xuthus' threat to the Athenian women that death awaits them if they do not keep quiet about Ion (666–67). The women immediately tell Creusa what has transpired between Xuthus and Ion. The circumstances surrounding Xuthus' recollection of how Ion might have been conceived (545–53) have many parallels in the New Comedy of later years, in which it is quite common for a child to be born after a young man, drunk at a religious festival, sexually assaults a maiden (compare especially PLAUTUS, *THE CASKET COMEDY* 156–87). The words and deeds of the aged tutor, with his complaints about the difficulty of making it up the mountain at Delphi and the laughter that he drew while serving the guests at Ion's banquet (1172), are balanced by the potentially tragic plot of which he is a part.

Overall, the tone of the play appears serious. Creusa's attempt on Ion's life and Ion's own threats to kill Creusa are certainly the stuff of tragedy, yet both attempts fail. Ion's threat to question Apollo directly about the god's actions and intent would put Ion in a dangerous relationship with the god, as he himself realizes (1385–86). This, too, never comes to pass. Apollo's rape of Creusa is of great concern in the play and is treated with seriousness. By the play's end, however, even Apollo's victim, Creusa, understands the god's actions and joyfully clings to the knocker on the door of Apollo's temple (1611–13).

The play's most dominant image, the serpent (either protective or destructive), is frequently linked with one of the play's most prominent themes, autochthony (originating from the earth). The root of the second half of the word *autochthony, chthon,* is a Greek word for "earth," and the people of Athens had a tradition that their ancestors sprang up from the earth. In the play's prologue, Hermes informs the audience that Creusa abandoned Ion in the same cave in which Apollo assaulted her. Thus, when Hermes rescues Ion, Ion experiences a figurative rebirth from the ground. Additionally, Creusa leaves a golden necklace with two intertwined serpents with Ion when she abandons him. She gives this necklace to him in accordance with a custom established by Athena, who placed two real serpents into a basket in which she had placed the infant ERICHTHONIUS, the future Athenian king (14–27). Not only does the serpent necklace serve as a protective charm for Ion, but it also links him with a past king of Athens who Euripides also tells us was born from the earth (20). Interestingly, Ion's foster father, Xuthus, also experiences a sort of birth from the ground: His visit to the oracle of Trophonius is mentioned several times in the play (300, 393, 405), and Euripides' audience was probably aware that a visit to this oracle involved a subterranean descent and reemergence. Note also that Xuthus' predecessor as king of Athens, Creusa's father, Erechtheus, was swallowed up by the earth (281–82) when Poseidon killed him for killing his (Poseidon's) son, Eumolpus.

Ion, figuratively reborn from the earth and under the protection of a golden-serpent necklace, is taken to Delphi, a place that also has several connections with serpents. Though the point is not mentioned in Euripides' play, his audience would have been aware that Delphi's lord, Apollo, was famous for killing a serpent known as the Python. On Apollo's temple, the chorus observe a depiction of Heracles' battling and defeating the HYDRA of Lerna, a dangerous water snake. Also on the temple, the chorus note a representation of Athena, who brandishes her shield at the Giant Enceladus. The women recognize the goddess from the protective image of a Gorgon, whose hair was composed of snakes (210). Later, Ion points out to the chorus Delphi's navel stone, which marked the center of the world as the Greeks knew it. This stone was ringed with the protective images of Gorgons (224).

Thus, surrounded by the images of protective serpents, Ion grew up at Delphi. After he learns that he will be adopted by Xuthus, Ion has further encounters with serpents. Some of the earliest Athenians were also said to be part human, part serpent. The cloth that covers the tent in which Ion celebrates his adoption has near its doorway the image of the early Athenian king CECROPS, whose dual aspects as a serpent and human are depicted on the tent's fabric and who, according to tradition, emerged from the earth (1163–64). As with the earlier necklace of Erichthonius, the image of Cecrops links Ion with another earth-born Athenian king. Furthermore, as with the necklace that protected Ion after his figurative rebirth from the cave in Athens, the image of Cecrops will protect Ion as he experiences a figurative rebirth from the tent as Xuthus' son and the future king of Athens. Ion will need this protection because his mother, Creusa, plots to take his life. According to Creusa, the poison she uses against him is from the blood of the serpentine Gorgon, which Athena killed whose skin she used for her shield (991–96). Furthermore, at line 989, Creusa notes that this Gorgon was born from the earth (or the goddess EARTH).

For Ion, however, the death-bearing poison from this serpentine creature is counterbalanced by the other protective serpent images at Delphi. A bird drinks the poison instead of Ion. When Ion realizes that Creusa has tried to poison him, he is enraged and calls her both an echidna (a monster that was part female, part serpent) and a serpent (1262–63). Now, Ion threatens to kill his mother. Eventually, however,

the serpent protects Creusa. When Apollo's priestess carries out the items that were left with Ion at his birth, Creusa identifies, among other things, a blanket that has the image of a Gorgon on it (1421) and the golden serpent necklace (1427–29). Thus, as did his father, Apollo, Ion overcomes the serpent, his mother, in a figurative way by avoiding being killed by the Gorgon's poison. At the same time, however, the images of the Gorgon and serpent protect Creusa herself.

BIBLIOGRAPHY
Burnett, A. P. "Human Resistance and Divine Persuasion in Euripides' *Ion*," *Classical Philology* 57 (1962): 98–103.
Goff, B. "Euripides' *Ion* 1132–1165: The Tent," *Proceedings of the Cambridge Philological Society* 34 (1988): 42–54.
Lee, K. H. *Euripides: Ion.* Warminster, U.K.: Aris & Phillips, 1997.
Loraux, N. "Autochthonous Kreousa: Euripides, *Ion.*" In *The Children of Athena.* Translated by C. Levine. Princeton, N.J.: Princeton University Press, 1993, 184–236.
Wolff, C. "The Design and Myth in Euripides' *Ion*," *Harvard Studies in Classical Philology* 69 (1965): 169–94.
Zeitlin, F. I. "Mysteries of Identity and Designs of the Self in Euripides' *Ion*," *Proceedings of the Cambridge Philological Society* 35 (1989): 144–97.

IONIAN SEA   The body of water by the coasts of southwestern Greece, southern Italy, and SICILY. According to legend, it took its name from IO, who traveled to this sea in the course of her wanderings. [ANCIENT SOURCES: Aeschylus, *Prometheus Bound* 840; Euripides, *Phoenician Women* 208; Seneca, *Agamemnon* 506, 565, *Hercules Oetaeus* 731, *Hippolytus* 1012, *Oedipus* 603, *Phoenician Women* 610, *Thyestes* 478]

IONIANS   One of the two major groups (the DORIANS were the other) who made up the Greek people. The Ionians spoke the Ionic dialect of Greek and inhabited the region around Athens, the island of EUBOEA, several AEGEAN islands, and the central part of the western coast of modern Turkey. The people of ATHENS regarded the Ionians as having descended from ION, the son of APOLLO, although even some ancients recognized that this lineage was inaccurate. Sometimes the playwrights make the name Ionians synonymous with Athenians. [ANCIENT SOURCES: Aeschylus, *Persians*

771; Aristophanes, *Ecclesiazusae* 883, 918, *Peace* 46, 577, 930, 933, *Thesmophoriazusae* 163; Euripides, *Ion* 1588; Herodotus, 1.455–48; Plautus, *Persian* 826, *Pseudolus* 1275, *Stichus* 769; Thucydides, 1.12]

IOPHON   Son of the tragic poet SOPHOCLES, Iophon himself also wrote tragedies (perhaps as many as 50), although his father was thought to have helped him in his writing. Iophon won a victory in competition in the 430s and finished second to EURIPIDES' HIPPOLYTUS in 428 B.C.E. [ANCIENT SOURCES: Argument to Euripides' *Hippolytus;* Aristophanes, *Frogs* 73–79; *Life of Sophocles; Suda* on "Iophon"]

IPHIANASSA   A daughter of AGAMEMNON and CLYTEMNESTRA, Iphianassa was the sister of ELECTRA, ORESTES, CHRYSOTHEMIS, and IPHIGENIA, although in the earliest reference to Iphianassa in Greek literature (in HOMER's *Iliad*), Iphianassa was probably another name for Iphigenia. [ANCIENT SOURCES: Homer, *Iliad* 9.145; Sophocles, *Electra* 157].

IPHIGENIA   The daughter of AGAMEMNON and CLYTEMNESTRA, Iphigenia was the sister of CHRYSOTHEMIS, ELECTRA, and ORESTES. AESCHYLUS wrote an *Iphigenia* (no longer extant), which presumably dealt with the same subject matter as EURIPIDES' IPHIGENIA AT AULIS. The fate of Iphigenia differs from playwright to playwright. In AESCHYLUS' AGAMEMNON, Agamemnon sacrifices Iphigenia at Aulis. In Euripides' IPHIGENIA AT AULIS, Iphigenia is rescued at the last moment by ARTEMIS' substitution of a deer at the altar. In Euripides' IPHIGENIA IN TAURIS, the events of which occur after Iphigenia's sacrifice, in which she vanishes as the blade falls on her neck, Iphigenia is alive and serves as the priestess of Artemis in the kingdom of Thoas, ruler of the Taurians. After her brother, ORESTES, and his friend, PYLADES, arrive in Tauris and are captured by the Taurians, the two men are taken to Iphigenia, who will participate in a ritual that will culminate in their sacrifice to Artemis. Before this horrific event happens, however, Iphigenia discovers their true identity and agrees to help them escape. Furthermore, she helps them steal a statue of Artemis that APOLLO's oracle had instructed Orestes to retrieve.

After escaping from Tauris with Orestes, Pylades, and the statue, Iphigenia returns to Greece and pays a visit to the DELPHIC ORACLE. Iphigenia's sister, Electra, also happens to be at Delphi because she had heard a rumor that Orestes and Pylades had been sacrificed in Tauris. When someone sees Iphigenia and tells Electra that she is the woman who had sacrificed the two men, Electra tries to blind Iphigenia. Fortunately, Orestes arrives in time to prevent her, and the three family members are reunited. Iphigenia takes the statue of Artemis to Brauron, a town not far east of Athens. At Brauron, Iphigenia resumes her life as a priestess of Artemis and there she dies.

As one would expect, the characterization of Iphigenia differs given the situation in which she finds herself. In *Iphigenia at Aulis,* Iphigenia is a noble young woman who willingly gives up her life to save Greece from the threat of Trojan aggression. In this respect, she most recalls two of Euripides' other sacrificial maidens: Macaria in CHILDREN OF HERACLES and POLYXENA in HECABE. In *Iphigenia in Tauris,* Iphigenia serves as perhaps the prototype for HELEN in Euripides' play of the same name, which was performed in the year after *Iphigenia in Tauris.* Iphigenia loyally serves as priestess of Taurian Artemis, but when she discovers that her brother, Orestes, will be sacrificed to the goddess she serves, she constructs a clever plot that takes advantage of the superstition of the barbarian king, Thoas. In Euripides' HELEN, the title character tricks the barbarian king, Theoclymenus, by concocting a false burial ritual that will allow her to escape with her husband, Menelaus, just as Iphigenia is able to escape with her brother in the earlier play.

In addition to the plays by Aeschylus and Euripides mentioned, works of several other playwrights treated Iphigenia's story. Aeschylus is said to have written an *Iphigenia,* but only a single line survives (fragment 94 Radt); Lloyd-Jones thinks the play was about Iphigenia's sacrifice at Aulis. The Greek comic poet Rhinthon wrote both *Iphigenia at Aulis* and *Iphigenia in Tauris,* of which only the title survives from the former play and a single line from the latter (fragment 7 Kaibel). Among Roman authors, NAEVIUS wrote an *Iphigenia,* of which four lines survive. Warmington thinks Naevius' play may have dealt with the events in Euripides'

Iphigenia in Tauris, and the few fragments that survive support this idea.

BIBLIOGRAPHY

Cropp, M. J. *Euripides: Iphigenia in Tauris.* Warminster, U.K.: Aris & Phillips, 2000, 43–56.

Kaibel, G. *Comicorum Graecorum Fragmenta.* Vol. 1.1 [*Poetarum Graecorum Fragmenta.* Vol. 6.1]. Berlin: Weidmann, 1899.

Smyth, H. W., and H. Lloyd-Jones. *Aeschylus.* Vol. 2. 1926. Reprint, Cambridge, Mass.: Harvard University Press, 1971.

Warmington, E. H. *Remains of Old Latin: Livius Andronicus, Naevius, Pacuvius, and Accius.* Vol. 2. Cambridge, Mass.: Harvard University Press, 1936.

IPHIGENIA AT AULIS EURIPIDES (405 B.C.E.)

EURIPIDES wrote *Iphigenia at Aulis* during the final years of his life. Euripides' son first staged the play after his father's death. The play deals with the gathering of the Greek fleet at AULIS, from which they would launch their expedition against TROY to recover HELEN. After the Greeks assembled, adverse weather prevented them from sailing. AGAMEMNON, commander of the Greek forces, consulted the prophet CALCHAS to discover a remedy for the weather. Calchas predicted ARTEMIS, the offended divinity, could be appeased only by the sacrifice of Agamemnon's daughter, IPHIGENIA.

The action of the play occurs outside Agamemnon's tent in the Greeks' camp at Aulis. The play opens just before dawn, as Agamemnon discusses with a family servant the dilemma of the prophecy about his daughter. Caught between his feelings as a father and the clamor of the Greek army, Agamemnon had sent a messenger to ARGOS to summon Iphigenia to Aulis with the pretext that she was to marry ACHILLES; Achilles himself knew nothing about this plot. Agamemnon now sends the family servant to Argos to tell CLYTEMNESTRA not to send Iphigenia to Aulis.

After the departure of the family servant, the CHORUS, consisting of women from Chalcis on the island of Euboea, enter. They have arrived to see the assembly of the Greek forces and sing an ode of almost 150 lines, in which they describe various Greek warriors. After the women's song, MENELAUS drags in Agamemnon's family servant, whom he has prevented from delivering his message. Menelaus and Agamemnon then debate whether Iphigenia should be sacrificed. Agamemnon decides to preserve his daughter's life, rather than yield to the desire of Menelaus and other Greeks to wage war against Troy. After Menelaus departs, a messenger enters, announcing the impending arrival of Clytemnestra and Iphigenia. After this announcement, Agamemnon again wavers in his resolve. Menelaus, after listening to his brother's concerns, changes his mind and now urges Agamemnon not to kill Iphigenia. Upon hearing Menelaus, however, Agamemnon has decided that the wishes of the army and the persuasive tongue of ODYSSEUS will compel them to sacrifice Iphigenia.

After Agamemnon and Menelaus depart to discuss the situation further, the chorus sing an ODE to APHRODITE in which they note the goddess' power and pray that she visits them in moderation. They also sing of the glories of virtue and recall PARIS' judgment of the goddesses, which caused the impending war. As their song concludes, they note the arrival of Iphigenia and Clytemnestra in their carriage.

The women are soon met by Agamemnon, whom Iphigenia greets excitedly in anticipation of her wedding to Achilles. Iphigenia notes that her father appears troubled, but Agamemnon does not reveal the truth. He does tell her, however, that before he departs for Troy he must offer a sacrifice at which Iphigenia will be present. At this, Agamemnon begins to break down into tears and sends his daughter into his tent. Next, Agamemnon turns to converse with his wife. Clytemnestra questions him about Achilles' ancestry and background and the preparations for the wedding. When Clytemnestra hears that Agamemnon intends to perform some of the roles customarily taken care of by the mother of the bride and that Agamemnon wants Clytemnestra to return to Argos, Clytemnestra is outraged by this potential breach of custom. Clytemnestra refuses to leave and enters Agamemnon's tent to make preparations for the wedding. Agamemnon, confused as to his next move, exits to consult with the prophet, Calchas. After Agamemnon's exit, the chorus sing an ode that anticipates the arrival of the Greek army at

Troy and the death and hardship the Greeks will inflict on the Trojans. The chorus also pray that they never experience abduction, as Menelaus' wife, Helen, has.

After the choral ode, Achilles enters and encounters his future mother-in-law, Clytemnestra. Agamemnon's plan now moves closer to disaster as Clytemnestra questions a baffled Achilles about his upcoming marriage to her daughter. When Achilles expresses ignorance of the wedding, Clytemnestra becomes troubled. Their ignorance ends, however, when an old servant of Clytemnestra's enters from Agamemnon's tent and informs Achilles and Clytemnestra that Agamemnon intends to sacrifice Iphigenia. Clytemnestra is horrified by this news and asks Achilles for help. Achilles is angered to hear that he has been implicated in this plot without his knowledge and vows to help Iphigenia. Clytemnestra is pleased by the words of Achilles, who urges Clytemnestra to beg Agamemnon not to kill Iphigenia. If Agamemnon rejects Clytemnestra's plea, then Clytemnestra should call in Achilles to help. These matters agreed upon, Achilles and Clytemnestra exit. The chorus then sing an ode that recalls the marriage of Achilles' parents, PELEUS and THETIS. At the wedding, which was attended by the gods themselves, APOLLO predicted that the couple would bear a son (Achilles), who would wage war successfully against the Trojans. The chorus then contrast the marriage of Peleus and Thetis with the "marriage" that Iphigenia will soon experience.

After the choral ode, Clytemnestra emerges from Agamemnon's tent and notes that Iphigenia has been informed of what her father intends. Agamemnon himself soon emerges and informs his wife that preparations have been made for the marriage sacrifice to ARTEMIS. Iphigenia, accompanied by the infant ORESTES, is summoned from the tent. At this point, Clytemnestra confronts Agamemnon about his true purpose and forces him to admit the truth. Clytemnestra goes on to plead for Iphigenia's life and Iphigenia pleads for compassion. Agamemnon, however, states that he must sacrifice her for the sake of all Greece. Hearing this, Iphigenia sings a lament that recalls that Paris should have died after his birth but was rescued and eventually grew up to judge the beauty of goddesses, a judgment that eventually led to PARIS' abduction of

Helen, which has in turn led to Iphigenia's current dire situation.

After Iphigenia's song, Achilles approaches and informs Clytemnestra and Iphigenia that the army is clamoring for the sacrifice of Iphigenia. Achilles states that he tried to argue against the sacrifice, but the army threatened to stone him. Still, Achilles tells Clytemnestra that he is willing to fight the entire army single-handedly, although the soldiers, led by Odysseus, intend to seize Iphigenia and drag her to the altar by force. At this point, Iphigenia breaks in, announces that she should not oppose the will of the gods, and states that for Greece to be saved she must give up her life. Achilles praises Iphigenia's nobility and tells her that he will be ready to defend her if she changes her mind. Clytemnestra weeps for her child, but Iphigenia tells her mother that her (Iphigenia's) sacrifice will yield glory for both her and her mother. Clytemnestra wants to accompany Iphigenia to the altar, but Iphigenia persuades her to stay behind. After Clytemnestra exits into Agamemnon's tent, Iphigenia, accompanied by the chorus, sings a song of procession as she prepares to depart for the altar.

Not long after Iphigenia exits to be sacrificed, a messenger enters, calls Clytemnestra from the tent, and informs her of the amazing events that occurred at the sacrifice. The messenger reports Iphigenia's bravery and noble words before the sacrifice and the various aspects of the ritual. When Calchas, however, attempted to strike Iphigenia, the young woman vanished from sight and a slain deer appeared on the altar. Upon seeing this, Calchas announced that Artemis was appeased and they could now sail for Troy. The messenger declares that Iphigenia must have been taken up by the gods. Soon, Agamemnon enters, tells Clytemnestra to be happy in Iphigenia's fate, and to take Orestes back to Argos, and says that it will be a long time before he sees her again. The play ends as the chorus wish Agamemnon good fortune at Troy.

COMMENTARY

When he wrote *Iphigenia in Aulis,* Euripides was more than 70 years old and had recently left Athens to live at the court of the Macedonian king, Archelaus. Athens was in the third decade of its war with Sparta and its allies, and in 404 Athens would surrender. With its subjects of war and the sacrifice of a young, unmarried person, *Iphigenia at Aulis* bears many similarities to earlier Euripidean plays such as CHILDREN OF HERACLES, HECABE, PHOENICIAN WOMEN, and the no-longer extant Erechtheus. Iphigenia at Aulis differs, however, because its title character is miraculously rescued at the play's conclusion. More than 50 years earlier, Aeschylus had treated the sacrifice of Iphigenia in *Agamemnon* (see ORESTEIA), but in that play Agamemnon kills Iphigenia.

As did Euripides' earlier HECABE, *Iphigenia at Aulis* gives much attention to slavery versus freedom. At line 330, Menelaus rejects his brother Agamemnon's outrage at his meddling by declaring that he is not his brother's slave. After Agamemnon decides that he will sacrifice his daughter, he laments that this sacrifice will occur because he, a nobleman and king, is actually a servant to the masses (449–50). Eventually, it is a slave whom Clytemnestra gave to Agamemnon as part of her dowry who reveals to Clytemnestra Agamemnon's plan to sacrifice Iphigenia (858ff.). After learning this, Clytemnestra appeals to Achilles for help. Achilles says he will assist her and declares that his free nature (930) allows him to fight both at Troy and at Aulis because Agamemnon has ceased to behave in a proper manner. When he agrees, Clytemnestra recognizes him as her powerful protector, and the queen of Argos declares that she must become a servant to Achilles (1033). Later, when Agamemnon is confronted with the truth, he explains to Iphigenia and Clytemnestra that it is not Menelaus who has enslaved him to this course of action, but Hellas (Greece) itself who demands Iphigenia's sacrifice whether he is willing or not and that he must preserve the freedom of Greece from the barbarians (1269–75). Ultimately, Iphigenia decides that she must lose her life. Setting the Greeks free from the barbarians will ensure her great fame (1383–84). Furthermore, Iphigenia declares that Greeks should rule barbarians rather than the converse because barbarians are slaves and Greeks are free (1400–1).

Another of the prominent topics dealt with in *Iphigenia at Aulis*, as Foley has well discussed, is marriage: the marriage ritual and the similarity between the marriage ritual and the sacrificial ritual. Foley writes: "The structure of the Iphigenia hangs on the performance of a sacrificial ritual that is disguised for a large part of the action as a fictitious marriage rite." Throughout the play, one finds references to unusual marriages. The marriage of Helen and Menelaus has some unusual features. At lines 68–69, Agamemnon recalls that Helen's father, TYNDAREUS, allowed his daughter to choose whichever suitor she wanted as a husband. This choice would have been unusual for a Greek woman, because a marriage was usually arranged by the father and prospective husband and the woman had virtually no say in the matter. A further unusual feature of Helen and Menelaus' marriage was that Helen's father, Tyndareus, persuaded Helen's suitors to take an oath that they would go to Menelaus' aid if anything happened to her (77–79). Such an oath would not have been a usual part of a marriage of Greeks.

Not only were the circumstances surrounding Helen and Menelaus' marriage unusual, but then that marriage bond was breached and the Trojan War was caused when their marriage was disrupted by the abduction of Helen by Paris, whom Agamemnon describes as a barbarian shepherd (71–77). Agamemnon also faults Helen, who he claims was in love with Paris (75). In Greek mythology, marriage unions between Greeks and barbarians are invariably doomed to failure and/or disaster. To repair the breach in Menelaus and Helen's marriage, Agamemnon will lead to Troy a coalition of Greeks, whose chief warriors were former suitors of Helen and who were bound to fight by their oath to Tyndareus.

When adverse weather prevents the Greeks from sailing, Calchas prophesies that Agamemnon must sacrifice his daughter to Artemis to resolve the situation. To achieve his purpose, Agamemnon decides to lure Iphigenia to Aulis under the pretense that she is to marry Achilles (100–5), a marriage that Agamemnon expects will actually be a marriage with the lord of the UNDERWORLD, Hades. Agamemnon's primary opposition will be his wife, Clytemnestra. The marriage of Clytemnestra and Agamemnon was not harmonious from the start. As Clytemnestra reminds Agamemnon at lines 1149–52, she did not marry him of her own free will; he forced her to marry him after he killed her husband, Tantalus. Agamemnon also killed Clytemnestra's child by Tantalus. Thus, not only does Agamemnon's brother, Menelaus, have a marriage that was the result of unusual circumstances, but Agamemnon's marriage to Helen's sister, Clytemnestra, also began in a bizarre way.

Agamemnon further perverts the marriage process by not informing Iphigenia's supposed future groom about the wedding. Achilles himself, as we learn in a choral ode (1036–79), was the product of an unusual union. Achilles' father was a mortal, and his mother was immortal. The chorus recall that their wedding was attended by, among others, gods and centaurs. Earlier in the play Clytemnestra was astonished to learn that the wedding occurred in the place where the centaurs lived (706).

When Clytemnestra and Iphigenia arrive at Aulis, their first encounter with Agamemnon is a happy one for the women, but bitter and filled with irony for Agamemnon. Before he leaves for Troy, he tells his daughter that he must offer a sacrifice at which Iphigenia will be present. Offering a sacrifice before marriage was a common part of the Greek ritual (Artemis herself received such sacrifices), and Iphigenia innocently wonders whether she will lead the dance around the altar (676). As we learn later, the altar will be circled, but Achilles, Iphigenia's false husband, will circle it and pray to Artemis to accept the Greeks' sacrifice of Iphigenia (1568–76).

The fact that the alleged wedding of Iphigenia and Achilles will be held in the midst of the Greek army also is unusual. Clytemnestra notes but accepts the necessity that the usual feast for the women will occur near the ships (722–24). Clytemnestra, however, is more troubled by Agamemnon's intention to give away the bride and for her to return to Argos (728–32). When Agamemnon also indicates that he will replace Clytemnestra in carrying the bridal torch, Clytemnestra declares, "This is not customary" (732–36). Clytemnestra is so upset by Agamemnon's perversion of marriage customs that she storms out and leaves Agamemnon worrying whether his scheme will succeed.

Ultimately, as Agamemnon's scheme begins to become reality, perversions of the marriage ritual continue. Animal victims were decked with garlands and flowers before sacrifice and new brides also wore gar-

lands. Accordingly, once Iphigenia learns of and accepts her role in this perverse marriage, she herself calls for flowers to crown her (1477–78). A purifying ritual bath was part of both the Greek wedding ritual and animal sacrifices and such a bath is alluded to several times in the play. Once Iphigenia discovers what her father actually has in mind for her, she bravely and willingly accepts her role in the sacrifice and calls for water for the bath (1479), although she now knows that the water anticipates a deadly, not a happy ritual.

Typically, the new bride would live in the house of her new husband, but because Iphigenia will die, the home of her new husband will be the underworld. Iphigenia's marriage will not result in the birth of her own children, but in the salvation of the children and marriage of all Greece.

BIBLIOGRAPHY

Foley, H. P. *Ritual Irony: Poetry and Sacrifice in Euripides.* Ithaca, N.Y.: Cornell University Press, 1985, 65–105.

Luschnig, C. A. E. *Tragic Aporia: A Study of Euripides' Iphigenia at Aulis.* Berwick, Australia: Aureal, 1988.

Schmidt, J. "Iphigenie in Aulis: Spiegel einer zerbrechenden Welt und Grenzpunkt der Dichtung?" *Philologus* 143, no. 2 (1999): 211–48.

Siegel, H. "Self-Delusion and the Volte-Face of Iphigenia in Euripides' *Iphigenia at Aulis,*" *Hermes* 108 (1980): 300–21.

Zeitlin, F. I. "Art, Memory, and Kleos in Euripides' *Iphigenia in Aulis.*" In *History, Tragedy, Theory: Dialogues on Athenian Drama.* Edited by B. Goff. Austin: University of Texas Press, 1995, 174–201.

IPHIGENIA IN TAURIS EURIPIDES (414 OR 413 B.C.E.)

The play concerns the reunion of IPHIGENIA and her brother, ORESTES. The drama's action occurs before the temple of ARTEMIS at Tauris, a town located in the Black Sea region. The play opens as Iphigenia enters from the temple and traces her descent from PELOPS. She also recalls her near-sacrifice by her father, AGAMEMNON, at Aulis, and her miraculous transportation by Artemis to Tauris, a barbaric land where the king, Thoas, sacrifices to Artemis all Greek males who land on his shores. Saved by Artemis at Aulis, Iphigenia in Tauris now serves the goddess as her priestess by consecrating the human victims for sacrifice. Iphigenia also informs the audience of a dream she had about her home in ARGOS. The house was destroyed except a single pillar that had golden hair and a human voice. Iphigenia dreamed that she consecrated the pillar for death in her usual way. Iphigenia concludes that the dream refers to her long-lost brother, ORESTES, and that she has participated in his sacrifice.

After Iphigenia's monologue, she returns to the interior of the temple. Next, Orestes and PYLADES enter from the direction of the sea and state their intention to steal the statue of Artemis, a task commanded of Orestes by the DELPHIC ORACLE. The two Greeks then exit to a hiding place from which they can make their next move. After their exit, Iphigenia and the chorus, composed of female Greek captives who serve Iphigenia, enter. When the chorus ask Iphigenia why she has summoned them, she informs them about her dream and her belief that her brother, Orestes, is dead. Iphigenia then proceeds to pour a libation to Hades for her brother and laments that she will not make offerings at his grave. The chorus and Iphigenia then sing laments in turn for the troubles experienced by Iphigenia's ancestors, such as ATREUS THYESTES, and by Iphigenia herself at Aulis, and by Orestes.

After their lament, a Taurian herdsman enters and informs Iphigenia that they have captured two Greeks whom they soon will be take to Artemis' temple for sacrifice. The herdsman says the name of one is Pylades, and the other's name is unknown. The unknown Greek, however, experienced an attack by the FURIES that helped him and the other herdsman to subdue the two Greeks. Upon hearing this story, Iphigenia tells the herdsman to take the Greeks to her. After the herdsman's departure, the thought of sacrificing these two Greeks reminds her of her own near sacrifice. She complains that Artemis does not permit someone who has had contact with blood or death to approach her altars yet demands human sacrifice in Tauris. After this, Iphigenia returns to the temple's interior and the chorus sing an ode in which they wonder who the two captive Greeks are and how they managed to make the dangerous voyage to the land of the Taurians. The women wish that HELEN had arrived in Tauris and been sacrificed.

After the choral ode, the two Greeks are taken in and meet Iphigenia, who, on learning that they are Greeks from Argos, questions them about various events and people (Helen, MENELAUS, CALCHAS, ODYSSEUS, and ACHILLES; her father, Agamemnon; her mother, CLYTEMNESTRA; her sister, ELECTRA). Iphigenia also questions Orestes about Orestes, but he does not reveal his identity. Hearing that Orestes knows so much about people in her family, she tells Orestes she will save him if he takes her letter to Argos. Orestes, however, refuses, because that would require Pylades' death. After Iphigenia says she will send Pylades with the letter, she reenters the temple to get the letter. Upon Iphigenia's departure, Orestes and Pylades marvel at how much Iphigenia knows about Greek affairs. Pylades also notes that he cannot allow Orestes to die and declares that he will stay with him. Orestes, however, convinces Pylades that he (Orestes) should die and Pylades return to Argos and to Electra, Orestes' sister, to whom Pylades is married.

At this point, Iphigenia returns from the temple with the letter. After making Pylades take an oath that he will take her letter back to Argos, she recites the letter's contents in case the letter is lost. In the letter, Iphigenia informs Orestes that she is alive and begs him to rescue her from Tauris. When Iphigenia gives Pylades the letter, Pylades immediately turns to Orestes and hands it to him. Orestes quickly greets Iphigenia as his sister and tries to embrace her. Iphigenia, however, is not convinced that he is her brother. After further interrogation, however, Iphigenia recognizes Orestes as her brother (Orestes' knowledge of a spear that Iphigenia had in her bedroom convinces her).

After a joyful reunion, Iphigenia's expression of horror that she had almost participated in the sacrifice of her brother, and the introduction to Iphigenia of Pylades, who she now learns is her brother-in-law, Orestes tells her further of his killing of their mother, his persecution by the Furies, and the reason why he is in Tauris. Upon hearing this, Iphigenia ponders how to help Orestes acquire Artemis' statue, avoid the wrath of Thoas, and escape from Tauris. Much as Helen does in Euripides' play of the next year, Iphigenia devises a plot to trick the barbarian king, Thoas. Iphigenia will tell Thoas that Orestes, who had killed his mother, defiled the statue. Accordingly, Iphigenia will say that she must take the statue and Orestes to be purified in the sea.

After the men agree to her plan, the trio enter the temple. The chorus then sing an ode in which they recall their enslavement and express their desire to return to Greece and rejoin their friends in their native land.

After the choral ode, Thoas enters in search of Iphigenia, who soon enters from the temple with the statue of Artemis in her arms. She tells Thoas that the statue turned on its base and averted its eyes because the two Greeks were defiled. When Iphigenia explains the need to purify the statue and the two Greeks, Thoas agrees to let this ritual take place. Iphigenia also warns Thoas to make sure that he and the Taurians remain inside their houses and avoid approaching the place of the ritual. At this point, Iphigenia instructs Thoas to cover his eyes while the Greeks are taken from the temple. After Iphigenia and Greek men leave the temple, they exit toward the seashore. After their departure, the chorus sing an ode in which they recall the birth of Apollo, his arrival at DELPHI and his destruction there of the Python, and his wresting of the Delphic oracle from the goddess THEMIS. To thwart Apollo's prophetic powers, Themis sent dreams to human beings. When Apollo complained about this to his father, ZEUS, Zeus put an end to Themis' sending dreams to mortals.

After the chorus' song, a messenger enters from the shore and informs the chorus and Thoas that Iphigenia, Orestes, and Pylades have taken the statue aboard Orestes' ship and attempted to sail away after battling a group of Taurians. The messenger also informs Thoas that an adverse sea and wind were preventing the ship from getting away, despite Iphigenia's prayers to Artemis. Upon hearing this, Thoas gives orders to pursue the Greeks, but any further hostility is prevented by the appearance of ATHENA, who stops Thoas. Athena also instructs Orestes to set up in Athenian territory a temple to house Artemis' statue on his return to Greece. Athena tells Iphigenia that she will be Artemis' priestess at this new temple. Finally, Athena orders Thoas to return the chorus to Greece. The play concludes with Thoas agreeing to all that Athena orders and the chorus wishing the Greeks a successful voyage and offering praise to Athena.

COMMENTARY

Iphigenia in Tauris is a drama whose action is lively but whose tone and themes lack the seriousness and pathos of other plays about Orestes and his family. Orestes is not faced with the horrific prospect of killing his mother and her lover, as in AESCHYLUS' *Libation Bearers* (see ORESTEIA) or the *Electra* plays by SOPHOCLES or Euripides; nor will Orestes experience the tension of a trial for his mother's death at the hands of the Furies, as in Aeschylus' *Eumenides* (see ORESTEIA). At the conclusion of *Iphigenia in Tauris,* Athena reveals that Orestes has already undergone this trial, but elsewhere in the play we hear that the Furies continue to pursue Orestes. Other than the short episode in the first part of the play (282–308), in which the Taurian herdsman describes Orestes' Fury-induced fit, the Furies have little visible role in the play and do not appear onstage as in *Eumenides.* Similarly, Iphigenia does not face the prospect of being sacrificed by her father, as alluded to several times in Aeschylus' AGAMEMNON and dramatized by Euripides himself several years after *Iphigenia in Tauris.*

Many scholars have noticed that the plot of *Iphigenia in Tauris* has several similarities to that of HELEN, staged the year after *Iphigenia.* Both plays involve women who have been transported by the gods into a land populated by barbarians who customarily do violence to Greek males. In both plays, the women are reunited with their loved ones. After the reunion, Greeks must escape from barbaric lands. In both plays, the women contrive the plot, which involves the falsification of a ritual, to escape the barbaric land. After the Greeks escape, the respective barbarian kings threaten violence but are prevented from carrying it out by the appearance of divinities. In both plays, the Greeks return to their native land with expectation of a "happy" life.

Helene Foley has classified *Iphigenia,* just as ALCESTIS and *Helen,* as an *anodos* drama. Foley thoroughly discusses this approach to the play with respect to *Alcestis* and *Helen* but does not elaborate on *Iphigenia* as an *anodos* drama. The Greek word *anodos* means "a way up," and Foley compares the plots of *Alcestis* and *Helen* to the experience of PERSEPHONE, her abduction by Hades, her eventual return from the UNDERWORLD, and her reunion with her mother, DEMETER. Thus, Iphigenia, as does Persephone, has a traumatic experience in which she is whisked away to a different world. This world is unlike her homeland and is a land where a cruel king (Thoas substitutes for Hades) detains a young woman. Eventually, the gods intervene and the young woman is restored to loved ones. We may note, however, that *Iphigenia in Tauris* does not correspond to the *anodos* drama model as well as *Alcestis* and *Helen* do. Although Tauris is a land of barbarians, Iphigenia's miraculous journey to Tauris saved her life; it did not end it. In addition, unlike in the case of Hades and Persephone or THEOCLYMENUS and Helen, Thoas does not want to marry Iphigenia.

One focal point in *Iphigenia* is salvation. Iphigenia's presence in Tauris is a result of Artemis' rescue of her at Aulis, a story to which reference is made several times in the play. In *Iphigenia in Tauris,* Euripides reverses the sequence of events at Aulis. At Aulis, the male tries to sacrifice the female. In Tauris, the female will sacrifice the male. Ironically, Orestes will be saved by Iphigenia in exchange for Pylades' taking her letter to Orestes (594). After the reunion of brother and sister, Pylades, whom Orestes calls his savior (923), urges Iphigenia and Orestes to consider how to effect their salvation from Tauris (905). Now Iphigenia comes to the rescue as she devises a plan to trick the king and acquire Artemis' statue, the key to Orestes' ultimate salvation from the Furies (979–80). Although Iphigenia's plan works, Iphigenia sees no hope of salvation (1412–13) if the sea and winds are not calmed. Eventually, Athena saves the Greeks as she arranges for POSEIDON to calm the storm. The goddess even arranges for the rescue of the chorus from the Taurians.

Added to the theme of salvation, we find several noteworthy references to purification and cleansing. Iphigenia's role in Tauris is to perform a purification ritual for those who will die. When Orestes and Pylades are first captured, the herdsmen were washing their cattle at the seashore. The herdsmen take the Greeks to Iphigenia for purification and sacrifice, but when she learns their true identity, she concocts a fake purification ritual to secure their escape. Interestingly, she returns to the same seashore where they were captured to cleanse both them (1191) and the statue (1199). Additionally, Iphigenia will keep Thoas busy by instructing him to purify Artemis' sacred precinct (1216). Eventually, Thoas learns that the purification

was a trick (1316). The near purification of Orestes and Pylades for sacrifice and their false purification for salvation are ironic when considered in light of Iphigenia's sacrifice at Aulis, another purification ritual (861), and the fact that both rituals are but preludes to rescue and transport to safety.

In addition to the focus on purification, *Iphigenia in Tauris,* as does *Helen,* provides some ironic contrasts between Greeks and barbarians. As the play progresses, we may wonder whether the Greeks are really more civilized than the so-called barbarians. At line 31, Iphigenia states that Thoas is a barbarian who rules a barbaric people. Iphigenia suggests that the Taurians are barbarians because they sacrifice Greeks to Artemis. Ironically, Iphigenia is a Greek whom Greeks tried to sacrifice to Artemis. After Iphigenia is reunited with her brother and Pylades, she prays to Artemis to accompany them "from the barbaric land" (1086) and thus live with them in Greece. For Artemis to join the Greeks, Iphigenia must create a false story that will convince the barbarian king that Artemis' statue has been defiled by Orestes and Pylades. Thoas wonders whether perhaps they killed one of the barbarians at the shore (1170). It would appear that Thoas considers his own people to be barbarians. Iphigenia's story is not a complete fabrication, however, as she tells Thoas that the statue was desecrated by Orestes, who killed his mother. A shocked Thoas says such an act would not even occur among barbarians (1174). Among Greeks, however, such an act has taken place. Thoas believes that Iphigenia has acted correctly and remarks that Greece raised her to be wise (*sophe,* 1180), although the Greek word here can also denote a sort of cleverness or cunning. In this instance, Iphigenia's Greek cunning preys upon the barbarian's gullibility. Iphigenia's Greek cunning leads her to tell the king a further partial truth when she declares that she hates all Greece, which destroyed her (1187). In a further ironical remark, Iphigenia, while using her Greek cunning against the barbarian, warns the king to bind Orestes and Pylades because Greeks cannot be trusted (1205).

Although Iphigenia's life has been preserved in a barbarian land, she tries to return to the land that destroyed her and begins to set her scheme in motion.

Artemis' statue is taken from the barbaric land and placed in the hold of a Greek ship (1292; cf. also 1345). Iphigenia goes to the shore and begins to chant, in the words of the barbarian messenger, barbaric songs (1337). Thus, in the course of a false ritual, the Greek Iphigenia's words become those of a barbarian. As the Greeks try to sail away, Iphigenia prays to Artemis to save her from the barbaric land (1400) and take her back to Greece. At the same time, however, she begs the goddess to forgive her theft of the statue (still another act one might consider barbaric). Once the theft of the statue is discovered, Thoas summons the citizens of "this barbaric land" (1422) to pursue the Greeks. The appearance of the Greek goddess, however, stops pursuit by the barbarians, and even this so-called barbarian king realizes that it is madness to struggle against the gods. The Greek Agamemnon launched ships to recover Helen; the barbarian Thoas will not launch ships to recover Iphigenia.

Thus, in *Iphigenia in Tauris,* the barbarians have been duped by the "civilized" Greeks, in particular a virgin priestess of Artemis who lies and creates a false religious ritual in order to steal the statue of a virgin goddess. Once in "civilized" Greece, the "barbarian" aspect of Artemis will not be completely wiped away: A temple called Taurian will be built to house Artemis' statue and a ritual will be established that will not kill the victim, but merely draw a small amount of blood.

BIBLIOGRAPHY

Burnett, A. P. *Catastrophe Survived: Euripides' Plays of Mixed Reversal.* Oxford: Clarendon Press, 1971, 47–75.

Cropp, M. J. *Euripides: Iphigenia in Tauris.* Warminster, U.K.: Aris & Phillips, 2000.

Foley, H. P. *Female Acts in Greek Tragedy.* Princeton, N.J.: Princeton University Press, 2001, 303–31.

O'Brien, M. J. "Pelopid History and the Plot of *Iphigenia in Tauris,*" *Classical Quarterly* 37 (1988): 98–115.

Platnauer, M. *Euripides: Iphigenia in Tauris.* Oxford: Clarendon Press, 1938.

Tzanetou, Angeliki. "Almost Dying, Dying Twice: Ritual and Audience in Euripides' *Iphigenia in Tauris,*" *Illinois Classical Studies* 24–25 (1999–2000): 199–216.

IPHITUS The son of EURYTUS, king of Oechalia, Iphitus was the brother of IOLE. After HERACLES had completed his labors for EURYSTHEUS, he decided to marry and talked to Eurytus to try to arrange a wedding to Iole. Eurytus agreed, provided that Heracles could defeat him and his sons in an archery contest. Heracles won the contest and Iphitus supported Heracles' claim to Iole, but Eurytus would not give Iole to Heracles because he was afraid that Heracles would kill any children he might have by Iole (Heracles had killed his children by his previous wife, MEGARA). Eventually, Heracles left Eurytus' kingdom without Iole and took up residence in TIRYNS. Not long after this, the notorious thief AUTOLYCUS stole cattle from Eurytus' kingdom and Eurytus thought Heracles, nursing a grudge, was the culprit. Iphitus, however, did not believe this allegation and went to question Heracles himself. Iphitus encountered Heracles and asked the hero to help him look for the cattle. Heracles agreed and took Iphitus to his house at Tiryns. At some point during the search, however, Heracles was again afflicted by insanity and threw Iphitus from the walls of Tiryns. According to SOPHOCLES' TRACHINIAN WOMEN, Heracles killed Iphitus in a fit of anger, not insanity. [ANCIENT SOURCES: Apollodorus, *Library* 2.6.1–2; Pausanias, 10.13.8; Plutarch, *Theseus* 6.5; Sophocles, *Trachinian Women* 38, 270, 357]

IRIS The daughter of Thaumas and Electra (not AGAMEMNON's daughter), Iris was the sister of the HARPIES and is the goddess who represents the rainbow; she also serves as a messenger for the gods. She appears in two extant plays, EURIPIDES' HERACLES and ARISTOPHANES' BIRDS. In *Heracles,* Iris, accompanied by MADNESS, goes to THEBES on behalf of HERA to make sure Madness attacks Heracles. The exchange between Iris and Madness is reminiscent of the exchange between Power and HEPHAESTUS in PROMETHEUS BOUND. Just as Hephaestus was reluctantly driven by Power to his task of binding PROMETHEUS to the mountain, Madness is reluctant to attack HERACLES. Iris, however, compels Madness to carry out the assignment. In *Birds,* Iris tries to pass through the birds' city on her way to Earth, but she is stopped by PEISETAERUS, who informs her that the gods she represents are no longer being worshiped by humans and that birds are the new masters of the heavens. Peisetaerus then drives Iris away. The Greek comic poet Achaeus wrote a SATYR PLAY entitled *Iris;* the brief extant fragments (19–23 Snell) reveal little about the play's content. [ANCIENT SOURCES: Apollodorus, *Library* 1.2.6; Aristophanes, *Birds* 575, 1202–61; Euripides, *Heracles* 822–74; Hesiod, *Theogony* 266, 775; Homer, *Iliad* 8.409, 18.166; Ovid, *Metamorphoses* 4.479, 845; Pausanias, 4.33.6; Vergil, *Aeneid* 5.620]

BIBLIOGRAPHY

Snell, B. *Tragicorum Graecorum Fragmenta.* Vol. 1. Göttingen, Ger.: Vandenhoeck & Ruprecht, 1971.

IRONY The occurrence of double meanings in words or deeds. In SOPHOCLES' *OEDIPUS TYRANNOS*, for example, King OEDIPUS puts a curse on the person who killed LAIUS, the previous king. The audience knows that Oedipus killed Laius, but the character Oedipus does not discover this until later in the play. Irony can also occur in COMEDY. In PLAUTUS' *AMPHITRUO*, several instances of irony occur because two gods, Jupiter/Jove (Greek: ZEUS) and Mercury (Greek: HERMES), are disguised as the mortals Amphitruo (see AMPHITRYON) and Sosia. At one point, for example, Sosia (in an encounter with Mercury/Sosia) swears by Jove that he is the real Sosia. Mercury/Sosia answers that he swears by Mercury that Jove does not believe him. The audience knows what the real Sosia does not know—that Sosia is in the presence of Mercury, the son of Jove.

ISLAND OF THE BLESSED A mythical land (free of sorrow) to which a few lucky persons (especially the heroes who fought in the Trojan War) might go after death. CRONUS was said to have ruled this land. At the conclusion of EURIPIDES' *HELEN*, it is predicted that MENELAUS will go to the Island of the Blessed after his death. [ANCIENT SOURCES: Hesiod, *Works and Days* 171: Josephus, *The Wars of the Jews* 2.154]

ISMENE The daughter of OEDIPUS and JOCASTA, Ismene was the sister of ETEOCLES, POLYNEICES, and ANTIGONE. Ismene has brief speaking parts in several extant dramas (AESCHYLUS' *SEVEN AGAINST THEBES*, SOPHOCLES' *ANTIGONE* and *OEDIPUS AT COLONUS*). In *Antigone,* Ismene's main function is to provide a con-

trast with the boldness of her sister, Antigone. Whereas Antigone advocates the burial of Polyneices, despite a decree promising death to anyone who does so, Ismene is unwilling to violate this decree. In *Oedipus at Colonus,* Ismene warns Oedipus and Antigone of CREON's evil intentions.

ISMENIAS A stereotyped name for a person from BOEOTIA, probably coined from the ISMENUS River of that region. [ANCIENT SOURCES: Aristophanes, *Acharnians* 861, *Lysistrata* 697]

BIBLIOGRAPHY

Sommerstein, A. H. *The Comedies of Aristophanes.* Vol. 1, *Acharnians.* Warminster, U.K.: Aris & Phillips, 1980, 200.

ISMENUS A river, arising from Mount CITHAERON and flowing into Lake Hylica, that has its course east of the town of THEBES. Pausanias says the river got its name from APOLLO's son Ismenus. The river is mentioned several times by the tragedians, especially EURIPIDES and SENECA. [ANCIENT SOURCES: Pausanias, 9.10.6]

ISTER The child of Tethys and OCEANUS, the mythic river Ister is identified with the modern Danube, Europe's longest river (more than 1,700 miles). [ANCIENT SOURCES: Hesiod, *Theogony* 339; Seneca, *Medea* 585, 736, *Thyestes* 629, *Hercules Oetaeus* 86, 515, 1365; Sophocles, *Oedipus Tyrannos* 1227]

ISTHMUS In Greek geography, Isthmus refers to the strip of land that connects the northern and southern halves of mainland Greece. CORINTH is the town usually associated with the Greek Isthmus and sometimes the word *Isthmus* is synonymous with Corinth. [ANCIENT SOURCES: Seneca, *Agamemnon* 564, *Hercules Furens* 336, *Hercules Oetaeus* 83, *Medea* 45, 299, *Phoenician Women* 375, *Thyestes* 112, 124]

ITHACA A small island (modern-day Thiaki), about 50 square miles in size, off the western coast of Greece. Ithaca was the home of ODYSSEUS, whom poets sometimes call "the Ithacan." [ANCIENT SOURCES: Euripides, *Cyclops* 103, *Trojan Women* 277; Seneca, *Trojan Women*]

ITYS   See TEREUS.

IXION   A king in the region of Thessaly, Ixion was
the son of Phlegyas (or Antion or ARES or Peision) and
Perimela. Ixion married Dia, daughter of Eioneus (or
Deioneus), and fathered PEIRITHOUS (although HOMER
says ZEUS was Peirithous' father). When Ixion failed to
deliver to his father-in-law, Eioneus, the bridal gifts that
he had promised, Eioneus took some horses from Ixion
instead. Later, Ixion, hoping to get back his horses,
invited his father-in-law to his house, pretending he
would give him the bridal gifts he had promised. When
Eioneus arrived, however, Ixion killed him by making
him fall into a pit filled with fire, thus making Ixion,
according to tradition, the first mortal to kill one of his
relatives. Ixion also became the first mortal to be purified of murder when Zeus cleansed him of his crime.
Zeus even took Ixion to Mount OLYMPUS, but the evil
fellow lusted after Hera and hoped to seduce her. Zeus,
however, created a cloud Hera and Ixion had intercourse with the cloud. According to some traditions,
the impregnated cloud gave birth to a CENTAUR. Zeus
then punished Ixion by sending him to the UNDER-
WORLD and binding him to a wheel that always turns.

AESCHYLUS wrote an *Ixion* (fragments 90–93 Radt),
which Lloyd-Jones thinks dealt with the purification of
Ixion. EURIPIDES also wrote an *Ixion* (fragments 424–26
Nauck), which is thought to have been staged shortly
after the death of Protagoras in 420 B.C.E., because
Philochorus identified a reference to his death in
Euripides' play. Surviving fragments reveal little about
the play's subject matter, though Webster supposes
Ixion had already killed his father-in-law. SOPHOCLES
also wrote an *Ixion,* but only a single word survives
from the play (fragment 296 Radt). The tragedians Callistratus and Timesitheus both composed an *Ixion,* of
which only the titles remain (see Snell). The comic
poet Eubulus wrote a play called *Ixion,* of which four
uninformative lines survive (fragment 36 Kock).
[ANCIENT SOURCES: Aeschylus, *Eumenides* 441, 718;
Apollodorus, *Library* 1.8.2, *Epitome* 1.20; Hyginus,
Fables 62; Pindar, *Pythian* 2; Seneca, *Hercules Furens*
750, *Medea* 744, *Octavia* 623]

BIBLIOGRAPHY
Kock, T. *Comicorum Atticorum Fragmenta.* Vol. 2. Leipzig:
    Teubner, 1884.
Radt, S. *Tragicorum Graecorum Fragmenta.* Vol. 3. Göttingen,
    Ger.: Vandenhoeck & Ruprecht, 1985.
————. *Tragicorum Graecorum Fragmenta.* Vol. 4. Göttingen,
    Ger.: Vandenhoeck & Ruprecht, 1977.
Smyth, H. W., and Lloyd-Jones, H. *Aeschylus.* Vol. 2. 1926.
    Reprint, Cambridge, Mass.: Harvard University Press,
    1971.
Snell, B. *Tragicorum Graecorum Fragmenta.* Vol. 1. Göttingen,
    Ger.: Vandenhoeck & Ruprecht, 1971.
Webster, T. B. L. *The Tragedies of Euripides.* London:
    Methuen, 1967.

J

JASON Famous for leading the quest for the Golden Fleece, Jason was the son of Aeson and Polymede (or Alcimede). Jason's uncle, Pelias, usurped the kingdom of Iolcus from Aeson, and then Pelias watched Aeson and his family closely. Pelias had heard a prophecy that he would be killed by a descendant of Aeson's, so when Aeson's wife became pregnant, Pelias planned to kill the child as soon as it was born. When Aeson's wife pretended the child was stillborn, Pelias did not investigate the matter carefully. The child, Jason, was smuggled out of Iolcus and taken to the centaur CHIRON, who raised the boy.

After Jason grew up, he returned to Iolcus in an attempt to regain the kingdom for his father. By this time, Pelias had been warned by another prophecy to beware of a man wearing one sandal. While Jason was traveling to Iolcus, he had helped an old woman (HERA in disguise) cross the Anaurus River. While crossing the river, Jason lost a sandal but gained Hera as an ally. When Jason arrived in Iolcus, he went to Pelias' palace and claimed the restoration of his father's kingdom. Pelias noticed Jason was wearing only one sandal and thought quickly of how to get rid of him. Pelias asked Jason what he would do if he were standing face to face with the person destined to kill him. Jason stated that he would send the person to fetch the Golden Fleece from COLCHIS. Pelias then gave Jason this assignment and promised to restore the kingdom to Jason's father were he successful.

Jason then invited the heroes of Greece to join him in his quest. A shipbuilder named ARGUS was commissioned to build the ship, which was subsequently named *Argo* ("fast") after its builder. The boat was equipped with an oracular beam, which Jason could consult in times of crisis. Thus, Jason's ship could actually speak to him. To pull this magical ship's 50 oars, an equal number of heroes were assembled, called Argonauts, "those who sail on the *Argo*." Sources differ as to the names of the 50, but most accounts include HERACLES; the famed musician ORPHEUS; ALCESTIS' husband, ADMETUS; ACHILLES' father, PELEUS; the keensighted LYNCEUS; Zetes and Calais, the winged sons of BOREAS; the helmsman Tiphys; and perhaps even THESEUS and ATALANTA.

During the voyage to Colchis, Jason and the Argonauts faced many obstacles and experienced many adventures. After sailing from Iolcus, the Argonauts landed on LEMNOS, an island where the women had recently killed almost the entire male population. By this time, however, the Lemnian women had decided in favor of male companionship and welcomed the Argonauts to their island. The Argonauts paired off with various women, and efforts to repopulate the island were soon under way. Jason impregnated HYPSIPYLE, the leader of the Lemnian women, and by him she had two sons, Euneus and Nebrophonus (or Deipylus). Jason, however, may have left Lemnos before these children were born, as Heracles eventually persuaded the Argonauts to end their delay on the island and continue their voyage.

After leaving Lemnos, Jason did not play an especially prominent role in the journey to Colchis. Jason accidentally killed Cyzicus, earlier their host, when bad weather drove them back to Cyzicus' land during the night. In the dark, the Argonauts defended themselves against an attack from Cyzicus' people, who did not realize they were attacking the Argonauts. Jason also won a rowing contest against the other Argonauts, but only because Heracles' oar broke. When the Argonauts landed at the Mysia to find fresh timber for Heracles' oar and collect fresh water, Heracles' comrade, Hylas, was abducted by water nymphs. When Heracles refused to continue on the voyage to search for Hylas, Jason was only too happy to leave Heracles behind. Many of the other Argonauts, however, did not want to set sail without Heracles. Fortunately, mutiny was averted by the appearance of the sea god Glaucus, who told them that Heracles was not destined to reach Colchis.

Jason's next significant appearance in the story does not occur until the Argonauts reach Colchis. There Jason met the Colchian king, AEETES, and requested the Golden Fleece. In exchange, Jason promised Aeetes that the Argonauts would help the Colchians wage war against their enemies, the Sauromatians. Aeetes, however, said that he would hand over the fleece if Jason would perform several tasks. First, Jason would yoke a pair of fire-breathing bulls; next, he would plough a certain field and sow it with dragon's teeth. From the dragon's teeth, armed men would spring up, and Jason would have to deal with them. If Jason failed, Aeetes threatened him and his comrades with death. Aeetes, of course, had no intention of handing over the fleece, even if Jason did succeed, and began to plot the destruction of the Argonauts.

Fortunately for Jason and the Argonauts, Hera arranged for APHRODITE to cause Aeetes' daughter, MEDEA, to fall in love with Jason. Medea helped Jason in his tasks by giving him a potion that would protect him against the fiery breath of the bulls and advice about how to deal with the warriors who would spring up from the dragon's teeth. With the help of Medea's magic, Jason was able to yoke the bulls, plow the field, and plant the dragon's teeth. When the armed men sprang up, he threw at them a boulder, which caused them to fight among themselves. Jason killed them after they had wounded one another.

Although Jason accomplished the tasks, Aeetes did not hand over the fleece but continued to plan to destroy the Argonauts. Medea, however, who knew her father's intentions, warned the Argonauts and guided them during the night to the grove in which the fleece was hanging. A dragon guarded the fleece, but Medea overcame this obstacle by giving it a potion that put it to sleep. Jason then snatched the fleece and the Argonauts, accompanied by Medea, made their way to the *Argo* and sailed away. The escape of Jason and company was not easy, as Aeetes gave chase. How Jason managed to end or avoid Aeetes' pursuit differs from source to source. The most common account is that either Jason or Medea killed Medea's brother, ABSYRTUS. SENECA (*MEDEA* 131–32, 911–12) follows the tradition that Absyrtus was taken aboard the *Argo,* and then, as Aeetes' ship was closing in on the *Argo,* Medea killed her brother, cut apart his body, and scattered the pieces across the sea in the expectation—one that ultimately proved correct—that Aeetes would stop and collect the body parts for a proper burial. Other sources indicate that Aeetes' pursuit did not end until Jason and Medea reached the island of Alcinous and Arete, where they were married. As Jason's wife, Medea was no longer under her father's "control," and therefore Aeetes gave up his pursuit.

The return voyage from Colchis to Iolcus held many other adventures for Jason and his crew. As did ODYSSEUS, Jason encountered CIRCE, the SIRENS, SCYLLA and CHARYBDIS, and the cattle of Helios (see SUN). Jason's encounters with these persons or creatures were far less eventful than those of Odysseus: Circe actually drove the Argonauts from her island; Orpheus prevented the Argonauts from being tempted by the Sirens; Thetis saved the ship from Scylla and Charybdis; and they left the cattle of Helios untouched. When a strange storm drove them into the Libyan desert, POSEIDON's son, TRITON, eventually pushed their ship back into the sea. When the giant Talus attacked their ship as they sailed past Crete, Medea's magic caused this creature's demise.

Upon reaching Iolcus, Jason handed over the Golden Fleece to Pelias. Pelias, however, did not turn over the kingdom as he had promised. Jason, still determined to acquire the throne, enlisted the help of Medea to destroy Pelias. Medea went to Pelias' house and pretended that she had left Jason. Pelias' daughters took Medea into the house and into their confidence. Medea convinced them that she could restore Pelias' youth by cutting up an aged ram, throwing his limbs into a magic cauldron, and then causing a frisky young lamb to emerge. Medea told Pelias' daughters to do that to their father. Unfortunately, when Pelias' daughters killed their father, Medea and her magic cauldron were nowhere to be found. With Pelias dead, Jason expected he would become king of Iolcus, but his hopes were thwarted when Pelias' son, ACASTUS, managed to drive Jason and Medea from the town.

Jason and Medea then made their way to Corinth and took up residence in the realm of CREON. Jason and Medea appear to have lived happily for some time and had two sons. Eventually, however, Jason's desire for kingship resurfaced, and he decided to divorce Medea and marry Creon's daughter. When Medea discovered this, she killed Creon's daughter with a deadly gown and diadem. Creon himself died when he tried to save his daughter from the lethal clothing. Medea also killed her children by Jason and then flew away to ATHENS on her grandfather, Helios', chariot. After the horrific events at Corinth, Jason was a shattered man. He wandered from town to town before finally returning to the place where he had beached the *Argo*. As Jason lay upon the shore beneath the ship's rotting hulk, he decided to kill himself. Before he could do so, a gust of wind blew the ship onto Jason's head (as Medea predicts at the conclusion of EURIPIDES' *MEDEA*).

Jason appears as a character in two extant dramas: Euripides' *Medea* and SENECA'S *MEDEA*. In each of these plays, he is characterized as a weakling, whose success in acquiring the Golden Fleece is a more the result of Medea's magic than of his own courage or prowess. In Euripides' play, the complaint most frequently made about Jason is that he has broken the oaths and promises to Medea that led her to leave her native land and go to Greece. The Greek tragedian Antiphon wrote a *Jason;* only a single word of this play survives (fragment 1a Snell). The Greek comic poet Antiphanes also wrote a *Jason,* of which only the title is extant (fragment 107 Kock). [ANCIENT SOURCES: Apollodorus, *Library* 1.9.16–28; Apollonius of Rhodes, *Argonautica;* Hyginus, *Fables* 13–25; Ovid, *Heroides* 6, *Metamorphoses* 7.1–403; Pindar, *Pythian* 4; Valerius Flaccus, *Argonautica*]

BIBLIOGRAPHY

Kock, T. *Comicorum Atticorum Fragmenta.* Vol. 2. Leipzig: Teubner, 1884.

Snell, B. *Tragicorum Graecorum Fragmenta.* Vol. 1. Göttingen, Ger.: Vandenhoeck & Ruprecht, 1971.

JOCASTA (IOCASTA)

The daughter of MENOECEUS, Jocasta (also known as Epicasta) was first the wife of LAIUS, king of THEBES. Despite a warning from the ORACLE at DELPHI, Laius had a child by Jocasta (OEDIPUS), but the child was to be exposed at its birth. The shepherd charged with exposing Oedipus did not do so, however, and Oedipus grew up in CORINTH. After Laius died (killed by Oedipus), Jocasta's brother, CREON, reigned as king. When Thebes was confronted by the SPHINX and no remedy could be found, Creon announced that whoever defeated the Sphinx would become not only king of Thebes but also the husband of Jocasta. When Oedipus arrived in Thebes and solved the Sphinx's riddle, he became Jocasta's husband. By Oedipus, Jocasta was the mother of two sons (ETEOCLES and POLYNEICES) and two daughters (ANTIGONE and ISMENE). She appears as a character in Sophocles' *OEDIPUS TYRANNOS*, Euripides' *PHOENICIAN WOMEN*, SENECA'S *OEDIPUS*, and Seneca's *PHOENICIAN WOMEN*. In Sophocles' play, Jocasta hangs herself when she realizes that Oedipus is on the verge of discovering his true identity. In Euripides' play, Jocasta remains alive after Oedipus' blinding and tries to persuade her sons to reconcile their differences. When her efforts fail, however, the sons fight in battle and kill one another, and Jocasta commits suicide when she discovers their bodies. Jocasta also plays the role of mediator in Seneca's *Phoenician Women,* but her fate is unknown because that play's manuscript breaks off during her negotiations with her sons. [ANCIENT SOURCES: Apollodorus, *Library* 3.5.7, 9; Homer, *Odyssey* 11.271–80; Hyginus, *Fables* 66, 67]

BIBLIOGRAPHY

Hind, J. "The Death of Agrippina and the Finale of the *Oedipus* of Seneca," *Journal of the Australasian Universities Language and Literature Association* 8 (1972): 204–11.

Scharffenberger, Elizabeth Watson. "A Tragic Lysistrata? Jocasta in the 'Reconciliation Scene' of the *Phoenician Women*," *Rheinisches Museum* 138, nos. 3–4 (1995): 312–36.

JOVE   See ZEUS.

JUDGMENT OF PARIS   When the Trojan PARIS was living as a shepherd outside TROY and was unaware that he was the son of PRIAM, HERMES. Three goddesses, HERA, ATHENA, and APHRODITE, took him. Paris was to make a judgment as to which of the goddesses was most beautiful. Each goddess offered Paris a bribe if he would choose her. Hera offered kingship, Athena prowess in war, and Aphrodite HELEN, the most beautiful woman in all the world. Paris' selection of Aphrodite led to the Trojan War.

Among the Greek dramatists, SOPHOCLES appears to have taken up this subject in his *Judgment.* Athenaeus writes that in Sophocles' play Aphrodite appeared on stage, anointed herself with perfume, and toyed with a mirror, while Athena anointed herself with olive oil and behaved as an athlete at a gymnasium would. [ANCIENT SOURCES: Apollodorus, *Epitome* 3.2; Athenaeus, 15.687c; Euripides, *Helen* 23–30, *Iphigenia at Aulis* 178–84; Hyginus, *Fables* 92]

JUNO   See HERA.

JUPITER   See ZEUS.

JUSTICE   The daughter of ZEUS and THEMIS, this divinity personifies and oversees justice and its administration. Her Greek name is *Dike,* which is often translated as "justice"; the Greek adjective *dikaios* means "just." Among Roman authors, the noun *iustitia* means "justice," and the adjective *iustus* means "just." Note, however, that the Greek noun *dike* can also mean "vengeance." Thus, although justice and vengeance seem to be completely different concepts to most moderns, the ancient Greeks considered them intertwined.

Although Justice does not appear as a character in any extant classical dramas, justice is a concept that figures prominently in both Greek TRAGEDY and COMEDY. This is not surprising given the civic climate of ATHENS, the birthplace of the extant Greek dramas, where court proceedings were common. The Athenian interest in justice was so commonplace that ARISTOPHANES names one of his heroes DICAEOPOLIS ("honest citizen"). ATHENS was a town in which courts were in session so frequently that Aristophanes portrays another of his characters, PHILOCLEON, as addicted to jury service. In Aristophanes' BIRDS, its heroes leave Athens because they are tired of their fellow citizens' constant legal wrangling. Aristophanes' CLOUDS has much of its focus on justice, as that play's hero, STREPSIADES, wants to become the best speaker in Greece so that he might defeat his creditors when they try to take him to court. By the play's end, Strepsiades fears for his life as his son has become such a clever speaker that he persuasively argues that it is just (*dikaios*) for him to beat his father.

The question What is justice? figures prominently in certain Greek tragedies, particularly those related to AGAMEMNON and ORESTES. In fact, AESCHYLUS' ORESTEIA may be considered an examination of the evolution of justice. Of course, in such dramas the answer to the question depends on the situation and the author. In Aeschylus' *Agamemnon* (see ORESTEIA), CLYTEMNESTRA thinks that the murder of her husband is in accordance with justice because he had sacrificed their daughter. In Aeschylus' *Libation Bearers* (see ORESTEIA), however, Orestes, ELECTRA, and the chorus think justice will be served by Orestes killing Clytemnestra and AEGISTHUS for their role in the death of his father. In Aeschylus' *Eumenides* (see ORESTEIA), the FURIES think they are acting in accordance with justice by persecuting Orestes for killing his mother. Eventually, the Furies agree to allow justice to be achieved not by violence, but in a legal proceeding in which persuasion will be the means by which it is attained. Of course, Aeschylus' definition of justice differs from that of SOPHOCLES or EURIPIDES. Euripidean Orestes and Electra believe that killing their mother is in accordance with justice, but at the end of Euripides' *ELECTRA* the DIOSCURI declare that although Clytemnestra has received justice, Orestes has not acted justly. Euripides' *ORESTES* deals with the trial of Orestes in a much more realistic and cynical way. Although at the end of the play APOLLO himself appears and declares Orestes will successfully undergo the sort of trial that Orestes underwent in Aeschylus' *Eumenides* (see *ORESTEIA*), for most of the play Orestes' killing of his mother is viewed in a negative light. TYNDAREUS argues that with respect to Clytemnestra Orestes should have pursued legal channels and had her banished from their house. Absent from Euripides' *Orestes* are the Furies as the prosecution, Athena as the judge, Apollo as Orestes' key witness, and the civilized Athenian citizens as the jury. Instead, Orestes is sentenced to death in a trial by a disorganized mob who are easily influenced by clever human speakers, some of whom are not even citizens of Argos, the town where the trial occurs. In contrast to Aeschylus' *Libation Bearers* (see *ORESTEIA*) and Euripides' *Electra,* Sophocles' *ELECTRA* looks at justice from a more feminine perspective. Sophocles' Clytemnestra declares that Justice killed Agamemnon, and Electra argues that her actions were unjust. When Electra declares that she will avenge her father's death, her sister, CHRYSOTHEMIS, declares that such justice will cause her harm. [ANCIENT SOURCES: Aeschylus, *Agamemnon* 733, 773–81, 911–13, 1431–32 (see *ORESTEIA*); *Libation Bearers* 983–90 (see *ORESTEIA*); *Eumenides* 511–15 (see *ORESTEIA*); Apollodorus, *Library* 1.3.1; Aristophanes, *Clouds* 1331–1438; Euripides, *Electra* 771; Hesiod, *Theogony* 901; Sophocles, *Electra* 528, 560–61, 1041–42, *Orestes* 500–3]

KATHARSIS   See CATHARSIS.

KERAUNOSKOPEION   A device used to produce lightning. Pollux says the *keraunoskopeion* was a swiveling panel (see PERIAKTOS) positioned above the stage. [ANCIENT SOURCES: Pollux, *Onomasticon* 4.127, 130]

KNIGHTS (Greek: *HIPPEIS*; Latin: *EQUITES*) ARISTOPHANES (424 B.C.E.)   *Knights* was staged at the LENAEA in ATHENS and won first prize. It was ARISTOPHANES' first play that he produced in his own name. The play's action occurs near the PNYX in ATHENS. The *SKENE* represents three houses: that of Demos in the center, that of Paphlagon on one side, and that of the Sausage Seller on the other. Demos personifies the Athenian people; Paphlagon (blusterer) represents CLEON, an Athenian leader, who, the year before the production of *Knights,* had astonishingly defeated the Spartans at the island of Sphacteria (near PYLOS). The CHORUS consist of well-to-do young Athenian men who compose the city's cavalry.

As the play opens, two SLAVES, DEMOSTHENES and NICIAS, the names of an Athenian politician and a military commander of the time, complain about beatings they received from Paphlagon, a new slave in Demos' house. After Demos bought Paphlagon, the latter quickly became the master's favorite by flattering him and by satisfying Demos' love of hearing oracles. Paphlagon also began to run a protection scheme with the other slaves, making them pay money to prevent Demos from beating them.

The fortunes of Demosthenes and Nicias seem so bleak that they consider suicide, then decide to become drunk. In their intoxication, the two decide to steal some of Paphlagon's oracles. From these prophecies they learn that ultimately Paphlagon will be bested by the lowest person in society—a sausage seller. Just as Demosthenes and Nicias wonder where they will find such a man, in walks the Sausage Seller, whom they hale as the savior of Athens. The Sausage Seller, of course, does not believe he can guide Athens, but Demosthenes points out that his lack of pedigree, education, character, and manners provides exactly the qualities that make a good politician. When the Sausage Seller wonders who among Athenian society will support him, Demosthenes points out that Paphlagon/Cleon's enemies, the Knights, will back him.

Soon Paphlagon bursts from the house and threatens to kill Demosthenes and Nicias for plotting against him. This threat prompts Demosthenes to call the Knights to help them. After the Knights enter, they and Paphlagon battle verbally. The Sausage Seller, spurred on by yelling, a familiar part of his trade, enters the fray. Now Paphlagon and the Sausage Seller trade insults, while the chorus of Knights serve as commentators for the action. After several rounds of verbal sparring, Paphlagon realizes he has met his match in the Sausage Seller. Their first battle ends as the two depart to denounce each other before the Athenian assembly.

After Paphlagon and the Sausage Seller exit, the chorus deliver the PARABASIS. First, the chorus, speaking in the voice of Aristophanes himself, address the question of why Aristophanes does not produce plays under his own name. They state that Aristophanes has seen the fates of other playwrights, whose plays are initially viewed with favor but later become unpopular. Next, the chorus sing a hymn to POSEIDON, patron divinity of the Knights; they praise their forefathers, who served Athens so well in war; they sing a hymn to ATHENA; and they end the parabasis with a song of thanksgiving for the service their horses have given them in war.

After the parabasis, the Sausage Seller returns triumphant from the assembly. The delighted Knights offer their congratulations and ask him to explain how he defeated Paphlagon. The Sausage Seller reveals that he proved himself more popular than Paphlagon by promising the assembly cheap sardines and then giving them free seasonings when they bought the fish. The Knights praise the Sausage Seller for his tricks and promise him their support.

At this point, an enraged Paphlagon returns from the assembly. Immediately, the Sausage Seller and Paphlagon renew their threats and verbal abuse of one another. They decide to have a contest to see which of them can win over Demos, who insists that the contest be held at the PNYX. For every benefit (financial and military) that Paphlagon claims he has conferred on Demos, the Sausage Seller points out a fault. Paphlagon argues that with his leadership Demos will rule all Greece, but the Sausage Seller claims that Paphlagon will benefit only financially while Demos is not paying attention. The Sausage Seller accuses Paphlagon of not providing Demos with such basic comforts as shoes and clothing. After the Sausage Seller promises Demos food, employment, and health care, Demos is persuaded and gives the Sausage Seller a ring that marks him as his favorite. The competition between the Sausage Seller and Paphlagon is not over, though, as the two next turn to oracles to win Demos' favor.

After Demos prefers the Sausage Seller's oracles, the two combatants leave to prepare food and drink for Demos. In their absence, Demos tells the chorus that he is making the Sausage Seller and Paphlagon compete for his affection in order to receive more good things. Thus, Demos is not as gullible as he appears. When the two rivals return, the banquet that the Sausage Seller provides for Demos defeats Paphlagon's feast when the Sausage Seller actually steals some food that Paphlagon had cooked and gives it to Demos. When Paphlagon protests, the Sausage Seller tells him that was what he (Cleon) did at Pylos (Cleon was accused of stealing the victory there from Demosthenes and, to a lesser extent, Nicias). Paphlagon then learns of the oracle regarding the Sausage Seller and realizes that he has been beaten. After Paphlagon's departure, Demos entrusts himself completely to the Sausage Seller's care.

At this point, Demos and the Sausage Seller exit behind the *skene* and a second parabasis of about 50 lines occurs in which the Knights, speaking on Aristophanes' behalf, defend his practice of making fun of public figures and, in the process, mock several prominent Athenians.

The play moves toward its conclusion with the reemergence of the Sausage Seller, who informs the audience that he has restored Demos to the good old days by boiling him in a magical potion (the tale is meant to recall MEDEA's rejuvenation of JASON's father, Aeson). Next, Demos, dressed in a costume fit for a king, is wheeled out on the ECCYCLEMA and hailed by the Knights as the ruler of the Greeks. Demos repents of his foolish behavior in the past, but the Sausage Seller blames the men who tricked Demos. As at the conclusion of Aristophanes' ACHARNIANS, in which DICAEOPOLIS ends the play with a pretty young woman under each arm, in *Knights* the Sausage Seller leads out two beautiful women, who represent peace treaties with SPARTA, and gives them to Demos. The sexually aroused Demos is eager to go back inside and enjoy his new-found "peace." Before Demos and the Sausage Seller exit, the Sausage Seller says Paphlagon will now perform the Sausage Seller's former job.

COMMENTARY

With only five speaking characters in the play other than the chorus (compare, for example, 18 in *Acharni-*

ans and 11 in C<small>LOUDS</small>), Aristophanes' *Knights* seems to be a rather simple play in terms of tension between the characters. Although a struggle obviously occurs between the Sausage Seller and Paphlagon, we must not lose sight of the fact that these two men are striving to be the favorite of Demos, the Athenian people. So powerful is Paphlagon/Cleon's influence on Demos that we almost forget that Demos is the master and Paphlagon is the slave. Although Demos does not make his appearance until the play is at its midpoint, the Athenian people have been a primary topic of conversation and are as much a focal point of *Knights* as Paphlagon/Cleon. Interestingly, about one-quarter of the occurrences of the word *demos* in Aristophanes' plays occur in *Knights*.

Thus, although considerable attention in *Knights* is paid to Aristophanes' attack on Cleon and much good fun is had as a professional politician is outwitted by the lowest huckster from the marketplace, one should not lose sight of the more subtle and, arguably, important issue of the play, namely, that the Athenian people can be easily manipulated by a single clever speaker. Cleon may have been defeated, but the Athenian people have been persuaded by someone who has an infinitely less impressive pedigree than Cleon and is equally capable of slinging verbal mud.

Accordingly, Aristophanes focuses not merely on the Athenian people, but in particular on their manipulation by the speech of others. Added to this is the issue of how Athenian politicians could manipulate the people with words supposedly issued from the mouths of their gods, that is, oracles. In Aristophanes' 11 surviving plays, more than half the references to oracles occur in *Knights*.

As the play opens, Demosthenes notes that Paphlagon gained control of Demos with flattering words (46–54) and the recitation of oracles (61) favorable to Demos, whose ignorance prevents him from seeing through Paphlagon's verbal tricks. Demosthenes believes, however, that they can be saved if they steal some of Paphlagon's oracles (116–54). Once the words of the gods are out of Paphlagon's control, then Demosthenes and Nicias can save themselves and the city (149). Once Demosthenes learns of the oracle about the Sausage Seller, he uses the oracle and his powers of per-

suasion to enlist the Sausage Seller's help (177, 195, 211). The Sausage Seller is impressed by the oracle but wonders how the ordinary huckster he is can be steward of the Athenian people (211–12). Demosthenes tells him that it can be accomplished through elegant and clever speech (216). Furthermore, Demosthenes tells him that he has all the other requisite qualities to lead the people (217), such as having "a repellent voice [and] low birth" (Sommerstein at line 218) and being a product of the marketplace (see A<small>GORA</small>).

When Paphlagon revives from his drunken stupor and roars out of Demos' house, he accuses Demosthenes and the Sausage Seller of being in a conspiracy against the Athenian people (236). When the Knights defend the Sausage Seller from Paphlagon's attacks, Paphlagon's attempt to manipulate the Knights with speech fails (266–72), and when the Knights turn to attack he calls on the Athenian people (273) to protect him. Once the Sausage Seller and Paphlagon square off against one another, the scene literally disintegrates into a war of words, as the Sausage Seller can match Paphlagon insult for insult. Although the two combatants say nothing of substance, Aristophanes' emphasis is on speech. For example, as the two begin their argument, between lines 337 and 50 forms of the Greek verb *legein* (to speak) occur seven times. Despite the Sausage Seller's ability to match Paphlagon' insults, Paphlagon says he has nothing to fear from him as long as the Athenian people (396) maintain their ignorant ways.

Although the Sausage Seller defeats Paphlagon when they appear before the Athenian Council, Paphlagon feels confident that he can get justice against the Sausage Seller from the Athenian people (710). The Sausage Seller is equally confident that his verbal skills will be sufficient to defeat Paphlagon (711), but Paphlagon feels confident that he can make a fool of the Athenian people (713) because he knows the sort of flattery on which they feed (714–15). The Sausage Seller realizes that Paphlagon even chews Demos' food for him and swallows most of it before handing over the remainder (716–18). Paphlagon even boasts that he "can make Demos expand and contract" (Sommerstein) through his clever ways (719–20). Accordingly, Paphlagon confidently declares, "Let's go to the *demos*" (723); when he calls Demos from his house Paphlagon summons him with the sort of flattering language that a lover might use with a beloved and at 726 addresses him as "Most beloved little Demos" (*Demidion . . . philtaton*).

Once Demos emerges from his house, the Sausage Seller presents himself as a rival for the love of Demos (733) and says he wants to do things that will benefit Demos. Paphalagon, of course, argues that he himself treats Demos well (741) and declares that no one has ever defended or loved Demos as much as he has (790). The Sausage Seller, however, hopes that someday Demos will realize that Paphlagon is manipulating him and using war as a means to prevent him (802) from discovering those tricks. As the Sausage Seller's arguments against Demos begin to have an effect, he feels confident enough to address Demos with the same sort of flattering language that Paphlagon used earlier. At line 827, the Sausage Seller addresses Demos as "my dear little big Demos" (*Demakidion*; Sommerstein's translation) and accuses Paphlagon of doing financial damage to the public treasury (826) and to the Athenian people (831). The Sausage Seller reiterates that Paphlagon does not love Demos (848) and asserts that Paphlagon is so tricky that Demos could not punish him if he wanted to (850).

When the Sausage Seller begins to provide Demos with the basic necessities of life, food and clothing, Demos moves closer allowing himself to move away from Paphlagon's influence. Upon receiving a new pair of shoes from the Sausage Seller, Demos declares him the best man for Demos (873). The Sausage Seller also says that Demos (882) should have a nice cloak at his age and then gives him one. When Paphlagon protests, the Sausage Seller quips that he is simply using the same sort of tactics that Paphlagon uses. The manipulative use of divine utterances in the form of oracles begins again as the play approaches its conclusion (997–1099). Once again, the Sausage Seller beats Paphlagon at his own game, manipulating the oracles as much as Paphlagon has. For every oracular utterance that Paphlagon issues, however, the Sausage Seller produces one that is even more favorable to Demos. Accordingly, Demos expresses his desire to entrust himself to the Sausage Seller's care.

When the Knights chastise Demos for being so gullible, Demos reveals that he just pretends to be foolish and that he is manipulating the two combatants for his own benefit. Upon hearing this, the Knights praise Demos' wisdom and remark that he is fattening up political leaders who try to manipulate Demos as if they are animals to be sacrificed for a public feast (*demosious,* 1136). Thus, whereas demogogues such as Cleon think they can prosper by fattening up Demos, Demos is actually fattening them up for his own meal.

The Sausage Seller ultimately proves the winner of the final contest for Demos' favor. When he shows Demos that his basket of goodies is empty and Paphlagon has held many things back in his basket, Demos declares the empty basket of the Sausage Seller has in mind "the things of the *demos*" (1216). After the defeated Paphlagon is sent off, a new and revitalized Demos goes forward. The Sausage Seller lectures Demos about being gullible and promises to punish those who try such tricks on him in the future.

So, although Aristophanes' attack on Cleon certainly seems to be the primary focus of *Knights,* the play also suggests that the Athenian people are susceptible to the manipulation of individual politicians, who influence them with flattery on both the human and the divine level. Aristophanes has every major character in the play comment on the foolishness and gullibility of the Athenian people, but he softens his criticism by having Demos claim that he knows what the politicians are doing to him and that he allows them to manipulate him verbally for his own advantages. Although Demos triumphed over Cleon in the fantasy world of Aristophanes' *Knights,* in the real world of Athens, the people again elected Cleon as one of their military commanders the next year.

BIBLIOGRAPHY

Bennett, L. J., and W. B. Tyrrell. "Making Sense of Aristophanes' *Knights,*" *Arethusa* 23 (1990): 235–54.

Edmonds, L. *Cleon, Knights, and Aristophanes' Politics.* Lanham, Md.: University Press of America, 1987.

Sommerstein, A. H. *The Comedies of Aristophanes.* Vol. 2, *Knights.* Warminster, U.K.: Aris & Phillips, 1981.

KOMMOS A Greek word derived from the verb *koptein,* "to beat" or "to strike," kommos (plural: *kom-*

moi) refers to the beating or striking of the breast in lamentation. In drama, the *kommos* is a song of wild lament in which the actor and CHORUS sing alternately. *Kommoi* occur twice in SOPHOCLES' *Ajax,* for example. In the first instance, TECMESSA and the chorus respond to the madness of Ajax. In the second, Ajax laments the calamity that has befallen him as the chorus try to comfort him. [ANCIENT SOURCES: Sophocles, *Ajax* 201–62, 348–429]

BIBLIOGRAPHY

Conacher, D. J. "Interaction between Chorus and Characters in the *Oresteia,*" *American Journal of Philology* 95 (1974): 323–43.
McDevitt, A. S. "The First *Kommos* of Sophocles' *Antigone,*" *Ramus* 11 (1982): 134–44.
Scott, W. C. "Musical Design in Sophocles' *Oedipus Tyrannus,*" *Arion* 4, no. 1 (1996–97): 33–44.

KORE   A name, meaning "maiden," for PERSEPHONE.

L

LACEDAEMON   See Sparta.

LACEDAEMONIA   See Sparta.

LACHES (1)   Not to be confused with the Athenian statesman Laches Laches is a fictional character in the plays of some comic poets after the time of Aristophanes, such as Menander's *Perinthia* and Terence's *Mother-in-Law*.

LACHES (2)   An Athenian statesman who served as a military commander in the early years of the Peloponnesian War. After Laches' mission in Sicily, Cleon prosecuted him for financial improprieties. Aristophanes parodies this prosecution in his *Wasps* in a trial involving two dogs, one of whom is named Labes ("snatcher"). In this mock trial, the dog Labes is prosecuted for stealing a Sicilian cheese from Philocleon's kitchen. [Ancient sources: Aristophanes, *Wasps* 240, 836, 895]

LACONIA   A region in southern Greece of which Sparta was the principal city. The Spartans are often called Laconians and a character called simply the Laconian appears in Aristophanes' *Lysistrata*. On a few occasions, Aristophanes mentions popular shoes, called Laconians, that were produced in this region. Several Greek comic poets—Cratinus (fragment 95 Kock 1), Eupolis (fragment 179 Kock 1), Plato the Comic (fragments 67–73 Kock 1), Eubulus (fragments 60–63 Kock 2), and Nichochares (Kock 1)—wrote plays entitled *Laconians*. Only the title of Nichochares' play survives and the short extant fragments of the plays of Cratinus and Eupolis reveal nothing of their content. Eubulus' play had the alternate title *Leda*, which indicates that the play had some relation to Helen's mother. The fragments, however, give little indication of the content. From Plato's *Laconians* (also known by the title *Poets*) about 20 lines survive, and three-quarters of these are found in fragment 69, in which two people, apparently slaves, discuss the dining that is ending and the entertainment that is beginning. [Ancient sources: Aristophanes, *Ecclesiazusae* 74, 269, 345, *Lysistrata* 1076ff., *Peace* 212, 282, 478, 622, *Wasps* 1158–62]

BIBLIOGRAPHY

Kock, T. *Comicorum Atticorum Fragmenta.* Vol. 1. Leipzig: Teubner, 1880.

Kock, T. *Comicorum Atticorum Fragmenta.* Vol. 2. Leipzig: Teubner, 1884.

LACRATEIDES   Perhaps a fictional character named as a member of the chorus in Aristophanes' *Acharnians* (220), although there was a historical Lacrateides who was an Archon in Athens during the last 20 years of the fifth century b.c.e.

BIBLIOGRAPHY

Sommerstein, A. H. *The Comedies of Aristophanes.* Vol. 1, *Acharnians.* Warminster, U.K.: Aris & Phillips, 1980, 167.

LAERTES The son of Arcesius, Laertes was the king of ITHACA and by Anticlea became the father of ODYSSEUS; however, sometimes Odysseus is called the son of the notorious trickster SISYPHUS. In extant drama, Laertes' name is heard almost exclusively in reference to Odysseus, whom the playwrights often call "Laertes' son." Ancient sources indicate that Laertes participated in the hunt for the Calydonian boar and JASON's quest for the Golden Fleece. [ANCIENT SOURCES: Apollodorus, *Library* 1.9.16, *Epitome* 3.12; Homer, *Odyssey;* Hyginus, *Fables* 95, 125]

LAIS A famous prostitute who, at the age of seven, was taken by the Athenian military from SICILY (ca. 422 B.C.E.) She was sold into slavery in CORINTH and became a prostitute. Apparently, Lais was still working in the profession in the 360s. [ANCIENT SOURCES: Aristophanes, *Wealth* 178; Epicrates, fragment 3 Kock 2; Pausanias, 2.2.5; Philetaerus, fragment 9.4 Kock 2; Plato Comicus, fragment 196; Plutarch, *Nicias* 15.4; Strattis, fragment 27 Kock 1]

BIBLIOGRAPHY
Kock, T. *Comicorum Atticorum Fragmenta.* Vol. 1. Leipzig: Teubner, 1880.
———. *Comicorum Atticorum Fragmenta.* Vol. 2. Leipzig: Teubner, 1884.
Sommerstein, A. H. *The Comedies of Aristophanes.* Vol. 11, *Wealth.* Warminster, U.K.: Aris & Phillips, 2001, 148.

LAISPODIAS An Athenian statesman and military commander who helped lead a military raid against Spartan territory in southeastern Greece in 414 B.C.E. In 411, the oligarchic government of the Four Hundred sent Laispodias to SPARTA as a diplomatic envoy. The comic poets made fun of Laispodias because of something unusual about the calves of his legs. [ANCIENT SOURCES: Aristophanes, *Birds* 1569; EUPOLIS, fragment 102 Kock; Thucydides, 6.105.2]

BIBLIOGRAPHY
Dunbar, Nan. *Aristophanes: Birds.* New York: Oxford University Press, 1995, 716–17.
Kock, T. *Comicorum Atticorum Fragmenta.* Vol. 1. Leipzig: Teubner, 1880.

LAIUS A king of THEBES, Laius was the son of Labdacus. Laius married JOCASTA, but at some point in his life he was attracted to CHRYSIPPUS, the son of PELOPS, and abducted him. Apparently the gods did not approve of their relationship: Some sources indicate that Laius and his fellow Thebans were punished by a visitation from the SPHINX; others say that Laius' punishment was to father a son, Oedipus, who would kill him. After hearing an oracle that he would be killed by his son, Laius avoided having intercourse with Jocasta. Jocasta, however, made Laius drunk one night, when Oedipus was conceived. After the child was born, Laius decided to expose the infant and gave him to a shepherd for this purpose. The Theban shepherd, however, gave the child to a Corinthian shepherd, who turned the child over to his masters, Polybus and MEROPE, the king and queen of Corinth. Polybus and Merope called the child Oedipus, "swollen foot," because Laius had arranged for the child's ankles to be bound together to ensure that he would not survive exposure. When Oedipus grew up, his parentage was questioned and he went to Delphi to ask Apollo's oracle about his identity. Told that he would kill his father and marry his mother, Oedipus decided not to return to Corinth. Instead, he traveled south from Delphi toward Thebes. At a place where three roads met, Oedipus encountered Laius. When the king tried to force Oedipus off the road and struck him with his staff, Oedipus, not realizing he was his true father, lashed out and killed Laius and most of his party.

Aeschylus wrote a *Laius* (the first play of his *Oedipus* tetralogy, which included SEVEN AGAINST THEBES); only two words survive (fragments 121–22 Radt). In SENECA's *OEDIPUS*, CREON reports to Oedipus that the ghost of Laius, conjured from the underworld, revealed that Oedipus was his killer and had married his mother. [ANCIENT SOURCES: Aeschylus, *Seven against Thebes;* Apollodorus, *Library* 3.5.5–8, 3.15.7; Euripides, *Phoenician Women;* Hyginus, *Fables* 66–67; Seneca, *Oedipus;* Sophocles, *Oedipus Tyrannos*]

BIBLIOGRAPHY
Halliwell, S. "Where Three Roads Meet: A Neglected Detail in the *Oedipus Tyrannus*," *Journal of Hellenic Studies* 106 (1986): 187–90.

Radt, S. *Tragicorum Graecorum Fragmenta.* Vol. 3. Göttingen, Ger.: Vandenhoeck & Ruprecht, 1985.

LAMACHUS (DIED 414 B.C.E.)

Lamachus, son of Xenophanes, was an Athenian general who lived in the latter half of the fifth century B.C.E. Forming a clear picture of Lamachus is difficult because he is characterized by both historians and comic poets. By the mid-430s, Lamachus had been elected *strategos* (general), and in his earliest appearance, described by THUCYDIDES, Lamachus sailed with 10 ships into the Pontus but subsequently lost his fleet in a flood on the river Calex. By the mid-420s, Lamachus was a recognizable enough figure to be a prominent character in ARISTOPHANES' ACHARNIANS (425 B.C.E.) and to be mentioned several times in his PEACE (421 B.C.E.). Lamachus' name also appears in a fragment of Aristophanes' *Georgoi* (Farmers). Aristophanes' *Acharnians* and *Peace* represent Lamachus as a warmonger who wants to continue the prosecution of the war with Sparta and its allies. In *Peace*, Aristophanes even puts onstage a young warrior who calls himself the son of Lamachus and has him sing about the glories of war—a performance that the play's peace-loving hero, Trygaeus, mocks. Although Thucydides mentions Lamachus as among the Athenians who signed the Peace of NICIAS in 421, in *Peace* Aristophanes describes the peace as a "day hateful to Lamachus" (O'Neill's translation).

In contrast to the negative portrayal by Lamachus' contemporary Aristophanes, the biographer Plutarch presents a fairly positive view of Lamachus. Plutarch says Lamachus "was a good soldier and a brave man; but he lacked authority and prestige because he was poor" (Perrin's translation). Plutarch also contrasts Lamachus' "roughness" or "ruggedness" with ALCIBIADES' daring and Nicias' caution. The combination of Lamachus' lack of financial resources and "ruggedness" and his high profile as a military commander would probably have made him an easy target for Aristophanes. Because Lamachus' name contains the root *machus-*, which means "warrior," Lamachus also would have been a logical candidate for Aristophanes' stereotypical warmonger. Despite Aristophanes' characterization of Lamachus in his early plays, a decade after Lamachus' death, Aristophanes' character Aeschylus singles out Lamachus as a fine example of a warrior.

Between the extremes of Aristophanes' and Plutarch's portrayals of Lamachus, Aristophanes' contemporary, Thucydides, gives a rather neutral picture of Lamachus. In 415, Lamachus, though well along in age, was appointed as one of the generals with Alcibiades and Nicias in the Athenians' expedition to SICILY, where Lamachus died in battle at Syracuse. At no point does Thucydides explicitly condemn Lamachus when he does not experience success or praise him when he does. [ANCIENT SOURCES: Aristophanes, *Frogs* 1038, *Peace* 304, 1270–90; Diodorus Siculus, 12.72.4, 12.84.3; Plutarch, *Alcibiades* 18.2, 21.9, *Nicias* 12.3–4; Thucydides, 4.75.1–2, 5.19.2, 5.24.1, 6.8.2, 6.101.6]

BIBLIOGRAPHY
Ketterer, R. C. "Lamachus and Xerxes in the Exodus of the *Acharnians*," *Greek, Roman, and Byzantine Studies* 32 (1991): 51–60.

LAMENTATION

An expression of sorrow or grief. In Greek culture, lamentation was often expressed by certain gestures and practices. In the case of lamentation of the dead, Greek mourners would extend their hand in a gesture of farewell. Women customarily made cries of wailing, tore at their face with their fingernails, and beat their breasts with their fists. Given the nature of tragic poetry, in these plays lamentation about a person's lot in life or about those who have died is common. Sometimes laments are sung by the CHORUS alone, as in EURIPIDES' HERACLES, at lines 1016–38, in which the chorus lament HERACLES' murder of his wife and children. Sometimes individual characters make lamentation, as in SOPHOCLES' AJAX, where at lines 974–1039, the title character's brother, TEUCER, laments the fate that awaits him after AJAX's death. In some cases, the chorus sang a responsive lament with another character in the play. In SOPHOCLES' OEDIPUS TYRANNOS, at lines 1297–1368, the chorus and OEDIPUS lament antiphonally over his blinding and the discovery of his crimes. In other cases, the chorus divided into two groups and lamented responsively, as at the conclusion of AESCHYLUS' SEVEN AGAINST THEBES.

BIBLIOGRAPHY
Foley, H. P. "The Politics of Tragic Lamentation." In *Tragedy, Comedy and the Polis.* Edited by Alan H. Sommerstein et al. Bari: Levante, 1993, 101–43.

LAMIA   The Lamiae were vampirelike creatures who were women from the waist up and serpents from the waist down. Their face glowed with fire, their body was smeared with blood, and some sources indicate they had feet made of either lead or iron. Some sources make them blind; others say they had a single eye. Lamiae are typically found in Africa or THESSALY (in which there was even a town called Lamia), where they attack those who travel along the main roads. They appear to have been attracted especially to the blood of young human beings, and they could either change their shape or hiss seductively to attract their victims.

According to one tradition, Lamia, daughter of POSEIDON, was a beautiful African queen. When HERA discovered that Lamia had had an affair with ZEUS, Hera destroyed her children. After that, Lamia killed the children of other women. Because of Lamia's cruel actions, the gods changed her into a wild animal. Lamia is mentioned a few times in the plays of ARISTO-PHANES, who seems to consider Lamia a male creature, twice referring to its unwashed testicles. EURIPIDES wrote a *Lamia,* of which only the title survives. In Euripides' *Busiris* (see BUSIRIS) a character named Lamia is a speaker. The comic poet Crates also wrote a *Lamia,* of which three brief fragments survive (19–21 Kock). Fragment 19 suggests that Thessaly may have been the play's setting. [ANCIENT SOURCES: Aristophanes, *Wasps* 1035, *Peace* 758; Pausanias, 10.12.1]

BIBLIOGRAPHY
Kock, T. *Comicorum Atticorum Fragmenta.* Vol. 1. Leipzig: Teubner, 1880.
Nauck, A. *Tragicorum Graecorum Fragmenta.* 1889. Reprint, Hildesheim: Olms, 1964.
Snell, B. *Tragicorum Graecorum Fragmenta: Supplementum.* Hildesheim, Ger.: Olms, 1964.

LAMIUS   The name or nickname of the husband of a woman mentioned by ARISTOPHANES at *ECCLESI-AZUSAE* 77. The ancient commentators on *Ecclesiazusae* 77 say that he was a poor man who made a living by carrying wood. These commentators also indicate that Lamius was the name of a jailer in COMEDY. The lexicographer Hesychius, at *lambda* 252, says Lamius was called the "Saw" (*priona*) or the "Axe" (*pelekus*) and that a certain comic poet also called him Mnesitheus.

Photius' lexicon, at *lambda* 206.21, also says Lamius' real name was Mnesitheus, a common name in ATHENS. Nothing else about this Lamius/Mnesitheus is known.

BIBLIOGRAPHY
Sommerstein, A. H. *The Comedies of Aristophanes.* Vol. 10, *Ecclesiazusae.* Warminster, U.K.: Aris & Phillips, 1998, 144–45.

LAMPON   An Athenian soothsayer who helped lead a group to colonize Thurii. The Greek comic poet Antiphanes wrote a *Lampon* from which two brief fragments (138–39 Kock) survive—the former about mullets, the latter about mixing of wine. [ANCIENT SOURCES: Aristophanes, *Birds* 521, 988, PEACE 1084; Athenaeus, 7.307d]

BIBLIOGRAPHY
Kock, T. *Comicorum Atticorum Fragmenta.* Vol. 2. Leipzig: Teubner, 1884.

LAOCOON   Famous for saying "I fear Greeks even bearing gifts," Laocoon was a Trojan priest who warned his fellow citizens not to take into their city the wooden horse, which the Greeks had left. Vergil says Laocoon threw his spear at the horse, which was dedicated to ATHENA, and that later Laocoon and his sons were killed by two sea serpents. The Trojans took this as an omen that the gods were angry that Laocoon had struck the horse and took it into their city. SOPHOCLES wrote a *Laocoon* of which more than a dozen lines survive (fragments 370–77 Radt). Fragment 371 may be a prayer to POSEIDON, perhaps by Laocoon. Fragment 373, spoken by a messenger, refers to Aeneas' carrying his father and leading a group of Trojans from the city. [ANCIENT SOURCES: Hyginus, *Fables* 135; Vergil, *Aeneid* 2]

BIBLIOGRAPHY
Kiso, A. *The Lost Sophocles.* New York: Vantage Press, 1984.
Lloyd-Jones, H. *Sophocles: Fragments.* Cambridge, Mass.: Harvard University Press, 1996.
Radt, S. *Tragicorum Graecorum Fragmenta.* Vol. 4. Göttingen, Ger.: Vandenhoeck & Ruprecht, 1977.
Sutton, D. F. *The Lost Sophocles.* Lanham, Md.: University Press of America, 1984.

LAODAMEIA   The daughter of ACASTUS, Laodameia married PROTESILAUS. After Protesilaus died in the Trojan War, the gods pitied Laodameia's grief and allowed Hermes to take him back from the UNDERWORLD for three hours. After conversing with his wife, Protesilaus returned to the underworld and Laodameia committed suicide. Other sources indicate that Laodameia missed her husband so much that she had a statue made of him. Laodameia placed the statue in her bed and spoke to it, caressed it, and even kissed it. When a servant saw Laodameia doing this, the servant, thinking Laodameia unfaithful to Protesilaus, reported her behavior to Acastus. Acastus had the statue burned, and Laodameia, unable to bear her grief, threw herself into the same flames and died. [ANCIENT SOURCES: Apollodorus, *Epitome* 3.30; Hyginus, *Fables* 103–4]

LAOMEDON

The son of Ilus, Laomedon was a king of TROY and the father of, among others, PRIAM and HESIONE. APOLLO and POSEIDON built walls for TROY during Laomedon's kingship but then inflicted hardship on the town when Laomedon did not give them the reward he had promised for this work. When a Poseidon-sent sea monster tormented the Trojans, Laomedon consulted an oracle about what to do. The oracle declared that Laomedon must sacrifice his daughter to the monster. Laomedon was obedient to the oracle, but HERACLES arrived in time to save Hesione and kill the monster. Again, however, Laomedon did not give Heracles the reward (horses) on which they had agreed. Accordingly, Heracles later returned to Troy, sacked the town, killed Laomedon, and took Hesione captive. Laomedon does not appear as a character in any surviving dramas, but he appears to have been a character in the Greek tragedian Demetrius' SATYR PLAY HESIONE. [ANCIENT SOURCES: Apollodorus, *Library* 2.5.9; Euripides, *Trojan Women* 814, 822; Hyginus, *Fables* 89; Ovid, *Metamorphoses* 11.194–220; Seneca, *Agamemnon* 864; Sophocles, *Ajax* 1302]

BIBLIOGRAPHY
Snell, B. *Tragicorum Graecorum Fragmenta*. Vol. 1. Göttingen, Ger.: Vandenhoeck & Ruprecht, 1971.

LAPITHS

A Greek tribe living in northeastern Greece. The Lapiths had a feud with the CENTAURS. PIRITHOUS was a member of the Lapith tribe when they fought and defeated the centaurs. [ANCIENT SOURCES:

Apollodorus, *Library* 2.5.4, 2.7.7; Euripides, *Andromache* 791; Hyginus, *Fables* 33; Ovid, *Metamorphoses* 12.210–535; Seneca, *Hercules Furens* 779]

LAR

Among the Romans, a Lar was a divinity who watched over a particular house. In PLAUTUS' POT OF GOLD, the Lar of Euclio's house delivers the PROLOGUE.

LARISA

A town in northeastern Greece in the region of THESSALY, Larisa would presumably have been the setting for SOPHOCLES' *Men of Larisa* (fragments 378–83 Radt), a play that may have dealt with PERSEUS' killing of his grandfather, ACRISIUS.

BIBLIOGRAPHY
Lloyd-Jones, H. *Sophocles: Fragments*. Cambridge, Mass.: Harvard University Press, 1996.
Radt, S. *Tragicorum Graecorum Fragmenta*. Vol. 4. Göttingen, Ger.: Vandenhoeck & Ruprecht, 1977.
Sutton, D. F. *The Lost Sophocles*. Lanham, Md.: University Press of America, 1984.

LASTHENES

A Theban whom ETEOCLES matches against AMPHIARAUS in the battle of the Seven against THEBES. [ANCIENT SOURCES: Aeschylus, *Seven against Thebes* 620]

LASUS

From the town of Hermione in southeastern Greece, the poet Lasus lived during the last half of the sixth century B.C.E. He went to ATHENS between 527 and 514 and may have helped institute competitions in dithyrambic poetry there. Lasus was famous for his wit and wisdom, as well as his research in acoustics and innovation in musical technique. [ANCIENT SOURCES: Aristophanes, *Wasps* 1410; Athenaeus, 8.338b–d, 10.455c; Herodotus, 7.6.3; pseudo-Plutarch, *Moralia* 1141c; *Suda,* "l" 139]

BIBLIOGRAPHY
Sommerstein, A. H. *The Comedies of Aristophanes*. Vol. 4, *Wasps*. Warminster, U.K.: Aris & Phillips, 1983, 241.

LATONA See LETO.

LEDA

The daughter of THESTIUS and Eurythemis, Leda married TYNDAREUS after he took refuge in her land of AETOLIA. Later, Tyndareus returned to his native SPARTA and became king. Their first child was Timandra (or Phoebe). Later, ZEUS and Tyndareus had intercourse with Leda on the same night—Zeus impregnated her when he appeared in the form of a swan—and Leda gave birth to four children, two boys and two girls. Polydeuces (or POLLUX) and HELEN were the children of Zeus; CASTOR and CLYTEMNESTRA were Tyndareus' children. In EURIPIDES' HELEN, the playwright says Leda committed suicide in shame about Helen's reputation. The Greek comic poet Sophilus wrote a *Leda* (alternatively entitled *Tyndareus*), of which only the title survives. The comic poet Eubulus also wrote a *Leda*, whose four short fragments (60–63 Kock) reveal little about the play's plot. [ANCIENT SOURCES: Apollodorus, 3.10.6–7; Euripides, *Iphigenia at Aulis* 49–51; Seneca, *Agamemnon* 125, 234, *Hercules Furens* 14, *Octavia* 205, 208, 764]

BIBLIOGRAPHY
Kock, T. *Comicorum Atticorum Fragmenta*. Vol. 2. Leipzig: Teubner, 1884.

LEIPSYDRIUM

A place in Athenian territory where, in the next-to-last decade of the sixth century B.C.E., the military forces of the tyrant, HIPPIAS, beseiged Athenians sympathetic to the Alcmeonid exiles. The sympathizers were defeated, but Hippias was eventually overthrown in 511/510. [ANCIENT SOURCES: Aristophanes, *Lysistrata* 665]

BIBLIOGRAPHY
Henderson, J. *Aristophanes: Lysistrata*. Oxford: Clarendon Press, 1987, 159.

LEMNOS

An island in the northern AEGEAN, Lemnos was the site of several tragic occurrences in Greek mythology. The god HEPHAESTUS, to whom the island was sacred, convalesced on the island after he was thrown from MOUNT OLYMPUS. PHILOCTETES was abandoned on this island for several years after the Greeks grew tired of the odor and commotion that occurred in connection with his snake-bitten foot (see SOPHOCLES, *PHILOCTETES*). The most famous occurrence on the island took place when the wives of Lemnos killed the husbands, one of the most notorious acts in classical mythology. Not long after the killings, the Argonauts arrived, were received hospitably by the Lemnian women, and helped repopulate the island by impregnating them. JASON himself fathered at least one child by their leader, HYPSIPYLE. ARISTOPHANES wrote a *Women of Lemnos* (*Lemniai*), from which 13 brief fragments survive (356–75 Kock). What aspect of the Lemnian women's story the play treated is not clear. The comic poet Nicochares also wrote a *Women of Lemnos* that may have dealt with the encounter of the Argonauts and the Lemnian women (fragments 11–14 Kock). [ANCIENT SOURCES: Homer, *Iliad* 1.468–69, 593; Seneca, *Agamemnon* 566, *Hercules Oetaeus* 1362]

BIBLIOGRAPHY
Kock, T. *Comicorum Atticorum Fragmenta*. Vol. 1. Leipzig: Teubner, 1880.

LENA

The *lena*, a madam or procuress, is a stock character in New Comedy. In two of PLAUTUS' extant comedies, *COMEDY OF ASSES* (Cleareta) and *BASKET COMEDY* (Melaenis), a *lena* appears.

BIBLIOGRAPHY
Morenilla Talens, C. "De lenae in comoedia figura," *Helmantica* 45 (1994) 81–106.

LENAEA

This Athenian festival, which honored the god DIONYSUS, took place on Gamelion 12 (roughly January). The festival was held at the Lenaeum, which was an important sanctuary of Dionysus in ATHENS. The derivation of the word Lenaea is not certain. Some think it was derived from *lenos* (wine vat); others think it was related to Lenai, a name for female worshipers of Dionysus. The Lenaea included a feast for the people that was paid for by the city. After the feast, the participants had a procession through the town, and, beginning around 442 B.C.E., festival goers were entertained by the performance of tragedies and beginning around 432, by commedies. In contrast to the City DIONYSIA, at which three tragedians staged three tragedies and a SATYR PLAY, the Lenaea was a competition of two tragedians, each presenting two tragedies. In the case of comedy, five playwrights each put on one play, as at the City Dionysia. Unlike the City Dionysia (held two months later), at which a large number of non-Athenians would have been present, the Lenaea apparently did not attract significant numbers of outsiders because the weather at that time of year was not conducive to travel. Although several of ARISTOPHANES' plays were staged at the Lenaea (ACHARNIANS, KNIGHTS, WASPS, FROGS, and probably LYSISTRATA), Pickard-Cambridge writes that the "great tragic poets seldom appeared" at this festival and it is clear that a victory at the Lenaea did not carry as much prestige as victory at the City Dionysia. Competition in TRAGEDY occurred at the Lenaea at least until 200 B.C.E., and competition in comedy is attested even after 150 B.C.E.

BIBLIOGRAPHY
Parke, H. W. Festivals of the Athenians. Ithaca, N.Y.: Cornell University Press, 1977, 104–6.
Pickard-Cambridge, A. W. Dithyramb, Tragedy, and Comedy, 2d ed. Revised by T. B. L. Webster. Oxford: Clarendon Press, 1962, 22–40.

LENO   See PIMP.

LEO   After HERACLES killed the lion of NEMEA, the animal's image was placed in the heavens as the zodiacal constellation Leo (the Latin word for "lion"). [ANCIENT SOURCES: Seneca, Hercules Furens 69, 83, 945, Thyestes 855]

LEOGORAS   A rich Athenian aristocrat who lived during the fifth century B.C.E. He was connected by marriage to PERICLES, and the famous orator Andocides was his son. [ANCIENT SOURCES: Aristophanes, Clouds 109, Wasps 1269; Plato Comicus, fragment 106.2 Kock]

BIBLIOGRAPHY
Kock, T. Comicorum Atticorum Fragmenta. Vol. 1. Leipzig: Teubner, 1880.

LEONIDAS (DIED 480 B.C.E.)   The Spartan king who died at Thermopylae leading a valiant defense of the coastal route there against a numerically superior Persian army. [ANCIENT SOURCES: Aristophanes, Lysistrata 1254; Herodotus, 7.205.2]

LEOTROPHIDES   A thin, weak-looking, and untalented playwright who was a contemporary of

ARISTOPHANES. [ANCIENT SOURCES: Aristophanes, Birds 1406; Hermippus, fragment 35.3 Kock]

BIBLIOGRAPHY
Kock, T. Comicorum Atticorum Fragmenta. Vol. 1. Leipzig: Teubner, 1880.

LEPREUS (LEPREON)   A town in southwestern Greece south of Olympia. [ANCIENT SOURCES: Aristophanes, Birds 149; Thucydides 5.34.1]

LERNA   A town on the southeastern coast of Greece, a few miles south of ARGOS, Lerna is famous in mythology as the home of the deadly Lernaean Hydra. This monster, the offspring of Typhon and Echidna, was a serpent that had numerous heads and haunted the swamps near the town of Lerna. Heracles was given the task of killing the Hydra as his second labor. Whenever Heracles tried to cut off one of the monster's heads, two more heads sprang up. Eventually, with the aid of his nephew, Iolaus, Heracles put an end to this exponential growth and killed the monster by cutting off a head and then burning the place where the head had been. After the Hydra's death, Heracles dipped his arrows into the monster's venom, an act that caused the arrows to cause certain death. Eventually Heracles himself was destroyed by venom from his own arrows. [ANCIENT SOURCES: Sophocles, Trachinian Women; Seneca, Hercules Furens 241–43; Seneca, Hercules Oetaeus]

LESBOS   An island off the northwest coast of what is today Turkey. The island was famous for its wine. The island's principal city was MYTILENE. [ANCIENT SOURCES: Aeschylus, Persians 882; Aristophanes, Ecclesiazusae 920; Plautus, Carthaginian 699; Seneca, Oedipus 496, Trojan Women 226]

LETHE   A body of water in the UNDERWORLD. Drinking the water of Lethe (which means "forgetfulness" in Greek) causes one to forget all memories of the upper world. [ANCIENT SOURCES: Seneca, Hercules Furens 680, 777, Hercules Oetaeus 936, 1162, 1208, 1550, 1985, Hippolytus 1202]

LETO   The daughter of Coeus and Phoebe, the goddess Leto (Latin: Latona) was the sister of Asteria. Some sources make Leto the sister of HECATE, although EURIPIDES calls her Hecate's mother. By ZEUS Leto became the mother of twins, APOLLO and ARTEMIS. When HERA discovered Leto's affair with Zeus, Leto was pregnant with Apollo and Artemis. Wanting to punish Leto, Hera sent a giant serpent, the Python, to pursue her. The pregnant Leto fled and wandered the world in search of refuge. She finally arrived at the island of DELOS, where she gave birth to Artemis, who then helped her mother deliver Apollo. After the birth of the twins, the three divinities, still harassed by the Python, traveled to DELPHI. There, Apollo killed the Python. While at Delphi, Leto was attacked by TITYUS, but Apollo and Artemis killed Tityus. Leto does not appear in any extant dramas, although she would have figured in some way in plays that dealt with NIOBE, who boasted that she was blessed with more children than Leto. This boast drew Leto's wrath on Niobe and Leto sent her two children, Apollo and Artemis, to kill Leto's children (who were at least 12 in number). [ANCIENT SOURCES: Apollodorus, *Library* 1.2.2, 1.4.1; Euripides, *Phoenician Women* 109–10]

LEUCOLOPHUS (LEUCOLOPHIDES)

Probably the son of Adeimantus of Scambonidae. Adeimantus was one of the few Athenian commanders not executed after the battle of Aegospotami in 405 B.C.E. In 352/351, Leucolophus was honored for service to the island of Imbros, which the Athenians had colonized. [ANCIENT SOURCES: Aristophanes, *Ecclesiazusae* 645, *Frogs* 1513; Eupolis, fragment 210.2 Kock]

BIBLIOGRAPHY
Kock, T. *Comicorum Atticorum Fragmenta*. Vol. 1. Leipzig: Teubner, 1880.
Sommerstein, A. H. *The Comedies of Aristophanes*. Vol. 10, *Ecclesiazusae*. Warminster, U.K.: Aris & Phillips, 1998, 195.

LIBATION   A liquid OFFERING (honey, milk, water, or wine), poured out on many solemn occasions. After a meal, for example, three libations were poured onto the ground—"The first to Olympian Zeus, the second to the heroes, and the third to Zeus the Saviour" (Brown). Libations were also poured out to the spirits of the dead at their grave or on their tomb. AESCHYLUS' *Libation Bearers* (see ORESTEIA) opens with the pouring of libations at the grave of AGAMEMNON. In EURIPIDES' *ION,* ION discovers that his wine has been poisoned when he pours the liquid onto the ground as a libation and a bird that drinks some of it dies. [ANCIENT SOURCES: Euripides, *Iphigenia in Tauris* 165; Sophocles, *Oedipus at Colonus* 466–90]

BIBLIOGRAPHY
Brown, A. *A New Companion to Greek Tragedy*. London: Croom Helm, 1983, 120.

LIBATION BEARERS   See ORESTEIA.

LIBRA   The constellation of the zodiac that represents a balance or scales. [ANCIENT SOURCES: Seneca, *Hippolytus* 839, *Thyestes* 858]

LIBYA   A region of northern Africa; sometimes the ancients used the name as a synonym for the entire continent of Africa. According to legend, the region took its name from Libya, the child of EPAPHUS and Memphis. HERACLES' labors took him through Libya. [ANCIENT SOURCES: Aeschylus, *Suppliant Women* 279, 317; Apollodorus, *Library* 2.1.4; Euripides, *Helen* 170, 404, 786, 1211, 1479; Seneca, *Hercules Furens* 482, 1171, *Hercules Oetaeus* 24]

LICHAS   A messenger who appears as a character in SOPHOCLES' *TRACHINIAN WOMEN* and SENECA'S *HERCULES OETAEUS*. Lichas does not have a speaking role in Seneca's play. In both plays, Lichas delivers to HERACLES the poisoned robe from DEIANEIRA that causes Heracles' destruction. In each play, Heracles, in a frenzy of pain-generated madness, kills Lichas. In Sophocles' play, which focuses to a great extent on communication and the accuracy of information, Lichas plays a more integral role with respect to the play's theme, as Sophocles' Lichas gives Deianeira false information about Heracles' actions against EURYTUS and his kingdom. Given Sophocles' concern with the accuracy of information, that the messenger Lichas, who delivers the poisoned robe, should meet his death seems only fitting. Lichas is the only messenger in extant TRAGEDY who dies.

LICYMNIUS (LIKYMNIOS)   Licymnius, the son of ELECTRYON and Midea, survived the cattle raid by the TELEBOANS that killed his brothers. After AMPHITRYON killed ELECTRYON, Licymnius traveled with Amphitryon and ALCMENA to THEBES. There, he grew up and eventually married Perimede, who was the daughter either of CREON or of Amphitryon and Alcmena. Licymnius had several sons, and he and his family were staunch supporters of HERACLES. While participating in an attack on ARGOS by Heracles' descendants, one of Heracles' sons, Tlepolemus, killed Licymnius accidentally or in a fit of anger. EURIPIDES wrote a *Licymnius* (fragments 473–78 Nauck) that was staged before 448 B.C.E. XENOCLES also wrote a *Licymnius;* in the surviving fragment of this play (2 Snell), Alcmena laments the death of Licymnius at the hands of Tlepolemus.

BIBLIOGRAPHY
Nauck, A. *Tragicorum Graecorum Fragmenta.* 1889. Reprint, Hildesheim, Ger.: Olms, 1964.
Snell, B. *Tragicorum Graecorum Fragmenta.* Vol. 1. Göttingen, Ger.: Vandenhoeck & Ruprecht, 1971.
Webster, T. B. L. *The Tragedies of Euripides.* London: Methuen, 1967.

LIGURIA   A region near the coast of northwestern Italy. The Romans called those who lived in this region Ligurians; the Greeks called them Ligyes or Ligystini. [ANCIENT SOURCES: Euripides, *Trojan Women* 437]

LIMNAE   A marshy area of uncertain location (perhaps south of the ACROPOLIS) in Athenian territory. The place had a sanctuary dedicated to DIONYSUS. [ANCIENT SOURCES: Aristophanes, *Frogs* 217]

BIBLIOGRAPHY
Dover, K. J. *Aristophanes: Frogs.* Oxford: Clarendon Press, 1993, 223.

LINUS   Various and numerous males (Amphimarus, APOLLO, Oeagrus) and females (Aethusa, Callipe, Psamathe, Urania) are named as the parents of Linus, a skilled musician, whose most famous pupil was the young HERACLES. Once, when Heracles was 12 years old, Linus struck him for playing poorly. The enraged Heracles struck his teacher and killed him. Later, the young Heracles was acquitted of Linus' murder because he convinced his judges that he had been struck wrongfully. Among the Greek dramatists, Achaeus wrote a satyric *Linus,* whose only surviving fragment (26 Snell) suggests that the play dealt with Linus' encounter with Heracles. [ANCIENT SOURCES: Apollodorus, *Library* 2.4.9; Hyginus, *Fables* 161, 273]

BIBLIOGRAPHY
Snell, B. *Tragicorum Graecorum Fragmenta.* Vol. 1. Göttingen, Ger.: Vandenhoeck & Ruprecht, 1971.

LIVIA (CA. 13 B.C.E.–CA. 31 C.E.)   Also known as Livilla, Claudia Livia was a Roman woman who was the wife of Drusus, the son of the emperor, Tiberius. Livia had an affair with Sejanus, the commander of Tiberius' Praetorian Guard, and the lovers poisoned Drusus, who died in 23 C.E. After the plot was discovered, both Livia and Sejanus were put to death. [ANCIENT SOURCES: Seneca, *Octavia* 942]

LIVIUS   See DRUSUS.

LOGEION   The *logeion,* Greek for "talking place," is the wooden platform that forms the roof of the PROSKENION. Thus, it is the stage. The Latin equivalent is *pulpitum.* [ANCIENT SOURCES: Plutarch, *Theseus* 16; Vitruvius, *On Architecture* 5.7.2]

LOTUS   A plant that, according to legend, caused those who consumed it to be forgetful. During the return of ODYSSEUS from TROY, he and his crew arrived in the land of the Lotus Eaters. Some of Odysseus' crew ate lotus and forgot their goal of returning home. Odysseus, however, forced the affected crew members to return to the ship and continue the voyage. [ANCIENT SOURCES: Apollodorus, *Epitome* 7.3; Euripides, *Phoenician Women* 1571, *Trojan Women* 439; Herodotus, 2.92, 4.177–78; Homer, *Odyssey* 9.82–104]

LOVE   See EROS.

LOVES   See EROTES.

LOXIAS   See APOLLO.

LUCINA See Eileithyia.

LUCRETIA A beautiful and virtuous Roman woman who was the wife of Tarquinius Collatinus. She was sexually assaulted by Sextus Tarquinius, son of the Roman king, Tarquinius Superbus. Lucretia told her husband and father what had happened and urged them to avenge her; she then committed suicide. Anger about the assault on Lucretia led to expulsion of Tarquinius Superbus as king in 510 B.C.E. [ANCIENT SOURCES: Diodorus Siculus, 10.20–21; Hyginus, *Fables* 256; Livy 1.57–59; Seneca, *Octavia* 302]

LUNA See Moon.

LYCABETTUS A rather tall hill (more than 900 feet high) situated east of the Acropolis in Athens. [ANCIENT SOURCES: Aristophanes, *Frogs* 1056]

LYCAEAN PRECINCT A sacred area dedicated to Zeus Lycaeus on Mount Lycaeon, between Olympia and Argos in southern Greece. [ANCIENT SOURCES: Euripides, *Electra* 1274]

LYCAEUS See Apollo.

LYCAON A son of Ares and the nymph Pyrene, Lycaon is mentioned by Euripides, at *Alcestis* 502, as having been overcome in battle by Heracles. Other details about this encounter are unknown.

LYCIA A region near the southwestern coast of what is modern-day Turkey. Apollo and Artemis were especially associated with this region. In the Trojan War, the Lycians were allies of the Trojans. [ANCIENT SOURCES: Aeschylus, *Libation Bearers* 346 (see *Oresteia*); Aristophanes, *Knights* 1240; Euripides, *Rhesus* 29, 224, 543; Sophocles, *Oedipus Tyrannos* 208]

LYCIS A comic playwright whom Aristophanes mocks at *Frogs* 14 for using the same old jokes in all his plays, although he may have won at the Dionysia in the latter part of the fifth century B.C.E.

BIBLIOGRAPHY
Dover, K. J. *Aristophanes: Frogs.* Oxford: Clarendon Press, 1993, 192.

LYCOMEDES A king on the island of Scyros. When Achilles was trying to avoid fighting at Troy, he hid at the court of Lycomedes. Achilles later impregnated Lycomedes' daughter, Deidamia, and fathered Neoptolemus. Eventually Achilles was discovered hiding at Lycomedes' palace and compelled to go to Troy. While Achilles was at Troy, Lycomedes served as a foster father to Neoptolemus. Elsewhere in classical mythology, Lycomedes does not seem to have been a pleasant fellow, as he is credited with killing Theseus. [ANCIENT SOURCES: Hyginus, *Fables* 96; Sophocles, *Philoctetes* 243]

LYCON From Thorikos (not far southeast of Athens), Lycon was the husband of Rhodia. Although Lycon appears friendly with Socrates in Xenophon, Plato makes him one of Socrates' accusers in the trial that led to his condemnation to death. [ANCIENT SOURCES: Aristophanes, *Lysistrata* 270, *Wasps* 1301; Eupolis, fragment 215, 273 Kock; Plato, *Symposium* 23e, 36a; Xenophon, *Symposium* 9.1]

BIBLIOGRAPHY
Henderson, J. *Aristophanes: Lysistrata.* Oxford: Clarendon Press, 1987, 102.
Kock, T. *Comicorum Atticorum Fragmenta.* Vol. 1. Leipzig: Teubner, 1880.

LYCURGUS (1) A king of Nemea. Lycurgus was the husband of Eurydice and the father of Opheltes. Euripides' *Hypsipyle* was set at the palace of Lycurgus.

BIBLIOGRAPHY
Page, D. L. *Select Papyri.* Vol. 3. 1941. Reprint, London: Heinemann, 1970, 77–109.

LYCURGUS (2) The son of Dryas, Lycurgus was the king of a Thracian tribe called the Edonians. When Dionysus passed through Lycurgus' kingdom and attempted to introduce his rites, Lycurgus rejected him and took prisoner some of the god's followers. Dionysus himself jumped into the sea and took refuge with Nereus' daughter, Thetis. Eventually Dionysus returned and caused Lycurgus to become mad. In his insanity, Lycurgus killed his son, Dryas, thinking the lad was turning into a vine. Lycurgus' killing of his son put a curse on his kingdom, which caused the land to be barren. Dionysus, however, revealed to the Edonians that their land's fertility would return if Lycurgus were killed. The Edonians then took Lycurgus to Mount Pangaeum and had him torn apart by horses. AESCHYLUS wrote an EDONIANS, which seems to have been about this story. He also wrote a *Lycurgus*, which was the SATYR PLAY that rounded off the Lycurgus trilogy of *Edonians, Bassarai,* and *Neaniskoi.* NAEVIUS wrote a TRAGEDY entitled *Lycurgus,* from which about three dozen lines survive. Naevius' play dealt with Lycurgus' encounter with Dionysus. [ANCIENT SOURCES: Hyginus, *Fables* 132; Seneca, *Hercules Furens* 903, *Oedipus* 471]

BIBLIOGRAPHY
Smyth, H. W., and H. Lloyd-Jones. *Aeschylus.* Vol. 2. 1926. Reprint, Cambridge, Mass.: Harvard University Press, 1971.

Warmington, E. H. *Remains of Old Latin: Livius Andronicus, Naevius, Pacuvius, and Accius.* Vol. 2. Cambridge, Mass.: Harvard University Press, 1936.

LYCUS (1)
A mythical person from the island of EUBOEA who took over the kingdom of THEBES by killing King CREON. He appears as a character in two plays, EURIPIDES' *HERACLES* and SENECA'S *HERCULES FURENS.* In both plays, Lycus tries to diminish the heroic status of HERACLES and threatens to kill Heracles' family but is killed by Heracles when the hero returns from the UNDERWORLD. EURIPIDES and SENECA give Lycus different motivations for the threats against Heracles' family. In Euripides' play, Lycus wants to kill Heracles' children so that they will not grow up and avenge his killing of their uncle, Creon (their mother was Creon's daughter). In Seneca's play, Lycus uses threats against the children to persuade their mother, a woman of royal blood, to marry him. MEGARA, however, rejects the proposed marriage.

LYCUS (2)
A person worshipped at ATHENS as a hero. [ANCIENT SOURCES: Aristophanes, *Wasps* 389, 819]

BIBLIOGRAPHY
Sommerstein, A. H. *The Comedies of Aristophanes.* Vol. 4, *Wasps.* Warminster, U.K.: Aris & Phillips, 1983, 180.

LYDIA
A region near the western coast of what is modern-day Turkey. Poets sometimes make the Lydians synonymous with the Trojans.

LYDIAS
A river in the region of Macedonia, north of Greece.

LYNCEUS
The son of Aphareus, Lynceus was the brother of Idas. Lynceus sailed with JASON and the Argonauts on their quest for the Golden Fleece. Lynceus had exceptional powers of sight and could see objects that were far away or even underground. CASTOR and POLLUX died after a cattle raid on which Lynceus and Idas accompanied them. When Idas tricked the brothers out of their share of the cattle and drove the animals to Messene, Castor and Pollux followed, recaptured the cattle, and then set up an ambush for Idas and Lynceus. Lynceus saw Castor and told Idas, who killed Castor. Pollux then pursued Lynceus and killed him. Pollux, who had suffered a head wound in his fight with Lynceus, fainted before he could attack Idas. Zeus, however, struck Idas with a lightning bolt. The Greek tragedian Theodectas wrote a *Lynceus,* of which only the title survives (3a Snell). [ANCIENT SOURCES: Apollodorus, *Library* 1.8.2, 1.9.16; Aristophanes, *Wealth* 210; Hyginus, *Fables* 14, 80; Pausanias, 3.13.1, 3.14.7, 4.2.7, 4.3.1; Seneca, *Medea* 232]

BIBLIOGRAPHY
Snell, B. *Tragicorum Graecorum Fragmenta.* Vol. 1. Göttingen, Ger.: Vandenhoeck & Ruprecht, 1971.

LYRE
A stringed musical instrument that is similar to a harp. The lyre had a base (usually round, and resembling a turtle's shell), to which were attached two arms in a U shape that had a connecting cross bar. The lyre's number of strings could vary; strings were seven most common. Softer tones were made by plucking the strings with the left hand; louder tones were produced by striking the strings with a plectrum (a stick, often of ivory or gold, whose function was similar to that of the modern guitar pick). According to legend, the lyre was invented by HERMES soon after he was born. Hermes later traded the lyre to his brother, APOLLO, who became the divinity most associated with

the instrument. ORPHEUS and AMPHION were mythical mortals famous for playing the lyre. Those who recited poetry often sang to the accompaniment of the lyre, hence the term *lyric poetry* (although not all lyric poetry was accompanied by the lyre). [ANCIENT SOURCES: *Homeric Hymn* 3, 4; Sophocles, *Searchers*]

LYSICLES
An Athenian sheep dealer who, after PERICLES died in 429 B.C.E., lived with PERICLES' mistress, ASPASIA. In 428, Lysicles lost his own life in Caria while in command of Athenian troops. [ANCIENT SOURCES: Aristophanes, *Knights* 765; Plutarch, *Pericles* 24.6; Thucydides, 3.19.2]

BIBLIOGRAPHY
Sommerstein, A. H. *The Comedies of Aristophanes.* Vol. 2, *Knights.* Warminster, U.K.: Aris & Phillips, 1981, 150–51.

LYSICRATES
In *BIRDS* (414 B.C.E.), ARISTOPHANES mentions a Lysicrates and suggests that he was an Athenian statesman who had taken bribes. The ancient commentator on the passage in *Birds* says Lysicrates was a military general, but no other ancient sources confirm this. In *ECCLESIASUZAE* of 392/391 B.C.E., Aristophanes mentions a Lysicrates who had an unusually shaped nose and who dyed his hair black. Whether the two men are the same is not certain. Dunbar notes that if Lysicrates had been a general around the time *Birds* was produced, he would have been at least 52 years old by the date of *Ecclesiazusae*. [ANCIENT SOURCES: Aristophanes, *Birds* 513, *Ecclesiazusae* 630, 736; Apostolius, 10.97]

BIBLIOGRAPHY
Dunbar, Nan. *Aristophanes: Birds.* New York: Oxford University Press, 1995, 513.
Sommerstein, A. H. *The Comedies of Aristophanes.* Vol. 10, *Ecclesiazusae.* Warminster, U.K.: Aris & Phillips, 1998, 193–94.

LYSISTRATA
Compared with ARISTOPHANES' heroes, Lysistrata ("the dissolver of armies") is most similar to DICAEOPOLIS (*ACHARNIANS*) and TRYGAEUS (*PEACE*). The most obvious difference between Lysistrata and these two heroes is that she is a woman and they are men. In fact, Lysistrata may have been the most powerful noblewoman to take a leading role in COMEDY up to the date of *LYSISTRATA*'s production (411 B.C.E.). Henderson and others have noted that Lysistrata may have been modeled on an actual Athenian woman, Lysimache ("the dissolver of battle"), who served as a priestess of ATHENA Polias at this time. Note also that Lysistrata is a more urban-centered hero than Dicaeopolis and Trygaeus, both of whom are explicitly linked to the Athenian countryside. As does that of the heroes of earlier plays, Lysistrata's proposed social reform involves a cessation of war between her native ATHENS and SPARTA. Unlike that of Dicaeopolis, whose peace treaty is only between him and the Spartans, and like that of Trygaeus, Lysistrata's goal is peace for all Greeks. Whereas Dicaeopolis enlists the god Amphitheus to arrange his peace treaty and Trygaeus flies on a dung beetle to heaven to return the goddess Peace to Earth, Lysistrata relies on the women of Greece and the power of love to effect her reform. In the case of Dicaeopolis and Trygaeus, after the establishment of their peace treaties, Aristophanes primarily examines the economic impact of their reforms. Lysistrata's peace plan does have an economic component, in that she has the older women seize the Athenian treasury, but the main challenges to the success of her peace depend on overcoming the desires of the flesh. The success of Lysistrata's plan depends on the women's being able to control their physical desires and the men's being unable to control theirs. The women triumph. Just as Trygaeus entered into a sacred marriage with the personification of the harvest season at the conclusion of *Peace,* at the conclusion of *Lysistrata,* the title character summons a women named Reconciliation. The Athenians and Spartans are ready to embrace, literally, Reconciliation. Unlike Dicaeopolis and Trygaeus, both of whom can expect the sexual favors of a new woman (or women, in the case of Dicaeopolis), Lysistrata and the other Greek women are to be reunited with their husband.

BIBLIOGRAPHY
Dover, K., and S. Tremewan. *Aristophanes: Clouds, Acharnians, Lysistrata: A Companion to the Penguin Translation of Alan H. Sommerstein.* Bristol, U.K.: Duckworth Publishing, 1989.

Foley, H. P. "The 'Female Intruder' Reconsidered: Women in Aristophanes' *Lysistrata* and *Ecclesiazusae*," *Classical Philology* 77 (1982): 1–21.

Henderson, Jeffrey. "Older Women in Attic Old Comedy," *Transactions of the American Philological Association* 117 (1987): 105–29.

Konstan, D. "Aristophanes' Lysistrata: Women and the Body Politic." In *Tragedy, Comedy and the Polis*. Edited by A. H. Sommerstein, S. Halliwell, J. Henderson, and B. Zimmerman. Bari, Italy: 1993, 431–44.

Martin, R. P. "Fire on the Mountain: Lysistrata and the Lemnian Women," *Classical Antiquity* 6 (1987): Italy: Levante Editori, 77–105.

Vaio, John. "The Manipulation of Theme and Action in Aristophanes' *Lysistrata*," *Greek Roman and Byzantine Studies* 14 (1973): 369–80.

Westlake, H. D. "The *Lysistrata* and the War," *Phoenix* 34 (1980): 38–54.

Wysocki, L. "Aristophanes, Thucydides, b. VIII, and the Political Events of 413–411 B.C.," *Eos* 76 (1988): 237–48.

LYSISTRATA ARISTOPHANES (411 B.C.E.)

We do not know at which festival ARISTOPHANES staged *Lysistrata* or how it placed in competition. The play appeared in the same year as Aristophanes' THEMOPHORIAZUSAE, but whether *Lysistrata* was performed earlier in 411 than *Thesmophoriazusae* is not known. Most scholars think that the *Lysistrata* was performed at the LENAEA, but others favor the DIONYSIA. Because the *Lysistrata* (with its focus on sexual relations) would be understood by a broader audience than *Thesmophoriazusae* (with its focus on the playwright EURIPIDES), it might seem logical that *Thesmophoriazusae* would have been performed at the LENAEA (where the spectators were predominantly Athenians), whereas *Lysistrata* would have been performed at the City DIONYSIA (at which more non-Athenians would have been present). Because the Lenaea was held about two months before the Dionysia, the *Thesmophoriazusae* should be the earlier of the two plays. Still, Henderson writes that internal evidence from *Lysistrata* "very strongly favours" its appearance at the Lenaea, especially because *Lysistrata* shows little awareness of the oligarchic revolution that was about to occur and the plans for which would have been known by the time of the Dionysia.

The play opens with Lysistrata' ("disolver of armies") impatiently waiting for the women of Greece to gather near the Athenian ACROPOLIS. When the women finally assemble, Lysistrata announces her radical plan for peace between the warring Athenians and Spartans—women must stop having sexual intercourse with their husbands. The women are initially reluctant to give up sex but decide that peace is worth the effort. To confirm their commitment, the women take an oath on a large bowl of wine (humorously appropriate because women were stereotyped as fond of alcoholic beverages). After the women drink of the wine, they hear a sound of triumph in the distance as the older women have captured the Acropolis. At this, Lysistrata sends the women off to their respective cities to put their plan into effect.

After the women's departure, a chorus of old Athenian men enter, carrying firewood and something to ignite it. They intend to smoke the women out of the Acropolis and smash through the gates of the citadel, but they are met by a chorus of old Athenian women, who fight back by pouring water on them. An Athenian magistrate enters to check on the old men's progress and finds them thoroughly drenched by the women. Lysistrata meets the magistrate, who threatens to arrest her. The women, however, fight back and prevent any of their number from being captured.

Eventually, the magistrate begins to question Lysistrata about why the women have seized the Acropolis. Lysistrata explains that they have seized it so that they can control the city's money, which Lysistrata suggests is the cause of the war. Furthermore, Lysistrata says the women will act as the city's treasurers. The magistrate scoffs at this idea, but Lysistrata explains that because women manage their household budget, they should be able to manage the city's finances just as well. Lysistrata compares the problems of Athens to a knotted and dirty tangle of thread and wool, which women, being experts in weaving, will untangle, wash, and weave into a garment that harmoniously incorporates all of the city's various constituents. When the magistrate rejects Lysistrata's logic, the women dress him as if he were going to be buried and drive him from their midst.

Next, the chorus of old men worry that the Spartans are somehow behind the women's plot. The women's chorus respond that they have even more at stake than the men because they contribute their sons to the city. They complain that the men have wasted the city's money. The men threaten to retaliate physically against the women, but the old women stand firm and threaten to fight back.

The struggle between the men and women is broken off by the entrance of Lysistrata, who complains that the younger women are trying to desert from the ranks because they want to have sex with their men. At this point, several women, eager to join their men, emerge and give various excuses at to why they need to leave the Acropolis. Lysistrata, however, rejects each of the deserting women's excuses and sends them back to the Acropolis. After Lysistrata puts an end to the women's efforts to desert, the two choruses engage in brief verbal and physical abuse.

The choruses' wrangling ends when Lysistrata sees a sex-starved male approaching. One of Lysistrata's companions, Myrrhine, recognizes him as her husband, CINESIAS, whose name is derived from the Greek word *kinein*, a verb that can denote the motion of sexual intercourse. Cinesias' erection is visible, so Myrrhine decides to torture her husband for a few moments. Cinesias begs his wife to return home, but Myrrhine refuses unless Cinesias promises to help put an end to the fighting with the Spartans. Cinesias wants to have sexual relations with his wife immediately, but Myrrhine torments him by gathering together a mattress, a pillow, ointment, and other things. Just as Myrrhine is about to satisfy her husband's lust, he expresses hesitation about voting for peace with Sparta. Thus, Myrrhine leaves her husband writhing in torment on the ground.

As the male chorus sympathize with Cinesias' plight, a Spartan herald, who also has an erection, enters in search of the Athenian assembly. He is met by the Athenian magistrate who appeared earlier in the play. The Spartan tells the magistrate about the sexual strike in Sparta and says that the Spartans are now ready to make peace. The Athenian magistrate agrees, and the two men exit for their respective political assemblies. After their exit, the two choruses again square off. The men express their hatred of women, but the women suggest that they are foolish to fight with them when they could just as easily be friends. The women then help the men arrange their clothing properly and brush annoying insects away from their eyes. The old men then decide to make peace with the women.

After the two choruses join to sing a song of celebration, ambassadors, who have erections, enter from Sparta. They are soon met by some Athenian men who are experiencing the same affliction. The two parties quickly note the need to make peace and summon Lysistrata to resolve the quarrel. Lysistrata, accompanied by her maidservant, Reconciliation, enters and chastises the men for fighting against one another when the two states had helped each other in the past. The men agree with Lysistrata's reasoning but still squabble over various territories that each wants restored. Lysistrata, however, manages to reconcile the two parties and then invites everyone to the Acropolis for a feast and a reunion with his wife.

After the exit of the men, the unified choruses rejoice about the approaching celebration and promise fine clothes and food to anyone in need. The choruses also arrange for a porter to drive away from the feast some lazy fellows from the Athenian AGORA who try to sneak into the feast. Next, some Athenians and a Spartan emerge from the feast in good spirits. The Athenians express interest in seeing the Spartan dance and the Spartan obliges them with a dance and a song that recalls the successful Athenian and Spartan alliance against the Persians and celebrates the new peace. After the Spartan's dance, Lysistrata enters and calls for the Athenian and Spartan men to pair off with their respective women and dance in honor of the gods. The play ends with celebratory songs to the gods from the united choruses and a song from the Spartans in praise of their native land and divinities.

COMMENTARY

Lysistrata is Aristophanes' most popular play with modern audiences, and its appeal is easily understood from the universality of its sexual content. The staging of the play is relatively unproblematic for scholars to reconstruct, but modern readers of the play should be aware that the ancient comic costume for men was equipped with an exaggerated PHALLUS (penis) and the visual humor of a play such as *Lysistrata* would have benefited greatly from this exaggerated appendage.

Although women take over the Athenian government in the play, *Lysistrata* should not be read as Aristophanes' endorsement of women's actually taking over the government or being empowered politically in any way. Aristophanes uses a female-controlled government and a peace treaty engineered by women to show the foolishness and stubborness of the men in his society, rather than highlight the plight of women in his society. Modern readers of *Lysistrata* should also be aware of one additional point: Although the success of a sexual strike between husbands and wives would be extremely far-fetched in our modern society, it might have been even more unlikely to be effective in ancient Greek society, in which married men were free to satisfy their lust with prostitutes. Furthermore, sexual contact between two men was also common in Greek society, even if the men were married. Aristophanes, however, asks his audience to play along with his scenario and does not raise the topics of prostitutes and male lovers.

Aristophanes' primary concern in Lysistrata is not women, but war, just as it had been for almost two decades, and specifically an interest in ending the war between Athens and Sparta. Although Athens had been weakened by the deaths of generals like NICIAS and LAMACHUS, the defection of ALCIBIADES to the Spartans, and the destruction of the SICILIAN EXPEDITION in 413, the Athenians remained resilient and in 411 gave little indication of being in jeopardy of losing the war to Sparta. Although an oligarchic revolution overthrew Athenian democracy in 411, it occurred after *Lysistrata* was produced and, as stated, Aristophanes shows little awareness of such a major change in *Lysistrata*.

Lysistrata can be compared with several of the playwright's other works. On one level, *Lysistrata* warrants comparison with Aristophanes' other two "women's plays," THESMOPHORIAZUSAE (411 B.C.E.) and ECCLESIAZUSAE (392/391). On another level, *Lysistrata* has much in common with Aristophanes' other two "peace plays," ACHARNIANS (425) and PEACE (421). As a "women's play," *Lysistrata* bears the least resemblance to *Thesmophoriazusae,* which primarily focuses on EURIPIDES and derives much of its humor from men

who resemble women or consciously dress as women. *Lysistrata* also would have derived humor from men's playing women's roles (all of the speaking actors were men) but does not make use of men who deliberately dress as women or are so effeminate that they are mistaken for women as does *Thesmophoriazusae. Lysistrata* is most similar to the later *Ecclesiazusae,* in which the women take on men's roles and overthrow the Athenian government but transform the city into a communist society in which food, possessions, and even men are shared. Note, however, that Lysistrata's reforms appear to be temporary, whereas PRAXAGORA's, in *Ecclesiazusae,* appear to be permanent. After Lysistrata's aim of peace between Athens and Sparta is achieved, relations between men and women return to normal. In Praxagora's case, Praxagora's communistic reforms remain.

As a "peace play," as do *Acharnians* and *Peace, Lysistrata* deals with the war between Athens and Sparta. *Lysistrata* follows a pattern seen in several other Aristophanic plays: An unlikely hero creates a fantastic plan to correct some social crisis, the plan is implemented, the plan is challenged (e.g., the women try to desert; Cinesias tries to tempt Myrrhine), and eventually the fantastic plan achieves its aim and those who embrace it are treated to food, drink, and a sexual encounter with a member of the opposite sex. Regarding the sexual aspect, *Lysistrata* differs from other Aristophanic plays because it is expected that the men will ultimately have sexual relations with their own wife. As does *Peace,* with the appearance of Opôra, *Lysistrata* concludes with the appearance of an allegorical woman, Reconciliation. Whereas Trygaeus will enter into a sacred marriage with Opôra, the men of *Lysistrata* merely gawk at and fondle Reconciliation.

The union of Trygaeus with the personification of the harvest points to another difference between *Lysistrata* and Aristophanes' other peace plays. The earlier peace plays have rustic heroes and are especially concerned with the effects of the war on the folk of the Athenian countryside. *Lysistrata* has a more urban aspect and Lysistrata seems more sophisticated than Dicaeopolis or Trygaeus.

In contrast to *Acharnians,* in which DICAEOPOLIS arranges for a personal peace between him and the

Spartans, Lysistrata's aim is, as is that of TRYGAEUS in *Peace,* peace for all Greeks. Unlike the challenges to the hero's plan in *Acharnians* and *Peace,* which mainly focus on the economic impact of peace upon those who benefit from war, in *Lysistrata* the main obstacle to the success of the title character's plan is the sexual drive of the respective genders. To be sure, for Lysistrata's plan to succeed, the women must gain control of the Athenian treasury, but otherwise economic obstacles to the hero's plan, such as informants (see especially *Acharnians*), will not trouble *Lysistrata.*

Lysistrata also has a different divine aspect from that of *Peace* or *Acharnians.* In *Acharnians,* Dicaeopolis employed the divinity AMPHITHEUS to arrange peace between him and the Spartans. In *Peace,* Trygaeus had to fly to heaven and negotiate with HERMES to take Peace back to Earth. In *Lysistrata,* no divinities speak during the play. The names of APHRODITE and EROS, however, are mentioned frequently. Thus, in some ways divine power is more evident in *Lysistrata* than in the other peace plays, because the power of Love produces peace between the Athenians and Spartans.

BIBLIOGRAPHY

Dillon, M. "The *Lysistrata* as a Post-Dekeleian Peace Play," *Transactions of the American Philological Association* 117 (1987): 97–104.

Henderson, J. "*Lysistrate:* The Play and Its Themes," *Yale Classical Studies* 26 (1980): 153–218.

———. *Aristophanes: Lysistrata.* Oxford: Clarendon Press, 1987.

Sommerstein, A. H. *The Comedies of Aristophanes.* Vol. 7, *Lysistrata.* Warminster, U.K.: Aris & Phillips, 1990.

LYSSA   See MADNESS.

MACARIA A daughter of HERACLES, Macaria is assumed to be the name of the woman who appears in EURIPIDES' *CHILDREN OF HERACLES* and, in accordance with an oracle, sacrifices herself to ensure victory over EURYSTHEUS.

MACISTUS A town in southwestern Greece. [ANCIENT SOURCES: Aeschylus, *Agamemnon* 289 (see *ORESTEIA*)]

MADNESS In EURIPIDES' *HERACLES*, HERA sends the goddess Madness (Greek: Lyssa) to drive HERACLES insane. As with HEPHAESTUS' binding of PROMETHEUS in AESCHYLUS' play, in Euripides' play Madness is reluctant to punish Heracles, but she does so in accordance with Hera's wishes. Madness also seems to have appeared as a character in AESCHYLUS' *Xantriai* (fragment 169 Radt), a play that concerned some aspect of DIONYSUS' travels through mainland Greece and an instance of madness that resulted from opposition to the god.

BIBLIOGRAPHY
Radt, S. *Tragicorum Graecorum Fragmenta*. Vol. 3. Göttingen, Ger.: Vandenhoeck & Ruprecht, 1985.

MAEANDER The Meander River, some 250 miles long, is located in western Turkey and flows into the AEGEAN SEA. [ANCIENT SOURCES: Seneca, *Hercules Furens* 684, *Phoenician Women* 606]

MAENADS Related to the Greek verb *mainomai* (to rave or to be beside oneself with madness), Maenads are female worshipers of DIONYSUS. The term *Maenads* is often synonymous with BACCHAE or Bacchants. Women in a state of madness or frenzy are often compared to Maenads and sometimes *maenad* is used as an adjective (see especially EURIPIDES' *BACCHAE,* in which the women who kill PENTHEUS are frequently called Maenads). [ANCIENT SOURCES: Seneca, *Hercules Oetaeus* 243, *Medea* 383, *Oedipus* 436, *Trojan Women* 674]

MAENALUS A mountain in southern Greece, Maenalus is associated with the stag that HERACLES had to capture as one of his labors. The divinities PAN and ARTEMIS are also associated with this mountain. [ANCIENT SOURCES: Euripides, *Phoenician Women* 1162; Seneca, *Hercules Furens* 222]

MAENIANUM In the Roman theater, a *maenianum* (plural: *maeniana*) is the lower, horizontal section of seats. The *maenianum* is also called the *cavea ima.*

MAEONIA A region near the coast of western Turkey and south of TROY. Maeonia is sometimes synonymous with the region of LYDIA. [ANCIENT SOURCES: Seneca, *Hercules Oetaeus* 665]

MAEOTIS North of the Black Sea, Maeotis is a body of water (often called a lake) that is today called the Sea of Azov. The AMAZONS and SCYTHIANS are sometimes said to live near Maeotis. [ANCIENT SOURCES: Aeschylus, *Prometheus Bound* 419, 731; Aristophanes, *Clouds* 273; Euripides, HERACLES 409]

MAGNES   A Greek comic poet who won more victories (11) at the City DIONYSIA than any other comic poet. Only some 50 words by Magnes survive (see Kock) and seven titles are known: *Barbiton-Playing Frogs, Birds, Dionysus, Gall-Flies, Grass-Cutters, Lydians,* and *Titakides.* One of Magnes' plays appeared in 472 B.C.E. [ANCIENT SOURCES: Aristophanes, *Knights* 520; Aristotle, *Poetics* 1448a34]

BIBLIOGRAPHY
Kock, T. *Comicorum Atticorum Fragmenta.* Vol. 1. Leipzig: Teubner, 1880.
Sommerstein, A. H. *The Comedies of Aristophanes.* Vol. 2, *Knights.* Warminster, U.K.: Aris & Phillips, 1981, 170.

MAGNESIA   One region and two towns in the classical world had this name. The region of Magnesia was east of THESSALY along the northeastern coast of Greece. There were two towns called Magnesia in what is today western Turkey: one located roughly between Mount SIPYLUS and the town of SARDIS, the other, south of the first, south of EPHESUS. [ANCIENT SOURCES: Aeschylus, *Persians* 492; Sophocles, *Electra* 705]

MAIA   The daughter of ATLAS and Pleione, Maia is a divinity (her name means "mother" in Greek) who joined with ZEUS to produce HERMES. [ANCIENT SOURCES: Apollodorus, *Library* 3.10.1–2; *Homeric Hymn to Hermes* 4]

MALIAN GULF   A body of water on the northeastern coast of Greece. The town of TRACHIS is on the southern shore of this gulf. During the PELOPONNESIAN WAR, the Spartans had strongholds in this area. [ANCIENT SOURCES: Aristophanes, *Lysistrata* 1169; Thucydides, 3.92–93, 8.3, 8.92.8]

BIBLIOGRAPHY
Henderson, J. *Aristophanes: Lysistrata.* Oxford: Clarendon Press, 1987, 205.

MALIS   A region along the northeast coast of Greece in which the town of TRACHIS was located. PHILOCTETES was from this region. [ANCIENT SOURCES: Sophocles, *Philoctetes* 4, *Trachinian Women* 635]

MANES   A common name of male slaves. [ANCIENT SOURCES: Aristophanes, *Birds* 1311, 1329, *Lysistrata* 1211, *Peace* 1146]

THE MAN FROM SICYON (Greek: SIKYONIOS) MENANDER (DATE UNKNOWN)
At least one of the five acts is completely missing. The play's setting is ELEUSIS, and the action takes place before two houses, one belonging to a soldier, Stratophanes, and the other to an elderly private citizen, Smicrines.

The PROLOGUE of the first act may is delivered by a divinity (perhaps DEMETER), who relates that Philoumene, the daughter of Kichesias, and Dromon, servant of Kichesias, were kidnapped by pirates and taken by Stratophanes. After Philoumene grew up, Stratophanes fell in love with Philoumene. In the play, Stratophanes has returned home from a foreign military campaign (as does Thrasonides in MAN SHE HATED). Other fragments from this act indicate that Philoumene and Dromon have taken refuge from Stratophanes at an altar and that a young man named Moschion, son of Smicrines, is also in love with Philoumene. A fragment from another act, a conversation between Stratophanes and his PARASITE, Theron, reveals that Stratophanes' property is in danger of falling into the hands of a Boeotian creditor. The two men are joined by Stratophanes' slave, Pyrrhias, who informs Stratophanes that his mother died while he was abroad, but that she was not actually his mother. Pyrrhias gives Stratophanes documents that will help him resolve his financial situation and items that will help him learn his true identity.

In the fourth act, of which about 150 lines survive, a man named Eleusinos tells Smicrines about a crowd who had gathered around Philoumene and Dromon at the altar. When people asked who the young woman's guardian was, Stratophanes stepped forward and claimed her. Stratophanes, however, agreed to place her under the protection of Demeter's priestess while her family could be sought. Stratophanes also told the crowd about the items he had recently acquired. Stratophanes believed they would lead to proof that he was a citizen of Eleusis. If her father were found, Stratophanes said that he would ask him for the right to marry Philoumene. Apparently, Moschion was in the crowd and had expressed his doubts about the soldier's claims to Eleusinian citizenship. After Eleusinos leaves, Moschion enters and tries to arrest Stratophanes. At this point, however, the manuscript contains a gap. Apparently, Stratophanes told Moschion he was looking for Smicrines; Moschion said Smicrines was his father; eventually, Stratophanes and Moschion discovered that they were brothers.

In the play's final act, Philoumene's father, Kichesias, and Theron quarrel. Theron apparently is trying to bribe Kichesias to say he knows who Philoumene's father is. Theron does not know who Kichesias is and Kichesias does not know Theron is talking about his daughter. Identifying Philoumene as an Athenian will allow Stratophanes (by now proved to be an Athenian citizen) to marry her. Theron, in supplying Kichesias with a story about the young woman, tells him the real history of Philoumene's abduction, which makes Kichesias think of his daughter. Kichesias soon discovers his daughter when Dromon arrives and recognizes Kichesias. Stratophanes enters, meets Kichesias, and proposes to marry Philoumene. The remainder of the play is largely missing. At one point, Moschion laments that he has to accept losing Philoumene to his brother. The play ends with Theron's calling for the wedding of Stratophanes and Philoumene to begin.

COMMENTARY

The play's setting in Eleusis and the likelihood that Demeter spoke the prologue invite an interpretation of the play that connects its characters and plot to the story of Demeter, her daughter PERSEPHONE, and HADES. In Menander's play, Philoumene obviously functions as the Persephone figure, and her abduction by pirates creates a rough parallel with Persephone's abduction by Hades. Stratophanes' acquisition of Philoumene casts him in the role of Hades. Moschion, in attempting to rescue Philoumene/Persephone from Hades/Stratophanes, would parallel Demeter's efforts to rescue her daughter

from the god of the underworld. Moschion, however, must put aside his Demeter-like qualities when he discovers that he is Stratophanes' brother. With Moschion no longer a threat, a second Demeter-figure appears in the form of Kichesias, who, like Demeter, is reunited with his long-lost daughter. As in the case of Demeter, in which an arrangement is reached that will allow Persephone and Hades to marry but still allow Persephone access to her parent, in Menander's play, Stratophanes and Philoumene will become as husband and wife and Philoumene will renew her relationship with her parent.

BIBLIOGRAPHY
Coles, R. A. "Notes on Menander's *Sikyonios.*" *Emerita* 34 (1966): 131–37.
Handley, E. W. "Notes on the *Sikyonios* of Menander." *Bulletin of the Institute of Classical Studies* 12 (1965): 38–62.
———. "Another Fragment of Menander's *Sikyonios.*" *Bulletin of the Institute of Classical Studies* 31 (1984): 25–31.
Kumaniecki, K. "Bemerkungen zu den neuentdeckten Fragmenten des *Sikyonios* von Menandros." *Athenaeum* 43 (1965): 154–66.
Lloyd-Jones, H. "Menander's *Sikyonios.*" *Greek, Roman, and Byzantine Studies* 7 (1966): 131–57.

MANIA   A name of a female slave. [ANCIENT SOURCES: Aristophanes, *Frogs* 1346, *Thesmophoriazusae* 728, 739, 754]

THE MAN SHE HATED (Greek: *MISOUMENOS*) MENANDER (DATE UNKNOWN)
The surviving fragments are not in good condition. The play's setting may be ATHENS; the action takes place before two houses, one belonging to a soldier, Thrasonides; the other, to a private citizen, Cleinias.

Fragments of the first act primarily involve a conversation between Thrasonides and his slave, Getas. Thrasonides has returned from a military campaign on CYPRUS and has taken back a captive woman, Krateia. The soldier loves her, but she will not sleep with him. Thrasonides and Getas puzzle over the reason for this. From the second act, only about 18 lines survive. Most of these involve a conversation between Cleinias' slave, Syra, and Demeas, in which Demeas discovers his daughter's whereabouts.

The text of the opening of the third act is in poor shape. Krateia's nurse may have attempted some sort of reconciliation of Krateia and Thrasonides. Geta describes seeing two men drinking and singing. Another 50 lines reveal the reunion between Krateia and Demeas, whom Getas initially mistakes for a rival lover. Krateia tells her father that she is sure her brother is dead and that Thrasonides killed him. After Krateia and Demeas enter Thrasonides' house to decide their next move, Thrasonides and Getas arrive. Getas has told him of the arrival of Krateia's father, and Thrasonides thinks this could be fortunate or unfortunate for him. The two men then enter Thrasonides' house. In the last few lines of the act, Cleinias is anxious about a dinner party that will include him, Demeas, and a young woman.

In the fourth act, Getas tells Demeas about Thrasonides' confession to Demeas that he loves Krateia. Thrasonides, however, received no sympathy from Demeas or Krateia, and Demeas demanded Krateia's return. The surviving part of the act reveals a despondent Thrasonides, who may be planning to pretend to kill himself. The surviving fragments from the play's final act indicate that Krateia's brother turned up alive, and his appearance led to Demeas' giving Krateia in marriage to Thrasonides.

BIBLIOGRAPHY

Davis, G. "Ovid's *Metamorphoses* 3.442 ff. and the Prologue to Menander's *Misoumenos*," *Phoenix* 32 (1978): 339–42.

Jarkho, V. N. "Menander's *Hated Man*," *Vestnik Drevnej Istorii* (Revue d'Histoire ancienne) 148 (1978): 24–40.

Katsouris, A. "Menander's *Misoumenos*: Problems of Interpretation," *Dodone* 14 (1985): 205–29.

Turner, E. G. *The Lost Beginning of Menander, Misoumenos.* London: British Academy, 1979.

Webster, T. B. L. "Woman Hates Soldier: A Structural Approach to New Comedy," *Greek, Roman, and Byzantine Studies* 14 (1973): 287–99.

MANTO   The daughter of the prophet TIRESIAS, Manto was also a prophet. She appears as a character in SENECA'S *OEDIPUS*. In this play, she accompanies her father to THEBES and acts as Tiresias' eyes, describing for her father the sacrificial victim they will use to try to determine who killed OEDIPUS' father, LAIUS. [ANCIENT SOURCES: Hyginus, *Fables* 128; Seneca, *Agamemnon* 319]

MARATHON   The site of one of the most famous battles in Greek history, Marathon is located about 25 miles northeast of ATHENS. At Marathon, in 490 B.C.E., some 5,000 Athenians and fewer than a thousand other troops, the majority from the town of PLATAEA, decisively defeated a force of Persians that was at least four times as numerous. This battle not only prevented the Persians from becoming the masters of Greece, but also vaulted Athens into prominence in Greece. In ancient drama, Marathon also has some significance. EURIPIDES' *CHILDREN OF HERACLES* has Marathon as its setting. Aristophanes often refers to Marathon in his comedies as an example of Athens' finest hour. Some of ARISTOPHANES' characters are described as veterans of the battle of Marathon. PHILOCLEON and the chorus of *WASPS* are veterans of Marathon.

MARDIANS   A nomadic tribe who are mentioned as part of the Persian force who invaded Greece under XERXES. [ANCIENT SOURCES: Aeschylus, *Persians* 993; Herodotus, 1.125]

MARDUS   AESCHYLUS calls him Mardus; HERODOTUS calls him Smerdis. Smerdis had the same name as and a resemblance to the son of the Persian king Cyrus. When Cyrus' son died, the other Smerdis pretended to be his son and ruled for only seven months before being murdered by Cambyses. [ANCIENT SOURCES: Aeschylus, *Persians* 774; Aristotle, *Politics* 1311b; Herodotus, 3.30–75]

BIBLIOGRAPHY

Hall, E. *Aeschylus: Persians.* Warminster, U.K.: Aris & Phillips, 1996, 162.

MARILADES   A fictional character who is a member of the chorus of ARISTOPHANES' *ACHARNIANS* (609). His name means "son of coal dust" (Sommerstein's translation).

BIBLIOGRAPHY

Sommerstein, A. H. *The Comedies of Aristophanes.* Vol. 1, *Acharnians.* Warminster, U.K.: Aris & Phillips, 1980, 187.

MARPSIAS   An orator, whose name means "gripper," who was said to be a noisy, argumentative, speaker of nonsense. EUPOLIS labeled him as a flatterer of a rich man named CALLIAS. [ANCIENT SOURCES: Aristophanes, *Acharnians* 701; Eupolis, fragment 166 Kock]

BIBLIOGRAPHY

Sommerstein, A. H. *The Comedies of Aristophanes.* Vol. 1, *Acharnians.* Warminster, U.K.: Aris & Phillips, 1980, 191.

MARS   See ARES.

MASKS

In Greek drama, the actors and CHORUS members wore masks made of linen that covered the face and even the entire head of those who wore them. The appearance of the masks ranged from realistic looking, in the case of Greek TRAGEDY, to various levels of distortion in the case of COMEDY. Several vase paintings, from the days when AESCHYLUS, SOPHOCLES, and EURIPIDES were producing tragedies, show persons holding masks, whose features do not differ much from those of the people holding them. The masks for players in comedy had features that were exaggerated for humorous effect. One can well imagine that a mask representing the Athenian statesman CLEON or the philosopher SOCRATES would have to be crafted to allow the audience to recognize the person and to evoke laughter. Of course, making a mask of a powerful Athenian political figure might be perilous, and ARISTOPHANES, at *KNIGHTS* 230–33, quips that no mask maker would dare to make the Cleon mask.

Occasionally, actors would have to change or alter masks during a performance. Someone who had been blinded, such as OEDIPUS, the Cyclops POLYPHEMUS, or POLYMESTOR in Euripides' *HECABE,* would need to represent blindness in some way. Sometimes in ancient drama people cut their hair as a sign of mourning (e.g., ORESTES, ADMETUS in Euripides' *ALCESTIS*). Accordingly, the hair on the mask would have to be altered. With regard to Greek New Comedy, which evolved after the end of the fourth century B.C.E., Pollux mentions 44 different kinds of masks that are used; archaeological evidence reveals that masks either are realistic in the case of women and young men or have exaggerated features with a large mouth in the case of the other characters. Also, with the advent of New Comedy, the crown of the forehead on some masks increasingly tapers upward. This "crown" is called an *oncus* (swelling).

Regarding Roman drama, the evidence for the use of masks in the time of PLAUTUS and TERENCE is unclear.

In the ancient literature, a few references to masks being used in some plays during this period exist, but modern scholars have disputed this idea and think that the Romans did not use masks until after 130 B.C.E. Duckworth, however, notes several references to masks in Plautus' plays. Furthermore, plays involving twins, such as *AMPHITRUO* and *MENAECHMI,* would be much easier to manage by using masks than by any sort of cosmetic alterations. Accordingly, Duckworth argues that "the evidence for the late introduction of masks in Roman comedy is weak" and asserts that they were used as early as the plays of Plautus.

BIBLIOGRAPHY

Duckworth, G. *The Nature of Roman Comedy.* Princeton, N.J.: Princeton University Press, 1952, 92–94.

Johnson, M. B. "The Mask in Ancient Greek Tragedy: A Reexamination Based on the Principles and Practices of the Noh Theater in Japan." Dissertation, University of Wisconsin at Madison, 1984.

Pickard-Cambridge, A. W. *Dithyramb, Tragedy, and Comedy,* 2d ed. Revised by T. B. L. Webster. Oxford: Clarendon Press, 1962, 177–212.

MATRONA

The Latin word *matrona* (plural: *matronae*) refers to a woman who is married. In Roman COMEDY, the *matrona* is a stock character, who is often stereotyped as a nag and an impediment to her husband's ability to enjoy himself with another woman (compare Artemona in the *COMEDY OF ASSES,* Cleostrata in *CASINA,* Matrona in *MENAECHMI,* Nausistrata in *PHORMIO*). Typically, the *matrona* catches her husband, puts an end to his affair, and forgives him. In *Menaechmi,* however, Menaechmus of Epidamnus sails away with his brother and leaves his wife at the play's conclusion. Not all *matronae* are characterized as nags, and as do most mothers they show great concern for their children (compare Phanostrata in *CASKET COMEDY,* Philippa in *EPIDICUS,* and the Sostratas in TERENCE'S *BROTHERS, MOTHER-IN-LAW,* and *SELF-TORMENTOR*). In *Mother-in-Law,* Sostrata even offers to move away from home to ensure the happiness of her daughter-in-law. Duckworth calls the faithful Alcmena in *AMPHITRUO* "Plautus' most noble woman character," although Christensen has recently cast some doubt on this characterization. The wives in *STICHUS* have remained faithful to their husband, despite their long absence and despite their father's advice that they divorce their husband and remarry.

BIBLIOGRAPHY

Christenson, David. "Grotesque Realism in Plautus' *Amphitruo*," *Classical Journal* 96, no. 3 (2000–1): 243–60.

Duckworth, G. *The Nature of Roman Comedy*. Princeton, N.J.: Princeton University Press, 1952, 255–58.

MAVORS   See ARES.

MECHANE (Latin: *MACHINA*)   In Greek drama, the *mechane* is a cranelike apparatus with which a character could be raised above the roof of the SKENE or swung out in front of the *skene* from behind that structure. Pollux, writing in the second century C.E., says the device was called a *mechane* in TRAGEDY, but a *krade* in COMEDY. The term *krade* refers to the end of a fig tree's branch, so some ancients conceived of the apparatus as having that appearance. Zenobius describes the apparatus as having a hook and ropes that attached to the actor's waist. The entrance of Socrates in ARISTOPHANES' CLOUDS, however, indicates the use of a basket (*kremathra*) to hold the actor. In some case, two persons (or a person and perhaps a manikin of some type) may have been in this basket, such as CASTOR and POLLUX at the conclusion of EURIPIDES' ELECTRA and HELEN or APOLLO and HELEN at the end of Euripides' ORESTES. A clear example of the use of the *mechane* occurs in Aristophanes' PEACE (421 B.C.E.), in which the hero, TRYGAEUS, flies to Mount OLYMPUS on a dung beetle. In this play, Trygaeus actually urges the operator of the *mechane* to be careful not to swing him too vigorously. PLATO and ARISTOTLE criticized tragedians for their frequent use of the *mechane* to introduce a divinity who would resolve a crisis in a rather artificial way. Euripides was especially fond of using the *mechane*. [ANCIENT SOURCES: Aristophanes, *Clouds* 218, *Peace* 173–76, fragment 188 Kock; Aristotle, *Poetics* 1454a36–b5; Oxyrhynchus Papyrus 2742.3–19; Plato, *Cratylus* 425d; Pollux, *Onomasticon* 4.128–29; Scholiast on Lucian, *Lover of Lies* 7; Zenobius, *Proverbs* 3.156]

BIBLIOGRAPHY

Foesel, K. R. *Der Deus ex machina in der Komödie*. Erlangen, Ger.: Palm & Enke, 1975.

Kock, T. *Comicorum Atticorum Fragmenta*. Vol. 1. Leipzig: Teubner, 1880.

Mastronarde, D. J. "Actors on High: The Skene Roof, the Crane, and the Gods in Attic Drama," *Classical Antiquity* 9 (1990): 247–94.

Newiger, H. "Ekkyklema e mechané nella messa in scena del dramma greco," *Dioniso* 59 (1989): 173–185.

———. "Ekkyklema und Mechané in der Inszenierung des griechischen Dramas," *Würzburger Jahrbücher für die Altertumswissenschaft* 16 (1990): 33–42.

Robkin, A. L. H. "That Magnificent Flying Machine: On the Nature of the Mechane of the Theatre of Dionysus at Athens," *Archaeological News* 8 (1979): 1–6.

MEDEA   One of the most notorious figures of classical mythology, Medea was the daughter of AEETES and Chalciope, king and queen of COLCHIS. When JASON arrives in Colchis in search of the Golden Fleece, Medea falls in love with him and helps him in the tasks that her father, Aeetes, assigns him. Medea gives Jason a potion to protect him against the fiery breath of the bulls he must yoke, gives him advice about how to deal with the armed warriors who spring up from the dragon's teeth he plants, and later charms to sleep the dragon that guards the Golden Fleece. EURIPIDES and SENECA make Medea the killer of her brother, ABSYRTUS, a brutal act that helps Jason and the Argonauts escape the pursuit of Aeetes.

After their arrival in Greece, Jason's men hand over the Golden Fleece to Pelias, who is supposed to turn over the kingdom of Iolcus to Jason. Pelias reneges on his promise, however, and Jason is deprived of the kingdom. At this point, Medea goes to Jason's aid and, pretending that she and Jason have had a quarrel, infiltrates the hearts and house of Pelias' daughters. Medea convinces Pelias' daughters that she can make their father young again through her magic. This rejuvenation, however, requires that Pelias be cut to pieces. Medea persuades Pelias' daughters to do this, but when they expect Medea to use her magic to restore his life and youth, Medea is nowhere to be found. Thus, with Pelias dead, Jason expects to become king of Iolcus. The people of Iolcus, however, led by Pelias' son, ACASTUS, drive Jason and Medea from their town.

After leaving Iolcus, Jason and Medea travel to CORINTH. They live happily there for several years and have two sons. Jason, still longing for a kingdom, decides to divorce Medea and marry the daughter of CREON, king of Corinth. An enraged Medea decides to take revenge on Jason, so she kills Creon's daughter (and Creon) by means of poisoned clothing. As an additional way of injuring Jason, Medea kills her sons by him. Medea then escapes from Corinth by means of the chariot of the SUN (her grandfather).

After leaving Corinth, Medea travels to ATHENS, where she marries King AEGEUS and has a child by him, MEDUS. When Aegeus' son, THESEUS, appears in Athens, Medea realizes that Theseus would stand to inherit the kingdom before her son, Medus, and plots to kill Theseus. She convinces Aegeus that Theseus plans to assassinate him and arranges for Aegeus to invite Theseus to a banquet, at which Aegeus will offer him poisoned wine. Before Theseus can drink the wine, however, Aegeus realizes that Theseus is his son and dashes the cup of poison from his hand.

Once again Medea escapes. She and her son return to her native land of Colchis, where her father has lost his kingdom. With Medea's help, Aeetes regains his throne. Medea's fate after this time becomes rather elusive. Some sources indicate that she becomes a goddess after her death; others say that she marries ACHILLES in the afterlife.

The Greek comic poet Strattis wrote a *Medea*, from which a few fragments survive (33–35 Kock). Fragment 34 suggests that Creon was a character in the play. Among Roman authors, ACCIUS wrote a *Medea*, about 30 of whose lines survive. The play's setting seems to have been Colchis. The fragments indicate that Jason and Medea had speaking roles. Aeetes and Absyrtus also may have appeared, and Absyrtus' death seems to have occurred during the course of the play. [ANCIENT SOURCES: Apollodorus, *Library* 1.9.16–28; Apollonius Rhodius, *Argonautica*; Hyginus, *Fables* 3, 12–25; Ovid, *Heroides* 6, 12, *Metamorphoses* 7.1–403; Pindar, *Nemean* 3, *Pythian* 4; Valerius Flaccus, *Argonautica*]

BIBLIOGRAPHY

Kock, T. *Comicorum Atticorum Fragmenta*. Vol. 1. Leipzig: Teubner, 1880.

MEDEA EURIPIDES (431 B.C.E.) The date of the play is significant as *Medea* was produced when EURIPIDES' fellow Athenians were in the initial stages of the PELOPONNESIAN WAR with SPARTA, a conflict that would last almost three decades and would end with the defeat of Athens. The play finished third (and last) in the competition that year. First place went to AESCHYLUS' son, Euphorion, and SOPHOCLES received second prize. The other plays that accompanied Euripides' *Medea* in its TETRALOGY in 431 are also known but have not survived to our time: *Philoctetes*, *Dictys*, and the SATYR PLAY *Theristai*.

The action of the play occurs before the palace of King CREON of CORINTH. With the exception of CYCLOPS and ALCESTIS, *Medea* is the only extant Euripidean play that can be performed by only two actors.

As the NURSE reveals in her opening monologue, MEDEA and JASON arrived in Corinth after they were exiled from IOLCUS. The daughters of Pelias, king of Iolcus, killed their father as part of Medea's plot. Medea and Jason's life in Corinth was a happy one until Jason decided to divorce Medea and marry Creon's daughter. Medea, who has learned of this, has become distraught, and the nurse worries she has some terrible deed in mind. After the nurse's monologue, a TUTOR enters with Jason and Medea's two sons. The tutor informs the nurse that Creon intends to exile Medea and her sons from Corinth. As the tutor and nurse talk, cries of anguish from Medea are heard from the palace. The tutor takes the boys into the house as Medea continues to wail inside.

After the departure of the tutor and the children, the CHORUS of Corinthian women enter in response to Medea's cries. The nurse informs the chorus of the situation, as Medea cries out a threat of suicide from within the house. The chorus urge her not to let anger overwhelm her. Medea breathes threats against Jason and his new bride and laments the loss of her father, her native land, and the brother, ABSYRTUS, whom she killed after leaving Colchis. The chorus urge Medea's nurse to persuade her to go outside so they can try to calm her temper. After a few moments, the nurse returns with Medea, who complains of the difficulties facing women, particularly barbarian women such as she, in their relationships with men. She states that the pain of childbirth is far worse than the dangers men face in war. Medea informs the chorus that she wants to avenge herself on Jason and asks the chorus to tell no one—a request to which the Corinthian women agree.

Next, Creon enters and informs Medea that she must leave Corinth. First, she successfully begs Creon, who threatens to exile her and her children from Corinth, for one more day in town. After Creon's exit, Medea informs the Corinthian women that she purposely fawned on Creon as part of her plot to destroy him, his daughter, and Jason. Medea then wonders how she will destroy them and in what city she can seek refuge after she carries out her plot. Medea remains on stage as the Corinthian women sing an ode in which they comment on the reversal of roles between men and women that appears to be unfolding—men, not women, are deceptive; stories of faithless women will fall out of favor and women will write poems about infamous men. The chorus lament that men's oaths are no longer valid and that a new woman occupies Medea's bed.

After the choral ode, Jason enters and criticizes Medea's words against Creon and his daughter. He promises to make sure that Medea and their children are provided for. Medea, filled with rage, calls him a coward and recalls all she has done for him: In Colchis, she helped him master the fire-breathing bulls and killed the dragon that guarded the Golden Fleece. She deceived her father, accompanied Jason to Iolcus, and brought about the death of Pelias. Medea recalls Jason's oaths to her and his begging her for help. Now, she will be exiled and friendless, although she saved Jason's life. Jason, in response, claims his success was due to the favor of APHRODITE, not Medea. He argues that he has done her a favor by taking her from a land of barbarians to Greece, where she is now famous. Jason also suggests that his marriage to Creon's daughter is actually in the best interest of Medea and the children, because such a marriage would allow them to live a life of wealth and privilege. After Jason exits, the Corinthian women sing an ode about the powers of Aphrodite. They hope that Aphrodite will never drive them to leave an old love for a new one and that they will never experience exile. They conclude their ode by sympathizing with Medea and expressing the hope that the man who disowns his friend will meet with ruin.

The choral song is followed by the arrival of AEGEUS, king of Athens, who happens to be passing through Corinth on his way home after consulting the DELPHIC ORACLE. Aegeus is traveling to Troezen to ask his wise friend, Pittheus, about the mysterious answer that the oracle gave him. When Medea hears that Aegeus had gone to Delphi to inquire about the possibility of having children, Medea, skilled in the ways of magic, promises to help him have children if he will allow her to stay at his house in Athens. Aegeus agrees but tells Medea that she will have to make her own way to Athens, as he does not want to cross purposes with Creon.

After the departure of Aegeus, Medea's plot against Jason begins in earnest. She begs Jason to arrange for her children to be allowed to stay in Corinth. Then she arranges to have her children give Jason's new bride a present—a gown and a diadem—both of which Medea has secretly poisoned. Ironically, the persuasive powers of Jason himself convince his new bride that she should put aside her anger, allow the children to stay in Corinth, and accept Medea's gift. Soon, a messenger enters and announces the death of Creon's daughter and of Creon, who tried to help his daughter when she put on the fatal garments and became stuck to the garments himself and was destroyed by their poison.

After the messenger's speech, Jason demands that the palace doors be opened so that he can see the horrors that Medea has wrought and kill her. Medea, however, appears above the palace in the chariot of her grandfather, Helios (see SUN). Jason curses Medea and wonders how she could have inflicted such injuries on her own sons. Medea retorts that Jason should have know better than to abandon her for another woman. After the two verbally abuse one another, Medea announces that she will bury her children in the precinct of Hera Acraea, that she will also establish an annual feast in their honor, and that she will depart for Athens. Medea then predicts that Jason will be killed when his head is crushed by a beam from his ship, *Argo*. Jason and Medea continue to argue; the play ends with Jason's continuing to complain bitterly about Medea, while she flies away in Helios' chariot.

COMMENTARY

Although *Medea* placed third in the competition in which it was staged, modern readers and critics almost universally rank it as one of the finest plays in extant Greek drama. The ancient HYPOTHESIS to the play (the information that accompanies the play in the ancient manuscript) says Euripides' *Medea* owed much to the *Medea* of Neophron, but Page, arguing on the basis of the language, meter, and style of the surviving fragments of Neophron's play, demonstrates that Neophron's *Medea* was actually written after Euripides' play. Euripides' play surely has some debt to AESCHYLUS' *Agamemnon* (see ORESTEIA). Both CLYTEMNESTRA, at *Agamemnon* 1233, and Medea, at *Medea* 1343, described as being like Scylla. Both women are also described as lionesses (*Agamemnon* 1258 (see ORESTEIA), *Medea* 1342). Additionally, Medea destroys the woman who becomes her sexual rival, just as Clytemnestra destroys CASSANDRA. Medea, however, uses magic, whereas Clytemnestra strikes down Cassandra with a blade, albeit one wielded by her own hands. Furthermore, Clytemnestra helps kill her husband, whereas Medea's punishment of Jason may be worse in some ways—she allows him to live.

The use of the poisoned robe in Euripides' *Medea* is also seen in SOPHOCLES' *TRACHINIAE,* as DEIANEIRA destroys HERACLES by the same means. Unlike Medea's act, however, Deianeira's destruction of Heracles was not intentional. One should also note that Deianeira delivers the robe to Heracles through the messenger Lichas (whom Heracles kills), whereas Medea has her children (whom she kills) deliver the robe to her rival. Whether Sophocles' play preceeded Euripides' play, or vice versa, is unknown.

Finally, the killing of children in *Medea* anticipates the killing of children in a later Euripidean play, *HERACLES,* in which the title character kills his children. In contrast to Medea, however, Madness, sent by HERA, leads Heracles to kill his children. Medea kills her children because she does not want them to be mocked and killed by her enemies after she has killed her rival in Corinth. Note, however, that in both *Medea* and *Heracles,* the title characters find refuge in Athens after their crimes have been committed. King Aegeus will take in Medea, and Aegeus' son THESEUS will take in Heracles.

The themes of parenthood and supplication are intertwined throughout *Medea,* and Jason and Medea's past, present, and future can be seen unfolding along the lines of these themes. At lines 496–98, Medea recalls that in Colchis, Jason gained her help by his supplications. Now, in Corinth, Medea successfully employs the same tactic to achieve her violent aims. At line 324, she begs Creon by his knees and his newlywed daughter. Creon says she will never persuade him,

but 25 lines later he yields to her request for one more day in Corinth. Having used supplication and appeal to Creon's child to manipulate the king of Corinth, Medea will use the same technique on the king of Athens. Although scholars have criticized the appearance of Aegeus as unmotivated, from a thematic point of view the scene does make sense. Medea's technique of supplication and manipulation will destroy Creon's child and even the king himself. Aegeus, however, has no children (that he knows of). Medea's powers help him; at lines 709–13, she becomes a supplicant, begging Aegeus for asylum in his kingdom. In exchange, she promises to put an end to his childlessness through her knowledge of drugs or remedies (*pharmaka,* 718). To many in Euripides' Athenian audience, the word *pharmaka* would have been ironic, because according to tradition Medea herself became the remedy for Aegeus' childlessness by bearing his son, MEDUS.

By this time, the chorus know that Medea is considering killing her children as well as the princess. At 853–55, the chorus try to use supplication and manipulation to dissuade her from killing her sons. They beg her by holding her knees not to kill them. At 862–65, they even predict that she will not be able to kill them when they are supplicants. Medea, however, has now become immune to the tactic she has used so successfully against the two kings. Even her own children's supplication will not succeed. With her plot approaching fulfillment, Medea must now stoop to the most degrading supplication yet. For her plan to succeed, she must appeal to the person she hates most—Jason. Her opening words to her former husband at lines 869–70 are "Jason, I beg you to forgive me for what I said." Medea wins over Jason and then sends her children as supplicants to the princess (971) to persuade her to accept the gifts that will cause her death. Thus Medea, who has used supplication and the promise of children to manipulate the Athenian king, makes her children employ the same tactic to destroy the Corinthian princess.

The playwright's portrait of Medea is both sympathetic and terrifying. Because one way a woman in the Greek world would be regarded as a "good" wife was through bearing male offspring, Medea succeeds from that perspective. Additionally, she has not been unfaithful to Jason. In Medea's view, she saved Jason's life when he was faced with various deadly forces in Colchis. One would not expect that many in Euripides' audience would have been sympathetic to Jason's argument that his success was due to Aphrodite rather than Medea. As Laurel Bowman's recent discussion of the play points out, Euripides' predominantly male audience of Athenians would probably have noticed that the union of the Greek Jason and the barbarian Medea could not have produced children who would recognized as citizens under Athenian citizenship laws. Furthermore, because Greek marriages were arranged by the bride's father and the prospective husband, the union of Jason and Medea would not accord with Athenian custom. Medea has betrayed her native land and left without her father's permission.

Although much about Medea could have prompted the audience's sympathies, we must not forget that she has committed numerous atrocities. By helping Jason, she has betrayed her father and her native land. When leaving Colchis, she also killed her brother. In Iolcus, she tricked Pelias' daughters into killing their own father. Although one could understand Medea's desiring to kill Jason, she instead directs her final revenge at Jason's new bride, the innocent object of a marriage arranged by Creon and Jason. As Bowman points out, Medea's destruction of Creon's daughter ensures that Jason will not be able to produce further male offspring to bear his name and maintain his family's reign in Corinth. Indeed, Medea destroys a woman who was going to have the sort of marriage that she should have had—one approved of and arranged by her father. Finally, and most horrifically, Medea kills her own children. Even the chorus of Corinthian women, who are generally sympathetic to her, beg her not to do this and at one point even express the belief that she will not be able to go through with the deed when she sees her own children begging for their lives. But Medea does kill her children. Then, perhaps most chilling of all for Euripides' Athenian audience, she flies away to Athens, where she will be taken in by Athens' king, Aegeus. Surely many in Euripides' audience would have been aware of the tradition that Medea later tried to kill Aegeus' son, Theseus, the greatest of Athenian heroes. Thus, in 431 B.C.E., as Euripides' audience stood on the

brink of war with Sparta and its allies, a war into which many Athenians would send their sons to die, Euripides presented his fellow citizens with the image of a childless king who has unwittingly granted asylum to a child killer.

BIBLIOGRAPHY

Bowman, Laurel. "Women and the *Medea.*" In *Approaches to Teaching the Dramas of Euripides.* Edited by R. Mitchell-Boyask. New York: Modern Language Association of America, 2002.

Mastronarde, D. J. *Euripides: Medea.* Cambridge: Cambridge University Press, 2002.

McDermott, E. A. *Euripides' Medea: The Incarnation of Disorder.* University Park and London: Pennsylvania State University Press, 1989.

Page, D. L. *Euripides: Medea.* Oxford: Clarendon Press, 1938.

Pucci, P. *The Violence of Pity in Euripides' Medea.* Ithaca, N.Y.: Cornell University Press, 1980.

MEDEA SENECA (WRITTEN BETWEEN 49 AND 65 C.E.?)

The plot of SENECA's *Medea* follows basically the same line as EURIPIDES' MEDEA. The play is set at CORINTH before the palace of that land's king, CREON. Unlike in Euripides' play, in which Medea's nurse delivers the opening monologue, in Seneca's play Medea herself delivers the prologue and explains that her husband, JASON, is divorcing her to marry Creon's daughter. Medea calls for the gods to take vengeance on Creon and his daughter and prays that Jason will experience harsh exile. Medea also hints at her intention to kill her children as part of her revenge on Jason.

Unlike in Euripides' play, where the Corinthian chorus are more sympathetic to Medea than Jason, in Seneca's the Corinthians enter and sing a marriage hymn in celebration of the marriage of Jason and Creon's daughter. They praise the beauty of Creon's daughter and approve of Jason's divorcing a barbarian. After Medea hears their song, she again indicates that she will take vengeance against Jason, his new bride, and Creon. Medea's nurse tries to calm her and urges her to leave Corinth. As Medea considers her next move, Creon enters and threatens to exile Medea, who pleads with him to grant her a place to live in his kingdom. Initially, Creon insists that Medea leave Corinth; later he grants her a one-day reprieve (as in Euripides). After Creon's exit, the chorus sing of the dangers encountered by sailors. They then describe the various obstacles that Jason and his crew overcame and note sarcastically that other than the Golden Fleece, the only "prize" acquired by the Argonauts was Medea. They conclude by noting that the sea no longer poses serious challenges to human beings and that the world's unexplored and unpopulated regions are becoming smaller and smaller.

After the choral ode, a furious Medea appears and again complains bitterly about her treatment by Jason and Creon. As Medea utters threats against her enemies, her nurse again tries to calm her. Next, Jason enters; he knows that Medea is furious and considers how to soothe her anger. Medea complains about the exile she faces and recalls to Jason all the help that she gave him and all that she has sacrificed for him during his adventures and since his return to Greece. Jason, however, does not retreat from his stance that Medea should accept exile and avoid the wrath of Creon, as well as that of Acastus, the son of Pelias, whose death Medea orchestrated in IOLCUS. Medea begs Jason to help her resist these enemies, but Jason refuses. Medea then asks to take her children into exile with her—again Jason refuses. After Jason's exit, Medea announces her plan to have her children take a poisoned gown and crown to Creon's daughter. Next, the chorus sing an ode about the dangerous effects of love. They pray that Jason will be safe and worry that Neptune (Greek: POSEIDON) is angry with Jason for sailing to Colchis and thus figuratively defeating the sea. The chorus recall that many of Jason's crew met a horrible fate during or since their participation in the voyage.

After the chorus' song, Medea's nurse enters and describes Medea's preparations and prayers for destroying Jason's new bride. Soon, Medea herself appears and prays to the divinities (especially HECATE), who she hopes will assist her in her plot. After Medea prays over the deadly gown and crown, she instructs her sons to take the gifts to Creon's daughter. The children's departure is followed by a choral ode in which the Corinthians marvel at Medea's savage behavior and wonder what the result of her anger will be. The chorus do not have long to wait for an answer: Soon, a messenger from the palace announces that both Creon and his daughter are dead. Next, Medea enters carrying a sword. At first, she won-

ders whether she should continue to wreak vengeance on Jason by killing her children. After a lengthy mental struggle with herself, Medea decides that she will.

Medea summons her children and kills one of them. When she hears Jason and some of the Corinthians, who are searching for her to kill her, she drags away her second son and the corpse of his brother. After Medea enters the palace, Jason appears and tells the Corinthians to tear down the house. Medea, however, appears on the roof of the palace in the chariot of the SUN. Medea has the corpse of one son with her and again debates with herself about killing the other. When Jason sees her, he urges the Corinthians to burn the palace. The play ends, with Medea's killing her second son, throwing the sons' bodies down to Jason, and flying away in the Sun's chariot.

COMMENTARY

As noted earlier, many similarities can be found in the *Medea* plays of Euripides and Seneca. Both playwrights examine the dangers of love's being tainted by anger, but for Seneca this combination has a particular significance. As a proponent of the Stoic philosophy (which did not exist in Euripides' day), Seneca, along with his fellow Stoics, believed that controlling anger was important to a happy life. Seneca's Medea perversely tries to achieve her aims by embracing anger.

As the play opens, when Medea speaks of girding herself with anger (51), Seneca uses language that invokes the image of girding oneself with a conventional weapon, such as a sword. Later, however, she denies that anger drove her to any of the crimes she has committed; she claims love drove her to them (136). As Medea's enemies corner her, her nurse urges her to control her anger (153, 381), but she recognizes in Medea the signs of an old anger that will soon burst forth (394). As Jason and his sailors conquered the seas; Medea, however, declares that the fury of no sea could equal her wrath (414).

Jason recognizes Medea's anger and attempts to soothe her with prayers (444). He urges her to go into exile and avoid the wrath of Creon (494), and he urges her to calm her wrath (506) for their children's sake. Medea cannot be moved, although as part of her plot to ruin Jason she pretends that she will put aside her anger and asks Jason to forget her outburst (556).

After Jason exits, Medea sets her plan in motion and the chorus note that love spurred on by anger cannot be controlled (591). They recall that MELEAGER's angry mother killed her own son (646), just as Medea will kill her children. As Medea prepares to kill her children, the chorus observe the anger on her face (853) and the deadly combination of love and anger present in her (866–68). When Medea wavers in her resolve to kill her children, as at the play's outset, she calls upon her anger to drive her toward the horrific deeds that will punish Jason (902). The wavering Medea wonders where her anger is going (916; cf. 927, 938). Earlier Medea's anger was more dangerous than a violent sea; now her anger and love are in conflict, as the winds and seas are. As Medea's anger conflicts with her maternal feelings (943–44), she considers not killing her children. Ultimately, the anger she feels toward her husband overcomes the love she has for her children. After killing one child, Medea again wavers and wonders that her anger has subsided (989). The sight of Jason again causes her wrath to seethe and she kills her other child. For the Stoics of Seneca's day, mastering one's anger could lead to happiness; for Seneca's Medea, harnassing her anger gives her the perverse pleasure of revenge.

BIBLIOGRAPHY

Hine, Harry M. *Medea: Seneca*. Warminster, U.K.: Aris & Phillips, 2000.
Nussbaum, Martha C. "Serpents in the Soul: A Reading of Seneca's *Medea*," In *Medea: Essays on Medea in Myth, Literature, Philosophy, and Art*. Edited by James J. Clauss and Sarah Iles Johnson. Princeton, N.J.: Princeton University Press, 1997, 219–49.
Ohlander, S. *Dramatic Suspense in Euripides' and Seneca's Medea*. New York: Lang, 1989.

MEDES   Often referred to by dramatists synonymously with Persians, the Medes were a group of people who inhabited the land of Media in what is today the northern part of Iran. At one time, the Medes had actually ruled the Persians; later the Persians overcame the Medes and made Media one of their provinces. According to legend, the Medes took their name from MEDEA, who fled to the area after her failed attempt to kill THESEUS. [ANCIENT SOURCES: Aeschylus, *Persians* 236; Herodotus, 5.77; Pausanias, 2.3.8]

MEDIA   See MEDES.

MEDUS   The son of MEDEA and AEGEUS, Medus was born in ATHENS and would have been the heir to Aegeus' throne had his half brother, THESEUS, not returned to Athens and driven out his mother and him. After they had been driven from Athens, Medus and Medea returned to Medea's native land of COLCHIS, although apparently by separate paths. Apollodorus states that Medus traveled east, defeated various barbarian tribes, and called the conquered land Media after himself. Apollodorus also says Medus died fighting against the natives of India.

The Greek comic poet Theopompus wrote a *Medus*, whose six extant lines tell us nothing of its plot. Among Roman authors, PACUVIUS wrote a tragic *Medus*, of which some two dozen fragments (mostly of a single line) survive. The setting for Pacuvius' play appears to be Colchis, its theme Medus' search for Medea. Medea's brother, Perses, had a speaking role in the play, and when Medus approached him, he was pretending to be Hippotes, the son of CREON. At some point in the play, a description detailed Medea's arrival in the serpent-drawn chariot of the SUN. Medea met with Perses and apparently told him that Hippotes was dead and that her son, Medus, was in his custody. At some point, Medea encountered her father, AEETES, who did not recognize her at first. [ANCIENT SOURCES: Apollodorus 1.9.28; Diodorus Siculus 10.27.1; Pausanias 2.3.8]

BIBLIOGRAPHY

Kock, T. *Comicorum Atticorum Fragmenta*. Vol. 1. Leipzig: Teubner, 1880.
Warmington, E. H. *Remains of Old Latin: Livius Andronicus, Naevius, Pacuvius, and Accius*. Vol. 2. Cambridge, Mass.: Harvard University Press, 1936.

MEDUSA   Phorcys and Ceto had two sets of daughters, one known as the Graiae (Dino, Enyo, Pephredo [or Pemphredo]), and the other known as the GORGONS (Euryale, Sthenno, and Medusa). Of the Gorgons, Medusa was the only mortal. According to some sources, Medusa was a beautiful woman until she angered the goddess ATHENA when she had sexual relations with POSEIDON in one of Athena's sanctuaries. Athena, in anger, changed Medusa into a hideous creature with snake-filled hair, savage tusks, and wings. Medusa's appearance was so horrible that people who saw her were turned to stone. Eventually, PERSEUS cut off Medusa's head and gave it to Athena, who put Medusa's terrifying face on her aegis or shield to frighten her enemies. Medusa was pregnant by POSEIDON when Perseus killed her, but from Medusa's body two creatures were born. The first was the male warrior Chrysaor. The second was the winged horse PEGASUS, of which BELLEROPHON later became the master. Medusa does not appear as a character in any extant dramas, although her story would have been a focus of AESCHYLUS' *Phorcides* (fragments 459a–461b Mette). [ANCIENT SOURCES: Apollodorus, *Library* 2.3.2, 2.4.2–3; Hesiod, *Theogony* 270–81; Ovid, *Metamorphoses* 4.612–5.249]

BIBLIOGRAPHY
Mette, H. J. *Die Fragmente der Tragödien des Aischylos.* Berlin: Akademie-Verlag, 1959.

MEGABAZUS

A person mentioned by ARISTOPHANES as a king of Persia. Dunbar, however, points out that no Persian king by this name existed, and that a Megabazus had been a Persian military commander in the 510s B.C.E. and another Megabazus was a naval commander during the second Persian invasion of Greece in 480 and in 456 may have tried to bribe the Spartans to attack the Athenians so that they would leave Egypt. [ANCIENT SOURCES: Aristophanes, *Birds* 484; Herodotus, 4.143–4, 5.1–26, 7.97; Thucydides, 1.109.3]

BIBLIOGRAPHY
Dunbar, Nan. *Aristophanes: Birds.* New York: Oxford University Press, 1995, 331–32.

MEGACLES

A man whom ARISTOPHANES calls the uncle of STREPSIADES' wife. His name means "very famous" and because Aristophanes is trying to portray Strepsiades' wife as a member of a wealthy family, this Megacles is unlikely to have been identified with the Athenian Megacles who served as a treasurer for ATHENA in 428/427 B.C.E. [ANCIENT SOURCES: Aristophanes, *Clouds* 46, 70, 124, 815]

BIBLIOGRAPHY
Dover, K. J. *Aristophanes: Clouds.* Oxford: Clarendon Press, 1989, 99.

MEGAENETUS

A man branded as ignorant by ARISTOPHANES at *FROGS* 965, but about whom nothing is known. Sommerstein suggested that he may have been "a military officer."

BIBLIOGRAPHY
Sommerstein, A. H. *The Comedies of Aristophanes.* Vol. 9, *Frogs.* Warminster, U.K.: Aris & Phillips, 1996, 242.

MEGAERA

Born when blood from the castrated genitalia of URANUS fell onto the Earth, Megaera was one of the FURIES. She was the sister of Tisiphone and Allecto. In SENECA's *HERCULES FURENS,* Juno (see HERA) summons Megaera to make HERACLES become mad. In the same author's *THYESTES,* ATREUS calls upon Megaera to help him take revenge on his brother. [ANCIENT SOURCES: Apollodorus, *Library* 1.1.4; Seneca, *Hercules Furens* 102, *Hercules Oetaeus* 1006, 1014, *Medea* 963, *Thyestes* 252]

MEGALENSIAN GAMES

The Megalensian Games, first celebrated in April 204 B.C.E., were held in honor of a divinity known as the Magna Mater ("great mother"). Beginning in 194 B.C.E., these games were arranged annually by the curule aediles; however, the production notice for PLAUTUS' *PSEUDOLUS* indicates that the urban praetor arranged the games in 191 B.C.E. In addition to *Pseudolus,* these games were the occasion for four other extant plays: TERENCE's *ANDRIA, MOTHER-IN-LAW, SELF-TORMENTOR,* and *EUNUCH.* Dramatic performances may have been held on as many as six days of the games.

MEGARA (1)

A town located a few miles west of ATHENS, which played a critical role in the outbreak of the PELOPONNESIAN WAR. In ARISTOPHANES' *ACHARNIANS* (425 B.C.E.), a trader from Megara arrives and does business with DICAEOPOLIS. The war has caused the Megarian such hardship that in exchange for Dicaeopolis' wares, the Megarian trades him his daughters (who are dressed as pigs). In 424/423, Megarians opposed to Athens destroyed the walls that connected Megara and Nisaea (a town under Athenian control just northwest of Megara). The Greek comic poet Simylus wrote a *Megarian Woman,* of which a single word survives (fragment 1 Kock). [ANCIENT SOURCES: Aristophanes, *Acharnians, Lysistrata* 1170, *Peace* 246, 481, 500, 609; Thucydides, 4.109.1]

BIBLIOGRAPHY

Henderson, J. *Aristophanes: Lysistrata*. Oxford: Clarendon Press, 1987, 205.

Kock, T. *Comicorum Atticorum Fragmenta*. Vol. 2. Leipzig: Teubner, 1884.

MEGARA (2)

The daughter of the Theban king CREON, Megara was given as a bride to HERACLES as a reward for his valor in leading the Thebans to victory over the MINYANS. Heracles later became insane and killed Megara and his children by her. Megara appears as a character in two extant plays, EURIPIDES' *HERACLES* and SENECA'S *HERCULES FURENS*. Although both plays treat the same general subject, Heracles' return from the UNDERWORLD, his killing of LYCUS, and his madness and killing of Megara and the children, the two playwrights treat the character of Megara in quite different ways. In Euripides' play, Megara is depicted as a beleaguered wife, who despairs that Heracles will return from the underworld. Seneca seems to integrate Megara into the action of his play in a more adept way than Euripides. For Seneca, Megara becomes the motivation for Lycus' threats against her and the children, as Lycus desires to marry Megara so that he can produce royal offspring. Megara staunchly resists Lycus' threats and remains loyal to Heracles.

MEGAREUS

The son of CREON and Eurydice, Megareus was the older brother of HAEMON. Megareus is mentioned in AESCHYLUS' *SEVEN AGAINST THEBES* as one of those chosen to defend THEBES' seven gates against POLYNEICES' invading army. Megareus was matched against Eteoclus (not to be confused with ETEOCLES, OEDIPUS' son) and killed him. In SOPHOCLES' *ANTIGONE,* we find references to Megareus' death and Creon's being blamed for his death. How Megareus died, however, is not clear. Perhaps he died in battle against Polyneices' forces, or he may be synonymous with MENOECEUS, who sacrificed himself to ensure that the Thebans would be victorious (see EURIPIDES' *PHOENICIAN WOMEN*). [ANCIENT SOURCES: Aeschylus, *Seven against Thebes* 474; Sophocles, *Antigone* 1303]

MELANION

A mythical person who hated women and spent his time hunting in the hills and countryside. The Greek comic poet Antiphanes wrote a *Melanion;* only two lines (about drinking to the goddess of health) survive (fragment 149 Kock). [ANCIENT SOURCES: Apollodorus, *Library* 3.9.2; Aristophanes, *LYSISTRATA* 785, 796, 806; Xenophon, *Cynegeticus* 1.2.7]

BIBLIOGRAPHY

Kock, T. *Comicorum Atticorum Fragmenta*. Vol. 2. Leipzig: Teubner, 1884.

MELANIPPE

The daughter of Aeolus and CHIRON's daughter, Hippo, Melanippe, whose name means "black horse," produced two sons, Aeolus and Boeotus, by POSEIDON. Melanippe's father, enraged by her producing the children out of wedlock, blinded and imprisoned Melanippe and had the two boys exposed. A cow suckled the boys, however, and herdsmen raised them. When the Icarian king, Metapontus, threatened to divorce his wife, Theano, because she had not borne children, Theano enlisted the same cowherds to find a child for her, and they gave her Aeolus and Boeotus, whom she raised as her own. Later, she had two children by Metapontus, but Aeolus and Boeotus remained in the house. When Metapontus showed favor to Aeolus and Boeotus, Theano became jealous and told her own children to kill them. Poseidon, their father, prevented this and in the fight that occurred among the four young men, Theano and Metapontus' sons died. Theano, in grief, committed suicide. Poseidon then told Aeolus and Boeotus to help their mother, Melanippe, who remained imprisoned by her father. Melanippe's sons rescued her and killed her father, and Poseidon restored her sight. When Aeolus and Boeotus returned with Melanippe to Icaria and told Metapontus what had happened, he married Melanippe and adopted Aeolus and Boeotus as his legitimate heirs. The brothers later founded towns that they named after themselves, Aeolia and Boeotia.

EURIPIDES wrote two plays about Melanippe, *Melanippe Sophe,* which means "Melanippe the wise" (fragments 480–88 Nauck), and *Melanippe Desmotis,* which means "Melanippe in chains" (fragments 489–513 Nauck). *Melanippe Sophe* apparently was about the birth, exposure, and recovery of Aeolus and Boeotus. As the play's title implies, *Melanippe Desmotis* seems to have treated Melanippe's imprisonment by Aeolus and her subsequent rescue by her sons. Among Roman authors, Ennius wrote a *Melanippa,* which Webster thinks was based on Euripides' *Melanippe Sophe.* [ANCIENT SOURCES: Hyginus, *Fables* 186].

BIBLIOGRAPHY

Webster, T. B. L. *The Tragedies of Euripides.* London: Methuen, 1967.

MELANIPPUS A son of Astacus, Melanippus of THEBES killed Mecisteus and mortally wounded TYDEUS in the battle of the Seven against Thebes. Some say that AMPHIARAUS killed Melanippus, cut off his head, and then persuaded the dying Tydeus to eat Melanippus' brain. [ANCIENT SOURCES: Aeschylus, *Seven against Thebes* 414; Apollodorus, *Library* 1.8.5–6, 3.6.8; Pausanias, 9.18.1]

MELEAGER The son of OENEUS (or ARES) and ALTHAEA, Meleager was a prince of CALYDON and the husband of Cleopatra. When Meleager was born his mother heard a prophecy that as long as a certain log on her hearth remained intact, Meleager would remain alive. Upon hearing this, Althaea took the log from the hearth and hid it inside a chest. Many years later, after Oeneus forgot to sacrifice to ARTEMIS, and Artemis sent a boar to ravage Calydon, Meleager was credited with dealing the fatal blow to the dangerous Calydonian boar. The famous female hunter ATALANTA had been first to wound the boar, however, and Meleager wanted to present the boar's pelt to Atalanta, with whom he had fallen in love (some sources say that Meleager had a son, PARTHENOPAEUS, by Atalanta). Two of Meleager's uncles, brothers of his mother, Althaea, opposed this, and when they tried to prevent Meleager from awarding the pelt to Atalanta, Meleager killed them both. According to some sources, when Althaea heard of her brother's deaths, she took the log from the chest and burned it, thus causing Meleager's death. Althaea, upset by her son's death, then committed suicide, as did Meleager's wife. Meleager's sisters mourned so much at their brother's death that Artemis changed them into guinea birds—the Greek name for these birds, *meleagrides,* is traced to Meleager's name.

Other sources say that after the boar hunt, some of Calydon's neighbors, the Curetes, waged war against the Calydonians. The Calydonians held out while Meleager fought for them, but when Meleager killed his maternal uncles, Althaea cursed him. This angered Meleager, who refused to fight longer. With Meleager out of the fighting, the Curetes began to smash their way into Calydon. Meleager's mother and father begged him to help the Calydonians, but he refused. Finally, at the pleas of his wife, Cleopatra, Meleager subdued his anger and returned to the fight. Most sources, except HOMER, say that Meleager died while repelling the Curetes, either because Althaea had cursed him or because APOLLO helped the Curetes.

Although Meleager does not appear as a character in any extant dramas, several dramatists, both tragedians and comic poets, wrote plays entitled *Meleager.* SOPHOCLES wrote a *Meleager* from which a few fragments survive (401–6 Radt); fragment 401 refers to the boar sent by Artemis. EURIPIDES wrote a *Meleager* (fragments 515–39 Nauck) known to date to before 414 B.C.E. because it is quoted in ARISTOPHANES' *Birds.* Euripides' play seems to have opened just before the hunt for the Calydonian boar and concluded with the death of Meleager and the suicide of Althaea. Webster thinks that Atalanta appeared and asked for Meleager's help in getting the boar's hide. Meleager then went out and killed Althaea's brothers when they refused to give the hide to a woman. Webster thought Meleager returned, tried to defend himself to Althaea, announced that he wanted to marry Atalanta, and debated with Althaea about the marriage. Althaea left after this debate and burned the log that preserved Meleager's life. Webster thinks that the play concluded with the appearance of a divinity, who prophesied that TYDEUS would eat the head of MELANIPPUS (fragment 537).

The tragedian Antiphon wrote a *Meleager,* from which the single brief surviving fragment refers to people chosen from among the Aetolians who went to the hunt for the Calydonian boar as witnesses to Meleager's valor (fragment 2 Snell). The tragedian Sosiphanes also composed a *Meleager,* of which a single, two-line fragment survives (fragment 1 Snell); it refers to the ability of every Thessalian maiden to charm the MOON down from the sky. The Roman ACCIUS also wrote a TRAGEDY entitled *Meleager,* which may have taken Euripides' play as its model. The play's 20 or so surviving lines indicate that the play concerned the hunt for the boar, the awarding of the hide to Atalanta, Meleager's killing of Althaea's brother, and Althaea's killing of Meleager.

Among the Greek comic poets, Antiphanes wrote a *Meleager,* from which a four-word fragment about a leather canteen survives (fragment 150 Kock). In Philetaerus' *Meleager,* the only surviving fragment is about an unnamed girl who is being told to return her home. Rhinthon wrote a *Slave Meleager* (*Doulos Meleagros*), whose single surviving line gives no hint at the play's content (fragment 8 Kaibel). Sciras also wrote a *Meleager,* whose single surviving fragment mentions a wild boar (fragment 1 Kaibel). Dinolochus may have written a *Meleager,* of which only the title survives (fragment 78.6 Austin). [ANCIENT SOURCES: Apollodorus, *Library* 1.8.2; Homer, *Iliad* 9.527–599; Hyginus, *Fables* 14, 70; 171–74; Ovid, *Metamorphoses* 8.268–546; Seneca, *Medea* 644, 779]

BIBLIOGRAPHY
Austin, C. *Comicorum Graecorum Fragmenta in Papyris Reperta.* Berlin: De Gruyter, 1973.
Kaibel, G. *Comicorum Graecorum Fragmenta.* Vol. 1.1 [*Poetarum Graecorum Fragmenta.* Vol. 6.1]. Berlin: Weidmann, 1899.
Kiso, A. *The Lost Sophocles.* New York: Vantage Press, 1984.
Kock, T. *Comicorum Atticorum Fragmenta.* Vol. 2. Leipzig: Teubner, 1884.
Lloyd-Jones, H. *Sophocles: Fragments.* Cambridge, Mass.: Harvard University Press, 1996.
Radt, S. *Tragicorum Graecorum Fragmenta.* Vol. 4. Göttingen, Ger.: Vandenhoeck & Ruprecht, 1977.
Segal, C. "Sacrifice and Violence in the Myth of Meleager and Heracles: Homer, Bacchylides, Sophocles," *Helios* 17 (1990): 7–24.
Snell, B. *Tragicorum Graecorum Fragmenta.* Vol. 1. Göttingen, Ger.: Vandenhoeck & Ruprecht, 1971.
Sutton, D. F. *The Lost Sophocles.* Lanham, Md.: University Press of America, 1984.
Webster, T. B. L. *The Tragedies of Euripides.* London: Methuen, 1967.

MELETUS A Greek who wrote erotic poetry and drinking songs. He may have lived during the sixth century B.C.E. [ANCIENT SOURCES: Aristophanes, *Frogs* 1302; Epicrates, fragment 4 Kock]

BIBLIOGRAPHY
Kock, T. *Comicorum Atticorum Fragmenta.* Vol. 2. Leipzig: Teubner, 1884.
Sommerstein, A. H. *The Comedies of Aristophanes.* Vol. 9, *Frogs.* Warminster, U.K.: Aris & Phillips, 1996, 273.

MELISTICHE A woman mentioned by ARISTOPHANES at *ECCLESIAZUSAE* 46 as the wife of an Athenian named SMICYTHION. Sommerstein thinks that both Smicythion and Melistiche were real persons, but nothing else is known about Melistiche.

BIBLIOGRAPHY
Sommerstein, A. H. *The Comedies of Aristophanes.* Vol. 10, *Ecclesiazusae.* Warminster, U.K.: Aris & Phillips, 1998, 142.

MELITE The name of a DEME in Athenian territory where a well-known sanctuary dedicated to HERACLES was located. [ANCIENT SOURCES: Aristophanes, *Frogs* 501]

BIBLIOGRAPHY
Dover, K. J. *Aristophanes: Frogs.* Oxford: Clarendon Press, 1993, 256.

MELITIDES The meaning of this name is uncertain. Stanford thinks it may be connected with the DEME of MELITE; Sommerstein says, "Melitides was a proverbial fool." [ANCIENT SOURCES: Aristophanes, *Frogs* 991; Menander, *Shield* 269]

BIBLIOGRAPHY
Sommerstein, A. H. *The Comedies of Aristophanes.* Vol. 9, *Frogs.* Warminster, U.K.: Aris & Phillips, 1996, 243.
Stanford, W. B. *Aristophanes: Frogs.* London: Bristol Classical Press, 1958, 160.

MELOS An island in the southern AEGEAN, due south of SERIPHUS. During the PELOPONNESIAN WAR, the Melians tried to remain neutral. The Athenians, under NICIAS' command, attacked Melos in 426 B.C.E. and in 416, after starving them into submission, slaughtered the men of the island and enslaved the women. Some scholars believe that the events depicted in EURIPIDES' *TROJAN WOMEN* allude to the destruction of Melos. Others, such as Peter Green, argue that Euripides' play was composed before the destruction of Melos. [ANCIENT SOURCES: Aristophanes, *Birds* 186; Thucydides, 5.84–116]

BIBLIOGRAPHY
Green, Peter. "War and Morality in Fifth-Century Athens: The Case of Euripides' *Trojan Women*," *Ancient History Bulletin* 13, no. 3 (1999): 97–110.

MEMNON   The son of Tithonus and Eos (Dawn), Memnon was a handsome Ethiopian king who became an ally of the Trojans in their war against the Greeks. Memnon killed NESTOR's son, Antilochus, and ACHILLES killed him soon after. Eos asked ZEUS to grant Memnon immortality. AESCHYLUS wrote a *Memnon* (fragments 127–30 Radt Vol. 3) that was part of a trilogy that included PSYCHOSTASIA (the third play is not known). The fragments from Aeschylus' play give little indication of its content. To SOPHOCLES is also attributed a *Memnon,* from which only the title survives; this drama, however, may be identical to his *Ethiopians.* The Greek tragedian Timesitheus also wrote a *Memnon,* of which only the title survives. [ANCIENT SOURCES: Apollodorus, *Library* 3.12.4; Hesiod, *Theogony* 984–85; Homer, *Odyssey* 11.522; Ovid, *Metamorphoses* 13.576–622; Seneca, *Agamemnon* 212, *Trojan Women* 239]

BIBLIOGRAPHY
Kiso, A. *The Lost Sophocles.* New York: Vantage Press, 1984.
Lloyd-Jones, H. *Sophocles: Fragments.* Cambridge, Mass.: Harvard University Press, 1996.
Radt, S. *Tragicorum Graecorum Fragmenta.* Vol. 3. Göttingen, Ger.: Vandenhoeck & Ruprecht, 1985.
———. *Tragicorum Graecorum Fragmenta.* Vol. 4. Göttingen, Ger.: Vandenhoeck & Ruprecht, 1977.
Snell, B. *Tragicorum Graecorum Fragmenta.* Vol. 1. Göttingen, Ger.: Vandenhoeck & Ruprecht, 1971.
Sutton, D. F. *The Lost Sophocles.* Lanham, Md.: University Press of America, 1984.

MENAECHMI (THE BROTHERS MENAECHMUS or THE TWO MENAECHMUSES)
PLAUTUS (CA. 200 B.C.E.)   The action takes place in Epidamnus (the only occurrence of this setting in an Roman COMEDY) before two houses, one belonging to a young nobleman named Menaechmus, the other to the prostitute Erotium. As the unnamed character who delivers the prologue explains, a merchant from Syracuse had identical twin sons, Menaechmus and Sosicles. When the boys were seven years old, their merchant father took them to Tarentum. During a crowded festival, another merchant abducted Menaechmus and took him to Epidamnus. The merchant from Syracuse soon died of a broken heart. Sosicles was raised by his grandfather, who changed the boy's name to Menaechmus, which also hap-

pened to be the grandfather's name. When the merchant from Epidamnus died, his money went to the Menaechmus whom he had abducted.

As the first act opens, the PARASITE Peniculus (whose name means "little brush") is going to Menaechus of Epidamnus' house. The two intend to have lunch at the home of a prostitute, Erotium (lovey). As Peniculus approaches Menaechmus' house, Menaechmus emerges in the midst of an argument with his wife, Matrona (matron or wife; see MATRONA). Menaechmus resents her constant questions about where he is going, what he is doing, and the like. When Menaechmus' tirade drives his wife back into the house, Menaechmus rejoices and displays an item of women's clothing—which he happens to be wearing—that he has stolen from his wife and intends to give to Erotium. At this point, Peniculus steps forward, Menaechmus reveals the stolen clothing, and the two men discuss their plans for dinner at Erotium's house. Once they arrive at Erotium's house, the prostitute herself greets them at the door. Menaechmus gives her the stolen garment and requests that she have dinner prepared for the three of them. Then, Menaechmus and Peniculus leave for the FORUM to have a few drinks before dinner. Erotium summons her cook, Cylindrus (mixing bowl), and gives him money to buy ingredients for the meal.

The second act opens with the arrival of Menaechmus Sosicles and his slave, Messenio. Sosicles has been searching for his long-lost brother for six years. As Sosicles and Messenio discuss their dwindling funds, the cook Cylindrus arrives and sees, he thinks, Menaechmus of Epidamnus. Cylindrus speaks to Sosicles as if he knows him and wonders where his parasite is. Sosicles thinks Cylindrus is insane, but Cylindrus attributes this to Sosicles' sense of humor. The cook goes inside Erotium's house to tell his mistress that Menaechmus is already back from the forum. Next, Erotium emerges from the house, addresses Sosicles as if she knows him, and invites him to dinner. Erotium also mentions the garment that Menaechmus had given her, which further baffles Sosicles, who denies having a wife or giving her the clothing. When Erotium, however, tells Sosicles his family history, Sosicles is amazed and decides that playing along with her may be of some advantage. Sosicles decides to enter her house and tells Erotium not to allow the parasite to enter if he arrives. Erotium also asks Sosicles to have the garment that he stole from his wife altered by an embroiderer. Sosicles agrees to this request, because he hopes he can get some money for the garment.

The third act begins with the arrival of Peniculus from the forum. In the confusion of a public meeting, Peniculus and Menaechmus became separated, and now Peniculus worries that he will miss the dinner at Erotium's house. Peniculus' fears seem to be confirmed when he sees Menaechmus Sosicles' emerging from Erotium's house, giving every indication that the feast has ended. Furthermore, Peniculus notices that Sosicles is carrying the clothing that Menaechmus had given to Erotium. As Sosicles leaves Erotium's house, rejoicing in his good fortune, Peniculus angrily confronts him. Sosicles, of course, has no idea who Peniculus is. When Peniculus threatens to tell his wife about the stolen garment, Sosicles denies having a wife, giving the clothing, or stealing it. As Peniculus storms off to Menaechmus' house, a maidservant arrives from Erotium's house, gives Sosicles a bracelet, and asks him to take it to the jeweler for refurbishing. After the maidservant returns to the house, Sosicles again rejoices in his good fortune, as he plans to steal the bracelet.

In the following act, Menaechmus' wife, Matrona, and Peniculus emerge from the house and discuss Menaechmus' behavior. Soon, Menaechmus of Epidamnus arrives, angry that he has been delayed in the forum on business. Matrona confronts him about the theft of her clothing, and Peniculus claims Menaechmus was going to take the garment to the embroiderer's shop and that he saw him at Erotium's house. Menaechmus denies all wrongdoing and tries to soothe his wife's feelings. Menaechmus tells Matrona that he let someone borrow the garment and promises to retrieve it. Menaechmus' wife tells him not to return home without the garment. As Matrona reenters the house, Peniculus asks for a reward from her but is refused. Peniculus then departs for the forum. Menaechmus, believing Erotium will welcome him, calls at the prostitute's door. Erotium invites him inside, but when Menaechmus asks for the clothing he had given her, Erotium says she just gave it to him a little earlier. When Menaechmus denies that he was given the garment, Erotium is angered and shuts the door in his face. Menaechmus, welcome neither at home nor at his girlfriend's, leaves to consult his friends about what he should do.

The play's final act begins with the arrival of Sosicles from the forum. As Sosicles looks for Messenio, Menaechmus' wife sees him and notices that he has the stolen clothing. Matrona, thinking Sosicles is her husband, questions him about the clothing, and Sosicles is baffled. When Matrona threatens to divorce Sosicles, he says he could not care less what she does. The infuriated wife then sends a servant to get her father and take him to the house. When her aged father, named Senex ("old man"; see SENEX) arrives, Matrona complains about Menaechmus' treatment of her. Senex, however, defends Menaechmus' visits to Erotium's house as the result of Matrona's nagging. Senex sympathizes with his daughter about the theft of her clothing and speaks to Sosicles about this charge. When Sosicles denies knowing Senex, the old man pronounces him insane. Hearing this claim, Sosicles pretends to be insane and threatens Matrona and Senex with bodily harm. Matrona exits into the house, and Senex runs off to call a doctor. Sosicles himself decides to leave the area to avoid further trouble.

After the arrival of the doctor, whose name is Medicus ("doctor"), the real Menaechmus arrives. Senex and Medicus eavesdrop on Menaechmus as he describes the misery he has experienced. Hearing this, Medicus approaches Menaechmus and begins to question him about his health. Menaechmus is so angered by the Medicus that the doctor, soon convinced that Menaechmus is insane, tells Senex to call for servants to carry Menaechmus to his house. After the Medicus leaves to make preparations and Senex departs to assemble the servants, Menaechmus remains onstage near his house to wait for nightfall, when he believes that he will be allowed inside. Next, Messenio arrives and goes to Erotium's doorway in search of Sosicles. Before Messenio can knock, however, he witnesses the arrival of Senex and some slaves, who try to haul Menaechmus away to the doctor's house. Messenio, thinking this is his master, goes to the aid of Menaechmus. With Messenio's help, Senex and the slaves are driven away. When Messenio addresses Menaechmus as master and suggests that he should set him free for saving his life, Menaechmus denies that he is his master. However, he humors the slave and tells him that he is free as far as he is concerned. Hearing this, the joyful Messenio thanks Menaechmus and departs to retrieve his master's luggage and money. At the mention of money, Menaechmus, as his profit-hungry brother was earlier, is excited. After Messenio departs, Menaechmus decides to go to Erotium's house to ask for the stolen garment.

Soon Messenio returns with Sosicles, telling him about how he rescued him from the slaves and how Sosicles had set him free. Before the two can argue about this, Messenio sees Menaechmus, who is leaving Erotium's house. Messenio immediately recognizes Menaechmus as the double of Sosicles, but the brothers, with Messenio's help, take almost 80 lines to reach the same conclusion. The play concludes with Messenio's being granted his freedom by Sosicles, the brothers' deciding to return to their native land, and Menaechmus' deciding to auction off all his property, including his wife.

COMMENTARY

Menaechmi is usually considered one of PLAUTUS' best plays, and its influence on Shakespeare's Comedy of Errors attests to its excellence. The scenes at the play's end in which Sosicles pretends to be insane to scare away the father-in-law and the appearance of the quack doctor are funny even "on paper" and would surely have been even more humorous on stage. The play is not perfect, however, and understanding why identical twins should take so long to recognize one another, especially because the goal of Sosicles' voyage was to find his long-lost twin, is difficult.

As AMPHITRUO does, Menaechmi exploits the comic possibilities of identical twins. As in Amphitruo, in Menaechmi a master and slave enter from abroad and soon find themselves in a confusing situation caused by the presence of a twin. Of course, in Amphitruo the confusion is multiplied exponentially because Jupiter (Greek: ZEUS) is Amphitruo's twin and Mercury (Greek: Hermes) is the slave, Sosia's, twin. In Amphitruo, the twins have two primary functions. Jupiter is a twin so

that he can have sexual relations with Amphitruo's wife. Mercury is a twin so that he can prevent the real Amphitruo and Sosia from interfering with his father's activities. In Menaechmi, the twins are unaware of one another until the conclusion.

In both Amphitruo and Menaechmi, married women become victims of the confusion created by the twins. Unlike in Amphitruo, however, in which the deceived wife, ALCMENA, is clearly a sympathetic figure, Menaechmus' nameless nagging wife would have received less sympathy than Alcmena from Plautus' audience. Even Menaechmus' father-in-law has little sympathy for his daughter until he finds out that Menaechmus has been stealing from her. Not only does the confusion created by the twins baffle the married woman, but, unlike Amphitruo, Menaechmi adds a prostitute who will also fall victim to the confusion. Erotium, however, maintains some sense of control throughout the confusion and by the play's end has essentially "broken even."

Unlike in Amphitruo, in which the arrival of the twins from abroad leads to their constantly being rejected from the house, in the Menaechmi, the introduction of a twin into Epidamnus creates instances of both acceptance and rejection. The foreign Menaechmus stumbles into acceptance as a result of the plans of the native Menaechmus, whereas the native Menaechmus is rejected because his brother has already enjoyed the fruits of preparations made by his brother. As Amphitruo does, Epidamnian Menaechmus knows how it feels to be shut out of a house in which he is accustomed to finding welcome. Epidamnian Menaechmus' exclusion is even worse than Amphitruo's, however, because Menaechmus is eventually shut out not only from his wife's house, but also from the house of his lover. Much of the audience's amusement in Menaechmi arises from the native Menaechmus' being shut out and the foreign Menaechmus' reaping the unexpected benefits of the delights that his twin brother has arranged. Also amusing is the zest with which Sosicles delves into the opportunities for pleasure and profit that present themselves. Epidamnian Menaechmus clearly illustrates Erich Segal's principle that much of Roman COMEDY concerns the goal of avoiding business in the forum. Activities in this area of the city prevent Epidamnian Menaechmus from enjoying the day that he has planned, and his presence in the forum gives his twin brother the opportunity to usurp the kingdom of pleasure that he wants to establish for himself.

Another result of the presence of twins in Epidamnus is the charge of insanity; *Menaechmi* has more references to sanity and insanity than any other Roman comedy, and *Amphitruo* also touches upon this theme as the husband Amphitruo questions the sanity of his slave and his wife and eventually even his own sanity. Eventually, the god Jupiter must heal Amphitruo and his household of insanity. No such divine intervention takes place in *Menaechmi.* As with *Amphitruo,* the twin who enters from abroad in *Menaechmi* encounters many people he thinks are insane (Cylindrus, Erotium, Peniculus, the Matrona, the Matrona's father) and who think that he is insane. Unlike Amphitruo, who is separated from his wife and his house by the insanity he perceives, Sosicles is able to play along with the mistakes being made about his identity, and the lack of obstacles (such as the divinities faced by Amphitruo) allows him to benefit. Not only does Sosicles take advantage of the Epidamnians' "insanity," he also uses "insanity" to escape from danger, as his pretense of insanity helps him elude Matrona's father. Once Sosicles escapes, the charge of insanity falls (as does all the other bad luck in the play) on Menaechmus, whom the doctor tries to carry away. Eventually, the insanity that plagues Menaechmus and his twin, Sosicles, is healed, not by a divinity (as in *Amphitruo*) or a doctor, but by the slave Messenio, who cures them with the remedy of recognition.

In addition to the great emphasis placed on insanity, *Menaechmi* differs from other Roman comedies in that it has no lovesick young bachelor who is desperately seeking a way to be with his beloved. Unlike most other young men in Roman comedy, Menaechmus is married (as is Amphitruo), and his relationship with the prostitute is well established. No PIMP will keep him away from the prostitute, and he has no intention of marrying her, as other young men in comedy do. Other young lovers in comedy seek the cash necessary to have their beloved prostitute; Menaechmus already has the money. His goal is "lunch" (*prandium*) and all of its accompanying pleasures. Almost one-third of the Plau-

tine references to "lunch" occur in *Menaechmi.* Because *prandium* and not *matrimonium* (marriage) is Epidamnian Menaechmus' goal, there is no need for Erotium to be discovered to be a freeborn woman as so many other beloved prostitutes in Roman comedy are. Unlike at the conclusion of Plautus' CARTHAGINIAN, in which the young man and his beloved, who was just liberated from prostitution by proof of her freeborn status, will sail away to Carthage, at the end of *Menaechmi,* Erotium will retain her status as a prostitute and Epidamnian Menaechmus will sail away with his brother. Whereas Erotium's social status will remain the same, Messenio will change from slave to free, and Epidamnian Menaechmus will be liberated from his oppressive wife.

BIBLIOGRAPHY

Gratwick, Adrian S. *Menaechmi: Plautus.* Cambridge: Cambridge University Press, 1993.

Jocelyn, H. D. "Anti-Greek Elements in Plautus' Menaechmi?" In *Papers of the Liverpool Latin Seminar.* Vol. 4. Liverpool: Cairns, 1984, 1–25.

Leach E. W. "*Meam Quom Formam Noscito:* Language and Characterization in the *Menaechmi,*" *Arethusa* 2 (1969): 30–45.

Moore, T. J. "Facing the Music: Character and Musical Accompaniment in Roman Comedy," *Syllecta Classica* 10 (1999): 130–53.

Segal, E. W. "*The Menaechmi:* Roman Comedy of Errors," *Yale Classical Studies* 21 (1969): 77–93.

MENANDER (342–292 B.C.E.)

MENANDER (342–292 B.C.E.)   The source of much of our knowledge about COMEDY between the time of ARISTOPHANES and that of PLAUTUS is from Menander, a writer of New Comedy. Before 1900, however, our knowledge of Menander was limited to fragments and no complete plays existed. During the 1900s, various ancient manuscripts and bits of manuscripts (some used as packing material for the cases of mummies) began to emerge from Egypt. These manuscripts yielded a virtually complete text of *DYSCOLUS* and substantial portions of four other plays. Not only were these discoveries important for what they reveal about Menander's art, but they also help us gain a better understanding of New Comedy and the art of PLAUTUS and TERENCE, who were influenced by Menander.

Menander, son of Deiopeithes and Hesgestrate, was from the DEME of Cephisia. He may have studied philosophy with Theophrastus and the art of writing plays with PHILEMON. Although Menander is linked with noble instructors, rumors about his personal life tended toward the ignoble, as tradition makes him the lover of various high-class prostitutes (such as Glycera and Thais). Modern scholars doubt the truth of this; however, because Menander's plays so frequently portray prostitutes (the names Glycera and Thais are even the titles of two Menandrian plays), it is not surprising that Menander should be linked with prostitutes. More credence is given to the story that Menander was prosecuted (unsuccessfully) in the Athenian courts for being a friend of the pro-Macedonian Demetrius of Phalerum, who was driven out of Athens in 307 after governing the city for a decade. Menander is said to have died during a swim in the PIRAEUS.

Both ancient and modern writers seem to make much of the fact that although Menander is said to have written as many as 109 plays (97 titles have survived), he achieved only eight victories in competition. Consider, however, that this surpasses the number of victories achieved by EURIPIDES and that being victorious in comedy was more difficult because five comic poets competed at the City DIONYSIA and the LENAEA, whereas three tragedians competed at the City Dionysia and only two at the Lenaea. Menander's first play, *Anger* (*Orge*), appeared between 323 and 320 B.C.E. and may have won first prize. Undisputed, however, is Menander's victory with *Dyscolus* in 317/316 at the Lenaea. *Dyscolus* is the only complete play that we possess from Menander, although *Samia* (The girl from Samos) and *Epitrepontes* (*THE ARBITRATION*) are almost complete. From the following plays more than 200 lines survive: *Aspis* (*SHIELD*), *Perikeiromene* (*GIRL WITH THE SHAVEN HEAD*), *Misoumenos* (*MAN SHE HATED*), and *Sikyonios* (*MAN FROM SICYON*). Fewer than 200 lines survive from *Dis Exapaton* (Twice a swindler), *Heros* (Hero), *Kitharistes* (Lyre player), *Georgos* (Farmer), *Phasma* (Apparition), *Kolax* (Flatterer), *Theophoroumene* (Girl possessed), *Leukadia* (Girl from Leukas), *Perinthia* (Girl from Perinthos), *Karchedonios* (Man from Carthage), and *Koneiazomenai* (Women drinking hemlock).

Perhaps the perception that Menander was not successful during his lifetime is due to the fact that his work was extremely popular with later generations.

Later authors (even Saint Paul at 1 Corinthians 15.33) often quoted individual lines from his plays as examples of sensible thought, good advice, or moral truths. Both PLAUTUS and TERENCE adapted Menander's plays for the Roman stage. Plautus' *BACCHIDES, CASKET COMEDY*, and *STICHUS* were adapted from (respectively) Menander's *Double Deceivers, Women at Luncheon*, and *Brothers*. Plautus' *POT OF GOLD* may have been adapted from Menander's *Apistos* (The distrustful man). Two-thirds of Terence's plays were based on Menandrian originals (*ANDRIA, BROTHERS, EUNUCH*, and *SELF-TORMENTOR*). The Menandrian *Brothers* on which Terence drew was a different *Brothers* from the one Plautus used for *Stichus*.

Menander's comedies were popular for a number of reasons. As stated, the plays contain a good bit of moralizing, so they were educational as well as entertaining. The literary critic Aristophanes of Byzantium placed only HOMER ahead of Menander in skill, and an ancient commentary on Hermogenes wondered whether Menander copied life or life copied Menander. Menander's plots are praised for their elegant construction, and his characters exhibit greater consistency than their Aristophanic predecessors. In addition to the perceived realism in Menander's plays, their appeal is to a broad audience. Compared with the plays of ARISTOPHANES, Menander's plays contain relatively little obscenity. Furthermore, unlike Aristophanes' plays, Menander's plays contain few contemporary and topical references. Menander's stock characters of fathers, sons, slaves, prostitutes, soldiers, parasites, and cooks appear in play after play. So enduring and broad has been the appeal of the scenarios and characters in these plays that Peter Brown has described Menander as "the founding father of European comedy." [ANCIENT SOURCES: Aristophanes of Byzantium, *Commentaria in Callimachi Pinaces* 5.1; Aulus Gellius, *Attic Nights* 2.23, 3.16, 17.4; Plutarch, *Comparison of Aristophanes and Menander; Suda*, "m" 589; see Arnott, Vol. 1, xiii–xxiii]

BIBLIOGRAPHY

Arnott, W. G. *Menander.* 3 vols. Cambridge, Mass.: Harvard University Press, 1979.

Balme, M. *Menander: The Plays and Fragments.* Introduction by P. Brown. Oxford: Oxford University Press, 2002.

Frost, K. B. *Exits and Entrances in Menander.* Oxford: Oxford University Press, 1988.

Gomme, A. W., and F. H. Sandbach. *Menander: A Commentary.* London: Oxford University Press, 1973.
Webster, T. B. L. *Studies in Menander.* 2d ed. Manchester: Manchester University Press, 1960.

MENELAUS The son of ATREUS (or Plisthenes) and AEROPE, Menelaus is the brother of AGAMEMNON and the husband of HELEN, by whom he had a daughter, HERMIONE. After his marriage to Helen, Menelaus eventually became the king of SPARTA. After Menelaus' cousin, AEGISTHUS, killed Menelaus' father, ATREUS (an act that allowed Aegisthus' father, THYESTES, to become king of MYCENAE), Menelaus and Agamemnon went into exile. Eventually the brothers, with the backing of Menelaus' future father-in-law TYNDAREUS, drove Thyestes from the kingship and into exile. After the expulsion of Thyestes, Agamemnon and Menelaus married Tyndareus' daughters, CLYTEMNESTRA and Helen, respectively. Agamemnon became king of Mycenae; Menelaus lived in Sparta and became king when Tyndareus turned over the throne to him.

Menelaus appears as a character in several dramas. Because almost all the surviving Greek dramas were written by Athenian playwrights for Athenians during a time in which either strained relations or war existed between ATHENS and Sparta, Menelaus, the king of Sparta, is depicted (not surprisingly) in a negative light. In SOPHOCLES' AJAX, Menelaus and Agamemnon oppose the burial of AJAX, whom Sophocles constantly links with Athens in that play. In EURIPIDES' ANDROMACHE, Menelaus tricks ANDROMACHE to leave the altar at which she has taken refuge and threatens to kill her and her son, Molossus. In Euripides' TROJAN WOMEN, Menelaus becomes the judge in a debate between HECABE and Helen over whether Helen should be put to death. In Euripides' ORESTES, Menelaus is characterized as the somewhat spineless uncle of ORESTES, as his support of his nephew buckles when pressure from his father-in-law, Tyndareus, becomes too great. In Euripides' IPHIGENIA AT AULIS, Menelaus at first ruthlessly drives his brother, Agamemnon, to sacrificing his niece, IPHIGENIA; later he reverses his position and urges Agamemnon not to sacrifice his child. Among the extant dramas, only Euripides' HELEN includes any degree of sympathetic treatment of Menelaus. In this play, Menelaus is a rather comic figure as he washes ashore in Egypt after he has been shipwrecked. The Spartan king, dressed in rags, makes his way to THEOCLYMENUS' house in search of assistance but is driven away by the old woman who answers the door. Later, Menelaus is baffled as he encounters his wife, Helen, whom he thought he had taken back from Troy with him. [ANCIENT SOURCES: Apollodorus, *Epitome* 2.15–16; Seneca, *Agamemnon* 273, *Thyestes* 327, *Trojan Women* 923].

BIBLIOGRAPHY
Galeotti Papi, D. "Victors and Sufferers in Euripides' *Helen*," *American Journal of Philology* 108 (1987): 27–40.
Kyriakou, P. "Menelaus and Pelops in Euripides' *Orestes*," *Mnemosyne* 51, no. 3 (1998): 282–301.

MENOECEUS (1) The father of CREON and JOCASTA.

MENOECEUS (2) Menoeceus was the son of CREON, king of THEBES. In EURIPIDES' PHOENICIAN WOMEN, Menoeceus sacrifices himself in accordance with a prophecy by TIRESIAS so that the Thebans will defeat the Argives in battle.

MEN OF CAMICUS See COCALUS.

MEN OF ELEUSIS See ADRASTUS.

MEN OF LARISA See LARISA.

MEN OF PROSPALTA See EUPOLIS.

MEN OF SCYROS See SCYROS.

MEN OF SERIPHUS See SERIPHUS.

***THE MERCHANT* (Latin: *MERCATOR*) PLAUTUS (206 B.C.E.?)** The play's setting is ATHENS (as is most common in Roman COMEDY), and its action occurs before the houses of two elderly citizens, Demipho and Lysimachus. The prologue informs the audience that Philemon (also the author behind the original of PLAUTUS' THREE-DOLLAR DAY) wrote the Greek original, which was entitled *Emporos.* The prologue is delivered by Demipho's son, Charinus, who relates that he has fallen in love with an Athenian prostitute and that by spending much of his father's money to gain her favors enraged his father, Demipho, a conservative gentleman trained through hard work on a farm. When Demipho's father dies, Demipho takes his inheritance, becomes a merchant, and recommends that Charinus enter the same line of work. Charinus, realizing that his riotous living made him hateful to his father, decides to respect Demipho's wishes. Accordingly, Demipho builds a ship, loads it with merchandise, and gives Charinus a talent of silver. Demipho sends along with Charinus a slave named Acanthio. Charinus and Acanthio sail to Rhodes and sell their cargo at a fine profit. While in Rhodes, Charinus encounters a friend, who invites him to dine and to lodge at his house. Later that night, Charinus' host sends to him a beautiful woman, who spends the night with him. The next day, Charinus, captivated by the woman, buys her from his host and then takes her back to Athens. Charinus' father, however, does not know about the young woman, whom Charinus has left at the harbor with his servant, Acanthio.

After Charinus' opening monologue, Acanthio runs in from the harbor and tells Charinus that Demipho saw the woman aboard the ship and asked questions about her. Acanthio told Demipho that Charinus had bought her as a maid for Charinus' mother. Acanthio reveals, however, that Demipho is attracted to the woman as well. Charinus worries that Demipho suspects the woman is his mistress, but Acanthio assures Charinus that Demipho believed his story. After the exit of Charinus and Acanthio, Demipho arrives and relates a strange dream he had the previous night. In Demipho's dream, he bought a beautiful she goat and entrusted her to a monkey so the she goat would not have problems with a she goat that he already had at home. The monkey later told Demipho that the she goat had consumed the dowry of the monkey's wife. The monkey then told Demipho that unless he took the she goat, the monkey would reveal the she goat to Demipho's wife. Next, a young male goat appeared and told Demipho that he had taken the beautiful she goat from the monkey, and started making fun of Demipho for lamenting the she goat's abduction. Demipho tells the audience that he cannot imagine how this dream

will play out but says that he just met the beautiful "she goat" down at the harbor and has fallen in love with her.

After Demipho's revelation about his dream, his neighbor, Lysimachus, leaves his house and makes a remark, which Demipho overhears, about castrating a goat. Demipho suspects that is what his wife will do to him. As Lysimachus leaves for the harbor, Demipho reveals to his neighbor that he has fallen in love. After Lysimachus leaves, Charinus returns from the harbor. At first, Demipho eavesdrops while his son laments the latest developments. Before Charinus reveals anything specific about his problems, he sees his father and converses with him. Eventually, Demipho questions his son about the maid whom Charinus bought for his mother. Demipho claims, however, that this maid's looks are not compatible with their household and that she should be sold to a friend of his. Charinus responds that he has a young friend who wants to buy her. Father and son then take turns outbidding one another for the young woman on behalf of their "friend." When Charinus claims he has shared ownership of the woman with another man, Demipho says he does not care and declares he will go down to the harbor and sell her. Demipho also forbids Charinus to go to the harbor. Demipho exits, telling the audience that he will arrange for Lysimachus to buy the woman. Charinus, after his father's departure, says he will kill himself. Before Charinus can act, his friend, Eutychus, son of Lysimachus, emerges and tells Charinus that he knows everything. Eutychus offers to buy the young woman for Charinus; Charinus, however, is not sure how he will find the money to pay Eutychus.

As the play's third act opens, the audience learn that Eutychus was too late, and that his father, Lysimachus, has bought the young woman, Pasicompsa ("totally elegant"). When Lysimachus tells Pasicompsa that he has purchased her to give her to her master, she thinks he means Charinus. After Lysimachus describes her master as old, married, and toothless, Pasicompsa is angry and puzzled. Before the conversation can proceed further, the two exit into Lysimachus' house. Soon Demipho returns and goes to Lysimachus' house to check on Pasicompsa. Lysimachus, however, delays Demipho and persuades his friend to go with him to the market, purchase supplies, and arrange for a cook to prepare a fine meal. Demipho agrees and they leave for the market. Next, Charinus returns, again laments his situation, and wonders how Eutychus is faring. Eutychus enters and informs him that Pasicompsa has been sold, but that he does not know who bought her. Charinus then declares his intention to go into exile. Eutychus tries to dissuade his friend, but Charinus' resolve is fixed.

In the next act, Lysimachus' wife, Dorippa, accompanied by the aged servant Syra, returns from their farm in the country. Syra enters Lysimachus' house but soon returns, shrieking about the presence of a strange woman in the house. Syra suggests to Dorippa that the woman is Lysimachus' mistress. Such remarks herald the arrival of Lysimachus, who has returned from the market, but without Demipho. Lysimachus sees his wife emerge from the house, hears her complaints, and realizes he is in trouble. Dorippa confronts Lysimachus about Pasicompsa, and Lysimachus lies, telling her that he has been made an arbitrator in a legal case concerning the woman. Lysimachus' lie is undermined, however, by the arrival of a cook, the cook's helpers, and the supplies for dinner. The cook mistakes Dorippa for the woman for whom Lysimachus was holding the dinner party. Lysimachus, of course, denies this and sends the cook away. Dorippa, who has heard enough by this time, sends Syra to summon her father. Lysimachus again tries to explain, but both Syra and Dorippa exit before he has a chance. Then Lysimachus, cursing Demipho, leaves for the FORUM to find his neighbor. When Syra returns, unable to find Dorippa's father, she encounters Eutychus, who has been searching for Pasicompsa. Syra informs Eutychus of what has been going on in the house. When Eutychus hears that the young woman is inside the house, he goes in to see her.

The play's final act begins with the arrival of Charinus, who continues to threaten to go into exile. His words are heard by a joyful Eutychus, who, for a few lines, listens from the balcony as Charinus pledges his love for Pasicompsa. Eutychus responds as if he were the forerunner of Shakespeare's Juliet. Finally, Eutychus recognizes Charinus and speaks with him. Eutychus, true to his name ("good fortune"), informs

Charinus that Pasicompsa is inside the house. When Charinus hears this, he takes off his traveling cloak and sword, puts down his luggage, and prepares to enter the house. When Eutychus delays him, Charinus puts on his traveling cloak and sword, picks up his luggage again, and threatens to leave. Finally, Eutychus calms his friend and informs him of the trouble between his mother and father, and Charinus agrees to set matters right between them.

After Eutychus and Charinus enter the house, Demipho and Lysimachus enter from the forum. As Demipho promises to rescue Lysimachus from his problem with his wife, Eutychus emerges from his house and encounters the two older men. Eutychus informs Demipho that Pasicompsa was actually Charinus' love. When Lysimachus hears this, he and Eutychus together criticize Demipho for trying to steal his own son's woman friend. Demipho then begs Eutychus to patch up matters between Charinus and him. Eutychus promises to help Demipho and informs Lysimachus that he has smoothed conditions over with Dorippa. After the two older men enter the house, Eutychus proposes a law that old men who pursue young women shall be considered fools; if they waste their fortune, they shall live in need. Young men, Eutychus proposes, shall be allowed to have love affairs.

COMMENTARY
Plautus' *Merchant* has attracted little attention from modern critics, although it is one of Plautus' more amusing plays. Duckworth classified *Merchant* as a play of "guileful deception" and grouped it with ASINARIA, BACCHIDES, CASINA, THE BRAGGART WARRIOR, THE HAUNTED HOUSE, THE PERSIAN, and PSEUDOLUS. *Merchant* is most like *Asinaria, Bacchides,* and *Casina,* in that it deals with a father and son who are rivals for the same woman. Unlike *Asinaria,* in which the father knows about the son's love affair and even supports it financially, *Merchant* is more typical in that the son tries to conceal the affair from his father. By hiding the love affair, however, the young man almost loses the young woman to his father.

Unlike in many Roman comedies, in which money must be acquired to purchase the beloved prostitute, in *Merchant* the woman has been paid for by the young lover only to be purchased again by the old lover. The young lover's goal in *Merchant* is to reacquire his purchase. Thus, instead of the usual PIMP whom the lover must defeat, in *Merchant* the young man's father must be overcome. Eventually, as in *Asinaria* and *Casina,* the father is defeated once his wife becomes aware of the old man's love affair. Unlike in *Asinaria* and *Casina,* in *Merchant* it is the neighbor's wife (Dorippa) who becomes aware of her old neighbor's (Demipho's) love, not the old lover's own wife (although Dorippa initially thinks that Pasicompsa is her husband's mistress). As in *Casina,* we encounter forgiveness between the wife and husband, but in *Merchant* the forgiveness is different because it primarily involves Dorippa and Lysimachus, who are only indirectly involved with Pasicompsa. In fact, we learn that Demipho's wife will not find out about Demipho's activities (1004). Thus, the criticism of Demipho at the play's conclusion is not voiced by his own wife or even his own son; this task is primarily performed by Lysimachus' son, Eutychus, who chastises the old man for behaving as a young man. The replacement of the wife as the person who chastises the husband with the son of the neighbor is perhaps in keeping with the play's conflict of old versus young, but some of the humorous tension is lost by the removal of Demipho's wife because Eutychus has little connection with Demipho.

In addition to the conflict between the older and younger generations, much of the play's humor and unity revolves around commerce, knowledge, and reality. Initially, Charinus' father does not know that Pasicompsa has been purchased to be his son's mistress. Once Demipho begins inquiring about the woman, Acanthio gives Demipho false information about Charinus' purchase. The situation becomes more complicated as father and son both reveal their true feelings about the purchase to a friend. Demipho makes Lysimachus aware of his intention in this purchase and Charinus makes Eutychus aware of his intentions. Although father and son make outsiders aware of their feelings for Pasicompsa, they continue to conceal this knowledge from one another. Because both father and son are merchants, they create an imaginary business deal that they hope will become real (compare the situation in Demipho's dream, which will also turn out to be real). Father and

son both claim to have friends, one old and the other young, who want to buy the woman and then make imaginary bids for their friend. This bidding war never takes place in reality because Lysimachus buys Pasicompsa before Eutychus can even make a bid. Charinus' loss of his purchase causes him great distress, but his claims that he will go into exile will not be realized.

The theme of knowledge and reality continues with the arrival of Pasicompsa. She thinks the man who owns her is a handsome young man, whereas in reality he is a rather ugly old man. Lack of accurate knowledge about the woman's purpose also leads to trouble for Lysimachus. Syra does not know who the strange woman is, but she incorrectly thinks that Pasicompsa is Lysimachus' mistress and informs his wife of her suspicion; as do Charinus and Demipho, Lysimachus creates a false story about her. The reality of the situation is revealed when Lysimachus' lie is undermined, when the cook mistakes Dorippa for Pasicompsa, a mistake that parallels Pasicompsa's earlier mistaking of Demipho for Charinus. Lysimachus then seems resolved to inform his wife about the reality of the situation (789), but Dorippa, who is also determined to acquire accurate knowledge about Pasicompsa (720), exits before he can provide accurate information about the strange woman.

Charinus' proposed journey into exile is postponed temporarily when Eutychus gives Charinus information about Pasicompsa's whereabouts. When Eutychus asks Charinus to delay awhile because of the quarrel between his parents, Charinus becomes frenzied and, as does the mad HERACLES in EURIPIDES' *HERACLES,* begins an imaginary journey into exile, until Eutychus agrees to let him enter the house. Although Charinus had become like the mad Heracles, he tells Eutychus that he will restore harmony between his friend's parents as if they were Jupiter (Heracles' father) and Juno (see ZEUS and HERA). One should also note that Charinus' madness here matches his father's declaration that he is madly in love with Pasicompsa earlier in the play (262–65). Not only are father and son merchants and lovers, they also lose sanity. Also noteworthy is Eutychus' remark that Charinus' madness seems to be the stuff of dreams (951), which parallels Demipho's earlier bizarre dream.

Once Charinus gives Dorippa accurate knowledge about the situation, marital harmony between Lysimachus and Dorippa is restored. Interestingly, at line 960, Demipho indicates to Lysimachus that he intends to patch up matters between Lysimachus and Dorippa. While Demipho is on his way to relay accurate information about his affair to Dorippa, Eutychus emerges from the house and becomes a source of accurate information for the two old men. He relates that Dorippa has been placated (965)—although later Lysimachus will ask his son to confirm this statement (1012)—and that Demipho has lost his woman friend (966). When Eutychus declares truly that Demipho had tried to take away his son's girlfriend, Demipho indicates that he was unaware that she was Charinus' beloved and recites the false story Charinus had fed him earlier about her being a maid for his mother (975). By now, however, Demipho knows that his deception is finished and confesses his wrongdoing (983). Demipho also begs Eutychus to persuade Charinus to forgive him and even offers to let Eutychus and Lysimachus beat him as if he were a slave. When Eutychus declares that he will let Demipho's wife do that, Demipho is terrified. Eutychus calms the old man's fears by telling him that his wife need not know about Demipho's affair (1004). Thus, just as *Merchant* began with one young man's concealing the truth from Demipho, the play will end with another young man's concealing the truth about Demipho. Unlike the wives in *Asinaria* and *Casina*, Demipho's wife will never know the truth.

BIBLIOGRAPHY

Lowe, J. C. B. "Notes on Plautus' *Mercator*," *Weiner Studien* 114 (2001): 143–56.

O'Bryhim, S. "The Originality of Plautus' *Casina*," *American Journal of Philology* 110 (1989): 81–103.

Woytek, E. "Sprach- und Kontextbeobachtung im Dienste der Prioritdtsbestimmung bei Plautus: Zur Datierung von *Rudens, Mercator* und *Persa*," *Weiner Studien* 114 (2001): 119–42.

MERCURY   See HERMES.

MERETRIX   See PROSTITUTE.

MEROPE   The wife of King POLYBUS of CORINTH, who OEDIPUS incorrectly believed was his mother. [ANCIENT SOURCES: Seneca, *Oedipus* 272, 661, 802; Sophocles, *Oedipus Tyrannos* 775, 990]

MESSALINA (24/25–48 C.E.)   Messalina was a wife of the Roman emperor CLAUDIUS. Claudius divorced Messalina and had her put to death after he learned of her numerous sexual affairs and her marriage to Gaius Silius, performed when she was married to Claudius. [ANCIENT SOURCES: Seneca, *Octavia* 10, 258, 265, 974; Suetonius, *Claudius* 26–39; Tacitus, *Annals* 11.2–13.32]

MESSAPIUM   A mountain north of Greece. [ANCIENT SOURCES: Aeschylus, *Agamemnon* 293]

MESSENE   A town in southern Greece to the west of SPARTA. [ANCIENT SOURCES: Aristophanes, *Lysistrata* 1142]

MESSENGER   In classical drama, the messenger reports events that ordinarily cannot be portrayed on stage. In TRAGEDY, messengers often give vivid reports of miraculous occurrences (e.g., the rescue of IPHIGENIA from death in EURIPIDES' *IPHIGENIA AT AULIS*), violent actions (e.g., the blinding of OEDIPUS in SOPHOCLES' *OEDIPUS TYRANNOS*), or deaths (HERACLES' killing of his wife and children). These reports, called messenger speeches, are often quite lengthy. The report of NEOPTOLEMUS' death in Euripides' *ANDROMACHE* is 81 lines. SENECA's messenger in *HIPPOLYTUS* spends 104 lines describing HIPPOLYTUS' death. Typically, a messenger speech is delivered by an otherwise nameless person called Messenger (Greek: *angelos* or *exangelos*; Latin: *nuntius*). Characters called Messenger appear in 14 of the 19 plays attributed to EURIPIDES, five of the seven extant tragedies of SOPHOCLES, and two of the seven plays of AESCHYLUS. One should note, however, that not every messenger speech is given by someone with the title *angelos*. Sometimes household servants give speeches that function as messenger speeches, as in EURIPIDES' *ALCESTIS*, when the title character's maidservant reports the activities of her mistress before her death. In Sophocles' *TRACHINIAN WOMEN*, HERACLES' son, HYLLUS, gives a messenger speech. That play is also interesting in that a messenger speech given by LICHAS is shown to be false by a second messenger. Messenger speeches also occur in COMEDY. In ARISTOPHANES' *CLOUDS*, for example, Strepsiades' speech about how his son struck him functions as a messenger speech. In Plautus' *Amphitruo*, Bromia's speech about the labor of ALCMENA also does.

BIBLIOGRAPHY

Buxton, R. G. A. "The Messenger and the Maenads: A Speech from Euripides' *Bacchae* (1043–1152)," *Acta Antiqua Academiae Scientiarum Hungaricae* 32 (1989): 225–34.

De Jong, Irene J. F. *Narrative in Drama: The Art of the Euripidean Messenger-Speech.* Leiden: Brill, 1991.

Rijksbaron A. "How Does a Messenger Begin His Speech?: Some Observations on the Opening Lines of Euripidean Messenger Speeches." In *Miscellanea Tragica in Honorem J. C. Kamerbeek.* Edited by J. M. Bremer, S. Radt, and C. J. Ruijgh. Amsterdam: Hakkert, 1976, 293–308.

METATHEATER

A term used by modern scholars for references in plays to the theater, plays that are about plays, and "plays" that occur within a play. For instance, in PLAUTUS' *AMPHITRUO*, Mercury (Greek: HERMES), who is disguised as the slave Sosia, runs in yelling for people to make way for him. In so doing, Mercury says it is fitting for him to behave as does the slave in comedy who runs in and announces that the ship has arrived safely or the arrival of an angry old man (896–98). In Plautus' *BACCHIDES* (214–15), the slave Chrysalus makes reference to the pleasure he feels from another of Plautus' plays, *EPIDICUS*.

In addition to references to theater within the plays, metatheater involves disguise, role playing, and schemes designed to deceive others in the play. Thus, a character in a play can become a playwright, director, actor, or audience within it. EURIPIDES' *IPHIGENIA IN TAURIS* and *HELEN* provide examples. In both plays, a female character contrives a scheme to trick a barbarian king. Thus, the female becomes a playwright and the king becomes an audience. Those who assist the female become her actors. In the case of *HELEN,* the title character even changes her clothing and cuts her hair to carry out her deception. ARISTOPHANES' plays have numerous examples of such role playing. In *Acharnians,* Dicaeopolis goes to the playwright Euripides' house in order to borrow a costume for a "play" that he wants to stage for the Acharnians, who become his audience within the play. Aristophanes' *THESMOPHORIAZUSAE* contains a series of plays within the play. Euripides and Mnesilochus play several different roles from Euripides' tragedies during *Thesmophoriazusae.* Many of Plautus' and Terence's plays can be read with a metatheatrical perspective, as the clever slaves in particular become playwrights as they deceive other characters in the play.

BIBLIOGRAPHY

Barrett, James. "Pentheus and the Spectator in Euripides' Bacchae," *American Journal of Philology* 119, no. 3 (1998): 337–60.

Batchelder, A. G. *The Seal of Orestes: Self-Reference and Authority in Sophocles' Electra.* Lanham, Md.: Rowman & Littlefield, 1995.

Dobrov, G. W. *Figures of Play: Greek Drama and Metafictional Poetics.* Oxford: Oxford University Press, 2001.

Ringer, Mark. *Electra and the Empty Urn: Metatheater and Role Playing in Sophocles.* Chapel Hill: University of North Carolina Press, 1998.

Slater, N. W. *Plautus in Performance.* Princeton, N.J.: Princeton University Press, 1985.

METER

Derived from a Greek word meaning "measure," *meter* is the arrangement of words in a pattern determined by the long and/or short syllables of each word. All classical drama is written in some metrical pattern, and the classical playwrights used many different patterns. Although modern translators of classical drama sometimes compose translations that rhyme at the end of the line, as many English poems do, the verse of classical playwrights does not have the regular end-of-line rhymes. Greek and Latin verse is one of rhythm, not rhyme. The meter most commonly found in Greek dramatic dialogue is iambic trimeter, which consists, in theory, of six iambs (a short syllable followed by a long syllable) that fall into three units (*metra*) of two iambs each. In the case of EURIPIDES, tendencies observed in his iambic trimeters over his career have helped modern scholars to date some of his plays with greater accuracy. Various types of tetrameters (lines that are divided into four metrical units) are also common in drama. In choral passages, metrical patterns can be extremely complex, and not uncommonly more than a half-dozen different meters are used in a single choral passage. As their Greek predecessors do, Latin comic playwrights commonly employ iambic rhythms, such as iambic senarius (based on six iambs), iambic septenarius (based on seven iambs), and iambic octonarius (based on eight iambs). The episodes in SENECA's tragedies commonly employ the iambic senarius, whereas he relies primarily on anapests (two short syllables followed by a long syllable) for his lyric passages.

BIBLIOGRAPHY

Dale, A. M. *The Lyric Metres of Greek Drama.* 2d ed. London: Cambridge University Press, 1968.

Halporn, J. W., M. Ostwald, and T. G. Rosenmeyer. *The Meters of Greek and Latin Poetry.* Norman: University of Oklahoma Press, 1980.

Lindsay, W. M. *Early Latin Verse.* London: Oxford University Press, 1968.

Maas, Paul. *Greek Metre.* Translated by Hugh Lloyd-Jones. Oxford: Clarendon Press, 1962.

West, M. L. *Greek Metre.* Oxford: Oxford University Press, 1982.

METIS (1) Another name for PROCNE, the wife of TEREUS. [ANCIENT SOURCES: Aeschylus, *Suppliant Women* 61]

METIS (2) A daughter of OCEAN, Metis (Prudence) had sexual relations with ZEUS and became pregnant. When Zeus discovered that a son by Metis would overthrow him, he swallowed the pregnant Metis. Eventually the child, ATHENA, was born by springing from Zeus' head. In AESCHYLUS' *PROMETHEUS BOUND*, Metis is also called the mother of PROMETHEUS. [ANCIENT SOURCES: Apollodorus, *Library* 1.2.1, 1.3.6; Hesiod, *Theogony* 471, 886; Plato, *Symposium* 203]

METON An Athenian astronomer of the fifth century B.C.E. who gained fame for observations on the summer solstice and his efforts to reconcile the lunar and solar calendars. Meton appears in ARISTOPHANES' *BIRDS* to survey the land of the new city in the clouds. Meton's interest in celestial matters, coupled with the fact that Meton's name recalls the Greek word *metron* (measure or rule), makes Meton the perfect character to survey the city. As he does to the others who try to infiltrate the new city, PEISETAERUS drives away Meton. [ANCIENT SOURCES: Aristophanes, *Birds* 992–1020]

BIBLIOGRAPHY

Depuydt, Leo. "The Egyptian and Athenian Dates of Meton's Observation of the Summer Solstice (431)," *Ancient Society* 27 (1996): 27–45.

Dunn, Francis M. "The Council's Solar Calendar," *American Journal of Philology* 120, no. 3 (1999): 369–80.

Pritchett, W. K. "The Calendar of the Athenian Civic Administration," *Phoenix* 30 (1976): 337–56.

MICON The son of Phnomachos, Micon was a painter and sculptor who was active in ATHENS in the second quarter of the fifth century B.C.E. Among his most famous paintings were those of THESEUS battling the CENTAURS and the AMAZONS. [ANCIENT SOURCES: Aristophanes, *Lysistrata* 679; Pausanias, 6.6.1]

BIBLIOGRAPHY

Henderson, J. *Aristophanes: Lysistrata.* Oxford: Clarendon Press, 1987, 160.

MIDAS (1) Also spelled Mida, Midas is the name of a fictional slave from the region of PHRYGIA (after the legendary King MIDAS, who ruled in that region). [ANCIENT SOURCES: Aristophanes, *Wasps* 433; Terence, *Phormio* 862]

MIDAS (2) A mythical king who received from DIONYSUS the ability to change into gold whatever he touched. When Midas' golden touch began to cause him great hunger and sorrow, he repented of his wish and Dionysus allowed him to rid himself of the golden touch by bathing in a certain river. Midas also heard a musical contest between Pan and APOLLO; when he declared Pan the better player, APOLLO changed the king's ears into those of an ass. [ANCIENT SOURCES: Aristophanes, *Wealth* 287; Hyginus, *Fables* 191; Ovid, *Metamorphoses* 11.85–193]

MIDDLE COMEDY See COMEDY.

MIDWIFE A person who helps someone who is about to give birth. In classical drama, midwives are always women. A midwife named Lesbia appears briefly in TERENCE's *ANDRIA*. [ANCIENT SOURCES: Plautus, *Captives* 629, *Casket Comedy* 141; Terence, *Andria* 299, 459–89, 515, *Brothers* 292, 354, 618, 620]

MILETUS A town on the western coast of what is today Turkey. In 494 B.C.E., the Greek tragedian PHRYNICHUS staged a historical drama entitled *Destruction of Miletus*. The play caused the Athenians such grief that they fined the playwright 1,000 drachmas.

ARISTOPHANES notes the Milesians' production of wool blankets. [ANCIENT SOURCES: Aristophanes, *Frogs* 543, *Knights* 361, 932, *Lysistrata* 108, 729; Herodotus, 6.21; Terence, *Brothers* 654–55]

MILTIADES (CA. 550–489 B.C.E.)

The son of CIMON, Miltiades was an Athenian statesman. Around 524 B.C.E., the Athenian tyrant, HIPPIAS, made Miltiades tyrant over the Thracian Chersonese, and during his rule Miltiades married Hegisipyle, the daughter of a Thracian king. Hegisipyle produced for him a son (also named Cimon). Miltiades returned to Athens in 493 and led forces to victory against the PERSIANS at MARATHON in 490. Miltiades died of a wound received while he was leading a naval attack on the island of Paros. [ANCIENT SOURCES: Aristophanes, *Knights* 1325; Cornelius Nepos, *Miltiades*; Herodotus, 4.137–38, 6.34–41, 6.103–40; Pausanias, 1.15.3]

MIMAS (1)

The child of EARTH, Mimas was one of the GIANTS who unsuccessfully waged war against ZEUS and the other gods. [ANCIENT SOURCES: Apollodorus, *Library* 1.6.1–2; Euripides, *Ion* 215; Seneca, *Hercules Furens* 981, *Hercules Oetaeus* 730, 1384]

MIMAS (2)

A mountain opposite the island of CHIOS on the coast of what is today western Turkey. [ANCIENT SOURCES: Aristophanes, *Clouds* 273]

MIME

Derived from the Greek word *mimos*, meaning both "imitation" and "imitator," mime can refer to a performance or performer that imitates something. Some mimes performed dances that imitated certain actions; others used gestures to imitate, as do modern mimes, who often imitate walking against the wind, pulling a rope, or being inside a box. Unlike modern mimes, who do not speak, ancient mimes could. Some mimes wore masks when they performed; some did not. In Greece, troupes of mimes composed of both male and female performers performed scenes from mythology or daily life or stock comic routines. The primary mime in a performance was called the archmime (masculine: *archmimus*, feminine: *archmima*).

About 150 brief fragments (see Kaibel) exist from the mimes of Sophron of Syracuse, who ancient sources believed invented mime in the fifth century B.C.E., are extant. Some of Sophron's mimes featured women's roles (such as his *Mother-in-Law*); others featured male roles (such as his *Tunnyfish-Catcher*). Sophron's son, Xenarchus, also composed mimes, but none of his work remains. About a dozen literary mimes from the third-century-B.C.E. writer Herodas (or Herodes) are also extant, although some are in fragmentary form. The complete mimes of Herodas range between 80 and 130 lines, involve conversations of two or three characters, and have titles such as *Matchmaker, Brothel Keeper, Schoolmaster, Offerings and Sacrifices, Jealous Lady, Private Chat, The Cobbler, The Dream,* and *Breaking Fast*.

In Rome, mime (also called *fabula riciniata*) appeared as early as the third century B.C.E. and became more popular than traditional stage plays. In some mimes, female characters (played by prostitutes) appeared nude. Among the known Roman writers of mime are Decimus Laberius, Gnaeus Matius, and Publilius Syrus, all of whom lived during the first century B.C.E. Only fragments of their mimes survive, however, only a handful of lines and two titles (*Murmurco, Pruners*) survive from Syrus. About a dozen lines and no titles of Matius' mimes survive. More than 180 lines from Laberius exist; his numerous titles include *Maiden, Poverty, Lake Avernus, Prison, The Pot of Gold,* and *Anna Peranna*. [ANCIENT SOURCES: Aristotle, *Poetics* 1447b8–13; Athenaeus, 14.621c; Plato, *Republic* 396b; Plutarch, *Quaestiones Conviviales* 712e]

BIBLIOGRAPHY
Beare, W. *The Roman Stage.* London: Methuen, 1950, 149–58.
Bonaria, M. *Romani Mimi.* Rome: In aedibus Athenaei, 1965.
Cunningham, I. C. *Herodas: Mimiambi.* Oxford: Clarendon Press, 1971.
Heitsch, E. *Die griechischen Dichterfragmente der römischen Kaiserzeit.* Vol. 1, 2d ed. Göttingen, Ger.: Vandenhoeck & Ruprecht, 1963.
Kaibel, G. *Comicorum Graecorum fragmenta.* Vol. 1.1 [*Poetarum Graecorum fragmenta.* Vol. 6.1. Berlin: Weidmann, 1899.
Knox, A. D. *Herodes, Cercidas, and the Greek Choliambic Poets.* Cambridge, Mass.: Harvard University Press, 1967.
Wiemken, H. *Der griechische Mimus; Dokumente zur Geschichte des antiken Volkstheaters.* Bremen: Schunemann Universitatsverlag, 1972.

MIMESIS   A Greek word whose basic meanings are "imitation" and "representation." With respect to literary criticism, when modern scholars speak of the concept of mimesis, they usually have in mind references to *mimesis* in Books 2, 3, and 10 of Plato's *Republic* and in ARISTOTLE's *Poetics*. PLATO and ARISTOTLE often mean different things when they employ the term *mimesis*. In *Republic,* Plato's concept of mimesis is shaped by the fact that Plato is theorizing about an ideal city-state. In the ideal city-state, Plato argues, poets (he primarily has HOMER in mind) should not represent gods or heroes behaving in an unseemly manner. When poets let their tales unfold through various characters, they are engaging in mimesis, as they imitate or represent what certain characters will say or do in a certain situation. Because poets often represent gods or people who are speaking or behaving in unseemly ways, Plato suggests that those who will take a lead in governing the ideal state should not be exposed to vile representations, but rather representations that will promote excellence, nobility, virtue, and the like. Plato also criticizes representations by persons such as poets. He claims that these representations cannot be accurate because poets are neither divinities nor experts in what they are attempting to represent. Poets are not experts in the gods or religion, yet they offer representations of what the gods and virtuous behavior are like, and the poets' audiences often accept what the poets say as accurate and true.

Aristotle's concept of mimesis responds and reacts to the earlier view of Plato. Aristotle says epic poetry, TRAGEDY, COMEDY, DITHYRAMB, most music, and even painting are representations (*mimeseis*). With respect to representations in drama, Aristotle says comedy tends to represent people who are worse than those in "real" life, and tragedy tends to represent people who are better. In Plato's *Republic,* poetic mimesis could deceive people about the truth, but Aristotle says that mimesis is natural to humans and that people take pleasure in and learn from representations. Aristotle's most famous remarks on mimesis occur at *Poetics* 1449b24–29. Here, Aristotle defines tragedy as a representation (*mimesis*) of action that is serious and complete, and possesses magnitude; that employs embellished language; that shows people who are acting; and that,

through pity and fear, brings about a CATHARSIS of such emotions. Thus, whereas Plato worries that poetic representation could create a harmful emotional response in the guardians of his ideal city-state, Aristotle in *Poetics* indicates that the form of mimesis known as tragic poetry can produce a catharsis of such emotions, which, Aristotle implies, is beneficial. [ANCIENT SOURCES: Plato, *Republic* 392–400, 597–607]

BIBLIOGRAPHY
Golden, Leon. *Aristotle on Tragic and Comic Mimesis.* Atlanta: Scholars Press, 1992.

Halliwell, Stephen. "Aristotelian Mimesis Reevaluated," *Journal of the History of Philosophy* 28 (1990): 487–510.

Woodruff, Paul. "Aristotle on Mimesis." In *Essays on Aristotle's Poetics.* Edited by Rorty Amélie Oksenberg. Princeton, N.J.: Princeton University Press, 1992, 73–95.

MINA   In the Athenian monetary system, a mina (plural: minae) was a coin of substantial value. One mina was worth one-tenth of a talent (or 6,000 OBOLS or 600 DRACHMAS). In PLAUTUS' *CAPTIVES,* Tyndarus' young son is sold as a slave for six minae. In the same playwright's *EPIDICUS,* a MUSIC GIRL is purchased for 40 minae. In TERENCE's *PHORMIO,* 30 minae are needed to purchase a music girl; in *BROTHERS,* Aeschinus says the PIMP, Sannio, paid 20 minae for a music girl.

MINERVA   See ATHENA.

MINOS   The son of ZEUS (or Asterius) and EUROPA, Minos was the brother of Sarpedon and RHADAMANTHYS. Minos became a king of CRETE, married PASIPHAE, and by her fathered Acacallis, Androgeus, ARIADNE, Catreus, Deucalion, Glaucus, PHAEDRA, and Xenodice. After the death of Asterius, Minos became king by driving Sarpedon and Rhadamanthys from the land. When rivals vied for the kingdom, Minos ended their claims by demonstrating that POSEIDON favored him. Claiming that the god would answer any request he made, Minos prayed for Poseidon to send him a bull, which Minos promised to sacrifice. Poseidon sent the bull, but the animal was so perfect that Minos kept it and sacrificed another in its place. Poseidon, angered by this act, caused Minos' wife to fall in love with the bull. Pasiphae, with the help of a hollow wooden cow built by DAEDALUS, managed to have intercourse with the bull, became pregnant, and produced the creature known as the MINOTAUR ("the bull of Minos"), which Minos concealed beneath his palace in a mazelike structure called the Labyrinth. Some sources say that Poseidon caused the bull that he sent to become enraged and thus a great danger to Minos' people. HERACLES, however, later subdued the bull and took it to mainland Greece.

When Athenians killed Minos' son, Androgeus, after he had defeated them in athletic competition, Minos waged war against ATHENS and was victorious. He then imposed a terrible tribute: Every nine years for a period of 27 years, they were required to send him a tribute of seven young men and seven young women. These young people were imprisoned in Minos' Labyrinth, where the Minotaur would kill them. When the tribute fell due for the third time, the Athenian hero THESEUS volunteered to go to Crete; there, with help from Minos' daughter, Ariadne, and DAEDALUS, who had built the Labyrinth, Theseus killed the Minotaur and escaped from Crete with Ariadne and his comrades.

Minos was apparently most angry with Daedalus, so he imprisoned him. Daedalus managed to escape the prison and Crete as well. Upon discovering Daedalus' escape, Minos pursued him. Wherever Minos searched, he took a conch shell and promised to reward the person who could pass a thread through the shell, thinking that the clever Daedalus would not be able to resist this challenge and would thus reveal himself. Upon reaching SICILY and the kingdom of COCALUS, where Daedalus was hiding, Minos showed the shell to Cocalus. Cocalus gave it to Daedalus, who threaded it. When Cocalus showed the shell to Minos, he realized Daedalus was nearby and demanded of Cocalus that Daedalus be turned over to him. Cocalus agreed to do so but stalled for time by inviting Minos to a banquet. Daedalus escaped Minos, however, because Cocalus' daughters killed Minos (some sources say they poured scalding water onto him). After Minos' death, he became a judge in the UNDERWORLD.

Minos does not appear as a character in any complete plays but is a character in EURIPIDES' Cretans (see the fragments in Page), in which he speaks of imprisoning his wife, Pasiphae, and discovering her sexual relationship with the bull. Sophocles wrote a Minos (which may be identical to his Daedalus), but the single line that survives (regarding fortune's not aiding the inactive) tells nothing of the play's content (fragment 407 Radt). Two Greek comic poets, Antiphanes (fragment 158 Kock) and Alexis (see Kock 2), wrote plays entitled Minos. Only the title of Alexis' play survives and the phrase about eating the root of a plant called moloche that survives from Antiphanes' play indicates nothing of that play's plot. Minos also is a character in ARISTOPHANES' Polyidos (fragments 1–4 Meineke). In fragment 2, Minos is apparently offering Phaedra in marriage to someone. Among Roman authors, ACCIUS (see Warmington) wrote a Minos (also called Minotaur), of which a single line survives ("Was the beast begotten from the seed of a bull or a human being?"). [ANCIENT SOURCES: Apollodorus, Library 2.5.7, 3.1.1–4, 3.15.7–9, Epitome 1.12–15; Hyginus, Fables 40–44; Ovid, Metamorphoses 8.152–262; Seneca, Agamemnon 24, Hercules Furens 733, Hippolytus 127, 149, 174, 245, 649, 1171, Thyestes 23]

BIBLIOGRAPHY

Kock, T. Comicorum Atticorum Fragmenta. Vol. 2. Leipzig: Teubner, 1884.

Lloyd-Jones, H. Sophocles: Fragments. Cambridge, Mass.: Harvard University Press, 1996.

Meineke, A. Fragmenta Comicorum Graecorum. Vol. 2.2. 1840. Reprint, Berlin: De Gruyter, 1970.

Page, D. L. Select Papyri. Vol. 3. 1941. Reprint, London: Heinemann, 1970.

Radt, S. Tragicorum Graecorum Fragmenta. Vol. 3. Göttingen, Ger.: Vandenhoeck & Ruprecht, 1985.

———. Tragicorum Graecorum Fragmenta. Vol. 4. Göttingen, Ger.: Vandenhoeck & Ruprecht, 1977.

Warmington, E. H. Remains of Old Latin: Livius Andronicus, Naevius, Pacuvius, and Accius. Vol. 2. Cambridge, Mass.: Harvard University Press, 1936.

MINOTAUR   See MINOS.

MINYANS   A mythical tribe who lived in north central Greece. HERACLES, before his labors, led THEBES to victory over the Minyans. JASON is sometimes referred to as a Minyan. The Greek tragedian Chaeremon wrote a Minyans; the single fragment (12 Snell) that survives gives no hint as to the play's plot. [ANCIENT SOURCES: Hyginus, *Fables* 14; Seneca, *Medea* 233]

BIBLIOGRAPHY
Snell, B. *Tragicorum Graecorum Fragmenta.* Vol. 1. Göttingen, Ger.: Vandenhoeck & Ruprecht, 1971.

MITYLENE A town on the island of LESBOS. In 427 B.C.E., the people of Mytilene revolted against the Athenians, the revolt was put down, and initially the Athenians, persuaded by CLEON, proposed to put the entire male population of Mytilene to death. This decision was reversed, however, and only the leaders of the revolt were executed. [ANCIENT SOURCES: Aristophanes, *Knights* 834; Thucydides, 3.2–51]

MOIRAI See FATES.

MOLON An actor of large bodily proportion. [ANCIENT SOURCES: Aristophanes, *Frogs* 55; Demosthenes, 19.246]

MOLOSSIA A region in northwestern Greece that, according to legend, took its name from MOLOSSUS, the son of NEOPTOLEMUS and ANDROMACHE, who became a king in the region. The region was famous for its hunting dogs. [ANCIENT SOURCES: Aeschylus, *Prometheus Bound* 829; Euripides, *Alcestis* 594, *Andromache* 1244, 1248; Plautus, *Captives* 86; Seneca, *Hippoltyus* 32]

MOLOSSUS The son of NEOPTOLEMUS and ANDROMACHE, Molossus appears as a young boy in EURIPIDES' *ANDROMACHE,* in which Neoptolemus' wife, HERMIONE, threatens to kill him and Andromache. Eventually, Andromache and Molossus are rescued by Neoptolemus' grandfather, PELEUS. Molossus went on to become a king in a region in northwestern Greece that bore his name (MOLOSSIA). [ANCIENT SOURCES: Apollodorus, *Epitome* 6.12; Pausanias, 1.11.1–2]

MOMUS Momus was the personification of faultfinding. SOPHOCLES wrote a satyric *Momus* from which six fragments survive. The play's plot is unknown; Lloyd-Jones thinks it may have involved ZEUS' decision to destroy humankind by fathering a woman over whom men would fight. A scholiast on HOMER, *Iliad* 1.5, says that Zeus' original plan of destruction had involved flood or lightning, but Momus found fault with this idea and suggested that Zeus produce the destructive woman. EURIPIDES' *HELEN* suggests that Zeus had caused the Trojan War to thin out the Earth's population; therefore, Lloyd-Jones' idea that the child produced was HELEN may well be correct. Sophocles' contemporary, Achaeus, also wrote a *Momus,* whose only surviving fragment contains a reference to the plundering ARES (fragment 29 Snell).

BIBLIOGRAPHY
Kiso, A. *The Lost Sophocles.* New York: Vantage Press, 1984.
Lloyd-Jones, H. *Sophocles: Fragments.* Cambridge, Mass.: Harvard University Press, 1996.
Radt, S. *Tragicorum Graecorum Fragmenta.* Vol. 4. Göttingen, Ger.: Vandenhoeck & Ruprecht, 1977.
Snell, B. *Tragicorum Graecorum Fragmenta.* Vol. 1. Göttingen, Ger.: Vandenhoeck & Ruprecht, 1971.
Sutton, D. F. *The Lost Sophocles.* Lanham, Md.: University Press of America, 1984.

MONODY A song delivered by a single character. An example is CREUSA's song about her sexual assault by APOLLO in EURIPIDES' *Ion.* In ARISTOPHANES' *FROGS,* Euripides is criticized for inserting "Cretan monodies" into his plays. This label appears to concern the subject matter of some of his plays (sexually "loose" women from CRETE such as PASIPHAE and PHAEDRA) rather than the composition of monodies using the meter called Cretic. Dover doubts "whether any Euripidean TRAGEDY contained anything which on formal grounds would be called 'a Cretan monody.'"

BIBLIOGRAPHY
Dover, K. J. *Aristophanes: Frogs.* Oxford: Clarendon Press, 1993, 298–99.

MOON Both the Greeks and the Romans worshiped a goddess of the Moon. Among the Greeks, her name was Selene or Phoebe; the Romans called her Luna or Phoebe. The name Phoebe is sometimes used for APOLLO's sister, ARTEMIS, who was considered a moon goddess. HECATE is also associated with the Moon. The Moon is often imagined as driving a chariot across the night sky and is also connected with witch-craft. [ANCIENT SOURCES: Aristophanes, *Clouds* 608, 614, *Peace* 406; Seneca, *Oedipus* 44, 253, *Hippolytus* 309–10, 422, 785, 790, *Thyestes* 838]

MOPSUS   The son of the nymph Chloris and Ampyx (or Ampycus), Mopsus accompanied JASON and the Argonauts on their quest for the Golden Fleece. During the journey (in Libya), Mopsus was bitten by a snake and died. SENECA indicates that Mopsus lived in THEBES; other sources make him a member of the LAP-ITH tribe in northeastern Greece. Pindar describes Mopsus as a prophet; as a result, he is sometimes con-fused with the prophetic Mopsus, who was the son of APOLLO and MANTO. [ANCIENT SOURCES: Pindar, *Pythian Odes* 4.191; Seneca, *Medea* 655; Strabo, 9.5.22]

MORSIMUS   The son of the Greek tragedian PHILOCLES, Morsimus himself was a Greek tragedian. ARISTOPHANES suggests that he was an unsuccessful playwright; as it happens, none of his work (or that of his father) survives. [ANCIENT SOURCES: Aristophanes, *Frogs* 151, *Knights* 401, *Peace* 803]

MORYCHUS   A person known only for his love of food and drink. [ANCIENT SOURCES: Aristophanes, *Acharnians* 887, *Peace* 1008, *Wasps* 506, 1142; Plato Comicus, fragment 106 Kock]

BIBLIOGRAPHY
Kock, T. *Comicorum Atticorum Fragmenta.* Vol. 1. Leipzig: Teubner, 1880.

MOSCHUS   A lyre player and singer. [ANCIENT SOURCES: Aristophanes, *Acharnians* 13]

MOSTELLARIA   See THE HAUNTED HOUSE.

THE MOTHER-IN-LAW **(Latin:** *HECYRA***)** TERENCE (160 B.C.E.)   A Greek play by Apol-lodorus provided the original for this play (as well as PHORMIO). *The Mother-in-Law* had a receptive audience after two unsuccessful productions. The play's first per-formance occurred at the MEGALENSIAN GAMES in 165 B.C.E.; the second and third performances were both in 160 B.C.E. Prologues for the second and third perform-

ances survive. In the former prologue, the speaker notes that a competing performance by a tightrope walker distracted the audience from Terence's play. The latter prologue begins by relating the difficulties the playwright has had in holding his audience's attention. This prologue also recalls the distractions that led to the demise of the first production and adds that a similar attraction, rumor of a gladiatorial show, lured away the audience of the second performance, which took place at the funeral games of Lucius Aemilius Paulus. On this third occasion, however, the prologue's speaker says, no such distractions exist, and he urges the audience to give the deserving playwright their quiet attention.

The play's setting is ATHENS (as in most Roman come-dies), and the action occurs before three houses: those of the elderly Athenian Laches, the elderly Athenian Phidippus, and a PROSTITUTE named Bacchis. This three-house configuration also appears in *Phormio,* the other Terentian play based on an original by Apollodorus, although in *Mother-in-Law* the house of the prostitute has replaced the house of the PIMP. In the play's opening scene, a prostitute named Philotis and an old woman named Syra discuss Pamphilus, son of Laches and Myr-rina, who has married Philumena despite his promise that he would not marry as long as Bacchis was alive. As they are talking, Parmeno, a slave in Laches' house-hold, emerges and announces that he is going to the harbor to find out when Pamphilus will arrive. Par-meno encounters Syra and Philotis, who informs him that she has spent the last two years in CORINTH in the company of a vile soldier. When Philotis questions Par-meno about Pamphilus' marriage, he informs her that Pamphilus is not happy about the marriage and that his father, Laches, forced it on him. Furthermore, Parmeno tells Philotis that Pamphilus has not yet had sexual rela-tions with his new wife (compare ELECTRA's husband in EURIPIDES' *ELECTRA*) and that Pamphilus is hoping that Philumena will divorce him. Parmeno also notes that Pamphilus continued to see Bacchis, but that she natu-rally resisted him after he was married.

Because Bacchis was rejecting Pamphilus and Philu-mena was tolerating Pamphilus' behavior in a noble fashion, Pamphilus' affections gradually turned to Philumena. Just as matters were settling down between Pamphilus and Philumena, Pamphilus' father, Laches, forced him to go to the island of Imbros to settle the affairs of a relative who had recently died. Pamphilus left Philumena with his mother, Sostrata; however, during his absence, Philumena began to hate Sostrata and to refuse to see her. When Laches learned of Philumena's behavior, he complained to her father, Phidippus. Parmeno, however, does not know the result of the conversation between Laches and Phidippus, so he tells Philotis he must leave to carry out his errand. Philotis and Syra also depart.

In the play's second act, Laches complains about his wife, Sostrata's, relationship with Philumena, while Sostrata claims she has done nothing wrong. Soon Phidippus emerges from his house, where Philumena is currently staying, and he and Laches discuss the breakdown in relations between Sostrata and Philumena. Phidippus reports that Philumena refuses to stay in Laches' house as long as Pamphilus is absent. Because Phidippus has business to attend to at the FORUM, Laches accompanies him, leaving Sostrata alone to declare again her innocence in the matter.

The third act begins with the arrival of Pamphilus and Parmeno from the harbor. Pamphilus laments the situation that has developed between his mother and his wife and wonders what could have caused their quarrel. As they pass Phidippus' house, they hear a scream from inside. Parmeno suggests that the scream may be related to a fever that Philumena claimed to have. Pamphilus declares that he will find out the truth and enters Phidippus' house. Next, Sostrata enters, wonders about the commotion from Phidippus' house, and declares her intention to enter Phidippus' house to find out what is going on. Parmeno, however, tells Sostrata not to bother because they will not allow her into the house. Sostrata is discouraged but is glad to hear that her son, Pamphilus, has returned. Soon Pamphilus emerges from the house and tells them that Philumena has a mild fever. After Pamphilus sends his mother back to their house and sends Parmeno to the harbor to help the other slaves with his baggage, Pamphilus informs the audience that he has discovered that Philumena was pregnant (she was raped before they were married) and is now in labor. Philumena's mother, Myrrina, had begged Pamphilus to keep Philumena's condition a secret from Laches and everyone

else. Myrrina also noted that if a child were born, she would arrange for the baby to be exposed (left to die). Pamphilus told Myrrina that he would keep Philumena's secret but tells the audience that he does not think it would be right for him to keep Philumena as his wife.

As Pamphilus ponders what he will do, he sees Parmeno approach and worries that Parmeno will hear Philumena's cries and realize that she is in labor. Pamphilus decides that he must get Parmeno out of the way until the baby is born. Accordingly, he sends him on an errand to find one of his traveling companions. After Parmeno exits, Pamphilus sees his father, Laches, and Phidippus approach. Pamphilus eavesdrops and hears his father say that because Pamphilus has returned, Philumena can return to their house; Pamphilus, however, wonders what he can say to prevent her return. Therefore, Pamphilus tells Laches and Phidippus that because Philumena and his mother cannot reconcile their differences, his duty as a son requires that he side with his mother. Laches and Phidippus urge Pamphilus to take Philumena back, but Pamphilus dashes off into his house. After this, Laches and Phidippus quarrel about what to do next. Phidippus declares that Pamphilus must decide whether he wants Philumena or not so that Phidippus can find another husband for his daughter if necessary. After Phidippus returns to his house, Laches enters to discuss the situation with his wife.

In the play's fourth act, Myrrina emerges from Phidippus' house and expresses her worries that Phidippus will find out that Philumena has just had a baby. Soon, an angry Phidippus emerges and questions his wife about the newborn child. Phidippus even accuses Myrrina of planning to expose the baby because she was angry that Pamphilus had kept Bacchis as his mistress after he was married to Philumena. Therefore, Phidippus gives orders not to take the baby outside their house. After Phidippus returns, Myrrina laments her situation: the possibility of having to raise the child of an unknown father and the difficulty of Pamphilus keeping Philumena's secret. Myrrina does note, however, that Philumena's rapist stole a ring that she was wearing at the time of the assault.

After Myrrina returns to her house, Sostrata and Pamphilus enter from their house. Sostrata tells Pamphilus that she has decided to live with Laches at their home in the country so that she will not be an obstacle to his marriage to Philumena. Pamphilus, however, does not want his mother to do this. At this point, Laches, who has been eavesdropping, confronts Sostrata about her plan to move to the country. As Pamphilus and his family discuss what they should do, Phidippus enters. When Laches tells Phidippus of Sostrata's plans to move to the country, Phidippus states that Sostrata, not his wife, Myrrina, was to blame for the current trouble. Phidippus also declares that Pamphilus must take Philumena's child. Laches then urges Pamphilus to take Philumena back and to raise the child. When Pamphilus blurts that he does not want to raise a baby whose father has disowned the child, Laches takes this remark as an excuse to reject Philumena because she has had an affair and as an opportunity to resume his relationship with Bacchis. Pamphilus vigorously denies this and rushes out after his father urges him to take Philumena's child. After Pamphilus' exit, Laches says that Phidippus can give him the child. Phidippus also suggests that they question Bacchis about the situation. Laches states that he will question Bacchis and sends Phidippus off to find a nurse for the baby.

The play's final act opens with an encounter between Bacchis and Laches. Bacchis denies that she has had anything to do with Pamphilus since he married. When Laches requests that Bacchis inform their women of this, Bacchis agrees, as she does not want Pamphilus to be suspected falsely. Before Bacchis can exit, Phidippus enters with a nurse, whom he sends into his house. Phidippus is doubtful that Bacchis will tell the truth and exits into his; Bacchis soon follows Phidippus. After their departure, Parmeno arrives after his unsuccessful attempt to find Pamphilus' traveling companion. He is soon met by Bacchis, who orders him to go find Pamphilus and tell him to go to Philumena. Bacchis also tells Parmeno to inform Pamphilus that Myrrina recognized a ring that Pamphilus once gave to Bacchis. After Parmeno exits, Bacchis informs the audience that nine months earlier an intoxicated Pamphilus had entered her house with the ring and admitted that he had raped a woman. The ring was in Bacchis' possession, Myrrina questioned her about it, and Bacchis told Myrrina about what Pamphilus had

done. Next, Pamphilus enters with Parmeno. Pamphilus is delighted because he has realized that Philumena is the woman he assaulted and that he is the father of her child. Pamphilus sees Bacchis, who indicates that she has not informed Laches and Phidippus about Pamphilus' actions. Pamphilus is relieved to hear this because he wants to keep them secret if possible. Myrrina, of course, knows the secret, but she will not tell Phidippus. It is assumed that Pamphilus will take Philumena back and raise the child. The play ends with Pamphilus' thanking a puzzled Parmeno for doing him a great favor.

COMMENTARY

Unlike *Mother-in-Law,* Terence's other five plays have a double plot in which two men pursue their beloved. In many other ways, *Mother-in-Law* differs not only from Terence's usual style, but also from that of other Roman comedies. In fact, contradicting the audience's expectations may well have been one of Terence's aims in this play.

In the case of the slave, Parmeno, the audience of a Roman COMEDY would expect the slave to be the architect of deception. In Terence's *Eunuch,* it is Parmeno who has the scheme of having Chaerea impersonate the eunuch. In *Mother-in-Law,* Parmeno plays no such role; he is relegated to helping explain the plot and running errands. Moreover, in the third act, Pamphilus sends Parmeno on a false errand that will keep him busy for more than 350 lines. Contrast Terence's BROTHERS, in which the slave, Syrus, sends Demea on a similiar errand. At the end of the play, when Syrus returns, Pamphilus' affairs have been resolved, the slave has had no part in that resolution, and that is one reason why Pamphilus succeeds. Although the slave has had no part in the young man's success, Pamphilus is overjoyed with Parmeno, as young men typically are when their slave helps them succeed. Such slaves are usually rewarded in some way. In *Mother-in-Law,* Pamphilus himself raises the subject of a reward without prompting from Parmeno. Unlike the typical slave in comedy, who would immediately take up his master on such an offer, Parmeno says he does not want anything (851). Moreover, the reward is not mentioned again and at the end of the play Parmeno has received nothing.

In addition to the audience's expectations with respect to Parmeno, expectations with respect to the relationship between the young man and the prostitute are thwarted. In the opening act, Syra complains about the difficulty of finding a lover who will remain faithful to his prostitute mistress. Typically, in Roman comedy, the lover remains hopelessly devoted to the prostitute even if she is involved with another lover. Furthermore, the prostitute's affections are more likely to go to the highest bidder or the person who offers money or presents. Additionally, in Roman comedy, a married man might cheat or attempt to cheat on his wife with a prostitute (cf. Menaechmus in TWO MENAECHMI), but the audience would not expect him to leave a willing mistress for his wife. Thus, Mother-in-Law contradicts the stereotypes. Pamphilus rejects the prostitute for his wife, with whom he is in love.

Mother-in-Law is unique because, unlike other Roman comedies, it focuses on the conflict between two wives. Additionally, whereas many Roman comedies end with the marriage of a young man, Mother-In-Law is about events that have occurred after a young man has already married. Whereas many Roman comedies present the struggle of a son torn between dutifulness (pietas) to his father and love of a prospective bride, Mother-in-Law depicts Pamphilus as enmeshed in a quarrel between his mother and his wife inclined to dutifulness (pietas, 481) to his mother, despite his father's advice that he rethink his attitude. Because of that dutifulness (pietati, 584), his mother decides to move to the country so that Pamphilus' wife will return. Usually, the wives (see MATRONA) of elderly gentlemen in Roman comedy are nags; Sostrata defies expectations. At the beginning of the second act, Laches complains that all mothers-in-law are alike and hate their daughters-in-law (201). Later, Laches says all mothers want their sons to marry, but after they have pushed them into marriage, they drive them out again. Earlier in the play, however, the audience has been told that Laches himself was the one who pushed Pamphilus into marry Philumena (116–24). Thus, Terence raises the expectation of a nagging wife only to undercut that expectation. Sostrata is willing to move out of her own house to keep Philumena happy. Such selflessness is rare in comedy, in either men or women.

In addition to overturning stereotypical expectations about the matrona, Terence has some surprises about the father (see SENEX) for his audience. Commonly, the father in Roman comedy finds out about his son's mischief. Sometimes, the son himself confesses his wayward behavior. As with other Roman comedies, in Mother-in-Law we find a contrast between knowing and not knowing, but as with other stereotypes in this play, Terence frustrates the audience's expectatations. In Mother-in-Law, the father is kept in the dark about Pamphilus' actions. At the end of the play, Bacchis tells Pamphilus that she has not revealed anything and Pamphilus wants to continue that way. In a metatheatrical moment, Pamphilus says he does not want what happens in comedies, in which everyone finds out everything, to happen in his situation. Pamphilus has no intention of revealing his actions to everyone (865–68).

This lack of knowledge extends to other characters as well. Sostrata swears she has no idea what she has done to make Philumena unhappy (579–81). The slave, Parmeno, the only person who knows Pamphilus has not consummated his marriage to Philumena, is sent off so that he will not reveal this knowledge. When he returns, Pamphilus thanks him for all his help, but the slave has no knowledge of how he has helped his master. This also contradicts the common practice; slaves are often the most aware characters in Roman comedy. They have to know everything because they are orchestrating plots against fathers or pimps. Parmeno, with the father, does not find out about Pamphilus' actions. At the play's conclusion, he exits with no idea how he has helped Pamphilus.

Pamphilus is unaware that he has impregnated Philumena. In Terence's Eunuch, Chaerea is fully aware that he has raped Pamphila and he intends to marry her. In Brothers, Aeschinus knows full well that he seduced Pamphila and wants to marry her. In Mother-in-Law, Terence changes the situation. Pamphilus does not know that he has raped Philumena. When she goes into labor, he is already married to her, but he does not intend to take her back. Both mothers and both fathers plead with Pamphilus to take Philumena back; none of these four is successful. Usually in Roman comedy, a young man agrees to marry his beloved instantly. He has been waiting for this the entire play. Pamphilus refuses to take back the woman he loves until a prostitute and fortune intervene. On two earlier occasions, Terence's *Mother-in-Law* had been interrupted by unexpected occurences. Finally, on his third attempt to stage the play, Terence found an audience. It could not have been what they expected.

BIBLIOGRAPHY
Gilula, D. "Terence's *Hecyra:* A Delicate Balance of Suspense and Dramatic Irony," *Scripta Classica Israelica* 5 (1979–80): 137–57.
Goldberg, S. M. "The Price of Simplicity." In *Understanding Terence.* Princeton, N.J.: Princeton University Press, 1986, 149–69.
Ireland, S. *Terence: Hecyra.* Warminster, U.K.: Aris & Phillips, 1990.
Konstan, D. "*Hecyra:* Ironic Comedy." In *Roman Comedy.* Ithaca, N.Y.: Cornell University Press, 1983, 130–41.
Slater, N. W. "The Fictions of Patriarchy in Terence's *Hecyra,*" *Classical World* 81 (1988): 249–60.

MOTHON   A wild, sexually suggestive dance. [ANCIENT SOURCES: Aristophanes, *Knights* 635, *Wealth* 279; Pollux, *Onomasticon* 4.101]

MULCIBER   See HEPHAESTUS.

MUNICHUS   A hero whose name was connected with Munichion, a port at ATHENS. [ANCIENT SOURCES: Euripides, *Hippolytus* 760–61]

MUNYCHION   According to the Athenian calendar, Munychion was the 10th month of the year. Munychion had 29 days and corresponds roughly to April in the modern calendar. [ANCIENT SOURCES: Aristophanes, *Birds* 1046–47]

MUSES   The daughters of ZEUS and Mnesmosyne, the Muses were nine women who each inspired a different type of writing. To SOPHOCLES is attributed a *Muses,* of which two uninformative fragments (407a–408 Radt) totaling seven words survive; however, this play may be identical to his *Thamyras.* Among the Greek comic poets, PHRYNICHUS (fragments 31–35 Kock 1) and Euphro (fragment 8 Kock 3) each wrote a play entitled *Muses.* The fragment from Euphro

describes a certain Phoenicides salivating over a seafood casserole. Fragment 31 from Phrynichus' play praises Sophocles; fragment 32 refers to a counting of votes.

BIBLIOGRAPHY
Kock, T. *Comicorum Atticorum Fragmenta.* Vol. 1. Leipzig: Teubner, 1880.
———. *Comicorum Atticorum Fragmenta.* Vol. 3. Leipzig: Teubner, 1888.
Radt, S. *Tragicorum Graecorum Fragmenta.* Vol. 4. Göttingen, Ger.: Vandenhoeck & Ruprecht, 1977.

MUSIC GIRL   A minor character in New Comedy, the music girl (Latin: *fidicina* or *tibicena*) is occasionally beloved by a male character. Because the music girl is not a freeborn person, a citizen could not enter a legal marriage with her unless she were freed or shown to be freeborn. Thus, music girls are much like the prostitutes who appear in these comedies. In PLAUTUS' EPIDICUS, plans are made to purchase the music girl, Acropolistis, from a PIMP, just as in other comedies prostitutes are purchased. In TERENCE'S BROTHERS, Ctesipho's beloved is a music girl owned by the pimp Dorio.

MYCALE   A Thessalian witch who was supposed to be able to charm the moon down from the sky. [ANCIENT SOURCES: Seneca, *Hercules Oetaeus* 525]

MYCENAE   Located close to the towns of ARGOS and TIRYNS near the southeast coast of Greece, Mycenae is famous in mythology as the home of AGAMEMNON; sometimes poets use the names Argos, Tiryns, and Mycenae interchangeably.

MYCONOS   One of the most beautiful islands in the southwestern AEGEAN SEA, Myconos is one of the Cycladic islands, a few miles east of DELOS. [ANCIENT SOURCES: Aeschylus, *Persians* 885; Euripides, *Trojan Women* 89]

MYRMEX   An otherwise unknown person on whom ARISTOPHANES wishes death at FROGS 1506. The Greek word *murmex* means "ant."

MYRMIDONS   A tribe of northeastern Greece, the Myrmidons are best known as the soldiers of

ACHILLES in the Trojan War. AESCHYLUS wrote a *Myrmidons* (fragments 131–42 Radt), which was part of a trilogy that included *Nereids* and *Phrygians* (also known as *Hector's Cleansing*). Aeschylus' *Myrmidons* would have been set at TROY and appears to have dealt with the death of PATROCLUS at the hands of HECTOR. As the play's title implies, Achilles' Myrmidons would have made up the play's chorus. Among the Greek comic poets, Strattis also wrote a *Myrmidons;* only a single two-line fragment (fragment 36 Kock vol. 1), which mentions bathing rooms and armies of iron, survives. Only the title survives from Philemon's *Myrmidons* (fragment 45 Kock vol. 2).

BIBLIOGRAPHY

Kock, T. *Comicorum Atticorum Fragmenta.* Vol. 1. Leipzig: Teubner, 1880.
———. *Comicorum Atticorum Fragmenta.* Vol. 2. Leipzig: Teubner, 1884.
Radt, S. *Tragicorum Graecorum Fragmenta.* Vol. 3. Göttingen, Ger.: Vandenhoeck & Ruprecht, 1985.

MYRONIDES   The son of Archinus, Myronides was an Athenian statesman and military commander between 458 and 456 B.C.E. He led the Athenians to victory over the Corinthians in the year 457. Myronides was known for being a tough soldier, but an honest and generous politician. Myronides' ghost may appear in EUPOLIS' *Demes* (fragments 90–134 Kock). [ANCIENT SOURCES: Aristophanes, *Ecclesiazusae* 304a, *Lysistrata* 801; Plutarch, *Aristides* 10.8, 20.1, *Pericles* 16.2, 24.6; Thucydides, 1.105.4]

BIBLIOGRAPHY

Henderson, J. *Aristophanes: Lysistrata.* Oxford: Clarendon Press, 1987, 171.
Kock, T. *Comicorum Atticorum Fragmenta.* Vol. 1. Leipzig: Teubner, 1880.

MYRRHA   The daughter of Cinyras, Myrrha conceived a passion for her father and managed to sleep with him (she entered his bed at night and pretended to be someone else). Myrrha became pregnant, and when Cinyras discovered what she had done, he tried to kill her. She fled from him, and before he caught up with her the gods changed her into a myrrh tree. Not only did the tree exude Myrrha's tears (drops of myrrh), but eventually it split open and an infant (ADONIS) emerged. [ANCIENT SOURCES: Hyginus, *Fables* 58; Ovid, *Metamorphoses* 10.311–518; Seneca, *Hercules Oetaeus* 196]

MYRSINE   See BYRSINE.

MYRTILUS   The son of HERMES, Myrtilus was the servant of OENOMAUS. Myrtilus was in love with Oenomaus' daughter, HIPPODAMEIA, but Oenomaus would allow her to marry only the man who defeated him (Oenomaus) in a chariot race. If Oenomaus won, then he would kill the suitor. When PELOPS became a suitor for Hippodameia, he realized that Myrtilus was in love with her and offered him a deal—he would allow Myrtilus to have sexual intercourse with Hippodameia if Myrtilus would help him defeat Oenomaus. Myrtilus agreed and sabotaged OENOMAUS' chariot. During the race with Pelops, Oenomaus' chariot fell apart and he was killed in the crash. After Myrtilus tried to collect his "reward" by force from Hippodameia, Pelops killed him. [ANCIENT SOURCES: Apollodorus, *Epitome* 2.6–8; Euripides, *Orestes* 991b, 1548; Hyginus, *Fables* 58, 84; Seneca, *Thyestes* 140, 660; Sophocles, *Electra* 509]

MYSIANS   A tribe who lived near the northwestern coast of Asia Minor (modern Turkey). The territory of the Mysians was home to TELEPHUS and the location where water NYMPHS abducted Hylas. AESCHYLUS wrote a *Mysians* (Greek: *Mysoi*), which may have treated Telephus' search for his true parents, a search that led him to Mysia (fragments 143–45 Radt vol. 3). SOPHOCLES also wrote a *Mysians,* which was about some aspect of the Telephus myth. The tragedians Agathon (fragment 3a Snell) and Nicomachus of Alexandria (fragment 6 Snell) also wrote plays entitled *Mysians,* of which only the titles survive. Among the comic poets, Eubulus wrote a *Mysians,* in whose lone fragment someone addresses Heracles, who has left THEBES (fragment 66 Kock).

BIBLIOGRAPHY

Kock, T. *Comicorum Atticorum Fragmenta.* Vol. 2. Leipzig: Teubner, 1884.
Lloyd-Jones, H. *Sophocles: Fragments.* Cambridge, Mass.: Harvard University Press, 1996.

Radt, S. *Tragicorum Graecorum Fragmenta.* Vol. 3. Göttingen, Ger.: Vandenhoeck & Ruprecht, 1985.
———. *Tragicorum Graecorum Fragmenta.* Vol. 4. Göttingen, Ger.: Vandenhoeck & Ruprecht, 1977.
Snell, B. *Tragicorum Graecorum Fragmenta.* Vol. 1. Göttingen, Ger.: Vandenhoeck & Ruprecht, 1971.
Sutton, D. F. *The Lost Sophocles.* Lanham, Md.: University Press of America, 1984.

MYSTERIES In the ancient world, mysteries consisted of knowledge, practices, and skills that were possessed by worshipers of a particular divinity or group of divinities. Persons who wanted to participate in these ceremonies had to be "initiated" into the mysteries and were not to reveal the knowledge, practices, or skills that they acquired to the uninitiated. People who were initiated into a divinity's mysteries expected special privileges, especially after they died. The most famous mysteries in the classical world, which honored DEMETER and PERSEPHONE, were called the Eleusinian Mysteries, because they took place at the town of ELEUSIS (see also CABEIRI). [ANCIENT SOURCES: Aristophanes, *Frogs* 420]

NAEVIUS A Roman poet who lived during the last three quarters of the third century B.C.E., Gnaeus Naevius composed an epic poem (*Bellum Poenicum*) about the First Punic War (264–241 B.C.E.), in which he himself served. Naevius had a falling out with the powerful Metelli family (because of a remark made onstage about their unworthiness for office), may have been jailed in the year 204, and died at Utica (perhaps in exile) in 201.

Naevius also wrote tragedies, comedies, and FABU-LAE PRAETEXTAE. The titles of 28 of Naevius' comedies are known, but only 100 or so verses survive. Two of Naevius' titles (*The Circumcised* and *A Play about Testicles*) suggest that Naevius' comedies were much bawdier than those of PLAUTUS. Names in the titles of two Naevian comedies, *Lampadio* and *Stalagmus,* appear as the names of slaves in Plautus' CASKET COM-EDY and CAPTIVES, respectively. From Naevius' tragedies, seven titles and about 60 verses have survived. More than half the verses are from *Lycurgus* (LYCURGUS was the Thracian king who had a deadly encounter with DIONYSUS). Of the *fabulae praetextae,* two titles and three verses are extant. *Romulus,* alternately titled *Wolf,* would have dealt with the birth of the title character; *Clastidium* is known to have treated the return of the Roman general Marcellus after his triumph over the Gaul Viridomarus in 222 B.C.E. [ANCIENT SOURCES: Aulus Gellius, 1.24, 7.8.6, 17.21.45; Cicero, *Against Verres* 1.29, *Brutus* 60]

BIBLIOGRAPHY
Goldberg, S. M. "Saturnian Epic: Livius and Naevius." In *Roman Epic.* Edited by A. J. Boyle. London and New York: Routledge, 1993, 19–36.
Marmorale, E. *Naevius Poeta.* Firenze: La Nuova Italia, 1953.
Warmington, E. H. *Remains of Old Latin: Livius Andronicus, Naevius, Pacuvius, and Accius.* Vol. 2. Cambridge, Mass.: Harvard University Press, 1936.

NAIAD A naiad (plural: naiads) is a minor female divinity who inhabits a body of water. A *Naiads* is attributed to SOPHOCLES, of which only the title survives (fragment 424 Radt). [ANCIENT SOURCES: Seneca, *Hippolytus* 780]

BIBLIOGRAPHY
Radt, S. *Tragicorum Graecorum Fragmenta.* Vol. 4. Göttingen, Ger.: Vandenhoeck & Ruprecht, 1977.

NAIS See LAIS.

NAUPACTUS An important harbor, southwest of DELPHI, on the northern shore of the Gulf Corinth. [ANCIENT SOURCES: Plautus, *Braggart Warrior* 102, 116]

NAUPLIA A port located on the southeastern coast of Greece, Nauplia served such towns as ARGOS, MYCENAE, and TIRYNS. Tradition regarded POSEIDON's son, NAUPLIUS, as the founder of this port. [ANCIENT SOURCES: Euripides, *Electra* 1278, *Helen* 1586, *Iphigenia in Tauris* 804, *Orestes* 242, 369, 472]

NAUPLIUS The son of POSEIDON and AMYMONE, Nauplius was the father of PALAMEDES and Oeax by Clymene, Hesione, or Philyra. After Palamedes was killed by his fellow Greeks at TROY, Nauplius demanded satisfaction. When the Greeks refused, he sailed to Greece and encouraged Greek wives to be unfaithful to their husbands. Furthermore, Nauplius lighted a false beacon that caused several of the Greeks' ships to run aground on the rocks near the southern end of Euboea at Cape Caphereus.

Four Greek tragedians wrote a *Nauplius,* of which only the titles survive from the plays of PHILOCLES, Astydamas, and Lycophron. To SOPHOCLES are attributed two plays about Nauplius, *Nauplius Pyrkaeus* (Nauplius lights a fire) and *Nauplius Katapleon* (Nauplius sails in), although some scholars believe that only one play existed. In either case, the fragments for the two plays are not grouped separately (fragments 425–38 Radt). The title of the first play suggests that it was about Nauplius' lighting the false beacon. The subject matter of the second play is less certain; some think it treated the voyage of Nauplius to Troy; others think that it may have dealt with Nauplius' traveling to various parts of Greece to encourage the Greek women to be unfaithful. The fragments from the plays give little help in establishing the subject of either play because, with one exception (fragment 432), they consist of no more than a dozen words. In fragment 432, Nauplius describes the various innovative contributions that Palamedes made to the Greek army. [ANCIENT SOURCES: Apollodorus, *Library* 2.1.5, 2.7.4, 3.2.2, *Epitome* 6.7–8; Pausanias, 2.38.2, 4.35.2, 8.47.7; Seneca, *Agamemnon* 567, *Medea* 659; Strabo, 8.6.2]

BIBLIOGRAPHY
Kiso, A. *The Lost Sophocles.* New York: Vantage Press, 1984.
Lloyd-Jones, H. *Sophocles: Fragments.* Cambridge, Mass.: Harvard University Press, 1996.
Radt, S. *Tragicorum Graecorum Fragmenta.* Vol. 4. Göttingen, Ger.: Vandenhoeck & Ruprecht, 1977.
Sutton, D. F. *The Lost Sophocles.* Lanham, Md.: University Press of America, 1984.

NAUSICAA The daughter of Alcinous and Arete, Nausicaa was a princess of Phaeacia. When ODYSSEUS was shipwrecked on Phaeacia, Nausicaa and her maidservants stumbled on him while they were at the shore washing clothes and playing a game with a ball. Nausicaa helped Odysseus make his way to the palace of her parents, who eventually arranged for him to be taken back to his native land. SOPHOCLES wrote a *Nausikaa* (also titled *The Women Washing Clothes*), which may have been a SATYR PLAY. The few fragments that survive, however, indicate nothing about the play's plot (439–41 Radt). The Greek comic poet Eubulus also wrote a *Nausicaa,* whose single fragment (68 Kock) refers to a person, presumably Odysseus, who has been washing himself for four days and has had nothing to eat. [ANCIENT SOURCES: Homer, *Odyssey* 6]

BIBLIOGRAPHY
Kiso, A. *The Lost Sophocles.* New York: Vantage Press, 1984.
Kock, T. *Comicorum Atticorum Fragmenta.* Vol. 2. Leipzig: Teubner, 1884.
Lloyd-Jones, H. *Sophocles: Fragments.* Cambridge, Mass.: Harvard University Press, 1996.
Radt, S. *Tragicorum Graecorum Fragmenta.* Vol. 4. Göttingen, Ger.: Vandenhoeck & Ruprecht, 1977.
Sutton, D. F. *The Lost Sophocles.* Lanham, Md.: University Press of America, 1984.

NAUSICYDES A wealthy Greek grain manufacturer from Cholargus (just north of ATHENS). [ANCIENT SOURCES: Aristophanes, *Ecclesiazusae* 426; Plato, *Gorgias* 487c; Xenophon, *Memorabilia* 2.7.6]

NAXOS A small island (about 215 square miles in size) in the southern AEGEAN, east of Paros and south of MYCONOS. The island was famous for its wine and almonds. THESEUS is said to have left (or lost) ARIADNE on Naxos. She was later rescued (or perhaps taken away) by DIONYSUS, who was devoutly worshiped by the people of Naxos. During the last three-quarters of the fifth century B.C.E., Naxos was part of the Athenian empire. [ANCIENT SOURCES: Aeschylus, *Persians* 884; Aristophanes, *Peace* 143, *Wasps* 355; Eupolis, fragment 253.1–2 Kock; Phrynichus Comicus, fragment 68.3 Kock; Thucydides, 1.98]

BIBLIOGRAPHY
Kock, T. *Comicorum Atticorum Fragmenta.* Vol. 1. Leipzig: Teubner, 1880.

NEANISKOI   See LYCURGUS (2).

NEISTAN GATE   One of the seven gates at the town of THEBES. The gate was defended by MEGAREUS of Thebes and attacked by ETEOCLUS in the battle of the Seven against Thebes. [ANCIENT SOURCES: Aeschylus, *Seven against Thebes* 460; Pausanias, 9.8.4, 9.25.1, 9.25.8]

NELEUS   A king of PYLOS and the father of NESTOR. [ANCIENT SOURCES: Euripides, *Helen* 849; Menander, *Arbitration* 326]

NEMEA   A town in southeastern Greece that is a few miles northwest of ARGOS, MYCENAE, and TIRYNS. Nemea was the site of HERACLES' first labor, against the Nemean lion, whose image was placed in the heavens as the constellation Leo after Heracles killed the creature. AESCHYLUS wrote a *Nemea,* which may have dealt with the institution of the Nemean Games by the Seven against Thebes after the death of Opheltes, son of Eurydice and Lycurgus. The Greek comic poet Theopompus wrote a *Nemea;* nothing of its plot can be derived from the surviving 11-line fragment, in which a man named Spinther (the son of HEPHAESTUS?) tries to force an old woman named Theolyte to kiss him. [ANCIENT SOURCES: Apollodorus, *Library* 3.6.4; Pausanias, 2.15.2–3; Seneca, *Hercules Furens* 224, *Hercules Oetaeus* 1193, 1235, 1665, 1885, *Oedipus* 40]

BIBLIOGRAPHY
Kock, T. *Comicorum Atticorum Fragmenta.* Vol. 1. Leipzig: Teubner, 1880.
Mette, H. J. *Die Fragmente der Tragvdien des Aischylos.* Berlin: Akademie-Verlag, 1959.

NEMESIS   The daughter of Night, Nemesis personifies both unmerited good fortune and retribution for evil actions. According to one tradition, ZEUS impregnated Nemesis, who produced HELEN. This story appears to have been the subject of CRATINUS' *Nemesis* (fragments 107–20 Kock). MENANDER also wrote a *Nemesis,* of which only the title survives (291 Körte). [ANCIENT SOURCES: Apollodorus, 3.10.7; Euripides, *Phoenician Women* 182; Hesiod, *Theogony* 223–24;

Hyginus, *Poetica Astronomica* 2.8; Pausanias, 1.33.2–8, 7.4.2–3; Sophocles, *Electra* 792]

BIBLIOGRAPHY
Kock, T. *Comicorum Atticorum Fragmenta.* Vol. 1. Leipzig: Teubner, 1880.
Körte, A., and A. Thierfelder. *Menandri Quae Supersunt.* Vol. 2, 2d ed. Leipzig: Teubner, 1959.

NEOCLEIDES   A frequent speaker in the assembly at ATHENS, Neocleides is accused by ARISTOPHANES of embezzlement and obstruction of public procedure. Aristophanes also says he had poor vision or even was blind. The ancient commentary on Aristophanes reports that Neocleides was an INFORMANT of foreign ancestry. [ANCIENT SOURCES: Aristophanes, *Ecclesiazusae* 254, 398, *Wealth* 665; scholiast on *Wealth,* 665]

BIBLIOGRAPHY
Sommerstein, A. H. *The Comedies of Aristophanes.* Vol. 11, *Wealth.* Warminster, U.K.: Aris & Phillips, 2001, 181.

NEOPTOLEMUS   The son of ACHILLES and LYCOMEDES' daughter, Deidamia. In the 10th year of the Trojan War, it was prophesied that the Greeks could not capture TROY without the help of Neoptolemus. At some point, Neoptolemus married HERMIONE, the daughter of MENELAUS and HELEN. After the war, Neoptolemus was awarded HECTOR's wife, ANDROMACHE, as a captive. By Andromache, Neoptolemus fathered Molossus. Neoptolemus was killed while consulting the DELPHIC ORACLE regarding the death of Achilles.

The death of Neoptolemus is related in great detail in EURIPIDES' *ANDROMACHE,* although he does not appear as a character in that play. In SOPHOCLES' *PHILOCTETES,* Neoptolemus is characterized as a thoughtful young man who must make a choice between duty to the Greek army and deception of an unfortunate man, Philoctetes. In this play, Neoptolemus characterizes himself as someone prepared to use force, *bia,* but not deception, *dolos* (90–91). He states that he prefers to fail and act nobly, rather than succeed and act in an evil manner (94–95). Eventually, Neoptolemus takes Philoctetes' bow from him by trickery, but then he changes his mind, returns the bow to Philoctetes, and promises to take him back to his native land.

BIBLIOGRAPHY

Belfiore, E. "*Xenia* in Sophocles' *Philoctetes*," *Classical Journal* 89 (1993–94): 113–29.

Blundell, M. W. "The *Phusis* of Neoptolemus in Sophocles' *Philoctetes*," *Greece and Rome* 35 (1988): 137–48.

Hamilton, R. "Neoptolemus' Story in the *Philoctetes*," *American Journal of Philology* 96 (1975): 131–37.

Roisman, H. M. "The Appropriation of a Son: Sophocles' *Philoctetes*," *Greek, Roman, and Byzantine Studies* 38, no. 2 (1997): 127–71.

Rose P. W. "Sophocles' *Philoctetes* and the Teachings of the Sophists," *Harvard Studies in Classical Philology* 80 (1976): 49–105.

NEPHELE   When Ixion was in love with Hera, Zeus took a cloud (Nephele) and shaped it to resemble Hera. Ixion had intercourse with this "cloud-woman." The cloud became impregnated, and produced a centaur, whom some sources name Nessus. [Ancient sources: Apollodorus, *Epitome* 1.20; Diodorus Siculus, 4.69.3–5; Pindar, *Pythian Odes* 2.21–48; Seneca, *Hercules Oetaeus* 492]

NEPTUNE   See Poseidon.

NEREIDS   The 50 daughters of Nereus and Doris were minor sea divinities called Nereids. The most famous Nereid was Thetis, the mother of Achilles. Aeschylus wrote a *Nereids* that may have dealt with the death of Patroclus, the reconciliation of Agamemnon and Achilles, and Achilles' subsequent killing of Hector. Nereids probably would have made up the chorus.

NEREUS   The son of Pontus (Sea) and Earth, Nereus was a sea divinity. He was sometimes called the Old Man because he was gentle, trustworthy, and righteous. He had two brothers (Phorcus and Thaumas) and two sisters (Ceto and Eurybia). Nereus married Doris and had numerous children, known as the Nereids. Nereus himself does not play a prominent role in many myths. As were many aquatic divinities, Nereus was able to change his form. This power, however, did not prevent Heracles from wrestling Nereus into submission and forcing him to reveal the location of the Hesperides' garden. Nereus does not appear as a character in any extant dramas, but two Greek comic poets, Anaxilas and Anaxandrides, wrote plays entitled *Nereus*. [Ancient sources: Apollodorus, *Library* 1.2.6–7, 2.5.11; Hesiod, *Theogony* 233–39]

NERIENE   A Roman goddess who is called the wife of Mars (see Ares). [Ancient sources: Plautus, *Truculentus* 515]

NERO (DECEMBER 15, 37–JUNE 68 C.E.)   The son of Gnaeus Domitius Ahenobarbus and Agrippina, Nero was emperor of Rome from the year 54 until his death. He followed Claudius as emperor. Nero's rule was greeted with optimism at first, and for some time the young man showed promise. As time passed, however, Nero's cruelty became manifest. In 59, Nero killed his mother, Agrippina, and married his stepsister, Octavia. Nero later divorced Octavia, had her murdered, and then married Poppaea, the daughter of the future emperor Otho. The events surrounding Nero's divorce of Octavia are dramatized in *Octavia,* a play incorrectly attributed to Seneca, although Seneca did write his tragedies during Nero's reign and did serve as Nero's tutor and political adviser for some time (he retired in 62 after about a dozen years of service). In 65, Seneca himself was forced to commit suicide by Nero after he was implicated in a plot to assassinate him. In *Octavia*, both Seneca and Nero appear as characters, Seneca in the role of Nero's adviser. In the play, Nero is shown as a savage ruler and a thoroughly arrogant man, who brutally eliminates both citizens and family who oppose him.

By the year 64, unpopular economic policies that Nero had crafted for his own benefit, as well as a fire in 64 that destroyed much of Rome (and that rumor said Nero himself started), led to a widespread hatred of the emperor. Nero, who loved its culture and art, toured Greece in 67 but was recalled to Rome because of a severe famine there. By the time Nero returned to Rome in 68, several prominent Roman governors were in open revolt against him, and when Nero's elite guard, the Praetorians, abandoned him, Nero committed suicide. [Ancient sources: Dio Cassius, 61–63; Seneca, *Octavia;* Suetonius, *Nero;* Tacitus, *Annals* 13–16]

BIBLIOGRAPHY

Champlin, E. *Nero.* Cambridge, Mass.: Belknap Press of Harvard University Press, 2003.

Elsner, J., and J. Masters, eds. *Reflections of Nero: Culture, History, and Representation.* Chapel Hill: University of North Carolina Press, 1994.

Grant, Michael. *Nero: Emperor in Revolt.* New York: American Heritage Press, 1970.

Holland, Richard. *Nero: The Man behind the Myth.* Stroud, U.K.: Sutton, 2000.

Warmington, B. H. *Nero: Reality and Legend.* New York: Norton, 1969.

NESSUS   A CENTAUR who tried to rape HERACLES' wife, DEIANEIRA. Heracles killed Nessus, but before the centaur died he persuaded Deianeira to take some of his blood and use it as a love charm on Heracles. Several years later, when Heracles' love for a female war captive, IOLE, came to light, Deianeira, hoping to regain Heracles' love, smeared some of the centaur's blood on one of Heracles' robes. Unfortunately, the centaur's blood contained venom from the Lernaean HYDRA, which Heracles had smeared on his arrows. This venom caused Heracles extreme torment when it touched his skin and eventually Heracles had himself burned alive to escape the torment of the poison. [ANCIENT SOURCES: Hyginus, *Fables* 34; Seneca, *Hercules Oetaeus*; Sophocles, *Trachinian Women*]

NESTOR   The son of Neleus and Chloris, Nestor was king of PYLOS. By his wife, Eurydice, Nestor had nine children. In his youth, Nestor was the only one of the brothers not killed by HERACLES. Nestor gained fame for killing a giant named Ereuthalion, fighting in the battle of the CENTAURS and LAPITHS, sailing with JASON and the Argonauts, and fighting in the Trojan War. Nestor's son, Antilochus, saved his father's life at Troy when Nestor was about to be killed by MEMNON. Nestor's greatest fame, however, was due to his speaking ability and wisdom. After the fall of TROY, Nestor was one of the few Greeks who returned home safely. [ANCIENT SOURCES: Apollodorus, *Library* 1.9.9, 2.7.3, 3.10.8, *Epitome* 3.12, 3.32, 6.1; Aristophanes, *Clouds* 1057; Euripides, *Iphigenia at Aulis* 273, fragment 899 Nauck; Homer, *Iliad, Odyssey;* Sophocles, *Philoctetes* 422, fragment 144a1, 855 Radt]

BIBLIOGRAPHY

Nauck, A. *Tragicorum Graecorum Fragmenta.* 1889. Reprint, Hildesheim, Ger.: Olms, 1964.

Radt, S. *Tragicorum Graecorum Fragmenta.* Vol. 4. Göttingen, Ger.: Vandenhoeck & Ruprecht, 1977.

NEW COMEDY   See COMEDY.

NICARCHUS   An otherwise unknown INFORMANT who is described as small in stature, he appears as a character in ARISTOPHANES' *ACHARNIANS* (908–58) to denounce the trading between DICAEOPOLIS and the Theban trader. Dicaeopolis packs up Nicarchus as a piece of pottery and trades him to the Theban.

NICIAS (1) (CA. 470–413 B.C.E.)   The son of Niceratus, Nicias was wealthy and a leading Athenian statesmen and military commander during the first half of the PELOPONNESIAN WAR. Nicias largely opposed the war with the Spartans and clashed especially with CLEON on this issue. In 425, Nicias relinquished his military command to Cleon at PYLOS, when Cleon accused him of not prosecuting an attack on the Spartans quickly enough. Cleon went on to achieve a major victory in this battle. In the next year, ARISTOPHANES' *KNIGHTS* portrayed Nicias as a slave oppressed by Cleon. After Cleon's death in 422, Nicias was able to craft a peace treaty with SPARTA in 421 B.C.E., a treaty that is alluded to in ARISTOPHANES' *PEACE*. This agreement disintegrated, however, a few years later, when the Athenians made a military expedition against SICILY in 415. Nicias was one of the Athenian commanders of this expedition, and his reliance on the advice of soothsayers about a lunar eclipse prevented the Athenians from escaping from Sicily in 413. Because Nicias took the soothsayers' advice that he should not move for 27 days, the Athenian forces were surrounded and eventually destroyed. Nicias lost his life in the massacre. [ANCIENT SOURCES: Aristophanes, *Birds* 363; Diodorus Siculus, 12.65–13.32; Eupolis, fragment 181 Kock; Phrynichus, fragment 22, 59; Plutarch, *Alcibiades, Nicias;* Teleclides, fragment 41.3 Kock; Thucydides, 3.54–7.86]

BIBLIOGRAPHY

Adkins, A. W. H. "The Arete of Nicias: Thucydides 7.86," *Greek, Roman, and Byzantine Studies* 16 (1975): 379–92.

Kagan, D. *The Peace of Nicias and the Sicilian Expedition.* Ithaca, N.Y.: Cornell University Press, 1981.

Kock, T. *Comicorum Atticorum Fragmenta.* Vol. 1. Leipzig: Teubner, 1880.

Tompkins, D. P. "Stylistic Characterization in Thucydides: Nicias and Alcibiades," *Yale Classical Studies* 22 (1972): 181–214.

Westlake, H. D. *Individuals in Thucydides.* London: Cambridge University Press, 1968.

NICIAS (2)

A handsome but pale-faced young Athenian whom ARISTOPHANES mentions as making a speech in favor of handing over the Athenian government to women. He may have been the grandson of the more famous NICIAS (see NICIAS (1)). [ANCIENT SOURCES: Aristophanes, *Ecclesiazusae* 428]

NICOMACHUS

A person on whom ARISTO-PHANES wishes death at FROGS 1506. According to Dover, Nichomachus was an *anagrapheus* (secretary), whose tasks in 410 B.C.E. and 403 were "the codification and public inscription of the laws." The Greek orator Lysias (speech 30) mentions a person of this name who was prosecuted in 399/398.

BIBLIOGRAPHY
Dover, Kenneth. *Aristophanes: Frogs.* Oxford: Clarendon Press, 1993, 382.

NICOSTRATUS (DIED 418 B.C.E.)

The son of Dieitrephes, Nicostratus was an Athenian military commander at least five times between 427 and 418 B.C.E. and "may have been a close associate of Nicias" (Sommerstein). Nicostratus died at the battle of Mantinea. [ANCIENT SOURCES: Aristophanes, *Wasps* 81; Thucydides, 3.75, 4.53, 4.119.2, 4.129.2, 4.133.4, 5.74.3]

BIBLIOGRAPHY
MacDowell, D. M. *Aristophanes: Wasps.* Oxford: Clarendon Press, 1971, 140–41.

Sommerstein, A. H. *The Comedies of Aristophanes.* Vol. 4, *Wasps.* Warminster, U.K.: Aris & Phillips, 1983, 159.

NIETZSCHE, FRIEDRICH WILHELM (OCTOBER 15, 1844–AUGUST 25, 1900)

Born near Leipzig, Germany, Nietzsche not only was a philosopher, but a scholar of classical literature. Nietzsche published extensively on philosophy and religion; his first book, *The Birth of Tragedy,* published in 1872, when Nietzsche was 28, has been of interest to scholars of classical drama and was criticized by scholars such as Ulrich von Wilamowitz-Möllendorff. In this work, Nietzsche suggested that the source of all reality and creativity is a nonrational "Dionysian" energy. Nietzsche considered this a healthy force that emerged from Greek culture but argued that after the heyday of the Greeks this "Dionysian" creative force had given way to the more logical and formal "Apollonian" forces, which he viewed as exerting an unhealthy dominance over European culture. Thus, Nietzsche believed, cultural rebirth could occur if society embraced its Dionysian side.

BIBLIOGRAPHY
Lenson, D. *The Birth of Tragedy: A Commentary.* Boston: Twayne, 1987.

Nietzsche, F. W. *The Birth of Tragedy.* Translated by D. Smith. Oxford: Oxford University Press, 2000.

Sallis, J. *Crossings: Nietzsche and the Space of Tragedy.* Chicago: University of Chicago Press, 1991.

Silk, M. S., and J. P. Stern. *Nietzsche on Tragedy.* Cambridge: Cambridge University Press, 1980.

Tanner, M. *Nietzsche: A Very Short Introduction.* Oxford: Oxford University Press, 2000.

NIGHT (Greek: *NUX*; Latin: *NOX*)

According to the Greeks, Night was one of the earliest things to exist in the universe. Night emerged from Chaos and (with EREBUS) produced Day and Upper Air (Ether). By herself, Night produced Death (Thanatos), Doom (Moros), the FATES, NEMESIS, and Sleep (Hypnos). Night is also said to be the mother of CHARON. [ANCIENT SOURCES: Aeschylus, *Eumenides* 745 (see *ORESTEIA*); Euripides, *Electra* 54; Hesiod, *Theogony* 123–25, 211–25, 744–66; Homer, *Iliad* 14.256–61; Seneca, *Octavia* 18; Sophocles, *Electra* 203]

NIKE (Latin: VICTORIA)

The daughter of the river STYX and a divinity named Pallas, Nike is the goddess of victory. She is often connected with ZEUS or ATHENA, to the latter of whose name Nike is sometimes added. Nike is the sister of Emulation (Zelus), Force (Bia), and Strength (Cratus). The poets themselves sometimes invoke Nike in their plays to help them win dramatic competition. [ANCIENT SOURCES: Aristophanes, *Birds* 574, *Knights* 589, *Lysistrata* 317; Euripides, *Ion* 1529, *Iphigenia in Tauris* 1497, *Orestes* 1691, *Phoenician Women* 1764; Hesiod, *Theogony* 383–88; Menander, *Dyscolus* 969, *The Man She Hated* 466, *Samia* 737, *Man from Sicyon* 423; Plautus, *Amphitruo* 42, *Merchant* 867; Sophocles, *Philoctetes* 134]

NILE   At almost 4,200 miles in length, the Nile, located in Africa, is the longest river in the world. The Nile has two sources: The White Nile originates from Lake Victoria, the Blue Nile originates from Lake Tana. Eventually these two branches connect in Sudan and the Nile's seven mouths eventually flow into the Mediterranean Sea. References to the Nile are common in AESCHYLUS' SUPPLIANT WOMEN and EURIPIDES' HELEN. Io's torment eventually ends near the Nile. [ANCIENT SOURCES: Herodotus, 2]

NIOBE   The daughter of TANTALUS and Dione, Niobe was the sister of PELOPS and became the wife of ZEUS' son, AMPHION, who was later king of THEBES. Niobe was a proud queen who boasted that she had more children than LETO, the mother of APOLLO and ARTEMIS. The offended Leto sent her divine twins to kill Niobe's children, usually 12 or 14 in number (six or seven boys, six or seven girls). After the death of her children, Niobe left Thebes and went to Mount Sipylus. When she prayed to the gods to relieve her of her grief, she was transformed into a stone, from which her tears continued to flow. Both AESCHYLUS and SOPHOCLES wrote plays entitled *Niobe*. As indicated by ARISTOPHANES' *FROGS,* Niobe remained silent for an extended period in Aeschylus' play. A fragment from Aeschylus' *Niobe* indicates that the children have been dead for three days when the play's action occurs. Sophocles' play dealt with the destruction of Niobe's children by Apollo and Artemis. In *FROGS,* ARISTOPHANES appears to mention Aeschylus' play as an example of that dramatist's practice of having a character onstage who does not speak for an extended period in order to build suspense. The Greek tragedian Melito also wrote a *Niobe,* of which only the title survives. [ANCIENT SOURCES:

Apollodorus, *Library* 3.5.6; Aristophanes, *Frogs* 911–13; Homer, *Iliad* 24.602–20; Hyginus, *Fables* 9; Ovid, *Metamorphoses* 6.146–312; Pausanias, 1.21.3; Seneca, *Agamemnon* 392–94, *Hercules Furens* 390, *Hercules Oetaeus* 185, 1849, *Oedipus* 613]

BIBLIOGRAPHY

Kiso, A. *The Lost Sophocles.* New York: Vantage Press, 1984.

Lloyd-Jones, H. *Sophocles: Fragments.* Cambridge, Mass.: Harvard University Press, 1996.

Page, D. L. *Select Papyri.* Vol. 3. 1941. Reprint, London: Heinemann, 1970.

Radt, S. *Tragicorum Graecorum Fragmenta.* Vol. 4. Göttingen, Ger.: Vandenhoeck & Ruprecht, 1977.

Snell, B. *Tragicorum Graecorum Fragmenta.* Vol. 1. Göttingen, Ger.: Vandenhoeck & Ruprecht, 1971.

Sutton, D. F. *The Lost Sophocles.* Lanham, Md.: University Press of America, 1984.

NIPTRA   See ODYSSEUS.

NIREUS   A handsome suitor of HELEN, Nireus fought in the Trojan War. [ANCIENT SOURCES: Euripides, *Iphigenia at Aulis* 205]

NISUS   The son of PANDION, Nisus was the brother of AEGEUS, Lycus, and Pallas. While Nisus, king of MEGARA, was at war with the Cretan king, MINOS, Nisus' daughter, Scylla, fell in love with Minos. Nisus had a purple lock of hair on his head; as long as this lock of hair remained, Nisus would live. Furthermore, as long as Nisus was alive, Minos was unable to defeat him. Scylla, however, hoping to win the favor of Minos, cut off her father's lock of hair, thus killing him, and presented it to Minos as a token of her love. Minos, appalled by this woman who had killed her father, rejected Scylla's advances. After Minos defeated Nisus' army and was on the point of sailing away, Scylla tried to swim after him and cling to his ship. She failed, however, and was transformed into a bird, the Ciris. Her father, Nisus, was changed into a sea eagle, who constantly tries to strike at the Ciris because of her crime against him. [ANCIENT SOURCES: Aeschylus, *Libation Bearers* 613–22 (see ORESTEIA); Apollodorus, *Library* 3.15.5; Ovid, *Metamorphosis* 8.1–151; Pausanias, 1.19.4]

NOCTURNUS   A Roman god of the NIGHT. [ANCIENT SOURCES: Plautus, *Amphitruo* 272]

NURSE   A character in both ancient TRAGEDY and COMEDY, the Nurse (Greek: *trophos;* Latin: *nutrix*) would have been a slave who helped raise a child and stayed with that child throughout his or her life. The earliest extant nurse (that of ORESTES) who has a speaking role appears in AESCHYLUS' *Libation Bearers* (see ORESTEIA). In EURIPIDES' extant plays, HERMIONE's nurse appears briefly in Euripides' ANDROMACHE; MEDEA's nurse has a more extensive role. She delivers the prologue of MEDEA and tries to calm the rage of her mistress, as she also does in SENECA'S *Medea*. In HIPPOLYTUS, PHAEDRA is persuaded to reveal her love for her stepson, HIPPOLYTUS, by her nurse, who attempts to arrange a love affair between them. In contrast, in Seneca's *Hippolytus*, Phaedra's nurse initially tries to persuade her to suppress her feelings for Hippolytus but later intercedes with Hippolytus on Phaedra's behalf. In SOPHOCLES' *Trachinian Women*, DEIANEIRA's nurse appears briefly. *Octavia,* incorrectly attributed to Seneca, is noteworthy in that two nurses appear in that play (the nurse of OCTAVIA and the nurse of POPPAEA) and both erroneously predict that the women will fare well at the hands of NERO.

NYCTELIUS   A name for DIONYSUS. Nyctelius is related to the Greek word for night (*nux*), when the mysteries of Dionysus took place. [ANCIENT SOURCES: Seneca, *Oedipus* 492]

NYMPHS   The Greek word *nymphe* means "young woman;" a nymph is a minor female divinity who lives in certain natural phenomena, objects, or places. Some nymphs, leimoniades, live in meadows; NAIADS live in bodies of water; oreads live in hills and mountains; others, such as meliae, dryads, and hamadryads, live in trees. The daughters of oceanus (OCEANIDS) and the daughters of NEREUS (NEREIDS) were also nymphs. The nymphs of Mount Nysa cared for the young DIONYSUS. In EURIPIDES' *Electra*, ORESTES kills AEGISTHUS while he is making a sacrifice to certain rock nymphs. [ANCIENT SOURCES: Aeschylus, *Eumenides* 22 (see ORESTEIA); Euripides, *Cyclops* 68, *Helen* 1317, *Heracles* 784, *Iphigenia at Aulis* 1292; Seneca, *Hercules Oetaeus* 1053, *Hippolytus* 784; Sophocles, *Antigone* 1128, *Philoctetes* 725, 1454, 1470]

NYSA   A name given to several places that were sacred to DIONYSUS. Some sources make Nysa a mountain in what is today western Turkey, where Dionysus was said to have been raised. Towns called Nysa were known in India, northern Africa, and central Greece (near the town of Thebes, where Dionysus was conceived). [ANCIENT SOURCES: Apollodorus, *Library* 3.4.3; Euripides, *Bacchae* 556, *Cyclops* 68; *Homeric Hymn,* 26.5; Sophocles, *Antigone* 1131]

NYX   A Greek word for NIGHT.

OBOL In the Athenian monetary system, the obol was the coin with the least value—one-sixth of a DRACHMA, one-six-hundredth of a MINA, and one-six-thousandth of a talent. By the time of ARISTOPHANES' *WASPS* (422 B.C.E.), jury pay in ATHENS was three obols per day. Similarly, in Aristophanes' *ECCLESIAZUSAE* (392/391 B.C.E.), we hear that those attending the assembly in Athens received three obols per day. At the end of the fourth century B.C.E., in MENANDER'S *ARBITRATION,* two obols per day is enough to feed someone who is starving.

OCEANIDS The daughters of OCEANUS and TETHYS, these minor divinities make up the CHORUS in AESCHYLUS' *PROMETHEUS BOUND.* Apollodorus names seven Oceanids, but Hesiod says there were 3,000. Perhaps the best-known of the Oceanids is STYX. [ANCIENT SOURCES: Apollodorus, *Library* 1.2.2; Hesiod, *Theogony* 346–66]

OCEANUS (OKEANOS) The son of EARTH and URANUS, Oceanus was the brother of CRONUS, RHEA, and many others. Oceanus personifies the ocean, which the ancients usually regarded as a river that encircled the world's various landmasses. Oceanus' wife was his sister, Tethys; they produced the world's rivers as well as several thousand water NYMPHS known as OCEANIDS. Oceanus appears as a character in AESCHYLUS' *PROMETHEUS BOUND.* His entrance in that play is one of the most spectacular in extant drama, as he appears from above in a hippogriff (a creature that was part horse and part GRIFFIN). In that play, Oceanus offers to help PROMETHEUS, but Prometheus refuses the offer, saying that he does not want Oceanus himself to risk offending ZEUS. [ANCIENT SOURCES: Hesiod, *Theogony* 133; Hyginus, *Fables* 182]

OCTAVIA (D. JUNE 9, 62 C.E.) Claudia Octavia was the daughter of the Roman emperor CLAUDIUS and his wife, Messalina. In 53 C.E., Octavia married her stepbrother, NERO, who had become emperor after the death of Claudius in 54. Nine years later, Nero, claiming Octavia was sterile, divorced her, married POPPAEA, and exiled Octavia from Rome. Initially, Octavia remained on the Italian mainland in the region of Campania, but the Roman people's sympathy for her plight and her popularity with them led Nero to send her to the island of Pandateria, where he had her killed. Octavia appears as a character in and is the subject of a TRAGEDY entitled *Octavia,* of which SENECA is incorrectly named as the author. The play is highly sympathetic to Octavia and deals with Nero's divorce of her in favor of Poppaea.

OCTAVIA (CA. 68–69 C.E.) *Octavia* is the only extant *FABULA PRAETEXTA* (Roman historical drama). Tradition makes SENECA the author, although he clearly was not because the play has some details of the death of the

Roman emperor Nero, which occurred three years after Seneca's death. The play's setting is Nero's palace at Rome, and the action deals with events of 62 C.E. in the life of Octavia, the wife and stepsister of Nero.

Octavia delivers an opening monologue and complains of her fate, which is worse than that of her mother (Messalina) and father (the previous emperor Claudius), and of the cruelty of her husband, Nero (he has taken a woman named Poppaea as his mistress). After her lament, Octavia goes back inside the palace. Next, Octavia's nurse enters, comments about the misfortune suffered by members of Octavia's family, and notes that they have tried to console Octavia. After hearing additional lamentation about her fate from within the palace, the Nurse is soon joined by Octavia, who suggests that her death is imminent. The Nurse encourages her to be calm and try to win over her husband with gentle behavior. Octavia, however, does not believe she will be able to win him over and notes that because her father, mother, and brother (Britannicus) are dead, she has no one to whom she can turn. Furthermore, Octavia fears Nero's mistress, Poppaea, will try to bring about her death. Octavia calls upon her father Claudius' spirit to help her, but the nurse tells her that such prayers are useless. Octavia suggests that she might try to kill Nero, but the nurse again urges her to save herself by bending to Nero's will and taking some comfort in the people's concern for her. Again, however, Octavia rejects the idea that she will accept Nero's will and wishes for Nero's death. The nurse suggests that some god may yet go to her aid, but Octavia doubts this will happen.

After Octavia and her nurse return to the palace's interior, a chorus of Romans enters and wonders at the rumors that Nero plans to take a new wife. They lament the loss of the Roman virtues of old and recall that Nero's unsuccessful attempt to kill his own mother was followed by her assassination. After the chorus' song, the aged Seneca, former tutor and current adviser of Nero, enters. He recalls the peace and prosperity of the Golden Age untold generations earlier and describes how humankind has become immoral, warlike, and greedy.

The play's second act opens with Seneca's being joined by Nero, who sends out his prefect to execute some of his enemies. Seneca tries to counsel Nero against this violent behavior, but Nero arrogantly rejects his advice. Nero argues that just as bloodshed eventually led to Augustus' triumphing over his enemies and becoming a divinity, he will follow a similar path. Seneca then urges Nero to be reconciled with his wife, Octavia, because she is of divine stock and can give Nero divine children. Nero claims that he never loved Octavia and that he has now found a woman worthy of him, who is as beautiful as Venus (see Aphrodite). Seneca warns Nero that beauty fades and that if Nero underestimates the power of love, then he will lose "love." Nero denies this and hopes that Love himself will bear the wedding torch at his marriage to Poppaea. Seneca argues that the Roman people do not want such a union and urges Nero to accede the people's will. Nero, of course, rejects this argument and leaves, suggesting that his wedding to Poppaea will take place the next day.

The third act begins with the appearance of the ghost of Agrippina, Nero's mother; who recalls her murder by Nero and expresses her hatred of her son. Agrippina's ghost imagines that she sees the ghost of her dead husband, Claudius, who threatens her because she brought about his death and demands that Nero be killed. Agrippina concludes her speech by regretting that she ever gave birth to Nero. After Agrippina's ghost disappears, Octavia returns and announces that Nero has divorced her. Before she departs from the palace, she worries what will happen to her. Next, the chorus enter and express their displeasure with Nero's marriage to Poppaea and consider violence against Poppaea and Nero.

The fourth act opens with the entrance of a tearful Poppaea and her nurse. Poppaea tells her nurse that she has had a troubling dream in which she saw her marriage bedroom crowded with mourners and Agrippina carrying a bloody torch. She then dreamed that the earth opened and swallowed up her marriage bed. She imagined that she saw her previous husband, Crispinus, and her son, Rufrius Crispinus. When the elder Crispinus tried to embrace her, Nero suddenly appeared and killed him. When Poppaea asks her nurse what this dream could mean, the nurse erroneously explains the dream as having positive implications for her future with Nero. Poppaea, however, is not so confident and sends the nurse out to make offerings to the gods so that she will not have more of such dreams and that her fears may become those of her enemies. After the exit of Poppaea and her nurse, a chorus of Roman women, who sympathize with Poppaea, praise her beauty above that of the most beautiful women in mythology. Next, a messenger enters and informs the chorus that a mob of citizens, who favor Octavia, are planning to overthrow Nero. The mob has toppled Poppaea's statues and are preparing to burn Nero's palace. After the messenger exits to inform Nero, the chorus comment briefly on the power of love.

The play's final act begins with the entrance of Nero, who expresses his anger at the mob for their love of Octavia and states that he will punish Octavia in a manner worse than death; he will also punish the mob. After this, Nero's prefect enters and announces that the mob has been put down forcefully and its leaders executed. When Nero tells the prefect that he wants Octavia to be executed as well, the prefect is horrified and tries to dissuade him from this order. Nero, however, refuses to yield and orders that Octavia be taken far away and killed. After the exit of Nero and the prefect, the chorus lament that the favor of the people has often proved the ruin of many.

Next, Octavia is dragged in by some of Nero's guards. Her lament about her impending punishment is answered sympathetically by the chorus, who recall that many royal Roman women have met a similar fate. The play ends with Octavia's declaring that she is ready to meet her fate and the chorus' praying that she will be rescued as IPHIGENIA was when she was at AULIS.

COMMENTARY

Octavia is an intriguing play for two major reasons: Because it is known that Seneca did not write the play, the question of who did compose it remains. This cannot be answered with certainty; the name of one Maternus, a person sympathetic to Octavia who had been present during these events, has been suggested. Perhaps more important than the question of authorship, however, is the fact that *Octavia* is the only surviving *fabula praetexta,* a Roman drama whose plot is derived from historical rather than mythological

events. Although based on historical events, *Octavia* still interweaves references and allusions to mythology with the playwright's representation of history. The play also employs some of the conventions of mythologically based tragedies, such as the presence of a chorus of citizens, an AGON (the debate between Nero and Seneca), messenger speeches, the appearance of a ghost, and the presentation of information through dreams.

The focal point of *Octavia* is the perversion of marriage within the house of Nero. Nero's divorce of Octavia in favor of Poppaea bears some resemblance to JASON's divorce of MEDEA for CREON's daughter and THESEUS' divorce of his AMAZON wife for PHAEDRA. Like Medea and the Amazon, Octavia has no relatives to whom she can turn after her husband divorces her. Unlike Medea, who kills her rival, Octavia does not possess magical power and has little chance of retaliating against Nero. Nero is more cruel than Jason in that the emperor plans to have Octavia killed. In this respect, Octavia is closer to Theseus' Amazon wife, who tried to kill Theseus but is instead killed by him. Still, the author of *Octavia* makes his title character appear much more helpless than the warrior princess to whom Theseus was married.

Like Phaedra and the ill-fated unions in which her mother, PASIPHAE, and sister, ARIADNE, were involved, Octavia has a family tradition of doomed marriages. Octavia recalls that her cruel stepmother (Agrippina) led the way to Octavia's bridal chamber (24) with Stygian torches. Just as Octavia's marriage was perverted by Agrippina's Stygian bridal torches, when Agrippina's ghost appears later in the play, she announces that she is carrying a Stygian torch to Nero's accursed marriage (*thalamis,* 595) with Poppaea. Thus, the tradition of Nero's cursed marriages will continue with Poppaea, who, as the ancient audience of *Octavia* would have known, was killed by Nero in 65 C.E.

Not only did the cruel stepmother's torches defile Octavia's bedchamber, but the spirit of Octavia's deceased brother (Britannicus), who carries dark torches, takes refuge there (120). As the audience of *Octavia* would have known, Nero was probably responsible for Britannicus' death by poison in 55 C.E. Octavia also notes that Nero, who killed his own mother, now threatens her own bedchamber (131). As did Phaedra's mother, who was possessed by a mad passion, Octavia's mother, Messalina, defiled her bridal chamber (252) by marrying Gaius Silius although she was already married to Octavia's father, Claudius. This drove an enraged Claudius to have Messalina killed and thus extinguish with blood the wedding torches stolen from his bridal chamber (264).

Although Octavia's family has had little happiness in marriage, the chorus is optimistic and pray that Poppaea will not enter the bridal chamber of the emperor (276). They note that Juno (see HERA) continues to occupy the bedchamber (282) of Jove (see ZEUS) and wonder why Octavia would be driven from Nero's house.

Although Octavia's nurse considered Nero unworthy of Octavia's bridal chamber (252), Nero tells Seneca that he has finally found someone worthy of his (544). Seneca tries to instruct Nero about the qualities a person should look for in a wife, but Nero is captivated by Poppaea, who he thinks is superior to Juno, Venus (see APHRODITE), and Minerva (see ATHENA). Thus, with such a statement, Nero clearly characterizes himself as someone more powerful than Jove, and, unlike the real Jove, he will expel his Juno (Octavia) from the bridal chamber. Seneca reinforces the chorus' earlier desires when he notes that the people will not stand for such a marriage (thalamos, 572), but Nero is determined and decides that the marriage (thalamis, 592) will occur the following day.

On that day, Octavia notes that she will no longer have to use the bedchamber in which she was treated as a slave (657). After Octavia departs, the chorus pity Octavia, who is being driven from the bedchamber of cruel Nero (671–72). Several of the wedding torches in this play have been perverse; the chorus of Roman people, angered by Nero's perversion of his marriage to Octavia, now threaten to assail Nero's palace with, among other things, flame (688).

After one wife has left Nero's bedchamber, a second wife makes her first appearance in the play from this same place (690) in a state of fear. As Octavia's bridal chamber was tainted by Agrippina's Stygian torches and visited by her brother's ghost, Poppaea dreams that her bridal chamber is visited by mourners (718). Additionally, she notes the presence of Agrippina, who again carries a blood-spattered marriage torch (722–23). Whereas the audience of the Octavia would have known that Poppaea's dream would refer to her own doom, Poppaea's nurse interprets the dreams incorrectly in a way that will soothe Poppaea. The nurse urges Poppaea to set aside her fear and return to her bridal chamber (755). Poppaea, however, will not return and decides to sacrifice to the gods instead.

After Poppaea's exit, a messenger announces news of the people's anger against Nero and their attempt to burn his palace. The perverse imaginary wedding torch (facem, 723) of Poppaea's dream has become real torches (faces, 822) which threaten to destroy Nero's palace. Eventually, however, the emperor suppresses the people, and the killing of their leaders ends their destructive flames. Furthermore, Nero makes Octavia a scapegoat for the people's rage and orders that she be killed. As Nero's guards drag Octavia away she imagines herself being carried away from Nero's bedchamber (909) on the same vessel that carried Nero's mother to her doom. The play ends with Octavia appearing to be a second Agrippina as she prays for Nero's destruction and calls upon the FURIES to carry out his punishment on her behalf.

BIBLIOGRAPHY

Ferri, R. "Octavia's Heroines: Tacitus, Annales 14, 63–64 and the 'Praetexta Octavia,'" Harvard Studies in Classical Philology 98 (1998): 339–56.
Poe, J. P. "Octavia Praetexta and its Senecan Model," American Journal of Philology 110 (1989): 434–59.
Williams, G. "Nero, Seneca and Stoicism in the Octavia." In Reflections of Nero: Culture, History, and Representation. Edited by Jas Elsner and Jamie Masters. Chapel Hill: University of North Carolina Press, 1994, 178–95.

ODE Its name derived from a Greek word meaning "song," an ode is a song by the chorus. A song by an individual is called a MONODY. Choral odes are divided into sections; the most common terms for the divisions are STROPHE, ANTISTROPHE, and EPODE. A typical pattern is strophe a, followed by antistrophe a; this pattern is repeated once. Sometimes the choral ode ends with an epode (concluding song). Some of the most famous choral odes are found in SOPHOCLES. At ANTIGONE

332–83, the Theban elders sing of humans' mastery of the world but note that humans have not devised a way to avoid death. In OEDIPUS AT COLONUS, lines 668–719, the elders of Colonus sing a lovely song in praise of the beauties of their city and the region where they live.

ODEUM   Built by PERICLES around 445 B.C.E. as a place for musical performances, the Odeum, east of the Theater of DIONYSUS at ATHENS, was also used for other civic functions, such as a law court. [ANCIENT SOURCES: Aristophanes, *Wasps* 1109; Demosthenes, 34.37; Xenophon, *Hellenica* 2.4.9–10]

BIBLIOGRAPHY
Sommerstein, A. H. *The Comedies of Aristophanes.* Vol. 4,
    Wasps. Warminster, U.K.: Aris & Phillips, 1983, 221–22.

ODOMANTI   A tribe living in THRACE east of the river Strymon and north of Mount Pangaeum. In ARISTOPHANES' *ACHARNIANS* (155–73), some of the Odomantians are hired by the Athenians as mercenaries to help them in the PELOPONNESIAN WAR. Aristophanes describes the Odomanti as being circumcised (a practice that the Athenians considered barbaric). The Odomanti in *Acharnians* steal DICAEOPOLIS' garlic. [ANCIENT SOURCES: Herodotus, 5.16.1; Thucydides, 2.101.3, 5.6.2]

ODRYSIA   The Odrysians were a tribe who lived in central Thrace. The name Odrysia is sometimes used as a synonym for Thrace. [ANCIENT SOURCES: Seneca, *Thyestes* 273]

ODYSSEUS (Latin: ULYSSES)   Odysseus, the son of the Ithacan king, Laertes, and Anticleia, was the father of Telemachus by PENELOPE. By CIRCE Odysseus fathered Telegonus. As a young man, Odysseus became one of HELEN's many suitors; when he realized he was not her favorite, he gave up his pursuit and offered Helen's father, TYNDAREUS, advice about choosing the correct husband on the condition that Tyndareus would persuade his brother, Icarius, to allow him to marry his daughter, Penelope. Tyndareus agreed and Odysseus told Tyndareus that before Helen

married he should make the suitors take an oath to defend her should anything happen to her. The suitors, including Odysseus, took this oath. Tyndareus married Helen to MENELAUS, but when PARIS abducted Helen a few years later, all the suitors had to go to TROY to help recover Menelaus' wife. Though Odysseus had taken the oath, when the Greeks went to ITHACA to get him, he tried to avoid military duty by pretending to be insane. The Greeks found Odysseus plowing a field with a horse and an ox and throwing salt into the furrows. The Greek PALAMEDES suspected Odysseus of trickery, so he took Odysseus' infant son, TELEMACHUS, and placed him in the plow's path. When Odysseus swerved to miss his son, his deception was uncovered and Odysseus was forced to go to Troy.

Odysseus soon had many opportunities for trickery, because ACHILLES was also trying to avoid going to Troy by disguising himself as a woman and hiding in the court of Lycomedes on SCYROS. Odysseus, however, tricked Achilles into revealing his true gender by arranging to have a battle trumpet blown while all the women of the court were gathered. When Achilles snatched up some arms that Odysseus had placed conveniently nearby, his identity was revealed. When at Aulis AGAMEMNON was told that he had to sacrifice his daughter, IPHIGENIA, to gain favorable weather for sailing to Troy, Odysseus was involved in the plot to lure Iphigenia to Aulis with the pretense that she was to marry Achilles.

Not only was Odysseus cunning, but he could also be cruel. After the Greeks sailed from Aulis and landed on Tenedos, PHILOCTETES was bitten by a snake. When the injured hero's wound caused him to cry out in pain constantly—cries that became bothersome to the Greeks—Odysseus is often said to have been the person who urged that Philoctetes be abandoned on LEMNOS.

During the Trojan War, Odysseus proved instrumental at several critical moments. In the 10th year of the war, he played a major role in the nocturnal raid on the Trojan camp that resulted in the slaughter of numerous enemy soldiers and the capture of the RHESUS' fabulous horses. It was prophesied that if these horses had fed on Trojan food first, the Trojans would win the war. Later in the same year, Odysseus and Diomedes managed to sneak into Troy and steal the Palladium. As long as the Trojans had this statue in their possession, their empire would remain intact. Finally, Odysseus is often given credit for the stratagem of the wooden horse, which led to Troy's destruction.

Odysseus, the versatile hero made famous in the verses of Homer's *Iliad* and *Odyssey,* remained equally versatile on the Greek stage. In SOPHOCLES' *PHILOCTETES,* he is portrayed as an unscrupulous trickster, who is willing to say or do anything to accomplish his mission of acquiring *PHILOCTETES'* bow. In EURIPIDES' *CYCLOPS,* Odysseus remains a trickster, but in this SATYR PLAY he is the trickster who triumphs over an uncivilized monster. In Sophocles' *AJAX,* Odysseus is shown in a different light: Although Ajax has tried to kill him, Odysseus pities Ajax, his enemy (121–22), and intervenes on his behalf at the end of the play to secure his burial, which Agamemnon and Menelaus oppose.

Many other dramas, tragedies, comedies, and satyr plays were written about Odysseus. Sophocles' *Niptra (Foot Washing)* and *Odysseus Akanthoplex (Odysseus Wounded by the Spine)* may have been the same play. Sophocles also wrote an *Odysseus Mainomenos (The Madness of Odysseus),* which was probably about Odysseus' attempt to avoid fighting at Troy by pretending to be insane. The Greek tragedian Chaeremon wrote an *Odysseus,* whose extant two-line fragment (13 Snell) describes women (NAUSICAA and her companions?) who have roses in their hair.

BIBLIOGRAPHY
Snell, B. *Tragicorum Graecorum Fragmenta.* Vol. 1. Göttingen, Ger.: Vandenhoeck & Ruprecht, 1971.

OEA   A place of uncertain location in the region of Attica, of which ATHENS is the principal city. [ANCIENT SOURCES: Sophocles, *Oedipus at Colonus* 1059]

OEAGRUS   Apparently an actor in tragedies in ARISTOPHANES' day. Aristophanes suggests that Oeagrus was a defendant in a court proceeding and that his acquittal resulted from his quoting lines from the play *Niobe,* probably the one by AESCHYLUS, although Sophocles also wrote a *Niobe.* [ANCIENT SOURCES: Aristophanes, *Wasps* 579]

BIBLIOGRAPHY
MacDowell, D. M. *Aristophanes: Wasps.* Oxford: Clarendon Press, 1971, 210–11.

OEAX   The son of NAUPLIUS and Clymene, Oeax was the brother of PALAMEDES and Nausimedon. Oeax was one of those who opposed ORESTES after he killed his mother. Oeax wanted revenge on Orestes because he blamed Orestes' father, AGAMEMNON, for the death of his brother, Palamedes. [ANCIENT SOURCES: Apollodorus, *Library* 2.1.5; Euripides, ORESTES 432]

OECHALIA   A town on the island of EUBOEA, where EURYTUS, father of IOLE and IPHITUS, was king when HERACLES destroyed the town by war. [ANCIENT SOURCES: Apollodorus, *Library* 2.6.1, 2.7.7; Euripides, *Heracles* 473, *Hippolytus* 545; Seneca, *Hercules Oetaeus;* Sophocles, *Trachinian Women*]

OECLES (OCLEUS)   The father of AMPHIA-RAUS, who was one of the Seven against THEBES. SOPHO-CLES appears to have written an *Oecles,* but the brief fragments (468–69 Radt) that survive give no indication of the play's subject matter. [ANCIENT SOURCES: Aeschylus, *Seven against Thebes* 382, 609; Euripides, *Suppliant Women* 925; Hyginus, *Fables* 70]

BIBLIOGRAPHY
Kiso, A. *The Lost Sophocles.* New York: Vantage Press, 1984.
Radt, S. *Tragicorum Graecorum Fragmenta.* Vol. 4. Göttingen, Ger.: Vandenhoeck & Ruprecht, 1977.
Sutton, D. F. *The Lost Sophocles.* Lanham, Md.: University Press of America, 1984.

OEDIPUS   The son of LAIUS and JOCASTA, Oedipus is one of the best known, most notorious characters of classical mythology. When Laius, king of THEBES, learned that he was destined to have a child who would kill him, he tried to avoid sexual relations with Jocasta. Jocasta, however, determined to have a child, made Laius drunk and had intercourse with him. Laius tried to get rid of the child by giving him to one of his shepherds, who was to leave the child on Mount CITHAERON to die. To ensure that the infant would not be able to crawl to safety, Laius had the child's feet pierced with a metal fastener. This fastener was later removed, however, but the injury gave the child his name—Oedipus ("swollen foot"). The Theban shepherd gave Oedipus to a Corinthian shepherd, who in turn gave him to POLYBUS and MEROPE, the king and queen of CORINTH. Having no children of their own, they raised Oedipus.

When Oedipus grew up, he was taunted by a drunken companion, who suggested that Polybus and Merope were not really his parents. Oedipus questioned his foster parents about the truth of this taunt and was told that he was their child. Unconvinced, Oedipus left home to consult the DELPHIC ORACLE. The oracle told Oedipus that he would kill his father and marry his mother. Wishing to avoid this horrific fate, Oedipus decided never to return to Corinth. As he traveled south from Delphi, he almost literally ran into his real father, Laius. At a narrow place in the road, Laius and his attendants had a traffic altercation with Oedipus. When Laius struck Oedipus, the young man retaliated, killing not only Laius, but almost all of his party (except one person).

Oedipus, not realizing he had killed his father, continued on to Thebes, where he became an instant hero by solving the riddle of the SPHINX, the monster who had been tormenting the Thebans. The Sphinx killed itself once its riddle was solved. The acting king of Thebes, CREON, had decreed that anyone who could solve this riddle would become king and marry Jocasta, whose husband, Laius, had recently died. Thus, Oedipus became king and married his mother, though neither knew the truth. The initial years of Oedipus' kingship and marriage seem to have been trouble-free. He and Jocasta had four children—ETEOCLES, POLYNEICES, ANTIGONE, and ISMENE.

Eventually Oedipus' happiness was shattered when a plague ravaged the Thebans. Oedipus sent Creon to consult the Delphic oracle and learned that the crisis could be resolved by driving out the killer of Laius, who the oracle declared was among the Thebans. Oedipus, determined to save his people from the plague, called upon the prophet TIRESIAS to reveal Laius' killer; unfortunately for Oedipus, Tiresias declared that he was Laius' killer. Oedipus, thinking that Tiresias and Creon were plotting to overthrow him, accused them of being in league with one another. That same day, a messenger arrived from Corinth and informed Oedipus that Polybus had died. For a moment, Oedipus believed that he had avoided Delphi's prophecy. Oedipus' relief was short-lived,

however, as the aged shepherd who had given him to the Corinthian herdsman was taken to the palace.

Oedipus appears as a character in several extant dramas: EURIPIDES' *PHOENICIAN WOMEN*, SOPHOCLES' *OEDIPUS TYRANNOS* and *OEDIPUS AT COLONUS*, and SENECA'S *OEDIPUS*. In *Phoenician Women*, Oedipus' blinding has already taken place and he appears at the end of the play, after the death of his sons, and goes into exile. Sophocles' *Oedipus Tyrannos* and Seneca's *Oedipus* both treat Oedipus' discovery that he has had sexual relations with his mother and his blinding of himself. *Oedipus at Colonus* deals with the arrival in Athenian territory of the blind and exiled Oedipus, the struggle between Polyneices and Eteocles to acquire Oedipus' favor so that they can be victorious in war over one another, Oedipus' rejection of his sons, and his eventual disappearance from the Earth. AESCHYLUS wrote an *Oedipus*, which was the second play of the tetralogy that included *Laius*, *Seven against Thebes*, and *Sphinx*. Aeschylus' *Oedipus* may have been about roughly the same events as Sophocles' *Oedipus the King*—Oedipus' discovery that he had killed his father, Laius. [ANCIENT SOURCES: Aeschylus, *Seven against Thebes* 742–1084; Apollodorus, *Library* 3.5.7–9; Homer, *Odyssey* 11.271–80; Hyginus, *Fables* 66–67; Pindar, *Olympian Odes* 38–42]

OEDIPUS SENECA (WRITTEN BETWEEN 49 AND 65 C.E.?)

The play follows the same story as SOPHOCLES' *OEDIPUS TYRANNOS*, but SENECA introduces several innovations before the final outcome is reached. The setting is THEBES at the palace of OEDIPUS and JOCASTA. The action of the play begins at dawn near an altar, as King Oedipus recalls APOLLO's prophecy that he would kill his father and marry his mother. Oedipus has difficulties that are more pressing at present, however, as he relates that his people are suffering through a terrible plague. Oedipus prays that he will not outlive all his citizens. Oedipus' wife, Jocasta, urges him not to make the situation worse by lamentation, but to face the crisis boldly. Oedipus, recalling his defeat of the SPHINX, declares that he never has and never will act as a coward does. He predicts that only Apollo can deliver them from the current trouble. Next, the chorus sing an ode in which they lament the destruction of the noble citizens of Thebes. They describe the stages by which the plague attacked the town, the symptoms of those who have the disease, and the prayers of those who long for death.

The play's second act opens with the arrival of CREON from DELPHI. As in SOPHOCLES' play, Creon tells Oedipus that Apollo's oracle has declared that to save the city from the plague they must expel the murderer of LAIUS, the previous king, because the killer (Oedipus) remains within the city limits and is causing pollution of the city. Oedipus declares that he is prepared to carry out what Apollo's oracle has commanded and puts a curse on Laius' killer (thus, unwittingly cursing himself). When Oedipus asks Creon to explain how Laius was killed, Creon does so. Before Oedipus can react to this story, the blind prophet TIRESIAS, accompanied by his daughter, MANTO (also a prophet), enters. Unlike in Sophocles' play, Tiresias states that to discover the killer of Laius, they must sacrifice a snow-white bull that has never been yoked and examine the heifer entrails. After the sacrifice of the heifer, Manto describes to her father the animal's entrails. In a lengthy description, Manto relates in gruesome detail the bull's internal organs, including the presence of a fetus in the womb of the animal, which was supposed to be a virgin. Despite this drawn-out ritual, Tiresias is unable to tell Oedipus who was Laius' killer. Accordingly, Tiresias declares that they must now raise the spirit of Laius from the UNDERWORLD so that he himself can name his killer. Because Tiresias says the king must not gaze on the dead, Oedipus sends Creon with Tiresias. After their departure, the chorus sing to Bacchus (Greek: DIONYSUS) a hymn, in which they summon him to Thebes. They also recall his birth, persecution by Juno (Greek: HERA), travels throughout the world, triumph over those who opposed him, and eventual marriage to ARIADNE.

In the play's third act, Creon returns from consulting the spirit of Laius. Creon describes in great detail the ritual that Tiresias performed to conjure up Laius, who named Oedipus as his killer, stated that Oedipus had married his own mother, and declared that Oedipus must be driven from Thebes and that his exile would be a miserable one. Oedipus, of course, is shocked by this revelation but continues to believe that

his parents are Polybus and Merope of CORINTH. Furthermore, Oedipus believes that Tiresias and Creon have conspired to make up this story so that Creon can become king. Creon denies this, and urges Oedipus to give up the kingship and go into exile. Oedipus refuses, however, and, despite Creon's claims of innocence, Oedipus has Creon arrested and imprisoned. After the exit of Oedipus and Creon, the chorus sing an ode in which they blame Oedipus' troubles on the gods' anger against Oedipus' family, an anger that the chorus trace to CADMUS' killing of the serpent of Mars (Greek: ARES). They also mention the destruction of Cadmus' grandson, ACTAEON, by the goddess Diana (Greek: ARTEMIS).

The drama's fourth act opens with a speech by Oedipus (who is joined on stage by Jocasta), in which he recalls killing a man at a crossroads between Delphi and Thebes. When Jocasta tells Oedipus the details of Laius' death, Oedipus begins to suspect that he may have been Laius' killer. Oedipus soon gains further information about his past when an old man from Corinth arrives and informs him that Polybus, who Oedipus thinks is his father, has died. The old man informs Oedipus that Polybus' wife, Merope, who Oedipus thinks is his mother, was not, in fact, his mother. The old man goes on to reveal that he himself had given the infant Oedipus to Polybus and Merope after he had received Oedipus from a Theban shepherd. As the old man tries to recall the shepherd's name, the person in question, Phorbas, enters. The old man questions Phorbas about his past, and Phorbas admits that he gave an infant to the old man. Phorbas also notes that an iron bolt pinned together the infant's feet. When Oedipus demands to know who the child's mother was, Phorbas does not want to answer. After Oedipus threatens him with torture, Phorbas reveals that Jocasta was the child's mother. On hearing this, Oedipus is horrified and realizes that he killed his father, Laius, and married his mother, Jocasta. Then, Oedipus and Jocasta exit into the palace.

In the final act, a messenger enters and describes to the chorus Oedipus' blinding of himself by tearing out his eyes with his bare hands (unlike Sophocles' method of blinding, in which he plunged Jocasta's brooches into his eyes). After the chorus lament that unalterable Fate has caused events, a blinded and bloody Oedipus emerges from the palace. In contrast to Sophocles' play, in which Jocasta commits suicide before Oedipus' blinding, Seneca's reverses the order of events. In Seneca's play, Jocasta now enters from the palace and addresses Oedipus but does not know whether she should call him her son. Oedipus, however, does not want to respond to her and suggests that never again should they have contact. Soon, Jocasta takes up a sword, the same one that killed her husband, Laius, and stabs herself in the womb. After Jocasta's suicide, Oedipus laments that he has been the cause of one more death than Fate had decreed. The play ends with the departure of Oedipus into exile.

COMMENTARY

Although readers of Seneca's play will note comparisons and contrasts with Sophocles' *Oedipus Tyrannos,* one should also keep in mind the political context in which Seneca's *Oedipus* was composed: NERO's rule at Rome. Thus, a Roman who encountered Seneca's *Oedipus* would be tempted to make connections between Laius and Nero's predecessor, CLAUDIUS, whose murder is usually ascribed to Nero's mother, AGRIPPINA. Thus, Seneca would also have linked Oedipus and Nero, who committed horrific atrocities such as having his mother murdered (59 C.E.).

In addition to the fascinating political background against which Seneca's play is set, Seneca's *Oedipus* provides a dramatic examination of the effects of fear on a person. As a Stoic, Seneca believed that emotions such as fear would impede a person's ability to be truly happy. For the Stoics, true happiness involved embracing one's fate and living one's life in acceptance of and in harmony with fate. Most people, however, would not be aware of their fate, and, even if they were to possess such awareness, few would have a fate as horrific as that of Oedipus.

Oedipus, however, is aware of his fate and tries to escape it. Leaving the kingdom of the man he thought was his father allowed him to leave behind his cares (*curis,* 13), because Oedipus feared (*timeo,* 15; *timor,* 22) that he would kill Polybus. Upon arriving in Thebes, Oedipus displayed his courage and lack of fear by facing the deadly Sphinx and solving its riddle.

These actions won Oedipus the kingship of Thebes, but after becoming king, Oedipus has different concerns, because his city suffers from a terrible plague. Jocasta, sounding as if she is a Stoic, advises him to be brave and not to run away from Fortune (86). Oedipus declares that his valor (*virtus,* 88) knows no fear, as his battle with the Sphinx proved. Still, Oedipus, speaking to himself, seems to long for death.

When Creon returns from Delphi, Oedipus expresses fear (*horrore . . . timens* 206) about what Creon will say and where fate will turn next. His unsure spirit longs to know, despite his fears (*timet,* 209). When Creon explains that Laius' killer must be expelled so that the plague will end, Creon suggests that their fear of the Sphinx prevented them from searching for Laius' killer earlier (245–46). Oedipus, behaving now as a fearless leader, declares that he will drive out Laius' killer.

After Tiresias and Manto perform their examination of the entrails, Oedipus still sounds confident as he declares that he will listen to their interpretation of the ritual without fear (*non timida,* 385). This ritual has failed, however, and Oedipus quickly and decisively orders Creon to carry out the ritual that will raise Laius' spirit. Upon Creon's return, Oedipus orders him to speak what fear (*metus,* 511) would prefer to remain silent. Compelled by Oedipus, Creon explains the terrifying ritual, which frightened both Creon and Manto, although Tiresias was unafraid (*intrepidus,* 596) because he could not see the horrific beings who were being conjured up (such as Horror, 591, and Fear, 594).

Oedipus had been confident before the ritual; the declaration from his father's ghost now causes him to fear (660) that he had done that which he was accused of doing. All the same, Oedipus then tries to shift the blame for Laius' death to Tiresias and Creon. Upon hearing this accusation, Creon protests that he is innocent, but Oedipus retorts that kings usually fear doubtful things as certain (700). Creon responds that a person who trembles over empty fears deserves real fears (700–1), and Oedipus argues that fear keeps kingdoms intact (704). Creon observes that when a tyrannical king fears his subjects (who fear him), then eventually the fear rebounds on the king. Oedipus' fears of conspiracy prevail, however, and he has Creon arrested.

As with Oedipus' previous appearance, when he next emerges from the palace he notes that his fears have been renewed (764). When he asks Jocasta to explain the circumstances surrounding Laius' death, he seems to recognize that the oracle has been fulfilled (782). The arrival of the old Corinthian, however, initially allays Oedipus' fears. Polybus' kingdom will dispel his fears (793), the old man suggests. Oedipus explains that despite Polybus' death, he still fears marriage to his mother (791–92, 794). The old man again tries to allay Oedipus' fears by informing him that Merope was not his mother (801). Once the old man explains how he knows this, Oedipus orders the Theban shepherd summoned to the palace. The old man, who sounds as if he is a Stoic, urges Oedipus to let the Fates unfold themselves (832), but Oedipus is determined to discover the truth.

After Oedipus learns the truth, his mind turns to thoughts of suicide, a form of death permissible for a Stoic in extreme circumstances. Fear, it seems, turns Oedipus from this course of action (933) and he decides to blind himself. Upon hearing of Oedipus' blinding, the chorus remark that fear itself causes harm for many people and that many have met their fate while fearing it (992–94). The suicide of Jocasta compounds Oedipus' misery. Because he blames himself for her death, he observes that he is now more guilty than he feared (1044), because he has, in essence, killed both of his parents.

Thus, Oedipus, by discovering his worst fears, has relieved his fellow Thebans of their fears, as his exile will mark the end of the plague. Oedipus departs as Tiresias enters, with a step that is slow and unsteady (289, 1047). Tiresias enters and departs with his daughter, Manto, as his companion (290); Oedipus will leave with violent Fates, Disease, Pestilence, Grief, and Wasting as his companions (1059–61). Now, both men are blind. Earlier in the play, Tiresias' blindness seems to have prevented him from being subject to the fear that gripped Manto and Creon. Henceforth, we might expect Oedipus to be fearless as well. After all, what more has he to fear?

BIBLIOGRAPHY

Bishop, J. D. "Seneca's *Oedipus*: Opposition Literature," *Classical Journal* 73 (1978): 289–301.

Konstan, D. "Oedipus and his Parents: The Biological Family from Sophocles to Dryden," *Scholia* 3 (1994): 3–23.

Mastronarde, D. J. "Seneca's *Oedipus*: The Drama in the Word," *Transactions of the American Philological Association* 101 (1970): 291–315.

Poe, J. P. "The Sinful Nature of the Protagonist of Seneca's *Oedipus*," *Ramus* 12 (1983): 140–58.

Tochterle, K. *Lucius Annaeus Seneca, Oedipus: Kommentar mit Einleitung, Text und Übersetzung.* Heidelberg: Universitatsverlag C. Winter, 1994.

OEDIPUS AT COLONUS SOPHOCLES (401 B.C.E.)

SOPHOCLES wrote this play, first produced by his son five years after his father's death. The drama's setting is COLONUS, just north of ATHENS, where Sophocles himself was born. The play's PROLOGUE opens with the arrival of the blind OEDIPUS, dressed in rags, and his daughter, ANTIGONE, who serves as his guide. After Oedipus sits down and wonders where they are, a citizen from Colonus approaches and tells Oedipus that he must not sit on ground sacred to the Eumenides (see FURIES). When Oedipus hears this, he declares himself a suppliant of these goddesses. Oedipus soon learns from the man that he is in Colonus and that the king in the region is THESEUS. Hearing this, Oedipus asks the man to summon the king to him. After the citizen departs, Oedipus prays to the Eumenides and declares that once APOLLO told him that after he had wandered many years the Eumenides would eventually give him rest and that the land in which he stopped would be blessed by his presence, and the land that rejected Oedipus would be cursed.

After Oedipus' prayer, the chorus, composed of old men from Colonus, enter in search of Oedipus. The chorus tell him that no one will drive him from his place of refuge against his will, but when they learn that he is Oedipus, they order him to leave their territory. Antigone pleads with the chorus, but they repeat that must Oedipus leave. Oedipus questions the reputation that their land has for hospitality to strangers and begs them to grant him a place of refuge. The chorus, however, state that they will defer to their king, whom a messenger has gone to seek.

As Oedipus anticipates the arrival of Theseus, his daughter ISMENE arrives from THEBES. She informs them that Oedipus' sons, ETEOCLES and POLYNEICES, whom Oedipus had cursed to be fated to destroy each other, have quarreled over the kingdom. Eteocles has driven Polyneices from Thebes; Polyneices has gone to ARGOS, has acquired allies there, and will march on Thebes to reclaim the throne. Ismene also reports that she has heard an oracle that Thebes will want to have Oedipus (whether dead or alive) returned to them because the power of Thebes will fall to whomever Oedipus supports. Ismene also informs Oedipus that CREON is now approaching to see him and to take him back to Theban territory—the Thebans will be blessed if Oedipus is buried near Thebes, but cursed if he is not. Ismene also says the oracle has indicated that someday the Thebans will be defeated in a battle near Oedipus' grave when they invade Athenian territory. When Ismene reports that both Eteocles and Polyneices are aware of these prophecies, Oedipus is outraged that his sons now want him back only to achieve their goal of kingship, yet they did nothing to help him when he was exiled from Thebes. Oedipus praises his daughters for their help and declares that he has no intention of returning to Thebes.

The chorus, upon hearing these things, now take pity on Oedipus and indicate that they will try to help him. They tell him that first he must perform a ceremony of atonement to the Eumenides for profaning their sacred grove and pray for their aid. Because of Oedipus' blindness, he cannot carry out all of their instructions, so he sends Ismene to attend to the ritual. After Ismene departs, the chorus ask Oedipus to recall the misfortunes that he has suffered. After Oedipus' recollection of incest with his mother and his killing of his father, King Theseus enters. Oedipus informs Theseus that his land will be blessed if they bury Oedipus there and that the Thebans will encounter destruction in Theseus' territory if they do not take Oedipus back to Thebes. After Theseus pledges to help Oedipus, he exits to make a sacrifice to POSEIDON. The chorus then sing an ode in which they praise the land to which Oedipus has travelled for refuge. They praise its beauty, its close association with the gods, the valiant men who are nurtured there, the benefits of ATHENA's olive tree, the might of the horse and sea that Poseidon has granted them.

After the choral ode, Creon enters and begs Oedipus to return with him to Thebes. Oedipus, of course, refuses and declares that his spirit will haunt the Thebans. Oedipus orders Creon to leave, but Creon informs Oedipus that his men have seized Ismene and are preparing to seize Antigone. As the Thebans drag away Antigone, Oedipus calls for help. Soon, Theseus returns and sends out some of his men to rescue Ismene and Antigone. Creon, however, declares that he was just in his actions. Creon expresses his surprise that Theseus' people would harbor a man who has committed incest and killed his father. Oedipus defends himself by stating that he did these acts unwittingly and suggests that if Creon had been assaulted by someone as he was, Creon would have killed his father as well. After this debate, Theseus urges that they set out in search of Oedipus' daughters and asks Creon to help show him the way.

After the departure of Creon and Theseus, the chorus sing an ode in which they anticipate the fight between Theseus and those who took hostage Oedipus' daughters. They boast of the fearsome nature of their warriors and of Theseus but worry that Oedipus' daughters may suffer something awful. No sooner have they prayed to the gods that matters will turn out well than Theseus returns with Antigone and Ismene. After the joyful reunion of the father and his daughters, Oedipus thanks Theseus for his help. Theseus also informs Oedipus that one of his relatives is now in the region and wants to speak with him. From Theseus' description of the man, Oedipus realizes that it is Polyneices. Oedipus does not want to speak with him, but Antigone urges her father to listen to Polyneices. Oedipus yields to Antigone's wishes and Theseus departs (apparently to inform Polyneices that Oedipus will speak with him).

After Theseus' exit, the chorus sing an ode about the inevitability of death and the hardship of the life of human beings, especially Oedipus. The choral ode is followed by the arrival of Polyneices, who describes to Oedipus how Eteocles drove him from Thebes, and how he traveled to Argos, married Adrastus' daughter, and enlisted the Argives' help in making a march on Thebes. Polyneices begs Oedipus for help because, as he tells his father, he has heard an oracle that victory will go to the side that has Oedipus as an ally. Furthermore, Polyneices promises to reinstate Oedipus at

Thebes if he is victorious. Oedipus rejects his son's plea and criticizes him for not helping him long ago. He declares that Eteocles and Polyneices are not his sons, and that Antigone and Ismene treat him as sons should. Additionally, Oedipus restates his curse that the brothers will kill each other in battle.

Hearing his father's harsh words, Polyneices departs in despair. He begs his sisters that if he falls in battle, they make sure he receives a proper burial. Antigone begs Polyneices not to lead his army against Thebes; Polyneices, however, does not want to continue living in exile and being mocked by his younger brother.

After Polyneices' exit, the chorus hear thunder, which signals to Oedipus that his life will soon end. As the thunder continues, Oedipus sends Antigone to summon Theseus. Upon Theseus' arrival, Oedipus informs him that his (Oedipus') death is approaching and proceeds to explain the blessings that he will confer Theseus' people. Oedipus tells Theseus, however, that what he tells him must remain a secret. After this, Oedipus, Theseus, and Oedipus' daughters depart. The chorus then pray that the powers of the underworld will be kind to Oedipus.

After the chorus' prayer, a messenger enters and informs the chorus that Oedipus, accompanied by his daughters, went to a certain rocky place, performed a ritual bathing, and bade farewell to his daughters. After his daughters mourned for him, a mysterious voice called Oedipus to hurry to meet the end of his life. Hearing this, Oedipus called for Theseus and made him promise to protect his daughters. Oedipus then sent his daughters out and allowed only Theseus to remain. The messenger helped escort Oedipus' daughters away, but when he looked back, he saw only Theseus, who was shading his eyes from something he had seen.

After the messenger's speech, Antigone and Ismene enter. Antigone expresses astonishment at her father's vanishing and Ismene wonders what fate has in store for her. Antigone then wants to go to the place where her father vanished and to die there herself, but Ismene dissuades her. As Antigone wonders where they will go next, Theseus enters. Antigone asks to see her father's tomb; Theseus tells her that Oedipus, before he died, commanded him not to allow anyone to approach his

tomb. The play ends with Antigone's acceding to his refusal and stating her intention to return to Thebes and deal with the strife between her brothers.

COMMENTARY

The staging of the play presents few difficulties. Oedipus spends most of the drama at or near the altar in the center of the orchestra to which the chorus direct him at 194–95 (they call it a block of natural stone). The door of the stage building would probably serve as the entrance to the grove. As for the thunder and lightning that accompany Oedipus' disappearance at the play's conclusion, Pollux, writing 600 years after *Oedipus at Colonus,* thought the Greeks of Sophocles' day had machines to create these effects, but modern scholars doubt the existence of such devices in Sophocles' day. Such effects, however, could have been created offstage by striking a blunt instrument on a metal surface. How three actors could have performed the play is difficult to imagine. For example, at lines 322–26, Antigone, Ismene, and Oedipus appear to be on stage together. At the end of the play, Antigone, Ismene, and Theseus seem to be on stage. At lines 1252–83, Antigone, Oedipus, and Theseus appear together. Obviously, the same actor could not have played the parts of Oedipus and Theseus; nor could the same actor play Antigone and Ismene. It appears that a fourth actor was needed for this play.

As can most other surviving Sophoclean plays, *Oedipus at Colonus* can be studied with Blundell's "helping friends and harming enemies" method. After Oedipus' exile from Thebes, most of his loved ones (*philoi*), with the exception of his daughters, treat him as an enemy. After Oedipus' sons, desirous of kingship, discover that they need Oedipus' help to gain mastery over Thebes, they try to reestablish their bond of friendship (*philia*) with him. In this sense, *Oedipus at Colonus* recalls Sophocles' *Philoctetes,* produced in 409, but written within about five years of the *Oedipus at Colonus.* In both plays, friends turned enemies try to reestablish their bond of *philia* with an exiled person for the purpose of gaining victory in war. In Philoctetes' case, however, he will eventually leave his place of exile and help the Greeks who exiled him win the Trojan War. Oedipus, however, will not return to help either of his sons. Oedipus establishes a bond of friendship not with his son, but with the stranger Theseus, and the stranger and his land will receive Oedipus' blessing.

Another major focal point of *Oedipus at Colonus* is the city: In *Oedipus Tyrannos,* Oedipus discovers that to save his city he has to leave it; In *Oedipus at Colonus,* Oedipus learns that to save himself he must find a new city. Unfortunately, because of Oedipus' past, no city in Greece will grant him asylum. Oedipus is a man without a city, as he himself states at line 207. The oracle that declares that victory for the brothers depends on Oedipus causes this man without a city suddenly to be courted by representatives from the city that drove him out. One representative defends the city, the other attacks the city, and victory will go to the side that gains the favor of the man without a city. Oedipus will side with neither of his sons and adopts a new city, Athens. The city that in drama had granted asylum to the child killer MEDEA in EURIPIDES' *MEDEA* and the child killer HERACLES in Euripides' *HERACLES,* will now become the final resting place for the man who killed his father and married his mother.

In Oedipus' search for a city that will grant him a place to rest, he moves from space that is uncivilized to space that is civilized, as Segal describes it. One facet of civilized society is ability to communicate with one's fellow human beings, and Segal shows that *logos,* speech, is one of the major concerns in the play. Oedipus' crimes, however, make him reluctant to speak. When confronted by the chorus about his identity, Oedipus does not want to reveal it. After he does speak, the men are horrified and demand that he leave. The desperate pleas of Antigone and Oedipus, however, move the chorus to pity, and they refer the matter to their king.

As Oedipus' words to the chorus reveal his horrific identity, his words on the arrival of Ismene show the love of this old blind man for his daughter. The daughter Ismene's words, however, inform Oedipus of the quarrel between his sons and the words of the gods regarding Oedipus, whose eagerness to hear Ismene reveal the oracle recalls the eagerness with which the chorus wanted to know Oedipus' identity. The assistance that Ismene's words give Oedipus contrasts with

the failure of speech of Oedipus' sons. After his fall from power, they did nothing in word or deed to help him. Although Oedipus had no political power, he did retain the power of speech, and with his curse he doomed the brothers to destroy one another.

The chorus, upon hearing the exchange between Oedipus and Ismene, is further moved to pity and now move to integrate him in their society. They explain the ritual he must perform for the Eumenides and detail the words that he must speak in prayer to them. Oedipus is delighted to hear these words, but when preparations for this ritual are being made, the chorus compel Oedipus to recount the horrors of his life.

The arrival of Theseus ends Oedipus' painful speech and the fact that Theseus himself was an exile once creates a bond between the two men. Accordingly, Oedipus feels he needs to offer little explanation and quickly explains what he wants from Theseus. Theseus' words in response prompt Oedipus to declare that he has no need for Theseus to take an oath to support his promise (650) and Theseus indicates that an oath would carry no less force than his word (651).

Theseus' word is put to the test when Creon arrives. Theseus' revelation that he, like Oedipus, was an exile created a bond between the two men. Creon tries to establish a bond between with Oedipus by noting that he (like Oedipus) is an old man, that he is related to Oedipus, and that he pities Oedipus (732–47). Creon declares that he was sent to persuade Oedipus to return to Thebes (736). Creon's rhetorical strategy fails, however, and Oedipus sees the hard thoughts that Creon has wrapped in soft words (774). Creon's hypocrisy is revealed when he exchanges soft words for harsh actions as he takes Ismene and Antigone hostage. Fortunately, Theseus is true to his word and Creon has failed in his mission.

Although the aged Creon's words fail to move Oedipus, the young Polyneices' words repel Oedipus. Even before Polyneices meets his father, Oedipus does not want to hear what his son will say (1173–74). Antigones' words, however, persuade Oedipus to listen to what Polyneices has to say. As is Oedipus (and as was Theseus at one point in his life), Polyneices points out that he is an exile. This attempt to create a bond with Oedipus does not succeed as it had in Theseus' case.

Initially, Oedipus remains silent and turns away from his son despite the young man's pleas to say something (1271–72). Antigone, however, urges Polyneices to explain his sufferings. Polyneices' detailed remarks on his quarrel with his brother do not move Oedipus, who reiterates his earlier curse. These are the last words from Oedipus that his son will ever hear and words that Polyneices will not dare to repeat to his Argive allies, lest they turn back from their march upon Thebes (1402–4).

Unmoved by the deceptive words of aged Creon and the pitiful words of young Polyneices, Oedipus at the play's end responds to divine sounds from the skies. The gods themselves are calling to him (1511), Oedipus tells Theseus. Unlike Creon and Polyneices, who were unable to persuade Oedipus, Oedipus persuades Theseus and Theseus urges him to speak (1516–17). Oedipus does speak, telling Theseus things that must remain unspoken afterward. Oedipus will not even allow Ismene or Antigone to know the mysteries that he would reveal to Theseus. In Oedipus' farewell to his daughters, he does, however, speak one word to them that will wipe away all the sufferings that they have experienced: *love* (1617). After expressing his love for his daughters, Oedipus again responds to a mysterious divine sound. This time, Oedipus does not need to interpret the sound of thunder, for the voice is intelligible to all. Oedipus sends his daughters away, and his final moments are spent in prayer in the presence of Theseus, the last person to hear Oedipus' words. Antigone wants to see her father's tomb, but Theseus honors the words of his pledge to her father and does not allow her to see it. Oedipus, the man who had committed unspeakable acts of horror, leaves the world after instructing Theseus with words that must not be spoken.

Oedipus at Colonus holds a special place in the history of classical drama, because it is the last surviving play written by one of the three great Athenian tragedians (AESCHYLUS, Sophocles, and EURIPIDES). As was the aged Oedipus, Sophocles himself was an old man (more than 80 years of age) when he wrote *Oedipus at Colonus*. As had Oedipus and Sophocles, Athens itself had undergone many trials and tribulations during the previous 80 years. As Oedipus had defeated the SPHINX, Athens had been instrumental in repelling the Persian invasions during the first quarter of the century. As had Oedipus, Sophocles and his fellow Athenians had survived a plague that ravaged their town. They had witnessed war, exile, and political upheaval. Sophocles died before Athens finally surrendered to Sparta in 404. As Oedipus would not have to witness the suffering of his daughter, Antigone, after the death of Polyneices, Sophocles would not have to witness the fall of his beloved city.

BIBLIOGRAPHY

Bernidaki-Aldous, E. A. *Blindness in a Culture of Light: Especially the Case of Oedipus at Colonus of Sophocles.* New York: Lang, 1990.

Blundell, M. W. *Helping Friends and Harming Enemies: A Study in Sophocles and Greek Ethics.* Cambridge: Cambridge University Press, 1989, 226–59.

Edmunds, L. *Theatrical Space and Historical Place in Sophocles' Oedipus at Colonus.* Lanham, Md.: Rowman & Littlefield, 1996.

Minadeo, R. "The Thematic Design of the *Oedipus at Colonus,*" *Studi Italiani di Filologia Classica* 8 (1990): 60–85.

Segal, C. *Tragedy and Civilization: An Interpretation of Sophocles.* Cambridge, Mass.: Harvard University Press, 1981, 362–408.

Travis, R. M. *Allegory and the Tragic Chorus in Sophocles' Oedipus at Colonus.* Lanham, Md.: Rowman & Littlefield, 1999.

OEDIPUS TYRANNOS SOPHOCLES (CA. 430–425 B.C.E.)

The date of the play is not certain but is thought to be between the years 430 and 425 B.C.E. the plague that affects THEBES in SOPHOCLES' play is often thought to be the plague in ATHENS that occurred soon after the beginning of the PELOPONNESIAN WAR in 431. Sophocles' play is set at Thebes at the palace of OEDIPUS and JOCASTA. As the play opens, Oedipus hears the pleas about the plague of the Theban elders, who compose the chorus. Oedipus promises to do everything he can to help his people and notes that he has sent his brother-in-law, Creon, to the Delphic oracle to learn how to remedy the plague.

Soon CREON returns from Delphi and informs Oedipus that Thebes suffers from the plague because the killer of their previous king, Laius, remains within the town's borders. The plague can only be remedied if

Laius' killer is driven from the town. Oedipus promises to do all in his power to discover Laius' killer. After Creon and Oedipus exit to begin the investigation, the chorus sing an ode in which they pray to the gods for guidance in their present crisis.

After the choral ode, Oedipus returns and calls upon the people of Thebes to reveal any information they have about Laius' killer. He even invokes a curse against the murderer (that the killer will live out his life in misery and suffer a miserable doom). The chorus swear that they have no information about Laius' killer and that they did not kill the king. They urge Laius to summon the prophet TIRESIAS for consultation. Oedipus has anticipated this and soon Tiresias arrives. Oedipus asks Tiresias for help in the present crisis, but Tiresias, who knows that Oedipus killed Laius, does not want to reveal what he knows. Oedipus, angered by Tiresias' reluctance, eventually prods him to make a statement. When Oedipus hears himself accused as Laius' killer, he is outraged and accuses Tiresias and Creon of plotting against him. An angry Tiresias also declares that Oedipus has married his mother and predicts that he will become a blind and miserable exile. After this, both Oedipus and Tiresias exit. Next, the chorus sing an ode in which they wonder who has killed Laius. They wonder at Tiresias' words and state that they cannot deny or approve of what he said. As their ode concludes, they remain faithful to Oedipus and demand solid proof if they are to believe the charges leveled against their king.

After the choral ode, Creon enters in response to Oedipus' accusation. Oedipus soon enters and repeats his charge against Creon, who tries to defend himself. Eventually, Jocasta emerges from the palace and chastises both men for airing their private griefs while the city is in crisis. Creon takes an oath and even curses himself if he is guilty of Oedipus' accusation. Both Jocasta and the chorus urge Oedipus to accept Creon's oath and he does so reluctantly.

After Creon exits, Jocasta remains with Oedipus and questions him about why he was so angry. Oedipus relates to her Tiresias' declaration that he killed Laius. Jocasta recalls a prophecy that Laius would be killed by his son but says Laius died at the hands of foreign robbers at a place where three roads meet and that he gave

his son to others to leave on a hillside to die. Accordingly, Jocasta tells Oedipus that he should pay no attention to such oracles because they have turned out to be false. When Oedipus hears Jocasta mention the crossroads, however, and describe Laius' appearance, he begins to suspect that he has unwittingly cursed himself. When Oedipus asked whether any of Laius' traveling companions survived the assault, Jocasta says that one man did. Oedipus desires to interrogate this man, and Jocasta says that he can be recalled.

When Jocasta probes Oedipus further about what is troubling him, Oedipus recalls growing up in Corinth at the home of their king and queen, Polybus and Merope. Once, during a dinner, a drunken fellow suggested to Oedipus that he was not the child of Polybus and Merope. When the king and queen denied such a charge, Oedipus went to DELPHI to consult the oracle. The oracle told Oedipus that he would have sexual relations with his mother and kill his father. To avoid this oracle, Oedipus decided to leave Corinth. As he traveled, Oedipus recalls, he arrived at a place where three roads meet and had a violent encounter with an old man and his traveling party. Oedipus states that he killed the old man and those with him and wonders fearfully whether he could have killed Laius and then married his widow. The chorus urge Oedipus to wait until he has heard from the slave before he reaches any final conclusions. Oedipus agrees and declares that he wants to question the man. Jocasta mentioned that several men attacked Laius, and Oedipus wants to verify the accuracy of this report. Jocasta confidently declares the truth of the servant's story and says she will send for the man.

After Oedipus and Jocasta depart, the chorus pray that they will always live in accordance with the laws of the gods; insolent people eventually are ruined. The chorus hope that those who are impious and prosper unjustly receive a terrible doom. Finally, however, the chorus express some doubt about the oracles concerning Laius.

After the choral ode, Jocasta, concerned for Oedipus, enters with an offering for the gods, especially APOLLO. As she stands there, a messenger from Corinth enters and informs her that the man Oedipus thinks is his father, Polybus, has died and that the people of Corinth want

Oedipus to be their king. When Oedipus is informed of this, he is initially relieved and scoffs at the validity of the oracles concerning him. Oedipus also tells the messenger that he fears a prophecy concerning the woman he believes is his mother, Merope of Corinth. The messenger then informs Oedipus that Polybus was not Oedipus' father and that he, the messenger, gave Oedipus to Polybus when Oedipus was a small child. The messenger states that once he was a shepherd in Polybus' service and that he received Oedipus from another shepherd who served Laius. When Oedipus asks whether anyone knows the shepherd in question, the chorus suggest that he may be the same servant whom Oedipus summoned earlier. Jocasta, on being questioned about this, begs Oedipus not to investigate the matter further. Hearing that Oedipus is determined to continue to investigate, Jocasta exits into the palace. The chorus worry that Jocasta's departure heralds some trouble, but Oedipus is determined to learn the secret of his birth. In Oedipus' presence, the chorus then sing a brief ode in which they wonder who Oedipus' parents were.

After the choral ode, the aged herdsman, earlier summoned by Oedipus, arrives. Both the messenger and the chorus confirm that this is the man for whom Oedipus was looking. After considerable prodding and even threats of physical violence, Oedipus compels the herdsman to reveal that he received a child from Jocasta with instructions to take him away to die. The herdman also relates that in pity for the child he gave it to another man, the messenger. Hearing this, a horrified Oedipus realizes that Apollo's oracles have been fulfilled and exits into the palace. After Oedipus' departure, the chorus lament Oedipus' fate. They recall his success in solving the SPHINX's riddle and receiving the highest honors in Thebes and note that now none has a worse fate than Oedipus.

As the chorus conclude their lamentation for Oedipus, another messenger arrives from the palace and informs the chorus that Jocasta has hanged herself with a rope in her bedroom. The messenger also reports that an enraged Oedipus had taken up a sword and was threatening to kill Jocasta, but by the time he broke through the doors to her bedroom, Jocasta was already dead. Oedipus then took the golden brooches from Jocasta's gown and plunged them into his eyes.

Soon, the blinded Oedipus appears. A horrified chorus gaze on their fallen king as he gropes to find his way. The chorus and Oedipus lament his fate and express the wish that Oedipus had died in infancy. The chorus state that he would have been better off dead than living and blind, but Oedipus says that when he reached the underworld he would not want to see Laius or Jocasta, so he blinded himself. Because he remains alive, he also does not want to be able to see his children (who are also his brothers and sisters), his city, or the city's people.

As Oedipus begs the chorus to cast him from their land, Creon, who will take Oedipus' place as king, enters and orders a servant to take Oedipus inside the palace so that the Sun will not be defiled by gazing on Oedipus. Oedipus begs Creon to cast him from Thebes and to bury Jocasta; he begs Creon to allow him to be with his daughters for a few moments, and the young women, ANTIGONE and Ismene, soon arrive from the palace and weep over their father. Oedipus expresses sorrow for his daughters because he expects no one will marry them, given their father's crimes. After this, Creon orders Oedipus to let go of his daughters and return the palace. After Creon, Oedipus, and his daughters return to the palace, the chorus call upon the people of Thebes to gaze on Oedipus, who once was looked on with envy and is now looked on with horror.

COMMENTARY

Sophocles' *Oedipus Tyrannos* is probably the most famous classical drama. Some of its fame is due to the opinion of ARISTOTLE in the *Poetics*. This work, written about 100 years after the staging of Sophocles' play, occasionally characterizes the play as a model for the way that a TRAGEDY should be constructed. At 1453b3–7, Aristotle says a play's plot "should be so constructed that even without seeing the play anyone hearing of the incidents happening thrills with fear and pity as a result of what occurs." Aristotle goes on to cite the story of Oedipus as one capable of generating such fear and pity in the audience. A dozen lines later Aristotle praises Sophocles' *Oedipus Tyrannos* as a skillfully constructed play because Oedipus commits his crimes unwittingly and discovers the horrifying truth later. At

1454b6–10, Aristotle says that in constructing a play anything that is inexplicable should remain outside the play, as in *Oedipus Tyrannos*. At 1455a16–18, Aristotle also considers Sophocles' handling of Oedipus' learning of the truth about his crimes the best way to deal with discovery (see ANAGNORISIS).

Aristotle's most controversial remark about Oedipus, however, occurs at *Poetics* 1453a7–12, in which Aristotle says the best sort of tragedy involves a person, such as Oedipus or THYESTES, who falls from good to bad fortune, not because of a vice or wickedness, but because of a major error (*megale hamartia*). Unfortunately, Aristotle does not elaborate on what he means by HAMARTIA, and the problem is made more complex because the play about Thyestes that Aristotle has in mind has not survived. Early critics of Sophocles' play thought that Aristotle's *hamartia* referred to a moral fault (the so-called tragic flaw) in Oedipus, such as his pride, overconfidence, or bad temper. In recent years, however, critics have understood Aristotle's *hamartia* as an error committed in ignorance. From the beginning of the play, Oedipus is a good man in the eyes of the chorus, who regard him as the savior of their city. Thus, Dodds writes, "The *hamartia* of Oedipus did not lie in losing his temper with Tiresias: it lay quite simply in parricide and incest—a *megale hamartia* indeed, the greatest a man can commit."

Sophocles' *Oedipus Tyrannos* has also received considerable attention as a result of SIGMUND FREUD'S interest in the play. In his *Interpretation of Dreams,* Freud wrote that Oedipus' fate captivates the male audience, who secretly feel that Oedipus' fate might have been their own fate, namely, that every man subconsciously desires to take his father's place and have sexual relations with his mother. Freud's theory was prompted by Jocasta' remark to Oedipus at lines 980–82 that he should not worry about marrying his mother because many men, in their dreams, have had sexual relations with their mother. Nothing in Sophocles' play, however, gives any hint that Oedipus wanted to kill his father or marry his mother. The drama gives every indication that Oedipus was trying to avoid these very events.

Modern students of the play have often been taught that Sophocles' play shows the human struggle against fate or destiny, and that Oedipus is merely trapped in the inescapable clutches of his fate. Such interpreters seem to feel that no matter what Oedipus does, he cannot avoid killing his father and marrying his mother. Oedipus is a mere plaything of the gods. Other modern scholars, however, have found this answer unsatisfying and simplistic.

In a famous essay on the play, E. R. Dodds wrote that "what fascinates us [about *Oedipus Tyrannos*] is the spectacle of a man freely choosing, from the highest motives, a series of actions which lead to his own ruin." For Dodds and others, Sophocles' play examines a person who must deal with appearance versus reality, a person who is face to face with the sort of man that God, in this case Apollo, has said he would be. The central question for Sophocles, in this line of interpretation, becomes, What is a man? or How does one define a human being? Oedipus had solved the riddle of the Sphinx with the answer "Man." In Sophocles' play, Oedipus learns that a human being's true definition lies in the divine view of that person, not in his or his peers' definition of him. In the play, the audience view the character of Oedipus from at least three different perspectives: Oedipus' view of himself, his peers' (Creon, Jocasta, and the people of Thebes) view of him, and the divine view of him, as represented by Apollo and Tiresias. For example, Oedipus and his peers think that he was born at Corinth, and the gods know that Oedipus was born at Thebes. At the beginning of the play, Oedipus and his peers do not think that he killed Laius, but the gods know that he did. Oedipus regards himself as the husband of Jocasta, but the gods know that he is also her son. Oedipus believes that he sees himself and his situation clearly, but Tiresias, God's representative, declares that Oedipus does not see the calamity in which he lives.

In the course of the play, Oedipus relentlessly pursues the question of who killed Laius but discovers that the truth of that mystery also contains the truth about who he is in the eyes of God. Throughout the play, people around Oedipus attempt to dissuade him from seeking this truth. First, Tiresias resists Oedipus' probe into the matter of Laius' death. Later in the play, Jocasta begs him not to investigate further the question of his birth (1056–68). Next, the herdsman, interrogated by

Oedipus, begs the king not to ask him more questions about the child that he was given. Despite the warnings, Oedipus continues to seek the truth about questions that people have sought and will always seek: Who am I? Unlike most people, however, Oedipus discovers in his own lifetime the truth about himself in the eyes of God. This is a self that Oedipus cannot bear to see.

BIBLIOGRAPHY

Dawe, R. D. *Oedipus Rex*. Cambridge: Cambridge University Press, 1982.

Dodds, E. R. "On Misunderstanding the *Oedipus Rex*." In *Oxford Readings in Greek Tragedy*. Edited by E. Segal. Oxford: Oxford University Press, 1983, 177–88.

Knox, B. *Oedipus at Thebes: Sophocles' Tragic Hero and His Time*. New Haven, Conn.: Yale University Press, 1957.

Segal, C. *Oedipus Tyrannus: Tragic Heroism and the Limits of Knowledge*. 2d ed. Oxford: Oxford University Press, 2001.

Vernant, J. P. "Ambiguity and Reversal: On the Enigmatic Structure of *Oedipus Rex*." In *Oxford Readings in Greek Tragedy*. Edited by E. Segal. Oxford: Oxford University Press, 1983, 177–88.

OENEUS

OENEUS The son of Porthaon (or Portheus) and Euryte, Oeneus, the husband of ALTHAEA, was the king of CALYDON. By Althaea Oeneus became the father of four sons, Clymenus, Thyreus, Toxeus (whom Oeneus himself killed because he jumped over a certain ditch), and MELEAGER (although some say his father was ARES). Oeneus also had two daughters, Gorge and DEIANEIRA. When Oeneus forgot to sacrifice to ARTEMIS, the angered goddess sent a boar to ravage his land. Oeneus' son Meleager not only killed the boar, but killed his maternal uncles, Toxeus and Plexippus, when they tried to prevent him from awarding the boar's hide to ATALANTA. In retaliation, Meleager's mother, Althaea, killed him and then committed suicide. After Althaea's death, Oeneus married Periboea, and by her he fathered TYDEUS.

Although Oeneus does not appear as a character in any extant dramas, among the Greek dramatists Sophocles may have written an *Oeneus,* but evidence for such a drama is not firm. Euripides staged an *Oeneus* that was produced by 426 B.C.E. at the latest. The tragedian Chaeremon also wrote an *Oeneus,* whose lone surviving fragment (14 Snell) contains a rather erotic description of Oeneus' gazing at some women (perhaps worshipers of Dionysus) who are asleep in the moonlight. [ANCIENT SOURCES: Apollodorus, *Library* 1.8.1; Aristophanes, *Acharnians* 418]

BIBLIOGRAPHY

Snell, B. *Tragicorum Graecorum Fragmenta*. Vol. 1. Göttingen, Ger.: Vandenhoeck & Ruprecht, 1971.

Webster, T. B. L. *The Tragedies of Euripides*. London: Methuen, 1967.

OENOMAUS The son of Alxion (or ARES) and Harpina (or Asterope), Oenomaus, king of PISA, was the husband of Evarete (or Asterope) and the father of Leucippus and HIPPODAMEIA. Oenomaus tried to prevent his daughter from marrying, either because he was in love with her or because a prophecy told him that her husband would kill him. Accordingly, Oenomaus challenged to a chariot race any man who presented himself as a suitor for Hippodameia. Defeating Oenomaus was difficult because Ares had given him a team of divine horses, and because he also made the suitor take Hippodameia in the chariot with him during the race. The penalty for losing to Oenomaus was death. Indeed, Oenomaus killed several suitors and then nailed the heads to his house. Oenomaus' reign of terror ended when PELOPS, with the help of Oenomaus' charioteer, MYRTILUS, defeated him. Oenomaus also died during the race as a result of a fall from the chariot. Sophocles wrote an *Oenomaus* that appears to have treated Oenomaus' chariot race against Pelops. To Euripides an *Oenomaus* is also attributed, but the fragments that survive (571–77 Nauck) provide little information about the plot. The Greek comic poets Antiphanes and Eubulus also wrote plays entitled *Oenomaus* (or *Pelops*); the single brief fragment that survives from each play provides no indication of their content. [ANCIENT SOURCES: Apollodorus, *Epitome* 2.4–7; Hyginus, *Fables* 84]

BIBLIOGRAPHY

Kiso, A. *The Lost Sophocles*. New York: Vantage Press, 1984.

Kock, T. *Comicorum Atticorum Fragmenta*. Vol. 2. Leipzig: Teubner, 1884.

Lloyd-Jones, H. *Sophocles: Fragments*. Cambridge, Mass.: Harvard University Press, 1996.

Radt, S. *Tragicorum Graecorum Fragmenta*. Vol. 4. Göttingen, Ger.: Vandenhoeck & Ruprecht, 1977.
Sutton, D. F. *The Lost Sophocles*. Lanham, Md.: University Press of America, 1984.
Webster, T. B. L. *The Tragedies of Euripides*. London: Methuen, 1967.

OENOPS A Theban, who was the father of HYPERBIUS. [ANCIENT SOURCES: Aeschylus, *Seven against Thebes* 504]

OEONICHUS A musician or poet mentioned by ARISTOPHANES at KNIGHTS 1287. He is otherwise unknown.

OETA A mountain in northeastern Greece, Oeta was the site of HERACLES' death. [ANCIENT SOURCES: Seneca, *Hercules Oetaeus*; Sophocles, *Trachinian Women*]

OGYGIAN According to legend, the founder of THEBES was named Ogyges, and so the Thebans are sometimes called Ogygians. DIONYSUS, whose mother, SEMELE, was from Thebes, is also sometimes called Ogygian. [ANCIENT SOURCES: Seneca, *Oedipus* 437, 589]

OILEUS The father of AJAX, who committed suicide during the Trojan War. At *MEDEA* 662, SENECA uses the name Oileus to refer to Ajax himself.

OLD COMEDY See COMEDY.

OLENUS A town in northwestern Greece. The Olenian goat, better known as Amalthea, was born in this area but was later taken to CRETE, where it suckled ZEUS when he was an infant. The goat's image was later set in the sky as the constellation Capricorn. [ANCIENT SOURCES: Seneca, *Medea* 313, *Oedipus* 283, *Trojan Women* 826]

OLYMPIA A town in southwestern Greece, Olympia was the home of the famous Olympic Games. Olympia was also a major center for the worship of ZEUS. [ANCIENT SOURCES: Aristophanes, *Lysistrata* 1131, *Wasps* 1382, 1387; Sophocles, *Oedipus Tyrannos* 901]

OLYMPUS (1) A musician, perhaps legendary, from PHRYGIA. According to tradition, Olympus founded "Greek flute music, and to him were attributed many famous melodies of great antiquity" (Sommerstein). [ANCIENT SOURCES: Aristophanes, *Knights* 8, *Lysistrata* 1131; pseudo-Plutarch, *Moralia* 1133d, 1135b]

BIBLIOGRAPHY
Sommerstein, A. H. *The Comedies of Aristophanes*. Vol. 2, *Knights*. Warminster, U.K.: Aris & Phillips, 1981, 145.

OLYMPUS (2) Located in northeastern Greece, Olympus is the country's tallest mountain and was considered the home of the gods.

OMEN An occurrence thought to indicate something that will happen in the future or reveal the nature of something or someone. The activities of certain animals (especially birds and snakes) were often considered omens. In EURIPIDES' *ELECTRA*, a deformity in a sacrificial animal serves as an omen of impending danger to AEGISTHUS. Dreams, words spoken at the wrong moment, and even sneezes were also considered omens. In AESCHYLUS' *PROMETHEUS BOUND*, PROMETHEUS claims that he taught humans how to interpret omens.

BIBLIOGRAPHY
Peradotto, J. J. "Cledonomancy in the *Oresteia*," *American Journal of Philology* 90 (1969): 1–21.

OMPHALE After HERACLES killed IPHITUS, to atone for his crime Heracles was sold as a slave to the Lydian queen, Omphale (whose name means "navel"). During Heracles' servitude to Omphale, the queen often dressed in his lion skin and carried his club, while Heracles was made to wear the queen's clothing or that of one of the queen's subjects, whom the Greeks regarded as barbarians. The Greek playwright Achaeus wrote a SATYR PLAY entitled *Omphale*, whose few brief fragments give no indication of the plot (fragments 32–25 Snell). Two Greek comic poets, Antiphanes (fragments 176–78 Kock) and the younger Carcinus (fragments 4–5 Kock), wrote plays entitled *Omphale*, but little if anything about their plots can be established. [ANCIENT SOURCES: Seneca, *Hercules Furens*

465–71, *Hercules Oetaeus* 371, 573, *Hippolytus* 317; Sophocles, *Trachinian Women* 252, 356]

BIBLIOGRAPHY

Kock, T. *Comicorum Atticorum Fragmenta.* Vol. 2. Leipzig: Teubner, 1884.

Snell, B. *Tragicorum Graecorum Fragmenta.* Vol. 1. Göttingen, Ger.: Vandenhoeck & Ruprecht, 1971.

ONCA   A title given to the goddess ATHENA. [ANCIENT SOURCES: Aeschylus, *Seven against Thebes* 164, 487, 501]

OPHELTES   The infant son of LYCURGUS and EURYDICE of NEMEA. He died of a snakebite while under the care of HYPSIPYLE, who was blamed for his death.

BIBLIOGRAPHY

Page, D. L. *Select Papyri.* Vol. 3. 1941. Reprint, London: Heinemann, 1970, 77–109.

OPHION   When CADMUS first arrived at the town of THEBES, he planted the ground with the teeth of ARES' dragon. A crop of men sprang up; one of these men was Ophion. The Thebans are sometimes referred to as Ophion's race. The death of the Theban PENTHEUS is once referred to as "Ophion's slaughter." [ANCIENT SOURCES: Seneca, *Hercules Furens* 268, *Oedipus* 485]

OPHIUCHUS   Also known as Anguitenens, Anguifer, or Serpentarius, this constellation represents a man who is grasping a serpent near its head. Originally, Ophiuchus was a man named Phorbas whom the people of Rhodes called in to rid their island of snakes. [ANCIENT SOURCES: Diodorus Siculus, 5.54; Seneca, *Medea* 693]

OPS   See RHEA.

OPUNTIUS   A man mocked in Greek COMEDY as having one eye and "a large, beaky nose" (Dunbar). [ANCIENT SOURCES: Aristophanes, *Birds* 152, 1294; Eupolis, fragment 282 Kock]

BIBLIOGRAPHY

Dunbar, Nan. *Aristophanes: Birds.* New York: Oxford University Press, 1995, 641.

Kock, T. *Comicorum Atticorum Fragmenta.* Vol. 1. Leipzig: Teubner, 1880.

ORACLE   In ancient times, a person who wanted to inquire into the future consulted an oracle. The most famous oracles were those of APOLLO at DELPHI and ZEUS at DODONA. The oracle of Trophonius, which was not far away from Delphi, is also mentioned occasionally in Greek drama (see especially EURIPIDES' *ION*). Several Greek tragedies involve the consequences of inquiries to oracles. In drama, oracles were often questioned about the possibility of having children. In Euripides' *MEDEA*, we hear that AEGEUS has traveled to Delphi to ask about having children, as does XUTHUS, in Euripides' *Ion*. Oedipus' question to the Delphic oracle about his real parents led him to avoid his foster parents and encounter his real parents. ORESTES kills his mother, CLYTEMNESTRA, in obedience to the Delphic oracle.

ORCHESTRA   Named from a Greek word meaning "place for dancing," the orchestra in a Greek theater is a flat area (usually circular), in which the chorus and actors move and dance. The size of an orchestra would vary from theater to theater. The orchestra in the theater of Dionysus in Athens was about 85 feet in diameter, the theater at Aigai was about 93 feet in diameter, and the theater at Megalopolis was almost 100 feet in diameter. In a Roman theater, the orchestra was semicircular and may not have been used by the performers after the days of PLAUTUS because Roman senators were allowed to sit in this space. [ANCIENT SOURCES: Aristotle, *Problems* 901b30; Heniochus, fragment 5.6–8 Kock; Juvenal, 7.47; Suetonius, *Caesar* 39, *Augustus* 35, 44, *Claudius* 21; Vitruvius, 5, 6]

BIBLIOGRAPHY

Gebhard, E. R. "The Form of the Orchestra in the Early Greek Theater," *Hesperia* 43 (1974): 428–40.

Kock, T. *Comicorum Atticorum Fragmenta.* Vol. 2. Leipzig: Teubner, 1884.

Ley, G., and M. Ewans. "The Orchestra as Acting Area in Greek Tragedy," *Ramus* 14 (1985): 75–84.

Tanner, R. G. "Problems in Plautus," *Proceedings of the Cambridge Philological Society* 15 (1969): 95–105.

West, M. L. "Heniochus and the Shape of the Athenian Orchestra," *Zeitschrift für Papyrologie und Epigraphik* 130 (2000): 12.

Wiles, D. *Tragedy in Athens: Performance Space and Theatrical Meaning*. Cambridge: Cambridge University Press, 1997, 44–52.

ORCUS   See HADES; UNDERWORLD.

ORESTEIA   AESCHYLUS (458 B.C.E.)   The *Oresteia* was originally a TETRALOGY that was comprised of *AGAMEMNON, LIBATION BEARERS, EUMENIDES,* and the SATYR PLAY *Proteus.* The three tragedies that begin this tetralogy constitute the only TRILOGY that survives from classical drama.

AGAMEMNON

The first play of the tetralogy, *Agamemnon,* deals with the return of the title character after the Trojan War. The play's setting is the town of ARGOS, and the action occurs at the palace of King AGAMEMNON. The play opens with a watchman looking for a signal fire that will indicate that the Greeks have captured TROY. Upon seeing this signal, the watchman rejoices, but he ends his speech with an allusion to trouble within the house.

After the watchman's departure, the chorus of elderly male Argives enter. In a lengthy and symbolically complex song, they recall the abduction of HELEN by ALEXANDER (Paris) and the war waged by AGAMEMNON, MENELAUS, and the Greeks to recover her. The chorus also sing how CALCHAS prophesied that to obtain fair winds for sailing to TROY, Agamemnon had to sacrifice IPHIGENIA to the goddess ARTEMIS. During the chorus' song, Agamemnon's wife, CLYTEMNESTRA, has entered. The chorus conclude their speech by asking Clytemnestra what news she has heard about the war. When Clytemnestra informs the men that the Greeks have captured Troy, they are skeptical at first, but they seem more convinced when Clytemnestra describes the elaborate torch relay that she had orchestrated to carry her news of this event. The chorus then sing an ode of thanksgiving to ZEUS for the victory over Alexander and the Trojans. They lament the extensive loss of Greek life—all for the sake of a single woman; the chorus also express some lingering doubt about whether Clytemnestra has jumped to conclusions about the end of the war.

The chorus' doubts, however, are put to rest as a messenger enters and announces the Greek victory. Clytemnestra reproaches the chorus for not believing her earlier. When the chorus question the messenger about the fate of Menelaus, the messenger tells them that a storm struck his ship and that he has not returned home. After the messenger's departure, the chorus sing an ode about Helen, whom they compare to a lion cub raised in captivity by human beings. Although cute and harmless at first, eventually the cub grew up and destroyed even those who had raised it. In the same way, Helen caused the destruction of both Greeks and Trojans. The chorus also warn about the sorrow that riches and pride ultimately produce. Righteousness, they declare, thrives in the houses of simple folk.

After the choral ode, Agamemnon, riding in a chariot, enters with his war captive, CASSANDRA, who is a prophet of the god APOLLO. After the chorus offer him their greeting, Agamemnon greets his native land and divinities, recalls the Greeks' destruction of Troy, and declares that he will now take steps to heal whatever ills may plague Argos. Next, Clytemnestra greets Agamemnon. She claims she spent many sleepless nights worrying about him while he was at war. She also informs Agamemnon that their son, ORESTES, is staying with Strophius of PHOCIS, a friend of the family's.

As she ends her speech, Clytemnestra urges Agamemnon to step down from his chariot onto certain red tapestries that she has prepared. Agamemnon fears what the people will think about this behavior and balks at accepting an honor he considers reserved for the gods, but he eventually is persuaded. After Agamemnon, accompanied by Clytemnestra, enters the house, the chorus express their amazement at seeing Agamemnon home again. The chorus, however, worry because they fear that misfortune will soon occur. After the chorus' speech, Clytemnestra arrives from the palace and urges Cassandra to enter the house. Cassandra, however, knowing that death awaits her inside the palace, refuses. Clytemnestra, angry with Cassandra, returns to the house, and Cassandra remains outside the palace for some time. In the presence of the chorus,

Cassandra predicts Agamemnon's and her deaths at the hands of Clytemnestra and her lover, Aegisthus.

Eventually, Cassandra also enters the house and her predictions are fulfilled. The chorus, who remain outside, hear the cries of anguish within, but before they can settle on a course of action Clytemnestra emerges from the house, with the bodies of her husband and Cassandra. Clytemnestra justifies her actions by saying that she has retaliated against Agamemnon for the killing of their daughter, Iphigenia. Soon, Clytemnestra's lover, Aegisthus, emerges from the house and explains his role in the murders. Aegisthus recalls that Agamemnon's father, ATREUS, fed his father, THYESTES, his own children at a banquet. This horrific action led Thyestes, who grew up in exile from Argos, to plot revenge on Agamemnon. As the play closes, Aegisthus and his attendants prepare to battle the chorus. Clytemnestra, however, intervenes and further violence is averted.

LIBATION BEARERS (Greek: *CHOEPHOROI*)

The second play in the *Oresteia* trilogy, *Libation Bearers,* like *Agamemnon,* is set in ARGOS. The play opens near the grave of Agamemnon and concludes before Agamemnon's palace, which is now occupied by Aegisthus and Clytemnestra. While Clytemnestra and Aegisthus were plotting the murder of Agamemnon, Agamemnon and Clytemnestra's son, ORESTES, was sent to live with a kinsman, Strophius of Phocis. After Agamemnon's murder, Orestes returns to Argos with the son of Strophius, PYLADES. As *Libation Bearers* opens, the audience see Orestes and Pylades at Agamemnon's grave. Orestes places a lock of his hair on the grave as an offering to his father. When Orestes and Pylades see a group of female mourners who are approaching, carrying liquid offerings from Clytemnestra to Agamemnon's grave, they conceal themselves nearby to watch the women. ELECTRA, daughter of Agamemnon and Clytemnestra and Orestes' sister, leads the group. Upon arriving, Electra prays to the gods for pity for her and her absent brother, Orestes; she also prays for vengeance against Clytemnestra and Aegisthus. After her prayer, Electra notices a lock of hair on the grave, which her brother, Orestes, has placed there as an offering. When Electra

sees the lock of hair and the footprints near her father's grave, she suspects that they are those of her brother, Orestes.

After Orestes and Pylades emerge from their hiding place, Electra is skeptical at first that Orestes is her brother, but then he shows her weaving that she herself made as a young girl. After Electra recognizes Orestes, Orestes prays to Zeus for guidance. He also tells Electra and the chorus about APOLLO's oracle, which directed him to kill his mother or otherwise suffer great torment and even death. Next, the chorus, Orestes, and Electra take turns singing prayers to the gods (especially Zeus) and the spirit of Agamemnon. They mourn Agamemnon and pray for guidance and strength in the vengeance that will be taken against Clytemnestra and Aegisthus.

After their prayers, Orestes wonders why Clytemnestra sent the libations to Agamemnon's grave. The chorus tell him that Clytemnestra had a terrifying dream: that she had given birth to a snake, that the snake suckled her breast, and that it drew out milk intermingled with blood. Clytemnestra, thinking that Agamemnon's angry spirit had caused the dream, sent drink offerings to Agamemnon's grave to appease his spirit. Orestes realizes that he is the snake in the dream and that he will kill Clytemnestra.

Next, Orestes announces his plot to enter the house of Clytemnestra and Aegisthus. Orestes knows that Aegisthus and Clytemnestra will be on guard against him, so he and Pylades will enter the palace disguised as strangers, imitating the dialect of Phocis. They will try to gain entry to the palace and, once inside, will make their attack. Orestes tells Electra to return to the palace and keep silent about the plot. After Orestes, Pylades, and Electra exit, the chorus sing an ode in which they recall several instances when women have committed horrific actions. They sing of ALTHAEA's killing of her son, MELEAGER; Scylla's killing of her father, NISUS; and the women of LEMNOS, who killed their husbands. They conclude by noting that at last vengeance has returned Orestes to his home.

After the choral ode, Orestes and Pylades call at the gates of the palace. When Clytemnestra answers the door, the disguised Orestes informs her that Orestes is dead. Clytemnestra expresses sadness at this news and admits the "strangers" to the palace. After Orestes and Pylades' entrance into the palace, a woman named Cilissa, who was Orestes' NURSE when he was a child, enters and expresses her sadness at the news of Orestes' death. Cilissa informs the chorus that she will inform Aegisthus. The chorus urge Cilissa not to give up hope that Orestes is still alive and tell her to encourage Aegisthus to go to the palace as quickly as possible and without his bodyguards. After Cilissa's exit, the chorus sing a prayer to Zeus, asking the god to protect and strengthen Orestes and for the blood feud in the house to end.

After the choral ode, Aegisthus enters in response to the news that Orestes is dead. He expresses his concern about this report and asks the chorus whether this news is true. The chorus send him into the palace to question "the strangers." After Aegisthus enters the palace, the chorus wonder what will happen next. Soon, they hear the cry of Aegisthus, who is being killed in the palace. Soon, one of Aegisthus' followers emerges and announces Aegisthus' death. Clytemnestra also arrives from the palace, questions Aegisthus' man, and begins to realize what is happening. No sooner does she call for someone to give her an ax than Orestes and Pylades enter. Clytemnestra pleads with Orestes not to kill her, and Orestes wavers in his resolve. Pylades, however, advises him not to make the gods his enemies and to keep in mind Apollo's oracle. Orestes accepts his advice and despite continued pleas by Clytemnestra, Orestes and Pylades eventually drag her back into the palace, where Orestes kills her.

After their exit, the chorus comment on the justice of Orestes' actions and express the hope that in time Agamemnon's house will be cleansed of its blood feud. After the chorus' remarks, Orestes emerges from the palace and displays the dead bodies of Aegisthus and Clytemnestra, as well as the cloth that was used to kill his father. Orestes comments on their death and the cloth. He is both satisfied and troubled by the killing of Clytemnestra, but the chorus approve of his actions. As *Libation Bearers* approaches its conclusion, Orestes, imagining that he sees the FURIES, who will torment him for killing his mother, flees Argos. The chorus end by recounting the course of the blood feud and wonder where it will end.

EUMENIDES

The third play of Aeschylus' tetralogy in 458 B.C.E., *Eumenides,* has two settings—it opens at Apollo's temple at DELPHI, then moves to ATHENS. As the play opens, APOLLO's priestess emerges from the temple at Delphi in horror at the sight of ORESTES, defiled by the blood of his mother, and the sleeping FURIES who surround him. Apollo goes to Orestes' aid and instructs him to travel to Athens and embrace the statue of the goddess ATHENA. Orestes, with HERMES as his guide, exits for Athens. After his departure, the ghost of CLYTEMNESTRA appears and urges the Furies to pursue him. After the Furies rouse themselves, Apollo confronts them, tells them to leave his temple precinct, and accuses them of defiling his temple by their presence. The Furies argue that Apollo himself has polluted his shrine by allowing Orestes, who killed his mother, to take refuge there. The Furies state that their persecution of Orestes is in accordance with their divine prerogative and express their intent to continue pursuing Orestes. After the departure of the Furies and Apollo, the scene changes to Athens, where the audience see Orestes, a supplicant at Athena's idol. Soon, the Furies enter and see Orestes, who calls on Athena to help him. The Furies surround Orestes, begin to dance around him, and sing a lengthy choral ode in which they state their prerogatives as divinities and their function as goddesses.

After the choral ode, Athena enters and asks the Furies the reason for their presence. After the Furies explain the reason for their persecution of Orestes, Athena asks Orestes to explain why he killed his mother. Because Athena realizes that both the Furies and Orestes have valid reasons for their actions, the goddess decides to conduct a legal trial to decide the matter and appoints the finest Athenian men to act as jurors for the case. The Furies follow with a song in which they protest Athena's decision as an encroachment on their rights as divinities. They urge people to respect their parents and strangers to their home. People who violate these customs will be punished.

After this ode, Athena calls the trial to order. The Furies begin the prosecution by questioning Orestes, who admits that he killed his mother, tells how he killed her, and states that he did so at Apollo's command. The

Furies claim that they have the advantage thus far in the trial, and Orestes appeals to Apollo for help. Apollo, who has followed Orestes to Athens, then testifies on Orestes' behalf. Apollo states that his oracle to Orestes was the result of Zeus' command to Apollo. Apollo argues that Clytemnestra's killing of Agamemnon was of greater consequence than Orestes' killing of Clytemnestra: that the killing of a male is worse than the killing of a female. The Furies then ask Apollo whether it is just for a son to kill his mother and then inherit his father's house. Apollo argues that men are the source of life and that women are merely nurses for the man's seed. As proof of his argument, Apollo points to Athena herself, who he says was born from Zeus alone without the benefit of a mother. At this point, Athena calls for the jurors to vote on the guilt or innocence of Orestes. Before the vote is taken, Athena explains the importance of the voting procedure to the history of the Athenian people and notes that henceforth the location of this trial, the hill of ARES, or AREOPAGUS, will be site of such trials.

As the jurors advance and cast their ballots into the two voting urns that stand on stage, the Furies threaten the jurors that the consequences for Athens will be dire if they acquit Orestes. Apollo tells the Furies that he will triumph over them. After this bickering, Athena tells Orestes that she will cast her vote in favor of Orestes, because she was swayed by Apollo's argument that the woman's death cannot be considered of more importance than that of the man. Athena then urges that the ballots be counted. The result of the count is a tie vote, which, in accordance with Athenian law, allows the defendant to be set free. Orestes celebrates his victory and promises the Athenian people that he and his descendants will always be their allies. The Furies, enraged by this verdict, lament their defeat by the younger divinities and the disrespect shown to their powers and threaten to release a plague on the Athenian land. Athena then tries to appease the Furies. She invites them to live in Athens and promises them that the Athenian people will show them great respect, but the Furies repeat their previous laments and threats. Eventually, however, Athena prevails upon the Furies and persuades them to accept a plot of sacred ground within Athens and the honor of the Athenian people. Athena tells some of her servants to give the Furies new crimson robes to replace their black ones; after the Furies don their new clothing, Athena leads them from the stage. As they exit, a group of Athenian women sing a hymn of praise to the Furies, who not only wear new clothing, but also are addressed by a new name—Eumenides, which means "the kindly goddesses."

COMMENTARY

AESCHYLUS' *Oresteia* is important for several reasons: First, it is the only surviving trilogy from antiquity. Although modern editors of collections of translations often group SOPHOCLES' *OEDIPUS THE KING, ANTIGONE,* and *OEDIPUS AT COLONUS,* one should keep in mind that these plays were staged in three different years over a period of four decades. All three plays of the *Oresteia* were staged on the same day in 458. The *Oresteia* gives us an idea of how ancient playwrights could have linked their plays when they grouped first three plays of a tetralogy. Note, however, that not all playwrights based the first three plays of the tetralogy on a single extended story line. For example, EURIPIDES' tetralogy of 431 B.C.E. was composed of *MEDEA, Philoctetes, Dictys,* and the satyr play *Theristae,* four plays that would have been taken from widely divergent mythological material.

The *ORESTEIA* is also important because its characters, content, and subject matter exerted considerable influence on later playwrights, especially Euripides. Regarding the matter of character, for example, Aeschylus' portrayal of Clytemnestra surely had some influence on Euripides' portrayal of MEDEA. Both women set out to destroy their husband, although Medea leaves JASON alive. Clytemnestra kills Agamemnon's concubine, Cassandra; Medea kills Jason's new bride, CREON's daughter. Both poets characterize the women as savage animals or monsters. At *Agamemnon* 1233, Clytemnestra is compared to the monster SCYLLA; Euripides also compares Medea to Scylla (*Medea* 1343), the only reference to the Scylla in Euripidean poetry. At *Agamemnon* 1258, Cassandra likens Clytemnestra to a lioness, and Medea is compared to a lioness four times in Euripides' play (187, 1342, 1358, 1407).

In the area of content and subject matter, we are fortunate to possess an *Electra* by both Sophocles and

Euripides, which have the same events as Aeschylus' *Libation Bearers* and reflect an awareness of Aeschylus' play but handle the material in a different manner. The recognition scene between Orestes and Electra in Euripides' *Electra,* though staged some 40 years after *Libation Bearers,* shows a clear awareness of Aeschylus' play. In Euripides' play, Electra rejects the very tokens (hair, footprints, clothing) that Aeschylus' Electra accepts as evidence or proof of her brother's presence. The trial of Orestes as presented within *Eumenides* is handled in quite a different way in Euripides' *Orestes,* as the latter playwright imagines that the people of Argos would not have allowed Orestes to escape from town. Accordingly, Euripides has Orestes tried by the people of Argos rather than the people of Athens, as Aeschylus does. The result is much different, as Euripidean Orestes is found guilty and condemned to death. Similarly, in Euripides' I PHIGENIA IN T AURIS, some of Euripides' Furies do not accept the solution arranged by Athena in Aeschylus' *Eumenides* and continue to persecute Orestes.

The major question raised by the O RESTEIA, one that still vexes us today, is, What is justice? During Aeschylus' day, the poet had witnessed some significant changes in the way that his fellow Athenians administered justice. In 461 B.C.E., just three years before the production of the O RESTEIA, changes to the Athenian system placed court cases before juries that were composed of a much broader group of the Athenian citizenry than before. The O RESTEIA itself examines changes in the way that justice is meted out. In the first two plays, we see a system of justice in which crimes are avenged by someone closely connected to the injured party (e.g., mother's avenging daughter, son's avenging father), and the shedding of blood is avenged by the shedding of blood. This cycle of vengeance continues from one generation to the next and in theory could continue without end. One stranger's killing another stranger is one matter, but Aeschylus further complicates this type of justice by creating close ties between those who seek revenge. Where does one draw the line between justice and injustice when brother takes vengeance against brother, wife against husband, or son against mother? Aeschylus further complicates the audience's ability to evaluate the right-

ness of such vengeance by portraying those who take revenge in animalistic terms. Although custom allowed people to take revenge on those who had wronged them, Aeschylus blurs the line between right and wrong as the avengers are often portrayed in language related to animal; thus, Aeschylus dehumanizes the avengers to some extent.

In *Agamemnon,* we find several references to the feud between Agamemnon's father, Atreus, and Aegisthus' father, Thyestes. According to tradition, Atreus' feeding of Thyestes' children to him was the result of Thyestes' seducing Atreus' wife and robbing him of the kingship. That feud continues and its actions are echoed in the conflict of Agamemnon, Aegisthus, and Clytemnestra. Another example of vengeance alluded to several times in *Agamemnon* is the story of the title character's fighting at Troy to liberate his brother Menelaus' wife, Helen, from the clutches of Paris. Such revenge by Agamemnon and the Greeks was perfectly within their rights and was even approved of by the gods. In abducting Helen from Menelaus, in whose house Paris was a guest at the time, Paris had violated the Greek custom of *xenia* (guest friendship). Zeus himself was the divinity who presided over this custom. The same custom would have been violated when Atreus served Thyestes the flesh of his own children.

Agamemnon, however, in attempting to carry out divinely sanctioned vengeance against Paris and the Trojans, finds himself faced with an extremely difficult choice. Adverse weather prevents the Greek fleet from sailing to Troy. An oracle, however, states that the winds will cease if Agamemnon sacrifices his daughter, Iphigenia, to the goddess Artemis. What does one do when a divinity calls for the killing of one's child? Abraham faced the same question regarding Isaac in Genesis. Unlike Abraham, whose sacrifice of Isaac was averted at the last minute, Agamemnon sacrifices Iphigenia. This sacrifice, however, leads to conflict between Agamemnon and Clytemnestra. While Agamemnon is away at Troy, Clytemnestra takes up with Aegisthus, just as Aegisthus' father had had an affair with Atreus' wife. Clytemnestra and Aegisthus have a shared hatred of Agamemnon. The wife wants to kill the husband for the sacrifice of their daughter;

the cousin, Aegisthus, wants to kill Agamemnon because of what Atreus did to Thyestes. Custom may justify their vengeance, but Aeschylus dehumanizes Aegisthus and Clytemnestra by descriptions that compare them to animals. Cassandra describes Aegisthus as a weak lion (*Agamemnon* 1224) and Clytemnestra as a fawning dog (1228–30), a serpent, and a SCYLLA (1233–34). Later, Cassandra describes the pair as a wolf and a lioness who bed together (*Agamemnon* 1258–59). Not only are they described as savage animals, but the perversity of their sexual relationship is made to cross the boundaries of species. On Agamemnon's return from Troy, the two avengers strike. To recall the encounter between Atreus and Thyestes and create a link between Agamemnon and Aegisthus, Cassandra speaks of Atreus' actions against Thyestes after Agamemnon has entered the house. Not only is Agamemnon killed, but Cassandra falls as well.

The cycle of violence does not end, however, and it continues in *Libation Bearers*. Orestes is well within his rights to take vengeance on someone who has killed his father. The killing of Aegisthus presents little legal difficulty as Orestes points out at lines 989–90: Aegisthus is an adulterer and as such he could be killed without any questions being asked by the community. Orestes' vengeance becomes complicated, however, by the fact that the other of his intended victims is his mother. Just as Artemis had called for Agamemnon to shed the blood of Iphigenia, Artemis' brother, Apollo, has called for Orestes to kill his mother. Orestes relates that Apollo has threatened him with terrible suffering and even death if he does not kill his mother (*Libation Bearers* 276–82). Of course, we also know that after Orestes kills his mother, her Furies torment him.

Aeschylus further complicates the audience's perception of Orestes' vengeance on his mother by comparisons of Orestes and Electra to animals: The chorus' description of the vengeance of Orestes and company as being like a double lion (*Libation Bearers* 938) could be taken as positive; Agamemnon was described as a proud lion in the previous play (1259). The Greek army who overwhelmed Troy was described as being like a hungry lion (827–28), who lapped at the blood of kings. Electra, at *Libation Bearers* 421–22, compares herself and her brother to bloody, savage wolves whose

mother was equally as savage. Recall that Aeschylus also compared Aegisthus to a wolf in *Agamemnon*. Later, in *Libation Bearers* (550), Orestes himself realizes that he is the snake about which Clytemnestra dreamed and that he would draw both milk and blood from her breast. The serpent image of Orestes seems appropriate, as Orestes later describes his mother in serpentine terms as well (994–96). The chorus also remark that by killing Aegisthus and Clytemnestra, Orestes decapitated two snakes with one stroke (1047). Although Apollo, Justice, and public opinion appear to be on Orestes' side, we note the irony that the serpent Orestes, who kills his serpent mother and her serpent lover, will eventually be tormented by her Furies, whom Orestes describes as being entwined with serpents (1049–50).

As the Furies note several times in *Eumenides*, the purpose of their existence is to persecute those who commit actions such as those of Orestes. Their torment of Orestes is well within their rights and prerogatives as divinities. In *Eumenides*, however, the mythical ancestors of Aeschylus' audience, the citizens of Athens, and not the Furies end the cycle of blood vengeance. In *Eumenides*, instead of Orestes' blood being shed as a result of the vengeance cycle, the Furies follow Orestes to Athens, where they agree to a trial, presided over by Athena and judged by a group of Athenian citizens. Victory in this contest will not be determined by physical strength, but by the persuasive power of one's words, just as in the Athenian court system of Aeschylus' day. Eventually, Apollo's persuasion wins the day for Orestes, as the god convinces Athena that the death of the woman, Clytemnestra, should not be considered to be of the same importance as the death of the man, Agamemnon (*Eumenides* 736–40). To modern readers of the play, Apollo's argument (that a woman is only the nurse of the child who grows within her womb, whereas the man is the one who plants the seed) is nonsense. One should also note that half the jury in Aeschylus' play voted to condemn Orestes. Most important, however, persuasion rather than violence effects a resolution to the conflict that had torn apart the family of Orestes. Such a resolution could not have been achieved under the custom of blood vengeance until every person involved in the feud lay dead. The system of justice based on persuasion was not without its flaws, but it did achieve its goal without violence.

BIBLIOGRAPHY
Oresteia
Bloom, H., ed. *Aeschylus's Oresteia.* New York: Chelsea House, 1988.
Conacher, D. J. *Aeschylus' Oresteia: A Literary Commentary.* Toronto: University of Toronto Press, 1987.
Goldhill, S. *Language, Sexuality, Narrative, the Oresteia.* Cambridge: Cambridge University Press, 1984.
———. *Aeschylus: The Oresteia.* Cambridge: Cambridge University Press, 1992.
Lebeck, A. *The Oresteia: A Study in Language and Structure.* Cambridge, Mass.: Harvard University Press, 1971.
Agamemnon
Denniston, J. D., and D. Page. *Aeschylus: Agamemnon.* Oxford: Clarendon Press, 1957.
Fraenkel, E. *Aeschylus: Agamemnon.* Oxford: Clarendon Press, 1950.
Lloyd-Jones, H. "The Guilt of Agamemnon," *Classical Quarterly* 12 (1962): 187–99.
Morrell, K. S. "The Fabric of Persuasion: Clytemnestra, Agamemnon, and the Sea of Garments," *Classical Journal* 92, no. 2 (1996–97): 141–65.
Smith, P. M. *On the Hymn to Zeus in Aeschylus' Agamemnon.* Chico, Calif.: Scholars Press, 1980.
Libation Bearers
Garvie, A. F. *Aeschylus: Choephoroi.* Oxford: Clarendon Press, 1986.
Halporn, J. W. "The Skeptical Electra," *Harvard Studies in Classical Philology* 87 (1983): 101–18.
Heath, J. "Disentangling the Beast: Humans and Other Animals in Aeschylus' *Oresteia,*" *Journal of Hellenic Studies* 119 (1999): 17–48.
O'Neill, K. N. "Aeschylus, Homer, and the Serpent at the Breast," *Phoenix* 52, no. 3 and 4 (1998): 216–29.
Podlecki, A. J. "Four Electras." *Florilegium* 3 (1981): 21–46.
Eumenides
Brown A. L. "The Erinyes in the *Oresteia*: Real Life, the Supernatural, and the Stage," *Journal of Hellenic Studies* 103 (1983): 13–34.
Henrichs, A. "'Why Should I Dance?': Choral Self-Referentiality in Greek Tragedy," *Arion* 3, no. 1 (1994–95): 56–111.
Podlecki, A. J. *Aeschylus: Eumenides.* Warminster, U.K.: Aris & Phillips, 1992.
Seaford, R. "Historicizing Tragic Ambivalence: The Vote of Athena." In *History, Tragedy, Theory: Dialogues on Athenian Drama.* Austin: University of Texas Press, 1995, 202–21.
Sommerstein, A. H. *Aeschylus: Eumenides.* Cambridge: Cambridge University Press, 1989.

ORESTES (1)   A highway robber noted for being insane, drunk, and stealing clothing from people at night. [ANCIENT SOURCES: Aristophanes, *Acharnians* 1167, *Birds* 712, 1491]

ORESTES (2)   The son of AGAMEMNON and CCLYTEMNESTRA, Orestes is one of the characters who appear most often in ancient drama. In EURIPIDES' *Telephus* (no longer extant), the title character took the infant Orestes hostage and threatened to kill him. In Euripides' IPHIGENIA AT AULIS, Orestes is taken as an infant to Aulis with his sister, IPHIGENIA. Orestes is best known, however, for avenging the murder of his father, Agamemnon, a story that occurs as early as HOMER'S *Odyssey.* The most famous dramatization of this action occurs in AESCHYLUS' *Libation Bearers* (see ORESTEIA), and was treated later by both Euripides (in his *Electra*) and SOPHOCLES (in his *Electra*). In these plays, Orestes, commanded to avenge his father's murder by Apollo's oracle at DELPHI, must kill his mother. He kills his mother's lover, AEGISTHUS, as well. In Euripides' *Electra,* Orestes appears in perhaps a more savage light than when he kills Aegisthus in Aeschylus' *Libation Bearers.* In Euripides' play, Orestes' killing of Aegisthus takes place during a sacrifice that Aegisthus is making to the NYMPHS of that locale. Furthermore, the unsuspecting Aegisthus has invited Orestes to join him in the sacrifice. In the course of this ritual, Orestes "sacrifices" Aegisthus.

After killing his mother, Orestes is tormented by her Furies. In Aeschylus' *Eumenides,* the Furies pursue him to Delphi and then to ATHENS, where they agree to have their grievance against him judged by Athena and a jury of Athenian citizens. In Aeschylus' play, Orestes is freed from the Furies' torment through this trial.

In Euripides' *Orestes,* however, the playwright has Orestes examined by the assembly at ARGOS, before he goes to Athens. The assembly at Argos decrees that Orestes must be put to death. Euripides' Orestes, however, is much more savage and erratic in his behavior than Aeschylean Orestes. In *Orestes,* the title character then enters into a plot with PYLADES to take MENELAUS' daughter, HERMIONE, hostage and kill his wife, HELEN. Apollo intervenes to rescue Helen; however, at the conclusion of *Orestes,* he appears on the roof of the palace threatening to kill Hermione. Apollo also resolves this situation by declaring that Orestes will marry Hermione.

Orestes appears again in Euripides' *Iphigenia in Tauris.* The events of this drama, perhaps invented by Euripides independently of any previous mythological tradition, occur after Orestes is put on trial in Athens. Some of the Furies refused to accept the verdict reached in Athens and therefore continue to pursue Orestes. To free himself of their torment, Orestes must travel to Tauris, steal a statue of ARTEMIS, and take it back to Athens. Arriving in Tauris with Pylades, Orestes is stricken with madness (induced by the Furies) and captured by the Taurians, who sacrifice all strangers to Artemis. Eventually Orestes escapes Tauris with the help of his sister, Iphigenia.

After he is freed from the Furies' torment, we hear little of Orestes. In Euripides' *Andromache,* he takes Hermione from the town of Pharsalus and seems to have some role in the murder of NEOPTOLEMUS. After the events described in *Andromache,* Orestes and Hermione appear to have married. Other sources say that Orestes married ERIGONE. Orestes fathered Tisamenus, and he died of snakebite at the town of Oresteum (or Oresthasium) in the region of ARCADIA. [ANCIENT SOURCES: Aeschylus, *Oresteia;* Apollodorus, *Epitome* 6.24–28; Euripides, *Electra, Iphigenia in Tauris, Orestes;* Sophocles, *Electra*]

ORESTES EURIPIDES (408 B.C.E.)

A scholiast's note informs us that the play was staged in the archonship of Diocles, thereby securely dating the play. The drama's setting is ARGOS, and its action occurs six days after ORESTES has killed his mother, CLYTEMNESTRA, and her lover, AEGISTHUS. As does AESCHYLUS' *Eumenides* (See ORESTEIA), *Orestes* deals with the trial of the title character after his killing of Clytemnestra. EURIPIDES, however, has removed much of the supernatural element from the story. Euripides does not allow Orestes to escape the FURIES and travel to ATHENS, as Aeschylus did. Instead, Euripides has the people of Argos prevent Orestes from leaving the town and condemn him to death. Furthermore, unlike that of Aeschylus' play, in which the Furies compose the chorus who prosecute Orestes in his trial and whom ATHENA later incorporates into Athens and Athenian worship, Euripides' play's audience only hear about the Furies and do not see them on stage. Euripides' chorus consist of women from Argos, who have little part in the play's action. Additionally, because Orestes is kept within Argos, Euripides has removed Athena as judge of Orestes' trial. Instead, Euripides' trial takes place in the Argive assembly without any clear presiding magistrate. In contrast to Aeschylus' divine judge, jury of Athenian citizens, Furies as prosecutors, and APOLLO's appearance as a witness for Orestes' defense, Euripides' trial has no single judge and no formal citizen jury, but a prosecution by the mob in which various speakers give opinions, and in which Apollo does not arrive to speak on Orestes' behalf.

As the play opens, Orestes' sister, ELECTRA, watches over her brother, who has fallen asleep in exhaustion from his torment by his mother's Furies. By having Orestes sleep, Euripides reverses the opening of Aeschylus' *Eumenides,* in which the Furies are asleep around Orestes, who scampers away to Athens and the protection of Athena. Electra tells the audience of the numerous horrific acts in her family's history. Electra also informs the audience that the Argives have decreed that Orestes and Electra are to be shunned and not given the basic necessities of life. Electra notes the Argives will decide whether she and Orestes will be stoned to death and states that their only hope lies in help from their uncle, MENELAUS, who has just arrived from Troy. Electra says HELEN has already arrived at the palace under the cover of darkness, so that she herself would not be stoned by those who lost sons at Troy. Electra also indicates that Helen and Menelaus' daughter is also within the palace.

Electra is then joined on stage by Helen, who laments Orestes' fate, as well as her own. Helen requests that Electra go to Clytemnestra's grave and make an offering on her behalf. Electra, however, does not want to go to her mother's grave, so Electra suggests that Helen send Hermione instead. When Hermione emerges from the palace, Helen gives her daughter the offerings, which include some short locks of her hair (a common offering to the dead among the Greeks). After Hermione exits for Clytemnestra's grave, Helen returns to the palace. After Helen leaves, Electra notes that Helen cut off little of her hair and curses her aunt.

At this point, the chorus of Argive women approach. When Euripides' chorus enter, Electra tells them to keep quiet so that they do not wake her brother. This call for silence to an entering chorus is unique in extant drama and contrasts with Aeschylus' *Eumenides,* in which the ghost of Clytemnestra, enraged by the sleeping Furies, appears and rouses the slumbering creatures. As the Argive women enter, they quietly ask how Orestes is faring and express their pity for the young man. As Orestes stirs, Electra continues to call for quiet from the women. Eventually Orestes awakens from his sleep in a state of confusion. Electra comforts him and cleans his face and hair. No sooner does Orestes reorient himself than he begins to imagine that he sees the Furies' tormenting him. He even imagines that Electra is a Fury. Orestes' hallucinations pass and he slumps down to the ground in exhaustion. Orestes urges Electra to rest, but she states her intention to stay by his side. At this point, the Argive women sing an ode begging the Furies to release Orestes from his torment; they lament that happiness among humans is fleeting, even in a family descended from ZEUS.

After the choral ode, Menelaus arrives from the harbor. He is soon met by Orestes, who begs him for help. Menelaus is horrified by Orestes' ghastly appearance. Orestes explains his torment by the Furies and mentions his persecution by the people of Argos, in particular Oeax (an enemy of AGAMEMNON's at Troy) and the friends of Aegisthus. As Orestes continues to beg his uncle for help, TYNDAREUS, the father of Helen and Clytemnestra and father-in-law of Menelaus, arrives. Tyndareus urges Menelaus not to help Orestes and argues that Orestes should have prosecuted Clytemnestra by legal means and banished her from the palace. Orestes, echoing the argument of APOLLO in Aeschylus' *Eumenides,* argues that his loyalty was to his father rather than his mother because the man is the prime giver of life. Orestes also claims his acts were justified because Clytemnestra was committing adultery with Aegisthus. Orestes declares his killing of

Clytemnestra benefited all of Greece, for it checked a potential trend of women killing their husbands without punishment. Orestes points out that if he had not avenged his father, his father's Furies would have persecuted him. Finally, he notes that Apollo ordered him to kill Clytemnestra. Tyndareus, angered by Orestes' words, states that he is all the more eager to speak against him in the Argive assembly. Tyndareus also threatens Menelaus, saying that if he supports Orestes, he should not return to Sparta.

After Tyndareus leaves, Menelaus begins to express doubts about helping Orestes. The troubled young man continues to beg him for help, and Menelaus agrees to try to persuade Tyndareus and the Argives to calm their anger. As Menelaus exits, he states that he will not use force, however. After Menelaus' departure, Orestes criticizes his uncle's cowardice and despairs that no hope exists for salvation from death. Next, Orestes' best friend, PYLADES, arrives. Orestes informs him of the situation, and Pylades notes that his father, Strophius, banished him because of his helping Orestes kill Clytemnestra. Pylades, however, promises to support Orestes despite any consequences from the Argives. After a discussion with Pylades, Orestes decides that he will address the Argive assembly. Thus, with Pylades supporting him, Orestes and his friend exit to the assembly. After their departure, the Argive women sing an ode about the feud over the kingdom of Argos of ATREUS and THYESTES, Orestes' grandfather and his grand uncle, respectively, that resulted in Atreus' feeding Thyestes some of his own children. This crime was followed by Orestes' killing of his mother, a deed by which the chorus is horrified.

The choral ode is followed by Electra's emergence from the palace. She is soon joined by a messenger, who announces that the Argive assembly has condemned her and her brother to die. The messenger also describes the speeches that were made in the assembly. Orestes' speech echoed his earlier statements to Tyndareus, namely, that his killing of Clytemnestra would prevent other women from murdering their husbands. The speech that was most persuasive was given by someone friendly to Tyndareus. This speech lacked substance but was full of charm and therefore was supported by the assembly. The brother and sister, however, will be given the opportunity to commit suicide rather than be stoned to death. Upon hearing this, Electra sings a MONODY lamenting her fate and that of her ancestors (TANTALUS, PELOPS, Atreus, Thyestes, and Agamemnon).

Although Euripides has removed the Furies as speakers in the play, he has added the prominent surviving members who are connected with Agamemnon's family: Helen and Menelaus; their daughter, Hermione; and Tyndareus, Helen's father. In the play's first half, each of these characters crosses the stage and reveal his or her true self. As Electra notes, Helen cut off little of her hair as a sign of mourning for Clytemnestra. Orestes eagerly anticipated the arrival of Menelaus, but Tyndareus' threats to Menelaus if he helps Orestes reveal Menelaus' unwillingness to support his nephew.

Pylades, who has a far more extensive speaking part in *Orestes* than in any of his other extant appearances in drama, does prove himself a true friend to Orestes: He decides that he also will commit suicide. Before the three kill themselves, Pylades suggests that they kill Helen and thus gain a glorious name for themselves. Pylades' plan proves agreeable and is soon set into motion.

The horrific mood established thus far in the play is soon confounded when an effeminate male slave from Phrygia rushes from the house to inform the audience of the attempt on Helen's life inside. The slave, terrified by the brutality of Orestes and Pylades, relates how the attempt was made on Helen's life. The attempt was not successful, however, because Apollo saved her from Orestes. Because the attempt to kill Helen fails, Hermione is taken hostage; Orestes climbs to the roof of the palace with her, threatens to kill her, and instructs Pylades to begin setting fire to the palace. Meanwhile, Menelaus arrives and tries to stop Orestes.

Before the standoff can proceed further, Apollo appears with Helen and tells Orestes and Menelaus to end their quarrel. Helen, the god says, will be taken to live with the gods and protect sailors such as her brothers, CASTOR and POLLUX. Apollo tells Menelaus to find another wife; he tells Pylades to marry Electra; and finally he tells Orestes to marry Hermione. Apollo informs Orestes that he will spend a year in exile in the land of PARRHASIA before eventually going to Athens to be prosecuted by the Furies in a trial in which, as in Aeschylus' *Eumenides,* he will be acquitted.

COMMENTARY

Orestes is another Euripidean play that has puzzled those who have encountered it. One problematic point of consideration is the puzzling statement in the play's ancient hypothesis, which suggested that *Orestes* was rather like a SATYR PLAY. Of course, the members of the chorus are not satyrs, but the play does contain a few humorous elements. The entry of the chorus is rather amusing as Electra tries to silence them so that they will not awaken her sleeping brother. This silent entry becomes more humorous when compared with Aeschylus' *Eumenides,* in which Clytemnestra had to wake the sleeping chorus. Another clearly humorous element occurs later in the play in the MESSENGER speech delivered by the effeminate Phrygian slave. To describe the play's ending as a happy one would be to push the definition of happy ending to its limits. No one actually dies in *Orestes* and Apollo does arrange two marriages at the play's conclusion, although Apollo's final speech does indicate that before Orestes marries Hermione, NEOPTOLEMUS, who intends to marry her, will be killed.

Other than a few elements, however, little about the play seems especially humorous, and *Orestes* is one of Euripides' more depressing plays. Talk of death dominates the drama. Consider that the Greek word root *than-,* which is found in the noun *thanatos* (death) and the verb *thanein* (to die), occurs about once every 19 lines in *Alcestis* and once every 26 lines in *Orestes* (compare Euripides' PHOENICIAN WOMEN at once every 70 lines and Euripides' *Medea* at once every 79 lines). In this respect, *Orestes* is similar to Euripides' ALCESTIS, which was staged 30 years earlier and occupied the position usually reserved for a satyr play.

Both *Alcestis* and *Orestes* deal with a cycle of death. In the prologue of *Alcestis,* we hear that Zeus killed Apollo's son, ASCLEPIUS, Apollo retaliated against his father by killing some CYCLOPES, and then Apollo, sentenced to become a servant to ADMETUS, arranged for him to avoid death by finding someone (ALCESTIS) to die in his place. In *Orestes,* we find a far more extensive cycle of death mentioned directly or alluded to: Tantalus killed his son, Pelops; Pelops, who was resurrected by the gods, killed Myrtilus; Atreus killed Thyestes' sons; Agamemnon had to kill his daughter, IPHIGENIA, to sail to Troy and wage war to rescue Helen, a mission that cost countless lives; Clytemnestra and Aegisthus killed Agamemnon; and Orestes (in accordance with Apollo's command) killed his father's murderers. Note also that at the conclusion of the play Apollo announces that ACHILLES' son, Neoptolemus, will die.

As at the beginning of *Alcestis* the title character was faced with death, in the opening of *Orestes,* the title character faces death. *Alcestis* will die a glorious death that will elevate her to an almost divine status. In Orestes' case, however, he and his sister face death and are treated as criminals. After Orestes' trial at Argos, he and Electra will be allowed to commit suicide rather than be stoned to death, and this sentence prompts Pylades to indicate that he also will take his life. *Orestes* careens off in an unexpected direction when Pylades proposes the killing of Helen. Electra chimes in and suggests that they take Hermione hostage and kill her if necessary. Whereas Alcestis' death would earn her glory, Pylades thinks that they will win glory by either killing Helen or by killing themselves if they fail (1151–52). None of these deaths takes place. Orestes, Pylades, Electra, Hermione, Menelaus, and Helen all escape Pylades' proposed assault. Whereas Alcestis' death is reversed when HERACLES wrestles her away from the god of death, at the conclusion of Orestes, Apollo does what he himself did not do for Alcestis and saves Helen from death. Unlike Helen, Alcestis was an eminently virtuous woman, and her husband, ADMETUS, although not an especially admirable figure, had certainly not committed or even contemplated committing the same deadly acts that Orestes had.

In addition to the frequent talk of death in *Orestes,* we find a focus on the concept of friendship (Greek: *philia*). For the Greeks, *philia* was expected from persons related to one another by marriage or blood. Thus, Electra, Orestes, Helen, Menelaus, and Tyndareus should be friends (*philoi*). These relations have become strained or broken by Clytemnestra's killing of Agamemnon and Orestes' killing of Clytemnestra. Although *philoi* have killed one another, Orestes still hopes that his *philoi* will go to his aid, because in addi-

tion to the madness caused by the Furies, Orestes is being vexed by the *philoi* of Aegisthus (435–36). Electra certainly proves her bond of *philia* with Orestes, and Pylades does as well. These *philoi* can provide Orestes comfort and support, but they have no political power in Argos. Orestes is counting on the *philia* of his paternal uncle, Menelaus (450–55), but Menelaus finds himself caught between two *philoi*, Tyndareus and Orestes. Tyndareus' threats lead Menelaus to turn his back on Orestes. For Tyndareus, the bond of *philia* is superseded by respect for the law, which he considers Orestes to have broken, and accordingly Tyndareus warns his son-in-law not to choose an ungodly person as his friend rather than a righteous person (672–28). Ultimately, Menelaus does not provide Orestes with any sort of useful friendship and in the Argive assembly the speaker under the control of Tyndareus gains a death sentence for Orestes and Electra. Pylades also declares that he will die with his friend (1095–96). Although the death of these three friends might have gained them some measure of honor, they taint their bond of *philia* by entering into a plot to kill one of their supposed *philoi,* Helen, in order to drive mad another of their supposed *philoi,* Menelaus. If necessary, they will kill another of their *philoi,* Hermione. Their rallying cry appears at line 1244: "For three friends, one struggle, one just vengeance." To gain access to Helen, Orestes can employ his bond of *philia* with Helen, which has not been completely disrupted; his aunt has not turned her back on him completely. The murderous and destructive intent of the three friends is thwarted by Apollo, who reorganizes and re-forms the bonds of *philia* among Electra, Orestes, Pylades, Hermione, and Menelaus. Pylades and Electra will now become *philoi* in a different sense, as husband and wife. *Philia* by marriage will also be created between Orestes and Hermione as husband and wife, and between Orestes and Menelaus as son- and father-in-law.

One final theme we shall mention is connected to Burnett's idea that *Orestes* is a play that makes failure its object. Everything Orestes attempts in the play fails: His effort to secure Menelaus' help, his effort to convince Tyndareus of the merits of his actions, his effort to win over the Argive assembly, and his attempt to kill Helen all fail. Inherent in many of Orestes' failures is the failure of speech. In Aeschylus' *Eumenides,* Apollo's defense of Orestes was able to convince enough Athenian jurors and Athena to allow Orestes to go free. Athena was even able to persuade the Furies to put aside their anger and take up residence in Athens.

In contrast, *Orestes* focuses on mortal speech, and in this play speech is often cut short, curbed, or altered or fails to achieve its object. Not only does Orestes fail to win support through his speech, but Menelaus also fails to defeat Tyndareus' arguments. In the PROLOGUE, Electra checks her own speech and refuses to elaborate on the some of most horrific aspects of her family's history. Orestes is onstage but does not speak until some 200 lines have passed. When the chorus enter, Electra commands them to be quiet several times. Interestingly, later in the play, after Orestes and Pylades have attacked Helen, the chorus tell themselves to keep quiet (1311) so they can hear what is going on. We also note that in *Orestes* the chorus only speak about 11 percent of the play's lines (20 to 25 percent is more usual). Interestingly, Pylades, who speaks a total of 72 lines in Aeschylus' *Libation Bearers* (see ORESTEIA), SOPHOCLES' ELECTRA, and Euripides' ELECTRA and IPHIGENIA IN TAURIS, speaks 110 lines in *Orestes* (only 84 fewer than the chorus).

When Orestes is trying to decide whether to plead his case before the assembly, he concludes that sitting in silence and not pleading his case would be cowardly (789) but decides not to tell Electra his plan in order to prevent her making a scene with her tears. After Orestes' speech in the assembly fails to persuade, Pylades persuades Orestes to try to kill Helen. Pylades proposes that they gain access to Helen through clever speech (they will pretend to be suppliants), and Orestes declares that they will lock up the servants and kill any of them who does not keep quiet (1128). Ironically, the MESSENGER speech is delivered by one of these very servants, and when Orestes threatens the Phrygian with death and asks him whether he was calling on Menelaus for help, the Phrygian lies: He says he was calling for help for Orestes. Orestes realizes that the Phrygian's words are designed to win him over and lets the man live because of his clever speech (1524); that, too, is ironic, because earlier Orestes had failed to save his own life with clever speech. At the end of the play,

Orestes makes another attempt to persuade Menelaus to speak on his behalf to the Argive assembly (1610). This time, Orestes makes his demand with a sword at the throat of Menelaus' daughter. Menelaus still is not persuaded by Orestes' words, but the standoff ends when Apollo appears and insists that the two men listen to his words (1628). Both Menelaus and Orestes are obedient to the god's words, and the two adversaries will, through divine arrangement, become in-laws.

BIBLIOGRAPHY

Euben, J. P. "Political Corruption in Euripides' *Orestes.*" In *Greek Tragedy and Political Theory.* Edited by J. P. Euben. Berkeley: University of California Press, 1986, 222–51.

Parry, H. "Euripides' *Orestes:* The Quest for Salvation," *Transactions and Proceedings of the American Philological Association* 100 (1969): 337–53.

Porter, J. R. *Studies in Euripides' Orestes.* Leiden, New York: Brill, 1994.

Willink, C. W. *Euripides: Orestes.* Oxford: Clarendon Press, 1986.

Zeitlin, F. I. "The Closet of Masks: Roleplaying and Myth-Making in the *Orestes* of Euripides," *Ramus* 9 (1980): 51–77.

OREUS   A town on the northern end of the island of EUBOEA. [ANCIENT SOURCES: Aristophanes, *Oeace* 1047, 1125]

ORION   Most sources make Orion the son of POSEIDON and Euryale; however, in one strange account Orion sprang up from the ground after a Thracian king named Hyrieus urinated on a bull's hide and buried it in the ground. The child was named Orion, which is similar to the Greek verb that means "to urinate." While Orion was a suitor for the daughter of Oenopion, king of CHIOS, Oenopion blinded Orion for an alleged sexual transgression with the young woman. Orion was later healed of his blindness by the SUN. Next, Orion went to CRETE, where he became a hunting partner of ARTEMIS. Apollo was not pleased by the relationship and tricked his sister into killing Orion. Other sources say that EARTH, upon hearing Orion boast that he would rid the Earth of animals, sent a giant scorpion to kill him. After Orion's death, his image and that of the scorpion were placed in the heavens as constellations. [ANCIENT SOURCES: Apollodorus, *Library* 1.4.3–5; Euripides, *Cyclops* 213, *Helen* 1476, *Ion* 1107; Homer, *Odyssey* 5.121–24, 11.572–75; Hyginus, *Fables* 195, *Poetica Astronomica* 2.21, 2.26, 2.33–34; Seneca, *Hercules Furens* 12]

ORNEAE   A town in southeastern Greece northwest of ARGOS. In 416/415 B.C.E., the Athenians and Argives attacked Orneae, whose people had aided the Spartans, in a nighttime siege, but the people actually escaped "under cover of night, leaving [the town] to be demolished by the Argives" (Dunbar). Thus, in 414 B.C.E., ARISTOPHANES mocks the "gallant" fighting at Orneae at *BIRDS* 399. The resemblance of the town's name to a Greek word for birds (*ornea*) gives Aristophanes the opportunity for added humor. [ANCIENT SOURCES: Thucydides, 6.7.1–2]

BIBLIOGRAPHY
Dunbar, Nan. *Aristophanes: Birds.* New York: Oxford University Press, 1995, 289.

ORPHEUS   The most famous musician and singer of classical mythology, Orpheus was the son of the Thracian king Oeagrus (or APOLLO) and the MUSE Calliope. Orpheus was such a skilled musician that his music was able to charm wild animals, as well as cause rocks and trees to move. He is said to have accompanied the Argonauts on their quest for the Golden Fleece; his most famous adventure involves his journey to the underworld. On the day that Orpheus married EURYDICE, his new bride was bitten by a serpent and died. Orpheus traveled to the underworld and with his music charmed the inhabitants and persuaded HADES and PERSEPHONE to release Eurydice. The rulers of the underworld did make one condition—Orpheus was not to look back as he traveled to the upper world. Unfortunately, Orpheus had cause to look back when he thought Eurydice had stumbled. When he turned Eurydice vanished, and Orpheus was unable to persuade Hades and Persephone to release his wife again. After returning from the underworld, Orpheus was so saddened by the loss of Eurydice that he refused to marry again. Some sources say that Orpheus turned his attention to the love of other males. At some point, a group of women became wild and tore Orpheus apart. Some say that DIONYSUS sent the women to destroy Orpheus because he honored Helios (see SUN) or did not honor Dionysus. Others state the women were angry with Orpheus because he refused to love anyone other than Eurydice, because he loved only men, or because they were fighting over him. The Muses buried Orpheus' body; his head, which had been thrown into the river Hebrus, continued to sing as it floated down the river.

Orpheus does not appear as a character in any extant dramas, but his name is mentioned by EURIPIDES about a dozen times. Often characters wish that they had the voice of Orpheus so that they could accomplish various aims. The Greek tragedian Aristias wrote an *Orpheus;* the only surviving line (fragment 5 Snell) mentions a wrestling ground and running ground. The Greek comic poet Antiphanes also wrote an *Orpheus,* from which a five-word fragment (about a "plug" of leaves) is extant (180 Kock). [ANCIENT SOURCES: Aeschylus, *Agamemnon* 1629 (see *ORESTEIA*); Aristophanes, *Frogs* 1032; Ovid, *Metamorphoses* 10.1–85, 11.1–84; Seneca, *Hercules Furens* 571, *Hercules Oetaeus* 1034, 1080, 1087, 1092, *Medea* 228, 348, 358]

BIBLIOGRAPHY
Kock, T. *Comicorum Atticorum Fragmenta.* Vol. 2. Leipzig: Teubner, 1884.
Snell, B. *Tragicorum Graecorum Fragmenta.* Vol. 1. Göttingen, Ger.: Vandenhoeck & Ruprecht, 1971.

ORTHIAN NOME   According to Sommerstein, this was "a famous melody composed by Terpander," a poet and singer from the island of LESBOS who went to SPARTA in the mid-seventh century B.C.E. [ANCIENT SOURCES: Aristophanes, *Acharnians* 16]

BIBLIOGRAPHY
Sommerstein, A. H. *The Comedies of Aristophanes.* Vol. 1, *Acharnians.* Warminster, U.K.: Aris & Phillips, 1980. 159.

OSSA   A mountain in northeastern Greece that the GIANTS used in their assault upon the gods of OLYMPUS. [ANCIENT SOURCES: Euripides, *Electra* 446]

OURANOS   See URANUS.

P

PACTOLUS A river in the region of LYDIA (southwestern Turkey today). The river's sands were supposedly made of gold. [ANCIENT SOURCES: Seneca, *Oedipus* 467, *Phoenician Women* 604; Sophocles, *Philoctetes* 393]

PACUVIUS (CA. 220–CA. 130 B.C.E.) A Roman playwright who composed tragedies and at least one *FABULA PRAETEXTA*. None of his plays survives complete, but 13 titles are known and about 440 lines of fragments exist. Pacuvius also wrote satires, but little is known about these. The known titles of Pacuvius' tragedies are *Antiope, Atalanta, Chryses, Orestes as a Slave (Dulorestes), Hermione, Iliona, Medus, The Washing (Niptra), Pentheus, Periboea, Protesilaus, Teucer*. Pacuvius' known *fabula praetexta*, entitled *Paulus*, must have treated Lucius Aemilius Paulus' victory at Pydna over the Macedonian king Perseus.

BIBLIOGRAPHY

Manuwald, G. ed. *Identität und Alterität in der frührömischen Tragödie*. Würzburg, Ger.: Ergon-Verl., 2000.

Warmington, E. H. *Remains of Old Latin: Livius Andronicus, Naevius, Pacuvius, and Accius*. Vol. 2. Cambridge, Mass.: Harvard University Press, 1936.

PAEAN A paean can be any sort of song or chant, but is best known as a song in honor of APOLLO. Sometimes Apollo is even called Paean. [ANCIENT SOURCES: Aeschylus, *Agamemnon* 146 (see *ORESTEIA*); Aristophanes, *Acharnians* 1212, *Wasps* 874; Euripides, *Alcestis* 92, 220, *Heracles* 820, *Ion* 125, 141; Seneca, *Hercules Oetaeus* 92; Sophocles, *Oedipus Tyrannos* 154, *Trachinian Women* 222]

PAEDAGOGUS See TUTOR.

PALAEMON Originally a mortal named Melicerta, the child of ATHAMAS and INO, Palaemon was transformed into a sea divinity after his mother (driven mad by Hera) jumped into the sea holding him. [ANCIENT SOURCES: Ovid, *Metamorphoses* 4.416–562; Plautus, *Rope* 160; Seneca, *Oedipus* 448]

PALAMEDES The son of NAUPLIUS and Clymene (or Philyra or Hesione), Palamedes sailed with the Greek forces who fought in the Trojan War. According to tradition, Palamedes was a great designer, inventor, and discoverer of skills previously unknown. He is said to have invented numbers, weights, and measures. He taught the Greek army how to count as high as 1,000 and how to use beacons. He designed the defensive wall that the Greeks built at TROY and methods for marshalling their troops. He also learned the movements of stars and revealed many facts previously unknown. ODYSSEUS, who hated Palamedes, plotted to kill him. In one version of the story Odysseus and DIOMEDES drown Palamedes; in another account, Palamedes, searching for treasure in a well, is crushed by stones. In a third version, Odysseus, having persuaded Agamemnon to move the Greek camp for a single day, secretly hides a large amount of gold in the ground where Palamedes had pitched his tent. Additionally, Odysseus made one of their captives write a letter to Priam, which stated that Palamedes would betray the Greek camp to the Trojans for a certain amount of gold.

AESCHYLUS wrote a *Palamedes,* from which a few fragments survive. In one fragment, the speaker, apparently Palamedes, describes his contribution to the organization of the Greek army. In another, Nauplius (?) asks ODYSSEUS why he killed his son. EURIPIDES also composed a tragic *Palamedes,* produced in 415 B.C.E. as part of the tetralogy that included *Alexandros, TROJAN WOMEN,* and *Sisyphus.* ARISTOPHANES, who criticized the play as "frigid," parodied Euripides' *Palamedes* in his *THESMOPHORIAZUSAE.* Euripides' play also dealt with the destruction of Palamedes through the efforts of Odysseus. In *Thesmophoriazusae,* Aristophanes parodies the Euripidean scene in which Palamedes' brother, Oeax, writes the news of Palamedes' death on oar blades and throws them into the sea. [ANCIENT SOURCES: Hyginus, *Fables* 105; Seneca, *Agamemnon* 568]

BIBLIOGRAPHY
Webster, T. B. L. *The Tragedies of Euripides.* London: Methuen, 1967.

PALLANTIDS
The sons of an Athenian, Pallas, who was the brother of AEGEUS, the Pallantids were political rivals of Aegeus and his son THESEUS. The Pallantids opposed Theseus' right to succeed Aegeus as king of ATHENS, and Theseus fought against and killed them. EURIPIDES, at *HIPPOLYTUS* 35, attributes HIPPOLYTUS' presence in TROEZEN as the result of his exile for killing the Pallantids.

PALLAS
Another name for ATHENA.

PAMPHILUS
Not to be confused with the fictional young man who is a character in New Comedy (see TERENCE's *ANDRIA* and *MOTHER-IN-LAW*), this Pamphilus was an Athenian politician and military commander from the DEME of Ceiriadae. Pamphilus

narrowly avoided being captured on AEGINA by the Spartans in 389 B.C.E. and the Athenians later tried and fined him for misappropriation of public funds. A famous painter named Pamphilus (from SICYON) also lived during the time of the politician Pamphilus, and ARISTOPHANES may refer to both of them in *WEALTH.* [ANCIENT SOURCES: Aristophanes, *Wealth* 173, 385; Demosthenes, 40.22; Lysias, 15.5; Pliny, *Natural History* 35.75–77, 123; Xenophon, *Hellenica* 5.1.2–5]

BIBLIOGRAPHY
Sommerstein, A. H. *The Comedies of Aristophanes.* Vol. 11, *Wealth.* Warminster, U.K.: Aris & Phillips, 2001, 146–47, 165–66.

PAN
The son of HERMES and PENELOPE (or the daughter of Dryops) or ZEUS and HUBRIS, Pan is a shepherd god usually associated with the wilds of ARCADIA. Pan has the legs and horns of a goat but an otherwise human physique. Pan is associated with singing, dancing, and playing the pipes, which he is said to have invented after a woman (Syrinx) he was pursuing was transformed into reeds. In some situations, Pan was thought to cause people to behave in unusual ways. The poisoned clothing MEDEA gives to CREON's daughter makes the young woman's servants think that Pan has afflicted her. Pan delivers the PROLOGUE in MENANDER's *DYSCOLUS* and a shrine dedicated to the god is represented onstage. [ANCIENT SOURCES: Aristophanes, *Frogs* 230, *Lysistrata* 2, 721, 912, 998, *Thesmophoriazusae* 978; Euripides, *Bacchae* 952, *Electra* 709, *Helen* 190, *Hippolytus* 142, *Ion* 492, 938, *Iphigenia in Tauris* 1126, *Medea* 1172, *Rhesus* 36; Sophocles, *Oedipus Tyrannos* 1100]

PANACEA
A daughter of ASCLEPIUS. [ANCIENT SOURCES: Aristophanes, *Wealth* 702]

PANAETIUS
It is uncertain whether Panaetius was a fictional or historical person. ARISTOPHANES indicates he was a member of the Athenian cavalry. A wealthy Athenian named Panaetius, who lived during Aristophanes' lifetime, is known. In 415 B.C.E., this Panaetius, as was ALCIBIADES, was implicated in the desecration of the Herms and profaning of the MYSTERIES of

DEMETER. Panaetius went into exile and his property was taken away, but he returned to ATHENS and his property had been restored by the year 400. [ANCIENT SOURCES: Aristophanes, *Knights* 243]

BIBLIOGRAPHY

Sommerstein, A. H. *The Comedies of Aristophanes.* Vol. 2, *Knights.* Warminster, U.K.: Aris & Phillips, 1981, 155–56.

PANATHENAEA

This annual festival, held in July of the modern calendar, honored ATHENS' patron divinity, ATHENA. That the Panathenaea was the oldest and most important of Athenian festivals is attested to by Athenians' tracing its origin to the mythical king ERICHTHONIUS. Every fourth year, from 566 B.C.E., the Panathenaea expanded to almost a week and became the Great Panathenaea, when athletic and musical competitions were held. Unlike winners at other major games such as those at Olympia, in which the prize was a crown of vegetation, winners in the musical competitions at the Great Panathenaea received a valuable golden crown, while the athletes received a crown of olive and large jar of olive oil. A major sacrifice to the goddess was made, and fire for this sacrifice was obtained via a relay torch race at night. Those present at the sacrifice received meat from the sacrificial animals. Athena's statue was given a new robe (*peplos*) on the next-to-last day of the festival, which was considered Athena's birthday. Scenes such as the gods' victory over the GIANTS were woven onto this robe. A grand procession transported the robe to the Athenian ACROPOLIS via a ship on wheels, the robe hanging from the ship's mast as a sail would. [ANCIENT SOURCES: Apollodorus, *Library* 3.14.6; Aristophanes, *Clouds* 386, 988, *Frogs* 1090, *Peace* 418; Pausanias, 1.29.1; Plato, *Euthyphro* 6b; Plutarch, *Theseus* 24]

BIBLIOGRAPHY

Neils, J. *Goddess and Polis: The Panathenaic Festival in Ancient Athens.* Princeton, N.J.: Princeton University Press, 1992.
Olson, S. D. *Aristophanes: Peace.* Oxford: Clarendon Press, 1998, 160–61.
Parke, H. W. *Festivals of the Athenians.* Ithaca, N.Y.: Cornell University Press, 1977, 33–50.

PANDATARIA (PANDATERIA)

A small, desolate island off the western coast of central Italy, Pandateria is best known as a place for exiles. Roman emperors such as AUGUSTUS, Tiberius, and NERO all exiled family members to Pandataria. To marry POPPAEA, Nero exiled his wife, OCTAVIA, at Pandataria in 62 C.E. [ANCIENT SOURCES: Seneca, *Octavia* 972; Tacitus, *Annals* 1.53]

PANDELETUS

A minor Athenian politician who initiated malicious legal prosecutions against others. [ANCIENT SOURCES: Aristophanes, *Clouds* 924]

BIBLIOGRAPHY

Sommerstein, A. H. *The Comedies of Aristophanes.* Vol. 3, *Clouds.* Warminster, U.K.: Aris & Phillips, 1982, 206.

PANDION

The mythological tradition regarding this king of ATHENS is confusing. Some make him the son of ERICTHONIUS and Praxithea and identify his children as PHILOMELA, PROCNE, ERECHTHEUS, and Butes. Other sources call Pandion the son of CECROPS and Metiadusa, and some sources say Pandion was the father of AEGEUS, Lycus, Nisus, and Pallas. Pandion had a statue in the AGORA at ATHENS, where he was regarded as one of the city's 10 eponymous heroes. [ANCIENT SOURCES: Aristophanes, *Peace* 1183; Pausanias, 1.5.2–4; Seneca, *Octavia* 8]

PANDORA

After PROMETHEUS stole fire from ZEUS and gave it to mortals, Zeus decided to punish not only Prometheus, but mortals. To punish the human race, Zeus had the gods create the first woman, Pandora, whose name indicates that all (*pan-*) the gods had given her gifts (*-dora*). Hephaestus crafted her body, Athena taught her arts and crafts, and Hermes gave her cunning. After Pandora was created, Zeus gave her to Prometheus' dim-witted brother, Epimetheus. Pandora had with her a jar, filled with various plagues and evils. Pandora was given instructions not to open the jar, but eventually curiosity got the better of her, she gave in to temptation, and all manner of evils were released into the world. Only delusive hope managed to be kept within the jar. The fate of Pandora is murky after this point. Pandora and Epimetheus are called the parents of Pyrrha and Deucalion.

Sophocles wrote a *Pandora* (also entitled *Hammerers*; Greek: *Sphyrokopoi*), which was surely a SATYR PLAY.

One fragment probably refers to molding the clay for Pandora's body; another mentions a male who, after drinking lots of wine, will have his penis massaged. The comic poet Nicophon also wrote a *Pandora,* but the 20 or so words that survive tell nothing about the play's plot (fragments 5–11 Kock). [ANCIENT SOURCES: Hesiod, *Theogony* 570–612, *Works and Days* 47–105]

BIBLIOGRAPHY
Kiso, A. *The Lost Sophocles.* New York: Vantage Press, 1984.
Kock, T. *Comicorum Atticorum Fragmenta.* Vol. 1. Leipzig: Teubner, 1880.
Lloyd-Jones, H. *Sophocles: Fragments.* Cambridge, Mass.: Harvard University Press, 1996.
Radt, S. *Tragicorum Graecorum Fragmenta.* Vol. 4. Göttingen, Ger.: Vandenhoeck & Ruprecht, 1977.
Sutton, D. F. *The Lost Sophocles.* Lanham, Md.: University Press of America, 1984.

PANHELLENES   A name given to the Greeks as a united group. [ANCIENT SOURCES: Aristophanes, *Peace* 302; Euripides, *Iphigenia at Aulis* 350, 414, *Suppliant Women* 526, 671, *Trojan Women* 413, 721; Homer, *Iliad* 2.530]

PANOPTES   Another name for the multieyed ARGUS, the guardian of IO. The name Panoptes means "all-seeing." [ANCIENT SOURCES: Aeschylus, *Suppliant Women* 304; Aristophanes, *Ecclesiazusae* 80; Euripides, *Phoenician Women* 1115]

PANTOMIME   A type of dramatic performance, popular among the Romans, that combined dancing and the acting of stories from mythology. The actor in pantomime wore a mask, danced, and acted but did not sing. The actor was accompanied, however, by a chorus, whose words explained the actor's gestures. In Lucian's *On the Dance* (67–68), the author marvels at how the actor in pantomime acted out all the various parts in a story, pretending to be ATHAMAS at one moment, INO the next, or ATREUS one moment and THYESTES the next.

BIBLIOGRAPHY
Csapo, E., and W. J. Slater. *The Context of Ancient Drama.* Ann Arbor: University of Michigan Press, 1995, 369–89.

PAPHOS   A town on the island of Cyprus, Paphos was a center for the worship of APHRODITE, who was said to have been born on the island. [ANCIENT SOURCES: Aeschylus, *Persians* 891; Aristophanes, *Lysistrata* 833; Euripides, *Bacchae* 406]

PARABASIS   A Greek word meaning "coming forward," the parabasis is an extended song in old COMEDY that was performed by the CHORUS and directly addressed the audience. No actors were onstage during the parabasis. The only surviving examples of the parabasis appear in ARISTOPHANES' plays, and two of his plays, KNIGHTS and BIRDS, contain two parabases. Some Aristophanic plays do not contain a parabasis (ECCLESIAZUSAE, WEALTH). The parabasis often contains the following structural elements: a farewell to the characters leaving the stage; a section in anapestic METER, in which the chorus leader speaks to the audience as if he were the poet; an ode to the gods; an epirrhema, in which the chorus leader gives advice to the audience; an antode, which has the same metrical pattern as the ode; and an antepirrhema, which has the same metrical pattern as the epirrhema.

The content of the parabasis varies from play to play; an Aristophanic parabasis often contains remarks on Athenian politicians or politics. In some instances, such as in WASPS, the parabasis contains a complaint from Aristophanes about the audience's reception of his previous play. In PEACE, the chorus argue that Aristophanes should be praised for not resorting to tired old routines in his comedies. Not all parabases focus on political matters or Aristophanes' concerns as a poet. The first parabasis in *Birds* presents an account of the creation of the universe in which birds play a central role.

BIBLIOGRAPHY
Bowie, A. M. "The Parabasis in Aristophanes: Prolegomena, *Acharnians,*" *Classical Quarterly* 32 (1982): 27–40.
Dover, K. J. *Aristophanic Comedy.* Berkeley: University of California Press, 1972, 49–53.
Hubbard, T. K. *The Mask of Comedy: Aristophanes and the Intertextual Parabasis.* Ithaca, N.Y.: Cornell University Press, 1991.
Sifakis, G. M. *Parabasis and Animal Choruses: A Contribution to the History of Attic Comedy.* London: Athlone Press, 1971.

PARALUS (1)   A special Athenian ship used for public business. The sailors on this ship were called the Paraloi. [ANCIENT SOURCES: Aristophanes, *Birds* 1204, *Frogs* 1071; Thucydides, 3.77, 8.73–74, 8.86]

PARALUS (2)   A coastal district in Athenian territory. [ANCIENT SOURCES: Aristophanes, *Lysistrata* 58; Euripides, *Suppliant Women* 659]

PARASITE (Greek: *KOLAX, PARASITOS*; Latin: *PARASITUS*)   Although parasites are usually thought of as stock characters only in New Comedy, those who behaved as parasites appeared in earlier Greek drama as well (for example, EUPOLIS' *Flatterers* of 421 B.C.E.). The Greek word *parasitos* literally means "food beside." Accordingly, the primary goal of the parasite is to find a free meal whenever possible. When a parasite takes the stage, the audience can expect to hear several jokes about food and the parasite's voracious hunger. In PLAUTUS' *STICHUS,* the first word the parasite Gelasimus speaks is *hunger,* who he claims is his mother. The cook in Plautus' *TWO MENAECHMI* (222–23) quips that a parasite can easily eat as much as eight people. In exchange for food, the parasite often performs various odd jobs for a patron. In Plautus' *CURCULIO,* for example, the parasite, Curculio, helps his patron, Phaedromus, in his efforts to acquire the young woman Planesium. In Plautus' *CAPTIVES,* the parasite, Ergasilus, characterizes himself as something of a witty jester and humorist whose delightful company would serve as "payment" for the food he would consume. In Plautus' *PERSIAN,* the appetite of the parasite, Saturio, so rules his life that he is willing to sell his daughter (albeit temporarily) to satisfy his belly.

BIBLIOGRAPHY
Damon, C. *The Mask of the Parasite: A Pathology of Roman Patronage.* Ann Arbor: University of Michigan Press, 1997.
Frangoulidis, Stavros A. "The Parasite as Poet-Playwright and the Slave as Parasite in Terence's *Phormio,*" *Bolletino di Studi Latini* 25, no. 2 (1995): 397–425.
———. "(Meta)theatre as Therapy in Terence's *Phormio,*" *Classica et Mediaevalia* 47 (1996): 169–206.
Leach, E. W. "Ergasilus and the Ironies of the *Captivi,*" *Classica et Mediaevalia* 30 (1969): 263–96.

PARASKENION   A Greek word (plural: *Paraskenia*) that means "beside the SKENE (stage building)." The term *paraskenion* can refer either to the space on stage to the sides of the *skene* or structures that project forward from either side of the *skene.* Pollux uses the term *paraskenion* in reference to a member of the chorus who serves as a fourth actor. [ANCIENT SOURCES: Demosthenes, 21.17; Pollux, *Onomasticon* 4.109]

BIBLIOGRAPHY
Csapo, E., and W. J. Slater. *The Context of Ancient Drama.* Ann Arbor: University of Michigan Press, 1995, 80–84.

PARCAE   A Roman name for the FATES.

PARIS (ALEXANDER)   Paris was the son of PRIAM and HECABE. Immediately before Hecabe gave birth to Paris, she dreamed that she gave birth to a blazing torch that was wriggling with serpents. When the dream was reported to the local prophets, they told Hecabe to kill the child because it would destroy the kingdom. Accordingly, after Paris' birth, he was exposed, but he was later rescued by a shepherd, who pitied the infant.

Once, after Paris grew up, HERMES took three goddesses (HERA, ATHENA, and APHRODITE) to him as he tended flocks on Mount Ida. Paris was told that he was to choose which goddess was the fairest. Each goddess tried to bribe Paris to choose her: Hera offered Paris the power of a king, Athena success as a great warrior, and Aphrodite the most beautiful woman in the world, HELEN of SPARTA, the wife of MENELAUS. When Paris chose Aphrodite as the fairest, the other two divinities left angry and began to plot Paris' ruin. Although Paris had chosen Aphrodite, he was still a simple shepherd living in the Trojan countryside, while Helen lived on the other side of the AEGEAN SEA at Sparta. That would soon change, however.

Not long afterward, Paris returned to Troy to compete in some funeral games that were held in honor of one of Priam's sons—ironically, Paris himself. Because the prize was to be a bull that Paris himself had raised and cared for, the young shepherd did not want to lose it. When Paris defeated the competition (ironically, his own brothers), they became enraged and threatened to kill him. After Paris took refuge at a nearby altar of Zeus Herceius (Zeus of the Oath), the prophetess CAS-SANDRA revealed that Paris was her brother. At this, Priam accepted Paris as his son and welcomed him to the royal palace.

As a Trojan prince, Paris now had the financial resources at his disposal to sail to Sparta. Once there, Paris made his way to Menelaus' home. The unsuspecting Menelaus entertained the exotic foreigner in his home and eventually left him alone with Helen when he attended a relative's funeral outside Sparta. With Menelaus out of the way, Paris abducted Helen and sailed with her to TROY.

During the ensuing Trojan War fought to recover Helen, we hear relatively little about Paris. In the war's 10th year, he fought a one-on-one combat with Menelaus, which would have decided the war and which Menelaus would have won had Aphrodite not rescued Paris. Eventually, PHILOCTETES killed Paris with a volley of arrows from the bow of HERACLES.

Although Paris is one of the most-often mentioned figures in classical mythology, he does not appear as a character in any extant classical drama. Paris would have been a character in tragedies, comedies, and SATYR PLAYS. Both EURIPIDES and SOPHOCLES wrote plays entitled *Alexander*. Euripides' play was part of the trilogy of 415 B.C.E. that included *Palamedes* (?) and *Trojan Women*. Sophocles' play seems to have treated the return of Paris to Troy and his recognition as Priam's son. ENNIUS wrote a tragic *Alexander*, of which about 40 lines are extant (fragments 17–26 Jocelyn). An 11-line fragment, perhaps the words of Cassandra in the prologue, mentions Hecabe's dream before Paris' birth and a prophecy by Apollo that Paris would be the ruin of Troy. Other fragments suggest that Ennius' play dealt with Paris' return to Troy for the games and his subsequent recognition as Priam's son. [ANCIENT SOURCES: Apollodorus, *Library* 3.12.5–6, *Epitome* 3.1–5, 5.8; *Cypria* 1, 9, 10; Euripides, *Andromache* 274–308, *Helen* 22–30, *Trojan Women* 920–32; Hyginus, *Fables* 91, 92, 110; Homer, *Iliad* 3, 6, 7.347–64, 11.368–83, 22.355–60; *Little Iliad* 1]

BIBLIOGRAPHY
Kiso, A. *The Lost Sophocles.* New York: Vantage Press, 1984.

Lloyd-Jones, H. *Sophocles: Fragments.* Cambridge, Mass.: Harvard University Press, 1996.
Radt, S. *Tragicorum Graecorum Fragmenta.* Vol. 4. Göttingen, Ger.: Vandenhoeck & Ruprecht, 1977.
Sutton, D. F. *The Lost Sophocles.* Lanham, Md.: University Press of America, 1984.
Warmington, E. H. *Remains of Old Latin: Ennius and Caecilius.* Vol. 1. Cambridge, Mass.: and London: Harvard University Press, 1935.
Webster, T. B. L. *The Tragedies of Euripides.* London: Methuen, 1967.

PARNASSUS   Both a mountain range and a twin-peaked mountain (almost 8,000 feet in height) in north central Greece. The town of DELPHI and APOLLO's temple and oracle are located on the southern slopes of Parnassus. For two extant plays, audiences must imagine Parnassus as the backdrop: AESCHYLUS' *Eumenides* (see ORESTEIA) opens at Apollo's temple on Parnassus; Euripides' *ION* is set at Apollo's temple at Delphi, and ION threatens to have CREUSA thrown from Parnassus after she tries to kill him. [ANCIENT SOURCES: Aeschylus, *Eumenides* 11 (see ORESTEIA; Aristophanes, *Frogs* 1057; Euripides, *Ion* 1267; Seneca, *Oedipus* 227, 281]

BIBLIOGRAPHY
McInerney, J. "Parnassus, Delphi, and the Thyiades," *Greek, Roman, and Byzantine Studies* 38, no. 3 (1997): 263–83.

PARNES   A well-forested mountain on the northern edge of Athenian territory. Parnes was close to the DEME of ACHARNAE, and charcoal producers would have used timber from Parnes to make their product. In the second century C.E., Pausanias noted a few altars to Zeus on Parnes and wrote that people hunted bears and wild boar on the mountain. [ANCIENT SOURCES: Aristophanes, *Acharnians* 348, *Clouds* 323; Pausanias, 1.32.1–2]

BIBLIOGRAPHY
Sommerstein, A. H. *The Comedies of Aristophanes.* Vol. 1, *Acharnians.* Warminster, U.K.: Aris & Phillips, 1980, 171.

PARODOS (1)   The song sung by the chorus when they first enter the ORCHESTRA. [ANCIENT SOURCES: Aristotle, *Poetics* 1452b22; Plutarch, *Old Men in Public Affairs* 785a]

BIBLIOGRAPHY

Calame, Claude. "From Choral Poetry to Tragic Stasimon: The Enactment of Women's Song," *Arion* 3, no. 1 (1994–95): 136–54.

Davidson, J. F. "The *Parodos* of Sophocles' *Ajax*," *Bulletin of the Institute of Classical Studies of the University of London* 22 (1975): 163–77.

Hoey, T. F. "Sun Symbolism in the *Parodos* of the *Trachiniae*," *Arethusa* 5 (1972): 133–54.

Verdenius, W. J. "Notes on the *Parodos* of Euripides' *Bacchae*," *Mnemosyne* 34 (1981): 300–15.

Zimmermann, B. "The *Parodoi* of the Aristophanic Comedies: Thoughts on the Typology and on the Function of the Entrance of the Chorus in the Comedies of Aristophanes," *Studi Italiani di Filologia Classica* 2, no. 3 (1984): 13–24.

***PARODOS* (2)**   Also called an *eisodos*, a *parados* is one of the two entry paths (plural: *parodoi*) into the ORCHESTRA from the sides of the theater. With the exception of entries and exits to and from the *skene*, entries and exits to the acting space occur via the *parodoi*. [ANCIENT SOURCES: Aristotle, *Nichomachean Ethics* 1123a23; Pollux, 4.108; Plutarch, *Precepts of Stagecraft* 805d]

PARODY   Imitation of an author's style or work for comic effect. ARISTOPHANES' plays frequently employ parody, especially of EURIPIDES and his plays. In *ACHARNIANS*, for example, DICAEOPOLIS' taking some charcoal hostage parodies Euripides' *Telephus*, in which the title character takes AGAMEMNON's son, ORESTES, hostage. Aristophanes' *THESMOPHORIAZUSAE* contains a series of parodies of Euripidean plays. Not only is parody found in COMEDY, but tragic poets could also employ this technique. Euripides' *ELECTRA* contains a parody of the recognition scene of ELECTRA and Orestes in AESCHYLUS' *Libation Bearers* (see *ORESTEIA*).

BIBLIOGRAPHY

Hammond, N. G. L. "Spectacle and Parody in Euripides' *Electra*," *Greek, Roman, and Byzantine Studies* 25 (1984): 373–87.

Marianetti, M. C. "Socratic Mystery-Parody and the Issue of *Asebeia* in Aristophanes' *Clouds*." *Symbolae Osloenses* 68 (1993): 5–31.

Nesselrath, H. "Parody and Later Greek Comedy," *Harvard Studies in Classical Philology* 95 (1993): 181–95.

Scharffenberger, E. W. "Parody, Satire, Irony, and Politics: From Euripides' *Orestes* to Aristophanes' *Frogs*," *Text and Presentation* 19 (1998): 111–22.

PAROS   A small island (with a circumference of about 36 miles) in the AEGEAN SEA west of NAXOS is famous for its marble. In the early fifth century B.C.E., the island fell to the Persians; later in the century, after XERXES' defeat, it was under ATHENS' control. [ANCIENT SOURCES: Aeschylus, *Persians* 884; Aristophanes, *Wasps* 1189]

PARRHASIA   A town in Arcadia (a region in southern Greece). Sometimes poets use the name Parrhasia as a synonym for Arcadia. According to one tradition, ORESTES spent some time in exile in Parrhasia after he killed his mother. [ANCIENT SOURCES: Euripides, *Orestes* 1645; Seneca, *Agamemnon* 831, *Hercules Oetaeus* 1281, *Hippolytus* 288]

PARTHENOPAEUS   The son of Melanion (or Hippomenes) and ATALANTA or MELEAGER and Atalanta, Parthenopaeus was exposed at birth on Mount Parthenius, but he survived and grew up to fight in the battle of the Seven against THEBES. Parthenopaeus died during the battle, but his son (variously named Promachus, Stratolaüs, Thesimenes, or Tlesimenes) later marched against the Thebans and was victorious. The Greek tragedian Astydamas wrote a *Parthenopaeus*, of which only the title survives (fragment 5b Snell). [ANCIENT SOURCES: Aeschylus, *Seven against Thebes* 547; Apollodorus, *Library* 1.9.13, 3.6.3; Euripides, *Suppliant Women* 889, *Phoenician Women* 150, 1106; Hyginus, *Fables* 70, 71, 100; Sophocles, *Oedipus at Colonus* 1320]

BIBLIOGRAPHY

Snell, B. *Tragicorum Graecorum Fragmenta*. Vol. 1. Göttingen, Ger.: Vandenhoeck & Ruprecht, 1971.

PASIAS   The name of a person mentioned by ARISTOPHANES at *CLOUDS* 21 as one of the people to whom STREPSIADES owes money. Later in the play, at line 1224, an unnamed creditor arrives and demands money from Strepsiades; some manuscripts of the play name this creditor Pasias. Pasias has not been identified with any actual historical person.

BIBLIOGRAPHY
Dover, K. J. *Aristophanes: Clouds.* Oxford: Clarendon Press, 1989, xxix–xxxii.

PASIPHAE   A daughter of Helius (see SUN) and Persies, Pasiphae, queen of Knossos, was the wife of MINOS and by him the mother of numerous children: Androgeus, Catreus, Deucalion, Glaucus, Acacallis, ARIADNE, PHAEDRA, and Xenodice. The most important of these children in drama are Ariadne and Phaedra. Having conceived a passion for a certain bull in the herds of MINOS, Pasiphae apparently related her feelings to the artisan DAEDALUS, who built a hollow wooden cow that Pasiphae could enter. With the aid of this wooden cow, Pasiphae was able to have her lust satisfied. She became pregnant and produced the MINOTAUR, a creature that was part human and part bull.

Pasiphae does not appear as a character in any extant play, although she is the speaker in a fragment of almost 40 lines from EURIPIDES' *Cretans* (see Page's edition). In this fragment, Pasiphae defends her passion for the bull and claims it was a madness caused by POSEIDON, whom Minos had offended. Thus, Pasiphae eventually blames her husband for her relationship with the bull and defiantly urges him to kill her if he wishes. Minos accepts her challenge, orders her to be imprisoned, and threatens her with death. Unfortunately, the rest of the play is lost and we do not know what eventually happened to Pasiphae in Euripides' play. Other sources indicate that she survived and released Daedalus from a similar imprisonment. The Greek comic poet Alcaeus wrote a *Pasiphae,* whose two lines that survive indicate nothing of the plot (fragments 26–27 Kock). [ANCIENT SOURCES: Apollodorus, *Library* 1.9.1, 3.1.2, 4, 3.15.1, 8; Euripides, *Hippolytus* 337–38; Hyginus, *Fables* proem 36, *Fables* 40]

BIBLIOGRAPHY
Kerényi, Karl. *Töchter der Sonne: Betrachtungen über griechische Gottheiten.* Stuttgart: Klett-Cotta, 1997.
Kock, T. *Comicorum Atticorum Fragmenta.* Vol. 1. Leipzig: Teubner, 1880.
Page, D. L. *Select Papyri.* Vol. 3. 1941. Reprint, London: Heinemann, 1970, 70–77.
Reckford, K. J. "Phaedra and Pasiphae: The Pull Backward," *Transactions of the American Philological Association* 104 (1974): 307–28.

PATROCLEIDES   An Athenian statesman mentioned by ARISTOPHANES as someone who defecated in his clothes while watching theatrical productions. Dunbar suggests that he may have proposed a decree in the 420s about trade with Aphytis, an ally of the Athenians' in Chalcidice, and in 405 proposed restoration of citizens' rights to many who had been disenfranchised. [ANCIENT SOURCES: Aristophanes, *Birds* 790]

BIBLIOGRAPHY
Dunbar, Nan. *Aristophanes: Birds.* Oxford: Clarendon Press, 1995, 482.
McDevitt, A. S. "Andocides I,78 and the Decree of Patrocleides," *Hermes* 98 (1970): 503–05.

PATROCLES   A wealthy miser mentioned by ARISTOPHANES in *WEALTH.* Because several persons named Patrocles were active when *Wealth* was staged, this Patrocles cannot be identified. [ANCIENT SOURCES: Aristophanes, *Wealth* 84, fragment 455 Kock]

BIBLIOGRAPHY
Sommerstein, A. H. *The Comedies of Aristophanes.* Vol. 11, *Wealth.* Warminster, U.K.: Aris & Phillips, 2001, 140.

PATROCLUS   The son of Menoetius and Sthenele (or Periopis or Perimele), Patroclus was famous as ACHILLES' best friend and, according to some, his lover. During the final year of the Trojan War, Patroclus was killed by HECTOR after Patroclus, to frighten the Trojans and to stem their rampage in the Greek camp, went into battle wearing Achilles' armor. After Achilles' death, the ashes of Achilles and Patroclus were buried together. Patroclus does not appear as a character in any surviving plays, but in AESCHYLUS' *Myrmidons* Patroclus and Achilles are portrayed as lovers. [ANCIENT SOURCES: Apollodorus, *Library* 3.13.8, *Epitome* 4.6–7, 5.5; Aristophanes, *Frogs* 1041; Athenaeus, 13.601a–b, 13.602e; Homer, *Iliad;* Hyginus, *Fables* 106, 114; Plato, *Symposium* 180a; Sophocles, *Philoctetes* 434]

PAUSON   A painter of caricature "and . . . novelty pictures that could be viewed upside down . . . or that gave the illusion of three-dimensionality" (Sommerstein). ARISTOPHANES mocks Pauson for his poverty, jokes, and riddles. [ANCIENT SOURCES: Aristophanes, *Acharnians* 854, *Thesmophoriazusae* 949, *Wealth* 602; Aristotle, *Metaphysics* 1050a19, *Poetics* 1448a6; Lucian, *Encomium of Demosthenes* 24; Plutarch, *Moralia* 396e]

BIBLIOGRAPHY
Sommerstein, A. H. *The Comedies of Aristophanes.* Vol. 11, *Wealth.* Warminster, U.K.: Aris & Phillips, 2001, 178.

PEACE (Greek: *EIRENE*; Latin: *PAX*)

ARISTOPHANES (421 B.C.E.) The second of ARISTOPHANES' three peace plays (see also *ACHARNIANS* and *LYSISTRATA*), *Peace* received the second prize at the City DIONYSIA. The play opens at the country house of an Athenian farmer, Trygaeus. As in *KNIGHTS* and *WASPS,* Aristophanes begins to unfold the plot through the conversation of two slaves, both unnamed in *Peace.* These slaves, who serve TRYGAEUS, have been given the task of preparing cakes of dung that are to be fed to a giant dung beetle. Trygaeus, upset by the hardships of the war between ATHENS and SPARTA, has grown angry with the gods. Thus, on the back of the giant dung beetle, he wants to fly to Mount OLYMPUS to try to arrange peace for the Greeks. Trygaeus has chosen the beetle because, according to one of AESOP's fables, the beetle was the only winged creature ever to reach the gods.

After bidding his household farewell, Trygaeus mounts the dung beetle and is raised into the air (using the MECHANE). When he lands, the audience must imagine that the scene has shifted to Mount Olympus and the palace of ZEUS, where Trygaeus is met by HERMES. Hermes informs him that the other gods have gone farther up into heaven because they do not want to see the Greeks' waging war. Hermes also tells Trygaeus that War has buried Peace in a deep cavern. Furthermore, War is planning to use a giant mortar to grind the Greek cities to bits. Soon, War himself emerges with his giant mortar and begins throwing various cities into it as if he were making a salad (PRASIAE, which represents the salad greens; MEGARA, famous for its garlic; SICILY, synonymous with cheese; and the region of Attica, known for its honey). After War throws the city ingredients into the mortar, he needs a pestle. Lacking one, War calls upon his slave, Riot, to go to Athens and get him a pestle (the demagogue CLEON is the "pestle"

of Athens). Riot soon returns and informs War that Cleon is dead. War sends Riot to Sparta to borrow their pestle, the Spartan leader, BRASIDAS, but he is also dead. Therefore, War goes off to make himself a pestle. Trygaeus, horrified by the prospect of another "pestle" like Cleon or Brasidas, calls on the people of Greece to help him pull Peace out of her cavern.

Trygaeus' call is answered by the CHORUS, who represent a group of farmers. Upon hearing what Trygaeus intends, the chorus gladly and excitedly agree to help him dig Peace out of her prison. As Trygaeus and the chorus begin the excavation, Hermes arrives and threatens them with death for what they are doing. When Trygaeus, however, tells Hermes that the Moon and Sun are plotting to betray Greece to the barbarians, who do not sacrifice to gods such as Hermes and Zeus, Hermes agrees to help Trygaeus and his fellow farmers dig out Peace. After a LIBATION and prayers to the gods against warmongers, the group (who are imagined to include men from several different Greek towns) begin to haul out Peace. Although some of the cities provide little or no help, Peace is eventually rescued when the farmers take the lead in the effort.

When the beautiful Peace emerges, she is accompanied by two beautiful attendants, Opôra (season for harvesting fruit) and Theoria (spectacle or delegation). As Trygaeus rejoices in Peace's sweet breath and fragrance, Hermes notes that the various cities are beginning to be reconciled. They also note, however, that those in the audience who work in professions that profit from war are unhappy, but those who work in professions that profit from farming are in good spirits. Next, the farmers are sent back home to return to their fields and the pleasures of peace. After the farmers rejoice in anticipation of all of life's simple pleasures to which they will return, they ask Hermes to explain why Peace has been absent for so long. On the Athenian side, Hermes blames the start of the trouble largely on the Athenian leader, PERICLES, and the Megarian Decree. On the Spartan side, Hermes suggests that they were bribed to enter the conflict by cities who were tired of paying tribute to the Athenians. The Spartans ravaged the Athenian countryside, compelling the rural population to seek refuge within the city walls of Athens, where clever Athenian politicians, especially Cleon, were able to hold the simple folks' attention.

After Hermes' explanation, Trygaeus notices that Peace herself has remained silent and asks Hermes the reason. Hermes states that Peace is angry with the people in the audience because they rejected earlier opportunities to make peace with the Spartans. With Hermes speaking on her behalf, Peace then asks about the politicians currently in favor with the citizens and how some of the poets are faring. Hermes then tells Trygaeus that he will arrange to have Opōra marry him so that together they can produce grapevines. Hermes asks that Theoria be given back to the town council in Athens, because she belonged to them long ago. With this, Hermes and Trygaeus prepare to leave. Zeus, however, is now using Trygaeus' dung beetle to pull his chariot, so Hermes tells Trygaeus that Peace will transport him back to his home.

Upon the departure of Hermes and Trygaeus, accompanied by Peace and her two attendants, the chorus deliver the PARABASIS. Here, the chorus argue that Aristophanes deserves praise because he has not resorted to tired old routines in his comedies. Instead, he has injected lofty thought and diction into his comedies. Furthermore, they note that Aristophanes has taken on the most powerful men of the day (namely, Cleon). The chorus go on to urge that Aristophanes be awarded the prize for this play. Next, the chorus invite the Muse to join them in a song, in which the chorus urge the Muse not to help Aristophanes' rival poets.

After the parabasis, the scene returns to Earth and the house of Trygaeus, who is met by one of his servants. The servant questions Trygaeus about his adventures and about the divine women who are with him. Trygaeus informs the slave that he is going to marry Opōra and tells him to prepare a bath for her and a marriage banquet and couch. Trygaeus says he will give Theoria back to the town council. As Trygaeus turns Theoria over to the men in the audience who occupy the seats reserved for the councilors, he gives a speech laced with sexual innuendo that anticipates the fun they will have with Theoria ("spectacle"). After Theoria is turned over to the council, Trygaeus and his slave perform a ritual to inaugurate the worship of Peace. Their ritual concludes with a lengthy prayer that asks Peace to allow the Greeks to get along with one another. Trygaeus then sends his servant into the house to sacrifice the sheep, because he claims Peace does not like the sight of blood. While the servant is gone, Trygaeus prepares a fire to roast the sheep, with which the servant soon arrives.

As the servant begins to roast the sheep, an ORACLE monger named Hierocles approaches and wants to know to whom Trygaeus and his servant are making sacrifice. Trygaeus tries to ignore the man, but the oracle monger begins to help them roast the various parts of the sheep. When the oracle monger learns that they are sacrificing to Peace, he calls them fools and with bizarre language prophesies that this is not the time for Peace. All the same, the oracle monger wants to partake of some of the sacrifice. Trygaeus, however, finally manages to drive away the pesky fellow.

After the oracle monger's exit, the chorus deliver a second parabasis. They rejoice in the simple pleasures of a life free of war, especially the fruits of the grapevine. They make fun of the man who dresses as a warrior but acts as a coward once a battle begins. They sympathize with the poor men from the countryside who are called upon to face the hardest fighting and complain about shameless people from the city who fare better in military service.

After the second parabasis, Trygaeus enters and prepares to enjoy his wedding feast. He is joined by a sickle maker and a seller of storage vessels for wine, whose businesses have been improved dramatically by the arrival of Peace. After these two men thank Trygaeus and give him wedding presents of sickles and storage vessels, Trygaeus invites them to join his celebration. Next, a parade of men, whose livelihood depended on war (e.g., a breastplate maker, a helmet maker), enter and complain to Trygaeus that their businesses have been ruined. Trygaeus mockingly tries to appease these men by suggesting new ways in which their products could be used (e.g., breastplates can be used as chamber pots). Eventually, however, those who profited from the business of war depart in anger from the banquet.

After the rejection of the war profiteers, Trygaeus calls upon the boys who have accompanied his guests to come out and practice their singing. After hearing the warlike song of the first boy, however, Trygaeus discovers that the boy is the son of the general LAMACHUS and drives him from the banquet. A second boy, the son of CLEONYMUS, sings a poem by the poet Archilochus about a coward who (as did Cleonymus himself) threw away his shield in battle. Trygaeus also does not like this song and chastises the boy for singing about a person who shamed his parents by being a coward. The play concludes with Trygaeus' urging his guests to partake of the feast. They chorus then call for Trygaeus' bride, Opôra, to be summoned, and then she and Trygaeus process out as Trygaeus sings the marriage hymn to the god HYMEN.

COMMENTARY

Of Aristophanes' three extant peace plays, *Peace* has received the least attention from modern scholars. In some ways, the play may have been anticlimactic because the Athenians and Spartans were on the verge of concluding a peace treaty when it was produced. The chief warmongers on the Athenian and Spartan sides (Cleon and Brasidas, respectively) had both died in the previous year, so public feeling in Athens must have been quite optimistic.

The staging of the play is problematic because of the travel between Earth and heaven and because the stage directions are not extant. Trygaeus uses the *mechane* to reach heaven, but where would heaven have been located in the Athenian theater? The wooden stage building had a second story, but how many characters could this second level have accommodated for the more than 500 lines that Trygaeus spends in heaven? Perhaps Hermes stands on the second story, while Trygaeus and the remaining characters appear below in the orchestra. Thus, in Trygaeus' ascent from the orchestra and then descent back into it, the spectators must simply imagine the change of scene as they were called upon to do in so many other Aristophanic plays.

The rescue of Peace and the way she was excavated from the "pit" are also somewhat problematic, but these actions probably would have been accomplished by workers' hauling Peace through the front doors of the SKENE by using the ECCYCLEMA. Regarding Peace, it appears that a statue was used rather than a human

being, but that the women who attend her were played by actors. It is uncertain, however, whether these actors were males dressed as women or women who would not have been Athenian citizens.

As noted, *Peace* is one of three surviving Aristophanic peace plays. As in *Lysistrata*, 10 years later, Trygaeus' peace extends to all Greeks, in contrast to the personal peace treaty into which Dicaeopolis entered in *Acharnians*. In other respects, however, *Peace* more closely resembles *Acharnians*. Both plays have heroes who are rustic males, both have choruses composed of rustic men, and both plays have an agrarian focus that is lacking in *Lysistrata*.

As *Acharnians* does, *Peace* focuses on the economic implications of war and peace. *Lysistrata* has more emphasis on the impact of war on husbands and wives; *Acharnians* and *Peace* focus on the economic benefits of peace. In *Peace*, Aristophanes pays some attention to those who benefit economically from the peace but spends more time allowing his audience to view the challenges that peace might create for those who have profited from war (the sickle maker, crest maker, breastplate seller, helmet seller, spear burnisher, and trumpeteer). Of course, Aristophanes has little sympathy for those who profit from the war-driven economy, and such men are not allowed to benefit from Trygaeus' peace.

The opening premise of *Peace*, Trygaeus' flying to heaven on a dung beetle, is far more humorous than the scheme of the personal peace treaty that Dicaeopolis arranges. The humor of this scheme has the additional fun of being a parody of EURIPIDES' character, BELLEROPHON, who attempted to fly to Olympus on the winged horse PEGASUS. Whereas Bellerophon's flight failed, Trygaeus' succeeds.

Trygaeus' journey between heaven and Earth also gives *Peace* an orientation different from that of *Acharnians* and *Lysistrata*. Other than the mission of the god between Dicaeopolis and the Spartans, the events of *Acharnians* generally move along an axis between the Athenian city and the Athenian countryside. In *Lysistrata*, the action begins with non-Athenians entering the city of Athens, returning to their respective towns to initiate the sex strike, and then sending their males back to the city of Athens. Trygaeus' journey from

Earth to heaven and back again gives a vertical dimension to *Peace* that is not present in the other peace plays. Dicaeopolis' peace was bought with money, and Lysistrata's peace was achieved through sexual deprivation. Trygaeus' peace is acheived through negotiation with a representative of the gods and the unified effort of farmers (*georgoi*). Trygaeus' peace is much more an accord between heaven and Earth, a notion given more attention in *Peace* than in the other plays. Furthermore, whereas *Acharnians* and *Lysistrata* conclude with the promise of sexual relations between men and women as a result of peace, *Peace* ends with a sacred marriage between Trygaeus and the divine Opôra. This union promises more than just physical pleasure: It points to a restoration of the fertility of the fields, whose fruits war destroyed and peace will allow to flourish again.

Although Aristophanes' *Peace* starts with an amusing premise, perhaps because its second half follows several of the formulae already seen in earlier Aristophanic plays, the play seems to lack the vitality and liveliness of *Acharnians*. Thus, Walton observes that despite the play's promising beginning, "the idea tails off. There is no confrontation with War, no follow-up to Hermes' conversion to the peace party, no new development in the plot to have purpose to any of the second half."

BIBLIOGRAPHY

McGlew, J. F. "Identity and Ideology: The Farmer Chorus of Aristophanes' *Peace*," *Syllecta Classica* 12 (2001): 74–97.

Newiger, H. J. "War and Peace in the Comedy of Aristophanes," *Yale Classical Studies* 26 (1980): 219–37.

Olson, S. D. *Aristophanes: Peace*. Oxford: Clarendon Press, 1998.

Sommerstein, A. H. *The Comedies of Aristophanes*. Vol. 5, *Peace*. Warminster, U.K.: Aris & Philips, 1985.

Walton, J. M. *Living Greek Theatre*. New York: Greenwood Press, 1987, 195.

PEACE OF NICIAS

Several days after ARISTOPHANES' *PEACE* was staged in 421 B.C.E., the Athenians and Spartans entered into a peace agreement known as the Peace of NICIAS (the treaty's chief architect). This treaty put a temporary halt to the PELOPONNESIAN WAR. The people of BOEOTIA, CORINTH, MEGARA, and ELIS,

allies of the Spartans, refused to sign the treaty. The peace was supposed to last for 50 years, but actually lasted only about five years. [ANCIENT SOURCES: Plutarch, *Nicias* 9.7; Thucydides, 5.17]

PEGASUS

The child of POSEIDON and MEDUSA and the brother of Chrysaor, Pegasus was a famous winged horse that helped BELLEROPHON. In ARISTOPHANES' *PEACE*, TRYGAEUS compares the dung beetle that he will fly to heaven to Pegasus. [ANCIENT SOURCES: Apollodorus, *Library* 2.4.2; Aristophanes, *Peace* 76, 135, 154; Seneca, *Trojan Women* 385]

PEIRAEUS

The name of the main harbor at ATHENS. [ANCIENT SOURCES: Aristophanes, *Peace* 145, 165]

PEIRENE

A famous spring at the town of CORINTH. [ANCIENT SOURCES: Pausanias, 2.3.2; Euripides, *Medea* 69, *Trojan Women* 205; Plautus, *Pot of Gold* 559; Seneca, *Medea* 745]

PEISANDER

The son of Glaucetes, Peisander, from the DEME of ACHARNAE, was a prominent Athenian in the last quarter of the fifth century B.C.E. Comic poets mocked him as a warmonger who was clumsy, fat, gluttonous, and cowardly. In 415, Peisander served as a commissioner "to bring to justice those responsible for mutilating the statues of Hermes [on the eve of the SICILIAN EXPEDITION] and parodying the Mysteries" (Dunbar). In 411, Peisander took part in the oligarchic revolution that overthrew the democracy in ATHENS; after the fall of the oligarchs Peisander left Athens and in his absence was sentenced to die. [ANCIENT SOURCES: Aelian, *Varia Historia* 1.27; Andocides 1.27, 36, 43; Aristophanes, *Birds* 1556, *Lysistrata* 490, *Peace* 395–99; Eupolis, fragments 31, 182 Kock; Phrynichus, fragment 20 Kock; Thucydides, 8.49–56, 63–68, 98.1; Xenophon, *Symposium* 2.14]

BIBLIOGRAPHY

Dunbar, Nan. *Aristophanes: Birds*. New York: Oxford University Press, 1995, 484–85.

Kock, T. *Comicorum Atticorum Fragmenta*. Vol. 1. Leipzig: Teubner, 1880.

Sommerstein, A. H. *The Comedies of Aristophanes*. Vol. 5,
  Peace. Warminster, U.K.: Aris & Phillips, 1985, 151.
Woodhead, A.G. "Peisander," *American Journal of Philology*
  75 (1954): 131–46.

PEISETAERUS

Peisetaerus ("he who persuades his comrades") is the hero of ARISTOPHANES' BIRDS (414 B.C.E.). The spelling of his name has been debated and some editors have "Peisthetaerus." Peisetaeurs and his friend, EUELPIDES, leave ATHENS and decide to live with the birds. Peisetaerus persuades the birds to build a city that will rival the home of the gods and cause the gods to hand over sovereignty to them. The birds agree to Peisetaerus' plan, and the gods eventually submit to Peisetaerus. Some scholars have seen similarities between Peisetaerus and the Athenian statesman ALCIB-IADES, who persuaded the Athenians to undertake an expedition to SICILY in 415. For more on the similarities between Alcibiades and Peisetaerus, see the Commentary section in the entry on Aristophanes' *Birds*.

BIBLIOGRAPHY
Dunbar, Nan. "*Sophia* in Aristophanes' *Birds*," *Scripta Classica
  Israelica* 15 (1996): 61–71.
Epstein, P. D. "The Marriage of Peisthetairos to Basileia in
  the *Birds* of Aristophanes," *Dionysius* 5 (1981): 6–28.
Pozzi, D. C. "The Pastoral Ideal in the *Birds* of Aristo-
  phanes," *Classical Journal* 81 (1986): 119–29.

PEISIAS, SON OF

An otherwise unknown person whom ARISTOPHANES, at BIRDS 766, characterizes as someone who would betray the city of the birds to its enemies. The son of Peisias may have been involved in the mutilation of the Herms at Athens in 415 B.C.E. He has also been identified with a person named Cleombrotus, whose nickname was "the son of Partridge" (a fitting nickname for someone criticized in *Birds*). [ANCIENT SOURCES: Athenaeus, 389a]

BIBLIOGRAPHY
Dunbar, Nan. *Aristophanes: Birds*. New York: Oxford University Press, 1995, 473.

PELARGICON

The name for the ancient walls that surrounded the ACROPOLIS at ATHENS. ARISTO-PHANES uses the name at BIRDS 832 in reference to the potential walls for the city of the birds because Pelargi-con originally may have meant "stork's nest." [ANCIENT SOURCES: Aristophanes, *Birds* 832; Herodotus, 5.64.2; Thucydides, 2.17.1]

BIBLIOGRAPHY
Dunbar, Nan. *Aristophanes: Birds*. New York: Oxford University Press, 1995, 497–98.

PELASGIA   See PELASGUS.

PELASGUS

According to some sources, Pelasgus was born from the earth itself. Other sources say Pelasgus was the son of Palaechthon, the son of Phoroneus, the son of POSEIDON and Larissa, or the son of ZEUS and a woman named Niobe, who was the first mortal woman with whom Zeus had sexual relations. Pelasgus was a king of ARGOS, who married Ocean's daughter, Meliboea (or the nymph Cyllene), and had a son named Lycaon. This region and the entire region of the Peloponnese is sometimes named Pelasgia, and its people Pelasgians, after him. Pausanias reports that the people of Arcadia considered Pelasgus the first to inhabit their land. Pelasgus was also credited with inventing huts and sheepskin coats, teaching people how to identify and avoid poisonous food, and teaching people to feed upon acorns from oak trees.

Pelasgus appears as a character in AESCHYLUS' SUPPLIANT WOMEN. In this play, Pelasgus, although king of Argos, appears as the precursor of such later Athenian kings as Theseus in EURIPIDES' SUPPLIANT WOMEN and in SOPHOCLES' OEDIPUS AT COLONUS, or Theseus' son, DEMOPHON, in Euripides' CHILDREN OF HERACLES. As such, Pelasgus must choose between granting asylum in his land to the daughters of Danaus or risking attack from the sons of AEGYPTUS, who pursue them for marriage. Eventually, Pelasgus takes the women's case before the people of Argos and persuades them to vote to allow Danaus and his daughters to enjoy the protection of Argos. [ANCIENT SOURCES: Apollodorus, *Library* 2.1.1, 3.8.1; Pausanias, 1.14.2, 2.14.3, 8.1.4–5]

BIBLIOGRAPHY
Burian, P. "Pelasgus and Politics in Aeschylus' Danaid Tril-
  ogy," *Weiner Studien* 8 (1974): 5–14.
Tarkow, T. A. "The Dilemma of Pelasgus and the Nautical
  Imagery of Aeschylus' *Suppliants*," *Classica & Mediaevalia*
  31 (1970): 1–13

Turner, Chad. "Perverted Supplication and Other Inversions in Aeschylus' 'Danaid' Trilogy," *Classical Journal* 97, no. 1 (2001–2): 27–50.

PELEUS The son of AEACUS and Endeis, Peleus was the king of PHTHIA. Peleus was born on AEGINA, where his father was king. After Peleus and his brother, TELAMON, killed their stepbrother, Phocus, Peleus exiled them. Telamon went to SALAMIS, and Peleus to Phthia, where he was purified of the murder. In Phthia, Peleus married Antigone, the daughter of Actor, who some sources say purified Peleus. Peleus and Antigone had a daughter, Polydora.

Later, while Peleus was in the town of TRACHIS, Psamathe, a sea nymph and the mother of the deceased Phocus, caused a wolf to ravage Peleus' herds. Peleus tried to appease Psamathe by various means, but he did not succeed. Eventually, Peleus' future wife, THETIS, one of Psamathe's sisters, persuaded Psamathe to stop the wolf; Psamathe did so by turning it to stone.

Peleus participated in several important adventures. First, he joined in the hunt for the Calydonian boar, although he accidentally killed one of his fellow hunters, Eurytion. Perhaps some further disgrace followed for Peleus, as he was defeated in wrestling by a woman, ATALANTA, at the funeral games held in honor of Pelias. After this time, Pelias' son, ACASTUS, exiled Peleus from THESSALY. Apollodorus relates that Acastus' wife, Astydameia, fell in love with Peleus and tried to seduce him. When Peleus refused, Astydameia told Peleus' wife (this was before his union with Thetis) that Peleus was planning to marry Acastus' daughter, Sterope. Hearing this, Peleus' wife hanged herself. Astydameia also informed Acastus that Peleus had attempted to rape her. Acastus took Peleus to hunt on Mount Pelion, and when Peleus fell asleep, Acastus, hoping Peleus would be killed, hid Peleus' sword and left him on the mountain. When the defenseless Peleus awoke, CENTAURS attacked him, but the centaur CHIRON saved him and gave him back his sword.

After this, Peleus married Polydora and had a son, Menesthius; Menesthius, however, was actually the Sperchius River's son. Peleus later married NEREUS' daughter, Thetis. ZEUS and POSEIDON had wanted to have sexual relations with Thetis, but when they learned of a prophecy that Thetis' son would be more powerful than his father, Zeus arranged for her to marry a mortal man, Peleus. Because Thetis was able to change her form, Peleus would have a difficult time catching her, but Chiron told Peleus to grab Thetis and hold her while she changed her shape. Although Thetis changed into fire, water, and a wild animal, Peleus held on to the goddess. Eventually, she returned to her human form and married Peleus. Their wedding took place on Mount Pelion and was attended by the gods. Chiron gave Peleus a spear made from an ash tree on PELION and Poseidon gave him a pair of immortal horses, Balius and Xanthus.

Peleus accompanied the Argonauts on their quest for the Golden Fleece. After marrying Thetis, Peleus became the father of ACHILLES, but Thetis left Peleus at some point not long after Achilles was born. At the end of EURIPIDES' ANDROMACHE, in which Peleus saves the title character from the cruelty of HERMIONE, Thetis appears and tells Peleus that he can live with her and attain immorality.

In addition to his appearance in Euripides' *Andromache*, Peleus would have appeared in numerous classical dramas. Euripides wrote a play entitled *Peleus* (fragments 617–24 Nauck), to which ARISTOPHANES appears to refer in the revised version of CLOUDS. The fragments give little indication of the play's content; Webster thinks the play most likely treated Astydameia's attempted seduction of Peleus. SOPHOCLES, before 424 B.C.E., wrote a *Peleus* (fragments 487–96 Radt), which appears to have been about the aged Peleus' exile from Iolcus by ACASTUS. [ANCIENT SOURCES: Apollodorus, *Library* 1.8.2, 3.9.2, 3.13.1–5; Aristophanes, *Clouds* 1063; Euripides, *Trojan Women* 1127–38; Hyginus, *Fables* 14; Ovid, *Metamorphoses* 11.221–409]

BIBLIOGRAPHY

Kiso, A. *The Lost Sophocles*. New York: Vantage Press, 1984.

Lloyd-Jones, H. *Sophocles: Fragments*. Cambridge, Mass.: Harvard University Press, 1996.

Radt, S. *Tragicorum Graecorum Fragmenta*. Vol. 4. Göttingen, Ger.: Vandenhoeck & Ruprecht, 1977.

Sutton, D. F. *The Lost Sophocles*. Lanham, Md.: University Press of America, 1984.

Webster, T. B. L. *The Tragedies of Euripides*. London: Methuen, 1967.

PELION A mountain near the northeast coast of mainland Greece in the region of Thessaly. In drama Pelion is perhaps most associated with PELEUS and his son, ACHILLES, whose spear was said to have been made from an ash tree cut from Mount Pelion. The pines of Mount Pelion also provided the timber for JASON's ship, *ARGO*.

PELLENE A Greek town on the southern coast of the Gulf of CORINTH. They sided with the Spartans in the PELOPONNESIAN WAR. [ANCIENT SOURCES: Aristophanes, *Birds* 1421]

PELOPONNESIAN WAR (431–404 B.C.E.)

The Peloponnesian War was between ATHENS and its allies and SPARTA and its allies (notably CORINTH and THEBES). The causes of the war were various; one was that the rising power of Athens in the region caused great alarm among the other cities in Greece. In the late 430s Corinth and Corcyra quarreled over the Corcyrean colony of Epidamnus. When the Corcyreans appealed to Athens for aid, the Athenians accepted, and soon the Corinthians and Athenians were involved in military hostilities. Likewise, when the Athenians suspected that the Corinthian colony of Potidaea, which they had made part of their empire, was planning to revolt and insisted that they expel various Corinthian public officials from Potidaea, the Potidaeans refused, revolted against Athenian control, and appealed to Corinth for military assistance (which they received). After the Athenians beseiged Potidaea in 432, the Corinthians appealed to the Spartans for help. Additionally, in ARISTOPHANES' *ACHARNIANS*, one of the primary causes given was the Megarian decree, a decree passed by the Athenian assembly that prevented the people of Megara from trading in Athenian markets. This decree severely damaged the Megarian economy, and the Megarians also appealed to Sparta for help at that time, when the Spartans and Athenians were in the midst of a 30-year peace treaty (agreed upon in 445). Sparta, however, decided that Athens had broken that treaty and the Spartans and their allies decided to go to war with Athens.

Because it was common practice for the Spartans to ravage their enemy's countryside during times of war,

PERICLES, the leading stateman in Athens, advised the Athenians to leave the countryside for the protection of the city's walls. Pericles also advised the Athenians to avoid fighting the Spartans on land, and to rely on their superior navy to make raids on Spartan territory and put a stranglehold on the ports on which the land-locked Spartans relied.

In the first years of the war, both Athens and Sparta followed their initial strategy. When Athens became crowded with people from the countryside and a horrific plague broke out in the city, of which Pericles himself died in 429, the Athenians began to waver in their resolve to pursue Pericles' strategy. The Athenians also faced trouble within their empire, as the Spartans were encouraging those of the empire to revolt. Thus, not only did the Athenians have to deal with the Spartans' ravaging their territory every summer, but they also had to suppress revolts within their empire (such as at MYTILENE in 428/427).

The plague and revolts within their empire had hampered the Athenians' ability to defeat the Spartans; the Spartans had their own problems as earthquakes in their territory in 426 postponed military operations. The Spartans also suffered a severe setback in 425 as the Athenians established a garrison in their territory at PYLOS and captured a large number of Sparta's finest soldiers on the island of Sphacteria (just off the coast from Pylos). So damaging was this setback that the Spartans tried to make peace with the Athenians. Athens' most influential statesman at this time, CLEON, persuaded his fellow citizens to reject this proposal and continue the war. In 422, however, Cleon and Brasidas (the leading proponent of war on the Spartan side) were killed in battle at Amphipolis, and in 421 the Athenians and Spartans agreed to the so-called PEACE OF NICIAS.

The peace was a tenuous one, as the Corinthians and Thebans would not agree to the treaty. Furthermore, some military hostilities continued between the Athenians and Spartans, such as the battle at Mantinea in 418, at which the Spartans were victorious. In 416, the Athenians destroyed the male population on the island of Melos, enslaved the women and children, and occupied the island because the Melians had remained neutral in the conflict between Athens and Sparta. In

415, the Athenians, persuaded by their leading states-man, ALCIBIADES, undertook the SICILIAN EXPEDITION, whose ultimate aim was nothing less than the conquest of that island. Alcibiades himself, because he was implicated in a scandal that occurred on the eve of the expedition's departure, was recalled to Athens, but he escaped and made his way to Sparta. The Athenian forces at Sicily were destroyed in 413. Meanwhile, Alcibiades advised the Spartans to establish a perma-nent garrison in Athenian territory so that they could inflict hardship on the Athenians through the year.

By now, the Peace of Nicias was all but forgotten and hostilities between Athens and Sparta began again in earnest. Despite the destruction of the Sicilian Expedi-tion, the Spartans' establishment of a garrison in Athenian territory (also in 413), and an oligarchic rev-olution in 411 that briefly overthrew the Athenian democracy, the Athenians continued to wage war effec-tively against the Spartans. The oligarchic revolution of 411 led to the recall of Alcibiades, who helped the Athenians achieve some success. After an Athenian loss at Notium in 406, however, Alcibiades was again exiled from Athens. Despite Alcibiades' absence, in 405 the Athenians inflicted a defeat so crushing at ARGINUSAE that the Spartans were prepared to pursue peace. As after the battle at Sphacteria, the Athenians refused the offer and the war continued. In 405, the Spartans defeated the Athenian navy at Aegospotami and laid seige to Athens. In 404, the Athenians were forced to surrender, tear down their fortification walls, and dismantle what was left of their navy.

The Peloponnesian War had an important impact on classical drama, especially on the works of EURIPIDES and ARISTOPHANES. Of the 18 plays accepted as gen-uinely Euripidean, 17 (ALCESTIS is the exception) were written during this war or on the eve of it (MEDEA was produced in 431). Euripidean plays such as ANDRO-MACHE, HECABE, SUPPLIANT WOMEN, TROJAN WOMEN, and PHOENICIAN WOMEN all focus on the hardships of war and are especially concerned with its effects on the lives of the noncombatants. Of the 11 surviving plays of Aristophanes, nine were produced during the war and three (ACHARNIANS, PEACE, and LYSISTRATA) focus on the war and its effects on the Athenians in particular. The influence of this war on SOPHOCLES' plays is less

clear because only seven Sophoclean plays survive, but certainly PHILOCTETES, which was produced during this time (409 B.C.), shows an awareness of the Athe-nians' dilemma about their statesman and military commander ALCIBIADES. Sophocles' TRACHINIAN WOMEN, which may have been produced during the war's first decade, demonstrates some concern with the effects of war on the household of HERACLES. [ANCIENT SOURCES: Diodorus Siculus, 12.30–13.107; Plutarch, Alcibiades, Lysander, Nicias, Pericles; Thucy-dides, History of the Peloponnesian War; Xenophon, Hellenica 1–2.2]

BIBLIOGRAPHY

Kagan, D. The Outbreak of the Peloponnesian War. Ithaca, N.Y.: Cornell University Press, 1969.
———. The Archidamian War. Ithaca, N.Y.: Cornell Univer-sity Press, 1974.
———. The Peace of Nicias and the Sicilian Expedition. Ithaca, N.Y.: Cornell University Press, 1981.
———. The Fall of the Athenian Empire. Ithaca, N.Y.: Cornell University Press, 1987.
———. The Peloponnesian War. New York: Viking, 2003.

PELOPS   The son of TANTALUS and Dione, Pelops experienced death and resurrection. After his father killed him, he served him as food to the gods. Although most of the gods did not partake of this vile meal, DEMETER ate Pelops' shoulder. The gods later restored Pelops to life and gave him an ivory shoulder. The rejuvenated Pelops was so handsome that he attracted the attention of POSEIDON. Later, when Pelops became a suitor for HIPPODAMEIA, daughter of OENO-MAUS, Poseidon gave Pelops a special team of horses and a chariot that could travel over land or sea. Because Hippodameia's father challenged all of her suitors to a chariot race and killed all those that he defeated, Poseidon's gift was quite useful.

To ensure victory, however, Pelops enlisted the help of Oenomaus' servant, MYRTILUS, who Pelops noticed was also attracted to Hippodameia. In exchange for Myrtilus' help, Pelops promised Myrtilus that he could sleep with Hippodameia if he were victorious in the chariot race. Myrtilus agreed and sabotaged his mas-ter's chariot, and in the middle of the race with Pelops, the chariot fell apart and Oenomaus was killed. Later, however, when Myrtilus tried to collect his "reward" from Hippodameia by force, Pelops went to his new bride's rescue and eventually killed Myrtilus by hurling him into the sea. As Myrtilus died, he cursed the descendants of Pelops. Pelops and Hippodameia seem to have lived happily after this time, as Pelops ruled over the region of southern Greece that bears his name to this day, the Peloponnese, which means "the island of Pelops." Pelops had numerous children. ATREUS and THYESTES are the most famous; Pelops is also said to have been the father of three daughters, Astydamia, Lysidice, Nicippe, and five other sons, Alcaeus, CHRYSIPPUS, Copreus, Pittheus and SCIRON.

Pelops does not appear as a character in any surviving dramas, but several ancient plays, both comedies and tragedies, dealt with him. The comic poet Nicochares wrote a *Pelops,* of which only the title survives. Among Roman authors, ACCIUS wrote *Pelops' Sons (Pelopidae),* which may have been about the murder of Pelops' son Chrysippus. The surviving fragments (lines 513–19 Warmington) tell us little about the play's content. Lines 516–17 refer to a man who seems to be coming to the realization of who his real father is; line 518 refers to someone whose spouse has just died. [ANCIENT SOURCES: Apollodorus, *Library* 2.5.1, 3.12.7, 3.15.6; Aristophanes, *Frogs* 1232; Euripides, *Helen* 387, *Iphigenia in Tauris* 1, *Orestes* 991a; Hyginus, *Fables* 83; Seneca, *Thyestes* 139–44]

BIBLIOGRAPHY
Warmington, E. H. *Remains of Old Latin: Livius Andronicus, Naevius, Pacuvius, and Accius.* Vol. 2. Cambridge, Mass.: Harvard University Press, 1936.

PENELOPE The daughter of Icarius and Periboea, Penelope, the wife of ODYSSEUS and mother of Telemachus, was a model of virtue for Greek wives. While Odysseus was involved in the Trojan War, Penelope remained on ITHACA and fended off a vast number of men who wanted to marry her. At one point, she told these men that she would marry as soon as she finished weaving a funeral garment for her father-in-law, Laertes. For three years she managed to deceive her suitors by weaving during the day and unraveling her work at night. Eventually, Penelope's deception

was revealed to the suitors by one of her own maidservants. Although Penelope's trickery was uncovered, she continued to keep her suitors at bay and remained faithful to her husband during his 20-year absence from home. AESCHYLUS wrote a *Penelope,* of which a single line survives (fragment 187 Radt). The Greek tragedian PHILOCLES also wrote a *Penelope,* of which only the title survives (fragment 1 Snell). The Greek comic poet Theopompus also wrote a *Penelope,* of which we have two brief, uninformative fragments (47–48 Kock). [ANCIENT SOURCES: Homer, *Odyssey;* Ovid, *Heroides* 1]

BIBLIOGRAPHY
Kock, T. *Comicorum Atticorum Fragmenta.* Vol. 1. Leipzig: Teubner, 1880.
Radt, T. *Tragicorum Graecorum Fragmenta.* Vol. 3. Göttingen, Ger.: Vandenhoeck & Ruprecht, 1985.
Snell, B. *Tragicorum Graecorum Fragmenta.* Vol. 1. Göttingen, Ger.: Vandenhoeck & Ruprecht, 1971.

PENTHEUS The son of Echion and AGAVE, Pentheus became king of THEBES while his grandfather, CADMUS, was still alive. In EURIPIDES' *BACCHAE,* the playwright connects his name with the Greek word *penthos,* which means "pain." In the same play, Pentheus incurs the wrath of the god DIONYSUS for rejecting his worship and is punished by being torn apart by his mother and aunts. Both Thespis and Aeschylus wrote plays entitled *Pentheus;* from each a single line survives (Thespis fragment 1c; Aeschylus fragment 183 Radt). Lycophon also wrote a *Pentheus,* of which only the title has survived. [ANCIENT SOURCES: Euripides, *Bacchae;* Hyginus, *Fables* 184; Plautus, *Vidularia* 17b; Ovid, *Metamorphoses* 511–733]

PERGASAE Two DEMES of uncertain location, which were probably "about eight miles north of" ATHENS. [ANCIENT SOURCES: Aristophanes, *Knights* 321]

BIBLIOGRAPHY
Sommerstein, A. H. *The Comedies of Aristophanes.* Vol. 2, *Knights.* Warminster, U.K.: Aris & Phillips, 1981, 160.

PERIAKTOS The Greek word *periaktos* (plural: *periaktoi*) refers to something that turns on a center or pivot. In the theater, Pollux indicates that a *periaktos* was placed near each of the entrances to the playing space. Pollux says the *periaktos* could display sea gods, things too heavy for the MECHANE, or changes of scenery. Vitruvius says the *periaktoi* were shaped as a three-sided prism. Use of the *periaktoi* probably did not occur until after the fourth century B.C.E. [ANCIENT SOURCES: Pollux, *Onomasticon* 4.160, 130, 131; Vitruvius, *On Architecture* 5.6.8]

PERICLEIDAS A Spartan who was sent to ATHENS to ask for aid when the Spartans' slaves, the Helots, and their allies attacked the Spartans after the earthquake of 464 B.C.E. [ANCIENT SOURCES: Aristophanes, *Lysistrata* 1138; Plutarch, *Cimon* 16.7]

PERICLES (CA. 495–429 B.C.E.) The son of Xanthippus and Agariste, Pericles was the most prominent public figure in ATHENS during the last three decades of his life. He served Athens as both a military commander and a political leader. Pericles' building program on the Athenian ACROPOLIS resulted in the construction of the famous Parthenon and other magnificent structures.

Although Pericles guided and shaped Athenian policies for some time, he was sometimes opposed. In 451/450, he had proposed a law that required that both of a person's parents be native Athenians in order for that person to be an Athenian citizen, but he later ran afoul of that very law. After Pericles divorced his wife, he lived with his mistress, ASPASIA, during the last 15 years or so of his life. Pericles and Aspasia had a son, but because Aspasia was not a native Athenian, their son was not recognized as a citizen during Pericles' lifetime.

Some Athenians blamed Pericles for the outbreak of the PELOPONNESIAN WAR, and his Megarian Decree (which prevented the Megarians from trading in Athenian markets) certainly contributed to the outbreak of war as the Megarians appealed to the Spartans for help. Athens' initial strategy during the first years of the war was crafted by Pericles, and it also drew opposition. Pericles wanted Athens to rely on its naval superiority and the protection of its city walls. When the Spartans raided the Athenian countryside, those who lived in the country moved to the city for protection. Not only did this cause crowded conditions in the city, but the country folk also longed for their former home. The influx of country people into the city led to increasingly unsanitary conditions, and not long after the war began a horrible plague broke out in Athens. Pericles received some blame for these hardships, and in 430 he was removed from office, tried for misappropriation of funds, and assessed a fine. In 429, Pericles was again chosen as a military commander, but he himself contracted plague and died.

Pericles had some connections with ancient drama and dramatists. He served as a CHOREGUS in 472 and had a close relationship with SOPHOCLES, with whom he had served as a military commander in 440 during the suppression of a revolt on SAMOS. Pericles died before ARISTOPHANES began producing plays; Aristophanes' *Acharnians* is critical of Pericles "Olympian" behavior with respect to the Megarian Decree. Aristophanes' criticism may have echoed a comment by the comic poet CRATINUS, who described Pericles as a ZEUS with a peaked head. During the 410s, the comic poet EUPOLIS, in his *Demes,* had Pericles as a character. [ANCIENT SOURCES: Aristophanes, *Acharnians* 530, *Clouds* 213, 859, *Knights* 283, *Peace* 606; Cratinus, fragment 71 Kock; Eupolis, fragment 98 Kock; Plutarch, *Pericles;* Thucydides 1.111–2.65]

BIBLIOGRAPHY

Burn, A. R. *Pericles and Athens.* London: English Universities Press, 1948.

Delcourt, M. *Pericles.* 3d ed. Paris: Gallimard, 1940.

Ehrenberg, V. *Sophocles and Pericles.* Oxford: Blackwell, 1954.

Kagan, D. *Pericles of Athens and the Birth of Democracy.* New York: Free Press, 1991.

Kock, T. *Comicorum Atticorum Fragmenta.* Vol. 1. Leipzig: Teubner, 1880.

Schubert, C. *Perikles.* Darmstadt, Ger.: Wissenschaftliche Buchgesellschaft, 1994.

PERIKEIROMENE See GIRL WITH THE SHAVEN HEAD.

PERIPETEIA In drama *peripeteia* (reversal) is a rapid change of circumstances or events. For example, in EURIPIDES' *IPHIGENIA IN TAURIS,* IPHIGENIA is on the verge of sending her brother, ORESTES, to his death when they recognize that they are brother and sister. The two then scheme as to how to escape together from the land of the Taurians.

PERRHAEBIA
A town in the region of THESSALY in northeastern Greece. AESCHYLUS wrote a *Women of Perrhaebia;* however, this may be an alternate title for Aeschylus' *Ixion* (184–86 Radt). The first two fragments are about drinking cups; the third mentions someone who has died a wretched death.

BIBLIOGRAPHY
Radt, S. *Tragicorum Graecorum Fragmenta.* Vol. 3. Göttingen, Ger.: Vandenhoeck & Ruprecht, 1985.

PERSEPHASSA
Another name for PERSEPHONE.

PERSEPHONE (Latin: PROSERPINA)
The daughter of ZEUS and DEMETER, Persephone is the wife of HADES and queen of the UNDERWORLD. While gathering flowers with some female companions, Persephone was abducted by Hades, who took her off to the underworld to be his bride. Although Hades had Zeus' permission to do this, Persephone's mother, Demeter, was unaware of this arrangement and missed her daughter. Demeter searched the world for Persephone, and when she learned that her daughter was in Hades' kingdom, she created barrenness on the Earth. Zeus, fearing the destruction of the human race, agreed to try to arrange for Persephone's release from the underworld. Hades, however, had fed Persephone pomegranate seeds. Apparently once Persephone ate food in the kingdom of the dead, she was required to remain in Hades' house. Zeus did, however, manage to arrange for Persephone to spend part of the year with Hades and part with Demeter. Despite this arrangement, references to Persephone after this time show her in the underworld and seemingly content in her role as queen of the underworld.

Aside from the story of her abduction by Hades, Persephone seldom appears in myths. THESEUS and PIRITHOUS traveled to the underworld in the hope of abducting Persephone and making her Pirithous' bride, but Hades thwarted this attempt. She is frequently mentioned in drama but does not appear as a character in any extant drama. Often, women who die "before their time," such as ALCESTIS, ANTIGONE, or IPHIGENIA, are called brides of Hades. In EURIPIDES' *CHILDREN OF HERACLES,* Demophon's daughter was to be sacrificed to Persephone to ensure victory over EURYSTHEUS and the Argives. The narrative pattern of the myth of Hades and Persephone—abduction, descent, and return—has been applied by modern scholars to various Greek dramas. Charles Segal has read SOPHOCLES' *ANTIGONE* with this pattern and Helene Foley has applied this method to the study of Euripides' *ALCESTIS, HELEN,* and *IPHIGENIA IN TAURIS.* [ANCIENT SOURCES: Apollodorus, *Library* 1.1.5–1.2.1, 1.5.1–3, 2.5.12, 3.6.8, 3.12.1, 3.14.7; Apollonius Rhodius, 4.986–90; Aristophanes, *Thesmophoriazusae;* Euripides, *Helen* 1301–68; Hesiod, *Theogony* 767–74, 908–11; Homer, *Iliad* 9.457, 568, *Odyssey* 10.492–95, 10.510, 11.213–18, 10.225–27, 10.632–35; *Homeric Hymn to Demeter,* 2; Hyginus, *Fables* 141, 146, 147; Ovid, *Metamorphoses* 5.341–571, 642–61, 6.118–19, 8.738–78, 9.422–23; Pausanias, 1.14.1–3, 1.37.2, 2.5.8; Seneca, *Hippolytus* 94, 244, 831, 1235

BIBLIOGRAPHY
Foley, H. P. *Female Acts in Greek Tragedy.* Princeton, N.J.: Princeton University Press, 2001, 303–31.
Segal, C. *Tragedy and Civilization: An Interpretation of Sophocles.* Cambridge, Mass.: Harvard University Press, 1981, 179–88.

PERSEUS
The son of ZEUS and DANAE, Perseus was famous for beheading the Gorgon MEDUSA. When Perseus was born, his grandfather, Acrisius, who had been told by an oracle that Perseus would destroy him, put Perseus and Danae into a wooden box and threw them into the sea. The box washed up on the island of SERIPHUS, where a fisherman, Dictys, found it. Dictys took Perseus and Danae to the house of his brother Polydectes who was king of Seriphus. Polydectes raised Perseus and over the years fell in love with Danae. After Perseus grew up, Polydectes wanted to marry Danae, but to get Perseus out of the way, he pretended that he instead wanted to marry Oenomaus' daughter HIPPODAMEIA. As part of Polydectes' plan, he required all the nobles of his island give him horses to

offer as an engagement present to Hippodameia. Perseus boasted that he would get even the GORGON Medusa's head for Polydectes. When Perseus was unable to provide the horses, Polydectes sent Perseus to take the Gorgon Medusa's head. Although this task was considered impossible because the sight of Medusa would turn a person to stone, Perseus had the gods on his side. Guided by HERMES and ATHENA, Perseus made his way to Phorcys' daughters, three old women who were the Gorgons' sisters and who also knew the location of certain NYMPHS. Phorcys' daughters were unusual in that they had only one eye and one tooth, which they shared. When Perseus took their eye and tooth, they revealed to him the nymphs' location. After leaving Phorcys' daughters, Perseus made his way to these nymphs, who provided him with winged sandals, HADES' helmet of invisibility, and a special knapsack in which he could carry Medusa's head. Hermes gave Perseus a sickle made of ADAMANT. Aided by this equipment, Perseus made his way to the Gorgons' lair. They were asleep when he found them, and he cut off Medusa's head with the aid of Athena and by looking at Medusa's reflection in a bronze shield. When Perseus cut off Medusa's head, the winged horse PEGASUS and a creature named Chrysaor were born from her body. After Perseus beheaded Medusa, he put her head into the special knapsack. The other Gorgons woke and chased Perseus, but he eluded them by putting on the helmet of invisibility.

After Perseus left the land of the Gorgons, he traveled to ETHIOPIA, where he found CEPHEUS' daughter, ANDROMEDA, exposed as a sacrifice to a sea monster. Perseus immediately fell in love with Andromeda and told Cepheus he would rescue her if he would allow him to marry her. Cepheus agreed, and Perseus rescued Andromeda and killed the monster. Afterward, however, when Cepheus' brother, Phineus, to whom Andromeda had been promised, tried to kill Perseus, Perseus turned him and his allies to stone by showing them Medusa's head. After leaving Ethiopia, Perseus and Andromeda returned to Seriphus. There, Perseus found his mother and Dictys besieged by Polydectes at an altar. Polydectes' threat was soon ended, as Perseus used Medusa's head to turn Polydectes to stone. After Polydectes' death, Perseus made Dictys king of Seri-

phus; he then left for Argos with Danae and Andromeda. When Acrisius heard of Perseus' return, he left Argos and went into exile in LARISA. Some time later, Perseus happened to go to Larisa to compete in the funeral games for the father of Teutamides, king of Larisa. Acrisius, who happened to be among the spectators, was hit in the foot and killed by an errant discus throw by Perseus.

After burying Acrisius, Perseus returned to Argos, but, given the way that his grandfather had died, he did not want to be king of the town. Therefore, Perseus arranged for an exchange of kingdoms with his cousin, Megapenthes, who ruled nearby Tiryns. Thus, Megapenthes became king of Argos, while Perseus ruled Tiryns. Perseus is also said to have fortified the towns of Midea and Mycenae. Perseus and Andromeda seem to have lived happily after this time. They had a daughter, Gorgophone, and several sons, Alcaeus, ELECTRYON, Heleus, Mestor, Perses, and Sthenelus.

Perseus does not appear as a character in any extant dramas, unless we include Aristophanes' parody of Euripides' *Andromeda* in *Thesmophoriazusae,* but Perseus was a character in TRAGEDY, COMEDY, and SATYR PLAYS. The tragedian Pratinas wrote a *Perseus,* of which only the title survives. The title of a satyric *Perseus* survives, but the name of its author does not. Aeschylus wrote a trilogy about Perseus: *Diktuoulkoi* (The net draggers), *Polydectes,* and *Phorcides* (The daughters of Phorcys). The first play would have treated Perseus' arrival on Seriphus, the second Polydectes' sending Perseus to get Medusa's head, the third his encounter with the daughters of Phorcys. [ANCIENT SOURCES: Apollodorus, *Library* 2.4.2–5; Ovid, *Metamorphoses* 4.604–803, 5.1–249]

THE PERSIAN (Latin: *PERSA*) PLAUTUS (CA. 186 B.C.E.)

The play's date is uncertain and the author of the Greek original for PLAUTUS' is not known. The play's setting is ATHENS, and the action occurs before a house belonging to the PIMP, Dordalus, and a house belonging to the master of the slave Toxilus (compare CARTHAGINIAN, COMEDY OF ASSES, and CURCULIO).

In the opening scene, Toxilus enters from the FORUM and complains about the difficulty of obtaining a loan. He is soon met by a slave owned by another family,

Sagaristio. Toxilus informs him that he is in love, but that he needs money to buy the prostitute Lemniselenis, whom he loves, because the pimp, Dordalus, owns her. Sagaristio, however, cannot help Toxilus, so he departs, leaving Toxilus to plot how to defeat the pimp. After Toxilus returns to his house, the PARASITE, Saturio, enters; he talks about the tradition in his family of being a parasite and complains about professional informants. As Saturio approaches Toxilus' house in search of food, Toxilus emerges and informs the audience that he has discovered a way to trick Dordalus out of the money he needs to purchase Lemniselenis. Toxilus also says he needs Saturio to help him with his plot and calls back to the slaves in his house to continue preparing a banquet. Saturio, hearing of the banquet preparations, immediately takes interest.

Soon, Saturio and Toxilus begin conversing. Toxilus asks Saturio to allow him to borrow his daughter to pretend to sell her to Dordalus. Saturio is horrified by this idea, but when Toxilus threatens that he will not allow Saturio to have any of their food, Saturio agrees to Toxilus' proposal. Before Saturio leaves to get his daughter, Toxilus instructs him that his daughter is to dress as a Persian and pretend that she was abducted from her birthplace and taken to Athens. Furthermore, Toxilus tells Saturio that he must dress as the merchant who will sell the young woman to Dordalus. After Dordalus gives the money for her to Saturio, Saturio will give it to Toxilus. After Toxilus buys Lemniselenis from Dordalus, Saturio (now out of disguise) will claim that the woman, Dordalus, is freeborn and therefore cannot legally be bought and sold.

In the play's second act, Lemniselenis and her maidservant, Sophoclidisca, emerge from Dordalus' house. Sophoclidisca is frustrated by her mistress' lovesickness, which is causing her to be angry (without good cause) at her. Sophoclidisca, however, soon exits with a letter from Lemniselenis that she will deliver to Toxilus. In the next scene, Toxilus and his fellow slave, Paegnium (plaything), enter from their house. Toxilus gives a letter to Paegnium and tells him to deliver it to Lemniselenis. After Toxilus returns to the house, Paegnium and Sophoclidisca encounter one another on the street. The two slaves, who dislike one another, wrangle verbally for some time but finally continue their

errands after learning that each carries a letter to the beloved of their respective masters. After their departure into the houses, Sagaristio enters and happily announces that his master has given him some money to buy some oxen, but that he plans to spend the money on something else. Sagaristio is soon met by Paegnium, who is returning from delivering the letter to Lemniselenis. Sagaristio wants to know where Toxilus is, but Paegnium refuses to tell him and exits into Toxilus' house. Sagaristio is rewarded, however, when Toxilus and Sophoclidisca emerge from his house. Toxilus tells her to inform Lemniselenis that he has made arrangements to purchase her from the pimp. After Sophoclidisca's departure, Sagaristio approaches Toxilus, who notices that Sagaristio has a wallet bulging with money. Sagaristio then turns the money over to Toxilus, who Sagaristio mentions had recently begged him for the loan of some money. Toxilus gleefully accepts the money and promises that he will soon return it to him after he has tricked Dordalus out of Lemniselenis and even more money. As Toxilus exits, he tells an agreeable Sagaristio that he needs his help in the plot.

The third act opens with the arrival of Saturio and his daughter, who is dressed as a Persian woman. Saturio's daughter is appalled that her father will sell her for the sake of his appetite, but Saturio argues that it is his right to do so and reminds her that the situation will only be temporary. Although Saturio's daughter tries to reason with her father, he persists and eventually she agrees to obey him. After Saturio and his daughter exit toward Toxilus' house, Dordalus emerges from his house. He is soon met by Toxilus, who abuses him verbally then angrily prepares to hand over the money that he owes Dordalus for Lemniselenis. Dordalus, in turn, verbally abuses Toxilus and demands his money. Eventually, Toxilus hands over the money and Dordalus promises to take Lemniselenis to him soon.

After Dordalus exits, Toxilus expresses satisfaction that matters are proceeding according to his plan. He then calls Sagaristio from the house with Saturio's disguised daughter and a letter that Toxilus pretends is from his master in Persia. Next, Dordalus enters and informs Toxilus that he has set Lemniselenis free and that she is currently at his house. In gratitude, Toxilus tells the pimp that his master has sent a certain female captive (Saturio's daughter) from Persia to be sold in Athens and that he would like to sell the Persian woman to Dordalus. Initially, Dordalus is skeptical about this transaction, but he changes his mind when he sees the woman. After several questions to her about her background and name (which she says is Lucris, meaning "profit") and some wrangling with Sagaristio about her price, Dordalus agrees to buy her. After Dordalus departs to get the money, Toxilus congratulates Saturio and his daughter on their performance. Soon Dordalus returns with the money and hands it over to Sagaristio, who states that he is eager to continue on his way and search for his twin brother, who was said to be in Athens. Toxilus takes Sagaristio's hint and says he thinks he has seen this person. After Sagaristio leaves, Toxilus congratulates Dordalus on his purchase, and the pimp thanks Toxilus for his help and returns to his house. Next, Saturio enters and Toxilus prepares him to confront Dordalus. Soon after the pimp emerges from his house, Saturio rushes up and declares that he will destroy the pimp. When Saturio's daughter greets him as her father, Dordalus realizes that he is in trouble for buying a free woman. With daughter and pimp accompanying him, Saturio sets out to find a government official who will deal with this crime.

The play's final act begins with Toxilus' giving thanks to the gods for a successful outcome to his scheme. He then invites Lemniselenis, Sagaristio, and his other fellow slaves to leave the house and begin celebrating. As their celebration begins, a thoroughly dejected Dordalus enters and laments his loss of money. By this time, Toxilus and the others have become somewhat intoxicated and invite Dordalus to join in their revelry. Dordalus, however, is quite angry and refuses, so Toxilus and the others taunt, insult, and physically harass the pimp. The play ends with Dordalus' departing in frustration at the treatment he has received and Toxilus' expressing delight in the destruction of the pimp.

COMMENTARY

Duckworth labels The Persian a play of "guileful deception" and groups it with COMEDY OF ASSES, BACCHIDES,

CASINA, MERCHANT, BRAGGART WARRIOR, HAUNTED HOUSE, and PSEUDOLUS. As in Pseudolus, the play's action revolves around the overthrow of a pimp by a wily slave. Both plays have the slaves employ disguised characters to fool the pimp, and in the final act of both plays we find the wily slaves celebrating their triumphs over the pimp. Unlike in Pseudolus, in which the slave is helping a young citizen acquire his beloved, who is a prostitute, in Persian we find a situation that Slater notes is "quite unparalleled in Plautus": The slave is both the helper and the lover, and his scheme aims to free his beloved, who is a prostitute. Thus, in Persian, we lack the sense of the forbidden that creates tension in so many Roman comedies. If a slave is in love with a prostitute, who cares? Indeed, Persian is unusual in its exclusively lower-class characters. In Persian, the slave has slaves who serve him, and, as Slater points out, "In his newly adopted role as master Toxilus must endure abuse from the slaves who serve him." Unlike in the several Roman comedies in which a parasite is devoted to a citizen, in Persian a parasite is devoted to a slave. The most noble character in Persian is the parasite's virgin daughter (also unique in Roman COMEDY). Indeed, behavior in Persian has sunk to such depths that the daughter of a parasite chides her father about proper behavior. Interestingly, however, Toxilus' plot, for all its success, does seem to have one flaw: He arranges for his beloved to be freed. Thus, whereas in Roman comedy it often turns out that the enslaved woman with whom the freeman is in love is actually freeborn and thus they are of the same social status and able to marry, in Persian Toxilus' beloved is freed, but he remains a slave at the end of the play.

Although several similarities exist between Persian and Pseudolus, the wily slave Toxilus lacks Pseudolus' liveliness, and the playwright's description of Toxilus is less elaborate than that of Pseudolus. Although both slaves have the potential to become kinglike, Toxilus' royal status is a result of his master's absence (see line 31), whereas Pseudolus' royal status will be a result primarily of his trickery. The military imagery and language associated with Pseudolus are less extensive and more subtle in the case of Toxilus. As Persian opens, Toxilus describes his struggle against Love as more difficult than the labors of HERACLES, but this characterization is not maintained throughout the play. As Pseudolus does, Toxilus becomes like a poet (although he is never called this in the play as Pseudolus is). In *Pseudolus,* the title character impersonates the pimp's slave and then arranges for another to impersonate the soldier's agent. In *Persian,* the tricky slave arranges for Sagaristio and Saturio's daughter to play the roles of Persians. Before the two "Persians" depart for the pimp, the "poet" Toxilus makes sure they know their roles and Sagaristio responds that no tragedian or comedian has ever known his role as well as they do (465–66). Both Pseudolus and Toxilus rely on letters to help them make their "plays" a success (compare also the wily Chrysalus in BACCHIDES). Pseudolus acquires his letter from the soldier's agent by impersonating the pimp's slave, whereas Toxilus himself composes the letter that will defeat his pimp and even gives the pimp direction as Dordalus reads the letter (500). Perhaps as the mythical BELLEROPHON unwittingly delivers a letter that calls for his own destruction, Dordalus unwittingly reads a letter that will bring about his own ruin. After Toxilus' "play" deceives the pimp, the two slaves and the freed prostitute have a "cast party," as Slater describes it, and invite the pimp to join them (792, 849). Dordalus, however, refuses and thus rejects the realm of comedy, as Slater comments. Just as in the final scene of ARISTOPHANES' ACHARNIANS the audience simultaneously watch DICAEOPOLIS enjoy a round of drinking and the company of women and the soldier, LAMACHUS, suffer through the miseries of war, in Plautus' *Persians* Toxilus and his companions enjoy the fruits of their comic victory while the defeated pimp is mired in "the world of tragedy" (Slater).

BIBLIOGRAPHY

Faller, S., ed. *Studien zu Plautus' Persa.* Tübingen, Ger.: Narr, 2001.

Hughes, D. "The Character of Paegnium in Plautus' *Persa,*" *Rheinisches Museum* 127 (1984): 46–57.

Lowe, J. C. B. "The *Virgo Callida* of Plautus, *Persa,*" *Classical Quarterly* 39 (1989): 390–99.

Marshall, C. W. "Shattered Mirrors and Breaking Class: Saturio's Daughter in Plautus' *Persa,*" *Text & Presentation* 18 (1997): 100–9.

Slater, N. W. "The Ruse of Persia, or, The Story-Telling Slaves." In *Plautus in Performance.* Princeton, N.J.: Princeton University Press, 1985, 37–54.

Woytek, E. *T. Maccius Plautus, Persa.* Einleitung, Text, Kommentar. Wien: Verlag der Österreichischen Akad. der Wissenschaften, 1982.

PERSIANS AESCHYLUS (472 B.C.E.) The only surviving Greek play that dramatizes a historical event, *Persians* was the second play of a TETRALOGY that won first prize at the City DIONYSIA. The other plays in the tetralogy were *Phineus, Glaucus of Potniae,* and the SATYR PLAY *Prometheus the Fire-Maker. Persians* deals with the aftermath of the Battle of SALAMIS, fought by the Persians and Greeks in 480 B.C.E. The play's hypothesis is that Aeschylus modeled his *Persians* on the *Phoenician Women* of PHRYNICHUS, which was also about the fall of XERXES. In contrast to those in Phrynichus' play, Aeschylus' CHORUS are aged Persian men.

Aeschylus' *Persians* is set in the Persian city of SUSA. Structures representing a meeting place for the Persian elders and a tomb of Xerxes' father, DARIUS, are visible to the audience. The play opens with the Persian chorus worrying about the fortunes of Xerxes and the Persian army in their war with the Greeks. They recite a lengthy catalog of the warriors and allies in the Persian army, noting the power of the army and the valor of Xerxes, whom they equate with a god. Still, the old men worry about the outcome of the war and sit down to await news of the war.

Next, a woman described as Xerxes' mother and Darius' wife enters. The chorus call her "Queen," but other ancient sources identify her as ATOSSA. The queen tells the Persian elders that she has had troubling dreams, which clearly indicate the defeat of the Persians by the Greeks and the fall of Xerxes. The Persian elders, however, tell the queen that they think matters will turn out well for her and advise her to pray to the gods and pour libations to EARTH and to her deceased husband, Darius. The queen agrees and then asks the Persian elders to tell her about the people of ATHENS, their style of fighting, and their form of government.

The Persian elders' report on the Athenians is followed by the arrival of a Persian MESSENGER, who describes in detail the Greek victory over the Persians at Salamis. The messenger relates how a certain Greek had fooled Xerxes into thinking that the Greeks would try to escape in the night. Instead, the Greek fleet had attacked at dawn and had thoroughly routed the Persian fleet. The messenger also reports that the Greek infantry had routed the Persians on another island near Salamis. The messenger tells how Xerxes, upon witnessing the Persian defeat, tore his robes (the fulfillment of one of the queen's dreams) and ordered his forces to retreat. After a brief lament by the queen over the fate of the Persians, the messenger tells her about the retreat of the Persian fleet.

After the messenger's exit, the queen again laments the army's defeat and complains that the Persian elders misinterpreted her dreams. She tells the elders of her intention to pray to the gods and pour libations to the Earth and Darius. She instructs the elders to comfort Xerxes if he arrives before she returns.

The queen departs and the Persian elders sing an ode in which they lament ZEUS' destruction of the Persian army and the sorrow that the Persian women will feel at the loss of their men. They lament the loss of life and worry that the defeat will weaken the Persians' grip on various parts of their empire.

After the choral ODE, the queen enters. In her first entrance, she had been dressed in royal robes and carried in a chariot. Now, she enters on foot and in clothing that may have been dark as an indication of mourning. She tells the Persian elders of her intent to pour libations and summon her husband's spirit from the grave and calls on them to join her in her prayers. The elders call on the gods to allow Darius' spirit to appear and to guide them in their present distress, because Darius was a wise leader in both civic and military matters.

After the CHORUS' invocation, Darius' ghost appears and asks to be informed about the crisis that faces the Persians. The chorus are afraid to speak to their former king, so the queen tells him about the defeat of Xerxes and the Persians. Darius informs her that Xerxes' defeat can be attributed to his arrogance and his angering of the god POSEIDON by trying to cross the Hellespont. Darius relates that Xerxes' youth has led him to act impetuously and unwisely. Darius also tells the Persian elders that they should not try to invade Greece again. Darius notes that Xerxes' army committed numerous atrocities against the Greeks' gods during their invasion

of Greece and predicts that the Persians will suffer an additional defeat at the town of PLATAEA. Darius sends the queen home to find fresh robes for Xerxes, who will soon arrive with his royal robes in tatters.

After Darius' ghost vanishes, the queen exits to fetch clothing for her son. The Persian elders then recall the glorious achievements of Darius at home and in war. They detail the extent of his empire and praise his wise rule.

The chorus' words are followed by the arrival of Xerxes. The Persian king laments his fate and his grief is echoed by the chorus. The Persian elders ask Xerxes what has happened to his friends and allies, and he notes that they have died at Salamis. Xerxes also points out that his royal robes are in tatters and that his arrows are gone. The play approaches its end with alternating lines of lamentation by Xerxes and the Persian elders and concludes with Xerxes' being escorted from the ORCHESTRA by the elders.

COMMENTARY

Because Aeschylus' *Persians* is the earliest surviving classical drama, the play deserves consideration for its position in the development of drama. Echoes of the grieving barbarian mother and queen, Atossa, may be detected in the figure of EURIPIDES' HECABE (*HECABE, TROJAN WOMEN*). The use of dreams as a forewarning of future events can also be seen in later plays (e.g., Aeschylus' *Libation Bearers* (see *ORESTEIA*), Euripides' *Hecabe* and, *IPHIGENIA IN TAURIS*). The appearance of a ghost occurs in Euripides' *Hecabe* and SENECA's *AGAMEMNON* and *THYESTES*. In Seneca's *OEDIPUS,* the murderer of Laius is discovered by conjuring up Laius' ghost from the dead. Whereas ARISTOPHANES, in *ACHARNIANS*, ridicules Euripides' presenting his leading characters in rags, Aeschylus' Xerxes, who enters with his robes torn, indicates that Euripides was not the first to reduce a king to ruined clothing. Xerxes himself also provides a "textbook" example of someone who has committed acts of HUBRIS (808, 821), as his army destroyed temples and other sacred objects during their invasion of Greece, and as someone whom the gods will punish for these acts.

In addition to the importance of *Persians* in the history of drama, the play, as noted, is the only surviving

Greek drama based on a historical event. Aeschylus' brother died fighting against the Persians at MARATHON in 490, and Aeschylus himself is also thought to have fought at both Marathon and Salamis.

Persians is unique in that it is the only extant drama whose characters are all non-Greek. The play takes its name from the male Persian elders who make up the chorus. Other than the chorus, only four actors speak: an unnamed Persian Messenger; Atossa, widow of DARIUS, former king of Persia; Darius' ghost; and XERXES, the son of Atossa and Darius and the king of Persia. The play's characters are all Persian, and Aeschylus frequently contrasts them with the Greeks (especially the Athenians). The Athenians are ruled by their citizens, whereas the Persians are ruled by one man. We also find a contrast between order (*kosmos*) and disorder (*akosmos*). The Greeks prepare for battle in an orderly manner (374), and their ships advance in an orderly fashion (400). In contrast, the Persias fleet is cast into disorder (422) and the Persians retreat in disorder (470, 481). Interestingly, the word *kosmos* can also refer to clothing, and at the end of the play Xerxes' mother is told to get appropriate *kosmos* for her son because he has torn the robes he was wearing in his anguish about the defeat (833). Thus, the Persian disorder is also manifested in the disorder of the clothing in which the Persian leader appears when the audience first see him.

The disarray of Xerxes' clothing has been prepared for earlier in the play. When the chorus enter, they describe the dark robes of their heart as being torn with fear (115). In Atossa's dream (182–83), she sees a woman dressed in Persian clothing (which would have been brightly colored) and a woman dressed in Greek clothing (which would have been monochrome). She dreams that after Xerxes' fall from his chariot, Xerxes sees his father and tears at his clothing (199). Later, when Xerxes sees that the Persians are being defeated, he tears his robes (468). When the defeated Xerxes enters at the play's conclusion, he notes that he has torn his robes (1016, 1030). As Xerxes and the chorus lament the defeat, Xerxes urges the chorus to tear at their robes as well (1060).

Also interesting is the play's contrast in modes of transportation. The victorious and orderly ships of the Greeks are juxtaposed not only with the disorderly Persian fleet, but also with the chariots of the Persians (29, 46, 82). We also note Atossa's dream about the chariot, to which Xerxes failed to yoke the woman who represented Greece and from which Xerxes falls (190). When Xerxes enters, it is not in a chariot, but in some sort of covered vehicle.

In addition to the contrast of Xerxes' clothing, we find contrasts in the two groups' military equipment. The Persians fight with bows, which allow them to attack their enemy from a distance, whereas the Athenians fight primarily with spears (contrast 460), which require that they fight at close quarters (compare the discussion of the bow's being the coward's weapon in Euripides' *HERACLES*). When the chorus ask for information about the outcome of the battle, they wonder whether the bow or the spear has won (147–49). After the battle, the messenger announces that the Persian bows were useless in the battle (278). When the broken Xerxes enters at the end of the play he calls attention to his quiver, which is probably empty of arrows (1020–22).

We also have a numerical contrast between the two groups. The Greeks have plenty of men who can inflict damage on the Persians (235); the Athenians have a sufficent number of men to defend their city (349), despite the numerical superiority of the Persian army (533). As for the Persians, under the rule of Xerxes' father, their land was rich in men and had an army of men who never rested (897–902). Because Xerxes has invaded Greece, however, Persia is empty of men (59–60, 119, 133, 166); the Persian defeat at Salamis will leave Persia empty of men, and thousands of Persian men have been killed (289, 730, 915, 920, 927, 993). The numerous references to Persia's being without men also carry a double connotation: The Greek words *anandros* and *anandria,* which occur several times in the play (119, 166, 289, 298, 730, 755), can denote not only a numerical lack of men, but a lacking of manly qualities. Thus, the underlying tone of some of Aeschylus' remarks may suggest Persian cowardliness. At 755, Atossa says accusations of *anandria,* unmanliness, led him to invade Greece. Thus, the charge of lacking manliness prompted Xerxes to empty Persia of men, and Xerxes' defeat will cause Persia to remain empty of men.

BIBLIOGRAPHY
Broadhead, H. D. *Aeschylus: Persians*. Cambridge, Mass.: Cambridge University Press, 1960.
Griffith, M. "The King and Eye: The Role of the Father in Greek Tragedy," *Proceedings of the Cambridge Philological Society* 44 (1998): 20–84.
Hall, E. *Aeschylus: Persians*. Warminster, U.K.: Aris & Phillips, 1996.
Harrison, T. *The Emptiness of Asia: Aeschylus' Persians and the History of the Fifth Century*. London: Duckworth, 2000.
Michelini, Ann M. *Tradition and Dramatic Form in the Persians of Aeschylus*. Cincinnati Classical Studies. Leiden: Brill, 1982.

PHAEACIANS The Phaeacians were a mythical people who lived on the island of Scherie. ODYSSEUS encountered them on his return from TROY, and JASON encountered them on his return from COLCHIS. The Phaeacians eventually transported Odysseus back to his native island of ITHACA and helped put an end to the Colchians' pursuit of Jason and MEDEA. SOPHOCLES wrote a play entitled *Phaeacians*, whose four surviving words indicate nothing of its content (fragments 675–76 Radt). [ANCIENT SOURCES: Homer, *Odyssey* 5–13; Apollonius Rhodius, 4.539–1211]

BIBLIOGRAPHY
Kiso, A. *The Lost Sophocles*. New York: Vantage Press, 1984.
Lloyd-Jones, H. *Sophocles: Fragments*. Cambridge, Mass.: Harvard University Press, 1996.
Radt, S. *Tragicorum Graecorum Fragmenta*. Vol. 4. Göttingen, Ger.: Vandenhoeck & Ruprecht, 1977.
Sutton, D. F. *The Lost Sophocles*. Lanham, Md.: University Press of America, 1984.

PHAEAX The son of Erasistratus, Phaeax was from the DEME of ACHARNAE and was a prominent figure in Athenian politics between 425 and 416 B.C.E. Phaeax had served as a diplomat to SICILY in 422 and even rivaled ALCIBIADES in popularity. Some of the Athenian people did not like Phaeax, however, and he was almost sent into exile. After the year 416, nothing more is heard about Phaeax. [ANCIENT SOURCES: Aristophanes, *Knights* 1377; Eupolis, fragment 95 Kock; Plutarch, *Alcibiades* 13; Andocides, 4; Thucydides, 5.4–5]

BIBLIOGRAPHY
Kock, T. *Comicorum Atticorum Fragmenta*. Vol. 1. Leipzig: Teubner, 1880.
Sommerstein, A. H. *The Comedies of Aristophanes*. Vol. 2, *Knights*. Warminster, U.K.: Aris & Phillips, 1981, 218.

PHAEDRA Phaedra was the daughter of MINOS and PASIPHAE and the sister of ARIADNE. Phaedra married THESEUS after he divorced the AMAZON Antiope (or Hippolyta). In EURIPIDES' *HIPPOLYTUS*, Phaedra becomes the victim of Aphrodite's wrath against Theseus' bastard son, HIPPOLYTUS. In *Hippolytus*, Phaedra falls in love with her stepson, Hippolytus, and confesses her feelings to her NURSE. The nurse then reveals Phaedra's feelings to Hippolytus. When Phaedra learns of Hippolytus' furious reaction to this news, Phaedra hangs herself, but before doing this she writes a letter to her husband, Theseus, accusing Hippolytus of sexually assaulting her.

Phaedra's story is also taken up in SENECA'S *HIPPOLYTUS*. Seneca changes some of the details of Euripides' play: Seneca's Phaedra is bolder in her feelings about Hippolytus than Euripides' Phaedra; in Seneca's play, Phaedra's nurse tries to persuade Phaedra not to reveal her love to Hippolytus, and Phaedra rejects her advice. Furthermore, in Seneca's play, Phaedra has a face-to-face, onstage encounter with Hippolytus in which she confesses her love for him. In Senecan Phaedra's defense, however (unlike in Euripides' play, in which Theseus was very much alive and merely absent from home), in Seneca's play Theseus has been in the underworld for four years and is not expected to return. Furthermore, unlike Euripides' Phaedra, who accuses Hippolytus of rape and then commits suicide, in Seneca's play the Nurse accuses Hippolytus of rape. Also, in Seneca's play, Theseus returns and converses with his wife before she commits suicide. At this point, Phaedra tells Theseus that Hippolytus tried to rape her. Whereas Euripides' Phaedra hanged herself before Hippolytus' death and made no lamentation over his body, Seneca's Phaedra falls on a sword after her lamentation.

SOPHOCLES wrote a play entitled *Phaedra* that may have treated the same subject as Euripides' *Hippolytus*. Sophocles' play appears to differ from Euripides' *Hippolytus,* however, in that Sophocles has Theseus return from the underworld during the drama. [ANCIENT SOURCES: Aristophanes, *Frogs* 1042, *Thesmophoriazusae* 547]

BIBLIOGRAPHY

Kiso, A. *The Lost Sophocles.* New York: Vantage Press, 1984.

Lloyd-Jones, H. *Sophocles: Fragments.* Cambridge, Mass.: Harvard University Press, 1996.

Radt, S. *Tragicorum Graecorum Fragmenta.* Vol. 4. Göttingen, Ger.: Vandenhoeck & Ruprecht, 1977.

Sutton, D. F. *The Lost Sophocles.* Lanham, Md.: University Press of America, 1984.

PHAEDRA SENECA   See *HIPPOLYTUS SENECA*.

PHAETHON

The son of the sun god (either HELIOS or APOLLO) and Clymene, Phaethon ("shining") became famous for his tragic attempt to drive his father's chariot. When one of Phaethon's playmates suggested that Phaethon was not really Helios' son, Phaethon questioned his mother about the claim. Clymene swore that the Sun was his father and urged her son to ask his father himself. Phaethon traveled to the Sun god's palace and asked his father for some favor that would prove he was his child. The sun god swore to grant whatever favor he might request. Unfortunately for Phaethon and the world, Phaethon asked to drive the chariot that his father used to pull the Sun across the sky. The Sun god tried to persuade Phaethon to ask for something else, but Phaethon insisted on driving his father's chariot. During the flight that followed, Phaethon lost control of the chariot and was in danger of setting the entire world ablaze. EARTH complained to ZEUS, who struck Phaethon with a lightning bolt, thus putting an end to him and his wild ride. Phaethon's sisters, known as the Heliades, were so upset by their brother's death that they wept continuously. Eventually, the sisters were transformed into poplar trees, from which their tears (now drops of amber) continued to ooze.

EURIPIDES wrote a *Phaethon* that appears to have been composed around 420 B.C.E. and from which fragments totaling some 300 lines exist (771–786 Nauck). The fragments reveal that Euripides' play follows roughly the same story line outlined previously. Euripides, however, introduces a few twists. The play's setting is the palace of Clymene's husband, Merops, an Ethiopian king, who believes Phaethon is his son. In fragment 773, the conversation of Clymene and Phaethon reveals that the young man is preparing to go to Helios' house. The exit of Clymene and Phaethon into Merops' palace is followed by the entrance of the chorus, who are servants in Merops' palace. Their song indicates that Phaethon is to be married on that day and concludes by announcing the entrance of Merops and Phaethon; then a herald calls for silence. After this, Merops gives a lengthy speech to Phaethon that has not survived. The remainder of the play's fragments are less complete. Fragment 779 contains a description of Phaethon's difficulty in controlling the chariot and indicates that Helios was following Phaethon and giving him instructions. In fragment 781, Clymene's speech indicates that Phaethon's burned body is being taken into Merops' palace and hidden from Merops. After Clymene and her attendants take Phaethon's body into the palace, Merops and the chorus enter. The chorus, who do not know of Phaethon's death, sings a hymn in anticipation of Phaethon's marriage. Soon, a servant emerges from the palace and informs Merops that a fire of unknown origin appears to be burning in the palace. When Merops enters the palace to investigate, he discovers that Phaethon has been killed by Zeus' lightning. Fragment 781a contains a lament by Merops. The content of the play after this point is uncertain. Merops would have been enraged on discovering that Phaethon was not his son, but Collard thinks that a divinity would have prevented any harm to Clymene, verified that Phaethon was Helios' son, and made some prophecy about Phaethon's future. [ANCIENT SOURCES: Plato, *Timaeus* 22c–d; Ovid, *Metamorphoses* 1.751–2.400; Seneca, *Hercules Oetaeus* 677–82]

BIBLIOGRAPHY

Collard, C., M. J. Cropp, and K. H. Lee. *Euripides: Selected Fragmentary Plays.* Vol. 1. Warminster, U.K.: Aris & Phillips, 1995.

Diggle, J. *Phaethon.* Cambridge: Cambridge University Press, 1970.

Nauck, A. *Tragicorum Graecorum Fragmenta.* 1889. Reprint, Hildesheim, Ger.: Olms, 1964.

Reckford, K. J. "Phaethon, Hippolytus, and Aphrodite," *Transactions of the American Philological Association* 103 (1972): 405–32.

PHALES Mentioned by Aristophanes at *Acharnians* 263 in connection with Dionysus, the Greek word *phales* means "penis." In *Acharnians*, Dicaeopolis, about to conduct a procession honoring Dionysus in which a *phales* would be carried, addresses Phales as if he were a god. Thus, Phales "is the personification of the processional phallus" (Sommerstein).

BIBLIOGRAPHY
Sommerstein. A. *The Comedies of Aristophanes*. Vol. 1, *Acharnians*. Warminster, U.K.: Aris & Phillips, 1980, 169.

PHALLUS The actors in satyr plays and comedy had costumes that had stitched onto them an oversized leather phallus (penis). The phallus does not seem to have been erect ordinarily. In Sophocles' *Searchers*, Cyllene tells one of the satyrs to stop extending his "smooth phallus in delight" (368). In Aristophanes' *Wasps*, Philocleon offers his phallus as a rope a flute girl may hold (1342–43). In Aristophanes' *Lysistrata*, in which Cinesias appears in a state of tremendous sexual excitement, the play's humor would have been enhanced by this exaggerated appendage. The oversized phallus was not part of the comic costume in New Comedy.

BIBLIOGRAPHY
Calder, W. M. "Aristophanes *Vespae* 68–69: An Unnoticed Obscenity," *Classical Philology* 65 (1970): 257.
Dickie, M. W. "A Joke in Old Comedy: Aristophanes Fragment 607 PCG," *Classical Philology* 90, no. 3 (1995): 241–45.
Seaford, R. A. "Silenus Erectus: Euripides, *Cyclops* 227," *Liverpool Classical Monthly* 12 (1987): 142–43.

PHANUS A friend of Cleon's, Phanus apparently aided Cleon in some of his prosecutions. [ancient sources: Aristophanes, *Knights* 1256, *Wasps* 1220]

BIBLIOGRAPHY
MacDowell, D. M. *Aristophanes: Wasps*. Oxford: Clarendon Press, 1971, 289.

PHARSALUS A Thessalian town near the coast of northeastern Greece. [ancient sources: Aristophanes, *Wasps* 1271; Euripides, *Iphigenia at Aulis* 812]

PHASIS A river in the Black Sea region on which the town of Colchis (the location of the Golden Fleece) was situated. [ancient sources: Euripides, *Andromache* 651; Seneca, *Agamemnon* 120, *Hercules Oetaeus* 950, *Hippolytus* 907, *Medea* 44, 211, 451, 762; Sophocles, *Oedipus Tyrannos* 1227]

PHAYLLUS A prize-winning athlete from the town of Croton in Italy, Phayllus won the pentathlon twice and the stadion (a foot race of about 200 meters) once at the Pythian Games. Phayllus commanded a ship at the battle of Salamis in 480 b.c.e. A statue of him existed at Delphi, as well as a monument on the Acropolis at Athens. [ancient sources: Aristophanes, *Acharnians* 215, *Wasps* 1206; Herodotus, 8.47.1; *Inscriptiones Graecae* i² 655; Pausanias, 10.9.2; Plutarch, *Alexander* 34]

BIBLIOGRAPHY
MacDowell, D. M. *Aristophanes: Wasps*. Oxford: Clarendon Press, 1971, 287.

PHEIDIPPIDES A character in Aristophanes' *Clouds*, Pheidippides is the son of Strepsiades. Pheidippides' name, which seems to mean something like "son of thrifty horse," alludes to the "disease" that Aristophanes gives his character—he loves horses and horse racing. This expensive interest causes his father much financial hardship. As other Aristophanic sons do, Pheidippides shows more restrained behavior than his father, the opposite of what a Greek audience would expect. Initially, Pheidippides refuses his father's request to become one of Socrates' pupils, but later he does submit to instruction by "Right Logic" and "Wrong Logic." Once indoctrinated into this new learning, Pheidippides becomes something of a monster and starts behaving in a manner that his father detests. Having learned Wrong Logic's method of arguing, Pheidippides attempts to convince his father that the son is within his rights to beat his father and proceeds to do so, and then also argues that the son is permitted to beat his mother as well. Tarrant and Vickers think that Aristophanes' audience would have identified Pheidippides with the Athenian statesman Alcibiades.

BIBLIOGRAPHY
Tarrant, H. "Alcibiades in Aristophanes' *Clouds* I and II," *Ancient History* 19 (1989): 13–20.
Vickers, M. "Alcibiades in Cloudedoverland." In *Nomodeiktes: Greek Studies in Honor of Martin Ostwald*. Edited by R. Rosen and J. Farrell. Ann Arbor: University of Michigan Press, 1993, 603–18.

PHERAE   A town near the coast of northeastern Greece. Pherae was the home of ADMETUS, ALCESTIS, and PHERES and the setting for EURIPIDES' *ALCESTIS*.

PHERECRATES   A Greek comic poet who was active in the latter half of the fifth century B.C.E. Pherecrates' first victory in competition is dated to 437. Some 250 fragments survive and 17 or 18 titles are known (*Cheiron* may not have been written by Pherecrates). A fragment from *Cheiron* contains a speech by Music to Justice about the way Music has been treated by recent musicians. Pherecrates' *Savages* (*Agrioi*), produced at the LENAEA in 420 B.C.E., in which some men leave civilization for a life among the savages, may have influenced ARISTOPHANES' *BIRDS* (414 B.C.E.), in which two men leave ATHENS to live among the birds. Pherecrates' *Ant-People* (*Myrmekanthropoi*) dealt with DEUCALION and PYRRHA's survival of the flood. Pherecrates appears to have been something of a pioneer in the realm of creating female characters in comedy (as his *Old Women* attests) and is often credited with inventing comedies that centered around a *hetaira* (high-class PROSTITUTE). [ANCIENT SOURCES: Aristophanes, *Lysistrata* 158; pseudo-Plutarch, *Moralia* 1141d–42a]

BIBLIOGRAPHY
Ceccarelli, P. "Life among the Savages and Escape from the City." In *The Rivals of Aristophanes: Studies in Athenian Old Comedy*. Edited by D. Harvey and J. Wilkins. London: Duckworth and the Classical Press of Wales, 2000, 453–71.
Dobrov, G. W., and E. Urios-Aparisi. "The Maculate Muse: Gender, Genre, and the *Chiron* of Pherecrates." In *Beyond Aristophanes: Transition and Diversity in Greek Comedy*. Atlanta: Scholars Press, 1995, 139–74.
Henderson, J. "Pherekrates and the Women of Old Comedy." In *The Rivals of Aristophanes: Studies in Athenian Old Comedy*. Edited by D. Harvey and J. Wilkins. London: Duckworth and the Classical Press of Wales, 2000, 135–50.
Urios-Aparisi, E. "Old Comedy Pherecrates' Way," *Itaca* 12–13 (1996–97): 75–86.

PHERES   The son of CRETHEUS and TYRO, Pheres was the brother of Aeson and Amythaon. Pheres is said to have founded the town of Pherae. By his wife, Periclymene, Pheres was the father of ADMETUS, Lycurgus, Idomene, and Periopis. Pheres was a king of Pherae, but after he became old he turned over the kingship to his son, Admetus. When Apollo gave Admetus the opportunity to avoid death, provided that he could find someone to die in his place, Admetus asked his father and mother, but they refused. Eventually, Admetus' wife, ALCESTIS, agreed to die in his place. Pheres' appearance in EURIPIDES' *ALCESTIS* has led him to be considered one of the more unpleasant characters in Greek TRAGEDY. Pheres arrives at his son's house after the death of Admetus' wife, Alcestis, carrying items of finery for Alcestis' burial. Because Pheres was unwilling to give up his life for Admetus, Admetus rejects Pheres and his gifts. Pheres responds to his son by declaring that he has given him everything a father should give a son; that he values life just as much as his son does and therefore should not have to die before his time; and that Admetus, and not he, is responsible for Alcestis' death. Pheres declares that he would be making a mistake if he died for his son. Pheres leaves with the declaration that someday Alcestis' relatives will avenge her death and punish Admetus. [ANCIENT SOURCES: Apollodorus, *Library* 1.9.11, 1.9.14, 3.10.4, 3.13.8; Euripides, *Alcestis*; Homer, *Odyssey* 11.258–59]

BIBLIOGRAPHY
Bradley, E. M. "Admetus and the Triumph of Failure in Euripides' *Alcestis*," *Ramus* 9 (1980): 112–27.

PHERSEPHATTA   A name for PERSEPHONE. [ANCIENT SOURCES: Aristophanes, *Frogs* 671]

PHIDIAS (CA. 490–432 B.C.E.)   The son of Charmides, Phidias was the greatest of Athenian sculptors. The gleam from Phidias' 30-foot high statue of ATHENA Promachus (ca. 456) was so bright that it could be seen from miles away, and EURIPIDES alludes to this statue in the opening of ION. Phidias also created the sculpture for the PROPYLAEA and the Parthenon in ATHENS, as well as the colossal gold and ivory statue of ATHENA (completed in the year 438) in the Parthenon. Phidias was later exiled from Athens for stealing material from these projects and went to the town of ELIS in southwestern Greece, where he made another colossal statue, this time of ZEUS (437–432 B.C.E.). He was again accused of stealing material from the project and was put to death. [ANCIENT SOURCES: Aristophanes, Peace 605, 616; Pausanias, 1.24.5; Plutarch, Pericles 13.4]

BIBLIOGRAPHY
Olson, S. D. Aristophanes: Peace. Oxford: Clarendon Press, 1998, 160–61.
Waldstein, C. Essays on the Art of Pheidias. 1885. Reprint, Washington, D.C.: McGrath, 1973.

PHILAENETE   A fictional Athenian woman mentioned at ARISTOPHANES, ECCLESIAZUSAE 42.

PHILBALIS   A Greek district famous for its figs. [ANCIENT SOURCES: Aristophanes, Acharnians 802]

BIBLIOGRAPHY
Sommerstein. A. The Comedies of Aristophanes. Vol. 1, Acharnians. Warminster, U.K.: Aris & Phillips, 1980, 196.

PHILEMON (1)   (CA. 365–CA. 265 B.C.E.)   A Greek playwright whose plays, as are those of MENANDER, are classified as New Comedy. Philemon was from SICILY or Cilicia and traveled to ATHENS, where he won a victory at the DIONYSIA in 327. Philemon is said to have written 97 plays; only some 60 titles and 200 fragments survive. At least two of PLAUTUS' plays were adapted from Philemon. Plautus' MERCHANT was based on Philemon's Emporos (Merchant) and Plautus' THREE-DOLLAR DAY was adapted from Philemon's Thesauros (Treasure). Plautus' HAUNTED HOUSE may have been adapted from Philemon's Phasma (Ghost).

BIBLIOGRAPHY
Fantham, E. "Philemon's Thesauros as a Dramatisation of Peripatetic Ethics," Hermes 105 (1977): 406–21.
Hunter, R. "Philemon, Plautus and the Trinummus," Museum Helveticum 37 (1980): 216–30.
Lefevre, Eckard. Plautus und Philemon. Tubingen, Ger.: G. Narr, 1995.

PHILEMON (2)   This person, who has not been identified, may have been an Athenian who was "accused . . . of not being a true-born citizen . . . or may have been a respectable citizen who bred or sold birds" (Dunbar). [ANCIENT SOURCES: Aristophanes, Birds 763]

BIBLIOGRAPHY
Dunbar, Nan. Aristophanes: Birds. New York: Oxford University Press, 1995, 472.

PHILEPSIAS   This Athenian politician, from the DEME of Lamptrae, was tried and jailed for misappropriation of public funds. Philepsias was apparently a clever public speaker who incorporated stories from mythology into his political speeches so that he could become popular with the people and thus become powerful politically. [ANCIENT SOURCES: Aristophanes, Wealth 177 and the scholia; Demosthenes, 24.134]

BIBLIOGRAPHY
Sommerstein, A. H. The Comedies of Aristophanes. Vol. 11, Wealth. Warminster, U.K.: Aris & Phillips, 2001, 148.

PHILIP (1)   (PHILIPPUS)   Although Philip is called the son of the famous sophist and rhetorician GORGIAS of Leontini, he may not have been Gorgias' child, but rather an imitator or student of his. Philip supposedly made a living by making malicious legal accusations against people. This Philip may also have prosecuted or denounced in writing "the anti-democratic intellectual and speech-writer Antiphon" (Sommerstein). [ANCIENT SOURCES: Aristophanes, Birds 1694–1705, Wasps 421; Isocrates, 15.156]

BIBLIOGRAPHY
MacDowell, D. M. Aristophanes: Wasps. Oxford: Clarendon Press, 1971, 192.
Sommerstein, A. H. The Comedies of Aristophanes. Vol. 4, Wasps. Warminster, U.K.: Aris & Phillips, 1983, 185.

PHILIP (2)   The name of several kings of the region of Macedon. The most famous of these was Philip II, who ruled from 359 to 336 B.C.E. and was the father of Alexander the Great. Under the rule of Philip II, the Macedonians conquered Greece. At the age of 46, Philip was preparing an attack against the Persians when he was assassinated. [ANCIENT SOURCES: Demosthenes, *Phillipics;* Diodorus Siculus, *Historical Library* 16; Isocrates, *Philippus;* Plautus, *Pot of Gold* 86, 704]

BIBLIOGRAPHY

Bradford, A. S. *Philip II of Macedon: A Life from the Ancient Sources.* Illustrated by P. M. Bradford. New York: Praeger, 1992.

Cawkwell, G. *Philip of Macedon.* London: Faber & Faber, 1978.

Ellis, J. R. *Philip II and Macedonian Imperialism.* London: Thames and Hudson, 1976.

Hammond, N. G. L. *Philip of Macedon.* Baltimore: Johns Hopkins University Press, 1994.

Hatzopoulos, M. B., and L. D. Loukopulos. *Philip of Macedon.* Athens: Ekdotike Athenon, 1980.

PHILIPICS   Named after the Macedonian king Philip, this gold coin (mentioned frequently in the plays of PLAUTUS), was worth 20 DRACHMAS.

PHILIPPI   A town in THRACE, Philippi was famous as the site where the forces of Octavian (AUGUSTUS) and Marcus ANTONIUS defeated the forces of Brutus and Cassius, the assassins of Julius CAESAR. [ANCIENT SOURCES: Seneca, *Octavia* 516]

PHILOCLEON   As are other leading Aristophanic characters such as DICAEOPOLIS, STREPSIADES, and TRYGAEUS, Philocleon, the focal point for the action in ARISTOPHANES' *WASPS,* is depicted as an unsophisticated older man. Unlike other Aristophanic heroes, though, Philocleon has a "disease"—he is addicted to serving on juries. Although Philocleon's son, Bdelycleon, tries to prevent his father from doing so, Philocleon keeps escaping from the house. Also unlike DICAEOPOLIS, STREPSIADES, and TRYGAEUS, Philocleon does not create a fantastic plan to solve some social problem, but he is the object of his son, Bdelycleon's, fantastic plan to cure him of his addiction to serving on juries. Not only is Philocleon not a social reformer, he may also be more uncouth and wild than these previously mentioned fellows. When his son asks him to recall the most manly deed of his youth, Philocleon responds that it was stealing the vine props of Ergasion (1201). Elsewhere, Philocleon says the best part of returning home from jury duty is his daughter's fishing his jury pay out of his mouth with her tongue (605–9). Philocleon also expresses pleasure in the power he exerts over defendants in court and is always prepared to condemn a defendant even before he has heard the case. Philocleon irreverently claims his life as a juror gives him dominion on the same level as that of ZEUS (620–21). Eventually, when Bdelycleon proves to his father that he is a slave to the demagogue CLEON, Philocleon agrees not to go to the law courts. Bdelycleon's cure, however, does not appear to work. Philocleon steals the MUSIC GIRL from the dinner party they are attending, assaults a baking girl on the way home from the party, and ends the play by dancing wildly.

BIBLIOGRAPHY

Bowie, A. M. "Ritual Stereotype and Comic Reversal. Aristophanes' *Wasps,*" *Bulletin for the Institute of Classical Studies* 34 (1987): 112–25.

Sidwell, Keith. "Was Philokleon Cured?: The *Nosos* Theme in Aristophanes' *Wasps,*" *Classica et Mediaevalia* 41 (1990): 9–31.

Vaio, J. "Aristophanes' *Wasps:* The Relevance of the Final Scenes," *Greek, Roman and Byzantine Studies* 12 (1971): 335–51.

PHILOCLES   The son of Philopeithes, Philocles was a Greek tragic poet and a nephew of AESCHYLUS'. Philocles' son, MORSIMUS, was also a tragic poet. Philocles is reported to have written some 100 plays and even defeated the production of SOPHOCLES that included *OEDIPUS TYRANNOS.* Comic poets made fun of Philocles' style, however, calling him "son of briny" (*almion*) and "gall" (*chole*). [ANCIENT SOURCES: Aristophanes, *Thesmophoriazusae* 168, *Wasps* 462; Cratinus, fragment 292 Kock; scholiast on Aristophanes, *Birds* 281; *Suda* on "Philocles"; Teleclides, fragment 14 Kock]

BIBLIOGRAPHY

Kock, T. *Comicorum Atticorum Fragmenta.* Vol. 1. Leipzig: Teubner, 1880.

Sommerstein, A. H. *The Comedies of Aristophanes.* Vol. 4, *Wasps.* Warminster, U.K.: Aris & Phillips, 1983, 185.

PHILOCRATES   An Athenian bird seller about whom ARISTOPHANES has two of his characters complain. [ANCIENT SOURCES: Aristophanes, *Birds* 13–16, 1076–83]

PHILOCTETES

The son of Poeas and Demonassa, Philoctetes was the king of the Malians, who lived near Mount OETA in northeastern Greece. Philoctetes made a brief appearance in the latter part of SENECA's *HERCULES OETAEUS*. In Seneca's play, when the hero, HERACLES, was in torment after he put on the poisoned robe given to him by his wife, DEIANEIRA, he told Philoctetes to build a pyre on Mount Oeta and then light it. As a reward, Heracles gave Philoctetes his bow and arrows.

When the Trojan War began, Philoctetes joined the other Greeks on the expedition because he had been one of HELEN's suitors. While he was on the island of Tenedos, just off the coast from TROY, a serpent bit Philoctetes in the foot. Hyginus reports that HERA sent the serpent because she was angry that Philoctetes was helping Heracles. When Philoctetes' wound did not heal, his cries of anguish and the stench of the wound were unbearable to the rest of the army, who then abandoned him on the island of LEMNOS. Later, when the Greeks learned that they could not defeat Troy without the help of Philoctetes and the bow and arrows of Heracles, which Philoctetes carried, some of the Greeks, led by ODYSSEUS, traveled to Lemnos to take Philoctetes back to Troy. Because Odysseus had been instrumental in the decision to abandon Philoctetes on Lemnos, Philoctetes did not want to return with the Greeks. In SOPHOCLES' play, the divine Heracles appeared and persuaded Philoctetes to return to Troy. After Philoctetes returned to Troy, he was healed of his wound and then killed PARIS in battle with arrows from Heracles' bow. After the war, Philoctetes traveled to Italy and eventually settled on SICILY at the town of Crimissa, where he established a shrine to APOLLO and dedicated Heracles' bow to the god.

In addition to the extant *PHILOCTETES*, Sophocles wrote a play entitled *Philoctetes at Troy*, which was probably about the healing of Philoctetes' wound on his return to Troy and Philoctetes' subsequent killing of Paris (fragments 697–703 Radt). Fragment 697, spoken by Philoctetes, begged more than one person not to be distressed by his odor. Fragment 701 described a staff that may have belonged to the healer ASCLEPIUS.

Several other Greek tragedians composed a *Philoctetes*. Only titles survive from the plays of Antiphon (fragment 3 Snell) and Philocles (fragment 1 Snell). One brief phrase survives from Theodectas' *Philoctetes*, a command to more than one person to "cut off my hand" (fragment 5b Snell). From Achaeus' *Philoctetes,* a four-line fragment (37 Snell) survives, in which AGAMEMNON appears to be calling Greek troops to aid someone.

AESCHYLUS (fragments 249–57 Radt) and EURIPIDES (fragments 787–803 Nauck) also wrote plays entitled *Philoctetes,* which had the same subject matter as Sophocles' play. Fortunately, Dio Chrysostomus (born 40 C.E.) compared the three plays by Aeschylus, Euripides, and Sophocles. Concerning Aeschylus' play, the chorus consisted of men from Lemnos and DIOMEDES accompanied Odysseus to Lemnos. In Aeschylus, Philoctetes' disease prevented him from recognizing Odysseus, who told him a false tale that Agamemnon and Odysseus were dead and the Greek army was in disarray. Dio reports that Aeschylus' Odysseus made such a persuasive argument that Philoctetes willingly went to Troy with the Greeks.

Euripides' *Philoctetes* appeared in the TETRALOGY of 431 with MEDEA. As in Aeschylus' play, Euripides' chorus consisted of Lemnians. Euripides appears to have added to the cast a Lemnian named Aktor, who may have been a supplier of food and information for Philoctetes (Webster). In Euripides' play both the Greeks and the Trojans sent teams (the former led by Odysseus, the latter by Paris) to Lemnos to try to persuade Philoctetes to aid their respective side. Apparently the Greeks, with the exception of Odysseus, did not enter until late in the play. Furthermore, Odysseus appears to have been in disguise as a Greek warrior returning from Troy. In this guise, Odysseus would have befriended Philoctetes and argued against Paris, who tried to persuade Philoctetes to aid the Trojans with the promise of riches. Near the play's conclusion, Odysseus would have revealed his true identity and Philoctetes would have left with the Greeks, but how Euripides brought this about is unknown.

Among the Greek comic poets, Antiphanes wrote a *Philoctetes;* the two lines that survive (fragment 219

Kock)—regarding wisdom in old age—tell us nothing about the play's plot. Strattis also wrote a *Philoctetes,* from which two fragments (43–44 Kock 2) survive. The first is about not casting treasure into dung; the second mentions people's entering a marketplace and buying fish and eels from COPAIS. Epicharmus also wrote a *Philoctetes* (fragments 132–34 Kaibel), whose fragments are uninformative.

Among Roman authors, ACCIUS wrote a *Philoctetes* (522–72 Warmington), in which DIOMEDES rather than NEOPTOLEMUS accompanied Odysseus to Lemnos. A Lemnian shepherd also appears to have been a character in Accius' play. [ANCIENT SOURCES: Apollodorus, *Library* 3.10.8, 3.12.6, *Epitome* 3.14, 3.27, 5.8, 6.15–15b; Dio Chrysostomus, *Orations* 52, 59; Homer, *Iliad* 2.716–25; Hyginus, *Fables* 102; Seneca, *Hercules Oetaeus* 1603–1757; Sophocles, *Philoctetes;* Strabo, 6.1.3]

BIBLIOGRAPHY

Kaibel, G. *Comicorum Graecorum Fragmenta.* Vol. 1.1 [*Poetarum Graecorum Fragmenta.* Vol. 6.1]. Berlin: Weidmann, 1899.

Kock, T. *Comicorum Atticorum Fragmenta.* Vol. 1. Leipzig: Teubner, 1880.

———. *Comicorum Atticorum Fragmenta.* Vol. 2. Leipzig: Teubner, 1884.

Radt, S. *Tragicorum Graecorum Fragmenta.* Vol. 3. Göttingen, Ger.: Vandenhoeck & Ruprecht, 1985.

Snell, B. *Tragicorum Graecorum Fragmenta.* Vol. 1. Göttingen, Ger.: Vandenhoeck & Ruprecht, 1971.

Warmington, E. H. *Remains of Old Latin: Livius Andronicus, Naevius, Pacuvius, and Accius.* Vol. 2. Cambridge, Mass.: Harvard University Press, 1936.

Webster, T. B. L. *The Tragedies of Euripides.* London: Methuen, 1967.

PHILOCTETES SOPHOCLES (409 B.C.E.)

The action of *Philoctetes* takes place near a double-mouthed cave on the island of LEMNOS (the only instance in extant drama in which this island serves as a setting). Nine years before to the play's action, the Greek archer Philoctetes was abandoned on the island of Lemnos by the Greek army as it was sailing to fight at TROY. When the Greek fleet had taken the island of Tenedos, a snake bit Philoctetes. When his wound did not heal, the stench of the wound and Philoctetes' moans became so annoying to his fellow Greeks that they abandoned him on Lemnos. Philoctetes has been on the island nine years when the Greeks learned through prophecy that Troy could not be captured without his aid and that of the weapons that he carried: a bow and arrows given to him by the great hero HERACLES.

As the action of SOPHOCLES' play opens, the Greek hero ODYSSEUS, accompanied by NEOPTOLEMUS, the son of ACHILLES, are searching for Philoctetes' cave. After they find it, Odysseus reveals to Neoptolemus that he wants Achilles' son to trick Philoctetes into giving him Philoctetes' weapons. Without Philoctetes' bow, Odysseus says, the Greeks will never capture Troy. Because Odysseus was one of the Greeks primarily responsible for Philoctetes' abandonment on Lemnos, Odysseus has enlisted Neoptolemus to try to trick Philoctetes to give his weapons to him. Neoptolemus would prefer even force to trickery, but Odysseus tells him that Philoctetes' arrows are too dangerous. Neoptolemus still does not want to lie to Philoctetes, but Odysseus again tells him that without the bow Troy cannot be taken. Odysseus also reveals that the presence of Neoptolemus is also required for victory at Troy. Eventually, Neoptolemus agrees Odysseus' plan. Before leaving Neoptolemus at the cave, Odysseus tells him that if he is taking longer than expected, he will send a scout disguised as the captain of a merchant ship to check on his progress.

After Odysseus' exit, a CHORUS of sailors from the island of Scyros (where Neoptolemus was raised) enter and ask what orders Neoptolemus has for them. Neoptolemus tells his sailors to watch for his signal and be ready to help him should the need arise. As Neoptolemus and his crew wait for Philoctetes, they express pity for the condition in which he lives. Soon they hear moaning, Philoctetes appears, and he asks the strangers who they are. When Philoctetes hears that Neoptolemus is Achilles' son, he is happy to meet the son of his old friend. When Neoptolemus feigns surprise on hearing that Philoctetes was a member of the force who sailed to Troy, Philoctetes is equally surprised that Neoptolemus has never heard of him. Philoctetes then explains to Neoptolemus who he is, how the serpent bit him on the island of Chryse, and how AGAMEMNON, MENELAUS, and Odysseus abandoned him on Lemnos. Philoctetes also tells how he was able to survive for the past 10 years. Neoptolemus claims (again falsely) that he too has suffered at the hands of Agamemnon, Menelaus, and Odysseus. Neoptolemus then tells of his father, Achilles', death—of which Philoctetes was unaware—and of how his father's guardian, Phoenix, had sailed to Scyros and told him of the prophecy that Neoptolemus would be the conqueror of Troy. Neoptolemus then says that he sailed for Troy, but when he arrived, his father's weapons had been given to Odysseus. Neoptolemus claims he was insulted by this; argued with Odysseus, who refused to give up Achilles' arms; and then sailed for Scyros.

Philoctetes is not surprised by the trickery of Odysseus and asks about some of the other warriors at Troy. Neoptolemus tells Philoctetes about the deaths of AJAX; NESTOR's son, Antilochus; and Patroclus. Philoctetes finds bitter irony in the fact that Thersites, who could never keep his mouth shut, was still alive. When Neoptolemus then states his intention to set sail from Scyros, Philoctetes begs to be taken along. After Neoptolemus agrees, two men, disguised agents of Odysseus', approach and tell Neoptolemus that the Greeks have sent out Phoenix and THESEUS' sons to track him down. When the disguised Merchant sees Philoctetes, he urges Neoptolemus to flee. When Neoptolemus tells the Merchant that he and Philoctetes are friends, the Merchant tells him that Odysseus and Diomedes have gone to track down Philoctetes. The Merchant explains that Odysseus had captured a son of PRIAM, HELENUS, who had informed the Greeks that they would not capture Troy without Philoctetes' help. When Philoctetes hears this, he suggests that he would never go with Odysseus. Upon hearing this, the Merchant exits. Philoctetes then urges Neoptolemus to set sail, but the young man delays, saying that the winds are not yet favorable. Neoptolemus tells Philoctetes to collect anything that he needs for the voyage. When Philoctetes mentions his bow and arrows, Neoptolemus asks to touch the bow. Philoctetes lets Neoptolemus handle the bow, and then the men enter Philoctetes' cave. Next, the chorus lament the sufferings of Philoctetes and express joy that Neoptolemus will help him.

After the choral ode, Neoptolemus and Philoctetes emerge from the cave. When Philoctetes experiences a spasm of pain, he asks Neoptolemus to hold his bow until the pain passes and makes him promise not to let anything happen to it. Neoptolemus takes the bow and watches in amazed horror as another spasm wracks Philoctetes. The wounded hero alternates between longing for death and begging Neoptolemus not to leave him. Eventually, after Philoctetes falls asleep, the chorus wonder whether they should now leave with the bow. Neoptolemus, however, says Troy cannot be taken without Philoctetes. The chorus again urge Neoptolemus to leave, however. Soon Philoctetes wakes and asks Neoptolemus to lift him up and take him to the ship. As they prepare to leave, Neoptolemus confesses that his mission is to take Philoctetes to Troy. Philoctetes is horrified by Neoptolemus' trickery and begs the young man for his bow.

Just as it seems that Neoptolemus will return the bow to Philoctetes, Odysseus appears and demands that Neoptolemus give the bow to him. Odysseus also demands that Philoctetes accompany them. Philoctetes, furious at this turn of events, threatens to hurl himself from a cliff but is restrained. After Philoctetes laments his fate and the trickery of Neoptolemus and Odysseus, Odysseus agrees to leave Philoctetes on the island, but says they will take the bow. Odysseus turns to go, but Neoptolemus tells his crew to stay with Philoctetes until he gives orders for them to go to the ship. After the departure of Odysseus and Neoptolemus, Philoctetes wonders how he will survive. The chorus, however, tell him that he could have left with Odysseus and Neoptolemus. Philoctetes continues to lament his lost bow and to wonder how he will survive. The chorus try to persuade Philoctetes to go to Troy, but Philoctetes refuses and begs the chorus to kill him.

After Philoctetes crawls back into his cave, Odysseus and Neoptolemus return. Neoptolemus states his intention to return the bow to Philoctetes. Odysseus threatens Neoptolemus, saying that he and the entire Greek army will prevent him. The two men then draw swords and threaten one another, but Odysseus backs down and exits for the ship. With Odysseus gone, Neoptolemus calls Philoctetes from the cave and gives him the bow. When Odysseus returns, Philoctetes threatens to shoot him with the bow, but Neoptolemus prevents him. After Odysseus runs away, however, Neoptolemus and Philoctetes are reconciled. Neoptolemus urges Philoctetes to go to Troy, promising that he will be healed if he does and that he and Philoctetes will triumph over Troy. Philoctetes, however, does not want to face Agamemnon, Menelaus, and Odysseus again and urges Neoptolemus to return to Scyros. The two continue to argue, and Philoctetes asks Neoptolemus to take him home, a request to which Neoptolemus eventually agrees.

Just as they are about to leave, however, the divine Heracles appears and tells Philoctetes that he must go to Troy, be healed of his wound, kill Paris in battle, and conquer Troy. Heracles also tells Neoptolemus that Philoctetes will not be successful without his help. As Heracles vanishes, Philoctetes and Neoptolemus agree to obey. After Philoctetes bids farewell to his island home, the chorus pray for smooth sailing.

COMMENTARY

Sophocles' *Philoctetes* is one of the more beautiful yet less appreciated plays in classical drama. The story of Philoctetes is mentioned briefly in HOMER, but Sophocles may have modeled the mission to Philoctetes on the embassy to Achilles in *Iliad* 9, a mission in which Odysseus played a key role that failed to achieve its aim of drawing Achilles back into battle. For the character of Neoptolemus, Sophocles may have drawn on the Homeric portrait of Odysseus' son, TELEMACHUS, in *Odyssey*. Just as Telemachus is educated in the ways of words and war in *Odyssey*, Neoptolemus learns how to seek a balance between persuasion and force in *Philoctetes*.

Although the more educated members of Sophocles' audience may have caught Sophocles' references to Homer, it is difficult to see how an Athenian audience in 409 B.C.E. would not draw parallels between Philoctetes and their own statesman ALCIBIADES, the most charismatic statesman and capable military commander in ATHENS during the last two decades of the fifth century B.C.E. In 415 B.C.E., Alcibiades was sent to SICILY as one of the commanders of a military expedition, but he was soon recalled when he was implicated in some religious crimes at Athens (compare Philoctetes, whose sufferings were attributed to his violation of a sacred shrine). Alcibiades escaped from the Athenians and went to SPARTA, where he aided the Spartans in their war against the Athenians. After Alcibiades' departure, the Athenian military was not successful and despite the help he gave to the enemy, the Athenian navy restored Alcibiades (compare Philoctetes) as commander, and in 410 (the year before *Philoctetes*) he led the Athenians to an important victory over Sparta.

In the case of Alcibiades, he had been a friend of the Athenians, he then became their enemy, and he then became their friend again. Instances when friends become enemies and enemies become friends had been of great interest to Sophocles. This is clear from his earliest extant play (*AJAX*), and, as Blundell has shown, such instances are important to almost all of Sophocles' plays. *Philoctetes* also explores such relationships. The Greeks and Philoctetes had been friends, but after they abandoned him on Lemnos they became enemies. An enemy of the Greeks, the Trojan prophet Helenus revealed to the Greeks that they could not capture Troy without Philoctetes and his bow. To take Philoctetes back to Troy, the Greeks send out Odysseus, the person whom Philoctetes regards as his greatest enemy and holds most responsible for his abandonment on Lemnos. Odysseus realizes that Philoctetes regards him as an enemy and thus enlists the aid of a person unknown to Philoctetes to trick him. To acquire the bow, Neoptolemus must gain Philoctetes' trust and convince him that he is his friend.

To win over Philoctetes, Neoptolemus employs both trickery and persuasion. As noted in the entry on Philoctetes, AESCHYLUS and EURIPIDES also wrote plays entitled *Philoctetes*. In each of the three dramas the way in which Philoctetes is compelled to depart Lemnos depends on persuasion. In Aeschylus, Odysseus made such a persuasive argument to Philoctetes that he willingly went to Troy with the Greeks. In Euripides, Odysseus, disguised as another Greek warrior, befriended Philoctetes and argued against Paris, who, with the promise of riches, tried to persuade Philoctetes to aid the Trojans. Thus, in contrast to Aeschylus and Euripides, Sophocles sends Odysseus into the background to some extent and places Neoptolemus opposite Philoctetes.

Interestingly, whereas Odysseus was a persuader in the plays of Aeschylus and Euripides, Sophocles' Odysseus rejects this tactic when Neoptolemus suggests using persuasion rather than trickery (102–3). Sophoclean Odysseus is convinced that trickery will be the only way to overcome Philoctetes. When Odysseus' scheme of having the disguised sailor approach Philoctetes is set in motion, the sailor declares that Odysseus and Diomedes are planning to take Philoctetes by persuasion or force (593–94). When this sailor reports the words of the prophet that prompted about this fictional mission of Odysseus', the fictional words of the prophet are that the Greeks could not capture Troy until Philoctetes was taken to Troy by persuasion (612). Philoctetes, of course, cannot believe that Odysseus swore he would take Philoctetes back to Troy by persuasion (623) and declares that he will not be persuaded by Odysseus (624) to return to Troy.

Eventually, however, the actors in Odysseus' play within the play fool Philoctetes, and he is persuaded to place his bow in Neoptolemus' hands. Now, however, Neoptolemus must be persuaded to hand over the bow to Odysseus, and he refuses to do so. Neoptolemus repents of his earlier trickery (1228) and tries again to win over Philoctetes, but the latter is wary after earlier having been persuaded to his detriment (1269). When Neoptolemus finds that he cannot persuade Philoctetes (1278–80), he ceases his attempt and returns the bow to him. The appearance of Odysseus, who declares his intent to take Philoctetes back to Troy by force (1297), prompts the bow-wielding Neoptolemus to use force, but Neoptolemus, who earlier in the play expressed a preference for force over trickery (90–91), now returns to persuasion to convince Philoctetes that the use of force would not be the proper course of action; Neoptolemus fails in a further attempt to persuade Philoctetes to return with him to Troy; instead, the two decide to return to Greece, where Philoctetes promises that the force of Heracles' bow will protect them from anyone in the Greek army who might use force against them.

Ultimately, force, trickery, and persuasion are at an impasse. Sophocles will not resolve his plot in the manner of his predecessors Aeschylus and Euripides. Because human beings do not succeed in winning over Philoctetes, Sophocles turns to divine persuasion in the person of Heracles, although the use of the divine appearance at the conclusion of the play was a favorite Euripidean practice. Ironically, Heracles, whose fame rested almost solely on his use of force, turns to the power of persuasion to convince Philoctetes and Neoptolemus that they should return to Troy, and as the play ends they both declare that they have been persuaded by his words (1447–48).

BIBLIOGRAPHY
Blundell, M. W. *Helping Friends and Harming Enemies: A Study in Sophocles and Greek Ethics.* Cambridge: Cambridge University Press, 1989, 184–225.
Poe, J. P. *Heroism and Divine Justice in Sophocles' Philoctetes.* Leiden: Brill, 1974.
Roisman, H. M. "The Appropriation of a Son: Sophocles' *Philoctetes,*" *Greek, Roman, and Byzantine Studies* 38.2 (1997): 127–71.
Rose P. W. "Sophocles' *Philoctetes* and the Teachings of the Sophists," *Harvard Studies in Classical Philology* 80 (1976): 49–105.
Webster. T. B. L. *Philoctetes.* Cambridge: Cambridge University Press, 1970.

PHILODORETUS   A probably fictional Athenian mentioned by ARISTOPHANES at *ECCLESIAZUSAE* 51. No historical Athenian of this name is known.

BIBLIOGRAPHY
Sommerstein, A. H. *The Comedies of Aristophanes.* Vol. 10, *Ecclesiazusae.* Warminster, U.K.: Aris & Phillips, 1998, 143.

PHILOMELA   See TEREUS.

PHILONIDES   An Athenian from the DEME of Milite, the wealthy Philonides was mocked by comic poets as ugly, uncouth, and ignorant and a lover of a Corinthian prostitute named Nais (or Lais). The comic poets also suggested he was the son of a camel or a donkey. The comic poet Aristophon wrote a play entitled *Philonides,* from which a five-line fragment survives (14 Kock). In this fragment, the speaker relates that his master gave him a special drinking bowl for his valuable service and then set him free after dousing him with wine. [ANCIENT SOURCES: Aristophanes, *Wealth* 179, 303; Nicochares, fragment 3 Kock; Philyllius, fragment 23 Kock; Plato Comicus, fragment 64.5 Kock; Theopompus, fragments 4–5 Kock]

BIBLIOGRAPHY

Kock, T. *Comicorum Atticorum Fragmenta.* Vol. 1. Leipzig: Teubner, 1880.

Sommerstein, A. H. *The Comedies of Aristophanes.* Vol. 11, *Wealth.* Warminster, U.K.: Aris & Phillips, 2001, 148.

PHILOSTRATUS   See CYANOPLEX.

PHILOXENUS   See ERYXIS.

PHINEUS   The son of Agenor (or Agenor's son, Phoenix, or POSEIDON), Phineus was king of Salmydessus, a town in THRACE. Phineus first married BOREAS' daughter CLEOPATRA by whom he fathered Plexippus and Pandion. Later, Phineus divorced Cleopatra and married Dardanus' daughter Idaea. When Idaea falsely accused Plexippus and Pandion of trying to seduce her, Phineus, believing the accusation, blinded both his sons. In *ANTIGONE,* SOPHOCLES says Idaea blinded her stepsons. Some sources say that the Argonauts and Boreas, who was the grandfather of Phineus' sons, saved the boys and blinded Phineus. The Argonauts then sent Idaea to her father, Dardanus, who sentenced her to die.

Other sources say that ZEUS blinded Phineus because he told mortals the future. As an additional punishment, the HARPIES were sent to steal Phineus' food anytime he tried to eat. His torment by the Harpies, however, ended after the arrival of JASON and the Argonauts. In exchange for information on how to reach COLCHIS, the Argonauts agreed to help Phineus, and the Harpies were driven away by the winged Argonauts, Zetes and Calais, who also happened to be Cleopatra's brothers. After this, Phineus told the Argonauts the route and dangers they would face on the way to Colchis. Some sources say that POSEIDON blinded Phineus for revealing this information.

AESCHYLUS wrote a *Phineus* (fragments 258–59a Radt), which appeared on the stage before *PERSIANS* in 472 B.C.E. The play appears to have dealt with the Argonauts' encounter with Phineus. To Sophocles are attributed two plays entitled *Phineus* (fragments 704–17a Radt), although Lloyd-Jones thinks that one of these plays may have been the same as *Drummers.* The Greek comic poet Theopompus also wrote a *Phineus* (fragment 62 Kock); the five lines that survive, in which a speaker gives another dietary advice, reveals nothing about the play's plot. [ANCIENT SOURCES: Aeschylus, *Eumenides* 50 (see ORESTEIA); Apollodorus, *Library* 3.15.3; Apollonius Rhodius, 2.178–489; Diodorus Siculus, 4.43.3–4.44.7; Sophocles, *Antigone* 969ff.]

BIBLIOGRAPHY

Kock, T. *Comicorum Atticorum Fragmenta.* Vol. 1. Leipzig: Teubner, 1880.

Lloyd-Jones, H. *Sophocles: Fragments.* Cambridge, Mass.: Harvard University Press, 1996, 334.

Radt, S. *Tragicorum Graecorum Fragmenta.* Vol. 3. Göttingen, Ger.: Vandenhoeck & Ruprecht, 1985.

PHLEGETHON   A river of flames by which the UNDERWORLD was bounded. [ANCIENT SOURCES: Seneca, *Agamemnon* 753, *Hippolytus* 848, 1227, *Oedipus* 162, *Thyestes* 73, 1018]

PHLEGRA   A plain where a battle between the gods and a certain group of Giants took place. Some sources thought Phlegra was a volcanic area near Naples in Italy; others thought it was near Pallene in northeastern Greece. [ANCIENT SOURCES: Apollodorus, *Library* 2.7.1; Aeschylus, *Eumenides* 295 (see ORESTEIA); Aristophanes, *Birds* 824; Euripides, *Heracles* 1192, *Ion* 988; Seneca, *Hercules Furens* 444, *Thyestes* 881]

PHOCIS   A region in north central Greece. The principal town of Phocis is DELPHI, and occasionally the dramatists use Phocis as a synonym for Delphi. Perhaps the most famous Phocians in drama are STROPHIUS and his son, PYLADES, with whom AGAMEMNON's son, ORESTES, lived for some time.

PHOEBE   See ARTEMIS.

PHOEBUS   See APOLLO.

PHOENICIAN WOMEN EURIPIDES (CA. 411–409 B.C.E.)

At 1,766 lines, this is the longest extant Euripidean play. The play's action takes place before the royal palace at THEBES. The general subject is the same as in AESCHYLUS' *SEVEN AGAINST THEBES*: the struggle between the sons of OEDIPUS, ETEOCLES and POLYNEICES, for the Theban kingdom. Unlike in Aeschylus' play, of which a substantial portion is occupied with describing the shields of the seven captains who march against Thebes, in EURIPIDES' more of the focus is on the family of Oedipus. In SOPHOCLES' *OEDIPUS TYRANNOS,* staged some two decades earlier than Euripides' play, JOCASTA commits suicide as Oedipus is discovering the truth about his identity. In Euripides' play, Jocasta is alive and frequently onstage during the first three-quarters of the drama, delivering the play's PROLOGUE, interacting with and mediating between Polyneices and Eteocles, and informing Antigone of the single combat between the brothers. Only the chorus have more lines than Jocasta in Euripides' play.

As the play begins, Jocasta tells of her family history: the horrific events that involved her, LAIUS, and Oedipus and the quarrel between her sons, Eteocles and Polyneices, that occurred after Oedipus had blinded himself. Jocasta informs the audience that she has persuaded her sons to agree to mediation before the battle. After Jocasta's monologue, she exits. Next, ANTIGONE and her TUTOR appear and gaze on Polyneices' advancing army. Over the next 70 lines, they comment on the captains of this force: Hippomedon, TYDEUS, PARTHENOPAEUS, Polyneices, ADRASTUS, AMPHIARAUS, and CAPANEUS. Antigone prays that ZEUS will destroy Capaneus, who Antigone suggests has boasted that he will enslave Theban women. At this, the tutor urges Antigone to go back indoors.

After Antigone and her tutor leave, the chorus, composed of war captives from a Phoenician island chosen to serve in APOLLO's temple at DELPHI, make their entry. These women were on their way to Delphi, but the outbreak of war apparently stopped their journey. After the chorus' entry, Polyneices approaches. He worries that the meeting with his brother is a trap. He questions the Phoenician women about who they are, and they ask him his name as well. When Polyneices tells them who he is, the women bow before him. The chorus then summon Jocasta from the palace. Jocasta embraces Polyneices, tells him of Oedipus, and asks about Polyneices' marriage to Adrastus' daughter, which Jocasta criticizes as marriage to a foreigner. Polyneices does not respond to this criticism and notes how much he has missed Thebes. Jocasta asks him about the life of an exile, and Polyneices explains the hardships of this life. He also tells Jocasta about his marriage to Adrastus' daughter and Adrastus' agreeing to help restore him to his native land.

At this point, Eteocles enters and urges that the discussion between him and Polyneices begin quickly, because he is busy with preparations for war. Jocasta urges Eteocles to relax and engage in face-to-face discussion with his brother. Polyneices speaks first and explains his side of the quarrel. He complains that Eteocles has not fulfilled the promise that he made—namely, to share the kingdom with him. Eteocles responds that his love of power compels him to hold on to the kingship and that it would be cowardly to hand it over because of the threat of war from Polyneices and his allies from ARGOS. Jocasta responds to Eteocles' remarks and tries to persuade him to give up his ambition for power. She also criticizes Polyneices for marching on his native land. She states that Polyneices' conquering Thebes will gain him no glory and that his defeat would make him unpopular should he return to Argos. Despite their mother's arguments, Eteocles and Polyneices refuse to compromise. At this point, the negotiation breaks down into name-calling by the two brothers, and the brothers threaten to kill one another in battle. After the departure of Eteocles and Polyneices, the Phoenician women sing an ode that recalls Cadmus' arrival in Greece and his founding of Thebes, the birthplace of Dionysus. They recall Cadmus' killing of ARES' serpent, his planting of the serpent's teeth, and his battle with the armed warriors who sprang up from the teeth. To protect and save Thebes, the women also call upon EPAPHUS, Zeus' son by their ancestor IO, PERSEPHONE, DEMETER, and GAIA.

After the choral ODE, Eteocles enters and summons his uncle, CREON, who informs him that Polyneices and his army are preparing an immediate attack on the city. The two men discuss possible strategies for attacking the enemy, who heavily outnumber the Thebans.

Because Creon has been told that the Argives plan to send each of their seven captains against one of Thebes' seven gates, Creon advises choosing seven men to lead the opposition against them. Before Eteocles leaves to see to these matters, he arranges for the marriage of Antigone and Creon's son HAEMON. Eteocles also notes that the prophet TIRESIAS should be consulted, and that Creon's son, MENOECEUS, should take Tiresias to the palace because he, Eteocles, and Tiresias do not get along. Eteocles also orders Creon not to allow Polyneices to be buried on Theban soil if he dies in battle and decrees death for anyone who tries to bury him. The departure of Eteocles and Creon is followed by another choral song, in which the Phoenician women sing of the intrusion of ARES, war, on the peaceful worship of divinities such as DIONYSUS and the Graces. The women lament the exposure of the infant Oedipus, the horrors of the SPHINX, and the new battle between brothers. They again recall the men who arose from the dragon's teeth, the gods attending the wedding of Cadmus and Harmonia, and the construction of the walls of Thebes through the power of AMPHION's music.

After the choral song, Creon's son, Menoeceus, and Tiresias, neither of whom appears in AESCHYLUS' *Seven against Thebes*, enter. Tiresias notes that he had warned Oedipus' sons not to be disrespectful to their father after the revelation of his crimes. Tiresias mentions the curse that Oedipus had placed on his sons and says that the brothers are destined to kill each other in battle. Tiresias also prophesies that Creon must sacrifice his son MENOECEUS to save Thebes. Because Menoeceus is descended from the men who arose from the serpent's teeth, Tiresias states, he must be sacrificed to appease Ares for the killing of his serpent. If Ares is appeased, he will help the Thebans. After Tiresias' departure, Creon says he himself will die to save the city and urges his son to go into exile. Initially Menoeceus agrees, but his agreement is meant to trick his father. Menoeceus, as do many other sacrificial victims in Euripides, states his intent to choose death and his country's salvation rather than his own safety. When Menoeceus leaves, the Phoenician women sing an ode that recalls the horrors of the Sphinx and Oedipus' ending the monster's reign of terror by solving his rid-

dle. They, praising Menoeceus for his valor, hope that they may have such noble sons.

The chorus' song is followed by the arrival of a MESSENGER, who summons Jocasta from the palace. The messenger states that Thebes remains safe and both her sons are alive, but that Creon's son is dead. The messenger goes on to describe the seven commanders who lead forces from Argos to Thebes (Parthenopaeus, Amphiaraus, Hippomedon, Tydeus, Polyneices, Capaneus, and Adrastus), the designs on their shields, and the various Theban gates against which they will make their assault. Next, the messenger describes the battle that takes place. First, Parthenopaeus is killed, then Capaneus, struck by a lightning bolt from Zeus. At this point, the messenger informs Jocasta that the Argive army has retreated and Eteocles and Polyneices have agreed to fight in single combat to decide the result of the war and determine who will become king. When Jocasta hears this, she summons Antigone from the palace and asks her to accompany her to the battlefield to try to persuade the brothers not to fight. After mother and daughter depart, the Phoenician women sing an ode of pity for a mother's misery. They wonder which of the brothers they will have to mourn and beg Fate for rescue from this vengeance.

After the choral ode, Creon enters, mentions that his son has died, and expresses the hope that his sister, Jocasta, will help prepare his corpse for burial. No sooner do the chorus tell Creon that Jocasta has gone to the battlefield than a messenger enters and announces that Eteocles and Polyneices have killed one another in battle and that Jocasta, who witnessed their deaths, committed suicide on the battlefield with a sword that she found near her sons' bodies. After the deaths of the brothers, the Theban army routes the Argives. After the messenger's speech, Antigone and some attendants enter, bearing the bodies of Eteocles, Polyneices, and Jocasta. Antigone laments over her mother and brothers, as well as the sufferings of her father. After Antigone's lament, Euripides has one final surprise for audience members who might have been familiar with Aeschylus' or SOPHOCLES' treatment of this myth: The blinded Oedipus emerges from the house. Once Antigone and Oedipus have mourned and Antigone tells him how Jocasta died, Creon enters;

announces that he is now king; informs Oedipus of the engagement of his son, Haemon, to Antigone; and banishes Oedipus from Thebes. Oedipus, recalling his horrific past, wonders who will accompany him into exile and tells Creon that his edict is like a death sentence. As in Sophocles' ANTIGONE, Creon decrees that Eteocles be given proper burial, but that Polyneices be thrown out beyond the city's boundaries and left unburied. Antigone declares her intent to bury Polyneices, but Creon meets this with threats of arrest and severe punishment. Antigone says she will refuse to marry Haemon, but Creon says he will make sure she does. Antigone then decides to accompany her father into exile. Before they depart, Oedipus notes the prophecy that he would die on Athenian soil at Colonus. Antigone also mentions that she will bury Polyneices secretly. As they exit, Oedipus urges Antigone to appeal to Dionysus for help, but Antigone suggests that that would be useless.

COMMENTARY

Phoenician Women has not received much attention from modern scholars, although the play appears to have been popular in antiquity. A few lines in the prologue and much of the last 180 lines of the play have often been thought to be written by someone other than Euripides. In general, scholars have criticized these lines either for not being Euripidean in style and METER or for having content that does not bear the mark of the skilled and veteran dramatist that Euripides was.

Modern readers of the play should note that ATHENS was still involved in the PELOPONNESIAN WAR when *Phoenician Women* was produced. Furthermore, Euripides produced this play when Athens either was in the midst of or had just emerged from an internal revolution that had witnessed both the overthrow and the restoration of its democracy within the space of a year (411). Thus, the concern in *Phoenician Women* with war and strife between brothers is not surprising given the period in which the play was produced.

The futility of war and war's impact on the entire family appear to be the play's focus. The curse of a father has put his two sons into a conflict that will ultimately result in the death of both. A sister watches as the army of one brother advances against that of the

other. A mother tries to reconcile the two brothers, but finds them both unbending in their desire for power. Eventually, the mother will add to her own the pleas of her daughter to stop the brothers from facing each other in combat. The effort of mother and daughter will fail, however. The mother will see her sons kill each other and the sister will see her brothers kill each other. Furthermore, the daughter will then see her mother kill herself in her grief about the sons' deaths.

In addition to the three corpses of Oedipus' immediate family, the conflict between the brothers spills over into the family of his former brother-in-law. As in other classical dramas (e.g., Aeschylus' *Agamemnon* or Euripides' fragmentary *Erechtheus*), in *Phoenician Women* the father, Creon, must choose between saving his country or city and sacrificing his child. Unlike in these other plays, in *Phoenician Women* the sacrificial virgin is a male rather than a female. From the Greek standpoint, the sacrifice of a male would have been more horrific than that of a female because, as another Euripidean sacrificial victim (IPHIGENIA) expresses it, "It is better that one man see the light than ten thousand women" (*Iphigenia at Aulis* 1394). As do his female sacrificial counterparts, the son, rejecting his father's suggestion that he flee the country, kills himself.

With four lives lost, a new king appears and begins wielding his power in a most unpleasant way. Oedipus' former brother-in-law declares that the old blind man must go into exile. He threatens death to his future daughter-in-law if she should try to bury her brother. In turn, the daughter-in-law threatens to kill her new husband, thus leading the new king to allow her to go into exile with her blind father/brother.

Theban kings and princes had come and gone, but the city of Thebes remained intact. Another approach to this play might be entitled "Salvation and the City." In the course of *Phoenician Women*, we hear of their efforts to avoid killing one another or being killed by one another, and the members of Oedipus' family have fled the city, only to return to the city and destroy one another. While the members of the family have died, the city has managed to ride out the cycle of death and violence. When the son, Oedipus, killed the father/king, LAIUS, the Sphinx threatened the city (46). Oedipus entered and saved the city by his wits.

After the father/king Oedipus was removed from the throne and badly treated by his sons, he cursed his sons. To avoid their father's curse, the sons decided to share the kingship. One son remained in the city; one son left the city. When Polyneices returned, he found himself barred from it and thus decided to try to force his way back into the city. Whereas the unwitting exile Oedipus became king of Thebes through his wits, the unwilling exile Polyneices will try to become king by force (629–30). His brother, Eteocles, will try to retain control of the city by meeting his brother with force. Their mother tries to persuade them to listen to reason. Unlike their father, who saved the city and then ruled it, the brothers will achieve their own destruction through their desire to rule. Polyneices, who leaves his city with the expectation of kingship and the goal of self-preservation, will lose the kingship and his life. Eteocles, who hopes to preserve his kingship and save the city (783) by force, will also lose the kingship and his life.

In addition to trying to save the city by military force, Eteocles turns to the interpreter of the gods' will, Tiresias, to save the city (864). Tiresias declares that the city will be destroyed (884) and Oedipus' sons will destroy it (888). When Creon asks what means of salvation (898) is available to the city and its citizens, he learns that to save the city (912) he must sacrifice his son. Creon, of course, does not want to do this, but Tiresias repeats his advice: "Either save your son or the city" (952). Creon urges that his son go into exile, but unlike Polyneices, Menoeceus has no expectation of kingship and refuses to go into exile just to save his life. He declares that he will save the city (997). After Menoeceus departs to sacrifice himself for the city, we hear of the onslaught of Polyneices' army, which has arrived to destroy the city. All these efforts fail and Thebes stands strong. While the seven towers of Thebes remain intact thanks to the sacrifice of Creon's son, the two sons of Oedipus destroy one another.

Although the city has been saved from Oedipus' sons, the new king, Creon, has been informed of an additional threat to the city if Oedipus remains in the city. Thus, to save the city from further trauma (1591), Creon orders Oedipus to go into exile. Although Polyneices is dead, even in this state he will pose a threat to the city's order. Before Polyneices dies, he begs Jocasta and Antigone to bury him in his fatherland and intercede on his behalf if the city is angry with him (1448). Creon, however, declares that Polyneices must not be buried and his corpse will experience a sort of second exile, for it will be cast beyond the borders of the land (1630). A defiant Antigone insists that she will bury his body, even if the city opposes the burial (1657). She begs Creon to allow her at least to bathe his body, but he declares that this would be forbidden by the city (1668).

An outraged Antigone, who is engaged to Creon's son, Haemon, declares that their marriage night will make her one of the DANAIDS, thus indicating that she intends to murder Creon's son. Interestingly, the Danaids lived in Argos when their infamous murders took place. So, just as Polyneices allied himself through marriage with the Argive king, Adrastus, and took a destructive Argive force to Thebes, Antigone threatens to become like the occupants of that city (Argos) and cause the destruction of a prince of her native city (Thebes). Upon hearing Antigone's threats, Creon declares that she must go into exile. As the play ends, Antigone and Oedipus go into exile. As must the exiled Polyneices, Oedipus will have to rely on another city to grant him shelter—Euripides' own Athens.

As had the mythical Thebes of Euripides' play, which had suffered through scandal, internal strife among its leading citizens, and war, Euripides' Athens experienced similar hardships around the time *Phoenician Women* was produced. While the major political players come and go, the city will survive. At the end of the play, the seven towers of Thebes remain intact, just as the city of Athens, behind its massive fortification walls, continues to press onward.

BIBLIOGRAPHY

Craik, E. *Euripides: Phoenician Women.* Warminster, U.K.: Aris & Phillips, 1988.

Luschnig, C. A. E. *The Gorgon's Severed Head: Studies of Alcestis, Electra, and Phoenissae.* Leiden: Brill, 1995.

Mastronarde, D. J. *Euripides: Phoenissae.* Cambridge: Cambridge University Press, 1994.

Saïd, S. "Tragedy and Politics." In *Democracy, Empire, and the Arts in Fifth-Century Athens.* Edited by D. Boedeker and K. A. Raaflaub. Cambridge, Mass.: Harvard University Press, 1998.

Scharffenberger, E. W. "A Tragic Lysistrata? Jocasta in the 'Reconciliation Scene' of the *Phoenician Women*," *Rheinisches Museum* 138, no. 3/4 (1995): 312–36.

PHOENICIAN WOMEN SENECA (WRITTEN BETWEEN 49 AND 65 C.E.?)

Only 664 lines survive from this play. The play's action takes place three years after OEDIPUS blinded himself. What remains of the play opens with the appearance of the blind Oedipus, now wandering in exile in the wilds outside THEBES and being guided by his daughter, ANTIGONE. Oedipus laments his fortune; imagines that he sees his dead father, LAIUS; and wonders why he continues to live. Antigone responds by declaring that she will not abandon him and encourages him to overcome his sorrow. Oedipus praises his daughter but begs her to help him die. Antigone, however, refuses and continues to urge him to calm himself and face adversity with courage. Oedipus will not take her advice, however, and continues to dwell on the horrific acts of his past. After he speaks of the war for the Theban throne that will take place between his sons, Antigone urges him to try to prevent the conflict. Oedipus argues that his sons have no care for him or Thebes and that they are both mad with a lust for power.

At this point, a gap in which a choral ODE would have taken place occurs. The play resumes with an announcement to Oedipus that the army of Oedipus' son POLYNEICES and his allies surround Thebes. Oedipus is called upon to help prevent the war, but he refuses. After this, another gap occurs and the next speech that appears may be from a different play. In this speech, JOCASTA laments the strife between her sons and gives some of the background to Polyneices' exile and his march on Thebes. Next, a MESSENGER enters, announcing that the battle between the Thebans and Polyneices' forces is about to take place. The messenger urges Jocasta to resolve the quarrel between her sons. Antigone, who, although she earlier said she would not leave Oedipus, now appears with her mother and echoes the messenger's words. As in EURIPIDES' play, Jocasta agrees to try to persuade the brothers to make peace. After Jocasta departs, the messenger relates that Jocasta has approached the brothers and that they have, for the moment, lowered their weapons.

At this point, a change of scene takes place and Jocasta, now on the battlefield between her sons, begs them to end their quarrel. The brothers are reluctant, but she does prevail upon ETEOCLES to put down his weapons. Jocasta then gives a lengthy speech in which she urges Polyneices not to wage war against his native land. Polyneices, however, thinks that if he gives in he will have to remain in exile or live in Thebes as if he is a servant to his brother. Jocasta argues that if he wants to be a king he can conquer a foreign land, and that he should not acquire a kingdom through civil war. When Polyneices complains that Eteocles receives no punishment for driving him from the kingdom, Jocasta argues that the burden of kingship is his penalty. Eteocles also breaks in and declares that Polyneices must continue his exile. Jocasta declares that exiling Polyneices will make Eteocles hated by the people. Jocasta and Eteocles continue to argue, but the text of the play ends at this point.

PHOENIX

The son of Amyntor, Phoenix was born at the foot of Mount PELION. When Phoenix's father took a concubine, Phoenix's mother became jealous and persuaded Phoenix to seduce the concubine. Phoenix did so, his father learned of it, and he cursed his son so that would have no children. Phoenix considered killing Amyntor but left home, escaping from his relatives, who had surrounded the house. Some sources say that Amyntor blinded Phoenix, and when Phoenix went into exile, PELEUS, granting him shelter, took him to the centaur CHIRON to heal him. Afterward, Peleus made Phoenix king of the DOLOPIANS. Phoenix also served as the tutor of Peleus' son, ACHILLES, and accompanied Achilles to TROY. Phoenix outlived his pupil but died on the voyage back from Troy.

Although Phoenix does not appear as a character in any surviving plays, he appeared in several ancient dramas. EURIPIDES wrote a *Phoenix* (fragments 804–18 Nauck), which was staged before ARISTOPHANES' *ACHARNIANS* (425 B.C.E.). The fragments indicate that Euripides' play dealt with Phoenix's seduction of Amyntor's concubine and the blinding of Phoenix. Aristophanes indicates that Phoenix appeared dressed in rags in Euripides' play, and this would have been his condition when he arrived at the house of Peleus. To SOPHOCLES is attributed a *Phoenix* (718–20 Radt), although Lloyd-Jones thinks this may be the same play as *Dolopians*. Phoenix also appeared as a character in Sophocles' SATYR PLAY *The Lovers of Achilles* (fragment 53 Radt). Two other Greek tragedians, Astydamas (fragment 5d Snell) and Athenodorus (fragment 1 Snell), wrote plays entitled *Phoenix,* of which only the titles survive. We also know that Phoenix appeared as a character in Chaeremon's *Achilles Thersitoktonos* (Achilles, the killer of Thersites) (see fragments 1c–3 Snell). The Greek comic poet Eubulus also wrote a *Phoenix* (fragment 114), whose single extant line (about the importation of peacocks) tells us nothing about the play's plot. Among Roman authors, ENNIUS wrote a *Phoenix,* whose fragments (306–18 Warmington) indicate that it was about the strife between Phoenix and Amyntor. [ANCIENT SOURCES: Apollodorus, *Library* 3.13.8, *Epitome* 4.3, 5.11; Aristophanes, *Acharnians* 421–22; Homer, *Iliad* 9.437–84]

BIBLIOGRAPHY

Kock, T. *Comicorum Atticorum Fragmenta.* Vol. 2. Leipzig: Teubner, 1884.

Lloyd-Jones, H. *Sophocles: Fragments.* Cambridge, Mass.: Harvard University Press, 1996, 336.

Nauck, A. *Tragicorum Graecorum Fragmenta.* 1889. Reprint, Hildesheim, Ger.: Olms, 1964.

Radt, S. *Tragicorum Graecorum Fragmenta.* Vol. 4. Göttingen, Ger.: Vandenhoeck & Ruprecht, 1977.

Snell, B. *Tragicorum Graecorum Fragmenta.* Vol. 1. Göttingen, Ger.: Vandenhoeck & Ruprecht, 1971.

Warmington, E. H. *Remains of Old Latin: Ennius and Caecilius.* Vol. 1. Cambridge, Mass.: Harvard University Press, 1935.

Webster, T. B. L. *The Tragedies of Euripides.* London: Methuen, 1967, 84–85.

PHORCIDES   The daughters of Phorcys and Ceto, the Phorcides, whose names were Dino, Enyo, and Pephredo, were the sisters of the GORGONS. The Phorcides are sometimes called the Gray Ones because they were already old when they were born. Among the three of them, the Phorcides had only one eye and one tooth, which they had to pass back and forth when they wanted to see or eat. PERSEUS, on a mission to acquire the Gorgon MEDUSA's head, went to the lair of the Phorcides and took the sisters' eye and tooth. Perseus gave the eye and tooth back to them only after they had given him directions to some NYMPHS who possessed some equipment that he would need to deal with Medusa. AESCHYLUS wrote a *Phorcides,* which seems to have dealt with Perseus' encounter with them. The Greek tragedian Timocles wrote a SATYR PLAY that dealt with the Phorcides, of which only the title survives. [ANCIENT SOURCES: Aeschylus, *Prometheus Bound* 794; Apollodorus, *Library* 1.2.6, 2.4.2; Hesiod, *Theogony* 270; Hyginus, *Fables* proem 9]

BIBLIOGRAPHY

Radt, S. *Tragicorum Graecorum Fragmenta.* Vol. 3. Göttingen, Ger.: Vandenhoeck & Ruprecht, 1985.

Snell, B. *Tragicorum Graecorum Fragmenta.* Vol. 1. Göttingen, Ger.: Vandenhoeck & Ruprecht, 1971.

PHORMIO (1)   (D. CA. 429/428 B.C.E.)   The son of Asopius, Phormio was an Athenian who had several successes as a naval commander in the first few years of the PELOPONNESIAN WAR. Phormio appeared as a character in *Taxiarch,* by ARISTOPHANES' contemporary, EUPOLIS (fragments 1–12 Meineke). In this play, Phormio "tried to teach the unwarlike and effeminate Dionysus how to be a soldier and perhaps also how to row" (Sommerstein). [ANCIENT SOURCES: Aristophanes, *Knights* 562, *Lysistrata* 804, *Peace* 348; Thucydides, 2.83–92, 3.7.1]

BIBLIOGRAPHY

Meineke, A. *Fragmenta Comicorum Graecorum.* Vol. 2.1. 1839. Reprint, Berlin: De Gruyter, 1970.

Sommerstein, A. H. *The Comedies of Aristophanes.* Vol. 2, *Knights.* Warminster, U.K.: Aris & Phillips, 1981, 174–75.

Wilson, A. M. "A Eupolidean Precedent for the Rowing Scene in Aristophanes' *Frogs,*" *Classical Quarterly* 24 (1974): 250–52.

PHORMIO (2)   The fictional title character of TERENCE's *PHORMIO.* See *PHORMIO.*

PHORMIO TERENCE (161 B.C.E.)   Performed at the ROMAN GAMES, this play is set in ATHENS, and the action occurs before three houses: those of Demipho (an elderly Athenian), Chremes (Demipho's brother), and the PIMP Dorio. In the prologue, TERENCE defends himself against the attacks of the veteran playwright Luscius Lanuvius. Terence also announces that he has adapted his play from a play entitled *The Claimant* (Greek: *Epidikazomenos*) by Apollodorus of Carystus, the same author who provided a model for Terence's Mother-in-Law.

In the opening act, Davus enters and gives Geta, a slave of Demipho ("people's voice"), money that he owes him. He suspects Geta needs the money to buy a present for his master's son, who has recently married. After Davus gives him the money, Geta informs Davus that when Demipho and his brother, Chremes, were out of the country, Geta was supposed to watch over their sons. Unfortunately, Chremes' son, Phaedria, fell in love with a music girl (Pamphila), whom the pimp Dorio owned, but Phaedria did not have enough money to purchase her. One day, Phaedria saw another young woman (Phanium, who is actually Chremes' daughter) crying over the death of her mother. When Phaedria told Demipho's son, Antipho ("opposing voice"), they went to see the woman. As soon as Antipho saw her, he fell in love and approached her guardian, an old woman named Sophrona, about her. Sophrona rejected Antipho, who then turned to help from the PARASITE, Phormio. Phormio devised a scheme (based on a law that required orphaned young women to marry a relative) that allowed Antipho to marry Phanium.

In the next scene, Antipho and Phaedria discuss Antipho's situation, as he is worried what will happen when his father finds out that he has married without his permission. Phaedria, however, says Antipho should be happy; he has the woman he loves, whereas the pimp is keeping Phaedria away from the MUSIC GIRL, Phanium. The two young men are interrupted by the arrival of Geta, who informs them that Antipho's father, Demipho, has returned from abroad. Upon hearing this, a terrified Antipho runs away. As Phaedria and Geta wonder what they will do next, Demipho enters. Phaedria and Geta eavesdrop as Demipho angrily discusses the rumor he has heard of Antipho's marriage. Soon, Phaedria and Geta approach Demipho and try to defend themselves and Antipho against the old man's wrath. Demipho, however, is determined to put a stop to the marriage and demands to be taken to Phormio's house. He also sends off Phaedria to find

Antipho. Phaedria promises to do so but instead sneaks into the pimp Dorio's house, where his own love, Pamphila, is. Demipho says he will pay respect to his household gods and then go to the FORUM to consult some friends about the current situation.

Next, Geta informs Phormio of Antipho's departure and Demipho's anger. Phormio declares he will rectify the situation by diverting Demipho's wrath onto himself. Soon, Demipho, accompanied by three advisers (Cratinus, Crito, and Hegio), returns from the forum. Phormio, knowing that Demipho can hear him, questions Geta about Demipho's denial that Phanium is related to him and that he knows Phanium's father (Stilpo, an alias for Chremes). Phormio also accuses Demipho of being greedy and of not acting as a gentleman would. Eventually, Demipho interrupts, denies knowing Stilpo (who is actually his brother, Chremes), and demands to know how he, Demipho, is related to Phanium. Phormio has no answer for this but challenges Demipho to take up the matter in court. Demipho tries to pay off Phormio to secure a divorce, but Phormio refuses Demipho's money. Ultimately, Demipho threatens to throw Phanium out of his house unless Phormio will take her. Phormio, in turn, threatens to sue Demipho if he uses force against a freeborn woman. After Phormio exits, Demipho sends Geta to find Antipho. Demipho then consults his advisers, but their opinions are divided about whether Demipho's case will stand up in court. Demipho then decides to wait for his brother, Chremes, and goes to the harbor to try to find out when he will return from abroad.

In the third act, Antipho, repenting of having run away from his responsibilities, returns. Geta informs him of the situation and tells him that Demipho has decided to follow Chremes' advice in the matter. Next, Phaedria enters from Dorio's house. Geta and Antipho listen as Phaedria begs the pimp, who has sold Pamphila to a soldier, to wait three days before completing the sale. Because the soldier is supposed to deliver the money the following day, Dorio says that if Phaedria can raise the money sooner, he can have Pamphila. Antipho and Geta sympathize with Phaedria and agree to help him find the money to buy Pamphila. Geta is appointed to devise a scheme to trick Demipho out of the money. After Geta and Phaedria send Antipho into his house to look after his wife, Phanium, Geta and Phaedria exit toward Phormio's house.

The fourth act opens with the arrival of Demipho and his brother, Chremes, from the harbor. Chremes had been on the island of LEMNOS to take back his daughter (a child by a woman other than his wife), but when he arrived on Lemnos, Chremes learned that she had already returned to Athens. Chremes worries that his wife will find out about this daughter, Phanium, and that he will have to leave home if she does. As the two brothers discuss these matters, Geta, who has returned from Phormio's, enters and informs the audience that he and Phormio have created a scheme to get the money from Demipho. When Geta sees Chremes, he announces that he will try to trick him if the plot against Demipho does not succeed. Soon, Antipho, looking for Geta, emerges but steps back unseen when he catches sight of his father and Chremes. As Antipho eavesdrops, Geta approaches Demipho and Chremes and, to trick the old men out of some money, tells them that he has encountered Phormio. Geta claims he has persuaded Phormio to accept a cash settlement to drop his lawsuit and accept a dowry to marry Antipho's wife. Although Antipho is furious that Geta has agreed to pay Phormio a substantial sum of money, Chremes decides that he will help Antipho raise the money. After Chremes and Demipho exit into Chremes' house, Antipho emerges from his hiding place and demands to know what Geta has done. Geta tells him that he has tricked the old men out of their money. When Antipho objects that Phormio will have to marry Phanium if he accepts the dowry, Geta tells him that Phormio will not actually marry Phanium, but that the preparations for the wedding will give Phaedria's friends time to deliver the money they promised. Using this money, Phormio will pay back the money Phaedria owes. In the act's final scene, Demipho and Chremes emerge from Chremes' house. Demipho, who carries a bag of money, tells Geta to take him to Phormio's house. Chremes instructs Demipho to see his wife after he finishes with Phormio so that they can explain that Phormio will marry Antipho's wife.

In the final act, Sophrona, agitated and looking for Chremes, emerges from Demipho's house. Sophrona, seeing Chremes, addresses him as Stilpo. Chremes tells her never to call him by that name again, because he used it long ago to prevent his wife from finding out the truth about his affair. Sophrona informs Chremes that his daughter's mother is dead and that his daughter, Phanium, is married to Antipho. When Chremes hears this, he thinks that Antipho has two wives. Sophrona, however, informs him that Phanium and the woman supposed to be Antipho's relative are the same person. Chremes is delighted to learn that his daughter is married to Antipho but does not want anyone to find out that Phanium is his daughter. After Sophrona and Chremes exit, Demipho and Geta enter. Demipho complains about the money that they have paid Phormio. As Demipho departs, he tells Geta to go to Demipho's house and advise them that Chremes' wife should talk with Phanium. After Demipho exits into Chremes' house, Geta informs the audience that Phormio has dropped his lawsuit and that they have found money for Phaedria to buy Pamphila.

In the next scene, Demipho and Chremes' wife, Nausistrata, emerge from Chremes' house. Nausistrata agrees to talk with Phanium about going with Phormio. As they set out, they see Chremes, who is leaving Demipho's house. Chremes takes Demipho aside and tells him that Phanium is a relative of theirs and that she should not be handed over to Phormio. At this point, Nausistrata is dismissed from the previous errand and reenters Chremes' house. After she leaves, Chremes takes Demipho into Demipho's house to inform him that Phanium is his daughter. After the brothers exit, Antipho enters and expresses his pleasure that Phaedria will have Pamphila. Next, Phormio enters and informs the audience that he has paid off the pimp and arranged for Phaedria to have Pamphila. Phormio tells Antipho that Phaedria is going to Phormio's house to do some drinking and asks Antipho to make an excuse to Chremes for him.

At this point, an excited Geta arrives from Demipho's house. He informs Antipho that he has learned that Chremes has been revealed as Phanium's father and that both Chremes and Demipho have agreed that Antipho can marry Phanium. After Geta takes a delighted Antipho into Demipho's house, Phormio announces that he now has the chance to trick Chremes and Demipho out of the money and give it to Phaedria. Next, Chremes and Demipho enter and announce their intention to get their money back from Phormio, who tells Demipho that he is ready to receive Phanium as his bride. Demipho and Chremes make various excuses why they do not want to give Phanium to him. Phormio says he will agree not to marry Phanium, but that he will keep the dowry because he had to break off an engagement with another woman to marry Phanium.

When Chremes and Demipho threaten to take Phormio to court, Phormio threatens to reveal Chremes' relationship with the woman on Lemnos. Upon hearing this, Chremes quickly agrees to let Phormio keep the money. Furthermore, Demipho suggests that Chremes tell his wife about the affair before she finds out from others. Phormio, hearing this, recognizes that his case will be weakened if Nausistrata knows the truth. Accordingly, Phormio declares that he will undermine any attempts to smooth matters over with Nausistrata. Hearing this, Chremes is furious, and he and his brother try to haul Phormio off to court. When Phormio cries out for Nausistrata, Chremes' wife responds, and she soon hears from Phormio about Chremes' secret love affair and daughter. Nausistrata is furious, but Demipho tries to calm her temper by explaining that Chremes was drunk at the time, that they only had sexual relations once, and that now the woman is deceased. As Nausistrata seems on the verge of forgiving Chremes, Phormio breaks in and reveals that their son, Phaedria, has purchased a prostitute. Chremes is enraged, but Nausistrata says he will not be able to chastise him because he himself has had two wives. Nausistrata then declares that Phaedria will be allowed to have his mistress, but that whether she forgives Chremes will be Phaedria's decision. Nausistrata also expresses her appreciation to Phormio and at his suggestion invites him to dinner. The play ends with Phormio's arranging to have Phaedria summoned to the house to act as arbiter between Chremes and Nausistrata.

COMMENTARY

Phormio is usually considered one of Terence's better plays, and Duckworth says that from a structural perspective it is "perhaps the best of Roman comedies." Harsh noted the play's influence on modern drama and pointed out that Terence's play influenced Molière's *Les Fourberies de Scapin* (Scapin's cheating) of 1671. Duckworth categorized *Phormio* as a play of "Mistaken Identity and Deception" (compare PLAUTUS' CAPTIVES, CARTHAGINIAN, CURCULIO, and EPIDICUS; Terence's ANDRIA, SELF-TORMENTOR, and EUNUCH). Konstan read the play as dealing with the tension between passion and the social code, as the lovesick sons have little concern for the social conventions that their fathers feel should separate them from their desired women. As shown by Frangoulidis' article, *Phormio* can be read by viewing Phormio as a playwright who is attempting to produce a play within Terence's play. Phormio's audience become the two fathers and Phormio himself, the slaves, and to a lesser extent the young men serve as the actors. For example, when Antipho wonders how Phaedria will be able to spend time with his beloved, Phormio speaks in theatrical terms as he informs him that Phaedria "is going to play your role" (*partis tuas acturus est,* 835) and run away from his father.

As commonly occurs in Terence's plays (except MOTHER-IN-LAW), *Phormio* has a double plot with the two love affairs of the two young men providing the two strands, although Chremes' love affair may be considered to provide a third plot line. The play's most unique feature is the title character. As does Plautus' *Curculio,* Terence's *Phormio* takes its name from a parasite. Although Phormio is twice called a parasite (27, 122), he is unlike any other parasite in Roman COMEDY, and Duckworth calls him "one of the cleverest scoundrels in ancient comedy." Usually, parasites in Roman comedy are interested only in the source of their next meal and food and drink dominate their conversation, but Phormio makes little mention of food (although by play's end he does receive a dinner invitation). Geta speaks with seriousness of his bravery (324–25), a trait seldom exhibited by parasites. Thus, with respect to the character Phormio modern translators usually prefer to translate *parasitus* as "adventurer." More appropriate is Konstan's description of Phormio as "a fixer, who bends the rules and softens the lines that define the social structure" (129). When Geta worries that Phormio's bravery will land him in jail, Phormio expresses a lack of concern and asks Geta

(327–28), "How many men do you think I've beaten to the point of death, foreigners and citizens?" (Barsby translation). One wonders how seriously to take this statement, but it makes Phormio seem more than an "adventurer."

In addition to the character of Phormio, this play is noteworthy for its frequent references to anxiety and fear, which help link the play's dual plots and affect its major characters. Davus' lack of awareness of the fear and danger that he and Geta face motivates Geta to reveal the crisis involving their respective households. Geta later reveals that Antipho is prevented from marrying his beloved because he is afraid of his father (118). Geta even warns Antipho that his apprehension threatens to expose the affair to his father (205). Note also that apprehension prevents Antipho from delivering a speech that was already prepared (284, 294). Not only does Antipho fear his father, but he also fears his uncle when he learns that his father will follow the advice of the uncle (482). Ironically, when the fearful Antipho listens to Geta's worries (555) about how he will help Phaedria, Antipho tells Geta not to be afraid (556) and says that the two young men will support him. After Geta collects his wits, he sends off Antipho to calm the fears of his beloved (564). Ultimately, Phormio will find the money for the woman and Phaedria's anxiety will be relieved (823).

As Antipho fears his father will find out about the woman, the father, Chremes, fears his wife will find out about his extramarital affair (743). After Phormio alleviates the anxiety of Phaedria, he turns to relieving Antipho's fears. To accomplish this, Phormio intensifies the anxiety of Chremes. Once Phormio learns of Chremes' affair, he threatens to reveal his knowledge to Chremes' wife. When Phormio, threatened by Chremes and Demipho, summons Chremes' wife from the house, Chremes' fear is mentioned four times in two lines (998–99). Once Chremes' secret is revealed, Antipho can be relieved of his fear. Even the young man's mother declares that he cannot be faulted for having one mistress when his father has two wives.

BIBLIOGRAPHY
Arnott, W. G. "Phormio Parasitus: A Study in Dramatic Methods of Characterization," Greece & Rome 17 (1970): 32–57.

Barsby, J. Terence. Vol. 2. Cambridge, Mass.: Harvard University Press, 2001, 49.
Duckworth, G. The Nature of Roman Comedy. Princeton, N.J.: Princeton University Press, 1952, 156–60.
Frangoulidis, S. A. "The Parasite as Poet-Playwright and the Slave as Parasite in Terence's Phormio," Bollettino di Studi Latini 25, no. 2 (1995): 397–425.
Harsh, P. W. A Handbook of Classical Drama. Stanford, Calif.: Stanford University Press, 1944, 389–92.
Konstan, D. "Phormio: Citizen Disorder." In Roman Comedy. Ithaca, N.Y.: Cornell University Press, 1983, 115–29.
Martin, R. H. Phormio: Terence. London: Methuen, 1959.

PHORMISIUS   A person mocked by the comic poet Plato for taking bribes from the Persians and by ARISTOPHANES for being a disciple of EURIPIDES and perhaps having a face resembling the female genitalia. If this Phormisius is the same person mentioned in a speech from Lysias, then he would have introduced a resolution (around 403 B.C.E.) that allowed Athenians exiled by the Thirty Tyrants to return but would grant citizenship only to those had land. [ANCIENT SOURCES: Aristophanes, Ecclesiazusae 97, Frogs 965; Plato Comicus, fragment 119.1 Kock; Lysias, 34]

BIBLIOGRAPHY
Dover, Kenneth. Aristophanes: Frogs. Oxford: Clarendon Press, 1993, 313.
Kock, T. Comicorum Atticorum Fragmenta. Vol. 1. Leipzig: Teubner, 1880.

PHRATRY   The phratry (brotherhood) was a religious association in which "in theory all male members were descended from a common male ancestor" (Parke). In Athens, under the constitution of SOLON, the original four tribes were each divided into three phratries, thus making 12 phratries. The members of a phratry were called fraters.

BIBLIOGRAPHY
Parke, H. W. Festivals of the Athenians. Ithaca, N.Y.: Cornell University Press, 1977, 89.

PHRIXUS   The son of ATHAMAS and Nephele, Phrixus was a noble young man who became the victim of his stepmother, INO's, plot against him—a plot that eventually led to his almost being sacrificed by his father, Athamas. At the last second, however, Phrixus' mother, Nephele, sent a ram with golden fleece to rescue him. Phrixus flew away to safety in the land of Colchis, where he sacrificed the ram; gave the fleece to the local king, Aeetes; and took up residence. Phrixus married Aeetes' daughter, Chalciope, and had several children by her: Argus, Cytisorus, Melas, and Phrontis.

Both SOPHOCLES (fragments 721–23a Radt) and EURIPIDES (fragments 819–38 Nauck) wrote plays entitled *Phrixus*. Regarding Sophocles' *Phrixus,* Lloyd-Jones thinks it may have been identical to one of Sophocles' two plays about ATHAMAS. The few brief fragments that survive of Sophocles' *Phrixus* give us little indication of the play's content. As for Euripides, he is known to have produced a *Phrixus* on two occasions. Webster thinks that *Phrixus A* dealt with the title character's experiences in Colchis, and *Phrixus B* treated Ino's plot against Phrixus and the young man's rescue by the ram. [ANCIENT SOURCES: Apollodorus, *Library* 1.9.1; Hyginus, *Fables* 3; Plautus, *Bacchides* 242; Seneca, *Agamemnon* 565, *Hercules Oetaeus* 776, *Medea* 471, *Trojan Women* 1034]

BIBLIOGRAPHY
Kiso, A. *The Lost Sophocles.* New York: Vantage Press, 1984.
Lloyd-Jones, H. *Sophocles: Fragments.* Cambridge, Mass.: Harvard University Press, 1996, 338–39.
Nauck, A. *Tragicorum Graecorum Fragmenta.* 1889. Reprint, Hildesheim, Ger.: Olms, 1964.
Radt, S. *Tragicorum Graecorum Fragmenta.* Vol. 4. Göttingen, Ger.: Vandenhoeck & Ruprecht, 1977.
Sutton, D. F. *The Lost Sophocles.* Lanham, Md.: University Press of America, 1984.
Webster, T. B. L. *The Tragedies of Euripides.* London: Methuen, 1967, 131–36.

PHRYGIANS

The Phrygians lived in what is today western Turkey. In classical drama, Phrygian is often synonymous with Trojan. One Greek stereotype of the Phrygians was that Phrygian men were not very masculine. This is evident from ZEUS' abduction of GANYMEDE and the effeminate Phrygian slave who delivers the messenger speech in EURIPIDES' ORESTES. SOPHOCLES wrote a *Phrygians,* from which a few fragments survive. Lloyd-Jones (339) suggests that this play may have been identical to Sophocles' *Priam.*

BIBLIOGRAPHY
Kiso, A. *The Lost Sophocles.* New York: Vantage Press, 1984.
Lloyd-Jones, H. *Sophocles: Fragments.* Cambridge, Mass.: Harvard University Press, 1996.
Radt, S. *Tragicorum Graecorum Fragmenta.* Vol. 4. Göttingen, Ger.: Vandenhoeck & Ruprecht, 1977.
Sutton, D. F. *The Lost Sophocles.* Lanham, Md.: University Press of America, 1984.

PHRYNICHUS (1)

The son of Polyphrasmon, Phrynichus was a Greek tragedian whose first victory in competition occurred in 510 B.C.E.; his last victory probably occurred around 476, the year in which the famous statesman THEMISTOCLES served as his CHOREGUS. Only about two dozen short fragments exist and the titles of nine plays (see Snell). Phrynichus' *Phoenician Women* was thought to be a model for AESCHYLUS' PERSIANS. Phrynichus' *Alcestis* may have influenced EURIPIDES' play of the same name. Phrynichus' historical drama *Destruction of Miletus* was said to have caused the Athenian audience such grief that Phrynichus was fined. In ARISTOPHANES' day, the plays of Phrynichus were considered old-fashioned and therefore were favored by the older generations. Aristophanes described Phrynichus' passages of lyric poetry as being like honey, and his dance steps were supposed to be quite varied and innovative in their day. [ANCIENT SOURCES: Aristophanes, *Birds* 748–51, *Frogs* 910, *Thesmophoriazusae* 164, *Wasps* 220, 269, 1490, 1523–24; Plutarch, *Themistocles* 5.5]

BIBLIOGRAPHY
MacDowell, D. M. *Aristophanes: Wasps.* Oxford: Clarendon Press, 1971, 160–61.
Snell, B. *Tragicorum Graecorum Fragmenta.* Vol. 1. Göttingen, Ger.: Vandenhoeck & Ruprecht, 1971.

PHRYNICHUS (2)

The son of Eunomides, Phrynichus was a Greek comic poet and a rival of ARISTOPHANES'. Phrynichus' first play appeared in 429 B.C.E., and he gained his first victory in competition in that year or the next. His last known production date is 405. In that year, Phrynichus' *Muses* finished second to Aristophanes' *Frogs.* Some 90 short fragments and 10 titles survive from Phrynichus' works. [ANCIENT SOURCES: Aristophanes, *Clouds* 556; *Inscriptiones Graecae* ii^2 2325.124]

BIBLIOGRAPHY

Kock, T. *Comicorum Atticorum Fragmenta.* Vol. 1. Leipzig: Teubner, 1880.

Sommerstein, A. H. *The Comedies of Aristophanes.* Vol. 3, *Clouds.* Warminster, U.K.: Aris & Phillips, 1982, 190.

PHRYNICHUS (3)   An Athenian statesman from the deme of Deiradiotae, Phrynichus, son of Stratonides, was a major player in the oligarchic overthrow of that city's democracy in 411 B.C.E. He was murdered in the same year and his bones were removed from Athenian territory. Phrynichus' murder appears to have led to the fall of the so-called Four Hundred oligarchs. [ANCIENT SOURCES: Aristophanes, *Frogs* 689; Lycurgus, *Against Leocrates* 112–14; Lysias, 13.70–72; Thucydides, 8.68.3, 8.92.2]

BIBLIOGRAPHY

Dover, Kenneth. *Aristophanes: Frogs.* Oxford: Clarendon Press, 1993, 73.

Sommerstein, A. H. *The Comedies of Aristophanes.* Vol. 9, *Frogs.* Warminster, U.K.: Aris & Phillips, 1996, 216.

PHRYNONDAS   Although it is unclear whether Phrynondas was a real or fictional person, his name was synonymous with wicked behavior. [ANCIENT SOURCES: Aeschines, 3.137; Aristophanes, *Thesmophoriazusae* 861, fragment 26, 484 Kock; Eupolis, fragment 45 Kock; Isocrates, 18.57; Plato, *Protagoras* 327d]

BIBLIOGRAPHY

Kock, T. *Comicorum Atticorum Fragmenta.* Vol. 1. Leipzig: Teubner, 1880.

Sommerstein, A. H. *The Comedies of Aristophanes.* Vol. 8, *Thesmophoriazusae.* Warminster, U.K.: Aris & Phillips, 1994, 213.

PHTHIA   A Thessalian town near the coast of northeastern Greece. Phthia was famous as the home of PELEUS and ACHILLES. Achilles' son, NEOPTOLEMUS, became a king of Phthia, EURIPIDES' *ANDROMACHE* is set in this area, and women from Phthia make up the chorus. SOPHOCLES wrote a *Women of Phthia* (Greek: *Phthiotides*), of which a handful of lines survive (fragments 694–96 Radt). Sutton thinks that the fragments indicate that two old men and a young man were among the play's characters, but nothing else about its content

is definitely known. Lloyd-Jones seems inclined to identify the young man as Neoptolemus.

BIBLIOGRAPHY

Kiso, A. *The Lost Sophocles.* New York: Vantage Press, 1984.

Lloyd-Jones, H. *Sophocles: Fragments.* Cambridge, Mass.: Harvard University Press, 1996.

Radt, S. *Tragicorum Graecorum Fragmenta.* Vol. 4. Göttingen, Ger.: Vandenhoeck & Ruprecht, 1977.

Sutton, D. F. *The Lost Sophocles.* Lanham, Md.: University Press of America, 1984.

PHYLE   A DEME in the northern part of Athenian territory. In 403 B.C.E., the Athenian general THRASYBULUS' occupation of Phyle eventually led to the overthrow of the government that the Spartans had installed in ATHENS after the PELOPONNESIAN WAR. [ANCIENT SOURCES: Aristophanes, *Acharnians* 1023, 1028, *Wealth* 1146]

BIBLIOGRAPHY

Sommerstein, A. H. *The Comedies of Aristophanes.* Vol. 11, *Wealth.* Warminster, U.K.: Aris & Phillips, 2001, 212.

PHYROMACHUS   An Athenian mentioned by ARISTOPHANES, apparently for mispronouncing a word. The circumstances for this blunder are unknown. It may have occurred during a speech in the public assembly or when Phyromachus was an actor in a TRAGEDY. [ANCIENT SOURCES: Aristophanes, *Ecclesiazusae* 22]

BIBLIOGRAPHY

Sommerstein, A. H. *The Comedies of Aristophanes.* Vol. 10, *Ecclesiazusae.* Warminster, U.K.: Aris & Phillips, 1998, 140.

PIMP   A stock character in New Comedy. Although our knowledge of pimps (Latin: *leno;* plural: *lenones*) in drama is gained primarily from the Roman comedies of PLAUTUS and TERENCE, pimps appeared in Greek comedies as early as the middle of the fourth century B.C.E. The Greek counterpart of the *leno* was the *pornoboskos* (plural: *pornoboskoi*), and two Greek comic poets wrote plays entitled *Pornoboskos*: Eubulus (fragments 88–89 Kock 1) and Posiddipus (fragment 22 Kock 3). The Greek comic poet Anaxilas (fragments 27–29 Kock 2) wrote *Hyakinthos Pornoboskos* (Hyacinthus the pimp), and Dioxippus (fragment 1 Kock 3) wrote *Antiporno-*

boskos (The pimp's enemy). Unfortunately, the fragments of these Greek plays are so brief that comparison with pimps in the later plays of Plautus and Terence is impossible. Additionally, the character of the *pornoboskos* is largely absent from the plays of MENANDER (with the exception of *Colax*), which influenced both Plautus and Terence.

In Roman comedy, *lenones* appear in two plays by Terence (Sannio in BROTHERS, Dorio in PHORMIO) and five plays by Plautus (Lycus in CARTHAGINIAN; Cappadox in CURCULIO; Dordalus in THE PERSIAN; Ballio in PSEUDOLUS; Labrax in ROPE). Although the buying and selling of other humans were considered vile, the *leno* was involved in legal business and expected to be paid for his service. Thus, as Duckworth notes, the term *leno* might be better translated as "slave dealer." However one translates *leno,* these persons are generally unpleasant fellows. Regarding Plautine pimps, Erich Segal writes, "Of all the people in the happy-go-lucky Plautine world, only the *leno* arouses the playwright's genuine indignation; Plautus hates this kind of spoilsport" (79). In Plautus' *Curculio,* the title character comments on *lenones:* "In my humble opinion, the whole pimp tribe occupies the social position of flies, gnats, bugs, lice, and fleas: you are a pest, a plague, a general nuisance, of no good to anybody, and no decent person dares stand beside you in the FORUM. If anyone does, he is censured, eyed, condemned" (Nixon translation). Sometimes, even the *lenones* themselves are made to admit their evil nature. In TERENCE'S BROTHERS, the *leno,* Sannio, states, "I'm a pimp, I admit it, the bane of all young men, a perjurer, a plague" (Barsby translation). As hinted at by Sannio's statement, the cause for hatred of the *leno* is that he is an obstacle to a man and the woman he loves. Accordingly, the *leno* must often be tricked (e.g., Ballio) or overcome in some way (e.g., Labrax) so that the man can have the woman. After the defeat of the *leno,* a celebration from which the *leno* will be excluded usually occurs. In two instances (*Persian, Rope*), the *leno* is invited to join the revelers, although in *Persian,* Dordalus rejects the invitation. In contrast to Plautine *lenones,* the two *lenones* in Terence's plays have minor roles, and in contrast to the common practice in Plautus "neither is cheated of money nor taken to court; on the contrary, they are each paid in full for their girls" (Duckworth).

Not all *lenones* were men, and in Plautus' COMEDY OF ASSES and CASKET COMEDY, women (Cleareta and Syra, respectively) take on this role (*lena;* plural: *lenae*). In *Casket Comedy,* Syra has a relatively minor role and is portrayed as a rather kindly old drunk. In *Comedy of Asses,* Cleareta's behavior is more like her male counterparts' as she stands between Argyrippus and the prostitute Philaenium, the woman he desires. Cleareta's role in this play is complicated, however, by the fact that she is also Philaenium's mother. Thus, Cleareta is both pimp and parent. In *Comedy of Asses,* the money to buy Philaenium is acquired easily enough and no tricking of the *lena* is required, unlike in other plays.

BIBLIOGRAPHY
Barsby, J. *Terence.* Vol. 2. Cambridge, Mass.: Harvard University Press, 2001, 271.
Duckworth, G. *The Nature of Roman Comedy.* Princeton, N.J.: Princeton University Press, 1952, 262–64.
Kock, T. *Comicorum Atticorum Fragmenta.* Vol. 2. Leipzig: Teubner, 1884.
———. *Comicorum Atticorum Fragmenta.* Vol. 3. Leipzig: Teubner, 1888.
Nixon, P. *Plautus.* Vol. 2. Cambridge, Mass.: Harvard University Press, 1938, 243.
Segal, Erich. *Roman Laughter: The Comedy of Plautus.* New York: Oxford University Press, 1987, 79–92.

PINAKES The Greek word *pinax* (plural: *pinakes*) can refer to boards, planks, or tablets on which things were written, drawn, or painted. In the classical theater (after the fifth century B.C.E.), wooden *pinakes,* painted to represent various types of scenery, could be inserted between pillars on the lower front (see PROSKENION) of the stage building (see SKENE). The theater at Aphrodisias (western Turkey) has spaces for *pinakes* more than eight feet tall and almost five feet wide. [ANCIENT SOURCES: Pollux, *Onomasticon* 4.131]

BIBLIOGRAPHY
Csapo, E., and W. J. Slater. *The Context of Ancient Drama.* Ann Arbor: University of Michigan Press, 1995, 86–87.

PINDAR (518–438 B.C.E.) A famous Greek lyric poet from BOEOTIA. Pindar wrote many different types of poetry, but his only surviving poems (called epinician odes) celebrate the victors at the four major athletic festivals of Greece (i.e., the games at OLYMPIA, DELPHI, NEMEA, and CORINTH). [ANCIENT SOURCES: Aristophanes, *Birds* 939]

BIBLIOGRAPHY
Bowra, C. M. *Pindar.* Oxford: Clarendon Press, 1964.
Race, W. H. *Pindar.* Boston: Twayne, 1986.

PINDUS   A mountain range in northern Greece that separates the regions of THESSALY and EPIRUS. The Pindus is mentioned frequently in Senecan TRAGEDY, especially in *HERCULES OETAEUS*.

PIRITHOUS   The son of IXION, Pirithous of LAR-ISA was the good friend of THESEUS. When Pirithous' bride, Hippodameia (or Deidameia), was killed on the day of their wedding during a fight between some CEN-TAURS and Pirithous' tribe of Lapiths, Pirithous and Theseus, whose wife PHAEDRA had committed suicide, both set out to find a wife. The two men decided that they would settle for no less than daughters of ZEUS. After their abduction of HELEN, Theseus' situation was settled. When Theseus and Pirithous could not find another daughter of Zeus' in the upper world, they traveled to the UNDERWORLD. Pirithous hoped that he could somehow acquire PERSEPHONE, wife of HADES, as his bride. Hades, however, trapped Theseus and Pirithous inside his house. HERACLES eventually rescued Theseus from the underworld, but an ominous earthquake prevented Heracles from rescuing Pirithous.

Although Pirithous does not appear as a character in any extant drama, several playwrights did treat his story. A TRAGEDY entitled *Pirithous,* from which more than 50 lines survive, is attributed to EURIPIDES, although in antiquity some doubted Euripides wrote the play (some assigned it to Critias). The play clearly deals with Pirithous' entrapment in the underworld and probably begins with a monologue by Pirithous. At some point, Heracles arrives on his quest to fetch CERBERUS and has an encounter with AEACUS, a meeting that ARISTOPHANES probably parodied in the *FROGS*. Another fragment reveals a discussion between Theseus and Heracles, in which Theseus seems to express

reluctance about leaving Pirithous in the underworld. The tragedian Achaeus also wrote a *Pirithous,* but the two words that survive tell us nothing about the plot. The comic poet Aristophon also wrote a *Pirithous,* from which four lines are extant. [ANCIENT SOURCES: Apollodorus, *Library* 1.8.2, 2.5.12, *Epitome* 1.21–23; Diodorus Siculus, 4.70.3; Hyginus, *Fables* 33; Ovid, *Metamorphoses* 12.210–535; Pausanias, 5.10.8; Plutarch, *Theseus* 30; scholiast on Homer, *Odyssey* 22.295; Servius on Vergil, *Aeneid* 7.304]

BIBLIOGRAPHY
Nauck, A. *Tragicorum Graecorum Fragmenta.* 1889. Reprint, Hildesheim, Ger.: Olms, 1964.
Page, D. L. *Select Papyri.* Vol. 3. 1941. Reprint, London: Heinemann, 1970.
Snell, B. *Tragicorum Graecorum Fragmenta.* Vol. 1. Göttingen, Ger.: Vandenhoeck & Ruprecht, 1971.

PITALLUS   Employed by the Athenian government, Pitallus was a doctor who treated his patients at no charge. [ANCIENT SOURCES: Aristophanes, *Acharnians* 1032, 1221, *Wasps* 1432]

BIBLIOGRAPHY
Sommerstein, A. *The Comedies of Aristophanes.* Vol. 1, *Acharnians.* Warminster, U.K.: Aris & Phillips, 1980, 207.
———. *The Comedies of Aristophanes.* Vol. 4, *Wasps.* Warminster: Aris & Phillips, 1980, 242.

PITCHER FEAST (Greek: *CHOAE*)   The Pitcher Feast occurred on the second day of a festival called the Anthesteria, which was held in about February of the modern calendar. In ARISTOPHANES' *ACHARNIANS*, DICAEOPOLIS becomes drunk and feasts at the Choae, while LAMACHUS suffers through the toils of war. [ANCIENT SOURCES: Aristophanes, *Acharnians* 961]

BIBLIOGRAPHY
Parke, H. W. *Festivals of the Athenians.* Ithaca, N.Y.: Cornell University Press, 1977, 107–20.
Sommerstein, A. H. *The Comedies of Aristophanes.* Vol. 1, *Acharnians.* Warminster, U.K.: Aris & Phillips, 1980, 203.

PLATAEA   A Greek town southwest of THEBES. In 490 B.C.E., the Plataeans had helped the Athenians defeat DARIUS' Persian forces at MARATHON. In 479,

Plataea was the site of an important Greek victory over the Persian forces of Darius' son, XERXES. During the PELOPONNESIAN WAR (427), the Spartans and their allies destroyed Plataea. Afterward, the Athenians granted the male Plataeans limited rights of citizenship. [ANCIENT SOURCES: Aeschylus, *Persians* 817; Aristophanes, *Frogs* 694; Demosthenes, 59.104; Herodotus, 9.19–75]

PLATO (CA. 429–347 B.C.E.)

The most famous of SOCRATES' students, Plato is the most extensive source on Socrates. Plato's numerous philosophical writings contain frequent references to and quotations from ancient drama. The comic poet ARISTOPHANES and the tragedian AGATHON are portrayed in Plato's *Symposium.* Plato's most conversial remarks on classical drama occur in his *Republic,* in which he discusses the role of poetry in an ideal society. In such a society, Plato writes, drama can corrupt its audience, because it portrays emotions that stir up such strong feelings that people have difficulty in maintaining control of their own emotions. [ANCIENT SOURCES: Plato, *Laws* 2.658, 2.667–70, 11.935–36; *Republic* 3.394–95, 3.398, 10.605–6]

BIBLIOGRAPHY

Annas, J. *An Introduction to Plato's Republic.* Oxford. Clarendon Press, 1981.

Else, G. F. *Plato and Aristotle on Poetry.* Edited with an introduction by P. Burian. Chapel Hill: University of North Carolina Press, 1986.

Field, G. C. *The Philosophy of Plato.* With appendix by R. C. Cross. 2d ed. Oxford: Oxford University Press, 1969.

Janaway, C. *Images of Excellence: Plato's Critique of the Arts.* Oxford: Clarendon Press, 1995.

Melling, D. J. *Understanding Plato.* Oxford: University Press, 1987.

PLAUTUS (CA. 254–184 B.C.E.)

Titus Maccius Plautus was born in the Umbrian town of Sarsina but later went to Rome, where he performed some sort of work in the theater (perhaps as an actor or producer). After making some money, he lost it all in a commercial venture and returned to Rome. After this, he is said to have worked in a baker's mill. He escaped this menial labor by writing plays, and as many as 130 plays were attributed to him, but even in ancient times

Roman scholars suspected that many plays attributed to Plautus were actually written by others. In the first century B.C.E., a scholar named Varro, trying to sort out this confusion, divided the so-called Plautine works into three lists. One of these lists, which contained 21 plays, he considered the genuine works of Plautus. As it turns out, 20 of these plays survive complete, and 120 lines survive from Plautus' VIDULARIA. The complete plays are AMPHITRUO, COMEDY OF ASSES (*Asinaria*), POT OF GOLD (*Aulularia*), BACCHIDES (*Two Bacchises*), CAPTIVES, CASINA, CASKET COMEDY (*Cistellaria*), CURCULIO, EPIDICUS, MENAECHMI (*Two Menaechmuses*), MERCHANT (*Mercator*), HAUNTED HOUSE (*Mostellaria*), BRAGGART WARRIOR (*Miles Gloriosus*), THE PERSIAN, THE CARTHAGINIAN (*Poenulus*), PSEUDOLUS, THE ROPE (*Rudens*), STICHUS, THREE-DOLLAR DAY (*Trinummus*), TRUCULENTUS, and *Vidularia*. Only three of Plautus' plays can be dated securely: *Braggart Warrior* (205), *Stichus* (200), and *Pseudolus* (191). None of Plautus' surviving plays appears to be earlier than the year 212 (*Comedy of Asses*), and he seems to have been producing plays until the time of his death.

The plays of Plautus, as those of TERENCE, were originally written by Greek playwrights and then adapted for Roman audiences. Unlike for Terence, for whom the Greek authors of all six of his plays' antecedents are known, for Plautus, only about half the Greek authors are known. *Asinaria* was adapted from a play by DEMOPHILUS; *Casina* and *Rope* were adapted from plays by PHILEMON. Plays from MENANDER provided the models for *Bacchides, The Casket Comedy,* and *Stichus,* and Philemon's originals also provided the source for three plays: *Haunted House, Merchant,* and *Three-Dollar Day.* How much material in Plautus' plays is his own work and how much is taken directly from his Greek sources are subject to debate. Clearly, however, Plautus did more than merely translate Greek originals into Latin. Compared with Terence, he is thought to have taken more liberties with the Greek plays.

Although staged for Roman audiences, almost all of Plautus' plays have settings on mainland Greece (*Rope* is the exception), and two-thirds of the plays are set in ATHENS. The action of Plautus' plays usually takes place before two houses, although in two plays (*Amphitruo,*

Captives) only a single structure is represented, and in two others three houses are present (*Pseudolus, Stichus*). In four plays, a temple or altar dedicated to a divinity is presented (*Pot of Gold, Curculio, Merchant, Rope*). In eight of the plays, one of the houses is occupied by a PIMP or one or more PROSTITUTES.

The primary building blocks of Plautus' plays are the stereotypical young Greek citizen (see ADULESCENS), the stereotypical old Greek citizen (see SENEX), and a male slave. Often the citizens are father and son and the slave is a member of their household. Usually the son is in love with a prostitute and spends his time trying to acquire her (contrast the double plots in most of Terence's plays, in which two young men seek to be united with two different women). Because the young man has little money, this lack is often an obstacle to purchasing the woman. Additional major obstacles to enjoyment of the beloved are the young man's father and/or the slave dealer (see PIMP) who owns her. Accordingly, the young man must have the assistance of the slave, who in some way will trick the father or the pimp so that his young master can be united with his beloved. Ultimately, the prostitute often turns out to be freeborn, so the young man can marry her.

Of course, variations on and complete divergences from this basic pattern occur. Sometimes the *senex* and/or *adulescens* is in love with the same woman (e.g., *Casina*). Sometimes a play has no love intrigue (e.g., *Captives*). In *Stichus,* the main goal of the play seems to be the title character's obtaining a meal. Sometimes a PARASITE rather than a slave aids the young man (e.g., *Curculio*) or a BRAGGART WARRIOR stands in the way of the young man and his beloved prostitute (e.g., *Braggart Warrior*). In *Menaechmi,* the twin brothers are reunited and leave behind Epidamnian Menaechmus' wife and his prostitute mistress.

In addition to being criticized for his often stereotypical characters, Plautus produces expository prologues, in which a single character explains the situation of the play, that are less elegant than those of Terence, who prefers to allow the story to unfold through the dialogue between the characters. Plautus' plot construction is also careless in some instances (e.g., *Stichus*), as he stitched together two Greek comedies to create a single play (see CONTAMINATIO). Some-

times, Plautus makes certain parts of a play much too long, such as Mercury's (see HERMES) prologue (152 lines) in *Amphitruo*. Plautus is also criticized for inserting Roman references into his Greek settings. For example, 21 times in Plautus' plays we find mention of a Roman magistrate called the praetor.

For all of Plautus' faults—his plot construction, character development, and style of language are certainly less polished than those of TERENCE—his language (filled with word play and alliteration), use of lyric passages, and overall tone are much more festive than Terence's. In terms of Plautus' brand of humor, he is closer to ARISTOPHANES than Terence. Of course, Plautus' comedies contain little political humor, but we do find instances of the coarser sort of humor present in Aristophanes: the belching of the drunken Pseudolus; men who gawk at and playfully paw a beautiful women; the use of coarse language (e.g., *cinaedus,* which means "sodomite" and never occurs in Terence). Plautus' humor also involves mistaken identity and deception. In several plays, the presence of twins causes confusion. Often, to carry out their schemes, the slaves pretend to be other people or arrange for their accomplices to pretend to be other people. Some modern scholars approach Plautus' plays as having plays within plays, as one character, usually the slave, produces a "play" whose aim is the deception of another character or characters within the play.

Although Plautus may not have been the most masterful playwright to grace the ancient stage, more of his plays survive than of any other ancient playwright. Furthermore, his type of COMEDY influenced the likes of Shakespeare, Molière, and Ben Jonson. So frequently redone was Plautus' *Amphitruo* that Jean Giraudoux entitled his version *Amphitryon 38.* The modern musical *A Funny Thing Happened on the Way to the Forum* is a reworking of several of Plautus' plays.

BIBLIOGRAPHY

Duckworth, G. E. *The Nature of Roman Comedy.* Princeton, N.J.: Princeton University Press, 1952.

Fraenkel, Edward. *Elementi plautini in Plauto (Plautinische im Plautus).* Translated by Franco Munari. Firenze: La Nuova Italia, 1960.

Konstan, D. *Roman Comedy.* Ithaca, N.Y.: Cornell University Press, 1983.

Segal, Erich. *Roman Laughter: The Comedy of Plautus.* 2d ed. London: Oxford University Press, 1987.

Slater, N. W. *Plautus in Performance.* Princeton, N.J.: Princeton University Press, 1985.

PLEBEIAN GAMES

The Plebeian Games, celebrated at least as early as November 220 B.C.E., were held in honor of Jupiter (see ZEUS). The games were arranged annually by the plebeian aediles. PLAUTUS' STICHUS was performed at these games in 200 B.C.E. In the second century B.C.E., dramatic performances appear to have been held on at least three days of the games.

PLEISTHENES

The name of several males with connections to the house of ATREUS. Some sources make Pleisthenes, rather than Atreus, the husband of AEROPE. Accordingly, MENELAUS and AGAMEMNON are sometimes called the sons of Pleisthenes rather than Atreus. Another tradition says that Pleisthenes was a son of Atreus, who killed him accidentally. In SENECA's *THYESTES*, Pleisthenes is a child of THYESTES. Atreus kills Pleisthenes and serves him as food to Thyestes. EURIPIDES wrote a *Pleisthenes,* which may have been produced in the final decade of the poet's life (fragments 625–33 Nauck). [ANCIENT SOURCES: Apollodorus, *Library* 3.2.2; Bacchylides, *Dithyramb* 1.48; Hyginus, *Fables* 86, 88; Seneca, *Thyestes* 726]

BIBLIOGRAPHY
Nauck, A. *Tragicorum Graecorum Fragmenta.* 1889. Reprint, Hildesheim, Ger.: Olms, 1964.

PLUTO

Another name for HADES.

PLUTUS

The son of DEMETER and Iasion, Plutus, the god of wealth, appears as a character in ARISTOPHANES' WEALTH. In this play, Plutus is initially blind (an attribute not found in other ancient sources) and because of this he gives his blessings to those who do not deserve them. Plutus' blindness, however, is remedied when an Athenian citizen named Chremylus decides that society's problems could be solved if Plutus could see. Accordingly, Chremylus takes Plutus to a temple of ASCLEPIUS for treatment. Once Plutus can see, he bestows his blessings on the "good" people in society. [ANCIENT SOURCES: Aristophanes, *Thesmophoriazusae* 299; Hesiod, *Theogony* 969–74]

PLUTUS See WEALTH.

PNYX

Mentioned frequently in ARISTOPHANES' plays (especially *KNIGHTS* and *ECCLESIAZUSAE*), the Pnyx was a rocky plateau near the Athenian ACROPOLIS that was the location for meetings of the assembly. In *Ecclesiazusae*, PRAXAGORA says she lived on the Pnyx and there learned how to speak by listening to the orators in the assembly. In that play, the women take over the government in Athens by dressing as men and infiltrating a meeting on the Pnyx. In the opening of Aristophanes' *Knights*, DEMOSTHENES says his master is "Demos [i.e., the Athenian people] of the Pnyx."

POEAS

The father of PHILOCTETES. [ANCIENT SOURCES: Seneca, *Hercules Oetaeus* 1485, 1604, 1649; Sophocles, *Philoctetes*]

POENULUS See THE CARTHAGINIAN.

POLIAS

A title of the goddess ATHENA as she was worshiped on the ACROPOLIS in ATHENS. The name Polias means "guardian of the city." [ANCIENT SOURCES: Aristophanes, *Birds* 828; Sophocles, *Philoctetes* 134]

POLLUX See CASTOR AND POLLUX.

POLYBUS

The king of CORINTH, who, along with his wife, MEROPE, raised OEDIPUS and who Oedipus mistakenly thought was his real father. [ANCIENT SOURCES: Aristophanes, *Frogs* 1192; Euripides, *Phoenician Women* 28, 45, 1607; Hyginus, *Fables* 67; Seneca, *Oedipus;* Sophocles, *Oedipus Tyrannos*]

POLYDEUCES See CASTOR AND POLLUX.

POLYIDUS

The son of Coeranus, Polyidus was a prophet from ARGOS. Other than his assistance of BELLEROPHON to tame PEGASUS, most of Polyidus' story is connected with MINOS and his son, Glaucus, who disappeared while chasing a mouse. When Minos consulted the DELPHIC ORACLE to learn of Glaucus' whereabouts, the oracle told him that the person who could find Glaucus would be the one to make the most appropriate simile to describe the strange occurrence on Crete. When Polyidus compared one of Minos' recently born calves, which every day had been changing colors from white to red to black, to the changes of a ripening mulberry, Minos sent Polyidus to find his son. When Polyidus saw some bees harassing an owl that was sitting on a wine cellar, Polyidus found Glaucus. Because bees make honey and the Greek word for owl, *glaux,* recalls the name Glaucus, Polyidus looked into a large jar of honey and discovered the body of Glaucus.

Despite Glaucus' death, Minos refused to give up his son for dead. Therefore, Minos enclosed Polyidus and Glaucus' body in a tomb and told the prophet to resurrect Glaucus. When a snake approached the body, Polyidus killed it. Soon, however, another snake appeared and used an herb to revive the first snake. Polyidus took some of this same herb and revived Glaucus. After Glaucus returned to life, Minos made Polyidus teach his son the art of prophecy. Polyidus did so, but just before his ship sailed from Crete, Polyidus told the boy to spit into his mouth. When Glaucus did so, he lost the prophetic art. The angered Minos then pursued Polyidus and invaded MEGARA, where Polyidus had gone to cleanse Alcathous of the killing of his own son, Callipolis. EURIPIDES wrote a *Polyidus* (fragments 634–46 Nauck), which appears to have dealt with Polyidus' discovery of Glaucus' body and his subsequent resurrection. [ANCIENT SOURCES: Apollodorus, *Library* 3.3.1; Aristophanes, *Frogs* 1477; Hyginus, *Fables* 136]

BIBLIOGRAPHY
Nauck, A. *Tragicorum Graecorum Fragmenta.* 1889. Reprint, Hildesheim, Ger.: Olms, 1964.
Webster, T. B. L. *The Tragedies of Euripides.* London: Methuen, 1967, 161–62.

POLYMESTOR

Polymestor was a Thracian king. During the Trojan War, Polymestor was friendly to TROY's king, PRIAM, who sent his son, POLYDORUS (and a large sum of gold), to stay with Polymestor so that the young man might not perish in the war as so many of his brothers had. Polymestor, however, desiring the young man's gold, murdered his guest. As the Greek fleet was preparing to sail from Troy, Polydorus' corpse was discovered near the shore. When HECABE, Polydorus' mother, learned of her son's death, she lured Polymestor into her tent with the promise of more gold and then blinded him. Polymestor appears as a character in EURIPIDES' *HECABE.* He is portrayed as a barbarian, and his blinding by Hecabe is modeled on ODYSSEUS' blinding of the CYCLOPS POLYPHEMUS. He appeals to AGAMEMNON for help after HECABE blinds him, but Agamemnon rejects Polymestor's appeals. At the conclusion of that play, Polymestor predicts that Hecabe will die before she reaches Odysseus' home on ITHACA.

POLYMNESTUS

From the town of Colophon (on the western coast of modern Turkey), Polymnestus was a musician who lived during the seventh century B.C.E. ARISTOPHANES suggests that he lacked moral restraint. [ANCIENT SOURCES: Aristophanes, *Knights* 1287; Cratinus, fragment 305 Kock; pseudo-Plutarch, *Moralia* 1132d, 1133a, 1134b–d, 1141b]

BIBLIOGRAPHY
Kock, T. *Comicorum Atticorum Fragmenta.* Vol. 1. Leipzig: Teubner, 1880.
Sommerstein, A. H. *The Comedies of Aristophanes.* Vol. 2, *Knights.* Warminster, U.K.: Aris & Phillips, 1981, 212.

POLYNEICES

The son of JOCASTA and the son and brother of OEDIPUS, Polyneices was the brother of ETEOCLES, ANTIGONE, and ISMENE. The name Polyneices means "much strife," and this meaning characterizes his life. After his father, Oedipus, discovered that he had killed his father and married his mother, Polyneices and his brother, Eteocles, did not treat him very kindly. This led Oedipus to curse his sons. To avoid this curse, Polyneices and Eteocles decided to share the kingship abdicated by their father. The brothers would take turns ruling THEBES. One brother would rule for one year, while the other went into exile. Eteocles assumed the kingship first and Polyneices went into exile at ARGOS. During that time, Polyneices stayed at the palace of King ADRASTUS and eventually married Adrastus' daughter, Argia (or Aegialeia), by whom he had a son (Thersander).

When Eteocles, after a year, did not hand over the throne, Polyneices appealed to his father-in-law, Adrastus, for help and with backing gathered an army and marched on Thebes. In the battle, Eteocles and Polyneices killed each other in single combat. After the brothers' deaths, it was decreed that Polyneices would not be buried and that anyone who buried him would be put to death. The person or persons who issue this decree varies. According to AESCHYLUS' SEVEN AGAINST THEBES a group of Theban nobles make the decree. In SOPHOCLES' ANTIGONE, the new Theban king, CREON, issues the decree.

Several extant plays deal with the strife between Polyneices and Eteocles. Although Polyneices does not have a speaking role in either Aeschylus' Seven or Sophocles' Antigone, he is, of course, much discussed in these plays, and in Aeschylus' play his words are reported. The story of Polyneices and the aftermath of his death from the Argive perspective are touched upon in EURIPIDES' SUPPLIANT WOMEN but are not the focal point of that play.

In Euripides' PHOENICIAN WOMEN, whose plot follows roughly the same lines as Aeschylus' Seven, Polyneices does have a substantial speaking role. In this play, Polyneices goes to Thebes for face-to-face negotiations with his brother, which are mediated by their mother, Jocasta. Euripides portrays Polyneices as extremely suspicious of his brother, hating the experience of exile, and longing to return to his native Thebes. Once Polyneices meets Eteocles, he claims nothing more than to share the throne in accordance with their arrangement and says he will send his army back if Eteocles will agree. Even the chorus of Phoenician women think Polyneices' claim is reasonable, although his mother condemns his march on his native land. Furthermore, after Eteocles proves fixed in his resolve for war, Polyneices becomes angry with his brother and declares his intent to kill him and become king of Thebes. Only part of Polyneices' declaration comes to pass, though, as he does kill his brother, but only after he has received a mortal wound from him.

Polyneices also makes an appearance toward the end of Sophocles' OEDIPUS AT COLONUS. In Sophocles' play, Polyneices goes to his father at Colonus and tries to gain his support so that he can gain victory over the Thebans (an ORACLE had indicated that Oedipus' support would determine the victor). Polyneices tries to gain his father's sympathy, emphasizing his plight as an exile. Oedipus, however, knows that his son has gone to him because of the oracle and angrily rejects Polyneices' pleas and curses him. Antigone tries to persuade Polyneices not to march against Thebes, but Polyneices refuses because doing so would undermine his authority in any future war.

Polyneices also appears in SENECA'S PHOENICIAN WOMEN. As in Euripides' play, he attends negotiations with his brother over which his mother presides. In Seneca's play, Jocasta does most of the talking, but the brief portrayal of Polyneices shows, as in Euripides, a mistrust of Eteocles, a loathing of exile, and a condemnation by Jocasta of his march against his native land. [ANCIENT SOURCES: Apollodorus, Library 3.5.8–3.7.2; Hyginus, Fables 68–72; Statius, Thebaid]

POLYPHEMUS This CYCLOPS is the son of POSEIDON and the nymph Thoosa. Polyphemus' encounter with ODYSSEUS is famous from HOMER'S Odyssey but was dramatized three centuries later in EURIPIDES' CYCLOPS. After Odysseus and his men near Polyphemus' home near Mount AETNA on SICILY, Polyphemus eats some of Odysseus' men. Odysseus retaliates by making the Cyclops drunk and then blinding him. In Euripides' Cyclops, the playwright makes the intoxicated Cyclops exhibit a sexual passion for SILENUS, the father of the SATYRS who had been serving Polyphemus. After Polyphemus' blinding, Odysseus and his surviving men escape from the monster's cave and make their way to their ship. In Homer's version of the story, Odysseus and his men escape the cave by tying themselves to the underbellies of Polyphemus' sheep. Such an escape would be difficult on the ancient stage, so this method obviously does not occur in Euripides' play. Instead, Odysseus and his men manage to slip past Polyphemus. Additionally, in Euripides' play, the satyrs leave with Odysseus. As Homer relates it, Odysseus, as he was sailing away, taunted the Cyclops and revealed his name to the monster. This led Polyphemus to throw large rocks at the ship and pray to his father, Poseidon, to destroy Odysseus. In Euripides' play, no rocks are thrown, but Polyphemus does predict that Odysseus will spend much time wandering the sea. [ANCIENT SOURCES: Homer, *Odyssey* 9; Hyginus, *Fables* 125]

POLYXENA   As the Greek fleet was preparing to sail from TROY, the ghost of ACHILLES appeared and demanded the sacrifice of Polyxena, daughter of PRIAM and HECABE. The wish of Achilles' ghost was granted and Polyxena was subsequently sacrificed at Achilles' grave. Details of Polyxena's death are given in three extant plays—EURIPIDES' *HECABE,* and *TROJAN WOMEN* and SENECA'S *TROJAN WOMEN.*

Polyxena has a fairly significant speaking role in Euripides' *Hecabe,* appears as a silent character in Seneca's play, and does not appear (but is talked about) in Euripides' *Trojan Women.* In Euripides' *Hecabe,* Polyxena gives a moving speech in which she expresses her preference to give up her life as a free Trojan woman rather than live as a slave among the Greeks.

Two other tragedians wrote plays entitled *Polyxena.* Only the title survives from the *Polyxena* of Nicarchus; several fragments are extant from SOPHOCLES' *Polyxena* (522–27 Radt). As in Euripides' *Hecabe,* Achilles' ghost has a speaking role in Sophocles' play. Unlike in Euripides' play, Menelaus appears as a character in Sophocles' play. [ANCIENT SOURCES: Apollodorus, *Epitome* 5.23; Hyginus, *Fables* 110; Ovid, *Metamorphoses* 13.439–80]

BIBLIOGRAPHY

Radt, S. *Tragicorum Graecorum Fragmenta.* Vol. 4. Göttingen, Ger.: Vandenhoeck & Ruprecht, 1977.

Snell, B. *Tragicorum Graecorum Fragmenta.* Vol. 1. Göttingen, Ger.: Vandenhoeck & Ruprecht, 1971.

PONTUS (1)   Another name for the Black Sea. In Greek, the word *pontos* means "sea." [ANCIENT SOURCES: Aeschylus, *Persians* 877]

PONTUS (2)   A region along the southern shore of the Black Sea in what is today northern Turkey. [ANCIENT SOURCES: Aristophanes, *Wasps* 700; Plautus, *Three-Dollar Day* 933–34, *Truculentus* 540]

POPPAEA (CA. 31–65 C.E.)   The daughter of Titus Ollius, Poppaea first married Rufrius Crispinus,

prefect of the praetorian guard of the emperor, CLAUDIUS. Next, she married Otho (before he became emperor), but by 58 C.E. she had become NERO'S mistress and is thought to have exerted considerable influence on him. In 59, Poppaea may have instigated Nero's murder of his mother, AGRIPPINA, and, as suggested by SENECA'S *OCTAVIA,* Poppaea was behind the divorce, exile, and execution of Nero's wife, OCTAVIA. Once Octavia was out of the way, Nero married Poppaea and the couple had a daughter, but the infant died at four months of age. Poppaea died in 65 after an angry Nero is said to have killed her (she was pregnant at the time). Poppaea was honored as a goddess after her death.

In Seneca's *Octavia,* Poppaea dreams that the earth opens and swallows her marriage bed. She also dreams that she has seen her previous husband, Crispinus, and her son, Rufrius Crispinus. When the elder Crispinus tries to embrace her, Nero suddenly appears and kills Crispinus. When Poppaea asks her NURSE what this dream could mean, her nurse incorrectly explains the dream as having positive implications for her future with Nero. [ANCIENT SOURCES: Seneca, *Octavia;* Suetonius, *Nero* 35; Tacitus, *Annals* 11, 13–16]

PORPHYRION   A son of EARTH, Porphyrion was a Giant, who, along with his brothers, tried to overthrow ZEUS and the other gods. The gods, with the help of HERACLES, eventually destroyed Porphyrion and the other GIANTS. In ARISTOPHANES' *BIRDS,* in which the birds rival the gods for power, the playwright takes advantage of the fact that a porphyrion is also a bird. Thus, at *Birds* 553, when Aristophanes mentions Porphyrion, his reference evokes both the name of the giant and that of the bird. [ANCIENT SOURCES: Apollodorus, *Library* 1.6.1; Aristophanes, *Birds* 707, 881, 1249, 1252; Pindar, *Pythian Ode* 8.17]

POSEIDON   The son of CRONUS and RHEA, Poseidon (Latin: Neptune) is the brother of ZEUS, HADES, DEMETER, HERA, and HESTIA. After the overthrow of CRONUS, Poseidon, Zeus, and Hades drew lots to divide the realms of the world, and Poseidon acquired the sea. Although Poseidon rules the waves, the Greeks also considered him the god of earthquakes. Accordingly, Poseidon is also called Ennosis, which means "earth shaker." Poseidon was also a god associated with horses and chariot racing.

Poseidon's wife is Amphitrite, but he had affairs with others. After sexually assaulting AMYMONE, Poseidon showed her LERNA's springs. By TYRO, Poseidon fathered JASON's nemesis, Pelias. By the nymph Thoosa, Poseidon also fathered the CYCLOPS POLYPHEMUS, whom ODYSSEUS blinded. As were several Greek divinities, Poseidon seems to have been attracted to both females and males. PELOPS, the grandfather of AGAMEMNON, attracted Poseidon's attention and Poseidon later gave the young man a splendid team of horses with which Pelops was able to defeat Oenomaus and win the hand of his daughter, HIPPODAMEIA. Poseidon was also famed as the father of the Athenian hero THESEUS. Although Poseidon does not appear as a character in EURIPIDES' *Hippolytus*, he does affect the outcome of that play, as Theseus uses one of three wishes given to him by Poseidon to curse his son, HIPPOLYTUS. This curse leads to Hippolytus' death.

Poseidon and APOLLO are said to have built the walls of TROY for King Laomedon. When Laomedon did not show the proper gratitude for this service, Poseidon sent a sea monster to ravage the town. Despite Laomedon's disrespect, Poseidon favored the Trojans in the Trojan War, and Poseidon appears as a character in the prologue of EURIPIDES' *TROJAN WOMEN*. In this play, he is leaving the ruined city when ATHENA approaches him and arranges for him to create a storm that will wreck the Greek fleet as they sail for home.

Poseidon also appears as a character in ARISTOPHANES' *BIRDS*, in which he, HERACLES, and a foreign god, Triballos, have been sent to arrange a peace with the birds. Poseidon opposes the peace treaty but eventually agrees to all of its terms. [ANCIENT SOURCES: Aristophanes, *Birds* 1565; Hyginus, *Fables* 157; Plautus, *Rope*]

POSTSCAENIUM   The part of the theater behind the stage building (see *SKENE*).

POT FEAST   See CHYTROI.

POTIDAIA   A town in northeastern Greece on the peninsula of Pallene. During the fifth century B.C.E. Potidaia was part of the Athenian empire. In 432, its people revolted against the Athenians, but the town was retaken in 429. [ANCIENT SOURCES: Aristophanes, *Knights* 438; Thucydides, 2.70]

THE POT OF GOLD (Latin: *AULU-LARIA*) PLAUTUS (CA. 191 B.C.E.)

The Greek model for PLAUTUS' play is unknown. Given Plautus' focus on the distrustful Euclio, MENANDER's *Apistos* (The distrustful man) is thought to have provided the source for Plautus' play. Several Greek comic poets, however, wrote plays entitled *Thesaurus* (Treasure), including DIPHILUS, MENANDER, and PHILEMON, all of whom Plautus is known to have drawn upon. Few fragments of these plays survive.

Plautus' play deals with a miser named Euclio, who is constantly on the lookout for anyone who might steal a pot of gold he keeps hidden in his house. The action takes places in ATHENS, before the houses of Euclio and Megadorus, both older gentlemen. The prologue is a little unusual in extant Plautine plays in that it is delivered by a divinity, the Lar Familiaris (HOUSEHOLD GOD) of Euclio's house. When Euclio's rich neighbor, Megadorus, proposes that he marry Euclio's daughter, Phaedria, Euclio suspects that Megadorus wants his gold. Euclio, however, agrees to marry his daughter to Megadorus, provided that Megadorus not expect her to provide a dowry. Megadorus, eager to marry, agrees, and the two men set the wedding for that very day.

Megadorus goes to the market and hires two cooks and two flute girls and orders food for the two families. When the provisions are taken to Megadorus' house, they are divided between the two houses. Euclio, who also goes to the market, returns with only incense and flowers for his daughter's wedding. When Euclio returns, he overhears one of the cooks' talking about a pot, thinks that the cook refers to his pot of gold, and dashes into his house to confront the cooks, whom he chases from the house. Euclio, having retrieved his pot of gold, then allows the cooks to return to work.

Euclio then conceals his pot of god at the shrine of Fides ("faith" or "trust") but is overheard addressing the divinity by Strobilus, a servant of Lyconides, the son of Eunomia and nephew of Megadorus. As it happens, Lyconides, who is in love with Euclio's daughter and had impregnated her nine months earlier, has just learned that Euclio has betrothed his daughter to his uncle. Lyconides' slave enters the shrine, intending to steal the gold, but Euclio catches him before he can do so. Euclio then decides to hide his gold in a grove of Silvanus, and Lyconides' slave decides to observe the old man.

After the exit of Euclio and Strobilus for the grove of Silvanus, Lyconides and Eunomia enter. Lyconides has told his mother of his love for Euclio's daughter and begs her to tell Megadorus that he is the father of Euclio's daughter's child. As the two talk, Euclio's daughter begins to cry out with labor pains. Hearing this, Eunomia urges Lyconides to go into Megadorus' house, so they can tell his uncle at once. After Eunomia and Lyconides go to Megadorus' house, Strobilus enters, carrying Euclio's pot of gold. Strobilus exits when he hears a frantic and enraged Euclio approach.

As Euclio rants about the loss of his gold, Lyconides enters. Perceiving Euclio's anger, Lyconides thinks that Euclio is angry about his daughter's pregnancy. Before Lyconides can escape, Euclio hears him, and Lyconides approaches the old miser. Soon Lyconides is confessing to some unspecified crime, but Euclio thinks he is confessing to stealing the gold. When Euclio says he wants back what Lyconides took, Lyconides is puzzled. When Euclio tells him about the pot of gold, Lyconides denies stealing it. When Lyconides continues to act ignorant about the gold, a desperate Euclio even offers him half the gold and promises not to take him to court. Lyconides denies taking the gold and manages to change the subject to Euclio's daughter. Lyconides informs Euclio that he is Megadorus' nephew and that Megadorus wants to break his engagement to Euclio's daughter. Euclio is furious at this news and curses Megadorus. Lyconides goes on to confess that he impregnated Euclio's daughter. He also informs Euclio that she has given birth and expresses his hope to marry her. An even angrier Euclio then goes into his house to find out the truth of the situation.

The play's final act begins with the arrival of Strobilus. Lyconides, who has been trying to decide his own next move, approaches his slave. When Strobilus claims he has found a pot of gold, Lyconides realizes that Strobilus has stolen Euclio's gold. Strobilus then suggests to Lyconides that he wants to buy his freedom with the gold. Lyconides rejects this idea, however, and demands that Strobilus hand over the gold. Unfortunately, at this point the manuscript breaks off. We expect, however, that Lyconides managed to retrieve the pot of gold and return it to Euclio, who forgave Lyconides' transgressions and gave the gold for his daughter's wedding dowry.

COMMENTARY

Duckworth classifies *Pot of Gold* as one of five extant Roman comedies (see also STICHUS, THREE-DOLLAR DAY, TRUCULENTUS, and TERENCE'S BROTHERS) that focus on character. As Duckworth points out, however, although while the character of the miser Euclio is the play's chief interest, Plautus has not created a study of avarice, but allowed comic situations to arise from Euclio's suspicion of those in his household and among his neighbors. Of the plays mentioned, *Three-Dollar Day* is probably most similar to *Pot of Gold*. In addition to the concern with character, both plays have prologues that are delivered by divinities and both have hidden treasures that are ultimately used to provide marriage dowries. Unlike in *Three-Dollar Day,* in which the treasure is unknown to the wasteful young Lesbonicus and is of secondary importance, in *Pot of Gold* the old miser is fully aware of the gold (of primary importance to the play) and spends all his effort keeping others away from it.

One of the major focal points of *Pot of Gold* is the concept of *fides,* a Latin word that embodies the concepts of trustworthiness, credibility, faithfulness, and the like. As Konstan points out, for the Romans *fides* was one of the bonds that linked the individual to the community, and Euclio's inability to enter into bonds of *fides* with others represents his withdrawal from the social life of his community. So important was *fides* to the members of Plautus' Roman audience that almost two centuries later the Roman poet Ovid, at *Metamorphoses* 1.90, would list it as one of the qualities that characterized people who lived during the Golden Age. Ovid also mentions that *fides* was absent during the Iron Age (1.129). In *Pot of Gold, fides* is a quality that Euclio values greatly but is incapable of fully embracing in others. Although it is not surprising that Euclio would not trust the unknown cooks who enter his house, he does not trust that his wealthy neighbor, Megadorus, does not want to acquire his gold even though Euclio acknowledges that his prospective son-in-law, Megadorus, is a person of good *fides* (213). Not only does Euclio not trust his fellow human beings, he does not even trust the gods.

The suspicious Euclio, not believing that his gold will be safe under the protection of his household god, eventually entrusts it to the divinity Fides. Euclio's lack of faith in the *fides* of his household god and the transfer of the gold to a different divinity, however, result in the loss of the gold. While Euclio has prayed to Fides to watch over his gold, Strobilus has overheard his prayer and utters a counterprayer to the Fides that the divinity not be more faithful (*fidelis,* 618) to Euclio than to him. Fortunately for Euclio, after Strobilus steals the gold, the old miser catches Strobilus and regains the gold. This theft, however, prompts Euclio not even to trust the divinity Fides—he does not even trust Trust. Accordingly, Euclio perversely decides that he will entrust the gold to the care of the divinity Silvanus rather than the divinity who represents trust (676). Thus, Euclio has gone from mistrusting a household divinity, to mistrusting a divinity of the city, to entrusting "his gold to the uncultivated precinct of a god of the wilderness. . . . And there, outside the city, he is treated like the outcast he has made himself" (Konstan).

When Strobilus steals the gold a second time, Euclio's character breaks down the invisible barrier that separates actor from spectator and begs the audience for help. He tells one audience member that he trusts him because he has an honest face (719). Although Euclio does not trust his neighbor or the gods, his desperation is so great that he goes outside the bounds of the play to find someone in whom he can have trust.

When the distraught Euclio accuses Lyconides of breaking the bonds of trust, the confused Lyconides almost confesses that he has sexually assaulted Euclio's daughter. When Lyconides realizes what Euclio is accusing him of and swears that he did not steal the gold, Euclio demands that he give him his word (literally, "speak with good *fides*," 772), an ironic statement from a person who does not even trust the divinity Fides. In this instance, however, Euclio does seem to trust (777) that Lyconides has not taken the gold. Any credibility Lyconides had with Euclio is shattered, however, when the young man reveals his uncle's desire to end the engagement to Euclio's daughter and then informs Euclio about the sexual assault. Although the rest of the play is lost, Lyconides apparently would have been able to regain his lost *fides* with Euclio by returning to him the gold that Strobilus has again stolen. Euclio, in turn, would have reciprocated this trust by giving the gold to Lyconides and his daughter as a wedding gift.

BIBLIOGRAPHY

Arnott, W. G. "The Greek Original of Plautus' *Aulularia,*" *Weiner Studien* 101 (1988): 181–91.

Hunter, R. L. "The *Aulularia* of Plautus and its Greek Original," *Proceedings of the Cambridge Philological Society* 27 (1981): 37–49.

Konstan, D. "*Aulularia:* City-State and Individual." In *Roman Comedy.* Ithaca, N.Y.: Cornell University Press, 1983, 33–47.

Marcovich, M. "Euclio, Cnemon, and the Peripatos," *Illinois Classical Studies* 2 (1977): 197–218.

PRAECINCTIO   In the seating area of the Roman theater, the *praecinctio* was a horizontal walkway that separated a lower block of seating from an upper block (see MAENIANUM). The Greek equivalent of *praecinctio* is *diazoma.* [ANCIENT SOURCES: *Corpus Inscriptionum Graecarum* 2755; Vitruvius, *On Architecture* 5.3.4, 5.6.2]

BIBLIOGRAPHY

Csapo, E., and W. J. Slater. *The Context of Ancient Drama.* Ann Arbor: University of Michigan Press, 1995, 432.

PRAMNIAN WINE   A famous wine produced in the eastern AEGEAN that was "noted for its strength and dryness." The meaning of the name Pramnian is not known. The Greek comic poet Ephippus (fragment 28 Kock 2) praised Pramnian wine made on the island of LESBOS. [ANCIENT SOURCES: Aristophanes, *Knights* 107; Athenaeus 1.30c; Homer, *Iliad* 11.639, *Odyssey* 10.235; Phrynichus Comicus, fragment 65 Kock]

BIBLIOGRAPHY

Kock, T. *Comicorum Atticorum Fragmenta*. Vol. 1. Leipzig: Teubner, 1880.

———. *Comicorum Atticorum Fragmenta*. Vol. 2. Leipzig: Teubner, 1884.

Sommerstein, A. H. *The Comedies of Aristophanes*. Vol. 2, *Knights*. Warminster, U.K.: Aris & Phillips, 1981, 150.

PRASIAE

A town in southern Greece. The Athenians attacked the town in 430 B.C.E. and planned to attack it again in the year 414. [ANCIENT SOURCES: Aristophanes, *Peace* 242; Thucydides, 2.56.6]

BIBLIOGRAPHY

Sommerstein, A. H. *The Comedies of Aristophanes*. Vol. 5, *Peace*. Warminster, U.K.: Aris & Philips, 1985, 144.

PRAXAGORA

The heroine of ARISTOPHANES' *ECCLESIAZUSAE*, Praxagora ("active in the marketplace") is a fictional Athenian woman who is similar to LYSISTRATA in Aristophanes' play of the same name. As does Lysistrata, Praxagora arranges for the women to take over the local government. Unlike Lysistrata, though, who aims to put an end to warfare between ATHENS and SPARTA, Praxagora is interested in social reform of Athens only, and the women Praxagora organizes are Athenians. Praxagora establishes a social system in which the people will share everything equally—food, property, sexual partners, and even children. Additionally, whereas the sex strike that Lysistrata organizes will end when peace is achieved, Praxagora's reforms will be permanent. Rothwell compares Praxagora with PERICLES' mistress, ASPASIA, and finds Praxagora a skilled speaker who is also skilled in the ways of love. This portrait also contrasts with Lysistrata, who is rather serious and chaste (appropriately so if she was modeled on Lysimache, a priestess of ATHENA).

BIBLIOGRAPHY

Foley, H. P. "The Female Intruder Reconsidered: Women in Aristophanes, *Lysistrata* and *Ecclesiazusae*," *Classical Philology* 77 (1982): 1–21.

Rothwell, Kenneth S. *Politics and Persuasion in Aristophanes' Ecclesiazusae*. Leiden: Brill, 1990, 77–101.

Taaffe, Lauren K. "The Illusion of Gender Disguise in Aristophanes' *Ecclesiazusae*," *Helios* 18 (1991): 91–112.

Ussher, R. G. *Aristophanes: Ecclesiazusae*. Oxford: Clarendon Press, 1973.

PREPIS

Perhaps the son of Eupherus, in 421 a Prepis may have served as secretary of the Athenian council during the year's first PRYTANY. [ANCIENT SOURCES: Aristophanes, *Acharnians* 843]

BIBLIOGRAPHY

Sommerstein, A. *The Comedies of Aristophanes*. Vol. 1, *Acharnians*. Warminster, U.K.: Aris & Phillips, 1980, 198.

PRIAM

The son of LAOMEDON and Strymo (or Leucippe or Placia), Priam was the husband of HECABE and the king of TROY during the famous Trojan War. Priam had 50 sons, 19 by Hecabe. The most famous of Priam's sons were PARIS, HECTOR, and POLYDORUS. Priam and Hecabe also had many daughters, the best known of whom are CASSANDRA and POLYXENA. When Priam was young, HERACLES conquered Troy and put most of the males to death. For the sake of Priam's sister, Hesione, however, Heracles spared Priam's life. In the course of the Trojan War, almost all of Priam's sons were killed. In the final year of the war, ACHILLES killed Hector, defiled his body, and threatened to leave the corpse to be eaten by dogs and birds. Priam, however, managed to make his way to the Greek camp and ransom Hector's body. After Hector's death, when Priam purified the Amazon Penthesileia of murdering one of her fellow AMAZONS, Penthesileia agreed to fight for the Trojans. She, too, was killed by Achilles. During the fall of Troy, Priam himself was killed, cut down by Achilles' son, Neoptolemus, while he was clinging to an altar and begging for his life. Priam would have appeared as a character in many Greek dramas but is seldom seen in the extant plays. SOPHOCLES wrote a *Priam*; only six words survive from the play (fragments 528a–32 Radt). The Greek tragedian Philocles also wrote a *Priam*, of which only the title survives (fragment 1 Snell). This play was the second in a TETRALOGY that included *Penelope, Tereus,* and *Philoctetes* (only the titles survive). [ANCIENT SOURCES: Aristophanes, *Birds* 512; Euripides, *Hecabe, Trojan Women;* Homer, *Iliad;* Plautus, *Bacchides* 926–78; Seneca, *Trojan Women;* Vergil, *Aeneid* 2]

BIBLIOGRAPHY
Kiso, A. *The Lost Sophocles*. New York: Vantage Press, 1984.
Lloyd-Jones, H. *Sophocles: Fragments*. Cambridge, Mass.: Harvard University Press, 1996.
Radt, S. *Tragicorum Graecorum Fragmenta*. Vol. 4. Göttingen, Ger.: Vandenhoeck & Ruprecht, 1977.
Snell, B. *Tragicorum Graecorum Fragmenta*. Vol. 1. Göttingen, Ger.: Vandenhoeck & Ruprecht, 1971.
Sutton, D. F. *The Lost Sophocles*. Lanham, Md.: University Press of America, 1984.

PRINIDES   A fictional character from ACHARNAE. His name means "son of holm oak." [ANCIENT SOURCES: Aristophanes, *Acharnians* 612]

BIBLIOGRAPHY
Sommerstein, A. *The Comedies of Aristophanes*. Vol. 1, *Acharnians*. Warminster, U.K.: Aris & Phillips, 1980, 187.

PROAGON   In the *proagon* (precontest), the playwrights made a public appearance to give a little information about their upcoming production. Aristophanes wrote a play entitled *Proagon* (461–70 Kock), of which little is known.

BIBLIOGRAPHY
Csapo, E., and W. J. Slater. *The Context of Ancient Drama*. Ann Arbor: University of Michigan Press, 1995, 432.
Kock, T. *Comicorum Atticorum Fragmenta*. Vol. 1. Leipzig: Teubner, 1880.

PROCNE   See TEREUS.

PROCRIS   The daughter of ERECHTHEUS, Procris was an Athenian princess who married CEPHALUS. According to one story about Procris, Cephalus left home for a lengthy period and then returned in disguise to test whether Procris would be faithful to him. As Procris was on the point of giving in to the temptation, Cephalus revealed his true identity. Another story says that when Cephalus went hunting, he was accustomed to rest in the forest and call upon Aura ("a breeze") or Nephele ("a cloud") to refresh him. Procris, who had heard rumors of Cephalus' having an affair, followed her husband on one of his hunts. Cephalus, while taking his accustomed rest, heard rustling near him. Cephalus threw his spear at the noise and fatally wounded Procris.

Sophocles wrote a *Procris,* but the three words that survive tell us nothing about the play's plot (fragment 533 Radt). The Greek comic poet Eubulus also wrote a *Procris* (fragments 90–92 Kock); and one of the fragments (90) describes how Procris' dog is to be treated in a royal fashion. [ANCIENT SOURCES: Apollodorus, *Library* 1.9.4, 2.4.7, 3.15.2; Athenaeus, 12.553b; Hyginus, *Fables* 189; Ovid, *Metamorphoses* 7.661–865; Pausanias, 1.37.4]

BIBLIOGRAPHY
Kiso, A. *The Lost Sophocles*. New York: Vantage Press, 1984.
Kock, T. *Comicorum Atticorum Fragmenta*. Vol. 2. Leipzig: Teubner, 1884.
Lloyd-Jones, H. *Sophocles: Fragments*. Cambridge, Mass.: Harvard University Press, 1996.
Radt, S. *Tragicorum Graecorum Fragmenta*. Vol. 4. Göttingen, Ger.: Vandenhoeck & Ruprecht, 1977.
Sutton, D. F. *The Lost Sophocles*. Lanham, Md.: University Press of America, 1984.

PROCRUSTES   Also called Damastes or Polypemon, Procrustes, son of POSEIDON, was an evil man who lived near the town of ELEUSIS. Procrustes had a lodge for travelers, whose bed or beds were unusual: If a traveler's limbs were too long for the bed, Procrustes would cut the traveler down to the bed's size. If the traveler were not tall enough for the bed, Procrustes would hammer them out to make them fit. During THESEUS' journey from TROEZEN to ATHENS, Theseus encountered Procrustes and made the villain "lie in his own bed": Theseus killed Procrustes in the same way he had killed others. [ANCIENT SOURCES: Apollodorus, *Epitome* 1.4; Aristophanes, *Ecclesiazusae* 1021; Bacchylides, *Dithyramb* 4.27–30; Hyginus, *Fables* 38; Pausanias, 1.38.5; Plutarch, *Theseus* 11.1; Seneca, *Hippolytus* 1170, *Thyestes* 1050]

PRODICUS   From the island of Ceos, Prodicus was best known for his interest in the proper use of words and, according to Sommerstein, "especially of distinguishing the meanings of near-synonyms." Prodicus' writings also deal with "ethics, the origin of religion, and apparently . . . human physiology." Prodicus also may have written about the universe's origins. [ANCIENT SOURCES: Aristophanes, *Birds* 692, *Clouds* 361, fragment 490.2 Kock; Plato, *Protagoras*]

BIBLIOGRAPHY
Kock, T. *Comicorum Atticorum Fragmenta.* Vol. 1. Leipzig: Teubner, 1880.
Sommerstein, A. H. *The Comedies of Aristophanes.* Vol. 3, *Clouds.* Warminster, U.K.: Aris & Phillips, 1982, 180.

PROHEDRIA This Greek word can refer either to front seats in the theater or to the privilege of sitting in these seats. [ANCIENT SOURCES: Aristophanes, *Knights* 575, 702, *Thesmophoriazusae* 834; Herodotus, 1.54, 9.73]

PROLOGUE According to ARISTOTLE (*Poetics* 1452b), the prologue is the part of the drama that takes place before the CHORUS' entrance (PARODOS). In some cases, however, the chorus is onstage from the play's outset, so these plays do not have a prologue in the Aristotelean sense of the word (compare AESCHYLUS' *PERSIANS,* and *SUPPLIANT WOMEN* and EURIPIDES' *RHESUS*). In TRAGEDY, especially Euripidean tragedy, prologues usually begin with a monologue in which a character provides a brief introduction to the characters and to events that have preceded the action of the play. This monologue may also point to themes that will emerge in the drama. Euripides' opening monologues are typically followed by dialogue between two characters about the emerging conflict in the play. In tragedy, a mortal usually delivers the opening speech, and sometimes a divinity leads off the play. Divinities who deliver prologues rarely return to the stage later (see DIONYSUS in EURIPIDES' *BACCHAE* for an exception).

In Aristophanic COMEDY, the prologues are not expository, as in Euripidean tragedy. Aristophanes begins most of his plays with a conversation between two characters and the crisis of the play emerges in a more natural way. Comedy after the time of Aristophanes, however, tended to revert to the Euripidean model. The prologues of both MENANDER and PLAUTUS are usually expository in nature, and occasionally a divinity (PAN in *DYSCOLUS;* Euclio's household divinity in *POT OF GOLD*) or the personification of some abstract concept (Misapprehension in Menander's *GIRL WITH THE SHAVEN HEAD*) makes the speech. In some cases, a play contains a delayed expository prologue, as in Plautus' *CASKET COMEDY.* The first 119 lines of the play involve a conversation between two prostitutes, but after their exit one prostitute's mother delivers a delayed prologue of some two dozen lines, then leaves stage before explaining the situation fully. Accordingly, the god Auxilium appears and continues the prologue for another 50 lines.

TERENCE'S prologues are the most unusual and in some ways the most interesting in the extant classical dramas. In each of the six Terentian plays, the prologue does not introduce the audience to the plot of the play, but rather focuses on the difficulties that the playwright has had with critics or the staging of his play. Thus, Terence's prologues are more like the PARABASIS in some of Aristophanes' comedies than a prologue. Goldberg has shown that Terence's prologues were modeled on Roman oratorical practice of the time. After Terence's prologues, the play begins in a manner more reminiscent of most of Aristophanes' plays, as the background to the plot is explained through the conversation of two characters.

BIBLIOGRAPHY
Goldberg, S. M. "The Style and Function of Menander's *Dyskolos Prologue,*" *Symbolae Osloenses* 53 (1978): 57–68.
———. "Terence, Cato, and the Rhetorical Prologue," *Classical Philology* 78 (1983): 198–211.
Hamilton, R. "Prologue Prophecy and Plot in Four Plays of Euripides," *American Journal of Philology* 99 (1978): 277–302.

PROMETHEUS The son of Iapetus and Clymene (or THEMIS), Prometheus was famous for stealing fire from the gods and giving it to mortals. For this crime, ZEUS had Prometheus bound to a mountain and sent an eagle to peck continually at his liver (which regrew every day). Eventually, Prometheus was freed of his bonds (and the eagle) by HERACLES.

He appears as a character in two surviving plays, AESCHYLUS' *PROMETHEUS BOUND* and ARISTOPHANES' *BIRDS.* In Aristophanes' *Birds,* Prometheus appears briefly to inform PEISETAERUS that Zeus is in danger of being overthrown. *Prometheus Bound* deals with Prometheus' punishment for giving fire to human beings. Despite this, Prometheus is confident that Zeus will someday need his help, because he knows how Zeus will eventually be overthrown and that he will eventually be freed from his punishment.

In addition to *Prometheus Bound,* Prometheus' name appears in three other plays attributed to Aeschylus: *Prometheus Unbound* (fragments 190–204 Radt), *Prometheus the Fire Bearer* (fragment 208 Radt), and *Prometheus the Fire Kindler* (fragments 204a–07 Radt). The last of these plays may have been satyric and have completed the TETRALOGY of 472 B.C.E., preceded by *Phineus,* PERSIANS, and *Glaucus Pontios. Prometheus the Fire Kindler* dealt with Prometheus' theft of fire, by which the satyrs would have been excited and amazed. Examination of the fragments of *Prometheus Unbound* reveals a chorus of TITANS, freed by Zeus from the underworld. As in *Prometheus Bound,* the chorus of *Prometheus Unbound* walk by and talk with Prometheus, who is still bound and tortured during the first part of the play. Also as in *Prometheus Bound,* in *Unbound* Prometheus describes he sufferings and the benefits he has conferred on humankind. Eventually, Heracles, during his quest for the apples of the HESPERIDES, appears. Presumably in exchange for information about his quest, Heracles shoots the eagle that torments Prometheus and releases him from his chains. The subject matter of *Prometheus the Fire-Bearer* is uncertain; Lloyd-Jones thinks that it may have preceded Aeschylus' *Prometheus Bound.*

Among Roman authors, ACCIUS wrote a *Prometheus,* from which two brief fragments survive (606–8 Warmington). Lines 606–7 refer to the eagle that pecked away at the hero. Line 608 appears to refer to the wintry weather that plagued the region where Prometheus was bound. [ANCIENT SOURCES: Apollodorus, *Library* 1.2.3, 1.3.6, 1.7.1–2, 2.5.4, 2.5.11, 3.13.5; Aristophanes, *Birds* 1494; Hesiod, *Theogony* 507–616, *Works and Days* 47–105; Hyginus, *Fables* 54, 144, *Poetica Astronomica* 2.6, 2.15, 2.42; Pausanias, 1.30.2, 2.19.5, 2.19.5]

BIBLIOGRAPHY

Radt, S. *Tragicorum Graecorum Fragmenta.* Vol. 3. Göttingen, Ger.: Vandenhoeck & Ruprecht, 1985.

Smyth, H. and Lloyd-Jones, H. *Aeschylus.* Vol. 2. 1926. Reprint, Cambridge, Mass.: Harvard University Press, 1971.

Warmington, E. H. *Remains of Old Latin: Livius Andronicus, Naevius, Pacuvius, and Accius.* Vol. 2. Cambridge, Mass.: Harvard University Press, 1936.

***PROMETHEUS BOUND* AESCHYLUS? (DATE UNCERTAIN)** West has argued that the play was staged between 445 and 435 B.C.E. on the basis of staging techniques and the configuration of the Theater of Dionysus in ATHENS that would have been required to perform the play. The play is attributed to AESCHYLUS, but many modern scholars doubt this, and West dates the play to a time after Aeschylus' death. The play's setting is a peak of the CAUCASUS Mountains. The CHORUS are OCEANUS' daughters. The play opens with the entrance of Might, Violence, and HEPHAESTUS, who have PROMETHEUS with them. Might reveals that the task Zeus has given to his trio is to bind Prometheus to a mountain peak because Prometheus has stolen fire and given it to humans. Hephaestus, however, is reluctant because he sympathizes with Prometheus as a fellow divinity. Nevertheless, Hephaestus knows that disobedience to Zeus is dangerous. Might and Hephaestus continue to argue about Prometheus as they bind him to the rock. Might believes that Prometheus is getting what he deserves, whereas Hephaestus continues to express pity for Prometheus.

After Prometheus is bound, the trio of divinities leave. Prometheus then laments his fate but recognizes that he must endure. He states that his punishment results from his helping humans. Prometheus' speech is cut short by the arrival of Oceanus' daughters, who express sorrow and sympathy for Prometheus. In the course of their encounter, Prometheus reveals to these immortal women that he has information about how Zeus will lose his kingdom. Prometheus declares that he will not reveal this information until Zeus sets him free. Oceanus' daughters worry that Prometheus' speech is too arrogant, but Prometheus predicts that one day Zeus will relent. Oceanus' daughters then ask Prometheus to explain how his conflict with Zeus occurred.

Prometheus explains that when the gods argued about whether Cronus or Zeus should rule, Prometheus advised those who supported Cronus to use cunning to defeat Zeus. When this advice was rejected, Prometheus, on the advice of THEMIS, joined Zeus' cause and helped him defeat Cronus and his supporters. After Zeus rose to power, he gave mortals no privilege or power and intended to destroy them. Prometheus helped mortals and thus was punished by Zeus. The chorus sympathize with Prometheus but urge him to recognize his mistake of opposing Zeus.

Next, the father of the chorus, Oceanus, enters and asks Prometheus how he can help him. Prometheus urges Oceanus not to become involved in his affairs, lest Oceanus also experience Zeus' wrath. Oceanus urges Prometheus to behave with greater moderation, but Prometheus persists in his self-pity. Given Prometheus' attitude, Oceanus departs. After the god's exit, the chorus lament Prometheus' fate and compare his misfortune to that of ATLAS. After their song, Prometheus recalls all the benefits that he gave to human beings and hints to the chorus that even Zeus himself will not be able to escape what the FATES have in store for him. The chorus then hope that they never have conflict with Zeus and note that they have learned not to oppose Zeus through the punishment Prometheus suffers.

After the chorus' comments, IO, a woman whom HERA has transformed into a cow, enters in a frenzy. She has been wandering the Earth, driven mad by a gadfly that is possessed by the Furies of a deceased herdsman named ARGUS. Prometheus recalls that she was a young woman with whom Zeus fell in love and whom Zeus' wife, Hera, is now helping to torment. Prometheus tells Io about his sufferings and then agrees to tell her what awaits her. At the chorus' request, Io tells how an oracle directed her father to drive her from her home. After this, she was transformed into a cow and pursued by the multieyed herdsman Argus. After Argus was killed (by HERMES according to other sources), a gadfly tormented her and drove her throughout the world.

After Io's speech, Prometheus gives a lengthy description of the various dangerous lands through which Io will wander. Upon hearing this, Io declares that she would be better off dead. Prometheus, however, says Io's sufferings are nothing compared to his, which will only end when Zeus falls from power. Io is astonished to hear that Zeus will lose power and declares that the only way Zeus can avoid this is by releasing Prometheus from his punishment. Prometheus also notes that one of Io's descendants will bring about Prometheus' release. When Io and the chorus beg to know more, Prometheus explains that Io's wanderings will eventually lead her to Egypt, where her descendants will found a colony. Furthermore, there Zeus will restore Io to her human form and his touch will cause her to bring forth a child, EPAPHUS. Eventually, a descendant of Epaphus', HERACLES, will free Prometheus from his chains. After she hears this, Io's spasms of torment return and she departs.

Upon Io's departure, the chorus pray that they will never find themselves the object of Zeus' lust. Prometheus comments that Zeus' downfall will result from one of his sexual unions. The chorus warn Prometheus that Zeus might inflict an even worse punishment on him, but Prometheus remains defiant.

Next, Hermes, sent by Zeus, appears and demands that Prometheus reveal how Zeus will fall from power. Prometheus, however, refuses to divulge what he knows regardless of what Zeus does to him. Hermes states that Zeus will send his lightning to shatter the mountain and hide his body; furthermore, Zeus will send an eagle to tear at Prometheus' body and feed on his liver. Although the chorus urge Prometheus to repent, Prometheus declares that Zeus can do whatever he likes but he will never destroy him. Hermes warns the chorus to depart, since if they remain, they may be terrified by the thunder, but they assert their intention to remain with Prometheus. After Hermes exits, the play concludes with Prometheus noting the onset of thunder and lightning and calling on his mother to see the injustice that he suffers.

COMMENTARY

In addition to the issue of its authorship and date, *Prometheus Bound* is unusual for several reasons. First, Prometheus is the only central figure in extant drama who remains on stage from the beginning of the play until its conclusion. Next, the action is unusual in that the play's central character, Prometheus, remains immobile throughout the drama, chained to the mountain peak. This also raises a question about the staging of the play: Where was the "rock" to which Prometheus was bound, and how was this rock constructed? Some scholars believe that the ancient theater in Athens, situated on the slopes of the ACROPOLIS, had a rock formation that jutted into the side of the ORCHESTRA and that Prometheus was attached to this rock and was able to disappear behind this rock at the play's conclusion. Others believe that Prometheus was bound to the THYMELE, a structure in the center of the orchestra.

In addition to the unique challenges of staging this play, with the exception of Io, all of the play's characters are divinities. This fact calls attention to the contrast between gods and mortals that occurs in the play. The Greek divinities live forever, whereas the play describes mortals as beings who live for a day. Zeus wants to destroy mortals, whereas Prometheus has helped them. When Io enters, we witness how Zeus' sexual intrusion into the world of mortals has caused not only the disruption of her father's house, but also the transformation of her physical self and extreme mental anguish. Interestingly, one of Io's descendants, Heracles, the person who will free Prometheus from his torment, will be the product of another union between Zeus and a mortal woman. Thus, the child of a mortal woman will become the savior of Prometheus, who claims to be the savior of humankind in this play.

Although *Prometheus Bound* is filled with mythical divine characters, the play still speaks to those who live in the modern world, especially the corporate world. As does Prometheus, modern workers may often feel that they are subject to tyrannical employers who wield absolute power over their employees. Zeus has saddled Atlas with the weight of the heavens (349–52) and crushed TYPHON beneath Mount Aetna (353–74), and Io is like a sexually harassed employee who finds herself oppressed by her boss. Might and Hermes are the corporate "yes men," who carry out the company president's orders even if those orders mean hardship for a fellow employee. Hephaestus is the compassionate but spineless middle manager who follows the company president's orders. Prometheus is like a middle manager who is caught between those he manages and the company's president. Unlike Hephaestus, however, Prometheus rebels against the company president and is punished for his insubordination.

Juxtaposed with the tyrannical power of Zeus is the knowledge of Prometheus. As for his modern counterparts in the corporate world, Prometheus' success and failure can be connected to his knowledge. Prometheus boasts that everything that human beings know and every skill they possess is a result of knowledge that he

has passed on to them (505–6). For all of Prometheus' great knowledge, however, Might notes that Prometheus' knowledge is nothing compared to that of Zeus (62). Prometheus' knowledge caused him to be in conflict with Zeus that same knowledge will comfort others and lead to both his torment and his freedom. In the case of Io, when she enters she says she is unable to discover how to escape her sufferings (609). Though Prometheus tells Io that not knowing her future is better than knowing it (624), Io still craves Prometheus' knowledge; indeed, this knowledge gives Io some comfort as she begins to understand the nature of her sufferings and their limit.

Just as Io takes comfort in Prometheus' knowledge, Prometheus is confident that his knowledge will protect him because he knows how Zeus will be overthrown. When this happens, Prometheus declares, Zeus will learn what it means to change from ruler to servant (926–27). Unfortunately for Prometheus, Zeus is aware that he possesses this knowledge and threatens him with additional punishment if he does not reveal what he knows to Hermes. Even the chorus think that Prometheus would be wise to take Hermes' advice not to be so stubborn and argue that it is not wise to continue being in error (1038–39). Stubbornness, however, is a trait shared by Prometheus and Zeus (see 907), and at the play's conclusion Zeus' power and Prometheus' knowledge remain at odds, although the audience is led to expect that ultimately Prometheus' knowledge will lead Zeus to relent.

BIBLIOGRAPHY

Conacher, D. J. *Aeschylus' Prometheus Bound: A Literary Commentary.* Toronto: University of Toronto Press, 1980.

Davidson, John. "*Prometheus Vinctus* on the Athenian Stage," *Greece and Rome* 41 (1994): 33–40.

Griffith, Mark. *The Authenticity of Prometheus Bound.* Cambridge: Cambridge University Press, 1977.

Hubbard, T. K. "Recitative Anapests and the Authenticity of *Prometheus Bound*," *American Journal of Philology* 112 (1991): 439–60.

West M. L. "The Prometheus Trilogy," *Journal of Hellenic Studies* 99 (1979): 130–48.

PRONOMUS An Athenian who Aristophanes jokes had his beard stolen by AGYRRHIUS. Sommerstein conjectures that he may have been a "politician whose sudden disappearance from the public eye (through death or exile) had coincided with a marked increase in the length of Agyrrhius' beard, leading to the joking suggestion that Agyrrhius' beard really belonged to Pronomus." [ANCIENT SOURCES: Aristophanes, *Ecclesiazusae* 102]

BIBLIOGRAPHY

Sommerstein, A. H. *The Comedies of Aristophanes.* Vol. 10, *Ecclesiazusae.* Warminster, U.K.: Aris & Phillips, 1998, 148.

PROPHET   A prophet (also called a seer or diviner) is one who is able to foresee events that have not happened or reveal things that are hidden. The process or art of discovering the future or revealing such secrets is called divination. The ancient Greeks and Romans used various methods of divination, such as casting lots, intepreting dreams, and observing the behavior of birds, atmospheric phenomena (such as lightning or thunder), patterns in flame, or the entrails of animals (see TIRESIAS in SENECA's *OEDIPUS*).

Prophets are connected with many plays in classical TRAGEDY. A female prophet named THEONOE appears as a character in EURIPIDES' *HELEN*. Calchas is referred to in plays about the Trojan War, such as AESCHYLUS' *Agamemnon* (see ORESTEIA), SOPHOCLES' *AJAX,* and EURIPIDES' *IPHIGENIA AT AULIS*. The prophecies of Calchas and the Trojan prophet HELENUS play an important role in Sophocles' *PHILOCTETES*. Regarding the battle of the Seven against THEBES, AMPHIARAUS participated both as a prophet and as a warrior. Usually, prophets are among the few people who escape unscathed from tragedy, but in the case of Amphiaraus his foreknowledge of his army's defeat did not allow him to save his own life and he died in battle (see Aeschylus, *SEVEN AGAINST THEBES*; Euripides, *PHOENICIAN WOMEN*). The most famous prophet of all, Tiresias, appears as a character in several surviving dramas: Sophocles' *ANTIGONE* and *OEDIPUS TYRANNOS,* Euripides' *PHOENICIAN WOMEN* and *BACCHAE,* and SENECA's *OEDIPUS*. In the Greek plays, he is almost always accused of making his forecasts for some financial gain and his advice is often rejected, but his predictions ultimately are fulfilled. Because prophets in actual society were often thought to be corrupt and

self-serving individuals, they are usually treated in a harsh way in ARISTOPHANES' plays (see especially *PEACE* and *BIRDS*).

PROPYLAEA   In ATHENS the Propylaea (gateway), was the western entrance to the ACROPOLIS. In ARISTOPHANES' *LYSISTRATA*, the Propylaea must be imagined as the backdrop for much of the play. [ANCIENT SOURCES: Aristophanes, *Knights* 1326, *Lysistrata* 265]

PROSERPINA   See PERSEPHONE.

PROSKENION   Called the *proscaenium* in Latin, the *proskenion* is the raised platform in front of the stage building (see SKENE). The roof of the *proskenion* is the STAGE. [ANCIENT SOURCES: Vitruvius, *On Architecture* 5.7.1]

PROSTITUTE (Greek: *HETAIRA*; Latin: *MERETRIX, PUELLA*)   Prostitutes (also called courtesans) are stock characters in New Comedy (see COMEDY). Music girls, who also appear in New Comedy, are essentially prostitutes who have musical skills. In the 26 complete plays of PLAUTUS and TERENCE, some 20 prostitutes are listed in the cast. Prostitutes appear in about half of both authors' plays. In four of Plautus' plays, two prostitutes appear (*BACCHIDES, BRAGGART WARRIOR, CASKET COMEDY, CARTHAGINIAN, ROPE*). In some comedies (e.g., Terence's *BROTHERS*), prostitutes do not appear onstage but remain behind the scenes. Prostitutes are of slave status and usually the property of a slave trader or PIMP. Some prostitutes, however, seem to operate independently of a pimp, such as Erotium in Plautus' *MENAECHMI*. Although the woman may be the property of a pimp, in a few plays she has not yet been sold to anyone and therefore her virginity remains intact (e.g., Planesium in *CURCULIO*; Adelphasium and Anterastilis in *Carthaginian*).

Many times in comedy, a young freeborn man (see ADULESCENS) is in love with a prostitute. Because she is a slave, he cannot marry her, but often she is discovered to be freeborn, and as a result a marriage can occur. In some cases, however, the prostitute is simply an object of affection and the male lover has no intention of marrying her. As Duckworth notes, prostitutes in Roman comedy are usually either mercenary (for example, the Bacchis sisters, Phronesium in *TRUCULEN-TUS,* or Thais in Terence's *SELF-TORMENTOR*) or devoted to their male suitors (for example, Pasicompsa in Plautus' *MERCHANT*). In *Braggart Warrior,* the prostitute Acroteleutium works to trick the soldier so that Pleusicles can run away with another prostitute, Philocomasium. Sometimes a prostitute in comedy has "a heart of gold," the so-called *bona meretrix* (the noble prostitute). Terence's Thais (*EUNUCH*) and Bacchis (*MOTHER-IN-LAW*) are of this sort. Duckworth observes that some of Plautus' prostitutes are *bonae meretrices* in the passive sense (they are eager to please their lover); however, Terence's Thais and Bacchis are active in their kindness. Bacchis succeeds in effecting the reconciliation of Pamphilus and his wife.

BIBLIOGRAPHY
Duckworth, G. E. *The Nature of Roman Comedy.* Princeton, N.J.: Princeton University Press, 1952, 258–61.

Edwards, C. "Unspeakable Professions: Public Performance and Prostitution in Ancient Rome." In *Roman Sexualities.* Edited by J. P. Hallett and M. B. Skinner. Princeton, N.J.: Princeton University Press, 1997, 66–95.

Fantham, E. "Sex, Status, and Survival in Hellenistic Athens: A Study of Women in New Comedy," *Phoenix* 29 (1975): 44–74.

Konstan, D. "Between Courtesan and Wife: Menander's *Perikeiromene,*" *Phoenix* 41 (1987): 122–39.

Wiles, David. "Marriage and Prostitution in Classical New Comedy." In *Themes in Drama.* Vol. 11. *Women in Theatre.* Edited by J. Redmond. Cambridge: Cambridge University Press, 1989, 31–48.

PROTAGONIST   His characterization derived from the Greek words *protos* (first) and *agonistes* (fighter, defender), the protagonist plays the leading role in a drama (e.g., OEDIPUS in SOPHOCLES' *OEDIPUS TYRANNOS;* LYSISTRATA in ARISTOPHANES' *LYSISTRATA*). The term *protagonist* can also refer to the first actor who converses with the CHORUS or the top-rated actor in an acting troupe. Csapo and Slater note that "only the protagonists could form contracts with the archon, receive payment from the state, or win the actor's prize." It is also said that the audience could usually identify a play's protagonist because he entered from the central door in the SKENE. This is not a strict rule,

however, and protagonists do make their initial entrance into the ORCHESTRA from places other than the central door (e.g., ORESTES in AESCHYLUS' *Libation Bearers* (see *ORESTEIA*)).

BIBLIOGRAPHY
Csapo, E., and W. J. Slater. *The Context of Ancient Drama.* Ann Arbor: University of Michigan Press, 1995, 223.

PROTESILAUS   Regarding the Trojan War, an ORACLE had stated that the first Greek to set foot on Trojan soil would die. Unfortunately, Protesilaus, the son of Iphiclus and Diomedeia, violated that prophecy and was killed by HECTOR. After Protesilaus' death, his wife, LAODAMEIA, missed him so much that she had a statue made of him. She would place the statue in her bed and caress it. EURIPIDES wrote a TRAGEDY entitled *Protesilaus* (fragments 647–57 Nauck), which was probably staged before 428 B.C.E. and probably dealt with Laodameia's grief after Protesilaus' death. Harmodius staged a satyric *Protesilaus,* of which only the title survives. Heliodorus (fragment 474 Lloyd-Jones) also wrote a *Protesilaus,* whose single extant line gives no indication of the plot. The comic poet Anaxandrides also wrote a *Protesilaus,* from which two fragments (40–41 Kock) totaling 73 lines survive. Brief fragment 40 is about perfume; in the lengthy fragment 41 Anaxandrides makes fun of the symposium at the wedding of a person named Iphicrates and lists the food served at the banquet. Among Roman authors, PACUVIUS wrote a *Protesilaus,* of which only the title survives. [ANCIENT SOURCES: Apollodorus, *Epitome* 3.30; Athenaeus, 553d–e; Hyginus, *Fables* 103–4; Ovid, *Heroides* 13]

BIBLIOGRAPHY
Kock, T. *Comicorum Atticorum Fragmenta.* Vol. 2. Leipzig: Teubner, 1884.

Lloyd-Jones, H. and Parsons, P. *Supplementum Hellenisticum.* Berlin: De Gruyter, 1983.

Nauck, A. *Tragicorum Graecorum Fragmenta.* 1889. Reprint, Hildesheim, Ger.: Olms, 1964.

Webster, T. B. L. *The Tragedies of Euripides.* London: Methuen, 1967.

PROTEUS (1)   Proteus was a shape-shifting sea divinity whom MENELAUS encountered on his return from TROY. Menelaus wrestled Proteus to make him tell him which divinity was preventing him from reaching his native land. Proteus told Menelaus that he must travel to Egypt and sacrifice to all the gods in order to return home. Other sources make Proteus an Egyptian king (see PROTEUS (2)). AESCHYLUS wrote a *Proteus*, which was the SATYR PLAY for the *ORESTEIA* trilogy of 458 B.C.E. The fewer than 20 words that survive indicate nothing about the plot. [ANCIENT SOURCES: Homer, *Odyssey* 4]

BIBLIOGRAPHY
Smyth, H. and H. Lloyd-Jones. *Aeschylus.* Vol. 2. 1926. Reprint, Cambridge, Mass.: Harvard University Press, 1971.

PROTEUS (2)   Proteus was an Egyptian king, the father of Theoclymenus. In EURIPIDES' *HELEN,* HELEN takes refuge at the tomb of Proteus when Theoclymenus tries to force her to marry him.

PROXENIDES   A person known for his boasting and physical weakness. [ANCIENT SOURCES: Aristophanes, *Birds* 1126, *Wasps* 325; Telecleides, fragment 18]

BIBLIOGRAPHY
Sommerstein, A. H. *The Comedies of Aristophanes.* Vol. 4, *Wasps.* Warminster, U.K.: Aris & Phillips, 1983, 228.

PRYTANAEUM   A building in ATHENS that served as a sort of town hall. The Prytanaeum takes its name "from the presiding prytaneis of Council and Assembly" (Dover). Certain distinguished persons, such as athletes who had won victories at the ancient Olympic Games, were honored with the privilege of having free meals at the Prytanaeum. [ANCIENT SOURCES: Aristophanes, *Acharnians* 125, *Frogs* 764, *Knights* 167]

BIBLIOGRAPHY
Dover, Kenneth. *Aristophanes: Frogs.* Oxford: Clarendon Press, 1993, 287.

PRYTANY   The people of Athens divided their legislative calendar into 10 prytanies of 36 days (the first four prytanies of the year) or 35 days (the last six prytanies of the year). During each prytany, one of the 10 Athenian tribes would supply 50 men to preside over governmental business. The Greek comic poet Telecleides wrote a *Prytaneis,* from which several brief fragments survive (22–30 Kock). Nothing of this play's plot is known.

BIBLIOGRAPHY
Kock, T. *Comicorum Atticorum Fragmenta.* Vol. 1. Leipzig: Teubner, 1880.

PSEUDOLUS PLAUTUS (191 B.C.E.)   The play was performed at the Megalensian Games in the city praetorship of Marcus Junius. The author of the Greek original for this play is not known. The action occurs in Athens before the houses of Simo, an elderly gentleman, and the PIMP Ballio. The house of Simo's friend, Callipho, may also be visible.

As the play opens, Simo's son, Calidorus, tells the SLAVE, Pseudolus ("liar"), that Ballio has sold Phoenicium, the woman he loves, to a Macedonian soldier, and that the transaction will be completed the next day. Calidorus begs Pseudolus for help. The slave agrees to assist his young master and promises to get 20 MINAE so that he, not the soldier, can buy her. Before the plan can progress further, the pimp, Ballio, emerges from his house with a group of slaves. Pseudolus and Calidorus eavesdrop as Ballio abuses the slaves physically and verbally. After the slaves depart for the FORUM, Ballio's prostitutes appear and the pimp tells them that unless they earn a lot of money for him he will prostitute them to the general populace. As Ballio continues to threaten the women, Calidorus becomes angry and more worried about losing his beloved. When Ballio begins to move off toward the forum, Pseudolus greets him. Pseudolus tells Ballio that Calidorus plans to pay him the money for the woman he loves in a few day, but does not have the money at that moment. Ballio has no pity on Calidorus despite Pseudolus' promises that they will obtain the money. Ballio continues to show no mercy to Calidorus and notes that he has sold Phoenicium to the Macedonian soldier. When Calidorus complains that Ballio had agreed to sell her to him, Ballio admits this but implies that the soldier's payment supercscedes any promise that he made to Calidorus. Finally, Calidorus persuades Ballio to agree to sell Phoenicium to him if he can acquire the money.

After Ballio departs for the forum, Pseudolus expresses his determination to defeat the pimp and tells Calidorus they need some clever, tricky fellow to help them. Pseudolus tells Calidorus to find such a person. After Calidorus' departure, Callipho and Simo, Calidorus' father, arrive. Pseudolus decides that he will trick Simo to obtain the necessary money, but first he eavesdrops on the two gentlemen's conversation. Simo laments that the whole city knows that Calidorus is trying to raise money to buy Phoenicium. Callipho points out, however, that many young men have done the same sort of thing. Simo, however, thinks that fathers should set a good example for their sons. Soon, Simo sees Pseudolus (who he knows is helping Calidorus). Pseudolus, knowing the old men are wary of him, approaches them. Simo confronts Pseudolus with Calidorus' situation and declares that he will not provide any money to finance his son's love affair, but Pseudolus boldly declares that Simo will give him the money. Pseudolus goes on to explain that he will trick Ballio to hand over Phoenicium and says he will need Callipho's help in his scheme. The act ends with Simo's leaving for the forum, Callipho's returning to his house, and Pseudolus' returning to Simo's house to collect his wits.

The second act opens with the appearance of Pseudolus, who announces that everything has been prepared for his assault on Ballio. Unexpectedly, however, Harpax ("snatcher"), the servant of the soldier, Polymachaeroplagides, arrives in search of Ballio's house. Pseudolus, eavesdropping on Harpax's comments, decides to change his strategy. Before Harpax can knock on Ballio's door, Pseudolus emerges from his hiding place; pretends to be Ballio's slave, Surus; and asks Harpax whether he has arrived to pay the balance of the money he owes for Phoenicium. Harpax is surprised that Pseudolus knows about his business but does not want to hand over the money he has when Pseudolus asks for it. Harpax says he will only give the money to Ballio himself and tells Pseudolus to give him a letter and token from the soldier.

After Harpax exits to rest at a local inn, Pseudolus rejoices that he has had the good fortune to encounter him and that his scheme will be successful. Pseudolus is soon joined by Calidorus and his friend, Charinus,

whom Calidorus has enlisted to help them trick Ballio. Pseudolus arranges for Charinus to dress as one of his father's slaves, Simia. Pseudolus also arranges to borrow from Charinus enough money to pay off Ballio. Pseudolus tells Charinus to dress up Simia, give him the letter and token from the soldier, and tell him to go to Ballio's house to make the final payment on Phoenicium, who will then be taken to Calidorus. After describing what he wants done, Pseudolus exits for the forum and the banker, Aeschinus; there he will meet Simia and go over the scheme.

The third act opens with the appearance of an unnamed slave boy from Ballio's house. The slave complains about the difficulties of working for the pimp and worries that he does not yet have a present for the pimp's birthday (that same day). As the slave reenters Ballio's house, Ballio, accompanied by a cook and the cook's helpers, arrives. After Ballio complains about the cook he has hired, the cook defends himself and argues that people will not hire him because he is the best and is therefore quite expensive. The cook even claims that those who eat his food can live for 200 years. After some further petty arguing between the cook and Ballio, the group finally exits into the pimp's house to prepare dinner. Before Ballio enters, however, he notes that Simo has recently told him to be on guard against the tricks of Pseudolus.

In the fourth act, Pseudolus and Simia, disguised as Harpax, enter. As the two slaves discuss the final details of Pseudolus' scheme, Ballio emerges from his house. At this, Simia approaches him and gives him the letter from the soldier. After Ballio reads the letter, which instructs him to accept the money from Harpax, Ballio and Simia enter the pimp's house. Pseudolus worries that the real Harpax will arrive, but eventually Simia and Phoenicium appear, and they set off with Pseudolus to find Calidorus. Next, Ballio emerges, declares his contentment now that Phoenicium is gone, and expresses his pleasure that Pseudolus has not tricked him. Ballio is soon joined by Simo, who arrives from the forum. Ballio tells Simo that his (Simo's) money is safe and says he will pay him 20 minae and give him Phoenicium if Pseudolus tricks him. When Simo agrees, Ballio announces that the soldier's slave has just taken the woman away.

Their conversation, however, is cut short by the arrival of the real Harpax. Ballio and Simo eavesdrop as Harpax complains that Syrus (Pseudolus earlier) did not go to the inn to get him when Ballio returned. Harpax also notes that he has money to give the pimp for a woman. Upon hearing this, the money-hungry Ballio emerges from his hiding place and approaches Harpax, who declares that he is ready to hand over the money from the soldier and take possession of Phoenicium. Ballio, however, thinks that Harpax has been sent by Pseudolus and after some interrogation confronts him with this change. An angry and confused Harpax denies that he knows Pseudolus and declares that earlier he gave the soldier's letter and token to Ballio's slave, Syrus. This information frightens Ballio, who (after questioning Harpax further) realizes that Pseudolus was pretending to be Syrus. Ballio wants Simo to hand over Pseudolus to him for punishment, but Simo refuses. Ballio and Harpax then exit for the forum to settle their business. Simo is left marveling at Pseudolus' trickery and says he will get the 20 minae that he promised Pseudolus.

In the play's final act, an intoxicated Pseudolus enters from a party with his master and Phoenicium. Soon, Simo enters and faces an assault of belches from Pseudolus, who also claims the money Simo promised. Simo begs Pseudolus not to make him pay the entire sum, but Pseudolus refuses. The play ends with Pseudolus' inviting Simo to the party from which he has just arrived.

COMMENTARY

Pseudolus is one of Plautus' most enjoyable plays, primarily because of its lively title character, who inspired the character of Pseudolus in the modern musical *A Funny Thing Happened on the Way to the Forum.* With its wily slave, destruction of an evil pimp, duped father, and young man who seeks money to buy his prostitute sweetheart, *Pseudolus* is a stereotypical Roman COMEDY. Duckworth labels *Pseudolus* a play of "guileful deception" and groups it with COMEDY OF ASSES, BACCHIDES, CASINA, MERCHANT, BRAGGART WARRIOR, HAUNTED HOUSE, and PERSIAN.

Despite its entertaining qualities, *Pseudolus* has some problems, including varying sums of money owed to

the pimp. Some critics have found fault with Callipho's failure to reappear in the play after line 560, despite his desire to continue watching Pseudolus' games (551–54). Harsh thought Plautus should have combined the roles of Callipho and Charinus. At 1,334 lines, *Pseudolus* is one of the longest Plautine plays; the first act, at more than 570 lines, testifies to the structural unwieldiness of the play. In the first act, Ballio spends almost 100 lines organizing his slaves and giving them orders (133–228). Although this emphasis contributes to the development of Ballio as a character, the audience already know that he is a pimp and therefore expect a specific type of behavior from him. Furthermore, these lines contribute little to the plot other than to inform the audience of Ballio's birthday and to introduce them to Phoenicium. Additionally, the entire third act, with its 100-line scene between Ballio and the cook, could have been omitted with virtually no damage to the plot.

Despite these shortcomings, the slave, Pseudolus, is one of the most delightful characters in ancient comedy and well illustrates Erich Segal's principle of reversal of social status in Roman comedy. In the course of Pseudolus' efforts to defeat the pimp, this slave becomes a wise man, a king, a poet, and a soldier. At lines 464–65, Simo compares Pseudolus to SOCRATES. A few lines later (480), Pseudolus tells Simo to regard an answer from him as if it were an answer from the ORACLE at DELPHI. The slave Pseudolus even achieves kingly status in the play. At line 458, Pseudolus stands before Simo and Callipho in a royal fashion (*basilicum*), and at line 532, Simo says Pseudolus will outdo King Agathocles if he accomplishes his aims. Pseudolus' elevation to kingly status is matched by the pimp, Ballio, who declares that he will have so much grain that the city will change his name to King Jason (not the JASON who sailed on the ARGO, but a tyrant in THESSALY).

At line 404, Pseudolus declares that he will turn himself into a poet in order to acquire the money his master needs. At line 388, Pseudolus acts as an onstage poet by refusing to recount material already mentioned in the play to Callipho because "plays are already long enough." Similarly, at line 720, when Charinus and Callipho are uninformed about the trickery that Pseudolus has carried out against the soldier, Pseudolus refuses to explain because the spectators already know about the trickery and he does not want them to have to sit through the explanation. At lines 562–73a, Pseudolus turns to the audience and tells them that he will carry out the tricks that he promised and directs them to listen to a flute player while he collects his thoughts.

The dominant image of Pseudolus, however, is that of a military leader, a characterization that he shares with several other Plautine slaves (e.g., Epidicus, Palaestrio in BRAGGART WARRIOR, Chrysalus in *Bacchides,* and Tranio in *Haunted House*). At line 447, Simo calls Pseudolus his son's leader *(dux),* thus making a free person subordinate to a slave. At lines 586 and 761, Pseudolus speaks of marshalling his legions. At line 384, Pseudolus transforms Ballio into a town to which he wants to lay siege. The meaning of the pimp's name (derived from the Greek verb *ballô*, which can be used in relation to hurling of weapons) is well suited to this military imagery, and at 585 Pseudolus declares that he will "ballistify" *(exballistabo)* Ballio. A few lines later, the house of Simo becomes "the old town" against which Pseudolus will lead his troops. Not only does Pseudolus plan to sack these two "towns," he also wants to plunder them. On several occasions, Pseudolus speaks of the plunder he will try to acquire (426, 588, 1029, 1138). At line 1198, Ballio describes Harpax as a military rival to Pseudolus as Ballio declares that Harpax ("snatcher") has reached the plunder before Pseudolus. Unfortunately for Ballio, Pseudolus became the "snatcher" before the arrival of the real snatcher and at line 1037, when Simia appears with Phoenicium, Pseudolus declares himself victor over those who have been guarding against him. Not surprisingly, Pseudolus is twice compared to the consummate Greek trickster-warrior, Ulysses (see ODYSSEUS; see also Chrysalus in *Bacchides* 946–58). At 1063–64, Simo compares Pseudolus' trickery to acquire the woman to Ulysses' theft of the Palladium (see also Chrysalus in *Bacchides* 958) during the Trojan War, and TROY becomes "Ballio's citadel" in Simo's words. Simo makes a similar comparison at 1244 as Pseudolus is again compared with Ulysses; this time the trick alluded to seems to be that of the wooden horse (see also Chrysalus in *Bacchides* 936–44). Interestingly and perhaps coincidentally, Ballio makes a

connection between himself and Venus (see APHRODITE), who favored the Trojan side in the war. Thus, in *Pseudolus,* we see the ever-changing slave defeat two towns, those of Ballio and Simo.

BIBLIOGRAPHY
Duckworth, G. *The Nature of Roman Comedy.* Princeton, N.J.: Princeton University Press, 1952, 160.
Goldberg, S. M. "Plautus on the Palatine," *Journal of Roman Studies* 88 (1998): 1–20.
Harsh, P. W.. *A Handbook of Classical Drama.* Stanford, Calif.: Stanford University Press, 1944, 365.
Lefevre, E. *Plautus' Pseudolus.* Tubingen, Ger.: G. Narr, 1997.
Lowe, J. C. B. "Pseudolus' 'Intrigue' against Simo," *Maia* 51, no. 1 (1999): 1–15.
Segal, E. *Roman Laughter: The Comedy of Plautus.* 2d ed. London: Oxford University Press, 1987, 99–136.
Sharrock, A. R. "The Art of Deceit: Pseudolus and the Nature of Reading," *Classical Quarterly* 46, no. 1 (1996): 152–74.
Wright, J. "The Transformation of Pseudolus," *Transactions of the American Philological Association* 105 (1975): 403–16.

PSOPHIS A town northeast of Olympia in southwestern Greece. Psophis was the setting for EURIPIDES' *Alcmeon at Psophis,* which survives only in fragments.

PTERELAS (PTERELAUS) A mythical king of the TELEBOANS (or Taphians). According to PLAUTUS' *AMPHITRUO,* AMPHITRYON and his Theban forces battled Pterelas' forces and Amphitryon killed Pterelas. Other sources say that POSEIDON had given Pterelas a lock of golden hair and that as long as Pterelas possessed it he would remain alive. At the arrival of Amphitryon, Pterelas' daughter, Comaetho, fell in love with the enemy commander, cut off her father's golden hair, and presented it to Amphitryon as a token of her love. Amphitryon, horrified by her killing her own father, put Comaetho to death. With Pterelas dead, his forces were no longer able to withstand Amphitryon's army and were defeated. [ANCIENT SOURCES: Apollodorus, 2.4.5–7; Plautus, *Amphitruo* 252ff.]

PULPITUM The Latin word (plural: *pulpita*) for the STAGE. The Greek equivalent is LOGEION. [ANCIENT SOURCES: Horace, *Epistles* 1.19.40, 2.1.174, *Ars Poetica* 215, 279; Suetonius, *Nero* 13]

PYLADES The son of STROPHIUS and Anaxibia, the sister of AGAMEMNON, Pylades is famous as the steadfast friend of Agamemnon's son, ORESTES. While Agamemnon was away during the Trojan War, his wife, CLYTEMNESTRA, took AEGISTHUS as a lover. Orestes, who posed a threat to Aegisthus, was sent (or smuggled away, according to some sources) to live with Strophius in the region of PHOCIS. Orestes and his cousin, Pylades, became inseparable, and when Orestes returned to his home to kill his mother, Pylades accompanied him. After Clytemnestra's death and during the FURIES' pursuit of Orestes, Pylades remained with Orestes. In EURIPIDES' ORESTES, when the people of ARGOS condemn Orestes to take his own life, Pylades declares that he will commit suicide as well. In *Orestes,* Pylades appears more bloodthirsty and desperate than in any of his other appearances in extant drama, as it is he who proposes that, instead of killing themselves, he, Orestes, and Electra try to kill HELEN. Failing that, Pylades suggests that they burn down the palace and kill themselves in the blaze. In Euripides' IPHIGENIA IN TAURIS, Pylades travels with Orestes to Tauris to help him steal the statue of ARTEMIS. When Orestes and Pylades first arrive in Tauris, Pylades even appears more brave than Orestes, who suggests that they leave before they are killed (102–3). Pylades, however, reminds him that they are not accustomed to avoiding danger and that they must be obedient to APOLLO's oracle. In this play, Pylades also expresses his willingness to die at Orestes' side. At some point after the death of Clytemnestra, Pylades married Orestes' sister, ELECTRA, by whom he had two children, Medon and Strophius. Although Pylades appears as a character in five extant plays, he speaks a total of 182 lines in these plays. In AESCHYLUS' *Libation Bearers* (see ORESTEIA), Pylades has only three lines (900–2), but with those three lines he convinces Orestes that he must be obedient to Apollo's oracle and kill his mother.

Other than in the plays of Aeschylus, SOPHOCLES, and Euripides, in Greek drama Pylades' name appears only in the title of a play by the Greek Timesitheus (*Orestes and Pylades*), from which no fragments survive. Among Roman authors, PACUVIUS wrote a *Dulorestes* (Orestes the slave) in which Orestes and Pylades are captured while plotting against Clytemnestra and Aegisthus. In Pacuvius' play, Pylades pretends to be Orestes so that his friend will not be killed (see 163–66 Warmington). In SENECA's *AGAMEMNON*, Pylades appears as a silent character. [ANCIENT SOURCES: Aeschylus, *Libation Bearers* (see ORESTEIA); Apollodorus, *Epitome* 6.24–28; Euripides, *Electra, Iphigenia in Tauris, Orestes;* Hyginus, *Fables* 119–20, 122; Pausanias, 2.16.7, 2.29.4; Seneca, *Agamemnon* 941; Sophocles, *Electra*]

BIBLIOGRAPHY
Snell, B. *Tragicorum Graecorum Fragmenta.* Vol. 1. Göttingen, Ger.: Vandenhoeck & Ruprecht, 1971.
Warmington, E. H. *Remains of Old Latin: Livius Andronicus, Naevius, Pacuvius, and Accius.* Vol. 2. Cambridge, Mass.: Harvard University Press, 1936.

PYLOS A town on the southwestern coast of Greece. In 425/424 B.C.E., the Athenians, under the command of DEMOSTHENES, captured the town and established a garrison there from which they could attack the Spartans. In mythology, Pylos is famous as the home of NESTOR. [ANCIENT SOURCES: Aristophanes, *Clouds* 185, *Knights* 55, 76, 355, 703, 846, 1058, 1167, *Lysistrata* 104, 1163, *Peace* 219, 665]

PYRILAMPES (CA. 480–420 B.C.E.) The son of Antiphon, Pyrilampes was the father of a certain Demos (by his first wife) and then another son, Antiphon (by his second wife). Pyrilampes' second wife, Perictione, had a child, PLATO, by a previous marriage, and so Pyrilampes was the stepfather of the famous philosopher. Pyrilampes was on friendly terms with PERICLES, served ATHENS as an ambassador, and in 424 B.C.E. may have fought (and been wounded) at the battle of Delium. Pyrilampes also gained notoriety for a collection of birds that included peacocks, which he received as a gift from the king of Persia while he was on a diplomatic mission there. [ANCIENT SOURCES: Aristophanes, *Wasps* 98; Athenaeus, 397c; Plato, *Charmides* 158a; Plutarch, *Pericles* 13.15, *On the Sign of Socrates* 581d]

BIBLIOGRAPHY
MacDowell, D. M. *Aristophanes: Wasps.* Oxford: Clarendon Press, 1971, 143–44.

Sommerstein, A. H. *The Comedies of Aristophanes*. Vol. 4, *Wasps*. Warminster, U.K.: Aris & Phillips, 1983, 160–61.

PYRRHA The daughter of Epimetheus and PANDORA, Pyrrha married her cousin, DEUCALION. After surviving a flood that destroyed the world, she and her husband helped repopulate the Earth by throwing stones behind their backs. These stones changed into human beings. Deucalion and Pyrrha had two sons, Amphictyon and Hellen, and a daughter, Protogenia. The Greek comic poets Diphilus (fragment 68 Kock) and Epicharmus (fragments 114–18 Kaibel) each wrote a play entitled *Pyrrha;* the surviving fragments are uninformative about their content. [ANCIENT SOURCES: Apollodorus, *Library* 1.7.2; Hyginus, *Fables* 153; Ovid, *Metamorphoses* 1.313–415; Seneca, *Trojan Women* 1038]

BIBLIOGRAPHY
Kaibel, G. *Comicorum Graecorum Fragmenta*. Vol. 1.1 [*Poetarum Graecorum Fragmenta*. Vol. 6.1]. Berlin: Weidmann, 1899.
Kock, T. *Comicorum Atticorum Fragmenta*. Vol. 2. Leipzig: Teubner, 1884.

PYRRHANDER An unknown Greek. Some modern scholars think Pyrrhander may have been another name for CLEON, but no proof of this exists. [ANCIENT SOURCES: Aristophanes, *Knights* 901]

BIBLIOGRAPHY
Sommerstein, A. H. *The Comedies of Aristophanes*. Vol. 2, *Knights*. Warminster, U.K.: Aris & Phillips, 1981, 192.

PYTHANGELUS A Greek tragic poet active apparently during the last decade of the fifth century B.C.E. ARISTOPHANES mentions his name in a mildly contemptuous way at *FROGS* 87, but nothing else is known of this playwright.

PYTHIA The title given to APOLLO's priestess at DELPHI. She appears as a character in AESCHYLUS' *Eumenides* (see *ORESTEIA*) and EURIPIDES' *ION*.

PYTHO Another name for the town of DELPHI or the ORACLE at Delphi.

PYTHON A giant serpent that the young APOLLO killed when he established himself as master of DELPHI. Tradition says that Apollo founded the Pythian Games to celebrate his defeat of the serpent. Some ancient sources said Pytho, a name sometimes given to Delphi, was derived from a Greek verb meaning "to rot" because Python's body was left to rot there. [ANCIENT SOURCES: Apollodorus, 1.4.1; Hyginus, *Fables* 140; Ovid, *Metamorphoses* 1.438, 460; Seneca, *Hercules Oetaeus* 94, *Medea* 700]

R

RED SEA In the fifth century B.C.E. the Greeks called the Indian Ocean by this name. [ANCIENT SOURCES: Aristophanes, *Birds* 145, *Knights* 1088; Herodotus, 1.202.4]

REVERSAL See *PERIPETEIA*.

RHADAMANTHYS The son of ZEUS and EUROPA and the brother of MINOS and Sarpedon, Rhadamanthys grew up on the island of CRETE, had a son named Gortys, and was a lawgiver for the people of the island. Later, he left Crete, went to BOEOTIA, and married ALCMENA after AMPHITRYON died. They lived in the town of Ocaleae. After Rhadamanthys' death, he became a judge in the UNDERWORLD because of the justice and discretion that he exhibited during his lifetime. EURIPIDES wrote a *Rhadamanthys* (fragments 658–60 Nauck), but the 12 lines that survive tell us nothing about the play's plot. Fragment 658 contains a reference to the island of EUBOEA, and Strabo recalls a line from HOMER's *Odyssey* (7.324) that mentions that Rhadamanthys went to talk to TITYUS on Euboea. [ANCIENT SOURCES: Apollodorus, *Library* 2.4.11, 3.1.1, 3.1.2; Pausanias, 8.53.4–5; Plato, *Laws* 948b–c; Strabo, 9.3.14]

BIBLIOGRAPHY
Nauck, A. *Tragicorum Graecorum Fragmenta*. 1889. Reprint, Hildesheim, Ger.: Olms, 1964.

RHEA Also known as Cybele (or Ops among the Romans), the goddess Rhea was the daughter of URANUS and EARTH (Gaia) and both the sister and the wife of Uranus. By Uranus, Rhea became the mother of ZEUS, POSEIDON, HADES, HESTIA, HERA, and DEMETER. When Uranus swallowed Rhea's first five children, Rhea, upon giving birth to Zeus, wrapped a stone in swaddling clothes and gave that to Uranus; she then had Zeus taken away to safety on the island of CRETE. Rhea is often called the Great Mother (Latin: Magna Mater), and her worship involved frenzied ritual. Rhea's priests were castrated. Her worship often took place on mountaintops and the rituals associated with DIONYSUS are often said to have been derived from those of Rhea. [ANCIENT SOURCES: Apollodorus, *Library* 1.1.3–7, 3.5.1; Hesiod, *Theogony* 135, 453–506; Homer, *Iliad* 14.201–4; Pausanias, 5.7.6, 8.8.2–3, 8.36.2–3; Seneca, *Hippolytus* 1136]

RHESUS The son of an unnamed MUSE and Eioneus, Rhesus was a Thracian king who went to TROY in the 10th year of the war as an ally of the Trojan forces. According to one prophecy, the Trojans would win the war if Rhesus' horses tasted Trojan food first. On the day that Rhesus arrived at Troy, the Greeks ODYSSEUS and DIOMEDES made a nighttime raid on the Greek camp, killed Rhesus, and led away his horses. As a result, the horses first were fed by the Greeks, who thus ensured that they would win the war. Rhesus appears briefly as a character in EURIPIDES' *RHESUS*. Although the play bears Rhesus' name, he speaks only

61 lines. [ANCIENT SOURCES: Euripides, *Rhesus;* Homer, *Iliad* 10; Seneca, *Agamemnon* 216, *Trojan Women* 8]

RHESUS EURIPIDES? (CA. 450? B.C.E.)

Rhesus is one of the more challenging plays in Greek drama because the drama's authorship and date are uncertain. Tradition assigns the play to EURIPIDES, but many modern scholars doubt this, primarily because they think that its quality is not worthy of Euripides. Those who believe EURIPIDES did write the play attribute its lack of quality to its being an early effort by playwright, and thus assign it to the early years of his career. Those who believe Euripides did not write the play date it to the fourth century B.C.E.

Although TROY is not an unusual setting for classical TRAGEDY, the events of this play occur during the night. Nighttime action may have presented a slight challenge for the playwright and the audience, because Greek dramas were performed in outdoor theaters during the day. The play's events are drawn from the 10th book of HOMER's *Iliad*. In this book, set in the 10th year of the Trojan War, the Thracian hero RHESUS has arrived as an ally of the Trojans.

Rhesus opens near the tent of the Trojan warrior HECTOR, who is camped with the rest of the Trojan army on the plain outside their city. The audience must also imagine that the Greek army is camped near the Trojan seashore. If Euripides did write the play, its lack of a prologue would be unique for a Euripidean play, and some scholars have thought that the prologue was lost. In *Rhesus,* the play's opening lines are spoken by the CHORUS, who consist of Trojan soldiers. They have gone to Hector's tent to urge him to prepare the sleeping army for battle. These soldiers have noticed numerous fires throughout the Greek camp and worry that the Greeks may be preparing something unusual. Hector, however, thinks that the Greeks are preparing to leave Troy and return to Greece.

Hector is soon joined by AENEAS, DOLON, and unnamed Trojan warriors. Hector tells Aeneas to arm for an attack on the Greeks, but Aeneas is skeptical that the Greeks are leaving Troy. Aeneas suggests that they send someone to spy the Greek camp and learn their true intent. Hector approves of this suggestion, and Dolon (whose name is derived from a Greek word that means "trickery") volunteers to undertake the mission in exchange for the horses of ACHILLES. After Hector agrees, Dolon announces that he will return to his home to fetch a wolf skin, with which he will cover himself during his mission. As Dolon departs, he boasts that he will return with the head of ODYSSEUS.

After Dolon's exit, the chorus pray to APOLLO to aid Dolon's mission and hope that Dolon will kill several of the leading Greeks. After the chorus' song, a shepherd enters and informs Hector that Rhesus, a Thracian ally of the Trojans', has just arrived at Troy. The shepherd notes especially the magnificent horses that draw Rhesus' chariot. Hector, however, suggests that the Trojans have no need of Rhesus' help, but the chorus and the shepherd urge Hector not to reject it. After Hector agrees, the chorus sing a song of welcome to Rhesus and pray that he will destroy Achilles. As the chorus' song concludes, Rhesus himself enters and is met by Hector, who chastises him for not aiding the Trojans earlier in the war. Rhesus apologizes for not helping sooner but notes that an attack on his own kingdom prevented him from traveling to Troy. Rhesus promises that he will now destroy the Greeks. Because it is night, Hector urges Rhesus to make camp and rest. Before he and Rhesus exit, Hector tells the chorus to be on the lookout for Dolon. The chorus take up the watch, but after some time they leave to summon the Lycians, who are supposed to take up the next watch. The departure of the chorus from the stage in the middle of a play occurs only a few times in Greek tragedy.

After the chorus' departure, the Greeks ODYSSEUS and DIOMEDES enter. As they make their way to the Trojans' camp, their conversation indicates that they have encountered and killed Dolon, who gave them the watchword required to enter the Trojan camp. As they search for the camp and consider whether they should attack or return to their own camp, they are met by the goddess ATHENA, who informs them that the Greeks will be victorious in the war provided that they kill Rhesus before dawn. Athena directs them to the place where Rhesus is camped and suggests that they capture his magnificent horses. As the two Greeks converse with Athena, the Trojan Alexander (see PARIS) approaches Hector's tent. Athena directs Odysseus and

Diomedes to pursue Rhesus while she, disguising her-self as APHRODITE, deals with Alexander.

After Odysseus and Diomedes' exit, Athena informs Alexander of the arrival of Rhesus as an ally for the Tro-jans and tells him that Hector has gone to help him set-tle his encampment. After Alexander exits, Athena tells Odysseus and Diomedes, who have by now killed Rhe-sus and captured his horses, to take care to avoid the Trojans, who are pursuing them. Next, Odysseus enters with the chorus of Trojans pursuing and threatening to kill him. When Odysseus gives the Trojans the watch-word, however, they end the pursuit. Odysseus then creeps away from the Trojan chorus, who are left won-dering who the man was and what scheme Odysseus might be contriving. The chorus also worry that Hec-tor will blame them for what has happened.

As the chorus ponder these events, Rhesus' wounded charioteer enters, lamenting the loss of Rhe-sus. The charioteer describes how Rhesus was killed, his horses were taken, and he, the charioteer, was wounded. The charioteer also voices his suspicion that the Trojans themselves were responsible for the attack. At this point, Hector enters and blames the Trojan cho-rus for Rhesus' misfortune. Both the chorus and Rhe-sus' charioteer deny the charge, however, and the charioteer goes so far as to blame Rhesus' death on Hec-tor himself. Hector responds correctly that Odysseus is responsible for the deed. Because the charioteer remains distraught, Hector takes him to stay at his own house in the city and gives orders that those killed by the Greeks be buried.

After the exit of Hector and the charioteer, the cho-rus lament Troy's fortune. Their lamentation is inter-rupted, however, by the appearance of the Muse, who is Rhesus' mother. She laments her son's death and curses Odysseus and Diomedes for their actions. The Muse recalls Rhesus' infancy and military prowess in Thrace. Though she was aware of Rhesus' fate, she did not warn him against going to Troy. The Muse goes on to blame Athena for Rhesus' death and threatens not to inspire anyone else in Athena's favorite city, ATHENS. Upon hearing the Muse's speech, the chorus note that Hector and Rhesus' charioteer had falsely accused them of plotting Rhesus' death. Hector, who has also heard the Muse, defends himself against the charge

that he had any responsibility in Rhesus' death and states that he is prepared to conduct a magnificent funeral for Rhesus. Before the Muse departs, she laments that she will not see her son again and predicts that THETIS' son, ACHILLES, will die soon. As the Sun rises, the play reaches its conclusion as the chorus and Hector prepare to go to battle with the Greeks.

COMMENTARY

Besides the debate about over the play's authorship and date, *Rhesus* is of interest because it is the only surviv-ing play derived from events in HOMER's *Iliad*. The 10th book of this epic was the model on which the author of *Rhesus* drew. *Rhesus* does not change the basic story (the Greek raid on the Trojan camp, the killing of Rhe-sus, and the capture of his horses), but the playwright does choose different focal points for his version. First, in contrast to Homer, the playwright focuses more on Hector and his poor decisions as a military com-mander. Additionally, Homer gives much more atten-tion (about 20 percent of Book 10) to Dolon than the playwright does. Rhesus appears only briefly in the play; he does not speak in *Iliad* 10 and his mother does not appear as a character.

Although the Homeric elements of *Rhesus* are note-worthy, one should observe that the tone of the play is not especially tragic. Burnett has discussed a number of humorous touches in *Rhesus*. The virgin goddess Athena's disguising of her voice as that of the love god-dess Aphrodite surely would have prompted some smiles in the audience. Most of the Trojans and their allies seem completely inept. Hector has his amusing moments as he incorrectly assesses the Greeks' inten-tions at the first of the play and incorrectly interprets Rhesus' purpose on his arrival. Dolon's disguising him-self as a wolf may have been humorous as well, because in Homer Dolon wears the wolf's skin only on his head. Dolon boasts that he will kill Odysseus, but he fails and is killed.

Rhesus, decked in gold armor and hymned as if he were a god, has been described as a BRAGGART WARRIOR by several scholars, and, as does Dolon, Rhesus prom-ises to cause the destruction of the Greeks, but he too is killed. The fact that Rhesus is a Thracian also may contribute to the humor of his characterization, if we compare him to the treacherous yet gullible barbarian POLYMESTOR in Euripides' HECABE. The GORGON on Rhesus' shield (306) may carry both humorous and ironic significance. In ACHARNIANS, ARISTOPHANES often mocks the warrior LAMACHUS for the Gorgon on his shield; yet, as the shepherd in *Rhesus* points out, Athena also has a Gorgon on her shield. In this play, only the truly divine bearer of the Gorgon will survive.

The chorus of *Rhesus* are simpletons. When they become sleepy (555–56), they leave their assigned posts and go off to find their replacements, an action that allows the Greeks to enter the camp and kill Rhesus. Later, of course, when threatened with punishment from Hector, they swear that they have not fallen asleep (824–28). The chase scene between Odysseus and the Trojan chorus is also amusing as they fail to catch Odysseus and then worry that Hector will blame them for Rhesus' death. The entrance of the chorus in their pursuit of Odysseus would also have been humorous, as their opening lines contain a chant that sounds rather ludicrous. At line 675, the pursuing chorus cries out, "Strike, strike, strike, strike, wound, wound" (*bale, bale, bale, bale, thene, thene*). The lines could be modeled on the FURIES' pursuit of ORESTES at *Eumenides* 130 (see ORESTEIA): "Seize, seize, seize, seize" (*labe, labe, labe, labe*). The lines have a closer parallel in COMEDY at ACHARNIANS 281–82 as the chorus pursue DICAEOPOLIS: "Strike, strike, strike, strike, hit, hit the wicked man" (*balle, balle, balle, balle, paie, paie ton miaron*). Although the chorus do not catch Odysseus, they set an ambush for and capture one of their own allies, Rhesus' charioteer (730–37).

Although the appearance of the Muse at the play's conclusion does belong to the realm of tragedy, Burnett takes the Muse's threats "as mean and ugly, as Dolon is." Furthermore, Burnett argues that the Muse's threats against Athens are actually amusing as the Muse declares she will deprive Athens of "the supply of mystics that have been coming down from Thrace." Thus, Burnett reasons that "by bringing about the death of Rhesus, the plot of this play has defeated an influx into Athens of a Thracian religion identified with the oracles of Musaeus, the mysteries of Orpheus, and the worship of Bacchus-Zagreus." Burnett further remarks that the killing of Rhesus has "not only supported the

Olympian scheme for the war and rescued Greece from a Thracian invasion, [but also] repulsed an exotic religion that rivaled accepted Greek beliefs."

BIBLIOGRAPHY

Bond, R. S. "Homeric Echoes in *Rhesus,*" *American Journal of Philology* 117 (1996): 255–73.

Burnett, A. P. "*Rhesus*: Are Smiles Allowed?" In *Directions in Euripidean Criticism: A Collection of Essays.* Edited by P. Burian. Durham, N.C.: Duke University Press, 1985, 13–51.

Kitto, H. D. F. "The *Rhesus* and Related Matters," *Yale Classical Studies* 25 (1977): 317–50.

Ritchie, W. *The Authenticity of the Rhesus of Euripides.* Cambridge: Cambridge University Press, 1964.

Walton, J. M. "Playing in the Dark: Masks and Euripides' *Rhesus,*" *Helios* 27 no. 2 (2000): 137–47.

RHIPAE Mythical mountains (also called Rhipaean) that were located far to the north of Greece and Italy. [ANCIENT SOURCES: Sophocles, *Oedipus at Colonus* 1248]

RHODOPE A high Thracian mountain range. DIONYSUS, ORPHEUS, and DIOMEDES (whom HERACLES killed) were sometimes associated with this range. [ANCIENT SOURCES: Seneca, *Hercules Oetaeus* 144, 1032, 1050, 1538]

ROMAN GAMES Every September the Romans honored Jupiter Optimus Maximus, Jupiter the Best and Greatest (see ZEUS). The games were arranged by the curule aediles and in 364 B.C.E. dramatic competition was added to the existing program of events that took place in the circus, especially chariot racing. Dramas were performed on four days of the festival by 214 B.C.E. TERENCE'S PHORMIO in 161 B.C.E. and the third production of MOTHER-IN-LAW took place at these games. [ANCIENT SOURCES: Livy, 24.43]

ROME Located on the Tiber River near the western coast of Italy, Rome has been one of the world's most important and powerful cities for more than 2,000 years. According to tradition, Rome was founded in 753 B.C.E., but the site had been inhabited as early as the Bronze Age. The government of Rome had three phases: Until 509 kings ruled Rome; after their expulsion a republican form of government developed; finally, in the last half of the first century B.C.E., Rome was ruled by emperors. By the middle of the second century B.C.E., Rome had become the unrivaled power in the Mediterranean region.

As Roman power expanded, the culture of those conquered by Rome began to influence the conquerors. Greek culture, in particular, had a powerful impacts. One aspect of Greek culture, literature, began to take hold in Rome in the middle of the third century B.C.E. Tradition maintains that in 240, a Greek COMEDY and a TRAGEDY were translated into Latin. Most of surviving Latin drama appeared in the two centuries that followed, as writers such as ENNIUS, CAECILIUS, PLAUTUS, TERENCE, NAEVIUS, PACUVIUS, and ACCIUS began to adapt Greek plays for Roman audiences. Although only FRAGMENTS remain from most of these authors, 26 complete comedies from Plautus and Terence are extant. Additionally, 10 tragedies (all attributed to SENECA) that were written about the middle of the first century C.E. survive. Although Roman audiences enjoyed the productions of such authors, one should note that the earliest theaters in Rome were temporary structures. The first permanant stone theater in Rome was not built until the 50s B.C.E.

Along with adaptations of Greek tragedy and comedy for Roman audiences, the Romans enjoyed MIME, PANTOMIME, and other types of theatrical productions. FABULA ATELLANA, said to have originated in the Italian town of Atella, appears to have revolved around the humorous situations of everyday life in "small-town" central Italy. FABULAE PRAETEXTAE were plays written in Latin that dramatized historical events (e.g., OCTAVIA). FABULAE TOGATAE were comedies written in Latin in which the characters dressed in Roman clothing (i.e., the toga).

BIBLIOGRAPHY

Beare, W. The Roman Stage. London: Methuen, 1950.

Brooks, R. A. Ennius and Roman Tragedy. New York: Arno Press, 1981.

Duckworth, G. E. The Nature of Roman Comedy. Princeton, N.J.: Princeton University Press, 1952.

Kenney, E. J., ed. The Cambridge History of Classical Literature. Vol. 2, Latin Literature. Cambridge: Cambridge University Press, 1982.

Shelton, J. As the Romans Did: A Source Book in Roman Social History. New York: Oxford University Press, 1988.

THE ROPE (Latin: RUDENS) PLAUTUS (CA. 189 B.C.E.)

At line 32, we learn that the original Greek play was authored by DIPHILUS. The title of Plautus' Greek model is not certain; it may have been Pera. The play's setting, the coast of northern African, near Cyrene, before a temple of Venus (see APHRODITE) and the cottage of Daemones ("guardian spirit"), an exile from ATHENS, is surely the most exotic among extant examples of Roman comedy. The play is slightly unusual for new comedy in that a divinity, Arcturus, delivers the PROLOGUE. In Plautus, this occurs also in AMPHITRUO (Mercury; see HERMES), POT OF GOLD (the Lar), and THREE-DOLLAR DAY (Luxury and her daughter, Poverty). Arcturus opens by discussing the power of Jupiter (see ZEUS) and especially his relationship with people who are good and evil. Arcturus informs the audience that Daemones' daughter was abducted and sold to a PIMP, Labrax ("ravenous seafish"), who transported her to Cyrene. A young Athenian, Plesidippus, saw the young woman, fell in love with her, and arranged with Labrax to buy her. Labrax, however, did not honor his agreement, and when a certain Sicilian, Charmides, who was visiting Labrax, heard about the woman, he promised Labrax that he could make a lot of money and persuaded him to go to SICILY. The pimp, after gathering his possessions and his women, then set sail for Sicily. When Arcturus saw Labrax sailing away, the divinity caused a storm to arise and wreck the ship. Labrax, Charmides, and the women swim to shore but take the stage at different times.

As the first act opens, Daemones' slave, Sceparnio, leaves the cottage to inspect the damage done by the storm. Next, Plesidippus and some companions enter in search of the temple of Venus (see APHRODITE), where Labrax had told Plesidippus he was going to offer a sacrifice before he set sail for Sicily. Plesidippus and his party are soon met by Daemones. Plesidippus asks Daemones whether he has seen Labrax, but Daemones says he has not. Soon, Daemones sees Labrax, Charmides, and two women. The exit of Daemones and Sceparnio is followed by the entrance of the shipwrecked Palaestra ("wrestling ground"), who laments her fate. Palaestra is soon joined by Ampelisca, who is in equally poor condition. As they make their way to Venus' shrine, Ptolemocratia, a priestess of Venus, leaves the temple. The two women see Ptolemocratia and beg her for help. The priestess promises to help them and accompanies them into the temple.

The second act begins with the arrival of a group of fishermen, who approach Venus' temple in the hope that the goddess will favor their efforts to catch fish. Next, Plesidippus' slave, Trachalio, enters in search of his master. Trachalio asks the fishermen about Plesidippus, but they have no information. After the fishermen exit, Trachalio expresses his belief that Labrax has left the country. Upon seeing Ampelisca emerge from the temple, Trachalio approaches her. Ampelisca recognizes Trachalio as Plesidippus' servant, tells him about the shipwreck, and relates how Venus' priestess had helped them. She also informs him about Labrax's attempt to sail for Sicily and states the belief that Labrax probably drowned. When Trachalio asks to see Palaestra, Ampelisca tells him that she is inside the temple and is upset because Labrax took from her a box with some items that would have helped her identify her long-lost parents. Ampelisca presumes that the box, which was aboard the ship, was lost at sea. After Trachalio enters the temple, Ampelisca approaches Daemones' house and asks for water. Sceparnio answers the door and tries to fondle the attractive stranger. Ampelisca fights Sceparnio off and finally persuades him to take the pitcher she carries and go inside to fill it with water. After Sceparnio leaves, Ampelisca sees that Labrax is approaching and rushes off to the temple to inform Palaestra. When Sceparnio returns, he finds that Ampelisca is gone. Then he also goes to the temple to return the pitcher to Ptolemocratia. After Sceparnio's departure, Labrax enters with Charmides. Labrax laments that he attempted the voyage to Sicily and looks for Palaestra and Ampelisca. Charmides suspects that the women have drowned. Labrax worries that Plesidippus will cause him trouble if he sees him. Next Sceparnio emerges from Venus' temple and reports that he saw Ampelisca and Palaestra clinging to Venus' statue. Labrax overhears Sceparnio and realizes that the two women are his women. Then Labrax enters the temple to retrieve the women. During Labrax's absence,

Charmides tries to get some hospitality from Sceparnio; the gruff slave will give him a covering but refuses to allow him into his house. When Sceparnio goes into his house, Charmides enters the temple to find out what Labrax is doing.

The next act opens with Daemones' reporting a dream that he had had the previous night. In his dream, Daemones saw a monkey, representing Labrax, trying to pull some swallows, representing Ampelisca and Palaestra, out of a nest. When the monkey failed, it asked Daemones for a ladder, but Daemones refused to contribute to the injury of the birds. The angry monkey then threatened Daemones and took him to court, but Daemones managed to grab the monkey and put the animal in chains. Daemones does not understand the meaning of his dream; that soon changes when Plesidippus' slave, Trachalio, rushes from the temple and calls upon the people of Cyrene for help, as Labrax is trying to drag Ampelisca and Palaestra from Venus' statue. Hearing this, Daemones calls for additional servants and enters the temple. Soon, Ampelisca and Palaestra emerge from the temple and tell of Labrax's actions. Trachalio approaches them and tries to offer comfort, seating the young women at an altar and promising to defend them. Next, Daemones emerges from the temple with Labrax, whom his servants are holding. Labrax complains that the women belong to him, but Daemones does not recognize his claim. When Trachalio points out that the women were freeborn and that Palaestra was born in Athens, Daemones notes that he is also from Athens and thinks that Palaestra would be about the same age as the three-year-old daughter he had lost a number of years earlier. Before this thought goes any further, Labrax continues to threaten violence against the women and Trachalio exits to retrieve his master, Plesidippus. After Trachalio's departure, Labrax and Daemones continue to argue over the women. Daemones reenters his house but leaves two of his slaves to guard Labrax. Soon, Plesidippus and Trachalio enter. When Plesidippus sees Labrax, he tells Trachalio to go to the harbor and fetch his friends so that they can help Plesidippus punish Labrax. Then Plesidippus puts a rope around Labrax's neck and starts to haul him off to court. Labrax calls for help, but even Charmides rejects him.

The fourth act opens with Daemones leaving his house and announcing that Ampelisca and Palaestra are safe inside. He wonders where his servant, Gripus, is, as Gripus had left for his fishing trip some time earlier. After Daemones goes back inside to lunch, Gripus arrives, carrying a trunk that he caught while fishing. Gripus imagines the great riches that the trunk must contain and plans to buy his freedom with the money. As Gripus starts to drag the trunk away, Trachalio sees him; recognizes the trunk as property of his master, Plesidippus; and begins negotiating with Gripus about the trunk. Gripus does not want to give up the trunk, and the negotiation deteriorates into a physical battle. Finally, Trachalio proposes that they submit their argument to Daemones for arbitration. Trachalio does not realize that Daemones is Gripus' master, so Gripus agrees to the arbitration because he expects Daemones will rule in his favor.

Next, Daemones emerges from his house with Ampelisca and Palaestra. He wants to help them but fears the wrath of his wife. Before this matter can proceed further, Gripus approaches Daemones and greets him. When Trachalio realizes that Gripus is Daemones' slave and tells him about the trunk, Trachalio tells Daemones that inside the trunk is a box that belonged to Ampelisca. Trachalio tells Gripus that he will renounce any claim to anything else in the trunk, that he merely wants Ampelisca's box, and he asks that Ampelisca and Palaestra be allowed to identify the trunk. Gripus protests, but eventually the women are called over, and they immediately identify the trunk. Palaestra then proceeds to identify the contents of the box in question. One of the items is a little gold sword inscribed with the names of Daemones and his wife, Daedalis. At this, Daemones realizes that Palaestra is his daughter, and Gripus curses his luck because he was seen finding the trunk. After the reunion of Palaestra, Daemones, and Daedalis, Daemones emerges from the house, expresses his delight at finding his daughter, and announces his plan to marry her to Plesidippus. Soon Trachalio enters and Daemones sends him out to find Plesidippus. Trachalio agrees and persuades Daemones to arrange for Plesidippus to set him free and marry him to Ampelisca once he is freed. After the departure of Trachalio, Gripus emerges from the house

and complains to Daemones about the loss of the trunk. Daemones sermonizes on greed but does not give in to Gripus' hopes of having the trunk's contents. After Gripus and Daemones exit, Plesidippus and Trachalio enter, discuss the impending marriage of Plesidippus and Palaestra, and enter Daemones' house.

In the play's final act, Labrax enters, complains about the loss of Palaestra, and sets out for Venus' temple to find Ampelisca. Before Labrax exits, he hears Gripus, who is still complaining about the trunk. Labrax, who claims the trunk as his property, approaches Gripus and tells him about the trunk that he lost. Gripus then bargains with Labrax for a reward for telling him where the trunk is. When the two agree on a price, Gripus leaves to retrieve the trunk from Daemones' house. After Gripus leaves, Labrax expresses his intent to give him no money. Soon Daemones enters, followed by Gripus with the trunk, which Labrax immediately claims as his own. Daemones also reveals that Palaestra, it has turned out, is his daughter. When Labrax receives the trunk, he refuses to pay Gripus the agreed-upon sum. After some argument, Labrax suggests that they choose an arbitrator for their quarrel. When Daemones serves as arbitrator, Labrax admits he promised money to Gripus. Eventually, Daemones persuades Labrax to agree to allow half the money he promised Gripus to be used to buy Ampelisca, and the other half to be given to Daemones himself to buy Gripus' freedom. After Labrax and Daemones conclude their agreement, Gripus still wants his money, but Daemones says he has the money and makes Gripus excuse Labrax's oath. As the play ends, Gripus ponders hanging himself, while Daemones invites the pimp and Gripus to dine with him.

COMMENTARY

Plautus' *Rope* has long been admired as one of the author's best plays and one of his most unique. The buildings that the audience must imagine are also unusual. Instead of a house or houses that belong to elderly gentlemen on an urban street, the setting of *Rope* is a seaside cottage and a shrine to Venus. The play is also unusual in that it contains a remnant of the original Greek chorus in the song of the fisherman at

290–305. As in *CASKET COMEDY,* the recognition depends on items contained in a certain box.

With its rather exotic setting on the northern coast of Africa and rescue from the perils of the sea, Plautus' *Rope* is in some ways reminiscent of the story of PERSEUS and DANAE, who were cast out to sea by ACRISIUS, washed ashore on the island of SERIPHUS, and rescued by a fisherman named DICTYS ("net"). Many years later, the king of Seriphus, Polydectes, tried to force Danae to marry him; she took refuge at an altar and was eventually rescued by her son, Perseus, who turned Polydectes to stone by showing him the head of MEDUSA. We may also compare *Rope* with EURIPIDES' *HELEN.* Just as Helen was transported by the gods to Egypt and oppressed by King THEOCLYMENUS, Palaestra is rescued by the god Arcturus, arrives in northern Africa, and is then beseiged by the pimp Labrax. Helen takes refuge at the tomb of Theoclymenus' father, PROTEUS; Palaestra takes refuge from Labrax in the temple of Venus. Eventually, Palaestra is protected from the pimp by Daemones, who she does not realize is her father. Whereas Helen is ultimately rescued by her own wits and some help from MENELAUS, who has arrived in Egypt after being shipwrecked, Palaestra is ultimately saved through the discovery of the trunk that washes ashore and her ability to identify its contents. The contents of the trunk lead to the discovery that Daemones is Palaestra's father. Just as the god-rescued Helen is eventually reunited with her husband, Menelaus, the reunion of Daemones and Palaestra will lead to her marriage to Plesidippus, who had actually arranged to purchase her from the pimp before the shipwreck. Finally, just as Helen's divine brothers appear at the end of the play to prevent Theoclymenus from pursuing Helen and Menelaus after their escape from Egypt, Palaestra's father, Daemones, acts as a divine rescuer and achieves a reconciliation with the pimp at the play's conclusion.

Despite its exotic setting, the main focus of *Rope,* as of *Carthaginian* and *Persian,* is the defeat of an evil pimp. *Rope* differs, however, in that in this play the pimp is not opposed by a wily slave (comparable to Milphio in *Carthaginian* or Toxilus in *Persian*), but by the gods themselves (especially Arcturus, Neptune [see POSEIDON], and Venus) and Daemones, who functions

as a substitute divinity. As Arcturus points out in the prologue, Jupiter employs him and other divinities to watch over the deeds of mortals. Arcturus ensures the audience that the gods will punish people who behave in evil ways. Accordingly, when Arcturus saw the pimp trying to make away with the women, he raised a storm that wrecked the pimp's ship but allowed the women to reach safety on the shore.

The storm that Arcturus claims to have raised is attributed to Neptune elsewhere in the play, and more than half the occurrences of Neptune's name in Plautus' plays appear in *Rope.* When asked what happened to the pimp, Ampelisca answers that he died of drinking and that Neptune gave him a lot to drink during the storm the previous night (361–62). When Labrax first enters, having washed ashore at last, he declares that anyone who wants to end up poor and miserable should entrust himself to Neptune (485–86). At 527, Labrax shivers because of the cold bath that Neptune has given him, and at 588 Labrax's friend, Charmides, complains about the dousing that Neptune gave them during the night.

Neptune has taken away everything that Labrax had and has entrusted Labrax's goods to others; the trunk that contained the tokens has also been preserved by Neptune, and after discovering it, Gripus praises Neptune as his patron (906). The women are preserved by Neptune and enter Venus' temple, where they will remain safe. Just as the name of Neptune appears more often in *Rope* than in any other extant Roman COMEDY (10 times), likewise *Rope* also contains more references to Venus than any other Roman comedy (50 times: 15 more than in the second, Plautus' *Carthaginian*). Thus, whereas Neptune ruins Labrax and preserves the women at sea, Venus shelters the women on land. Indeed, the plight of the women invites some comparison to Venus' birth. Venus was born from the sea after an act of violence (the castration of URANUS) and stepped ashore safely on the island of Cyprus. In *Rope,* the pimp's violent attempt to carry the women off to Sicily results in their being cast into the sea and then stepping ashore near Cyrene and taking refuge in Venus' temple. Interestingly, when Sceparnio first sees Ampelisca, he compares her to Venus (420–21). Most importantly, however, at line 704, Trachalio compares the birth of Venus to the plight of Ampelisca and Palaestra.

When Labrax learns that his women are in Venus' temple, he declares that he will burst into the temple (570). This violence prompts Trachalio to call for help. When Daemones responds (true to the meaning of his name, "guardian spirit"), Trachilo reports that Venus' priestess has been badly treated and that the women are clinging to Venus' statue (644–48). Upon hearing this, Daemones enters the temple with two of his burly slaves and drives Labrax out. After Labrax is expelled from the temple, Trachalio promises to defend the women with the aid of Venus (693). In turn, Palaestra prays to Venus for protection (694). When Daemones declares that he will defend the women, Labrax shows his opposition to Venus by threatening to burn Venus' temple because Vulcan (fire) is the enemy of Venus (761). Labrax's effort to appropriate the weapon of Vulcan, however, is thwarted by Daemones. Still, Labrax shows his opposition to the gods again when he declares that he will drag the women away from the altar by the hair even if Venus and Jupiter are unwilling (783). Once again, the guardian spirit Daemones arranges to protect them with two men whom Labrax compares to Hercules (822). The opposition that Labrax faces from heaven's representatives on Earth intensifies when Plesidippus learns that Labrax has tried to drag his beloved from Venus' temple. Thus, Plesidippus in turn drags Labrax off to court.

After Labrax, who has lost his case, returns from court, the pimp encounters Gripus and strikes a deal to reward him in exchange for the trunk. Ironically, Gripus makes Labrax swear to uphold his agreement by swearing to Venus, the very divinity whom Gripus has so opposed during the play. Labrax even prays that if he violates his oath, Venus will cause all pimps to be miserable (1348–49). Of course, as soon as Gripus exits to retrieve the trunk, Labrax declares that he will not pay Gripus anything. Fortunately for Gripus, the guardian spirit Daemones arbitrates the dispute between Gripus and Labrax and arranges for Gripus to be set free. Daemones then forces Gripus to release Labrax from his oath and invites both the evil pimp and Gripus to dinner. Although the play ends happily, during most of the action Labrax has been buffeted severely by Neptune, Venus, and the guardian spirit Daemones.

BIBLIOGRAPHY

Henderson, M. M. "Structural Anomaly in Plautus' *Rudens*," *Akroterion* 22 (1977): 8–14.

Konstan, D. "*Rudens*: City-State Utopia." In *Roman Comedy.* Ithaca, N.Y.: Cornell University Press, 1983, 73–95.

Leach, E. W. "Plautus' *Rudens*: Venus Born from a Shell," *Texas Studies in Literature & Language* 15 (1974): 915–31.

Lefèvre, E. *Diphilos und Plautus: Der Rudens und sein Original.* Wiesbaden, Ger.: Steiner, 1984.

Lowe, J. C. B. "Plautus' Choruses," *Rheinisches Museum* 133 (1990): 274–97.

RUDENS   See ROPE.

S

SABAZIUS A god worshiped especially in the region of PHRYGIA, who was known in ATHENS in ARISTOPHANES' day. In a play of Aristophanes that no longer survives, perhaps *Seasons,* Sabazius "and other foreign gods are tried and expelled from the state" (MacDowell). [ANCIENT SOURCES: Aristophanes, *Birds* 873–75, *Lysistrata* 388, *Wasps* 9–10, fragment 566; Cicero, *On Laws* 2.37]

BIBLIOGRAPHY
MacDowell, D. M. *Aristophanes: Wasps.* Oxford: Clarendon Press, 1971, 128–29.

SACAS Another name for the land of SCYTHIA. [ANCIENT SOURCES: Aristophanes, *Birds* 31]

SACRIFICE Among the Greeks and Romans, a sacrifice was usually an offering to a divinity or the spirit of a dead person. Whereas modern scholars debate the purpose of offerings, in the plays they are made to gain the favor of a divinity (e.g., the sacrifice of IPHIGENIA at AULIS) or spirit (e.g., the sacrifice of POLYXENA at ACHILLES' grave), to offer thanks to a divinity (HERACLES' sacrifice to ZEUS in SOPHOCLES' *TRACHNIAN WOMEN*), to ratify a treaty or agreement (see ARISTOPHANES' *LYSISTRATA*), and even to achieve a prophetic purpose (e.g., TIRESIAS in SENECA's *OEDIPUS*). In some cases, people swear that they will make offerings if the gods answer their prayers. The shedding of blood from a sacrifice was thought to have a purifying

effect, and in the Greek theater victims were sacrificed before the performances of plays to purify the theater.

Offerings could consist of an animal (e.g., sheep or bulls), some sort of food, or drink (see LIBATION). When making a sacrifice, often only part of the offering would go to the divinity or spirit, and those making the offering would consume the rest of it. In some cases the offering would be burned so that the smoke from the sacrifice would rise to the sky (the home of the gods). In ARISTOPHANES' *BIRDS,* the city built by the birds in the clouds prevents sacrifices from reaching the gods, who begin to starve.

People who wanted to make an offering did not have to hold any religious office, although the Greeks and Romans did have priests who presided over certain sacrifices. In the plays, those who offer and preside over sacrifices are often important males or females in a household. In EURIPIDES' *HERACLES,* Heracles leads his family and household in a sacrificial ritual; then, after madness strikes him, he kills his family. In Euripides' *IPHIGENIA AT AULIS,* the prophet, CALCHAS, wields the blade for the sacrifice of Iphigenia, but ACHILLES offers a prayer to ARTEMIS before the blade is used. Sometimes one person would have another make an offering on his or her behalf, as in AESCHYLUS' *Libation Bearers* (see *ORESTEIA*), when CLYTEMNESTRA sends ELECTRA to pour a libation at AGAMEMNON's grave.

During sacrifices decorum was observed. Silence had to be maintained during the sacrifice, and often someone present would call for holy silence to be observed before a prayer to the divinity or spirit was spoken. The participants in the sacrifice cleansed themselves with water beforehand. Fire, considered to have purifying elements, was often nearby. In the case of an animal sacrifice, the blade was initially placed in a basket of barley meal and some of the barley was scattered upon the victim and the altar before the cut was made. The sacrificial victim had to be without blemish and had to move willingly toward the altar.

After the scattering of barley, some of the victim's hair was cut and an initial nonfatal cut into the victim was made to signify that the victim was being consecrated for death. The next cut was intended to kill, and failure to kill with this blow was considered a bad omen. The victim was raised above the altar before the blow; when the blow was struck, the blood would spill into a vessel on the altar. Unlike the elaborate altars in some modern churches and cathedrals, ancient altars did not have to be elaborate (and could even consist of piled-up turf) and could be made almost anywhere.

Once the fatal blow was struck, the animal would be cut open and its entrails inspected for defects (see especially Tiresias in Seneca's *Oedipus*). Internally blemished animals would be a cause for alarm, as in the case of the sacrifice made by AEGISTHUS in Euripides' ELECTRA, and would necessitate that another victim be killed. Once a healthy victim was killed and the entrails inspected successfully, the animal would be carved up. The participants in the sacrifice would eat the "good" meat, and the animal's thigh bones would be wrapped in its fat and burned.

Whereas animal were common sacrifices in actual practice, in the ancient tragedies the sacrificial victim was often a human, usually a young woman. Several of Euripides' plays involve a deliberate human sacrifice: Heracles' daughter in CHILDREN OF HERACLES, Polyxena in HECABE and TROJAN WOMEN, Iphigenia in *Iphigenia at Aulis*, MENOECEUS in PHOENICIAN WOMEN. In such human sacrifices, the victim had to have the characteristics and behavior of an animal victim. The victim had to be pure (i.e., unmarried) and had to go to the altar willingly. In addition to the sacrifice of human victims, Euripides likes to pervert sacrificial rituals by the shedding of human blood. During AEGISTHUS' sacrifice to the local nymphs of ARGOS in Euripides' ELECTRA,

Orestes kills him. In Euripides' *Heracles,* Heracles' sacrifice to purify his house of his killing of Lycus is turned upside down when Heracles is inflicted with madness and kills his wife and children.

BIBLIOGRAPHY
Burkert, W. *Homo Necans. The Anthropology of Greek Sacrificial Ritual and Myth.* Translated by P. Bing. Berkeley: University of California Press, 1983.

Foley, H. P. *Ritual Irony: Poetry and Sacrifice in Euripides.* Ithaca, N.Y.: Cornell University Press, 1985.

SALABACCHO   A well-known Athenian PROSTITUTE. [ANCIENT SOURCES: Aristophanes, *Knights* 765, *Thesmophoriazusae* 805]

SALAMINIA   Like PARALUS, the *Salaminia* was a special Athenian ship used for public business. [ANCIENT SOURCES: Aristophanes, *Birds* 147, 1204]

SALAMIS   A small island off the coast of ATHENS, Salamis was the site of a famous naval battle between the Greeks and Persians in 480 B.C.E.—a battle in which the Greeks were victorious, as described in AESCHYLUS' PERSIANS. In legend, Salamis' most famous inhabitants were AJAX and TEUCER, the sons of TELAMON. In SOPHOCLES' *AJAX,* the chorus consist of Ajax's comrades from Salamis. AESCHYLUS wrote a play entitled *The Women of Salamis* (*Salaminiai*), which may have dealt with the return of Teucer to Salamis after the fall of TROY. The 10 words that survive from this play give us no indication of the plot (see fragments 216–20 Radt). As the title indicates, the play's chorus was probably composed of women from Salamis. Lloyd-Jones thinks that in the play Telamon, grief-stricken by Ajax's death, banished Teucer from Salamis.

BIBLIOGRAPHY
Radt, S. *Tragicorum Graecorum Fragmenta.* Vol. 3. Göttingen, Ger.: Vandenhoeck & Ruprecht, 1985.

Smyth, H. W., and H. Lloyd-Jones. *Aeschylus* Vol. 2. 1926. Reprint, Cambridge, Mass.: Harvard University Press, 1971.

SALMONEUS   The son of AEOLUS, Salmoneus fathered TYRO by Alcidice. When Alcidice died, Salmoneus married Sidero. When Tyro produced

Neleus and Pelias by Poseidon, Salmoneus did not believe Tyro's claim that the god was their father, and subsequently Salmoneus and Sidero treated Tyro in a cruel manner. Although Salmoneus was born in Thessaly, at some point he became king of Elis in southwestern Greece. Salmoneus tried to convince his subjects that he was Zeus by driving through town in a chariot and dragging behind him bronze cauldrons, whose noise he claimed was thunder. Zeus himself blasted Salmoneus with a lightning bolt. Sophocles wrote a satyric *Salmoneus,* of which a few fragments survive (537–41 Radt). Two of the fragments seem to refer to the thunder and lightning that Salmoneus manufactured. [Ancient sources: Apollodorus, *Library* 1.9.8; Hyginus, *Fables* 61; Vergil, *Aeneid* 6.585–94]

BIBLIOGRAPHY

Kiso, A. *The Lost Sophocles.* New York: Vantage Press, 1984.
Lloyd-Jones, H. *Sophocles: Fragments.* Cambridge, Mass.: Harvard University Press, 1996.
Radt, S. *Tragicorum Graecorum Fragmenta.* Vol. 4. Göttingen, Ger.: Vandenhoeck & Ruprecht, 1977.
Sutton, D. F. *The Lost Sophocles.* Lanham, Md.: University Press of America, 1984.

SALMYDESSUS A town in the northeastern part of Thrace near the entrance to the Black Sea. Io is said to have wandered past Salmydessus. [Ancient sources: Aeschylus, *Prometheus Bound* 726; Sophocles, *Antigone* 970]

SAMIA (THE GIRL FROM SAMOS)

MENANDER (315–309 B.C.E.) The action takes place in Athens before two houses, one belonging to Demeas, the adoptive father of a young Athenian gentleman named Moschion, and the other belonging to Niceratus, Demeas' neighbor. Although the text of the first two acts is damaged, it seems clear that Moschion delivered the prologue.

The existing manuscript picks up in the prologue with Moschion's speech. The young man speaks of how he grew up well treated by his father, Demeas, and how he behaved himself in return. Moschion explains that Demeas fell in love with a young woman named Chrysis from Samos and that Moschion persuaded him to allow her to stay in their house.

Although about two dozen lines are missing at this point, Moschion apparently explained that Chrysis became pregnant and Demeas instructed Moschion to get rid of the child when it was born. When the manuscript resumes, Moschion says their neighbor, Niceratus, had a daughter named Plangon, whom Moschion impregnated during a celebration of the festival of Adonis. After Moschion learned of the child, he promised to marry Plangon, who Moschion notes has recently given birth to their child. Moschion also states that Chrysis has given birth to a child by his father, Demeas. At this point, the manuscript breaks off again. It is thought that Moschion mentioned that the child of Chrysis died, and that Chrysis was given Plangon's child to nurse. In the missing lines, Moschion concluded his speech and Chrysis entered.

When the manuscript resumes, Parmenon, a servant of Demeas and Moschion's, has joined Moschion and Chrysis. Moschion and Parmenon discuss Moschion's upcoming marriage with Plangon and assert that Chrysis should be allowed to continue nursing Plangon's child. Here, another two-dozen-line gap in the manuscript occurs. When the text resumes, Moschion concludes a speech about the difficulties of his situation and then exits. Demeas and Niceratus then enter and start to make plans for Moschion's wedding to Plangon.

The play's second act opens with an encounter between Moschion and his father, Demeas. Demeas is upset about the child whom he has seen Chrysis nursing, but then the manuscript becomes garbled again. Apparently, Moschion persuaded his father to raise the child. When the manuscript becomes legible again, Moschion and Demeas confirm plans for the marriage of Moschion and Plangon that day. The manuscript remains spotty for the remainder of the act, but the dozen or so lines that survive involve a discussion involving Demeas, Parmenon, and Niceratus about preparations for the wedding.

In the third act, Demeas emerges from the house and reports that a conversation he has overheard has led him to doubt that the baby is Chrysis' and that Moschion may be the child's father. Demeas soon questions Parmenon about this possibility and compels his slave to admit that Moschion is the father. Demeas incorrectly concludes however, after Parmenon exits, that Chrysis seduced Moschion and that she will have to leave the house. Accordingly, Demeas drives Chrysis from the house but does not specifically accuse her of having relations with Moschion. Niceratus, who is leaving his house while this argument is taking place, takes Chrysis and the baby into his house.

As the fourth act begins, Niceratus encounters Moschion and tells the young man what Demeas has done. When Demeas arrives from his house, Moschion confronts his father. Moschion admits that the child is his, but the initial conversation between the two does not confirm that Chrysis is not the child's mother. Niceratus overhears and thinks that Moschion and Chrysis have slept together. Niceratus is horrified by this idea and threatens to throw Chrysis out. When Niceratus reenters his house, Moschion reveals to Demeas that Niceratus' daughter is the child's mother. Niceratus also discovers the truth. He emerges from the house and reports that he has just found Plangon nursing the child. Niceratus rushes back into the house uttering threats against the child. When Niceratus returns, he reports that Plangon and his wife will admit nothing, and that Chrysis refuses to hand over the baby. Soon Chrysis (with the baby) rushes from Niceratus' house and is directed back to Demeas' house. This events puts Niceratus and Demeas on the brink of blows. The two fathers resolve the situation, however, when Demeas persuades Niceratus to act as if ZEUS were the child's father.

The play's final act begins with the entrance of Moschion, who tells the audience that he will trick his father and pretend that he is leaving town, so that his father will not doubt his word. As Moschion speaks, Parmenon enters. Moschion asks Parmenon to get him a cloak and sword, as if he is preparing to leave town. Demeas emerges from the house and thinks Moschion intends to leave. He apologizes to his son for doubting him and urges him to forgive him. Niceratus enters, sees Moschion dressed for traveling, and threatens to arrest Moschion as an adulterer. This threat is half-hearted, however, and soon Niceratus summons Plangon from the house and gives her to Moschion as his wife. The play ends with the marriage of Moschion and Plangon.

COMMENTARY

One problem in MENANDER's play involves the identity of the baby. It is not clear whether Chrysis was the mother of Demeas' child or whether Chrysis might have stolen the child from Plangon or whether two babies existed. Because much of the play is lost, this issue will continue to be debated. Recent scholarly opinion seems to favor Chrysis' pretending to be the mother of Plangon's baby.

Regarding themes, as with many other plays in New Comedy, the relationship between father and son is central. Clearly, father and son care for one another and do not want to upset each other. Both men have done things of which they are ashamed (27, 47). Unfortunately for Moschion, although the young man had intended to tell his father the truth about his relationship as soon as his father returned from abroad, Moschion's first encounter with his father confuses him and he leaves Demeas apparently thinking that his father knows the truth. Whereas the father's absence from home led to the son's gaining accurate information about his father's affair, the son's absence led the father to obtain inaccurate information about his son's affair.

In contrast to the mythical father THESEUS, however, who curses his son immediately when HIPPOLYTUS is charged with raping his wife and declares that the young man must go into exile, Demeas' wrath falls not on his son, but on his mistress, and he drives her from the house. The wrath of the other father, Niceratus, has a more Theseus-like quality, as he wants Demeas to punish him severely and then drives Chrysis from his house. Although Demeas does believe Moschion when the young man finally reveals the truth, Moschion is still upset by his father's thinking that he had slept with Chrysis. Thus, Moschion takes on the role of a comic Hippolytus and pretends to go into exile in order to make his father treat him more fairly in the future. Moschion's ruse works. Unlike Hippolytus, Moschion does not go into exile; as Theseus and Hippolytus are at the conclusion of EURIPIDES' play, Moschion and his father are reconciled. Hippolytus, unfortunately, died after he was reconciled with his father. Moschion will marry his beloved Plangon.

Another prominent theme in the play is anger, whose importance to the play Groton has well outlined. For example, when Demeas incorrectly thinks that Chrysis seduced Moschion, he angrily drives Chrysis from the house. Demeas' anger at Chrysis creates a feeling of pity for the woman; when the cook recognizes Demeas' anger (383) and tries to mediate, Demeas turns that anger on him. The anger at the cook provides comic relief from the tense anger at Chrysis. Additionally, Demeas' anger drives the woman from the house but drives the cook back into it.

Demeas' wrong conclusions lead to his wrath against Chrysis; the play's other father becomes angry when he also incorrectly thinks that Moschion and Chrysis have slept together. At line 463, Niceratus had concurred with Moschion's advice to Demeas that he should not give in to anger; by line 499, however, Niceratus is urging Demeas to allow his anger to reach a level heard of only in mythology and blind his son. Now the angry Niceratus drives Chrysis out of his house and threatens to kill her and the child. When Demeas tries to calm Niceratus, Niceratus becomes even angrier and thinks Demeas is involved in the deception. Fortunately, before Niceratus and Demeas come to blows, the two fathers reach a mutual understanding.

Whereas the fathers have quelled their rage, young Moschion is angry at his father's accusations against him (621) and decides to pretend to leave town. Moschion worries, however, that perhaps his father will be so angry (683) with him that he will let him go. When Demeas perceives Moschion's intention he states, "Because you are angry, I love you" (695) and goes on to become reconciled with his son. Now that the anger between father and son has ended, Demeas and Moschion decide to have a bit of fun with Niceratus and stir up his anger by pretending that Moschion is leaving town. When Niceratus' rage begins to boil, Demeas orders his son not to stir up Niceratus further (720–21).

BIBLIOGRAPHY

Grant, John M. "The Father-Son Relationship and the Ending of Menander's *Samia*," *Phoenix* 40 (1986): 172–84.
Groton, A. "Anger in Menander's *Samia*," *American Journal of Philology* 108 (1987): 437–43.
Ireland, S. *Menander, Dyskolos, Samia and Other Plays: A Companion to the New Penguin Translation by Norma Miller.* Bristol, U.K.: Classical Press, 1992.

Jaeger, G. *Menander: Samia.* Bamberg, Ger.: Buchner, 1979.
Lloyd-Jones, H. "Menander's *Samia* in the Light of the New Evidence," *Yale Classical Studies* 22 (1972): 119–44.

SAMOS   A Greek island in the AEGEAN SEA less than a mile off the coast of modern Turkey. The people of Samos were allies of the Athenians in the fifth century B.C.E. and had been incorporated into the Athenian empire but had unsuccessfully tried to revolt against ATHENS in 440/439. In 411, an attempt to overthrow the democracy on Samos, encouraged by the exiled Athenian ALCIBIADES, also failed. [ANCIENT SOURCES: Aeschylus, *Persians* 882–83; Aristophanes, *Lysistrata* 313; Thucydides, 8.46–81]

SAMOTHRACE   An island off the coast of THRACE between Thasos and Imbros. Samothrace was home to the mysteries of the CABEIRI. The Greek comic poet Athenio wrote a *Samothracians*, from which a 46-line fragment survives (fragment 1 Kock). The fragment, spoken by a COOK, lectures someone of a nationality different from his own about the civilizing benefits that the cook's arts have given to humankind. [ANCIENT SOURCES: Aristophanes, *Peace* 277; Athenaeus, 14660e–661d; Herodotus, 2.51]

BIBLIOGRAPHY

Kock, T. *Comicorum Atticorum Fragmenta.* Vol. 3. Leipzig: Teubner, 1888.

SARDANAPALUS   Living in the seventh century B.C.E., Sardanapalus was a famous effeminate Assyrian king who, after his enemies besieged him for two years at Nineveh, assembled his wives, concubines, and treasures and burned both them and himself. [ANCIENT SOURCES: Aristophanes, *Birds* 1021; Cicero, *Tusculan Disputations* 5.35.101; Diodorus Siculus, 2.21]

SARDIS   Located in what is now western Turkey, Sardis, on the Pactolus River at the foot of Mount TMOLUS, was the principal city of the region of Lydia. Sardis was said to possess extensive deposits of gold and was famous for its dye. [ANCIENT SOURCES: Aeschylus, *Persians* 45, 321; Aristophanes, *Peace* 1174, *Wasps* 1139; Euripides, *Bacchae* 463; Sophocles, *Antigone* 1037]

SARDO   Another name for the island of Sardinia. [ANCIENT SOURCES: Aristophanes, *Wasps* 700]

SARONIC GULF   This horseshoe-shaped body of water is located on mainland Greece's east central shore. The city of ATHENS is on its northern shore, the town of TROZEN on its southern shore. According to some sources, THESEUS' wife, PHAEDRA, while sitting in Athens, lustfully watched her stepson, HIPPOLYTUS, as he exercised in Trozen.

SATURN   See CRONUS.

SATYR   A satyr is a semidivine creature that has the horns and legs of a goat and the tail of a horse. The rest of the body is human. Satyrs live in fields and forests and are depicted as lusty creatures and even thieves. Satyrs are typically found in the company of the wine god DIONYSUS. A satyr named SILENUS was often called the father of these creatures. In the SATYR PLAY, satyrs usually made up the chorus. [ANCIENT SOURCES: Euripides, *Cyclops*; Sophocles, *Searchers*]

SATYR PLAY   One of the more controversial and elusive kinds of ancient drama was the satyr play, so called because typically the chorus was comprised of SATYRS. EURIPIDES' *ALCESTIS,* which occupies the position usually reserved for a satyr play, provides an exception to this rule. Satyr plays have essentially the same features as tragedies (PROLOGUE, *PARODOS,* EPISODE, *AGON,* choral songs, and an EXODUS).

In the fourth chapter of *Poetics,* ARISTOTLE says TRAGEDY developed from the satyr play, but modern scholars doubt the accuracy of this assertion, and the earliest satyr plays seem to have been staged after the appearance of tragedy. According to tradition, the first person to compose satyr plays was the tragedian Pratinas of Phleius, who is said to have written 32 satyr plays, although only four titles are known and only one of these can positively be identified as satyric (*Wrestling Satyrs*). Additionally, only four fragments of Pratinas' works survive, although one of these fragments (3 Snell) is clearly from a satyr play. The only known date for Pratinas in competition is between 499 and 496 B.C.E. We also know that AESCHYLUS was producing satyr plays at least as early as 472 B.C.E.

Thus, beginning at some point during the late sixth or early fifth century B.C.E., at the City DIONYSIA (satyr plays were not staged at the LENAEA), after a Greek tragedian had put on the stage three tragedies, he presented a fourth play, a satyr play. Why the Greeks wanted or felt a need to put on a satyr play after three tragedies is not clear. A common reason given is the desire for comic relief after sitting through three tragedies over several hours. Such a motive is understandable, but no proof of this notion exists.

Knowledge of the satyr play is also hampered because we have only one complete satyr play, Euripides' *CYCLOPS,* although 400 lines survive from SOPHOCLES' *SEARCHERS.* Satyr plays were generally humorous in content (again with the exception of Euripides' *Alcestis*) and, to be sure, provided a contrast to the tragedies that preceded them to the stage. Besides these two plays, numerous extant titles and fragments of satyr plays help us gain a better understanding of this elusive genre's themes.

In addition to the frequent portrayal of lusty sexuality and the consumption of or eagerness to consume wine, in many satyr plays, the satyrs appear to have sought liberation from an oppressive master (e.g., Euripides' *CYCLOPS*). Also common seems to have been the satyrs' encounter with some sort of novelty (e.g., HERMES' lyre in *SEARCHERS*) or new person (e.g., the infant Hermes in *Searchers*). Athletic activities, especially wrestling (cf. Aeschylus' *Cercyon*; HERACLES and Death in Euripides' *Alcestis*), seem to have been common in satyr plays, although the satyrs themselves were spectators to the events rather than participants. Encounters with persons going to or from the UNDERWORLD also appear to have been common, as reflected by Euripides' *Alcestis.* Heracles, ORPHEUS, and SISYPHUS, all of whom had journeyed to the underworld, were common subjects of satyr plays. In addition to the satyrs, other sorts of unusual creatures or beings with unusual powers were the subjects of satyr plays (cf. Aeschylus' *Circe, Proteus, Sphinx;* Euripides' *Cyclops*).

Heracles was a frequent character in satyr plays, and one can imagine that this brawny, ever-hungry, wine-loving fellow would be at home in humorous situations. Also, in the case of Sophocles' *Searchers,* one can easily see that the subject matter of that play, the infant HERMES' theft of APOLLO'S cattle, might be humorous. In some instances, however, the subject of a satyr play might not seem to lend itself to humor. Euripides' *Cyclops* humorously recasts the story made famous by Homer in *Odyssey* 9, in which the Cyclops brutally kills and eats several of Odysseus' men. Odysseus then makes the Cyclops drunk and blinds the monster by driving a stake into his single eye. As Odysseus escapes from the Cyclops' land, he foolishly reveals his name to the Cyclops, who prays to his father, POSEIDON, to destroy Odysseus. Accordingly, Poseidon causes Odysseus great hardship during his efforts to return to his native land. In Euripides' play, however, satyrs are introduced into the story as slaves of the Cyclops; the monster's drinking is accompanied by an aroused sexual passion for the father of the satyrs, SILENUS; and the play ends with Odysseus and the satyrs' sailing away happily without any reference or allusion to the trials that await Odysseus at the hands of Poseidon.

BIBLIOGRAPHY
Krumeich, R., N. Pechstein, and B. Seidensticker. *Das griechische Satyrspiel.* Darmstadt, Ger.: Wissenschalftliche Buchgesselschaft, 1999.

Seaford, Richard. *Euripides: Cyclops.* Oxford: Oxford University Press, 1984. 10–44.

Sutton, D. F. "A Handlist of Satyr Plays," *Harvard Studies in Classical Philology* 78 (1974): 107–43.

———. *The Greek Satyr Play.* Meisenheim am Glan, Ger.: Hain, 1980.

SAUSAGE SELLER   See AGORACRITUS.

SCAENA   See SKENE.

SCALES   A constellation of the zodiac. The Scales represent the time of the year when the lengths of day and night are balanced equally. [ANCIENT SOURCES: Seneca, *Hercules Furens* 842]

SCAMANDER   One of two rivers (the other is the SIMOIS) near the town of TROY.

SCELLIAS' SON   An Athenian named Aristocrates was the son of Scellias. Aristocrates signed the PEACE OF NICIAS in 421 and 10 years later became one of the 400 oligarchs who replaced the democracy in ATHENS; he later participated in removing extremist oligarchs. In 406, an Aristocrates was one of the commanders executed after the battle of ARGINUSAE, but it is not certain whether this was the same Aristarchus. [ANCIENT SOURCES: Aristophanes, *Birds* 126; Thucydides, 5.19.2, 8.9.2, 8.89, 8.92; Xenophon, *Hellenica* 1.7.2, 1.7.34]

BIBLIOGRAPHY
Dunbar, Nan. *Aristophanes: Birds.* New York: Oxford University Press, 1995, 173.

SCHOLIA   Scholia (singular: scholion), is a Greek word that means "crooked" or "bent," are comments written in the margins of the manuscripts of ancient dramas. The writers of these comments are called scholiasts.

SCIONE   A town in northeastern Greece on the westernmost peninsula of Chalcidike. In 423 B.C.E. the people of Scione revolted against the Athenian empire. The Athenians beseiged the Scionians, who surrendered in 421. [ANCIENT SOURCES: Aristophanes, *Wasps* 210; Thucydides, 4.120–34, 5.32.1]

SCIRA   See SCIROPHORIA.

SCIRON   The son of PELOPS or POSEIDON, Sciron was a cruel and powerful man who lurked about the rugged cliffs near MEGARA. These cliffs were called the Scironian Rocks. When people passed by, Sciron forced them to wash his feet; after they finished, Sciron kicked them down the cliffs into the water below. If the fall did not kill them, then some sort of creature (some say a dangerous turtle) ate them. Sciron's reign of terror ended when THESEUS threw him down the same cliffs. Euripides wrote a SATYR PLAY entitled *Sciron,* of which a few uninformative fragments survive (675–81 Nauck). The comic poet Epicharmus wrote a *Sciron,* whose single two-line extant fragment tells nothing about the play's plot (fragment 125 Kaibel). [ANCIENT

SOURCES: Apollodorus, *Epitome* 1.2; Euripides, *Children of Heracles* 860, *Hippolytus* 979, 1208; Hyginus, *Fables* 38; Seneca, *Hippolytus* 1025, 1225]

BIBLIOGRAPHY

Kaibel, G. *Comicorum Graecorum Fragmenta.* Vol. 1.1 [*Poetarum Graecorum Fragmenta,* Vol. 6.1]. Berlin: Weidmann, 1899.

Nauck, A. *Tragicorum Graecorum Fragmenta.* 1889. Reprint, Hildesheim, Ger.: Olms, 1964.

SCIROPHORIA   This Athenian festival, held on the 12th day of the month Scirophorion (June–July), honored Athena (or, according to some, DEMETER and PERSEPHONE), who was called Sciras, after Sciron, a place on the Sacred Way between ATHENS and ELEUSIS. The name Scirophoria is derived from the large white sunshade (*skiron*) beneath which Athena's priestess, the priest of ERECHTHEUS, and the priest of Helios (see SUN) traveled to Sciron to offer sacrifice. The sunshade symbolized divine protection from the sun, whose heat was more intense during the month of the festival. In this, as in other festivals of invocations, offerings of atonement also took place; for this reason they carried in the procession the hide of a ram that had been sacrificed to Zeus. In ARISTOPHANES' *ECCLESIAZUSAE,* PRAXAGORA's plan for the women to take over the Athenian government is launched during the Scirophoria. [ANCIENT SOURCES: Aristophanes, *Thesmophoriazusae* 834, *Ecclesiazusae* 18, 59]

SCITALOI   A name called upon as the "powers of impudence." Sommerstein translates the word as "Saucies." [ANCIENT SOURCES: Aristophanes, *Knights* 634]

BIBLIOGRAPHY

Sommerstein, A. H. *The Comedies of Aristophanes.* Vol. 2, *Knights.* Warminster, U.K.: Aris & Phillips, 1981, 178.

SCORPION   A constellation of the zodiac whose stars represent the scorpion that ORION killed. [ANCIENT SOURCES: Seneca, *Thyestes* 859]

SCYLLA   A monster with six heads on long necks or a woman's head and six dogs in the place of legs. Various fathers (Phorcys, Trienus, TRITON, or Typhon) and mothers (Crataeis, Echidna, Hecate, or LAMIA) are named as Scylla's parents. Scylla had been a beautiful woman, but CIRCE, who was jealous because the sea divinity GLAUCUS fell in love with Scylla, changed her into a monster. The Scylla had her lair opposite the whirlpool CHARYBDIS, and these obstacles were often thought to be located between the toe of Italy's boot and SICILY. Both ODYSSEUS and JASON passed the Scylla during their adventures. AESCHYLUS compares CLYTEMNESTRA to a Scylla; EURIPIDES compares MEDEA to a Scylla. [ANCIENT SOURCES: Aeschylus, *Agamemnon* 1233 (see *ORESTEIA*); Euripides, *Medea* 1343, 1359; Homer, *Odyssey* 12.85–110, 222–59; Ovid, *Metamorphoses* 13.730–41, 13.898–14.74; Seneca, *Hercules Furens* 376, *Hercules Oetaeus* 235, *Medea* 408, *Thyestes* 579]

SCYROS   An island in the western AEGEAN, Scyros was the site of several unusual events in mythology. THESEUS died on Scyros when LYCOMEDES pushed him off a cliff. The same Lycomedes raised ACHILLES when he was hidden on Scyros so that he could avoid fighting in the Trojan War. When Achilles eventually did go to TROY, Lycomedes also raised Achilles' son, NEOPTOLEMUS, on this island, and it is from there that Neoptolemus arrives in SOPHOCLES' *Philoctetes.*

Sophocles wrote a play entitled *The Men of Scyros,* whose the subject matter is uncertain (fragments 553–61 Radt). Some have thought the play dealt with the departure of Achilles to the Trojan War. Because Neoptolemus addresses an elderly man in one fragment, the more accepted view is that the drama was about Neoptolemus' departure for the war.

BIBLIOGRAPHY

Kiso, A. *The Lost Sophocles.* New York: Vantage Press, 1984.

Lloyd-Jones, H. *Sophocles: Fragments.* Cambridge, Mass.: Harvard University Press, 1996, 29.

Radt, S. *Tragicorum Graecorum Fragmenta.* Vol. 4. Göttingen, Ger.: Vandenhoeck & Ruprecht, 1977.

Sutton, Dana. *The Lost Sophocles.* Lanham, Md.: The University Press of America, 1984.

SCYTHIA   The region of Scythia was located in the Black Sea. From an Athenian perspective, the nomadic Scythians were barbarians. Some Scythians were enslaved by the Athenians and employed as a sort of police squad. In ARISTOPHANES' *THESMOPHORIAZUSAE*, a Scythian, who speaks broken Greek, guards Mnesilochus. SOPHOCLES wrote a *Scythians* (Greek: *Skythai*), which may have treated MEDEA's killing of her brother, ABSYRTUS, after *Argo* left COLCHIS (fragments 546–52 Radt). Lloyd-Jones suggests the possibility that this play may have formed a trilogy with *WOMEN OF COLCHIS* and *Root Cutters*.

BIBLIOGRAPHY

Kiso, A. *The Lost Sophocles.* New York: Vantage Press, 1984.

Lloyd-Jones, H. *Sophocles: Fragments.* Cambridge, Mass.: Harvard University Press, 1996, 275.

Pinney, G. F. "Achilles, Lord of Scythia." In *Ancient Greek Art and Iconography.* Edited by W. G. Moon. Madison: University of Wisconsin Press, 1983, 127–46.

Radt, S. *Tragicorum Graecorum Fragmenta.* Vol. 4. Göttingen, Ger.: Vandenhoeck & Ruprecht, 1977.

Sutton, Dana. *The Lost Sophocles.* Lanham, Md.: The University Press of America, 1984.

SEARCHERS (Greek: *ICHNEUTAI*)

SOPHOCLES   The date of this play is unknown. Other than EURIPIDES' *CYCLOPS*, the remains of SOPHOCLES' *Searchers* (a little fewer than 400 lines) provide the most extensive example of a Greek SATYR PLAY. The action of the play occurs near a cave (compare Euripides' *Cyclops*) on Mount Cyllene in Arcadia and SATYRS constitute the CHORUS. Sophocles' play deals with the theft of APOLLO's cattle by the infant HERMES, a subject covered by the earlier *Homeric Hymn to Hermes*.

As the surviving fragment opens, Apollo is searching for his stolen cattle. He encounters SILENUS and a group of SATYRS and asks for their help in searching for the cattle. Apollo promises the satyrs freedom (although it is not clear from what, because the ancient manuscript is muddled at this point), and they agree to undertake the search. In Euripides' *Cyclops*, the satyrs were slaves of the CYCLOPS until the arrival of ODYSSEUS, and his triumph over the Cyclops led to release from their bondage.

Silenus and the satyrs begin their search and see reversed hoofprints on the ground (Hermes has driven the cattle backward to disguise his course), and then an unfamiliar sound (the young Hermes has invented the LYRE) frightens them. Next, the NYMPH Cyllene, who

has been watching over Hermes, emerges from the cave and asks the satyrs about the noise they are making. The satyrs tell Cyllene of their search for the stolen cattle and she tells them of the birth of Hermes and his invention of the lyre. The news of this wondrous child leads the satyrs to believe that Hermes has stolen the cattle, but Cyllene denies this and defends the young god. The satyrs and Cyllene continue their argument, and the manuscript breaks off at this point.

BIBLIOGRAPHY

Lloyd-Jones, H. *Sophocles: Fragments.* Cambridge, Mass.: Harvard University Press, 1996.

Zagagi, N. "Comic Patterns in Sophocles' *Ichneutae*." In *Sophocles Revisited: Essays Presented to Sir Hugh Lloyd-Jones.* Edited by J. Griffin. Oxford: Oxford University Press, 1999, 177–218.

SEER   See PROPHECY.

SELENE   See MOON.

SELEUCIA   The name of several cities in western Asia. [ANCIENT SOURCES: Plautus, *Three-Dollar Day* 112, 771, 845, 901]

THE SELF-TORMENTOR (Greek: *HEAUTON TIMOROUMENOS*)

TERENCE   The attached production notice (see DIDASCALIA) reveals that the play was performed at the MEGALENSIAN GAMES in 163 B.C.E., that the original was MENANDER's *Self-Tormentor*, and that this was TERENCE's third play. The drama's setting is a rural town in the region of Attica; the action takes place before two houses, belonging to Chremes and Menedemus. The play's prologue, delivered by an unnamed old man, explains that the drama has been transformed into a "double play" from "a single plot" (line 6). The speaker of the prologue says Terence has enlisted him to try to refute rumors that the author has "contaminated" (see CONTAMINATIO) many Greek dramas but has produced few Latin dramas. The prologue's speaker urges the audience to be open-minded about the play they are about to see and not to interrupt the actors.

The drama opens with the appearance of two old farmers, Chremes and Menedemus. Menedemus explains that his son, Clinia, fell in love with Antiphila, the daughter of a poor old Corinthian woman. Menedemus states that his constant criticism of Clinia for treating the woman as if she were his wife caused the young man to leave as a mercenary for military service in Asia, where he has been for three months. Menedemus felt so bad about his son's leaving that he decided to punish himself by selling all his goods and buying a humble farm. Chremes tries to comfort Menedemus and invites him to celebrate the Rural DIONYSIA with him at his house. Menedemus, however, insistent on tormenting himself, refuses the invitation.

After Menedemus exits into his house, Clitipho, the son of Chremes, emerges from his. Clitipho encounters his father and reveals to him that Clinia has returned from Asia and is staying in their house. Chremes wants to tell Menedemus, but Clitipho rejects this idea. Clitipho mentions that Clinia is worried about Menedemus' anger and Antiphila's feelings about him. Clitipho adds that Clinia has sent his servant to take Antiphila to Chremes' house. Clitipho worries that Menedemus will lose his temper with Clinia, but Chremes defends Menedemus' right to be strict with his son. Chremes then reenters his house.

As the second act opens, Clitipho complains that fathers expect sons to behave as if they were born into maturity. He notes that he too has a girlfriend (the prostitute Bacchis), but that he has not told his father about her. Clinia, who is worried about his situation with Antiphila, soon joins Clitipho. His worries are allayed, however, as Dromo (Clinia's servant) and Syrus (Clitipho's servant) approach and say that Antiphila will soon arrive. Clinia worries that Antiphila has been living a luxurious mode of life in his absence, but Syrus tells him not to worry. Syrus has seen that Antiphila is living a life of moderation and sensibility. Syrus adds that the old woman who was said to be Antiphila's mother was not her mother and has died. Syrus also notes that when he told Antiphila of Clinia's return, the young woman was overjoyed. Syrus has also mentioned that another young woman (Bacchis) will accompany Antiphila. Clitipho worries about how his father will react, but Syrus says he has a plan for outwitting Chremes. They will pretend that Bacchis is Clinia's beloved, and they will take Antiphila to Cli-

tipho's mother, Sostrata, for safekeeping. Clitipho is skeptical about the plan, but eventually he agrees to it. As Clitipho and Syrus finalize their plans, Antiphila and Bacchis approach. Clitipho wants to embrace Bacchis, but Syrus restrains him because doing so might undermine their plan. After Syrus sends Clitipho back into his father's house, Bacchis, Antiphila, and their servants enter. Bacchis commends Antiphila for remaining faithful to Clinia and keeping other potential lovers at a distance. Clinia, eavesdropping on the conversation, notes his approval of Antiphila's behavior to Syrus. Soon, the women see Clinia. He approaches and embraces Antiphila, and then Syrus sends them into Chremes' house.

Whereas the action of most classical plays takes place during a single day, the third act of Terence's play begins at daybreak on the morning of the next day. Chremes emerges from his house and decides to tell Menedemus that Clinia has returned, despite the young man's wish to keep this news quiet for the moment. When Menedemus hears this, he is eager to become reconciled with Clinia and says he intends to be less strict with his son. Chremes, however, urges Menedemus not to go to extremes because doing so will cost him a substantial amount of money, as Chremes informs Menedemus that Clinia's young woman has expensive taste. Chremes recommends finding some clever way of supplying Clinia with a modest amount of money. Menedemus agrees with Chremes' reasoning but urges him to tell Clinia and his friends to speed up their scheme to deceive him so that he and his son can be reconciled as quickly as possible. Chremes agrees and then sends Menedemus back to his own house.

Chremes then meets Syrus, who is arriving from Chremes' house. Syrus, trying to acquire money for Clinia, sets out to try to trick Chremes, who is already aware of this scheme. Chremes, accordingly, urges Syrus to trick Menedemus so that Clinia can find money to support his girlfriend. Chremes exits into his house, then returns dragging Clitipho with him. Chremes is angry with Clitipho, because he saw the young man fondling a woman (Bacchis) who he thinks is Clinia's girlfriend. After some argument, Clitipho exits and Chremes and Syrus return to their plot against Menedemus. Syrus tells Chremes that his mistress lent an old Corinthian woman 1,000 DRACHMAS, but when the old woman died, she left a young woman, Antiphila, as collateral for the debt. According to Syrus, Bacchis wants Clinia to pay her and says she will not give him Antiphila until he does so. Syrus then says he will go to Menedemus, tell him that Antiphila is a captive from Caria, and try to persuade him to buy her. When Chremes says Menedemus will never agree, Syrus says this will actually play into his plan. Chremes is baffled, but before Syrus can explain, Chremes' wife, Sostrata, and a NURSE emerge from the house.

Sostrata and the nurse are examining a ring, which is the one Sostrata's daughter (who is Antiphila) was wearing when she was given away at birth. Chremes approaches and Sostrata confesses that she once gave an infant daughter of theirs to an old Corinthian woman to raise (Chremes had ordered that the child be exposed). Chremes is angry but forgives Sostrata. Sostrata then shows Chremes the ring that the nurse gave her. Sostrata and Chremes are eager to learn more about the ring, so they enter the house to question Antiphila. After they leave, Syrus worries that Chremes will be angry if he finds out that Bacchis is Clitipho's girlfriend. After Syrus announces that he has just thought of a plan to save himself, Clinia enters and announces that he will marry Antiphila, who has been discovered to be Chremes' daughter. Syrus tells Clinia that they must now make sure that Clitipho's situation turns out well. To accomplish this, Syrus tells Clinia that he cannot leave Bacchis behind at their house, because if he does, Chremes will discover the truth. Clinia, however, does not want to take Bacchis with him, because he is set to marry Antiphila. Clinia wonders how his father would view this behavior. When Syrus suggests that Clinia tell Menedemus the truth, Clinia thinks that Syrus is insane. Syrus says this is part of his plan, because he thinks that when Menedemus tells Chremes that Bacchis is Clitipho's girlfriend, Chremes will not believe him. Clinia does not want to do this, because this will ruin his plan to marry Antiphila. Syrus argues that they will keep up this pretense only one day.

As Clinia agrees, Bacchis and her maid, Phrygia, enter. Bacchis mentions that Syrus has promised her

10 MINAE and that if Syrus does not honor his promise, she will take revenge on him. As she is talking, Bacchis sees Clinia and Syrus but pretends that she does not and decides to trick them. Accordingly, Bacchis sends Phrygia off to find a certain soldier to tell him that she is being kept there against her will. Syrus, hearing this, fears punishment by the soldier, approaches Bacchis to tell her to call Phrygia back, and says he will give her the money that he promised. Syrus then arranges for Bacchis and her attendants to go over to Menedemus' house so he can arrange for the payoff.

After the transfer of Bacchis, Chremes emerges from his house and talks with Syrus, who informs him that Clinia has told Menedemus that Bacchis is Clitipho's girlfriend and that Clinia took Bacchis along so that Chremes would not discover Clitipho's secret. Syrus also tells Chremes that Clinia is pretending that he is in love with Chremes' daughter, Antiphila, and wants to marry her. When Chremes says he does not want to marry Antiphila to Clinia, Syrus suggests that Chremes pretend to allow Clinia to marry her. Chremes, however, rejects this idea. After Syrus reminds Chremes about the money owed to Bacchis for Antiphila, Chremes declares that he himself will take the money to her. Syrus, however, urges Chremes to tell Clitipho to take the money to Bacchis, as this will help the scheme he has in mind. Chremes agrees to this and returns to his house to get the money.

Next, Clitipho enters and is met by Syrus. At first, Clitipho is angry with Syrus because his scheming has separated him from Bacchis. Clitipho's mood changes, however, when Syrus informs him that he will be able to give Bacchis the money, which Chremes will soon give them. At this point, Chremes emerges from his house and gives the money to Clitipho, whom Syrus accompanies into Menedemus' house. After their departure, Chremes complains about the money that Antiphila has cost him and about the money she will cost him in the future. Next, Menedemus, reconciled with Clinia, emerges and tells Chremes that Clinia wants to marry Antiphila. Chremes, however, tells Menedemus that he has been tricked and that Clinia is just pretending to want to marry to get money from Menedemus. Chremes suggests that they try to trick Clinia by telling him that Chremes agreed to Menedemus' proposal that Clinia and Antiphila marry. According to Chremes, this will make Clinia ask for the money he wants sooner. After Menedemus agrees, he and Chremes exit into their respective houses.

A short time later, Menedemus emerges and announces his realization that Chremes has been tricked. When Chremes enters, he still believes that Menedemus is the one who has been tricked. Chremes soon discovers the truth when Menedemus informs him that Bacchis is Clitipho's girlfriend and not Clinia's. Chremes is furious at this news and Menedemus playfully gives him the same advice on how to deal with his son that Chremes gave him earlier in the play. Given the change in situation, Chremes now agrees to Menedemus' proposal to marry Clinia to Antiphila. Chremes declares that he will chastise his son and give Syrus a proper beating. Soon, Menedemus takes Clitipho and Syrus from his house. Chremes expresses his anger at Clitipho and Syrus and then exits into his house. Clitipho, prompted by a comment from Syrus, begins to suspect that his parents may try to get rid of him because they have found their long-lost daughter, Antiphila. At Syrus' urging, Clitipho reenters the house to confront his parents and find out whether he is actually their son. Syrus then sets out for Menedemus' house to ask him to help him with Chremes. Next, Chremes and Sostrata enter and argue about Clitipho. Sostrata is concerned that Chremes' treatment of Clitipho will alienate their son. Clitipho himself soon enters and questions Chremes and Sostrata about the identity of his parents. Sostrata tries to convince Clitipho that he is their son. Chremes, however, expresses his anger with Clitipho about his trickery and demands that the young man change his ways. Menedemus enters and reconciles Chremes and Clitipho. Chremes says he will forgive Clitipho on the condition that he marry the daughter of their neighbor, Archonides. Clitipho agrees, provided that Chremes will forgive Syrus. Chremes' agreement concludes the play.

COMMENTARY

As commonly occurs with Terence's plays, scholars have been at pains to determine how Terence altered his original Greek material. The statement in the prologue that the play has been transformed into a "dou-

ble play" from "a single plot" has vexed modern scholars. Because Menander's *Self-Tormentor* must have centered around Menedemus, Clinia, and Antiphila, some scholars have surmised that Terence himself added the Clitipho-Bacchis relationship. A. J. Brothers has argued that removing Clitipho and Bacchis would cause the play's plot to disintegrate and suggests, therefore, that in Menander's play Antiphila and Bacchis were silent characters. Thus, when Terence gives them speaking roles, he "doubles" the play in this way.

When we consider Terence's play on its own merits, we find that *Self-Tormentor* is most similar to his BROTHERS, which would appear three years later. In both plays, the sons are involved in love affairs. In both plays, one of the women is freeborn, and the other is of slave status. As does *Brothers*, *Self-Tormentor* focuses on the relationships between two fathers and two sons. As in *Brothers*, one of the fathers is strict with his son and the other is more lenient. In *Self-Tormentor*, however, the strict father has repented of his earlier behavior at the beginning of the play, whereas in *Brothers* the strict father does not moderate his strictness until the end of the play. Also, in *Self-Tormentor* the more lenient father tries to prevent the more strict father from becoming too indulgent with his son. Ultimately, as in *Brothers*, the more lenient father discovers that his son has been lying to him. In both plays, the son of the more strict father will marry the freeborn young woman; however, whereas in *Brothers* the son of the more indulgent father will be allowed to keep his slave-concubine, in *Self-Tormentor* the son of the more indulgent father will have to take a wife and marry a freeborn woman. Both *Self-Tormentor* and *Brothers* have the message that fathers must seek a middle ground in dealing with sons.

The major difference between *Self-Tormentor* and *Brothers* is the role of the slave, Syrus, who is much more prominent in *Self-Tormentor*. In *Brothers*, Syrus aids the young men, but he is not an architect of deception as in *Self-Tormentor*. As in several Roman comedies, a metatheatrical approach may be useful in the analysis of the *Self-Tormentor*. In this play, we may consider Syrus, Chremes, and Bacchis (to a lesser extent) as the rival playwrights. Syrus' first attempt to produce a play within the play occurs in the second act as Syrus plots to outwit Chremes. In Syrus' initial play, they will pretend (*adsimulabimus,* 332; *adsimulet,* 358) that Bacchis is Clinia's girlfriend and Clitipho's mother will literally and figuratively keep Antiphila offstage. The illusion of Syrus' play is almost dissolved when Clitipho wants to embrace Bacchis, but Syrus prevents him from shattering the illusion and sends Clitipho back into his father's house.

In the play's third act, Chremes' play begins to take shape as he directs Menedemus on how to play the role of father. Menedemus wants to play the indulgent father, but Chremes directs him instead to play the moderate father. Chremes knows that he wants to incorporate trickery into his play so that Clinia can have some money, but this part of his play has not yet developed fully. Thus, Chremes sends Menedemus offstage so that he can develop his plot.

At this point, the two rival playwrights meet and the playwright Syrus treats Chremes as if he is the typical gullible father of comedy and wants to trick him out of some money. The playwright Chremes, however, will not allow himself to be cast in this role and, already aware of Syrus' plot, decides to incorporate Syrus into his own play. Thus, Chremes tells Syrus that Menedemus will play the role of gullible father and directs Syrus to trick him. Chremes' play appears to be moving forward nicely, but he is becomes entangled in Syrus' play when he sees Clitipho fondling Bacchis. After father and son argue, Chremes and Syrus return to their plot. Syrus offers a suggestion to Chremes on how to construct the plot of his play (tell Menedemus that Antiphila is a captive from Caria and try to persuade him to buy her), but Chremes does not think their intended audience (Menedemus) will be fooled by that. Syrus argues that this will work, but before their collaboration can advance Chremes again becomes entangled in Syrus' play as the presence of Antiphila in his house will lead to the discovery that she is his daughter.

The playwright Syrus does not yet know this, however, and decides to rewrite his play. Clinia will continue to play the role of the young man in love with the prostitute, but they must change the setting of the play to Menedemus' house. Clinia is not the same actor he was earlier in the play, though. He is on the verge of

becoming a husband and casting aside the role of young man (see ADULESCENS). Just as Chremes did not think Syrus' modification of his (Chremes') plot would succeed against Menedemus, Clinia does not think Syrus' suggestion that Clinia tell Menedemus the truth will work. Syrus, insisting that he can fool both fathers and the young man, reluctantly agrees to play the role Syrus has in mind.

At this point, however, Syrus' play is again threatened as Bacchis emerges as a rival playwright. Because Syrus has not paid her for her services, she sets out to trick Syrus. Bacchis' play involves a fictional BRAGGART WARRIOR who will punish Syrus for not paying her. Bacchis' impromptu play fools Syrus, who agrees to pay her. While taken in by Bacchis' play, Syrus also keeps sight of his own play and tells Bacchis and her attendants to go to Menedemus' house in accordance with the recent revisions to his play.

Syrus continues to try to produce his play as Chremes emerges from his house. Syrus lies to Chremes, telling him that Menedemus has been told that Bacchis is Clitipho's mistress, but he tells Chremes that Clinia is pretending to want to marry Antiphila. Chremes does not want this marriage but rejects Syrus' suggestion that Chremes pretend to allow Clinia to marry her. Chremes, however, will not allow himself to be cast in this role. Ironically, the playwright Chremes remarks that pretense (*simulatio,* 782) is not in his nature. Chremes is eager to play the role of "bag man" as he offers to take the money to Bacchis. Syrus, however, wants Clitipho to play this part and Chremes agrees to take him the money.

Just as Syrus' play is on the verge of succeeding, one of his cast members, Clitipho, becomes enraged at his playwright. Syrus quickly calms his cast member, and Clitipho reintegrates himself into Syrus' play as he goes off with the money for Bacchis. After surviving this threat, Syrus' play meets an additional challenge as Chremes again takes on the role of playwright. When Chremes tells Menedemus that Clinia pretended (*adsimulat,* 888) to be happy at the prospect of marriage in order to get money from Menedemus, Chremes devises the plot of tricking Clinia. Menedemus agrees to play the role of the agreeable father to make Clinia ask for the money.

Chremes' second play fails, however, when Menedemus realizes that Chremes has been playing the gullible father. In turn, Chremes thinks that Menedemus has been playing that role, but Menedemus soon convinces him otherwise. Upon learning the truth, Chremes moves into a new role, *senex iratus,* the angry old man (see SENEX), as he threatens to chastise his son and beat his slave.

In danger of physical punishment, Syrus tries one last desperate attempt as a playwright. This time, however, Syrus' play is not a comedy, but a TRAGEDY, as he prompts Clitipho to confront his parents and find out whether he is actually their son. Syrus' latest play causes conflict between Chremes and Sostrata, as well as between Chremes and Clitipho. Fortunately, Menedemus defuses Syrus' final play by reconciling Chremes and Clitipho. Now, the play reverts to comedy and Clitipho will enter a proper marriage. Chremes forgives Syrus, but the play ends with the failure of all of Syrus' efforts as a playwright.

BIBLIOGRAPHY

Brothers, A. J. "The Construction of Terence's *Heautontimorumenos," Classical Quarterly* 30 (1980): 94–119.

———. *Terence: The Self-Tormentor.* Warminster, U.K.: Aris & Phillips, 1988.

Fantham, E. "*Heautontimorumenos* and *Adelphoe:* A Study of Fatherhood in Terence and Menander," *Latomus* 30 (1971): 970–98.

Goldberg, S. M. "The *Duplex Comoedia.*" In *Understanding Terence.* Princeton, N.J.: Princeton University Press, 1986, 135–48.

Jocelyn. H. D. "*Homo Sum: Humani Nil a Me Alienum Puto* (Terence, *Heauton Timorumenos* 77)," *Antichthon* 7 (1973): 14–46.

Konstan, D. "Self-Tormentor." In *Greek Comedy and Ideology.* New York: Oxford University Press, 1995, 120–30.

Lowe, J. C. B. "The Intrigue of Terence's *Heauton Timorumenos,*" *Rheinisches Museum* 141 (1998): 163–71.

SEMELE   The mortal daughter of CADMUS and HARMONIA, Semele was the mother of DIONYSUS by ZEUS. When Semele was pregnant with Dionysus, Zeus' wife, HERA, discovered her husband's affair, disguised herself as Semele's maidservant, and persuaded Semele to ask Zeus to have sexual intercourse with her in the same way that he did with his wife, Hera. The disguised Hera told Semele that this would prove to Semele that Zeus was the god he claimed to be, but in reality it would result in Semele's death because Hera and Zeus' lovemaking involved thunder and lightning. When Semele asked Zeus for a favor, he swore an inviolable oath to grant her request before she had specified the favor she wanted. Semele was destroyed by Zeus' lightning, but Zeus rescued the unborn Dionysus from her body and sewed Dionysus into his thigh, from which he was later reborn. According to some sources, after Dionysus became a god, he rescued Semele from the underworld and she joined him on Mount OLYMPUS.

Semele does not appear as a character in any existing plays, but much of her story is told in the prologue of EURIPIDES' BACCHAE. AESCHYLUS wrote a *Semele,* also titled *Hydrophoroi,* but only seven words survive (fragments 221–24 Radt). Three other Greek tragedians also wrote plays whose title includes Semele's name. Only the title survives of Spintharus' *Semele Struck by Thunder* (see Snell). Two brief fragments (2–3 Snell) of Carcinus Junior's *Semele* survive. An 11-line fragment (1 Snell) of Diogenes' *Semele* is extant. In this fragment, the speaker reports hearing about the ecstatic style of the worship of Cybele (see RHEA) and ARTEMIS. [ANCIENT SOURCES: Apollodorus, *Library* 3.4.4, 3.5.3; Aristophanes, *Birds* 559, *Thesmophoriazusae* 991; Euripides, *Hippolytus* 454, *Phoenician Women* 1754–55; Hyginus, *Fables* 167, 179; Ovid, *Metamorphoses* 3.253–315; Pausanias, 2.31.2, 9.2.3]

BIBLIOGRAPHY

Radt, S. *Tragicorum Graecorum Fragmenta.* Vol. 3. Göttingen, Ger.: Vandenhoeck & Ruprecht, 1985.

Snell, B. *Tragicorum Graecorum Fragmenta.* Vol. 1. Göttingen, Ger.: Vandenhoeck & Ruprecht, 1971.

Smyth, H. W., and H. Lloyd-Jones. *Aeschylus.* Vol. 2. 1926. Reprint, Cambridge, Mass.: Harvard University Press, 1971.

SEMNAI THEAI   Sometimes referred to as the Semnai, these two (or three) "Revered Goddesses" were worshiped at ATHENS, where they, as did the EUMENIDES, lived in a cave beneath the AREOPAGUS. Classical works sometimes equate the Semnai Theai with the FURIES. [ANCIENT SOURCES: Aeschylus,

Eumenides 1041 (see ORESTEIA); Sophocles, *Oedipus at Colonus* 458]

SENATE   In Rome senators were former holders of public office. In theaters, senators had reserved seats in the orchestra. [ANCIENT SOURCES: Dio Cassius, 58.4.4; Livy, 33.44.5; Suetonius, *Augustus* 44.1]

SENECA (BORN BETWEEN 4 B.C.E. AND 1 C.E.; DIED 65 C.E.)   Lucius Annaeus Seneca, son of a father of the same name, was born in Corduba (Córdoba), Spain. An author of tragedies, Seneca was also a Stoic philosopher. When he went to Rome is not clear, but in 39 C.E. he is said to have offended the emperor, Caligula, and in 41 he was exiled to the island of Corsica under the charge of committing adultery with Caligula's sister, Julia Livilla. Seneca returned from exile in 49, and from 51 he served as tutor (and later political adviser) to NERO. Seneca retired from this service around 62. In 65 Nero accused Seneca of being involved in a conspiracy against him and forced him to commit suicide.

In addition to several philosophical works, 77 epigrams, and *Apocolocyntosis* (a satire of the deification of the emperor CLAUDIUS), 10 tragedies attributed to Seneca have survived: AGAMEMNON, HERCULES FURENS, HIPPOLYTUS, MEDEA, OEDIPUS, PHOENICIAN WOMEN (of which only 664 lines survive), THYESTES, TROJAN WOMEN, HERCULES OETAEUS, and OCTAVIA (however, most scholars do not believe Seneca wrote the last two plays). With the exception of *Octavia*, which is based on actual events in Roman history, and *Thyestes,* eight of the plays attributed to Seneca were influenced by earlier plays by Greek authors. AESCHYLUS wrote an *Agamemnon;* SOPHOCLES wrote a play about Oedipus' fall from power (OEDIPUS TYRANNOS) and HERACLES' final hours on Earth (TRACHINIAN WOMEN); and EURIPIDES composed a MEDEA, PHOENICIAN WOMEN, TROJAN WOMEN, a play about HERACLES' madness (HERACLES), and a play about PHAEDRA's lust for HIPPOLYTUS (HIPPOLYTUS). The dates of composition for Seneca's plays are uncertain; *Octavia,* which was written a few years before his death, is the exception. The other plays may tentatively be dated between the years 49 and 65.

Instances that seem to have little regard to visual plausibility before an audience have led some modern scholars to debate whether Seneca's plays were written to be performed. For example, Senecan choruses enter and exit much more frequently than in Greek TRAGEDY. Staging them may have been possible, however, if the Senecan chorus was smaller than the Greek chorus. Indeed, some scholars believe the Senecan chorus was no more than half the size of its Greek counterpart. If Seneca's plays were not performed, they may have been composed for private recitation. They were performed after Seneca's lifetime, however, and are occasionally performed today. Senecan tragedy differs from Greek tragedy in its use of a five-act structure and asides (some of which are extended monologues).

Seneca's plays are marked by an extreme psychological darkness and despair. He frequently makes obscure mythological references that seemingly serve little purpose other than to demonstrate his vast learning and the depth of his reading of ancient literature. Seneca's tragedies often contain lengthy descriptions that do not advance the plot. In *Oedipus,* for example, the playwright lengthily describes a ritual undertaken by TIRESIAS that fails to determine the killer of LAIUS; accordingly, another ritual must be performed. In *Hercules Furens,* THESEUS' extensive description of the UNDERWORLD is valuable for its information but does not make for "good" drama. Whereas modern scholars have a lower opinion of Seneca's tragedies than those of his Greek predecessors, his plays exerted significant influence on Elizabethan drama. [ANCIENT SOURCES: Dio Cassius, 59.19–62.25; Suetonius, *Nero* 7, 35, 52; Tacitus, *Annals* 13–15]

BIBLIOGRAPHY
Anderson, W. S. *Anger in Juvenal and Seneca.* Berkeley: University of California Press, 1964.

Griffin, Miriam. *Seneca: A Philosopher in Politics.* 2d ed. Oxford: Clarendon Press, 1992.

Segal, Charles. *Language and Desire in Seneca's Phaedra.* Princeton, N.J.: Princeton University Press, 1986.

Veyne, P. *Seneca: The Life of a Stoic.* Translated by D. Sullivan. New York: Routledge, 2003.

SENEX   His name the Latin word for "old man," the *senex* (plural: *senes*) is one of the most common characters in Roman COMEDY. Only three of the surviving Roman comedies (AMPHITRUO, CURCULIO, and PERSIAN) do not have a *senex* listed among their cast of characters. Although the *senex* is a stock character, *senes* behave in a variety of ways. The relationship of primary interest to the *senex* is that with his son (see ADULESCENS), who is often in love with a woman of lower social class. In PLAUTUS' COMEDY OF ASSES, the *senex* knows about his son's affair and even helps him achieve his desires; however, the *senex* usually opposes to his son's quest for a good time. This sort of *senex* is the *senex iratus* ("the angry old man"; see especially Demea in TERENCE'S BROTHERS), although not all *senes* (e.g., Euclio in POT OF GOLD) are angered by their son's love affair. Accordingly, the son, aided by a SLAVE or PARASITE, tries to conceal his affair from the *senex* while he is authorizing that deception to acquire money to continue the affair. *Senes* are often portrayed as foolish; such a *senex* is the *senex credulus* (gullible old man; e.g., Periphanes in EPIDICUS). Eventually, the *senex* discovers his son's affair and becomes angry, but then forgives him because he behaved the same way when he was young. In some cases, the *senex* and his son are in love with the same young woman (e.g., PLAUTUS' *Casina*). In such situations, the *senex* is called the *senex amator* (old lover) and must be on guard against his wife, who will spoil his fun. Some *senes* are facilitators of other people's love affairs (e.g., Alcesimus for Lysidamus in *Casina;* Periplectomenus in BRAGGART WARRIOR). Another common role for the *senex* is that of the father who searches for and is ultimately reunited with a long-lost son or daughter (e.g., Hanno in CARTHAGINIAN, Hegio in CAPTIVES, Daemones in ROPE).

BIBLIOGRAPHY

Cody, J. M. "The *Senex Amator* in Plautus' *Casina,*" *Hermes* 104 (1976): 453–76.

Duckworth, G. *The Nature of Roman Comedy.* Princeton, N.J.: Princeton University Press, 1952, 242–49.

Ryder, K. C. "The *Senex Amator* in Plautus," *Greece and Rome* 31 (1984): 181–89.

SERIANS A nation of eastern Asia famous for their silken fabrics. They are now identified as the Chinese. [ANCIENT SOURCES: Seneca, *Hercules Oetaeus* 414, *Hippolytus* 389, *Thyestes* 379]

SERIPHUS A small Greek island in the southern AEGEAN SEA, south of Cythnos and north of Siphnos. PERSEUS and his mother, DANAE, washed ashore on this island; were found by a fisherman, DICTYS; and were cared for in the palace of the local king, POLYDECTES (Dictys' brother). During ARISTOPHANES' time, the people of Seriphus were allies of the Athenians. Aristophanes' contemporary and rival comic poet CRATINUS wrote *Men of Seriphus* (205–14 Kock), whose fragments give little indication of the play's content. [ANCIENT SOURCES: Apollodorus, *Library* 1.9.6, 2.4.1–2; Aristophanes, *Acharnians* 542; Hyginus, *Fables* 63]

BIBLIOGRAPHY

Kock, T. *Comicorum Atticorum Fragmenta.* Vol. 1. Leipzig: Teubner, 1880.

SEVEN AGAINST THEBES (Greek: *HEPTA EPI THEBAS;* Latin: *SEPTEM CONTRA THEBAS*) AESCHYLUS (467 B.C.E.) This play was the third in a Theban TETRALOGY that included *Laius, Oedipus,* and the SATYR PLAY *Sphinx.* The setting is the ACROPOLIS at THEBES, but what the stage building represented (if there was one for this play) is not clear. Apparently, statues of the gods were used either in front of the stage building or around the edge of the ORCHESTRA farthest from the audience.

The play's subject is the war between OEDIPUS' sons, ETEOCLES and POLYNEICES, for control of the Theban throne. The prologue begins as the king of Thebes, Eteocles (the son of Oedipus and JOCASTA), addresses a group of Theban citizens about the status of their current war with his brother, Polyneices, and his allies from ARGOS. Eteocles says that a recent prophecy indicates that the Argives are preparing an attack on the walls of Thebes and urges the people to prepare to defend them. Next, a Theban scout enters and describes what he has seen in the Argive camp. He declares that the army is led by seven chieftains who are prepared to destroy Thebes or die trying. The chieftains had drawn lots to determine which would attack each of Thebes' seven gates. After the scout departs, Eteocles prays to the gods that Thebes will be saved.

After the exit of Eteocles and the Theban citizens, a CHORUS of distraught Theban women enter and express their fear at the approach of the enemy. They pray to the gods to protect them and repel the enemy. After their prayers, Eteocles enters and chastises the chorus for behaving in such an agitated manner and causing panic in the city. Eteocles threatens death to anyone who disobeys him. The women try to explain their actions, but Eteocles suggests that they rely on their might and weapons to save them rather than the gods. He also tells them not to become overly troubled if they hear the horrific sounds of war and to remain quiet. Eteocles then vows sacrifices to the gods if the Thebans are victorious and announces his intention to lead six Theban champions against the seven Argive chieftains.

After Eteocles exits, the chorus worry about the impending battle and again call upon the gods to help their city. They are also concerned that Theban women may be taken captive and subjected to violence. As their song ends, Eteocles, accompanied by the six Theban champions, and the scout enter from opposite directions. The scout announces the approach of the Argive army and begins to describe their seven chieftains. After the scout describes TYDEUS and his shield in some detail, Eteocles declares that he has no fear of what a person has on his shield and then sends out MELANIPPUS to match up with Tydeus.

The scout then describes Argive CAPANEUS and mentions his boast that he will take the city even against the will of the gods. He describes Capaneus' shield, which declares Capaneus' intention to burn the city. Again, ETEOCLES scoffs at Capaneus' proud attitude, and he sends out Polyphontes to face his attack. Next, the scout describes Eteoclus of ARGOS, whose shield shows a man scaling city walls; against him Eteocles sends MEGAREUS. The scout then describes the Argive HIPPOMEDON, whose shield is emblazoned with the image of the fire-breathing monster TYPHON. Eteocles matches against him Hyperbius, whose shield bears the image of ZEUS, who, according to legend, defeated TYPHON.

The fifth Argive chieftain is PARTHENOPAEUS, whose shield has an image of the SPHINX, the monster that harassed the Thebans before Oedipus caused its downfall. Against him Eteocles sends Hyperbius' brother, ACTOR. Next, the scout describes the Argive warrior-prophet AMPHIARAUS, who the scout says opposed the war against Thebes and predicted disaster for himself and his fellow Argives. The scout notes that Amphiaraus, a man of deeds and not boasts, carries a shield that has no decoration. The scout warns Eteocles about the danger of having a man devoted to the gods as an enemy. Eteocles responds that he has no fear of Amphiaraus and sends Lasthenes against him.

The final champion described by the scout is Eteocles' brother, Polyneices, who declares that he will retake the kingdom and either kill Eteocles or send him into exile. Polyneices' shield bears the image of Lady JUSTICE leading a golden warrior and an inscription that states that Justice will restore Polyneices to his rightful kingdom of Thebes. Eteocles scoffs at the notion of Polyneices having Justice as an ally and declares that he himself will go out to face his brother.

The chorus warn Eteocles about the implications of killing one's brother, but Eteocles is determined to gain victory even if it means the destruction of his own brother and his own household. The chorus suggest that a sacrifice might appease the gods who oppose Eteocles' house, but Eteocles believes the gods have forsaken him and his family. The Theban women beg Eteocles not to go out into battle against his brother, but he refuses.

After Eteocles exits, the chorus recall Oedipus' curse that his sons would destroy each other. They wonder how the stain of brother's killing brother can be cleansed; the women recall APOLLO's warning to Oedipus' father, LAIUS, that he should remain childless, and Laius' having sexual relations with his wife and producing the child Oedipus, whose curse has led them to the current crisis. The women wonder how their city can be saved now. They remember that Oedipus saved the city when they were faced with the threat of the Sphinx, but that after Oedipus' murder and incest were discovered his sons barred him from the company of their table and he cursed them.

After the choral ode, the scout enters and informs the Theban women that the Theban army has held, but that Eteocles and Polyneices have killed one another in battle. Hearing this news, the Theban women wonder how they should react. They are happy that Thebes is safe but lament the deaths of the brothers and the fulfillment of Oedipus' curse. As the chorus continue their lament, the bodies of Polyneices and Eteocles are carried in. The brothers' sisters, ANTIGONE and ISMENE, accompany the mourners who have entered. The Theban women express their sorrow for the sisters' loss and make a lengthy lamentation over the brothers. Eventually, the sisters join in the lamentation.

After this lament, a herald enters and informs the mourners that the Theban councilors have decreed that Eteocles, as a defender of the town, will be buried with all appropriate honor, but that Polyneices, as one who waged war against Thebes, will not be given burial and his body will be left out for the wild animals. Upon hearing this, Antigone declares that she will bury Polyneices whatever the penalty the Thebans impose on her. The herald warns her against this, but Antigone persists.

After the herald's exit, the play reaches its conclusion as half the chorus wonder what they should do with respect to Polyneices, while the other half declare that they will mourn him. They also state that they will accompany his body to the grave because he helped save them from falling into the hands of the enemy.

COMMENTARY

As noted, *Seven against Thebes* followed *Laius* and *Oedipus* to the stage. Although neither of the first two plays has survived, the fragments give some indication of their content. In *Laius,* Oedipus had apparently been born, and his birth violated an ORACLE in which Laius had been directed not to have a child. This play may have dealt with Laius' death but did not reveal that Oedipus was the killer. As did SOPHOCLES' *OEDIPUS* some four decades later, Aeschylus' *Oedipus* apparently treated the discovery of Oedipus as Laius' killer, his blinding, and his curse on Eteocles and Polyneices. How and/or when Polyneices' exile to Argos and his marriage to Adrastus' daughter was made known to the audience is not clear. Perhaps Aeschylus expected the audience to know of these events already. What images or themes connected *Seven* with the two plays that preceded it are unknown. We might guess that in each play the king (Laius, Oedipus, Eteocles) was faced with an oracle that would lead to his own downfall and danger to the city.

Oedipus' sons are the principal individuals in this play; however, the city of Thebes could well be considered a character: The audience of *Seven* would hear the word *brother* (*adelphos, kasignetos*) 11 times in the play, whereas the word *city* (*polis*) is spoken more than 60 times. In *Seven,* the goal is the defense of the city and the play focuses on how Eteocles will defend Thebes. The city's king likens himself to an alert captain of a ship (nautical and water imagery is commonly used in *Seven*) and begins the drama by calling upon the Theban citizens and the gods to defend the city. In contrast to Eteocles, who is confident, the Theban women are terrified for their city.

Eteocles may be an alert ship's captain, but the chorus view the approaching army as like a rushing river (80). They wonder who will save them and their city and pray to the gods. Eteocles chastises them and suggests that their panic does not help the city (183). The panicked cries of the women within the city are juxtaposed with the sounds of war outside the city. Within the city, Eteocles tries to silence the women so that they will not spread their fear to others. Although Eteocles prayed to the gods to protect the city earlier, he criticizes the women's frenzied worship of the gods. Eteocles argues that men should conduct sacrifice and consult the gods in an orderly fashion. Still, after Eteocles departs to select six other Theban champions to defend the gates from those who threaten the city from the outside, inside the city the women continue to call upon the gods to save the city and imagine what will happen to the city's inhabitants if it is captured.

While the chorus focus on affairs inside the city, the messenger and Eteocles now give their full attention to business outside the city and the seven gates of Thebes. The Argive champions do not speak; their shields speak for them. The perceived arrogance of the various Argive champions is contrasted with the nobility of the Thebans who will oppose them. Capaneus, for example, has boasted that he will sack the city whether the gods will it or not (427–28), and his shield bears the inscription "I shall burn the city" (434). As Capaneus does, Parthenopaeus threatens to destroy the city even if he opposes Zeus' will (531–32). Furthermore, the image of the Sphinx on his shield serves as an insult to the city (539).

The arrogance of the Argive champions Capaneus and Parthenopaeus is contrasted with the attitude of Amphiaraus, who is not concerned with the destruction of the Theban city, but of the Argive city. He labels TYDEUS a source of confusion to the Argive city (572) and criticizes Polyneices for waging war against his native city (581). Even Eteocles recognizes Amphiaraus' piety and, in keeping with the nautical imagery elsewhere in the play, likens him to a pious sailor who travels with rascals. Ultimately, the pious and the impious will perish together (602–8).

Finally, Eteocles' brother is described and the messenger notes how Polyneices curses the city (632). Polyneices wants to take control of the city and either kill or exile Eteocles in the process. Polyneices also calls upon the gods to help him take the city, and his shield's inscription bears the words of the goddess Justice: "I will escort this man and he will have his father's city and the occupation of his house" (647–48). Eteocles has been rational and methodical in his previous selection of champions; with full awareness of his father's curse he decides to stand against his brother. Earlier in the play, Eteocles had criticized the women for their irrational behavior; now the women beg Eteocles to reject the madness that is driving him on.

Eteocles will not accept the women's advice, however, and goes out to defend his city. Just as his father, Oedipus, saved the city but experienced his own downfall, Eteocles' strategy helps save the city but results in his own death. The city sails on smooth water again (795–96), but it has lost its captain. The city prospers, but the brothers have perished (816–18). Earlier in the play, the women were emotional, but were certain about what sort of prayers they would address to the gods. Now they are not sure whether to rejoice for the city's safety (826) or mourn for Eteocles and Polyneices. The arrival of Antigone and Ismene determines their decision, and the women mourn the brothers.

The concerns of the city return, however, with the arrival of the herald. The city's counselors (1006) have decided that Eteocles will be buried on the city's soil, but that Polyneices' body will be unburied because he led an army against the city (1019). This announcement upsets Antigone, who declares she will bury Polyneices in defiance of the city (1030). The herald responds, "I forbid you to exert force on the city in this matter" (1042). He also marvels that Antigone will

honor with burial someone whom the city hates (1046). Just as Polyneices used force against his native land, Antigone is now determined to wage her own sort of war against Thebes. Earlier Eteocles had tried to silence the Theban women and persuade them to return to their home. Now Eteocles' own sister will not be silent and threatens to involve herself in the affairs of the city, an uncommon role for a Greek female. As Polyneices visited violence on the city from the outside, Antigone's intent to defy the city's decree causes a rift within the city. The women of the chorus now become divided, some opposing the city (1066–67) and others speaking in favor of the city's decree (1072–73).

BIBLIOGRAPHY
Adkins, A. W. H. "Divine and Human Values in Aeschylus' *Seven against Thebes*," *Antike und Abendland* 28 (1982): 32–68.
Cameron, H. D. *Studies on the Seven against Thebes of Aeschylus*. Den Haag: Mouton, 1971.
Hutchinson, G. O. *Aeschylus: Seven against Thebes*. Oxford: Clarendon Press, 1985.
Thalmann, W. G. *Dramatic Art in Aeschylus' Seven against Thebes*. New Haven, Conn.: Yale University Press, 1978.
Zeitlin, F. I. *Under the Sign of the Shield: Semiotics and Aeschylus' Seven against Thebes*. Roma: Edizioni dell' Ateneo, 1982.

THE SHIELD (Greek: ASPIS) MENANDER (DATE IS UNKNOWN)

Most of the final two acts is lost. The drama's setting is ATHENS, and its action takes place before the houses of Smicrines, the uncle of Cleostratus, and Chairestratus, the younger brother of Smicrines. The first act opens with the appearance of Daos, a servant of Smicrines and the former tutor of Cleostratus. Daos has returned from Lycia with Lycian captives and various spoils of war. Daos, who carries Cleostratus' shield, informs the audience that he thinks Cleostratus has died in battle. Smicrines overhears this declaration and asks Daos to explain how he died. Daos explains how Cleostratus acquired the spoils of war and describes an unexpected attack by the Lycians. A number of Greeks were killed, and Daos presumes that Cleostratus was among them, but he could not identify his body because the corpses were already a few days old. Daos did, however, find

Cleostratus' shield beside one of the bodies. After this, Smicrines and Daos enter their respective houses to break the news of Cleostratus' death to the others.

After their departure, the goddess Chance (Greek: TYCHE) appears and delivers a delayed prologue. She informs the audience that Cleostratus is not dead and that another man grabbed his shield in the confusion of the sudden Lycian attack and was killed. The goddess tells the audience that Cleostratus will soon return. She also points out that Smicrines is an evil person who wants to get his hands on the spoils of war and will try to do so by arranging a marriage with Cleostratus' sister (heir to the spoils of war and living in Chairestratus' house). Cleostratus' sister, however, has already been engaged to Chaireas, Chairestratus' stepson. The goddess, however, lets the audience know that she will prevent Smicrines from carrying out his evil plot and will reveal his true nature.

After the goddess exits, Smicrines enters from his house and goes to speak with Daos, who has emerged from Chairestratus' house. Smicrines complains to Daos about Chairestratus' treatment of him, including not consulting him about the man to whom Chairestratus will marry Cleostratus' sister. Smicrines suggests that he himself should marry Cleostratus' sister. Daos, however, does not want to become involved in Smicrines' business and returns to Chairestratus' house. Smicrines departs for the city to seek further advice on the matter. After his exit, a cook and his waiter are run out of Chairestratus' house by Daos, because the apparent death of Cleostratus has cancelled the wedding of Chaireas and Cleostratus' sister that was to occur.

The play's second act begins with the arrival of Smicrines; his brother, Chairestratus; and Chairestratus' stepson, Chaireas. They discuss arrangements for Cleostratus' funeral and Smicrines' proposal to marry Cleostratus' sister. Chairestratus is opposed to the plan because Smicrines is much older than Cleostratus' sister and is engaged to Chaireas. The debate, however, is not settled. An angry Smicrines exits to his house, while Chairestratus and Chaireas lament the current situation. Daos then emerges from Chairestratus' house and tells Chairestratus that he has a scheme for thwarting Smicrines. Chairestratus will pretend to be ill and

to die suddenly. With Chairestratus dead, Smicrines will forget Cleostratus' sister and attempt to marry Chairestratus' daughter, who stands to inherit more money than Cleostratus' sister. Chairestratus agrees to Daos' plan, and Chaireas offers to help. The act closes as the three plan to put the scheme into action.

In Act 3, Daos arrives from Chairestratus' house, sees Smikrines, and begins to lament the illness of Chairestratus. Soon one of Chaireas' friends, pretending to be a doctor, arrives and enters Chairestratus' house. After a short time, the doctor emerges and informs Smicrines of Chairestratus' illness and impending death. At this point, the manuscript breaks off for more than 200 lines. As Daos predicted earlier, however, Smicrines apparently decides to marry Chairestratus' daughter.

Most of the fourth act is also lost; it appears that Chairestratus' "death" occurred, and that Smicrines agreed to the marriage of Chaireas and Cleostratus' sister. About a dozen lines that do survive reveal that Cleostratus returned alive from the war and was met by a stunned Daos. The last dozen lines of act 4 are lost; presumably Daos explained the plot against Smicrines to Cleostratus. The final act is also largely missing, but presumably Cleostratus would have married Chairestratus' daughter, Chaireas would have married Cleostratus' sister, and Smicrines, discovering that Chairestratus was not dead, would have had neither a wife nor the financial rewards for which he hoped.

COMMENTARY

The issues at the forefront of scholarly discussion of MENANDER's Shield are the role of Tyche ("fortune" or "chance") and the playwright's treatment of the law. Although the divinity Tyche delivers the play's prologue of the play and does not appear again, the goddess and her power drive the play's development. When Smicrines chances to overhear Daos lamenting the death of Cleostratus, this leads him to question the slave about the fate of Cleostratus and he learns about the plunder with which Daos has returned. This knowledge leads Smicrines to plot to marry Cleostratus' sister. When Daos leans of Smicrines' plan, the slave laments that Tyche intends to give him an awful master (Smicrines) and wonders how he has wronged the goddess (213–15). In the second half of the play, Smicrines again chances to overhear Daos lamenting a death. This time, however, Daos knows that Smicrines is listening and has concocted a false death that he hopes will lead Smicrines away from his plan to marry Cleostratus's sister. Ultimately, Daos' creation of a false occurrence of Tyche prevents Smicrines' from carrying out his evil plan.

In addition to the play's concern with Tyche, the issue of law has dominated scholarly modern criticism of the *Shield*. In 1977, Karnezis posited that Menander's representation of inheritance law in the *Shield* did not correspond completely to actual practice in Athenian law. In 1982, MacDowell argued that although Smicrines had a legal right to pursue Cleostratus' sister and thus acquire the property of her brother, *Shield* reveals Menander's opposition to Athenian laws regarding inheritance. In the following year, Brown attempted to rebut MacDowell's argument, returning to the line of argument first set forth by Karnezis, namely that because the characters in *Shield* do not accurately cite Athenian law on inheritance, the play does not show that Menander opposes Athenian law on this matter.

BIBLIOGRAPHY

Brown, P. G. M. "Menander's Dramatic Technique and the Law of Athens." *Classical Quarterly* 33 (1983): 412–20.
Groton, A. H. *A Commentary on Menander's Aspis 1–163.* Ph.D. dissertation, University of Michigan at Ann Arbor, 1982.
Karnezis, J. E. "Misrepresentation of Attic Laws in Menander's Aspis." *Platon* 29 (1977): 152–55.
Lloyd-Jones, H. "Menander's Aspis." *Greek, Roman, and Byzantine Studies* 12 (1971): 175–95.
MacDowell, D. M. "Love Versus the Law. An Essay on Menander's Aspis." *Greece and Rome* 29 (1982): 42–52.

SIBYL (SIBYLLA) A female prophet who made frenzied prophecies under the inspiration of APOLLO. She became so famous that eventually the name Sibyl was applied to other female prophets; the best known of these was on the eastern coast of Italy at Cumae. [ANCIENT SOURCES: Aristophanes, *Peace* 1095, 1116; Pausanias, 10.12.1–7; Plato, *Phaedrus* 244b]

SICILIAN EXPEDITION In 415 B.C.E., the Athenians sent a substantial naval force to SICILY. On the surface, the expedition's aim was to provide support to the people of Egesta (also known as Segesta), with whom the Athenians had an alliance, against any Sicilian cites that might try to aid the Spartans. The city of Syracuse, which had a large fleet, posed the greatest threat to the Athenians. In reality, the Athenians probably hoped to exploit the vast natural resources of the island, as well as its strategic trading location in the Mediterranean Sea. The expedition started badly, as its most skilled military commander, ALCIBIADES, was recalled to Athens for an inquiry into his involvement in a scandal about the MYSTERIES of Demeter. Alcibiades eluded the ship sent to take him back and escaped to SPARTA. In 414, another of the expedition's commanders, Lamachus, was killed. This left the mission in the charge of NICIAS, a capable but overly cautious commander. In 413, when it became clear that the Athenians could not win, Nicias decided to leave SICILY. As the Athenians were preparing to sail away, a lunar eclipse occurred. This prompted Nicias to consult the army's soothsayers, who recommended that they not move for 27 days. Nicias followed their advice and the Athenian fleet was surrounded and eventually destroyed.

SICILY A large, triangular island in the Mediterranean Sea located just off the toe of Italy's boot. The island had been colonized by Greeks as early as the eight century B.C.E. AESCHYLUS lived in Sicily for some time, produced a few of his plays there, and died there. In classical drama, Sicily and its volcanic mountain Aetna were the setting for EURIPIDES' CYCLOPS. In 415 B.C.E., the Athenians launched a military expedition to the island, which was defeated two years later.

SICINNIS A type of dance in SATYR PLAYS. Athenaeus says a barbarian named Sicinnus invented the dance. A person who danced the *sicinnis* was called a *sicinnistes*. According to Eustathius' source, the Phrygians originally performed this dance in honor of DIONYSUS Sabazius, and it was named after a nymph, Sicinnis, a follower of Cybele (see RHEA). [ANCIENT SOURCES: Athenaeus, 1.20e; Euripides, *Cyclops* 37; Eustathius on *Iliad,* 16.617; Lucian, *On Dance* 22]

SICYON A town on the Greek coast northwest of CORINTH. ZEUS' lover ANTIOPE is said to have fled here after her father, Nycteus, discovered that she was pregnant with Zeus' children. [ANCIENT SOURCES: Aristophanes, *Birds* 968]

SIDON A Phoenician town just north of TYRE on the coast of the eastern Mediterranean. Playwrights sometimes mention Sidon as the birthplace of EUROPA and CADMUS. [ANCIENT SOURCES: Aristophanes, *Frogs* 1225; Euripides, *Bacchae* 171; Seneca, *Oedipus* 163, 713, *Octavia* 206]

SIGEUM The name of the harbor at TROY. [ANCIENT SOURCES: Sophocles, *Philoctetes* 355; Seneca, *Agamemnon* 436, *Trojan Women* 75, 141, 932]

SIKYONIOS See MAN FROM SICYON.

SILANUS, L. JUNIUS A Roman politician engaged to OCTAVIA, who was killed so that she could marry NERO. [ANCIENT SOURCES: Seneca, *Octavia* 145]

SILENUS (SILEN) The son of HERMES, PAN, or Gaea (see EARTH), Silenus is often called the father of the SATYRS. One source makes him the father of the centaur Pholus by a Melian NYMPH. As were satyrs, Silenus was part human, but had the horns and legs of a goat and the tail of a horse. He was quite lusty and usually quite drunk. Unlike the satyrs, though, Silenus had a gift for prophecy. Some sources attribute the invention of the pipes to Silenus, and some refer to multiple Sileni.

Silenus was a common character in the SATYR PLAY. Silenus appears as a character in EURIPIDES' CYCLOPS. In this play, Silenus is loyal to DIONYSUS and had searched for the god when pirates abducted him, but is also a double-crossing, cowardly fellow. When ODYSSEUS and his men arrive at the CYCLOPS' cave, where Silenus and his sons are slaves, Silenus agrees to trade Odysseus some food in exchange for Odysseus' wine. When the Cyclops returns, however, Silenus, fearing his evil master will punish him, claims that Odysseus and his men were trying to steal the food. Eventually, Silenus is punished, when Odysseus makes the Cyclops drunk and the Cyclops drags Silenus into his cave to have his way (sexually) with the old satyr. Silenus also appeared as a character in SOPHOCLES' satyr play SEARCHERS. [ANCIENT SOURCES: Apollodorus, *Library* 2.5.4; Hyginus, *Fables* 191; Ovid, *Metamorphoses* 11.90, 99; Seneca, *Oedipus* 429]

SILVANUS A Roman god of forests. [ANCIENT SOURCES: Plautus, *Pot of Gold* 674, 676, 766]

SIMAETHA A prostitute supposedly loved by ALCIBIADES. [ANCIENT SOURCES: Aristophanes, *Acharnians* 524]

BIBLIOGRAPHY
Sommerstein, A. H. *The Comedies of Aristophanes.* Vol. 1, *Acharnians.* Warminster, U.K.: Aris & Phillips, 1980, 182.

SIMOIS One of two rivers (the other is the SCAMANDER) near the town of TROY.

SIMON (1) An Athenian, perhaps fictional, who may have been a cavalry commander. One known Simon "wrote a treatise on horsemanship and . . . dedicated a bronze statue of a horse at the Eleusinium in Athens with his . . . achievements . . . displayed in relief on the plinth" (Sommerstein). [ANCIENT SOURCES: Aristophanes, *Clouds* 351, *Knights* 242; Xenophon, *On Horsemanship* 1.1]

BIBLIOGRAPHY
Sommerstein, A. H. *The Comedies of Aristophanes.* Vol. 2, *Knights.* Warminster, U.K.: Aris & Phillips, 1981, 155.

SIMON (2) An Athenian, probably a politician and a supporter of CLEON, whom the comic poets labeled a debtor, embezzler, and perjurer. [ANCIENT SOURCES: Aristophanes, *Clouds* 351; Eupolis, fragment 218 Kock]

BIBLIOGRAPHY
Kock, T. *Comicorum Atticorum Fragmenta.* Vol. 1. Leipzig: Teubner, 1880.
Sommerstein, A. H. *The Comedies of Aristophanes.* Vol. 3, *Clouds.* Warminster, U.K.: Aris & Phillips, 1982. 179.

SIMONIDES (556–457 B.C.E.) From the island of Ceos, Simonides wrote various types of lyric poetry. Sometime before 514 B.C.E., Simonides went to

ATHENS, where he is said to have been victorious 56 times in competitions for dithyrambic poetry (see DITHYRAMB). In 514 Simonides traveled to THESSALY, but he had returned to Athens by 490 B.C.E., and his epitaph written in honor of those who died at the battle of MARATHON was selected instead of that composed by AESCHYLUS. [ANCIENT SOURCES: Aristophanes, *Birds* 919, *Clouds* 1356, 1362, *Knights* 406, *Peace* 697–98, *Wasps* 1410; Eupolis, fragment 139.1 Kock]

BIBLIOGRAPHY

Bowra, C. M. *Greek Lyric Poetry from Alcman to Simonides.* 2d rev. ed. Oxford: Clarendon Press, 1961.

Kock, T. *Comicorum Atticorum Fragmenta.* Vol. 1. Leipzig: Teubner, 1880.

SINIS The son of Polypemon (or Lytaeus) and Sylea, Sinis was an outlaw who lived near the town of CORINTH and whose nickname was the Pine Bender. According to some sources, Sinis forced those who passed by to bend pine trees. The trees then snapped back and threw the people into the air. Other sources say that Sinis made people bend two pines or tied their limbs to two bent pines, and then let the pines snap back, tearing people apart and killing them when they fell to the ground. THESEUS, however, ended Sinis' reign of terror by forcing him to bend his own pines. Pausanias says that Theseus was related to Sinis through Theseus' grandfather, Pittheus, and that Theseus had a son, Melanippus, by Sinis' daughter, who Plutarch says was named Perigune. [ANCIENT SOURCES: Apollodorus, *Library* 3.16.2; Baccylides, *Ode* 18.19–24; Euripides, *Hippolytus* 977–78; Pausanias, 1.37.4, 2.1.4, 10.25.7; Plutarch, *Theseus* 8.2–3, 25.6, 29.1; Seneca, *Hercules Oetaeus* 1393, *Hippolytus* 1169, 1223]

SINON The son of Aesimus, Sinon was a spy left behind by the Greeks after they deposited the wooden horse outside TROY and pretended to sail for Greece. Sinon allowed the Trojans to capture him and told them a false tale to persuade them to taken the horse into their city. Sophocles wrote a *Sinon,* of which four words survive (fragments 542–44 Radt). [ANCIENT SOURCES: Apollodorus, *Epitome* 5.15–19; Hyginus, *Fables* 108; Seneca, *Agamemnon* 626, *Trojan Women* 39; Vergil, *Aeneid* 2.57–198]

BIBLIOGRAPHY

Kiso, A. *The Lost Sophocles.* New York: Vantage Press, 1984.

Lloyd-Jones, H. *Sophocles: Fragments.* Cambridge, Mass.: Harvard University Press, 1996.

Radt, S. *Tragicorum Graecorum Fragmenta.* Vol. 4. Göttingen, Ger.: Vandenhoeck & Ruprecht, 1977.

Sutton, D. F. *The Lost Sophocles.* Lanham, Md.: University Press of America, 1984.

SINOPE An important Greek colony on the Black Sea's southern coast. [ANCIENT SOURCES: Plautus, *Curculio* 443]

SIPARIUM (Plural: SIPARIA) A curtain before which MIMES performed; according to Csapo and Slater, it "blocked the view of the stage."

BIBLIOGRAPHY

Csapo, E., and W. J. Slater. *The Context of Ancient Drama.* Ann Arbor: University of Michigan Press, 1995.

SIPYLUS A mountain in what is today western Turkey. NIOBE was said to have been transformed into a stone that was on Sipylus. [ANCIENT SOURCES: Apollodorus, *Library* 3.5.6; Euripides, *Iphigenia at Aulis* 952; Pausanias, 1.21.3; Seneca, *Agamemnon* 394, *Hercules Furens* 391, *Hercules Oetaeus* 185; Sophocles, *Antigone* 825]

SIRENS The daughters of the river ACHELOUS, the Sirens were a group of creatures who had the body of a bird and the face of a woman. Apollodorus gives their names as Aglaope, Pisinoe, and Thelxiepia. When sailors ventured past their island, they sang an alluring song that would cause the sailors to venture too close to their island, which was ringed by treacherous reefs that wrecked the ships. Some sailors jumped off their ship and were killed by smashing on the reefs. ODYSSEUS' encounter with the Sirens on his journey home from TROY is the best-known story involving these creatures. Odysseus managed to save his crew from the Sirens by telling them to put wax into their ears before they sailed past. Odysseus told his crew to tie him to the ship's mast and thereby heard their song. It was prophesied that the Sirens would die if a ship escaped them and some traditions say they perished after Odysseus sailed past. The comic poet Nicophon wrote a *Sirens,* whose three brief extant fragments tell nothing about the play's plot or characters (fragments 12–14 Kock). [ANCIENT SOURCES: Apollodorus, *Epitome* 7.18–19; Ovid, *Metamorphoses* 5.552–562]

BIBLIOGRAPHY

Kock, T. *Comicorum Atticorum Fragmenta.* Vol. 1. Leipzig: Teubner, 1880.

SISYPHUS   The son of AEOLUS and Aenarete, Sisyphus was the husband of MEROPE and the father of GLAUCUS, Ornytion, Thersander, and Almus. Sisyphus was also credited with founding CORINTH. Because the name of Sisyphus was synonymous with deception, ODYSSEUS is sometimes called the son of Sisyphus. In EURIPIDES' *MEDEA,* MEDEA links JASON, who had reneged on his oath to her, with Sisyphus. When Sisyphus revealed to the river Asopus that ZEUS had carried off his daughter, Aegina, Sisyphus was punished in the UNDERWORLD, where he was forced to push a rock up a hill, only to have it roll down again once he reached the top. Another story about Sisyphus is that he bound Death himself and that people ceased to die. ARES released Death, captured Sisyphus, and took the rascal to the underworld. Sisyphus, however, who had instructed his wife not to make proper offering to HADES, persuaded the underworld's ruler to allow him to return to the upper world to arrange for appropriate offerings. After he was above ground, however, Sisyphus refused to return to the underworld.

Sisyphus was the subject of several dramas that are not extant. Aeschylus may have written two plays about him, *Sisyphus Drapetês* (The runaway) and *Sisyphus Petrokylistês* (The stone roller) (fragments 225–34 Radt); Lloyd-Jones seems inclined to think that they were actually the same play. The few fragments that survive indicate that Aeschylus' *Sisyphus* was a SATYR PLAY about Sisyphus' return from the underworld. Sophocles may also have written a *Sisyphus,* but only one uninformative fragment survives (fragment 545 Radt). Euripides also wrote a *Sisyphus,* in which HERACLES seems to have been a character and perhaps encountered Sisyphus when Heracles journeyed to the underworld to take CERBERUS (fragments 673–74

Nauck) back. [ANCIENT SOURCES Apollodorus, *Library* 1.9.3, 3.12.6; Euripides, *Heracles* 1103; Homer, *Odyssey* 11.593–600; Hyginus, *Fables* 60; Pausanias, 2.4.3]

BIBLIOGRAPHY

Nauck, A. *Tragicorum Graecorum Fragmenta.* 1889. Reprint, Hildesheim, Ger.: Olms, 1964.
Radt, S. *Tragicorum Graecorum Fragmenta.* Vol. 3. Göttingen, Ger.: Vandenhoeck & Ruprecht, 1985.
Smyth, H. W., and H. Lloyd-Jones. *Aeschylus.* Vol. 2. 1926. Reprint, Cambridge, Mass.: Harvard University Press, 1971.

SITALCES (DIED 424 B.C.E.)   King of a Thracian tribe called the Odrysae, Sitalces was an ally of ATHENS in the first years of the PELOPONNESIAN WAR. In the year 429/498, the Athenians did not give Sitalces the naval support he needed to invade Macedonia, and the cordial relations of the Athenians and Sitalces appear to have ended. After Sitalces' death, his nephew, Seuthes, who was well disposed toward the Macedonians, succeeded him. [ANCIENT SOURCES: Aristophanes, *Acharnians* 134; Thucydides 2.95–101]

BIBLIOGRAPHY

Sommerstein, A. H. *The Comedies of Aristophanes.* Vol. 1, *Acharnians.* Warminster, U.K.: Aris & Phillips, 1980, 164.

SKENE (SCAENA) (Plural: SKENAI/ SCAENAE)   The *skene* is the stage building that is situated at the side of the ORCHESTRA that is farthest from the audience. The English word *scene* is derived from this Greek word, which literally means "tent." In the fifth century B.C.E., the *skene* was made of wood; it appears to have been in use as early as AESCHYLUS' *ORESTEIA* of 458 B.C.E. Around 430 B.C.E., permanent *skenai* of stone were first built. The *skene* was rectangular, and its width would have varied from theater to theater but could have been more than 60 feet. The *skene* had as many as three doors; the surviving Greek tragedies probably needed only one door, whereas the surviving Greek comedies seem to have made use of three doors. The *skene* had an opening in the roof of its lower story that allowed actors access to the skene's roof. In the fifth century B.C.E., the roof appears to have been flat, but as stone theaters were built second levels with roofs, sides, and doors were constructed.

In Greek TRAGEDY, the *skene* usually represents the palace of a ruler but can also represent a temple (e.g., EURIPIDES' *ION*, *IPHIGENIA IN TAURIS*) or cave (e.g., SOPHOCLES' *PHILOCTETES*, Euripides' *Cyclops*). Among the surviving Greek tragedies, change of scene is not common. Aeschylus' *Eumenides* (see *ORESTEIA*) opens at the temple of APOLLO at DELPHI, then moves to ATHENS. Sophocles' *Ajax* begins near Ajax's tent, but Ajax kills himself near the seashore. How these changes would have been represented—if they were—on stage is not clear. The *skene* may have been equipped with slots into which painted panels could be placed and removed as the scene required, but it is doubted whether such panels were available in the fifth century B.C.E.

Although changes of scene did occur in Greek tragedy, in Aristophanic COMEDY, the audience must have had to pay more careful attention, as what the *skene* represented might change multiple times in a play. In ARISTOPHANES' *ACHARNIANS*, the audience must imagine DICAEOPOLIS at the meeting place of the Athenian assembly, at his own house in the country, at the house of Euripides, and at an imaginary marketplace. In Aristophanes' *PEACE* and *FROGS*, the scene changes between the Earth and heaven in the former play and between Earth and the UNDERWORLD in the latter. In New Comedy, the *skene* most often represents two houses (usually either the houses of two citizens or the house of a citizen and that of a PIMP or PROSTITUTE). Less often in New Comedy, the *skene* represents one or three houses. Sometimes, New Comedy has a temple or altar near the "houses" (e.g., PLAUTUS' *CURCULIO*, *POT OF GOLD*, *ROPE*).

BIBLIOGRAPHY

Csapo, E., and W. J. Slater. *The Context of Ancient Drama.* Ann Arbor: University of Michigan Press, 1995, 79–88.

Mastronarde, D. J. "Actors on High: The Skene Roof, the Crane, and the Gods in Attic Drama," *Classical Antiquity* 9 (1990): 247–94.

Taplin, O. "Sophocles in His Theatre." In *Sophocle.* Edited by J. de Romilly. Geneva: Vandœuvres Fondation Hardt, 1982, 155–83.

Townsend, R. F. "The Fourth Century *Skene* of the Theater of Dionysos at Athens," *Hesperia* 55 (1986): 421–38.

SKENOGRAPHIA *Skenographia*, scene painting, was, according to ARISTOTLE, introduced in drama by SOPHOCLES. Vitruvius, however, writing in the last quarter of the first century B.C.E., says it first appeared in ATHENS during the time of AESCHYLUS and that an artist named Agatharchus introduced it. Apparently, the front of the stage building (see *SKENE*) had an apparatus that allowed panels to be attached to its front. These panels could be painted so that the stage building might better represent a palace, temple, cave, or other setting required by a particular play. According to Vitruvius different forms of scene painting were used in TRAGEDY, COMEDY, and the SATYR PLAY. [ANCIENT SOURCES: Aristotle, *Poetics* 1449a11; Vitruvius, *On Architecture* 5.6, 7 preface 11]

SKENOTHEKE (SKANOTHEKA) An area near or within the stage building (see *SKENE*) used for dressing or storage. [ANCIENT SOURCES: *Inscriptions de Délos* 444 B 103, 104; *Inscriptiones Graecae* 5(1).879.2, 5(2).469.5]

SLAVES In the Greek and Roman world, slaves were usually people captured through the conquest of their land, victims of abduction by slave traders or pirates, or persons whose financial situation led them to sell themselves into slavery. Slaves included not only those who performed manual labor, such as herders of cattle, but also tutors and nurses in classical drama. In Greek drama of the fifth century, especially TRAGEDY, slaves usually do not have extensive speaking roles. In the seven surviving plays attributed to AESCHYLUS, slaves deliver fewer than 100 total lines. After the time of Aeschylus, however, the speaking roles for slave characters increased. In ARISTOPHANES' *FROGS*, EURIPIDES is criticized for expanding the speaking roles of members of the lower classes in tragedy. Euripides' surviving plays (some of which have no speaking roles for slaves), however, suggest that Aristophanes exaggerated. It is true, however, that slaves speak more than 15 percent of the lines in *HIPPOLYTUS*, *ION*, and *IPHIGENIA IN TAURIS*.

In Aristophanes' early plays, slaves have fairly limited speaking roles. WASPS and PEACE both begin with dialogues between slaves that help introduce the subject matter of the play, but these slaves have no significance after the PROLOGUE. In Aristophanic comedy slaves seem to have had more speaking parts as time went on. The wise-cracking slave Sosias, who accompanies DIONYSUS to the UNDERWORLD in *Frogs* (405 B.C.E.), and the rather clever Cario in Aristophanes' WEALTH (388 B.C.E.) are often regarded as predecessors of the wily slaves who would become commonplace in the centuries after Aristophanes.

Although slaves appear frequently in MENANDER's comedies, they usually do not have the cleverness and trickery that would become a hallmark of Plautine comedy. Three of PLAUTUS' comedies, *Epidicus, PSEUDOLUS,* and *STICHUS,* take their name from slaves. In several Plautine plays, slaves control and dominate the action: Chrysalus (BACCHIDES), Palaestrio (BRAGGART WARRIOR), Tranio (HAUNTED HOUSE). None of TERENCE's six plays is named after a slave, but Terence does have important roles for slaves (e.g., Davus in ANDRIA; Parmeno in EUNUCH; Geta in PHORMIO).

Most slaves in Roman comedy, although they often grumble about their job and fear punishment, do attend to their duties, are loyal to their master and mistress, and reject improper or immoral behavior. The most memorable slaves in Roman comedy, however, are that small number who, although loyal to at least their master or their mistress, engage in trickery and deception. Terms used to describe such slaves are *servus callidus* (shrewd slave) and *servus dolosus* (tricky slave). The most common target for these slaves' deceptions is either an old citizen (SENEX) or a pimp. The clever slave usually embarks on such deceptions at the request of a young man (ADULESCENS) who is the son of his master. Thus, to be loyal to his young master the slave must deceive his old master. Often, to carry out their schemes, slaves pretend to be other people or arrange for their accomplices to pretend to be others. In carrying out their schemes, the clever slaves often reverse their social roles in literal and figurative ways. They order freeborn people to perform tasks and take on roles to help them accomplish their schemes. In a figurative sense, the slaves are often characterized as kings, generals, or heroes of mythology. Some modern scholars have characterized Plautus' plays as containing plays within plays in which one character, usually the slave, produces a "play" whose aim is the deception of another character or characters within the play.

BIBLIOGRAPHY
Duckworth, G. *The Nature of Roman Comedy.* Princeton, N.J.: Princeton University Press, 1952, 249–53.
Ehrenberg, V. *The People of Aristophanes: A Sociology of Old Attic Comedy.* 2d rev. ed. Oxford: Blackwells, 1951, 165–91.
Fitzgerald, William. *Slavery and the Roman Literary Imagination: Roman Literature and Its Contexts.* Cambridge: Cambridge University Press, 2000.
MacCary, W. T. "Menander's Slaves: Their Names, Roles, and Masks," *Transactions and Proceedings of the American Philological Society* 100 (1969): 277–94.
McCarthy, K. *Slaves, Masters and the Art of Authority in Plautine Comedy.* Princeton, N.J.: Princeton University Press, 2000.

SLEEP (Greek: *HUPNOS*; Latin: *SOMNUS*)

The son of NIGHT, this divinity personifies sleep. In EURIPIDES' CYCLOPS (601), when ODYSSEUS prepares to blind the monster, he prays to HEPHAESTUS, a god of fire, and to Sleep to help him in his task. In SOPHOCLES' PHILOCTETES (827), the chorus pray for Sleep to fall upon the eyes of PHILOCTETES. See also SENECA's HERCULES FURENS (1066), in which the chorus invoke Sleep after Hercules' (see HERACLES) fit of madness.

SMICYTHION

Sommerstein suggests that this man, whom ARISTOPHANES calls the husband of MELISTICHE and suggests was impotent, may have been a frequent prosecutor in the Athenian court system and identical with Smicythion of Halae, who "was secretary to the board of control for Eleiusis in 407/6 [B.C.E.]." Aristophanes' elder contemporary the comic poet Pherecrates mentions a gluttonous Smicythion. [ANCIENT SOURCES: Aristophanes, *Ecclesiazusae* 46, *Wasps* 401; Pherecrates, fragment 32]

BIBLIOGRAPHY
Kock, T. *Comicorum Atticorum Fragmenta.* Vol. 1. Leipzig: Teubner, 1880.
Sommerstein, A. H. *The Comedies of Aristophanes.* Vol. 10, *Ecclesiazusae.* Warminster, U.K.: Aris & Phillips, 1998, 142.

SMICYTHUS (SMICYTHES) A person mentioned by ARISTOPHANES at KNIGHTS 969, who the ancient commentators on the line say was effeminate. In the Athenian inscriptions of that time, the name Smicythus occurs twice—once in reference to a councilor of 427/426 B.C.E. and once in 424/423 in reference to a "secretary to the Treasurers of Athena" (Sommerstein). Which Smicythus Aristophanes had in mind is unknown. They may have been the same person.

BIBLIOGRAPHY
Sommerstein, A. H. *The Comedies of Aristophanes.* Vol. 2, *Knights.* Warminster, U.K.: Aris & Phillips, 1981, 195.

SMINTHEUS An epithet of APOLLO.

SMOIUS A man mentioned by ARISTOPHANES at *ECCLESIAZUSAE* 846 as someone who performed oral sex on women. No other information about Smoius exists, however.

BIBLIOGRAPHY
Sommerstein, A. H. *The Comedies of Aristophanes.* Vol. 10, *Ecclesiazusae.* Warminster, U.K.: Aris & Phillips, 1998, 211.

SOCCUS (Plural: ***SOCCI***) A special slipper or shoe worn by the actors in comedy. The *soccus* fit both feet. [ANCIENT SOURCES: Horace, *Ars Poetica* 80; Pliny the Elder, 7.30.31; Pliny the Younger, *Letters* 9.7.3; Quintilian, 10.2.22]

SOCRATES (469–399 B.C.E.) The son of Sophroniscus and Phaenarete, Socrates was an Athenian citizen from the DEME of Alopece. Socrates fought bravely during the 420s in the PELOPONNESIAN WAR, opposed the motion to try as a group the generals at ARGINUSAE (406), and avoided being linked with the crimes of the Thirty Tyrants who ruled Athens after its fall to SPARTA in 404. Socrates was married to Xanthippe, who gained a reputation (probably undeserved) as a difficult person with whom to live.

At some point in his life, perhaps before the Peloponnesian War, Socrates, prompted by his friend CHAEREPHON's question to the DELPHIC ORACLE ("Is anyone wiser than Socrates?"), made it his mission to discover the meaning behind the response that Chaerephon was given (that no one was wiser than Socrates). Accordingly, Socrates began to question his fellow Athenians to determine whether he was, in fact, wiser than they were. Socrates' questioning of his fellow citizens also attracted the attention of numerous young men (such as ALCIBIADES and PLATO), who found Socrates' method of inquiry into the wisdom of others fascinating. This activity angered many of Socrates' fellow citizens, who no doubt felt that he was trying to subvert societal values. Eventually, Socrates' enemies prosecuted him in court on charges of corrupting the youth of ATHENS, not believing in the divinities worshiped by the Athenian state, and introducing new divinities. In 399, Socrates was put to death by the Athenians.

The charges against Socrates in 399 were not new, as Socrates himself mentions in Plato's *Apology*. In ARISTOPHANES' *CLOUDS* (first staged in 423 B.C.E.), Aristophanes characterizes Socrates along these same lines. In *Clouds*, Socrates' first entrance depicts him as "walking on air." In this play, he also advocates the worship of unusual divinities (such as Vortex, Chaos, and Tongue) and is shown as being involved in unusual intellectual inquiry into matters above and below the Earth. This Socrates also advocates the use of a sort of argumentation that would allow the person who employed it to defeat an opponent's argument even if the opponent's argument were stronger. Aristophanes has Socrates teaching this sort of argumentation to young men at a school called the Phrontesterion. The real Socrates had no such school and was not the head of any philosophical school, although his follower, Plato, did become the head of a school of philosophical thought. At the conclusion of *Clouds*, STREPSIADES, blaming Socrates for teaching his (Strepsiades') son the sort of lessons that led him to behave unbearably, tries to kill Socrates by burning down his school. Although Aristophanes' portrayal of Socrates is clearly comic and should be regarded as a caricature, this portrayal did have a lasting impression on some members of the Athenian public, and in Plato's *Apology* the author has Socrates make a few remarks to discount Aristophanes' portrayal of him. If Socrates and Aristophanes did have entertain hard feelings about each other, they are not readily apparent in Plato's *Symposium*. *Symposium* is set at a dinner party in 416 B.C.E. (nine years after the initial appearance of *Clouds*), at which both Aristophanes and Socrates participate in the conversation.

BIBLIOGRAPHY

Benson, H. H., ed. *Essays on the Philosophy of Socrates*. New York: Oxford University Press, 1991.

Gooch, P. W. *Reflections on Jesus and Socrates: Word and Silence*. New Haven, Conn.: Yale University Press, 1996.

Kraut, R. *Socrates and the State*. Princeton, N.J.: Princeton University Press, 1984.

Smith, N. D., and P. B. Woodruff, eds. *Reason and Religion in Socratic Philosophy*. Oxford: Oxford University Press, 2000.

Taylor, C. C. W. *Socrates*. Oxford: Oxford University Press, 1998.

SOL   See SUN.

SOLON
An Athenian poet and statesman, Solon held the office of the chief archon in 594/593 B.C.E. Solon is credited with introducing sweeping social, legislative, judicial, and economic reforms, many of which benefited the lower classes. Although his reforms did not solve all the problems of his day, later generations regarded him as one of ATHENS' wisest citizens. [ANCIENT SOURCES: Aristophanes, *Birds* 1660, *Clouds* 1187; Aristotle, *Constitution of the Athenians*; Diogenes Laertius, 1.45–67; Plutarch, *Solon*]

BIBLIOGRAPHY

Gerber, D. E., ed. *Greek Elegiac Poetry: From the Seventh to the Fifth Centuries B.C.* Cambridge, Mass.: Harvard University Press, 1999.

Linforth, I. M. *Solon the Athenian*. Berkeley: University of California Press, 1919.

Rexine, J. E. *Solon and His Political Theory*. New York: William-Frederick Press, 1958.

Woodhouse, W. J. *Solon the Liberator*. London: Oxford University Press, H. Milford, 1938.

SOMATION
A padded garment worn by an actor on the upper body. In COMEDY, the *somation* would be used to make an actor appear grotesquely overweight. [ANCIENT SOURCES: Lucian, *Juppiter Tragoedus* 41; Pollux, *Onomasticon* 2.235, 4.115]

SOMNUS   See SLEEP.

SOPHISTS
Around the middle of the fifth century B.C.E. in Greece, some men began to make their living by traveling from town to town and charging young men for lessons in how to succeed in public life. These teachers became known as sophists, and their primary subject of instruction was rhetoric, although not all sophists taught the same subjects or skills. One sophist, Hippias of ELIS, taught people to improve their memory (among other attributes). Protagoras claimed to be able to teach people how to be virtuous. Other sophists taught astronomy, geometry, grammar, history, mathematics, music, philosophy, poetry, and a host of other subjects and skills. After some time, sophists began to gain a reputation for teaching people to win arguments by using rhetorical strategies and tactics that the sophists considered clever, but that others would term as irrelevant. The orator Demosthenes, in his speech *Against Aphobus* (29.32), speaks of sophists in the same breath as magicians. PLATO, in *Sophist* (234e), compares the sophist to a juggler. In *CLOUDS,* ARISTOPHANES described their technique as making the weaker argument stronger. In this play, Aristophanes portrays SOCRATES as a sophist (although he was not) who teaches young men this line of argumentation, as well as other subjects such as astronomy, geology, geography, grammar, meteorology, and natural history. Aristophanes was not the only comic poet to attack sophists, as shown by the comic poet Plato's *Sophists* (fragments 134–47 Kock). Aristophanes also links EURIPIDES with the sophists; although Euripides was not a sophist, some of his characters make remarks that sound like those of sophists. The sophist GORGIAS of Leontini composed as a rhetorical exercise a defense of MENELAUS' wife, HELEN (*Encomium of Helen*), which may have influenced the defense that Euripides' Helen offers in *TROJAN WOMEN* (914–65). [ANCIENT SOURCES: Plato, *Hippias Major, Hippias Minor, Protagoras, Sophist*]

BIBLIOGRAPHY

Conacher, D. J. *Euripides and the Sophists*. London: Duckworth, 1998.

Guthrie, W. K. C. *The Sophists*. Cambridge: Cambridge University Press, 1971.

Kerferd, G. B. *The Sophistic Movement*. London: Cambridge University Press, 1981.

Kock, T. *Comicorum Atticorum Fragmenta*. Vol. 1. Leipzig: Teubner, 1880.

Romilly, J. de. *The Great Sophists in Periclean Athens*. Translated by Janet Lloyd. Oxford: Clarendon Press; New York: Oxford University Press, 1992.

SOPHOCLES (CA. 496–406 B.C.E.)

The son of Sophilus, Sophocles was born at COLONUS, a DEME a little more than a mile northwest of ATHENS. Sophocles was not only a playwright, he also served as a priest on several occasions, was head of the Athenian treasury in 443/442 B.C.E., was elected to a military command in 440 (supposedly on the success of his *ANTIGONE*), and was appointed to a special commission after disaster befell the SICILIAN EXPEDITION in 413. Sophocles had two sons (Iophon and Sophocles the younger) by Nicostrata and a third son (Ariston) by Theoris. Both his sons by Nicostrata were playwrights. Sophocles had a reputation as being good-natured and being a true gentleman. After the death of EURIPIDES, Sophocles is said to have honored Euripides by wearing mourning clothes and by presenting his chorus before the play without their usual garlands. In ARISTOPHANES' *FROGS*, Sophocles is portrayed as not contesting the recognition of AESCHYLUS as the greatest of tragedians. In that play, after Aeschylus leaves the underworld, he turns over his title of best tragedian to SOPHOCLES rather than EURIPIDES.

Sophocles wrote 123 plays, of which seven survive: *AJAX, Antigone, TRACHINIAN WOMEN, OEDIPUS TYRANNOS, ELECTRA, PHILOCTETES,* and *OEDIPUS AT COLONUS*. We also have some 400 lines from a Sophoclean SATYR PLAY, *Ichneutae* (*SEARCHERS*). The dating of Sophocles' plays is difficult, and the preceding list reflects a likely order of production. Only the dates of *Philoctetes* (409), and *Oedipus at Colonus* (produced in 401, after Sophocles' death) are securely established. *Antigone* is usually dated to 442/441, but this date is based on the anecdote about the link between Sophocles' military command in 440 and the success of *Antigone*. *Ajax* is usually dated to the 440s, *Oedipus Tyrannos* to around the time of the plague in Athens (430/429), *Electra* to about the same period as Euripides' *ELECTRA* (420–410). The date of *Trachinian Women* ranges between 450 and 425; most scholars now favor a date in the last decade of that period. The date of *Searchers* is unknown.

Tradition and inscriptional evidence confirm that Sophocles won first prize in competition 18 times, perhaps more than AESCHYLUS and Euripides combined. Sophocles is said never to have finished in last place in a dramatic competition. His first victory was in 468 (with the no longer extant *Triptolemus*) against Aeschylus. Early in his career, Sophocles took roles in some of his own plays, but he is said to have stopped because of a weak voice. According to ARISTOTLE in *Poetics*, Sophocles was the first to use three actors and scene painting (see SKENOGRAPHIA). Sophocles is also credited with increasing the number of the chorus from 12 to 15. The effects of increasing the choral number are not clear, and scene painting would not have added much to the powerful messages contained in Sophocles' surviving plays; however, the use of a third actor did allow Sophocles to explore his heroes and heroines from an additional perspective. Instead of only ANTIGONE versus CREON, we have ISMENE's added perspective on Antigone's actions. Instead of only Electra versus CLYTEMNESTRA, we have CHRYSOTHEMIS' view of Electra's attitude.

Other than their inclusion of a third actor, Sophocles' surviving plays seem fairly conventional with respect to staging and spectacle. His *Ajax,* however, is one of two Greek tragedies that have a change of scene (Aeschylus' *Eumenides* [see ORESTEIA] is the other); some scholars think the title character may have committed suicide before the audience rather than dying offstage and his death later being reported. Sophocles' plays seem fairly conventional when compared with the numerous problems that occur in Euripides'. Powerful visual images do occur in Sophocles, to be sure, such as AJAX's sword, PHILOCTETES' bow, and Electra's urn, but Sophocles does not have Euripidean extremes of spectacle. Divinities appear before the audience only twice in Sophocles' tragedies (*Ajax, Philoctetes*), and only one of Sophocles' tragedies (*Philoctetes*) ends with the appearance of a divinity; in contrast, Euripides ends many of his plays in this way.

Sophocles also lets the action of his plays unfold in a more natural way than Euripides and avoids the expository prologues of his contemporary. The seven tragedies show a more consistent use of the chorus than do the works of Euripides; Sophoclean choruses deliver between 15 and 25 percent of the lines. Five of Sophocles' seven tragic choruses represent men (the exceptions are *Trachinian Women* and *Electra*). Two of Sophocles' choruses (*Ajax, Philoctetes*) represent sailors, unlike in the tragedies of Aeschylus or Euripides. Sophocles' choruses are also considered to deliver some of the finest lyric poetry, such as the beautiful little ode to the beauty of Athens in *Oedipus at Colonus* and the famous ode in *Antigone* on the wonders of humankind.

Whereas Euripides was stereotyped as allowing a greater stage presence to women, common people, and slaves, Sophocles relegates most of his commoners to the chorus or to the function of MESSENGER; however, the role of the messenger, Lichas, in *Trachinian Women* is an important one and the unnamed guard in *Antigone* adds some levity to an otherwise serious play. Only one NURSE (*Trachinian Women*) and one TUTOR (*Electra*) have speaking roles in Sophocles' extant tragedies. Sophocles' tragedies have several prominent female roles, especially *Antigone, Electra,* and *Trachinian Women,* but none of Sophocles' surviving plays has onstage a seductive PHAEDRA or STHENEBOEA, as do Euripides'. In the lost plays, however, Sophocles did treat wicked women such as ERIPHYLE and MEDEA.

Sophocles' primary interest are kings, queens, princes, and princesses and the struggles they experience within themselves, with their fellow human beings, and with the gods. Whereas Euripides' characters often express a cynical attitude about the behavior of their fellow humans and the divinities, Sophocles is usually perceived as less pessimistic and more accepting of the religious system of his day. Scholars often think of Sophocles as a pious person, and he even helped introduce the cult of Asclepius to Athens. Most of Sophocles' plays contain prophecies that lead the play's characters to grapple with their own relationship to the gods. As Blundell's study shows, most of Sophocles' surviving plays deal with instances in which expected friends become one's enemies. AJAX turns against his fellow Greeks at TROY; Antigone and CREON, niece and uncle, oppose one another; ORESTES and Electra oppose their mother; PHILOCTETES is rejected and then sought out by his fellow Greeks; OEDIPUS is rejected and then sought out by his sons. Such oppositions cause the questions taken up by Sophocles' play to become far more complicated and tension filled. In *Ajax* and *Antigone*, Sophocles poses the following question: "Does a deceased person have a right to be buried?" The answer seems simple, but the question becomes far more complex when the deceased person has tried to wage war against his native land or kill his commanding officers. Similar complex questions are raised in *Oedipus at Colonus:* "Should a country grant asylum to a refugee?" "If so, how far should that country go to protect that refugee?" The answer becomes more complicated when the refugee is Oedipus, one of the most abhorrent figures in mythology. Further complicating the issue is that this abhorrent figure must be defended by the host nation's military might. Finally, Sophocles' *Oedipus Tyrannos* may ask the most profound and complex question of any ancient work: "What is the definition of a man?" [ANCIENT SOURCES: Anonymous, *Vita Sophoclis;* Aristophanes, *Birds* 100, *Frogs* 82, *Peace* 531, 695; Aristotle, *Poetics, Rhetoric* 1419a25; Athenaeus 13.603e–604d; Diodorus Siculus, 10.103.4; *Inscriptiones Graecae* ii¹202, ii²2325; *Parian Marble* 56; Plutarch, *Cimon* 8, *Nicias* 15, *Numa* 3, *Pericles* 8; Suda, s815]

BIBLIOGRAPHY

Blundell, M. W. *Helping Friends and Harming Enemies: A Study in Sophocles and Greek Ethics.* Cambridge: Cambridge University Press, 1989.

Knox, B. M. W. *The Heroic Temper.* Berkeley and Los Angeles: University of California Press, 1964.

Segal, Charles P. *Sophocles' Tragic World: Divinity, Nature, Society.* Cambridge, Mass.: Harvard University Press, 1995.

———. *Tragedy and Civilization.* Cambridge, Mass., and London: Harvard University Press, 1981.

Segal, Erich (ed.). *Oxford Readings in Greek Tragedy.* Oxford: Oxford University Press, 1983.

Winnington-Ingram, R. P. *Sophocles: An Interpretation.* Cambridge: Cambridge University Press, 1980.

SOSTRATE A woman mentioned by ARISTOPHANES at *ECCLESIAZUSAE* 41. She is not identified with any historical person.

SPARTA Located in the central part of southern Greece in the region of Laconia, Sparta (also called Lacedaemon or Lacedaemonia) was one of that country's two most important cities (the other was ATHENS) in ancient times. The Spartans were known for their austere mode of life and military prowess. The most famous Spartans in mythology are TYNDAREUS; his wife, LEDA; and their children, CASTOR, POLLUX, HELEN, and CLYTEMNESTRA. Because MENELAUS married Helen, he became king of Sparta. During the fifth and fourth centuries B.C.E., Sparta vied with Athens for supremacy in Greece, and from 431 to 404 Sparta and their allies waged war with and eventually defeated the Athenians (see PELOPONNESIAN WAR). Accordingly, some plays written during this time that have characters from Sparta are regarded as having a negative view of the Spartans (e.g., EURIPIDES' ANDROMACHE). Three of ARISTOPHANES' comedies (ACHARNIANS, PEACE, LYSISTRATA) deal with aspects of this war and reveal some Athenian stereotypes of the Spartans. [ANCIENT SOURCES: Herodotus 1, 5–9; Homer, *Odyssey* 4; Pausanias, 3.11–20; Plutarch, *Agis, Agesilaus, Cleomenes, Lycurgus, Apophthegmata Laconica*; Strabo, 8.4–6; Thucydides, *Histories*; Xenophon, *De republica Lacedaemoniorum, Hellenica*]

BIBLIOGRAPHY
Jones, A. H. M. *Sparta.* Oxford: Blackwell, 1967.

SPHINX The offspring of the monsters Echidna and Typhon (or the dog Orthus), the Sphinx had a woman's face, a lion's body, an eagle's wings, and a serpent's tail. HERA, angered at the Theban king LAIUS for his violation of his marriage to JOCASTA, sent the Sphinx to terrorize the people of THEBES. The Sphinx sat upon Mount Phicium outside the town and asked those who passed by a riddle: "What creature walks on four legs in the morning, two legs at noon, and three legs in the evening?" Another version of the riddle is, "What has one voice, but becomes four-footed, two-footed, and three-footed?" An ORACLE had told the Thebans that if they solved the Sphinx's riddle, they would be rid of the monster. If the person could not answer the riddle, the Sphinx would kill him. After several had died in this way, CREON, who became king after Oedipus killed Laius, declared that whoever solved the rid-

dle would be given the kingdom of Thebes and be allowed to marry Laius' widow, Jocasta. When OEDIPUS provided the correct answer to the riddle ("a human being"), the Sphinx hurled itself from the Theban citadel and died. AESCHYLUS' SATYR PLAY *Sphinx* completed the TETRALOGY in which the extant *SEVEN AGAINST THEBES* was staged (fragments 235–37 Radt). Unfortunately, little is known about the content of this play. Presumably it dealt with Oedipus' solution of the Sphinx's riddle. [ANCIENT SOURCES: Apollodorus, *Library* 3.5.8; Euripides, *Phoenician Women* 45–54, 806–11; Hesiod, *Theogony* 326–27; Pausanias, 9.26.2–4; Seneca, *Oedipus*; Sophocles, *Oedipus Tyrannos* 130]

BIBLIOGRAPHY
Radt, S. *Tragicorum Graecorum Fragmenta.* Vol. 3. Göttingen, Ger.: Vandenhoeck & Ruprecht, 1985.
Smyth, H. W., and H. Lloyd-Jones. *Aeschylus.* Vol. 2. 1026. Reprint, Cambridge, Mass.: Harvard University Press, 1971.

SPINTHARUS An unknown man from PHRYGIA mentioned by ARISTOPHANES at *BIRDS* 762.

SPONGER See PARASITE.

SPORGILUS A barber with whom Athenian audiences were familiar. [ANCIENT SOURCES: Aristophanes, *Birds* 300 and the scholia on 299a; Plato Comicus, fragment 144 Kock]

BIBLIOGRAPHY
Kock, T. *Comicorum Atticorum Fragmenta.* Vol. 1. Leipzig: Teubner, 1880.

STAGE The Greek word for "stage" is *logeion*; the Latin is *pulpitum*. In Greek productions of the late sixth and the first half of the fifth century, it is not clear whether the theater had a stage. Thus, in the early days of Greek drama, both the chorus and the actors performed in the ORCHESTRA or occasionally an actor appeared on top of the stage building (see SKENE). By the time of ARISTOPHANES' WASPS (422 B.C.E.), some sort of stage, raised a few steps above the orchestra, does seem to have been used. At *Wasps* 1341–44, Philocleon leads a slave woman toward his house (the *skene*) and orders her to "come up here" (*anabaine deuro*), an instruction that seems to indicate the presence of something above the level of the orchestra. If a stage did exist in the fifth century, the center of the orchestra, rather than the stage, appears to have been the focal point of the action. By the fourth century B.C.E., however, a wooden stage in the Greek theater was well established and occupied by the actors, while the chorus remained in the orchestra. The second phase of the theater construction at Epidaurus, 170–60 B.C.E., had a stage that was almost 66 feet wide and about 13 feet deep.

No doubt exists about the presence of a stage in the Roman theater, although Rome's first permanent theater did not exist until the middle of the first century B.C.E. Because the Roman orchestra was semicircular, rather than circular as in the Greek theater, and occupied by seating for dignitaries, the stage would need to be larger to accommodate the performers. Csapo and Slater estimate that the average Roman stage during the imperial period was about 160 feet wide and 25 feet deep. The stage at Aphrodisias (in western Turkey), built in the first century B.C.E., was almost 100 feet wide and stood almost 12 feet above the orchestra.

BIBLIOGRAPHY

Arnott, P. D. *Public and Performance in the Greek Theatre.* London: Routledge, 2003.

Csapo, E., and W. J. Slater. *The Context of Ancient Drama.* Ann Arbor: University of Michigan Press, 1995, 79–88.

Dover, K. J. *Aristophanic Comedy.* Berkeley: University of California Press, 1972, 18–19.

Webster, T. B. L. *Greek Theatre Production.* 2d ed. London: Methuen, 1970.

Wiles, D. *Greek Theatre Performance: An Introduction.* Cambridge: Cambridge University Press, 2000, 104.

STAGE DIRECTIONS

The ancient manuscripts of dramas rarely contain stage directions. These are provided by modern editors, sometimes on the basis of evidence from the text itself. For example, in EURIPIDES' ALCESTIS, we know APOLLO carries a bow because Thanatos mentions it at line 35. Sometimes ancient commentators on texts tell us of a gesture, state property, or the like. As for the direction from which a character enters the ORCHESTRA (the flat, circular space

on which most of the drama takes place), this cannot be known for certain, and is inferred in modern theories.

BIBLIOGRAPHY

Wiles, D. *Tragedy in Athens: Performance Space and Theatrical Meaning.* Cambridge: Cambridge University Press, 1997, 158–60.

STASIMON (Plural: *STASIMA*)

A stasimon (standing or stationary) was an ode sung by the CHORUS that occurred after their entry song, PARODOS, and before their exit song (EXODOS).

STENIA

Celebrated in October of the modern calendar, the Stenia was a nighttime festival (two days before the THESMOPHORIA), in which only women participated. The Stenia honored DEMETER, and the women engaged in jokes about and verbal abuse of one another in imitation of a woman named Iambe, who is said to have made Demeter laugh (when she was saddened by the loss of PERSEPHONE). [ANCIENT SOURCES: Aristophanes, *Thesmophoriazusae* 833]

STHENEBOEA

See BELLEROPHON or IOBATES.

STICHOMYTHIA

Stichomythia ("line talking") usually involves single-line exchanges of dialogue between two characters but can include half-line, two-line, and three-line conversation.

STICHUS PLAUTUS (200 B.C.E.)

PLAUTUS' play, staged at the PLEBEIAN GAMES in the plebeian aedileship of Gnaeus Baebius and Gnaeus Terentius, in the consulship of Gaius Sulpicius and Gaius Aurelius, was adapted from MENANDER's *Adelphoi* (*Brothers*) and another *Adelphoi* by an unknown poet. Plautus' play was produced by Titus Publilius Pellio and its musical accompaniment on the pipes by a certain Marcipor. The play's setting is Athens, and the action occurs before three houses: that of Antipho, an elderly Athenian gentleman, and the two houses of Epignomus and Pamphillipus, young Athenian gentlemen who are brothers.

The play opens at the house of Epignomus with a conversation between Panegyris and her sister (unnamed). Panegyris and her sister are the daughters of Antipho. Panegyris is married to Epignomus; her sister is married to Pamphillipus. The sisters lament that their father has been behaving badly and that their husbands have been away from home for three years. As the sisters sympathize with one another, their father, Antipho, emerges from his house. The women greet their father, who tells them that his friends are advising him that his daughters should move back into his house (because their husbands have been gone for so long). The sisters, however, resist this idea because they both remain true to their husband. After their father departs, the unnamed sister exits to Pamphillipus' house, and Panegyris send her maid, Crocotium, to find the PARASITE, Gelasimus, whom Panegyris wants to send to the harbor to find out whether any ship has arrived with news of her husband. In the next scene, Gelasimus enters, describing his constant hunger and the origin of his name, which is derived from the Greek word for laughter. Crocotium sees Gelasimus and eavesdrops on his conversation, which involves further complaints about his hunger. Finally, Crocotium steps forward and asks him to go to Panegyris' house. After Crocotium exits, Gelasimus promises to follow but stops when he sees Panegyris' male servant, Pinacium.

The second act opens as Gelasimus eavesdrops on Pinacium, who indicates that he has good news for Panegyris. Pinacium knocks on the door of Panegyris' house, but before the door is answered Gelasimus approaches and wants to know what Pinacium is doing. At this point, Panegyris herself enters from the house. Pinacium tells Panegyris that he has just arrived from the harbor, where he claims he has seen her husband, Epignomus, and his servant, Stichus. Pinacium also says that the ship in which they were traveling is loaded with gold, silver, wool, purple cloth, various female musicians, and even a few parasites. Furthermore, Pinacium says that Pamphillipus, her sister's husband, is with Epignomus. Delighted by this news, Panegyris tells Pinacium to go inside and prepare a sacrifice. After Panegyris reenters the house, Gelasimus expresses disappointment, as it appears that he will not be fed.

In the third act, Epignomus and Stichus arrive, express thanks to the gods for their safe and profitable

journey, and discuss preparations to celebrate their return. After these two exit into Epignomus' house, Gelasimus arrives and encounters Epignomus. Gelasimus wants to dine at Epignomus' house, but Epignomus tells him that he already has plans to entertain some public speakers from Ambracia. At this, Epignomus returns to his house and an upset Gelasimus departs.

The following act begins with the entrance of Antipho and Pamphillipus. Antipho expresses his delight that Pamphillipus has returned home. The two are soon joined by Epignomus, who discusses dinner plans with Pamphillipus. Before the brothers leave, Antipho asks them to give him one of the MUSIC GIRLS who have accompanied them. After making his request, which Antipho assumes will be granted, Antipho leaves to congratulate his daughters on the arrival of their husbands and to prepare for dinner. After Antipho's exit, Epignomus tells Pamphillipus that he will grant their father-in-law's request. Then, as the brothers see Gelasimus approach, they decide to tease the parasite. Because Epignomus had rejected Gelasimus as a dinner companion, Gelasimus tries to get an invitation from Pamphillipus. Pamphillipus claims that he also has a previous dinner engagement that he cannot break. After much teasing of the parasite, the two brothers exit and leave Gelasimus out in the street. Gelasimus departs, threatening to kill himself.

The play's fifth act starts with the arrival of Stichus, who is waiting for his fellow slave, Sangarinus, on whose behalf Stichus was supposed to greet Stephanium, a female friend of Sangarinus and Stichus'. When Sangarinus arrives, Stichus informs him that dinner is being prepared for them in Pamphillipus' house. After the two exit into Pamphillipus' house, Stephanium emerges from Epignomus' house, where she has been helping to clean. After she exits to Pamphillipus' house, Sangarinus and Stichus reemerge from it. Both men are fairly well intoxicated and enjoying themselves. Soon, they summon Stephanium from the house to dance for them. Stephanium, more than happy to please the two men, indulges their flirtation. As the play ends the two men are trying to steal kisses from Stephanium and the three are taking turns dancing.

COMMENTARY

Stichus is one of Plautus' most unique plays, and Duckworth rightly noted that it "almost defies classification; there is nothing quite like it in Roman comedy." The play is unique in its initial premise of the reunion of two husbands with their wives. Thus, in this play we shall not find the lovestruck young man, the scheming slave, the befuddled father, or the treacherous PIMP. Trickery and misdirection are lacking from *Stichus*. The concept of two husbands' and two wives' reuniting could have opened the door for a play involving twins—the return of AMPHITRUO from war and his reunion with ALCEMA in Plautus' *AMPHITRUO* has excellent use of twin husbands and twin slaves, but no twins are present in *Stichus*. Even without twins, the play's opening allusion to ODYSSEUS' faithful and enduring wife, PENELOPE, hints at the success that the reunion premise could have. The only potential threat to the success of this reunion, the father of the women, is removed quickly, however, and Antipho never poses much of a threat at any rate. In contrast to Odysseus' Penelope, there are no suitors for Plautus' wives to provide dramatic tension; no sons searching for their long-lost father as Odysseus' son does for him; and no obstacles to the return of the husbands such as threaten Odysseus. By the third act, the husbands have returned and the audience does not even witness the reunion with the wives. Neither the husbands nor the wives even take the stage in the play's final act. Thus, any unity of subject matter the play might have is extremely difficult to discern, and Harsh rightly notes that the play "has less plot than any other Roman comedy."

The play's greatest concern is whether Geta will eat dinner. Even this theme, however, does not emerge until the arrival of Gelasimus. Although it is one of the shortest of the Roman COMEDY plays, *Stichus* has far more references to dining and hunger than any other Roman comedy. Compared with Plautus' *CURCULIO*, the other Plautine play named after a parasite and of comparable length with *Stichus*, *Stichus* has almost 10 times more references to dining. Unlike Curculio, though, who is quite busy helping young Phaedromus win his beloved, Stichus is busy with nothing other than begging for his dinner. Additionally, in contrast to Plautus' *MENAECHMI*, which successfully exploits the comic potential of

Menaechmus' being thwarted in his desire to attend a dinner party by his unwitting twin brother, *Stichus* generally involves a substantial amount of complaining by the parasite about not having dinner and being threatened with the possibility of not having dinner.

Indeed, Gelasimus, who complains that he has carried hunger in his belly for more than 10 years (160), sounds more "Odyssean" than the brothers who have been absent for three years. If the wives in the play are the Penelope figures, then Gelasimus is more of an Odysseus figure than the brothers. For the last three-quarters of the play, the audience watch as Gelasimus struggles as Odysseus does to reintegrate himself into the home on which he depended for his meals. Gelasimus is rejected by the maidservant, Crocitium; the fisherman, Pinacium; and the matron, Panegyris. The return of Epignomus improves Gelasimus' fortunes as Epignomus endorses the parasite's plans for dinner with Stephanium and Sangarinus, but when Epignomus decides to dine with his brother, hunger again threatens Gelasimus. As Gelasimus despairs, dinner plans for the other males in the play are shaping up nicely as Antipho and Pamphillipus make plans to dine together. Finally, Gelasimus must face both Epignomus and Pamphillipus, who decide that they will torment him a little longer, and as the fourth act closes neither brother has extended Gelasimus a dinner invitation. Despite this rejection, however, the audience soon witness Gelasimus' having a grand time dining, dancing, and singing with his fellow slaves, Stephanium and Sangarinus. Thus, although Gelasimus may not have enjoyed the company of the upper-class brothers, the parasite has no lack of enjoyment at the dinner party he does attend.

BIBLIOGRAPHY

Arnott, W. G. "Targets, Techniques, and Tradition in Plautus' Stichus," *Bulletin for the Institute of Classical Studies* 19 (1972): 54–79.

Duckworth, G. *The Nature of Roman Comedy.* Princeton, N.J.: Princeton University Press, 1952, 146.

Harsh, Philip Whaley. *A Handbook of Classical Drama.* Stanford, Calif.: Stanford University Press, 1944, 369.

Owens, William M. "Plautus' *Stichus* and the Political Crisis of 200 B.C.," *American Journal of Philology* 121, no. 3 (2000) 385–407.

Petersmann, H. von *T. Maccius Plautus: Stichus*. Heidelberg: Winter, 1973.

Petrone, G. *Morale e Antimorale Nelle Commedie di Plauto: Ricerche Sullo Stichus*. Palermo: Palumbo, 1977.

STILBIDES (DIED 413 B.C.E.)

A prophet of considerable fame during the first half of the PELOPON-NESIAN WAR. Plutarch says that the Athenian statesman NICIAS relied on Stilbides, who accompanied Nicias on the SICILIAN EXPEDITION. Stilbides died, however, before a critical prophetic moment in the expedition. After a lunar eclipse on August 27, 413, the other prophets recommended to Nicias that the Athenian army delay leaving SICILY for 27 days. Nicias took their advice and the delay led to the Athenians' being trapped and slaughtered. [ANCIENT SOURCES: Aristophanes, *Peace* 1031; Eupolis, fragment 211 Kock; Plutarch, *Nicias* 23.5]

BIBLIOGRAPHY

Kock, T. *Comicorum Atticorum Fragmenta*. Vol. 1. Leipzig: Teubner, 1880.

Platnauer, M. *Aristophanes: Peace*. Oxford: Clarendon Press, 1964, 153.

Sommerstein, A. H. *The Comedies of Aristophanes*. Vol. 5, *Peace*. Warminster, U.K.: Aris & Philips, 1985, 182.

STOICISM

This philosophical school of thought emerged around 300 B.C.E. and Zeno of Citeum is regarded as its founder. The Stoics' name was derived from their original meeting place in ATHENS, a public building called the Stoa Poikile. The key to happiness for the Stoics was to live in harmony with nature, which was synonymous with God and became manifest in the form of fate and divine providence. For the Stoics, nature was not random and unpredictable, but perfect, ordered, and rational. Because fate was a part of nature, and nature was rational, the Stoics were not supposed to struggle against fate, but try to live in harmony with it and by so doing have an ordered and rational life. The major obstacle to such an ordered and rational life was anxiety. To rid oneself of anxiety, the Stoics constantly struggled to master emotions such as anger, fear, and passion. The weapon of the Stoics against these emotions was *virtus* (which embodies courage, excellence, and valor), which the Stoics regarded as a person's only true possession, which

could never be taken. SENECA, both a tragedian and the author of treatises on Stoicism, called *virtus* "perfect Reason." Because a person's *virtus* could never be taken away, the Stoics were taught not to fear death, but to welcome it as a release from the body, which is subject to anxiety. If Stoics found themselves in such dire emotional circumstances that they were prevented from pursuing a life in accordance with nature, then they were allowed to commit suicide to separate themselves from the burden of the body. Seneca himself, under pressure from the Roman emperor, NERO, committed suicide in 65 C.E. Because Seneca was a Stoic, his tragedies often examine characters who struggle with the sort of emotions and passions against which the Stoics battled.

BIBLIOGRAPHY

Bobzien, S. *Determinism and Freedom in Stoic Philosophy*. Oxford: Clarendon Press, 1998.

Ierodiakonou, K., ed. *Topics in Stoic Philosophy*. New York: Oxford University Press, 1999.

Rist, J. M. *Stoic Philosophy*. Cambridge: Cambridge University Press, 1969.

———. "Seneca and Stoic Orthodoxy," *Aufstieg und Niedergang der römischen Welt* 36, no. 3 (1989): 1993–2012.

Rosenmeyer, T. G. "Seneca and Nature," *Arethusa* 33, no. 1 (2000): 99–119.

STRATO (STRANTON)

A man with an effeminate appearance who is linked with CLEISTHENES in ARISTOPHANES' *Knights*. [ANCIENT SOURCES: Aristophanes, *Acharnians* 122, *Birds* 942, *Knights* 1374]

BIBLIOGRAPHY

Sommerstein, A. H. *The Comedies of Aristophanes*. Vol. 1, *Acharnians*. Warminster, U.K.: Aris & Phillips, 1980, 163.

STREPSIADES

The central character of ARISTO-PHANES' *CLOUDS*, Strepsiades has a name derived from the Greek verb that means "twist." The name is fitting, as his goal in the play is to "twist" his way out of debts that he owes to people who have lent him money to support his son's love of horses. As several Aristophanic heroes are, Strepsiades is portrayed as a simple man from the Athenian countryside. Aristophanic heroes often concoct a grand scheme to solve a pressing social problem. Strepsiades, however, aims to avoid paying his creditors by telling his son, Pheidippides, to enroll in SOCRATES' school and learn how to argue his way out of the money Strepsiades owes. Initially Pheidippides refuses to study with Socrates, so Strepsiades decides to attend the school himself. Unlike other Aristophanic heroes, such as DICAEOPOLIS or LYSISTRATA, Strepsiades is not clever enough to carry out his scheme. Strepsiades' actions at the conclusion of *Clouds* are unusually violent in comparison to those in other Aristophanic plays. Most Aristophanic plays end with intoxication, dancing, and the expectation of sexual pleasure. At the conclusion of *Clouds,* Strepsiades sets fire to Socrates' school in an effort to kill Socrates and CHAEREPHON.

BIBLIOGRAPHY
Green, P. "Strepsiades, Socrates and the Abuses of Intellectualism," *Greek, Roman, and Byzantine Studies* 20 (1979): 15–25.
Reckford, K. J. "Strepsiades as a Comic Ixion," *Illinois Classical Studies* 16 (1991): 125–36.

STROPHE A strophe (turning) is a section of a lyric ODE that precedes an ANTISTROPHE. In the strophe, the chorus sang while moving to the right.

STROPHEION A revolving device used to transport deceased heroes to the gods or to represent persons' dying at sea or in battle. The *stropheion* was not in use until after the fifth century B.C.E. [ANCIENT SOURCES: Pollux, *Onomasticon* 4.127, 132]

STROPHIUS The father of PYLADES, who was the cousin and best friend of ORESTES. Strophius lived in the region of PHOCIS and took care of Orestes, who was in danger from his mother, CLYTEMNESTRA, and her lover AEGISTHUS. Strophius appears as a character in SENECA's *AGAMEMNON,* in which he goes to congratulate AGAMEMNON on his success at TROY only to find that the king has been murdered. ELECTRA then arranges for Strophius to take Orestes to safety, because Agamemnon's son will probably be the next target of Clytemnestra and Aegisthus. [ANCIENT SOURCES: Aeschylus, *Agamemnon* 880 (see ORESTEIA), *Libation Bearers* 679 (see ORESTEIA); Euripides, *Electra* 18, *Iphigenia in Tauris* 60, 917, 921, *Orestes* 765, 1403; Sophocles, *Electra* 1111]

STRYMODORUS A name given to a farmer at ARISTOPHANES' *ACHARNIANS* 273, one of PHILOCLEON's fellow jurors at *WASPS* 233, and a member of the CHORUS of old men at *LYSISTRATA* 259. The orator Demosthenes (36.29) mentions a Strymodorus who was a banker from AEGINA, and Aristophanes may have known of this person.

BIBLIOGRAPHY
Sommerstein, A. H. *The Comedies of Aristophanes.* Vol. 4, *Wasps.* Warminster, U.K.: Aris & Phillips, 1983, 170.

STYGIAN Pertaining to the river STYX.

STYMPHALIA A town located west of Argos in southern Greece, Stymphalia was the site of HERACLES' encounter with the Stymphalian birds. These unusual creatures had metallic feathers and fed on the flesh of human beings. Heracles drove the birds from the region by using a bronze rattle (made by HEPHAESTUS) given to him by ATHENA. [ANCIENT SOURCES: Seneca, *Hercules Furens* 243–44]

STYX The Styx ("hated") is a river or marsh in the UNDERWORLD. Styx was a daughter of OCEANUS and TETHYS'. Styx's union with the Titan Pallas produced Bia (Force), Cratus (Power), NIKE (Victory), and Zelus (Emulation). Divinities who wished to take an unbreakable oath swore by the Styx. When such an oath was broken, the divinity fell into a coma for a year and on awaking had to spend nine years in exile from the other divinities. When a person died, his or her soul descended to the underworld and was usually said to have to cross the Styx (some sources mention another body of water such as the ACHERON). [ANCIENT SOURCES: Aristophanes, *Frogs* 470; Hesiod, *Theogony* 360–63, 383–403, 775–806; Homer, *Iliad* 2.751–55, *Odyssey* 10.513–15; Seneca's tragedies, passim, but especially *Hercules Oetaeus*; Sophocles, *Oedipus at Colonus* 1564]

SUBSELLIA (SINGULAR: *SUBSELLIUM*) In Roman theaters, *subsellia* (low steps) were located in the orchestra and were reserved as seats for persons of special importance. [ANCIENT SOURCES: Plautus,

Amphitruo 65, *Carthaginian* 5; Suetonius, *Augustus* 43, 44, *Claudius* 41, *Nero* 26]

SUN (Greek: HELIOS; Latin: SOL)

The son of Hyperion and Theia and the brother of Eos (Dawn) and Selene (Moon). The Sun had a wife, Perse (or Perseis); by her he had a son, AEETES, and two daughters, CIRCE and PASIPHAE. The Sun was also the father of PHAETHON by OCEANUS's daughter, Clymene. He is sometimes synonymous with APOLLO. Each day the Sun drove his four-horse chariot across the sky from east to west. Because the Sun saw everything from this vantage point, he was often invoked as a witness to oaths and other events. In the evening, the Sun would return to his starting point in a cauldron that sailed upon the ocean. The Sun allowed HERACLES to use this cauldron during his quest for the cattle of GERYON and his journey to the garden of the Hesperides. After MEDEA kills her children, she flees CORINTH in the Sun's chariot (he was her grandfather through Aeetes). [ANCIENT SOURCES: Apollodorus, *Library* 1.6.1, 2.5.10–11, *Epitome* 2.12; Apollonius Rhodius, 4.964–74; Hesiod, *Theogony* 371–74, 956–62; Homer, *Odyssey* 1.8–9, 8.270–71, 8.302, 11.104–115, 12.260–419; *Homeric Hymn to Demeter* 2.26–27, 62–89; Hyginus, *Fables* 154; Ovid, *Metamorphoses* 1.750–2.400; Pausanias, 2.1.6, 2.3.10, 2.4.6, 8.29.4, 9.25.5; Pindar, *Olympian Odes* 7.54–76]

SUNIUM

The cape on the southeastern coast of Athenian territory. [ANCIENT SOURCES: Aristophanes, *Clouds* 401; Euripides, *Cyclops* 293; Sophocles, *Ajax* 1220]

SUPPLIANT WOMEN AESCHYLUS (CA. 463 B.C.E.)

The date of the play is uncertain; *Suppliant Women* was the first play of a TETRALOGY and was followed by *Egyptians, Danaids,* and the SATYR PLAY *Amymone.* AESCHYLUS' production defeated those of SOPHOCLES and Mesatus. The play's action centers around an altar to the gods at ARGOS. The CHORUS consist of the daughters of DANAUS, an African king. The number of members in this particular chorus has been debated: Ancient sources state that Danaus had 50 daughters, but the CHORUS in ancient TRAGEDY at this

time is usually thought to be 12 in number. The drama begins with the chorus explaining that with their father they have left Africa to avoid marriage to their cousins, the 50 sons of AEGYPTUS, king of Egypt. They have chosen Argos because they are related to an Argive woman, IO. The women's opening ode also calls upon Io, ZEUS, and other gods for protection. The women threaten to kill themselves if the gods do not hear their prayer.

After the choral ode, Danaus, perceiving that the leader of Argos is approaching, urges his daughters to take up positions as suppliants at a nearby altar. After Danaus' daughters do so, PELASGUS, king of Argos, arrives with a band of armed men and questions the women about why they have taken refuge in Argos. The chorus explain that they are descended from Io, state that they have fled to avoid marriage with Aegyptus' sons, and beg Pelasgus not to turn them over to Aegyptus' sons. Pelasgus wants to help the women, because suppliants are protected by the gods, but does not want his land to suffer any military hardships that might result from war with Aegyptus' sons. Pelasgus wavers as to whether to act, and the women eventually threaten to kill themselves at the altar if he will not help them. Pelasgus does not reject the women, however, and urges Danaus and his daughters to leave their present location and to place suppliant branches at other altars throughout the land.

At this point, Pelasgus exits to assemble his people so that they can consider the course of action they should follow. Danaus accompanies Pelasgus to help make their case before the assembly. Once again, the chorus call upon Zeus for help and recall the sufferings of their ancestor, Io. After the choral ode, Danaus returns and announces that the Argive assembly have decreed that the women should receive protection from Aegyptus' sons. The chorus respond with an ode of praise and gratitude to Pelasgus and his people. They pray that war will not descend on the land and that Zeus will shower Pelasgus' people with blessings.

The chorus' happiness is short lived, however, as Danaus announces that he has seen Aegyptus' sons' ship in the harbor. The women are fearful, but Danaus encourages them to trust Pelasgus and his people. After Danaus exits to seek help from Pelasgus' people, the women fearfully wonder what will happen next and what will become of them. Their ode is cut short as they catch sight of a herald from the Egyptian ship. The herald enters and attempts with threats to force the women to board the ship. The arrival of Pelasgus prevents this, as the king declares that he will protect the women and drives off the herald.

After the women thank Pelasgus for his help, the king exits and Danaus enters. Danaus tells his daughters to give thanks to the people of Argos and regard their chastity as more precious than life itself. The play concludes as the Danaids and their maidservants, who form a secondary chorus, praise the Argives and ask the gods for protection from marriage with Aegyptus' sons.

COMMENTARY

Suppliant Women has received little attention in modern times; perhaps the appearance of Charles L. Mee's *Big Love,* a modern adaptation of the play, will renew interest in Aeschylus' work. Aeschylus' play is, however, an important example of early Greek tragedy. The chorus deliver more than 60 percent of the play's lines and only three other characters have speaking parts. Despite the lack of attention of modern readers, the play clearly influenced EURIPIDES' *CHILDREN OF HERACLES* and *SUPPLIANT WOMEN.* Several other extant tragedies also deal with suppliants, such as SOPHOCLES' *OEDIPUS AT COLONUS* and Euripides' *ANDROMACHE, HERACLES,* and *HELEN.* The figure of the "good king" would appear again in *Children of Heracles, Suppliant Women,* and *Oedipus at Colonus.* These kings would be from ATHENS; Argive Pelasgus is similar to these Athenian kings, as he is also a protector of suppliants.

Like Aeschylus' PERSIANS, *Suppliant Women* is a play of contrasts: Greek versus barbarian, civilized versus uncivilized, male versus female, stranger versus kinsman, purity versus impurity, chastity versus love. In some instances, however, these contrasts become blurred, especially with respect to the Danaids. From the Greek perspective, the Danaids are people of a barbarian land. At the same time, these barbarian women claim that Aegyptus' sons threaten them with barbarous violence, and they seek the civil protection of the Greeks. One of the primary relationships within

Greek civilization is the marriage of a man and a woman, but the Danaids refuse marriage with Aegyptus' sons because they consider such marriage abhorrent. Thus, the Danaids threaten to become like Hippolytus, inclined toward Artemis to the exclusion of Aphrodite. The Danaids are strangers to the Argives, yet they also claim to be related to them.

As does *Children of Heracles,* in which IOLAUS tries to persuade the Athenian king, DEMOPHON, son of THESEUS, to protect HERACLES' children by demonstrating how they are related to Demophon's family, Aeschylus' *Suppliant Women* often calls attention to family links. On one hand, the Danaids want to avoid marriage because the prospective grooms are related to them. On the other hand, they argue that the Argives should protect them because they are related to them. Their argument is based on their being descendants of Io, who was originally from Argos but later went to Africa. In the case of the Danaids, they seek to avoid becoming like their ancestor, Io. Zeus' sexual relationship with Io caused her tremendous pain and suffering, and the Danaids want to avoid the pain and suffering that marriage to Aegyptus' sons might cause them. At the same time, the Danaids long for the aid that Zeus gave to Io when he freed her from her distress with the touch of his hand.

The concept of touch is an interesting one in this play. Zeus' touch freed Io from her torment, but Zeus' initial sexual touching of Io enraged HERA, who transformed the young woman into a cow. Thus, Zeus' touch had both dangerous and liberating consequences for Io. The Danaids face a similar conflict with respect to touch: They long for the liberating hand of Zeus, the god who planted their race with his own hand (592), but abhor the violent touch of Aegyptus' sons (392, 756, 820–21), who threaten to sow their seed within them. They regard the violent touch of Aegyptus' sons as impious (9, 755–56) and pray to the gods for help, but they threaten violence against themselves if the gods will not help.

Not only do the Danaids pray for the touch of the divine male and abhor the touch of their mortal male cousins, but also they flee the barbarous hands of their fellow Africans for the civilized hands of the Argives, who are simultaneously strangers and kinsmen. The

Danaids will welcome the hands of the Argives, who, in this play, use their hands not for sexual purposes, but in the context of civil assembly and the righteous protection of suppliants. The Danaids benefit from the Argives' hands when Danaus reports that the Argive assembly supported the proposal to help the Danaids by holding their right hands in the air (607–8, 621). Eventually, the hands of civil assembly must become protective when the herald of Aegyptus' sons tries to drive the Danaids by force to the Egyptian ship. The words of the king that persuaded his fellow citizens to vote to protect the Danaids now threaten serious force if the herald touches the women (925).

The civil and righteous hands of the Greeks protect the Danaids in *Suppliant Women;* later in Aeschylus' tragic TRILOGY hands would play a much different role. Eventually the sons of Aegyptus would marry the Danaids and attempt to place their hands on them. The Danaids, however, would respond with violence to perceived violence against their bodies. Aeschylus' audience probably would have known the legend of the Danaids' murder of Aegyptus' sons when they saw Aeschylus' production, but Aeschylus hints at the horror ahead early in *Suppliant Women.* When the Danaids arrive in Argos, they carry suppliant boughs in their hands. At line 21, Aeschylus uses the word *encheiridia* to refer to these boughs. This word can refer to anything carried in the hand, but it sometimes means "dagger." Additional foreshadowing occurs when the Danaids hear the song of the nightingale, which reminds them of TEREUS' wife, who was transformed into this bird after she killed her son by Tereus with her own hand (66). This reference foreshadows the vengeance that the Danaids will take on Aegyptus' sons.

Later in the trilogy, the Danaids, with one exception, would strike down Aegyptus' sons with their hands. The suppliant boughs the Danaids hold in the trilogy's first play will be replaced with death-dealing blades later. It is also interesting that when the Danaids hold the boughs of supplication, they grasp them in the left hand (193), in contrast with right hand (607) raised by the Argives to approve of the proposal to protect the Danaids. When the Danaids killed their husbands later in the trilogy, they would have held the blade in their right hand. *Suppliant Women* frequently raises the anticipation of men's

employing their hands in violent ways; later in the trilogy women will use their hands violently. The civilized right hand of the male Argives raised to protect the women will be replaced by the violent right hand of the women. Io's human hands would have been perversely altered when Hera transformed her into a cow. The Danaids' hands will be perverted by shedding the blood of Aegyptus' sons on their wedding night.

BIBLIOGRAPHY
Caldwell, R. S. "The Psychology of Aeschylus' *Supplices,*" *Arethusa* 7 (1974): 45–70.
Gantz, T. "Love and Death in the Suppliants of Aeschylus," *Phoenix* 32 (1978): 279–87.
Garvie, A. F. *Aeschylus' Supplices: Play and Trilogy.* Cambridge: Cambridge University Press, 1969.
Rehm, Rush. "The Staging of Suppliant Plays," *Greek, Roman, and Byzantine Studies* 29 (1988): 263–307.

SUPPLIANT WOMEN EURIPIDES (CA. 421 B.C.E.)

The subject matter of EURIPIDES' *Suppliant Women* differs from AESCHYLUS' SUPPLIANT WOMEN. Aeschylus' play deals with the flight of DANAUS and his daughter from Africa to Greece; Euripides', with the burial of the Argive warriors who died in battle against Thebes. The action of the play occurs before the temple of DEMETER in ELEUSIS, a town several miles west of Athens. This play treats the aftermath of the famous expedition known as the Seven against Thebes. The chorus consist of mothers of the deceased Argive captains and their attendants. The Argive mothers are also accompanied by the sons of the deceased men. After the battle, the mothers of the deceased Argive warriors attempt to recover the bodies of their sons for burial, because the victorious Thebans had refused to allow this rite. Aethra, mother of the Athenian king, THESEUS, delivers the play's opening monologue from the altar steps at Demeter's temple. Aethra describes the circumstances, and notes that she has been urged by the Argive king, ADRASTUS, to take up the cause of the Argive mothers. Aethra and Adrastus urge Theseus to help the Argives. Aethra also mentions that she has sent a herald to summon Theseus either to help the Argive mothers or to send them from Athenian territory.

After Aethra's speech, the CHORUS beg her for help and ask her to urge Theseus to march against the Thebans so that their sons can have a proper burial. The women's lament is heard by Theseus, who enters after their song. Aethra explains who the women are and points out that Adrastus is with them. Theseus questions Adrastus, who explains about why he and his fellow Argives marched on Thebes. Adrastus begs Theseus for help in recovering the bodies of his fallen comrades. Theseus criticizes Adrastus' decision to march on Thebes and initially rejects Adrastus' plea for help. Adrastus then tells the Argive women to leave the altar and go. The Argive women plead with Theseus and argue that because Theseus' grandfather, Pittheus, was of the same blood as they are, he should not refuse them. Then Theseus' mother, Aethra, takes up the Argives' case and characterizes her son as a coward for rejecting Adrastus and the Argive women. Theseus, won over by his mother, decides that he will try to persuade the Thebans to return the Argives' dead to them. If persuasion fails, then, Theseus states, he is prepared to use force.

At this, Theseus, Aethra, and Adrastus depart to consult the assembly of Athenian citizens. After their departure, the Argive women sing a song that prays for Theseus' success. They also pray that Justice will go to their aid. After the choral song, Theseus, Adrastus, and an Athenian herald enter. Theseus instructs the herald to go to CREON and request that he give up the Argive dead for burial. If Creon refuses this request, then the Thebans should expect an attack by the Athenians. Before the Athenian herald can set out, a Theban herald enters. Before the herald states his business, he and Theseus engage in a debate on the virtues of kingship versus democracy. After the argument, the Theban herald states that the Athenians should expel Adrastus from their land and should not threaten to use force to remove the Argive corpses for burial. Theseus, refusing to be threatened by the Thebans, argues that the Thebans should not deny the right of burial to the Argives (a right granted by all Greeks). Theseus declares that he and his citizens will take up arms to defend the Argives' right to bury their dead. The Theban herald, however, states that the Athenians will never take the Argive dead from Theban soil. After the herald departs, Theseus calls his citizens to arms and tells them to prepare to march on Thebes.

After Theseus departs, the Argive women are fearful, wondering what the outcome of the struggle will be. They pray to ZEUS for aid. After the choral song, a MES-

SENGER enters and announces the victory of Theseus and the Athenians. The messenger explains that Theseus did not enter Thebes, but simply demanded the Argive dead for burial. The messenger also informs Adrastus that Theseus buried the fallen Argives on the slopes of Mount CITHAERON. After the messenger's announcement, the chorus comment on the intermingled joy and sorrow created by the Athenian victory and the burial. They regret that they had children because now they have to face the sorrow of losing them. The chorus and Adrastus then exchange laments about the death of their loved ones and the sorrow that they must endure.

After this exchange, Theseus enters and asks Adrastus to comment on the several dead captains whose bodies lie before them. Whereas AESCHYLUS' *SEVEN AGAINST THEBES* provided a detailed description of the shields of these warriors as they marched on Thebes, Adrastus now describes the qualities of the fallen leaders: CAPANEUS, ETEOCLUS, Hippomedon, Parthenopaeus, and TYDEUS. After Adrastus' comments, Theseus declares that most of the captains will be burned on a common pyre, but that Capaneus will be burned separately because he died when struck by a lightning bolt from Zeus. At this point, the funeral procession begins to move the bodies toward the funeral pyres. While they do so, the Argive women lament the loss of their sons and the joyless life that awaits them.

As the Argive women conclude their lament, they notice Capaneus' wife, Evadne, who is standing above the funeral pyre of her husband. She announces her intention to throw herself upon into the same flames that burn her husband's body. Before Evadne can act, her father, Iphis, enters and tries to prevent her from killing herself. Unfortunately, he cannot persuade Evadne, who views her death as a noble victory and throws herself into the flames. After Evadne's death, Iphis laments the loss of his daughter, as well as of his son, Eteoclus, who also died while fighting against the Thebans. Iphis grieves that he will have no one to care for him in his old age. After the departure of Iphis, the sons of the dead Argive captains approach, carrying the ashes of their fathers in urns. The Argive women and the young men exchange lamentation for the loss of their sons and the loss of their fathers. The young men boast that they will someday avenge their fathers' deaths.

After the Argive mothers and sons bid farewell to their loved ones, Theseus calls Adrastus and the Argives to witness the gift that Athens has given to them and urges Adrastus to teach his people to remember what Athens has done for them. Adrastus expresses his thanks and Theseus prepares to allow the Argives to depart when ATHENA suddenly appears. Athena urges Theseus not to allow the Argives to leave until they swear that they will not march on Athens and that they will help defend Athens should others attack the city. Athena also tells Theseus to inscribe the oath on a tripod and deposit the tripod at APOLLO's temple at DELPHI. Athena then predicts the future victory of the Argives' sons over the Thebans. After Theseus promises to obey Athena's commands, the chorus promise they will give Theseus the oath prescribed by Athena.

COMMENTARY

The staging of Euripides' play poses little challenge until the unexpected arrival of Evadne. How her suicide would have been staged is a matter of debate. The actor playing Evadne apparently would have appeared on top of the stage building and would have had to drop onto the "pyre" (which appears to be within the spectators' view). Perhaps a hollow structure crafted to resemble a pyre with padding in the middle would have allowed an athletic actor to jump down from the upper level of the stage building. An opening in the back of this structure could allow the actor to exit the "pyre" unseen by the audience.

Euripides' *Suppliant Women* is one of at least five extant plays within about a 10-year period that comment on the subject of war. As do CHILDREN OF HERACLES, HECABE, and TROJAN WOMEN, and, to a lesser extent, ANDROMACHE, *Suppliant Women* deals with the effects of war on the loved ones of fallen warriors. At the time *Suppliant Women* was produced, Euripides' fellow Athenians were involved in a war with the Spartans and their allies. Because the people of Thebes were also fighting Athenians in this war, the hostilities between the mythical Athenians and Thebans also would have been quite real to Euripides' audience. Indeed, *Suppliant Women* would have touched on several themes to which Euripides' audience could relate. In *Suppliant Women*, Euripides allows the audience to see the grief of mothers who have lost their sons in

war, the suicidal grief of a wife who has lost her husband, the grief of a father whose daughter has committed suicide because she lost her husband, and the grief of sons who have lost their fathers. Other "war" plays usually deal with the hardships of war for the female and child survivors; *Suppliant Women* adds the component of the downtrodden king and his state. Thus, in Euripides' play, we see the grief not only of individuals, but also of entire communities. As must Danaus in Aeschylus' *Suppliant Women*, Adrastus must turn to another king for help. Euripides' play, however, reverses the situation of Aeschylus' play. Whereas Aeschylus' Danaus sought help from the king of Argos, Euripides' Adrastus, king of Argos, seeks help from the king of Athens. Although the cities that Aeschlyus' Pelasgus and Euripides' Theseus represent are different, the democratic forms of government that they represent are essentially the same. Pelasgus and Theseus may be kings, but they represent themselves as representatives of the people's will.

As Aeschylus' *Suppliant Women*, Euripides' *Children of Heracles*, *Andromache*, *Heracles*, and *Helen*, and SOPHOCLES' OEDIPUS AT COLONUS do, Euripides' *Suppliant Women* treats a group of people taking refuge at an altar. Unlike *Helen*, however, Euripides' *Suppliant Women* is completely serious in its tone and subject matter. The evil oppressor in Euripides' *Suppliant Women* is the Theban king, Creon, who does not take the stage in the play. Unlike in other plays of supplication, the Argive suppliants in Euripides' play are not physically threatened by Creon, but the corpses of their loved ones are. As in other suppliant plays, the refugees seek the assistance of a protector, and, as in other such plays (especially *Children of Heracles* and *Oedipus at Colonus*), the Athenians are the protectors. Additionally, just as in *Children of Heracles*, the protectors in *Suppliant Women* will fight a battle against the oppressors to secure the wishes of the suppliants. Unlike in *Children of Heracles*, however, in which one of the suppliants, the aged Iolaus, undergoes a miraculous rejuvenation and plays a key role in the battle, no Argive males in *Suppliant Women* will contribute to the battle in which Theseus and his fellow Athenians show their valor and attain victory.

For all the superficial praise of Theseus and the Athenian way of government and conducting of military operations, Euripides' audience would have recognized many of their own actions in those of Adrastus and the Argives. Early in the play, Theseus asks Adrastus whether he consulted prophets before going to war against the Thebans. Adrastus says he did, but that he ignored the warnings of the prophets and was carried away by the clamor of the younger men for war (160). Later, at lines 737–41, Adrastus notes that the Theban leader, ETEOCLES, had offered them fair terms of peace, but that because they were young and superior in number, they did not accept the offer. Such statements surely would have reminded some of Euripides' audience of the Athenian demagogue CLEON. In 425 B.C.E., when the Athenians had a significant number of Spartans pinned down at Sphacteria, the Spartans tried to negotiate a peace, but the counterdemands of Cleon and the Athenians were excessive and the war continued. It was certainly no coincidence that after Cleon's death a peace agreement between Athens and SPARTA was reached in 421.

BIBLIOGRAPHY

Burian, P. "Logos and Pathos: The Politics of the Suppliant Women." In Directions in Euripidean Criticism: A Collection of Essays. Edited by P. Burian. Durham, N.C.: Duke University Press, 1985, 129–55.

Goff, B. "The Women of Thebes," Classical Journal 90, no. 4 (1994–95): 353–65.

Scully, S. P. "Orchestra and Stage in Euripides' Suppliant Women," Arion 4, no. 1 (1996–97): 61–84.

SUPPLICATION   The act of begging someone. In Greek custom, the person who begs, the supplicant, kneels on the ground, places one arm around the other person's knees, and with the other arm reaches up and touches the person's chin. Supplication plays an important role in Greek TRAGEDY. Extant plays by both AESCHYLUS and EURIPIDES are entitled SUPPLIANT WOMEN. In Euripides' MEDEA, the title character uses supplication to achieve mastery over JASON, who had originally been a supplicant to her in COLCHIS (cf. lines 496–98). MEDEA is a supplicant to CREON to gain one more day in CORINTH (324); she is a supplicant to AEGEUS to secure a place to stay when she leaves Corinth (709–11); and finally she arranges for her children to be supplicants to Creon's daughter so that she will receive the deadly gifts that Medea has prepared for her.

SUSA   The capital city of Persia. [ANCIENT SOURCES: Aeschylus, Persians]

SYBARIS   A Greek town in southern Italy whose inhabitants were famous for their ignorance and their luxurious mode of life. The Sybarites were supposed to be so foolish that people told humorous stories about them, comparable to the jokes people make today. [ANCIENT SOURCES: Aristophanes, Peace 344, Wasps 1259, 1427, 1435, 1438; Herodotus, 5.44, 6.21, 6.127.1]

SYCOPHANT   See INFORMANT.

SYMPLEGADES   See CLASHING ROCKS.

SYNAGONIST (Greek: SYNAGONISTES; Plural: SYNAGONISTAI)   A synagonist (one with whom one competes) was the actor who served as either the DEUTERAGONIST or the TRITAGONIST, as opposed to the PROTAGONIST, in the dramatic company.

SYNCHOREGIA (Plural: SYNCHOREGIAI)   A Greek word used to refer to two or more people who perform the duty of a CHOREGIA.

SYRA   A common name of female slaves. [ANCIENT SOURCES: Aristophanes, Peace 1146; Plautus, Merchant; Terence, Mother-in-Law]

SYRACUSE   An important city on the eastern coast of SICILY. In PLAUTUS' MENAECHMI, one of the Menaechmus twins grew up in Syracuse.

SYRIA   A country near the eastern shore of the Mediterranean Sea. The Greeks' conception of Syria's borders changed over time. AESCHYLUS' description of Syria suggests that its borders were rather close to northern Africa. By the days of SENECA, Syria was a Roman province, whose borders were similar to, but more expansive than, those of the modern country of Syria. [ANCIENT SOURCES: Aeschylus, Suppliant Women 5]

T

TAENARUS (TAENARUM) A place near the southern tip of Greece. According to legend, one could gain entrance to the UNDERWORLD through a cavern at Taenarus. SOPHOCLES wrote a play whose title may have been *Satyrs at Taenarus* (fragments 198a–e Radt); however, this may have been an alternate title for Sophocles' *Heracles, Infant Heracles,* or *Cerberus.* [ANCIENT SOURCES: Aristophanes, *Acharnians* 510, *Frogs* 187; Euripides, *Cyclops* 292, HERACLES 23]

BIBLIOGRAPHY
Lloyd-Jones, H. *Sophocles: Fragments.* Cambridge, Mass.: Harvard University Press, 1996, 98–99.
Radt, S. *Tragicorum Graecorum Fragmenta.* Vol. 4. Göttingen, Ger.: Vandenhoeck & Ruprecht, 1977.

TAGUS A river in Spain in which sand of gold was supposed to be found. [ANCIENT SOURCES: Seneca, *Hercules Furens* 1325, *Hercules Oetaeus* 626, *Thyestes* 354]

TALAUS Talaus was the father of ADRASTUS (according to some sources) or HIPPOMEDON (according to others). Both Adrastus and Hippomedon were members of the Seven against THEBES expedition. [ANCIENT SOURCES: Apollodorus, *Library* 3.6.1, 3; Euripides, *Iphigenia at Aulis* 245, *Phoenician Women* 422; Sophocles, *Oedipus at Colonus* 1318]

TALTHYBIUS The primary herald for the Greek army during the Trojan War. He appears as a character in EURIPIDES' HECABE and TROJAN WOMEN and delivers messages between the Greek army and the Trojan captives. In Euripides' ORESTES, Talthybius' speech against ORESTES is reported by a MESSENGER. [ANCIENT SOURCES: Apollodorus, *Epitome* 3.9, 3.22; Euripides, *Iphigenia at Aulis* 95, 1563, *Orestes* 888; Plautus, *Stichus* 305; Seneca, *Trojan Women* 164]

BIBLIOGRAPHY
Dyson, M., and K. H. Lee. "Talthybius in Euripides' *Troades,*" *Greek, Roman, and Byzantine Studies* 41, no. 2 (2000): 141–74.

TANAUS A river located in the southern part of mainland Greece that formed a border between Argive and Spartan territory. [ANCIENT SOURCES: Euripides, ELECTRA 410; Seneca, *Agamemnon* 680, *Hercules Furens* 1323, *Hercules Oetaeus* 86, *Hippolytus* 715, *Trojan Women* 9]

TANTALUS (1) The son of ZEUS and a woman named Pluto, Tantalus had a son named PELOPS, and some sources make him the father of NIOBE, although others call Niobe the daughter of Pelops. Tantalus suffered one of the more fascinating punishments in the UNDERWORLD. After having the privilege of sharing in the feasts of the gods, Tantalus gave some of the food to his fellow humans. Furthermore, when the gods dined at the house of Tantalus, he killed his son, Pelops, and mixed his flesh with the food. For this, the gods killed Tantalus, and in the underworld he was compelled always to be hungry and thirsty. Tantalus was immobilized in a pool of water and positioned near a fruit tree; whenever Tantalus tried to get a drink, the water receded; whenever he tried to reach for fruit, a gust of wind whisked it from his grasp. Thus, he was always "tantalized" (SENECA, THYESTES 149–75).

In Greek drama, Tantalus does not appear as a character in any surviving plays, although he appears to have been a character in AESCHYLUS' Niobe. Several dramatists wrote plays entitled Tantalus. Among the Greek tragedians, a single word survives from PHRYNICHUS' Tantalus (fragment 7 Snell); a title is known from Pratinas (fragment 2 Snell); and five lines (that the wise know no more than those who are not wise) survive from Aristarchus' Tantalus (fragment 1b Snell). SOPHOCLES wrote a Tantalus; its two brief extant fragments, about the brevity of life and the revelation of an ORACLE by HERMES, indicate little about the play's content (fragments 572–73 Radt). Among Roman works, Tantalus' ghost appears as a character in SENECA's Thyestes. In that play, a FURY drives Tantalus' ghost to goad the brothers ATREUS and THYESTES to savage and brutal conflict. Tantalus does not want to do this, but eventually such madness does manifest itself in the play, although Tantalus' ghost does not take the stage again after line 121. [ANCIENT SOURCES Hyginus, Fables 82; Seneca, Thyestes]

BIBLIOGRAPHY

Kiso, A. The Lost Sophocles. New York: Vantage Press, 1984.
Lloyd-Jones, H. Sophocles: Fragments. Cambridge, Mass.: Harvard University Press, 1996.
Radt, S. Tragicorum Graecorum Fragmenta. Vol. 4. Göttingen, Ger.: Vandenhoeck & Ruprecht, 1977.
Snell, B. Tragicorum Graecorum Fragmenta. Vol. 1. Göttingen, Ger.: Vandenhoeck & Ruprecht, 1971.
Sutton, D. F. The Lost Sophocles. Lanham, Md.: University Press of America, 1984.

TANTALUS (2) A son of THYESTES, this Tantalus appears as a character in SENECA's THYESTES, as a young man who tries to persuade his father to trust his brother, ATREUS, and to sieze the opportunity to become king. Atreus later kills this Tantalus and serves him as food to his father.

TANTALUS (3) This Tantalus was CLYTEMNESTRA's first husband, who was killed by AGAMEMNON, who also killed Clytemnestra's child by him. [ANCIENT SOURCES: Euripides, Iphigenia at Aulis 1148–52]

TAPHIANS Another name for the TELOBOIANS.

TARTARUS Another name for the UNDERWORLD.

TARTESIAN LAMPREY A type of eel from Tartessos (in the southwestern part of the Iberian peninsula). [ANCIENT SOURCES: Aristophanes, Frogs 475]

TAURIS The land of Tauris was located on the peninsula on the northern part of the Black Sea. According to one tradition, IPHIGENIA, just as she was to be sacrificed by her father, AGAMEMNON, was miraculously transported to Tauris. There, she became a priest of ARTEMIS and prepared human victims for sacrifice to the goddess. Tauris provides the setting for EURIPIDES' IPHIGENIA IN TAURIS, which deals with Iphigenia's reunion with her brother, ORESTES, and escape from that land.

TAUROPOLIA A festival in ATTICA (the region where ATHENS is located) that honored ARTEMIS. [ANCIENT SOURCES: Menander, Arbitration 451, 472, 477, 517, 863, 1119]

TAUROPOLOS An epithet of ARTEMIS which refers to her mastery over bulls (taur-). [ANCIENT SOURCES: Euripides, Iphigenia in Tauris 1457; Sophocles, Ajax 172]

TAURUS The constellation representing the bull. Tradition says that this bull was the form adopted by ZEUS when he abducted EUROPA from CRETE. [ANCIENT SOURCES: Seneca, Hercules Furens 9, 952, Thyestes 852]

TAYGETUS A mountain located southwest of SPARTA. [ANCIENT SOURCES: Aristophanes, Lysistrata 117, 1296]

TECHNITES (Plural: TECHNITAI) From the latter half of the fourth century B.C.E. onward, a *technites* (artist) was a member of an acting guild. [ANCIENT SOURCES: *Inscriptiones Graecae* 9.1.694, 76ff., 12.9.207, and p. 176, 12 Supplement p. 178; *Sylloge Inscriptionum Graecarum* 3.690]

TECMESSA
This woman became the war prize of AJAX during the Trojan War and by him produced a son, EURYSACES. Tecmessa appears as a character in SOPHOCLES' *Ajax*, in which she gives a speech modeled on that of ANDROMACHE to HECTOR in the sixth book of HOMER's *Iliad*, as Tecmessa worries about what will happen to her and her son if Ajax dies. In Sophocles, however, the dynamic differs from that of the Homeric Andromache and Hector because Tecmessa is a war captive rather than a legitimate bride; she is also a Trojan woman who has come to care for a Greek man, rather than a Trojan woman involved with a fellow Trojan.

TEIRESIAS
See TIRESIAS.

TELAMON
Telamon accompanied HERACLES when that hero sacked TROY during the reign of LAOMEDON. After the battle, Heracles gave Laomedon's daughter, HESIONE, as a battle prize to Telamon. By his concubine, Hesione, Telamon became the father of TEUCER; by his wife, Eriboea, he became the father of AJAX. ENNIUS wrote a *Telamon*, from which about a dozen lines survive. [ANCIENT SOURCES: Apollodorus, *Library* 2.6.4, 3.12.6–7; Euripides, *Helen* 87–94; Hyginus, *Fables* 89; Pindar, *Isthmian Odes* 6.26–54, *Nemean Odes* 3.36–39; Pausanias, 8.15.6–7]

TELEAS
The son of Telenicus, Teleas was a wealthy Athenian who served as "Secretary . . . of the Treasurers of Athena for 415/4" (Dunbar) but who must have been familiar to the Athenian public as early as 421 B.C.E. ARISTOPHANES calls him a fickle person, an embezzler, and a glutton. The ancient commentators on Aristophanes noted that the comic poets also mocked Teleas as a coward and a passive homosexual. The comic poet PHRYNICHUS calls him a big ape. [ANCIENT SOURCES: Aristophanes, *Birds* 168 and the scholia at 167, 1025, *Peace* 1008; *Inscriptiones Graecae* i³.331.23, 370.62; Phrynichus, fragment 20.2 Kock]

BIBLIOGRAPHY
Dunbar, Nan. *Aristophanes: Birds.* New York: Oxford University Press, 1995, 189.

TELEBOANS (TELOBOIANS)
Also known as the Taphians, the Teleboans were a mythical tribe who lived in the so-called Taphian islands off the western coast of Greece. AMPHITRYON and his Theban forces defeated the Teleboans and their king, PTERELAS (or Pterelaus), in a war that was prompted by the Teleboans' theft of cattle that belonged to Amphitryon's uncle, ELECTRYON. Electryon's sons were killed while trying to fend off the raiders. [ANCIENT SOURCES: Plautus, *Amphitruo* 101ff]

TELEPHUS
Telephus was the son of HERACLES and AUGE. Telephus was born in the Greek town of Tegea and left to die after his birth. He survived by being suckled by a deer. Upon the Greeks' first attempt to sail for Troy to recover HELEN, they landed in Mysia and fought with Telephus and his people, in the course of which ACHILLES wounded him. The Greeks then returned to Greece in need of someone to guide them to Troy. Later, when Telephus' wound would not heal, Telephus went to Greece in accordance with an ORACLE, which stated that he could only be healed by the one who had wounded him. Telephus made his way to ARGOS and the court of AGAMEMNON. When Telephus did not receive the help he desired from Agamemnon, he took Agamemnon's infant son, ORESTES, hostage and threatened to kill him. Ultimately, Agamemnon relented and Telephus was put in contact with ACHILLES, who healed him with the rust from his spear. In thanks, Telephus agreed to guide the Greeks to Troy.

EURIPIDES wrote a play entitled *Telephus*, which was produced in 438 B.C.E. along with *Alcmeon in Psophis, Cretan Women,* and *Alcestis.* We possess rather substantial fragments from the play that give us some understanding of it. Our knowledge of Euripides' *Telephus* is also augmented by ARISTOPHANES' parody of the hostage scene in his ACHARNIANS and THESMOPHORIAZUSAE. In *Acharnians*, DICAEOPOLIS takes charcoal hostage and threatens to "kill" it if the Acharnians do not end their threats to stone him. In *Thesmophoriazusae*, Mnesilochus takes hostage a woman's baby—

which turns out to be a skin of wine—and threatens to kill it if the women do not leave him alone. In Euripides' *Telephus,* Telephus apparently took the infant Orestes hostage and threatened to kill him. SOPHOCLES is also said to have written a *Telephus* and appears to have treated Telephus' story in *Mysians.* [ANCIENT SOURCES: Hyginus, *Fables* 101]

BIBLIOGRAPHY
Lloyd-Jones, H. *Sophocles: Fragments.* Cambridge, Mass.: Harvard University Press, 1996.

Radt, S. *Tragicorum Graecorum Fragmenta.* Vol. 4. Göttingen, Ger.: Vandenhoeck & Ruprecht, 1977.

Sutton, D. F. *The Lost Sophocles.* Lanham, Md.: University Press of America, 1984.

TEMENUS   The son of Aristomachus, Temenus was one of the descendants of HERACLES known as the Heraclids. When Heracles' son, HYLLUS, trying to restore the Heraclids to the kingdom of the Peloponnese, led an army against ORESTES' son TISAMENUS, Temenus' father, Aristomachus, was killed in battle. Temenus blamed his father's death on an ORACLE of APOLLO, with which Temenus claimed the Heraclids had complied in attacking the Peloponnesians. Apollo, however, declared that the Heraclids had misinterpreted the oracle. When Temenus learned the proper interpretation of the oracle, he assembled an army and built a fleet at the town of Naupactus.

While at Naupactus, Temenus' army suffered terrible hardship. At one point, a soothsayer appeared, reciting oracles. The army thought the soothsayer was a magician sent by their enemies to cause their ruin, and one of the soldiers, Hippotes, killed him. Because of this killing, the sailors and the fleet were destroyed and the army fell apart after a terrible famine. Temenus again consulted the oracle and learned that the soothsayer's death had caused the disaster and that his killer, Hippotes, must be exiled for 10 years. Furthermore, Temenus learned that he and his surviving forces should use "the Three-Eyed One" as their guide. After Hippotes' exile, Temenus and his companions searched for the Three-Eyed One. Upon encountering Oxylus, a man sitting on a one-eyed horse, they realized he must be the one meant by the oracle. With Oxylus as his guide, Temenus and his army defeated the Peloponnesians and killed ORESTES' son, Tisamenus. After establishing their mastery over the Peloponnese, Temenus and three other chieftains (CRESPHONTES and Aristodemus' sons, EURYSTHENES and Procles) drew lots to determine who would rule which city (ARGOS, Messenia, and SPARTA). They cast their lots into a pitcher of water. Temenus and Aristodemus' sons used stones as lots, but Cresphontes, who wanted to obtain Messenia as his kingdom, used a clod of dirt as his because the clod's dissolution would cause the other two lots to be taken first.

After the lottery, in which Cresphontes won Messenia, Aristodemus' sons won Sparta, and Temenus won Argos, Temenus began to show favor to his daughter, Hyrnetho, and her husband, Deiphontes, over his sons, Agelaus, Callias, and Eurypylus. This behavior angered Temenus' sons, who hired men to kill their father. After Temenus' murder, however, his army decided to hand over the kingdom to Deiphontes and Hyrnetho.

EURIPIDES wrote a *Temenus* (fragments 742–51 Nauck) that probably dates to the last five years of his life. Fragment 742 may refer to the lottery of the three lands; fragments 743–44, which refer to the qualities of a good general, may point to Deiphontes, who was the general of Temenus' army. Euripides also wrote a *Daughters of Temenus* (fragments 728–41 Nauck), which may have been part of a trilogy with his *Temenus* and *Archelaus* and may have dealt with the death of Hyrnetho, whose brothers tried to carry her off from Deiphontes. Deiphontes pursued the brothers and in the subsequent battle they and Hyrnetho were killed. [ANCIENT SOURCES: Apollodorus, *Library* 2.8.2–5; Hyginus, *Fables* 219; Pausanias, 2.18.7–2.19.1, 2.26.2, 2.28.3–7]

BIBLIOGRAPHY
Harder, M. Annette. "Euripides' *Temenos* and *Temenidai.*" In *Fragmenta Dramatica: Beiträge zur Interpretation der griechischen Tragikerfragmente und ihrer Wirkungsgeschichte.* Edited by M. A. Harder. Göttingen, Ger.: Vandenhoeck & Ruprecht, 1991, 117–35.

Nauck, A. *Tragicorum Graecorum Fragmenta.* 1889. Reprint, Hildesheim, Ger.: Olms, 1964.

Webster, T. B. L. *The Tragedies of Euripides.* London: Methuen, 1967.

TERENCE (CA. 190–159 B.C.E.)   According to tradition, Publius Terentius Afer was born in the north African town of CARTHAGE. At a young age he went to Rome as the slave of a senator, Terentius Lucanus. This senator, apparently impressed by the young Terence, provided him with an education and later freed him. Eventually, Terence made his way into a literary circle that formed around the Roman statesman Scipio Aemilianus and the comic poet CAECILIUS, to whom Terence is said to have read his first play. Terence is said to have died on a trip to Greece, but the exact date his death is not known.

The six surviving plays that we have represent Terence's entire output: *Eunuchus* (EUNUCH), *Adelphoi* (BROTHERS), *Andria* (GIRL FROM ANDROS), *Phormio*, *Hecyra* (MOTHER-IN-LAW), and *Heauton Timorumenos* (SELF-TORMENTOR). The plays of Terence, like those of PLAUTUS, were originally written by Greek playwrights and then adapted for Roman audiences. All of Terence's plays are set in ATHENS. Unlike Plautus, though, who inserted Roman references and terms into his plays, Terence does not allow Roman elements to intrude in his Greek setting.

MENANDER provided models for four of Terence's plays (*Andria, Brothers, Eunuch, Self-Tormentor*); Terence took the other two from Apollodorus of Carystus (*Mother-in-Law, Phormio*). As did Plautus, Terence took liberties with his Greek sources. In the prologue of his *Andria* (13–14), for example, Terence admits that he has combined elements from Menander's *Perinthia* (*Woman of Perinthos*) and Menander's *Andria*. Whereas Terence was criticized in his own day for this practice (see CONTAMINATIO), modern scholars usually praise his relatively seamless integration of such material, especially when compared to that of Plautus. The plots of Terence's plays are generally more complicated than those of Plautus. With the exception of *Mother-in-Law*, Terence's plays have a double plot, in which two lovers pursue their love interests.

Terence's PROLOGUES are certainly different from those of Plautus. Plautus' were usually expository in nature, with a character appearing at the beginning of the play to explain the background to the action. Terence's prologues are slightly reminiscent of the PARABASIS in ARISTOPHANES as Terence often defends himself against his critics and comments on the challenges he faces in winning over an audience. Whereas Plautus usually explains the background to a play in the rather artificial, expository fashion, Terence allows the background to his plays to emerge in a more natural way through the conversation of the play's characters. Terence also differs from Plautus in his avoidance of song and lyric passages. Terence's language is regarded as closer to everyday speech than that of Plautus and his characters as more realistically and sensitively drawn than those of Plautus. Although they were more elegant in style and realistic in characterization than those of Plautus, Terence's plays were not as popular as Plautus'. They lack the spirited fun of Plautus' plays and some of Plautus' stock characters (e.g., the evil PIMP and the aged male lover). In fact, Terence's most popular play, *Eunuch*, is Terence's most Plautine play in its content, as it includes a stereotypical food-obsessed PARASITE and a BRAGGART WARRIOR. Terence's dramas had significant influence on Augustine, given their lack of moral value in Augustine's opinion. Likewise, the plays of the medieval writer Hrothswitha tried to counteract the perceived immorality in Terence's work.

BIBLIOGRAPHY
Arnott, W. G. *Menander, Plautus, and Terence.* Oxford: Clarendon Press, 1975.
Buchner, K. *Das Theater des Terenz.* Heidelberg: Winter, 1974.
Forehand, W. E. *Terence.* Boston: Twayne, 1985.
Goldberg, S. M. *Understanding Terence.* Princeton, N.J.: Princeton University Press, 1986.
Norwood, G. *The Art of Terence.* Oxford: Blackwell, 1923.

TEREUS   The son of ARES, the Thracian Tereus committed one of the greatest atrocities recorded in classical mythology. Tereus, who had married Pandion's daughter, PROCNE, and fathered a son, Itys, by her, raped Procne's sister, PHILOMELA; cut out her tongue and then imprisoned her in a hut in the Thracian countryside. Eventually, however, Philomela was able to reveal what had happened to her by weaving a cloth depicting her horrific experience and arranging for the cloth to be smuggled to Procne. When Procne understood what had happened to her sister, she managed to release her from her confinement. After she had taken Philomela into her own house, Procne proceeded to kill her own son, Itys, and serve the child as food to her husband. When Tereus realized that he had consumed the vile dish, he tried to kill Procne and Philomela. The women, however, who had prayed to the gods for salvation, were changed into birds. Procne became a nightingale, and Philomela became a swallow. Tereus also became a bird—the hoopoe.

SOPHOCLES wrote a *Tereus,* of which about a dozen fragments survive (581–95b Radt). Because ARISTOPHANES jokes about Sophocles' *Tereus* in his BIRDS of 414 B.C.E., Sophocles' play appeared before this date. Among Roman authors, ACCIUS wrote a *Tereus* (lines 639–55 Warmington). Shakespeare's *Titus Andronicus* was heavily influenced by the story of Tereus. [ANCIENT SOURCES: Apollodorus, *Library* 3.14.8; Aristophanes, *Birds* 15, 201, 665, *Lysistrata* 562; Euripides, *Heracles* 1021; Hyginus, *Fables* 45; Ovid, *Metamorphoses* 6.401–674; Seneca, *Thyestes* 56]

BIBLIOGRAPHY

Kiso, A. *The Lost Sophocles.* New York: Vantage Press, 1984.

Lloyd-Jones, H. *Sophocles: Fragments.* Cambridge, Mass.: Harvard University Press, 1996.

Radt, S. *Tragicorum Graecorum Fragmenta.* Vol. 4. Göttingen, Ger.: Vandenhoeck & Ruprecht, 1977.

Sutton, D. F. *The Lost Sophocles.* Lanham, Md.: University Press of America, 1984.

Warmington, E. H. *Remains of Old Latin: Livius Andronicus, Naevius, Pacuvius, and Accius.* Vol. 2. Cambridge, Mass.: Harvard University Press, 1936.

TETHYS   The daughter of URANUS and Gaia (see EARTH), Tethys became the wife of her brother, OCEANUS. With Oceanus, Tethys had some 3,000 children. Sometimes playwrights use the name of Tethys as a synonym for the sea. [ANCIENT SOURCES: Apollodorus, *Library* 1.1.3; Hesiod, *Theogony* 136, 337; Seneca, *Hercules Furens* 887, 1328, *Hercules Oetaeus* 1252, 1902, *Hippolytus* 571, 1161, *Medea* 378, *Trojan Women* 879]

TETRALOGY   This term refers to a group of four plays offered by Greek tragedians at a single dramatic festival. The first three plays of the tetralogy were tragedies; the last play was usually a SATYR PLAY. No extant tetralogy survives, but the names of the plays that several tetralogies comprised are known. The closest to a complete tetralogy is AESCHYLUS' ORESTEIA. The first three plays of the tetralogy (*Agamemnon, Libation Bearers,* and *Eumenides* [see ORESTEIA]) are extant, but the satyr play that followed them, *Proteus,* has not survived. The plays that constitute some tetralogies, such as Aeschylus' Theban tetralogy (composed of *Laius, Oedipus, Seven against Thebes,* and the satyr play *Sphinx*), have clear connections in subject matter. Other tetralogies, however, seemingly have little connection in the subject matter of the various plays. We shall never know what, if any, connections Aeschylus might have established in the tetralogy that consisted of *Phineus, Persians,* and *Glaucus Potnieus* and its satyr play, *Prometheus Pyrkaeus.*

TEUCER   The son of TELAMON and PRIAM's daughter, HESIONE, Teucer is the half brother of AJAX. Teucer, a skilled archer, fought on the Greek side during the Trojan War. Teucer appears as a character in SOPHOCLES' AJAX and EURIPIDES' HELEN. In *Ajax,* the title character gives Teucer custody of his son, EURYSACES, before he commits suicide. After Ajax's death, Teucer argues unsuccessfully with AGAMEMNON and MENELAUS about the burial of Ajax. Eventually, ODYSSEUS intervenes and secures burial for Ajax, but Teucer prevents Odysseus from participating in the burial because he feels this would not have been in accordance with Ajax's wishes. Euripides' *Helen* is about the life of Teucer after the fall of TROY. Apparently, when Teucer returned to his native island of SALAMIS, his father, Telamon, blaming Teucer for the fate of Ajax, banished him from Salamis. Accordingly, Teucer set out to find a new home. According to Euripides' *Helen,* Teucer makes a stop in Egypt to consult the female prophet THEONOE. Eventually, Teucer arrives at the island of Cyprus, where he settles and founds a town called Salamis, after his native land. SOPHOCLES wrote a *Teucer,* from which about a dozen lines survive (fragments 576–79 Radt); Telamon seems to have appeared as a character. [ANCIENT SOURCES: Aristophanes, *Frogs* 1041; Homer, *Iliad* 8.266–344, 12.370–403, 13.169–85, 15.437–83, 23.859–83; Pausanias, 1.3.2, 1.28.11, 2.29.4, 8.15.6–7; Vergil, *Aeneid* 1.619–22]

BIBLIOGRAPHY

Kiso, A. *The Lost Sophocles.* New York: Vantage Press, 1984.

Lloyd-Jones, H. *Sophocles: Fragments.* Cambridge, Mass.: Harvard University Press, 1996.

Radt, S. *Tragicorum Graecorum Fragmenta.* Vol. 4. Göttingen, Ger.: Vandenhoeck & Ruprecht, 1977.

Sutton, D. F. *The Lost Sophocles.* Lanham, Md.: University Press of America, 1984.

TEUCRIAN

Pertaining to Teucer, an early king in the region where TROY is located. The classical playwrights sometimes call Troy either Teucria or the Teucrian land. The Trojans are sometimes called Teucrians.

TEUMESSUS

A mountain or range of hills near THEBES. [ANCIENT SOURCES: Euripides, *Phoenician Women* 1100; Pausanias, 9.19]

THALES

A Greek scientist of the sixth century B.C.E. whom ARISTOTLE considered one of the Seven Sages of the world. Thales was regarded as the founder of geometry and was said to have predicted correctly a solar eclipse in the year 585. [ANCIENT SOURCES: Aristophanes, *Clouds* 180, *Birds* 1009; Aristotle, *Metaphysics* 983b20; Herodotus, 1.74; Plautus, *Bacchides* 122]

THAMYRIS (THAMYRAS)

The son of Philammon and Argiope, Thamyris was a handsome musician who had a musical contest with the MUSES. The goddesses agreed that if Thamyris won, he could have sexual relations with them, but if he lost, then they would take away from him whatever they wished. When the Muses won the contest, they blinded him and robbed him of his musical ability. SOPHOCLES wrote a *Thamyras,* of which a few fragments survive (237–45 Radt). The fragments have many references to music and musical instruments but reveal little else about the play's content. The Greek comic poet Antiphanes also wrote a *Thamyras,* from which three lines (fragment 105 Kock) about someone who will be named after the STRYMON River survive. [ANCIENT SOURCES: Euripides, *Rhesus* 924–25]

BIBLIOGRAPHY

Kiso, A. *The Lost Sophocles.* New York: Vantage Press, 1984.

Kock, T. *Comicorum Atticorum Fragmenta.* Vol. 2. Leipzig: Teubner, 1884.

Lloyd-Jones, H. *Sophocles: Fragments.* Cambridge, Mass.: Harvard University Press, 1996.

Radt, S. *Tragicorum Graecorum Fragmenta.* Vol. 4. Göttingen, Ger.: Vandenhoeck & Ruprecht, 1977.

Sutton, D. F. *The Lost Sophocles.* Lanham, Md.: University Press of America, 1984.

THANATOS

The personification of death, Thanatos appears at the beginning of EURIPIDES' *Alcestis.*

THEAGENES

The identification of this Greek is uncertain, as the name is common in ATHENS. ARISTOPHANES makes fun of a person named Theagenes on several occasions and labels him a braggart, a person with filthy habits, and someone who had suffered the penalty for adultery. Thucydides mentions two people named Theagenes, one a "fact finder" (Dunbar), the other one of those who in 421 B.C.E. ratified the PEACE OF NICIAS. Xenophon mentions a Theagenes who in 409 had a diplomatic mission to Persia. [ANCIENT SOURCES: Aristophanes, *Birds* 822, 1127, 1295, *Lysistrata* 64, *Peace* 928, *Wasps* 1183–84, fragment 582 Kock; Thucydides, 4.27.3, 5.19.2, 5.24.1; Xenophon, *Hellenica* 1.3.13]

BIBLIOGRAPHY

Dunbar, Nan. *Aristophanes: Birds.* New York: Oxford University Press, 1995. 492–93.

THEATRON (Plural: THEATRA; Latin: CAVEA [sg.], CAVEAE [pl.])

The *theatron* ("place for viewing") was the space from which the spectators watched a play. In the early days of Greek drama, the *theatron* was nothing more than the side of a hill or wooden bleachers on a hillside. From the fourth century B.C.E. onward, the *theatra* became permanent structures made of stone. By 160 B.C.E., the *theatron* at EPIDAURUS had been expanded to 55 rows of seats, which could accommodate about 12,000 spectators. The *theatron* at Aphrodias (in western Turkey), which was dedicated in 28 B.C.E., could seat 8,000 spectators.

BIBLIOGRAPHY

Csapo, E., and W. J. Slater. *The Context of Ancient Drama.* Ann Arbor: University of Michigan Press, 1995, 79–88.

THEBES A town about 30 miles northwest of ATHENS. Two foundation stories are connected with Thebes. The better involves CADMUS, whom the DELPHIC ORACLE told to follow a cow until it stopped walking and on that site found a town. Cadmus did as he was told and followed the cow into the region of BOEOTIA (whose name contains the Greek word for "cow," *bous*). The other foundation story connected with Thebes involves the twin sons of ZEUS and ANTIOPE, AMPHION and Zethus. Amphion, an excellent musician, and Zethus, a strong fellow, served as corulers of Thebes and built walls for the city by using their skills. Zethus moved stones into place by sheer strength, but Amphion's music caused stones to roll into place. The town of Thebes had seven gates, which became strategic points of battle in the famous Seven against Thebes conflict. Numerous persons with a connection to classical TRAGEDY lived at Thebes: ANTIGONE, CREON, ETEOCLES, HERACLES, LAIUS, OEDIPUS, PENTHEUS, POLYNEICES. Several classical tragedies have Thebes as their setting: AESCHYLUS' *SEVEN AGAINST THEBES*, SOPHOCLES' *ANTIGONE* and *OEDIPUS TYRANNOS*, EURIPIDES' *BACCHAE*, *HERACLES*, and *PHOENICIAN WOMEN*.

THEMIS The daughter of URANUS and Gaia (see EARTH), Themis personifies that which is "right" (the meaning of her name), customary, ethical, and established by law. Before the arrival of APOLLO, Themis was the divinity who controlled the oracle at DELPHI. [ANCIENT SOURCES: Apollodorus, *Library* 1.3.1, 4.1; Hesiod, *Theogony* 135, 901; Homer, *Iliad* 15.87, 20.4, *Odyssey* 2.68; Ovid, *Metamorphoses* 1.321, 4.642; Pausanias, 1.22.1, 5.14.8, 9.22.1, 9.25.4, 10.5.3]

THEMISCYRA A plain near the Thermodon River in the Black Sea region. AMAZONS were said to inhabit Themiscyra. [ANCIENT SOURCES: Aeschylus, *Prometheus Bound* 724; Herodotus, 4.86]

THEMISTO See ATHAMAS.

THEMISTOCLES (CA. 528–462 B.C.E.) An important Athenian politician and military leader in the first quarter of the fifth century B.C.E. In the late 480s, Themistocles persuaded the Athenians to use some of the revenue from their silver mines to build up their navy. Themistocles commanded the Athenian naval forces that helped repel the Persian invasion of 480. After this, Themistocles persuaded the Athenians to build massive fortification walls to protect Athens' main harbor, PIRAEUS. Although Themistocles had advised his fellow Athenians well, he had many political enemies, and they managed to secure his exile in 471. He first traveled to Argos but then had to flee to what is now western Turkey after he was accused of consorting with the Persians. In Themistocles' absence, the Athenians sentenced him to die, and he is known to have died in 462. The Greek comic poet Philiscus wrote a *Themistocles*, of which only the title survives. [ANCIENT SOURCES: Aristophanes, *Knights* 84, 812, 813, 818, 884; Hermippus, fragment 6 Kock; Herodotus, 7–8; Plutarch, *Themistocles*; Thucydides, 1.74, 1.93, 1.135–38]

BIBLIOGRAPHY

Anderson, C. A. "Themistocles and Cleon in Aristophanes' *Knights*, 763ff.," *American Journal of Philology* 90 (1989): 10–16.

Frost, F. J. *Plutarch's Themistocles: A Historical Commentary.* Princeton, N.J.: Princeton University Press, 1980.

Marr, John. *Plutarch: Life of Themistocles.* Warminster, U.K.: Aris & Phillips, 1998.

Podlecki, A. J. *The Life of Themistocles: A Critical Survey of the Literary and Archaeological Evidence.* Montreal: McGill-Queen's University Press, 1975.

THEOCLYMENUS The son of PROTEUS and the NEREID Psamathe, Theoclymenus was the brother of THEONOE (also called Eido). Theoclymenus became the king of Egypt after his father's death, and in EURIPIDES' *HELEN,* he pressures HELEN to marry him. In that play, Theoclymenus is characterized as a hater of Greeks, but it is his trust of Greeks (Helen and MENELAUS) that ultimately leads to his being tricked by them. His fate after the action of Euripides' *Helen* is unknown.

THEOGNIS A Greek tragedian whose work was considered so "frigid" that his nickname was "Snow." Only two words of his work survive (fragment 1 Snell). He may have been the same Theognis who was one of the Thirty Tyrants whom the Spartans installed to rule

ATHENS after their victory in 404 B.C.E. [ANCIENT SOURCES: Aristophanes, *Acharnians* 11, 140, *Thesmophoriazusae* 170, *Wasps* 1183; Lysias, 12.6.13; Xenophon, *Hellenica* 2.3.2]

BIBLIOGRAPHY
Snell, B. *Tragicorum Graecorum Fragmenta.* Vol. 1. Göttingen, Ger.: Vandenhoeck & Ruprecht, 1971.

THEOLOGEION (Plural: *THEOLOGEIA*)

The *theologeion* ("place from which a divinity speaks") was a space on the roof of the SKENE where ACTORS, usually portraying gods, could appear. [ANCIENT SOURCES: Pollux, *Onomasticon* 4.130]

THEONOE

The daughter of NEREUS, Theonoe ("divine mind") was a prophetess and the sister of the Egyptian king Theoclymenus. Theonoe appears in EURIPIDES' HELEN, in which she predicts that HELEN's husband, MENELAUS, is still alive. After Menelaus arrives on the scene, Theonoe indicates that she will tell her brother, King THEOCLYMENUS, that Menelaus has arrived. This will mean death for Menelaus, because Theoclymenus hates Greeks, but Helen pleads with Theonoe not to tell her brother and wins her over. After Helen and Menelaus escape from Egypt, Theoclymenus threatens to kill Theonoe, but the gods CASTOR and POLLUX order him not to do this. [ANCIENT SOURCES: Aristophanes, *Thesmophoriazusae* 896; Euripides, *Helen*]

BIBLIOGRAPHY
Sansone, D. "Theonoe and Theoclymenus," *Symbolae Osloenses* 60 (1985): 17–36.

THEORIKON (Plural: *THEORIKA*)

Public funds held in the Athenian treasury that was given to Athenian citizens so that all could afford entry to public entertainment events such as plays. Until most of the fourth century B.C.E. the *theorikon* was usually two OBOLS or one DRACHMA, but in the last quarter of that century the *theorikon* increased to five drachmas. [ANCIENT SOURCES: Demosthenes, *On the Crown* 28.5; Dinarchus, *Against Demosthenes* 56; Harpocration on *theorika*; Hyperides, *Against Demosthenes* 26; *Inscriptiones Graecae* ii².1176; Lucian, *Timon* 49 and the scho-

lia; Plutarch, *Pericles* 9; Ulpian on Demosthenes, *Olynthiacs* 1.1]

BIBLIOGRAPHY
Csapo, E., and W. J. Slater. *The Context of Ancient Drama.* Ann Arbor: University of Michigan Press, 1995, 287–97.

THEORUS

An Athenian statesman who supported CLEON and jurors. In 426 B.C.E., Theorus may have traveled to THRACE on a diplomatic mission to King Sitalces, and in ARISTOPHANES' ACHARNIANS Theorus gives a brief report on his mission. In 409, Theorus may have died near SAMOS while serving as a naval commander. ARISTOPHANES calls him a flatterer, imposter, and perjurer. The ancient commentators say that other comic poets labeled him an adulterer and a glutton. [ANCIENT SOURCES: Aristophanes, *Acharnians* 134, 155, *Clouds* 400, *Knights* 608 and the scholia, *Wasps* 42 and the scholia, 599, 1220, 1236]

BIBLIOGRAPHY
MacDowell, D. M. *Aristophanes: Wasps.* Oxford: Clarendon Press, 1971, 133.
Sommerstein, A. H. *The Comedies of Aristophanes.* Vol. 4, *Wasps.* Warminster, U.K.: Aris & Phillips, 1983, 155.

THERAMENES (D. 404/403 B.C.E.)

A prominent Athenian statesman and military figure, Theramenes, son of Hagnon, in the year 411 played an important role in the overthrow of Athenian democracy and the establishment of the oligarchy of the Four Hundred. A few months later, Theramenes helped overthrow the Four Hundred and establish the rule of the Five Thousand; within a year he helped remove the Five Thousand and reestablish democracy. Although Theramenes commanded a ship in 405 in the Athenian loss to the Spartans at ARGINUSAE, a battle after which six Athenian naval commanders were executed by their fellow citizens, Theramenes managed to avoid death. Theramenes' luck ran out a year or so later, when after he had helped negotiate the peace treaty that ended the war between ATHENS and SPARTA in 404, the Spartans appointed him one of the Thirty Tyrants who would govern Athens. When the Athenians overthrew the rule of the Thirty, Theramenes was put to death. The younger Cratinus wrote a *Theramenes,* of which only the title survives (see Kock 2). [ANCIENT SOURCES: Aristophanes, *Frogs* 541, 967–68, fragment 549 Kock 1; Thucydides, 8.68.4, 8.89.2–94.1; Xenophon, *Hellenica* 1.6.35, 1.7.5–8]

BIBLIOGRAPHY

Dover, K. J. *Aristophanes: Frogs.* Oxford: Clarendon Press, 1993, 262.

Kock, T. *Comicorum Atticorum Fragmenta.* Vol. 1. Leipzig: Teubner, 1880.

————. *Comicorum Atticorum Fragmenta.* Vol. 2. Leipzig: Teubner, 1884.

Lang, M. L. "Theramenes and Arginousai," *Hermes* 120, no. 3 (1992): 267–79.

Pesely, G. E. *Theramenes and Athenian Politics: A Study in the Manipulation of History.* Berkeley: University of California Press, 1983.

THERMODON   A river in the Black Sea region. Amazon women were said to live along the Thermodon, and HERACLES went to this area to obtain the belt of the Amazon queen. [ANCIENT SOURCES: Aeschylus, *Prometheus Bound* 725; Seneca, *Hercules Furens* 246, *Hercules Oetaeus* 21, *Medea* 215, *Oedipus* 481]

THERSITES   The son of Agrius, Thersites was the brother of Celeutor, Lycopeus, MELANIPPUS, Onchestus, and Prothous. With his brothers, Thersites helped usurp the kingdom of CALYDON from OENEUS and transfer it to their father, Agrius. Eventually, however, DIOMEDES killed most of Thersites' brothers and drove Agrius from the kingdom. Thersites and Onchestus escaped to the Peloponnese. When Oeneus left Calydon and arrived in the Peloponnese, Thersites and Onchestus killed him. Later Thersites went to TROY as part of the mission to rescue HELEN. He was universally hated by his fellow Greeks (his name means "brawler" and he was ugly). Thersites was eventually killed by ACHILLES after Achilles killed the Amazon PENTHESILEIA in the 10th year of the war. Thersites made fun of Achilles, because he then fell in love with her. The Greek tragedian Chaeremon wrote an *Achilles Thersitoktonos* (Achilles, the killer of Thersites); among the brief remains of this play (fragments 1c–3 Snell) is a list of the play's characters. The presence of PAN and HERMES on the list suggests that Chaeremon's treatment of Thersites' death was not somber. [ANCIENT SOURCES: Apollodorus, *Library* 1.8.6, *Epitome* 5.1; Homer, *Iliad* 2.212ff.]

BIBLIOGRAPHY

Snell, B. *Tragicorum Graecorum Fragmenta.* Vol. 1. Göttingen, Ger.: Vandenhoeck & Ruprecht, 1971.

THESEUM   The name of a sacred precinct, perhaps on the eastern end of the Athenian ACROPOLIS, in which the bones of THESEUS were said to have been placed. The Theseum was sometimes used as a place of refuge for slaves, who "could demand to be sold to a new master" (Sommerstein). [ANCIENT SOURCES: Aristophanes, *Knights* 1312, fragment 567 Kock; Plutarch, *Cimon* 8.5–7, *Theseus* 36.2–4]

BIBLIOGRAPHY

Kock, T. *Comicorum Atticorum Fragmenta.* Vol. 1. Leipzig: Teubner, 1880.

Sommerstein, A. H. *The Comedies of Aristophanes.* Vol. 2, *Knights.* Warminster, U.K.: Aris & Phillips, 1981, 214.

THESEUS   The son of POSEIDON (or AEGEUS) and AETHRA, Theseus was born in TROEZEN. By the AMAZON ANTIOPE, Theseus fathered HIPPOLYTUS. By PHAEDRA, Theseus was the father of DEMOPHON and Acamas. When Theseus grew up, his mother, Aethra, led him to a large rock under which his father, Aegeus, had placed a sword and a pair of sandals. If Theseus could lift the rock and retrieve these objects, he was to travel to ATHENS, Aegeus' kingdom. Theseus succeeded, put the sandals on his feet, strapped the sword to his side, and set out for Athens over land, although the sea route was faster and much safer.

Because travel over land presented six challenges, Theseus decided to take this route, so that he could gain a reputation for valor. On the way to Athens, Theseus killed six persons or creatures who were accustomed to kill passersby: Periphetes, SINIS, the sow of Crommyon, SCIRON, CERCYON, and PROCRUSTES. In each instance, Theseus killed the person or creature in the way in which it had killed others.

When Theseus arrived in Athens, he found Aegeus married to the dangerous MEDEA, who with Aegeus had a son, MEDUS. Through her magic powers, Medea knew that Theseus was Aegeus' son. Medea convinced

Aegeus that Theseus was going to try to kill him and accordingly tried to kill Theseus. First, she challenged Theseus to capture the deadly bull of Marathon. When Theseus subdued the bull, led it to Athens, and sacrificed it, Medea arranged for Aegeus to poison him at a banquet. Fortunately for Theseus, Aegeus recognized Theseus' sword as the one he had placed under the rock at Troezen and dashed the cup of poisoned wine from Theseus' lips. Medea managed to escape Athens with her son.

After the departure of Medea, the joyful reunion of Theseus and Aegeus was short lived, as the tribute that the Athenians owed to MINOS, the king of CRETE, fell due. After Minos' son, Androgeus, was killed in Athens, Minos had waged war successfully against Athens. After the victory, Minos imposed a penalty on the Athenians—every nine years they had to send to Crete seven young men and seven young women. When they reached Crete, the young Athenians were imprisoned in a labyrinth beneath Minos' palace, where they either starved to death or were killed by a monster called the MINOTAUR. Not long after Theseus' arrival in Athens, the tribute fell due a third time. Theseus volunteered to go to Crete as one of the sacrificial victims. Despite Aegeus' fears for his son, Theseus sailed with the other young people to Crete. Upon his arrival in Crete, APHRODITE aided Theseus by causing Minos' daughter, ARIADNE, to fall in love with him. Ariadne gave Theseus a special ball of thread to take with him into the labyrinth. This thread, the property of the labyrinth's architect, DAEDALUS, could guide Theseus through this deadly maze. With Ariadne's thread and the favor of the gods, Theseus led his companions through the labyrinth. Theseus also managed to kill the Minotaur in the process. Before Theseus left Crete, he sabotaged the Cretan ships so that they could not pursue him. Then, accompanied by Ariadne and his fellow Athenians, Theseus made his escape.

On the journey back to Athens, the ship stopped on the island of NAXOS. Theseus and his fellow Athenians left Naxos; Ariadne did not. Sources give different reasons for this: Some say that ARTEMIS killed Ariadne; others that DIONYSUS took Ariadne away from Theseus; others that Theseus simply left Ariadne on the island. Whatever the reason, Theseus' life after his departure

from Naxos was not a happy one. When Theseus had left Athens, the ship was flying a dark-colored sail. Aegeus had told Theseus to change the sail to a light-colored one if he had been successful on Crete. On his return to Athens, however, Theseus forgot to change the ship's sail. When Aegeus, anxiously awaiting Theseus' return from Crete, saw that the ship was flying a dark-colored sail, he assumed that Theseus had died on Crete and threw himself into the sea. Although Theseus had freed his fellow Athenians from the tribute they paid to Crete, his forgetfulness had caused his father's death.

After Aegeus' death, Theseus became the king of Athens. He soon instituted a democracy, which allowed him to participate in other adventures. Some say he joined in the hunt for the Calydonian boar, the quest for the Golden Fleece, and HERACLES' journey to get the Amazon's girdle. In this latter adventure, Theseus is said to have abducted the Amazon Antiope (or Hippolyta). After Theseus' return to Athens, the other Amazons traveled to Athens and waged war against Theseus and his people. Some say that Antiope was killed in this battle, others that she fought alongside Theseus against her former tribe. In either case, Theseus triumphed over the Amazons, and by Antiope he fathered a son, Hippolytus. Some time later, Theseus married Phaedra, the daughter of Minos and sister of Ariadne. Some sources say that to do this he divorced Antiope, and perhaps even killed her when the angered Amazon tried to attack him. Theseus' marriage to Phaedra also ended in disaster, as she fell in love with Hippolytus. When an attempt to arrange a union with Hippolytus failed, Phaedra committed suicide. Before her suicide, however, Phaedra wrote a note to Theseus accusing Hippolytus of trying to assault her sexually. When Theseus read Phaedra's note, he used one of three curses his father, Poseidon, had given him to cause Hippolytus' death.

Accounts of Theseus' life after the deaths of Phaedra and Hippolytus vary. It appears, however, that Theseus attended his friend, PIRITHOUS the Lapith, at Pirithous' marriage to HIPPODAMEIA. When CENTAURS tried to attack Hippodameia during the wedding festivities, a battle broke out between the centaurs and the Lapiths. With the help of Theseus, Pirithous and the Lapiths defeated the centaurs. Hippodameia, however, was killed accidentally during the battle. Because Pirithous and Theseus were both unmarried now, the two set out to find brides for themselves and decided that they would settle for nothing less than daughters of ZEUS. The first woman the two pursued was young HELEN, the daughter of Zeus and LEDA. When they abducted Helen from SPARTA, they decided that Theseus would eventually marry her. After Theseus left Helen in Troezen with his mother, Aethra, Theseus and Pirithous then set out to find another daughter of Zeus for Pirithous. After consulting the DELPHIC ORACLE, Theseus and Pirithous descended to the UNDERWORLD to inquire about PERSEPHONE, who was a daughter of Zeus, but who was also married to HADES himself. Hades took the two undead heroes into his house and offered them a seat on the Couch of Forgetfulness. When the unsuspecting pair sat on the couch, not only did they forget why they had gone to the underworld, they also became stuck to the couch. Some time later Theseus was rescued from the couch by Heracles during his labor to fetch CERBERUS. Pirithous, however, was not so lucky, as an earthquake occurred while Heracles tried to remove him from the couch. Heracles took this as an omen that the gods were displeased with the rescue, and so Pirithous remained in the underworld.

When Theseus returned to Athens, he found that the government had changed hands during his absence. Now, Mnestheus was king and Theseus found himself regarded as an outlaw. Theseus then left Athens and traveled to SCYROS, where his family had some land. Unfortunately for Theseus, LYCOMEDES, king of Scyros, was a friend of Mnestheus', and when Theseus arrived on the island Lycomedes killed him by pushing him off a cliff into the sea. Thus, Theseus died in roughly the same manner as his father, Aegeus, had.

Theseus appears as a character in several extant plays: EURIPIDES' *HIPPOLYTUS, SUPPLIANT WOMEN, HERACLES*; SOPHOCLES' *OEDIPUS AT COLONUS*; and SENECA's *HERCULES FURENS* and *HIPPOLYTUS*. In Euripides' *Hippolytus*, Theseus is portrayed as the unfortunate king who rushes to a judgment that results in the death of a loved one. In Euripides' *Suppliant Women* and *Heracles*, as well as Sophocles' *Oedipus at Colonus*, Theseus rep-

resents the compassionate side of Athens, the Athens that helps the downtrodden mothers of fallen Argive warriors recover the bodies of their sons for burial or who provides a place of refuge for Heracles or OEDIPUS, who will be or are cast out of their native lands for horrific crimes or actions.

In addition to those plays, Theseus would have appeared in a number of other ancient dramas. Euripides wrote a *Theseus,* and Sophocles may have written one. Webster thinks that Euripides' *Theseus* treated Theseus' encounter on Crete with the Minotaur. The Greek tragedian Achaeus also wrote a *Theseus,* but the four words that survive give no firm information about the play's content (fragments 18–18a Snell). Four Greek comic poets, Aristonymous (fragment 1 Kock 1), Theopompus (fragments 17–20 Kock 1), Anaxandrides (fragments 19–20 Kock 2), and DIPHILUS (fragment 49 Kock 2) also produced plays entitled Theseus, but the fragments are too brief to give any hint at their plots. [ANCIENT SOURCES: Aristophanes, *Frogs* 142; Euripides, *Heracles, Hippolytus, Suppliant Women*; Hyginus, *Fables* 37–38, 40–43, 47–48, 79, 187; Plutarch, *Life of Theseus*; Seneca, *Hercules Furens, Hippolytus*; Sophocles, *Oedipus at Colonus*]

BIBLIOGRAPHY

Kock, T. *Comicorum Atticorum Fragmenta.* Vols. 1 and 2. Leipzig: Teubner, 1880, 1884.

Snell, B. *Tragicorum Graecorum Fragmenta.* Vol. 1. Göttingen, Ger.: Vandenhoeck & Ruprecht, 1971.

Webster, T. B. L. *The Tragedies of Euripides.* London: Methuen, 1967.

THESMOPHORIAZUSAE ARISTOPHANES (411 B.C.E.)

The play was produced (perhaps at the City DIONYSIA) in the same year as LYSISTRATA. How the play finished in the competition is not known. The play is set in ATHENS and the audience has to imagine at least two different locations: The play opens at the house of the poet Agathon and later moves to the place where the women are celebrating the Thesmophoria.

At the festival of the Thesmophoria, the women decree that EURIPIDES must be put to death because of what he says about them in his plays. As the play opens, Euripides, who would have been close to 70 years old when *Thesmophoriazusae* was staged, is accompanied by one of his kinsman, Mnesilochus, to the house of Agathon, a tragic poet. Because Agathon behaves and dresses in an effeminate manner, Euripides hopes that Agathon will be able to infiltrate the all-female Thesmophoria and plead his case before the women. When Agathon refuses, Euripides dresses Mnesilochus as a woman and has his kinsman go to the festival. Mnesilochus pleads Euripides' case, but the women eventually discover his true gender, thanks to the information of Cleisthenes, whose womanlike appearance has gained him entry to the Thesmophoria. Mnesilochus tries to escape by taking one woman's baby as a hostage; he soon discovers, however, that what the woman had wrapped in a blanket was not a baby, but a skin of wine. This scene parodies Euripides' *Telephus*, originally staged 27 years earlier, in which the title character took the infant ORESTES as a hostage. Mnesilochus, after the failure of this tactic, is taken into custody by an Athenian policeman.

The remainder of the play consists of Euripides' attempts to free Mnesilochus from captivity. These attempts involve parodies of various Euripidean plays. First, Mnesilochus takes a page from *Palamedes,* in which Oeax, the brother of PALAMEDES, threw into the sea oar blades inscribed with news of Palamedes' death. In *Palamedes*, Oeax hoped news of Palamedes' death would reach Palamedes' father in Greece. In *Thesmophoriazusae,* Mnesilochus does not have oar blades; instead he throws wooden voting tablets into the audience in the hope that news of his capture will reach Euripides. When this tactic fails, an attempt to free Mnesilochus is made by using tactics from Euripides' *Andromeda,* staged not long before *Thesmophoriazusae.* The aged Mnesilochus plays ANDROMEDA, and Euripides pretends to be PERSEUS. The humor of the parody is further intensified as Andromeda/Mnesilochus' opening lament is echoed by the goddess ECHO herself. Aristophanes enhances the effect by making Echo respond to the comments of the Scythian who is guarding Mnesilochus. Thus, Echo does double duty by echoing an old man who is pretending to be a young woman, as well as echoing a foreigner who speaks imperfect Greek. The attempt to free Mnesilochus with scenes from *Andromeda* fails. Next, Mnesilochus and Euripides turn to Euripides' HELEN. Again,

Mnesilochus plays the role of Helen, and Euripides pretends to be her shipwrecked husband, MENELAUS. When Euripides' tragedies fail to rescue his kinsman, he (dressed as an old woman) approaches the women at the Thesmophoria and promises not to slander them any longer. The women accept Euripides' proposal but tell him that if he wants to set Mnesilochus free, he himself will have to take care of the Scythian. To do this, Euripides finally resorts to a trick from the comic genre: He induces the Scythian to chase a dancing girl. With the Scythian out of the way, Euripides rescues Mnesilochus and the play swiftly ends.

COMMENTARY

ARISTOPHANES' *Thesmophoriazusae* has not received as much critical attention as other Aristophanic plays, but the more often one reads the play, the more one appreciates its cleverness and consistency of theme and structure. Moreover, *Thesmophoriazusae* is one of the most unique plays among Aristophanes' surviving works. As in *Lysistrata* and ECCLESIAZUSAE, women play a central role in *Thesmophoriazusae*. Unlike those two plays, however, *Thesmophoriazusae* does not suggest sweeping social or political reform. Furthermore, other than the decree of death against Euripides, the women's role in the play is not as substantial as in *Lysistrata* or *Ecclesiazusae*. Unlike *Lysistrata*, *Thesmophoriazusae* does not focus on how war affects not only women but the whole of society, but on how a particular poet affects a specific group in society.

The "concern" that faces Euripides and Mnesilochus in this play is one of stereotype. Euripides is claimed to stereotype women as evil, and therefore the women of the Thesmophoria decide to kill him. What the audience should note about this play, however, is the means by which Euripides tries to extricate himself from this situation. To save himself, Euripides relies on his skills as a creator of dramatic plots, especially tragic ones. Almost from start to finish, *Thesmophoriazusae* consists of a series of plays within the play. First, Euripides tries to enlist the help of the poet Agathon to plead his case with the women. Although the effeminate poet already has the appropriate costume to address a group of women, unlike Euripides in Aristophanes' ACHARNIANS (who let Dicaeopolis borrow a costume from one of his plays), Agathon refuses to participate in Euripides' "play." Because Euripides' attempt to organize this play has failed, he must recast the role for the character who will plead his case and settles on his relative. Unfortunately for Euripides but fortunately for COMEDY, Euripides' relative will need more preparation to become a woman. He does not already dress as a woman or resemble a woman; accordingly, he must be shaved (all over his body). Eventually, however, this "play" fails. The women are outraged by Mnesilochus' speech, and eventually his male identity is revealed to them by another man who can pass as a woman.

Trapped, Mnesilochus turns to Euripidean drama for escape. Just as in *Acharnians* Dicaeopolis had turned to a parody of Euripides' *Telephus* and had taken charcoal hostage when faced with an assault from the Acharnians, likewise in *Thesmophoriazusae* Mnesilochus takes a skin of wine hostage. Mnesilochus, however, performs the role of TELEPHUS incorrectly, and, unlike Telephus, Euripides' relative "kills" his hostage by pouring out the wine. Thus, Mnesilochus remains trapped and Euripidean drama has failed to extricate him from this situation.

Thus, Mnesilochus is trapped and the remainder of the play functions almost as a tetralogy, with the performance of three tragedies and a satyr play. The first TRAGEDY to which Mnesilochus resorts is Euripides' *Palamedes*. Mnesilochus' attempt to call for help fails, however, as no one responds to the messages that he casts out to the audience. Next, Mnesilochus hopes performing *Helen* will save him, but again the audience onstage (the women of the chorus and the woman, Critylla, who guards him) are not taken in by Euripidean drama.

The arrival of a new member for the audience on stage, the Scythian, marks the beginning of the third tragedy in the tetralogy. Once again, however, Euripidean tragedy fails to achieve its object, as Mnesilochus and Euripides, cast in the roles of Andromeda and Perseus, cannot fool the barbarian to whom they are playing.

With the failure of these three tragedies (*Palamedes*, *Helen*, and *Andromeda*), Euripides concludes the tetralogy with a comedy. Although no satyrs are present, Euripides clearly employs tactics from comedy as he lures the Scythian into chasing the dancing girl. Thus, each time Mnesilochus or Euripides tries to employ tactics from one of Euripides' tragedies to escape from a threatening situation, his effort fails. Ultimately, Euripides must turn to a gag from comedy, in the form of a seductive woman, to free Mnesilochus. Thus, it would appear that Aristophanes' purpose in *Thesmophoriazusae* is to demonstrate the triumph of comedy over tragedy. Perhaps Aristophanes felt some sympathy for his fellow poet Euripides, however. Just as the internal audiences of *Thesmophoriazusae* failed to appreciate the Euripidean tragedies that were being performed before them, so, too, audiences had not appreciated Aristophanes' plays at times in his career (see the PARABASIS of *WASPS*).

BIBLIOGRAPHY

Habash, M. "The Odd Thesmophoria of Aristophanes' *Thesmophoriazusae*," *Greek, Roman, and Byzantine Studies* 38, no. 1 (1997): 19–40.

Hall, E. M. "The Archer Scene in Aristophanes' *Thesmophoriazusae*," *Philologus* 133 (1989): 38–54.

Hansen, H. "Aristophanes' *Thesmophoriazusae*: Theme, Structure, and Production," *Philologus* 120 (1976): 165–85.

Sommerstein, A. H. "Aristophanes and the Events of 411," *Journal of Hellenic Studies* 97 (1977): 112–26.

———. *The Comedies of Aristophanes*. Vol. 8, *Thesmophoriazusae*. Warminster, U.K.: Aris & Phillips, 1994.

THESPIADES   The 50 daughters of Thespius, a king in central Greece. When HERACLES was a young man, he had sexual relations with all of them. This was arranged by their father, who wanted to have grandchildren by the great hero. [ANCIENT SOURCES: Hyginus, *Fables* 162; Seneca, *Hercules Oetaeus* 369]

THESPIS (CA. 550–500 B.C.E.)   Considered by some the inventor of drama, Thespis is said to have won the first competition for TRAGEDY at the City DIONYSIA in ATHENS (from 535 to 533). Thespis is also credited with the introduction of an ACTOR to accompany the CHORUS and even the invention of the mask, although other ancient sources say that Thespis' actors smeared wine lees on their faces. Modern scholars are skeptical that Thespis was either the inventor of the mask or introduced the first actor. Four titles of Thespis' plays exist, including a *Pentheus,* but even the ancient sources did not believe Thespis wrote these plays (for the dozen lines that survive from Thespis' plays, see Snell, fragments 1–5). [ANCIENT SOURCES: Diogenes Laertius, 1.59, 5.92; Horace, *Ars Poetica* 275–77; Plutarch, *Solon* 29; Suda on "Thespis"]

BIBLIOGRAPHY

Snell, B. *Tragicorum Graecorum Fragmenta.* Vol. 1. Göttingen, Ger.: Vandenhoeck & Ruprecht, 1971.

THESPROTIA   A region along the northwestern coast of Greece. ZEUS' oracle at DODONA was located in Thesprotia. The Greek comic poet Alexis wrote a play entitled *Thesprotians,* of which only two lines survive (fragment 89 Kock). [ANCIENT SOURCES: Aeschylus, *Prometheus Bound* 831; Euripides, *Phoenician Women* 982]

BIBLIOGRAPHY

Kock, T. *Comicorum Atticorum Fragmenta.* Vol. 2. Leipzig: Teubner, 1884.

THESSALY   A region between Boeotia and Macedonia in mainland Greece. In drama and elsewhere, Thessaly is described as being a good place to breed horses, an area where exotic animals such as the lion and lynx can be found, and a region inhabited by persons and creatures with unusual powers, especially magical ones. Among the extant plays, EURIPIDES' *ALCESTIS* and *ANDROMACHE* are both set in Thessaly; SOPHOCLES' *TRACHINIAN WOMEN* has a town on the southern border of Thessaly as its setting. Many other plays would have had Thessalian settings, particularly those dealing with the arrival of MEDEA in COLCHIS.

THESTIUS   The son of ARES and Demonice or Demonice's father, Agenor, and Epicaste. Thestius was a king in the region of AETOLIA and the father of ALTHAEA, Hypermnestra, LEDA, and at least two sons. Thestius' nephew, MELEAGER, killed Thestius' son in a quarrel after the hunt for the Calydonian boar. [ANCIENT SOURCES: Apollodorus, *Library* 1.7.7, 1.7.10, 1.8.2–3, 3.10.5; Hyginus, *Fables* 14; Ovid, *Metamorphoses* 8.434–87; Pausanias, 3.13.8]

THETIS   The daughter of NEREUS and Doris, Thetis was a beautiful NYMPH who attracted the attention of ZEUS. When Zeus learned through prophecy that Thetis would produce a child who would be mightier than his father, Zeus arranged for her to marry the mortal PELEUS. When Thetis and Peleus had a son, ACHILLES, Thetis tried to make him immortal but was not completely successful: His body was invulnerable except for his right heel. She was prevented from completing the process because Peleus discovered what she was doing. Thetis was so angry with Peleus that she left him and returned to the sea.

When the Trojan War began, Thetis tried to prevent Achilles from taking part because she knew that he would die if he went to TROY. Thetis' efforts to hide Achilles on the island of SCYROS failed, however, and Achilles eventually went to Troy. When Achilles' friend, PATROCLUS, was killed while wearing Achilles' armor and the armor was lost, Thetis arranged for HEPHAESTUS to create new armor for Achilles. Hephaestus owed Thetis a favor because she had taken care of him after he was thrown off Mount OLYMPUS by Zeus or HERA.

After Achilles fell in battle, a furious struggle occurred on the battlefield over Achilles' body and his armor. The Greeks managed to take Achilles and his armor off the battlefield, and Thetis declared that the armor should be given to the Greek who had done most to help retrieve Achilles' body from the battlefield. The armor was awarded to ODYSSEUS.

Thetis appears as a character in EURIPIDES' *ANDROMACHE.* She arrives at the conclusion of that play and becomes reconciled with PELEUS. Unlike the other marriages or unions alluded to in the play, such as those of NEOPTOLEMUS and HERMIONE, PARIS and HELEN, or MENELAUS and Helen, the reunion of Peleus and Thetis is a happy one, and Thetis' return to Peleus is described as a reward for Peleus' virtue. [ANCIENT SOURCES: Apollodorus, *Library* 1.2.2, 3.13.5; Homer, *Iliad* 1.359, 500, 18.395, 434, 24.60, 535, *Odyssey* 11.495; Hyginus, *Fables* 54; Pausanias, 3.14.4, 3.22.2, 8.18.1; Pindar, *Isthmian Odes* 8.58, *Nemean Odes* 3.60; Plautus, *Epidicus* 35, *Truculentus* 731; Seneca, *Agamemnon* 615, *Hercules Furens* 734, *Medea* 657, *Octavia* 707, *Trojan Women* 346, 880]

THOAS   The son of Dionysus and Ariadne, Thoas was the father of Hypsipyle. He was the brother of Oenopion, Peparethus, and Staphylus. Thoas, whose name means "swift," lived on the island of LEMNOS until that island's women rose up and killed all the men except him, because his daughter, Hypsipyle, was the leader of the uprising. Hypsipyle arranged for her father's life to be spared but placed him on a raft on which he left the island. According to one tradition, Thoas arrived at the Cycladic island of Oenoe, where he had a child by the island's namesake, Oenoe, who was a water NYMPH. Another tradition says that the women from Lemnos found him and killed him. According to another tradition Thoas reached Tauris. In EURIPIDES' IPHIGENIA IN TAURIS, Thoas is the king of the Taurians. As Theoclymenus is in Euripides' HELEN, Thoas is portrayed as a hater of strangers, someone who kills all Greeks who enter his land. Another parallel to Theoclymenus is that a Greek female tricks Thoas. In *Iphigenia in Tauris*, IPHIGENIA tricks Thoas to allow her to take to the seashore a sacred statue of ARTEMIS, as well as two Greeks, ORESTES and PYLADES, the former of whom is her brother. Once at the shore, Iphigenia, Orestes, and Pylades board a ship and sail away with the statue. Thoas threatens to pursue, but the appearance of the goddess ATHENA puts an end to this. [ANCIENT SOURCES: Apollodorus, *Library* 1.9.17, *Epitome* 1.9; Hyginus, *Fables* 15, 254]

THORICUS   A DEME on the Greek coast between ATHENS and SUNIUM. A fortress at Thoricus helped protect the Athenians' silver mines at Laurium. A stone at COLONUS, just north of Athens, was called the Thorician Stone. Because CEPHALUS, who was abducted by EOS, was from Thoricus, the people of Colonus may have called this stone Thorician because they thought of it as a place from which one could be carried off to the gods. OEDIPUS is near this stone at Colonus when he vanishes from the Earth. [ANCIENT SOURCES: Apollodorus, *Library* 2.4.7; Sophocles, *Oedipus at Colonus* 1595]

THORYCION   ARISTOPHANES suggests that Thorycion was a tax collector from the island of AEGINA and that he was involved in smuggling material used to help Athens' enemies. Aristophanes' ideas about Tho-

rycion cannot be verified. [ANCIENT SOURCES: Aristophanes, *Frogs* 362, 382]

BIBLIOGRAPHY
Dover, Kenneth. *Aristophanes: Frogs.* Oxford: Clarendon Press, 1993, 241.

THOUPHANES   A crony of CLEON's, Thouphanes was a public clerk who apparently had proposed a free or cheap distribution of grain to the Athenians, but either the distribution had not occurred or it did not live up to expectations. [ANCIENT SOURCES: Aristophanes, *Knights* 1103 and the scholia]

BIBLIOGRAPHY
Sommerstein, A. H. *The Comedies of Aristophanes.* Vol. 2, *Knights.* Warminster, U.K.: Aris & Phillips, 1981, 203.

THRACE   A region in the extreme northeastern part of Greece. Thrace is often associated with cold weather, good land for breeding horses, a region where gold could be found, and wild or savage behavior. Among the Greeks who lived in ATHENS, the Thracians were considered barbarians. The DIOMEDES who fed strangers to his horses was a Thracian king, as was LYCURGUS, who opposed DIONYSUS and eventually killed his own son. TEREUS, who raped his wife's sister and cut out her tongue, was also from Thrace. POLYMESTOR, another barbaric Thracian, appears in EURIPIDES' HECABE. In lust for gold, Polymestor killed PRIAM's son, POLYDORUS. Eventually, Priam's wife, HECABE, took revenge on Polymestor, blinding him. AESCHYLUS wrote a *Thracian Women* (Greek: *Threissai*), a TRAGEDY set at TROY, that appears to have treated the same subject as SOPHOCLES' *AJAX*, namely, the suicide of the title character. The chorus presumably would have been composed of Thracian women who were the captives of Ajax (see fragments 83–85 Radt).

BIBLIOGRAPHY
Radt, S. *Tragicorum Graecorum Fragmenta.* Vol. 3. Göttingen, Ger.: Vandenhoeck & Ruprecht, 1985.

THRASYBULUS (D. 388 B.C.E.)   One of ATHENS' most important political and military figures from the year 411 B.C.E. until his death, Thrasybulus, the son of Lycus, was from the DEME of Steiria. In 411,

Thrasybulus took the lead in suppressing an oligarchic revolt by the Athenian fleet at SAMOS. Around the same time, Thrasybulus was also a leading advocate for the recall of the exiled statesman and military leader ALCIBIADES. After the Athenians' naval defeat at ARGINUSAE in 405 and during the trial of the Athenian generals that followed it, Thrasybulus, who had commanded a ship in the battle, did much to prevent himself and his fellow ship commanders from being executed. After Athens fell to the Spartans in 404, Thrasybulus was exiled from Athens, but a year later he and a band of supporters returned, overthrew the puppet government established by the Spartans, and restored democracy in Athens. At this point, Thrasybulus was a major hero among the Athenians, but his popularity began to decrease somewhat in the decade that followed. When hostilities with the Spartans began again, Thrasybulus served again as a military commander around 394 and was put in charge of the main forces of the Athenian navy in 390. In 388, while camped at Aspendus (near the southern coast of modern Turkey), Thrasybulus lost his life during a raid on the camp by the local people. [ANCIENT SOURCES: Aristophanes, *Ecclesiazusae* 203, 356, *Wealth* 550; Diodorus Siculus, 14.94.2–4; Isocrates, 18.23; Lysias, 2.59–66, 16.15; Thucydides, 8.73–76, 8.81; Xenophon, *Hellenica* 2.3.42, 3.5.16, 4.8.25–30]

BIBLIOGRAPHY

Buck, R. J. *Thrasybulus and the Athenian Democracy.* Stuttgart: F. Steiner, 1998.

Sommerstein, A. H. *The Comedies of Aristophanes.* Vol. 11, *Wealth.* Warminster, U.K.: Aris & Phillips, 2001, 174–75.

THRATTA   A Greek name meaning "Thracian woman," Thratta was a common name for slaves. [ANCIENT SOURCES: Aristophanes, *Acharnians* 273, *Peace* 1138, *Thesmophoriazusae* 280–93, *Wasps* 828]

THREE-DOLLAR DAY (Latin: *TRINUMMUS*) PLAUTUS (BEFORE 192 B.C.E.)   As the audience is informed in the prologue, the Greek original for PLAUTUS' play was Philemon's *Thesaurus* (Treasure), which has been dated tentatively to the rule of Demetrius Poliorcetes in Athens (392–287 B.C.E.); *Three-Dollar Day* was staged before 192 B.C.E. The

Latin title of Plautus' play, *Three-Dollar Day,* refers to a sum of money worth three nummi (singular: *nummus*). Among the Romans, the nummus was a silver coin of relatively low value. The setting of the play is ATHENS, and the drama's action occurs before the houses of Charmides and Megaronides. The house of Philto is also nearby. Behind Charmides' house is an additional space in which Lesbonicus lives. The brief prologue is delivered by the goddess Luxury (Latin: Luxuria), who is accompanied by her daughter, Poverty (Latin: Inopia). No sooner do the pair of divinities take the stage than Luxury sends Poverty into the house of Lesbonicus. As indicated, Luxury tells the audience about the Greek original for Plautus' play, but the goddess does not reveal any information about the plot other than that she has sent Poverty to live with Lesbonicus because he wasted his father Charmides' fortune.

After the departure of Luxury, Megaronides, an old Athenian gentleman, enters and informs the audience that he is going to chastise his friend, Callicles, another elderly Athenian. After Megaronides complains about the lax morality of his times, Callicles appears and Megaronides begins to express his disappointment with Callicles, whom people around town are criticizing for being greedy for profit and uncaring about the people he harms. Callicles, however, responds that Charmides, when he realized that he was becoming poor, entrusted his son, Lesbonicus, and his daughter to Callicles and left town. Megaronides wonders why Callicles did not try to reform Lesbonicus, because the young man had spent so much money on wild living and why Callicles paid Lesbonicus a large sum of money for the house in which Callicles currently lives. Megaronides complains that Callicles' giving Lesbonicus this money made the young man's behavior worse. At this point, Callicles breaks down and tells Megaronides why he paid such a large sum of money for the house; as it turns out, Charmides had shown Callicles a treasure that was hidden in the house: 3,000 gold coins. If Charmides returns, Callicles will give the money back to him; if he does not return, Callicles will use the money to provide a dowry for Charmides' daughter when she is married. Callicles further notes that the reason he bought the house was that Lesbonicus was going to try to sell the house, and that would have allowed Charmides' treasure to fall into someone else's hands. Hearing this changes Megaronides' attitude about Callicles, who also informs him that Lesbonicus is now living in an apartment behind Charmides' house and that Callicles is taking good care of Charmides' daughter. After Callicles exits, Megaronides repents that he had believed the rumors about Callicles.

The play's second act opens with the arrival of Lysiteles, a young Athenian gentleman, who gives a lengthy and poetic speech about the dangerous powers of love. Lysiteles hopes that he can avoid such love and expresses a desire to live a virtuous life. Soon, Lysiteles' father, Philto, emerges from their house in search of his son. Philto urges his son to emulate him and live a virtuous life, and Lysiteles tells him that he has tried to live such a life. The young man also asks his father to allow him to help Lesbonicus, who has wasted his father's fortune. Philto is upset by this proposal, but Lysiteles says he wants to marry Lesbonicus' sister and not ask for a dowry. Philto is reluctant to give his permission, but eventually he accedes to his son's wishes. Lysiteles also requests that Philto himself approach Lesbonicus with this proposal. Again, Philto balks at this, but soon he agrees and approaches Lesbonicus' door.

Before Philto approaches Lesbonicus, however, he stops to eavesdrop on a conversation between Lesbonicus and Stasimus, a slave of Lesbonicus and Charmides'. The pair discuss how Lesbonicus has already spent the money that Callicles gave him for the house. Philto, after listening to Lesbonicus and Stasimus discuss the squandered money, finally approaches the two men. When Philto proposes that Lysiteles marry Lesbonicus' sister, Lesbonicus initially rejects this proposal, as his family and Philto's family are not of equal social status. Stasimus, however, urges Lesbonicus not to refuse the proposal. After further discussion between Lesbonicus and Philto, Philto adds that he is not requesting a dowry. Lesbonicus, however, insists that his sister should not be married without a dowry and offers a farm that his family owns. At this point, Stasimus takes Philto aside and advises him not to accept the farm, because it suffers from extreme bad luck and is therefore unprofitable. Philto agrees not to accept the farm

but still refuses to accept a dowry for Lesbonicus' sister. Finally, Lesbonicus relents, and Philto and he prepare to plan the wedding date. Before Lesbonicus leaves, he tells Stasimus to arrange for Callicles to meet him.

The third act opens with Stasimus' informing Callicles that Lesbonicus has arranged for his sister to marry without a dowry. Callicles is astonished by this news and goes off to consult Megaronides. When Stasimus hears this, he thinks that Callicles will try to persuade Lesbonicus to sell him the farm. As Stasimus ponders the difficulty of finding a friend one can trust, he sees Lesbonicus and Lysiteles' approaching and eavesdrops on them. Lysiteles criticizes Lesbonicus for his wild living and tells him not to let his judgment become clouded by love. Lesbonicus acknowledges his wrongdoing but says that marrying his sister without a dowry will add to his shame. Lysiteles thinks that if Lesbonicus turns over the farm as a dowry, then he will not have more ties to the community and will leave his family and country behind. The argument finally ends when Stasimus interrupts. After this, Lysiteles insists that the marriage take place without a dowry and Lesbonicus exits without responding. Lysiteles also exits, leaving Stasimus alone on stage. Stasimus expects that soon Lesbonicus will leave to become a soldier and he will have to serve him in some foreign land.

After Stasimus leaves for the FORUM, Megaronides and Callicles enter and discuss the problem of Lesbonicus' sister's marrying without a dowry. After rejecting various ideas for obtaining a dowry for her, the two old men decide to hire a con man, dress him as a foreigner from Seleucia, and have him claim to have money from Charmides to give to Lesbonicus as a dowry for his sister. In actuality, though, the money will be from the treasure that Charmides had hidden in the house. After agreeing on these matters, Megaronides sends Callicles to dig up Charmides' treasure. Megaronides himself heads out to the forum to find a con man.

In the play's fourth act, Charmides returns from his journey abroad and expresses his thanks to Neptune (Greek: Poseidon) for a safe return. As Charmides looks forward to resting, he sees the con man whom Megaronides has hired, who is approaching on the street. Charmides is puzzled by the man's strange appearance and decides to eavesdrop on him. The con man tells the audience that he has been paid a *trinummus* to trick Lesbonicus. Charmides is troubled when he sees that the con man is knocking on the door of his house. Before anyone can answer the door, Charmides approaches the man and asks what he wants. After receiving uncooperative answers, Charmides realizes that the fellow is a con man and decides to try a little trickery himself. When the con man reveals that he has been sent by the father of Lesbonicus, Charmides, Charmides asks him what the father's name is. After some prompting by Charmides, the forgetful con man finally remembers the father's name and even curses Charmides, not realizing that he is standing in the man's presence. When Charmides asks the man whether he would recognize Charmides, the con man lies, saying that he would. In another lie, he says that Charmides has entrusted to him a vast sum of money. Upon hearing this, Charmides demands that the man hand over the money then, because he is Charmides. The con man is astounded, and soon Charmides drives him away from the house. As Charmides watches the man leave, he wonders why he had gone to his house and what his claims about the money may mean. While Charmides ponders these matters, an intoxicated Stasimus approaches and begins philosophizing that morality in the past was better than in the present. Charmides eavesdrops on his slave for some time before emerging and greeting him. Stasimus is delighted to see his master, but when Charmides moves toward the house Stasimus informs him that Lesbonicus sold it to Callicles. Hearing this, Charmides begins to gasp for breath. Callicles, perceiving the commotion outside, arrives from the house and explains that he has been digging up Charmides' treasure to provide a dowry for Charmides' daughter. An apparently relieved Charmides then sends Stasimus to the harbor to watch over the unloading of the ship. Charmides then goes into the house with Callicles.

The play's final act begins with the appearance of Lysiteles, who expresses his delight at the news that Charmides has returned. Next, Charmides and Callicles enter. Charmides thanks Callicles for being such a faithful friend. When Callicles tells him that his daughter will marry Lysiteles and explains the trick involving the con man, Lysiteles, who has been eavesdropping on the conversation, steps forward and greets Charmides. The

men greet each other warmly and Charmides gives Lysiteles permission to marry his daughter and offers him a vast dowry. Lysiteles initially rejects the offer of the dowry, but he agrees when Charmides says he will not allow his daughter to marry without the dowry. Charmides expresses his displeasure with Lysiteles, however, saying that Lysiteles allowed Lesbonicus to waste his money. Lysiteles urges Charmides not to be angry with his son and summons Lesbonicus from the house. As soon as Charmides sees Lesbonicus, he forgets his anger at his son, who indicates that he is willing to behave properly. The play ends with Charmides' announcement that Lesbonicus will marry Callicles' daughter—a proposition to which Lesbonicus readily agrees.

COMMENTARY

Three-Dollar Day has attracted less scholarly attention than other Plautine plays. Indeed, the moral tone of the play seems closer to that of TERENCE than of Plautus, and Duckworth classifies *Three-Dollar Day* as a play that focuses on character (see also POT OF GOLD, STICHUS, TRUCULENTUS, and TERENCE'S BROTHERS). *Three-Dollar Day* contains several passages in which characters (even the slave Stasimus) comment on the way people ought to behave and lament the lack of morals of current times.

The absence of a lovesick youth or old man pining for a PROSTITUTE, as well as the absence of a woman who has had a child as a result of being assaulted sexually, contribute to the play's more serious tone. Lysiteles' desire to marry Lesbonicus' sister is not motivated by an all-consuming passion or a desire to prevent a child from being born out of wedlock. In fact, other than the brief appearance (22 lines) of the female divinities at the first of the play, women are heard of but not seen for the rest of the performance. *Three-Dollar Day* also lacks the rollicking fun generated by the scheming slaves of such plays as PSEUDOLUS or the HAUNTED HOUSE and the delightful confusion created by twins as in MENAECHMI or AMPHITRUO.

The deception in *Three-Dollar Day* is not orchestrated by a wily slave or young man for the purpose of deceiving an evil PIMP, BRAGGART SOLDIER, or old man for a young woman or money. Instead, in *Three-Dollar Day*, two rather altruistic old men try trick the prodigal young Lesbonicus accept money. Unlike the stingy, rich old Euclio (*Pot of Gold*), who would be more than happy to provide the smallest possible dowry for his daughter, Lesbonicus, a young man who has squandered his father's money does not want to accept the efforts of Lysiteles to enter into a marriage with Lesbonicus' sister.

Although *Three-Dollar Day* has a more serious tone than most of Plautus' other plays, it is not without its attractive qualities. The play's preponderance of moralizing (in comparison to that in other Plautine plays) offers instruction, rather than pure entertainment. At the opening of the second act, Lysiteles' 50-line speech on love and its pitfalls contains some of the most extensive remarks on love in Plautus. Indeed, the speech is quite enjoyable, even if it does seem trite in places.

In many ways, *Three-Dollar Day* is a play about the friendship of men, as it has more occurrences of the Latin words for friend (*amicus*) and friendship (*amicitia*) than any extant Roman COMEDY. The first word from Megaronides' mouth when he enters is *friend* (*amicum*, 23) as he worries about how to confront his friend, Callicles, rumors about whom are causing him extreme grief. Once Megaronides learns that Callicles has only been acting in the best interest of another friend (Charmides; cf. lines 106–7), however, the friendship of the men is repaired. Megaronides' confrontation of Callicles is so disturbing to Callicles that he feels compelled to reveal to him the secret of the treasure, which Charmides entrusted to him in the name of friendship (153). After Callicles exits, Megaronides regrets that he allowed rumors to affect their friendship (216).

When Lysiteles enters, part of his speech about love comments on the disruption of a person's friendships that love can cause (262) and declares that he does not want love to become a friend (268) of his. Just as the friendship between the elder men, Megaronides and Callicles, was strained by the financial irresponsibility of Lesbonicus, Lysiteles wants to help his friend, Lesbonicus (326), by marrying his sister without a dowry. Philto does not want Lysiteles to be the friend of such an irresponsible person (337), but Lysiteles suggests that it is disgraceful not to help a friend (347). Philto, realizing that Lysiteles intends to create a bond of friendship that will benefit their family (382), agrees to his son's wishes to help Lesbonicus.

Unfortunately, Lesbonicus does not want to be helped, despite Stasimus' advice that he should not reject this friend he has found (456). Lesbonicus even accuses Lysiteles of trying to injure a friend by proposing a union with his sister that requires no dowry (630). Thus, Lysiteles' efforts to help his friend are actually damaging the friendship. Lysiteles tries to reason with Lesbonicus and urges him to pay attention to his male friends in the FORUM rather than his female friends in bed (651). Lysiteles also fears his acceptance of Lesbonicus' farm would eventually cause Lesbonicus to leave town and his friends (702), and that as a result people would consider Lysiteles greedy. Accordingly, Lysiteles insists that Lesbonicus accept his proposed conditions for the marriage because if he does not, he declares, he will no longer be his friend (716).

After the two young friends exit with their friendship on the verge of disintegration, Megaronides and Callicles return and try to concoct a plan that will allow the various bonds of friendship to remain intact. Megaronides suggests that Callicles, because of his friendship with Charmides (737), might offer a dowry on behalf of Lesbonicus' sister. Megaronides rules out the idea, however, because people would think that Callicles had ulterior motives. Eventually, Megaronides and Callicles settle on the plot involving the con man, who unwittingly declares to Charmides that he is Charmides' friend (895). Of course, when Charmides challenges the man to recall Charmides' name, the con man does so only after considerable prompting from Charmides. Amusingly, the con man then unknowingly curses Charmides to his face (923), to which Charmides ironically responds that one should not speak badly of a friend who is not present (924, 926). After toying with his alleged friend for some time, Charmides finally reveals his identity to the dumbfounded man.

After driving away this false friend, Charmides approaches his own house and soon has the wrong impression about Callicles, a person whom he considered his friend (1095). The confrontation of Callicles by Megaronides earlier in the play is now matched by

Charmides' confrontation of Callicles, whom Charmides discovers digging up the secret treasure. Once Charmides learns the reason for Callicles' actions, their friendship is repaired and Stasimus declares that Callicles was the only person who was a true friend to Charmides. Indeed, just as Charmides had advised the con man that he should not speak badly of an absent friend, Charmides discovers that Callicles has been a friend to him in his absence. Soon, Charmides himself declares to Callicles what a faithful friend his neighbor has been to him (1126). Thus, once Charmides and Callicles' friendship has been reestablished, the wedding of Charmides' daughter and Lysiteles can go forward. Equally importantly, however, the friendship of Lysiteles and Lesbonicus is repaired (cf. 1177).

BIBLIOGRAPHY

Anderson, W. S., "Plautus' Trinummus: The Absurdity of Officious Morality," Traditio 35 (1979): 333–45.

Fantham, E. "Philemon's Thesauros as a Dramatisation of Peripatetic Ethics," Hermes 105 (1977): 406–21.

Hunter, R. "Philemon, Plautus and the Trinummus," Museum Helveticum 37 (1980): 216–30.

Riemer, P. Das Spiel im Spiel: Studien zum plautinischen Agon im Trinummus und Rudens. Stuttgart: Teubner, 1996.

Segal, E. "The Purpose of the Trinummus," American Journal of Philology 95 (1974): 252–64.

Slater, N. W. "The Dates of Plautus' Curculio and Trinummus Reconsidered," American Journal of Philology 108 (1987): 264–69.

THUCYDIDES (1)

The son of Melesias, the Athenian statesman Thucydides opposed PERICLES in the middle of the fifth century B.C.E. Thucydides was exiled from ATHENS for 10 years in 443 B.C.E. but returned and on his resumption of political life prosecuted Pericles' friend, the philosopher Anaxagoras, for impiety. When Thucydides was approaching 80 years of age, from 432 to 426, he was prosecuted by a certain CEPHISODEMUS and is said to have been unable to defend himself in court. [ANCIENT SOURCES: Aristophanes, Acharnians 703, Wasps 946–48; Diogenes Laertius, 2.12]

BIBLIOGRAPHY

MacDowell, D. M. Aristophanes: Wasps. Oxford: Clarendon Press, 1971, 255.

Sommerstein. A. The Comedies of Aristophanes. Vol. 1, Acharnians. Warminster, U.K.: Aris & Phillips, 1980, 191–92.

THUCYDIDES (2) (CA. 460–CA. 400 B.C.E.)

The son of Olorus, Thucydides was an Athenian who wrote a history of the PELOPONNESIAN WAR in eight books. Although Thucydides' history is incomplete, it remains our most important source of knowledge for this war. Many ancient historians lived after (sometimes hundreds of years after) the events about which they write. Thucydides, however, lived during the Peloponnesian War and served as a military commander in 424 B.C.E. When Thucydides was unable to prevent the Spartan commander, BRASIDAS, from taking Amphipolis, he was exiled from ATHENS. After two decades in exile, Thucydides returned to ATHENS after the city's fall to SPARTA in 404. Thucydides died soon afterward.

BIBLIOGRAPHY

Finley, John H. Thucydides. Ann Arbor: University of Michigan Press, 1963.

Gomme, A. W. Essays in Greek History and Literature. Oxford: Blackwell, 1937.

Hornblower, S. Thucydides. London: Duckworth, 1987.

Hunter, V. Past and Process in Herodotus and Thucydides. Princeton, N.J.: Princeton University Press, 1982.

Romilly, Jacqueline de. Thucydides and Athenian Imperialism. Translated by Philip Thody. Oxford: Blackwell, 1963.

Stahl, Hans-Peter. Thukydides: Die Stellung des Menschen im geschichtlichen Prozess. Munich: Beck, 1966.

THULE

The mythical island that is farthest away from civilization as the Greeks and Romans understood it. Some equated it with Iceland; others thought it was the largest of the Shetland Islands. [ANCIENT SOURCES: Seneca, Medea 379]

THYESTES

The son of PELOPS and HIPPODAMEIA, Thyestes was the brother of ATREUS. After the brothers quarreled over the kingship and Atreus tricked his brother by serving him a dish made from Thyestes' own children, Thyestes sought revenge on Atreus. After consulting the DELPHIC ORACLE about how to accomplish this, Thyestes disguised himself and sexually assaulted his own daughter, Pelopea, who was a virgin priestess. Pelopea became pregnant and gave birth to AEGISTHUS. Euripides wrote an *Oeneus,* which was produced by 426 B.C.E. at the latest. The Greek tragedian Chaeremon wrote a *Thyestes;* the single line (8 Snell) that survives, a reference to roses and lilies, gives no hint as to the play's plot.

BIBLIOGRAPHY

Snell, B. *Tragicorum Graecorum Fragmenta.* Vol. 1. Göttingen, Ger.: Vandenhoeck & Ruprecht, 1971.

Webster, T. B. L. *The Tragedies of Euripides.* London: Methuen, 1967.

THYESTES SENECA (WRITTEN BETWEEN 49 AND 65 C.E.?)

As SENECA'S *AGAMEMNON* does, his *Thyestes* begins with the appearance of a ghost from the UNDERWORLD, as the spirit of THYESTES' grandfather, TANTALUS, demands to know who has summoned him to the upper world. Tantalus' query is answered by a FURY, who urges Tantalus to feast on the blood that will be shed in the house of his descendants. As MADNESS in EURIPIDES' *HERACLES* is reluctant to drive HERACLES insane, Tantalus does not want any part in the blood that will be shed. The Fury, however, compels him to set the two brothers, ATREUS and Thyestes, at one another. The Fury and Tantalus' ghost give way to the arrival of the chorus of Mycenean citizens, whose initial song recalls the sins of Tantalus and Myrtilus and the respective punishment and fate each suffered because of his actions.

Atreus opens the second act with a speech in which he considers how to take vengeance on his brother, Thyestes, who has stolen the kingdom from him. A minister who accompanies Atreus questions the morality of acting against one's brother, but Atreus recalls that Thyestes once cheated him of the throne by stealing from him a golden lamb, whose ownership the people of Mycenae decided would determine who became king of their town. Atreus explains that initially he had the lamb, but after Thyestes seduced his wife, she helped Thyestes acquire the lamb. In this way, Thyestes became king of Mycenae and exiled his brother, Atreus. Although Atreus does not mention this, other versions of this myth relate that because the gods did not want Thyestes to be king, they managed to persuade Thyestes to turn the kingdom over to Atreus if the Sun should reverse its course in the sky.

To Thyestes' amazement, the Sun reversed course and he was obliged to give up the kingdom.

Atreus, determined to take vengeance, asks the minister for advice about how to punish his brother. Atreus rejects the suggestion of killing him as too lenient for Thyestes. Finally, Atreus decides to devise a way to make Thyestes eat his own children. Atreus decides to lure Thyestes to his palace with the pretext of inviting him back to Mycenae to share the kingdom. Atreus sends his sons, AGAMEMNON and MENELAUS, to invite Thyestes to a banquet. The minister urges Atreus to reconsider what he is about to do, but Atreus is determined to go through with the plot.

At this point, Atreus and the minister appear to exit. The CHORUS, who appear to be unaware of what Atreus is planning, sing a choral ODE in which they speculate on why kings use sinful means to acquire kingdoms. They conclude that the perfect king is not rich; the true king is one who fears nothing and wants nothing. The chorus wish that they themselves might live in peace and obscurity.

The third act begins with the arrival of Thyestes, looking disheveled and dressed in rags, and three of his young sons (Plisthenes, Tantalus the younger, and another son, who is not named). Thyestes is glad to see Mycenae again but has doubts about whether he should trust his brother. His son Tantalus, however, urges his father to consider the kingdom that he might have. Thyestes responds that kingship has its difficulties and that his current life carries few concerns. Tantalus continues to urge his father to the kingship, and eventually Thyestes decides to approach his brother, who has apparently been waiting in silence onstage for some time. Before Thyestes speaks, Atreus, in an aside, notes that his brother is falling into his trap. Atreus then greets his brother in a friendly manner and proposes that they put aside harsh feelings. Thyestes agrees to forget their differences and reluctantly agrees to share the kingship. After Atreus and Thyestes enter the palace, the chorus sing an ode in which they marvel that Atreus and his brother have become reconciled. They note that a person's life is cyclical, alternating between good times and bad, and that FATE controls and sets all things in motion.

The appearance of a distraught MESSENGER opens the fourth act. The messenger explains to the chorus that

Atreus butchered Thyestes' sons as if they were sacrificial victims. After Atreus killed the children, he cooked them and fed them to their unwitting father. Upon hearing this, the chorus sing an ode in which they wonder why the gods have turned away from them. They wonder whether the universe has fallen into chaos; they fear that the world will be destroyed and that the stars will fall from the sky.

In the play's final act, Atreus arrives from the palace and congratulates himself on taking revenge on his brother. Atreus then anticipates with glee seeing his brother's face when he finds out what he has done. Next, Thyestes emerges and happily imagines that he has good fortune again. At the same time, he wonders whether these happy feelings will last and cannot help but feel that he will soon face trouble and danger. After Thyestes asks Atreus to see his sons, Atreus displays the children's heads to him. When a horrified Thyestes asks what has happened to their bodies, Atreus tells him that he has eaten his children and explains in gruesome detail how he killed the children. The play ends with Thyestes' hoping that the gods will avenge the evils that Atreus has done. [ANCIENT SOURCES: Aeschylus, *Agamemnon* 1583–1611]

COMMENTARY

Seneca's *Thyestes* is interesting in that, other than *OCTAVIA*, it is the only Senecan TRAGEDY that does not have a corresponding Greek tragedy to which we can compare it. Whereas Seneca's *Agamemnon* focuses on fathers and their children, *Thyestes,* as does Seneca's *PHOENICIAN WOMEN,* takes as its the focal point the struggle of brother against brother for a kingdom. As in *Phoenician Women,* in *Thyestes* questions about the desirability of kingship are taken up, but in *Thyestes* the younger Tantalus does not so much debate his father as question Thyestes about why he is reluctant to be king. Unlike the struggle of ETEOCLES and POLYNEICES, which takes place on the battlefield and will result in the death of both brothers, the struggle between Atreus and Thyestes occurs inside the house and both brothers remain alive after the "battle." Although fault can be found with both brothers in Seneca's *Phoenician Women,* the portrait of Thyestes is fairly sympathetic and Thyestes' seduction of Atreus'

wife, which plays a prominent role in the strife between the two brothers elsewhere in mythology, is somewhat downplayed in *Thyestes* (235, 1099). The atrocities of these two brothers against one another are perpetrated in bed (Thyestes committed adultery with Atreus' wife) and at the table of hospitality.

Given the method of Atreus' revenge on Thyestes, it is not surprising that references to hunger and thirst are frequent in the play. The perversion of hospitality that Atreus unleashes against Thyestes has been anticipated by their ancestor Tantalus, who tried to feed his son, Pelops, Atreus and Thyestes' father, to the gods (149). Tantalus' punishment for his perversion of food was torment by the lure of food and drink throughout eternity (2). Despite Tantalus' reluctance to drive Atreus to commit such a heinous crime, the Fury wants the brothers to thirst for each other's blood (103). With the entry of the chorus, the subject again turns to the horrific banquet at which Tantalus served up his son and the eternal hunger and thirst to which Tantalus has been subjected in the underworld. Tantalus served to the gods a banquet that was not fit to be touched, and the gods punish Tantalus by serving to him a delicious banquet that they do not allow him to touch 121–75). Ultimately, Atreus lures his brother to the feast by using as bait the kingdom. Thyestes, however, is not especially interested in the kingship. Thyestes notes the benefits of living a simple life and points out that he does not, as a king would, feed his wicked belly (460–61) on the tribute of nations. Despite his fears, Thyestes accepts his brother's invitation.

Intertwined with the themes of hunger and thirst is the concept of wilderness versus civilization. Hospitality is something shared between civilized persons; in *Thyestes* civilization is turned upside down. By the end of the play, we are left to wonder whether greater savagery exists in the wilderness or in the palace of a king. The contrast between civilization and savagery appears when the chorus describe the food that Tantalus served to the gods as savage (*feris,* 150). Tantalus perverts the banquet, a gathering place for civilized beings, by serving savage food. As punishment, Tantalus is placed in a fruit-filled wood (*silva,* 168), where he cannot reach the food. Thus, the gods punish Tantalus by placing him in a bountiful grove (*nemus,* 162) that is located in a savage place (the underworld) preventing him from enjoying the fruits of civilization.

Tantalus is exiled to a place where savagery and civilization are intermingled. Similarly, Thyestes' exile has compelled him to live in a woodland (*silvestres,* 412) retreat, a place usually inhabited by wild beasts (*feris,* 413). Thyestes returns to Argos, deceived by the prospect of becoming reintegrated into society and partaking of a civilized meal with his brother. Instead, Thyestes will find savagery beneath the facade of civilization. Thyestes left a space filled with wild animals only to be transformed into an animal by his brother. When Atreus realizes that Thyestes will accept his invitation, he describes his brother as like a wild animal caught in a net (491) and himself as like a hound on the trail of wild animals (*feras,* 497). Not only is Thyestes transformed into an animal, Atreus also becomes an animal. Atreus, when he kills Thyestes' sons, leaves the palace and enters a gloomy forest that bears a striking resemblance to the underworld (see especially 651–82). Not only has Atreus entered a place like the one occupied by his grandfather, Tantalus; as Atreus prepares the ghastly feast, Seneca dehumanizes him, describing him as like a tiger trying to decide which bull to attack first (707–13) and a lion in the Armenian forest who rages on even after he has satisfied his hunger (732–34).

After hearing of Atreus' perversion of hospitality, the chorus express horror and comment at length on the complete overturning of everything in the universe. In contrast to the chorus' knowledge of his horrible banquet, an unaware Thyestes appears in the costume of and exhibits the behavior of a civilized man. His brother welcomes him into the house by placing a crown on his head (544–55); he has unguent in his hair (780); he drinks wine and reclines on a couch decked with the colors of royalty, gold and purple (909–10); he even sings a joyous song (918–19). After the banquet, Thyestes appears to have reached a state for which Seneca's fellow Stoics longed, as Thyestes declares that he has now put aside his usual cares (*curas,* 921). Soon, however, Thyestes' worries return and the marks of civilization begin to recede. The garlands of roses fall from his head, and his hair, wet with unguent, stands on end in horror (947–51). Thyestes recomposes himself, however, and happily accepts a cup of wine (or so he

thinks) from his brother. When he tastes the wine, Thyestes' anxiety returns, and his brother soon confirms his worst fears. Now Thyestes wishes that he were with his grandfather, Tantalus, in the underworld (1011–16). The play concludes with Atreus suggesting to his brother that Thyestes would have tried to serve him a similar feast (1107) if he had not believed that Atreus' children were actually his own. Thus, Atreus avenges Thyestes' crimes against his marriage bed at the table of hospitality, and in this play Thyestes discovers that civilization can be more savage than wilderness.

BIBLIOGRAPHY
Giancotti, Francesco. *Tieste: Seneca.* Torino: G. Giappichelli, 1989.
Littlewood, C. "Seneca's *Thyestes:* The Tragedy with No Women?" *Materiali e discussioni per l'analisi dei testi classici* 38 (1997): 57–86.
Poe, J. P. "An Analysis of Seneca's *Thyestes,*" *Transactions and Proceedings of the American Philological Association* 100 (1969): 355–76.
Schiesaro, A. "Seneca's *Thyestes* and the Morality of Tragic Furor." In *Reflections of Nero.* Edited by J. Elsner and J. Masters. Chapel Hill: University of North Carolina Press, 1994.
Tarrant, R. J., ed. *Seneca's Thyestes.* Atlanta: Scholars Press, 1985.

THYIADS A name given to women who are inspired or possessed, especially by DIONYSUS. [ANCIENT SOURCES: Aeschylus, *Seven against Thebes* 498, 836, *Suppliant Women* 564; Seneca, *Hercules Oetaeus* 701; Sophocles, *Antigone* 1151]

THYMELE In the classical Greek theater, the *thymele* was an altar or podium in the center of the ORCHESTRA. Wiles has argued that the *thymele* would have been a focal point for the spectators of Greek TRAGEDY. Such an altar would have been used by supplicants in plays such as AESCHYLUS' SUPPLIANT WOMEN and EURIPIDES' ANDROMACHE, CHILDREN OF HERACLES, and SUPPLIANT WOMEN. [ANCIENT SOURCES: Pollux, *Onomasticon* 4.123]

BIBLIOGRAPHY
Wiles, D. *Tragedy in Athens: Performance Space and Theatrical Meaning.* Cambridge: Cambridge University Press, 1997, 63–86.

THYRSUS   The thyrsus was a staff carried by worshipers of DIONYSUS. In ancient vase paintings, the thyrsus is typically taller than a person and is tipped with something that resembles a pine cone. The thyrsus often has a strand of ivy wrapped around it as well. Dionysus' worshipers usually tapped the ground with the thyrsus; it could also be employed as a weapon.

TIMON   It is uncertain whether Timon was an actual person. In ARISTOPHANES, his name is synonymous with misanthropy, and if he was a real person, he died before the production of *LYSISTRATA* in 411 B.C.E. Six centuries after Aristophanes, Lucian mentions a Timon, son of Echecrates, from the DEME of Collytus, and Pausanias knew of a tower in ATHENS named after a misanthropic Timon. [ANCIENT SOURCES: Aristophanes, *Birds* 1549, *Lysistrata* 808 and the scholia; Lucian, *Timon* 7; Pausanias, 1.30.4; Plutarch, *Antonius* 70]

BIBLIOGRAPHY
Henderson, J. *Aristophanes: Lysistrata.* Oxford: Clarendon Press, 1987, 172.

TIMOTHEUS   The son of Cimon, Timotheus, an Athenian from the DEME of Anaphlystus, was a prominent politician and military commander in the first half of the fourth century B.C.E. When Timotheus' father died around 392 or 391, Timotheus used some of his inheritance to build a large house that had a tall tower. From the early 380s until mid-350s, Timotheus had a successful military career, but lack of success in the Social War of 357–355 led to Timotheus' exile. He died not long after. [ANCIENT SOURCES: Aristophanes, *Wealth* 180; Cornelius Nepos, *Timotheus*; Diodorus Siculus, 15.29.7; Isocrates, 15.101–39; Lysias, 19.40]

BIBLIOGRAPHY
Sommerstein, A. H. *The Comedies of Aristophanes.* Vol. 11, *Wealth.* Warminster, U.K.: Aris & Phillips, 2001, 149.

TIPHYS   The son of Hagnias, Tiphys served as the helmsman for JASON and the Argonauts. Tiphys died in the land of the Mariandynians, before the Argonauts acquired the Golden Fleece. [ANCIENT SOURCES: Apollodorus, *Library* 1.9.16, 1.9.23; Apollonius Rhodius,

Argonautica; Hyginus, *Fables* 14; Seneca, *Medea* 3, 318, 346, 617]

TIRESIAS (TEIRESIAS)   The son of Everes and the NYMPH Chariclo, Tiresias was the famous blind Theban prophet of APOLLO. Various reasons are given for his blindness: Some say that he saw the goddess ATHENA naked and that when she covered his eyes with her hands, he became blind. Others say the gods blinded him for revealing their secrets to humans. Still others, such as Ovid, say that when HERA and ZEUS argued over which gender derived more pleasure from intercourse, they called on Tiresias to settle their dispute, because Tiresias had been transformed into a woman for part of his life. Tiresias, having struck a pair of snakes that he saw mating, was changed into a woman. Some time later, after he had observed the same pair of snakes mating, he struck them again and became a man once more. When Tiresias, who had said that women enjoy intercourse 10 times more than men, took Zeus' side in the argument with Hera, Hera blinded him.

Tiresias appears as a character in several extant plays: SOPHOCLES' *OEDIPUS TYRANNOS AND ANTIGONE*, EURIPIDES' *PHOENICIAN WOMEN AND BACCHAE*, and SENECA's *OEDIPUS*. In *Phoenician Women*, Tiresias prophesies that CREON must sacrifice his son, MENOECEUS, to save Thebes. Menoeceus follows Tiresias' advice and sacrifices himself despite Creon's desire to the contrary. In *Antigone, Bacchae,* and the two Oedipus plays, Tiresias' advice or warnings to various kings are scorned initially and later discovered to be true. The kings who hear Tiresias' advice often accuse him of making his prophecies for the purpose of financial gain. In Sophocles' *Oedipus,* Tiresias, after much prodding from OEDIPUS, declares that Oedipus killed his father and married his mother. In Seneca's *Oedipus,* Tiresias tries to determine the killer of LAIUS by consulting the entrails of a sacrificial victim. Because of Tiresias' blindness, his daughter, MANTO, describes the entrails to him. After a lengthy description, this form of prophecy fails to reveal Laius' killer. Tiresias then says they must discover Laius' killer by raising his spirit from the UNDERWORLD. This method is successful and Oedipus is named as the killer.

Tiresias' presence in *Bacchae* differs from that in the other plays. In this play, he has not been called in to offer prophecy; he is present to accompany CADMUS in worshiping DIONYSUS. Tiresias' initial appearance in this play must have provoked some laughter from the audience as the blind and aged Tiresias and the elderly Cadmus are dressed as worshipers of Dionysus and test some of the gestures used in that god's worship. When Cadmus' grandson, King PENTHEUS, arrives, he is repulsed by their behavior and indicates his disapproval of Dionysus. Tiresias then goes on to warn Pentheus about the dangers of opposing the god's worship and speaks to him of the benefits that Dionysus has given to humankind. Pentheus ignores Tiresias' advice and is eventually destroyed by the god. [ANCIENT SOURCES: Apollodorus, *Library* 2.4.8, 3.6.7, 3.7.3–4; Homer, *Odyssey* 10.488–95, 11.90–151; Hyginus, *Fables* 75; Ovid, *Metamorphoses* 3.322–50; Pausanias, 7.3.1, 9.11.3, 9.33.1–2]

TIRYNS A town in southeastern Greek that is near ARGOS and MYCENAE. According to one tradition, its walls were built by the CYCLOPES. In EURIPIDES' *ALCESTIS,* EURYSTHEUS is said to be king of Tiryns.

TISIPHONE One of the FURIES. [ANCIENT SOURCES: Apollodorus, *Library* 1.1.4; Ovid, *Metamorphoses* 4.474, 481; Seneca, *Hercules Furens* 984, *Hercules Oetaeus* 1012; Vergil, *Aeneid* 6.555, 571, 10.761]

TITAN The Titans were a group of divinities who existed in the generation before ZEUS and his brothers and sisters. Most of the Titans were children of Gaia (EARTH) and URANUS, but Iapetus' sons, PROMETHEUS and ATLAS, are also called Titans. The name Titan is derived from the Greek verb *titainein,* "to strain." After Gaia gave birth to the children, Uranus, who hated them, put them back into Gaia's womb; thus, Gaia was caused to strain. Eventually the children emerged when one of the Titans, CRONUS, castrated his father, Uranus. After this, Cronus ruled the gods until his son Zeus (and Zeus' brothers and sisters) defeated him and the other Titans in a war known as the Titanomachy. PROMETHEUS' mother, THEMIS, was a Titan, and the Titan Phoebe was said to have controlled the ORACLE at

DELPHI before the arrival of APOLLO. In SENECA's plays, the divinities representing the SUN and MOON are frequently referred to as Titans. [ANCIENT SOURCES: Aeschylus, *Eumenides* 6 (see ORESTEIA), *Prometheus Bound* 205, 427, 874; Apollodorus, 1.2.1; Aristophanes, *Birds* 469; Euripides, *Hecabe* 472, *Helen* 382, *Ion* 455, *Iphigenia in Tauris* 224, *Phoenician Women* 1122; Hesiod, *Theogony* 617–735; Pausanias, 8.37.3; Sophocles, *Oedipus at Colonus* 56]

TITHONUS The son of Laomedon and Strymo (or Placia or Leucippe), Tithonus was the brother of PRIAM. The goddess of the dawn, EOS, became attracted to Tithonus, carried him off, and made him her lover. By Tithonus, Eos produced two sons, Emathion and MEMNON. Some sources also make Phaethon their son. Eos arranged with ZEUS to make Tithonus immortal, but she forgot to request that he remain eternally youthful. Accordingly, when Tithonus continued to age, Eos was no longer attracted to him. According to one tradition, Eos imprisoned the aged Tithonus in a room so she would not have to hear his senile chatter. In another tradition Eos changes Tithonus into a grasshopper.

TITINIUS See FABULA TOGATA.

TITYUS The son of EARTH, Tityus was a giant who tried to rape LETO, the mother of APOLLO and ARTEMIS. The divine twins avenged their mother by killing him. In the UNDERWORLD, Tityus was punished by a vulture that pecked out his liver, which regrew every month. [ANCIENT SOURCES: Apollodorus, *Library* 1.4.1; Homer, *Odyssey* 7.321–24, 11.576–81; Hyginus, *Fables* 55; Ovid, *Metamorphoses* 4.457–58; Pausanias, 10.4.5–6; Pindar, *Pythian Odes* 4.46; Seneca, *Hercules Furens* 756, 977, *Hercules Oetaeus* 1070, *Hippolytus* 1233, *Octavia* 622, *Thyestes* 9, 807]

TLEPOLEMUS (TLEMPOLEMUS) The son of HERACLES, Tlepolemus killed his grandmother ALCMENA's half brother, LICYMNIUS. This occurred while Tlepolemus was participating in an attack on Argos by Heracles' descendants. Some traditions said the killing was accidental, others that it was deliberate. Tlepolemus went into exile after killing Licymnius and settled on the island of Rhodes. Tlepolemus fought on the Greek side during the Trojan War and was killed by Sarpedon. [ANCIENT SOURCES: Aristophanes, *Clouds* 1266; Homer, *Iliad* 2.658]

TMOLUS   A mountain ridge in what is now western Turkey. Female followers of DIONYSUS are often associated with the Tmolus. [ANCIENT SOURCES: Aeschylus, *Persians* 49; Euripides, *Bacchae* 55, 65, 154, 462; Seneca, *Phoenician Women* 602]

TORCH RACE   A foot race held at night during several festivals at ATHENS. In some festivals, an individual runner would carry the torch; in others, one runner would pass a torch to the next in a relay fashion. [ANCIENT SOURCES: Aristophanes, *Frogs* 1087; Herodotus, 8.98.3; Pausanias, 1.30.2]

BIBLIOGRAPHY
Dover, Kenneth. *Aristophanes: Frogs.* Oxford: Clarendon Press, 1993, 206–7.

TOXEUS   A brother of IOLE. HERACLES killed him when he sacked Iole's town of OECHALIA. [ANCIENT SOURCES: Seneca, *Hercules Oetaeus* 214]

TRACHINIAN WOMEN (Greek: TRACHINIAI) SOPHOCLES (DATE UNKNOWN)

The play is generally thought to have been staged between 450 and 425 B.C.E. The drama's setting is TRACHIS, a town on the northeast coast of Greece. As the play's title indicates, women from Trachis make up the chorus. Whereas the action of the play itself is simple, its background is quite extensive and complex. After the conclusion of HERACLES' labors, the hero won the right to marry a Calydonian woman, DEIANEIRA, after he defeated the river god ACHELOUS in a wrestling match. After leaving CALYDON, Heracles and Deianeira had to cross the river Evenus. Here Heracles enlisted the help of the CENTAUR NESSUS to carry Deianeira across the river. When Nessus tried to assault Deianeira sexually, Heracles shot Nessus with an arrow. Because Heracles' arrows were tinged with lethal venom from the LERNEAN HYDRA, Nessus would soon die. With his dying words, though, he told Deianeira

to save some of his blood to use as a love charm on Heracles. Deianeira followed the centaur's instructions.

Initially Heracles and Deianeira resided in Argos, and Deianeira gave birth to a son, Hyllus. After Heracles murdered Iphitus, however, Heracles went into exile and the family moved to Trachis. To atone for his crime, Heracles was commanded by the DELPHIC ORACLE to become a servant to the queen Omphale of Lydia. After serving Omphale, Heracles returned to Greece and waged war against EURYTUS, king of Oechalia. Eurytus was the father of Iphitus, whom Heracles had killed, and Heracles blamed Eurytus for his exile and servitude to Omphale. When Heracles sacked Eurytus' kingdom, he took a number of prisoners, one of whom was Eurytus' daughter, Iole.

As Sophocles' play opens, Deianeira recalls how she first became Heracles' wife, the battle between Heracles and Achelous, Heracles' killing of Iphitus, and Heracles' exile to Trachis. Now, however, Deianeira has not seen Heracles for 15 months and wonders what has happened to him. Deianeira's NURSE advises her to send her son, Hyllus, to find out about Heracles. Mention of Hyllus heralds his arrival, and the young man tells his mother that he knows where his father is. He informs Deianeira that Heracles had been a servant to Omphale for a year, had returned to Greece, and had been waging war against Eurytus, king of Oechalia on Euboea. Deianeira tells Hyllus that Heracles had told her an oracle regarding Euboea—Heracles would find either death or the end of his labors and peace there. Deianeira asks Hyllus to try to help Heracles, a request that Hyllus says he will honor.

The departure of Hyllus is followed by the entry of the chorus of Trachinian women. They also wonder where Heracles is, express their pity for Deianeira, lament the pain that all humans face, and wonder whether Zeus cares for his sons. Deianeira reveals to the chorus another oracle that Heracles had revealed to her the last time he had seen her: In 15 months, he would die or have a peaceful life. Deianeira tells the chorus that the 15 months are reaching their completion at that moment. Deianeira's fears, however, are temporarily put to rest, when an aged MESSENGER arrives and announces that Heracles is alive and victorious. The messenger also tells Deianeira that he has heard the news from the herald Lichas. Deianeira is overjoyed by the news and the chorus sing a brief ode of praise to Apollo and Artemis. Soon the herald Lichas, accompanied by some of Heracles' female captives from Euboea, arrives and also informs Deianeira that Heracles is alive and is dedicating an altar at Cenaeum on Euboea. Lichas also tells Deianeira that Heracles had served Omphale for a year, and that because Heracles blamed this servitude on Eurytus, he had vowed to destroy Eurytus' kingdom. As ODYSSEUS feels pity for his enemy, AJAX, in SOPHOCLES' *AJAX,* Deianeira pities the captive women. One young woman in particular catches Deianeira's eye, and she suspects the woman may be Eurytus' daughter, Iole. Lichas, however, is not able to confirm this suspicion.

After Lichas and the female captives begin their exit, the aged messenger tells Deianeira that Lichas was lying, and that Heracles attacked Eurytus' kingdom because he was in love with the captive. The aged messenger claims he heard Lichas himself say so in the marketplace in Trachis. The messenger confirms that the captive Deianeira noticed is Eurytus' daughter, Iole. Deianeira is distraught at this news, and the chorus urge her to question Lichas. In the presence of the aged messenger and Deianeira, Lichas soon emerges from the house. The aged messenger challenges Lichas' account of the story to Deianeira, and eventually Lichas admits that he lied to Deianeira. Lichas admits that Heracles' sacking of Eurytus' kingdom was motivated by Heracles' passion for Iole. Hearing this, Deianeira enters the house with Lichas to prepare gifts and a message for Heracles. During Deianeira's absence, the chorus sing an ode to the power of APHRODITE and recall that she presided over the match between Heracles and Achelous for Deianeira's hand in marriage.

After the choral ode, Deianeira emerges from the house with a small box, inside of which is a robe that she will send to Heracles. Deianeira expresses the realization that Heracles will take Iole as a concubine, and at this point, Deianeira resorts to using the "love potion" about which the centaur Nessus had told her. Deineira recalls her encounter with Nessus and now tells the chorus that she has placed some of the centaur's blood on a robe that Heracles would wear while making a sacrifice in the hope that she may secure Her-

acles' love for herself. Deianeira then gives the box to Lichas and tells him to take it to Heracles. With the robe sent to Heracles, still at Oechalia, Deianeira sees that a piece of wool, tinged with the centaur's blood, catches on fire when exposed to sunlight. Deianeira realizes that she will become her husband's killer. After Lichas exits and Deianeira reenters the house, the chorus sing an ode hoping that Heracles will return and that he will love Deianeira.

After the choral ode, an alarmed Deianeira leaves the house and informs the chorus that the substance she had put on Heracles' robe had just caused a piece of wool to vanish into nothing when it was exposed to the sun. Deianeira realizes that she will have caused Heracles' death, and she decides that if he dies, she will kill herself. The chorus advise Deianeira against rash behavior, but before anything further can happen, Hyllus enters to tell Deianeira that she has destroyed Heracles. Hyllus says he himself has witnessed Heracles' sufferings and relates to her that when Heracles put on the robe, it stuck to his skin and he began to be tormented. In his pain and rage, Heracles killed the messenger, Lichas, who gave the robe to him. Heracles then begged Hyllus to take him to Trachis. Hyllus then calls upon Justice and the FURIES to punish Deianeira. Upon hearing this, Deianeira turns in silence and goes into the house, while Hyllus exits. Next, the chorus sing an ode that expresses the realization that the unfortunate side of the prophecies associated with Heracles is coming true; they lament Deianeira and the accident she has caused; and they state their belief that Aphrodite is behind these events.

The chorus' song is followed by the appearance of Deianeira's nurse, who announces that Deianeira has committed suicide with a sword. Hyllus, who has witnessed Deianeira's suicide, weeps for his mother and blames himself for his words against her. After the nurse's announcement, the chorus lament the death of Deianeira and the almost certain death of Heracles and wonder what they should do and what will happen to them. Soon an old man, Hyllus, and Heracles, carried on a litter, enter. In his agony, Heracles longs for death and laments that a woman has destroyed him. Heracles wants to see Deianeira so that he can punish her, but Hyllus tells him that she has committed suicide. Heracles is not displeased to learn of Deianeira's death but seems to relent somewhat when Hyllus tells him that Nessus' trickery actually caused Heracles' agony. Heracles reveals to Hyllus that he had heard a prophecy that he could be killed only by someone who was already dead. Realizing that Nessus has fulfilled this prophecy, Heracles makes Hyllus promise to marry Iole and take him to Mount Oeta and there burn his body on a funeral pyre. Hyllus is horrified by his father's demands but agrees to carry them out. As the play concludes, Hyllus and some attendants exit with the body of Heracles.

COMMENTARY

Trachinian Women has not received as much critical acclaim as other Sophoclean plays such as OEDIPUS TYRANNOS or ANTIGONE. The structure of the play has been considered uneven, and Sophocles' handling of Heracles' character may seem somewhat unorthodox to a modern reader of the play. Heracles is the most talked about character in the play, yet the audience do not see him until three-quarters of the drama have been completed. This, however, may be in keeping with the drama's themes of communication and first-hand experience of events. Additionally, such an arrangement is not completely without parallel because in EURIPIDES' ANDROMACHE, produced in the 420s B.C.E., NEOPTOLEMUS is the most talked about character, but the spectators see only his corpse near the end of the play.

As Euripides' *Andromache* is set in the region of THESSALY, Sophocles' play is set near the southern border of this region. Thessaly was famous for witchcraft, and whereas ANDROMACHE is accused of using witchcraft to destroy the marriage of HERMIONE and NEOPTOLEMUS, Deianeira actually engages in witchcraft to preserve her marriage with Heracles. As does Neoptolemus, Heracles threatens his marriage with his desire to have two women under the same roof, one his wife, the other a war captive who will be his concubine. Unlike Neoptolemus and Andromache, however, Heracles will be prevented from having a child with Iole by his death.

Sophocles' play also shows some similarities to AESCHYLUS' *Agamemnon* (see ORESTEIA). Both Agamem-

non and Heracles are conquering heroes who return home from their conquests with a captive slave. Both Clytemnestra and Deianeira have a chance to observe their female rival, who remains silent throughout the scrutiny of the wife. Rival or no rival, Clytemnestra has been plotting to kill Agamemnon for some time, and her stated motivation is Agamemnon's sacrifice of Iphigenia. Eventually, Clytemnestra will also kill CASSANDRA, whereas Deianeira has no intention of killing Iole. In fact, Deianeira feels sorry for Iole, whose beauty has led to her capture and the destruction of her city. In expressing her sympathy for the young woman, Deianeira perhaps parallels ODYSSEUS in Sophocles' AJAX, in which Odysseus shows sympathy for AJAX, who had tried to kill him. Although Iole threatens to destroy Deianeira's marriage with Heracles, Deianeira still shows pity for her.

Euripides' MEDEA, staged in 431 B.C.E., also bears some similarities to Sophocles' play. As is Heracles, JASON is an exile from his native land and decides that he will take a new bride. Unlike Heracles, who intends to keep both Deianeira and Iole under the same roof, Jason will divorce MEDEA and she will leave town. As Deianeira does, Medea decides to create a magic robe. Deianeira intends that her robe will ensure Heracles' love; Medea intends that her robe will kill her rival, Creon's daughter. Deianeira tells the messenger, Lichas, to deliver the robe to her husband; Medea has her children deliver the robe to her rival, Creon's daughter. The robes torment both Heracles and Creon's daughter physically. Creon's daughter dies and Heracles is on the verge of death as Sophocles' play ends.

As in Euripides' *Medea,* in Sophocles' play the power of love is mentioned frequently. Medea, however, suffers tremendous and destructive anguish as a result of Jason's rejection. To be sure, Deianeira does not brush aside Heracles' introduction of another woman into their house, but she tries to win back Heracles' devotion through magic rather than destroy her rival as Medea does. Furthermore, for all of Jason's faults in Euripides' *Medea,* Jason does not appear as physically violent as Heracles does. Sophocles' play describes Heracles as being involved in a series of violent encounters, most of them motivated by love or, perhaps more properly, brutish lust. Heracles' exile to Trachis was a result of his murder of Iphitus, Iole's brother. Heracles' marriage to Deianeira was the result of his successful physical battle with the shape-shifting river god, Achelous. At lines 515–16, the chorus sing that Aphrodite served as the umpire for their bizarre battle. Although Deianeira says she would rather have died than marry such a creature, ultimately a marriage to Achelous probably would have been happier than her marriage to Heracles.

Soon after Heracles' marriage to Deianeira, she is again associated with violent lust as the centaur Nessus tries to rape her. Again, as in his violent defeat of Achelous, Heracles takes the centaur's life with one of his arrows. After Heracles has twice secured Deianeira by violently defeating bizarre creatures, Heracles' lust for Iole emerges in his assault on Eurytus' kingdom. As with Achelous and Heracles, at lines 351–55, the messenger says Love (Eros) was Heracles' sole motivation for attacking Eurytus' kingdom; at lines 860–61, again the chorus note Aphrodite as the driving force in this action.

Deianeira, won by violence, a victim of violence, and now threatened with a rival because of Heracles' violence, turns to magic to win back Heracles. Her source for her love charm, however, is the beast who tried to rape her. Primed with false information from the centaur and motivated by love, Deianeira uses a charm that is deadly. When she realizes what she has done, she employs violence against herself. Heracles, now the victim of violence that was motivated by love, is carried onstage in agony. Even in the throes of death, Heracles arranges the marriage of Iole and his son, Hyllus, a union by which Hyllus is horrified, but into which the dutiful son promises he will enter, although he considers Iole the cause of his mother's death and the cause of his father's suffering. Paralleling Deianeira's reaction to marrying Achelous, Hyllus says he would rather die than live with his worst enemy (1233–37).

Intertwined with the theme of violent love throughout *Trachinian Women* is Sophocles' emphasis on how knowledge is acquired and how characters, especially Deianeira, evaluate that knowledge. For example, when Deianeira tells of Heracles' wrestling match with Achelous, she notes that she had not witnessed the bout. Later, when trying to learn where Heracles is, Hyllus says that if it is possible to believe the rumors

(67), "they say" (70) Heracles served Omphale for a year and informs her that "they say" (74) he is off waging war against Eurytus. Once again, Heracles' wife has, at best, secondhand information about her husband. She does, however, make Hyllus aware of reliable oracles (77) that Heracles had told her before he left Trachis: After accomplishing this final task, either he would meet death or he would live the rest of his life peacefully. Thus, Hyllus, previously unaware of this information, leaves his mother and sets out to learn "the whole truth" (91).

After Iole is sent to Heracles' house at Trachis, Deianeira's knowledge of this woman is based on information she gains secondhand, through messengers, not through direct communication with her husband, Heracles. The messenger, Lichas, informs her of Heracles' construction of an altar to Zeus near Eurytus' kingdom and of Heracles' servitude to Omphale. Furthermore, Lichas links Heracles' anger at serving Omphale with Heracles' war against Eurytus. After hearing Lichas' report, both the chorus and Deianeira express their joy at Heracles' return. After Lichas' exit, however, a second messenger arrives and declares that Lichas' report was false. The second messenger claims that he and many others heard Lichas declare that Heracles had captured Iole for no other reason than his love for her. Deianeira's previous joy turns to unhappiness at this secondhand report, and the chorus urge her to question Lichas. Accordingly, Lichas returns, is interrogated by both Deianeira and the second messenger, and eventually admits his lie, saying that he was trying to protect Deianeira from being hurt.

Once Deianeira learns the truth, she decides to apply the love potion to Heracles' robe. The chorus tell her that if she has some assurance that the potion will work, then they think she should use it. Deianeira, however, has not tested the charm and the sources of her information about this potion is a half-human, half-beast who had attempted to rape her. Deceived earlier by Lichas' information, Deianeira later discovers that the information given to her by the centaur was also unreliable. Given the dominance of secondhand information in this play, it is no accident that Heracles receives the robe not from Deianeira's hands, but from those of the messenger, Lichas. Furthermore, when the deadly poison begins to take effect on Heracles, he kills the messenger. One should also note that Deianeira learns that the robe has caused Heracles to suffer from Heracles' son, Hyllus. Typically, persons who are not so intimately connected to the events they are describing deliver "messenger speeches" in Greek TRAGEDY. Finally, when Heracles is carried on at the end of the play and Hyllus informs him of Deianeira's love charm that she had learned from the centaur, Heracles informs Hyllus of an oracle that he had heard from his father, Zeus, that he would be killed by one who lived in the realm of the dead (1159–63). Heracles also realizes that this prophecy was linked to the one Deianeira had mentioned earlier in the play, but that what Heracles considered a happy life was actually death, which is a release from one's labors (1164–73). Thus, in Sophocles' *Trachinian Women*, both Heracles and Deianeira fall victim to information they are given. Deianeira fails to see through the centaur's deception; Heracles is unable to avoid the prophecy regarding the centaur. Ultimately, however, it appears that communication from the gods, although difficult to interpret, turns out to be true, whereas communication from human mouths must be tested before one acts on it.

BIBLIOGRAPHY

Bowman, L. M. "Prophecy and Authority in the *Trachiniai*," *American Journal of Philology* 120, no. 3 (1999): 335–50.

Conacher, D. J., "Sophocles' *Trachiniae*: Some Observations," *American Journal of Philology* 118, no. 1 (1997) 21–34.

Davies, M. *Sophocles: The Trachiniae*. Oxford: Clarendon Press, 1991.

Easterling, P. E., ed. *Trachiniae*. Cambridge: Cambridge University Press, 1982.

Hoey, T. F. "The Date of the Trachiniae," *Phoenix* 33 (1979): 210–32.

Kraus, Christina S., "'*LOGOS MEN EST' ARCHAIOS*: Stories and Storytelling in Sophocles' *Trachiniae*," *Transactions of the American Philological Association* 121 (1991): 75–98.

Segal, C. P. "Sophocles' *Trachiniae*: Myth, Poetry, and Heroic Values." *Yale Classical Studies* 25 (1977): 99–158.

TRACHIS

A town near the coast of northeastern Greece, Trachis is the setting for SOPHOCLES' *TRACHINIAN WOMEN* and SENECA'S *HERCULES OETAEUS*. The town's name appears to be related to the Greek word *trachus*, which means "rough" or "rugged."

TRAGEDY

The word *tragedy* is derived from a Greek word, *tragoidia*, which literally means "goat song." Although we can easily see the connection between tragedy and song (tragedies contained songs), the connection of goats to tragedy is not clear. Wiles notes the suggestion that a goat was originally "the prize . . . for which the first tragic choruses competed." As for COMEDY, the two main festivals at which Greek tragedies were performed were the LENAEA and the City DIONYSIA. Both festivals honored the god DIONYSUS, who is often associated with goats. Dionysus is often found in the company of SATYRS, who were part human and part goat, and in one ancient tradition ZEUS changed Dionysus into a goat to hide him from HERA.

Just as we do not fully understand the history behind the word *tragoidia*, we also are on uncertain ground regarding the origins of tragedy. Both the towns of ATHENS and SICYON (northwest of CORINTH) claimed to be the birthplace of Greek tragedy. The *Suda*, a lexicon compiled in the 10th century C.E., credits a certain Arion of Corinth with inventing the tragic mode (*tropos*), but it may refer to the music later included in tragedy. Although modern scholars do not accept Arion as the inventor of tragedy, most acknowledge the presence of a Doric (a term connected with those living in southern Greece) element in Greek tragedy, especially in its lyric passages. The most famous remarks about the origins of tragedy appear in ARISTOTLE's *Poetics*. Intense controversy exists over these remarks, because Aristotle makes seemingly contradictory statements. At one point, he says tragedy began from improvisation; at another, he says tragedy evolved from DITHYRAMB; at still another, he appears to suggest that tragedy developed from the SATYR PLAY. That tragedy would develop from satyr play seems highly unlikely, because the earliest satyr plays were staged after the emergence of tragedy. In the case of dithyramb and satyr play, both employed choruses and both honored Dionysus. Perhaps we may safely conclude that tragedy evolved from choral singing and dancing in honor of Dionysus.

Our knowledge of Greek tragedy is primarily based on 32 complete plays that are attributed to three playwrights: AESCHYLUS, SOPHOCLES, and EURIPIDES. We also have hundreds of FRAGMENTS from the plays of these three tragedians, as well as hundreds more fragments from the works about 80 other tragic playwrights. Compare Greek comedy, in which fragments survive from about 150 playwrights. Some, but not all, of the discrepancy in these numbers may be attributed to the fact that at the City Dionysia three tragedians staged three tragedies and a satyr play, whereas five comic poets staged only one play each.

The earliest tragedies were said to have been produced by a certain THESPIS between 535 and 532 B.C.E. We have little evidence to verify this, however, and only a dozen lines of Thespis' plays are extant. Ancient sources also credit Thespis with introducing the first ACTOR, and Aeschylus is said to have added a second, and Sophocles a third. None of these ancient assertions can be confirmed, however, and a few episodes in Aeschylus' ORESTEIA clearly need three actors. Sophocles' OEDIPUS AT COLONUS surely needed four actors. Because most Greek tragedies have seven or eight speaking roles in addition to the chorus, actors would play multiple roles. As in Greek comedy, males took the speaking roles of both genders.

The tragic chorus consisted of 12 members originally, but Sophocles is credited with increasing the number to 15. Why the increase was felt necessary is not clear. The chorus both sang and danced. As in comedy, in tragedy the words the actors and chorus spoke or sang followed a fixed patterns of rhythm (see METER) rather than rhyme and were accompanied by musical pipes (see AULOS). As in comedy, the speaking parts of the chorus decreased over time, but, unlike in comedy, the chorus never vanished from tragedy. As in comedy, in tragedy both the chorus and the actors wore MASKS. In contrast to fifth-century comedy, in which the costumes could be quite elaborate (e.g., choruses dressed as birds, clouds, goats, wasps), in tragedy costumes for the players were simple. In ACHARNIANS, ARISTOPHANES stereotyped Euripides as introducing his characters in rags. Not all tragic costumes were simple, however: The text of Aeschylus' PERSIANS indicates that the Persian royalty in that play were elaborately dressed, and the costumes of the FURIES in Aeschylus' *Eumenides* (see ORESTEIA) must have been quite remarkable.

Tragedy and comedy were staged in the same theater. The plays were all performed outdoors and during the daytime. Tragedy and comedy also employed the same special effects devices, such as the ECCYCLEMA (a rolling platform used to show interior scenes) and the MECHANE (a crane used to suspend characters above the ground). Compared with fifth-century comedy, tragedy used few stage properties (e.g., a scepter, sword, bow, vessel to carry water, and funeral urn).

Tragedy and comedy also have many of the same structural features, such as the PROLOGUE, EPISODE, choral songs, and EXODUS. Tragedy, however, did not have a PARABASIS (in which the chorus addressed the audience as if the playwright were speaking to them). Tragedy did employ an AGON (debate), whose structure was less formalized than in comedy. Unlike fifth-century comedy, tragedy, with the exception of the few historical dramas, did not make explicit reference to real people, such as CLEON or SOCRATES. Greek tragedy also did not deal with politics, intellectual trends, or social concerns as explicitly as fifth-century comedy, though treatment of contemporary issues certainly lies beneath the surface of many Greek tragedies. In Aristophanes' *FROGS,* Dionysus restores Aeschylus from the UNDERWORLD so that the playwright can instruct the city on how to deal with its political problems. Whereas comedy exaggerates, some kernel of truth is present in the idea that in some way tragedians attempted to instruct the public about contemporary issues.

With a few exceptions (such as tragedies based on historical events, such as Aeschylus' *Persians*), Greek tragedy took its stories from mythology. HOMER's *Iliad* and *Odyssey* were fertile sources of material: The name of the most prominent hero in *Iliad*, ACHILLES, appears in the title of at least eight plays by Greek tragedians, and Aeschylus' *Agamemnon* and *Libation Bearers* (see ORESTEIA), Sophocles' *AJAX*, and Euripides' ANDROMACHE, CYCLOPS, HECABE, RHESUS, and TROJAN WOMEN all have connections to the Homeric epics. CADMUS and his descendants, who ruled THEBES, were also the subject of many Greek tragedies. At least a dozen known plays have the name of OEDIPUS in their title, and at least four plays entitled *Niobe* are known. JASON's barbarian bride, MEDEA, was also a popular subject for tragedy, and at least eight Greek tragedies carry her name in the title.

Because the subject matter of Greek tragedy was relatively limited, playwrights often used the same subject previous poets had. In the fifth century, Aeschylus, Sophocles, and Euripides produced plays entitled *Philoctetes;* all three wrote plays about Orestes' killing of his mother. Thus, it is not surprising that during the last few decades of the fifth century an apparent struggle for new material begins to emerge. The tragedian Agathon wrote a tragedy, *Antheus* (or *Athos*), in which the characters were fictional and not based on characters from mythology. Euripides' IPHIGENIA IN TAURIS, HELEN, and ION, all produced in the 410s, make use of mythological traditions that either were not well known (*Helen* and *Ion*) or may have been largely invented by Euripides himself (*Iphigenia in Tauris*). These three plays all begin on a tragic tragectory but, at least on the surface, have "happy" endings. Euripides' *Ion* is often cited as anticipating the content of new comedy. In *Ion,* CREUSA is raped, she abandons her child (Ion), the child is raised by someone else, and eventually Creusa and Ion recognize one another through items left with the infant. Compare MENANDER's *Arbitration,* in which Pamphile is raped, becomes pregnant, marries Charisius, and exposes the child during Charisius' absence from home. Slaves find the child, and items left with the infant reveal that the baby is Pamphile's and that Charisius was the rapist.

In Aristophanes' FROGS, Dionysus complains that Athens no longer possesses any "good" tragedians since the deaths of Aeschylus, Euripides, and Sophocles. Although Aristophanes' assessment may have been accurate, tragedies continued to be written. There are extant fragments from some 20 tragedians of the fourth century; however, there are only fragments from about that number for the three centuries that followed. As the number of tragedians apparently dwindled, the plays of Aeschylus, Euripides, and Sophocles continued to be performed in the Greek world.

According to tradition, Greek tragedy was first performed in Rome in 240 B.C.E., when Livius Andronicus translated a Greek tragedy and comedy into Latin. After the time of Livius Andronicus, three important writers of tragedy in Latin emerged: ENNIUS, PACUVIUS, and ACCIUS. Although none of their plays survives, several hundred fragments and about 80 titles are known. Their titles show the influence of Aeschylus, Sophocles, and especially Euripides. A handful of titles by these three authors are from Roman historical tragedies (see FABULA PRAETEXTA). After Accius' death early in the first century B.C.E., tragedy continued to be written, but few prominent playwrights emerged. Ovid wrote a *Medea* (no longer extant), and even the emperor AUGUSTUS tried his hand (unsuccessfully) at an *Ajax.* In the first century C.E., Pomponius Secundus gained some fame, but only two titles (*Aeneas, Atreus*) and about a dozen lines survive of his works.

Although understanding of Greek tragedy is hampered by the survival of only 32 plays by only three poets, knowledge of Roman tragedy is made even more limited because only 10 tragedies written in Latin survive: AGAMEMNON, HERCULES FURENS, HERCULES OETAEUS, HIPPOLYTUS, MEDEA, OEDIPUS REX, PHOENICIAN WOMEN (of which only 664 lines survive), THYESTES, TROJAN WOMEN, and OCTAVIA. Furthermore, these surviving plays are attributed to the same author, SENECA, although it is unlikely that he wrote both the *Octavia* and the *Hercules Oetaeus.* Most of the Senecan plays (with the exception of *Thyestes* and *Octavia*) were influenced by the Greek tragedies of Aeschylus, Sophocles, and Euripides. Even *Octavia,* which is based on historical events, owes a debt to Greek plays written on mythological themes. Senecan tragedy differs from Greek tragedy in that its choruses enter and exit much more frequently. The smaller size of the Senecan chorus may have permitted this, however, and some scholars believe the Senecan chorus was no more than half the size of its Greek counterpart. Senecan tragedy also differs from Greek tragedy in its use of a five-act structure and asides (some are extended monologues). Senecan tragedy is not read or performed extensively today; however, Seneca's influence in the Renaissance and during the 17th century was considerable, and he was regarded more highly than the greatest Greek tragedians. [ANCIENT SOURCES: Aristophanes, *Acharnians, Frogs, Thesmophoriazusae;* Aristotle, *Poetics, Politics* 8.7; Athenaeus, *Deipnosophists* passim; Plato, *Republic* 3.394–95, 3.398, 10.605–6; Pollux, *Onomasticon* 4.99–154; Horace, *Ars Poetica;* Lucian, *On Dance* 26–30, 65–67, 78–79; Vitruvius, *On Architecture* 5.6–7]

BIBLIOGRAPHY
Brooks, R. A. *Ennius and Roman Tragedy.* New York: Arno Press, 1981.

Csapo, E., and W. J. Slater. *The Context of Ancient Drama.* Ann Arbor: University of Michigan Press, 1995.

Pickard-Cambridge, A. W. *Dithyramb, Tragedy, and Comedy,* 2d ed. Revised by T. B. L. Webster. Oxford: Clarendon Press, 1962.

———. *The Dramatic Festivals of Athens,* 2d ed. Revised by J. Gould and D. M. Lewis. Oxford: Clarendon Press, 1968.

Rehm, R. *Greek Tragic Theatre.* London: Routledge, 1992.

Wiles, D. *Greek Theatre Performance: An Introduction.* Cambridge: Cambridge University Press, 2000, 34.

TRAGICOMEDY

A term used by modern scholars to describe plays that have a mixture of tragic and comic elements. Some of EURIPIDES' plays are often called tragicomedies: *ALCESTIS, IPHIGENIA IN TAURIS, HELEN,* and *ION.* The prologue of PLAUTUS' *AMPHITRUO* describes that play as a tragicomedy (lines 59, 63). Three Greek comic playwrights wrote plays entitled *Comoidotragoidia,* a title that indicates a mixture of comic and tragic elements. See Alcaeus (fragments 19–21 Kock 1), Anaxandrides (fragment 25 Kock 2), Dinolochus (fragment 3 Kaibel). We know nothing about the content of these plays.

BIBLIOGRAPHY

Kaibel, G. *Comicorum Graecorum Fragmenta.* Vol. 1.1 [*Poetarum Graecorum Fragmenta,* Vol. 6.1]. Berlin: Weidmann, 1899.

Kitto, H. D. F. *Greek Tragedy: A Literary Study.* London: Methuen, 1939, 311–29.

Knox, B. M. W. *Word and Action: Essays on the Ancient Theater.* Baltimore: Johns Hopkins University Press, 1986, 250–74.

Kock, T. *Comicorum Atticorum Fragmenta.* Vol. 1. Leipzig: Teubner, 1880.

———. *Comicorum Atticorum Fragmenta.* Vol. 2. Leipzig: Teubner, 1884.

TRIBALLIAN

The Triballians were a fierce and savage tribe of Thracians. They lived "in what is now W[estern] Bulgaria and the former Yugoslav Macedonia" (Dunbar). In 424 B.C.E., the Triballians had killed their fellow Thracian and Athenian ally Sitacles. The Greek comic poet ALEXIS claimed that the Triballians had the unusual custom of feeding sacrificial meat to those who had no food after showing the meat to guests whom he had invited to dine (a practice that would run contrary to that of "civilized" Greeks).

In ARISTOPHANES' *BIRDS,* a Triballian god appears in the divine delegation who negotiate with PEISETAERUS. Because the Triballian speaks gibberish, his response to the question of whether to allow Basileia to marry Peisetaerus is subject to interpretation. HERACLES votes for the proposal; POSEIDON votes against it. Peisetaerus then turns to the Triballian to cast the tie-breaking vote. Peisetaerus interprets the Triballian's response as voting with Heracles' position. Although Poseidon interprets Triballos' response as agreeing with his view, at this point he agrees to Peisetaerus' terms. [ANCIENT SOURCES: Alexis, fragment 241 Kock; Aristophanes, *Birds* 1529–1629; Demosthenes, 54.39; Herodotus, 4.49.2; Isocrates, Panathenaicus, 227; Thucydides, 2.96.4, 4.101.5]

BIBLIOGRAPHY

Dunbar, Nan. *Aristophanes: Birds.* New York: Oxford University Press, 1995, 702.

Kock, T. *Comicorum Atticorum Fragmenta.* Vol. 2. Leipzig: Teubner, 1884.

TRICORYTHUS

A town on the eastern coast of Greece not far north of MARATHON. Because Tricorythus was located in a marshy area, it had a reputation for its insects. [ANCIENT SOURCES: Aristophanes, *Lysistrata* 1032]

TRILOGY

A group of three plays by a tragedian that were performed at the same dramatic festival. AESCHYLUS' *ORESTEIA* is the only surviving trilogy from ancient times, although many others are known. The *Oresteia* is unified in its subject matter (the return of AGAMEMNON from TROY, his murder by AEGISTHUS and CLYTEMNESTRA, the revenge taken by ORESTES against Aegisthus and Clytemnestra, and the trial of Orestes for his killing of Clytemnestra), whereas the first three plays of a TETRALOGY were not always unified.

TRINUMMUS

See *THREE-DOLLAR DAY.*

TRIPTOLEMUS

The son of CELEUS and Metaneira, Triptolemus was a prince from ELEUSIS. DEMETER, in mourning after the loss of PERSEPHONE, was hired to nurse the infant Triptolemus. Demeter tried to make him immortal by holding the infant in the fire, but a terrified Metaneira interrupted the goddess. Instead, Demeter honored Triptolemus by teaching him about the cultivation of grain. SOPHOCLES wrote a *Triptolemus,* from which several fragments survive (fragments 596–617a Radt). Demeter speaks in at least one of the fragments, but little else is known about the play. [ANCIENT SOURCES: Aristophanes, *Acharnians* 48; Seneca, *Hippolytus* 838]

BIBLIOGRAPHY

Kiso, A. *The Lost Sophocles.* New York: Vantage Press, 1984.

Lloyd-Jones, H. *Sophocles: Fragments.* Cambridge, Mass.: Harvard University Press, 1996.

Matheson, Susan B., "The Mission of Triptolemus and the Politics of Athens," *Greek, Roman, and Byzantine Studies* 35 (1994) 345–72.

Radt, S. *Tragicorum Graecorum Fragmenta.* Vol. 4. Göttingen, Ger.: Vandenhoeck & Ruprecht, 1977.

Simms, R. M., "The Eleusinia in the Sixth to Fourth Centuries B.C.," *Greek, Roman, and Byzantine Studies* 16 (1975) 269–79.

Sutton, D. F. *The Lost Sophocles.* Lanham, Md.: University Press of America, 1984.

TRITAGONIST   Most extant Greek tragedies and comedies can be performed by only three actors. The third actor is called the tritagonist and probably performed the minor roles in a drama; for example, the character of PYLADES in the extant plays connected with ORESTES would have been performed by the tritagonist. Several ancient sources credit SOPHOCLES with introducing the third actor, although an ancient biography of AESCHYLUS attributes the innovation to him. [ANCIENT SOURCES: Aristotle, *Poetics* 1449a15–19; Diogenes Laertius, 3.56; Hesychius, t1435; *Life of Aeschylus* 15; Suda, t1012]

TRITON (1) (TRITONIS)   A body of water, both a river and a lake, in Libya, beside which the goddess ATHENA was said to have been born. [ANCIENT SOURCES: Aeschylus, *Eumenides* 293 (see *ORESTEIA*); Apollodorus, *Library* 1.3.6; Euripides, *Ion* 872; Herodotus, 4.178.1]

TRITON (2)   Triton was the son of POSEIDON and Amphitrite. Triton's favorite body of water was the Libyan lake TRITON. Tritons were sea divinities who were part human (they had a human nose and hands) and part fish (a scaly body and dolphin's tail). SENECA says Tritons sang the chorus at ACHILLES' wedding. [ANCIENT SOURCES: Euripides, *Cyclops* 263; Pausanias, 8.2.7, 9.20.4–21.1; Seneca, *Trojan Women* 202]

TRIVIA   Another name for ARTEMIS.

TROEZEN (TROIZEN; TROZEN)   A town on the southeastern coast of mainland Greece, Troezen was situated east of Epidaurus and on the opposite shore of the Saronic Gulf from ATHENS. In mythology, Troezen is the home of Pittheus; his daughter, Aethra; and THESEUS, the son of Aethra. In drama, Troezen is the setting for EURIPIDES' *HIPPOLYTUS,* but not SENECA's *HIPPOLYTUS.*

TROILUS   The son of PRIAM (or APOLLO) and HECABE, Troilus was a Trojan prince. According to an oracle, the Trojans would win their war against the Greeks if Troilus reached a certain age. ACHILLES, however, killed Troilus before that time. SOPHOCLES wrote a *Troilus,* of which a few fragments survive, which seems to have been produced in 418 B.C.E. One of the fragments indicates that a eunuch was a speaking character in the play. The comic poet Strattis also wrote a *Troilus,* from which about 20 words survive; in one fragment, a child of ZEUS is addressed. [ANCIENT SOURCES: Apollodorus, *Epitome* 3.32; Seneca, *Agamemnon* 748]

BIBLIOGRAPHY

Kiso, A. *The Lost Sophocles.* New York: Vantage Press, 1984.

Kock, T. *Comicorum Atticorum Fragmenta.* Vol. 1. Leipzig: Teubner, 1880.

Lloyd-Jones, H. *Sophocles: Fragments.* Cambridge, Mass.: Harvard University Press, 1996.

Radt, S. *Tragicorum Graecorum Fragmenta.* Vol. 4. Göttingen, Ger.: Vandenhoeck & Ruprecht, 1977.

Sutton, D. F. *The Lost Sophocles.* Lanham, Md.: University Press of America, 1984.

TROJAN HORSE   In the 10th year of the famous war fought over HELEN, wife of MENELAUS, the Greeks finally defeated the Trojans by the stratagem of the wooden horse, or Trojan horse, as it is called. Epeus built the horse, but ODYSSEUS, inspired by ATHENA, is usually credited with the idea. The Greeks filled the horse with a group of selected warriors and burned their camp to the ground. Those not within the horse sailed to the western side of the island of Tenedos, just off the coast from Troy. When the Trojans found the horse outside their city walls, they debated whether to take it into the city or destroy it. The Greeks left a spy, SINON, to persuade the Trojans to take in the horse. A Trojan priest, LAOCOON, warned the Trojans about a possible trick and even hurled his spear at the horse. Not long afterward, however, when Laocoon and his sons were killed by sea serpents, the Trojans were convinced that destroying the horse would be dangerous. Accordingly, they took the horse into their city. After the Trojans went to sleep that night, the Greeks emerged from their hiding place, burned Troy, and began to slaughter their enemies. This stratagem resulted in the destruction of Troy and the recovery of Helen. Several playwrights mention the stratagem of the Trojan horse. Naevius wrote a play entitled *Trojan Horse* (Latin: *Equos Troianus*); the single line that survives tells us nothing about the play's plot other than what is implied by the title.

TROJAN WOMEN (Greek/Latin: *TRO-IADES*) EURIPIDES (415 B.C.E.) In Aelian's *Varia Historia* (2.8), the author indicates the play's date and remarks that EURIPIDES' production finished second to the plays of XENOCLES in that year. Aelian also writes that *Trojan Women* was the third play of the TETRALOGY that included *Alexander, Palamedes,* and the SATYR PLAY *Sisyphus.* Little of *Sisyphus* survives (fragments 673–74 Nauck), but HERACLES appears to have been a character in the play. About a dozen fragments of *Palamedes* survive (578–90 Nauck), and ARISTOPHANES parodies this play in *THESMOPHORIAZUSAE.* *Palamedes* treated ODYSSEUS' destruction of his fellow warrior, PALAMEDES, during the Trojan War; *Alexander,* of which some fairly substantial fragments are extant (42–63 Nauck), recalled the events surrounding the birth and return of the title character (see PARIS) to TROY and his recognition as PRIAM and HECABE's son. The clearly interconnected subject matter of the three

tragedies was unusual compared with what is known about Euripides' other productions, and full appreciation of *Trojan Women* is hampered by the fragmentary condition of the two plays that preceded it.

The play's action occurs after the fall of Troy outside the walls of Troy before AGAMEMNON's tent (139). The play opens with a monologue by POSEIDON, who built the walls of Troy. Poseidon laments the troubles of a city from which he himself is about to depart. Poseidon mentions the stratagem of the TROJAN HORSE, the death of Priam, the looting of Troy by the Greeks, and the wailing of captive Trojan women who will become the property of Greek masters. Poseidon notes that Helen remains in the tent that the SKENE represents. In front of the "tent" lies Hecabe, Priam's wife. Poseidon relates that Hecabe's daughter, POLYXENA, will be sacrificed at ACHILLES' tomb and that another daughter, CASSANDRA, will be given to Agamemnon. As Poseidon's monologue concludes, ATHENA, to whom Poseidon attributes the destruction of Troy, enters. Athena proposes that she and Poseidon put aside their differences and make an alliance. Athena expresses her anger at the desecration of one of her temples by AJAX, who dragged Cassandra from it when she was seeking refuge there. Because Ajax had not been punished by the Greeks, Athena requests that Poseidon cause the Greek ships to be wrecked at sea so that they will respect the gods in the future. Poseidon agrees to Athena's request and the divinities exit.

Next, Hecabe rises from her prone position and begins a lament for the fate of her town, husband, and children. She also laments her fate, as she will be led away as a captive. After Hecabe's monologue, the CHORUS of captive Trojan women, divided into two groups, enter. The chorus ask Hecabe why she is crying out and what is happening. Hecabe tells them that soon the Greeks will set sail and that their situation is probably hopeless. When the first choral group summons the other half of the chorus, Hecabe begs that Cassandra not appear in her bacchantlike state of mind. When the second half of the chorus enter from Agamemnon's quarters, they ask Hecabe about their fate. The chorus and Hecabe wonder to which Greek they will be allotted. The united chorus then lament their departure from Troy and wonder what their arrival in Greece will present.

After the choral ode, the chief herald of the Greek army, TALTHYBIUS, enters to tell Hecabe that Cassandra has been assigned to Agamemnon; Polyxena will be sacrificed at Achilles' tomb; Hector's wife, ANDROMACHE, will become the prize of Achilles' son, NEOPTOLEMUS; and Hecabe herself has been assigned to ODYSSEUS, a fate that Hecabe considers the worst of all. Talthybius then tells a servant to take Cassandra from Agamemnon's quarters. Cassandra emerges from the tent carrying burning torches and singing the wedding hymn in mockery of Greek marriage ritual. At the chorus' urging, Hecabe persuades Cassandra to put aside the torches. Cassandra does so and then in a lengthy speech tries to demonstrate that Troy is more blessed than Greece. The Greeks, Cassandra argues, tracked down Helen and killed thousands of Trojans. Many Greeks died in a land not their own, while members of their families died in Greece without anyone to attend their funeral. The Trojans, on the other hand, died fighting for their country and were buried by their loved ones. Trojans who survived returned from battle to their family. Fighting against the Greeks may have caused Hector's death, but it also earned him glory. Paris also would not have become famous had he not abducted and "married" Helen. Cassandra ends her speech by promising that her own "marriage" to Agamemnon will cause his destruction.

Talthybius dismisses Cassandra's words as the ravings of a madwoman and orders the Trojan women to follow him to the Greek ships. Cassandra mocks Talthybius as a servant to powerful men and goes on to state that Hecabe is destined to die at Troy. Cassandra also predicts the wanderings of Odysseus and the troubles that await him when he finally reaches home. Cassandra then ends her prophetic words, welcomes her impending fatal marriage, tells her mother good-bye, and exits for the Greek ships. Hecabe, in her distress, falls to the ground and recalls the blessings she experienced in her life. She notes the irony that whereas once she was a queen, now she will become a slave. She then laments the fate of her daughters, Cassandra and Polyxena.

Hecabe's lamentation is followed by a choral ode that recalls the arrival of the fatal wooden horse in their city. They recall that the Trojans thought their troubles were over and took the horse into Troy amid celebration, only to discover that the horse was filled with destruction. The chorus end their song by announcing the arrival of Hector's wife, Andromache, and her son, ASTYANAX. For several lines Andromache and Hecabe exchange laments for their loved ones and city. In the course of their grief, Andromache reveals to Hecabe that Polyxena has been sacrificed at Achilles' grave. Andromache then makes a speech that, in terms of the play's structure, parallels the earlier speech by Cassandra. Just as Cassandra spoke of the blessings Troy experienced in spite of the war, Andromache claims that Polyxena is fortunate to be dead and that she herself was a virtuous wife to Hector. She concludes by stating that Polyxena's fate is more fortunate than her own—Polyxena is dead; she will be taken as a slave to Greece. Hecabe tells Andromache to cease mourning Hector and honor her new master and "husband."

Next, Talthybius enters and informs Andromache that the Greeks are going to kill her son, Astyanax. Talthybius tells Andromache, to whom the young boy is clinging, not to resist or do anything rash, lest they not allow him to be buried. Andromache mourns for her son and curses Helen for the destruction that her beauty has caused the Trojans. Talthybius takes Astyanax from his mother and sends him off to be thrown down from the walls of Troy. After the departure of Talthybius and Astyanax, Hecabe laments the fate of Astyanax and Troy. In the choral ode that follows, the Trojan women sing of the earlier destruction of Troy by Heracles and his allies, among whom was Telamon of SALAMIS. They recall the abduction of the Trojan GANYMEDE by ZEUS, and the union of the goddess EOS and the Trojan TITHONUS. The divinities loved these Trojan males; the chorus assert that the gods no longer love Troy.

After the choral ode, MENELAUS enters, utters threats against HELEN's life, and then summons his wife from the tent. Hecabe hears these prayers, expresses her approval of Menelaus' decision to kill Helen, but urges Menelaus not to set eyes on her. When Helen walks out of the tent, she offers a lengthy argument as to why it would be unjust for Menelaus to put her to death. Hecabe persuades Menelaus to allow her to offer a rebuttal. Helen argues that Paris was to blame for the

Trojan War, that Priam should have killed him as soon
as he was born, and that APHRODITE helped Paris to
abduct her when he judged Aphrodite as more beautiful than Athena or HERA. Hecabe argues that these goddesses would never have behaved in such a manner,
that Aphrodite never went with Paris to Menelaus'
house, and that Paris' good looks and wealth persuaded Helen to leave Menelaus and Sparta. Hecabe
says Helen enjoyed her life with Paris at Troy and
rejected Hecabe's offer to help her leave Troy. After
Hecabe's speech, Menelaus states that he will kill Helen
when he reaches Greece. Hecabe urges Menelaus not
to allow Helen to travel on the same ship as he does,
but Menelaus departs with Helen.

After the departure of Menelaus and Helen, the chorus sing an ode that begins by questioning whether
Zeus cares about Troy, a city that had worshiped him
faithfully. The chorus lament the loss of their husbands
and the cries of their children as they are being taken
away and hope that Menelaus will never reach home.
As their song concludes, the chorus see the body of
Astyanax, the son of Hector and Andromache, carried
in upon Hector's shield. Talthybius enters and reports
that Neoptolemus' ship has sailed with Andromache
and that Astyanax was thrown from the walls of Troy.
Talthybius says that he cleaned the child's wounds and
that he is going to break ground for the child's grave.
Hecabe is appalled that the Greeks would kill a child
and recalls that the child had promised to care for her
when she died. Now, however, the grandmother will
bury the grandchild. Next, some of Hecabe's servants
arrive with clothing in which to bury Astyanax.
Hecabe clothes the corpse, she and the chorus sing a
dirge for the child, and then Astyanax's body is carried
out for burial.

Next the chorus see Greeks waving torches that will
burn Troy. Talthybius enters again and announces that
the city will be burned and that Hecabe must go with
Odysseus as his slave. Hecabe laments her fate, as well
as that of the city. She urges the chorus to accompany
her and throw themselves into the pyre. The suicide is
prevented, however, by Talthybius, who summons soldiers to take Hecabe to Odysseus. As the play ends
Hecabe and the chorus exchange laments as they are
led away to the ships of the Greeks.

COMMENTARY

Whereas modern scholars have preferred to analyze
dramas such as *ALCESTIS*, *MEDEA*, *HIPPOLYTUS*, and *BAC-
CHAE*, those who stage ancient Euripidean dramas seem
most inclined to present *Trojan Women*. Euripides' *Trojan Women* may be "one of the greatest tragedies," as
Shirley Barlow has written, but it is also one of the
author's most disturbing and depressing plays. The
play's structure is not balanced, and Francis Dunn has
made sense of this imbalance by interpreting *Trojan
Women* as a series of exits. Even when characters enter
the orchestra, they enter with a view to their departure.
The exit of Poseidon from Troy begins the play; it is followed by the exit of Cassandra; the exit of Andromache and her child, Astyanax; the exit of Helen; and
finally the exit of Hecabe and the chorus.

In addition to being a play of exits, *Trojan Women* is
filled with groaning and lamentation, references to and
images of slavery, destruction of family and home, and
brutal death. Such images were familiar to Euripides'
fellow Athenians, and some scholars believe that the
Athenian slaughter of the men of MELOS and enslavement of their women (in the year before *Trojan Women*)
is reflected in the events of Euripides' play. Even if
Euripides did not have the destruction of Melos in
mind, the Athenians, as the mythical Greeks had at
Troy, had violently put down the rebellions of several
cities in their empire during the past two decades, and
the killing of males and the enslavement of females
were not practices with which Euripides' Athenian
audience was unfamiliar. In 427 B.C.E., for example,
the people of MYTILENE revolted against the Athenians,
the revolt was put down, and initially the Athenians
voted to put the entire male population of Mytilene to
death. This decision was reversed, however, and only
the leaders of the revolt were executed.

Thus, set against a backdrop of the now-ruined hulk
of the once fabulous city of Troy, Euripides not only
represents the death of an entire city, but focuses on
the misery and death of the inhabitants of that city
who are least able to defend themselves, women and
children. Not only does Euripides have his fellow
Greeks watch what mythical Greeks have done and are
doing to this mythical city, but he makes his audience
witness this largely through Hecabe, a lone old

woman, for whom the action that unfolds is of the greatest concern. Those in Euripides' audience see what Hecabe sees and hear what Troy's once glorious queen, now Odysseus' wretched slave, hears. Euripides' audience imagine what the pitiful Hecabe is made to imagine.

Whereas Euripides' SUPPLIANT WOMEN, staged within the decade before *Trojan Women*, deals with the recovery of corpses after a war, *Trojan Women*, in general, focuses on those who are about to become corpses. Of course, *Trojan Women* does mention the deaths of Priam and Hector, but unlike *Suppliant Women*, in which mothers retrieve the corpses of the Argive men who died in battle, *Trojan Women* primarily deals with consequential casualties of war. In *Trojan Women*, various persons will die because of the violence of others or their connection to certain warriors. In the prologue, the audience hear that the Greeks, conquerors of Troy, will have their corpses (84, 91) strewn about the AEGEAN SEA because of Ajax's rape of Hecabe's daughter, Cassandra. Cassandra herself later enters and predicts that she will be cast out as a naked corpse (448) from Agamemnon's home but also predicts that she will triumphantly enter Hades, the land of corpses (460), after she has ruined those who ruined Troy. Another daughter of Hecabe also becomes a corpse: Polyxena dies at the grave of Achilles; thus, she must become a corpse herself to appease a lifeless corpse (623). Next, Hecabe's daughter-in-law, Andromache, and grandson, Astyanax, enter. Astyanax will be hurled from the city walls. Talthybius warns Andromache not to do anything that will anger the Greeks, lest they forbid that his corpse be buried (738). Later, Astyanax's corpse is carried in on Hector's shield after it was hurled from Troy's walls as a discus (1121). Before this event Andromache herself is carried away to the Greek ships and therefore is not allowed to bury her own son. The Greek messenger Talthybius has bathed the child's corpse (1152) and will break ground for the grave. The final preparations for Astyanax's corpse will be left to his grandmother, Hecabe, who complains that he should have been the one to bury her. Earlier in the play, Hecabe had described herself as being like a corpse (191); now she is one of the few Trojans alive and must bury the corpse of someone whose life was just beginning.

As for Andromache, Euripides' audience may have known that she would survive but that she would spend the next few years of her life as the concubine of Neoptolemus, the son of the man who killed her husband, Hector, another of Hecabe's sons. Interestingly, the body of Helen, the woman that Dunn calls "the symbol of this war, and the symbol of the Greek cause," will not become a corpse. In earlier plays such as SOPHOCLES' *AJAX* and *ANTIGONE*, kings and their subordinates debated whether to bury the corpse of a fallen warrior. In *Trojan Women*, two queens, who have now become captives, debate what to do about the body of a woman. The Trojan queen wants the woman to become a corpse; the Greek queen wants the body, her own, to remain alive. Menelaus tells Hecabe that he will kill Helen, but the audience know that Helen will survive.

Perhaps the lone comfort of which Euripides' audience knew, but of which Hecabe herself is not made aware in the course of the play, is that Hecabe would not survive much longer but would leap from the ship of her new master, Odysseus, to her death. Death would be a welcome relief to a woman whose entire family had been destroyed. Moreover, as play ends, the Greeks will make a corpse of the last of the *Trojan Women*, Troy herself, as they burn the once proud city. In *Alexander*, the first play of Euripides' tragic TRILOGY of 415, Hecabe, before the birth of Paris, had dreamed she was giving birth to a burning brand that would destroy the city. Although Paris himself is now a corpse, many burning brands are being applied to Troy as Euripides' trilogy ends.

BIBLIOGRAPHY

Barlow, Shirley A. *Euripides: Trojan Women,* Warminster, U.K.: Aris & Phillips, 1986.

Conacher, D. J. *Euripidean Drama.* Toronto: University of Toronto Press, 1967, 127–45.

Croally, N. T. *Euripidean Polemic: The Trojan Women and the Function of Tragedy.* Cambridge and New York: Cambridge University Press, 1994.

Dunn, Francis. *Tragedy's End.* Oxford: Oxford University Press, 1996.

Green, Peter. "War and Morality in Fifth-Century Athens: The Case of Euripides' *Trojan Women*," Ancient History Bulletin 13, no. 3 (1999): 97–110.

Nauck, A. *Tragicorum Graecorum Fragmenta.* 1889. Reprint, Hildesheim, Ger.: Olms, 1964.

Walton, J. M. *Living Greek Theatre.* New York: Greenwood Press, 1987, 138–42.

TROJAN WOMEN (Latin: *TROADES*)
SENECA (WRITTEN BETWEEN 49 AND 65 C.E.?)

As is Euripides' *Trojan Women,* Seneca's drama is set at Troy and its chorus are Trojan women whom the victorious Greeks have taken captive. Unlike in Euripides' play, which begins with Poseidon's departure from Troy and his encounter with Athena, in Seneca's Hecuba (Greek: Hecabe) delivers the prologue. Hecuba begins with a lengthy lament of her fallen city, in which she recalls the deaths of her many children and describes the death of her husband, Priam. Hecuba notes that now the various Greeks are choosing Trojan women to be their slaves, but that she herself remains to be chosen. As her monologue concludes, Hecuba invites the chorus of Trojan women to join her in lamentation. For the next 100 lines, Hecuba and the chorus take turns lamenting Troy, Hector, and Priam.

The play's second act opens with the arrival of several Greeks: the herald Talthybius; Achilles' son, Pyrrhus (see Neoptolemus); Agamemnon; and the prophet Calchas. Talthybius informs the Trojan women that Achilles' ghost demanded that Hecuba's daughter, Polyxena, be sacrificed to him by his son, Pyrrhus. Pyrrhus then defends his father's right to such a sacrifice by listing all that Achilles did for the Greek army. In contrast to Euripides' *Hecabe,* in which the debate about Polyxena's sacrifice occurs between Hecabe and Ulysses (Greek: Odysseus), Seneca's play presents a debate between two Greeks, and Agamemnon opposes Pyrrhus and the shedding of innocent blood to appease Achilles' ghost. Agamemnon suggests, rather, that the finest Trojan animals be sacrificed to Achilles. Pyrrhus, however, declares that he will sacrifice Polyxena as his father wished. Agamemnon and Pyrrhus continue to debate this issue and eventually summon Calchas to settle the argument. Calchas declares that Polyxena, dressed in the manner of a bride from Thessaly (Achilles' native land), must be sacrificed to Achilles. Calchas also states that Hector's son must be hurled from the heights of Troy. After

Calchas' speech, the Trojan women sing an ode in which they wonder what sort of life remains for them. They also conclude that nothing awaits human beings after they die.

The third act opens with a lament by Andromache, who recalls the death of her husband, Hector, and says she herself would die if it were not for her responsibility to her child, Astyanax. A Trojan elder, who accompanies Andromache, questions her about further worries she might have. Andromache relates that in a dream Hector appeared and urged her to save Astyanax from danger. Now, however, Andromache wonders what safe place can be found for her son. After some deliberation, Andromache sends Astyanax to take refuge inside his father's tomb. Soon Ulysses arrives and demands from Andromache that Astyanax be handed over to be put to death, because the Greeks believe that someday Astyanax will become a second Hector and wage war against them. Andromache pretends that Astyanax is already dead, but Ulysses suspects that she is lying and threatens to torture her to learn the truth. Andromache swears that Astyanax is dead; Ulysses is convinced that he is hiding.

When Ulysses' henchmen find the boy hiding in his father's tomb, Ulysses declares that Astyanax must be dragged from this place, although a grave is sacred ground. Andromache wonders whether she should allow the Greek to tear apart her husband's burial place so that they can find Astyanax. Eventually Ulysses' threats to destroy her husband's tomb become more than Andromache can bear, and she begs Ulysses not to bury her son with her husband. At Ulysses' command, Andromache calls Astyanax from the tomb and urges him to beg Ulysses for mercy. Andromache's pleas do move Ulysses somewhat, but he states that he is more concerned about what Astyanax might do someday to the sons of Greek mothers and about Calchas' prophecy. Andromache continues to beg Ulysses for mercy, and Astyanax tries to cling to his mother, but eventually Ulysses orders his henchmen to pull the boy away. After Ulysses departs with Astyanax, the Trojan women sing an ode in which they wonder what awaits them in Greece and what Hecuba's fate will be.

In the fourth act, Helen announces that she will tell Andromache about her "marriage" to Pyrrhus. Andromache, hearing Helen's statement, laments over this news, but Helen herself worries what Menelaus will do to her. Helen also reveals that Polyxena, who is also onstage, is to be sacrificed to the spirit of Achilles; that CASSANDRA will become Agamemnon's slave; and that Hecuba will become Ulysses' slave. The act ends with the approach of Pyrrhus, who has arrived to take Polyxena for sacrifice, and a choral ode in which the Trojan women lament that they will soon be parted from one another.

The play's final act begins with the arrival of a MESSENGER, who informs Hecuba and Andromache of the deaths of Polyxena and Astyanax. First, the messenger relates that Ulysses led Astyanax to a high tower and the boy jumped to his death. Next the messenger describes the mock wedding ritual, led by Helen, in which Pyrrhus killed Polyxena at the grave of Achilles. After the messenger's report, Hecuba declares an end to the war and wonders what fate awaits her. The messenger ends the play by telling the captive Trojan women to hurry to the ships, which are waiting to set sail from Troy.

COMMENTARY

As alluded to in the preceding paragraphs, in this play Seneca has combined elements of Euripides' *Hecabe* and *Trojan Women*. All the same, Seneca has not merely copied from his Greek predecessor, but has crafted a situation in which the dead affect the living. Seneca's play is entitled *Trojan Women,* but the names of two Trojan men, Hector and Priam, appear more frequently than that of any woman in the play. Hector is mentioned by name 40 times, twice as often as in Euripides' *Trojan Women,* and Priam is mentioned by name 23 times, compared with 10 times in Euripides' play. We note also that in Seneca's play the name Achilles occurs 23 times. Thus, one approach may be to view Seneca's *Trojan Women* from the perspective of the influence of these deceased warriors and fathers on the living.

In the first part of the play Hecuba and the chorus in more than 60 lines deliver a lament that focuses not on their own fate, but that of Hector and Priam (98–164). For Hecuba, Hector's death meant the fall of Troy (129), and though Hector's death occurred before

Priam's eyes (238), father and son will have a happy reunion in the UNDERWORLD (157–64).

With Priam and Hector dead, the Greeks turn to the destruction of the rest of their family. First, the ghost of Achilles has demanded that Priam's daughter (247) be sacrificed at his grave. Achilles' son argues for the sacrifice, but he is opposed by his commanding officer, Agammemnon. Ultimately the brutal Pyrrhus wins and Polyxena will be sacrificed at his father's grave.

Next the focus turns to Astyanax, Hector's son and Priam's grandson (369). The appearance of Achilles' ghost to the Greeks is paralleled by the appearance of Hector in the dream of his wife, Andromache. Whereas Achilles' ghost demanded the blood of Hector's sister, Hector's image will urge his wife to prevent the shedding of their son's blood. Andromache prays to her dead husband to protect her and their son (501). Even in death, Hector becomes a protector of his son as Andromache hides the child in Hector's tomb. Soon, however, Ulysses arrives for Hector's son. Ulysses is well aware of the sort of warrior that Hector was and fears the sort of man Hector's son will become (535, 551). Andromache falsely tells Ulysses that Hector's son is dead (597). Eventually Ulysses sees through Andromache's deception and threatens to tear down Hector's tomb. Just as Achilles' son wanted to honor his father's grave, Andromache does not want her husband's tomb to be dishonored in this way. Furthermore, Ulysses forces Andromache to choose to protect one of two Hectors—the one buried in the tomb or the one hiding in the tomb, who is the youthful embodiment of her dead father (658–59). When Ulysses orders his men to tear down Hector's tomb, a frantic Andromache calls upon her dead husband to stop them (682, 684). Ulysses discovers the boy, however, and Andromache predicts that the walls of Troy will now witness a death even sadder than that of Hector (784).

The play concludes with the surviving women of Priam and Hector taken to the ships. Hector's mother, as Hecuba calls herself (986), will become the property of Ulysses. Soon messengers enter to relate in detail the deaths of these two young people. Hector's son leaps into the midst of his grandfather's kingdom (1103) from the same tower on which his grandfather used to hold him in his arms and gaze on the efforts of his father in battle (1168–1174). As the scene of Astyanax's death is closely linked with the royal splendor of his dead grandfather and the military prowess of his dead father, Polyxena's death is the result of the dead Achilles' ability to influence the living. As does her nephew, Astyanax, Polyxena bravely faces death. After Hecuba hears the report of the deaths of her grandson and daughter, she marvels that she herself has not yet died, although she had often stood close to Priam (1177).

BIBLIOGRAPHY

Ahl, F. *Trojan Women*. Ithaca, N.Y.: Cornell University Press, 1986.

TROPHONIUS

An ORACLE of Trophonius, a local Greek hero in the region of BOEOTIA, existed in the Lebadeia (near THEBES). In EURIPIDES' *ION*, XUTHUS consults this oracle on his way to DELPHI. Consultation of this oracle entailed a descent underground, and in ARISTOPHANES' *CLOUDS* STREPSIADES compares his entrance into SOCRATES' school to the descent. Several Greek comic poets wrote plays entitled *Trophonius*. The fragments of Cratinus' *Trophonius* hint that some consultation of Trophonius' oracle took place in the play (fragments 218–25 Kock 1). The fragments from the *Trophonius* of Aristophanes' younger contemporary, Cephisodorus (fragments 3–4 Kock 1), preserve a conversation between a master and a slave named Xanthias about the anointing of the master's body and three lines about some elegant sandals. Among the fragments (236–38 Kock 2) of Alexis' *Trophonius* we find reference to a parasite named Moschion and a command to some men to remove their clothing. Among the fragments (397–98 Körte) of Menander's *Trophonius* are preserved several lines of a conversation about the relationship of the dinner menu to the nationality of the guest. [ANCIENT SOURCES: Aristophanes, *Clouds* 508; Euripides, *Ion* 300, 393, 405; Pausanias, 8.10.2, 9.11.1, 9.37.4–7, 9.39.1–9.40.2]

BIBLIOGRAPHY

Betz, H. D. "The Problem of Apocalyptic Genre in Greek and Hellenistic Literature: The Case of the Oracle of Trophonius, I." In *Gesammelte Aufsätze*. I, *Hellenismus und Urchristentum*. Tübingen, Ger.: Mohr, 1990, 184–208.

Clark, R. J. "Trophonius: The Manner of His Revelation," *Transactions and Proceedings of the American Philological Association* 99 (1968): 63–75.

Kock, T. *Comicorum Atticorum Fragmenta*. Vol. 1. Leipzig: Teubner, 1880.

———. *Comicorum Atticorum Fragmenta*. Vol. 2. Leipzig: Teubner, 1884.

Körte, A., and A. Thierfelder. *Menandri Quae Supersunt*. Vol. 2, 2d ed. Leipzig: Teubner, 1959.

TROY

Located in what is today the northwest corner of Turkey, Troy (also called ILIUM or ILION) was the site of the famous Trojan War and the home of numerous figures of classical drama, such as ANDROMACHE, CASSANDRA, HECABE, HECTOR, HESIONE, PARIS, and PRIAM. Troy is also the setting for five extant dramas—SOPHOCLES' *AJAX*, EURIPIDES' *HECABE*, *RHESUS*, and *TROJAN WOMEN*; and SENECA'S *TROJAN WOMEN*—but would have been the setting for many other dramas that have not survived.

TRUCULENTUS PLAUTUS (CA. 190–189 B.C.E.)

The play's date cannot be established with certainty. The author of the Greek original for *Truculentus* is not known. The play's setting is ATHENS, and the action takes place before two houses: that of Phronesium ("wisdom"), a PROSTITUTE, and that of Strabax's father, who is not named in the play. The 20-line prologue is delivered by an unnamed character, who informs the audience that Phronesium has pretended to give birth to the son of a certain soldier, Stratophanes of Babylon.

After the prologue, Diniarchus enters and gives a long speech about the difficulties of being in love. In particular, he focuses on the financial hardships of loving a prostitute. Diniarchus complains that when Phronesium found someone (the soldier) from whom she could gain more wealth, she forgot about him. Diniarchus' speech is cut short when he sees Phronesium's maidservant, Astaphium. After eavesdropping on her conversation and hearing that she is going to take a man to the house, Diniarchus approaches Astaphium and asks where she is going. She tells him that she is going to take a midwife named Archillis to the house. Diniarchus says that he heard her mention a man and wants to know who it is. Astaphium initially refuses to tell him but eventually admits that the soldier is said to be on his way to the house. Astaphium, however, does allow Diniarchus to enter and visit Phronesium, who she claims, still cares for him.

After Diniarchus enters Phronesium's house, Astaphium informs the audience that Phronesium really does not care for him any longer, and that he has already lost all his money after promising his fortune to Phronesium in exchange for her sexual favors. Astaphium also states that prostitutes must always be on the lookout for generous new clients and notes that their young neighbor, Strabax, is such a man, but that the young man's slave (Truculentus) always tries to keep anyone from Phronesium's house away from their own house. Truculentus himself then arrives from Strabax's house and encounters Astaphium, who says she wants to speak with the women of the house. Truculentus tells Astaphium that no women live at the house and tries to drive her away, because he knows that Strabax has visited Phronesium's house. Astaphium, however, lies, telling him she does not know Strabax. After further comments criticizing Astaphium and those of Phronesium's house, Truculentus says he will go to the FORUM to find Strabax's father and tell him what is going on.

In the next scene Diniarchus enters from Phronesium's house and complains that he has not seen Phronesium because she has not yet returned from her bath. Diniarchus realizes that Phronesium is interested in the soldier now. His complaints are interrupted by the arrival of Phronesium, who greets him in a flattering manner and invites him to dinner. Diniarchus realizes that Phronesium is toying with him and slyly inquires about her new baby. Phronesium admits that the baby is fictitious and tells Diniarchus that once she has obtained what she wants from the soldier, she will figure out a way to get rid of him so she and Diniarchus can be together. Diniarchus is delighted by this idea, and when Phronesium asks him for a present, he says he will send over one of his servants with the gift. After Phronesium exits into her house, Diniarchus sets out to arrange for her present.

Some time later, Phronesium emerges from her house, dressed as if she has recently given birth. She reclines on a couch and prepares for the arrival of the soldier. Soon Stratophanes enters, boasting of his valor. Astaphium, who attends Phronesium, converses with the soldier about the newborn son. Stratophanes gives Phronesium two captive women, a fine purple cloak, and Arabian balsam. When Phronesium pretends the gifts do not please her, Stratophanes is troubled and decides to leave. When he sees Diniarchus' slave, Cyamus, who is approaching with all sorts of gifts and food, Stratophanes decides to watch and find out what is happening. When Cyamus approaches Phronesium and offers her the presents, she praises them and Diniarchus. Phronesium knows that Stratophanes is watching her and deliberately speaks loudly enough for the soldier to hear. Eventually Stratophanes charges forward and demands to know what Phronesium is doing. Cyamus advances to intervene and he and the soldier almost come to blows. Soon Cyamus surrenders and exits. Phronesium reenters her house, while an angry Stratophanes predicts that after a few days she will change her mind about him.

The third act opens with the arrival of Strabax, who has just returned from performing an errand for his father. In the course of these activities, Strabax was approached by a man who owed some money to his father. Strabax took the money and now states that he will give it to Phronesium. When he knocks on her door, Astaphium quickly admits him to the house. Next Truculentus enters, worried that Strabax has not returned from the farm. He also worries that Strabax has entered Phronesium's house. When Truculentus sees Astaphium emerge from the house, he approaches her in a friendly fashion and offers her money in exchange for a night with her. A surprised Astaphium invites Truculentus into Phronesium's house, but Truculentus says he wants to stay outside and wait for Strabax to return. When Astaphium tells Truculentus that Strabax is inside Phronesium's house, Truculentus is enraged, but Astaphium manages to persuade him to enter Phronesium's house.

In the fourth act Diniarchus enters and expresses delight over the news that Phronesium is pleased with his gifts and rejects those of the soldier. Astaphium returns outside and sees Diniarchus, who wants to know whom Phronesium has in the house. When Astaphium informs him that Strabax, who is Phronesium's favorite, is inside, Diniarchus laments that his presents have gained him nothing in return. Astaphium, however, has little sympathy for Diniarchus and drives him away from Phronesium's door. Astaphium departs, but Diniarchus remains before the house and complains about Phronesium and her treatment of him. Diniarchus' tirade is cut short, however, by the arrival of the aged Callicles, an Athenian gentleman who was to have become Diniarchus' father-in-law. When Diniarchus sees Callicles, he fears his affair with Phronesium has been discovered.

As Diniarchus hides in fear, Callicles, accompanied by two women (one a maidservant, the other a hairdresser), approaches Phronesium's house and demands to know what happened to the son to whom his daughter gave birth. The maidservant claims Callicles' daughter gave the boy to her and that she then gave the child to the hairdresser. The hairdresser says that she gave the child to her mistress (Phronesium), who pretended that the child was her own. The maidservant also notes that the child's father sexually assaulted Callicles' daughter. When Callicles demands to know who the man was, the maidservant points to Diniarchus. Hearing this, Diniarchus emerges from his hiding place, begs for Callicles' mercy, and asks to marry Callicles' daughter. Callicles wants to take Diniarchus to court but decides to subtract the financial penalty from his daughter's dowry. Before Callicles exits, he demands that Diniarchus retrieve his son from Phronesium's house. As Diniarchus approaches Phronesium's house, she emerges because she has heard from her hairdresser that the child was Diniarchus' son. Diniarchus goes to meet her and demands his son be handed over. When Phronesium begs to keep the child for a few more days so that she can continue to trick the soldier, Diniarchus foolishly agrees because her feminine charms have softened his anger. After Diniarchus leaves, Phronesium admits that she is fond of the soldier but that she wants to get all the money she can from him.

The play's final act opens with the arrival of the soldier, who approaches with money in hand to win over Phronesium. The prostitute feigns reluctance and complains about all the expenses involved in raising a child. The soldier promises he will do everything he

can and tries to kiss her. As Stratophanes does this, Strabax arrives from Phronesium's house. When Stratophanes demands to know the man's identity, Phronesium claims she cares for Strabax more than she cares for him and starts to embrace Strabax. An infuriated Stratophanes draws his sword and threatens Strabax, who is not particularly troubled by the soldier's hostile actions. Finally when Stratophanes hands Phronesium his entire money belt, she agrees to allow him to enter her house—but she also invites Strabax. Stratophanes is angry, but Phronesium tells him that she wants the rest of Strabax's money. After both men enter the house, Phronesium congratulates herself on how she has managed the situation and the play ends.

COMMENTARY

Although Cicero, in his treatise *On Old Age* (section 50), says that *Truculentus* was one of Plautus' favorite plays, *Truculentus* has not attracted much attention from modern scholars or readers. The creation of humor from a grumpy character was successfully exploited by Plautus in POT OF GOLD and has remained successful in modern times. In *Truculentus,* however, the character of the grumpy slave is not especially well integrated into the play. Truculentus' indication that he will get Strabax's father remains unfulfilled, and we are ill-prepared for Truculentus' change of attitude and desire to enter the house of Phronesium with Astaphium. Indeed, the role of Truculentus seems an intrusion in the play. Truculentus is onstage for less than one-tenth of play and has no effect on its outcome. Truculentus' presence is mainly a comic diversion from the otherwise dominating presence of Phronesium, around whom the play's action revolves.

Duckworth regarded *Truculentus* as a play that focuses on character and customs and grouped it with Plautus' *Pot of Gold,* STICHUS, and THREE-DOLLAR DAY and TERENCE's BROTHERS. The character and customs focused on in *Truculentus,* however, are not those of the title character, but those of the prostitute, Phronesium, and her effect on her three suitors (compare a similar situation in in Plautus' COMEDY OF ASSES). Duckworth notes that some critics have found the play a clever, cynical satire of "an unpleasant aspect of ancient society." Others consider *Truculentus* rather depressing, and

Duckworth writes that the play "is primarily concerned with the delineation of characters who are unattractive and unsympathetic, and presents a serious and rather sordid picture of the life of a courtesan and her treatment of three foolish rivals for her favor." Even Harsh, who admired the play for its stark realism, noted that "few tragedies are so depressing" as *Truculentus*. Unlike in other Plautine plays, such as ROPE, in which a prostitute is eventually discovered to be a freeborn woman and then marries a freeborn nobleman, Phronesium remains a prostitute at the end and has no intention of marrying anyone. She will remain a prostitute and continue to bilk foolish men out of their money. As Konstan writes, Phronesium's "overriding preoccupation is with cash" (147). As *Truculentus* concludes, all three of Phronesium's lovers remain interested in her affections.

Thus, *Truculentus* is a play about manipulation and exchange between men and women. It is worth noting that the Latin word for "please" (*amabo*), which literally means "I shall love," occurs more often in *Truculentus* than in any other Roman COMEDY. With one exception, we find this verb on the lips of either Astaphium or Phronesium as they try to persuade the men play to yield to their will. What the leading women (Phronesium and Astaphium) in Plautus' *Truculentus* have to exchange are sexual favors, and in exchange for these favors they want men to give them items of tangible value. Nouns denoting gift and verbs of giving are especially common in *Truculentus,* as Phronesium manipulates her suitors to give her gifts and they vie with each other to give her presents that will win her. Phronesium's skills in manipulation recall those of MEDEA in EURIPIDES' play. Just as in Euripides' play Medea manipulates three men, CREON, AEGEUS, and JASON, to grant her various favors so that she can accomplish her plan, Plautus' Phronesium manipulates three men to enhance her wealth. Just as Medea manipulated Euripides' Aegeus with the lure of a child who has yet to be born, Phronesium manipulates Stratophanes with a fictitious child and then uses the real child of another lover, Diniarchus, to continue her manipulation of Stratophanes so that she can gain mastery over "everything he owns" (400). As Medea's ruthlessness leads her to use her children to deliver the poisoned gifts that destroy her rival for Jason's love,

Phronesium displays extreme callousness toward her borrowed child. At one point, Phronesium orders her maidservants to make sure that the borrowed child is fed because the child's death would ruin her scheme against Stratophanes (456). Indeed, Phronesium's fictitious pregnancy and her use of one lover's child (even with the knowledge of the child's father) to manipulate another lover seem extremely distasteful and comparable with Saturio's sale of his own daughter in Plautus' PERSIAN. Although the audience do not know how Phronesium will rid herself of this child, one could well imagine that after she has what she wants from Stratophanes she will pretend that the child has died.

Although Phronesium bears some resemblance to Medea, Harsh compared her to CIRCE, who turned ODYSSEUS' men into pigs. Part of Circe's power over men appears to have been predicated on their entering her house. With the exception of Plautus' *Pot of Gold* and BRAGGART WARRIOR (a much longer play than *Truculentus*), *Truculentus* has more references to going inside a house than any other Roman comedy. Indeed, the goal of Phronesium's three suitors is to enter her house, while keeping other suitors out. In *Truculentus,* the suitors fail to achieve this aim. Even Truculentus, whose mission in life is to keep people from Phronesium's house out of Strabax's house, leaves his post and enters Phronesium's house. Phronesium and Astaphium's goal is to keep as many men as possible in their house, while not allowing the men who are inside to take what other men have given (cf. lines 95–111). Although Strabax's house is also visible to the audience, the house seems almost nonexistent and by the end of *Truculentus* Strabax's house is essentially empty, as Stratophanes, Strabax, and Strabax's slave, Truculentus, have all been lured into Phronesium's house and are under the control of Phronesium and Astaphium, the two comic Circes. Unlike in the case of Odysseus' men and Circe, those who have entered the house of Phronesium do not have an Odysseus to rescue them from her clutches and restore them to their human state. The men who enter Phronesium's house remain in her control when the play concludes. Even Diniarchus, who does not enter Phronesium's house and is to marry another, declares with his final words that he will go to her when he has the chance (883). Indeed, the total and utter defeat of the men in *Truculentus* makes this a bleak play. Perhaps if the play is read as either the willingness of men to give up everything they have to acquire wisdom, the meaning of Phronesium's name, or the triumph of wisdom over ignorance, some redeeming quality in the play might be found. As it stands, however, even if one accepts *Truculentus* as biting satire and exultant comedy, as Konstan does (164), the Circe-like Phronesium maintains firm control over the men who have fallen into her orbit. They have been transformed into her pigs, and rescue does not appear to be forthcoming.

BIBLIOGRAPHY

Broccia, G. "Appunti sull'ultimo Plauto: Per l'interpretazione del Truculentus," *Wiener Studien* 16 (1982): 149–64.

Dessen, C. S. "Plautus' Satiric Comedy: The Truculentus," *Philological Quarterly* 56 (1977): 145–68.

Duckworth, G. *The Nature of Roman Comedy.* Princeton, N.J.: Princeton University Press, 1952, 145.

Grimal P. "Le Truculentus de Plaute et l'esthétique de la palliata," *Dioniso* 45 (1971–74): 532–43.

Harsh, P. W. *A Handbook of Classical Drama.* Stanford, Calif.: Stanford University Press, 1944, 373.

Konstan, D. "Truculentus: Satiric Comedy." In *Roman Comedy.* Ithaca, N.Y.: Cornell University Press, 1983, 142–64.

Kruse K. H. *Kommentar zu Plautus Truculentus.* Ph.D. dissertation, Heidelberg, 1974.

Lefèvre, E. "Truculentus oder Der Triumph der Weisheit." In *Plautus Barbarus: Sechs Kapitel zur Originalität des Plautus.* Edited by E. Lefèvre et al. Tübingen, Ger.: Narr, 1991, 175–200.

Musso, O. "Sulla Datazione del Truculentus di Plauto," *Studi Italiani di Filologia Classica* 41 (1969): 135–38.

TRYGAEUS   The hero of ARISTOPHANES' *PEACE*, Trygaeus ("harvester of grapes"), when compared with other Aristophanic heroes, is most similar to DICAEOPOLIS of *ACHARNIANS*. Both men are from the Athenian countryside and seek peace from the Athenians' war with SPARTA. Trygaeus' plan of flying to heaven on a dung beetle to take the goddess Peace back to Earth is far more fantastic than the peace treaty that Dicaeopolis makes. Additionally, Trygaeus' plan creates peace for all Greeks, not for him only as Dicaeopolis' does. In this respect Trygaeus anticipates Aristophanes' heroine, LYSISTRATA, who also orchestrates a peace for all Greeks.

As does Dicaeopolis', Trygaeus' peace causes changes in the Athenian economy: Dicaeopolis' peace allows him to trade with persons formerly banned from Athenian markets; Trygaeus' poses challenges for those who have been profiting from the war. Eventually, however, as do most Aristophanic heroes, Trygaeus overcomes all the obstacles to his reforms. At the play's conclusion, Trygaeus enters into a sacred marriage with Opôra (compare PEISETAERUS and Basilea in *BIRDS*), who personifies the harvest season.

TULLIA   The daughter of the Roman king Servius Tullius, Tullia was married to Aruns Tarquinius. She entered into a plot with Aruns' brother, Lucius, to murder Lucius' wife (Tullia's sister of the same name), Aruns, and Servius Tullius. After this, Lucius would become king of Rome and Tullia would marry him and become queen. After the murders, Tullia drove a chariot over her father's corpse. Aruns' brother became king (Rome's last) and was known by the name Tarquinius Superbus. When Tarquinius Superbus was overthrown, Tullia escaped from the palace and wherever she went people cursed her. [ANCIENT SOURCES: Seneca, *Octavia* 304; Livy, 1.46–48, 59]

TUTOR   A character in classical drama who would have overseen a person's education as a youth and would have continued as an adviser to a person who had reached maturity. In EURIPIDES' plays, the tutor of JASON and MEDEA's sons appears in the prologue of *MEDEA*. In Euripides' *ION*, the tutor of CREUSA's father, ERECHTHEUS, accompanies Creusa to DELPHI and attempts to carry out Creusa's plot to poison ION. In EURIPIDES' *PHOENICIAN WOMEN*, ANTIGONE's tutor informs her about the warriors who are approaching THEBES. In SOPHOCLES' *ELECTRA*, ORESTES' tutor helps him plot against AEGISTHUS and CLYTEMNESTRA. COMEDY had its tutors as well, such as Lydus in PLAUTUS' *BACCHIDES*, who warns his young charge about associating with prostitutes.

THE TWO BACCHISES   See *BACCHIDES*.

TYCHE   A Greek word with a wide range of meanings, among which are "fortune," "chance," and "fate."

Of course, a person's fortune can be good or bad, and *tyche* is that element in the universe that allows people to have good fortune or bad fortune. Thus, *tyche* is beyond human control. In SOPHOCLES' OEDIPUS TYRANNOS, line 776, OEDIPUS indicates that *tyche* caused a drunken person at a party to question whether POLYBUS was really Oedipus' father. In EURIPIDES' ION, at lines 1512–15, the title character, whose mother tried to kill him and when he had threatened to kill before he discovered that she was his mother, marvels that *tyche* can change the lot of mortals from grievous to joyous. In Euripides' MEDEA, line 671, AEGEUS says that he and his wife are childless because of the *tyche* of some god. Sometimes *tyche* is personified as a goddess; in MENANDER's *Shield*, Tyche delivers a delayed PROLOGUE. Tyche's Roman counterpart is Fortuna.

TYDEUS The son of OENEUS, Tydeus was the brother of MELEAGER and DEIANEIRA. After killing one of his relatives, Tydeus went into exile from his native CALYDON and traveled to ARGOS, where he took asylum with King ADRASTUS. When Adrastus wondered to whom he should marry his daughters, he consulted the DELPHIC ORACLE, who told him to yoke his daughters to a lion and a boar. When Adrastus returned from Delphi, he saw Tydeus and POLYNEICES quarreling. When Adrastus noticed Tydeus' shield bore the image of a boar and Polyneices' shield had the image of a lion, he married his daughters to them. Not long afterward, Tydeus aided Polyneices in his quest to regain the throne of THEBES and Tydeus became one of the Seven against Thebes. In the battle the Theban MELANIPPUS wounded Tydeus. When Melanippus was killed, the wounded Tydeus was given the chance to have some measure of revenge against his enemy by eating Melanippus' brain. Just as Tydeus was doing this, the goddess ATHENA was on her way to make Tydeus immortal. When Athena saw Tydeus eating Melanippus' brain, the disgusted goddess withheld the gift of immortality and allowed Tydeus to die. By Adrastus' daughter, Tydeus became the father of DIOMEDES, who fought in the Trojan War and in the war against Thebes waged by the sons of the Seven. The Greek tragedian Theodectas wrote a *Tydeus,* of which only the title survives (fragment 5a Snell). [ANCIENT SOURCES: Aeschylus, *Seven against Thebes* 377, 380, 407, 571; Apollodorus, *Library* 1.8.4–5, 3.6.1–8; Euripides, *Phoenician Women* 134, 419, 428, 1120, 1144, 1165, *Suppliant Women* 136, 144, 148, 901, 1208; Homer, *Iliad* 4.376–98; Hyginus, *Fables* 69–71a; Sophocles, *Oedipus at Colonus* 1316]

BIBLIOGRAPHY
Snell, B. *Tragicorum Graecorum Fragmenta.* Vol. 1. Göttingen, Ger.: Vandenhoeck & Ruprecht, 1971.

TYMPANUM A small handheld drum that resembles a tambourine. The tympanum is especially associated with the worship of DIONYSUS and RHEA. According to legend, the sounds of the tympanum were used by those who watched over the infant ZEUS to conceal his wailing. The drum was then passed on to Rhea, who not only used it in her worship, but also seems to have shared the instrument with Dionysus and his worshipers. [ANCIENT SOURCES: Euripides, *Bacchae* 59, 120–34, *Cyclops* 65, 205, *Heracles* 892; Herodotus, 4.76; Plautus, *Carthaginian* 1317; Seneca, *Hercules Furens* 470]

TYNDAREUS The son of Oebalus (or Perieres) and PERSEUS' daughter, Gorgophone (or the NAIAD Bateia), Tyndareus was the husband of LEDA and the king of SPARTA. Tyndareus and Leda raised four children, CASTOR, POLYDEUCES, HELEN, and CLYTEMNESTRA. Polydeuces and Helen were the children of Zeus and Leda; Castor and Clytemnestra were the children of Tyndareus and Leda. When Helen grew up and numerous suitors arrived in Sparta asking for her hand in marriage, Tyndareus was afraid of offending any of the powerful nobles. Before giving Helen away, Tyndareus made Helen's suitors swear an oath (later known as the oath of Tyndareus) that they would go to the defense of Helen and her husband if anything ever happened to Helen. After Helen's suitors took the oath, Tyndareus married Helen to MENELAUS. When PARIS abducted Helen, her former suitors led the expedition against Troy.

Although Tyndareus is mentioned numerous times in extant drama, he appears as a character only in EURIPIDES' ORESTES. In this play he condemns ORESTES' killing of Clytemnestra and warns Menelaus not to help Orestes. Euripides also portrays Tyndareus as having little remorse for the death of Clytemnestra. In the assembly in which Orestes and Electra are condemned to die, a pawn of Tyndareus' delivers the speech that persuades the assembly to vote for their condemnation. SOPHOCLES wrote a *Tyndareus,* whose several surviving lines provide no information about the play's plot. The Greek tragedian Nicomachus also wrote a *Tyndareus,* of which only the title survives.

BIBLIOGRAPHY
Kiso, A. The Lost Sophocles. New York: Vantage Press, 1984.
Lloyd-Jones, H. *Sophocles: Fragments.* Cambridge, Mass.: Harvard University Press, 1996.
Radt, S. *Tragicorum Graecorum Fragmenta.* Vol. 4. Göttingen, Ger.: Vandenhoeck & Ruprecht, 1977.
Sutton, D. F. *The Lost Sophocles.* Lanham, Md.: University Press of America, 1984.

TYNDARIDAE   Another name for CASTOR and POLLUX, which means "the sons of TYNDAREUS." [ANCIENT SOURCES: Aristophanes, *Lysistrata* 1301; Seneca, *Hercules Furens* 14, 552]

TYNDARIS   A name that means "the daughter of TYNDAREUS," which some playwrights, especially EURIPIDES, sometimes use to refer to either HELEN or occasionally her sister, CLYTEMNESTRA.

TYPHO   Also known as Typhon, Typho was the child of Typhoeus, who was the son of HERA or Tartarus and Mother EARTH. By Echidna, Typho became the father of the CERBERUS, the CHIMAERA, the Hydra of LERNA, the dog Orthus, and the SPHINX. Typho, the embodiment of a hurricane, was a giant creature that had the wings of an eagle, the head and upper torso of a man, and the lower body of a serpent. When Typho attacked the gods, ZEUS blasted him with a lightning bolt and threw an island (either SICILY or Inarime) onto him. Some ancient sources do not distinguish between Typho and Typhoeus, but in those who do Typhoeus is associated with winds, battles with and is defeated by Zeus, and is buried beneath Sicily (Mount AETNA). [ANCIENT SOURCES: Aeschylus, *Prometheus Bound* 354, 370, *Seven against Thebes* 493, 511, 518, *Suppliant Women* 560; Aristophanes, *Clouds* 336, *Knights* 511;

Euripides, *Heracles* 1272; Herodotus, 3.5.2; Hesiod, *Theogony* 821, 869; Homer, *Iliad* 2.782; Seneca, *Hercules Oetaeus* 1155, 1733, *Medea* 773, *Octavia* 238, *Thyestes* 809]

TYPHOEUS   See TYPHO.

TYPHON   Another name for TYPHO.

TYRANNOS   A word meaning "absolute ruler," *tyrannos* (plural: *tyrannoi*) appears in the title of SOPHOCLES' *OEDIPUS TYRANNOS.* A *tyrannos* was someone whose rule was not limited by a constitution or laws. Whereas our modern understanding of the words *tyrant* and *tyranny* has a negative connotation, this is not always the case in ancient Greek literature. Sometimes playwrights use *tyrannos* as a synonym for *king.* In EURIPIDES' *HELEN,* line 4, the Egyptian king Proteus is called a *tyrannos,* but nothing negative is said about him. In general, however, when the Greek playwrights use the words *tyrannos* and *tyrannis* (absolute ruler), they do so with a negative connotation. The word *tyrannos* is negatively applied even to ZEUS many times in AESCHYLUS' *PROMETHEUS BOUND.* In writing about mortals, Greek dramatists often apply the term *tyrannos* to non-Athenian rulers, such as EURYSTHEUS, PRIAM, and the king of Persia. The Athenians themselves had at times been ruled by tyrants, but the last of these had been driven out at the end of the sixth century B.C.E., and in the following century, when most surviving Greek plays appear, ATHENS was a democracy. Thus, it is not surprising that to the Athenians of the fifth century, the word *tyrannos* had a negative connotation.

TYRE   A Phoenician town on the coast of the eastern Mediterranean. The people of Tyre are called Tyrians. CADMUS is often associated with Tyre and its neighboring city of SIDON. The CHORUS in EURIPIDES' *PHOENICIAN WOMEN* speak of being from Tyre.

TYRO   The daughter of SALMONEUS and Alcidice, Tyro married her paternal uncle, CRETHEUS, by whom she became the mother of Aeson, Amythaon, and PHERES. POSEIDON fell in love with Tyro; disguised as the Enipeus River, with whom Tyro was in love, the god impregnated her. After giving birth to twins, Neleus and Pelias, she exposed the boys, but a shepherd rescued and raised them. When Salmoneus discovered that Tyro had given birth, he considered her at fault. To make matters worse, Tyro's stepmother, Sidero, treated her badly. When Neleus and Pelias grew up, they learned the truth about their birth and the abuse of Sidero. Therefore, they saved Tyro and took vengeance on Sidero by killing her. Pelias killed Sidero as she took refuge at HERA's altar, an act that caused Hera to hate Tyro.

SOPHOCLES is said to have written two plays entitled *Tyro*. Lloyd-Jones (313) thinks that the second *Tyro* was a revision of the first, and that the second play was produced before ARISTOPHANES' *BIRDS*, in which the play is quoted. In *Poetics*, ARISTOTLE appears to refer to Sophocles' *Tyro* as an example of a play in which recognition occurs by means of tokens; in the case of *Tyro*, the title character's children apparently were recognized by means of the small boat in which they were exposed. [ANCIENT SOURCES: Apollodorus, *Library* 1.9.7; Aristotle, *Poetics* 1454b25; Diodorus Siculus, 4.68; Homer, *Odyssey* 2.120, 11.235; Hyginus, *Fables* 60, 239, 254; Lucian, *Timon or Misanthrope* 2; Propertius, 1.13.21; Strabo, 8.3.33; Virgil, *Aeneid* 6.585]

BIBLIOGRAPHY

Kiso, A. "*Tyro*: Sophocles' Lost Play." In *Studies in Honour of T. B. L. Webster*. Edited by J. H. Betts, J. T. Hooker, and J. R. Green. Bristol, U.K.: Bristol Classical Press, 1986. 161–69.
Magistrini, S. "La/e perduta/e *Tyro* di Sofocle," *Dioniso* 56 (1986): 65–86.
Martino, G. "La Tyro e l'Elettra di Sofocle: Due tragedie a lieto fine?" *La parola del passato* 51 (1996 51): 198–212.

TYRRHENIANS The Greek name for the Etruscans, a race who inhabited Italy. The Greeks associated the Tyrrhenians with the invention of the trumpet. DIONYSUS was said to have been abducted by Tyrrhenian pirates. The monster SCYLLA is also called Tyrrhenian. The Greek comic poet Antiphanes wrote a *Tyrrhenian*, from which two fragments survive (210–11 Kock). The first deals with virtue; the second with a man from the DEME of Halae. Another Greek comic poet, Axionicus, also wrote a *Tyrrhenian*, which has two surviving fragments (1–2 Kock); the first describes a prodigal named Pythodelus; the second, a PARASITE named Gryllion. [ANCIENT SOURCES: Euripides, *Children of Heracles* 830, *Cyclops* 11, *Medea* 1342]

BIBLIOGRAPHY

Kock, T. *Comicorum Atticorum Fragmenta*. Vol. 2. Leipzig: Teubner, 1884.

U

ULYSSES See ODYSSEUS.

UNDERWORLD According to most ancient Greeks and Romans, when a human being died, the spirit descended to the underworld, a region below the Earth. In classical drama, the playwrights use seveal different names to refer to the underworld: HADES (the same name as the divinity who rules over the underworld), the house of Hades, or the house of Pluto (another name for the god Hades). Sometimes the underworld is called Erebus or Tartarus; on occasion the name ACHERON (also the name of a body of water in the underworld) is synonymous with the underworld. The Romans also called the underworld Orcus.

In addition to the Acheron, several bodies of water were said to be in the underworld, such as the COCYTUS, LETHE, PHLEGETHON, and STYX. When a person's spirit reached the underworld, it had to be taken across one of these bodies of water. Ancient sources differ on which body this was, but usually the Acheron or Styx are named. At the banks of this water, a rough-looking sailor, CHARON, waited with a small boat to ferry spirits across. The Greeks and Romans buried people with coins in the mouth so that they could pay Charon for his service. In ARISTOPHANES' *FROGS,* when DIONYSUS enters the underworld, he pays Charon two OBOLS.

Once across the water, the spirit went to one of three judges, MINOS, RHADAMANTHYS, or AEACUS. After judgment, the spirit was assigned to a region of the underworld. One region was assigned for eternal punishment, one for eternal reward. Various horrible punishments are known for the most wicked persons. IXION was bound to an ever-spinning wheel throughout eternity; SISYPHUS had to push a stone up a hill only to have it roll back again; TITYUS had his liver pecked out by vultures every day; the DANAIDS had to transport vessels of water that had holes in them. TANTALUS was fixed in a pool whose waters always receded when he tried to drink; nearby was a tree whose fruit was always blown out of grasp when he tried to reach for it.

As for those who escaped punishment, these spirits resided in the Elysian Fields. Some writers mention a place called the ISLAND OF THE BLESSED as a place inhabited by a select few heroes (such as MENELAUS) after death. Other sources mention a fabulous White Island (Leuce), where persons such as HELEN and ACHILLES went after their life had ended. In *Odyssey,* however, HOMER places ACHILLES in the underworld with the rest of the spirits and Achilles tells ODYSSEUS that he would rather be the servant of a poor farmer on Earth than the ruler of the underworld.

Several ancient heroes traveled to and from the underworld while they were still alive, such as AENEAS, HERACLES, ODYSSEUS, ORPHEUS, and THESEUS and PIRITHOUS. Aeneas and Odysseus went to learn about their respective futures; Orpheus tried (unsuccessfully) to retrieve his deceased wife; Theseus and Pirithous tried (unsuccessfully) to arrange for Pirithous to marry Hades' wife, PERSEPHONE. Heracles, as his final labor for EURYSTHEUS, went to the underworld to take back CER-

BERUS, the dog that guarded the entrance and exit to the underworld. While in the upper world, Heracles also wrestled (successfully) THANATOS, the personification of death, to prevent him from taking ALCESTIS to the underworld.

In classical drama, the underworld is the setting for most of ARISTOPHANES' *FROGS* and Charon, Aeacus, and Pluto (Hades) appear as characters. In several tragedies, beings from the underworld or spirits of the dead appear or are conjured. The FURIES make up the chorus of AESCHYLUS' *Eumenides* (see *ORESTEIA*). In AESCHYLUS' *PERSIANS*, the spirit of XERXES' father, DARIUS, is conjured, and in SENECA's *OEDIPUS*, the spirit of OEDIPUS' father, LAIUS, is raised. In Seneca's *AGAMEMNON*, the ghost of THYESTES appears from the underworld; in his *THYESTES*, the ghost of Tantalus and a Fury appear. [ANCIENT SOURCES: Euripides, *Alcestis, Heracles;* Hesiod, *Theogony;* Homer, *Odyssey* 11; Seneca, *Hercules Furens;* Vergil, *Aeneid* 6]

URANUS
The son of Gaia (EARTH), Uranus, whose name means "sky," also fathered numerous children by his mother: Coeus, Crius, CRONUS, Hyperion, Iapetus, OCEANUS, Mnemosyne, Phoebe, RHEA, Thea, THEMIS, Tethys, the CYCLOPES (Arges, Brontes, Steropes), and the Hecatoncheires (Briareus, Cottus, and Gyes). Uranus hated his children, and when they were born he put them back into Gaia's womb. Gaia finally retaliated and enlisted the help of her youngest son, Cronus, against Uranus. Gaia created a sharp sickle and gave it to Cronus, who then cut off his father's testicles and threw them into the sea. From the foam that surrounded Uranus' genitalia, APHRODITE was born. From the blood of Uranus' wound were born the Meliae (ash tree NYMPHS), some giants, and the FURIES. After Uranus' castration, Cronus replaced him as master of the sky and Uranus seems to have been exiled to the UNDERWORLD.

USURER
Someone who loans money to others and charges interest, a usurer (Latin: *danista*) is a stock character in New Comedy. As are PIMPS and bankers, usurers are detested characters. At *Mostellaria* (Haunted house) 657–58, PLAUTUS' Tranio calls usurers the most despicable and dishonest race on Earth. The term *danista* does not occur in TERENCE, but Plautus has two *danistae* who appear as characters. In Plautus' *Mostellaria*, Misargyrides ("son of bad silver") hopes to collect the money owed to him by Philolaches, who used it to purchase Philematium. A similar scenario occurs in Plautus' *Epidicus*, as Stratippocles borrows money from an unnamed *danista* to purchase a woman who turns out to be his sister.

V

VENETI Also called the Enetoi, this tribe, who lived on the northern shore of the Adriatic Sea, were famous for their horses. [ANCIENT SOURCES: Euripides, *Hippolytus* 231, 1131; Herodotus, 1.196; Homer, *Iliad* 2.852; Livy, 1.1, 5.33, 10.2; Polybius, 2.17; Strabo, 5.212, 12.543]

VENUS See APHRODITE.

VERSE See METER.

VICTORY See NIKE.

VIDULARIA (THE TALE OF A TRAVELING BAG) PLAUTUS (DATE UNKNOWN) Little more than 100 lines has survived from this play. The extant fragments indicate that two fishermen (one named Gorgines, the other Cacistus), two young gentlemen (one named Nicodemus), a farmer named Dinia (who is Gorgines' neighbor), an unnamed woman, a maiden named Soteris, and a PIMP were in the play's cast. The town in which the play is set is unknown, but the action probably took place before the houses of Gorgines and Dinia. At some point in the play, Dinia hired Nicodemus, who was living with Gorgines, to work on his farm. In PLAUTUS' ROPE a trunk hauled from the sea helped reunite a father and daughter; in *Vidularia*, Cacistus seems to have found a certain bag while fishing. Eventually Nicodemus

would have been discovered as the owner of the bag, and presumably its contents would have revealed that he was the son of Dinia.

BIBLIOGRAPHY

Dér, Katalin. "*Vidularia*: Outlines of a Reconstruction," *Classical Quarterly* 37 (1987): 432–43.

VIRGINIA A Roman woman, the daughter of Virginius. In the middle of the fifth century B.C.E., Virginius killed her to prevent her enslavement by Appius Claudius. Eventually Appius himself was imprisoned and in prison committed suicide. [ANCIENT SOURCES: Dionysius of Halicarnassus, 11.28–46; Livy, 3.44–58; Seneca, *Octavia* 296]

VIRGO (1) The daughter of Jove (ZEUS) and THEMIS, Virgo was originally named as Astraea (starry). When the divinities began to leave the earth because of the sins of humankind, Astraea was the last to leave. She became the constellation Virgo (maiden). [ANCIENT SOURCES: Seneca, *Thyestes* 857]

VIRGO (2) Also called a *puella* (plural: *puellae*), the *virgo* (maiden, young woman; plural: *virgines*), a freeborn unmarried young woman, is a stock character in Roman COMEDY. These women do not have extensive speaking roles, and only 10 such women appear in the list of characters in the plays of PLAUTUS (eight) and TERENCE (two). Plautus' CARTHAGINIAN and ROPE have two *puellae* in each play. In several instances, a *virgo* is present offstage but not listed in the cast of characters. Although the English word *virgin* is derived from *virgo,* sometimes a *virgo* has been sexually violated and is pregnant (e.g., Euclio's daughter in POT OF GOLD, Pamphila in Terence's BROTHERS and MOTHER-IN-LAW). The man who violated the woman eventually marries her. In some cases, the *virgo* or *puella* is the property of a PIMP, but then is discovered to be the daughter of a freeborn man and therefore freed (e.g., Planesium in CURCULIO; Hanno's daughters in CARTHAGINIAN; Palaestra in ROPE). In Terence's ANDRIA and SELF-TORMENTOR, the *virgines* are discovered to be freeborn and are reunited with their parents. The discovery of the *virgo's* freeborn status allows a young freeborn male (see ADULESCENS) to marry her. The most unusual *virgo* in surviving comedy is the unnamed maiden in Plautus' PERSIAN, who is unusual in that her father, Saturio, is a PARASITE (most *virgines* are the daughters of respectable citizens). Furthermore, she is part of a scheme to trick the pimp, Dordalus, and her father pretends to sell her and has her dress as a Persian woman. Usually in Roman comedy freeborn young women do not take such active roles in deception.

BIBLIOGRAPHY
Duckworth, G. E. *The Nature of Roman Comedy.* Princeton, N.J.: Princeton University Press, 1952, 253–54.
Lowe, J. C. B. "The *Virgo Callida* of Plautus, *Persa,*" *Classical Quarterly* 39 (1989): 390–99.
Packman, Zola M. "*Adulescens* as *Virgo:* A Note on Terence's *Eunuch* 908," *Akroterion* 42, no. 1 (1997): 30–35.

VULCAN   See HEPHAESTUS.

WASPS (Greek: *SPHEKES*; Latin: *VES-PAE*) ARISTOPHANES (422 B.C.E.)

Wasps placed second in the competition for comic poets at the LENAEA. Philonides' *Preview* (*Proagon*) took first place and Leucon's *Ambassadors* finished third. The action of *Wasps* takes place in ATHENS at the house of the elderly PHILOCLEON ("CLEON lover") and his son, BDELYCLEON ("Cleon hater"). Like do ARISTOPHANES' KNIGHTS and PEACE, the play begins at dawn with the conversation of two slaves, whose master, Bdelycleon, has stationed himself on the roof of the house. The two slaves discuss the problems that Bdelycleon has been having with his aged father, Philocleon. Philocleon is overly keen on serving on juries, and Bdelycleon has ordered the servants not to allow Philocleon out of the house. From the perspective of staging, *Wasps* is quite unusual in that when the play opens the stage building has all of its points of entrance and access blocked and covered with nets. Soon Philocleon, with incredible energy for an old man, tries various methods to escape from the house, including trying to climb out the chimney (claiming he is "smoke") and, in the manner of ODYSSEUS, trying to escape by clinging to the underbelly of a donkey.

Eventually the CHORUS, composed of old men who also serve on juries, enter to summon their companion, Philocleon, to jury duty. The chorus are dressed in costumes that make them resemble wasps, because the "sting" of jurors is formidable. When they find that Bdelycleon is preventing his father from leaving, the chorus urge Philocleon to escape from the house. Philocleon tries again to escape, but he is blocked by his son. The chorus threaten to summon their patron, CLEON, but Bdelycleon appeals to the feisty jurors to listen to his side of the issue.

After some further scuffling between the chorus and Bdelycleon and his slaves, an AGON between Philocleon and Bdelycleon occurs: Philocleon argues that his life as a juror is a glorious one and gives him power that rivals that of ZEUS himself; Bdelycleon argues that Philocleon and his juror friends are nothing more than slaves of politicians such as Cleon. Bdelycleon manages to convince both Philocleon and the chorus that they are Cleon's pawns. Furthermore Bdelycleon persuades his father to agree to stop going to town to serve on juries. Bdelycleon proposes that Philocleon instead set up a court at home and judge disputes that occur there. Philocleon agrees to this arrangement and Bdelycleon quickly takes out things that his father will need for his new "home court." The first "case" that Philocleon hears involves the theft from the kitchen of Sicilian cheese by a dog named Labes. This case parodies the actual trial of an Athenian politician named LACHES for embezzlement while he was a military commander in SICILY between 427 and 425 B.C.E. At the trial's conclusion Bdelycleon tricks his father into acquitting the dog.

After Bdelycleon and his father enter the house, the chorus deliver the PARABASIS. Here the chorus, speaking for Aristophanes, complains that the audience has not treated the playwright fairly. They complain that Aristophanes has used his plays to attack such prominent figures as Cleon and SOCRATES (in his *CLOUDS*), but that Aristophanes did not win the prize for that play despite its clever premise. The chorus then go on to explain why they are dressed as wasps. They recall that they are the men who repelled the Persian invaders many years earlier and that the same waspish nature that they exhibited then is employed in their service as jurors. They complain that "stingless drones" reap the financial rewards of jury duty but do nothing to earn their pay.

After the parabasis Philocleon and Bdelycleon emerge from the house and prepare to leave for a dinner party. Despite his father's objections, Bdelycleon dresses his father in suitable clothing and tries to school him in ways to engage in sophisticated conversation at the party. Father and son then leave for the party. After some time passes, the SLAVE, Xanthias, appears and tells the chorus about Philocleon's unsophisticated behavior at the party. Next a drunken Philocleon enters, accompanied by the nude flute girl from the party and followed by some angry party guests whom Philocleon has insulted. Bdelycleon also follows his father and accuses him of stealing the flute girl from the party. Philocleon denies this and claims that she is actually a torch (a claim that provides the opportunity for a few sexual jokes about her anatomy).

These jokes are followed by the arrival of a baking woman (accompanied by CHAEREPHON as her witness), who claims Philocleon has assaulted her. After Philocleon scorns the baking woman and Chaerephon, another complainant enters and charges Philocleon with outrage against him. Again Philocleon scoffs at the accusations and finally he is dragged inside the house by his son. After their exit, the chorus praise and marvel at Philocleon's transformation.

After the chorus' remarks, Xanthias emerges from the house and informs them that Philocleon has become more drunk and has declared that he will outdance the modern tragedians. Soon a wildly dancing Philocleon emerges from the house and challenges any tragedian to a dance competition. This challenge draws a response from three sons of the tragedian Carcinus (the sons are also tragic poets). This poet's name, which means "crab" in Greek, provides the opportunity not only for crablike dancing but also for several jokes about crabs. The play ends with Philocleon's dancing wildly in competition with Carcinus' sons.

COMMENTARY

Wasps achieved only moderate success when it was produced and has not been especially popular with modern scholars or audiences. At the least, *Wasps* is an important source of information on the workings of the Athenian courts. Although Americans are quite familiar with rampant lawsuits, the premise that a person would be overly keen on jury duty is difficult for Americans to understand because most people do everything they can to avoid jury duty. The premise that a substantial segment of a population should be loyal to a political leader by whom they are being used is easier for modern audiences to appreciate. Although the combined humor of both premises is largely lost on modern audiences, both were tried and true standards in ancient Athens. Aristophanes had attacked Cleon two years earlier in *KNIGHTS* and Athenians who constantly sat on juries were a staple of humor. In *CLOUDS*, STREPSIADES cannot recognize Athens on a map because he does not see any juries in session.

In addition to its information about the Athenian court system, *Wasps* may provide insight about rivalry between poets in antiquity. In 425 and 424, Aristophanes' *ACHARNIANS* and *Knights* had defeated the offerings of his elder rival, Cratinus. In *Knights*, Aristophanes had described Cratinus as a washed-up drunk (526–36). In 423, Cratinus' *Putine* (*Wine Flask*), which parodied Cratinus' alleged drinking problem, defeated Aristophanes' *Clouds*. In 422, in the parabasis of *Wasps*, Aristophanes complains about his audience's failure to grasp the fresh COMEDY of *Clouds* and urges them to show more appreciation to poets who have something new to say (1043–57). At the same time, Aristophanes spends much of the first part of the parabasis of *Wasps* recalling that his attacks on Cleon made him successful (1029–42).

In 422, Aristophanes hoped to return to his winning ways. To do so, he may have tried to refurbish some old approaches and ideas as well as blend the old and the new. Aristophanes' attacks on Cleon had yielded success in previous years, so in 422 he obviously decided to return to this technique. To further his chances of winning with *Wasps,* Aristophanes may also have taken a page from Cratinus' work in the previous year by transforming Cratinus' addiction to alcohol into Philocleon's undue fondness for jury service. Ironically, perhaps, Philocleon's keenness for jury service has passed and he now abuses alcohol, just as Cratinus was alleged to have. Just as the drunken old Cratinus had defeated the younger Aristophanes in 423, drunken old Philocleon uses dance steps from old dramatists to defeat the younger dramatists. Cratinus had defeated Aristophanes in 423; Aristophanes may have turned to Cratinus to help him win in 422.

Aristophanes' *Wasps* may reflect the poet's rivalry with Cratinus; however, its structure seems at odds with itself. In the first half of *Wasps,* some clear themes emerge. The contrast between freedom and slavery appears in *agon* between Philocleon and Bdelycleon, and the theme of Philocleon's sickness also stands out. After the parabasis, however, the play moves into a series of comic routines that seemingly have little relation to the first half. Philocleon has been prevented from going to court; his son convinces him that he is a pawn of Cleon; he has been tricked into acquitting a defendant. So far, matters have gone Bdelycleon's way. After the parabasis, however, Bdelycleon's efforts to integrate his father into polite society fail. An old man's behaving in an unsophisticated way at a dinner party of arrogant young aristocrats is a classic comic premise. The same old man's running off from the party with a sexy young woman and then scoffing at the efforts of his victims to take him to justice are also great comic fun. Finally, this old man's dance contest with people whose dance steps imitate crabs was also undoubtedly hilarious but seems to have little connection with the first half of the play.

The unity of *Wasps* may appear in the evolution of Philocleon's character as he experiences life in reverse. A young Athenian would learn how to become an adult citizen who exercises political power in a positive way. *Wasps* begins with an old citizen whose political power has become uncontrolled. Thus, his son tries to strip away this unbridled power and integrate him into the society of young men. Bdelycleon does rejuvenate

his father, who, however, remains out of control among the younger generation. As an old man, Philocleon abused the law established in the courts. As a "young man," Philocleon abuses the customs of symposium. Although Bdelycleon shows his father that he was a slave to Cleon, the liberating experience of the symposium has not proved to be a better solution for Philocleon. In the first half of the play, Philocleon declared that his "kingdom" as a juror rivaled that of Zeus himself; in the second half the drunken Philocleon has embraced the realm of Zeus' son, Dionysus. In both realms, Philocleon is out of control. The sickness that Philocleon had in the first half of the play has become a mania at its end.

BIBLIOGRAPHY

MacDowell, D. M. *Aristophanes: Wasps.* Oxford: Clarendon Press, 1971.

Olson, S. Douglas. "Politics and Poetry in Aristophanes' *Wasps,*" *Transactions of the American Philological Association* 126 (1996): 129–50.

Reckford, K. J. "Catharsis and Dream-Interpretation in Aristophanes' *Wasps,*" *Transactions of the American Philological Association* 107 (1977): 283–312.

Sidwell, Keith. "Poetic Rivalry and the Caricature of Comic Poets: Cratinus' *Pytine* and Aristophanes' *Wasps.*" In *Stage Directions: Essays in Ancient Drama in Honour of E. W. Handley.* Edited by A. Griffiths. *Bulletin for the Institute of Classical Studies.* Supplement 66. London: Institute of Classical Studies 1995, 56–80.

Slater, N. W. "Bringing Up Father: *Paideia* and *Ephebeia* in the *Wasps.*" In *Education in Greek Fiction.* Edited by A. H. Sommerstein and C. Atherton. Bari, Italy: Levante, 1996, 27–52.

WEALTH (Greek: *PLOUTOS*) ARISTOPHANES (388 B.C.E.)

Wealth is ARISTOPHANES' last extant play. Both the festival at which the play appeared and the play's success there are unknown. In 408 B.C.E., Aristophanes also produced a *Wealth* whose subject matter was apparently quite different. The *Wealth* of 388 B.C.E. was produced again later with Aristophanes' own minor revisions by Aristophanes' son, Araros.

The play's setting is ATHENS, and the action takes place before the house of Chremylus, an elderly Athenian gentleman. The PROLOGUE opens with the appearance of Plutus, the blind god of wealth; Chremylus;

and his slave, Cario. Chremylus explains to Cario that he was frustrated that he had lived a virtuous life but had no riches, whereas evil people appeared to have plenty of money. Accordingly, Chremylus went to APOLLO's oracle at DELPHI to ask the god whether his (Chremylus') son should live a virtuous or evil life. The oracle told Chremylus to leave the shrine, take the first person he met back home with him, and make that person his constant friend (compare XUTHUS in EURIPIDES' *ION*). The first person whom Chremylus encountered was the blind and dirty Plutus whose name Chremylus does not yet know.

When Chremylus does learn that the blind man is the god of wealth, he is stunned that a god should appear in such a condition. Plutus explains that ZEUS made him blind so that he (Plutus) would not know whether he was blessing virtuous or evil people. Chremylus asks Plutus whether he would help the virtuous people if he could see. When Plutus says that he would, Chremylus decides to find a cure for Plutus' blindness. The god fears the punishment of Zeus, but Chremylus argues that Zeus is the ruler of the gods only because he is the richest of the gods. If Plutus wills it, he can make sure that people do not have money to pay for sacrifices to the gods. Everything in the world revolves around money, Chremylus argues, and Plutus can control the world and the gods if he acts boldly.

Thus, Chremylus sends out Cario to summon his fellow poverty-stricken farmers so that they can have a share in Plutus. After Cario exits, Chremylus takes Plutus into his house. Later Cario returns with the CHORUS, who are poor old Athenian farmers. Cario explains to them that Plutus is in Chremylus' house and that he is going to make them all wealthy. The chorus rejoice and dance with Cario in anticipation of this blessing. After Cario's exit to find his supper, Chremylus enters and welcomes the chorus. Chremylus' friend, Blepsidemus, who has heard the news that Chremylus is rich, soon joins them. Chremylus informs Blepsidemus that he also can share in the wealth, but that the plan is not yet complete. Chremylus tells Blepsidemus that they must first take Plutus to the temple of ASCLEPIUS to be cured of his blindness. After Plutus is cured, they will be rich.

Before Chremylus can exit, however, Poverty, a wild-looking woman, enters and expresses her outrage that she may be driven from the land. Blepsidemus, fearing he will be struck by Poverty, threatens to leave. Poverty argues that they will be doing a great injustice by driving her from their country because she claims she actually helps people. At this point, a debate (see AGON) occurs between Chremylus and Poverty. Chremylus argues that if Plutus regains his sight, virtuous people will receive financial rewards. Poverty counters: If good people become wealthy, then people will no longer work or be creative. When Chremylus suggests that slaves will perform work for them, Poverty retorts that slaves and the slave trade will cease to exist when slave traders have no need of money. Without slaves, Poverty responds, Chremylus' work will be twice as difficult. All the goods and products Chremylus buys will not exist, because there will be no one to make them once the good workers all have money. Poverty argues that she drives people to struggle and work, whereas Plutus allows people to become fat and lazy. Chremylus argues that Zeus himself is wealthy, but Poverty asserts that Zeus is poor because victors at the Olympic Games, held in Zeus' honor, receive only a crown of olive leaves. If Zeus were rich, winners at his games would receive a crown of gold. Chremylus, however, argues that Zeus is just hoarding his money for himself, but Poverty chastises Chremylus for suggesting that Zeus behaves in such a way. Eventually the debate ends with Chremylus' refusing to accept Poverty's logic and, with the help of Blepsidemus, driving her away. After Poverty's exit, Chremylus and Blepsidemus announce that they will take Plutus to Asclepius' temple to try to cure his blindness.

In the next scene, the audience is to imagine that a night has passed. First, Cario enters and informs the chorus that Plutus has been cured of his blindness. Chremylus' wife, hearing the celebration of the chorus, emerges from the house and is also informed of the good news in Cario's lengthy description of the healing ceremony. Cario also tells Chremylus' wife that Plutus, followed by a throng of just people, is now on his way to the house. After Chremylus' wife returns to the house to prepare gifts to welcome Plutus, the newly healed god enters, gives thanks for his sight, and promises to give wealth to good people. When Chremylus' wife enters to give the god gifts of welcome,

Plutus refuses them and states that he should be the one to give gifts.

After Chremylus, his wife, Cario, and Plutus enter the house, Cario reemerges and informs the audience of the riches and abundance that are now enjoyed in the house. Next a just man enters with a worn old cloak and a similarly worn pair of shoes. The just man tells Cario that he is going to offer these articles of clothing to Plutus in thanks for granting him wealth. Their conversation is interrupted by the arrival of an INFORMANT, who laments his situation now that Plutus has been healed. When the informant threatens to make accusations against them, Cario drives him off by wrapping him in the just man's old cloak and then tacking his old shoes to his forehead. After the departure of the informant, the just man and Cario enter Chremylus' house. Chremylus then emerges and is met by an old woman, who enters and complains that Plutus' change has caused her to lose the young male lover she had enjoyed. The young man, who had spent time with the old woman because of her riches, soon enters and, because he himself is now wealthy, scorns her. Chremylus has some sympathy for the old woman, however, and produces some measure of reconciliation between the old woman and the young man.

After Chremylus escorts the pair into his house, Cario reappears and soon encounters HERMES, who informs him that Zeus intends to punish the household because the healing of Plutus has resulted in the end of sacrifices to the gods. Hermes notes that he himself is going hungry and begs Cario for some food. Hermes even begs Cario to allow him to stay in their house and claims that he could help them in a number of ways. Eventually Cario allows Hermes to enter, although he immediately puts him to work at menial labor. After the exit of Cario and Hermes, Chremylus returns and encounters a priest of Zeus, who also complains of hunger because now no one makes sacrifices, of which the priest would get a share. The priest suggests that he desires to leave the service of Zeus and devote himself to Plutus. Chremylus, however, tells the priest that even Zeus himself is now present in the house. The play ends with Chremylus arranging a procession to take Plutus to the Athenian ACROPOLIS to establish him as guard of the city's treasury.

COMMENTARY

As in *Ecclesiazusae* of 392/391, in *Wealth* Aristophanes' attacks on and caricatures of contemporary political figures, which were very common in Aristophanes' early plays, have almost completely disappeared, and the role of the chorus has been greatly diminished. The play does not contain a PARABASIS. The expanded role of the slave, Cario, also shows similarities to the slaves one finds in the comedy of MENANDER. As they have *Ecclesiazusae,* modern scholars have described *Wealth* as a transitional play between the Old Comedy of plays such as *ACHARNIANS* and *KNIGHTS* and the New Comedy of Menander, which would emerge in the last quarter of the fourth century B.C.E. Thus, *Wealth* is sometimes considered an example of Middle Comedy.

Despite this classification, the play follows the pattern commonly found in Aristophanes' earlier plays. As in *BIRDS* of 414, in *Wealth* the hero has a fantastic plan that will ultimately have an effect on the gods. Just as PEISETAERUS' plan for a city in the clouds creates a disruption in relations between human beings and gods, Chremylus' plan does. The gods in *Birds* send representatives to strike a deal with Peisetaerus; in *Wealth* hungry Hermes, whom Zeus has sent to negotiate with Chremylus, has replaced hungry HERACLES of *Birds*. As in *Birds* (and *Acharnians*), an informant is not allowed to enjoy the benefits of the hero's fantastic plan.

As *Ecclesiazusae* does, *Wealth* deals with a revolution within the Athenian economy; those who benefit from Plutus will receive the basic comforts of life such as food, clothing, and, to some extent, the promise of sex, although this latter reward is emphasized less than it is in *Ecclesiazusae*. Both plays, however, use the humorous situation of a relationship between a young man and an old woman. In *Wealth,* the young man is the party in control; in *Ecclesiazusae* the young men seem rather helpless victims of the old women. Unlike *Ecclesiazusae,* which has numerous references to the city (*polis*) and allusions to specific problems of the distribution of wealth among people, *Wealth* contains few references to Athens itself and seems more general in its outlook. At line 461, Chremylus indicates that he is trying to do something good for all people. Also in contrast with *Ecclesiazusae,* in which virtually everyone will be included in Praxagora's reforms, in theory only the just (*dikaioi*) will enjoy the benefits of Plutus. Whereas plays such as ACHARNIANS and CLOUDS frequently refer to what is just, *Wealth* is more concerned with who is just.

Chremylus complains that he is a man who has revered the gods and who is just (28), but that he suffers and is poor. When Plutus later explains that this is so because Zeus made him blind so that he could not know which people were wise, orderly, and just (89), Chremylus responds that good and just people (94) are the only ones who worship the gods. If Chremylus can restore Plutus' sight, then Plutus promises he will visit only the just (97). Chremylus is gladdened by this response and pledges that he and other just men (219) who are like him will work to carry out this plan. The just men to whom Chremylus refers make up the chorus. Thus, although the chorus of *Wealth* are less exotic than the choruses of *Clouds* or *Wasps,* they do fit well with the play's focus on distributing wealth to the just.

Upon learning that Plutus' sight is to be restored, Poverty arrives and argues against making just men (475). Chremylus, of course, argues that it is only just that the good succeed, whereas the wicked should suffer the opposite (490–91). Poverty later counters that when the just become wealthy they no longer benefit the people or the city (568). Poverty eventually leaves amid Chremylus' curses but has made a number of valid points and Walton judges that Poverty has won the argument.

After Plutus regains his sight, Cario announces that Chremylus is returning with a happy crowd of just men (751), who were previously poor. In contrast, those who previously acquired their riches through unjust means (755) are now unhappy. As proof of the success of Chremylus' plan, a person once poor but now wealthy arrives. He is simply called Dikaios (823), Just Man, and his wealth is manifested by his new suit of clothing. The Just Man is contrasted in the arrival of the Informant, whose way of life has been ruined by Plutus' newfound sight. Ironically the Informant states that if justice still exists (859), then Plutus' blindness will return. Justice does exist, but not for the unjust, and the Informant is driven away. The line between just and unjust becomes somewhat blurred in the case of the old woman and her young lover, who has no

intention of continuing in the relationship now that Plutus has made him wealthy. The old woman complains that it would only be just for Plutus to compel the young man to treat her well again; otherwise it is unjust for the young man to experience good fortune (1028–30). Eventually, however, the old woman will have her way, and as the play ends Chremylus promises her that the young man will visit her that night (1201).

Finally, because poor, just persons have been made rich, then the previously rich must become poor. This includes the gods and their priests. This premise holds true, not surprisingly, for the priest of Zeus. Corrupt religious officials were as common in ancient society as they are in modern society. As a result of Plutus' new condition those who formerly called on the priest, such as those who had escaped justice (1181), no longer do so. The suggestion that Hermes, one of the gods, is unjust, however, seems quite bold, and interestingly the servant of the gods is called unjust by the servant of a mortal (1124). Furthermore, this same mortal servant determines the grounds on which the servant of the gods should be allowed to participate in the blessings of Plutus.

So, although Aristophanes' *Wealth* may not be as lively or humorous as Aristophanes' earlier plays, it does raise questions that continue to vex humankind: Why do the wicked prosper, while the just struggle to survive? Aristophanes creates a scenario that allows the audience to see what might happen if life worked out in the way people often expect that it should. Poverty admirably argues against such a system, but during the space of this play Aristophanes does not allow his audience to see Chremylus' plan fail.

BIBLIOGRAPHY

Sfyroeras, P. "What Wealth Has to Do with Dionysus: From Economy to Poetics in Aristophanes' *Plutus*," *Greek, Roman, and Byzantine Studies* 36, no. 3 (1995): 231–62.

Sommerstein, A. H. *The Comedies of Aristophanes.* Vol. 11, *Wealth.* Warminster, U.K.: Aris & Phillips, 2001.

Walton, J. M. *Living Greek Theatre.* New York: Greenwood Press, 1987, 218.

WOMEN   Because men played the parts of women in classical drama, any consideration of female roles in classical drama must keep this fact in mind. The activities of women in Greece and Rome were largely centered around the home. Women had no voting rights in political matters, and even appearing alone in public, much less on stage, would not have been considered appropriate behavior. Not only did women not play parts in ancient TRAGEDY or COMEDY, but some debate exists as to whether women were even allowed to attend theater productions in Greece. Women in Rome could apparently attend theater productions, but in some cases their seating was separate from the men's and on the fringes of the seating area. In both Greece and Rome, the exception to these practices would have been certain priestesses, who not only were allowed to attend theater productions, but also given preferential seating.

Regarding tragedy, with the exception of SOPHOCLES' *PHILOCTETES* and SENECA'S *THYESTES,* all the surviving plays had female characters. A little more than half of the speaking roles in the surviving tragedies, both Greek and Roman, are royal women. The most common female speaking role (22 of the 32 complete Greek tragedies) is the princess, who is the daughter of a king or former king (e.g., ANTIGONE, ISMENE, ELECTRA) or the wife of a prince (ANDROMACHE). The life of a princess in Greek tragedy is rarely happy, as she usually suffers as a result of the dominant male figure (her father and/or brother) in her life. In the case of Antigone, she commits suicide as a result of her treatment at the hands of CREON. Some princesses allow themselves to be sacrificed for the sake of their family (MACARIA) or country (IPHIGENIA). The most notable exceptions to the "suffering princess" rule are AETHRA, the mother of THESEUS, who champions the cause of the suppliant mothers in EURIPIDES' *SUPPLIANT WOMEN,* and MEDEA, who killed her father (king of COLCHIS) and brother, married JASON, and then was divorced by Jason. Medea then killed her child and the princess Jason intended to marry and escaped unscathed.

Of Sophocles' surviving plays, five of the seven have two princesses (the exceptions are *AJAX* and *PHILOCTETES*). In the three Theban plays, Antigone and Ismene are the princesses; Electra and CHRYSOTHEMIS appear in *ELECTRA,* and DEIANEIRA and IOLE appear in *TRACHINIAN WOMEN.* In the case of Antigone and Ismene

and Electra and Chrysothemis, Sophocles likes to contrast the attitude of the sisters toward the crisis that they face. Deianeira and Iole are interesting in that the former is the wife and the latter is the concubine of the same man, HERACLES. Outside those of Sophocles, only four plays have two princesses who have speaking roles: AESCHYLUS' *SEVEN AGAINST THEBES* (Antigone and Ismene) and EURIPIDES' *CHILDREN OF HERACLES* (ALCMENA, MACARIA), *TROJAN WOMEN* (CASSANDRA, Andromache), and *ORESTES* (Electra, HERMIONE). Alcmena, in *Children of Heracles,* is difficult to classify, as her age and behavior in that play make her seem queenly, but her husband, AMPHITRYON, never became king according to common tradition, although her father was a king.

With the exception of the CHORUS, the next common female speaking role (17 of the 32 complete Greek tragedies) is that of the queen, who is the wife of a king or former king (e.g., ATOSSA, HECABE, CLYTEMNESTRA). As does the princess, the queen suffers from her connection with an unfortunate male (her husband and/or son). Sometimes the queen commits suicide (JOCASTA, EURYDICE, PHAEDRA); at other she is enslaved (Hecabe). The most notorious queen in surviving tragedy is Clytemnestra, who helps kill her husband and then is killed by her son. Surely the most pitiable queen is Hecabe, who outlives her husband, sons, daughters, and grandson only to become a slave. The most noble queen and the one who experiences the most amazing reversal of fortune is ALCESTIS, who dies for her king and then is rescued from the dead.

Regarding the chorus, in 21 of the 32 complete tragedies the chorus are women. Only two of Sophocles' seven tragic choruses are female (*Trachinian Women, Electra*). Most often these choruses represent freeborn females of a particular town (e.g., Sophocles' *Trachinian Women,* the Corinthian women in Euripides' *MEDEA*) or women who are slaves (e.g., Euripides' *HECABE, Trojan Women*). In Aeschylus' *SUPPLIANT WOMEN,* the women who make up the chorus are the central focus of the play. The women of the chorus also play a prominent role and are greatly involved in the action of Aeschylus' *Eumenides* (see *ORESTEIA*) and Euripides' *BACCHAE.* In contrast to male choruses, female choruses often serve as confidantes or sympathetic allies of other women onstage (e.g., Euripides'

Ion, IPHIGENIA IN TAURIS). In some Euripidean plays, the female choruses are only loosely connected to the play's action. In *IPHIGENIA IN AULIS,* for example, the chorus go to AULIS for the purpose of watching the Greek army assemble. In two plays, Aeschylus' *PROMETHEUS BOUND* and *Eumenides* (see *ORESTEIA*), the chorus are divinities.

Two divine choruses are female, and some 14 individual female divinities have speaking roles in the extant Greek tragedies, 11 of these in Euripidean plays. Not surprisingly, ATHENA makes half of these appearances, in tragedies written by Athenian playwrights for Athenian audiences. Most often the divine female appears at the play's conclusion to lead the play to a resolution. In Euripides' *Heracles,* Iris and Madness appear in the middle of the play to cause disaster as Madness will cause Heracles to kill his wife and children. In Euripides' *HIPPOLYTUS,* APHRODITE and ARTEMIS appear at the beginning and end, respectively, and their presence reinforces the play's conflict between love and chastity. *RHESUS* also has two divine appearances. In the middle of the play, Athena enters to aid the Greeks and baffle the Trojans; at the play's conclusion RHESUS' mother, a MUSE, arrives to mourn her son's death and to express her anger at the Greeks and Athena's favorite city, ATHENS. *PROMETHEUS BOUND* has a most unusual divine figure in that IO, the daughter of a river god, arrives after she has been transformed into a cow and while she is being tormented by a gadfly. She gallops away after PROMETHEUS tells her about her future.

Other than the chorus, queens, princesses, and divinities, few other female speaking parts exist in Greek tragedy. A few NURSES (*Libation Bearers* [see *ORESTEIA*], *Trachinian Women, Hippolytus, Andromache*), priestesses (*Eumenides* [see *ORESTEIA*], *Ion*), female prophets (*AGAMEMNON, HELEN*), and slaves appear. Clytemnestra's ghost has a speaking role in *Eumenides* (see *ORESTEIA*).

Because most Senecan tragedies (except *Thyestes* and *Octavia*) are based on Greek plays for which the original survives, women's roles in the Latin plays are basically the same. Unlike Aeschylus, SENECA does give Electra a speaking role in his *Agamemnon*. To *HERCULES OETAEUS,* based on Sophocles' *Trachinian Women,* Seneca adds speaking roles for Iole and ALCMENA. Into

his *Oedipus,* Seneca introduces the role of Tiresias' daughter, MANTO. In two plays, Seneca has two female choruses (*Agamemnon, Hercules Oetaeus*), one native to the town, another consisting of outsiders. *OCTAVIA* is unique in that it has two nurses, one for Octavia, the other for POPPAEA. Only one female divinity, Juno (Greek: HERA), appears in Senecan tragedy (*Hercules Furens*), and the ghost of AGRIPPINA appears in *Octavia.*

In the realm of COMEDY, ARISTOPHANES' surviving plays have few speaking parts for women until 411 B.C.E. Other than the female chorus of *CLOUDS* and a brief appearance by IRIS in *BIRDS,* the female characters who do appear on the Aristophanic stage before this time are usually silent and are the object of sexual gawking and pawing by the males onstage. Women in the SATYR PLAY seem to have experienced the same sort of treatment (e.g., Cyllene in Sophocles' *SEARCHERS*; AMYMONE in Aeschylus' satyr play of that name). In 411, however, two female-centered plays appeared, *LYSISTRATA* and *THESMOPHORIAZUSAE*. *ECCLESIAZUSAE,* produced in 392/391, also has prominent female roles. In these three plays, we find a female chorus, and in *Lysistrata* and *Ecclesiazusae,* a freeborn female is the architect of the social reform. *Ecclesiazusae* also marks the first extant appearance of the sex-crazed old woman and her young male love interest. This role is reprised in Aristophanes' *WEALTH* (388). Also in *Wealth,* the goddess Poverty vigorously defends the necessity of her presence in society.

Beginning in the latter half of the fourth century B.C.E., the roles of both women and men in comedy become stereotyped. In the so-called New Comedy of authors such as MENANDER, PLAUTUS, and TERENCE, the chorus is no longer involved in the action and the women in such plays are usually either freeborn maidens (see VIRGO), the wives of citizens (see MATRONA), SLAVES, and PROSTITUTES or MUSIC GIRLS (who are almost synonymous with prostitutes). Occasionally a woman serves as the PIMP for a prostitute. With the exception of Alcmena in Plautus' *AMPHITRUO,* royal women are largely absent from New Comedy. Goddesses rarely have speaking roles, and even in those cases they deliver only the PROLOGUE, as in the case of TYCHE (Chance) in Menander's *SHIELD,* Agnoia (Misapprehension) in *THE GIRL WITH THE SHAVEN HEAD,* or Luxury (and her daughter, Poverty) in Plautus' THREE-DOLLAR DAY. Although the speaking roles for women do not increase markedly for female characters, the freeborn maidens and prostitutes do provide the catalyst for males in New Comedy. The action of most of the these plays is set in motion as a result of a man's love for a maiden or prostitute, and the remainder of the play usually focuses on his hope of marrying his beloved or, at the least, spending an afternoon or evening of sexual bliss with her.

BIBLIOGRAPHY

Bouvrie, S. Des. *Women in Greek Tragedy: An Anthropological Approach.* Oslo: Norwegian University Press; Oxford: Oxford University Press, 1990.

Foley, H. P. *Female Acts in Greek Tragedy.* Princeton, N.J.: Princeton University Press, 2001.

Loraux, N. *Tragic Ways of Killing a Woman.* Translated by A. Forster. Cambridge, Mass.: Harvard University Press, 1987.

Rosivach, V. J. *When a Young Man Falls in Love: The Sexual Exploitation of Women in New Comedy.* London: Routledge, 1998.

Taaffe, L. K. *Aristophanes and Women.* London: Routledge, 1993.

WOMEN OF AETNA   See Aeschylus; Aetna.

WOMEN OF ARGOS   See Adrastus; Argos.

WOMEN OF BACCHUS   See Bacchae.

WOMEN OF COLCHIS   See Colchis.

WOMEN OF LEMNOS   See Lemnos.

WOMEN OF PERRHAEBIA   See Perhaebia.

WOMEN OF PHTHIA   See Phthia.

WOMEN OF SALAMIS   See Salamis.

WOODEN HORSE   See Trojan horse.

X

XANTHIAS A common name (meaning "golden-haired") of slaves in Aristophanic COMEDY. The most extensive role for a Xanthias occurs in ARISTOPHANES' FROGS (405 B.C.E.), in which a wisecracking Xanthias accompanies DIONYSUS on his journey to the UNDERWORLD. [ANCIENT SOURCES: Aristophanes, *Acharnians, Clouds, Frogs, Wasps*]

XENOCLES A son of the elder CARCINUS, Xenocles was a Greek tragedian active in the last quarter of the fifth century B.C.E. ARISTOPHANES had a poor opinion of his work; however, in 415 Xenocles' plays defeated EURIPIDES' offerings (one of which was TROJAN WOMEN). [ANCIENT SOURCES: Aristophanes, *Frogs* 86, *Clouds* 1259–66; *Thesmophoriazusae* 169, 441; Plato Comicus, fragment 134 Kock]

BIBLIOGRAPHY
Kock, T. *Comicorum Atticorum Fragmenta.* Vol. 1. Leipzig: Teubner, 1880.

XENOPHANTES See HIERONYMUS.

XUTHUS The husband of CREUSA and the adoptive father of ION. See EURIPIDES' ION.

Z

ZEPHYR The son of Astraeus and Eos, Zephyr personifies the west wind. Zephyr receives frequent mention in SENECA's plays. [ANCIENT SOURCES: Aeschylus, *Agamemnon* 692 (see *ORESTEIA*); Euripides, *Iphigenia in Tauris* 434, *Phoenecian Women* 211; Hesiod, *Theogony* 378–80; Homer, *Iliad* 16.148–51; Pausanias, 1.37.2, 3.19.5]

ZETES A son of BOREAS and ORITHYIA, Zetes was the brother of Calais. The two brothers had wings and accompanied JASON on his quest for the Golden Fleece. During that voyage, the brothers were instrumental in ridding PHINEUS of the Harpies that plagued him. [ANCIENT SOURCES: Apollodorus, *Library* 1.9.16, 21, 3.15.2; Hyginus, *Fables* 14, 19; Seneca, *Medea* 634, 782]

ZETHUS See AMPHION.

ZEUS His Roman counterpart is Jupiter (also known as Jove). Zeus is the son of CRONUS and RHEA. He is the brother of POSEIDON, HADES, HERA, DEMETER, and HESTIA. Cronus, warned by an oracle that he would be overthrown by one of his children, swallowed them whole as soon as they were born. After giving birth to Zeus, Rhea tricked her husband by giving him a stone wrapped in swaddling clothes, and Zeus himself was carried off to Crete and hidden in the Dictaean cave. Eventually Zeus returned and managed to rescue his brothers and sisters by giving Cronus a potion that made him vomit. After this Zeus and his siblings waged war against Cronus, overthrew him, and banished him to the UNDERWORLD. After Zeus defeated Cronus, he and his brothers cast lots to divide the world. Zeus became master of the sky, Poseidon the sea, and Hades the underworld. After the overthrow of Cronus, Zeus faced other challenges as well. Zeus blasted TYPHON with a lightning bolt and imprisoned him under Mount AETNA.

Zeus' main female companion is HERA, by whom he had ARES, HEBE, and EILYTHIA. Zeus had numerous relationships with other women, both goddesses and mortals. By his sister, Demeter, he produced PERSEPHONE; by the goddess LETO he fathered the twins APOLLO and ARTEMIS; by the goddess Maia he fathered HERMES; by SEMELE he became the father of DIONYSUS; by the goddess Mnemosyne he produced the nine MUSES. Zeus' affair with IO resulted in extreme hardships for her, and ultimately she had a child, EPAPHUS. Zeus disguised himself as a swan to impregnate LEDA; he turned into a SATYR to impregnate ANTIOPE and become the father of AMPHION and ZETHUS; he disguised himself as AMPHITRYON to impregnate ALCMENA and become the father of HERACLES.

Zeus appears as a character in only one surviving classical play, PLAUTUS' *AMPHITRUO*. In this play, appearing under his Roman name of Jupiter, the god and his son, Mercury (Greek: Hermes), are in THEBES at the house of Amphitruo (Greek: Amphitryon). Jupiter is disguised as Amphitruo and Mercury is disguised as Amphitruo's slave, Sosia. Plautus takes up the story after Jupiter has impregnated Alcmena and is now leaving his unwitting lover. Humor ensues as Jupiter is mistaken for the real Amphitruo, who arrives after Jupiter's departure from the house and quarrels with his wife about her alleged infidelity. Ultimately Jupiter sets matters right between husband and wife and makes sure that Alcmena delivers her children safely.

Although Zeus appears only in Plautus' *Amphitruo,* he is mentioned hundreds of times in classical drama. Zeus' name frequently occurs in ARISTOPHANES' *CLOUDS,* in which SOCRATES convinces STREPSIADES that Zeus (Dios) has been overthrown and replaced by a divinity named Vortex (Dinos). In Aristophanes' *BIRDS,* PEISETAERUS' city in the clouds threatens Zeus' kingdom, and eventually the king of the gods must send an embassy to negotiate a settlement with Peisetaerus and the birds. Similarly in Aristophanes' *WEALTH,* the cure of Plutus' blindness results in a loss of power for Zeus and the other gods. The Greek comic poet Plato wrote a play entitled *Zeus Kakoumenos* (Zeus outraged); the surviving fragments (46–54 Kock) reveal that a PIMP and HERACLES were characters and that the drinking game cottabos was played at some point in the action.

In TRAGEDY Zeus is a focal point of AESCHYLUS' *PROMETHEUS BOUND,* as the title character's punishment is a result of his opposing Zeus' wishes and giving fire to mortals. In this play Zeus is portrayed as an oppressive tyrant (see TYRANNOS) over both gods and human beings. As in *Amphitruo,* Zeus' name is often heard in plays that deal with Heracles, such as SOPHOCLES' *TRACHINIAN WOMEN,* EURIPIDES' *CHILDREN OF HERACLES* and *HERACLES,* and SENECA's *HERCULES FURENS* and *HERCULES OETAEUS.* When Heracles suffers from tragic circumstances, he often feels abandoned by his divine father.

BIBLIOGRAPHY

Cook, A. B. *Zeus: A Study in Ancient Religion.* New York: Biblo & Tannen, 1964–1965.

Kerenyi, C. *Zeus and Hera: Archetypal Image of Father, Husband, and Wife.* Translated by C. Holme. Princeton, N.J.: Princeton University Press, 1975.

Kock, T. *Comicorum Atticorum Fragmenta.* Vol. 1. Leipzig: Teubner, 1880.

Kovacs, D. "Zeus in Euripides' *Medea,*" *American Journal of Philology* 114 (1993): 45–70.

Mikalson, J. D. "Zeus the Father and Heracles the Son in Tragedy," *Transactions and Proceedings of the American Philological Association* 96 (1986): 89–98.

Smith, P. M. *On the Hymn to Zeus in Aeschylus' Agamemnon.* Chico, Calif.: Scholars Press, 1980.

APPENDIX I

PLAYS ATTRIBUTED TO THE EIGHT CLASSICAL PLAYWRIGHTS WITH SURVIVING WORKS

Plays marked in CAPITAL LETTERS have survived in complete form or substantially complete form. The presence of a question mark (?) indicates some doubt about the play's authorship, genre, or title. In some cases, playwrights produced more than one version of a play. Such instances are accompanied by a letter of the alphabet (e.g., *Hippolytus A*, *Hippolytus B*).

AESCHYLUS OF ATHENS (GREEK: TRAGEDY)

Modern Title	Ancient Title
AGAMEMNON	AGAMEMNON
EUMENIDES	EUMENIDES
LIBATION BEARERS	CHOÊPHOROI
PERSIANS	PERSAI
PROMETHEUS BOUND?	PROMÊTHEUS DESMOTÊS?
SEVEN AGAINST THEBES	HEPTA EPI THÊBAS
SUPPLIANT WOMEN	HIKETIDES
Aetnaeans	Aitnaiai
Alcmena	Alcmênê
Amymone (satyr?)	Amumonê
Archers	Toxotides
Argive Men or Argive Women	Argeioi or Argeiai

Argo	Argô
Atalanta	Atalanta
Athamas	Athamas
Bacchae	Bakchai
Bassarids	Bassarai
Bone Gatherers	Ostologoi
Cabiri (satyr?)	Kabeiroi
Callisto (satyr?)	Kallistô
Carians or Europa	Kares or Europa
Cercyon (satyr)	Kerkuôn
Children of Heracles	Herakleidai
Children of the Sun	Hêliades
Circe (satyr)	Kirkê
Cycnus?	Kuknos?
Danaids	Danaides
Edonians	Êdônoi
Egyptians	Aiguptioi
Eleusianians	Eleusinioi
Epigoni	Epigonoi
Glaucus of Potniae	Glaukos Potnieus
Glaucus of the Sea (satyr?)	Glaukos Pontios
Heralds (satyr)	Kêrukes
Hypsipyle	Hupsipulê
Iphigenia	Iphigeneia
Ixion	Ixiôn
Judgment of Arms	Hoplôn Krisis
Laius	Laios
Lion (satyr)	Leôn
Lycurgus (satyr)	Lukourgos
Memnon	Memnon

Men of Lemnos or Women of Lemnos	Lêmnioi or Lêmniai
Myrmidons	Murmidones
Mysians	Musoi
Nemea	Nemea
Nereids	Nêreides
Net Draggers (satyr)	Diktuoulkoi
Niobe	Niobê
Nurses of Dionysus or Nurses (satyr)	Dionusou Trophoi or Trophoi
Oedipus	Oidipous
Oreithyia	Oreithuia
Palamedes	Palamêdês
Paraders	Propompoi
Penelope	Pênelopê
Pentheus	Pentheus
Perrhaebians	Perraibides
Philoctetes	Philoktêtês
Phineus	Phineus
Phorcides (satyr?)	Phorkides
Phrygians	Phrugioi
Phrygians or Ransom of Hector	Phruges or Hektoros Lutra
Polydectes	Poludektês
Preparers of the Bed Chamber	Thalamopoioi
Priestesses	Hiereiai
Prometheus the Fire Bringer	Promêtheus Purphoros
Prometheus the Fire Maker (satyr)	Promêtheus Purkaeus
Prometheus Unbound	Promêtheus Luomenos
Proteus (satyr)	Proteus
Semele or Water Carriers	Semelê or Hudrophoroi
Sisyphus Runaway (satyr?)	Sisuphos Drapetês
Sisyphus Stone Pusher (satyr)	Sisuphos Petrokulistês
Soul Attendants	Psuchagogoi
Spectators or Spectators of the Isthmian Games (satyr)	Theôroi or Isthmiastai
Sphinx (satyr)	Sphinx
Telephus	Têlephos
Weighing of Lives	Psuchostasia
Women of Crete	Krêssai
Women of Salamis	Salaminiai
Women of Thrace	Thêissai
Xantriai (satyr?)	Xantriai
Youths	Neaniskoi

SOPHOCLES (GREEK; TRAGEDY)

Modern Title	Ancient Title
AJAX (WITH THE WHIP)	AIAS MASTIGOPHOROS
ANTIGONE	ANTIGONE
ELECTRA	ÊLEKTRA
OEDIPUS AT COLONUS	OIDIPOUS EPI KOLÔNÔI
OEDIPUS TYRANNUS	OIDIPOUS TYRANNOS
PHILOCTETES	PHILOKTÊTÊS
TRACHINIAN WOMEN	TRACHINIAI
Acrisius	Akrisios
Aegeus	Aigeus
Ajax the Locrian	Aias Lokros
Alcmeon	Alkmeôn
Alexander	Alexandros
Amphiaraus (satyr)	Amphiareôs
Amphitryon	Amphitruôn
Amycus (satyr)	Amukos
Andromeda	Andromeda
Antigone	Antigonê
Athamas A	Athamas A
Athamas B	Athamas B
Atreus or Women of Mycenae	Atreus or Mukênaiai
Captive Women	Aichmalotides
Cassandra	Kassandra
Cedalion (satyr)	Kedalion
Cerberus (satyr?)	Kerberos
Chryses	Chrusês
Clytemnestra	Klutaimestra
Colchian Women	Kolchides
Creusa	Kreousa
Daedalus	Daidalos
Danae	Danaê
Demand for Helen's Return	Helenês Apaitesis
Dolopians	Dolopes
Drummers	Tumpanistai
Electra	Êlektra
Erigone	Êrigonê
Eriphyle	Eriphulê
Eris (satyr?)	Eris
Ethiopians	Aithiopes
Eumelus	Eumelos
Euryalus	Eurualos
Eurypylus	Eurupulos
Eurysaces	Eurusakes
Foot Washing	Niptra
Gathering of Achaeans	Achaiôn Sullogos
Helen's Marriage (satyr?)	Helenês Gamos
Hipponous	Hipponous
Hubris (satyr)	Hubris
Inachus (satyr?)	Inachos
Infant Dionysus (satyr)	Dionusiskos
Infant Heracles (satyr)	Herakleiskos
Iobates	Iobates
Ion	Iôn

Iphigenia	Iphigeneia
Ixion	Ixiôn
Judgment (satyr)	Krisis
Laocoon	Laokoon
Lovers of Achilles (satyr?)	Achilleôs Erastai
Meleager	Meleagros
Memnon	Memnon
Men of Camicus	Kamikoi
Men of Larissa	Larisaioi
Minos	Minôs
Momus	Mômos
Muses	Mousai
Mute Ones (satyr)	Kôphoi
Mysians	Musoi
Nauplius Sailing In	Nauplios Katapleôn
Nauplius the Fire Maker	Nauplios Purkaeus
Nausicaa or Women Washing Clothes (satyr?)	Nausikaa or Pluntriai
Niobe	Niobê
Odysseus Wounded by the Spine	Odusseus Akanthoplêx
Odysseus' Madness	Odusseus Mainomenos
Oedipus at Colonus	Oidipous epi Kolônôi
Oedipus Tyrannus	Oidipous Tyrannos
Oeneus (satyr?)	Oineus
Oenomaus	Oinomaos
Pandora (satyr?)	Pandôra
Phaeacians	Phaiakes
Phaedra	Phaidra
Philoctetes	Philoktêtês
Philoctetes at Troy	Philoktêtês en Troiai
Phineus A	Phineus A
Phineus B	Phineus B
Phoenix (or Dolopians)	Phoinix (or Dolopians)
Phrixus	Phrixos
Phrygians	Phruges
Prophets or Polyidus	Manteis or Poluidos
Salmoneus (satyr)	Salmôneus
Satyrs at Taenarum (satyr)	Epi Tainaroi Saturoi
Scythians	Skuthai
Shepherds	Poimenes
Sons of Aleus	Aleadai
Sons of Antenor	Antenoridai
Telephus, Telepheia	Têlephos, Têlepheia
Tereus	Têreus
Thamyras	Thamuras
Theseus	Thêseus
Those Who Dine Together (satyr?)	Sundeipnoi
Thyestes A	Thuestês A
Thyestes B	Thuestês B
Thyestes C	Thuestês C
Trackers (satyr)	Ichneutai
Triptolemus	Triptolemus
Tyndareus	Tundareôs
Tyro A	Turô A
Tyro B	Turô B
Water Carriers	Hudrophoroi
Women of Laconia	Lakainai
Women of Lemnos A	Lemniai A
Women of Lemnos B	Lemniai B
Women of Phthia	Phthiôtides
Women of Trachis	Trachiniai

EURIPIDES (GREEK; TRAGEDY)

Modern Title	Ancient Title
ALCESTIS	ALKESTIS
ANDROMACHE	ANDROMACHÊ
BACCHAE	BAKCHAI
CHILDREN OF HERACLES	HERAKLEIDAI
CYCLOPS (SATYR)	KUKLÔPS
ELECTRA	ÊLEKTRA
HECABE	HÊKABÊ
HELEN	HELENÊ
HERACLES	HÊRAKLÊS
HIPPOLYTUS B	HIPPOLUTOS B
ION	IÔN
IPHIGENIA AT TAURIS	IPHIGENEIA HÊ EN TAUROIS
IPHIGENIA IN AULIS	IPHIGENEIA HÊ EN AULIDI
MEDEA	MÊDEIA
ORESTES	ORESTÊS
PHOENICIAN WOMEN	PHOINISSAI
RHESUS?	RHÊSOS?
SUPPLIANT WOMEN	HIKETIDES
TROJAN WOMEN	TRÔIADES
Aegeus	Aigeus
Aeolus	Aiolos
Alcmena	Alcmêenê
Alcmeon at Psophis	Alcmeôn dia Psôphidos
Alexander	Alexandros
Alope	Alopê
Andromeda	Andromeda
Antigone	Antigonê
Antiope	Antiopê
Archelaus	Archelaos
Auge	Augê
Autolycus (satyr)	Autolukos

Bellerophon	Bellerophontês
Busiris (satyr)	Bousiris
Cadmus	Kadmos
Chrysippus	Chrusippos
Cresphontes	Kresphontês
Cretans	Krêtês
Cretan Women	Krêssai
Danae	Danaê
Daughters of Pelias	Peliades
Dictys	Diktus
Epeus	Epeios
Erechtheus	Erechtheus
Eurystheus (satyr)	Eurustheus Saturikos
Hippolytus A	Hippolutos A
Hypsipyle	Hupsipulê
Ino	Inô
Ixion	Ixiôn
Lamia (satyr)	Lamia
Licymnius	Likumnios
Melanippe the Prisoner	Melanippê Hê Desmotis
Melanippe the Wise	Melanippê Hê Sophê
Meleager	Meleagros
Mysians	Musoi
Oedipus	Oidipous
Oenomaus	Oinomaos
Palamedes	Palamêdês
Peirithous	Peirithous
Peleus	Pêleus
Phaethon	Phaethôn
Philoctetes	Philoktêtês
Phoenix	Phoinix
Phrixus	Phrixos
Pleisthenes	Pleisthenês
Polyidus	Poluidos
Protesilaus	Prôtesilaos
Reapers (satyr)	Theristai
Rhadamanthys	Rhadamanthus
Sciron (satyr)	Skirôn
Scylla	Skulla
Scyrians	Skurioi
Sisyphus (satyr)	Sisuphos
Stheneboea	Stheneboia
Syleus (satyr)	Suleus Saturikos
Telephus	Têlephos
Temenos	Têmenos
Teminidae	Têmenidai
Tennes	Tennês
Theseus	Thêseus
Thyestes	Thuestês

SENECA [LUCIUS ANNAEUS SENECA] (LATIN; TRAGEDY)

Modern Title	Ancient Title
AGAMEMNON	AGAMEMNON
HERCULES' MADNESS	HERCULES FURENS
HERCULES ON OETA?	HERCULES OETAEUS?
HIPPOLYTUS or PHAEDRA	HIPPOLYTUS or PHAEDRA
MEDEA	MEDEA
OCTAVIA?	OCTAVIA?
OEDIPUS	OEDIPUS
THYESTES	THYESTES
TROJAN WOMEN	TROADES
Phoenician Women	Phoenissae[1]

ARISTOPHANES (GREEK; COMEDY)

Modern Title	Ancient Title
ACHARNIANS	ACHARNÊS
BIRDS	ORNITHES
CLOUDS B	NEPHELAI B
FROGS	BATRACHOI
KNIGHTS	HIPPEIS
LYSISTRATA	LUSISTRATA
PEACE A	EIRÊNÊ A
WASPS	SPHÊKES
WEALTH B	PLOUTOS B
WOMEN AT THE THESMOPHORIA A	THESMOPHORIAZUSAI A
WOMEN IN ASSEMBLY	EKKLESIAZUSAI
Aeolus as Sicon	Aiolosikôn
Amphiaraus	Amphiareôs
Anagyrus	Anaguros
Apparel?	Skeuai
Babylonians	Babulônioi
Banqueters	Daitalês
Boilers	Tagênistai
Clouds A	Nephelai A
Cocalus	Kôkalos
Daedalus	Daidalos
Danaides	Danaides
Dramas or Centaur	Dramata or Kentauros
Dramas or Niobos	Dramata or Niobos
Farmers	Geôrgoi
Gerytades	Gêrutadês
Heroes	Hêrôes

[1]About half of this play has survived.

Islands	Nêsoi	False Accuser	Katapseudomenos
Old Age	Gêras	Farmer	Georgos
Peace B	Eirênê B	Fishermen	Halieis
Phoenician Women	Phoinissai	Flatterer	Kolax
Poetry	Poiêsis	Flute Girl	Aulêtris
Polyidus	Poluidos	Ghost	Phasma
Preview	Proagôn	Groom	Hippokomos
Seasons	Hôrai	Guardian Spirit	Heros
Seat Stealers	Skênas Katalambanousai	Half Brothers	Homopatrioi
Storks	Pelargoi	Hated Man	Misoumenos
Telemessians	Telemêssês	Headdress	Kekruphalos
Traders	Olkades	Heiress	Epiklêros
Triple Phallus	Triphalês	Hymnis	Humnis
Twice Shipwrecked	Dis Nauagos	Imbrians	Imbrioi
Wealth A	Ploutos A	Ladies at Lunch	Sunaristôsai
Women at the	Thesmophoriazusai B	Lawgiver	Nomothetês
Thesmophoria B		Lyre Player	Kitharistês
Women of Lemnos	Lêmniai	Man from Sicyon	Sikuônios
		Man Woman or Cretan	Androgunos or Krês

MENANDER (GREEK; COMEDY)

Modern Title	Ancient Title	Misogynist	Misogunês
		Mistruster	Apistos
ARBITRATION	EPITREPONTES	Necklace	Plokion
BAD-TEMPERED MAN	DUSKOLOS	Noise-Shy Man	Psophodeês
WOMAN OF SAMOS	SAMIA	Once Married	Progamôn or Progamoi
Accuser	Proenkalôn	Peplos Bearer	Arrêphoros
Anger	Orgê	Phanion	Phanion
Basket Bearer	Kanêphoros	Pilots	Kubernêtai
Beggar Priest	Mênagurtês	Pretend Heracles	Pseudêraklês
Boeotian Woman	Boiôtia	Priestess	Hiereia
Bridal Manager	Dêmiourgos	Promiser	Epangelomenos
Brothers A	Adelphoi A	Recruiting Officer	Xenologos
Brothers B	Adelphoi B	Ring	Daktulios
Brothers in Love	Philadelphoi	Self-Pitier	Hauton Penthôn
Captain	Nauklêros	Self-Tormentor	Heauton Timôroumenos
Carian Wailing Woman	Karinê	Sex	Aphrodisia
Carthaginian	Karchêdonios	Shield	Aspis
Charioteer	Hêniochos	Slapped Woman	Rhapizomenê
Concubine	Pallakê	Slave	Paidion
Cousins	Anepsioi	Smiths' Festival	Chalkeia
Dagger	Encheiridion	Soldiers	Stratiôtai
Dardanus	Dardanos	Superstitious Man	Deisidaimôn
Deposit	Parakatathêkê	Suppositious Baby	Hupobolimaios
Doorman	Thurôros	Thais	Thais
Double Deceiver	Dis Exapatôn	Those Offered for Sale	Pôloumenoi
Drunkenness	Methê	Thrasuleon	Thrasuleôn
Entrusted Woman	Anatithemenê	Treasure	Thêsauros
Ephesian	Ephesios	Trophonius	Trophônios
Eunuch	Eunouchos	Twin Women	Didumai
		Urn	Hudria

Wet-Nurse	Titthê
Widow	Chêra
Woman in Flames	Empimpramenê
Woman of Andros	Andria
Woman of Chalcis	Chalkis
Woman of Cnidus	Knidia
Woman of Leucas	Leukadia
Woman of Olynthus	Olunthia
Woman of Perinthus	Perinthia
Woman of Thessaly	Thettalê
Woman Possessed by a Divinity	Theophoroumenê
Woman Who Was Shorn	Perikeiromenê
Woman with Two Lovers	Sunerôsa
Women Dosed with Hemlock	Kôneiazomenai
Young Comrades	Sunephêboi

PLAUTUS (LATIN; COMEDY)

Modern Title	Ancient Title
AMPHITRUO	AMPHITRUO
BRAGGART WARRIOR	MILES GLORIOSUS
CAPTIVES	CAPTIVI
CARTHAGINIAN	POENULUS
CASINA	CASINA
CASKET COMEDY	CISTELLARIA
COMEDY OF ASSES	ASINARIA
CURCULIO	CURCULIO
EPIDICUS	EPIDICUS
HAUNTED HOUSE	MOSTELLARIA
MERCHANT	MERCATOR
PERSIAN (WOMAN)	PERSA
POT OF GOLD	AULULARIA
PSEUDOLUS	PSEUDOLUS
ROPE	RUDENS
STICHUS	STICHUS
THREE DOLLAR DAY	TRINUMMUS
TRUCULENTUS	TRUCULENTUS
TWO BACCHISES	BACCHIDES
TWO MENAECHMUSES	MENAECHMI
Acharistio	Acharistio
Artemo	Artemo
Bacaria	Bacaria
Bad-Tempered Man	Dyscolus

Bagatelle	Frivolaria
Blind Man or Bandits	Caecus or Praedones
Bondman	Addictus
Bucket Cleaner	Sitellitergus
Cesistio?	Cesistio?
Charcoal Woman	Carbonaria
Epidicus	Epidicus
Flatterer	Colax
Fugitives	Fugitivi
Glutton	Phago
Lazy Parasite	Parasitus Piger
Lipargus	Lipargus
Little Crow	Cornicula
Little Garden	Hortulus
Little Ring	Condalium
Male Triplets	Trigemini
Pack Saddle	Astraba
Parasite Doctor	Parasitus Medicus
Plocinus	Plocinus
Rustic	Agroecus
Saturio	Saturio
Schematicus (Pertaining to Phrases?)	Schematicus
Small Shoe	Calceolus
Strait	Fretum
Tale of a Traveling Bag	Vidularia
Tale of the Cords?	Nervolaria
Those Dying Together	Commorientes
Twin Pimps	Lenones Gemini
Woman Moneylender	Faeneratrix
Woman of Boeotia	Boeotia

TERENCE [PUBLIUS TERENTIUS AFER] (LATIN; COMEDY)

Modern Title	Ancient Title
BROTHERS	ADELPHOE
EUNUCH	EUNUCHUS
MOTHER-IN-LAW	HECYRA
PHORMIO	PHORMIO
SELF-TORMENTOR	HEAUTON TIMOROUMENOS
WOMAN OF ANDROS	ANDRIA

APPENDIX II

LIST OF CLASSICAL PLAYWRIGHTS

Authors who have a play or mime that survives in complete form or substantially complete form have been marked in CAPITAL LETTERS. The presence of a question mark (?) indicates that some doubt exists regarding the author's name or the time in which he wrote.

Author Name	Language	Genre(s)	Date
Accius, Lucius	Latin	Tragedy	170–ca. 86 B.C.E.
		Fabulae praetextae	
Acestor	Greek	Tragedy	fifth century B.C.E.
Achaeus of Eretria	Greek	Tragedy	fifth century B.C.E.
Achaeus of Syracus	Greek	Tragedy	fourth century B.C.E.
Aeantides	Greek	Tragedy	third century B.C.E.
Aelius Amphichares, Publius of Athens	Greek	Tragedy	second century C.E.
Aelius Lamia?	Latin	*Fabulae togatae*	first century B.C.E.–first century C.E.?
Aemilius Hymettus, Marcus	Greek	Tragedy	second century C.E.
Aemilius Scaurus, Mamercus	Latin	Tragedy	first century B.C.E.–first century C.E.
Aemilius Severianus Tarraconensis	Latin	Mime	Uncertain
Aeschylus of Alexandria	Greek	Tragedy	third century B.C.E.?
AESCHYLUS of Athens	Greek	Tragedy	525/4–456/5 B.C.E.
Afranius, Lucius	Latin	*Fabulae togatae*	active 160–120 B.C.E.
Agathon	Greek	Tragedy	ca. 450–400 B.C.E.
Agathenor	Greek	Comedy	first century B.C.E.
Agathocles	Greek	Comedy	second century B.C.E.
Alcaeus	Greek	Comedy	fourth century B.C.E.
Alcimenes of Athens	Greek	Comedy	Uncertain
Alcimenes of Megara	Greek	Tragedy	Uncertain (earliest reference 10th century C.E.)
Alexander	Greek	Comedy	first century B.C.E.
Alexander of Aetolia	Greek	Tragedy	fourth–third century B.C.E.
Alexander of Tanagra	Greek	Tragedy	first century B.C.E.
Alexis	Greek	Comedy	ca. 375–275 B.C.E.

(continues)

(continued)

Author Name	Language	Genre(s)	Date
Aminias	Greek	Comedy	fourth–third century B.C.E.
Amipsias	Greek	Comedy	fifth–fourth century B.C.E.
Amphichares	Greek	Comedy	second century C.E.
Aminias of Thebes	Greek	Tragedy	first century B.C.E.
Amymon	Greek	Tragedy	third century B.C.E.
Anaxandrides	Greek	Comedy	fourth century B.C.E.
Anaxilas	Greek	Comedy	fourth century B.C.E.
Anaxion of Mytilene	Greek	Tragedy	Uncertain
Anaxippus	Greek	Comedy	fourth–third century B.C.E.
Annaeus Lucanus, Marcus	Latin	Tragedy	39–65 C.E.
Antheas	Greek	Comedy	Uncertain (earliest reference second–third century C.E.)
Antidotus	Greek	Comedy	fourth century B.C.E.
Antigenes?	Greek	Comedy	second century B.C.E.
Antiochus	Greek	Comedy	second century C.E.
Antiochus	Greek	Tragedy	second century B.C.E.
Antiphanes	Greek	Comedy	fourth century B.C.E.
Antiphanes II	Greek	Comedy	third century B.C.E.
Antiphanes of Carystos	Greek	Tragedy	Uncertain (earliest reference tenth century C.E.)
Antiphilus?	Greek	Tragedy	third century B.C.E.
Antiphon	Greek	Tragedy	fifth–fourth century B.C.E.
Anubion	Greek	Comedy	second century C.E.
Aphareus	Greek	Tragedy	fourth century B.C.E.
Apollinaris	Greek	Comedy	fourth century C.E.
Apollinaris	Greek	Tragedy	fourth century C.E.
Apollodorus Carystius	Greek	Comedy	fourth–third century B.C.E.
Apollodorus of Gela (perhaps same as Apollodorus of Carystos)	Greek	Comedy	fourth–third century B.C.E.
Apollodorus of Tarsus	Greek	Tragedy	fourth century B.C.E.
Apollonides	Greek	Tragedy	third–second century B.C.E.
Apollonius Aspendius	Greek	Tragedy	second century C.E.
Apollonius	Greek	Comedy	Uncertain
Apollonius	Greek	Tragedy	second century B.C.E.
Apollophanes	Greek	Comedy	fifth–fourth century B.C.E.
Aprissius	Latin	Fabulae atellanae	second–first century B.C.E.
Aquilius	Latin	Fabulae palliatae	second century B.C.E.
Araros (son of Aristophanes)	Greek	Comedy	fifth–fourth century B.C.E.
Arcesilaus	Greek	Comedy	fifth century B.C.E.
Archedicus	Greek	Comedy	fourth–third century B.C.E.
Archenomus	Greek	Tragedy	second century B.C.E.
Archestratus	Greek	Tragedy	fourth century B.C.E.
Archippus	Greek	Comedy	fifth century B.C.E.
Archytas?	Greek	Tragedy	third century B.C.E.
Ariphron	Greek	Tragedy	fourth century B.C.E.
Aristaenetus?	Greek	Tragedy	first century B.C.E.
Aristagoras	Greek	Comedy	fifth century B.C.E.?
Aristarchus of Tegea	Greek	Tragedy	fifth century B.C.E.
Aristias	Greek	Tragedy	fifth century B.C.E.
Aristides	Greek	Comedy	third century B.C.E.
Aristius Fuscus	Latin	Fabulae palliatae	first century B.C.E.
Aristocles?	Greek	Comedy	second century B.C.E.
Aristocrates	Greek	Comedy	third or second century B.C.E.

Author Name	Language	Genre(s)	Date
Aristocrates?	Greek	Tragedy	first century B.C.E.
Aristomenes of Athens	Greek	Tragedy	second century B.C.E.
Aristomenes	Greek	Comedy	fifth–fourth B.C.E.
Ariston I	Greek	Comedy	second century B.C.E.
Ariston II	Greek	Comedy	first century B.C.E.
Ariston III	Greek	Comedy	first century B.C.E.
Ariston (son of Menelaus)	Greek	Tragedy	second century B.C.E.
Aristonymus	Greek	Comedy	fifth–fourth century B.C.E.
ARISTOPHANES of Athens	Greek	Comedy	ca. 450–385 B.C.E.
Aristophon	Greek	Comedy	fourth century B.C.E.
Artabazes	Greek	Tragedy	first century B.C.E.
Artemon of Athens	Greek	Tragedy	second century C.E.
Asclepiades I	Greek	Tragedy	fourth century B.C.E.
Asclepiades II	Greek	Tragedy	second century B.C.E.
Asinius Pollio, Gaius	Latin/Greek	Tragedy	76 B.C.E.–4 C.E.
Astydamas I	Greek	Tragedy	fourth century B.C.E.
Astydamas II	Greek	Tragedy	fourth century B.C.E.
Astydamas III	Greek	Tragedy	third century B.C.E.
Athenias of Anthedon	Greek	Tragedy	first century B.C.E.
Athenio	Greek	Comedy	third century B.C.E.
Athenodorus? or Zenodorus? or Menodorus?	Greek	Tragedy	second century B.C.E.
Atilius	Latin	Tragedy _Fabulae palliatae_	second century B.C.E.?
Atta, Titus Quinctius	Latin	_Fabulae togatae_	second century B.C.E.–first century B.C.E.
Atticus	Latin	Mime	first century C.E.?
Augeas of Athens	Greek	Comedy	Uncertain (earliest reference second–third century C.E.)
Augustus (Caesar Octavianus Augustus)	Latin	Tragedy	63 B.C.E.–14 C.E.
Autocrates	Greek	Comedy	fifth–fourth century B.C.E.
Axionicus	Greek	Comedy	fourth century B.C.E.
Bassus	Latin	Tragedy	first century B.C.E.–first century C.E.?
Baton	Greek	Comedy	third century B.C.E.
Bion	Greek	Tragedy	Uncertain (earliest reference third century C.E.)
Biottus	Greek	Comedy	second century B.C.E.
Biotus	Greek	Tragedy	second century B.C.E.?
Blaesus of Capri	Greek	Comedy	second or first century B.C.E.?
Caecilius Statius	Latin	_Fabulae palliatae_	died 168 B.C.E.
Caerius	Greek	Tragedy	fourth B.C.E.
Callias	Greek	Comedy	fifth century B.C.E.
Callicrates	Greek	Comedy	Uncertain (earliest reference second–third century C.E.)
Callippus? of Athens	Greek	Comedy	Uncertain (earliest reference second–third century C.E.)
Callipus of Thebes	Greek	Tragedy	first century B.C.E.
Callistratus	Greek	Tragedy	fifth century B.C.E.
Canius Rufus	Latin	Tragedy	first century C.E.–second century C.E.?
Cantharus	Greek	Comedy	fifth century B.C.E.
Carcinus (son of Xenotimus)	Greek	Tragedy	fifth century B.C.E.
Carcinus the Younger (son of Xenocles)	Greek	Tragedy	fourth century B.C.E.

(continues)

(continued)

Author Name	Language	Genre(s)	Date
Cassius Parmensis	Latin	Tragedy	first century B.C.E.
Catullus	Latin	Mime	first century C.E.
Cephisodorus	Greek	Comedy	fifth–fourth century B.C.E.
Chaeremon	Greek	Tragedy	fourth century B.C.E.
Chaerion	Greek	Comedy	Uncertain
Chariclides	Greek	Comedy	Uncertain (earliest reference second–third century C.E.)
Chionides	Greek	Comedy	fifth century B.C.E.
Choerilus of Athens	Greek	Tragedy	sixth–fifth century B.C.E.
Cleaenetus	Greek	Tragedy	fourth century B.C.E.
Clearchus	Greek	Comedy	fourth century B.C.E.
Cleophon of Athens	Greek	Tragedy	fourth century B.C.E.
Clitus	Greek	Tragedy	second century B.C.E.
Clodius, Quintipor	Latin	*Fabulae palliatae*	second century B.C.E.?
Cordus	Latin	Tragedy	first century C.E.–second century C.E.?
Cornelius Balbus, Lucius	Latin	*Fabulae praetextae*	first century B.C.E.
Cornelius Sulla, Lucius	Latin	*Fabulae atellanae*	second century B.C.E.–first century B.C.E.
Crates of Athens	Greek	Comedy	fifth century B.C.E.
Crates	Greek	Tragedy	fourth century B.C.E.
Cratinus	Greek	Comedy	fifth century B.C.E.
Cratinus Junior	Greek	Comedy	fourth century B.C.E.
Critias of Athens	Greek	Tragedy	ca. 460–403 B.C.E.
Crito	Greek	Comedy	second century B.C.E.
Crobylus	Greek	Comedy	fourth century B.C.E.
Damoxenus	Greek	Comedy	fourth or third century B.C.E.
Datis	Greek	Tragedy	fifth century B.C.E.
Demetrius	Greek	Comedy	fifth or fourth century B.C.E.
Demetrius	Greek	Tragedy	fifth century B.C.E.?
Demetrius Junior	Greek	Comedy	fourth or third century B.C.E.
Demetrius of Tarsus	Greek	Tragedy	Uncertain (earliest reference third century C.E.)
Democrates of Sicyon	Greek	Comedy	third century B.C.E.
Demonax	Greek	Tragedy?	Uncertain (earliest reference 5th century C.E.)
Demonicus	Greek	Comedy	fifth or fourth century B.C.E.?
Demophilus	Greek	Comedy	third–fourth century B.C.E.
Dexicrates	Greek	Comedy	fourth or third century B.C.E.?
Dicaeogenes	Greek	Tragedy	fourth century B.C.E.
Dieuches	Greek	Comedy	first century B.C.E.
Dinolochus	Greek	Comedy	fifth century B.C.E.
Diocles	Greek	Comedy	fifth–fourth century B.C.E.
Diodorus of Sinope	Greek	Comedy	third century B.C.E.
Diogenes of Athens	Greek	Tragedy	fifth century B.C.E.
Diogenes of Sinope	Greek	Tragedy	fourth century B.C.E.
Diogenes of Thebes	Greek	Tragedy	first century B.C.E.
Diogenes	Greek	Tragedy	second century B.C.E.
Dionysius of Tarsus	Greek	Tragedy	second century B.C.E.
Diognetus	Greek	Tragedy	third century B.C.E.
Diomedes	Greek	Comedy	second or first century B.C.E.
Dionysiades	Greek	Tragedy	third century B.C.E.
Dionysius of Anaphlystus	Greek	Tragedy	second century B.C.E.
Dionysius of Athens	Greek	Tragedy	second century B.C.E.
Dionysius of Cyprus	Greek	Tragedy	second century B.C.E.
Dionysius of Heraclea	Greek	Tragedy	third century B.C.E.

Author Name	Language	Genre(s)	Date
Dionysius Scymnaeus	Greek	Tragedy	Uncertain
Dionysius of Sicily	Greek	Tragedy	fourth century B.C.E.
Dionysius of Sinope	Greek	Comedy	fifth or fourth century B.C.E.
Dionysius II	Greek	Comedy	fourth century B.C.E.
Dionysius III	Greek	Comedy	second century B.C.E.
Diophantus	Greek	Comedy	Uncertain
Dioxippus	Greek	Comedy	fourth century B.C.E.?
Diphilus of Sinope	Greek	Comedy	ca. 360–ca. 300 B.C.E.
Dorillus or Dorilaus	Greek	Tragedy	fifth century B.C.E.
Dorotheus of Chalcis	Greek	Tragedy	first century B.C.E.
Dromo	Greek	Comedy	fourth century B.C.E.
Dymas	Greek	Tragedy	second century B.C.E.
Euaretus	Greek	Tragedy	fourth century B.C.E.
Ecphantides	Greek	Comedy	fifth century B.C.E.
Emmenides?	Greek	Comedy	second century B.C.E.
Empedocles	Greek	Tragedy	fourth century B.C.E.
Ennius, Quintus	Latin	Tragedy	239–169 B.C.E.
		Fabulae praetextae	
		Fabulae palliatae	
Ephippus	Greek	Comedy	fourth century B.C.E.
Epicharmus of Syracuse	Greek	Comedy	fifth century B.C.E.
Epicrates I	Greek	Comedy	fourth century B.C.E.
Epicrates II?	Greek	Comedy	second century B.C.E.
Epigenes	Greek	Comedy	fourth century B.C.E.
Epilycus	Greek	Comedy	fifth or fourth century B.C.E.?
Epinicus	Greek	Comedy	third or second century B.C.E.
Eriphus	Greek	Comedy	fourth century B.C.E.
Euaeon (son of Aeschylus)	Greek	Tragedy	fifth century B.C.E.
Euages	Greek	Comedy	uncertain
Euandridas	Greek	Tragedy	third century B.C.E.
Euangelus	Greek	Comedy	fourth century B.C.E. (after)
Euaretus	Greek	Tragedy	fourth century B.C.E.
Eubulides I	Greek	Comedy	fourth century B.C.E.?
Eubulides II?	Greek	Comedy	third century B.C.E.
Eubulus	Greek	Comedy	fourth century B.C.E.
Eudoxus	Greek	Comedy	fourth–third century B.C.E.?
Euetes	Greek	Comedy	uncertain
Euetes	Greek	Tragedy	fifth century B.C.E.
Eumedes	Greek	Comedy	fourth century B.C.E. (after?)
Eunicus	Greek	Comedy	fifth century B.C.E.
Euphanes	Greek	Comedy	fourth century B.C.E.
Euphantus	Greek	Tragedy	third century B.C.E.
Euphorion (son of Aeschylus)	Greek	Tragedy	fifth century B.C.E.
Euphron	Greek	Comedy	third century B.C.E.
Euphronius	Greek	Comedy	fifth century B.C.E.
Euphonius?	Greek	Tragedy	third century B.C.E.
Eupolis	Greek	Comedy	died. ca. 411 or 410 B.C.E.
Euripides I	Greek	Tragedy	fifth century B.C.E.
Euripides II	Greek	Tragedy	fifth century B.C.E.
EURIPIDES III (son of Mnesarchus)	Greek	Tragedy	ca. 484–406 B.C.E.
Euthias	Greek	Comedy	fourth century B.C.E.

(continues)

(continued)

Author Name	Language	Genre(s)	Date
Euthycles	Greek	Comedy	fifth or fourth century B.C.E.?
Euthycrates?	Greek	Comedy	third century B.C.E.
Euxenides	Greek	Comedy	fifth century B.C.E.
Ezechiel	Greek	Tragedy	second century B.C.E.?
Faustus	Latin	Tragedy	first century C.E.?
Fundanius	Latin	*Fabulae palliatae*	first century B.C.E.
Gnesippus	Greek	Tragedy	fifth century B.C.E.
Gorgippus of Chalcis	Greek	Tragedy	first century B.C.E.
Gracchus	Latin	Tragedy	first century B.C.E.?
Harmodius of Tarsus	Greek	Tragedy	first century B.C.E.
Hegemon	Greek	Comedy	fifth century B.C.E.
Hegesippus	Greek	Comedy	third century B.C.E.
Heliodorus of Athens	Greek	Tragedy	first century B.C.E. (before)
Heniochus of Athens	Greek	Comedy	fourth century B.C.E.
Heraclides of Athens	Greek	Tragedy	first century B.C.E.
Heraclides	Greek	Comedy	fourth century B.C.E.
Heraclides?	Greek	Tragedy	fifth century B.C.E.
Heraclitus?	Greek	Comedy	fourth century B.C.E.
Hermippus of Athens	Greek	Comedy	fifth century B.C.E.
Hermocrates of Miletus	Greek	Tragedy	first century B.C.E.
Herodas or Herondas	Greek	Mime	third century B.C.E.
Hipparchus	Greek	Comedy	third century B.C.E.
Hippias	Greek	Tragedy	fifth century B.C.E.
Hippothoon? or Hippothous?	Greek	Tragedy	Uncertain (earliest reference fifth century C.E.)
Hieronymus	Greek	Tragedy	fifth century B.C.E.
Homerus	Greek	Tragedy	third century C.E.
Hostilius	Latin	Mime	first century C.E.?
Iolaus	Greek	Comedy	second century B.C.E.
Ion	Greek	Comedy	fifth century B.C.E.
Ion of Chios	Greek	Tragedy	fifth century B.C.E.
Iophon	Greek	Tragedy	fifth century B.C.E.
Isagoras	Greek	Tragedy	second century C.E.
Isidorus	Greek	Tragedy	Uncertain (earliest reference fifth century C.E.)
Iuventius	Latin	*Fabulae palliatae*	*second century B.C.E.?*
Julius Caesar Strabo, Gaius	Latin	Tragedy	second century B.C.E.–first century B.C.E.
Julius Caesar, Gaius	Latin	Tragedy	100–44 B.C.E.
Julius Caesar, Germanicus	Greek	Comedy	16 or 15 B.C.E.–19 C.E.
Julius Longianus, Gaius	Greek	Tragedy	second century C.E.
Julius Magnus, Gaius	Greek	Tragedy	first century C.E.
Laberius, Decimus	Latin	Mime	second–first century B.C.E.
Laines	Greek	Comedy	second century B.C.E.
Lampytus	Greek	Comedy	second century B.C.E.
Laon	Greek	Comedy	third century B.C.E.?
Lentulus	Latin	Mime	first century C.E.?
Leuco	Greek	Comedy	fifth–fourth century B.C.E.
Licinius Imbrex	Latin	*Fabulae palliatae*	second century B.C.E.?
Livius Andronicus, Lucius	Latin	Tragedy	third century B.C.E.
		Fabulae palliatae	
Lucilius	Latin	Mime	first century C.E.?
Lucius Varius Rufus	Latin	Tragedy	first century B.C.E.–first century C.E.?
Luscius Lanuvius	Latin	*Fabulae palliatae*	second century B.C.E.
Lycis	Greek	Comedy	fifth century B.C.E.

Author Name	Language	Genre(s)	Date
Lycophron	Greek	Tragedy	fourth–third century B.C.E.
Lynceus	Latin	Tragedy	first century B.C.E.?
Lynceus of Samos	Greek	Comedy	fourth or third century B.C.E.
Lysimachus	Greek	Tragedy	second century B.C.E.
Lysippus	Greek	Comedy	fifth century B.C.E.
Lysistratus of Chalcis	Greek	Tragedy	first century B.C.E.
Machon	Greek	Comedy	third century B.C.E.
Maecenas Melissus, Gaius	Latin	*Fabulae trabeatae*	first century B.C.E.–first century C.E.
Magnes	Greek	Comedy	fifth century B.C.E.
Mamercus	Greek	Tragedy	fourth century B.C.E.
Marius Antiochus, Lucius of Corinth	Greek	Tragedy	second century C.E.
Marullus	Latin	Mime	first century B.C.E.–first century C.E.?
Maternus, Curiatus	Latin	Tragedy *Fabulae praetextae*	first century C.E.
Melanthius of Athens	Greek	Tragedy	fifth century B.C.E.
Melanthius of Rhodes	Greek	Tragedy	second century B.C.E.
Meletus I	Greek	Tragedy	fifth–fourth century B.C.E.
Meletus II	Greek	Tragedy	fifth–fourth century B.C.E.
Meliton	Greek	Tragedy	first century C.E.
Memor, Scaevus	Latin	Tragedy	first century C.E.–second century C.E.
MENANDER of Athens	Greek	Comedy	344/3–392/1 B.C.E.
Menecrates	Greek	Comedy	fifth century B.C.E. (after)
Menelaus	Greek	Tragedy	second century B.C.E.
Menippus?	Greek	Comedy	Uncertain
Mesatus	Greek	Tragedy	fifth century B.C.E.
Metagenes	Greek	Comedy	fifth century B.C.E.
Miletus	Greek	Tragedy	first century C.E.
Mimnermus	Greek	Tragedy	fourth century B.C.E. (before?)
Mnesimachus	Greek	Comedy	fourth century B.C.E.
Morsimus of Athens	Greek	Tragedy	fifth century B.C.E.
Morychus	Greek	Tragedy	fifth century B.C.E.
Moschion	Greek	Tragedy	third century B.C.E.
Moschus	Greek	Tragedy	third century B.C.E.
Mummius	Latin	*Fabulae atellanae*	first century B.C.E.
Myrtilus	Greek	Comedy	fifth century B.C.E.
Naevius, Gnaeus	Latin	Tragedy *Fabulae praetextae* *Fabulae palliatae*	died 201 B.C.E.
Nausicrates	Greek	Comedy	fourth century B.C.E.
Neophron	Greek	Tragedy	fifth century B.C.E.
Nico	Greek	Comedy	fifth century B.C.E. (after)
Nicochares	Greek	Comedy	fourth century B.C.E.
Nicolaus	Greek	Comedy	fourth century B.C.E.?
Nicolaus of Damascus	Greek	Tragedy	first century B.C.E.
Nicomachus	Greek	Comedy	third century B.C.E.
Nicomachus of Alexandria (in the Troad)	Greek	Tragedy	third century B.C.E.
Nicomachus of Athens	Greek	Tragedy	fifth century B.C.E.
Nicophon of Athens	Greek	Comedy	fifth–fourth century B.C.E.
Nicostratus	Greek	Comedy	fourth century B.C.E.
Nothippus	Greek	Tragedy	fifth century B.C.E.
Novius	Latin	*Fabulae atellanae*	first century B.C.E.

(continues)

(continued)

Author Name	Language	Genre(s)	Date
Oenomaus of Gadaris	Greek	Tragedy	second century C.E.
Ophelio	Greek	Comedy	fourth century B.C.E.
Ovid (Publius Ovidius Naso)	Latin	Tragedy	43 B.C.E.–17 C.E.
Paccius	Latin	Tragedy	first century C.E.?
Pacuvius, Marcus	Latin	Tragedy	ca. 220–ca. 130 B.C.E.
		Fabulae praetextae	
Pamphilus of Athens	Greek	Tragedy	fourth century B.C.E.
Paramonus	Greek	Comedy	Uncertain
Patrocles of Athens	Greek	Tragedy	fourth century B.C.E.
Patrocles of Thuria	Greek	Tragedy	fourth century B.C.E.
Persius Flaccus, Aulus	Latin	*Fabulae praetextae*	34–62 C.E.
Phaenippus	Greek	Tragedy	third century B.C.E.
Phanes	Greek	Tragedy	third century B.C.E.
Phanostratus	Greek	Tragedy	fourth century B.C.E.
Pharadas of Athens	Greek	Tragedy	first century B.C.E.
Pherecrates	Greek	Comedy	fifth century B.C.E.
Philemon of Syracuse	Greek	Comedy	368/60–267/63 B.C.E.
Philemon the Younger	Greek	Comedy	third century B.C.E.
Philetaerus	Greek	Comedy	fourth century B.C.E.
Philinus	Greek	Tragedy	fourth century B.C.E.
Philippides	Greek	Comedy	fourth century B.C.E.
Philippus	Greek	Comedy	fourth century B.C.E.
Philiscus of Aegina	Greek	Tragedy	fourth century B.C.E.
Philiscus of Corcyra	Greek	Tragedy	third century B.C.E.
Philiscus	Greek	Comedy	fourth century B.C.E.?
Philocles I	Greek	Tragedy	fifth century B.C.E.
Philocles II	Greek	Tragedy	fourth century B.C.E.
Philocles	Greek	Comedy	Uncertain
Philonides	Greek	Comedy	fifth century B.C.E.
Philostephanus	Greek	Comedy	Uncertain (earliest reference second–third century C.E.)
Philostratus of Lemnos	Greek	Tragedy	second century C.E.
Philoxenides Oropius	Greek	Tragedy	first century B.C.E.
Philyllius	Greek	Comedy	fifth–fourth century B.C.E.
Phoenicides	Greek	Comedy	third century B.C.E.
Phormis (or Phormus)	Greek	Comedy	fifth century B.C.E.?
Phrynichus II of Athens	Greek	Tragedy	Uncertain (earliest reference 10th century C.E.)
Phrynichus of Athens	Greek	Comedy	fifth century B.C.E.
Phrynichus of Athens	Greek	Tragedy	sixth–fifth century B.C.E.
Plato	Greek	Tragedy	fifth century B.C.E.
Plato of Athens	Greek	Comedy	fifth–fourth century B.C.E.
Plautius	Latin	*Fabulae palliatae*	second century B.C.E.?
PLAUTUS, Titus Maccius	Latin	*Fabulae palliatae*	ca. 254–184 B.C.E.
Pliny the Younger	Greek	Tragedy	ca. 61–ca.112 C.E.
Polemaeus of Ephesus	Greek	Tragedy	first century B.C.E.
Polemon	Greek	Tragedy	second century B.C.E.
Poliochus	Greek	Comedy	fifth or third century B.C.E.
Polychares	Greek	Tragedy	fourth century B.C.E.
Polyidus? of Selymbria	Greek	Tragedy	fourth century B.C.E.
Polyphrasmon	Greek	Tragedy	fifth century B.C.E.
Polyzelus	Greek	Comedy	fifth–fourth century B.C.E.
Pompeius Capito	Greek	Tragedy	first century C.E.

Author Name	Language	Genre(s)	Date
Pompeius Macer, Gnaeus	Greek	Tragedy	first century C.E.
Pompilius	Latin	Tragedy	second or first century B.C.E.?
Pomponius Bassulus, Marcus	Latin	*Fabulae palliatae*	first century C.E.–second century C.E.?
Pomponius Bononiensis, Lucius	Latin	*Fabulae atellanae*	second century B.C.E.–first century B.C.E.
Pomponius Secundus, Publius	Latin	Tragedy *Fabulae praetextae*	first century C.E.
Posidippus	Greek	Comedy	third century B.C.E.
Pratinas of Phlius	Greek	Tragedy	sixth–fifth century B.C.E.
Protarchus of Thebes	Greek	Tragedy	first century B.C.E.
Ptolomaeus IV Philopator	Greek	Tragedy	ca. 244–205 B.C.E.
Publius Romanus	Greek	Tragedy	first century B.C.E.
Publilius Syrus	Latin	Mime	first century B.C.E.
Pupius, Publius	Latin	Tragedy	first century B.C.E.
Pythangelus	Greek	Tragedy	fifth century B.C.E.
Python	Greek	Tragedy	fourth century B.C.E.
Rhinthon (or Rhinton) of Syracuse	Greek	Comedy	third century B.C.E.
Rubrenus Lappa	Latin	Tragedy	first century C.E.?
Rufus, Antonius?	Latin	*Fabulae togatae*	first century B.C.E.–first century C.E.?
Sannyrion	Greek	Comedy	fifth century B.C.E.
Santra	Latin	Tragedy	first century B.C.E.
Sciras	Greek	Comedy	third century B.C.E.
Sclerias?	Greek	Tragedy	Uncertain (earliest reference fifth century C.E.)
SENECA, Lucius Annaeus	Latin	Tragedy	ca. 4 B.C.E.–65 C.E.
Serapion	Greek	Tragedy	first century C.E.
Silenus	Greek	Tragedy	second century B.C.E.
Simylus	Greek	Comedy	fourth or third century B.C.E.
Sogenes	Greek	Comedy	Uncertain
Sopater of Paphos	Greek	Comedy	fourth–third century B.C.E.
Sophilus	Greek	Comedy	fourth century B.C.E.?
SOPHOCLES I	Greek	Tragedy	ca. 496–406 B.C.E.
Sophocles II	Greek	Tragedy	fourth century B.C.E.
Sophocles III	Greek	Tragedy	second century B.C.E.
Sophron	Greek	Mime	fifth century B.C.E.
Sosicrates	Greek	Comedy	third century B.C.E.?
Sosipater	Greek	Comedy	third century B.C.E.?
Sosiphanes I	Greek	Tragedy	fourth century B.C.E.
Sosiphanes II	Greek	Tragedy	third century B.C.E.
Sosistratus	Greek	Tragedy	second century B.C.E.
Sositheus	Greek	Tragedy	third century B.C.E.
Sostratus of Chalcis	Greek	Tragedy	first century B.C.E.
Sotades	Greek	Comedy	fourth century B.C.E.
Spintharus of Heraclea	Greek	Tragedy	fifth or fourth century B.C.E.
Stephanus	Greek	Comedy	fourth–third century B.C.E.
Sthenelus	Greek	Tragedy	fifth century B.C.E.
Straton	Greek	Comedy	fourth or third century B.C.E.
Strattis of Athens	Greek	Comedy	fifth century B.C.E.
Susarion of Megara	Greek	Comedy	sixth or fifth century B.C.E.
Synesius of Cyrene	Greek	Tragedy	fifth century C.E.
Teleclides	Greek	Comedy	fifth century B.C.E.
TERENCE (Publius Terentius Afer)	Latin	*Fabulae palliatae*	ca. 190–159 B.C.E.
Theaetetus?	Greek	Tragedy	third century B.C.E.

(continues)

(continued)

Author Name	Language	Genre(s)	Date
Theodectas of Phaselis	Greek	Tragedy	fourth century B.C.E.
Theodorides	Greek	Tragedy	fourth century B.C.E.
Theodorus	Greek	Tragedy	second century B.C.E.
Theognetus	Greek	Comedy	third century B.C.E.?
Theognis	Greek	Tragedy	fifth century B.C.E.
Theophilus	Greek	Comedy	fourth century B.C.E.
Theopompus	Greek	Comedy	fifth–fourth century B.C.E.
Thespis of Athens	Greek	Tragedy	ca. 550–500 B.C.E.
Theudotus?	Greek	Tragedy	first century B.C.E.
Thrasycles of Athens	Greek	Tragedy	first century B.C.E.
Thugenides	Greek	Comedy	fifth century B.C.E.
Thymoteles?	Greek	Tragedy	second century B.C.E.
Tiberius Claudius Alexander of Laodicea	Greek	Tragedy	third century C.E.
Timesitheus	Greek	Tragedy	Uncertain (earliest citation tenth century C.E.)
Timocles	Greek	Comedy/tragedy	fourth century B.C.E.
Timon	Greek	Comedy	third century B.C.E.
Timon	Greek	Tragedy	third century B.C.E.
Timostratus of Athens	Greek	Comedy	second century B.C.E.
Timostratus	Greek	Tragedy	fourth century B.C.E.
Timotheus of Athens	Greek	Comedy	fourth or third century B.C.E.?
Timotheus of Gaza	Greek	Tragedy	fifth century C.E.
Timoxenus	Greek	Comedy	Uncertain
Titinius	Latin	*Fabulae togatae*	second century B.C.E.
Titius, Gaius	Latin	Tragedy	second or first century B.C.E.
Trabea	Latin	*Fabulae palliatae*	third–second century B.C.E.?
Tullius Cicero, Quintus	Latin	Tragedy	first century B.C.E.
Turpilius, Sextus	Latin	*Fabulae palliatae*	second century B.C.E.
Turranius	Latin	Tragedy	first century B.C.E.–first century C.E.?
Valerius	Latin	Mime	first century B.C.E.?
Varro	Latin	Tragedy	first century C.E.?
Vatronius	Latin	*Fabulae palliatae*	second century B.C.E.?
Vergilius Romanus	Latin	*Fabulae palliatae*	first–second century C.E.?
Vespasianus, Titus Flavius	Greek	Tragedy	9–79 C.E.
Volnius	Latin	Tragedy	second century B.C.E.?
Xenarchus	Greek	Comedy	fourth century B.C.E.
Xeno	Greek	Comedy	third century B.C.E.
Xenocles	Greek	Tragedy	fifth century B.C.E.
Xenocrates	Greek	Tragedy	third century B.C.E.
Xenophilus	Greek	Comedy	fifth century B.C.E.
Xenophon	Greek	Comedy	fifth century B.C.E.
Zenodotus	Greek	Tragedy	Uncertain (earliest reference fifth century C.E.)
Zopyrus	Greek	Tragedy	third century B.C.E.?
Zotion	Greek	Tragedy	second century B.C.E.

APPENDIX III

LIST OF ALL TITLES ATTRIBUTED TO CLASSICAL PLAYWRIGHTS

The following is a list, organized by playwright, of all fragmentary or nonsurviving plays whose titles can be identified. The presence of a question mark (?) indicates some doubt about the spelling of the author's name, translation of the work's title, or the name of the work. In some cases, playwrights produced more than one version of a play. Such instances are accompanied by a letter of the alphabet (e.g., *Hippolytus A, Hippolytus B*).

ACCIUS, LUCIUS (LATIN; *FABULA PRAETEXTA*)

Translation	Ancient Title
Aeneadae or *Decius*	Aeneadae or Decius
Brutus	Brutus

ACCIUS, LUCIUS (LATIN; TRAGEDY)

Translation	Ancient Title
Achilles	Achilles
Aegisthus	Aegisthus
Agamemnon's Children	Agamemnonidae
Alcestis	Alcestis
Alcmaeon	Alcimeo
Alphesiboea	Alphesiboea
Amphitryon	Amphitryon
Andromeda	Andromeda
Antigone	Antigona
Astyanax	Astyanax
Athamas	Athamas
Atreus	Atreus
Bacchae	Bacchae
Battle at the Ships	Epinausimache
Chrysippus	Chrysippus
Clytemnestra	Clytemnestra
Deiphobus	Deiphobus
Diomedes	Diomedes
Epigoni	Epigoni
Erigone	Erigona
Eriphyle	Eriphyla
Eurysaces	Eurysaces
Hecuba	Hecuba
Hellenes	Hellenes
Io	Io
Judgment of Arms	Armorum Iudicium
Medea	Medea
Melanippus	Melanippus
Meleager	Meleager
Minos or *Minotaur*	Minos or Minotaurus
Myrmidons	Myrmidons
Neoptolemus	Neoptolemus
Night Alarm	Nyctegresia
Oenomaus	Oenomaus
Philoctetes	Philocteta
Phoenician Women	Phoenissae
Prometheus	Prometheus
Rebels or *Trophy of Bacchus*	Stasiastae or Tropaeum Liberi

Sons of Antenor	Antenoridae
Sons of Pelops	Pelopidae
Sons of Perseus	Persidae
Sons of Phineus	Phinidae
Tale of Thebes	Thebais
Telephus	Telephus
Tereus	Tereus
Trojan Women	Troades

ACHAEUS (GREEK; TRAGEDY)

Translation	Ancient Title
Adrastus	Adrastos
Aethon (satyr)	Aithôn Saturikos
Alcmeon (satyr)	Alkmeôn Saturikos
Alphesiboea	Alphesiboia
Attack (of disease)	Katapeira
Cycnus	Kuknos
Erginus	Erginos?
Fates (satyr)	Moirai (Saturoi)
Games (satyr)	Athla or Athloi (Saturoi)
Hephaestus (satyr)	Hêphaistos Saturikos
Iris (satyr)	Iris Saturoi
Linus (satyr)	Linos Saturikos
Momus	Mômos
Oedipus	Oidipous
Omphale (satyr)	Omphalê Saturikê
Peirithous	Peirithous
People of Zan	Azanes
Philoctetes	Philoktêtês
Phrixus	Phrixos
Theseus	Thêseus

AESCHYLUS OF ALEXANDRIA (GREEK; TRAGEDY)

Translation	Ancient Title
Amphitryon	Amphitruôn

AFRANIUS, LUCIUS (LATIN; *FABULA TOGATA*)

Translation	Ancient Title
Auction	Auctio
Augur	Augur
Betrayed Man	Proditus
Compitalia	Compitalia
Cousins	Consobrini
Crime?	Crimen
Deposit	Depositum
Divorce	Divortium
Divorced Man	Repudiatus
Enemies	Inimici
Filth	Purgamentum
Fire	Incendium
Freedman	Libertus
Just Alike	Aequales
Letter	Epistula
Maiden	Virgo
Man Who Curled Hair	Cinerarius
Man Who Was Emancipated	Emancipatus
Man Who Was Excepted?	Exceptus
Married Couple	Mariti
Maternal Aunts	Materterae
Megalensia	Megalensia
Notice of Sale	Titulus
Omen	Omen
Pantelius	Pantelius
Pretender	Simulans
Procession	Pompa
Prodigal	Prodigus
Prosa?	Prosa?
Retaliation	Talio
Seat	Sella
Sisters	Sorores
Sisters-in-Law	Fratriae
Stepson	Privignus
Steward	Promus
Surrender	Deditio
Surviving Twin	Vopiscus
Thais	Thais
Thoughtless Man	Temerarius
Woman of Brundisium	Brundisiae
Woman Who Was Abducted	Abducta
Woman Who Was Suspected	Suspecta

AGATHENOR (GREEK; COMEDY)

Translation	Ancient Title
Woman of Miletus	Milêsia

AGATHOCLES (GREEK; COMEDY)

Translation	Ancient Title
Unity	Homonoia

AGATHON (GREEK; TRAGEDY)

Translation	Ancient Title
Aerope	Aeropê
Alcmeon	Alkmeôn
Flower	Anthos or Antheus
Mysians	Musoi
Telephus	Têlephos
Thyestes	Thuestês

ALCAEUS (GREEK; COMEDY)

Translation	Ancient Title
Adulterous Sisters	Adelphai Moicheuomenai
Callisto	Kallistô
Endymion	Endumiôn
Ganymede	Ganumêdês
Pasiphae	Pasiphaê
Sacred Marriage	Hieros Gamos
Seriocomedy	Kômôidotragôidia
Wrestling School	Palaistra

ALCIMENES (GREEK; COMEDY)

Translation	Ancient Title
Women Diving	Kolumbôsai

ALEXANDER (GREEK; COMEDY)

Translation	Ancient Title
Cicada	Titigonion
Dionysus	Dionusos
Drinking Bout	Potos
Goatherds	Aipoloi
Helen	Helenê
Tigonion?	Tigonion

ALEXANDER (GREEK; TRAGEDY)

Translation	Ancient Title
Dice Players	Astragalistai?

ALEXIS (GREEK; COMEDY)

Translation	Ancient Title
Aesop	Aisôpos
Agonis or Scarf	Agônis or Hippiskos
Altar	Bômos
Anteia	Anteia
Archilochus	Archilochos
Asclepiocleides	Asklêpiokleidês
Atalanta	Atalantê
Attis	Atthis
Baskets	Sôrakoi
Brothers	Adelphoi
Captive	Aichmalôtos
Carthaginian	Karchêdonios
Cauldron	Lebês
Cithara Player	Kitharôidos
Cleobouline	Kleoboulinê
Concubine	Pallakê
Crateias or Druggist	Krateuas or Pharmakopôlês
Cup Maker	Ekpômatopoios
Cycnus	Kuknos
Cyprian	Kuprios
Dancing Girl	Orchêstris
Demetrius or True Friend	Dêmêtrios or Philetairos
Dominion of Women	Gunaikokratia
Dorcis or Woman Who Smacks	Dorkis or Poppuzousa
Dropides	Drôpidês
Epidaurian	Epidaurios
Eretrian	Eretrikos
Fair Measure	Isostasion
Female Athletic Trainer	Aleiptria
Female Follower of Pythagoras	Puthagorizousa
First Chorus	Prôtochoros
Fugitive	Phugas
Galatea	Galateia
Gamblers	Kubeutai
Garment with Tassels	Kalasiris
Goatherds	Aipoloi
God-Possessed	Theophorêtos
Guardian	Epitropos
Hairdresser	Kouris
Harvest Season	Opôra
Healing	Iasis
Heiress	Epiklêros
Helen	Helenê
Helen's Abduction	Helenês Harpagê
Helen's Suitors	Helenês Mnêstêres
Helmsman	Kubernêtês
Hesione	Hêsionê
Knight	Hippeus
Laborers	Thêteuontes
Letter	Epistolê
Leucadia or Runaway Girls	Leukadia or Drapetai

Translation	Ancient Title
Leuce	Leukē
Liar	Pseudomenos
Libation Bearer	Spondophoros
Linus	Linos
Lock of Hair	Bostruchos
Locrians	Lokroi
Lovelorn Woman	Ponēra
Lover of Athenians	Philathēnaios
Lover of Beauty or Nymphs	Philokalos or Numphai
Lover of Tragedies	Philotragōidos
Lyciscus	Lukiskos
Man Lighting a Fire	Puraunos
Man of Pontus	Pontikos
Man of Sicyon	Sikuōnios
Man Who Was a Herald?	Kēruttomenos
Man Banished by Proclamation	Ekkēruttomenos
Man Who Was Cut Loose	Apokoptomenos
Man Who Was Falsely Accused	Katapseudomenos
Man With a Cataract	Apeglaukōmenos
Mandrake-Drugged Woman	Mandragorizomenē
Meeting at Pylae	Pulaia
Men of Caunus	Kaunioi
Meropis	Meropis
Midon	Midōn
Milcon	Milkōn
Miller	Mulōthros
Minos	Minōs
Moneylender or Man Who Was Falsely Accused	Tokistēs or Katapseudomenos
New Tenant	Eisoikizomenos
Noose	Ankuliōn
Odysseus Being Washed	Odusseus Aponiptomenos
Odysseus the Weaver	Odusseus Huphainōn
Olympiodorus	Olumpiodōros
Orestes	Orestēs
Pail	Amphōtis
Pamphile	Pamphilē
Pancratiast	Pankratiastēs
Parasite	Parasitos
Pezonike	Pezonikē
Phaedrus	Phaidros
Phaidon or Phaidrias	Phaidōn or Phaidrias
Philiscus	Philiskos
Phrygian	Phrux
Picture	Graphē
Plasterer	Koniatēs
Poetess	Poiētria
Poets	Poiētai
Polycleia	Polukleia
Profligacy Teacher	Asōtodidaskalos
Prophets	Manteis
Raised Together	Suntrophoi
Reapers	Erithoi
Rhodian or Woman Who Smacks	Rhodion or Poppuzousa
Ring	Daktulios
Running Mates	Suntrechontes
Scattered (or Scattering) Before?	Proskedannumenos
Sciron	Skeirōn
Seven against Thebes	Hepta Epi Thēbais
Similarity	Homoia
Sleep	Hupnos
Soldier	Stratiōtēs
Suitors	Mnēsthres
Suppositious Baby	Hupobolimaios
Syracusan	Surakosios
Tarentines	Tarantinoi
Thebans	Thēbaioi
Those Dying Together	Sunapothnēiskontes
Thrason	Thrasōn
Thresprotians	Thesprōtoi
Torch	Lampas
Trick Rider	Apobatēs
Trophonius	Trophōnios
True Friend	Philetairos
Twice Mourning	Dis Penthōn
Twins	Didumoi or Didumai
Tyndareus	Tundareōs
Vigil or Reapers	Pannuchis or Erithoi
Vine Dresser	Ampelourgos
Wet-Nurse	Titthē
Woman in Love	Philousa
Woman in the Well	Hē eis to phrear
Woman of Achaea	Achaiis
Woman of Bruttia	Brettia
Woman of Cnidus	Knidia
Woman of Hellas	Hellēnis
Woman of Lemnos	Lēmnia
Woman of Miletus	Milēsia
Woman of Olynthus	Olunthia
Woman Who Plays the Pipes	Aulētris
Woman Choregus	Chorēgis
Women Sailing Through	Diapleousai
Wounded Man	Traumatias

AMINIAS (GREEK; COMEDY)

Translation	Ancient Title
Adulterers	Moichoi
Woman Leaving Her Husband	Apoleipousa

AMIPSIAS (GREEK; COMEDY)

Translation	Ancient Title
Connus	Konnos
Devourer	Katesthiôn
Playing at Cottabus	Apokottabizontes
Revelers	Kômastai
Sappho	Sapphô
Sling	Sphendonê

AMPHIS (GREEK; COMEDY)

Translation	Ancient Title
Alcmeon	Alkmeôn
Amphicrates	Amphikrtês
Athamas	Athamas
Bath	Balaneion
Brotherly Love	Philadelphoi
Callisto	Kallistô
Deceiver	Planos
Dexidemides	Dexidêmidês
Dithyrambus	Dithurambos
Dominion of Women	Gunaikokratia
Female Athletic Trainer	Aleiptria
Gamblers	Kubeutai
Hairdresser	Kouris
Harvest Season	Opôra
Lamentation	Ialemos
Leucadia or Leucas	Leukadia or Leukas
Odysseus	Odusseus
Pan	Pan
Plasterer	Koniatês
Reapers	Erithoi
Ring	Daktulios
Sappho	Sapphô
Seven against Thebes	Hepta Epi Thêbais
Silly Woman	Akkô
True Friend	Philetairos
Uranus	Ouranos
Vine Dresser	Ampelourgos
Woman Madness	Gunaikomania

ANAXANDRIDES (GREEK; COMEDY)

Translation	Ancient Title
Achilles	Achilleus
Amprakiôtis	Amprakiôtis
Anchises	Anchisês
Anteros	Anterôn
Basket Bearer	Kanêphoros
Cities	Poleis
Dionysus' Birth	Dionusou Gonai
Drill Sergeant	Hoplomachos
Drug Prophet	Pharmakomantis
Erechtheus	Erechtheus
Female Cithara Player	Kitharistria
Helen	Helenê
Heracles	Hêraklês
Honey Clover? or Melilot?	Melilôtos
Hubris	Hubris
Hunters	Kunêgetai
Io	Iô
Kerkios	Kerkios
Lycurgus	Lukourgos
Man Driven Mad?	Mainomenos?
Nereids	Nêrêides
Nereus	Nêreus
Odysseus	Odusseus
Old Man's Madness	Gerontomania
Painters or Geographers	Zôgraphoi or Geôgraphoi
Pandarus	Pandaros
Pious	Eusebeis
Protesilaus	Prôtesilaos
Rustics	Agroikoi
Satyrias	Saturias
Seriocomedy	Kômôidotragôidia
Sosippus	Sôsippos
Tereus	Têreus
Theseus	Thêseus
Thessalians	Thettaloi
Treasure	Thêsauros
Twins	Didumoi
Ugly?	Aischra
Urn Carrier	Phialêphoros
Woman of Samos	Samia
Women of Locria	Lokrides

ANAXILAS (GREEK; COMEDY)

Translation	Ancient Title
Botrulion	Botruliôn
Calypso	Kalupsô
Chick	Neottis
Circe	Kirkê
Cooks	Mageiroi
Cyclops	Kuklôps
Exchange?	Antidosis?
Glaucus	Glaukos
Goldsmith	Chrusochoos

Graces	Charites
Hyacinthus	Huakinthos
Io	Iô
Lyre Maker	Luropoios
Manliness	Euandria
Misanthrope	Monotropos
Nereus	Nêreus
Pimp	Pornoboskos?
Player of the Pipes	Aulêtês
Poultry Keepers	Ornithokomoi
Rich	Plousioi or Plousiai
Rustic Man	Agroikos
Seasons	Hôrai

ANAXION (GREEK; TRAGEDY)

Translation	Ancient Title
Persians (satyr)	Persai Saturoi

ANAXIPPUS (GREEK; COMEDY)

Translation	Ancient Title
Cithara Player	Kitharôidos
Lightning or Man Who Was Struck By Lightning	Keraunos or Keraunoumenos
Man Who Hid His Face	Enkaluptomenos
Man Who Was Sued	Epidikazomenos
Well	Phrear

ANTIDOTUS (GREEK; COMEDY)

Translation	Ancient Title
Faultfinder	Mempsimoiros
First Chorus	Prôtochoros
Similarity	Homoia

ANTIPHANES (GREEK; COMEDY)

Translation	Ancient Title
Adonis	Adônis
Adulterers	Moichoi
Aeolus	Aiolos
Alcestis	Alkêstis
Amorous	Aphrodisios
Andromeda	Andromeda
Antaeus	Antaios
Anteia	Anteia
Aphrodite's Birth	Aphroditês Gonai

Arcadian	Arkas
Archestrata	Archestratê
Asclepius	Asklêpios
Athamas	Athamas
Augur	Oiônistês
Bacchae	Bakchai
Bag	Kôrukos
Begetting of Men	Anthrôpogonia
Begging Priest of Cybele	Mêtragurtês
Boutalion	Boutaliôn
Bumblebee or Gurgling Pitcher	Bombulios
Bursiris	Bousiris
Caeneus	Kaineus
Carian Wailing Woman	Karinê
Carians	Kares
Charioteer	Hêniochos
Chick	Neottis
Cithara Player	Kitharistês
Cithara Player	Kitharôidos
Cleophanes	Kleophanês
Cyclops	Kuklôps
Deucalion	Deukalôn
Doctor	Iatros
Egyptians	Aiguptioi
Elimination of Money	Arguriou Aphanismos
Epidaurian	Epidaurios
Etruscan	Turrênos
Euthydicus	Euthudikos
Fair Voyage	Euploia
Female Athletic Trainer	Aleiptria
Fuller	Knapheus
Gamblers	Kubeutai
Ganymede	Ganumêdês
Gardener	Kêpouros
Glaucus	Glaukos
Golden Vessel	Chrusis
Gorgythus	Gorguthos
Grazier	Probateus
Hairdresser	Kouris
Half Brothers	Homopatrioi
Hard to Sell	Duspratos
Heiress	Epiklêros
Homonyms	Homônumoi
Image Maker	Koroplathos
Jason	Iasôn
Just Alike	Homoioi or Homoiai
Knave Hater	Misoponêros
Knights	Hippeis
Lampon	Lampôn

Translation	Ancient Title
Leonides	Leônidês
Little Leptines	Leptiniskos
Lover of Boys	Paiderastês
Lover of Father	Philopatôr
Lover of Mother	Philomêtôr
Lover of Thebans	Philothêbaios
Lycon	Lukôn
Lydian	Ludos
Magistrate	Archôn
Man Killing Himself by Abstinence	Apokarterôn
Man Lighting a Fire?	Puraunos?
Man of Byzantium	Buzantios
Man of Cnoethe or Belly	Knoithideus or Gastrôn
Man of Leucas	Leukadios
Man of Phrearrus	Phrearrios
Man of Pontus	Pontikos
Man Who Loved Himself	Autou Erôn
Marriage	Gamos or Gamoi
Matricide	Mêtrophôn
Medea	Mêdeia
Melanion	Melaniôn
Meleager	Meleagros
Melissa	Melitta
Memorials	Mnêmata
Midon	Midôn
Mill House	Mulôn
Minos	Minôs
Mystic	Mustis
Oenomaus or Pelops	Oinomaos or Pelops
Omphale	Omphalê
Orpheus	Orpheus
Painter	Zôgraphos
Parasite	Parasitos
People of Thoricus or Digger	Thorikioi or Dioruttôn
Phaon	Phaôn
Philiscus	Philiskos
Philoctetes	Philoktêtês
Philotis	Philôtis
Player of the Pipes	Aulêtês
Player Who Took the Third Part	Tritagônistês
Poetry	Poiêsis
Profligates	Asôtoi
Proverbs	Paroimiai
Rescued Men	Anasôizomenoi
Resident Alien	Metoikos
Restorer of Runaways	Drapetagôgos
Rich Men	Plousioi
Riddle	Problêma
Rival in Love	Anterôsa
Rustic Man	Agroikos
Sappho	Sapphô
Scythians or Taurians	Skuthai or Tauroi
Seamstress	Akestria
Sisters	Adelphai
Sleep	Hupnos
Soft Woman	Malthakê
Soldier or Tychon	Stratiôtês or Tuchôn
Speechless	Enea
Stepchildren	Progonoi
Stutterer	Batalos
Terrible	Obrimos
Thamyras	Thamuras
Theogony	Theogonia?
Timon	Timôn
Torch	Lampas
True Friend	Philetairos
Twice as Much	Diplasioi
Twins	Didumoi
Unhappy Lovers	Duserôtes
Urn	Hudria
Woman Fishing	Halieuomenê
Woman Hit by a Javelin	Akontizomenê
Woman of Boeotia	Boiôtia
Woman of Corinth	Korinthia
Woman of Delos	Dêlia
Woman of Dodona	Dôdônis
Woman of Ephesus	Ephesia
Woman Who Plays the Pipes or Female Twins	Aulêtris or Didumai
Woman Who Was Abducted	Harpazomenê
Woman Wrongly Wed	Parekdidomenê
Women of Lemnos	Lêmniai
Women of Tough Town	Sklêriai
Wounded Man	Traumatias
Youths	Neaniskoi
Zacynthian	Zakunthios

ANTIPHON (GREEK; TRAGEDY)

Translation	Ancient Title
Andromache	Andromachê
Jason	Iasôn
Meleager	Meleagros
Philoctetes?	Philoktôtôs?

APHAREUS (GREEK; TRAGEDY)

Translation	Ancient Title
Auge	Augê

Translation	Ancient Title
Daughters of Pelias	Peliades
Orestes	Orestês

APOLLODORUS (GREEK; TRAGEDY)

Translation	Ancient Title
Child Murderer	Teknoktonos
Hellenes	Hellênes
Odysseus	Odusseus
Suppliant Women	Hiketides
Thyestes	Thuestês
Wounded by a Spine	Akanthoplêx

APOLLODORUS OF CARYSTOS (GREEK; COMEDY)

Translation	Ancient Title
Amphiaraus	Amphiareôs
Man Returning a Kindness	Anteuergetôn
Man Who Was Sued	Epidikazomenos
Men Killing Themselves by Abstinence	Apokarterountes
Mother-in-Law	Hecura
Priestess	Hiereia
Slanderer	Diabolos
Speechless	Enea
Tablet Maker	Grammateidiopolos
Woman Given a Dowry or Female Clothes Dealer	Proikizomenê or Himatiopôlis
Woman Leaving Her Husband	Apoleipousa or Apolipousa
Woman Who Was Slaughtered	Sphattomenê

APOLLODORUS OF GELA (GREEK; COMEDY)

Translation	Ancient Title
Brotherly Love or Man Killing Himself by Abstinence	Philadelphoi or Apokarterôn
Brothers	Adelphoi
Dyer	Deusopoios
Priestess	Hiereia
Pseudaias?	Pseudaias
Sisyphus	Sisuphos
Tablet Maker	Grammateidiopoios

Translation	Ancient Title
Uglier?	Aischriôn
Woman Leaving Her Husband	Apoleipousa

APOLLODORUS OF CARYSTOS OR GELA (GREEK; COMEDY)

Translation	Ancient Title
Brothers	Adelphoi
Celts	Galatai
Cithara Player	Kitharôidos
Imposters	Paralogizomenoi
Man Going Wrong	Diamartanôn
Man Who Disappeared	Aphanizomenos
Slave	Paidion
Woman of Laconia	Lakaina
Young Comrades	Sunephêboi

APOLLONIUS (GREEK; COMEDY)

Translation	Ancient Title
Free from Blame or Invited	Anepiklêtos or Epiklêtos

APOLLOPHANES (GREEK; COMEDY)

Translation	Ancient Title
Bride	Dalis
Centaurs	Kentauroi
Cretans	Krêtês
Danae	Danaê
Iphigeron	Iphigerôn

AQUILIUS (LATIN; COMEDY)

Translation	Ancient Title
Misogynist	Misogynos

ARAROS (GREEK; COMEDY)

Translation	Ancient Title
Adonis	Adônis
Caeneus	Kaineus
Hunchback	Kampuliôn
Hymenaeus	Humenaios
Pan's Birth	Panos Gonai

ARCHEDICUS
(GREEK; COMEDY)

Translation	Ancient Title
Man Going Wrong	Diamartanōn
Treasure	Thēsauros

ARCHESTRATUS
(GREEK; TRAGEDY)

Translation	Ancient Title
Antaeus?	Antaios?

ARCHICLES (GREEK; COMEDY)

Translation	Ancient Title
Captain or Heiress	Nauklēros or Epiklēros

ARCHIPPUS (GREEK; COMEDY)

Translation	Ancient Title
Amphitryon	Amphitruōn
Ass's Shadow	Onou Skia
Fish	Ichthues
Heracles' Marriage	Hēraklēs Gamōn
Rhinon	Rhinōn
Wealth	Ploutos

ARISTAGORAS
(GREEK; COMEDY)

Translation	Ancient Title
Blockhead	Mammakuthos

ARISTARCHUS
(GREEK; TRAGEDY)

Translation	Ancient Title
Achilles	Achilleus
Asclepius	Asklēpios
Tantalus	Tantalos

ARISTIAS (GREEK; TRAGEDY)

Translation	Ancient Title
Antaeus	Antaios
Atalanta	Atalantē

Cyclops (satyr)	Kuklōps Saturoi
Fates	Kēres
Orpheus	Orpheus

ARISTOMENES
(GREEK; COMEDY)

Translation	Ancient Title
Admetus	Admētos
Assistants	Boēthoi
Dionysus Artisan	Dionusos Askētēs
Witch	Goētes
Wood Carriers	Hulophoroi

ARISTONYMUS
(GREEK; COMEDY)

Translation	Ancient Title
Shivering Helios	Hēlios Rigōn
Theseus	Thēseus

ARISTOPHON
(GREEK; COMEDY)

Translation	Ancient Title
Babias	Babias
Callonides	Kallōnidēs
Deposit	Parakatathēkē
Doctor	Iatros
Follower of Pythagoras	Puthagoristēs
Peirithous	Peirithous
Philonides	Philōnidēs
Plato	Platōn
Twins or Man Lighting a Fire	Didumoi or Didumai or Puraunos

ASTYDAMAS
(GREEK; TRAGEDY)

Translation	Ancient Title
Achilles	Achilleus
Alcmene	Alkmēnē
Alcmeon	Alkmeōn
Antigone	Antigonē
Athamas	Athamas
Bellerophon	Bellerophontēs
Epigoni	Epigonoi

Hector	*Hektōr*
Heracles (satyr)?	*Hēraklēs Saturikos?*
Hermes (satyr?)	*Hermēs Saturoi?*
Lycaon	*Lukaōn*
Madness of Ajax	*Aias Mainomenos*
Nauplius	*Nauplios*
Palamedes	*Palamēdēs*
Parthenopaeus	*Parthenopaios*
Phoenix	*Phoinix*
Tyro	*Turō*

ATHENIO (GREEK; COMEDY)

Translation	Ancient Title
Samothracians	*Samothraikes*

ATHENODORUS? (GREEK; TRAGEDY)

Translation	Ancient Title
Phoenix	*Phoinix*

ATILIUS (LATIN; COMEDY)

Translation	Ancient Title
Woman of Boeotia	*Boeotia*

AUGEAS (GREEK; COMEDY)

Translation	Ancient Title
Purple Shell	*Porphura*
Rustic	*Agroikos*
Twice Accused	*Dis Katēgoroumenos*

AUTOCRATES (GREEK; COMEDY)

Translation	Ancient Title
Drummers	*Tumpanistai*

AXIONICUS (GREEK; COMEDY)

Translation	Ancient Title
Etruscan	*Turrēnos*
Lover of Euripides	*Phileuripidēs*
Man of Chalcis	*Chalkidikos*
Philinna	*Philinna*

BATO (GREEK; COMEDY)

Translation	Ancient Title
Aetolian	*Aitōlos*

Benefactors	*Euergetai*
Fellow Cheater	*Sunexapatōn*
Murderer	*Androphonos*

BIOTTUS (GREEK; COMEDY)

Translation	Ancient Title
Ignorant Man	*Agnoōn*
Poet	*Poiētēs*

BIOTUS (GREEK; TRAGEDY)

Translation	Ancient Title
Medea	*Mēdeia*

BLAESUS (GREEK; COMEDY)

Translation	Ancient Title
Mesotribas	*Mesotribas*
Saturnus	*Satournos*

CAECILIUS STATIUS (LATIN; COMEDY)

Translation	Ancient Title
Bastard Nicasio	*Nothus Nicasio*
Boxer	*Pugil*
Captain	*Nauclerus*
Carian Wailing Woman	*Karine*
Carrier	*Portitor*
Chrysion	*Chrysion*
Comrades in Youth	*Synephebi*
Coppersmiths' Holiday	*Chalcia*
Cratinus	*Kratinus?*
Dardanus	*Dardanus*
Davus	*Davos*
Debauchee	*Asotus*
Ephesio	*Ephesio*
Ethereal	*Aethrio* or *Aetherio*
Exile	*Exul*
Fiancée	*Philumena*
Fraud	*Fallacia*
Heiress	*Epicleros*
Hymnis	*Hymnis*
Imbrians	*Imbrii*
Letter	*Epistula*
Makepeace	*Pausimachus*
Man Woman	*Androgynos*
Marriage	*Gamos*
Men for Sale	*Polumeni*
Moneylender	*Obolostates* or *Falenerator*

Necklace	Plocium
Prostitute	Meretrix
Quartermaster	Epistathmos
Suppositious	Hypobolimaeus or
	Subditivos
Suppositious Aeschinus	Hypobolimaeus
	Aeschinus
Suppositious Chaerestratus	Hypobolimaeus
	Chaerestratus
Suppositious, A Tale of the Hoe	Hypobolimaeus Rastraria
Syracusans	Syracusii
Token	Symbolum
Triumph	Triumphus
Wards	Demandati
Wedding Preliminaries	Progamos
Wet-Nurse	Titthe
Wise in His Own Conceit	Ex Hautu Hestos
Woman of Andros	Andrea
Woman Who Was Abducted	Harpazomenē
Women at Lunch	Synaristosae

CALLIAS (GREEK; COMEDY)

Translation	Ancient Title
Atalanta	Atalantē
Cyclopes	Kuklōpes
Egyptian	Aiguptios
Frogs	Batrachoi
Guts? or Pestles? of Iron	Entera? or Hupera? Sidēra
Men at Leisure	Scholazontes
Prisoners	Pedētai

CALLICRATES (GREEK; COMEDY)

Translation	Ancient Title
Moschion	Moschiōn

CALLIPPUS? (GREEK; COMEDY)

Translation	Ancient Title
Vigil?	Pannuchis

CALLISTRATUS (GREEK; TRAGEDY)

Translation	Ancient Title
Amphilochus	Amphilochōi
Ixion?	Ixiōn?

CANTHARUS (GREEK; COMEDY)

Translation	Ancient Title
Alliance	Summachia
Ants	Murmēkes
Medea	Mēdeia
Singers	Aēdones
Tereus	Tēreus

CARCINUS (GREEK; TRAGEDY)

Translation	Ancient Title
Mice?	Mues?

CARCINUS JUNIOR (GREEK; TRAGEDY)

Translation	Ancient Title
Achilles	Achilleus
Aerope or Thyestes	Aeropē or Thuestēs
Ajax	Aias
Alope	Alopē
Amphiaraus	Amphiareōs
Medea	Mēdeia
Oedipus	Oidipous
Orestes	Orestēs
Semele	Semelē
Tyro?	Turō?

CATULLUS (LATIN; MIME)

Translation	Ancient Title
Ghost	Phasma

CATULLUS, QUINTUS LUTATIUS (LATIN; MIME)

Translation	Ancient Title
Laureolus	Laureolus

CEPHISODORUS (GREEK; COMEDY)

Translation	Ancient Title
Amazons	Amazones
Anti-Lais	Antilais
Boar	Hus
Trophonius	Trophōnios

CHAEREMON (GREEK; TRAGEDY)

Translation	Ancient Title
Alphesiboea	Alphesiboia
Centaur	Kentauros
Dionysus	Dionusos
Io	Iô
Minyans	Minuai
Odysseus	Odusseus
Oeneus	Oineus
Thersites or Achilles, Killer of Thersites	Thersitês or Achilleus Thersitoktonos
Thyestes	Thuestês
Wounded Man	Traumatias

CHAERION (GREEK; COMEDY)

Translation	Ancient Title
Man Who Falsely Accused Himself	Autou Katapseudomenos

CHARICLIDES (GREEK; COMEDY)

Translation	Ancient Title
Chain	Alusis

CHIONIDES (GREEK; COMEDY)

Translation	Ancient Title
Beggars	Ptôchoi
Guardian Spirits	Hêrôes
Persians or Assyrians	Persai or Assurioi

CHOERILUS (GREEK; TRAGEDY)

Translation	Ancient Title
Alope	Alopê

CLEAENETUS (GREEK; TRAGEDY)

Translation	Ancient Title
Hypsipyle	Hupsipulêi

CLEARCHUS (GREEK; COMEDY)

Translation	Ancient Title
Cithara Player	Kitharôidos

| Corinthians | Korinthioi |
| Pandrosus | Pandrosos |

CLEOPHON (GREEK; TRAGEDY)

Translation	Ancient Title
Achilles	Achilleus
Actaeon	Aktaiôn
Amphiaraus	Amphiaraos
Bacchae	Bakchai
Dexamenus	Dexamenos
Erigone	Êrigonê
Leucippus	Leukippos
Mandroboulus	Mandroboulos
Persian Woman	Persis
Telephus	Têlephos
Thyestes	Thuestês

CRATES (GREEK; COMEDY)

Translation	Ancient Title
Beasts	Thêria
Daring Deeds	Tolmai
Dionysus	Dionusos
Games of Childhood	Paidiai
Guardian Spirits	Hêrôes
Holidays	Heortai
Lamia	Lamia
Neighbors	Geitones
Resident Aliens	Metoikoi
Samians	Samioi
Speakers	Rhêtores

CRATES II (GREEK; COMEDY)

Translation	Ancient Title
Birds	Ornithes
Misers	Philarguros
Treasure	Thêsauros
Woman Who Dreams?	Enupniastria?

CRATINUS (GREEK; COMEDY)

Translation	Ancient Title
Archilochoi	Archilochoi
Busiris	Bousiris
Caught in a Storm	Cheimazomenoi
Chirons	Cheirônes
Cleobulinas or Tellers of Riddles	Kleoboulinai
Descendants of Euneus	Euneidai

Translation	Ancient Title
Dionysalexandros	Dionusalexandros
Dionysuses	Dionusoi
Eumenides	Eumenides
Fugitives	Drapetides
Herdsmen	Boukoloi
Laconians	Lakōnes
Laws	Nomoi
Meeting at Pylae	Pulaia
Men in Flames or Idaeans	Empimpramenoi or Idaioi
Men of Ida	Idaioi
Nemesis	Nemesis
Odysseus	Odusseus
Rehearsals?	Didaskaliai
Satyrs	Saturoi
Seasons	Hōrai
See Everythings	Panoptai
Seriphians	Seriphioi
Softies	Malthakoi
Trophonius	Trophōnios
Wealths	Ploutoi
Wine Flask	Putinē
Woman of Thrace	Thraittai
Women of Delos	Dēliades

CRATINUS JUNIOR (GREEK; COMEDY)

Translation	Ancient Title
Chiron	Cheirōn
Falsely Suppositious	Pseudupobolimaios
Female Follower of Pythagoras	Puthagorizousa
Giants	Gigantes
Omphale	Omphalē
Tarentines	Tarantinoi
Titans	Titanes
Woman Who Was Hunted	Thērōmenē

CRITIAS (GREEK; TRAGEDY)

Translation	Ancient Title
Peirithous	Peirithous
Rhadamanthys	Rhadamanthus
Sisyphus (satyr)	Sisuphos Saturikos
Tennes	Tennēs

CRITO (GREEK; COMEDY)

Translation	Ancient Title
Aetolian	Aitōlos
Busybody	Philopragmōn

Translation	Ancient Title
Ephesians	Ephesioi
Woman of Messenia	Messēnia

CROBYLUS (GREEK; COMEDY)

Translation	Ancient Title
Falsely Suppositious	Pseudupobolimaios
Strangled Man	Apanchomenos
Woman Leaving Her Husband	Apoleipousa or Apolipousa

DAMOXENUS (GREEK; COMEDY)

Translation	Ancient Title
Man Who Pitied Himself	Auton Penthōn
Raised Together	Suntrophoi

DECIMUS LABERIUS (LATIN; MIME)

Translation	Ancient Title
Anna Peranna	Anna Peranna
Athuae Caldae	Athuae Caldae
Augur	Augur
Basket	Cophinus
Belonistria	Belonistria
Birthday Festival	Natal
Braggart?	Late Loquens
Bull	Taurus
Catularius	Catularius
Compitalia	Compitalia
Crab	Cancer
Cretan	Cretensis
Etrurian	Tusca
Fisherman	Piscator
Flatterer	Colax
Forgetful	Cacomnemon
Fuller	Fullo
Gauls	Galli
Image or Ghost?	Imago
Lake Avernus	Lacus Avernus
Little Blind Men?	Caeculi
Maiden	Virgo
Maker of Patchwork	Centonarius
Men at the Pales?	Parilicii
Polisher	Colorator
Pot of Gold	Aularia
Poverty	Paupertas
Prison	Carcer

Translation	Ancient Title
Prostitute	Hetaera?
Ram?	Aries
Rope Maker	Restio
Salt Dealer	Salinator
Saturnalia	Saturnalia
Scylax	Scylax
Sisters	Sorores
Six-Fingered Man	Sedigitus
Staminariae	Staminariae
Stricturae	Stricturae?
Summoning of the Dead	Necyomantia
Twins	Gemelli
Wedding	Nuptiae
Woman of Alexandria?	Alexandrea
Youth	Ephebus

DEMETRIUS (GREEK; TRAGEDY)

Translation	Ancient Title
Hesione (satyr)	Hêsionê? Saturoi

DEMETRIUS I (GREEK; COMEDY)

Translation	Ancient Title
Dionysus' Birth	Dionusou Gonai?
Woman of Sicily or Men of Sicily	Sikelia or Sikelikoi

DEMETRIUS II (GREEK; COMEDY)

Translation	Ancient Title
Members of the Areopagus	Areopagitês

DEMONICUS (GREEK; COMEDY)

Translation	Ancient Title
Achelonius or Achelous	Achelônios or Achelous

DEMOPHILUS (GREEK; TRAGEDY)

Translation	Ancient Title
Ass Driver	Onagos?

DEXICRATES (GREEK; COMEDY)

Translation	Ancient Title
Self-Deceivers	Huph' Eautôn Planômenoi

DICAEOGENES (GREEK; TRAGEDY)

Translation	Ancient Title
Cyprians	Kuprioi
Medea	Mêdeia

DINOLOCHUS (GREEK; COMEDY)

Translation	Ancient Title
Althea	Althaia
Amazons	Amazones
Medea	Mêdeia
Seriocomedy	Kômôidotragôidia
Telephus	Têlephos

DIOCLES (GREEK; COMEDY)

Translation	Ancient Title
Bacchae	Bakchai
Bees?	Melittai
Cyclopes	Kuklôpes
Dreams	Oneiroi
Sea	Thalatta
Thyestes B	Thuestês B

DIODORUS (GREEK; COMEDY)

Translation	Ancient Title
Attenders of the Assembly	Panêguristai
Corpse	Nekros
Heiress	Epiklêros
Madman	Mainomenos
Woman Who Plays the Pipes	Aulêtris

DIOGENES OF ATHENS (GREEK; TRAGEDY)

Translation	Ancient Title
Achilles	Achilleus
Atreus	Atreus
Chrysippus	Chrusippos
Helen	Helenê
Heracles	Hêraklês
Medea	Mêdeia
Oedipus	Oidipous
Semele	Semelê
Thyestes	Thuestês

DIONYSIUS (GREEK; COMEDY)

Translation	Ancient Title
Homonyms	Homônumoi
Hunger	Limos
Lawgiver	Thesmophoros
Man Hit by a Javelin	Akontizomenos
Woman Savior	Sôizousa or Sôteira

DIONYSIUS I (GREEK; TRAGEDY)

Translation	Ancient Title
Adonis	Adônis
Alcmena	Alkmênê
Hunger (satyr)	Limos Saturikos
Leda	Lêda
Ransom of Hector	Hektoros Lutra

DIOPHANTUS (GREEK; COMEDY)

Translation	Ancient Title
Man Who Emigrated	Metoikizomenos

DIOXIPPUS (GREEK; COMEDY)

Translation	Ancient Title
Arbitrants	Diadikazomenoi
Historian	Historiographos
Miser	Philarguros
Pimp Opposer	Antipornoboskos
Treasure	Thêsauros

DIPHILUS (GREEK; COMEDY)

Translation	Ancient Title
Accusers	Enkalountes
Amastris	Amastris
Anagyrus or Penniless	Anaguros or Anarguros
Ass Driver	Onagos
Bath	Balaneion
Boat?	Schedia
Brick Carrier	Plinthophoros
Brotherly Love	Philadelphoi or Philadelphos
Brothers	Adelphoi
Busybody	Polupragmôn
Casting Lots	Klêroumenoi
Cithara Player	Kitharôidos
Concubine	Pallakis
Danaids	Danaides
Daughters of Pelias	Peliades
Eunuch	Eunouchos
Female Athletic Trainer	Aleiptria
Goldsmith	Chrusochoos
Grandmother	Têthê
Greedy	Aplêstos
Guardian	Epitropeus
Guardian Spirit	Hêrôs
Hecate	Hekatê
Heiress	Epiklêros
Helen's Guardians	Elenêphorountes
Heracles	Hêraklês
Ignorance	Agnoia
Leucadia	Leukadia
Lovers of Boys	Paiderastai
Man Driven Mad	Mainomenos
Man Exempt from or Discharged from Military Service? or Paralyzed Man?	Paraluomenos
Man of Boeotia	Boiôtios
Man of Sicily	Sikelikos
Man Who Was Slaughtered	Sphattomenos
Man Who Was Sued	Epidikazomenos
Marriage	Gamos
Men Dosed with Hellebore	Helleborizomenoi
Merchant	Emporos
Olive Orchard or Guardians	Ela[i]ôn or Phrourountes
Painter	Zôgraphos
Pancratiast	Pankratiastês
Parasite	Parasitos
Pouch?	Pêra
Pyrrha	Purra
Raised Together	Suntrophoi
Sappho	Sapphô
Soldier	Stratiôtês
Souvenir	Mnêmation
Synoris	Sunôris
Taker of Cities	Airêsiteichês
Telesias	Telesias
Theseus	Thêseus
Those Dying Together	Sunapothnêiskontes
Those Making Offerings to the Dead or Offerings to the Dead	Enagizontes or Enagismata

Those Who Were Rescued	Anasôizomenoi or Anasôizomenai
Tithraustes	Tithraustēs
Treasure	Thēsauros
Trick Rider	Apobatēs
Well	Phrear
Woman Going Wrong	Diamartanousa
Woman of Boeotia	Boiōtis
Woman Who Left Her Husband	Apoleipousa or Apolipousa
Women of Lemnos	Lēmniai

DROMO (GREEK; COMEDY)

Translation	Ancient Title
Female Harper	Psaltria

ECPHANTIDES (GREEK; COMEDY)

Translation	Ancient Title
Attempts or Trials?	Peirai
Satyrs	Saturoi

ENNIUS, QUINTUS (LATIN; COMEDY)

Translation	Ancient Title
Little Hostess	Caupuncula
Pancratiasts	Pancratiastes

ENNIUS, QUINTUS (LATIN; FABULA PRAETEXTA)

Translation	Ancient Title
Ambracia	Ambracia
Sabine Women	Sabinae

ENNIUS, QUINTUS (LATIN; TRAGEDY)

Translation	Ancient Title
Achilles	Achilles
Achilles Aristarchi	Achilles Aristarchi
Ajax	Aiax
Alcmeon	Alcumeo
Alexander	Alexander
Andromache the Captive	Andromacha Aechmalotis

Andromeda	Andromeda
Athamas	Athamas
Cresphontes	Cresphontes
Erechtheus	Erechtheus
Eumenides	Eumenides
Hecuba	Hecuba
Iphigenia	Iphigenia
Medea	Medea
Medea the Exile	Medea Exul
Melanippe	Melanippa
Nemea	Nemea
Phoenix	Phoinix
Ransom of Hector	Hectoris Lutra
Telamon	Telamo
Telephus	Telephus
Thyestes	Thyestes

EPHIPPUS (GREEK; COMEDY)

Translation	Ancient Title
Artemis	Artemis
Busiris	Bousiris
Circe	Kirkē
Cydon	Kudōn
Geryon	Gēruonēs
Just Alike or Obeliaphoroi	Homoioi or Obeliaphoroi
Merchandise	Empolē
Philyra	Philura
Sappho	Sapphō
Shipwreck Victim	Nauagos
Targeteer	Peltastēs
Youths	Ephēboi

EPICHARMUS (GREEK; COMEDY)

Translation	Ancient Title
Alcyoneus	Alkuoneus
Amycus	Amukos
Atalantas	Atalantai
Bacchae	Bakchai
Busiris	Bousiris
Chiron	Chirōn
Chorus Members	Xoreuontes or Xoreutai
Citizens	Politai
Cyclops	Kuklōps
Deucalion or Leukarion	Deukaliōn or Leukariōn
Dionysuses	Dionusoi
Earth and Sea	Ga kai Thalassa

Hebe's Marriage	Hēbas Gamos
Heracles at the House of Pholus	Hēraklēs Ho Para Pholōi
Heracles at Zoster	Hēraklēs Ho Epi ton Zōstēra
Holiday and Islands (see Islands)	Heorta kai Nasoi (see Nasoi)
Hope or Wealth	Elpis or Ploutos
Islands	Nasoi
Medea	Mēdeia
Months or Moons	Mēnes
Mr. and Mrs. Logos	Logos kai Logina
Muses	Mousai
Odysseus the Deserter	Odusseus Automolos
Odysseus the Shipwreck Victim	Odusseus Nauagos
Periallus	Periallos
Persians	Persai
Philoctetes	Philoktētas
Pithon?	Pithōn
Plunder?	Harpagai
Pots	Chutrai
Pyrrha and Prometheus	Purra kai Promatheus
Revelers or Hephaestus	Kōmastai or Haphaistos
Rustic Man	Agrōstinos
Sausage	Orua sive Oroua
Sciron	Skirōn
Sirens	Seirēnes
Spectators	Thearoi
Sphinx	Sphinx
The Thirtieth Days of the Month	Triakades
Trojans	Trōes
Victorious?	Epinikios
Woman of Megara	Megaris

EPICRATES (GREEK; COMEDY)

Translation	Ancient Title
Amazons	Amazones
Anteros	Anterōs
Anti-Lais or Antillis	Antilais or Antillis
Chorus	Choros
Hard to Sell	Duspratos
Merchant	Emporos
Trident or Maker of Petty Wares	Triodous or Rōpopōiēs

EPIGENES (GREEK; COMEDY)

Translation	Ancient Title
Bacchis	Bakchis?
Elimination of Money	Arguriou Aphanismos

Female Guardian Spirit	Hērōinē
Man of Pontus	Pontikos
Souvenir	Mnēmation

EPILYCUS (GREEK; COMEDY)

Translation	Ancient Title
Coraliscus	Kōraliskos

EPINICUS (GREEK; COMEDY)

Translation	Ancient Title
Mnesiptolemus	Mnēsiptolemos
Suppositious Babies	Hupoballomenai

ERIPHUS (GREEK; COMEDY)

Translation	Ancient Title
Aeolus	Aiolos
Meliboea	Meliboia
Targeteer	Peltastēs

EUANGELUS (GREEK; COMEDY)

Translation	Ancient Title
Unveiled Woman	Anakaluptomenē

EUARETUS (GREEK; TRAGEDY)

Translation	Ancient Title
Achilles?	Achillei?
Alcmeon?	Alkmeōn?
Teucer	Teukrōi

EUBULIDES (GREEK; COMEDY)

Translation	Ancient Title
Revelers	Kōmastai

EUBULUS (GREEK; COMEDY)

Translation	Ancient Title
Amalthea	Amaltheia
Anchises	Anchisēs
Antiope	Antiopē
Attachment? or Cycnus	Prosousia or Kuknos
Auge	Augē
Basket Carriers	Kalathēphoroi
Bellerophon	Bellerophontēs

Cercopes	Kerkôpes
Chick	Neottis
Chrysilla	Chrusilla
Clepsydra	Klepsudra
Daedalus	Daidalos
Damaleia	Damaleia
Danae	Danaê
Deucalion	Deukaliôn
Dionysian	Dionusios
Dolon	Dolôn
Echo	Êchô
Europa	Eurôpe
Female Harper	Psaltria
Gamblers	Kubeutai
Ganymede	Ganumêdês
Glaucus	Glaukos
Glued Together	Katakollômenos
Graces	Charites
Happy Woman	Olbia
Hunchback	Kampuliôn
Impotent Men	Astutoi
Ion	Iôn
Ixion	Ixiôn
Laconians or Leda	Lakônes or Lêda
Lark	Korudallos
Leather Worker	Skuteus
Little Parmeno	Parmeniskos
Medea	Mêdeia
Mysians	Musoi
Nannion	Nannion
Nausicaa	Nausikaa
Noose	Agkuliôn
Odysseus or All-Seeing Ones	Odusseus or Panoptai
Oedipus	Oidipous
Oenomaus or Pelops	Oinomaos or Pelops
Orthanês	Orthanês
Pamphilus	Pamphilos
Peace	Eirênê
Pentathlete	Pentathios
Phoenix	Phoinix
Pimp	Pornoboskos
Plangon	Plangôn
Procris	Prokris
Rescued Men	Anasôizomenoi
Semele or Dionysus	Semelê or Dionusos
Sphinx Cario	Sphingokariôn
Titans	Titanes
Vigil?	Pannuchis
Wet-Nurses or Wet-Nurse	Titthai or Titthê
Woman Dealing in Chaplets	Stephanopôlides
Woman of the Mill	Mulôthris
Xuthus	Xouthos

EUDOXUS (GREEK; COMEDY)

Translation	Ancient Title
Captain	Nauklêros
Suppositious Baby	Hupobolimaios

EUETES (GREEK; COMEDY)

Translation	Ancient Title
Heiress	Epiklêros

EUMEDES (GREEK; COMEDY)

Translation	Ancient Title
Man Who Was Slaughtered	Sphattomenos

EUNICUS (GREEK; COMEDY)

Translation	Ancient Title
Anteia	Anteia
Cities	Poleis

EUPHANES (GREEK; COMEDY)

Translation	Ancient Title
Man Lighting a Fire	Puraunos
Muses	Mousai

EUPHRO (GREEK; COMEDY)

Translation	Ancient Title
Brothers	Adelphoi
Gods' Marketplace	Theôn Agora
Muses	Mousai
Spectators	Theôroi
Twins	Didumoi
Ugly?	Aischra
Woman Who Gave It Back	Apodidousa
Woman Who Was Surrendered	Paradidomenê
Young Comrades	Sunephêboi

EUPOLIS (GREEK; COMEDY)

Translation	Ancient Title
Abusers of Law	Hubristodikai
Autolycus A	Autolukos A

Autolycus B	Autolukos B
Bathers	Baptai
Cities	Poleis
Demes	Dêmoi
Flatterers	Kolakes
Friends	Philoi
Goats	Aiges
Golden Race	Chrusoun Genos
Helots	Eilôtes
Laconians	Lakônes
Maricas	Marikas
Men of Prospalta	Prospaltioi
New Moons	Noumêniai
Out of the Army or	Astrateutoi or
Man Women	Androgunai
Taxiarchs	Taxiarchoi
Thefts	Klopai

EURIPIDES II (GREEK; TRAGEDY)

Translation	Ancient Title
Medea	Mêdeia
Orestes	Orestês
Polyxena	Poluxenê

EUTHYCLES (GREEK; COMEDY)

Translation	Ancient Title
Atalanta	Atalantê

EUTHYCLES (GREEK; COMEDY)

Translation	Ancient Title
Profligates or Letter	Asôtoi or Epistolê

EZECHIEL (GREEK; TRAGEDY)

Translation	Ancient Title
Exodus	Exagôgê

GRACCHUS (LATIN; TRAGEDY)

Translation	Ancient Title
Atalanta	Atalanta
Daughters of Pelias	Peliades
Thyestes	Thyestes

HARMODIUS (GREEK; TRAGEDY)

Translation	Ancient Title
Protesilaus (satyr)	Prôtesilaos Saturoi

HEGEMON (GREEK; COMEDY)

Translation	Ancient Title
Philinna	Philinna

HEGESIPPUS (GREEK; COMEDY)

Translation	Ancient Title
Brothers	Adelphoi
True Friends	Philetairoi

HELIODORUS (GREEK; TRAGEDY)

Translation	Ancient Title
Protesilaus	Prôtesilaos

HENIOCHUS (GREEK; COMEDY)

Busybody	Polupragmôn
Gorgons	Gorgones
Heiress	Epiklêros
Polyeuctus	Polueuktos
Thorikion	Thôrukion?
Trochilus	Trochilos
True Friend	Philetairos
Twice Deceived	Dis Exapatômenos

HERACLITUS? (GREEK; COMEDY)

Translation	Ancient Title
Man Who Was a Stranger	Xenizôn

HERMIPPUS (GREEK; COMEDY)

Translation	Ancient Title
Agamemnon	Agamemnôn
Athena's Birth	Athênas Gonai
Bread Women	Artopôlides
Cercopes	Kerkôpes
Demesmen	Dêmotai
Europa	Eurôpe
Fates	Moirai

Translation	Ancient Title
Gods	Theoi
Porters	Phormophoroi
Soldiers	Stratiōtai or Stratiōtides

HIPPARCHUS (GREEK; COMEDY)

Translation	Ancient Title
Painter	Zōgraphos
Rescued Men	Anasōizomenoi
Thais	Thais
Vigil?	Pannuchis

ION (GREEK; TRAGEDY)

Translation	Ancient Title
Agamemnon	Agamemnōn
Alcmene	Alkmēnē
Argive Men	Argeioi
Big Drama	Mega Drama
Caeneus (see Phoenix)	Kaineus (see Phoinix)
Guards	Phrouroi
Laertes	Laertēs
Oeneus	Oineus?
Omphale (satyr)	Omphalē Saturoi
Phoenix A	Phoinix A
Phoenix B	Phoinix B
Sons of Eurytus	Eurutidai
Teucer	Teukros

IOPHON (GREEK; TRAGEDY)

Translation	Ancient Title
Achilles	Achilleus
Actaeon	Aktaiōn
Bacchae (or Pentheus?)	Bakchai (or Pentheus?)
Dexamenus	Dexamenos
Sack of Troy	Iliou Persis
Satyrs Who Sing to the Pipes (satyr)	Aulōidoi Saturoi
Telephus	Tēlephos

IUVENTIUS (LATIN; COMEDY)

Translation	Ancient Title
Woman Who Was Recognized	Anagnorizomenē

JULIUS CAESAR STRABO, GAIUS (LATIN; TRAGEDY)

Translation	Ancient Title
Adrastus	Adrastus

| Tecmessa | Tecmesa |
| Teuthras | Teuthras |

LAON (GREEK; COMEDY)

Translation	Ancient Title
Dispositions?	Diathēkai

LENTULUS (LATIN; MIME)

Translation	Ancient Title
Inhabitants of Catina	Catinenses

LEUCO (GREEK; COMEDY)

Translation	Ancient Title
Ambassadors	Presbeis
Ass Bearing Wineskins	Onos Askophoros
Clansmen	Phrateres

LICINIUS IMBREX (LATIN; COMEDY)

Translation	Ancient Title
Neaera	Neaera

LIVIUS ANDRONICUS, LUCIUS (LATIN; COMEDY)

Translation	Ancient Title
Circumcised Man	Verpus
Man of Lydia	Ludius
Small Sword	Gladiolus

LIVIUS ANDRONICUS, LUCIUS (LATIN; TRAGEDY)

Translation	Ancient Title
Achilles	Achilles
Aegisthus	Aegisthus
Ajax with the Whip	Ajax Mastigophorus
Andromeda	Andromeda
Danae	Danae
Hermione	Hermiona
Ino	Ino
Tereus	Tereus
Trojan horse	Equos Troianus

LUCIUS VARIUS RUFUS (LATIN; TRAGEDY)

Translation	Ancient Title
Thyestes	Thyesta

LUSCIUS LANUVINUS (LATIN; COMEDY)

Translation	Ancient Title
Ghost	Phasma
Treasure	Thensaurus

LYCOPHRON (GREEK; TRAGEDY)

Translation	Ancient Title
Aeolus	Aiolos
Aletes?	Alētēs
Allies	Summachoi
Andromeda	Andromeda
Cassandreis	Kassandreis
Chrysippus	Chrusippos
Elpenor	Elephēnōr
Heracles	Hēraklēs
Hippolytus	Hippolutos
Laius	Laios
Marathonians	Marathōnioi
Menedemus (satyr)	Menedēmos Saturoi
Nauplius	Nauplios
Oedipus A	Oidipous A
Oedipus B	Oidipous B
Orphan	Orphanos
Pentheus	Pentheus
Sons of Aeolus	Aioidēs
Sons of Pelops	Pelopidai
Suppliants	Hiketai
Telegonus	Tēlegonos

LYNCEUS (GREEK; COMEDY)

Translation	Ancient Title
Centaur	Kentauros

LYSIPPUS (GREEK; COMEDY)

Translation	Ancient Title
Bacchae	Bakchai
Charms?	Katachēnai?
Thysus Keeper	Thursokomos

MACHON (GREEK; COMEDY)

Translation	Ancient Title
Ignorance	Agnoia
Letter	Epistolē

MAGNES (GREEK; COMEDY)

Translation	Ancient Title
Babiton Players	Barbitistai
Birds	Ornithes
Dionysus A	Dionusos A
Dionysus B	Dionusos B
Frogs	Batrachoi
Gall Insects	Psēnes
Grass Cutters	Poastriai
Lydians	Ludoi

MELANTHIUS (GREEK; TRAGEDY)

Translation	Ancient Title
Medea	Mēdeia?

MELETUS JUNIOR (GREEK; TRAGEDY)

Translation	Ancient Title
Oedipus' Tale	Oidipodeia

MELITO (GREEK; TRAGEDY)

Translation	Ancient Title
Niobe	Niobē

MENECRATES (GREEK; COMEDY)

Translation	Ancient Title
Hector the Slave?	Manektōr
Hemioneus	Hermioneus

MENIPPUS (GREEK; COMEDY)

Translation	Ancient Title
Cercopes	Kerkōpes

METAGENES (GREEK; COMEDY)

Translation	Ancient Title
Breezes or *Blockhead*	*Aurai* or *Mammakuthos*
Homer or *Artisans* or *Sophists*	*Omêros* or *Askêtai* or *Sophistai*
Lover of Sacrifices	*Philothutês*
Thurio Persians	*Thouriopersai*

METRODORUS (GREEK; COMEDY)

Translation	Ancient Title
Just Alike	*Homoioi*

MIMNERMUS (GREEK; TRAGEDY)

Neoptolemus	*Neoptolemos*

MNESIMACHUS (GREEK; COMEDY)

Translation	Ancient Title
Alcmeon	*Alkmaiôn* or *Alkmeôn*
Bad-Tempered Man	*Duskolos*
Busiris	*Bousiris*
Druggist	*Pharmakopôiês*
Horse Breeder	*Hippotrophos*
Philippus	*Philippos*
Winners in the Isthmian Games	*Isthmionikês*

MORSIMUS (GREEK; TRAGEDY)

Translation	Ancient Title
Medea	*Mêdeia?*

MOSCHION (GREEK; TRAGEDY)

Translation	Ancient Title
Pheraeans	*Pheraioi*
Telephus	*Têlephos*
Themistocles	*Themistoklês*

MYRTILUS (GREEK; COMEDY)

Translation	Ancient Title
Loves	*Erôtes*
Titanopanes	*Titanopanes*

NAEVIUS, GNAEUS (LATIN; COMEDY)

Translation	Ancient Title
Astiologa	*Astiologa*
Branded Slave	*Stigmatias*
Cataract	*Glaucoma*
Charlatan	*Technicus*
Circumcised	*Appella*
Collier Maid	*Carbonaria*
Commotria	*Commotria*
Concubine	*Paelex*
Demetrius	*Demetrius*
Driver	*Agitatoria*
Flatterer	*Colax*
Fraud	*Dolus*
Garland Maid	*Corollaria*
Gym Master	*Gumnasticus*
Lampadio	*Lampadio*
Leon	*Leon*
Madmen	*Dementes*
Man Hit by a Javelin	*Acontizomenos*
Masked Play	*Personata*
Nagido	*Nagido*
Nervolaria	*Nervolaria*
Outcast	*Proiectus*
Potter	*Figulus*
Quadruplets	*Quadrigemini*
Sailors?	*Nautae?*
Soothsayer	*Ariolus*
Stalagmus	*Stalagmus*
Tale of a Cloak	*Clamidaria*
Tale of Testicles	*Testicularia*
Tale of the Little Coat	*Tunicularia*
Tribacelus?	*Tribacelus*
Triple Phallus	*Triphallus*
Wide Awakes	*Agrypnuntes*
Woman of Tarentum	*Tarentilla*

NAEVIUS, GNAEUS (LATIN; FABULA PRAETEXTA)

Translation	Ancient Title
Clastidium	*Clastidium*
Romulus (= Wolf?)	*Romulus (= Lupus?)*
Wolf (= Romulus?)	*Lupus (= Romulus?)*

NAEVIUS, GNAEUS (LATIN; TRAGEDY)

Translation	Ancient Title
Andromache	Andromacha
Danae	Danae
Hector's Departure	Hector Proficiscens
Hesione	Hesiona
Iphigenia	Iphigenia
Lycurgus	Lycurgus
Trojan Horse	Equos Troianus

NAUSICRATES (GREEK; COMEDY)

Translation	Ancient Title
Captains	Nauklēroi
Persian Woman	Persis

NEOPHRON (GREEK; TRAGEDY)

Translation	Ancient Title
Medea	Mēdeia

NICO (GREEK; COMEDY)

Translation	Ancient Title
Cithara Player	Kitharōidos

NICOCHARES (GREEK; COMEDY)

Translation	Ancient Title
Agamemnon	Agamemnōn
Amymone or Pelops	Amumonē or Pelops
Centaur	Kentauros
Cretans	Krētēs
Galatea	Galateia
Heracles' Marriage	Hēraklēs Gamōn
Heracles the Chorus Leader	Hēraklēs Chorēgos
Laconians	Lakōnes
Poet	Poiētēs
Women of Lemnos	Lēmniai

NICOMACHUS (GREEK; COMEDY)

Translation	Ancient Title
Eileithyia	Eileithuia
Sea fight	Naumachia
Women Passing From One Place to Another	Metekbainousai

NICOMACHUS OF ALEXANDRIA (GREEK; TRAGEDY)

Translation	Ancient Title
Alcmeon or Tyndareus	Alkmaiōn or Tundareōs
Aletides?	Aletides?
Alexander	Alexandros
Eriphyle	Eriphulē
Geryon	Gēruonēs
Mysians	Musoi
Neoptolemus	Neoptolemos
Oedipus	Oidipous
Persian Woman	Persis
Polyxena	Poluxenē
Teucer	Teukros
Trilogy	Trilogia

NICOMACHUS OF ATHENS (GREEK; TRAGEDY)

Translation	Ancient Title
Amymone and Oedipus	Amumōnē et Oidipous

NICOPHON (GREEK; COMEDY)

Translation	Ancient Title
Adonis	Adōnis
Aphrodite's Birth	Aphroditēs Gonai
Manual Laborers	Encheirogastores
Pandora	Pandōra
Returning from Hades	Ex Aidou Aniōn
Sirens	Seirēnes

NICOSTRATUS (GREEK; COMEDY)

Translation	Ancient Title
Antyllus	Antullos
Banished Man	Apelaunomenos
Bird Catcher	Ornitheutēs
Bustard?	Hōtis?
Cook	Mageiros
Couch	Klinē
Falsely Branded	Pseudostigmatias
Fellow Countrymen	Patriōtai

Translation	Ancient Title
Hecate	Hekatê
Hesiod	Hêsiodos
Hierophant	Hierophantês
Kings	Basileis
Moneylender	Tokistês
Pandrosus	Pandrosos
Pet	Habra
Public Speaker	Rhêtôr?
Rival in Love	Anterôsa
Slanderer	Diabolos
Syrian	Suros
Wealth	Ploutos
Wine Maker	Oinopoios
Woman Swimming Alongside	Parakolumbôsa

NOVIUS (LATIN; *FABULA ATELLANA*)

Translation	Ancient Title
Andromache	Andromacha
Blockhead	Asinus
Bubulcus the Laborer?	Bubulcus Cerdo
Bucculus	Bucculus
Buffoons	Sanniones
Choice	Optio
Conclusion	Exodium
Deaf Man	Surdus
Doctor Mania	Mania Medica
Enemies	Malivoli
Farmer	Agricola
Fate	Parcus
Fig Planter	Ficitor
Fullers	Fullones
Fuller's Trade	Fullonicum
Funeral	Funus
Girdle	Zona
Grand?	Dapatici?
Grape Pickers	Vindemiatores
Hercules the Money Collector	Hercules Coactor
In Three Parts	Tripertita
Inquiry	Quaestio
Judgment of Death and Life	Mortis et Vitae Iudicium
Maccus	Maccus
Maccus the Exile	Maccus Exul
Maccus the Tradesman	Maccus Copo
Pacilius	Pacilius
Pappus the Departed	Pappus Praeteritus
Phoenician Women	Phoenissae
Picus	Picus
Pregnant Maiden	Virgo Praegnans

Translation	Ancient Title
Prostitute	Hetaera
Slave	Paedium
Soldier of Pometia	Milites Pometinenses
Tale of a Little Toga	Togularia
Tale of the Hen House	Gallinaria
Tale of the Tablets?	Tabellaria
Tithe	Decuma
Twins	Gemini
Two Dossennuses	Duo Dossenni
Unoccupied Fullers	Fullones Feriati
Woman Richly Endowed	Dotata
Wood Dealer	Lignaria
Young Horse	Eculeus

OPHELIO (GREEK; COMEDY)

Translation	Ancient Title
Callaeschrus	Kallaischros
Deucalion	Deukaliôn
Lamentation	Ialemos
Putacides? or Titacides?	Putakidês or Titakidês

PACUVIUS, MARCUS (LATIN; *FABULA PRAETEXTA*)

Translation	Ancient Title
Paulus	Paulus

PACUVIUS, MARCUS (LATIN; TRAGEDY)

Translation	Ancient Title
Antiope	Antiopa
Atalanta	Atalanta
Chryses	Chryses
Foot Washing	Niptra
Hermione	Hermiona
Iliona	Iliona
Judgment of Arms	Armorum Iudicium
Medus	Medus
Orestes as a Slave	Dulorestes
Pentheus	Pentheus
Periboea	Periboea
Teucer	Teucer

PAMPHILUS (GREEK; TRAGEDY)

Translation	Ancient Title
Children of Heracles	Hêrakleidai

PARAMONUS (GREEK; COMEDY)

Translation	Ancient Title
Chorus Leader	Chorêgôn
Shipwrecked	Nauagos

PHERECRATES (GREEK; COMEDY)

Translation	Ancient Title
Ant Men	Murmêkanthrôpoi
Chiron	Cheirôn
Corianno	Koriannô
Deserters	Automoloi
Forgetful or Thalatta	Epilêsmôn or Thalatta
Good Men	Agathoi
Heracles the Human Being	Anthrôphêraklês
Miners	Metallês
Mullets or Flounders	Krapataloi
Old Women	Graes
Oven or Vigil	Ipnos or Pannuchis
Persians	Persai
Petale	Petalê
Pseudo-Heracles	Pseudêraklês
Resident Aliens	Metoikoi
Savages	Agrioi
Teacher of Slaves	Dou123odidaskalos
Triflers	Lêroi
Tyranny	Turannis

PHILEMON (GREEK; COMEDY)

Translation	Ancient Title
Addicted to Wine	Paroinos
Adulterer	Moichos
Aetolian	Aitôlos
Babylonian	Babulônios
Bastard	Nothos
Beggar Woman or Rhodia	Ptôchê or Rhodia
Brothers	Adelphoi
Butting In	Pareisiôn
Dagger	Encheiridion
Distributed?	Nemomenoi
Doctor	Iatros
Doorman	Thurôros
Ephedrismos Players	Ephedritai or Ephedrizontes
Euripus?	Euripos
Fire Bringer	Purphoros
Flatterer	Kolax
Ghost	Phasma
Graces	Charites
Guard	Phulakê
Guardian Spirits	Hêrôes
Little Boy	Paidarion
Little Wing	Pterugion
Man in Exile?	Apollôn
Man Killing Himself by Abstinence	Apokarterôn
Man of Sicily	Sikelikos
Man Who Was Abducted	Harpazomenos or Harpazomenê
Man Who Was Banished	Exoikizomenos
Man Who Was Falsely Accused	Katapseudomenos
Man Who Was Sued	Epidikazomenos
Man Whose Hair Was Removed by Pitch	Pittokopoumenos
Marriage	Gamos
Merchant	Emporos
Murderer	Adrophonos
Myrmidons	Murmidones
Mystic	Mustis
Neaera	Neaira
Night	Nux
Palamedes	Palamêdês
Pancratiast	Pankratiastês
Panegyris or Assembly	Panêguris
Partners	Koinônoi
Philosophers	Philosophoi
Player of the Pipes	Aulêtês
Priest of Cybele or Eunuch	Gallos?
Pursuer or Soupy	Metiôn or Zômion
Pyrrhus	Purros
Resident Alien	Metoikos
Ring	Daktulios
Rustic Man	Agroikos
Sardian	Sardios
Sculptor	Lithogluphos
Slaves	Paides
Soldier	Stratiôtês
Suppositious Baby	Hupobolimaios
Thebans	Thêbaioi
Those Dying Together	Sunapothnêiskontes
Treasure	Thêsauros
Unveiled	Anakaluptontes
Vagabond	Agurtês
Widow	Chêra
Woman of Corinth	Korinthia
Woman Who Renewed Herself	Ananeoumenê
Young Comrade	Sunephêbos
Youth	Ephêbos

PHILEMON JUNIOR (GREEK; COMEDY)

Translation	Ancient Title
Phocians	Phôkeis

PHILEMON III (GREEK; COMEDY)

Translation	Ancient Title
Woman of Miletus	Miêsia

PHILETAERUS (GREEK; COMEDY)

Translation	Ancient Title
Achilles	Achilleus
Antullos	Antullos
Asclepius	Asklêpios
Atalanta	Atalantê
Cephalus	Kephalos
Huntress	Kunagis
Lover of the Pipes	Philaulos
Meleager	Meleagros
Months or Moons	Mênes
Oenopion	Oinopiôn
Tereus	Têreus
Torch Bearers	Lampadêphoroi
Whoremonger	Korinthiastês

PHILIPPIDES (GREEK; COMEDY)

Translation	Ancient Title
Amphiaraus	Amphiareôs
Brotherly Love	Philadelphoi
Cup Maker	Ekpômatopoios
Elimination of Money	Arguriou Aphanismos
Lover of Athenians	Philathênaios
Lover of Euripides	Phileuripidês
Lover of Power	Philarchos
Miser	Philarguros
Pimp	Mastropos
Pipes	Auloi
Renewal	Ananeôsis
Renewed Woman	Ananeousa
Woman Who Was Tortured	Basanizomenê
Women of Laconia?	Lakiadai
Women Sailing Along	Sunekpleouosai
Women Worshiping Adonis	Adôniazousai

PHILIPPUS (GREEK; COMEDY)

Translation	Ancient Title
Daedalus	Daidalos
Money Testers?	Kôdôniastai
Nannion	Nannion
Woman of Olynthus	Olunthia

PHILISCUS (GREEK; COMEDY)

Translation	Ancient Title
Adonis	Adôonis
Birth of Artemis and Apollo	Artemidos kai Apollônos Gonai
Birth of Hermes and Aphrodite	Hermou kai Aphroditês Gonai
Birth of Pan	Panos Gonai
Birth of Zeus	Dios Gonai
Misers	Philarguroi
Olympus	Olumpos
Themistocles	Themistoklês

PHILOCLES (GREEK; COMEDY)

Translation	Ancient Title
Wounded Man	Traumatias

PHILOCLES (GREEK; TRAGEDY)

Translation	Ancient Title
Erigone	êrigonê
Nauplius	Nauplios
Oedipus	Oidipous
Oeneus	Oineus
Penelope	Pênelopê
Philoctetes	Philoktêtês
Prian	Priamos
Tereus or Epops	Têreus or Epops
Tetralogy of Pandion	Pandionis Tetralogia

PHILONIDES (GREEK; COMEDY)

Translation	Ancient Title
Buskins	Kothornoi
Mule Cart	Apênê
Preview	Proagôn
True Friend	Philetairos

PHILOSTEPHANUS (GREEK; COMEDY)

Translation	Ancient Title
Man of Delos	Dêlios

PHILYLLIUS (GREEK; COMEDY)

Translation	Ancient Title
Aegeus	Aigeus
Anteia	Anteia
Atalanta	Atalantē
Auge	Augē
Cities	Poleis
Helen	Helenē
Heracles	Hēraklēs
Twelfth	Dōdekatē
Washerwomen or Nausikaa	Pluntriai or Nausikaa
Well Sinker	Phreōruchos

PHOENICIDES (GREEK; COMEDY)

Translation	Ancient Title
Cavalry Commander	Phularchos
Hated Woman	Misoumenē
Poet	Poiētēs
Those Who Were Rescued	Anasōizomenoi
Women Who Play the Pipes	Aulētrides

PHORMIS (GREEK; COMEDY)

Translation	Ancient Title
Atalantas	Atalantai

PHRYNICHUS (GREEK; COMEDY)

Translation	Ancient Title
Connus	Konnos
Cronus	Kronos
Ephialtes	Ephialtēs or Epialtēs
Grass Cutters	Poastriai
Initiates	Mustai
Misanthrope	Monotropos
Muses	Mousai
Revelers	Kōmastai
Satyrs	Saturoi
Tragedians or Freedmen	Tragōidoi or Apeleutheroi

PHRYNICHUS (GREEK; TRAGEDY)

Translation	Ancient Title
Actaeon	Aktaiōn
Alcestis	Alkēstis
Antaeus or Libyans	Antaios or Libues
Capture of Miletus	Milētou Alōsis
Danaids	Danaides
Egyptians	Aiguptioi
Just Men or Persians or Partners	Dikaioi or Persai or Sunthōkoi
Phoenician Women	Phoinissai
Tantalus	Tantalos
Women of Pleuron	Pleurōniai

PHRYNICHUS II (GREEK; TRAGEDY)

Translation	Ancient Title
Andromeda	Andromeda
Erigone	Ērigonē

PLATO (GREEK; COMEDY)

Translation	Ancient Title
Adonis	Adōnis
Alliance	Summachia
Ambassadors	Presbeis
Amphiaraus	Amphiareōs
Ants	Murmēkes
Apparel?	Skeuai
Blockheads	Mammakuthoi
Cleophon	Kleophōn
Daedalus	Daidalos
Europa	Eurōpe
Griffins	Grupes
Hellas or Islands	Hellas or Nēsoi
Holidays	Heortai
Hyperbolus	Huperbolos
Io	Iō
Laconians	Lakōnes
Laconians or Poets	Lakōnes or Poiētai
Laius	Laios
Little Boy	Paidarion
Long Night	Nux Makra
Menelaus	Meneleōs
Mob or Scum of the Earth	Surphax
Peisander	Peisandros
Person in Extreme Pain	Perialgēs
Phaon	Phaōn
Poet	Poiētēs
Resident Aliens	Metoikoi
Sophists	Sophistai
Staff Bearer	Rhabdouchoi

Victories	Nikai
Woman after Festival	Hai aph' Hierôn
Xantriai or Cercopes	Xantriai or Kerkôpes
Zeus Outraged	Zeus Kakoumenos

POLEMAEUS (GREEK; TRAGEDY)

Translation	Ancient Title
Ajax (satyr)	Aias Saturoi
Clytemnestra	Klutaimestra

POLIOCHUS (GREEK; COMEDY)

Translation	Ancient Title
Whoremonger	Korinthiastês

POLYIDUS? (GREEK; TRAGEDY)

Translation	Ancient Title
Iphigenia at Tauris	Iphigeneia Hê en Taurois?

POLYPHRASMON (GREEK; TRAGEDY)

| Lycurgus Tetralogy | Lukourgeia Tetralogia |

POLYZELUS (GREEK; COMEDY)

Translation	Ancient Title
Aphrodite's Birth	Aphroditês Gonai
Dionysus' Birth	Dionusou Gonai
Foot Washing	Niptra
Muses' Birth	Mousôn Gonai
Tyndareus of the People	Dêmotundareôs

POMPONIUS BONONIENSIS, LUCIUS (LATIN; *FABULA ATELLANA*)

Translation	Ancient Title
Agamemnon Supplositious	Agamemno Suppositus
Augur	Augur
Baker	Pistor
Brothers	Adelphi
Bucco Adopted	Bucco Adoptatus
Bucco Given as a Pledge	Bucco Auctoratus
Cake	Placenta
Campanians	Campani
Conch Shell	Concha
Doctor	Medicus
Earlier Maccus Twins?	Macci Gemini Priores?
Emasculated Man	Maialis
Fates	Parci
Fisherman	Piscatores
Fullers	Fullones
Gamesters	Aleones
Guild	Collegium
Household God	Lar Familiaris
Inferior Herald?	Praeco Posterior
Inferior Ring?	Anulus Posterior
Judgment of Arms	Armorum ludicium
Kalends of March	Kalendae Martiae
Maccus	Maccus
Maccus the Go-Between	Maccus Sequester
Maccus the Maiden	Maccus Virgo
Maccus the Soldier	Maccus Miles
Maccus' Twins	Macci Gemini
Male Prostitute	Prostibulum
Man Bound by Obligation	Auctoratus
Marsyas	Marsya
Medley	Satura
Mevia	Mevia
Munda	Munda
Painters	Pictores
Pappus' Bride	Sponsa Pappi
Pappus' Jug	Hirnea Pappi
Pappus the Departed	Pappus Praeteritus
Pappus the Farmer	Pappus Agricola
Paternal Uncle	Patruus
Petitioning Heir	Heres Petitor
Philosophy	Philosophia
Pimp	Leno
Player on the Cithara	Citharista
Prefect of Morals	Praefectus Morum
Pytho the Gorgon?	Pytho Gorgonius
Quinquatrus	Quinquatrus
Ragged Men	Pannuceati
Rich	Dives
Rustic Man	Rusticus
She Ass	Asina
She Goat	Capella
Soothsayer or Pexor the Rustic	Aruspex or Pexor Rusticus
Sow Who has Given Birth	Porcetra
Syrians	Syri
Tale of a Dowry?	Dotalis
Tale of the Light Hoe	Sarcularia

Temple Caretaker	Aeditumus
Terms of the Agreement	Condiciones
Tithe	Decuma
Tithe of the Fuller	Decuma Fullonis
Transalpine Gauls	Galli Transalpini
Vaca or Purse	Vaca or Marsuppium
Verniones?	Verniones
Verres Diseased	Verres Aegrotus
Verres Healthy	Verres Salvos
Wedding	Nuptiae
White Clay or Petitioner	Cretula or Petitor
Woman Richly Endowed	Dotata
Workhouse Foreman	Ergastilus
Young Comrades	Synephebi

POSIDIPPUS (GREEK; COMEDY)

Translation	Ancient Title
Arsinoe	Arsinoē
Bell	Kôdōn
Celts	Galatēs
Changed Men	Metapheromenoi
Demesmen	Dēmotai
Female Chorus Members	Choreuousai
Hermaphroditus	Hermaphroditos
Just Alike	Homoioi
Lover of Father	Philopatōr
Man Who Regained His Sight	Anablepōn
Myrmex or Ant	Murmēx
Pimp	Pornoboskos
Quartermaster	Epistathmos
Raised Together	Suntrophoi
Slave	Paidion
Woman of Ephesus	Ephesia
Woman Shut Out	Apokleiomenē
Women of Locria	Lokrides

PRATINAS (GREEK; TRAGEDY)

Translation	Ancient Title
Bacchae or Women of Caryae	Dusmainiai or Karuatides
Perseus	Perseus
Tantalus	Tantalos
Wrestlers (satyr)	Palaistai Saturoi

PTOLEMAEUS IV PHILOPATOR (GREEK; TRAGEDY)

Translation	Ancient Title
Adonis	Adōnis

PUBLILIUS SYRUS (LATIN; MIME)

Translation	Ancient Title
Murmurco	Murmurco
Tree Pruners	Putatores

PUBLIUS OVIDIUS NASO (LATIN; TRAGEDY)

Translation	Ancient Title
Medea	Medea

PUBLIUS POMPONIUS SECUNDUS (LATIN; FABULA PRAETEXTA)

Translation	Ancient Title
Aeneas	Aeneas

PUBLIUS POMPONIUS SECUNDUS (LATIN; TRAGEDY)

Translation	Ancient Title
Atreus	Atreus

PYTHON (GREEK; TRAGEDY)

Translation	Ancient Title
Agen (satyr)	Agēn Saturikos

RHINTHON (GREEK; COMEDY)

Translation	Ancient Title
Amphitryon	Amphitruôn
Eunobatai	Eunobatai
Heracles	Hēraklēs
Iphigenia at Tauris	Iphigeneia Ha En Taurois
Iphigenia in Aulis	Iphigeneia Ha En Aulidi
Medea	Mêdeia
Meleager the Slave	Doulos Meleagros
Orestes	Orestas
Telephus	Tēlephos

SANNYRION (GREEK; COMEDY)

Translation	Ancient Title
Danae	Danaê
Io	Iô
Laughter	Gelôs

SANTRA (LATIN; TRAGEDY)

Translation	Ancient Title
Wedding of Bacchus	Nuptiae Bacchi

SCIRAS (GREEK; COMEDY)

Translation	Ancient Title
Meleager	Meleagros

SEXTUS TURPILIUS (LATIN; COMEDY)

Translation	Ancient Title
Assistants?	Boethuntes
Basket Bearer	Canephorus
Chief Magistrate	Demiurgus
Demetrius	Demetrius
Heiress	Epiclerus
Leucadia	Leucadia
Lover of Father	Philopatōr
Paraterusa	Paraterusa
Prostitute	Hetaera
Slave	Paedium
Thrasyleon	Thrasuleon
Woman of Lindus	Lindia
Women of Lemnos	Lemniae

SILENUS (GREEK; TRAGEDY)

Translation	Ancient Title
Chryses?	Chru[s]—

SIMYLUS (GREEK; COMEDY)

Translation	Ancient Title
Woman of Ephesus	Ephesia
Woman of Megara	Megarikē

SOGENES (GREEK; COMEDY)

Translation	Ancient Title
Lover of Master	Philodespotos

SOPATER (GREEK; COMEDY)

Translation	Ancient Title
Bacchis	Bakchis
Bacchis' Marriage	Bakchidos Gamos
Bacchis' Suitors	Bakchidos Mnēstēres
Bookworms	Silphai
Celts	Galatai
Eubulus the Godlike Mortal	Euboulotheombrotos
Gates	Pulai
Ghost-Summoning Rite	Nekuia
Hippolytus	Hippolutos
Lentil Soup	Phakē
Natural Philosopher	Phusiologos
Orestes	Orestēs
Slavery of Mystacus	Mustakou Thēteion
Woman of Cnidus	Knidia

SOPHILUS (GREEK; COMEDY)

Translation	Ancient Title
Androcles	Androklēs
Cavalry Commander or Lover of Power	Phularchos or Philarchos
Cithara Player	Kitharōidos
Dagger	Encheiridion
Deposit	Parakatathēkē
Marriage	Gamos
Running Mates	Suntrechontes
Tyndareus or Leda	Tundareōs or Lēda
Woman of Delos	Dēlia

SOPHRON (GREEK; MIME)

Translation	Ancient Title
Busy with the Bride	Numphoponos
Fisherman versus the Farmer	Hōlieus ton agroiōtan
Messenger	Angelos
Moral Prefixed to a Fable	Promuthion
Mother-in-Law	Penthera
Puffing Passion	Paidika poiphuxeis
Seamstresses	Akestriai
The Women Going to Attend? the Isthmian Games	Tai thamenai ta Isthmia
The Women Who Drove Out the Goddess By Speaking?	Tai gunaikes hai tan theon phanti exelan
Tuna Catcher	Thunnothēras

SOSICRATES (GREEK; COMEDY)

Translation	Ancient Title
Brotherly Love	Philadelphoi
Deposit	Parakatathēkē

SOSIGENES? (GREEK; COMEDY)

Translation	Ancient Title
Ransomed Man	Lutroumenos

SOSIPATER (GREEK; COMEDY)

Translation	Ancient Title
Man Who Was Falsely Accused	Katapseudomenos

SOSIPHANES (GREEK; TRAGEDY)

Translation	Ancient Title
Meleager	Meleagros

SOSIPPUS (GREEK; COMEDY)

Translation	Ancient Title
Woman Leaving Her Husband	Apoleipousa

SOSITHEUS (GREEK; TRAGEDY)

Translation	Ancient Title
Translation	Ancient Title
Aethlius	Aethlios
Daphnis or Lityersas (satyr?)	Daphnis or Lituersês Saturoi

SOTADES (GREEK; COMEDY)

Translation	Ancient Title
Man Who Was Ransomed	Paralutroumenos
Shut-Ins	Enkleiomenai or Enkleiomenoi

SPINTHARUS (GREEK; TRAGEDY)

Translation	Ancient Title
Heracles in Flames	Perikaiomenos Hêraklês
Semele Struck by Lightning	Semelê Keraunoumenê

STEPHANUS (GREEK; COMEDY)

Translation	Ancient Title
Lover of Laconians	Philolakôn

STRATO (GREEK; COMEDY)

Translation	Ancient Title
Sons of Phoenix	Phoinikidês

STRATTIS (GREEK; COMEDY)

Translation	Ancient Title
Atalanta, Atalantas, or Atalantus	Atalantê, Atalantai, or Atalantos
Callipides	Kallipidês
Chrysippus	Chrusippos
Cinesias	Kinêsias
Elimination of Money	Arguriou Aphanismos
Good Men	Agathoi
Iphigeron	Iphigerôn
Lemnomeda	Lêmnomeda
Macedonians or Pausanias	Makedones or Pausanias
Man Orestes	Anthrôporestês
Medea	Mêdeia
Men of Riverside	Potamioi
Myrmidons	Murmidones
Philoctetes	Philoktêtês
Phoenician Women	Phoinissai
Putisus?	Putisos?
Those Who Cool Themselves in the Shade	Psuchastai
Troilus	Trôilos
Zopyrus Engulfed in Flame	Zôpuros Perikaiomenos

TELECLIDES (GREEK; COMEDY)

Translation	Ancient Title
Hesiods	Hêsiodoi
Islanders?	Nêsiôtai?
Members of the Amphictyonic Council	Amphiktuones
Prytanes	Prutaneis
Sicilians or Soldiers	Sikeliôtai or Stratiôtai
Stubborn Men	Sterroi
Truthful	Apseudeis

THEODECTAS (GREEK; TRAGEDY)

Translation	Ancient Title
Ajax	Aias
Alcmeon	Alkmeôn
Helen	Helenê

Lynceus	Lunkeus
Mausolus	Mausôlos
Oedipus	Oidipous
Orestes	Orestês
Philoctetes	Philoktêtês
Tydeus	Tudeus

THEODORIDES (GREEK; TRAGEDY)

Translation	Ancient Title
Medea	Mêdeiai
Phaethon	Phaethonti

THEODORUS (GREEK; TRAGEDY)

Translation	Ancient Title
Hermione	Hermionê
Satyrs as Sacrificers	Thutês Saturoi

THEOGNETUS (GREEK; COMEDY)

Translation	Ancient Title
Centaur	Kentauros
Ghost or Miser	Phasma or Philarguros
Lover of Master	Philodespotês

THEOPHILUS (GREEK; COMEDY)

Translation	Ancient Title
Abroad	Apodêmoi
Cithara Player	Kitharôidos
Daughters of Proteus	Proitides
Doctor	Iatros
Epidaurian	Epidaurios
Lover of the Pipes	Philaulos
Neoptolemus	Neoptolemos
Pancratiast	Pankratiastês
Woman of Boeotia	Boiôtia

THEOPOMPUS (GREEK; COMEDY)

Translation	Ancient Title
Admetus	Admêtos
Althea	Althaia
Aphrodite	Aphroditê
Callaeschrus	Kallaischros
Hedychares	Hêducharês
Mede	Mêdos
Nemea	Nemea
Odysseus	Odusseus
Pamphile	Pamphilê
Pantaleon	Pantaleôn
Peace	Eirênê
Penelope	Pênelopê
Phineus	Phineus
She Dwarf	Batulê
Sirens	Seirênes
Slaves	Paides
Soldier Women	Stratiôtides
Theseus	Thêseus
Tisamenus	Teisamenos
Tisamenus	Tisamenos
Women Hucksters	Kapêlides

THESPIS (GREEK; TRAGEDY)

Translation	Ancient Title
Games for Pelias or Phorbas	Athla Peliou or Phorbas
Pentheus	Pentheus
Priests	Hiereis
Unmarried Youth?	Êitheoi

THEUDOTUS? (GREEK; TRAGEDY)

Translation	Ancient Title
Palamedes (satyr)	Palamêdês Saturoi

THUGENIDES (GREEK; COMEDY)

Translation	Ancient Title
Jurors	Dikastai

TIMESITHEUS (GREEK; TRAGEDY)

Translation	Ancient Title
Capaneus	Kapaneus
Castor and Polydeuces	Kastôr kai Poludeukês
Danaids B	Danaides B
Demand for Helen's Return	Helenês Apaitêsis

Heracles	Hēraklēs
Ixion	Ixiōn
Memnon B	Memnōn B
Orestes and Pylades	Orestēs Puladēs
Ransom of Hector	Hektoros Lutra
Suitors	Mnêsthres
Zeus' Birth	Zēnos Gonai

TIMOCLES (GREEK; COMEDY)

Translation	Ancient Title
Bath	Balaneion
Boxer	Puktēs
Busybody	Polupragmôn
Centaur or Dexamenus	Kentauros or Dexamenos
Consilaus	Konisalos
Coworkers	Sunergoi
Dionysus	Dionusos
Dracontium	Drakontion
Egyptians	Aiguptioi
Farmer	Geôrgos
Forgetfulness	Lêthê
Guardian Spirits	Hêrôes
Satyrs of the People	Dēmosaturoi
Helpmates	Sunerithoi
Letters	Epistolai
Lover of Being a Judge	Philodikastēs
Man of Delos	Dēlos
Man of Pontus	Pontikos
Marathonians	Marathônioi
Men of Gaunus	Kaunioi
Neaera	Neaira
Orestautocleides	Orestautokleidēs
Person Who Rejoiced Over the Neighbor's Bad Fortune	Epichairekakos
Pseudorobbers	Pseudolêistai
Purple Shell	Porphura
Ring	Daktulios
Sappho	Sapphô
Satyrs	Saturoi
Women Worshiping Dionysus	Dionusiazusai

TIMOCLES (GREEK; TRAGEDY)

Translation	Ancient Title
Icarians (satyr)	Ikarioi Saturoi
Lycurgus (satyr)	Lukourgôi Saturikôi
Oedipus	Oidipodi

Phorcides (satyr)	Phorkisi Saturikoi
Phrixus	Phrixôi

TIMOSTRATUS (GREEK; COMEDY)

Translation	Ancient Title
Deposit	Parakatathêkê
Lover of Master	Philodespotos
Lover of One's Relations	Philoikeios
Made a Citizen	Dēmopoiētos
Pan	Pan
Profligate	Asôtos
Ransomed Man	Lutroumenos

TIMOTHEUS (GREEK; COMEDY)

Translation	Ancient Title
Boxer	Puktēs
Deposit	Parakatathêkê
Man Who Was Changed	Metaballomenos or Metapheromenos
Puppy	Kunarion

TIMOTHEUS (GREEK; TRAGEDY)

Translation	Ancient Title
Alcmeon	Alkmeôn
Alphesiboea	Alphesiboia

TIMOTHEUS II (GREEK; COMEDY)

Translation	Ancient Title
Man Returning a Kindness	Anteuergetôn

TIMOXENUS (GREEK; COMEDY)

Translation	Ancient Title
Concealing Man	Sunkruptôn

TITINIUS (LATIN; FABULA TOGATA)

Translation	Ancient Title
Bearded Man?	Barbatus
Blind Man	Caecus
Female Harper or Ferentine	Psaltria or Ferentinatis
Flute Girl	Tibicina

Fuller's Trade	Fullonia
Hortensius	Hortensius
Prilia	Prilia
Quintus?	Quintus
Stepdaughter	Privigna
Twin	Gemina
Varus	Varus
Woman of Insubria?	Insubra?
Woman of Setia?	Setina
Woman of Velitrae	Veliterna
Woman Skilled in the Law	Iurisperita

TITUS QUINCTIUS ATTA (LATIN; *FABULA TOGATA*)

Translation	Ancient Title
Father-in-Law or Mother-in-Law	Socrus
Hot Springs	Aquae Caldae
Joy	Gratulatio
Matchmaker	Conciliatrix
Maternal Aunts	Materterae
Medley	Satura
Megalensia	Megalensia
Night Work	Lucubratio
Nurse	Nurus
Supplication	Supplicatio
Tale of an Aedile?	Aedilicia
Tiro's Departure	Tiro Proficiscens

UNKNOWN AUTHOR (GREEK; COMEDY)

Translation	Ancient Title
Beggary	Ptōcheia
Braggart	Alazōn
Calling of Mormoluke?	Anaklēsis Mormolukēs?
Competitors	Sunagōnistai
Cousins	Anepsioi
Dream or Once Married	Oneiros or Progamōn
Erchians?	Erchieis
Homonyms	Homōnumoi
Ignorant Man	Agnoōn
Liar	Pseudomenos?
Mother of the Gods	Mētēr Theōn
Nemesis	Nemesis
Once Married	Progamōn
Raised Together	Suntrophoi?
Ring	Daktulios

Sisters	Adelphai
Thumoitadai	Thumoitadai
Widow	Chēra
Woman Agreeing or Confessing?	Homologousa
Woman of Peparethia?	Peparēthia
Women of Salamis	Salaminiai
Young Comrades	Sunephēboi?
Zeuses?	Dies

UNKNOWN AUTHOR (GREEK; TRAGEDY)

Translation	Ancient Title
Aegisthus	Aigisthos
Agamemnon?	Agamemnōn?
Ajax	Aias?
Ajax the Locrian	Aias Lokros?
Aletes? or Sinner?	Aleitēs
Amphiareōs	Amphiareōs?
Amymone (satyr)	Amumōnē Saturikē
Andromache	Andromachē?
Argo (satyr)	Argō Saturikē
Athamas	Athamas
Atlas (satyr)	Atlas Saturikos
Bacchae	Bakchai?
Gassandra	Kassandra
Chryses	Chrusēs
Chrysippus	Chrusippos
Cinyras	Kinuras
Croesus	Kroisos?
Disciples (satyr)	Mathētai Saturoi
Epigoni	Epigonoi
Erigone	Êrigonē?
Eriphyle or Amphiaraus?	Eriphulē or Amphiareōs?
Eurypylus	Eurupulos
Gyges	Gugēs?
Hecabe	Hekabē?
Hector	Hektōr?
Helios (satyr)	Hêlios Saturikos?
Helle	Hellê
Hephaestus (satyr)	Hêphaistos Saturikos?
Heracles (satyr)	Hêraklēs Saturikos?
Heracles Oetaeus	Hêraklēs (Oitaios)?
Hermes (satyr)	Hermês Saturikos
Hylas	Hulas?
Iberians	Ibêres
Io (satyr)	Io Saturikē?
Iphigenia	Iphigeneia?
Iris (satyr)	Iris Saturikē?

Ixion	Ixiôn
Medea	Mêdeia
Melanippus or Merops	Melanippos or Merops?
Meleagros	Meleagros?
Merops	Merops?
Mute Ones	Kôphoi
Mysians	Musoi?
Neoptolemus	Neoptolemos
Niobe	Niobê
Odysseus	Odusseus
Odysseus the False Messenger	Odusseus Pseudangelos
Oedipus	Oidipous
Oeneus	Oineus?
Oenopion	Oinopiôn
Oresteia	Oresteia
Orestes	Orestês?
Orpheus	Orpheus?
Parthenopaeus	Parthenopaios?
Peirithous	Peirithous?
Persephone (satyr)	Persephonê Saturikê?
Perseus (satyr)	Perseus Saturikos?
Persians	Persai
Philoctetes (satyr)	Philoktêtês Saturikos?
Philoctetes?	Philoktêtês?
Phoenician Women	Phoinissai?
Phorcides (satyr)	Phorkides Saturoi
Prometheus (satyr)	Promêtheus Saturikos?
Rhesus	Rhêsos
Scylla	Skulla
Scyrians	Skurioi
Seasons	Hôrai
Seven against Thebes or Phoenician Women?	Hepta Epi Thêbas or Foinissai?
Sons of Phineus	Phineidai
Sphinx (satyr)	Sphinx Saturikê
Telephus (satyr)	Têlephos Saturikos
Triptolemus (satyr)	Triptolemos Saturikos?
Tyro	Turô
Tyro	Turô?
Voyage	Apoplous
Women of Locria	Lokrides?

UNKNOWN AUTHOR (LATIN; COMEDY)

Translation	Ancient Title
Brothers?	Adelphoi?
Farmer	Georgos
Urn	Hydria

UNKNOWN AUTHOR (LATIN; MIME)

Translation	Ancient Title
Bean	Faba
Laserpiciarius	Laserpiciarius
Tutor	Tutor

UNKNOWN AUTHOR (LATIN; TRAGEDY)

Translation	Ancient Title
Chorus of Proserpina	Chorus Proserpinae
Laomedon	Laomedon
Penthesilea	Penthesilea
Song of Neleus	Nelei Carmen
Trojan Horse	Equus Troianus

VALERIUS (LATIN; MIME)

Translation	Ancient Title
Phormio	Phormio

VATRONIUS (LATIN; COMEDY)

Translation	Ancient Title
Burra	Burra

XENARCHUS (GREEK; COMEDY)

Translation	Ancient Title
Boutalion	Boutaliôn
Pentathlete	Pentathlos
Priapus	Priapos
Purple Shell	Porphura
Scythians	Skuthai
Sleep	Hupnos
Soldier	Stratiôtês
Twins	Didumoi

XENOCLES (GREEK; TRAGEDY)

Translation	Ancient Title
Athamas (satyr)	Athamas Sat.
Bacchae	Bakchai
Licymnius	Likumnios
Lycaon	Lukaôn
Mice?	Mues?

APPENDIX IV

CHRONOLOGY

753 B.C.E.
Traditional date for founding of Rome

534–32
First tragedy produced by Thespis

525
Birth of Aeschylus

510
Tyrant Hippias driven from Athens

496
Birth of Sophocles

490
Athenian victory over Persians at Marathon

486
First competition in comedy at the City Dionysia

485–480
Birth of Euripides

484
Aeschylus' first victory at Dionysia

480
Greeks defeat Persians at Salamis

472
Aeschylus' *Persians*

469
Birth of Socrates

468
Sophocles' first victory in dramatic competition

467
Aeschylus' *Seven against Thebes*

463?
Aeschylus' *Suppliant Women*

458
Aeschylus victorious with *Agamemnon*, *Libation Bearers*, *Eumenides*, (see ORESTEIA), *Proteus*

456
Death of Aeschylus

455
Euripides' first play (*Peliades*)

ca. 445?
Sophocles' *Ajax*

442/441
Sophocles' *Antigone*

441
Euripides' first victory in dramatic competition

438
Euripides' *Cretan Women*, *Alcmeon in Psophis*, *Telephus*, *Alcestis*

435?
Sophocles' *Trachinian Women*

432
Parthenon completed

644

431
Outbreak of Peloponnesian War between Athens and Sparta

431
Euripides' *Medea*

ca. 430
Euripides' *Children of Heracles*

429
Death of Pericles; Sophocles' *Oedipus Tyrannos?*

428
Euripides' *Hippolytus*

427
Aristophanes' first play, *Banqueters* (*Daitales*); birth of the philosopher Plato

426
Aristophanes' *Babylonians*; Euripides' *Andromache?*

425
Aristophanes' *Acharnians*

424
Aristophanes' *Knights*; Euripides' *Hecabe?*

423
Aristophanes' *Clouds* (first production)

422
Aristophanes' *Wasps*; Euripides' *Suppliant Women?*; death of Athenian Cleon

421
Aristophanes' *Peace*; Peace of Nicias between Athens and Sparta

ca. 417
Euripides' *Electra, Heracles*

415
Euripides' *Alexander, Palamedes, Trojan Women*; departure of Alcibiades from Athens

414
Aristophanes' *Birds*

413
Athenian expedition to Sicily destroyed; death of Athenian statesman Nicias

414–412
Euripides' *Ion, Iphigenia in Tauris*

412
Euripides' *Andromeda, Helen*

411
Aristophanes' *Lysistrata, Thesmophoriazusae*; oligarchic revolution in Athens

410
Athenian victory over Spartans at Cyzicus led by Alcibiades

ca. 409
Euripides' *Phoenician Women, Cyclops*

409
Sophocles' *Philoctetes*

ca. 408
Euripides' *Antiope*

408
Euripides' *Orestes*; Aristophanes' *Wealth* (lost version)

407
Euripides' *Archelaus*

406
Death of Euripides; death of Sophocles; Battle of Arginusae

405
Aristophanes' *Frogs*; Euripides' *Bacchae, Iphigenia at Aulis*

404
Defeat of Athens by Sparta in Peloponnesian War

401
Sophocles' *Oedipus at Colonus*

399
Socrates put to death

392/391
Aristophanes' *Ecclesiazusae*

388
Aristophanes' *Wealth*

ca. 385
Death of Aristophanes

384
Birth of Aristotle

347
Death of the philosopher Plato

342/341
Birth of Menander

336
Alexander becomes king of Macedon

ca. 330
Aristotle's *Poetics*

323
Death of Alexander

322
Death of Aristotle

316
Menander's *Dyscolus*

ca. 291
Death of Menander

ca. 250
Birth of Plautus

240
First Greek plays adapted for Roman audiences

218
Beginning of Second Punic War (Rome versus Carthage)

205
Plautus' *Braggart Warrior*

201
Roman defeat of Carthage in Second Punic War

200
Plautus' *Stichus*

191
Plautus' *Pseudolus*

c. 190
Birth of Terence

166
Terence's *Andria*

165
Terence's first production of *Mother-in-Law*

163
Terence's *Self-Tormentor*

161
Terence's *Eunuch, Phormio*

160
Terence's *Brothers,* second and third productions of *Mother-in-Law*

c. 159
Death of Terence

55–52
First stone theater built in Rome

44
Julius Caesar assassinated

31
Defeat of Antony at Actium by Octavian (later named Augustus)

20–10
Horace's *Ars Poetica* written

ca. 4 B.C.E.
Birth of Seneca

14 C.E.
Death of Augustus; beginning of reign of Tiberius

37
Death of Tiberius; beginning of reign of Caligula

41
Assassination of Caligula; beginning of reign of Claudius; Seneca exiled

48
Claudius' wife, Messalina, put to death

49
Seneca returns from exile; becomes Nero's tutor; begins writing his tragedies (?)

53
Nero's marriage to Octavia

54
Death of Claudius; beginning of reign of Nero

58
Nero takes Poppaea as mistress

59
Nero kills his mother, Agrippina

62
Seneca retires from political service; Nero divorces Octavia; Octavia is murdered

65
Suicide of Seneca; death of Poppaea

68 C.E.
Suicide of Nero

APPENDIX V

SELECTED BOOKS ON CLASSICAL DRAMA

TRANSLATIONS WITHOUT COMMENTARY OR WITH LIMITED COMMENTARY

General Works

Duckworth, G. E. *The Complete Roman Drama.* 2 vols. New York: Random House, 1942.

Grene, D., and R. Lattimore, eds. *The Complete Greek Tragedies.* 4 vols. Centennial ed. Chicago: University of Chicago Press, 1992.

Aeschylus

Fagles, R., trans. *Aeschylus: The Oresteia.* New York: Viking Penguin, 1979.

Aristophanes

Barrett, D. *Aristophanes: The Birds, The Assemblywomen.* Harmondsworth, U.K.: Penguin, 1978.

———. *Aristophanes: The Frogs, and Other Plays.* Baltimore: Penguin, 1964.

Sommerstein, A. H. *Aristophanes: The Knights, Peace, Wealth.* Harmondsworth, U.K.: Penguin, 1978.

———. *Aristophanes: Lysistrata and Other Plays.* Rev. ed. New York: Penguin, 2002.

Euripides

Davie, J. *Euripides: Heracles and Other Plays.* London: Penguin, 2002.

Vellacott, P. *The Bacchae, and Other Plays: Ion, The Women of Troy, Helen, The Bacchae.* Harmondsworth, U.K: Penguin, 1961.

Menander

Balme, M. *Menander: The Plays and Fragments.* Oxford: Oxford University Press, 2001.

Miller, N. *Menander: Plays and Fragments.* London: Penguin, 1987.

Plautus

Watling, E. R. *Plautus: The Pot of Gold, and Other Plays.* Baltimore, Penguin, 1972.

———. *Plautus: The Rope, and Other Plays.* Baltimore, Penguin, 1964.

Seneca

Watling, E. F. *Seneca: Thyestes, Phaedra, The Trojan Women, Oedipus, with Octavia.* Harmondsworth, U.K.: Penguin, 1972.

Sophocles

Fagles, R. *Sophocles: The Three Theban Plays.* Introductions and notes by Bernard Knox. Harmondsworth, U.K.: Penguin, 1984.

Watling, E. F. *Sophocles: Electra, and Other Plays.* Baltimore: Penguin Books, 1953.

Terence

Radice, B. *Terence: The Comedies.* Harmondsworth, U.K.: Penguin Books, 1976.

ANCIENT TEXT AND TRANSLATION

Aeschylus

Smyth, H. W. *Aeschylus, with an English Translation.* 2 vols. London, W. Heinemann, 1922–1926.

Aristophanes

Henderson, J. *Aristophanes.* 3 vols. Cambridge, Mass.: Harvard University Press, 1998–2002.

Euripides

Kovacs, D. *Euripides.* Cambridge, Mass.: Harvard University Press, 1994–2002.

Menander

Arnott, W. G., ed. and trans. *Menander.* 3 vols. Cambridge, Mass.: Harvard University Press, 1979.

Plautus

Nixon, P. *Plautus, with an English Translation.* 5 vols. London: W. Heinemann, 1916–1938.

Seneca

Fitch, J. G. *Seneca: Tragedies.* 2 vols. Cambridge, Mass.: Harvard University Press, 2002.

Herrmann, L. *Seneque: Tragedies.* Paris: Les Belles Lettres, 1961.

Sophocles

Lloyd-Jones, H. L. *Sophocles: Fragments.* Cambridge, Mass.: Harvard University Press, 1996.

Storr, F. *Sophocles; with an English translation.* 2 vols. London: W. Heinemann, 1928.

Terence

Barsby, J. *Terence.* 2 vols. Cambridge, Mass.: Harvard University Press, 2001.

Fragments

Page, D. L. *Select Papyri.* Vol. 3. 1941. Reprint, London: Heinemann, 1970.

Warmington, E. H. *Remains of Old Latin: Ennius and Caecilius.* Vol. 1. Cambridge, Mass.: Harvard University Press, 1935.

———. *Remains of Old Latin: Livius Andronicus, Naevius, Pacuvius and Accius.* Vol. 2. Cambridge: Harvard University Press, 1936.

ANCIENT TEXT AND COMMENTARY

Aeschylus

Broadhead, H. D. *Aeschylus: Persians.* Cambridge: Cambridge University Press, 1960.

Conacher, D. J. *Aeschylus Oresteia: A Literary Commentary.* Toronto: University of Toronto Press, 1989.

———. *Aeschylus' Prometheus Bound: A Literary Commentary.* Toronto: University of Toronto Press, 1980.

Denniston, D., and D. Page. *Aeschylus: Agamemnon.* Oxford: Clarendon Press, 1957.

Fraenkel, E. *Aeschylus: Agamemnon.* 3 vols. Oxford: Clarendon Press, 1950.

Garvie, A. F. *Aeschylus: Choephoroi.* Oxford: Clarendon Press, 1986.

Hutchinson, G. O. *Aeschylus: Seven against Thebes.* Oxford: Clarendon Press, 1985.

Sommerstein, A. H. *Aeschylus: Eumenides.* Cambridge, Mass.: Cambridge University Press, 1989.

Aristophanes

Dover, K. J. *Aristophanes: Clouds.* Oxford: Clarendon Press, 1989.

———. *Aristophanes: Frogs.* Oxford: Clarendon Press, 1993.

Dunbar, Nan. *Aristophanes: Birds.* New York: Oxford University Press, 1995.

Henderson, J. *Aristophanes: Lysistrata.* Oxford: Clarendon Press, 1987.

MacDowell, D. M. *Aristophanes: Wasps.* Oxford: Clarendon Press, 1971.

Olson, S. D. *Aristophanes: Peace.* Oxford: Clarendon Press, 1998.

Ussher, R. G. *Aristophanes: Ecclesiazusae.* Oxford: Clarendon Press, 1973.

Ennius

Jocelyn, H. D. *The Tragedies of Ennius.* Cambridge: Cambridge University Press, 1969.

Euripides

Bond, G. W. *Euripides: Heracles.* London: Oxford University Press, 1981.

———. *Euripides: Hypsipyle.* Oxford: Clarendon Press, 1963.

Dale, A. M. *Euripides: Alcestis.* Oxford: Clarendon Press, 1954.

———. *Euripides: Helen.* Oxford: Clarendon Press, 1967.

Denniston, J. D. *Euripides: Electra.* Oxford: The Clarendon Press, 1954.

Diggle, J. *Phaethon.* Cambridge: Cambridge University Press, 1970.

Dodds, E. R. *Euripides. Bacchae.* 2d ed. Oxford: Clarendon Press, 1960.

Ferguson, J. *Euripides: Medea and Electra: A Companion to the Penguin Translation.* Bristol, U.K.: Bristol Classical Press, 1987.

Mastronarde, D. J *Euripides: Medea.* Cambridge: Duckworth, 2002.

———. *Euripides: Phoenissae.* Cambridge: Cambridge University Press, 1994.

Page, D. L. *Euripides: Medea.* Oxford: Oxford University Press, 1938.

Seaford, R. *Euripides: Cyclops.* Oxford: Oxford University Press, 1984.

Stevens, P. T. *Euripides: Andromache.* Oxford: Clarendon Press, 1971.

Wilkins, J. *Euripides: Heraclidae.* Oxford: Clarendon Press, 1993.

Willink, C. W. *Euripides. Orestes.* Oxford: Clarendon Press, 1986.

Menander

Gomme, A. W. *Menander: A Commentary.* London: Oxford University Press, 1973.

Plautus

Christenson, D. *Plautus: Amphitruo.* Cambridge: Cambridge University Press, 2000.

Gratwick, A. S. *Plautus: Menaechmi.* Cambridge: Cambridge University Press, 1993.

Ussing, J. L. *Commentarius in Plauti Comoedias: Denuo edendum curavit indicibus auxit Andreas Thierfelder.* Hildesheim: G. Olms, 1972.

Seneca

Costa, C. D. N. *Seneca: Medea.* Oxford: Clarendon Press, 1973.

Fitch, J. G. *Seneca's Hercules Furens.* Ithaca, N.Y.: Cornell University Press, 1987.

Sophocles

Davies, M. *Sophocles: Trachiniae.* Oxford: Oxford University Press, 1991.

Easterling, P. E. *Trachiniae.* Cambridge: Cambridge University Press, 1982.

Griffith, M. *Sophocles: Antigone.* Cambridge: Cambridge University Press, 1999.

Kells, J. H. *Sophocles: Electra.* Cambridge: Cambridge University Press, 1973.

Pearson, A. C. *The Fragments of Sophocles.* 3 vols. With additional notes from the papers of Sir R. C. Jebb and W. G. Headlam. Cambridge: Cambridge University Press, 1917.

Webster, T. B. L. *Philoctetes.* Cambridge: Cambridge University Press, 1970.

Wilkins, J., and M. Macleod. *Sophocles, Antigone and Oedipus the King: A Companion to the Penguin Translation of Robert Fagles.* Bristol, U.K.: Bristol Classical Press, 1987.

Terence

Barsby, J. *Terence: Eunuchus.* Cambridge: Cambridge University Press, 1999.

Martin, R. H. *Terence: Adelphoe.* Cambridge: Cambridge University Press, 1976.

Wessner, P., ed. *Donatus: Aeli Donati quod Fertur Commentum Terenti.* 2 vols. Leipzig: Teubner, 1902, 1905.

ANCIENT TEXT, TRANSLATION, AND COMMENTARY

Aeschylus

Hall, E. *Aeschylus: Persians.* Warminster, U.K.: Aris & Phillips, 1996.

Lloyd-Jones, H. *Aeschylus: Agamemnon.* Englewood Cliffs, N.J.: Prentice-Hall, 1970.

Podlecki, A. J. *Aeschylus: Eumenides.* Warminster, U.K.: Aris & Phillips, 1992.

Aristophanes

Sommerstein, A. H. *The Comedies of Aristophanes.* 11 vols. Warminster, U.K.: Aris & Phillips, 1980–2001.

Euripides

Allan, W. *Euripides: The Children of Heracles.* Warminster, U.K.: Aris & Phillips, 2001.

Barlow, S. A. *Euripides: Heracles.* Warminster, U.K.: Aris & Phillips, 1996.

Collard, C. *Euripides: Hecuba.* Warminster, U.K.: Aris & Phillips, 1991.

Collard, C., M. J. Cropp, and K. H. Lee. *Euripides: Selected Fragmentary Plays.* Vol. 1. Warminster, U.K.: Aris & Phillips, 1995.

Conacher, D. J. *Euripides: Alcestis.* Warminster, U.K.: Aris & Phillips, 1988.

Craik, E. *Euripides: Phoenician Women.* Warminster, U.K.: Aris & Phillips, 1988.

Cropp, M. J. *Euripides: Electra.* Warminster, U.K.: Aris & Phillips, 1988.

———. *Euripides: Iphigenia in Tauris.* Warminster, U.K.: Aris & Phillips, 2000.

Halleran, M. *Euripides: Hippolytus.* Warminster, U.K.: Aris & Phillips, 1995.

Lee, K. F. *Euripides: Ion.* Warminster, U.K.: Aris & Phillips, 1997.

Lloyd, M. *Euripides: Andromache.* Warminster, U.K.: Aris & Phillips, 1994.

Seaford, R. *Euripides: Bacchae.* Warminster, U.K.: Aris & Phillips, 1996.

Menander

Bain, D. M. *Menander: Samia.* Warminster, U.K.: Aris & Phillips, 1983.

Ireland, S. *Menander: The Bad-Tempered Man Dyskolos*. Warminster, U.K.: Aris & Phillips, 1995.

Plautus

Barsby, J. *Plautus: Bacchides*. Warminster, U.K.: Aris & Phillips, 1986.

Seneca

Boyle, A. J. *Seneca: Troades*. Leeds, U.K.: Cairns, 1994.

Hine, H. M. *Seneca: Medea*. Warminster, U.K.: Aris & Phillips, 2000.

Sophocles

Garvie, A. F. *Sophocles. Ajax*. Warminster, U.K.: Aris & Phillips, 1998.

Sutton, D. F. *The Lost Sophocles*. Lanham, Md.: University Press of America, 1984.

Ussher, R. G., *Sophocles: Philoctetes*. Warminster, U.K.: Aris & Phillips, 1990.

Terence

Brothers, A. J. *Terence: The Eunuch*. Warminster, U.K.: Aris & Phillips, 2000.

———. *Terence: The Self-Tormentor*. Warminster, U.K.: Aris & Phillips, 1988.

Gratwick, A. S. *Terence: The Brothers*. Warminster, U.K.: Aris & Phillips, 1999.

Ireland, S. *Terence: The Mother-in-Law*. Warminster, U.K.: Aris & Phillips, 1990.

Martin, R. H. *Terence: Phormio*. London: Methuen, 1959.

SCHOLARLY INTERPRETATION: AESCHYLUS

Bloom, H. *Aeschylus: Comprehensive Research and Study Guide*. New York: Chelsea House Publishing, 2001.

Cameron, H. D. *Studies on the Seven against Thebes of Aeschylus*. Den Haag: Mouton, 1971.

Conacher, D. J. *Aeschylus: The Earlier Plays and Related Studies*. Toronto: University of Toronto Press, 1996.

Finley, J. H. *Pindar and Aeschylus*. Martin Classical Lectures 14. Cambridge, Mass.: Harvard University Press, 1966.

Gagarin, M. *Aeschylean Drama*. Berkeley: University of California Press, 1976.

Golden, L. *In Praise of Prometheus: Humanism and Rationalism in Aeschylean Thought*. Chapel Hill: University of North Carolina Press, 1966.

Goldhill, S. *Aeschylus: The Oresteia*. Cambridge: Cambridge University Press, 1992.

———. *Language, Sexuality, Narrative, the Oresteia*. Cambridge: Cambridge University Press, 1984.

Griffith, M. *The Authenticity of Prometheus Bound*. Cambridge: Cambridge University Press, 1977.

Harrison, T. *The Emptiness of Asia: Aeschylus' Persians and the History of the Fifth Century*. London: Duckworth, 2000.

Herington, C. J. *Aeschylus*. New Haven, Conn.: Yale University Press, 1986.

Ireland, S. "Aeschylus." In *Greece and Rome: New Surveys in the Classics 18*. Oxford: Oxford University Press, 1986.

Konishi, H. *The Plot of Aeschylus' Oresteia: A Literary Commentary*. Amsterdam: Hakkert, 1990.

Kuhns, R. *The House, The City and The Judge: The Growth of Moral Awareness in the Oresteia*. Indianapolis: Bobbs-Merrill, 1962.

Lebeck, A. *The Oresteia: A Study in Language and Structure*. Cambridge, Mass.: Harvard University Press, 1971.

McCall, M., ed. *Aeschylus: A Collection of Critical Essays*. Englewood Cliffs, N. J.: Prentice Hall, 1972.

Michelini, A. N. *Tradition and Dramatic Form in The Persians of Aeschylus*. Leiden: Brill, 1982.

Murray, G. *Aeschylus: The Creator of Tragedy*. 1940. Reprint, Oxford: Clarendon Press, 1978.

Otis, Brooks. *Cosmos and Tragedy: An Essay on the Meaning of Aeschylus*. Chapel Hill: University of North Carolina Press, 1981.

Owen, E. T. *The Harmony of Aeschylus*. Toronto: Clarke, Irwin, 1952.

Podlecki, A. J. *The Political Background of Aeschylean Tragedy*. Ann Arbor: University of Michigan Press, 1966.

Prag, A. J. N. W. *The Oresteia: Iconographic and Narrative Tradition*. Chicago: Bolchazy-Carducci, 1985.

Roberts, D. H. *Apollo and His Oracle in the Oresteia*. Gottingen, Ger.: Vandenhoeck & Ruprecht, 1984.

Rosenmeyer, T. G. *The Art of Aeschylus*. Berkeley: University of California Press, 1982.

Scott, W. C. *Musical Design in Aeschylean Theater*. Hanover, N.H.: University Press of New England, 1984.

Smith, P. M. *On the Hymn to Zeus in Aeschylus' Agamemnon*. Chico, Calif.: Scholars Press, 1980.

Smyth, H. W. *Aeschylean Tragedy*. 1924. Reprint, Berkeley: University of California Press, 1969.

Solmsen, F. *Hesiod and Aeschylus*. With a new foreword by G. M. Kirkwood. Ithaca, N.Y.: Cornell University Press, 1995.

Sommerstein, A. H. *Aeschylean Tragedy*. Bari, Italy: Levante, 1996.

Spatz, L. *Aeschylus*. Boston: Twayne, 1982.

Sullivan, S. D. *Aeschylus' Use of Psychological Terminology: Traditional and New*. Montreal: McGill-Queens University Press, 1997.

Taplin, O. *The Stagecraft of Aeschylus: The Dramatic Use of Exits and Entrances in Greek Tragedy.* Oxford: Oxford University Press, 1990.

Thalmann, W. G. *Dramatic Art in Aeschylus' Seven against Thebes.* New Haven, Conn.: Yale University Press, 1978.

Thomson, G. D. *Aeschylus and Athens: A Study in the Social Origins of Drama.* 1941. Reprint, London: Lawrence & Wishart, 1969.

Vellacott, P. *The Logic of Tragedy. Morals and Integrity in Aeschylus' Oresteia.* Durham, N.C.: Duke University Press, 1984.

Wartelle, A. *Bibliographie historique et critique d'Eschyle et de la tragedie grecque,* 1518–1974. Paris: Les Belles Lettres, 1978.

West, M. L. *Studies in Aeschylus.* Stuttgart: B. G. Teubner, 1990.

Whallon, W. *Problem and Spectacle: Studies in the Oresteia.* Heidelberg: C. Winter, 1980.

Winnington-Ingram, R. P. *Studies in Aeschylus.* Cambridge: Cambridge University Press, 1983.

Zeitlin, F. I. *Under the Sign of the Shield: Semiotics and Aeschylus' Seven against Thebes: Filologia e Critica.* Roma: Edizioni dell' Ateneo, 1982.

SCHOLARLY INTERPRETATION: ARISTOPHANES

Bowie, A. M. *Aristophanes: Myth, Ritual, and Comedy.* Cambridge: Cambridge University Press, 1994.

Cartledge, P. *Aristophanes and His Theatre of the Absurd.* London: Bristol Classical Press, 1990.

Croiset, M. *Aristophanes and Political Parties at Athens.* Translated by J. Loeb. London: Macmillan, 1909.

Dearden, C. W. *The Stage of Aristophanes.* London: Athlone Press, 1976.

Dover, K. J. *Aristophanic Comedy.* Berkeley: University of California Press, 1972, 49–53.

Ehrenberg, V. *The People of Aristophanes: A Sociology of Old Attic Comedy.* 3d rev. ed. New York: Schocken Books, 1962.

Harriot, R. M. *Aristophanes: Poet and Dramatist.* London: Croom Helm, 1986.

Harvey, D., and J. Wilkins, eds. *The Rivals of Aristophanes: Studies in Athenian Old Comedy.* London: Duckworth and the Classical Press of Wales, 2000.

Heath, M. *Political Comedy in Aristophanes.* Göttingen, Ger.: Vandenhoeck & Ruprecht, 1987.

Henderson, J. *Aristophanes: Essays in Interpretation.* Cambridge: Cambridge University Press, 1980.

———. *The Maculate Muse.* 2d ed. New York: Oxford University Press, 1991.

———. *Yale Classical Studies.* Vol. 26, Aristophanes. New Haven, Conn.: Yale University Press, 1980.

Hubbard, T. K. *The Mask of Comedy: Aristophanes and the Intertextual Parabasis.* Ithaca, N.Y.: Cornell University Press, 1991.

Lada-Richards, I. *Initiating Dionysus: Ritual and Theatre in Aristophanes' Frogs.* Oxford: Clarendon Press, 1999.

Lord, L. E. *Aristophanes: His Plays and Influence.* New York: Cooper Square, 1963.

MacDowell, D. M. *Aristophanes and Athens: An Introduction to the Plays.* Oxford: Oxford University Press, 1995.

McLeish, K. *The Theatre of Aristophanes.* London: Thames and Hudson, 1980.

Moulton, C. *Aristophanic Poetry.* Göttingen, Ger.: Vandenhoeck & Ruprecht, 1981.

Murray, G. *Aristophanes: A Study.* Oxford: Clarendon Press, 1933.

Parker, L. P. E., *The Songs of Aristophanes.* Oxford: Clarendon Press, 1996.

Quicke, A. C. *Aristophanes and Athenian Old Comedy. A Survey and Bibliography of Twentieth-Century Criticism.* Thesis: London Library Association, 1982.

Rabinowitz, N. S. *Anxiety Veiled: Euripides and the Traffic in Women.* Ithaca, N.Y.: Cornell University Press, 1993.

Reckford, K. J. *Aristophanes' Old and New Comedy.* Chapel Hill: University of North Carolina Press, 1987.

Rothwell, K. S. *Politics and Persuasion in Aristophanes' Ecclesiazusae.* Leiden: Brill, 1990.

Russo, C. F. *Aristophanes, an Author for the Stage.* London and New York: Routledge, 1994.

Segal, Erich, ed. *Oxford Readings in Aristophanes.* Oxford: Oxford University Press, 1996.

Silk, M. S. *Aristophanes and the Definition of Comedy.* Oxford: Oxford University Press, 2000.

Spatz, L. *Aristophanes.* Boston: Twayne, 1978.

Stone, L. M. *Costume in Aristophanic Poetry.* New York: Arno Press, 1981.

Strauss, L. *Socrates and Aristophanes.* Chicago: University of Chicago Press, 1980.

Sutton, D. F. *Self and Society in Aristophanes.* Washington, D.C.: University Press of America, 1980.

Taaffe, L. K. *Aristophanes and Women.* New York: Routledge, 1993.

Ussher, R. G. *Aristophanes.* Greece and Rome New Surveys in the Classics 13. Oxford: Clarendon Press, 1979.

Van Steen, G. *Venom in Verse.* Princeton, N.J.: Princeton University Press, 2000.

Vickers, M. *Pericles on Stage: Political Comedy in Aristophanes' Early Plays.* Austin: University of Texas, 1997.

Whitman, C. H. *Aristophanes and the Comic Hero*. Cambridge, Mass.: Harvard University Press, 1964.

SCHOLARLY INTERPRETATION: EURIPIDES

Ahl, F. *Trojan Women*. Ithaca, N.Y.: Cornell University Press, 1986.

Allan, W. *Euripides: Medea*. London: Duckworth, 2002.

Barlow, S. A. *The Imagery of Euripides*. 2d ed. London: Methuen, 1986.

Burian, P., ed. *Directions in Euripidean Criticism*. Durham, N.C.: Duke University Press, 1985.

Burnett, A. P. *Catastrophe Survived: Euripides' Plays of Mixed Reversal*. Oxford: Oxford University Press, 1971.

Collard, C. *Euripides*. Greece and Rome New Surveys in the Classics No. 14. Oxford: Clarendon Press, 1981.

Conacher, D. J. *Euripidean Drama: Myth, Theme and Structure*. Toronto: University of Toronto Press, 1967.

———. *Euripides and the Sophists*. London: Duckworth 1998.

Cropp, M., and G. Fick. *Resolutions and Chronology in Euripides: The Fragmentary Tragedies*. London: Institute of Classical Studies, University of London, 1985.

Cropp, M., and K. Lee, eds. *Euripides and Tragic Theatre in the Late Fifth Century*. Champaign, Ill.: Stipes, 2000.

Dunn, F. *Tragedy's End: Closure and Innovation in Euripidean Drama*. Oxford: Oxford University Press, 1996.

Foley, H. P. *Ritual Irony: Poetry and Sacrifice in Euripides*. Ithaca, N.Y.: Cornell University Press, 1985.

Goff, B. *The Noose of Words: Readings of Desire, Violence and Language in Euripides, Hippolytus*. Cambridge: Cambridge University Press, 1990.

Gregory, J. *Euripides and the Instruction of the Athenians*. Ann Arbor: University of Michigan Press, 1991.

Grube, G. M. A. *The Drama of Euripides*. London: Methuen, 1941.

Halleran, M. *Stagecraft in Euripides*. London: Croom Helm, 1985.

Jong, I. de. *Narrative in Drama: The Art of the Euripidean Messenger-Speech*. Leiden: Brill, 1991.

Kirk, G. S. *The Bacchae*. Cambridge: Cambridge University Press, 1979.

Kovacs, D. *Euripidea*. Leiden: Brill, 1994.

———. *The Heroic Muse: Studies in the Hippolytus and Hecuba of Euripides*. Baltimore: Johns Hopkins University Press, 1987.

Lloyd, M. *The Agon in Euripides*. Oxford: Clarendon Press, 1992.

Luschnig, C. A. E. *The Gorgon's Severed Head: Studies in Alcestis, Electra, and Phoenissae*. Leiden: Brill, 1995.

———. *Tragic Aporia: A Study of Euripides' Iphigenia at Aulis*. Berwick, Australia: Aureal, 1988.

McDermott, E. A. *Euripides' Medea: The Incarnation of Disorder*. London: Pennsylvania State University Press, 1989.

Michelini, A. N. *Euripides and the Tragic Tradition*. Madison: University of Wisconsin Press, 1987.

Mossman, J., ed. *Oxford Readings in Euripides*. Oxford: Oxford University Press, 2003.

———. *Wild Justice: A Study of Euripides' Hecuba*. Oxford: Clarendon Press, 1995.

Murray, G. *Euripides and His Age*. 2d ed. New York and London: Oxford University Press 1946.

Norden, E. *Ennius und Vergilius: Kriegsbilder aus Roms grosser Zeit*. Leipzig: Teubner, 1915.

Oranje, H. *Euripides' Bacchae. The Play and Its Audience*. Leiden: Brill, 1984.

Porter, J. R. *Studies in Euripides' Orestes*. Leiden and New York: Brill, 1994.

Powell, A., ed. *Euripides, Women and Sexuality*. London: Routledge, 1989.

Pucci, P. *The Violence of Pity in Euripides' Medea*. Ithaca, N.Y.: Cornell University Press, 1980.

Riemer, P. *Die Alkestis des Euripides: Untersuchungen zur tragischen Form*. Frankfurt am Main, Ger.: Athenaum, 1990.

Ritchie, W. *The Authenticity of the Rhesus of Euripides*. Cambridge: Cambridge University Press, 1964.

Segal, Charles. *Dionysiac Poetics and Euripides' Bacchae*. Expanded ed. Princeton, N.J.: Princeton University Press, 1997.

———. *Euripides and the Poetics of Sorrow: Art, Gender, and Commemoration in Alcestis, Hippolytus, and Hecuba*. Durham, N.C.: Duke University Press, 1993.

Segal, Erich, ed. *Twentieth Century Interpretations of Euripides*. Englewood Cliffs, N.J.: Prentice-Hall, 1968.

Vellacott, P. *Ironic Drama: A Study of Euripides' Method and Meaning*. Cambridge: Cambridge University Press, 1975.

Webster, T. B. L. *The Tragedies of Euripides*. London: Methuen, 1962.

Whitman, C. H. *Euripides and the Full Circle of Myth*. Cambridge, Mass.: Harvard University Press, 1974.

Winnington-Ingram, R. P. *Euripides and Dionysus: An Interpretation of the Bacchae*. Amsterdam: Hakkert, 1969.

Yunis, H. A. *New Creed: Fundamental Religious Beliefs in the Athenian Polis and Euripidean Drama*. Göttingen, Ger.: Vandenhoeck & Ruprecht, 1988.

SCHOLARLY INTERPRETATION: MENANDER

Blundell, J. *Menander and the Monologue*. Göttingen, Ger.: Vandenhoeck & Ruprecht, 1980.

Frost, K. B. *Exits and Entrances in Menander.* Oxford: Oxford University Press, 1988.

Goldberg, S. M. *The Making of Menander's Comedy.* Berkeley: University of California Press, 1980.

Handley, E. and A. Hurst, eds. *Relire Ménandre.* Geneva: Droz, 1990.

Henry, M. M. *Menander's Courtesans and the Greek Comic Tradition.* Frankfurt: P. Lang, 1985.

Katsouris, A. G. *Tragic Patterns in Menander.* Athens: Hellenic Society for Humanistic Studies, 1975.

Walton, J. M., and P. D. Arnott. *Menander and the Making of Comedy.* Westport, Conn.: Greenwood Press, 1996.

Webster, T. B. L. *An Introduction to Menander.* Manchester: Manchester University Press, 1974.

———. *Studies in Menander.* 2d ed. Manchester: Manchester University Press, 1960.

Wiles, D. *The Masks of Menander: Sign and Meaning in Greek and Roman Performance.* Cambridge: Cambridge University Press, 1991.

Zagagi, N. *The Comedy of Menander: Convention, Variation, and Originality.* Bloomington, Ind.: Duckworth, 1995.

SCHOLARLY INTERPRETATION: PLAUTUS

Anderson, W. S. *Barbarian Play: Plautus' Roman Comedy.* Toronto: University of Toronto Press, 1993.

Auhagen, U., ed. *Studien zu Plautus' Epidicus.* ScriptOralia 125. Reihe A, Altertumswissenschaftliche Reihe 33. Tübingen, Ger.: 2001.

Benz, L., E. Stärk, and G. Vogt-Spira, eds. *Plautus und die Tradition des Stegreifspiels.* Tübingen, Ger.: Gunter Narr, 1995.

Brix, J., and M. Niemeyer, eds. *Ausgewählte Komödien des T. Maccius Plautus.* Leipzig: Teubner, 1907.

Bubel, F. *Bibliographie zu Plautus, 1976–1989.* Bonn: R. Habelt, 1992.

Buck, C. H., Jr. *A Chronology of the Plays of Plautus.* Baltimore, 1940.

Chiarini, G. *La recita: Plauto, la farsa, la festa.* Bologna: Patròn Editore, 1979.

Cole, H. E. W. *Deception in Plautus: A Study in the Technique of Roman Comedy.* Boston: R. G. Badger, 1920.

Corte, F. della. *Da Sarsina a Roma: Ricerche Plautine.* Genova: Instituto Universitario di Magistero, 1952.

Fraenkel, E. *Elementi plautini in Plauto.* Firenze: La Nuova Italia, 1960.

Heidelberg, M. G. *Poenulus.* Heidelberg: Winter, 1975.

Hughes, J. D. *A Bibliography of Scholarship on Plautus.* Amsterdam: A. M. Hakkert, 1975.

Langen, P. *Beiträge zur Kritik und Erklärung des Plautus.* 1880. Reprint, Hildesheim, Ger.: G. Olms, 1973.

Lefèvre, Eckard. *Plautus und Philemon.* Tübingen, Ger.: G. Narr, 1995.

Lefèvre, E., E. Stärk, and G. Vogt-Spira. *Plautus barbarus: Sechs Kapitel zur Originalität des Plautus.* ScriptOralia 25. Tübingen: Gunter Narr, 1991.

Leo, F. *Plautinische Forschungen zur Kritik und Geschichte der Komödie.* Berlin, 1912.

Lindsay, W. M. *An Introduction to Latin Textual Emendation Based on the Text of Plautus.* New York and London: MacMillan, 1896.

———. *The Syntax of Plautus.* 1907. Reprint, New York: G. E. Stechert, 1936.

Lodge, G. *Lexicon Plautinum.* Leipzig: Teubner, 1904–1938.

McCarthy, K. *Slaves, Masters, and the Art of Authority in Plautine Comedy.* Princeton, N.J.: Princeton University Press, 2000.

Moore, T. J. *The Theater of Plautus: Playing to the Audience.* Austin: University of Texas Press, 1998.

Petrone, G. *Morale e antimorale nelle commedie di Plauto: Ricerche sullo Stichus.* Palermo: G. B. Palumbo, 1977.

———. *Teatro antico e inganno: Finzioni Plautine.* Palermo: G. B. Palumbo, 1983.

Questa, C. *Introduzione alla metrica di Plauto.* Bologna: R. Patron, 1967.

Schaaf, L. *Der Miles Gloriosus des Plautus und sein griechisches Original. Ein Beitrag zur Kontaminationsfrage.* München: Fink, 1977.

Schutter, K. H. E. *Quibus annis comoediae Plautinae primum actae sint quaeritur.* Groningen, Ger.: De waal, 1952.

Segal, Erich. *Roman Laughter: The Comedy of Plautus.* 2d ed. London: Oxford University Press, 1987.

Slater, N. W. *Plautus in Performance.* Princeton, N.J.: Princeton University Press, 1985.

Taladoire, B. A. *Essai sur le comique de Plaute.* Monte Carlo: L'Imprimerie Nationale de Monaco, 1956.

Thierfelder, A. *De rationibus interpolationum Plautinarum.* 1929. Reprint, Hildesheim, Ger.: G. Olms, 1971.

Zagagi, N. *Tradition and Originality in Plautus: Studies of the Amatory Motifs in Plautine Comedy.* Göttingen, Ger.: Vandenhoeck & Ruprecht, 1980.

Zwierlein, O. *Zur Kritik und Exegese des Plautus.* Vol. I, *Poenulus und Curculio.* Stuttgart: Steiner, 1990.

SCHOLARLY INTERPRETATION: SENECA

Billerbeck, M. *Seneca: Hercules Furens.* Leiden: Brill, 1999.

Bishop, J. D. *Seneca's Daggered Stylus: Political Code in the Tragedies.* Königstein, Ger.: Hain, 1985.

Boyle, A. J., ed. *Seneca Tragicus*. Berwick, Australia: Aureal, 1983.

———. *Tragic Seneca: An Essay in the Theatrical Tradition*. London: Routledge, 1997.

Braden, G. *Renaissance Tragedy and the Senecan Tradition*. New Haven, Conn.: Yale University Press, 1985.

Braginton, M. V. *The Supernatural in Seneca's Tragedies*. Menasha, Wis.: Banta, 1933.

Costa, C. D. N., ed. *Seneca*. London and Boston: Routledge & K. Paul, 1974.

Davis, P. *Shifting Song: The Chorus in Seneca's Tragedies*. New York: Olms-Weidmann, 1993.

Fantham, E. *Seneca's Troades*. Princeton, N.J.: Princeton University Press, 1982.

Griffin, M. *Seneca: A Philosopher in Politics*. Oxford: Clarendon Press, 1976.

Henry, D., and E. Henry. *The Mask of Power: Seneca's Tragedies and Imperial Rome*. Warminster, U.K.: Aris & Phillips, 1985.

Herington, C. J. *Senecan Tragedy*. Boston: Twayne, 1966.

Keulen, A. J. L. *Annaeus Seneca: Troades*. Leiden: Brill, 2001.

Lucas, F. L. *Seneca and Elizabethan Tragedy*. Cambridge: Cambridge University Press, 1922.

Marcucci, S. *Analisi e interpretazione dell'Hercules Oetaeus*. Pisa: Istituti Editoriali e Poligrafici Internazionali, 1997.

Mendell, C. W. *Our Seneca*. New Haven, Conn.: Yale University Press, 1941.

Motto, A. L. *Seneca: A Critical Bibliography 1900–1980*. Amsterdam: A.M. Hakkert, 1989.

Ormand, K. *Exchange and the Maiden: Marriage in Sophoclean Tragedy*. Austin: University of Texas Press, 1999.

Pratt, N. T. *Dramatic Suspense in Seneca and in his Greek precursors*. Princeton, N.J.: Princeton University Press, 1939.

———. *Seneca's Drama*. Chapel Hill, N.C.: University of North Carolina Press, 1983.

Rosenmeyer, T. G. *Senecan Drama and Stoic Cosmology*. Berkeley: University of California Press, 1989.

Shelton, J. A. *Seneca's Hercules Furens: Theme, Structure and Style*. Göttingen, Ger.: Vandenhoeck & Ruprecht, 1978.

Sutton, D. F. *Seneca on the Stage*. Leiden: Brill, 1986.

SCHOLARLY INTERPRETATION: SOPHOCLES

Adams, S. M. *Sophocles the Playwright*. Toronto: University of Toronto Press, 1957.

Ahl, F. *Sophocles' Oedipus*. Ithaca, N.Y.: Cornell University Press, 1991.

Batchelder, A. G. *The Seal of Orestes: Self-Reference and Authority in Sophocles' Electra*. Lanham, Md.: Rowman & Littlefield, 1995.

Blundell, M. W. *Helping Friends and Harming Enemies: A Study in Sophocles and Greek Ethics*. Cambridge: Cambridge University Press, 1989.

Bowra, C. M. *Sophoclean Tragedy*. Oxford: Clarendon Press, 1944.

Brown, A. L., ed. *Sophocles: Antigone*. Warminster, U.K.: Aris & Phillips, 1987.

Budelmann, F. *The Language of Sophocles*. Cambridge: Cambridge University Press, 2000.

Burton, R. W. B. *The Chorus in Sophocles' Tragedies*. Oxford: Oxford University Press, 1980.

Buxton, R G. A. *Sophocles*. Greece and Rome New Surveys in the Classics, No. 16. Oxford: Clarendon Press, 1984.

Ditmars, E. van nes. *Sophocles' Antigone: Lyric Shape and Meaning*. Pisa: Giardinia Editori e Stampatori, 1992.

Ehrenberg, V. *Sophocles and Pericles*. Oxford: Blackwell, 1954.

Gardiner, C. P. *The Sophoclean Chorus*. Iowa City: University of Iowa Press, 1987.

Gellie, G. *Sophocles: A Reading*. Melbourne: Melbourne University Press, 1972.

Goheen, R. F. *The Imagery of Sophocles' Antigone*. Princeton, N.J.: Princeton University Press, 1951.

Greengard, C. *Theatre in Crisis: Sophocles' Reconstruction of Genre and Politics in Philoctetes*. Amsterdam: Hakkert, 1987.

Griffin, J. *Sophocles Revisited*. Oxford: Oxford University Press, 1999.

Kamerbeek, J. C. *The Plays of Sophocles: Commentaries*. 7 vols. Leiden: Brill, 1953–84.

Kirkwood, G. M. *A Study of Sophoclean Drama*. Ithaca, N.Y.: Cornell University Press, 1994.

Kiso, A. *The Lost Sophocles*. New York: Vantage Press, 1984.

Knox, B. M. W. *The Heroic Temper: Studies in Sophoclean Tragedy*. Berkeley: University of California Press, 1966.

Long, A. A. *Language and Thought in Sophocles*. London: Athlone Press, 1968.

Minadeo, R. *The Thematic Sophocles*. Amsterdam: Hakkert, 1994.

Opstelten, J. C. *Sophocles and Greek Pessimism*. Amsterdam: North-Holland, 1952.

Oudemans, C. W., and A. P. M. H. Lardinois. *Tragic Ambiguity: Anthropology, Philosophy and Sophocles' Antigone*. Leiden: Brill, 1987.

Poe, J. P. *Heroism and Divine Justice in Sophocles' Philoctetes*. Leiden: Brill, 1974.

Reinhardt, K. *Sophocles*. Translated by H. Harvey and D. Harvey. Oxford: Blackwell, 1979.

Ringer, Mark. *Electra and the Empty Urn: Metatheater and Role Playing in Sophocles*. Chapel Hill: University of North Carolina Press, 1998.

Scodel, R. *Sophocles.* Boston: Twayne, 1984.

Seale, D. *Vision and Stagecraft in Sophocles.* Chicago: Croom Helm, 1982.

Segal, Charles. *Oedipus Tyrannus: Tragic Heroism and the Limits of Knowledge.* 2d ed. New York: Oxford University Press, 2001.

———. *Sophocles' Tragic World: Divinity, Nature, Society.* Cambridge, Mass.: Harvard University Press, 1995.

———. *Tragedy and Civilization: An Interpretation of Sophocles.* Cambridge, Mass.: Harvard University Press, 1981.

Sutton, D. F. *The Lost Sophocles.* Lanham, Md.: University Press of America, 1984.

Tyrrell, W. B., and L. J. Bennett. *Recapturing Sophocles' Antigone.* Lanham, Md.: Rowman & Littlefield, 1998.

Waldock, A. J. A. *Sophocles the Dramatist.* Cambridge: Cambridge University Press, 1951.

Webster, T. B. L. *Philoctetes.* Cambridge: Cambridge University Press, 1970.

Whitman, C. H. *Sophocles.* Cambridge, Mass.: Harvard University Press, 1951.

Winnington-Ingram, R. P. *Sophocles: An Interpretation.* Cambridge: Cambridge University Press, 1980.

Woodard, T., ed. *Sophocles: A Collection of Critical Essays.* Englewood Cliffs, N.J.: Prentice-Hall, 1966.

SCHOLARLY INTERPRETATION: TERENCE

Büchner, K. *Das Theater des Terenz.* Heidelberg: C. Winter, 1974.

Cupaiuolo, G. *Terenzio, teatro e societa.* Naples: Lofredo, 1991.

Denzler, B. *Der Monolog bei Terenz.* Zürich: P. G. Keller, 1908.

Forehand, W. E. *Terence.* Boston: Twayne, 1985.

Goldberg, S. M. *Understanding Terence.* Princeton, N.J.: Princeton University Press, 1986.

Laidlaw, W. A. *The Prosody of Terence: A Relational Study.* London: Oxford University Press, 1938.

McGlynn, P. *Lexicon Terentianum.* London: Blackie and Son, 1963 and 1967.

Norwood, G. *The Art of Terence.* Oxford: B. Blackwell, 1923.

SCHOLARLY INTERPRETATION: COMEDY AND SATYR PLAY

Arnott, W. G. *Menander, Plautus, Terence.* Greece and Rome. New Surveys in the Classics, No. 9. Oxford: Clarendon Press, 1975.

Astorga, J. A. "The Art of Diphilus: A Study of Verbal Humor in New Comedy." Dissertation, University of California Berkeley, 1990.

Cornford, F. M. *The Origin of Attic Comedy.* 2d ed. Gloucester, Mass.: P. Smith, 1934.

Damen, M. L. "The Comedy of Diphilos Sinopeus in Plautus, Terence and Athenaeus." Dissertation, University of Texas at Austin, 1985.

Davidault, A. *Comoedia Togata: Fragments.* Paris: Les Belles Lettres, 1981.

Dobrov, G., ed. *Beyond Aristophanes: Transition and Diversity in Greek Comedy.* Atlanta: Scholars Press, 1995.

Duckworth, G. E. *The Nature of Roman Comedy.* 2d ed. With a Foreword and Bibliographical Appendix by Richard Hunter. Norman: University of Oklahoma Press, 1994.

Echard, L. *Prefaces to Terence's Comedies and Plautus's Comedies.* Los Angeles: William Andrews Clark Memorial Library, University of California, 1968.

Fields, D. E. *The Technique of Exposition in Roman Comedy.* Chicago, 1938.

Green, J. R., A. Seeberg, and T. B. L. Webster. *Monuments Illustrating New Comedy.* 3d rev. ed. Bulletin for the Institute of Classical Studies Suppl. 50. London: Institute of Classical Studies, 1995.

Handley, E. W. *Menander and Plautus: A Study in Comparison.* London: Published for the College by H. K. Lewis, 1968.

Hunter, R. L. *The New Comedy of Greece and Rome.* Cambridge: Cambridge University Press, 1985.

Konstan, D. *Greek Comedy and Ideology.* New York: Oxford University Press, 1995.

———. *Roman Comedy.* Ithaca, N.Y.: Cornell University Press, 1983.

Krumeich, R., N. Pechstein, and B. Seidensticker. *Das griechische Satyrspiel.* Darmstadt, Ger.: Wissenschalftliche Buchgesselschaft, 1999.

Manuwald, G. *Fabulae Praetextae: Spuren einer literarischen Gattung der Romer.* Munich: 2001.

Miola, R. S. *Plautus and Terence.* New York: Longmans, Green, 1932.

———. *Shakespeare and Classical Comedy: The Influence of Plautus and Terence.* Oxford: Clarendon Press, 1994.

Norwood, G. *Greek Comedy.* London: Methuen, 1931.

Redmond, J., ed. *Themes in Drama. 10, Farce.* Cambridge: Cambridge University Press, 1988.

Ritschl, F. *Parerga zu Plautus und Terenz.* 1845. Reprint, Amsterdam: Hakkert, 1965.

Rosen, R. *Old Comedy and the Iambographic Tradition.* Atlanta: Scholars Press, 1988.

Rosivach, V. J. *When a Young Man Falls in Love: The Sexual Exploitation of Women in New Comedy.* London: Routledge, 1998.

Sandbach, F. H. *The Comic Theatre of Greece and Rome.* New York: Norton, 1977.

Saunders, C. *Costume in Roman Comedy.* New York: The Columbia University Press, 1909.

Segal, Erich, ed. *Oxford Readings in Menander, Plautus, and Terence.* Oxford: Oxford University Press, 2001.

Sifakis, G. M. *Parabasis and Animal Choruses: A Contribution to the History of Attic Comedy.* London: Athlone Press, 1971.

Slater, N. W., and B. Zimmermann, eds. *Intertextualität in der griechisch-römischen Komödie.* Stuttgart: M & P Verl. für Wiss. & Eorsch., 1993.

Spranger, P. P. *Historische Untersuchungen zu den Sklavenfiguren des Plautus und Terenz.* 2d ed. Stuttgart: Franz Steiner, 1984.

Sutton, D. F. *Ancient Comedy: The War of the Generations.* New York: Twayne, 1993.

———. *The Greek Satyr Play.* Meisenheim am Glan, Ger.: Hain, 1980.

Webster, T. B. L. *Monuments Illustrating Old and Middle Comedy.* 3d ed. Revised and enlarged by J. R. Green. London: Institute of Classical Studies, 1978.

———. *Studies in Later Greek Comedy.* 2d ed. Manchester: Manchester University Press, 1970.

Willi, A., ed. *The Language of Greek Comedy.* Oxford: Oxford University Press, 2002.

Wright, J. *Dancing in Chains: The Stylistic Unity of the Comoedia Palliata.* Rome: American Academy in Rome, 1974.

SCHOLARLY INTERPRETATION: TRAGEDY

Arnott, P. D. *An Introduction to the Greek Theatre.* London: Macmillan, 1959.

Baldock, M. *Greek Tragedy: An Introduction.* Bristol: Bristol Classical Press, 1989.

Baldry, H. C. *The Greek Tragic Theatre.* New York: Chatto & Windus, 1971.

Belfiore, E. *Murder among Friends: Violations of Philia in Greek Tragedy.* Oxford: Oxford University Press, 2000.

Bouvrie, S. Des. *Women in Greek Tragedy: An Anthropological Approach.* Oslo: Norwegian University Press and Oxford: Oxford University Press, 1990.

Bremer, J. M., et al., eds. *Miscellanea Tragica in honorem J.C. Kamerbeek.* Amsterdam: Hakkert, 1976.

Brooks, R. A. B. *Ennius and Roman Tragedy.* New York: Arno Press, 1981.

Brown, A. *A New Companion to Greek Tragedy.* London: Beckenham, 1983.

Burnett, A. P. *Revenge in Attic and Later Tragedy.* California: University of California Press, 1998.

Bushnell, R. W. *Prophesying Tragedy.* Ithaca, N.Y. and London: Cornell University Press, 1988.

Buxton, R. G. A. *Persuasion in Greek Tragedy.* Cambridge: Cambridge University Press, 1982.

Carpenter, T. H., and C. A. Faraone. *Masks of Dionysus.* Ithaca, N.Y.: Cornell University Press, 1993.

Clauss, J. J., and S. I. Johnston, eds. *Medea: Essays on Medea in Myth, Literature, Philosophy, and Art.* Princeton, N.J.: Princeton University Press, 1997.

Cropp, M. J., E. Fantham, and S. E. Scully, eds. *Greek Tragedy and its Legacy: Essays Presented to D. J. Conacher.* Calgary: University of Calgary Press, 1986.

Dale, A. M. *Collected Papers.* Cambridge: Cambridge University Press, 1969.

Dawe, R. D., J. Diggle, and P. E. Easterling, eds. *Dionysiaca: Nine Studies in Greek Poetry by Former Pupils, Presented to Denys Page on His Seventieth Birthday.* Cambridge: Cambridge Faculty Library, 1978.

Devereux, G. *Dreams in Greek Tragedy: An Ethno-Psycho-Analytical Study.* Berkeley: University of California Press, 1976.

Easterling, P. E. ed. *The Cambridge Companion to Greek Tragedy.* Cambridge: Cambridge University Press, 1997.

Else, G. F. *The Origin and Early Form of Greek Tragedy.* Cambridge, Mass.: Harvard University Press, 1965.

Erp Taalman Kip, A.M. van. *Reader and Spectator: Problems in the Interpretation of Greek Tragedy.* Amsterdam: Gieben, 1990.

Etman, A. M. *The Problem of Heracles' Apotheosis in the Trachiniae of Sophocles and in Hercules Oetaeus of Seneca: A Comparative Study of the Tragic and Stoic Meaning of the Myth.* Athens: University of Athens, 1974.

Euben, J. P. *The Tragedy of Political Theory: The Road Not Taken.* Princeton, N.J.: Princeton University Press, 1990.

Falkner, T. M. *The Poetics of Old Age in Greek Epic, Lyric and Tragedy.* Norman: University of Oklahoma Press, 1995.

Foley, H. P. *Female Acts in Greek Tragedy.* Princeton, N.J.: Princeton University Press, 2001.

Garrison, E. P. *Groaning Tears: Ethical and Dramatic Aspects of Suicide in Greek Tragedy.* Leiden: Brill, 1995.

Gibert, J. C. *Change of Mind in Greek Tragedy.* Gottingen, Ger.: Vandenhoeck & Ruprecht, 1995.

Goff, B., ed. *History, Tragedy, Theory: Dialogues on Athenian Drama.* Austin: University of Texas Press, 1995.

Goldhill, S. *Reading Greek Tragedy.* Cambridge: Cambridge University Press, 1986.

Gould, T. F. & C. J. Herington, eds. *Yale Classical Studies.* Vol. 25, *Greek Tragedy.* New Haven, Conn.: Yale University Press, 1977.

Goward, B. *Telling Tragedy: Narrative Technique in Aeschylus, Sophocles, and Euripides.* London: Focus, 2003.

Hall, E., F. Macintosh, and O. Taplin, eds. *Medea in Performance 1500–2000.* Oxford: Legenda, 2000.

Hartigan, K. V. *Greek Tragedy on the American Stage: Ancient Drama in the Commercial Theater, 1882–1994.* Westport, Conn.: Greenwood Press, 1995.

Heath, M. *The Poetics of Greek Tragedy.* London: Duckworth, 1987.

Jepsen, L. *Ethical Aspects of Tragedy: A Comparison of Certain Tragedies by Aeschylus, Sophocles, Euripides, Seneca, and Shakespeare.* Gainseville: University of Florida Press, 1953.

Jones, J. *On Aristotle and Greek Tragedy.* London and New York: Oxford University Press, 1962.

Kerrigan, J. *Revenge Tragedy: Aeschylus to Armageddon.* Oxford University Press, 1998.

Kitto, H. D. F. *Greek Tragedy: A Literary Study.* Garden City, N.Y.: Doubleday, 1954.

Knox, B. M. W. *Word and Action.* Baltimore: Johns Hopkins University Press, 1979.

Lattimore, R. *Story-Patterns in Greek Tragedy.* Ann Arbor: University of Michigan Press, 1964.

———. *The Poetry of Greek Tragedy.* Baltimore: Johns Hopkins Press, 1958.

Lesky, A. *Greek Tragedy.* Translated by H. Frankfort. London: E. Benn, 1967.

———. *Greek Tragic Poetry.* Translated by M. Dillon. New Haven, Conn.: Yale University Press, 1983.

Loraux, N. *Mothers in Mourning.* Ithaca, N.Y.: Cornell University Press, 1998.

———. *Tragic Ways of Killing a Woman.* Translated by A. Forster. Cambridge, Mass.: Harvard University Press, 1987.

Mackinnon, K. *Greek Tragedy into Film.* London: Croom Helm, 1986.

McAuslan, I., and P. Walcot, eds. *Greek Tragedy.* Oxford: Oxford University Press, 1993.

Meier, C. *The Political Art of Greek Tragedy.* Translated by A. Webber. Baltimore: Johns Hopkins University Press, 1993.

Mikalson, J. D. *Honor thy Gods: Popular Religion in Greek Tragedy.* Chapel Hill: University of North Carolina Press, 1991.

Mills, S. *Theseus, Tragedy and the Athenian Empire.* Oxford: Oxford University Press, 1997.

Mueller, M. *Children of Oedipus and Other Essays on the Imitation of Greek Tragedy 1550–1800.* Toronto: University of Toronto Press, 1980.

Nussbaum, M. C. *The Fragility of Goodness: Luck and Ethics in Greek Tragedy and Philosophy.* Cambridge: Cambridge University Press, 1986.

Ohlander, S. *Dramatic Suspense in Euripides' and Seneca's Medea.* New York: Lang, 1989.

Padel, R. *In and Out of the Mind: Greek Images of the Tragic Self.* Princeton, N.J.: Princeton University Press, 1992.

———. *Whom Gods Destroy: Elements of Greek and Tragic Madness.* Princeton, N.J.: Princeton University Press, 1995.

Pelling, C., ed. *Greek Tragedy and the Historian.* Oxford: Oxford University Press, 1997.

Porter, D. H. *Only Connect: Three Studies in Greek Tragedy.* Lanham, Md.: University Press of America, 1987.

Pucci, P., ed. *Language and the Tragic Hero.* Atlanta: Scholars Press, 1988.

Rehm, R. *Greek Tragic Theatre.* London: Routledge, 1992.

———. *Marriage to Death: The Conflation of Wedding and Funeral Rituals in Greek Tragedy.* Princeton, N.J.: Princeton University Press, 1994.

Ribbeck, O. *Die römischen Tragödie im Zeitalter der Republik.* 1870. Reprint, Hildesheim, Ger.: G. Ohms, 1968.

Seaford, R. *Reciprocity and Ritual: Homer and Tragedy in the Developing City-State.* Oxford: Oxford University Press, 1994.

Segal, Charles. *Interpreting Greek Tragedy.* Ithaca, N.Y.: Cornell University Press, 1986.

Segal, Erich, ed. *Greek Tragedy: Modern Essays in Criticism.* New York: Harper & Row, 1983.

———. *Oxford Readings in Greek Tragedy.* Oxford: Oxford University Press, 1983.

Sheppard, J. T. *Aeschylus and Sophocles.* New York: Cooper Square, 1963.

Silk, M. ed. *Tragedy and the Tragic: Greek Theatre and Beyond.* Oxford: Clarendon Press, 1996.

Simon, B. *Tragic Drama and the Family: Psychoanalytic Studies from Aeschylus to Beckett.* New Haven, Conn.: Yale University Press, 1988.

Sommerstein, A. H. *Greek Drama and Dramatists.* London: Routledge, 2002.

Sommerstein, A. H., S. Halliwell, J. Henderson, and B. Zimmerman, eds. *Tragedy, Comedy and the Polis.* Bari, Italy: Levante editori, 1993.

Stanford, W. B. *Greek Tragedy and the Emotions.* London: Routledge & Kegan Paul, 1983.

Steiner, G. *Antigones.* Oxford: Oxford University Press, 1984.

Stinton, T. C. W. *Collected Papers on Greek Tragedy.* Oxford: Clarendon Press, 1990.

Suerbaum, W. *Untersuchungen zur Selbstdarstellung älterer römischer Dichter: Livius Andronicus, Naevius, Ennius.* Hildesheim, Ger.: G. Olms, 1968.

Taplin, O. *Greek Tragedy in Action.* Berkeley: University of California Press, 1978.

Vernant, J. P. *Tragedy and Myth in Ancient Greece.* Translated by J. Lloyd. Sussex, Ger.: Harvester Press, 1990.

Vickers, B. *Towards Greek Tragedy.* London: Longman, 1973.

Webster, T. B. L. *Greek Tragedy.* Greece and Rome Series. *New Surveys 5.* Oxford, U.K.: Clarendon Press, 1971.

———. *Monuments Illustrating Tragedy and Satyr Play.* 2d ed. London: Institute of Classical Studies, 1967.

Wiles, D. *Tragedy in Athens: Performance Space and Theatrical Meaning.* Cambridge: Cambridge University Press, 1997.

Winkler, J. J., and F. I. Zeitlin eds. *Nothing to Do with Dionysus?* Princeton, N.J.: Princeton University Press, 1990.

Zeitlin, F. I. *Playing the Other: Gender and Society in Classical Greek Literature.* Chicago: University of Chicago Press, 1996.

Zimmermann, B. *Greek Tragedy: An Introduction.* Baltimore: Johns Hopkins University Press, 1991.

SCHOLARLY INTERPRETATION: ANCIENT THEATER

Arnott, P. D. *Greek Scenic Conventions in the Fifth Century B.C.* Oxford: Clarendon Press, 1962.

———. *Public and Performance in the Greek Theatre.* London: Routledge, 1989.

Beacham, R. C. *The Roman Theatre and Its Audience.* Cambridge, Mass.: Harvard University Press, 1992.

Beare, W. *The Roman Stage: A Short History of Latin Drama in the Time of the Republic.* 3d ed. London: Methuen, 1964.

Betts, J. H., J. T. Hooker, and J. R. Green, eds. *Studies in Honour of T. B. L. Webster.* Vol. I. Bristol: Bristol Classical Press, 1986.

Bieber, M. *The History of the Greek and Roman Theater.* 2d ed. Princeton, N.J.: Princeton University Press, 1961.

Csapo, E., and W. J. Slater. *The Context of Ancient Drama.* Ann Arbor: The University of Michigan Press, 1995.

Dorey, T. A., and D. K. Dudley, K. Donald, eds. *Roman Drama.* London: Routledge & Kegan Paul, 1965.

Dudley, D. R., and T. A. Dorey, eds. *Roman Drama.* London: Routledge & K. Paul, 1965.

Dupont, F. *L'acteur-roi: Le théatre à Rome. Collection Realia.* Paris: Les Belles Lettres, 1985.

Finley, M. I. *The Idea of a Theatre: The Greek Experience.* London: British Museum Publications, 1980.

Fitton-Brown, A. D. *Greek Plays as First Productions.* Leicester: Leicester University Press, 1970.

Forman, R. J. *Classical Greek and Roman Drama: An Annotated Bibliography.* Pasadena, Calif.: Salem Press, 1989.

Garton, C. *Personal Aspects of the Roman Theatre.* Toronto: Hakkert, 1972.

Gredley, B., ed. *Essays on Greek Drama.* London: Bulletin of the Institute of Classical Studies 34, 1987.

Green, J. R. *Theatre in Ancient Greek Society.* London: Routledge, 1994.

Green, J. R., and E. Handley, eds. *Images of the Greek Theatre.* London: University of Texas Press, 1995.

Griffiths, A., ed. *Stage Directions: Essays in Ancient Drama in Honour of E. W. Handley.* London: Institute of Classical Studies, 1995.

Harsh, P. W. *A Handbook of Classical Drama.* Stanford, Calif.: Stanford University Press, 1944.

Hartigan, K. V. ed. *Legacy of Thespis: Drama Past and Present.* Vol. IV. Lanham, Md.: University Press of America, 1984.

Kranz, W. *Stasimon.* Berlin: Weidmann, 1933.

Lefèvre, E., ed. *Das römische Drama.* Darmstadt, Ger.: Wissenschaftliche Buchgesellschaft, 1978.

O'Connor, J. B. *Chapters in the History of Actors and Acting in Ancient Greece.* Chicago: University of Chicago Press, 1966.

Pickard-Cambridge, A. W. *Dithyramb, Tragedy, and Comedy.* 2d ed. Revised by T. B. L. Webster. Oxford: Clarendon Press, 1962.

———. *The Dramatic Festivals of Athens.* 2d ed. Revised by J. Gould and D. M. Lewis. Oxford: Clarendon Press, 1968.

———. *The Theatre of Dionysus at Athens.* Oxford: Clarendon Press, 1946.

Redmond, J., ed. *Themes in Drama. 7, Drama, Sex and Politics.* Cambridge: Cambridge University Press, 1985.

———. *Themes in Drama. 13, Violence in Drama.* Cambridge: Cambridge University Press, 1991.

Scodel, R., ed. *Theater and Society in the Classical World.* Ann Arbor: University of Michigan Press, 1993.

Scullion, J. S. *Three Studies in Athenian Dramaturgy.* Stuttgart: Teubner, 1994.

Simon, E. *The Ancient Theatre.* Translated by C. E. Vafopoulou-Richardson. London: Methuen, 1982.

Soubiran, Jean. *Essai sur la versification dramatique des Romains: senaire iambique et septenaire trochaique.* Paris: Editions du Centre national de la recherche scientifique, 1988.

Taplin, O. *Comic Angels: And Other Approaches to Greek Drama through Vase-Paintings.* Oxford: Oxford University Press, 1993.

Taylor, D. *Acting and the Stage.* London: Allen & Unwin, 1978.

Traina, A. *Vortit barbare. Le traduzioni poetiche da Livio Andronico a Cicerone.* Rome: Edizioni dell' Ateneo, 1970.

Trendall, A. D., and T. B. L. Webster. *Illustrations of Greek Drama.* London: Phaidon, 1971.

Walcot, P. *Greek Drama in its Theatrical and Social Context.* Cardiff: University of Wales Press, 1976.

Walton, J. M. *The Greek Sense of Theatre.* London: Methuen, 1984.

———. *Greek Theatre Practice.* Westport, Conn.: Greenwood Press, 1980.

————. *Living Greek Theatre*. Westport, Conn: Greenwood Press, 1987.

Webster, T. B. L. *Greek Theatre Production*. 2d ed. London: Methuen, 1970.

Whitman, C. H. *The Heroic Paradox: Essays on Homer, Sophocles, and Aristophanes*. Ithaca, N.J.: Cornell University Press, 1982.

Wilson, P. *The Athenian Institution of the Khoregia*. Cambridge: Cambridge University Press, 2000.

Zimmermann, B., ed. *Antike Dramentheorien und ihre Rezeption*. Stuttgart: M & P Verlag fur Wissenschaft und Forschung, 1992.

MISCELLANEOUS

Austin, N. *Helen of Troy and Her Shameless Phantom*. Ithaca, N.Y.: Cornell University Press, 1994.

Boedeker, D., and K. Raaflaub, eds. *Democracy, Empire and the Arts in Fifth-Century Athens*. Cambridge, Mass.: Harvard University Press, 1998.

Boegehold, A., and A. Scafuro, eds. *Athenian Identity and Civic Ideology*. Baltimore: The Johns Hopkins University Press, 1994.

Bonaria, M. *I mimi romani*. Rome: In aedibus Athenaei, 1965.

Bowersock, G. W., W. Burkert, and M. C. J. Putnam, eds. *Arktouros*. Berlin, New York: W. De Gruyter, 1979.

Bremer, J. M. *Hamartia*. Amsterdam: Hakkert, 1969.

Brock, R., and A. J. Woodman, eds. *Papers of the Leeds International Latin Seminar*. Leeds, U.K.: Cairns, 1995.

Burkert, W. *Greek Religion*. Oxford: Oxford University Press, 1985.

Bury, J. B., and R. Meiggs. *A History of Greece to the Death of Alexander the Great*. 4th ed. London: St. Martin's Press, 1975.

Cairnes, F., ed. *Papers of the Leeds International Latin Seminar*. Liverpool: Cairns, 1981.

————. *Papers of the Liverpool Latin Seminar, Fifth Volume 1985*. Liverpool: Francis Cairns, 1986.

Cohen, C., ed. *Not the Classical Ideal: Athens and the Construction of the Other in Greek Art*. Leiden: Brill, 2000.

Cook, A. B. *Zeus: A Study in Ancient Religion*. New York: Biblo & Tannen, 1964–1965.

Corti, L. *The Myth of Medea and the Murder of Children*. Westport, Conn.: Greenwood Press, 1998.

Craik, E. M., ed. *Owls to Athens: Essays on Classical Subjects Presented to Sir Kenneth Dover*. Oxford: Clarendon Press, 1990.

Damon, C. *The Mask of the Parasite: A Pathology of Roman Patronage*. Ann Arbor: University of Michigan Press, 1997.

DeForest, M., ed. *Woman's Power, Man's Game: Essays on Classical Antiquity in Honor of Joy K. King*. Wauconda, Ill.: Bolchazy-Carducci, 1993.

Deroux, C., ed. *Studies in Latin Literature and Roman History*. Bruxelles: Latomus, 1979–2000.

Derrida, J. *The Post Card: From Socrates to Freud and Beyond*. Translated by A. Bass. Chicago: University of Chicago Press, 1987.

Detienne, M. *The Gardens of Adonis: Spices in Greek Mythology*. Translated from the French by Janet Lloyd. Introduction by J. P. Vernant. Hassocks, U.K.: Harvester Press, 1977.

Dodds, E. R., ed. *The Ancient Concept of Progress and Other Essays on Greek Literature and Belief*. Oxford: Clarendon Press, 1973.

Donlan, W., ed. *The Classical World Bibliography of Roman Drama and Poetry and Ancient Fiction*. New York: Garland, 1978.

Dover, K. J. *Ancient Greek Literature*. Oxford: Oxford University Press, 1980.

————. *Greek Popular Morality*. Oxford: Blackwell, 1974.

Edmunds, L., ed. *Approaches to Greek Myth*. Baltimore: Johns Hopkins University Press, 1990.

Else, G. F. *Aristotle's Poetics: The Argument*. Cambridge, Mass.: Harvard University Press, 1957.

Foley, H. P., ed. *Reflections of Women in Antiquity*. London: Gordon and Breach Science, 1981.

Fox, R. *Reproduction and Succession*. New Brunswick, N.J.: Transaction, 1993.

Frassinetti, P. *Atellanae Fabulae*. Rome: In aedibus Athenai, 1967.

Gentili, B. *Theatrical Performance in the Ancient World: Hellenistic and Early Roman Theatre*. Amsterdam: Gieben, 1979.

Goldhill, S., and R. Osborne, eds. *Art and Text in Ancient Greek Culture*. Cambridge: Cambridge University Press, 1994.

Griffith J. G. *Festinat Senex or An Old Man in a Hurry*. Oxford: Oxbow Books, 1988.

Griffith, M., and D. J. Mastronarde, eds. *Cabinet of the Muses*. Atlanta: Scholars Press, 1989.

Grube, G. M. A. *The Greek and Roman Critics*. London: Methuen, 1965.

Gruen, E. S. *Culture and National Identity in Republican Rome*. Ithaca, N.Y.: Cornell University Press, 1992.

————. *Studies in Greek Culture and Roman Policy*. Leiden: Brill, 1990.

Hall, E. *Inventing the Barbarian*. Oxford: Clarendon Press, 1989.

Halliwell, S. *Aristotle's Poetics*. Chapel Hill: University of North Carolina Press, 1986.

Halliwell, S. et al., eds. *Aristotle, Poetics: Longinus, On the Sublime. Demetrius, On Style*. Cambridge, Mass.: Harvard University Press, 1996.

Harrison, J. E. *Themis.* Cambridge: Cambridge University Press, 1912.

Hawley, R., and B. Levick, eds. *Women in Antiquity: New Assessments.* London: Routledge, 1995.

Herington, J. *Poetry into Drama.* Berkeley: University of California Press, 1985.

Holst-Warhaft, G. *Dangerous Voices: Women's Laments and Greek Literature.* London and New York: Routledge, 1995.

Hornblower, S., and A. Spawforth, eds. *The Oxford Classical Dictionary.* 3d ed. Oxford: Oxford University Press, 1996.

———. *The Oxford Companion to Classical Civilization.* Oxford: Oxford University Press, 1998.

Howatson, M. C., ed. *The Oxford Companion to Classical Literature.* 2d ed. Oxford and New York: Oxford University Press, 1989.

Hutchinson, G. O. *Latin Literature from Seneca to Juvenal.* Oxford: Clarendon Press, 1993.

Kenney, E. J., ed. *The Cambridge History of Classical Literature.* Vol. 2, *Latin Literature.* Cambridge: Cambridge University Press, 1982.

Kerenyi, C. *Zeus and Hera: Archetypal Image of Father, Husband, and Wife.* Translated by C. Holme. Princeton, N.J.: Princeton University Press, 1975.

Kuntz, M. *Narrative Setting and Dramatic Poetry.* Leiden: Brill, 1993.

Leffingwell, G. W. *Social and Private Life at Rome in the Time of Plautus and Terence.* Columbia University: Studies in History, Economics and Public Law, Vol. 81, No. 1. New York: Longmans, Green, 1918.

Lesky, A. *A History of Greek Literature.* New York: Crowell, 1966.

Lindsay, W. M. *Early Latin Verse.* Oxford: Clarendon Press, 1922.

Lloyd-Jones, H. L. *Blood for the Ghosts.* London: Duckworth, 1982.

———. *The Justice of Zeus.* Berkeley: University of California Press, 1984.

Loraux, N. *The Children of Athena.* Translated by Caroline Levine. Princeton, N.J.: Princeton University Press, 1993.

Luce, T. J., ed. *Ancient Writers: Greece and Rome.* Vol. 1, *Homer to Caesar.* New York: Charles Scribner's Sons, 1982.

Mandel, O. *Philoctetes and the Fall of Troy.* Lincoln: University of Nebraska Press, 1981.

Marmorale, E. V. *Naevius Poeta.* 3d ed. Florence: La Nuova Italia, 1953.

Maurach, G. *Untersuchungen zum Aufbau plautinischer Lieder.* Hypomnemata 10. Göttingen, Ger.: Vandenhoeck & Ruprecht, 1964.

Meagher, R. E. *Helen: Myth, Legend, and the Culture of Misogyny.* New York: Continuum, 1995.

Merkelbach, R. *Hestia und Erigone: Vorträge und Aufsätze.* Edited by Blümel, B. Kramer, J. Kramer, and C. E. Römer. Stuttgart: Teubner, 1996.

Mylonas, G. *Studies Presented to David Moore Robinson.* St. Louis: Washington University, 1951.

Osborne, R., and S. Hornblower, eds. *Ritual, Finance, Politics: Athenian Democratic Accounts Presented to David Lewis.* Oxford: Oxford University Press, 1994.

Parke, H. W. *Festivals of the Athenians.* London: Cornell University Press, 1977.

Pelling, C., ed. *Characterization and Individuality in Greek Literature.* Oxford: Clarendon Press, 1990.

Poulter, A. G. *Literature and Art.* Vol. 1, *Ancient Bulgaria.* Papers Presented to the International Symposium on the Ancient History and Archaeology of Bulgaria, University of Nottingham, 1981. Nottingham, 1983.

Pozzi, D. C., and J. M. Wickersham, eds. *Myth and the Polis.* Ithaca, N.Y.: Cornell University Press, 1991.

Rabinowitz, N. S., and A. Richlin, eds. *Feminist Theory and the Classics.* New York: Routledge, 1993.

Ribbeck, O. *Scaenicae Romanorum Poesis Fragmenta.* Leipzig: Teubner, 1897–98.

Richlin, A., ed. *Pornography and Representation in Greece and Rome.* Oxford: Oxford University Press, 1991.

Rudd, N. *The Classical Tradition in Operation.* Toronto: University of Toronto Press, 1994.

Rudnytsky, P. L., and E. H. Spitz, eds. *Freud and Forbidden Knowledge.* New York: New York University Press, 1994.

Russell, D.A., and M. Winterbottom. *Ancient Literary Criticism.* Oxford: Clarendon Press, 1972.

Santas, G. X. *Plato and Freud: Two Theories of Love.* Oxford: Blackwell, 1988.

Skinner, M., ed. *Rescuing Creusa. Helios* 13, no. 2 (1987).

Skutsch, O. *Studia Enniana.* London, Athlone, 1968.

Stanford, W. B. *The Ulysses Theme: A Study in the Adaptability of a Traditional Hero.* 2d ed. Oxford: B. Blackwell, 1963.

Ste. Croix, G. E. M. de. *The Origins of the Peloponnesian War.* London: Duckworth, 1972.

Strauss, B. S. *Fathers and Sons in Athens: Ideology and Society in the Era of the Peloponnesian War.* Princeton, N.J.: Princeton University Press, 1993.

Sutton, R. F., Jr., ed. *Daidalikon: Studies in Memory of Raymond V. Schoder.* Wauconda, Ill.: Bolchazy-Carducci, 1989.

Travlos, J. *Pictorial Dictionary of Ancient Athens.* New York: Hacker, 1971.

West, D., and T. Woodman, eds. *Creative Imitation and Latin Literature.* Cambridge: Cambridge University Press, 1979.

White, M., ed. *Studies in Honour of Gilbert Norwood.* Toronto: University of Toronto Press, 1952.

Williams, B. *Shame and Necessity.* Berkeley: University of California Press, 1993.

INDEX

REFERENCE